COMMUNICACT
200

Updated as of March 26, 2018

THE LAW LIBRARY

TABLE OF CONTENTS

Introductory Text

Communications Act 2003

2003 CHAPTER 21

An Act to confer functions on the Office of Communications; to make provision about the regulation of the provision of electronic communications networks and services and of the use of the electro-magnetic spectrum; to make provision about the regulation of broadcasting and of the provision of television and radio services; to make provision about mergers involving newspaper and other media enterprises and, in that connection, to amend the Enterprise Act 2002; and for connected purposes.

[17th July 2003]

Be it enacted by the Queen's most Excellent Majesty, by and with the advice and consent of the Lords Spiritual and Temporal, and Commons, in this present Parliament assembled, and by the authority of the same, as follows:—

Modifications etc. (not altering text)

C1. Act: amendment to earlier affecting provision SI 2004/1944, art. 4 (22.1.2010) by The Community Radio (Amendment) Order 2010 (S.I. 2010/118), arts. 1, 2-5

C2. Act applied (with modifications) (20.7.2004) by Community Radio Order 2004 (S.I. 2004/1944), art. 4, Sch.

C3. Act: specified provisions extended (Isle of Man) (with modifications) (with effect in accordance with art. 1. (3)(4) of the amending S.I.) by Communications (Isle of Man) Order 2003 (S.I. 2003/3198), art. 6, Sch. 2 (as amended (27.2.2004) by Broadcasting and Communications (Isle of Man) Order 2004 (S.I. 2004/309), art. 2. (2), Sch. Pt. 2; and (26.3.2004) by Broadcasting and Communications (Isle of Man) (No.2) Order 2004 (S.I. 2004/718), art. 2)

C4. Act: specified provisions extended (Guernsey) (with modifications) (27.2.2004) by Communications (Bailiwick of Guernsey) Order 2004 (S.I. 2004/307), art. 4, Sch. (with art. 1. (2))

C5. Act: specified provisions extended (Jersey) (with modifications) (with effect in accordance with art. 1. (3)-(5) of the amending S.I.) by Communications (Jersey) Order 2003 (S.I. 2003/3197), art. 6, Sch. 2 (as amended (27.2.2004) by Broadcasting and Communications (Jersey) Order 2004 (S.I. 2004/308), art. 6. (3), Sch. 2; and (26.3.2004) by Broadcasting and Communications (Jersey) (No.2) Order 2004 (S.I. 2004/716), art. 3; and (23.4.2004) by Broadcasting and Communications (Jersey) (No.3) Order 2004 (S.I. 2004/1114), art. 2; and (31.3.2005) by The Communications (Jersey) (Amendment) Order 2005 (S.I. 2005/855), art. 2)

C6. Act: specified provisions extended (Guernsey) (with modifications) (with effect in accordance with art. 1. (4)(5) of the amending S.I.) by Communications (Bailiwick of Guernsey) Order 2003 (S.I. 2003/3195), art. 6, Sch. 2 (as amended (26.3.2004) by Communications (Bailiwick of Guernsey) (No.2) Order 2004 (S.I. 2004/715), art. 3, Sch.; and (23.4.2004) by Communications (Bailiwick of Guernsey) (No.3) Order 2004 (S.I. 2004/1116), art. 2; and (31.3.2005) by The Communications (Bailiwick of Guernsey) (Amendment) Order 2005 (S.I. 2005/856), art. 2)

C7. Act: amendment to earlier affecting provision SI 2003/3198 art. 6 Sch. 2 (8.2.2007) by Wireless Telegraphy (Isle of Man) Order 2007 (S.I. 2007/278), art. 3, Sch. 2 Pt. 1

C8. Act modified (3.5.2007) by National Assembly for Wales Commission (Crown Status) Order 2007 (S.I. 2007/1118), art. 7

C9. Act applied (with modifications) (5.12.2012) by The Community Radio (Guernsey) Order 2012 (S.I. 2012/2690), art. 4, Sch.

C10. Act: amendment to earlier affecting provision. SI 2003/3195 Sch. 2 (5.12.2012) by The Communications (Bailiwick of Guernsey) (Amendment) Order 2012 (S.I. 2012/2688), arts. 2, 3

C11. Act modified (Guernsey) (19.3.2013) by The Community Radio (Guernsey) Order 2013 (S.I. 2013/243), art. 5, Sch. Pt. 2

C12. Act: amendment to earlier affecting provision SI 2004/1944 art. 4 Sch. (27.3.2015) by The Community Radio (Amendment) Order 2015 (S.I. 2015/1000), arts. 3, 8 (with art. 9)

Part 1. Functions of OFCOM

Part 1. Functions of OFCOM

1. Functions and general powers of OFCOM

(1) The Office of Communications ("OFCOM") shall have the following functions—
  (a) the functions transferred to OFCOM under section 2; and
  (b) such other functions as may be conferred on OFCOM by or under any enactment (including this Act).

(2) OFCOM shall also have any functions in relation to telephone numbers that are conferred on them by the law of the Isle of Man or of any of the Channel Islands.

(3) OFCOM may do anything which appears to them to be incidental or conducive to the carrying out of their functions, including borrow money.

(4) OFCOM are not to borrow money except with the consent of the Secretary of State, or in accordance with a general authorisation given by him.

(5) OFCOM's powers under subsection (3) include, in particular—
  (a) power to undertake research and development work in connection with any matter in relation to which they have functions;
  (b) power to promote the carrying out of such research and development by others, or otherwise to arrange for it to be carried out by others;
  (c) power to institute and carry on criminal proceedings in England and Wales or Northern Ireland for an offence relating to a matter in relation to which they have functions; and
  (d) power, in such cases and in such circumstances as they may think fit, to make payments (where no legal liability arises) to persons adversely affected by the carrying out by OFCOM of any of their functions.

(6) In exercise of their powers under subsection (3), OFCOM must establish and maintain separate offices in each of the following parts of the United Kingdom—
  (a) England;
  (b) Wales;
  (c) Scotland; and
  (d) Northern Ireland.

(7) Part 2 of the Deregulation and Contracting Out Act 1994 (c. 40) (contracting out) is to have effect in relation to the functions conferred on OFCOM by or under any enactment as if—
  (a) OFCOM were an office holder within the meaning of that Part; and
  (b) a power of OFCOM to make subordinate legislation were excluded from section 69 of that Act to the extent only that it is exercisable by statutory instrument.

(8) In this section "telephone numbers" has the same meaning as in Chapter 1 of Part 2.

Commencement Information

I1. S. 1. (1) (2) (4) (5)(a) (b) (d) (6)-(8) in force at 29.12.2003 by S.I. 2003/3142, art. 3. (1), Sch. 1

(with art. 11)

12. S. 1. (3) in force at 25.7.2003 for specified purposes by S.I. 2003/1900, arts. 1. (2), 2. (1), Sch. 1 (with art. 3) (as amended by S.I. 2003/3142, art. 1. (3))

13. S. 1. (3) in force at 29.12.2003 in so far as not already in force by S.I. 2003/3142, art. 3. (1), Sch. 1 (with art. 11)

14. S. 1. (5)(c) in force at 25.7.2003 for specified purposes by S.I. 2003/1900, arts. 1. (2), 2. (1), Sch. 1 (with art. 3) (as amended by S.I. 2003/3142, art. 1. (3))

15. S. 1. (5)(c) in force at 29.12.2003 in so far as not already in force by S.I. 2003/3142, art. 3. (1), Sch. 1 (with art. 11)

2. Transfer of functions of pre-commencement regulators

(1) As from such date as the Secretary of State may appoint for the coming into force of this section, the functions that are set out in Schedule 1 (functions of the Secretary of State and of the pre-commencement regulators) shall become functions of OFCOM in accordance with that Schedule.

(2) References in any enactment to a person who is a person from whom functions are transferred by virtue of this section are to have effect, so far as necessary for the purposes of the transfers, as references to OFCOM.

(3) The functions of OFCOM are to include the carrying out of the transferred functions, at times after the time when they become functions of OFCOM, in relation to anything occurring before that time.

(4) The provisions of this section have effect subject to—

(a) the modifications made by this Act of the enactments relating to the transferred functions; and

(b) any express transitional or consequential provisions made by or under this Act in relation to those enactments.

Commencement Information

16. S. 2 in force at 29.12.2003 for specified purposes by S.I. 2003/3142, art. 3. (1)(3), Sch. 1 (with art. 11)

17. S. 2 in force at 1.4.2004 in so far as not already in force by S.I. 2003/3142, art. 4. (2), Sch. 2 (with art. 11) (as amended (4.3.2004) by S.I. 2004/545, art. 2. (2)(3)(a))

General duties in carrying out functions

3. General duties of OFCOM

(1) It shall be the principal duty of OFCOM, in carrying out their functions—

(a) to further the interests of citizens in relation to communications matters; and

(b) to further the interests of consumers in relevant markets, where appropriate by promoting competition.

(2) The things which, by virtue of subsection (1), OFCOM are required to secure in the carrying out of their functions include, in particular, each of the following—

(a) the optimal use for wireless telegraphy of the electro-magnetic spectrum;

(b) the availability throughout the United Kingdom of a wide range of electronic communications services;

(c) the availability throughout the United Kingdom of a wide range of television and radio services which (taken as a whole) are both of high quality and calculated to appeal to a variety of tastes and interests;

(d) the maintenance of a sufficient plurality of providers of different television and radio services;

(e) the application, in the case of all television and radio services, of standards that provide adequate protection to members of the public from the inclusion of offensive and harmful material in such services;

(f) the application, in the case of all television and radio services, of standards that provide adequate protection to members of the public and all other persons from both—

(i) unfair treatment in programmes included in such services; and

(ii) unwarranted infringements of privacy resulting from activities carried on for the purposes of such services.

(3) In performing their duties under subsection (1), OFCOM must have regard, in all cases, to—

(a) the principles under which regulatory activities should be transparent, accountable, proportionate, consistent and targeted only at cases in which action is needed; and

(b) any other principles appearing to OFCOM to represent the best regulatory practice.

(4) OFCOM must also have regard, in performing those duties, to such of the following as appear to them to be relevant in the circumstances—

(a) the desirability of promoting the fulfilment of the purposes of public service television broadcasting in the United Kingdom;

(b) the desirability of promoting competition in relevant markets;

(c) the desirability of promoting and facilitating the development and use of effective forms of self-regulation;

(d) the desirability of encouraging investment and innovation in relevant markets;

(e) the desirability of encouraging the availability and use of high speed data transfer services throughout the United Kingdom;

(f) the different needs and interests, so far as the use of the electro-magnetic spectrum for wireless telegraphy is concerned, of all persons who may wish to make use of it;

(g) the need to secure that the application in the case of television and radio services of standards falling within subsection (2)(e) and (f) is in the manner that best guarantees an appropriate level of freedom of expression;

(h) the vulnerability of children and of others whose circumstances appear to OFCOM to put them in need of special protection;

(i) the needs of persons with disabilities, of the elderly and of those on low incomes;

(j) the desirability of preventing crime and disorder;

(k) the opinions of consumers in relevant markets and of members of the public generally;

(l) the different interests of persons in the different parts of the United Kingdom, of the different ethnic communities within the United Kingdom and of persons living in rural and in urban areas;

(m) the extent to which, in the circumstances of the case, the furthering or securing of the matters mentioned in subsections (1) and (2) is reasonably practicable.

(5) In performing their duty under this section of furthering the interests of consumers, OFCOM must have regard, in particular, to the interests of those consumers in respect of choice, price, quality of service and value for money.

(6) Where it appears to OFCOM, in relation to the carrying out of any of the functions mentioned in section 4. (1), that any of their general duties conflict with one or more of their duties under sections 4, 24 and 25, priority must be given to their duties under those sections.

[F1. (6. A)Where it appears to OFCOM, in relation to the carrying out of any of their functions in relation to postal services, that any of their general duties conflict with their duty under section 29 of the Postal Services Act 2011 (duty to secure provision of universal postal service), priority must be given to their duty under that section.]

(7) Where it appears to OFCOM that any of their general duties conflict with each other in a particular case, they must secure that the conflict is resolved in the manner they think best in the circumstances.

(8) Where OFCOM resolve a conflict in an important case between their duties under paragraphs (a) and (b) of subsection (1), they must publish a statement setting out—

(a) the nature of the conflict;

(b) the manner in which they have decided to resolve it; and

(c) the reasons for their decision to resolve it in that manner.

(9) Where OFCOM are required to publish a statement under subsection (8), they must—

(a) publish it as soon as possible after making their decision but not while they would (apart from a statutory requirement to publish) be subject to an obligation not to publish a matter that needs to be included in the statement; and

(b) so publish it in such manner as they consider appropriate for bringing it to the attention of the persons who, in OFCOM's opinion, are likely to be affected by the matters to which the decision relates.

(10) Every report under paragraph 12 of the Schedule to the Office of Communications Act 2002 (c. 11) (OFCOM's annual report) for a financial year must contain a summary of the manner in which, in that year, OFCOM resolved conflicts arising in important cases between their general duties.

(11) A case is an important case for the purposes of subsection (8) or (10) only if—

(a) it involved one or more of the matters mentioned in subsection (12); or

(b) it otherwise appears to OFCOM to have been of unusual importance.

(12) Those matters are—

(a) a major change in the activities carried on by OFCOM;

(b) matters likely to have a significant impact on persons carrying on businesses in any of the relevant markets; or

(c) matters likely to have a significant impact on the general public in the United Kingdom or in a part of the United Kingdom.

(13) This section is subject to sections 370. (11) and 371. (11) of this Act and to section 119. A(4) of the Enterprise Act 2002 (c. 40) (which applies to functions conferred on OFCOM by Chapter 2 of Part 5 of this Act).

(14) In this section—

"citizens" means all members of the public in the United Kingdom;

"communications matters" means the matters in relation to which OFCOM have functions;

"general duties", in relation to OFCOM, means—

 - their duties under subsections (1) to (5); and

 - the duty which, under section 107. (5), is to rank equally for the purposes of subsections (6) and (7) with their duties under this section;

"relevant markets" means markets for any of the services, facilities, apparatus or directories in relation to which OFCOM have functions.

Amendments (Textual)

F1. S. 3. (6. A) inserted (1.10.2011) by Postal Services Act 2011 (c. 5), s. 93. (2)(3), Sch. 12 para. 57; S.I. 2011/2329, art. 3

Modifications etc. (not altering text)

C1. S. 3 excluded by 2002 c. 40, s. 119. (4) (as inserted (29.12.2003) by Communications Act 2003 (c. 21), ss. 385, 411. (2) (with Sch. 18); S.I. 2003/3142, art. 3. (1), Sch. 1 (with art. 11))

Commencement Information

I8. S. 3 in force at 29.12.2003 by S.I. 2003/3142, art. 3. (1), Sch. 1 (with art. 11)

4. Duties for the purpose of fulfilling [F2. EU] obligations

(1) This section applies to the following functions of OFCOM—

(a) their functions under Chapter 1 of Part 2;

(b) their functions under the enactments relating to the management of the radio spectrum;

(c) their functions under Chapter 3 of Part 2 in relation to disputes referred to them under section 185;

(d) their functions under sections 24 and 25 so far as they relate to information required for purposes connected with matters in relation to which functions specified in this subsection are conferred on OFCOM; and

(e) their functions under section 26 so far as they are carried out for the purpose of making information available to persons mentioned in subsection (2)(a) to (c) of that section.

(2) It shall be the duty of OFCOM, in carrying out any of those functions, to act in accordance with the six Community requirements (which give effect, amongst other things, to the requirements of Article 8 of the Framework Directive and are to be read accordingly).

(3) The first Community requirement is a requirement to promote competition—

(a) in relation to the provision of electronic communications networks and electronic communications services;

(b) in relation to the provision and making available of services and facilities that are provided or made available in association with the provision of electronic communications networks or electronic communications services; and

(c) in relation to the supply of directories capable of being used in connection with the use of electronic communications networks or electronic communications services.

(4) The second Community requirement is a requirement to secure that OFCOM's activities contribute to the development of the European internal market.

(5) The third Community requirement is a requirement to promote the interests of all persons who are citizens of the European Union (within the meaning of [F3. Article 20 of the Treaty on the Functioning of the European Union]).

(6) The fourth Community requirement is a requirement to take account of the desirability of OFCOM's carrying out their functions in a manner which, so far as practicable, does not favour—

(a) one form of electronic communications network, electronic communications service or associated facility; or

(b) one means of providing or making available such a network, service or facility,

over another.

[F4. (6. A)The fourth Community requirement does not apply to—

(a) the imposition, in relation to a wireless telegraphy licence, of a limitation of a kind falling within section 9. ZA(1) of the Wireless Telegraphy Act 2006; or

(b) the review, variation or removal of such a limitation.]

(7) The fifth Community requirement is a requirement to encourage, to such extent as OFCOM consider appropriate for the purpose mentioned in subsection (8), the provision of network access and service interoperability.

(8) That purpose is the purpose of securing—

(a) efficiency and sustainable competition F5...; F6...

[F7. (aa)efficient investment and innovation; and]

(b) the maximum benefit for the persons who are customers of communications providers and of persons who make [F8associated facilities] available.

(9) The sixth Community requirement is a requirement to encourage such compliance with the standards mentioned in subsection (10) as is necessary for—

(a) facilitating service interoperability; and

(b) securing freedom of choice for the customers of communications providers.

(10) Those standards are—

(a) standards or specifications from time to time drawn up and published in accordance with Article 17 of the Framework Directive;

(b) the standards and specifications from time to time adopted by—

(i) the European Committee for Standardisation;

(ii) the European Committee for Electrotechnical Standardisation; [F9and]

(iii) the European Telecommunications Standards Institute; and

(c) the international standards and recommendations from time to time adopted by—

(i) the International Telecommunication Union;

(ii) the International Organisation for Standardisation; F10...

[F11. (iia)the European Conference of Postal and Telecommunications Administrations; and]

(iii) the International Electrotechnical Committee.

(11) Where it appears to OFCOM that any of [F12. European Union] requirements conflict with each other, they must secure that the conflict is resolved in the manner they think best in the circumstances.

(12) In this section—

F13...

"network access" and "service interoperability" each has the same meaning as in Chapter 1 of Part 2.

[F14. (13)In this section and sections 4. A and 5, "the Framework Directive" has the same meaning as in Chapter 1 of Part 2.]

Amendments (Textual)

F2. Words in Act substituted (22.4.2011) by The Treaty of Lisbon (Changes in Terminology) Order 2011 (S.I. 2011/1043), arts. 2, 3, 6 (with art. 3. (2)(3), 4. (2), 6. (4)(5))

F3. Words in s. 4. (5) substituted (1.8.2012) by The Treaty of Lisbon (Changes in Terminology or Numbering) Order 2012 (S.I. 2012/1809), art. 2. (1), Sch. Pt. 1 (with art. 2. (2))

F4. S. 4. (6. A) inserted (26.5.2011) by The Electronic Communications and Wireless Telegraphy Regulations 2011 (S.I. 2011/1210), reg. 1. (2), Sch. 1 para. 5. (a) (with Sch. 3 para. 2)

F5. Words in s. 4. (8)(a) omitted (26.5.2011) by virtue of The Electronic Communications and Wireless Telegraphy Regulations 2011 (S.I. 2011/1210), reg. 1. (2), Sch. 1 para. 5. (b)(i) (with Sch. 3 para. 2)

F6. Word in s. 4. (8) omitted (26.5.2011) by virtue of The Electronic Communications and Wireless Telegraphy Regulations 2011 (S.I. 2011/1210), reg. 1. (2), Sch. 1 para. 5. (b)(ii) (with Sch. 3 para. 2)

F7. S. 4. (8)(aa) inserted (26.5.2011) by The Electronic Communications and Wireless Telegraphy Regulations 2011 (S.I. 2011/1210), reg. 1. (2), Sch. 1 para. 5. (b)(ii) (with Sch. 3 para. 2)

F8. Words in s. 4. (8)(b) substituted (26.5.2011) by The Electronic Communications and Wireless Telegraphy Regulations 2011 (S.I. 2011/1210), reg. 1. (2), Sch. 1 para. 5. (b)(iii) (with Sch. 3 para. 2)

F9. Word in s. 4. (10)(b) substituted (26.5.2011) by The Electronic Communications and Wireless Telegraphy Regulations 2011 (S.I. 2011/1210), reg. 1. (2), Sch. 1 para. 5. (c)(i) (with Sch. 3 para. 2)

F10. Word in s. 4. (10)(c)(ii) omitted (26.5.2011) by virtue of The Electronic Communications and Wireless Telegraphy Regulations 2011 (S.I. 2011/1210), reg. 1. (2), Sch. 1 para. 5. (c)(ii) (with Sch. 3 para. 2)

F11. S. 4. (10)(c)(iia) inserted (26.5.2011) by The Electronic Communications and Wireless Telegraphy Regulations 2011 (S.I. 2011/1210), reg. 1. (2), Sch. 1 para. 5. (c)(ii) (with Sch. 3 para. 2)

F12. Words in Act substituted (22.4.2011) by The Treaty of Lisbon (Changes in Terminology) Order 2011 (S.I. 2011/1043), arts. 2, 3, 4 (with art. 3. (2)(3), 4. (2), 6. (4)(5))

F13. Words in s. 4. (12) omitted (26.5.2011) by virtue of The Electronic Communications and Wireless Telegraphy Regulations 2011 (S.I. 2011/1210), reg. 1. (2), Sch. 1 para. 5. (d) (with Sch. 3 para. 2)

F14. S. 4. (13) inserted (26.5.2011) by The Electronic Communications and Wireless Telegraphy Regulations 2011 (S.I. 2011/1210), reg. 1. (2), Sch. 1 para. 5. (e) (with Sch. 3 para. 2)

Commencement Information

I9. S. 4 in force at 25.7.2003 for specified purposes by S.I. 2003/1900, arts. 1. (2), 2. (1), Sch. 1 (with art. 3) (as amended by S.I. 2003/3142, art. 1. (3))

I10. S. 4 in force at 29.12.2003 in so far as not already in force by S.I. 2003/3142, art. 3. (2) (with art. 11)

[F154. A.Duty to take account of European Commission recommendations for harmonisation

(1) This section applies to the following functions of OFCOM—

(a) their functions under Chapter 1 of Part 2;

(b) their functions under the enactments relating to the management of the radio spectrum;

(c) their functions under Chapter 3 of Part 2 in relation to disputes referred to them under section 185;

(d) their functions under sections 24 and 25 so far as they relate to information required for purposes connected with matters in relation to which functions specified in this subsection are conferred on OFCOM; and

(e) their functions under section 26 so far as they are carried out for the purpose of making information available to persons mentioned in subsection (2)(a) to (c) of that section.

(2) In carrying out those functions, OFCOM must take due account of all applicable recommendations issued (whether before or after the coming into force of this section) by the European Commission under Article 19. (1) of the Framework Directive.

(3) Where OFCOM decide not to follow such a recommendation they must notify the Commission of their decision, and of the reasons for it.]

Amendments (Textual)

F15 S. 4. A inserted (26.5.2011) by The Electronic Communications and Wireless Telegraphy Regulations 2011 (S.I. 2011/1210), reg. 1. (2), Sch. 1 para. 6 (with Sch. 3 para. 2)

5. Directions in respect of networks and spectrum functions

(1) This section applies to the following functions of OFCOM—

(a) their functions under Part 2; and

(b) their functions under the enactments relating to the management of the radio spectrum that are not contained in that Part.

(2) It shall be the duty of OFCOM to carry out those functions in accordance with such general or specific directions as may be given to them by the Secretary of State.

(3) The Secretary of State's power to give directions under this section shall be confined to a power to give directions for one or more of the following purposes—

(a) in the interests of national security;

(b) in the interests of relations with the government of a country or territory outside the United Kingdom;

(c) for the purpose of securing compliance with international obligations of the United Kingdom;

(d) in the interests of the safety of the public or of public health.

[F16. (3. A)The Secretary of State may not give a direction under this section in respect of a function that Article 3. (3a) of the Framework Directive requires OFCOM to exercise without seeking or taking instructions from any other body.]

(4) The Secretary of State is not entitled by virtue of any provision of this section to direct OFCOM to suspend or restrict—

(a) a person's entitlement to provide an electronic communications network or electronic communications service; or

(b) a person's entitlement to make available associated facilities.

[F17. (4. A)Before giving a direction under this section, the Secretary of State must take due account of the desirability of not favouring—

(a) one form of electronic communications network, electronic communications service or associated facility, or

(b) one means of providing or making available such a network, service or facility,

over another.]

(5) The Secretary of State must publish a direction under this section in such manner as appears to him to be appropriate for bringing it to the attention of the persons who, in his opinion, are likely to be affected by it.

(6) The Secretary of State is not required by subsection (5) to publish a direction, and he may exclude matter from a direction he does publish, if he considers the publication of the direction or matter to be—

(a) against the interests of national security; or

(b) against the interests of relations with the government of a country or territory outside the United Kingdom.

(7) Subsection (4) does not affect the Secretary of State's powers under section 132.

Amendments (Textual)

F16. S. 5. (3. A) inserted (26.5.2011) by The Electronic Communications and Wireless Telegraphy Regulations 2011 (S.I. 2011/1210), reg. 1. (2), Sch. 1 para. 7. (a) (with Sch. 3 para. 2)

F17. S. 5. (4. A) inserted (26.5.2011) by The Electronic Communications and Wireless Telegraphy Regulations 2011 (S.I. 2011/1210), reg. 1. (2), Sch. 1 para. 7. (b) (with Sch. 3 para. 2)

Commencement Information

I11. S. 5 in force at 25.7.2003 for specified purposes by S.I. 2003/1900, arts. 1. (2), 2. (1), Sch. 1 (with art. 3) (as amended by S.I. 2003/3142, art. 1. (3))

I12. S. 5 in force at 18.9.2003 in so far as not already in force by S.I. 2003/1900, art. 2. (2), Sch. 2

I13. S. 5 in force at 29.12.2003 in so far as not already in force by S.I. 2003/3142, art. 3. (2) (with art. 11)

6. Duties to review regulatory burdens

(1) OFCOM must keep the carrying out of their functions under review with a view to securing that regulation by OFCOM does not involve—

(a) the imposition of burdens which are unnecessary; or

(b) the maintenance of burdens which have become unnecessary.

(2) In reviewing their functions under this section it shall be the duty of OFCOM—

(a) to have regard to the extent to which the matters which they are required under section 3 to further or to secure are already furthered or secured, or are likely to be furthered or secured, by effective self-regulation; and

(b) in the light of that, to consider to what extent it would be appropriate to remove or reduce regulatory burdens imposed by OFCOM.

(3) In determining for the purposes of this section whether procedures for self-regulation are effective OFCOM must consider, in particular—

(a) whether those procedures are administered by a person who is sufficiently independent of the persons who may be subjected to the procedures; and

(b) whether adequate arrangements are in force for funding the activities of that person in relation to those procedures.

(4) OFCOM must, from time to time, publish a statement setting out how they propose, during the period for which the statement is made, to secure that regulation by OFCOM does not involve the imposition or maintenance of unnecessary burdens.

(5) The first statement to be published under this section—

(a) must be published as soon as practicable after the commencement of this section; and

(b) shall be a statement for the period of twelve months beginning with the day of its publication.

(6) A subsequent statement—

(a) must be published during the period to which the previous statement related; and

(b) must be a statement for the period of twelve months beginning with the end of the previous period.

(7) It shall be the duty of OFCOM, in carrying out their functions at times during a period for which a statement is in force under this section, to have regard to that statement.

(8) OFCOM may, if they think fit, revise a statement under this section at any time before or during the period for which it is made.

(9) Where OFCOM revise a statement, they must publish the revision as soon as practicable.

(10) The publication under this section of a statement, or of a revision of a statement, must be in such manner as OFCOM consider appropriate for bringing it to the attention of the persons who, in their opinion, are likely to be affected by the matters to which it relates.

Commencement Information

I14. S. 6 in force at 29.12.2003 by S.I. 2003/3142, art. 3. (1), Sch. 1 (with art. 11)

7. Duty to carry out impact assessments

(1) This section applies where—

    (a) OFCOM are proposing to do anything for the purposes of, or in connection with, the carrying out of their functions; and

    (b) it appears to them that the proposal is important;

but this section does not apply if it appears to OFCOM that the urgency of the matter makes it impracticable or inappropriate for them to comply with the requirements of this section.

(2) A proposal is important for the purposes of this section only if its implementation would be likely to do one or more of the following—

    (a) to involve a major change in the activities carried on by OFCOM;

    (b) to have a significant impact on persons carrying on businesses in the markets for any of the services, facilities, apparatus or directories in relation to which OFCOM have functions; or

    (c) to have a significant impact on the general public in the United Kingdom or in a part of the United Kingdom.

(3) Before implementing their proposal, OFCOM must either—

    (a) carry out and publish an assessment of the likely impact of implementing the proposal; or

    (b) publish a statement setting out their reasons for thinking that it is unnecessary for them to carry out an assessment.

(4) An assessment under subsection (3)(a) must set out how, in OFCOM's opinion, the performance of their general duties (within the meaning of section 3) is secured or furthered by or in relation to what they propose.

(5) An assessment carried out under this section—

    (a) may take such form, and

    (b) must relate to such matters,

as OFCOM consider appropriate.

(6) In determining the matters to which an assessment under this section should relate, OFCOM must have regard to such general guidance relating to the carrying out of impact assessments as they consider appropriate.

(7) Where OFCOM publish an assessment under this section—

    (a) they must provide an opportunity of making representations to them about their proposal to members of the public and other persons who, in OFCOM's opinion, are likely to be affected to a significant extent by its implementation;

    (b) the published assessment must be accompanied by a statement setting out how representations may be made; and

    (c) OFCOM are not to implement their proposal unless the period for making representations about it has expired and they have considered all the representations that were made in that period.

(8) Where OFCOM are required (apart from this section)—

    (a) to consult about a proposal to which this section applies, or

    (b) to give a person an opportunity of making representations about it,

the requirements of this section are in addition to, but may be performed contemporaneously with, the other requirements.

(9) Every report under paragraph 12 of the Schedule to the Office of Communications Act 2002 (c. 11) (OFCOM's annual report) must set out—

    (a) a list of the assessments under this section carried out during the financial year to which the report relates; and

(b) a summary of the decisions taken during that year in relation to proposals to which assessments carried out in that year or previous financial years relate.

(10) The publication of anything under this section must be in such manner as OFCOM consider appropriate for bringing it to the attention of the persons who, in OFCOM's opinion, are likely to be affected if their proposal is implemented.

Commencement Information

I15. S. 7 in force at 29.12.2003 by S.I. 2003/3142, art. 3. (1), Sch. 1 (with art. 11)

8. Duty to publish and meet promptness standards

(1) It shall be the duty of OFCOM to publish a statement setting out the standards they are proposing to meet with respect to promptness in—

(a) the carrying out of their different functions; and

(b) the transaction of business for purposes connected with the carrying out of those functions.

(2) This section does not require standards to be set out with respect to anything which (apart from this section) is required to be done by a time, or within a period, provided for by or under an enactment.

(3) OFCOM may, if they think fit, at any time revise the statement for the time being in force under this section.

(4) It shall be the duty of OFCOM—

(a) in carrying out their functions, and

(b) in transacting business for purposes connected with the carrying out of their functions,

to have regard to the statement for the time being in force under this section.

(5) Where OFCOM revise a statement under this section, they must publish the revision as soon as practicable.

(6) The publication under this section of a statement, or of a revision of a statement, must be in such manner as OFCOM consider appropriate for bringing it to the attention of the persons who, in their opinion, are likely to be affected by the matters to which it relates.

(7) OFCOM's report under paragraph 12 of the Schedule to the Office of Communications Act 2002 (c. 11) (annual report) for each financial year must contain a statement by OFCOM summarising the extent to which they have complied during that year with the standards set out under this section.

Commencement Information

I16. S. 8 in force at 29.12.2003 by S.I. 2003/3142, art. 3. (1), Sch. 1 (with art. 11)

9. Secretary of State's powers in relation to promptness standards

(1) Where the Secretary of State considers that the statement published by OFCOM under section 8 is not adequate for securing that they meet satisfactory promptness standards, he may give them a notification to that effect.

(2) If the period of three months after the date of the giving of a notification under subsection (1) expires without OFCOM taking steps which the Secretary of State is satisfied remedy the situation, he may give them a direction under this section.

(3) A direction under this section is one requiring OFCOM to issue a new or revised statement under section 8 in accordance with the direction.

(4) Before giving a direction under this section, the Secretary of State must—

(a) give OFCOM an opportunity of making representations to him about his proposed direction; and

(b) have regard to any representations made to him by them.

(5) Where the Secretary of State gives a direction to OFCOM under this section, he must publish a copy of it in such manner as he considers appropriate for bringing it to the attention of persons

who, in his opinion, are likely to be affected by OFCOM's promptness standards.

(6) It shall be the duty of OFCOM to revise their statement under section 8 in accordance with any direction of the Secretary of State under this section.

(7) In this section "promptness standards" means standards of promptness in—

(a) the carrying out by OFCOM of their different functions; and

(b) the transaction by them of business for purposes connected with the carrying out of those functions.

(8) No notification is to be given under subsection (1) at any time in the period of twelve months beginning with the commencement of section 8.

Commencement Information

I17. S. 9 in force at 29.12.2003 by S.I. 2003/3142, art. 3. (1), Sch. 1 (with art. 11)

Accessible domestic communications apparatus

10. Duty to encourage availability of easily usable apparatus

(1) It shall be the duty of OFCOM to take such steps, and to enter into such arrangements, as appear to them calculated to encourage others to secure—

(a) that domestic electronic communications apparatus is developed which is capable of being used with ease, and without modification, by the widest possible range of individuals (including those with disabilities); and

(b) that domestic electronic communications apparatus which is capable of being so used is as widely available as possible for acquisition by those wishing to use it.

(2) It shall be the duty of OFCOM from time to time to review whether they need to take further steps, or to enter into further arrangements, for the purpose of performing their duty under this section.

(3) OFCOM must not do anything under this section that would be inconsistent with [F12. European Union] requirements set out in section 4.

(4) In this section "electronic communications apparatus" means apparatus that is designed or adapted for a use which consists of or includes the sending or receiving of communications or other signals that are transmitted by means of an electronic communications network.

(5) For the purposes of this section electronic communications apparatus is domestic electronic communications apparatus except to the extent that it is designed or adapted for use solely for the purposes of, or in connection with, a business.

(6) In this section "signal" includes—

(a) anything comprising speech, music, sounds, visual images or communications or data of any description; and

(b) signals serving for the impartation of anything between persons, between a person and a thing or between things, or for the actuation or control of apparatus.

Amendments (Textual)

F12. Words in Act substituted (22.4.2011) by The Treaty of Lisbon (Changes in Terminology) Order 2011 (S.I. 2011/1043), arts. 2, 3, 4 (with art. 3. (2)(3), 4. (2), 6. (4)(5))

Commencement Information

I18. S. 10 in force at 29.12.2003 by S.I. 2003/3142, art. 3. (1), Sch. 1 (with art. 11)

Media literacy

11. Duty to promote media literacy

(1) It shall be the duty of OFCOM to take such steps, and to enter into such arrangements, as appear to them calculated—

(a) to bring about, or to encourage others to bring about, a better public understanding of the nature and characteristics of material published by means of the electronic media;

(b) to bring about, or to encourage others to bring about, a better public awareness and understanding of the processes by which such material is selected, or made available, for publication by such means;

(c) to bring about, or to encourage others to bring about, the development of a better public awareness of the available systems by which access to material published by means of the electronic media is or can be regulated;

(d) to bring about, or to encourage others to bring about, the development of a better public awareness of the available systems by which persons to whom such material is made available may control what is received and of the uses to which such systems may be put; and

(e) to encourage the development and use of technologies and systems for regulating access to such material, and for facilitating control over what material is received, that are both effective and easy to use.

(2) In this section, references to the publication of anything by means of the electronic media are references to its being—

(a) broadcast so as to be available for reception by members of the public or of a section of the public; or

(b) distributed by means of an electronic communications network to members of the public or of a section of the public.

Commencement Information

I19. S. 11 in force at 29.12.2003 by S.I. 2003/3142, art. 3. (1), Sch. 1 (with art. 11)

OFCOM's Content Board

12. Duty to establish and maintain Content Board

(1) It shall be the duty of OFCOM, in accordance with the following provisions of this section, to exercise their powers under paragraph 14 of the Schedule to the Office of Communications Act 2002 (c. 11) (committees of OFCOM) to establish and maintain a committee to be known as "the Content Board".

(2) The Content Board shall consist of—

(a) a chairman appointed by OFCOM; and

(b) such number of other members appointed by OFCOM as OFCOM think fit.

(3) The chairman of the Content Board must be a non-executive member of OFCOM but is not to be the chairman of OFCOM.

(4) At least one of the other members of the Content Board must also be a non-executive member of OFCOM other than the chairman of OFCOM.

(5) In appointing persons to be members of the Content Board, OFCOM must secure that, for each of the following parts of the United Kingdom—

(a) England,

(b) Scotland,

(c) Wales, and

(d) Northern Ireland,

there is a different member of the Board capable of representing the interests and opinions of persons living in that part of the United Kingdom.

(6) In appointing a person for the purposes of subsection (5)(a), OFCOM must have regard to the desirability of ensuring that the person appointed is able to represent the interests and opinions of persons living in all the different regions of England.

(7) The validity of any proceedings of the Content Board shall not be affected by any failure by OFCOM to comply with subsection (5) or (6).

(8) It shall be the duty of OFCOM when appointing members of the Content Board to secure, so far as practicable, that a majority of the members of the Board (counting the chairman) consists of persons who are neither members nor employees of OFCOM.

(9) The following shall be disqualified from being the chairman or another member of the Content Board—

(a) governors and employees of the BBC;

(b) members and employees of the Welsh Authority; and

(c) members and employees of C4. C.

(10) Before appointing a person to be the chairman or another member of the Content Board, OFCOM must satisfy themselves that he will not have any financial or other interest which would be likely prejudicially to affect the carrying out by him of any of his functions as chairman or member of the Content Board.

(11) A person is not to be taken to have such an interest by reason only that he is or will be a member or employee of OFCOM.

(12) Every person whom OFCOM propose to appoint to be the chairman or another member of the Content Board, shall, whenever requested to do so by OFCOM, furnish OFCOM with any information they consider necessary for the performance of their duty under subsection (10).

(13) In addition to paying remuneration and expenses under paragraph 14. (4) of the Schedule to the Office of Communications Act 2002 (c. 11), OFCOM may—

(a) pay to, or in respect of, any member of the Content Board who is not a member or employee of OFCOM, such sums by way of pensions, allowances or gratuities as OFCOM may determine; and

(b) provide for the making of such payments to or in respect of any such member of the Content Board.

(14) In subsection (13)—

(a) the reference to pensions, allowances and gratuities includes a reference to similar benefits payable on death or retirement; and

(b) the reference to providing for the payment of a pension, allowance or gratuity to, or in respect of, a person includes a reference to the making of payments towards the provision or payment of a pension, allowance or gratuity, or of any such similar benefits, to or in respect of that person.

Commencement Information

I20. S. 12 in force at 29.12.2003 by S.I. 2003/3142, art. 3. (1), Sch. 1 (with art. 11)

13. Functions of the Content Board

(1) The Content Board shall have such functions as OFCOM, in exercise of their powers under the Schedule to the Office of Communications Act 2002 (c. 11), may confer on the Board.

(2) The functions conferred on the Board must include, to such extent and subject to such restrictions and approvals as OFCOM may determine, the carrying out on OFCOM's behalf of—

(a) functions in relation to matters that concern the contents of anything which is or may be broadcast or otherwise transmitted by means of electronic communications networks; and

(b) functions in relation to the promotion of public understanding or awareness of matters relating to the publication of matter by means of the electronic media.

(3) In determining what functions to confer on the Content Board, OFCOM must have particular regard to the desirability of securing that the Board have at least a significant influence on decisions which—

(a) relate to the matters mentioned in subsection (2); and

(b) involve the consideration of different interests and other factors as respects different parts of the United Kingdom.

(4) It shall be the duty of the Content Board to ensure, in relation to—

(a) the carrying out of OFCOM's functions under Part 3 of this Act, Parts 1 and 3 of the 1990 Act and Parts 1 and 2 of the 1996 Act,

(b) the matters with respect to which functions are conferred on the Board, and

(c) such other matters mentioned in subsection (2) as OFCOM may determine,

that OFCOM are aware of the different interests and other factors which, in the Board's opinion, need to be taken into account as respects the different parts of the United Kingdom in relation to the carrying out of OFCOM's functions.

(5) The power of OFCOM to determine the Content Board's functions includes power to authorise the Board to establish committees and panels to advise the Board on the carrying out of some or all of the Board's functions.

(6) The power of OFCOM to authorise the establishment of a committee or panel by the Content Board includes power to authorise the establishment of a committee or panel that includes persons who are not members of the Board.

(7) In this section references to the publication of anything by means of the electronic media are references to its being—

(a) broadcast so as to be available for reception by members of the public or of a section of the public; or

(b) distributed by means of an electronic communications network to members of the public or of a section of the public.

Commencement Information

I21. S. 13 in force at 29.12.2003 by S.I. 2003/3142, art. 3. (1), Sch. 1 (with art. 11)

Functions for the protection of consumers

14. Consumer research

(1) OFCOM must make arrangements for ascertaining—

(a) the state of public opinion from time to time about the manner in which electronic communications networks and electronic communications services are provided;

(b) the state of public opinion from time to time about the manner in which associated facilities are made available;

(c) the experiences of consumers in the markets for electronic communications services and associated facilities, in relation to the manner in which electronic communications networks and electronic communications services are provided and associated facilities made available;

(d) the experiences of such consumers in relation to the handling, by communications providers and by persons making such facilities available, of complaints made to them by such consumers;

(e) the experiences of such consumers in relation to the resolution of disputes with communications providers or with persons making associated facilities available; and

(f) the interests and experiences of such consumers in relation to other matters that are incidental to, or are otherwise connected with, their experiences of the provision of electronic communications networks and electronic communications services or of the availability of associated facilities.

(2) The matters to which the arrangements must relate do not include the incidence or investigation of interference (within the meaning of [F18the Wireless Telegraphy Act 2006]) with wireless telegraphy.

(3) The matters to which the arrangements must relate do not (except so far as authorised or required by subsections (4) to (6)) include public opinion with respect to—

(a) the contents of anything broadcast or otherwise published by means of an electronic communications network; or

(b) the experiences or interests of consumers in any market for electronic communications services with respect to anything so broadcast or published.

(4) OFCOM must make arrangements for ascertaining—

(a) the state of public opinion from time to time concerning programmes included in television and radio services;

(b) any effects of such programmes, or of other material published by means of the electronic media, on the attitudes or behaviour of persons who watch, listen to or receive the programmes or material; and

(c) so far as necessary for the purpose mentioned in subsection (5), the types of programmes that members of the public would like to see included in television and radio services.

(5) That purpose is the carrying out by OFCOM of their functions under Chapter 4 of Part 3 of this Act.

(6) OFCOM must make arrangements for the carrying out of research into the following—

(a) the matters mentioned in section 11. (1);

(b) matters relating to, or connected with, the setting of standards under section 319 of this Act;

(c) matters relating to, or connected with, the observance of those standards by persons providing television and radio services;

(d) matters relating to, or connected with, the prevention of unjust or unfair treatment in programmes included in such services; and

(e) matters relating to, or connected with, the prevention of unwarranted infringements of privacy resulting from activities carried on for the purposes of such services.

[F19. (6. A)OFCOM must make arrangements for ascertaining—

(a) the state of public opinion from time to time about the way in which postal services are provided;

(b) the experiences of consumers in the markets for postal services, in relation to the way in which those services are provided;

(c) the experiences of such consumers in relation to the handling, by persons providing postal services, of complaints made to them by such consumers;

(d) the experiences of such consumers in relation to the resolution of disputes with persons providing postal services;

(e) the interests and experiences of such consumers in relation to matters that are incidental to or otherwise connected with their experiences of the provision of postal services.]

(7) Arrangements made by OFCOM for the purposes of this section may include arrangements for the carrying out of research in one or more of the following ways—

(a) by members or employees of OFCOM;

(b) by the Content Board;

(c) in accordance with arrangements made by that Board;

(d) by persons who are neither members nor employees of OFCOM.

(8) In this section references to the publication of anything by means of the electronic media are references to its being—

(a) broadcast so as to be available for reception by members of the public or of a section of the public; or

(b) distributed by means of an electronic communications network to members of the public or of a section of the public.

(9) This section does not restrict OFCOM's power to make any arrangements they consider to be incidental or conducive to the carrying out of any of their functions.

Amendments (Textual)

F18. Words in s. 14. (2) substituted (8.2.2007) by Wireless Telegraphy Act 2006 (c. 36), s. 126. (2), Sch. 7 para. 26

F19. S. 14. (6. A) inserted (1.10.2011) by Postal Services Act 2011 (c. 5), s. 93. (2)(3), Sch. 12 para. 58; S.I. 2011/2329, art. 3

Commencement Information

I22. S. 14 in force at 29.12.2003 by S.I. 2003/3142, art. 3. (1), Sch. 1 (with art. 11)

15. Duty to publish and take account of research

(1) It shall be the duty of OFCOM—

(a) to publish the results of any research carried out by them or on their behalf under section 14; and

(b) to consider and, to such extent as they think fit, to take account of the results of such research in the carrying out of their functions.

(2) OFCOM are not required under this section—

(a) to publish any matter that is confidential in accordance with subsection (3) or (4); or

(b) to publish anything that it would not be reasonably practicable to publish without disclosing such a matter.

(3) A matter is confidential under this subsection if—

(a) it relates specifically to the affairs of a particular body; and

(b) publication of that matter would or might, in OFCOM's opinion, seriously and prejudicially affect the interests of that body.

(4) A matter is confidential under this subsection if—

(a) it relates to the private affairs of an individual; and

(b) publication of that matter would or might, in OFCOM's opinion, seriously and prejudicially affect the interests of that individual.

(5) The publication of research under this section must be in such manner as OFCOM consider appropriate.

Commencement Information

I23. S. 15 in force at 29.12.2003 by S.I. 2003/3142, art. 3. (1), Sch. 1 (with art. 11)

16. Consumer consultation

(1) It shall be the duty of OFCOM to establish and maintain effective arrangements for consultation about the carrying out of their functions with—

(a) consumers in the markets for the services and facilities in relation to which OFCOM have functions;

(b) consumers in the markets for apparatus used in connection with any such services or facilities [F20. (other than postal services)] ;

(c) consumers in the markets for directories capable of being used in connection with the use of an electronic communications network or electronic communications service.

(2) The arrangements must include the establishment and maintenance of a panel of persons (in this Act referred to as "the Consumer Panel") with the function of advising both—

(a) OFCOM; and

(b) such other persons as the Panel think fit.

(3) The arrangements must secure that the matters about which the Consumer Panel are able to give advice include the interests of domestic and small business consumers in relation to the following matters—

(a) the provision of electronic communications networks;

(b) the provision and making available of the services and facilities mentioned in subsection (4);

(c) the supply of apparatus designed or adapted for use in connection with [F21a service or facility mentioned in subsection (4)(a) to (e)] ;

(d) the supply of directories capable of being used in connection with the use of an electronic communications network or electronic communications service;

(e) the financial and other terms on which [F22services or facilities mentioned in subsection (4)] are provided or made available, or on which such apparatus or such a directory is supplied;

(f) standards of service, quality and safety for such services, facilities, apparatus and directories;

(g) the handling of complaints made by persons who are consumers in the markets for such services, facilities, apparatus or directories to the persons who provide the services or make the facilities available, or who are suppliers of the apparatus or directories;

(h) the resolution of disputes between such consumers and the persons who provide such services or make such facilities available, or who are suppliers of such apparatus or directories;

(i) the provision of remedies and redress in respect of matters that form the subject-matter of such complaints or disputes;

(j) the information about service standards and the rights of consumers that is made available by persons who provide or make available such services or facilities, or who are suppliers of such apparatus or directories;

(k) any other matter appearing to the Panel to be necessary for securing effective protection for persons who are consumers in the markets for any such services, facilities, apparatus or directories.

(4) Those services and facilities are—

(a) electronic communications services;

(b) associated facilities;

(c) directory enquiry facilities;

(d) a service consisting in the supply of information for use in responding to directory enquiries or of an electronic programme guide; F23...

(e) every service or facility not falling within any of the preceding paragraphs which is provided or made available to members of the public—

(i) by means of an electronic communications network; and

(ii) in pursuance of agreements entered into between the person by whom the service or facility is provided or made available and each of those members of the public.

[F24. (f)postal services.]

(5) The matters about which the Consumer Panel are to be able to give advice do not include any matter that concerns the contents of anything which is or may be broadcast or otherwise transmitted by means of electronic communications networks.

(6) The arrangements made by OFCOM under this section must also secure that the Consumer Panel are able, in addition to giving advice on the matters mentioned in subsection (3), to do each of the following—

(a) at the request of OFCOM, to carry out research for OFCOM in relation to any of the matters in relation to which OFCOM have functions under section 14;

(b) to make arrangements for the carrying out of research into such other matters appearing to the Panel to be relevant to the carrying out of the Panel's functions as they think fit;

(c) to give advice to OFCOM in relation to any matter referred to the Panel by OFCOM for advice;

(d) to publish such information as the Panel think fit about the advice they give, about the carrying out of the Panel's other functions and about the results of research carried out by them or on their behalf.

(7) It shall be the duty of OFCOM, in the carrying out of their functions, to consider and, to such extent as they think appropriate, to have regard to—

(a) any advice given to OFCOM by the Consumer Panel; and

(b) any results notified to OFCOM of any research undertaken by that Panel.

(8) It shall also be the duty of OFCOM (subject to subsection (9))—

(a) to provide the Consumer Panel with all such information as, having regard, in particular, to the need to preserve commercial confidentiality, OFCOM consider appropriate to disclose to the Panel for the purpose of enabling the Panel to carry out their functions; and

(b) to provide the Panel with all such further information as the Panel may require.

(9) OFCOM are not required to provide information by virtue of subsection (8)(b) if, having regard to—

(a) the need to preserve commercial confidentiality, and

(b) any other matters that appear to OFCOM to be relevant,

it is reasonable for OFCOM to refuse to disclose it to the Panel.

(10) It shall be the duty of OFCOM, in the case of any advice or opinion received from and

published by the Panel which OFCOM propose to disregard in whole or in part, or with which OFCOM disagree in whole or in part—

(a) to ensure that the Panel know OFCOM's reasons for disregarding or disagreeing with the advice or opinion; and

(b) to ensure that those reasons are or have been published in such manner as OFCOM consider appropriate for bringing them to the attention of persons who are aware of the Panel's advice or opinion.

(11) The Consumer Panel must—

(a) as soon as practicable after the end of the period of twelve months beginning with the commencement of this section, and

(b) as soon as practicable after the end of each subsequent period of twelve months, prepare a report on the carrying out of their functions in that period.

(12) The Consumer Panel must publish each report—

(a) as soon as practicable after its preparation is complete; and

(b) in such manner as they consider appropriate.

(13) In this section—

"domestic and small business consumer" means a person who—

- is a consumer in the market for services or facilities mentioned in subsection (4) or for apparatus designed or adapted for use in connection with [F25a service or facility mentioned in subsection (4)(a) to (e)] ; but

- is neither—

a communications provider or a person who makes associated facilities available; nor

a person who is a consumer in the market in respect of an undertaking carried on by him for which more than ten individuals work (whether as employees or volunteers or otherwise);

"electronic programme guide" means a service which consists of—

- the listing or promotion, or both the listing and the promotion, of some or all of the programmes included in any one or more programme services the providers of which are or include persons other than the provider of the guide; and

- a facility for obtaining access, in whole or in part, to the programme service or services listed or promoted in the guide.

Amendments (Textual)

F20. Words in s. 16. (1)(b) inserted (1.10.2011) by Postal Services Act 2011 (c. 5), s. 93. (2)(3), Sch. 12 para. 59. (2); S.I. 2011/2329, art. 3

F21. Words in s. 16. (3)(c) substituted (1.10.2011) by Postal Services Act 2011 (c. 5), s. 93. (2)(3), Sch. 12 para. 59. (3)(a); S.I. 2011/2329, art. 3

F22. Words in s. 16. (3)(e) substituted (1.10.2011) by Postal Services Act 2011 (c. 5), s. 93. (2)(3), Sch. 12 para. 59. (3)(b); S.I. 2011/2329, art. 3

F23. Word in s. 16. (4)(d) omitted (1.10.2011) by virtue of Postal Services Act 2011 (c. 5), s. 93. (2)(3), Sch. 12 para. 59. (4)(a); S.I. 2011/2329, art. 3

F24. S. 16. (4)(f) inserted (1.10.2011) by Postal Services Act 2011 (c. 5), s. 93. (2)(3), Sch. 12 para. 59. (4)(b); S.I. 2011/2329, art. 3

F25. Words in s. 16. (13) substituted (1.10.2011) by Postal Services Act 2011 (c. 5), s. 93. (2)(3), Sch. 12 para. 59. (5); S.I. 2011/2329, art. 3

Commencement Information

I24. S. 16 in force at 29.12.2003 by S.I. 2003/3142, art. 3. (1), Sch. 1 (with art. 11)

17. Membership etc. of the Consumer Panel

(1) The members of the Consumer Panel shall be appointed by OFCOM and shall comprise a chairman and such other members as OFCOM may determine.

(2) The approval of the Secretary of State is required for the appointment of a person to be the chairman or to be another member of the Panel.

(3) In appointing persons to be members of the Consumer Panel, OFCOM must secure that, for each of the following parts of the United Kingdom—

(a) England,

(b) Scotland,

(c) Wales, and

(d) Northern Ireland,

there is a different member of the Panel capable of representing the interests and opinions of persons living in that part of the United Kingdom.

(4) In appointing persons to be members of the Consumer Panel, OFCOM must secure, so far as practicable, that the Panel are able to give informed advice about matters referable to each of the following—

(a) the interests of persons living in rural areas;

(b) the interests of persons living in urban areas;

(c) the interests of small businesses;

(d) the interests of disadvantaged persons, persons with low incomes and persons with disabilities; and

(e) the interests of the elderly.

[F26. (4. A) The Secretary of State may direct OFCOM to appoint as a member of the Consumer Panel a person specified by the Secretary of State who—

[F27. (a)is an employee of the National Association of Citizens Advice Bureaux ("Citizens Advice"), and

(b) is nominated for the purposes of this subsection by Citizens Advice after consultation with OFCOM.]

(4. B) Only one person may, at any time, be a member of the Consumer Panel appointed in accordance with a direction under subsection (4. A); but that does not prevent OFCOM appointing as a member of the Consumer Panel any person who is also [F28an employee of Citizens Advice]

.

[F29. (4. BA)The Secretary of State may direct OFCOM to appoint as a member of the Consumer Panel a person specified by the Secretary of State who—

(a) is an employee of the Scottish Association of Citizens Advice Bureaux ("Citizens Advice Scotland") Citizens Advice Scotland, and

(b) is nominated for the purposes of this subsection by Citizens Advice Scotland after consultation with OFCOM.

(4. BB)Only one person may, at any time, be a member of the Consumer Panel appointed in accordance with a direction under subsection (4. BA); but that does not prevent OFCOM appointing as a member of the Consumer Panel any person who is also an employee of Citizens Advice Scotland.]

[F30. (4. C)A person appointed in accordance with a direction under subsection (4. A) or (4. BA) ceases to be a member of the Consumer Panel—

(a) on ceasing to be an employee of Citizens Advice or, as the case may be, Citizens Advice Scotland, or

(b) if Citizens Advice or, as the case may be, Citizens Advice Scotland decide that the person is no longer to be on the Consumer Panel.]]

(5) The validity of any proceedings of the Consumer Panel shall not be affected by any failure by OFCOM to comply with [F31subsections (3) to (4. A)][F32and (4. BA)] .

(6) It shall be the duty of the Consumer Panel, in carrying out their functions, to have regard to the following interests—

(a) the interests of persons from the different parts of the United Kingdom; and

(b) the interests specified in subsection (4).

(7) A person shall be disqualified from being the chairman or a member of the Consumer Panel if he is a member or employee of OFCOM.

(8) The chairman and every member of the Consumer Panel—

(a) shall be appointed for a fixed period specified in the terms of his appointment but shall be eligible for re-appointment at the end of that period; and

(b) may at any time be removed from the Panel by a notice given by OFCOM with the approval of the Secretary of State.

(9) OFCOM may pay to the chairman and to any other member of the Consumer Panel such remuneration and allowances as OFCOM consider appropriate.

Amendments (Textual)

F26. S. 17. (4. A)-(4. C) inserted (21.12.2007) by Consumers, Estate Agents and Redress Act 2007 (c. 17), ss. 40. (a), 66. (2) (with s. 6. (9)); S.I. 2007/3546, art. 3, Sch.

F27. S. 17. (4. A)(a)(b) substituted (1.4.2014) by The Public Bodies (Abolition of the National Consumer Council and Transfer of the Office of Fair Trading's Functions in relation to Estate Agents etc) Order 2014 (S.I. 2014/631), art. 1. (3), Sch. 1 para. 11. (2)(a) (with Sch. 1 para. 28, Sch. 2 paras. 13-15)

F28. Words in s. 17. (4. B) substituted (1.4.2014) by The Public Bodies (Abolition of the National Consumer Council and Transfer of the Office of Fair Trading's Functions in relation to Estate Agents etc) Order 2014 (S.I. 2014/631), art. 1. (3), Sch. 1 para. 11. (2)(b) (with Sch. 1 para. 28, Sch. 2 paras. 13-15)

F29. S. 17. (4. BA)(4. BB) inserted (1.4.2014) by The Public Bodies (Abolition of the National Consumer Council and Transfer of the Office of Fair Trading's Functions in relation to Estate Agents etc) Order 2014 (S.I. 2014/631), art. 1. (3), Sch. 1 para. 11. (2)(c) (with Sch. 1 para. 28, Sch. 2 paras. 13-15)

F30. S. 17. (4. C) substituted (1.4.2014) by The Public Bodies (Abolition of the National Consumer Council and Transfer of the Office of Fair Trading's Functions in relation to Estate Agents etc) Order 2014 (S.I. 2014/631), art. 1. (3), Sch. 1 para. 11. (2)(d) (with Sch. 1 para. 28, Sch. 2 paras. 13-15)

F31. Words in s. 17. (5) substituted (21.12.2007) by Consumers, Estate Agents and Redress Act 2007 (c. 17), ss. 40. (b), 66. (2) (with s. 6. (9)); S.I. 2007/3546, art. 3, Sch.

F32. Words in s. 17. (5) inserted (1.4.2014) by The Public Bodies (Abolition of the National Consumer Council and Transfer of the Office of Fair Trading's Functions in relation to Estate Agents etc) Order 2014 (S.I. 2014/631), art. 1. (3), Sch. 1 para. 11. (2)(e) (with Sch. 1 para. 28, Sch. 2 paras. 13-15)

Commencement Information

I25. S. 17 in force at 29.12.2003 by S.I. 2003/3142, art. 3. (1), Sch. 1 (with art. 11)

18. Committees and other procedure of the Consumer Panel

(1) The Consumer Panel may make such arrangements as they think fit for committees established by the Panel to give advice to them about matters relating to the carrying out of the Panel's functions.

(2) The Consumer Panel may make such other arrangements for regulating their own procedure, and for regulating the procedure of the committees established by them, as they think fit.

(3) Those arrangements may include arrangements as to quorums and as to the making of decisions by a majority.

(4) The committees established by the Panel may include committees the membership of which includes persons (including persons constituting a majority of the committee) who are not members of the Panel.

(5) The membership of every committee established by the Consumer Panel must contain at least one person who is a member of the Panel.

(6) Where a person who is not a member of the Consumer Panel is a member of a committee established by the Panel, OFCOM may pay to that person such remuneration and expenses as OFCOM may determine.

Commencement Information

I26. S. 18 in force at 29.12.2003 by S.I. 2003/3142, art. 3. (1), Sch. 1 (with art. 11)

19. Power to amend remit of Consumer Panel

(1) The Secretary of State may by order modify subsection (3) of section 16 so as to add to the matters about which the Consumer Panel are required to be able to give advice.

(2) Before making an order under this section the Secretary of State must consult OFCOM and such other persons as he thinks fit.

(3) No order is to be made containing provision authorised by this section unless a draft of the order has been laid before Parliament and approved by a resolution of each House.

(4) The power to amend or revoke an order under this section does not include power to provide for a matter to cease to be a matter about which the Consumer Panel are required to be able to give advice.

Commencement Information

I27. S. 19 in force at 29.12.2003 by S.I. 2003/3142, art. 3. (1), Sch. 1 (with art. 11)

Advisory committees

20. Advisory committees for different parts of the United Kingdom

(1) It shall be the duty of OFCOM, in accordance with the following provisions of this section, to exercise their powers under paragraph 14 of the Schedule to the Office of Communications Act 2002 (c. 11) (committees of OFCOM) to establish and maintain a committee for each of the following parts of the United Kingdom—

  (a) England;
  (b) Wales;
  (c) Scotland; and
  (d) Northern Ireland.

(2) Each committee shall consist of—

  (a) a chairman appointed by OFCOM; and
  (b) such number of other members appointed by OFCOM as OFCOM think fit.

(3) In appointing a person in accordance with this section to be a member of a committee, OFCOM must have regard to the desirability of ensuring that the person appointed is able to represent the interests and opinions, in relation to communications matters, of persons living in the part of the United Kingdom for which the committee has been established.

(4) The function of each committee shall be to provide advice to OFCOM (including other committees established by OFCOM) about the interests and opinions, in relation to communications matters, of persons living in the part of the United Kingdom for which the committee has been established.

(5) A committee established under this section may also, at the request of the Consumer Panel, provide advice about those interests and opinions to the Consumer Panel.

(6) The consent of OFCOM is required for the giving of advice under subsection (5).

(7) In this section "communications matters" has the same meaning as in section 3.

Commencement Information

I28. S. 20 in force at 29.12.2003 by S.I. 2003/3142, art. 3. (1), Sch. 1 (with art. 11)

21. Advisory committee on elderly and disabled persons

(1) It shall be the duty of OFCOM, in accordance with the following provisions of this section, to exercise their powers under paragraph 14 of the Schedule to the Office of Communications Act

2002 (c. 11) (committees of OFCOM) to establish and maintain a committee to provide the advice specified in this section.

(2) The committee shall consist of—

    (a) a chairman appointed by OFCOM; and

    (b) such number of other members appointed by OFCOM as OFCOM think fit.

(3) In appointing persons to be members of the committee, OFCOM must have regard to the desirability of ensuring that the members of the committee include—

    (a) persons who are familiar with the needs of the elderly; and

    (b) persons who are familiar with the needs of persons with disabilities.

(4) The function of the committee shall be to provide advice to OFCOM (including other committees established by OFCOM) about the interests, in relation to communications matters, of—

    (a) the elderly; and

    (b) persons with disabilities.

(5) The committee may also, at the request of the Consumer Panel, provide advice about those interests to the Consumer Panel.

(6) The consent of OFCOM is required for the giving of advice under subsection (5).

(7) In this section "communications matters" has the same meaning as in section 3.

Commencement Information

I29. S. 21 in force at 29.12.2003 by S.I. 2003/3142, art. 3. (1), Sch. 1 (with art. 11)

International matters

22. Representation on international and other bodies

(1) It shall be the duty of OFCOM to do, as respects the United Kingdom, such of the following things as they are required to do by the Secretary of State—

    (a) provide representation on behalf of Her Majesty's Government in the United Kingdom on international and other bodies having communications functions;

    (b) become or serve as a member of an international or other body having such functions;

    (c) subscribe to such a body;

    (d) provide representation on behalf of Her Majesty's Government in the United Kingdom at international meetings about communications.

(2) OFCOM shall also have the power, if requested to do so by the Secretary of State, to do one or more of those things as respects any of the Channel Islands, the Isle of Man or a British overseas territory.

(3) It shall be the duty of OFCOM to carry out their functions under this section in accordance with such general or specific directions as may be given to them by the Secretary of State.

(4) The Secretary of State—

    (a) is not entitled to direct OFCOM to comply with a request made under subsection (2); but

    (b) may give directions about how OFCOM are to carry out any representative role that they undertake in accordance with such a request.

(5) In this section—

"communications functions" means—

    - functions relating to the use of the electro-magnetic spectrum for wireless telegraphy;

    - functions relating to the regulation of television or radio broadcasting or the provision of television and radio services ; F33...

    - [F34functions relating to postal services; and]

    - any other function which relates to, or is connected with, a matter in respect of which OFCOM have functions;

"international meetings about communications" means international meetings relating to, or to matters connected with, one or more of the following—

   - the use of the electro-magnetic spectrum for wireless telegraphy;

   - the regulation of television or radio broadcasting or of the provision of television and radio services;

   - [F35the regulation of postal services;]

   - any other matter in respect of which OFCOM have functions.

(6) In relation to—

   (a) a part of the British Islands outside the United Kingdom, or

   (b) a British overseas territory,

the references in subsection (5) to matters in respect of which OFCOM have functions include references to matters corresponding, in the case of that part of those Islands or of that territory, to matters in respect of which OFCOM's functions are confined to the United Kingdom.

(7) In subsection (5) "television or radio broadcasting" includes the provision by means other than broadcasting of services similar to those provided by television or radio broadcasts.

Amendments (Textual)

F33. Word in s. 22. (5) omitted (1.10.2011) by virtue of Postal Services Act 2011 (c. 5), s. 93. (2)(3), Sch. 12 para. 60. (2); S.I. 2011/2329, art. 3

F34. Words in s. 22. (5) inserted (1.10.2011) by virtue of Postal Services Act 2011 (c. 5), s. 93. (2)(3), Sch. 12 para. 60. (2); S.I. 2011/2329, art. 3

F35. Words in s. 22. (5) inserted (1.10.2011) by Postal Services Act 2011 (c. 5), s. 93. (2)(3), Sch. 12 para. 60. (3); S.I. 2011/2329, art. 3

Commencement Information

I30. S. 22 in force at 29.12.2003 by S.I. 2003/3142, art. 3. (1), Sch. 1 (with art. 11)

23. Directions for international purposes in respect of broadcasting functions

(1) This section applies to—

   (a) OFCOM's functions under the enactments relating to broadcasting; and

   (b) the matters in relation to which those functions are conferred.

(2) It shall be the duty of OFCOM—

   (a) to carry out those functions in accordance with any general or specific directions given to them by the Secretary of State for the purpose mentioned in subsection (3); and

   (b) to carry out such other functions in relation to the matters to which this this section applies as they are required to carry out by any general or specific directions so given.

(3) The Secretary of State is not to give a direction under this section except for the purpose of securing compliance, in relation to a matter to which this section applies, with an international obligation of the United Kingdom.

(4) A direction under this section must be contained in an order made by the Secretary of State.

(5) In this section "the enactments relating to broadcasting" means—

   (a) the 1990 Act;

   (b) the 1996 Act;

   (c) Part 3 of this Act; and

   (d) the other provisions of this Act so far as relating to the 1990 Act, the 1996 Act or that Part.

Commencement Information

I31. S. 23 in force at 29.12.2003 by S.I. 2003/3142, art. 3. (1), Sch. 1 (with art. 11)

General information functions

24. Provision of information to the Secretary of State

(1) It shall be the duty of OFCOM to comply with a direction by the Secretary of State to provide him with information falling within subsection (2).

(2) The information that may be the subject of a direction under this section is any information reasonably required by the Secretary of State for the purpose of enabling him to secure compliance with an international obligation of the United Kingdom.

(3) Information that is required to be provided by a direction under this section must be provided in such manner and at such times as may be required by the direction.

Commencement Information

I32. S. 24 in force at 25.7.2003 for specified purposes by S.I. 2003/1900, arts. 1. (2), 2. (1), Sch. 1 (with art. 3) (as amended by S.I. 2003/3142, art. 1. (3))

I33. S. 24 in force at 29.12.2003 in so far as not already in force by S.I. 2003/3142, art. 3. (2) (with art. 11)

25. Community requirement to provide information

(1) This section applies if—

(a) the European Commission requires OFCOM to provide it with information for the purpose of enabling it to perform any of its functions in relation to electronic communications networks, electronic communications services or associated facilities; and

(b) the information is information obtained by OFCOM in the course of carrying out any of their functions under—

(i) Part 2; or

(ii) the enactments relating to the management of the radio spectrum that are not contained in that Part.

(2) It shall be the duty of OFCOM to comply with the requirement.

(3) If information provided to the European Commission under this section has been obtained by OFCOM from a person who is or, at the time the information was obtained from him, was—

(a) a communications provider, or

(b) a person making associated facilities available,

OFCOM must notify him that they have provided the information to the Commission.

(4) It shall be for OFCOM to determine the manner in which a notification is given under subsection (3).

Commencement Information

I34. S. 25 in force at 25.7.2003 for specified purposes by S.I. 2003/1900, arts. 1. (2), 2. (1), Sch. 1 (with art. 3) (as amended by S.I. 2003/3142, art. 1. (3))

I35. S. 25 in force at 29.12.2003 in so far as not already in force by S.I. 2003/3142, art. 3. (2) (with art. 11)

26. Publication of information and advice for consumers etc.

(1) OFCOM [F36must] arrange for the publication of such information and advice about matters in relation to which they have functions as it appears to them to be appropriate to make available to the persons mentioned in subsection (2).

(2) Those persons are—

(a) the customers of communications providers;

(b) the customers of persons who make associated facilities available;

[F37. (ba)any person affected by the application of the electronic communications code (within the meaning of section 106. (1));]

(c) persons who use electronic communications networks, electronic communications services or associated facilities; F38...

(d) persons to whom radio and television services are provided or who are otherwise able or likely to take advantage of any of those services.

[F39. (e)the customers of persons who provide postal services.]

[F40. (2. A)In subsection (2)(e) the reference to customers of persons who provide postal services includes—

(a) persons who wish to be provided with such services,

(b) persons who are likely to seek to be provided with such services, and

(c) addressees.]

(3) In arranging for the publication of information or advice under this section, OFCOM must have regard to the need to exclude from publication, so far as that is practicable, the matters which are confidential in accordance with subsections (4) and (5).

(4) A matter is confidential under this subsection if—

(a) it relates specifically to the affairs of a particular body; and

(b) publication of that matter would or might, in OFCOM's opinion, seriously and prejudicially affect the interests of that body.

(5) A matter is confidential under this subsection if—

(a) it relates to the private affairs of an individual; and

(b) publication of that matter would or might, in OFCOM's opinion, seriously and prejudicially affect the interests of that individual.

(6) The publication of information or advice under this section must be in such manner as OFCOM consider appropriate.

Amendments (Textual)

F36. Word in s. 26. (1) substituted (26.5.2011) by The Electronic Communications and Wireless Telegraphy Regulations 2011 (S.I. 2011/1210), reg. 1. (2), Sch. 1 para. 8. (a) (with Sch. 3 para. 2)

F37. S. 26. (2)(ba) inserted (26.5.2011) by The Electronic Communications and Wireless Telegraphy Regulations 2011 (S.I. 2011/1210), reg. 1. (2), Sch. 1 para. 8. (b) (with Sch. 3 para. 2)

F38. Word in s. 26. (2)(c) omitted (1.10.2011) by virtue of Postal Services Act 2011 (c. 5), s. 93. (2)(3), Sch. 12 para. 61. (2)(a); S.I. 2011/2329, art. 3

F39. S. 26. (2)(e) inserted (1.10.2011) by Postal Services Act 2011 (c. 5), s. 93. (2)(3), Sch. 12 para. 61. (2)(b); S.I. 2011/2329, art. 3

F40. S. 26. (2. A) inserted (1.10.2011) by Postal Services Act 2011 (c. 5), s. 93. (2)(3), Sch. 12 para. 61. (3); S.I. 2011/2329, art. 3

Commencement Information

I36. S. 26. (1)(2)(a)-(c)(3)-(6) in force at 25.7.2003 for specified purposes by S.I. 2003/1900, arts. 1. (2), 2. (1), Sch. 1 (with art. 3) (as amended by S.I. 2003/3142, art. 1. (3))

I37. S. 26. (1) (2)(a)-(c) (3)-(6) in force at 29.12.2003 in so far as not already in force by S.I. 2003/3142, art. 3. (1), Sch. 1 (with art. 11)

I38. S. 26. (2)(d) in force at 29.12.2003 by S.I. 2003/3142, art. 3. (1), Sch. 1 (with art. 11)

Employment in broadcasting

27. Training and equality of opportunity

(1) It shall be the duty of OFCOM to take all such steps as they consider appropriate for promoting the development of opportunities for the training and retraining of persons—

(a) for employment by persons providing television and radio services; and

(b) for work in connection with the provision of such services otherwise than as an employee.

(2) It shall be the duty of OFCOM to take all such steps as they consider appropriate for promoting equality of opportunity in relation to both—

(a) employment by those providing television and radio services; and

(b) the training and retraining of persons for such employment.

(3) It shall also be the duty of OFCOM, in relation to such employment, training and retraining, to

take all such steps as they consider appropriate for promoting the equalisation of opportunities for disabled persons.

(4) The reference in subsection (2) to equality of opportunity is a reference to equality of opportunity—

(a) between men and women; and

(b) between persons of different racial groups.

(5) In this section—

"disabled" has the same meaning as in [F41the Equality Act 2010 or, in Northern Ireland,] the Disability Discrimination Act 1995 (c. 50);

"racial group" has the same meaning as in the [F42. Race Relations Act 1976 (c. 74)] [F42. Equality Act 2010] or, in Northern Ireland, the Race Relations (Northern Ireland) Order 1997 (S.I. 1997/869 (N.I. 6)).

(6) The Secretary of State may by order amend subsection (4) by adding any other form of equality of opportunity that he considers appropriate.

(7) No order is to be made containing provision authorised by subsection (6) unless a draft of the order has been laid before Parliament and approved by a resolution of each House.

Amendments (Textual)

F41. Words in s. 27. (5) inserted by 2010 c. 15, Sch. 26 Pt. 1 para. 54. (a) (as inserted (E.W.S.) (1.10.2010) by The Equality Act 2010 (Consequential Amendments, Saving and Supplementary Provisions) Order 2010 (S.I. 2010/2279), art. 1. (2), Sch. 1 para. 5) (see S.I. 2010/2317, art. 2)

F42. Words in s. 27. (5) substituted by 2010 c. 15, Sch. 26 Pt. 1 para. 54. (b) (as inserted (E.W.S.) (1.10.2010) by The Equality Act 2010 (Consequential Amendments, Saving and Supplementary Provisions) Order 2010 (S.I. 2010/2279), art. 1. (2), Sch. 1 para. 5) (see S.I. 2010/2317, art. 2)

Commencement Information

I39. S. 27 in force at 29.12.2003 by S.I. 2003/3142, art. 3. (1), Sch. 1 (with art. 11)

Charging

28. General power to charge for services

(1) OFCOM may provide a service to which this section applies to any person on such terms as to the making of payments to OFCOM—

(a) as they may determine in advance; or

(b) as may be agreed between that person and OFCOM.

(2) This section applies to a service which is provided by OFCOM to a person in the course of carrying out their functions and is neither—

(a) a service which OFCOM are under a duty to provide to that person; nor

(b) one in respect of which express provision is made by or under an enactment for authorising or forbidding the payment of fees or charges.

(3) In this section references to providing a service to a person include references to a service consisting in—

(a) the giving of advice to that person;

(b) the entry of his particulars in a register or other record kept by OFCOM otherwise than in pursuance of an express statutory duty to keep the register or record; or

(c) the taking of steps for the purposes of determining whether to grant an application for an entry in a register or record so kept.

Commencement Information

I40. S. 28 in force at 18.9.2003 by S.I. 2003/1900, art. 2. (2), Sch. 2

Guarantees

29. Secretary of State guarantees for OFCOM borrowing

(1) The Secretary of State may guarantee—
    (a) the repayment of the principal of any borrowing by OFCOM;
    (b) the payment of interest on any such borrowing; and
    (c) the discharge of other financial obligations incurred by OFCOM in connection with any such borrowing.
(2) The power of the Secretary of State to give a guarantee under this section is a power (subject to subsection (3)) to give it in such manner and on such conditions as he thinks fit.
(3) The Secretary of State must not give a guarantee under this section if the aggregate of—
    (a) the amounts that he may be required to pay for fulfilling that guarantee, and
    (b) the amounts that he may be required to pay for fulfilling other guarantees previously given under this section and still in force,
exceeds £5 million.
(4) The Secretary of State may by order substitute another amount for the amount for the time being specified in subsection (3).
(5) No order is to be made containing provision authorised by subsection (4) unless a draft of the order has been laid before Parliament and approved by a resolution of the House of Commons.
(6) Immediately after a guarantee is given under this section, the Secretary of State must lay a statement of the guarantee before each House of Parliament.
(7) Where any sum is paid by the Secretary of State under a guarantee given under this section, he must lay a statement relating to that sum before each House of Parliament as soon as practicable after the end of each of the financial years—
    (a) beginning with the one in which the sum is paid; and
    (b) ending with the one in which OFCOM's liabilities under subsection (8) in respect of that sum are finally discharged.
(8) If sums are paid by the Secretary of State in fulfilment of a guarantee given under this section OFCOM must pay him—
    (a) such amounts in or towards the repayment to him of those sums as he may direct; and
    (b) interest, at such rates as he may determine, on amounts outstanding under this subsection.
(9) Payments to the Secretary of State under subsection (8) must be made at such times and in such manner as he may determine.
Commencement Information
I41. S. 29 in force at 18.9.2003 by S.I. 2003/1900, art. 2. (2), Sch. 2

Provisions supplemental to transfer of functions

30. Transfers of property etc. from pre-commencement regulators

(1) The Secretary of State may, by a direction to any of the pre-commencement regulators, require that regulator to make one or more schemes for the transfer from that regulator to OFCOM of such of the regulator's property, rights and liabilities as may be specified or described in the direction.
(2) Where a pre-commencement regulator is required to make a scheme, the scheme must be made by such date as may be specified in the direction.
(3) Before making a scheme in pursuance of a direction under subsection (1), a pre-commencement regulator must consult OFCOM.
(4) A pre-commencement regulator who makes a scheme in pursuance of a direction under subsection (1) shall submit that scheme to the Secretary of State for approval.

(5) A scheme that is required to be so submitted shall have effect only if, and to the extent that, it is approved by the Secretary of State.

(6) The Secretary of State, in approving a scheme, may do so subject to such modifications as he thinks fit.

(7) Where the Secretary of State approves a scheme subject to modifications specified by him, it shall have effect with those modifications.

(8) A scheme approved by the Secretary of State under this section shall come into force either—

(a) if no time is appointed under paragraph (b), at the time when the approval is given; or

(b) if the Secretary of State appoints a later time for the coming into force of the scheme (whether when approving the scheme or by subsequently varying a time appointed under this paragraph), at that later time.

(9) Where a scheme is submitted to the Secretary of State under this section, he must—

(a) consult OFCOM about any proposal of his to approve the scheme; and

(b) consult both OFCOM and the pre-commencement regulator in question about any modifications subject to which he proposes to give his approval, or about any proposal of his to refuse approval.

(10) The Secretary of State may, after consulting OFCOM, himself make a scheme for the transfer of property, rights and liabilities—

(a) from a pre-commencement regulator to OFCOM; or

(b) from himself to OFCOM;

and such a scheme shall come into force on such day as the Secretary of State may appoint (whether in the scheme or subsequently).

(11) The Secretary of State is not to make a scheme for the transfer of property, rights and liabilities from a pre-commencement regulator to OFCOM unless—

(a) that regulator has failed to comply with a direction under subsection (1); or

(b) that regulator has complied with such a direction by submitting a scheme to the Secretary of State that he has decided not to approve (with or without modifications).

(12) Schedule 2 (which makes further provision about schemes under this section) shall have effect.

Commencement Information

I42. S. 30 in force at 18.9.2003 by S.I. 2003/1900, art. 2. (2), Sch. 2

31. Transitional functions and abolition of pre-commencement regulators

(1) It shall be the duty of the pre-commencement regulators to take all such steps as are necessary or expedient for ensuring that OFCOM are able effectively to carry out OFCOM's functions from the time when they are vested in OFCOM.

(2) The pre-commencement regulators, in taking those steps, must comply with every direction given to them by the Secretary of State.

(3) The pre-commencement regulators and OFCOM shall each have a duty to provide the Secretary of State with all such information and assistance as he may require for the purposes of, or in connection with—

(a) his power to give directions under subsection (1) of section 30; and

(b) his powers and duties in relation to the approval and making of schemes under that section.

(4) On such day as the Secretary of State may by order appoint—

(a) the office of the Director General of Telecommunications shall be abolished; and

(b) the Broadcasting Standards Commission, the Independent Television Commission and the Radio Authority shall cease to exist.

(5) Section 54 of the Telecommunications Act 1984 (c. 12) (which provides for the establishment of advisory bodies) shall cease to have effect; and each of the bodies established under that section shall cease to exist on such day as the Secretary of State may by order appoint.

(6) Different days may be appointed under this section for the Director General of Telecommunications and for each of the different bodies mentioned in subsections (4)(b) and (5). Commencement Information

I43. S. 31 partly in force; s. 31. (1)(2)(3)(4)(6) in force at Royal Assent see s. 411. (3)

I44. S. 31. (5) in force at 29.12.2003 by S.I. 2003/3142, art. 3. (1), Sch. 1 (with art. 11)

Part 2. Networks, services and the radio spectrum

Part 2. Networks, services and the radio spectrum

Chapter 1. Electronic communications networks and services

32. Meaning of electronic communications networks and services

(1) In this Act "electronic communications network" means—

(a) a transmission system for the conveyance, by the use of electrical, magnetic or electro-magnetic energy, of signals of any description; and

(b) such of the following as are used, by the person providing the system and in association with it, for the conveyance of the signals—

(i) apparatus comprised in the system;

(ii) apparatus used for the switching or routing of the signals; F1...

(iii) software and stored data[F2; and

(iv) (except for the purposes of sections 125 to 127) other resources, including network elements which are not active.]

(2) In this Act "electronic communications service" means a service consisting in, or having as its principal feature, the conveyance by means of an electronic communications network of signals, except in so far as it is a content service.

[F3. (3)In this Act "associated facility" means a facility, element or service which is available for use, or has the potential to be used, in association with the use of an electronic communications network or electronic communications service (whether or not one provided by the person making the facility, element or service available) for the purpose of—

(a) making the provision of that network or service possible;

(b) making possible the provision of other services provided by means of that network or service; or

(c) supporting the provision of such other services.]

(4) In this Act—

(a) references to the provision of an electronic communications network include references to its establishment, maintenance or operation;

(b) references, where one or more persons are employed or engaged to provide the network or service under the direction or control of another person, to the person by whom an electronic communications network or electronic communications service is provided are confined to references to that other person; and

(c) references, where one or more persons are employed or engaged to make facilities available under the direction or control of another person, to the person by whom any associated facilities are made available are confined to references to that other person.

(5) Paragraphs (a) and (b) of subsection (4) apply in relation to references in subsection (1) to the provision of a transmission system as they apply in relation to references in this Act to the provision of an electronic communications network.

(6) The reference in subsection (1) to a transmission system includes a reference to a transmission system consisting of no more than a transmitter used for the conveyance of signals.

(7) In subsection (2) "a content service" means so much of any service as consists in one or both of the following—

(a) the provision of material with a view to its being comprised in signals conveyed by means of an electronic communications network;

(b) the exercise of editorial control over the contents of signals conveyed by means of a such a network.

(8) In this section references to the conveyance of signals include references to the transmission or routing of signals or of parts of signals and to the broadcasting of signals for general reception.

(9) For the purposes of this section the cases in which software and stored data are to be taken as being used for a particular purpose include cases in which they—

(a) have been installed or stored in order to be used for that purpose; and

(b) are available to be so used.

(10) In this section "signal" includes—

(a) anything comprising speech, music, sounds, visual images or communications or data of any description; and

(b) signals serving for the impartation of anything between persons, between a person and a thing or between things, or for the actuation or control of apparatus.

Amendments (Textual)

F1. Word in s. 32. (1)(b)(ii) omitted (26.5.2011) by virtue of The Electronic Communications and Wireless Telegraphy Regulations 2011 (S.I. 2011/1210), reg. 1. (2), Sch. 1 para. 9. (a)(i) (with Sch. 3 para. 2)

F2. S. 32. (1)(b)(iv) and word inserted (26.5.2011) by The Electronic Communications and Wireless Telegraphy Regulations 2011 (S.I. 2011/1210), reg. 1. (2), Sch. 1 para. 9. (a)(ii) (with Sch. 3 para. 2)

F3. S. 32. (3) substituted (26.5.2011) by The Electronic Communications and Wireless Telegraphy Regulations 2011 (S.I. 2011/1210), reg. 1. (2), Sch. 1 para. 9. (b) (with Sch. 3 para. 2)

Commencement Information

I1. S. 32 in force at 25.7.2003 for specified purposes by S.I. 2003/1900, arts. 1. (2), 2. (1), Sch. 1 (with art. 3) (as amended by S.I. 2003/3142, art. 1. (3))

I2. S. 32 in force at 29.12.2003 in so far as not already in force by S.I. 2003/3142, art. 3. (2) (with art. 11)

Notification by providers

33. Advance notification to OFCOM

(1) A person shall not—

(a) provide a designated electronic communications network,

(b) provide a designated electronic communications service, or

(c) make available a designated associated facility,

unless, before beginning to provide it or to make it available, he has given a notification to OFCOM of his intention to provide that network or service, or to make that facility available.

(2) An electronic communications network, electronic communications service or associated facility is designated for the purposes of this section if it is of a description of networks, services or facilities that is for the time being designated by OFCOM as a description of networks, services or facilities for which notification under this section is required.

(3) A person who has given a notification for the purposes of subsection (1) must, before—

(a) providing or making available the notified network, service or facility with any significant differences, or

(b) ceasing to provide it or to make it available,

give a notification to OFCOM of the differences or (as the case may be) of his intention to cease to provide the network or service or to make the facility available.

(4) A notification for the purposes of this section must—

(a) be sent to OFCOM in such manner as OFCOM may require; and

(b) contain all such information as OFCOM may require.

(5) The only information OFCOM may require a notification to contain is—

(a) a declaration of the relevant proposal of the person giving the notification;

(b) the time when it is intended that effect should be given to the relevant proposal;

(c) particulars identifying the person giving the notification;

(d) particulars identifying one or more persons with addresses in the United Kingdom who, for the purposes of matters relating to the notified network, service or facility, are authorised to accept service at an address in the United Kingdom on behalf of the person giving the notification;

(e) particulars identifying one or more persons who may be contacted if there is an emergency that is caused by or affects the provision of the notified network, service or facility;

(f) addresses and other particulars necessary for effecting service on or contacting each of the persons mentioned in paragraphs (c) to (e).

(6) The declaration of the relevant proposal that may be required under subsection (5) is whichever of the following is appropriate in the case of the person giving the notification—

(a) a declaration of his proposal to provide the network or service described in the notification or to make available the facility so described;

(b) a declaration of his proposal to make the modifications that are so described of the network, service or facility specified in the notification; or

(c) a declaration of his proposal to cease to provide the network or service so specified or to cease to make available the facility so specified.

(7) Requirements imposed under subsection (4) are not to require a notification by a person to contain particulars falling within subsection (5)(d) in a case in which—

(a) that person is resident in a member State or has a place of business in a member State;

(b) the notification contains a statement under subsection (8);

(c) the notification sets out an address in a member State at which service will be accepted by the person who, in accordance with that statement, is authorised to accept it; and

(d) OFCOM are satisfied that adequate arrangements exist for effecting service on that person at that address.

(8) That statement is one which—

(a) declares that the person authorised, for the purposes of matters relating to the notified network, service or facilities, to accept service on behalf of the person giving the notification is that person himself; or

(b) identifies another person who is resident in a member State, or has a place of business in such State, as the person so authorised.

(9) The reference in subsection (3) to providing or making available a notified network, service or facility with significant differences is a reference to continuing to provide it, or to make it available, after a change in whatever falling within subsection (5)(a) to (f) was last notified to OFCOM under this section.

(10) References in this section to accepting service at an address are references—

(a) to accepting service of documents or process at that address; or

(b) otherwise to receiving notifications at that address;

and the reference in subsection (7) to effecting service at an address is to be construed accordingly.

(11) Where a description of electronic communications network, electronic communications service or associated facility is designated for the purposes of this section at a time when a network, service or facility of that description is already being provided or made available by a person—

(a) that person's obligation under this section to give a notification before beginning to provide or make available that network, service or facility shall have effect as an obligation to give a notification within such period after the coming into force of the designation as may be specified in the notice in which the designation is contained; and

(b) that notification is to be one stating that that person is already providing the network or service, or making the facility available (rather than that it is his intention to do so).

(12) Subsection (11) has effect subject to any transitional provision—

    (a) which is contained in the notification setting out the designation; and

    (b) treats a person as having given the notification required by that subsection.

Commencement Information

13. S. 33 in force at 25.7.2003 for specified purposes by S.I. 2003/1900, arts. 1. (2), 2. (1), Sch. 1 (with art. 3) (as amended by S.I. 2003/3142, art. 1. (3))

14. S. 33 in force at 29.12.2003 in so far as not already in force by S.I. 2003/3142, art. 3. (2) (with art. 11)

34. Designations and requirements for the purposes of s. 33.

(1) Before—

    (a) making or withdrawing a designation for the purposes of section 33, or

    (b) imposing or modifying a requirement under subsection (4) of that section,

OFCOM must consult such of the persons who, in their opinion, are likely to be affected by it as they think fit.

(2) Before making or withdrawing a designation for the purposes of section 33 OFCOM must also consult the Secretary of State.

(3) The way in which a designation for the purposes of section 33 or a requirement under subsection (4) of that section—

    (a) is to be made or imposed, or

    (b) may be withdrawn or modified,

is by a notice published in such manner as OFCOM consider appropriate for bringing the designation, requirement, withdrawal or modification to the attention of the persons who, in their opinion, are likely to be affected by it.

(4) A designation for the purposes of section 33 may be framed by reference to any such description of networks, services or facilities, or such other factors, as OFCOM think fit.

(5) Requirements imposed under section 33. (4) may make different provision for different cases.

Commencement Information

15. S. 34 in force at 25.7.2003 for specified purposes by S.I. 2003/1900, arts. 1. (2), 2. (1), Sch. 1 (with art. 3) (as amended by S.I. 2003/3142, art. 1. (3))

16. S. 34 in force at 29.12.2003 in so far as not already in force by S.I. 2003/3142, art. 3. (2) (with art. 11)

35. Notification of contraventions of s. 33.

(1) Where OFCOM determine that there are reasonable grounds for believing that a person has contravened section 33, they may give him a notification under this section.

(2) A notification under this section is one which—

    (a) sets out the determination made by OFCOM; F4...

    [F5. (b)specifies the contravention in respect of which the determination has been made;

    (c) specifies the period during which the person notified has an opportunity to make representations;

    (d) specifies information to be provided by the person to OFCOM; and

    (e) specifies any penalty which OFCOM are minded to impose in accordance with section 35. A.]

F6. (3). . . . .

F6. (4). . . . .

F6. (5). . . . .

F6. (6). . . . .

F6. (7). . . . .

(8) A notification under this section—

    (a) may be given in respect of more than one contravention of section 33; and

    (b) if it is given in respect of a continuing contravention, may be given in respect of any period during which the contravention has continued.

(9) Where a notification under this section has been given to a person in respect of a contravention

of section 33, OFCOM may give a further notification in respect of the same contravention if, and only if—

(a) the subsequent notification is in respect of so much of a period during which the contravention in question was continuing as falls after a period to which the earlier notification relates; or

(b) the earlier notification has been withdrawn without a penalty having been imposed by reference to the notified contravention.

F7. (10). . . . .

Amendments (Textual)

F4. Word in s. 35. (2)(a) omitted (26.5.2011) by virtue of The Electronic Communications and Wireless Telegraphy Regulations 2011 (S.I. 2011/1210), reg. 1. (2), Sch. 1 para. 10. (a) (with Sch. 3 paras. 2, 3)

F5. S. 35. (2)(b)-(e) substituted for s. 35. (2)(b) (26.5.2011) by The Electronic Communications and Wireless Telegraphy Regulations 2011 (S.I. 2011/1210), reg. 1. (2), Sch. 1 para. 10. (a) (with Sch. 3 paras. 2, 3)

F6. S. 35. (3)-(7) omitted (26.5.2011) by virtue of The Electronic Communications and Wireless Telegraphy Regulations 2011 (S.I. 2011/1210), reg. 1. (2), Sch. 1 para. 10. (b) (with Sch. 3 paras. 2, 3)

F7. S. 35. (10) omitted (26.5.2011) by virtue of The Electronic Communications and Wireless Telegraphy Regulations 2011 (S.I. 2011/1210), reg. 1. (2), Sch. 1 para. 10. (b) (with Sch. 3 paras. 2, 3)

Commencement Information

I7. S. 35 in force at 25.7.2003 for specified purposes by S.I. 2003/1900, arts. 1. (2), 2. (1), Sch. 1 (with art. 3) (as amended by S.I. 2003/3142, art. 1. (3))

I8. S. 35 in force at 29.12.2003 in so far as not already in force by S.I. 2003/3142, art. 3. (2) (with art. 11)

[F835. A.Penalties for contravention of section 33.

(1) This section applies where a person is given a notification under section 35 which specifies a proposed penalty.

(2) Where the notification relates to more than one contravention, a separate penalty may be specified in respect of each contravention.

(3) Where the notification relates to a continuing contravention, no more than one penalty may be specified in respect of the period of contravention specified in the notification.

(4) But, in relation to a continuing contravention, a penalty may be specified in respect of each day on which the contravention continues after—

(a) the giving of a confirmation decision under section 36. (4)(c) which requires immediate action; or

(b) the expiry of any period specified in the confirmation decision for complying with a requirement so specified.

(5) The amount of a penalty under subsection (4) is to be such amount not exceeding £100 per day as OFCOM determine to be—

(a) appropriate; and

(b) proportionate to the contravention in respect of which it is imposed.

(6) The amount of any other penalty specified in a notification under section 35 is to be such amount not exceeding £10,000 as OFCOM determine to be—

(a) appropriate, and

(b) proportionate to the contravention in respect of which it is imposed.

(7) The Secretary of State may by order amend this section so as to substitute a different maximum penalty for the maximum penalty for the time being specified in subsection (6).

(8) No order is to be made containing provision authorised by subsection (7) unless a draft of the order has been laid before Parliament and approved by a resolution of each House.]

Amendments (Textual)

F8. S. 35. A inserted (26.5.2011) by The Electronic Communications and Wireless Telegraphy

Regulations 2011 (S.I. 2011/1210), reg. 1. (2), Sch. 1 para. 11 (with Sch. 3 paras. 2, 3)

36 [F9. Confirmation decision] for contravention of s. 33.

(1) This section applies where—

(a) a person ("the notified provider") has been given a notification under section 35;

(b) OFCOM have allowed the notified provider an opportunity of making representations about the notified determination; and

(c) the period allowed for the making of the representations has expired.

[F10. (2)OFCOM may—

(a) give the notified provider a decision (a "confirmation decision") confirming the imposition of requirements in accordance with the notification under section 35; or

(b) inform the notified provider that they are satisfied with the notified provider's representations and that no further action will be taken.

(3) OFCOM may not give a confirmation decision to the notified provider unless, after considering any representations, they are satisfied that the notified provider has, in one or more of the respects notified, been in contravention of section 33.]

[F11. (4)A confirmation decision—

(a) must be given to the person without delay;

(b) must include reasons for the decision;

(c) may require immediate action by the person to comply with requirements imposed by virtue of section 35. (2)(d), or may specify a period within which the person must comply with those requirements; and

(d) may require the person to pay—

(i) the penalty specified in the notification under section 35, or

(ii) such lesser penalty as OFCOM consider appropriate in the light of the person's representations or steps taken by the person to comply with the condition or remedy the consequences of the contravention, and

may specify the period within which the penalty is to be paid.]

(5) It shall be the duty of a person to whom [F12a confirmation decision] has been given to comply with [F13any requirement imposed by it] .

(6) That duty shall be enforceable in civil proceedings by OFCOM—

(a) for an injunction;

(b) for specific performance of a statutory duty under section 45 of the Court of Session Act 1988 (c. 36); or

(c) for any other appropriate remedy or relief.

[F14. (7)A penalty imposed by a confirmation decision—

(a) must be paid to OFCOM; and

(b) if not paid within the period specified by them, is to be recoverable by them accordingly.]

Amendments (Textual)

F9. Words in s. 36 heading substituted (26.5.2011) by The Electronic Communications and Wireless Telegraphy Regulations 2011 (S.I. 2011/1210), reg. 1. (2), Sch. 1 para. 12. (e) (with Sch. 3 paras. 2, 3)

F10. S. 36. (2)(3) substituted (26.5.2011) by The Electronic Communications and Wireless Telegraphy Regulations 2011 (S.I. 2011/1210), reg. 1. (2), Sch. 1 para. 12. (a) (with Sch. 3 paras. 2, 3)

F11. S. 36. (4) substituted (26.5.2011) by The Electronic Communications and Wireless Telegraphy Regulations 2011 (S.I. 2011/1210), reg. 1. (2), Sch. 1 para. 12. (b) (with Sch. 3 paras. 2, 3)

F12. Words in s. 36. (5) substituted (26.5.2011) by The Electronic Communications and Wireless Telegraphy Regulations 2011 (S.I. 2011/1210), reg. 1. (2), Sch. 1 para. 12. (c)(i) (with Sch. 3 paras. 2, 3)

F13. Word in s. 36. (5) substituted (26.5.2011) by The Electronic Communications and Wireless Telegraphy Regulations 2011 (S.I. 2011/1210), reg. 1. (2), Sch. 1 para. 12. (c)(ii) (with Sch. 3 paras. 2, 3)

F14. S. 36. (7) inserted (26.5.2011) by The Electronic Communications and Wireless Telegraphy Regulations 2011 (S.I. 2011/1210), reg. 1. (2), Sch. 1 para. 12. (d) (with Sch. 3 paras. 2, 3)
Commencement Information
I9. S. 36 in force at 25.7.2003 for specified purposes by S.I. 2003/1900, arts. 1. (2), 2. (1), Sch. 1 (with art. 3) (as amended by S.I. 2003/3142, art. 1. (3))
I10. S. 36 in force at 29.12.2003 in so far as not already in force by S.I. 2003/3142, art. 3. (2) (with art. 11)
F1537. Penalties for contravention of s. 33.
. . . .
Amendments (Textual)
F15. S. 37 omitted (26.5.2011) by virtue of The Electronic Communications and Wireless Telegraphy Regulations 2011 (S.I. 2011/1210), reg. 1. (2), Sch. 1 para. 13 (with Sch. 3 paras. 2, 3)
Commencement Information
I11. S. 37 in force at 25.7.2003 for specified purposes by S.I. 2003/1900, arts. 1. (2), 2. (1), Sch. 1 (with art. 3) (as amended by S.I. 2003/3142, art. 1. (3))
I12. S. 37 in force at 29.12.2003 in so far as not already in force by S.I. 2003/3142, art. 3. (2) (with art. 11)

Administrative charges imposed on providers

38. Fixing of charges

(1) A person who, at any time in a charging year, is a person to whom this section applies shall—

(a) in respect of the network, service or facility provided or made available by him,

(b) in respect of the application to him of a universal service condition relating to matters mentioned in section 66. (3),

(c) in respect of the application to him of an SMP apparatus condition, or

(d) in respect of the application of the electronic communications code in his case,

pay to OFCOM the administrative charge (if any) that is fixed by them for the case that is applicable to him.

(2) This section applies to a person at a time if, at that time, he is—

(a) providing an electronic communications network of a description which is, at that time, designated for the purposes of this section;

(b) providing an electronic communications service of a description which is, at that time, so designated;

(c) making available an associated facility of a description which is, at that time, so designated;

(d) a person who without being a communications provider is designated in accordance with regulations under section 66;

(e) a supplier of apparatus to whom an SMP apparatus condition applies; or

(f) a person in whose case the electronic communications code applies by virtue of a direction given under section 106 otherwise than for the purposes of the provision by him of an electronic communications network of a designated description.

(3) OFCOM are not to fix the administrative charge for a charging year unless—

(a) at the time the charge is fixed there is in force a statement by OFCOM of the principles that OFCOM are proposing to apply in fixing charges under this section for that year; and

(b) the charge is fixed in accordance with those charging principles.

(4) Those principles must be such as appear to OFCOM to be likely to secure, on the basis of such estimates of the likely costs as it is practicable for them to make—

(a) that, on a year by year basis, the aggregate amount of the charges payable to OFCOM is sufficient to meet, but does not exceed, the annual cost to OFCOM of carrying out the functions mentioned in subsection (5);

(b) that the cost of carrying out those functions is met by the imposition of charges that are objectively justifiable and proportionate to the matters in respect of which they are imposed;

(c) that the relationship between meeting the cost of carrying out those functions and the amounts of the charges is transparent;

(d) that the charges fixed for persons who are liable to charges by reason only of being persons to whom SMP apparatus conditions apply are referable only to things done in, or in connection with, the setting, modification or enforcement of SMP apparatus conditions or the carrying out of the functions mentioned in subsection (6)(l); and

(e) that the charges fixed for persons who are liable to charges by reason only of being persons falling within subsection (2)(f), are referable only to costs incurred in, or in connection with, the carrying out of the functions mentioned in subsection (6)(g) and (l).

(5) Those functions are—

(a) the relevant Chapter 1 functions;

(b) the carrying out for a Chapter 1 purpose of any research by OFCOM or the Consumer Panel into any of the matters mentioned in section 14. (1)(c) to (f);

(c) the publication under section 26 of any information or advice that it appears to OFCOM to be appropriate to make available to the persons mentioned in subsection (2)(a) to (c) of that section; and

(d) the function of taking any steps that OFCOM consider it necessary to take—

(i) in preparation for the carrying out of any of the functions mentioned in paragraphs (a) to (c) of this subsection; or

(ii) for the purpose of facilitating the carrying out of those functions or otherwise in connection with carrying them out.

(6) The relevant Chapter 1 functions are—

(a) OFCOM's functions under sections 33 to 37 and 44;

(b) the setting, modification and enforcement of conditions under section 45;

(c) the supervision, as respects the requirements of sections 33 to 37 and of any such conditions, of communications providers and of persons who make associated facilities available;

(d) the monitoring of compliance with those requirements and with any such conditions;

(e) the functions conferred on OFCOM by or under section 55;

F16. (f). . . . .

(g) their functions under sections 106 to 119;

(h) their functions under sections 185 to 191;

(i) securing international co-operation in relation to the regulation of electronic communications networks, electronic communications services and associated facilities;

(j) securing the harmonisation and standardisation of the regulation of electronic communications networks, electronic communications services and associated facilities;

(k) market analysis and any monitoring of the controls operating in the markets for electronic communications networks, electronic communications services and associated facilities;

(l) OFCOM's functions under this section and sections 39 to 43.

(7) A purpose is a Chapter 1 purpose for the purposes of subsection (5)(b) if it is the purpose of ascertaining the effectiveness of one or more of the following—

(a) the regulation of the provision of electronic communications networks or electronic communications services;

(b) the regulation of the making available of associated facilities;

(c) the mechanisms in place for the handling, by communications providers and by persons making such facilities available, of complaints made to them by consumers in markets for such services or facilities;

(d) the mechanisms in place for resolving disputes between such consumers and communications providers or persons who make such facilities available.

(8) OFCOM's power to fix charges for a particular case includes—

(a) power to provide that the charges in that case are to be equal to the amounts produced by a computation made in the manner, and by reference to the factors, specified by them;

(b) power to provide for different charges to be imposed in that case on different descriptions of persons; and

(c) power to provide for particular descriptions of persons falling within subsection (2)(d) to (f) to be excluded from the liability to pay charges in that case.

(9) As soon as reasonably practicable after the end of each charging year, OFCOM must publish a statement setting out, in respect of that year—

(a) the aggregate amounts of the administrative charges for that year that have been received by OFCOM;

(b) the aggregate amount of the administrative charges for that year that remain outstanding and are likely to be paid or recovered; and

(c) the cost to OFCOM of carrying out the functions mentioned in subsection (5).

(10) Any deficit or surplus shown (after applying this subsection for all previous years) by a statement under subsection (9) shall be carried forward and taken into account in determining what is required to satisfy the requirement imposed by virtue of subsection (4)(a) in relation to the following year.

(11) Section 34 applies in relation to the making and withdrawal of a designation for the purposes of this section as it applies to the making and withdrawal of a designation for the purposes of section 33.

(12) In this section "charging year" means—

(a) the period beginning with the commencement of this section and ending with the next 31st March; or

(b) any subsequent period of twelve months beginning with 1st April.

Amendments (Textual)

F16. S. 38. (6)(f) omitted (26.5.2011) by virtue of The Electronic Communications and Wireless Telegraphy Regulations 2011 (S.I. 2011/1210), reg. 1. (2), Sch. 1 para. 14 (with Sch. 3 para. 2)

Commencement Information

I13. S. 38 in force at 25.7.2003 for specified purposes by S.I. 2003/1900, arts. 1. (2), 2. (1), Sch. 1 (with art. 3) (as amended by S.I. 2003/3142, art. 1. (3))

I14. S. 38 in force at 29.12.2003 in so far as not already in force by S.I. 2003/3142, art. 3. (2) (with art. 11)

39. Supplemental provision about fixing charges

(1) OFCOM's power to fix a charge under section 38—

(a) is to be exercisable only by the publication or giving of such notification as they consider appropriate for bringing the charge to the attention of the persons who, in their opinion, are likely to be affected by it; and

(b) includes power, by setting it out in that notification, to fix the time at which the charge is to become due to OFCOM.

(2) A charge fixed under section 38 for a charging year may be fixed in terms providing for a deduction from the charge on a proportionate basis to be made for a part of the year during which—

(a) the network, service or facility in respect of which it is fixed is not provided or made available by the person otherwise liable to the charge;

(b) the universal service condition in respect of which it is fixed does not apply in that person's case;

(c) the SMP apparatus condition in respect of which it is fixed does not apply in that person's case; or

(d) the electronic communications code does not apply in that person's case.

(3) Such a charge may also be fixed (subject to subsection (4)) so that it is referable, in whole or in part—

(a) to the provision or making available of a network, service or facility during a part of the year falling before the fixing of the charge;

(b) to the application of a universal service condition to a person for a part of the year so falling;

(c) to a person's being a person to whom an SMP apparatus condition applies for a part of the year so falling; or

(d) to the application of the electronic communications code in a person's case during a part of the year so falling.

(4) A charge may be fixed so as to be referable to a time before it is fixed to the extent only that both—

    (a) the imposition of the charge, and

    (b) the amount of the charge,

are required by, and consistent with, the statement of charging principles in force at the beginning of the charging year.

(5) Before making or revising a statement of charging principles, OFCOM must consult such of the persons who, in OFCOM's opinion, are likely to be affected by those principles as they think fit.

(6) The way in which a statement of charging principles must be made or may be revised is by the publication of the statement or revised statement in such manner as OFCOM consider appropriate for bringing it to the attention of the persons who, in their opinion, are likely to be affected by it.

(7) References in this section to a statement of charging principles are references to a statement by OFCOM of the principles that they are proposing to apply in fixing charges under section 38 for a charging year.

(8) In this section "charging year" has the same meaning as in section 38.

Commencement Information

I15. S. 39 in force at 25.7.2003 for specified purposes by S.I. 2003/1900, arts. 1. (2), 2. (1), Sch. 1 (with art. 3) (as amended by S.I. 2003/3142, art. 1. (3))

I16. S. 39 in force at 29.12.2003 in so far as not already in force by S.I. 2003/3142, art. 3. (2) (with art. 11)

40. Notification of non-payment of charges

(1) OFCOM are not entitled to bring proceedings for the recovery from a person of an administrative charge fixed for any year under section 38 unless they have given that person a notification under this section with respect to the amount they are seeking to recover.

(2) Where OFCOM determine that there are reasonable grounds for believing that a person is in contravention (whether in respect of the whole or a part of a charge) of a requirement to pay such an administrative charge, they may give him a notification under this section.

(3) A notification under this section is one which—

    (a) sets out the determination made by OFCOM; and

    (b) specifies the period during which the person notified has an opportunity of [F17making representations about the notified determination] .

F18. (4). . . . .

F18. (5). . . . .

F18. (6). . . . .

F18. (7). . . . .

F18. (8). . . . .

(9) A notification under this section—

    (a) may be given in respect of contraventions of more than one requirement to pay an administrative charge; and

    (b) if it is given in respect of a continuing contravention, may be given in respect of any period during which the contravention has continued.

(10) Where a notification under this section has been given to a person in respect of an amount outstanding, OFCOM may give a further notification in respect of the whole or a part of that amount if, and only if—

    (a) the subsequent notification is in respect of so much of a period during which that amount was outstanding as falls after a period to which the earlier notification relates; or

    (b) the earlier notification has been withdrawn without a penalty having been imposed in respect of the matters notified.

F19. (11). . . . .

Amendments (Textual)

F17. Words in s. 40. (3)(b) substituted (26.5.2011) by The Electronic Communications and

Wireless Telegraphy Regulations 2011 (S.I. 2011/1210), reg. 1. (2), Sch. 1 para. 15. (a) (with Sch. 3 paras. 2, 4)

F18. S. 40. (4)-(8) omitted (26.5.2011) by virtue of The Electronic Communications and Wireless Telegraphy Regulations 2011 (S.I. 2011/1210), reg. 1. (2), Sch. 1 para. 15. (b) (with Sch. 3 paras. 2, 4)

F19. S. 40. (11) omitted (26.5.2011) by virtue of The Electronic Communications and Wireless Telegraphy Regulations 2011 (S.I. 2011/1210), reg. 1. (2), Sch. 1 para. 15. (b) (with Sch. 3 paras. 2, 4)

Commencement Information

I17. S. 40 in force at 25.7.2003 for specified purposes by S.I. 2003/1900, arts. 1. (2), 2. (1), Sch. 1 (with art. 3) (as amended by S.I. 2003/3142, art. 1. (3))

I18. S. 40 in force at 29.12.2003 in so far as not already in force by S.I. 2003/3142, art. 3. (2) (with art. 11)

41. Penalties for non-payment of charges

(1) This section applies where—

(a) a person ("the notified charge payer") has been given a notification under section 40;

(b) OFCOM have allowed the notified charge payer an opportunity of making representations about the notified determination; and

(c) the period allowed for the making of the representations has expired.

(2) OFCOM may impose a penalty on the notified charge payer if he—

(a) has, in one or more of the respects notified, been in contravention of a requirement to pay an administrative charge fixed under section 38; F20...

F20. (b). . . . .

(3) Where a notification under section 40 relates to more than one contravention, a separate penalty may be imposed in respect of each contravention.

(4) Where such a notification relates to a continuing contravention, no more than one penalty may be imposed in respect of the period of contravention specified in the notification.

(5) The amount of a penalty imposed under this section is to be such amount, not exceeding twice the amount of the charge fixed for the relevant year, as OFCOM determine to be—

(a) appropriate; and

(b) proportionate to the contravention in respect of which it is imposed.

(6) In making that determination OFCOM must have regard to—

(a) any representations made to them by the notified charge payer; and

(b) any steps taken by him towards paying the amounts that he was notified under section 40 were outstanding.

(7) Where OFCOM impose a penalty on a person under this section, they shall—

(a) [F21without delay,] notify that person of that decision and of their reasons for that decision; and

(b) in that notification, fix a reasonable period after it is given as the period within which the penalty is to be paid.

(8) A penalty imposed under this section—

(a) must be paid to OFCOM; and

(b) if not paid within the period fixed by them, is to be recoverable by them accordingly.

(9) In this section "the relevant year", in relation to a contravention of a requirement to pay the whole or a part of the administrative charge fixed for any year, means that year.

(10) The provisions of this section do not affect OFCOM's power, apart from those provisions, to bring proceedings (whether before or after the imposition of a penalty under this section) for the recovery of the whole or part of an amount due to them under section 38. (1).

Amendments (Textual)

F20. S. 41. (2)(b) and preceding word omitted (26.5.2011) by virtue of The Electronic Communications and Wireless Telegraphy Regulations 2011 (S.I. 2011/1210), reg. 1. (2), Sch. 1 para. 16. (a) (with Sch. 3 paras. 2, 4)

F21. Words in s. 41. (7)(a) substituted (26.5.2011) by The Electronic Communications and

Wireless Telegraphy Regulations 2011 (S.I. 2011/1210), reg. 1. (2), Sch. 1 para. 16. (b) (with Sch. 3 paras. 2, 4)

Commencement Information
I19. S. 41 in force at 25.7.2003 for specified purposes by S.I. 2003/1900, arts. 1. (2), 2. (1), Sch. 1 (with art. 3) (as amended by S.I. 2003/3142, art. 1. (3))
I20. S. 41 in force at 29.12.2003 in so far as not already in force by S.I. 2003/3142, art. 3. (2) (with art. 11)

42. Suspending service provision for non-payment

(1) OFCOM may give a direction under this section to a person who is a communications provider or who makes associated facilities available ("the contravening provider") if they are satisfied—

(a) that he is or has been in [F22serious or repeated] contravention of requirements to pay administrative charges fixed under section 38 (whether in respect of the whole or a part of the charges);

(b) that the contraventions are not contraventions relating only to charges in respect of the application to the contravening provider of SMP apparatus conditions;

[F23. (ba)that, in the case of a single serious contravention, a notification has been given to the contravening provider under section 40 and the period for making representations under that section has expired;]

(c) that [F24, in the case of a repeated contravention,] the bringing of proceedings for the recovery of the amounts outstanding has failed to secure complete compliance by the contravening provider with the requirements to pay the charges fixed in his case, or has no reasonable prospect of securing such compliance;

(d) that [F25, in the case of a repeated contravention,] an attempt, by the imposition of penalties under section 41, to secure such compliance has failed; and

[F26. (e)that the giving of the direction is appropriate and proportionate to the contravention in respect of which it is given.]

(2) A direction under this section is—

(a) a direction that the entitlement of the contravening provider to provide electronic communications networks or electronic communications services, or to make associated facilities available, is suspended (either generally or in relation to particular networks, services or facilities); or

(b) a direction that that entitlement is restricted in the respects set out in the direction.

(3) A direction under this section—

(a) must specify the networks, services and facilities to which it relates; and

(b) except so far as it otherwise provides, takes effect for an indefinite period beginning with the time at which it is notified to the person to whom it is given.

(4) A direction under this section—

(a) in providing for the effect of a suspension or restriction to be postponed may provide for it to take effect only at a time determined by or in accordance with the terms of the direction; and

(b) in connection with the suspension or restriction contained in the direction or with the postponement of its effect, may impose such conditions on the contravening provider as appear to OFCOM to be appropriate for the purpose of protecting that provider's customers.

(5) Those conditions may include a condition requiring the making of payments—

(a) by way of compensation for loss or damage suffered by the contravening provider's customers as a result of the direction; or

(b) in respect of annoyance, inconvenience or anxiety to which they have been put in consequence of the direction.

(6) OFCOM are not to give a direction under this section unless they have—

(a) notified the contravening provider of the proposed direction and of the conditions (if any) which they are proposing to impose by that direction;

(b) provided him with an opportunity of making representations about the proposals and of proposing steps for remedying the situation; and

(c) considered every representation and proposal made to them during the period allowed by them for the contravening provider to take advantage of that opportunity.

[F27. (7)That period is such reasonable period as OFCOM may specify, beginning with the day of the giving of the notification.]

(8) If OFCOM consider it appropriate to do so (whether or not in consequence of any representations or proposals made to them), they may revoke a direction under this section, or modify its conditions—

(a) with effect from such time as they may direct;

(b) subject to compliance with such requirements as they may specify; and

(c) to such extent and in relation to such networks, services or facilities, or parts of a network, service or facility, as they may determine.

(9) For the purposes of this section there are repeated contraventions by a person of requirements to pay administrative charges to the extent that—

(a) in the case of a previous notification given to that person under section 40, OFCOM have determined for the purposes of section 41. (2) that such a contravention did occur; and

(b) in the period of [F2824] months following the day of the making of that determination, one or more further notifications have been given to that person in respect of the same or different failures to pay administrative charges.

Amendments (Textual)

F22. Words in s. 42. (1)(a) substituted (26.5.2011) by The Electronic Communications and Wireless Telegraphy Regulations 2011 (S.I. 2011/1210), reg. 1. (2), Sch. 1 para. 17. (a)(i) (with Sch. 3 paras. 2, 4)

F23. S. 42. (1)(ba) inserted (26.5.2011) by The Electronic Communications and Wireless Telegraphy Regulations 2011 (S.I. 2011/1210), reg. 1. (2), Sch. 1 para. 17. (a)(ii) (with Sch. 3 paras. 2, 4)

F24. Words in s. 42. (1)(c) inserted (26.5.2011) by The Electronic Communications and Wireless Telegraphy Regulations 2011 (S.I. 2011/1210), reg. 1. (2), Sch. 1 para. 17. (a)(iii) (with Sch. 3 paras. 2, 4)

F25. Words in s. 42. (1)(d) inserted (26.5.2011) by The Electronic Communications and Wireless Telegraphy Regulations 2011 (S.I. 2011/1210), reg. 1. (2), Sch. 1 para. 17. (a)(iv) (with Sch. 3 paras. 2, 4)

F26. S. 42. (1)(e) substituted (26.5.2011) by The Electronic Communications and Wireless Telegraphy Regulations 2011 (S.I. 2011/1210), reg. 1. (2), Sch. 1 para. 17. (a)(v) (with Sch. 3 paras. 2, 4)

F27. S. 42. (7) substituted (26.5.2011) by The Electronic Communications and Wireless Telegraphy Regulations 2011 (S.I. 2011/1210), reg. 1. (2), Sch. 1 para. 17. (b) (with Sch. 3 paras. 2, 4)

F28. Word in s. 42. (9)(b) substituted (26.5.2011) by The Electronic Communications and Wireless Telegraphy Regulations 2011 (S.I. 2011/1210), reg. 1. (2), Sch. 1 para. 17. (c) (with Sch. 3 paras. 2, 4, 5)

Commencement Information

I21. S. 42 in force at 25.7.2003 for specified purposes by S.I. 2003/1900, arts. 1. (2), 2. (1), Sch. 1 (with art. 3) (as amended by S.I. 2003/3142, art. 1. (3))

I22. S. 42 in force at 29.12.2003 in so far as not already in force by S.I. 2003/3142, art. 3. (2) (with art. 11)

43. Enforcement of directions under s. 42.

(1) A person is guilty of an offence if he provides an electronic communications network or electronic communications service, or makes available any associated facility—

(a) while his entitlement to do so is suspended by a direction under section 42; or

(b) in contravention of a restriction contained in such a direction.

(2) A person guilty of an offence under subsection (1) shall be liable—

(a) on summary conviction, to a fine not exceeding the statutory maximum;

(b) on conviction on indictment, to a fine.

(3) The duty of a person to comply with a condition of a direction under section 42 shall be a duty

owed to every person who may be affected by a contravention of the condition.

(4) Where a duty is owed by virtue of subsection (3) to a person—

  (a) a breach of the duty that causes that person to sustain loss or damage, and

  (b) an act which—

(i) by inducing a breach of the duty or interfering with its performance, causes that person to sustain loss or damage, and

(ii) is done wholly or partly for achieving that result,

shall be actionable at the suit or instance of that person.

(5) In proceedings brought against a person by virtue of subsection (4)(a) it shall be a defence for that person to show that he took all reasonable steps and exercised all due diligence to avoid contravening the condition in question.

(6) Sections [F2996. A] to 99 apply in relation to a contravention of conditions imposed by a direction under section 42 as they apply in relation to a contravention of conditions set under section 45.

Amendments (Textual)

F29. Word in s. 43. (6) substituted (26.5.2011) by The Electronic Communications and Wireless Telegraphy Regulations 2011 (S.I. 2011/1210), reg. 1. (2), Sch. 1 para. 18 (with Sch. 3 paras. 2, 4)

Commencement Information

I23. S. 43 in force at 25.7.2003 for specified purposes by S.I. 2003/1900, arts. 1. (2), 2. (1), Sch. 1 (with art. 3) (as amended by S.I. 2003/3142, art. 1. (3))

I24. S. 43 in force at 29.12.2003 in so far as not already in force by S.I. 2003/3142, art. 3. (2) (with art. 11)

Register of providers required to notify or to pay charges

44. Duty of OFCOM to keep publicly accessible register

(1) It shall be the duty of OFCOM to establish and maintain a register for the purposes of section 33.

(2) OFCOM must record in the register—

  (a) every designation by them for the purposes of section 33 or 38;

  (b) every withdrawal by them of such a designation;

  (c) every notification given to them under section 33; and

  (d) every notification treated as given to them under that section by a transitional provision made under subsection (12) of that section.

(3) Information recorded in the register must be so recorded in such manner as OFCOM consider appropriate.

(4) It shall be the duty of OFCOM to publish a notification setting out—

  (a) the times at which the register is for the time being available for public inspection; and

  (b) the fees that must be paid for, or in connection with, an inspection of the register.

(5) The publication of a notification under subsection (4) must be in such manner as OFCOM consider appropriate for bringing it to the attention of the persons who, in their opinion, are likely to be affected by it.

(6) OFCOM must make the register available for public inspection—

  (a) during such hours, and

  (b) on payment of such fees,

as are set out in the notification for the time being in force under subsection (4).

Commencement Information

I25. S. 44 in force at 25.7.2003 for specified purposes by S.I. 2003/1900, arts. 1. (2), 2. (1), Sch. 1 (with art. 3) (as amended by S.I. 2003/3142, art. 1. (3))

I26. S. 44 in force at 29.12.2003 in so far as not already in force by S.I. 2003/3142, art. 3. (2) (with art. 11)

Conditions of entitlement to provide network or service etc.

45. Power of OFCOM to set conditions

(1) OFCOM shall have the power to set conditions under this section binding the persons to whom they are applied in accordance with section 46.

(2) A condition set by OFCOM under this section must be either—

 (a) a general condition; or

 (b) a condition of one of the following descriptions—

(i) a universal service condition;

(ii) an access-related condition;

(iii) a privileged supplier condition;

(iv) a significant market power condition (an "SMP condition").

(3) A general condition is a condition which contains only provisions authorised or required by one or more of sections 51, 52, 57, 58 or 64.

(4) A universal service condition is a condition which contains only provisions authorised or required by section 67.

(5) An access-related condition is a condition which contains only provisions authorised by section 73.

(6) A privileged supplier condition is a condition which contains only the provision required by section 77.

(7) An SMP condition is either—

 (a) an SMP services condition; or

 (b) an SMP apparatus condition.

(8) An SMP services condition is a condition which contains only provisions which—

 (a) are authorised or required by one or more of sections 87 to [F3091] ; or

 (b) in the case of a condition applying to a person falling within section 46. (8)(b), correspond to provision authorised or required by one or more of sections 87 to [F3189. A] .

(9) An SMP apparatus condition is a condition containing only provisions authorised by section 93.

(10) OFCOM's power to set a condition under this section making provision authorised or required by this Chapter includes each of the following—

 (a) power to impose a requirement on the person or persons to whom the condition is applied to comply with such directions with respect to the matters to which the condition relates as may be given from time to time by OFCOM or by another person specified in the condition;

 (b) power to impose an obligation with respect to those matters that is framed by reference to, or is conditional upon, the giving of a consent or of an approval, or on the making of a recommendation, by OFCOM or by another person so specified;

 (c) power, for the purposes of provision made by virtue of either of the preceding paragraphs, to confer a discretion exercisable from time to time by OFCOM or by another person specified in the condition or determined in accordance with provision contained in it;

 (d) power (subject to section 51. (3)) to set different conditions for different cases (including different conditions in relation to different parts of the United Kingdom); and

 (e) power to revoke or modify the conditions for the time being in force.

(11) The directions that may be authorised by virtue of subsection (10) do not include directions withdrawing, suspending or restricting a person's entitlement—

 (a) to provide, in whole or in part, any electronic communications network or electronic communications service; or

 (b) to make available, in whole or in part, any associated facilities.

Amendments (Textual)

F30. Word in s. 45. (8)(a) substituted (26.5.2011) by The Electronic Communications and Wireless Telegraphy Regulations 2011 (S.I. 2011/1210), reg. 1. (2), Sch. 1 para. 19. (a) (with Sch. 3 para. 2)

F31. Word in s. 45. (8)(b) substituted (26.5.2011) by The Electronic Communications and Wireless Telegraphy Regulations 2011 (S.I. 2011/1210), reg. 1. (2), Sch. 1 para. 19. (b) (with Sch. 3 para. 2)

Commencement Information

I27. S. 45 in force at 25.7.2003 for specified purposes by S.I. 2003/1900, arts. 1. (2), 2. (1), Sch. 1 (with art. 3) (as amended by S.I. 2003/3142, art. 1. (3))

I28. S. 45 in force at 29.12.2003 in so far as not already in force by S.I. 2003/3142, art. 3. (2) (with art. 11)

46. Persons to whom conditions may apply

(1) A condition set under section 45 is not to be applied to a person except in accordance with the following provisions of this section.

(2) A general condition may be applied generally—

(a) to every person providing an electronic communications network or electronic communications service; or

(b) to every person providing such a network or service of a particular description specified in the condition.

(3) A universal service condition, access-related condition, privileged supplier condition or SMP condition may be applied to a particular person specified in the condition.

(4) A privileged supplier condition may also be applied generally—

(a) to every person to whom such a condition is required to apply under section 77; or

(b) to every such person who is of a particular description specified in the condition.

(5) The particular person to whom a universal service condition is applied—

(a) except in the case of a condition relating to matters mentioned in subsection (3) of section 66, must be a communications provider designated in accordance with regulations under that section; and

(b) in that excepted case, must be a communications provider so designated or a person who is not such a provider but who is so designated for the purposes only of conditions relating to those matters.

(6) The particular person to whom an access-related condition is applied—

(a) in the case of a condition falling within section 74. (1), may be any person whatever; and

(b) in any other case, must be a person who provides an electronic communications network or makes associated facilities available.

(7) The particular person to whom an SMP services condition is applied must—

(a) be a communications provider or a person who makes associated facilities available; and

(b) fall within subsection (8).

(8) A person falls within this subsection if—

(a) he is a person whom OFCOM have determined to be a person having significant market power in a specific market for electronic communications networks, electronic communications services or associated facilities (a "services market"); or

(b) it appears to OFCOM that he is a person on whom it is necessary, for the purpose of securing compliance with an international obligation of the United Kingdom, to impose a condition containing provision that corresponds to provision which, in the case of a person falling within paragraph (a), must be made (or may be made) under any of sections 87 to [F3289. A] .

(9) The particular person to whom an SMP apparatus condition is applied must be—

(a) a person who supplies electronic communications apparatus; and

(b) a person whom OFCOM have determined to be a person having significant market power in a specific market for electronic communications apparatus (an "apparatus market").

Amendments (Textual)

F32. Word in s. 46. (8)(b) substituted (26.5.2011) by The Electronic Communications and Wireless Telegraphy Regulations 2011 (S.I. 2011/1210), reg. 1. (2), Sch. 1 para. 20 (with Sch. 3 para. 2)

Commencement Information

I29. S. 46 in force at 25.7.2003 for specified purposes by S.I. 2003/1900, arts. 1. (2), 2. (1), Sch. 1

(with art. 3) (as amended by S.I. 2003/3142, art. 1. (3))

I30. S. 46 in force at 29.12.2003 in so far as not already in force by S.I. 2003/3142, art. 3. (2) (with art. 11)

47. Test for setting or modifying conditions

(1) OFCOM must not, in exercise or performance of any power or duty under this Chapter—

    (a) set a condition under section 45, or

    (b) modify such a condition,

unless they are satisfied that the condition or (as the case may be) the modification satisfies the test in subsection (2).

(2) That test is that the condition or modification is—

    (a) objectively justifiable in relation to the networks, services, facilities, apparatus or directories to which it relates [F33. (but this paragraph is subject to subsection (3))] ;

    (b) not such as to discriminate unduly against particular persons or against a particular description of persons;

    (c) proportionate to what the condition or modification is intended to achieve; and

    (d) in relation to what it is intended to achieve, transparent.

[F34. (3)Subsection (2)(a) does not apply in relation to the setting of a general condition.]

Amendments (Textual)

F33. Words in s. 47. (2)(a) inserted (26.5.2011) by The Electronic Communications and Wireless Telegraphy Regulations 2011 (S.I. 2011/1210), reg. 1. (2), Sch. 1 para. 21. (a) (with Sch. 3 para. 2)

F34. S. 47. (3) inserted (26.5.2011) by The Electronic Communications and Wireless Telegraphy Regulations 2011 (S.I. 2011/1210), reg. 1. (2), Sch. 1 para. 21. (b) (with Sch. 3 para. 2)

Commencement Information

I31. S. 47 in force at 25.7.2003 for specified purposes by S.I. 2003/1900, arts. 1. (2), 2. (1), Sch. 1 (with art. 3) (as amended by S.I. 2003/3142, art. 1. (3))

I32. S. 47 in force at 29.12.2003 in so far as not already in force by S.I. 2003/3142, art. 3. (2) (with art. 11)

48. Procedure for setting, modifying and revoking conditions

(1) Subject to the following provisions of this Chapter—

    (a) the way in which conditions are to be set or modified under section 45 is by the publication of a notification setting out the conditions or modifications; and

    (b) the way in which such a condition is to be revoked is by the publication of a notification stating that the condition is revoked.

[F35. (2)Where section 48. A applies, OFCOM must comply with the applicable requirements of that section and section 48. B before—

    (a) setting conditions under section 45; or

    (b) modifying or revoking a condition so set.

(2. A)Where section 48. A does not apply to the setting, modification or revocation of conditions because of subsection (2) of that section—

    (a) the conditions, or their modification or revocation, must be temporary; and

    (b) the notification published under subsection (1) of this section must state the period for which the conditions, or their modification or revocation, are to have effect.

(2. B)Where OFCOM propose to extend or make permanent any such temporary conditions, modification or revocation—

    (a) sections 48. A and 48. B(1) do not apply in relation to the proposal; and

    (b) subsections (2) to (9) of section 48. B apply in relation to the proposal as if the words from the beginning of subsection (2) to "appropriate" were omitted.]

(4) In the case of a [F36proposal by OFCOM] with respect to an SMP condition, the applicable requirements of sections 79 to 86 must also be complied with.

F37. (5). . . . .

(6) The publication of a notification under this section [F38or section 48. A] must be in such manner as appears to OFCOM to be appropriate for bringing the contents of the notification—

(a) in the case of a notification setting general conditions, to the attention of such persons as OFCOM consider appropriate; and

(b) in any other case, to the attention of the persons who, in OFCOM's opinion, are likely to be affected by the contents of the notification.

(7) Nothing in the following provisions of this Chapter imposing a duty on OFCOM to set or modify a condition shall be taken as dispensing with any of the requirements of this section [F39, section 48. A or section 48. B] .

Amendments (Textual)

F35. S. 48. (2)-(2. B) substituted for s. 48. (2)(3) (26.5.2011) by The Electronic Communications and Wireless Telegraphy Regulations 2011 (S.I. 2011/1210), reg. 1. (2), Sch. 1 para. 22. (a) (with Sch. 3 paras. 2, 6)

F36. Words in s. 48. (4) substituted (26.5.2011) by The Electronic Communications and Wireless Telegraphy Regulations 2011 (S.I. 2011/1210), reg. 1. (2), Sch. 1 para. 22. (b) (with Sch. 3 paras. 2, 6)

F37. S. 48. (5) omitted (26.5.2011) by virtue of The Electronic Communications and Wireless Telegraphy Regulations 2011 (S.I. 2011/1210), reg. 1. (2), Sch. 1 para. 22. (c) (with Sch. 3 paras. 2, 6)

F38. Words in s. 48. (6) inserted (26.5.2011) by The Electronic Communications and Wireless Telegraphy Regulations 2011 (S.I. 2011/1210), reg. 1. (2), Sch. 1 para. 22. (d) (with Sch. 3 paras. 2, 6)

F39. Words in s. 48. (7) inserted (26.5.2011) by The Electronic Communications and Wireless Telegraphy Regulations 2011 (S.I. 2011/1210), reg. 1. (2), Sch. 1 para. 22. (e) (with Sch. 3 paras. 2, 6)

Commencement Information

I33. S. 48 in force at 25.7.2003 for specified purposes by S.I. 2003/1900, arts. 1. (2), 2. (1), Sch. 1 (with art. 3) (as amended by S.I. 2003/3142, art. 1. (3))

I34. S. 48 in force at 29.12.2003 in so far as not already in force by S.I. 2003/3142, art. 3. (2) (with art. 11)

[F4048. A.Domestic consultation for section 45 conditions

(1) This section applies where OFCOM propose to set, modify or revoke—

(a) SMP apparatus conditions; or

(b) any other conditions set under section 45 where what is proposed would, in OFCOM's opinion, have a significant impact on a market for any of the services, facilities, apparatus or directories in relation to which they have functions under this Chapter.

(2) But this section does not apply where the proposal is of EU significance and in OFCOM's opinion—

(a) there are exceptional circumstances; and

(b) there is an urgent need to act in order to safeguard competition and to protect the interests of consumers.

(3) OFCOM must publish a notification—

(a) stating that they are proposing to set, modify or revoke the conditions that are specified in the notification;

(b) setting out the effect of those conditions, modifications or revocations;

(c) giving their reasons for making the proposal; and

(d) specifying the period within which representations may be made to OFCOM about their proposal.

(4) That period must end no less than one month after the day of the publication of the notification.

(5) But where OFCOM are satisfied that there are exceptional circumstances justifying the use of a shorter period, the period specified as the period for making representations may be whatever shorter period OFCOM consider reasonable in those circumstances.

(6) OFCOM must—

(a) consider every representation about the proposal made to them during the period specified in the notification; and

(b) have regard to every international obligation of the United Kingdom (if any) which has been notified to them for the purposes of this paragraph by the Secretary of State.

(7) Where the proposal is not of EU significance, OFCOM may then give effect to it, with any modifications that appear to OFCOM to be appropriate.

Amendments (Textual)

F40. Ss. 48. A-48. C inserted (26.5.2011) by The Electronic Communications and Wireless Telegraphy Regulations 2011 (S.I. 2011/1210), reg. 1. (2), Sch. 1 para. 23 (with Sch. 3 paras. 2, 6)

48. B. EU consultation for section 45 conditions

(1) This section applies where, after complying with section 48. A(6) in relation to a proposal of EU significance, OFCOM wish to proceed with the proposal.

(2) After making any modifications of the proposal that appear to OFCOM to be appropriate, OFCOM must send a copy of the proposal, and of a statement setting out the reasons for it, to—

(a) the European Commission;

(b) BEREC; and

(c) the regulatory authorities in every other member State.

(3) If at the end of the period of one month referred to in Article 7. (3) of the Framework Directive no notification has been given to OFCOM by the Commission under Article 7a(1) of that Directive, OFCOM may give effect to the proposal, with any modifications that appear to OFCOM to be appropriate.

(4) Before giving effect to the proposal under subsection (3), OFCOM must consider any comments made by—

(a) the Commission;

(b) BEREC; and

(c) any regulatory authority in any other member State.

(5) Subsections (6) to (9) apply where such a notification is given by the Commission to OFCOM during that period.

(6) During the period of 3 months beginning with the notification, OFCOM must co-operate with the Commission and BEREC to identify the most appropriate and effective measure.

(7) OFCOM may give effect to the proposal, with any modifications that appear to them to be appropriate, within one month (or such longer period as may be allowed under paragraph (6) of Article 7a of the Framework Directive) of the Commission—

(a) issuing a recommendation to amend or withdraw the proposal in accordance with paragraph (5)(a) of that Article; or

(b) taking a decision to lift its reservations in accordance with paragraph (5)(b) of that Article.

(8) In a case in which OFCOM give effect to the proposal despite a recommendation of the Commission to amend or withdraw the proposal, OFCOM must send to the Commission a copy of a reasoned justification for their decision.

(9) If at the end of the period of one month referred to in paragraph (5) of Article 7a of the Framework Directive the Commission has neither issued a recommendation nor lifted its reservations in accordance with that paragraph, OFCOM may give effect to the proposal, with any modifications that appear to them to be appropriate.

Amendments (Textual)

F40. Ss. 48. A-48. C inserted (26.5.2011) by The Electronic Communications and Wireless Telegraphy Regulations 2011 (S.I. 2011/1210), reg. 1. (2), Sch. 1 para. 23 (with Sch. 3 paras. 2, 6)

48. C.Delivery of copies of notifications etc. in respect of section 45 conditions

(1) OFCOM must send to the Secretary of State a copy of every notification published under section 48. (1) or 48. A(3).

(2) OFCOM must send to the European Commission a copy of every notification published under section 48. (1) with respect to—

(a) a universal service condition;

(b) an access-related condition falling within section 73. (2);

(c) an SMP services condition.

(3) OFCOM must send to BEREC a copy of every notification published under section 48. (1) with respect to a proposal of EU significance.

(4) Where a notification published under section 48. (1) relates to a proposal to which section 48. A did not apply because of subsection (2) of that section, OFCOM must send a copy of a statement setting out the reasons for the proposal and for the urgent need to act to—

    (a) the Commission;

    (b) BEREC; and

    (c) the regulatory authorities in every other member State.]

Amendments (Textual)

F40. Ss. 48. A-48. C inserted (26.5.2011) by The Electronic Communications and Wireless Telegraphy Regulations 2011 (S.I. 2011/1210), reg. 1. (2), Sch. 1 para. 23 (with Sch. 3 paras. 2, 6)

49. Directions and approvals for the purposes of a s. 45 condition

(1) This section applies where—

    (a) a condition set under section 45 has effect by reference to directions, approvals or consents given by a person (whether OFCOM themselves or another); and

    (b) that person [F41. (referred to in this section and sections 49. A to 49. C as "the responsible person")] is proposing to give a direction, approval or consent that affects the operation of that condition or to modify or withdraw a direction, approval or consent so as to affect the condition's operation.

(2) [F42. The responsible person] must not give, modify or withdraw the direction, approval or consent unless he is satisfied that to do so is—

    (a) objectively justifiable in relation to the networks, services, facilities, apparatus or directories to which it relates [F43. (but this paragraph is subject to subsection (2. A))] ;

    (b) not such as to discriminate unduly against particular persons or against a particular description of persons;

    (c) proportionate to what it is intended to achieve; and

    (d) in relation to what it is intended to achieve, transparent.

[F44. (2. A)Subsection (2)(a) does not apply in relation to a direction, approval or consent affecting a general condition.]

(3) [F45. Where the responsible person is a person other than OFCOM, that person shall in giving, modifying or withdrawing the direction] be under the same duty as OFCOM to act in accordance with the six Community requirements set out in section 4.

[F46. (4)Where section 49. A applies, the applicable requirements of that section and section 49. B must be complied with before the direction, approval or consent is given, modified or withdrawn.

(4. A)Where section 49. A does not apply because of subsection (2) of that section—

    (a) the direction, approval or consent given, or its modification or withdrawal, must be temporary; and

    (b) the instrument that gives, modifies or withdraws the direction, approval or consent must state the period for which it is to have effect.

(4. B)Where it is proposed to extend or make permanent any such temporary direction, approval or consent, or modification or withdrawal—

    (a) sections 49. A and 49. B(1) do not apply in relation to the proposal; and

    (b) subsections (2) to (10) of section 49. B apply in relation to the proposal as if for the words from the beginning of subsection (2) to "the person" were substituted "The responsible person".

(4. C)Where the responsible person is a person other than OFCOM, that person must refer to OFCOM such of the following questions as are relevant in the case in question—

    (a) whether OFCOM is of the opinion mentioned in section 49. A(1)(b);

    (b) whether OFCOM is of the opinion mentioned in section 49. A(2); and

    (c) whether the proposal is of EU significance.

(4. D)OFCOM must immediately determine any question so referred to them.]

Amendments (Textual)

F41. Words in s. 49. (1)(b) inserted (26.5.2011) by The Electronic Communications and Wireless Telegraphy Regulations 2011 (S.I. 2011/1210), reg. 1. (2), Sch. 1 para. 24. (a) (with Sch. 3 paras.

2, 7)

F42. Words in s. 49. (2) substituted (26.5.2011) by The Electronic Communications and Wireless Telegraphy Regulations 2011 (S.I. 2011/1210), reg. 1. (2), Sch. 1 para. 24. (b)(i) (with Sch. 3 paras. 2, 7)

F43. Words in s. 49. (2)(a) inserted (26.5.2011) by The Electronic Communications and Wireless Telegraphy Regulations 2011 (S.I. 2011/1210), reg. 1. (2), Sch. 1 para. 24. (b)(ii) (with Sch. 3 paras. 2, 7)

F44. S. 49. (2. A) inserted (26.5.2011) by The Electronic Communications and Wireless Telegraphy Regulations 2011 (S.I. 2011/1210), reg. 1. (2), Sch. 1 para. 24. (c) (with Sch. 3 paras. 2, 7)

F45. Words in s. 49. (3) substituted (26.5.2011) by The Electronic Communications and Wireless Telegraphy Regulations 2011 (S.I. 2011/1210), reg. 1. (2), Sch. 1 para. 24. (d) (with Sch. 3 paras. 2, 7)

F46. S. 49. (4)-(4. D) substituted for s. 49. (4)-(10) (26.5.2011) by The Electronic Communications and Wireless Telegraphy Regulations 2011 (S.I. 2011/1210), reg. 1. (2), Sch. 1 para. 24. (e) (with Sch. 3 paras. 2, 7)

Commencement Information

I35. S. 49 in force at 25.7.2003 for specified purposes by S.I. 2003/1900, arts. 1. (2), 2. (1), Sch. 1 (with art. 3) (as amended by S.I. 2003/3142, art. 1. (3))

I36. S. 49 in force at 29.12.2003 in so far as not already in force by S.I. 2003/3142, art. 3. (2) (with art. 11)

[F4749. A.Domestic consultation for directions, approvals and consents

(1) This section applies where the responsible person is proposing to give, modify or withdraw a direction, approval or consent for the purposes of—

   (a) an SMP apparatus condition; or

   (b) any other condition set under section 45 where what is proposed would, in OFCOM's opinion, have a significant impact on a market for any of the services, facilities, apparatus or directories in relation to which they have functions under this Chapter.

(2) But this section does not apply where the proposal is of EU significance and in OFCOM's opinion—

   (a) there are exceptional circumstances; and

   (b) there is an urgent need to act in order to safeguard competition and to protect the interests of consumers.

(3) The responsible person must publish a notification—

   (a) stating that there is a proposal to give, modify or withdraw the direction, approval or consent;

   (b) identifying the responsible person;

   (c) setting out the direction, approval or consent to which the proposal relates;

   (d) setting out the effect of the direction, approval or consent or of its proposed modification or withdrawal;

   (e) giving reasons for the making of the proposal; and

   (f) specifying the period within which representations may be made about the proposal to the responsible person.

(4) That period must be one ending not less than one month after the day of the publication of the notification.

(5) But where the responsible person is satisfied that there are exceptional circumstances justifying the use of a shorter period, the period specified as the period for making representations may be whatever shorter period that person considers reasonable in those circumstances.

(6) The responsible person must—

   (a) consider every representation about the proposal made to that person during the period specified in the notification; and

   (b) have regard to every international obligation of the United Kingdom (if any) which has been notified to OFCOM for the purposes of this paragraph by the Secretary of State.

(7) Where the proposal is not of EU significance, the responsible person may then give effect to the proposal, with any modifications that appear to that person to be appropriate.

(8) The publication of a notification under this section must be in such manner as appears to the responsible person to be appropriate for bringing the contents of the notification to the attention of such persons as that person considers appropriate.

Amendments (Textual)

F47. Ss. 49. A-49. C inserted (26.5.2011) by The Electronic Communications and Wireless Telegraphy Regulations 2011 (S.I. 2011/1210), reg. 1. (2), Sch. 1 para. 25 (with Sch. 3 paras. 2, 7)

49. B. EU consultation for directions, approvals and consents

(1) This section applies where, after complying with section 49. A(6) in relation to a proposal of EU significance, the responsible person wishes to proceed with it.

(2) After the responsible person has made any modifications of the proposal that appear to the person to be appropriate, the person must send a copy of the proposal, and of a statement setting out the reasons for it, to—

    (a) the European Commission;

    (b) BEREC; and

    (c) the regulatory authorities in every other member State.

(3) If at the end of the period of one month referred to in Article 7. (3) of the Framework Directive no notification has been given to the responsible person by the Commission under Article 7a(1) of that Directive, the responsible person may give effect to the proposal, with any amendments that appear to the responsible person to be appropriate.

(4) Before giving effect to the proposal under subsection (3), the responsible person must consider any comments made by—

    (a) the Commission;

    (b) BEREC; and

    (c) any regulatory authority in any other member State.

(5) Subsections (6) to (10) apply where such a notification is given by the Commission to the responsible person during that period.

(6) During the period of 3 months beginning with the notification, the responsible person must co-operate with the Commission and BEREC to identify the most appropriate and effective measure.

(7) The responsible person may give effect to the proposal, with any modifications that appear to that person to be appropriate, within one month (or such longer period as may be allowed under paragraph (6) of Article 7a of the Framework Directive) of the Commission—

    (a) issuing a recommendation to amend or withdraw the proposal in accordance with paragraph (5)(a) of that Article; or

    (b) taking a decision to lift its reservations in accordance with paragraph (5)(b) of that Article.

(8) In a case in which the responsible person is a person other than OFCOM and the Commission has recommended that the proposal be amended or withdrawn, the responsible person may give effect to the proposal only with the agreement of OFCOM.

(9) In a case in which the responsible person gives effect to the proposal despite a recommendation of the Commission to amend or withdraw it, the responsible person must send to the Commission a copy of the responsible person's reasoned justification for the decision.

(10) If at the end of the period of one month referred to in paragraph (5) of Article 7a of the Framework Directive the Commission has neither issued a recommendation nor lifted its reservations in accordance with that paragraph, the responsible person may give effect to the proposal, with any modifications that appear to that person to be appropriate.

Amendments (Textual)

F47. Ss. 49. A-49. C inserted (26.5.2011) by The Electronic Communications and Wireless Telegraphy Regulations 2011 (S.I. 2011/1210), reg. 1. (2), Sch. 1 para. 25 (with Sch. 3 paras. 2, 7)

49. C.Delivery of copies of notifications etc. in respect of directions, approvals and consents

(1) The responsible person must send to the Secretary of State—

    (a) a copy of every notification published under section 49. A(3);

    (b) a copy of every direction, approval or consent given for the purposes of a condition set under section 45; and

(c) a copy of every instrument modifying or withdrawing such a direction, approval or consent.

(2) The responsible person must send to the European Commission—

(a) a copy of every direction, approval or consent given for the purposes of a universal service condition, an access-related condition falling within section 73. (2) or an SMP services condition; and

(b) a copy of every instrument modifying or withdrawing such a direction, approval or consent.

(3) The responsible person must send to BEREC—

(a) a copy of every direction, approval or consent given for the purposes of a condition set under section 45 where the proposal to give the direction, approval or consent was a proposal of EU significance;

(b) a copy of every instrument modifying or withdrawing a direction, approval or consent given for the purposes of a condition set under section 45 where the proposal to modify or withdraw the direction, approval or consent was a proposal of EU significance.

(4) In a case in which the responsible person is a person other than OFCOM, the responsible person must send to OFCOM—

(a) a copy of every notification published under section 49. A(3);

(b) a copy of every direction, approval or consent given for the purposes of a condition set under section 45;

(c) a copy of every instrument modifying or withdrawing such a direction, approval or consent;

(d) a copy of every proposal and statement to which section 49. B(2) applies;

(e) a copy of any comments about such a proposal made by the Commission, BEREC or any regulatory authority in any other member State;

(f) a copy of every notification given to the responsible person by the Commission under Article 7a(1) of the Framework Directive;

(g) a copy of every recommendation made in respect of the proposal by the Commission under Article 7a(5)(a) of the Framework Directive.

(5) Where because of subsection (2) of section 49. A, that section did not apply in relation to a proposal to give a direction, approval or consent for the purposes of a condition, or to modify or withdraw such a direction, approval or consent, the responsible person must send a copy of a statement setting out the reasons for the proposal and for the urgent need to act to—

(a) the Commission;

(b) BEREC; and

(c) the regulatory authorities in every other member State.

(6) In a case in which the responsible person is a person other than OFCOM, references to OFCOM in section 395. (4), (5) and (6. A) are to be read as references to the responsible person in relation to copies of directions, approvals, consents, instruments and statements to which subsections (2), (3) and (5) of this section apply.]

Amendments (Textual)

F47. Ss. 49. A-49. C inserted (26.5.2011) by The Electronic Communications and Wireless Telegraphy Regulations 2011 (S.I. 2011/1210), reg. 1. (2), Sch. 1 para. 25 (with Sch. 3 paras. 2, 7)

F4850. Delivery of copies of notifications etc.

. . . .

Amendments (Textual)

F48. S. 50 omitted (26.5.2011) by virtue of The Electronic Communications and Wireless Telegraphy Regulations 2011 (S.I. 2011/1210), reg. 1. (2), Sch. 1 para. 26 (with Sch. 3 paras. 2, 8)

Commencement Information

I37. S. 50 in force at 25.7.2003 for specified purposes by S.I. 2003/1900, arts. 1. (2), 2. (1), Sch. 1 (with art. 3) (as amended by S.I. 2003/3142, art. 1. (3))

I38. S. 50 in force at 29.12.2003 in so far as not already in force by S.I. 2003/3142, art. 3. (2) (with art. 11)

General conditions: subject-matter

51. Matters to which general conditions may relate

(1) Subject to sections 52 to 64, the only conditions that may be set under section 45 as general conditions are conditions falling within one or more of the following paragraphs—

(a) conditions making such provision as OFCOM consider appropriate for protecting the interests of the end-users of public electronic communications services;

(b) conditions making such provision as OFCOM consider appropriate for securing service interoperability and for securing, or otherwise relating to, network access;

(c) conditions making such provision as OFCOM consider appropriate for securing the proper and effective functioning of public electronic communications networks;

(d) conditions for giving effect to determinations or regulations made under section 71;

(e) conditions requiring F49... the provision, availability and use, in the event of a disaster, of electronic communications networks, electronic communications services and associated facilities;

(f) conditions making such provision as OFCOM consider appropriate for securing the protection of public health by the prevention or avoidance of the exposure of individuals to electro-magnetic fields created in connection with the operation of electronic communications networks;

(g) conditions requiring compliance with relevant international standards.

(2) The power under subsection (1)(a) to set conditions for protecting the interests of the end-users of public electronic communications services includes power to set conditions for that purpose which—

(a) relate to the supply, provision or making available of goods, services or facilities in association with the provision of public electronic communications services; F50...

(b) give effect to [F51. EU] obligations to provide protection for such end-users in relation to the supply, provision or making available of those goods, services or facilities.

[F52. (c)specify requirements in relation to the provision of services to disabled end-users;

(d) require the provision, free of charge, of specified information, or information of a specified kind, to end-users;

(e) in order to prevent the degradation of service and the hindering or slowing down of traffic over networks, impose minimum requirements in relation to the quality of public electronic communications networks;

(f) require a communications provider, in specified circumstances, to block access to telephone numbers or services in order to prevent fraud or misuse, and enable them to withhold fees payable to another communications provider in those circumstances;

(g) impose a limit on the duration of a contract between an end-user and a communications provider; and

(h) ensure that conditions and procedures for the termination of a contract do not act as a disincentive to an end-user changing communications provider.]

[F53. (2. A)Where OFCOM propose to set a general condition of a kind specified in subsection (2)(e), they must—

(a) notify the European Commission and BEREC, and

(b) take due account of comments and recommendations made by the Commission.]

(3) The power to set general conditions in relation to a description of electronic communications network or electronic communications service does not include power—

(a) to set conditions that are made applicable according to the identity of the provider of a network or service; or

(b) to set conditions that differ according to the identity of the provider of the networks or services to which they relate.

(4) The power to set general conditions falling within subsection (1)(b) does not include power to set conditions containing provision which under—

(a) section 73, or

(b) any of sections 87 to [F5491] ,

must be or may be included, in a case in which it appears to OFCOM to be appropriate to do so, in an access-related condition or SMP condition.

(5) The conditions falling within subsection (1)(c) include conditions making such provision as OFCOM consider appropriate for the purpose, in accordance with [F51. EU] obligations, of preventing or restricting electro-magnetic interference—

(a) with the provision of an electronic communications network or electronic communications service; or

(b) with, or with the receipt of, anything conveyed or provided by means of such a network or service.

(6) In this section "electro-magnetic interference" means interference by means of the emission or reflection of electro-magnetic energy in the course of, or in connection with, the provision any electronic communications network or electronic communications service.

(7) In this section "disaster" includes any major incident having a significant effect on the general public; and for this purpose a major incident includes any incident of contamination involving radioactive substances or other toxic materials.

Amendments (Textual)

F49. Words in s. 51. (1)(e) omitted (26.5.2011) by virtue of The Electronic Communications and Wireless Telegraphy Regulations 2011 (S.I. 2011/1210), reg. 1. (2), Sch. 1 para. 27. (a) (with Sch. 3 para. 2)

F50. Word in s. 51. (2)(a) omitted (26.5.2011) by virtue of The Electronic Communications and Wireless Telegraphy Regulations 2011 (S.I. 2011/1210), reg. 1. (2), Sch. 1 para. 27. (b)(i) (with Sch. 3 para. 2)

F51. Words in Act substituted (22.4.2011) by The Treaty of Lisbon (Changes in Terminology) Order 2011 (S.I. 2011/1043), arts. 2, 3, 6 (with art. 3. (2)(3), 4. (2), 6. (4)(5))

F52. S. 51. (2)(c)-(h) inserted (26.5.2011) by The Electronic Communications and Wireless Telegraphy Regulations 2011 (S.I. 2011/1210), reg. 1. (2), Sch. 1 para. 27. (b)(ii) (with Sch. 3 para. 2)

F53. S. 51. (2. A) inserted (26.5.2011) by The Electronic Communications and Wireless Telegraphy Regulations 2011 (S.I. 2011/1210), reg. 1. (2), Sch. 1 para. 27. (c) (with Sch. 3 para. 2)

F54. Word in s. 51. (4)(b) substituted (26.5.2011) by The Electronic Communications and Wireless Telegraphy Regulations 2011 (S.I. 2011/1210), reg. 1. (2), Sch. 1 para. 27. (d) (with Sch. 3 para. 2)

Commencement Information

I39. S. 51 in force at 25.7.2003 for specified purposes by S.I. 2003/1900, arts. 1. (2), 2. (1), Sch. 1 (with art. 3) (as amended by S.I. 2003/3142, art. 1. (3))

I40. S. 51 in force at 29.12.2003 in so far as not already in force by S.I. 2003/3142, art. 3. (2) (with art. 11)

General conditions: customer interests

52. Conditions relating to customer interests

(1) It shall be the duty of OFCOM to set such general conditions (if any) as they consider appropriate for securing that—

(a) public communications providers, or

(b) such descriptions of them as OFCOM consider appropriate,

establish and maintain procedures, standards and policies with respect to the matters mentioned in subsection (2).

(2) Those matters are—

(a) the handling of complaints made to public communications providers by any of their domestic and small business customers [F55, where the complaint relates to contractual conditions, or to the performance of a contract for the supply of an electronic communications network or service] ;

(b) the resolution of disputes between such providers and any of their domestic and small business customers [F56, where the complaint relates to contractual conditions, or to the performance of a contract for the supply of an electronic communications network or service] ;

(c) the provision of remedies and redress in respect of matters that form the subject-matter of such complaints or disputes;

[F57. (ca)the payment of compensation to a person in respect of delay in porting a number to another public communications provider, or abuse of the process for porting a number;]

(d) the information about service standards and about the rights of domestic and small business customers that is to be made available to those customers by public communications providers;

(e) any other matter appearing to OFCOM to be necessary for securing effective protection for the domestic and small business customers of such providers.

(3) It shall be the duty of OFCOM, in setting conditions in accordance with subsection (1), to secure so far as they consider appropriate—

(a) that the procedures established and maintained for the handling of complaints and the resolution of disputes are easy to use, transparent [F58, non-discriminatory] and effective;

(b) that domestic and small business customers have the right to use those procedures free of charge; and

(c) that where public communications providers are in contravention of conditions set in accordance with the preceding provisions of this section, the providers follow such procedures as may be required by the general conditions.

(4) Subject to section 55, OFCOM's duties under subsections (1) and (3) so far as relating to procedures for the handling of complaints are to be performed, to such extent as they consider appropriate, by the setting of general conditions requiring public communications providers to establish and maintain procedures that conform with a code of practice which is—

(a) applicable to the providers to whom the conditions apply; and

(b) for the time being approved by OFCOM for the purposes of this subsection.

(5) Subject to section 55, OFCOM's duties under subsections (1) and (3) so far as relating to procedures for resolving disputes are to be performed, to such extent as they consider appropriate, by the setting of general conditions requiring public communications providers—

(a) to establish and maintain procedures for resolving disputes; and

(b) to secure that those procedures are, and continue to be, approved by OFCOM.

(6) In this section "domestic and small business customer", in relation to a public communications provider, means a customer of that provider who is neither—

(a) himself a communications provider; nor

(b) a person who is such a customer in respect of an undertaking carried on by him for which more than ten individuals work (whether as employees or volunteers or otherwise).

Amendments (Textual)

F55. Words in s. 52. (2)(a) inserted (26.5.2011) by The Electronic Communications and Wireless Telegraphy Regulations 2011 (S.I. 2011/1210), reg. 1. (2), Sch. 1 para. 28. (a) (with Sch. 3 para. 2)

F56. Words in s. 52. (2)(b) inserted (26.5.2011) by The Electronic Communications and Wireless Telegraphy Regulations 2011 (S.I. 2011/1210), reg. 1. (2), Sch. 1 para. 28. (b) (with Sch. 3 para. 2)

F57. S. 52. (2)(ca) inserted (26.5.2011) by The Electronic Communications and Wireless Telegraphy Regulations 2011 (S.I. 2011/1210), reg. 1. (2), Sch. 1 para. 28. (c) (with Sch. 3 para. 2)

F58. Words in s. 52. (3)(a) inserted (26.5.2011) by The Electronic Communications and Wireless Telegraphy Regulations 2011 (S.I. 2011/1210), reg. 1. (2), Sch. 1 para. 28. (d) (with Sch. 3 para. 2)

Commencement Information

I41. S. 52 in force at 25.7.2003 for specified purposes by S.I. 2003/1900, arts. 1. (2), 2. (1), Sch. 1

(with art. 3) (as amended by S.I. 2003/3142, art. 1. (3))

142. S. 52 in force at 29.12.2003 in so far as not already in force by S.I. 2003/3142, art. 3. (2) (with art. 11)

53. Approval of codes of practice for the purposes of s. 52.

(1) Where a code of practice is submitted to OFCOM for approval, they shall approve that code if and only if, in their opinion, it makes all such provision as they consider necessary in relation to the matters dealt with in the code for the protection of the domestic and small business customers of the public communications providers to whom the code applies.

(2) It shall be the duty of OFCOM to keep under review the codes of practice for the time being approved by them.

(3) OFCOM may at any time, by a notification given or published in such manner as they consider appropriate—

(a) approve modifications that have been made to an approved code;

(b) withdraw their approval from a code; or

(c) give notice that the withdrawal of their approval will take effect from such time as may be specified in the notification unless such modifications of the code as are specified in the notification are made before that time.

(4) In considering—

(a) whether to approve a code of practice, or

(b) whether or in what manner to exercise their powers under subsections (2) and (3) of this section,

OFCOM must have regard to the matters mentioned in subsection (5).

(5) Those matters are—

(a) the need to secure that customers are able readily to comprehend the procedures that are provided for by an approved code of practice;

(b) the need to secure that there is consistency between the different codes for the time being approved by OFCOM; and

(c) the need to secure that the number of different codes so approved is kept to a minimum.

(6) In this section—

"approval" means approval for the purposes of section 52. (4) and "approve" and "approved" are to be construed accordingly; and

"domestic and small business customer" has the same meaning as in section 52.

Commencement Information

143. S. 53 in force at 25.7.2003 for specified purposes by S.I. 2003/1900, arts. 1. (2), 2. (1), Sch. 1 (with art. 3) (as amended by S.I. 2003/3142, art. 1. (3))

144. S. 53 in force at 29.12.2003 in so far as not already in force by S.I. 2003/3142, art. 3. (2) (with art. 11)

54. Approval of dispute procedures for the purposes of s. 52.

(1) Before giving their approval to any dispute procedures, OFCOM must consult the Secretary of State.

(2) OFCOM are not to approve dispute procedures unless they are satisfied that the arrangements under which the procedures have effect—

(a) are administered by person who is for practical purposes independent (so far as decisions in relation to disputes are concerned) of both OFCOM and the communications providers to whom the arrangements apply;

(b) give effect to procedures that are easy to use, transparent [F59, non-discriminatory] and effective;

(c) give, in the case of every communications provider to whom the arrangements apply, a right to each of his domestic and small business customers to use the procedures free of charge;

(d) ensure that all information necessary for giving effect to the procedures is obtained;

(e) ensure that disputes are effectively investigated;

(f) include provision conferring power to make awards of appropriate compensation; and

(g) are such as to enable awards of compensation to be properly enforced.

(3) OFCOM may approve dispute procedures subject to such conditions (including conditions as to the provision of information to OFCOM) as they may think fit.

(4) It shall be the duty of OFCOM to keep under review the dispute procedures for the time being approved by them.

(5) OFCOM may at any time, by a notification given or published in such manner as they consider appropriate—

(a) modify the conditions of their approval of any dispute procedures or withdraw such an approval; or

(b) give notice that the modification of those conditions, or the withdrawal of such an approval, will take effect from such time as may be specified in the notification unless the procedures (or the arrangements under which they have effect) are modified before that time in the manner required by the notification.

(6) In considering—

(a) whether to approve dispute procedures, or

(b) whether or in what manner to exercise their powers under subsections (3) to (5),

OFCOM must have regard to the matters mentioned in subsection (7).

(7) Those matters are—

(a) the need to secure that customers are able readily to comprehend dispute procedures;

(b) the need to secure that there is consistency between the different procedures for the time being approved by OFCOM; and

(c) the need to secure that the number of different sets of procedures so approved is kept to a minimum.

(8) In this section—

"approval" means approval for the purposes of subsection (5) of section 52 and "approve" and "approved" are to be construed accordingly;

"dispute procedures" means any such procedures as may fall to be approved for the purposes of that subsection; and

"domestic and small business customer" has the same meaning as in section 52.

Amendments (Textual)

F59. Words in s. 54. (2)(b) inserted (26.5.2011) by The Electronic Communications and Wireless Telegraphy Regulations 2011 (S.I. 2011/1210), reg. 1. (2), Sch. 1 para. 29 (with Sch. 3 para. 2)

Commencement Information

I45. S. 54 in force at 25.7.2003 for specified purposes by S.I. 2003/1900, arts. 1. (2), 2. (1), Sch. 1 (with art. 3) (as amended by S.I. 2003/3142, art. 1. (3))

I46. S. 54 in force at 29.12.2003 in so far as not already in force by S.I. 2003/3142, art. 3. (2) (with art. 11)

55. Orders by OFCOM in the absence of conditions under s. 52.

(1) OFCOM may make an order under this section if, at any time, they consider in relation to any one or more public communications providers—

(a) that it is not practicable, or at least not appropriate, for OFCOM's duties under subsections (1) and (3) of section 52 to be performed in a particular respect by the setting of general conditions; and

(b) that it is necessary to make the order for the purpose—

(i) of securing the necessary protection for the customers of that provider or of those providers; or

(ii) of securing compliance with a [F51. EU] obligation.

(2) An order under this section may make such of the following provisions as OFCOM think fit—

(a) provision imposing requirements with respect to the complaints and disputes mentioned in section 52. (2);

(b) provision for the enforcement of those requirements;

(c) provision making other arrangements for the purposes of those requirements.

(3) The power to make provision by an order under this section includes, in particular—

(a) power to establish a body corporate with the capacity to make its own rules and to establish its own procedures;

(b) power to determine the jurisdiction of a body established by such an order or, for the purposes of the order, of any other person;

(c) power to confer jurisdiction with respect to any matter on OFCOM themselves;

(d) power to provide for a person on whom jurisdiction is conferred by the arrangements to make awards of compensation, to direct the reimbursement of costs or expenses, or to do both;

(e) power to provide for such a person to enforce, or to participate in the enforcement of, any awards or directions made under such an order; and

(f) power to make such other provision as OFCOM think fit for the enforcement of such awards and directions.

(4) An order under this section may require such public communications providers as may be determined by or under the order to make payments to OFCOM in respect of expenditure incurred by OFCOM in connection with—

(a) the establishment and maintenance, in accordance with such an order, of a body corporate or of a procedure; or

(b) the making of any other arrangements for the purposes of the requirements of such an order.

(5) The consent of the Secretary of State is required for the making by OFCOM of an order under this section.

(6) Section 403 applies to the power of OFCOM to make an order under this section.

(7) A statutory instrument containing an order made by OFCOM under this section shall be subject to annulment in pursuance of a resolution of either House of Parliament.

Amendments (Textual)

F51. Words in Act substituted (22.4.2011) by The Treaty of Lisbon (Changes in Terminology) Order 2011 (S.I. 2011/1043), arts. 2, 3, 6 (with art. 3. (2)(3), 4. (2), 6. (4)(5))

Commencement Information

I47. S. 55 in force at 25.7.2003 for specified purposes by S.I. 2003/1900, arts. 1. (2), 2. (1), Sch. 1 (with art. 3) (as amended by S.I. 2003/3142, art. 1. (3))

I48. S. 55 in force at 29.12.2003 in so far as not already in force by S.I. 2003/3142, art. 3. (2) (with art. 11)

General conditions: telephone numbers

56. The National Telephone Numbering Plan

(1) It shall be the duty of OFCOM to publish a document (to be known as "the National Telephone Numbering Plan") setting out—

(a) the numbers that they have determined to be available for allocation by them as telephone numbers;

(b) such restrictions as they consider appropriate on the adoption of numbers available for allocation in accordance with the plan; F60...

[F61. (ba)such requirements as they consider appropriate, for the purpose of protecting consumers, in relation to the tariff principles and maximum prices applicable to numbers so adopted or available for allocation; and]

(c) such restrictions as they consider appropriate on the other uses to which numbers available for allocation in accordance with the plan may be put.

(2) It shall be OFCOM's duty—

(a) from time to time to review the National Telephone Numbering Plan; and

(b) to make any revision of that plan that they think fit in consequence of such a review; but this duty must be performed in compliance with the requirements, so far as applicable, of section 60.

(3) OFCOM must also keep such day to day records as they consider appropriate of the telephone numbers allocated by them in accordance with the National Telephone Numbering Plan.

(4) The publication of the National Telephone Numbering Plan, or of a revision of it, must be in such manner as appears to OFCOM to be appropriate for bringing the contents of the Plan, or of

the revised Plan, to the attention of such persons as OFCOM consider appropriate.

(5) In this Chapter references to a telephone number are (subject to subsection (7)) references to any number that is used (whether or not in connection with telephony) for any one or more of the following purposes—

    (a) identifying the destination for, or recipient of, an electronic communication;

    (b) identifying the origin, or sender, of an electronic communication;

    (c) identifying the route for an electronic communication;

    (d) identifying the source from which an electronic communication or electronic communications service may be obtained or accessed;

    (e) selecting the service that is to be obtained or accessed, or required elements or characteristics of that service; or

    (f) identifying the communications provider by means of whose network or service an electronic communication is to be transmitted, or treated as transmitted.

(6) In this Chapter references to the adoption of a telephone number by a communications provider are references to his doing any of the following in relation to a number allocated (whether or not to that provider) by OFCOM—

    (a) allocating or transferring that number to a particular customer or piece of apparatus;

    (b) using that number for identifying a service or route used by that provider or by any of his customers;

    (c) using that number for identifying a communication as one to be transmitted by that provider;

    (d) designating that number for use in selecting a service or the required elements or characteristics of a service;

    (e) authorising the use of that number by others for any of the purposes mentioned in subsection (5).

(7) The Secretary of State may by order exclude such numbers as may be described in the order from the numbers that are to be treated as telephone numbers for the purposes of this Chapter.

(8) No order is to be made containing provision authorised by subsection (7) unless a draft of the order has been laid before Parliament and approved by a resolution of each House.

(9) References in this section to the allocation of a number are references to its allocation for the purposes of general conditions under section 58 or in accordance with conditions under section 59.

(10) In this section—

"electronic communication" means a communication for transmission by means of an electronic communications network; and

"number" includes data of any description.

Amendments (Textual)

F60. Word in s. 56. (1)(b) omitted (26.5.2011) by virtue of The Electronic Communications and Wireless Telegraphy Regulations 2011 (S.I. 2011/1210), reg. 1. (2), Sch. 1 para. 30 (with Sch. 3 para. 2)

F61. S. 56. (1)(ba) inserted (26.5.2011) by The Electronic Communications and Wireless Telegraphy Regulations 2011 (S.I. 2011/1210), reg. 1. (2), Sch. 1 para. 30 (with Sch. 3 para. 2)

Commencement Information

I49. S. 56 in force at 25.7.2003 for specified purposes by S.I. 2003/1900, art. 2. (1), Sch. 1 (with art. 3) (as amended by S.I. 2003/3142, art. 1. (3))

I50. S. 56 in force at 29.12.2003 in so far as not already in force by S.I. 2003/3142, art. 3. (1), Sch. 1 (with art. 11)

[F6256. A.Conditions for limitations on allocation of telephone numbers

(1) When OFCOM allocate telephone numbers in accordance with the National Telephone Numbering Plan, they must specify whether an allocation may be transferred from one person to another, and may set out the conditions under which the allocation may be transferred.

(2) If OFCOM allocate telephone numbers for a limited period of time, the limitation must be objectively justifiable in relation to the services to which it relates, taking account of the need to allow for an appropriate period of investment amortisation.]

Amendments (Textual)

F62 S. 56. A inserted (26.5.2011) by The Electronic Communications and Wireless Telegraphy Regulations 2011 (S.I. 2011/1210), reg. 1. (2), Sch. 1 para. 31 (with Sch. 3 para. 2)

57. Conditions to secure access to telephone numbers

(1) General conditions may impose such requirements as OFCOM consider appropriate for securing that every end-user of a public electronic communications service is able, by means of that service—

(a) to make calls or otherwise transmit electronic communications to every normal telephone number; and

(b) to receive every call or other electronic communication that is made or transmitted to him using such a service from apparatus identified by a normal telephone number.

(2) A normal telephone number is one which—

(a) has been made available, in accordance with the National Telephone Numbering Plan, as a number to be used for the purpose of identifying the destination for, or the recipient of, electronic communications; and

(b) is for the time being—

(i) a number adopted by a communications provider to be used for such a purpose; or

(ii) a number in use for such a purpose by a person other than a communications provider to whom it has been allocated in accordance with conditions under section 59.

(3) In this section "electronic communication" has the same meaning as in section 56.

Commencement Information

I51. S. 57 in force at 25.7.2003 for specified purposes by S.I. 2003/1900, art. 2. (1), Sch. 1 (with art. 3) (as amended by S.I. 2003/3142, art. 1. (3))

I52. S. 57 in force at 29.12.2003 in so far as not already in force by S.I. 2003/3142, art. 3. (1), Sch. 1 (with art. 11)

58. Conditions about allocation and adoption of numbers

(1) General conditions may include conditions which—

(a) prohibit the adoption of telephone numbers by a communications provider except in cases where the numbers have been allocated by OFCOM to a person;

[F63. (aa)impose tariff principles and maximum prices for the purpose of protecting consumers in relation to the provision of an electronic communications service by means of telephone numbers adopted or available for use;]

(b) regulate the use by a communications provider, for the purpose of providing an electronic communications network or electronic communications service, of telephone numbers not allocated to that provider;

(c) impose restrictions on the adoption of telephone numbers by a communications provider, and on other practices by communications providers in relation to telephone numbers allocated to them;

(d) impose requirements on a communications provider in connection with the adoption by him of telephone numbers;

(e) require an allocation of particular telephone numbers to be transferred from one communications provider to another in the circumstances provided for in the conditions;

(f) impose such requirements and restrictions on a communications provider from whom an allocation is required to be transferred as may be provided for, in relation to the transfer, in the conditions;

(g) require payments of such amounts as may be determined by OFCOM to be made to them by a person in respect of the allocation to him of telephone numbers;

(h) require payments of such amounts as may be determined by OFCOM to be made to them by a person in respect of transfers of allocations from one person to another; and

(i) require communications providers to secure compliance with such rules relating to the use of telephone numbers by their customers as OFCOM may set out in general conditions or determine in accordance with provision made by the general conditions.

(2) General conditions may also—

(a) provide for the procedure to be followed on the making of applications to OFCOM for the allocation of telephone numbers;

(b) provide for the information that must accompany such applications and for the handling of such applications;

(c) provide a procedure for telephone numbers to be reserved pending the making and disposal of an application for their allocation;

(d) provide for the procedure to be followed on the making of applications for telephone numbers to be reserved, and for the handling of such applications;

(e) regulate the procedures to be followed, the system to be applied and the charges to be imposed for the purposes of, or in connection with, the adoption by a communications provider of telephone numbers allocated to that provider;

(f) regulate the procedures to be followed, the system to be applied and the charges to be imposed for the purposes of, or in connection with, the transfer of an allocation from one person to another.

(3) The conditions that may be set under subsection (1)(d) include conditions imposing requirements with respect to the provision of information for purposes connected with—

(a) the compilation of directories; and

(b) the provision of directory enquiry facilities.

(4) The procedure to be followed on the making of an application for the allocation of numbers that are available for allocation in accordance with the National Telephone Numbering Plan must require OFCOM's determination of the application to be made—

(a) in the case of an application made in response to an invitation in accordance with subsection (5), before the end of six weeks after the day on which the application is received; and

(b) in any other case, before the end of three weeks after that day.

(5) Where OFCOM are proposing to allocate any telephone numbers, they may—

(a) invite persons to indicate the payments each would be willing to make to OFCOM if allocated the numbers; and

(b) make the allocation according to the amounts indicated.

(6) General conditions providing for payments to be made to OFCOM in respect of anything mentioned in subsection (1)(g) or (h)—

(a) must set out the principles according to which the amounts of the payments are to be determined;

(b) may provide for the payments to consist of a lump sum in respect of a particular allocation or transfer or of sums payable periodically while an allocation remains in force, or of both;

(c) may provide for the amounts to be determined by reference to—

(i) any indication according to which the allocation has been made as mentioned in subsection (5); or

(ii) any other factors (including the costs incurred by OFCOM in connection with the carrying out of their functions by virtue of section 56 and this section) as OFCOM think fit.

(7) General conditions may—

(a) make modifications from time to time of, or of the method of determining, the amounts of periodic payments falling to be made by virtue of conditions containing provision authorised by this section; and

(b) make different provision in relation to different descriptions of communications provider and different descriptions of telephone number.

(8) Nothing in subsection (7) authorises the modification, after it has been fixed, of the amount of a periodic payment fixed in accordance with arrangements made in relation to numbers allocated as mentioned in subsection (5)(b).

(9) Payments that are required to be made to OFCOM in respect of anything mentioned in subsection (1)(g) or (h)—

(a) must be paid to them as soon as they become due in accordance with the conditions imposing the obligation to pay; and

(b) if not so paid, are to be recoverable by them accordingly.

Amendments (Textual)

F63. S. 58. (1)(aa) inserted (26.5.2011) by The Electronic Communications and Wireless Telegraphy Regulations 2011 (S.I. 2011/1210), reg. 1. (2), Sch. 1 para. 32 (with Sch. 3 para. 2)

Commencement Information

153. S. 58 in force at 25.7.2003 for specified purposes by S.I. 2003/1900, art. 2. (1), Sch. 1 (with art. 3) (as amended by S.I. 2003/3142, art. 1. (3))

154. S. 58 in force at 29.12.2003 in so far as not already in force by S.I. 2003/3142, art. 3. (1), Sch. 1 (with art. 11)

59. Telephone numbering conditions binding non-providers

(1) OFCOM may set conditions under this section that apply to persons other than communications providers and relate to—

(a) the allocation of telephone numbers to such persons;

(b) the transfer of allocations to and from such persons; and

(c) the use of telephone numbers by such persons.

(2) The conditions that may be set under this section include conditions imposing obligations corresponding to any of the obligations that may be imposed on communications providers by general conditions making provision for, or in connection with—

(a) the allocation of telephone numbers;

(b) the transfer of allocations; or

(c) the use of telephone numbers.

(3) Subsection (10) of section 45 applies to OFCOM's power to set a condition under this section as it applies to their power to set a condition under that section.

(4) Sections 47 to 49 apply in relation to—

(a) the setting of conditions under this section and the modification and revocation of such conditions; and

(b) the giving, modification or withdrawal of any direction, approval or consent for the purposes of a condition under this section,

as they apply in the case of general conditions and in the case of directions, approvals and consents given for the purposes of general conditions.

(5) It shall be the duty of a person who—

(a) is not a communications provider, but

(b) applies for the allocation of a telephone number, or is allocated such a number,

to comply with any conditions set under this section.

(6) That duty shall be enforceable in civil proceedings by OFCOM—

(a) for an injunction;

(b) for specific performance of a statutory duty under section 45 of the Court of Session Act 1988 (c. 36); or

(c) for any other appropriate remedy or relief.

(7) Subsection (6) does not apply in the case of a person against whom the obligations contained in the condition in question are enforceable (by virtue of his having become a communications provider) as obligations imposed by general conditions.

Commencement Information

155. S. 59 in force at 25.7.2003 for specified purposes by S.I. 2003/1900, art. 2. (1), Sch. 1 (with art. 3) (as amended by S.I. 2003/3142, art. 1. (3))

156. S. 59 in force at 29.12.2003 in so far as not already in force by S.I. 2003/3142, art. 3. (1), Sch. 1 (with art. 11)

60. Modification of documents referred to in numbering conditions

(1) This section applies where numbering conditions for the time being have effect by reference to provisions, as they have effect from time to time, of—

(a) the National Telephone Numbering Plan; or

(b) another document published by OFCOM.

(2) OFCOM must not revise or otherwise modify the relevant provisions unless they are satisfied that the revision or modification is—

(a) objectively justifiable in relation to the matters to which it relates;

(b) not such as to discriminate unduly against particular persons or against a particular description of persons;

(c) proportionate to what the modification is intended to achieve; and

(d) in relation to what it is intended to achieve, transparent.

(3) Before revising or otherwise modifying the relevant provisions, OFCOM must publish a notification—

(a) stating that they are proposing to do so;

(b) specifying the Plan or other document that they are proposing to revise or modify;

(c) setting out the effect of their proposed revisions or modifications;

(d) giving their reasons for making the proposal; and

(e) specifying the period within which representations may be made to OFCOM about their proposal.

(4) That period must be one ending not less than one month after the day of the publication of the notification.

(5) OFCOM may give effect, with or without modifications, to a proposal with respect to which they have published a notification under subsection (3) only if—

(a) they have considered every representation about the proposal that is made to them within the period specified in the notification; and

(b) they have had regard to every international obligation of the United Kingdom (if any) which has been notified to them for the purposes of this paragraph by the Secretary of State.

(6) The publication of a notification under this section must be in such manner as appears to OFCOM to be appropriate for bringing the contents of the notification to the attention of such persons as OFCOM consider appropriate.

(7) In this section—

"numbering conditions" means—

- general conditions the making of which is authorised by section 57 or 58;

- conditions set under section 59;

"the relevant provisions", in relation to the Plan or document, means the provisions of the Plan or document by reference to which (as they have effect from time to time) the numbering conditions in question have effect.

Commencement Information

I57. S. 60 in force at 25.7.2003 for specified purposes by S.I. 2003/1900, art. 2. (1), Sch. 1 (with art. 3) (as amended by S.I. 2003/3142, art. 1. (3))

I58. S. 60 in force at 29.12.2003 in so far as not already in force by S.I. 2003/3142, art. 3. (1), Sch. 1 (with art. 11)

61. Withdrawal of telephone number allocations

(1) Where OFCOM have allocated telephone numbers for the purposes of any numbering conditions, they may withdraw that allocation if, and only if, the case is one in which the withdrawal of an allocation is authorised by this section.

(2) The withdrawal of an allocation is authorised (subject to section 62) if—

(a) consent to the withdrawal is given by the person to whom the numbers are for the time being allocated;

(b) the withdrawal is made for the purposes of a transfer of the allocation required by numbering conditions;

(c) the withdrawal is made for the purposes of a numbering reorganisation applicable to a particular series of telephone numbers;

(d) the withdrawal is made in circumstances specified in the numbering conditions and for the purpose of securing that what appears to OFCOM to be the best and most efficient use is made of the numbers and other data that are appropriate for use as telephone numbers;

(e) the allocated numbers are numbers that have not been adopted during such period after their allocation as may be specified in the numbering conditions; or

(f) the allocated numbers are comprised in a series of numbers which have not to a significant extent been adopted or used during such period as may be so specified.

(3) The withdrawal of an allocation is also authorised where—

(a) there have been [F64serious or repeated] contraventions, by the person to whom the allocation is for the time being allocated, of the numbering conditions; and

(b) it appears to OFCOM that the taking of other steps in respect of the contraventions is likely to prove ineffective for securing future compliance.

(4) The withdrawal of an allocation is also authorised where—

(a) the person to whom the allocation is for the time being allocated is not a communications provider; and

(b) it appears to OFCOM that contraventions by that person of numbering conditions makes the withdrawal of the allocation appropriate.

(5) OFCOM's power to set conditions specifying circumstances for the purposes of subsection (2)(d), and their power to withdraw an allocation in the specified circumstances, are each exercisable only in a manner that does not discriminate unduly—

(a) against particular communications providers;

(b) against particular users of the allocated numbers; or

(c) against a particular description of such providers or users;

and the purposes for which those powers may be exercised do not include the carrying out of a numbering reorganisation of the sort mentioned in subsection (2)(c).

(6) Where OFCOM are proposing to withdraw an allocation in exercise of the power conferred by virtue of subsection (2)(e) or (f), they must—

(a) give a notification of their proposal;

(b) consider any representations made to them about the proposal within the period of one month following the day on which the notification is given; and

(c) ensure that the withdrawal (if OFCOM decide to proceed with it after considering those representations) does not take effect until the end of the three months beginning with the end of the period mentioned in paragraph (b).

(7) A notification for the purposes of subsection (6) must be given in such manner as OFCOM consider appropriate for bringing it to the attention of—

(a) the person to whom the numbers to which the proposed withdrawal relates are for the time being allocated;

(b) every person appearing to OFCOM to be a person to whom communications are or may be transmitted using one of those numbers for identifying the destination or route;

(c) every person who uses one or more of those numbers for obtaining access to services or for communication; and

(d) every other person who, in OFCOM's opinion, is likely to be affected by the proposal.

(8) For the purposes of this section there are repeated contraventions by a person of numbering conditions to the extent that—

[F65. (a)in the case of a previous notification of a contravention given to that person under section 96. A, OFCOM have given a confirmation decision to that person under section 96. C(2) in respect of the contravention; and

(b) in the period of 24 months following the giving of that confirmation decision, one or more further confirmation decisions have been given to the person in respect of contraventions of numbering conditions;]

and for the purposes of this subsection it shall be immaterial whether the [F66confirmation decisions] related to the same contravention or to different contraventions of the same or different conditions.

(9) In this section "numbering conditions" means—

(a) general conditions the making of which is authorised by section 58; or

(b) conditions set under section 59.

Amendments (Textual)

F64. Words in s. 61. (3)(a) substituted (26.5.2011) by The Electronic Communications and Wireless Telegraphy Regulations 2011 (S.I. 2011/1210), reg. 1. (2), Sch. 1 para. 33. (a) (with Sch. 3 paras. 2, 9)

F65. S. 61. (8)(a)(b) substituted (26.5.2011) by The Electronic Communications and Wireless Telegraphy Regulations 2011 (S.I. 2011/1210), reg. 1. (2), Sch. 1 para. 33. (b)(i) (with Sch. 3 paras. 2, 9)

F66. Words in s. 61. (8) substituted (26.5.2011) by The Electronic Communications and Wireless Telegraphy Regulations 2011 (S.I. 2011/1210), reg. 1. (2), Sch. 1 para. 33. (b)(ii) (with Sch. 3 paras. 2, 9, 10)

Commencement Information

I59. S. 61 in force at 25.7.2003 for specified purposes by S.I. 2003/1900, art. 2. (1), Sch. 1 (with art. 3) (as amended by S.I. 2003/3142, art. 1. (3))

I60. S. 61 in force at 29.12.2003 in so far as not already in force by S.I. 2003/3142, art. 3. (1), Sch. 1 (with art. 11)

62. Numbering reorganisations

(1) This section applies to the withdrawal of an allocation for the purposes of a numbering reorganisation that is applicable to a particular series of telephone numbers.

(2) The allocation is to be withdrawn only if the reorganisation, so far as it relates to numbers of any description, is not such as to discriminate unduly—

(a) against particular communications providers;

(b) against particular users of the allocated numbers; or

(c) against a particular description of such providers or users.

(3) The allocation must not be withdrawn if the reorganisation fails to provide for withdrawn allocations to be replaced by allocations of telephone numbers so nearly resembling the numbers to which the withdrawal relates as the purpose of the reorganisation allows.

(4) Where a replacement allocation is made for the purposes of the re-organisation—

(a) no payment is to be made to OFCOM in respect of the making of the replacement allocation; but

(b) subsection (5) is to apply.

(5) Where this subsection applies—

(a) a provision for the making of periodic payments in respect of the withdrawn allocation is to be treated, to the extent that OFCOM determine that it should, as a provision requiring the making of periodic payments in respect of the replacement allocation; and

(b) OFCOM may, if they think fit, make such repayments or adjustments of a provision for payment as appear to them to be appropriate in consequence of differences between—

(i) the numbers to which the withdrawn allocation relates; and

(ii) the numbers to which the replacement allocation relates.

Commencement Information

I61. S. 62 in force at 25.7.2003 for specified purposes by S.I. 2003/1900, art. 2. (1), Sch. 1 (with art. 3) (as amended by S.I. 2003/3142, art. 1. (3))

I62. S. 62 in force at 29.12.2003 in so far as not already in force by S.I. 2003/3142, art. 3. (1), Sch. 1 (with art. 11)

63. General duty as to telephone numbering functions

(1) It shall be the duty of OFCOM, in the carrying out of their functions under sections 56 to 62—

(a) to secure that what appears to them to be the best use is made of the numbers that are appropriate for use as telephone numbers; and

(b) to encourage efficiency and innovation for that purpose.

(2) It shall also be the duty of OFCOM, in carrying out those functions, to secure that there is no undue discrimination by communications providers against other communications providers in relation to the adoption of telephone numbers for purposes connected with the use by one communications provider, or his customers, of an electronic communications network or electronic communications service provided by another.

(3) In this section "number" has the same meaning as in section 56.

Commencement Information

I63. S. 63 in force at 25.7.2003 for specified purposes by S.I. 2003/1900, art. 2. (1), Sch. 1 (with art. 3) (as amended by S.I. 2003/3142, art. 1. (3))

I64. S. 63 in force at 29.12.2003 in so far as not already in force by S.I. 2003/3142, art. 3. (1), Sch. 1 (with art. 11)

General conditions: must-carry obligations

64. Must-carry obligations

(1) General conditions may include conditions making any provision that OFCOM consider appropriate for securing that particular services are broadcast or otherwise transmitted by means of the electronic communications networks described in the conditions.

(2) A general condition containing provision authorised by this section is not (subject to subsection (4)) to require a service to be broadcast or otherwise transmitted by means of an electronic communications network unless—

(a) the service is included in the list of must-carry services; and

(b) the effect of the requirement is confined to networks by means of which public electronic communications services are provided that are used by a significant number of end-users as their principal means of receiving television programmes.

(3) That list is as follows

(a) any service of television programmes provided by the BBC so far as it is provided in digital form and is a service in relation to which OFCOM have functions;

(b) the Channel 3 services so far as provided in digital form;

(c) Channel 4 so far as provided in digital form;

(d) Channel 5 so far as provided in digital form;

(e) S4. C Digital;

(f) the digital public teletext service.

(4) General conditions making provision authorised by this section in relation to a listed service must, to such extent as OFCOM consider appropriate (and subject to subsection (5))—

(a) apply the requirement to broadcast or otherwise transmit that service to every service which is an ancillary service by reference to the listed service [F67. (including, but not limited to, a service enabling access for disabled end-users)] ; and

(b) provide for the listed service to be treated for the purposes of the conditions as constituting such other services comprised in or provided with that service as may be determined by OFCOM.

(5) General conditions making provision authorised by this section must also comply with all such restrictions (if any) as may be imposed by order made by the Secretary of State as to the maximum and minimum amounts, or proportions, of available capacity that are to be required by such conditions to be used in the case of a network for the broadcasting or other transmission of particular services, or descriptions of service.

(6) In making an order under subsection (5) the Secretary of State must have regard to—

(a) the objective of securing that services included in the list of must-carry services, and the other services to which conditions set in accordance with this section are likely to be applied by virtue of subsection (4), are available for reception by as many members of the public in the United Kingdom as practicable; and

(b) the need to secure that the amount of capacity available in the case of every network for making other services available is reasonable and, accordingly, that the burden of complying with conditions set in accordance with this section is proportionate to the public benefit to be secured by that objective.

(7) It shall be the duty of the Secretary of State from time to time to review—

(a) the list of must-carry services; and

(b) any requirements for the time being in force under this section with respect to the terms on which services must be broadcast or otherwise transmitted.

(8) Where the Secretary of State carries out such a review, he must consult the following about the matters under review—

(a) OFCOM; and

(b) such persons who, in his opinion, are likely to be affected by a modification of the list of must-carry services, or who represent any of those persons, as he thinks fit.

(9) If, on such a review, he considers it appropriate to do so, the Secretary of State may by order modify the list of must-carry services.

(10) In determining whether it is appropriate for the purposes of subsection (9) to add a service to the list of must-carry services or to remove it, the Secretary of State must have regard, in particular, to—

(a) the public benefit to be secured by the addition of the service to the list, or by its retention in the list;

(b) the extent to which the service (if it were not included in the list) would nevertheless be made available to an acceptable technical standard by means of the networks to which conditions set in accordance with this section apply;

(c) the capacity left available, after the requirements of those conditions have been complied with, for the broadcasting or other transmission of material by means of each of those networks; and

(d) the need to secure that the burden of complying with conditions so set is proportionate to the objective of securing that the services in the list of must-carry services, and the other services to which conditions set in accordance with this section are likely to applied by virtue of subsection (4), are available for reception by as many members of the public in the United Kingdom as practicable.

(11) The Secretary of State may also, if (whether on such a review or in any other circumstances) he considers it appropriate to do so, by order make provision imposing requirements as to what, as between—

(a) the person providing a must-carry service, and

(b) the person providing a network by means of which it is to be provided,

are to be the terms on which the service is to be broadcast or otherwise transmitted, in pursuance of general conditions set in accordance with this section, by means of that network.

(12) An order under subsection (11) may provide for the terms to be determined by OFCOM in accordance with the provisions of the order.

(13) Before making an order under subsection (5), and before making an order under subsection (11) in a case in which there has been no review under subsection (7), the Secretary of State must consult—

(a) OFCOM, and

(b) such persons who, in his opinion, are likely to be affected by the order, or who represent any of those persons, as he thinks fit.

(14) Section 362 applies for construing this section as it applies for the purposes of Part 3.

Amendments (Textual)

F67. Words in s. 64. (4)(a) inserted (26.5.2011) by The Electronic Communications and Wireless Telegraphy Regulations 2011 (S.I. 2011/1210), reg. 1. (2), Sch. 1 para. 34 (with Sch. 3 para. 2)

Commencement Information

I65. S. 64 in force at 25.7.2003 for specified purposes by S.I. 2003/1900, arts. 1. (2), 2. (1), Sch. 1 (with art. 3) (as amended by S.I. 2003/3142, art. 1. (3))

I66. S. 64 in force at 29.12.2003 in so far as not already in force by S.I. 2003/3142, art. 3. (2) (with art. 11)

Universal service conditions

65. Obligations to be secured by universal service conditions

(1) The Secretary of State must by order ("the universal service order") set out the extent to which the things falling within subsection (2) must, for the purpose of securing compliance with [F51. EU] obligations for the time being in force, be provided, made available or supplied throughout the United Kingdom.

(2) Those things are—

(a) electronic communications networks and electronic communications services;

(b) facilities capable of being made available as part of or in connection with an electronic communications service;

(c) particular methods of billing for electronic communications services or of accepting payment for them;

(d) directories capable of being used in connection with the use of an electronic communications network or electronic communications service; and

(e) directory enquiry facilities capable of being used for purposes connected with the use of such a network or service.

(3) The universal service order may contain guidance about matters relating to the pricing of things that the order says must be provided, made available or supplied.

(4) Before making or varying the universal service order, the Secretary of State must consult OFCOM and such other persons as he considers appropriate.

[F68. (5)Before making or varying the universal service order, the Secretary of State must take due account of the desirability of not favouring—

(a) one form of electronic communications network, electronic communications service or associated facility, or

(b) one means of providing or making available such a network, service or facility,

over another.]

Amendments (Textual)

F51. Words in Act substituted (22.4.2011) by The Treaty of Lisbon (Changes in Terminology) Order 2011 (S.I. 2011/1043), arts. 2, 3, 6 (with art. 3. (2)(3), 4. (2), 6. (4)(5))

F68. S. 65. (5) inserted (26.5.2011) by The Electronic Communications and Wireless Telegraphy Regulations 2011 (S.I. 2011/1210), reg. 1. (2), Sch. 1 para. 35 (with Sch. 3 para. 2)

Modifications etc. (not altering text)

C1. S. 65 excluded (11.12.2003) by The Privacy and Electronic Communications (EC Directive) Regulations 2003 (S.I. 2003/2426), regs. 1, 35. (2) (with regs. 4, 15. (3), 28, 29)

Commencement Information

I67. S. 65 in force at 25.7.2003 for specified purposes by S.I. 2003/1900, arts. 1. (2), 2. (1), Sch. 1 (with art. 3) (as amended by S.I. 2003/3142, art. 1. (3))

I68. S. 65 in force at 29.12.2003 in so far as not already in force by S.I. 2003/3142, art. 3. (2) (with art. 11)

66. Designation of universal service providers

(1) OFCOM may by regulations make provision for the designation of the persons to whom universal service conditions are to be applicable.

(2) Subject to subsection (3), those regulations are not to authorise the designation of a person other than a communications provider.

(3) The regulations may provide for a person other than a communications provider to be designated for the purposes only of conditions relating to—

(a) the supply of directories capable of being used in connection with the use of an electronic communications network or electronic communications service; and

(b) the making available of directory enquiry facilities capable of being used for purposes connected with the use of such a network or service.

(4) OFCOM may from time to time—

(a) review the designations for the time being in force in accordance with regulations under this section; and

(b) on such a review, consider what (if any) universal service conditions should continue to apply to each of the designated persons.

(5) The procedure to be followed in the case of every such review must be the procedure provided for in regulations made by OFCOM.

(6) Regulations made by OFCOM under this section must provide for a person's designation as a person to whom universal service conditions are to be applicable to cease to have effect where, in

any such case as may be described in the regulations, the universal service conditions applied to him are all revoked.

(7) Regulations made by OFCOM under this section providing a procedure for the designation of persons, or for the conduct of a review under subsection (4), must not provide for any procedure other than one appearing to OFCOM—

(a) to be efficient, objective and transparent; and

(b) not to involve, or to tend to give rise to, any undue discrimination against any person or description of persons.

(8) Where—

(a) OFCOM designate a person in accordance with regulations under this section, or

(b) a designation of a person in accordance with any such regulations ceases to have effect,

they must give a notification of that designation, or of that fact, to the European Commission.

(9) A notification under this section must identify the person who has been designated, or the person whose designation has ceased to have effect.

(10) Section 403 applies to the power of OFCOM to make regulations under this section.

Commencement Information

I69. S. 66 in force at 25.7.2003 for specified purposes by S.I. 2003/1900, arts. 1. (2), 2. (1), Sch. 1 (with art. 3) (as amended by S.I. 2003/3142, art. 1. (3))

I70. S. 66 in force at 29.12.2003 in so far as not already in force by S.I. 2003/3142, art. 3. (2) (with art. 11)

67. Subject-matter of universal service conditions

(1) OFCOM may set any such universal service conditions as they consider appropriate for securing compliance with the obligations set out in the universal service order.

[F69. (1. A)OFCOM may also set universal service conditions which apply to a designated universal service provider who proposes to make a disposal to another person of a substantial part or all of the designated universal service provider's local access network assets.

(1. B)But subsection (1. A) does not apply where the disposal is made by a company to a connected company (within the meaning given by section 1122. (2) of the Corporation Tax Act 2010).]

(2) Universal service conditions applied to a person must include a condition requiring him to publish information about his performance in complying with the universal service conditions that apply to him.

(3) A condition set in accordance with subsection (2) must contain provision which—

(a) requires information published in accordance with it to be updated from time to time and published again;

(b) requires information so published to satisfy the requirements that OFCOM consider appropriate for securing that it is adequate; and

(c) requires information so published to be framed by reference to the quality of service parameters, definitions and measurement methods for the time being set out in Annex III to the Universal Service Directive.

(4) A condition set in accordance with that subsection may impose requirements as to—

(a) the times at which information published in accordance with it is to be published; and

(b) the manner in which that information is to be published.

(5) Universal service conditions may impose an obligation on a person to whom they apply to do one or both of the following, if required to do so by OFCOM—

(a) to make facilities available for enabling information published in pursuance of a condition applied to that person under subsection (2) to be independently audited;

(b) to meet the costs of any independent auditing of that information that is required by OFCOM.

(6) The reference in subsection (5) to the independent auditing of information is a reference to its being audited by a qualified auditor—

(a) for accuracy; and

(b) for its usefulness in the making of comparisons with information published by other designated universal service providers.

(7) Universal service conditions may impose performance targets on designated universal service providers with respect to any of the matters in relation to which obligations may be imposed by such conditions.

(8) In setting a universal service condition, OFCOM must have regard to any guidance about matters relating to pricing that is contained in the universal service order.

[F70. (9)In this section "qualified auditor" means a person who—

(a) is eligible for appointment as a statutory auditor under Part 42 of the Companies Act 2006, and

(b) if the appointment to carry out such auditing as is mentioned in subsection (5) were an appointment as a statutory auditor, would not be prohibited from acting by section 1214 of that Act (independence requirement).]

Amendments (Textual)

F69. S. 67. (1. A)(1. B) inserted (26.5.2011) by The Electronic Communications and Wireless Telegraphy Regulations 2011 (S.I. 2011/1210), reg. 1. (2), Sch. 1 para. 36 (with Sch. 3 para. 2)

F70. S. 67. (9) substituted (6.4.2008) by The Companies Act 2006 (Consequential Amendments etc) Order 2008 (S.I. 2008/948), art. 2. (2), Sch. 1 para. 30. (2) (with arts. 6, 11, 12)

Commencement Information

I71. S. 67 in force at 25.7.2003 for specified purposes by S.I. 2003/1900, arts. 1. (2), 2. (1), Sch. 1 (with art. 3) (as amended by S.I. 2003/3142, art. 1. (3))

I72. S. 67 in force at 29.12.2003 in so far as not already in force by S.I. 2003/3142, art. 3. (2) (with art. 11)

68. Tariffs etc. for universal services

(1) It shall be the duty of OFCOM—

(a) to keep under review universal service tariffs; and

(b) to monitor changes to those tariffs.

(2) Universal service conditions may require one or more of the following—

(a) the use of a common tariff, or of common tariffs, in relation to anything mentioned in section 65. (2);

(b) the use, in such cases as may be specified or described in the conditions, of such special tariffs in relation to anything so mentioned as may be so specified or described;

(c) the fixing of tariffs used in accordance with the conditions by the use of such methods, and by reference to such methods of computing costs, as may be so specified or described.

(3) Universal service conditions must secure that the terms on which a person is provided with anything required by the universal service order do not require him—

(a) to pay for an unnecessary additional service; or

(b) to pay, in respect of anything required by the order, any amount that is attributable to the provision to him of such a service.

(4) The references in subsection (3), in relation to a person, to an unnecessary additional service are references to anything the provision of which—

(a) he has to accept by reason of his being provided, at his request, with something required by the order ("the requested service"); and

(b) is not necessary for the purpose of providing him with the requested service.

(5) It shall be the duty of OFCOM, in setting a universal service condition about universal service tariffs, to have regard to anything ascertained by them in the performance of their duty under subsection (1).

(6) References in this section to a universal service tariff are references to any of the tariffs used by designated universal service providers [F71or, where there is no designated universal service provider, by other persons,] in relation to the things for the time being required by the universal service order.

(7) References in this section to providing a person with anything include references to making it available or supplying it to him.

(8) In this section "tariff" includes a pricing structure.

Amendments (Textual)
F71. Words in s. 68. (6) inserted (26.5.2011) by The Electronic Communications and Wireless Telegraphy Regulations 2011 (S.I. 2011/1210), reg. 1. (2), Sch. 1 para. 37 (with Sch. 3 para. 2)
Commencement Information
173. S. 68 in force at 25.7.2003 for specified purposes by S.I. 2003/1900, arts. 1. (2), 2. (1), Sch. 1 (with art. 3) (as amended by S.I. 2003/3142, art. 1. (3))
174. S. 68 in force at 29.12.2003 in so far as not already in force by S.I. 2003/3142, art. 3. (2) (with art. 11)

69. Directories and directory enquiry facilities

(1) This section applies where universal service conditions require a designated universal service provider—

(a) to supply a directory capable of being used in connection with the use of an electronic communications network or electronic communications service; or

(b) to make available directory enquiry facilities capable of being used for purposes connected with use of such a network or service.

(2) The universal service conditions applied to the provider must include the conditions that OFCOM consider appropriate for securing that the provider does not unduly discriminate against a source of relevant information—

(a) in the compiling of the directory or the answering of directory enquiries; or

(b) in the treatment in the directory, or for the purposes of the facilities, of any relevant information from that source.

(3) In this section—

(a) references to relevant information are references to information provided for inclusion in the directory or for use in the answering of directory enquiries; and

(b) references to a source of relevant information are references to a communications provider or designated universal service provider who provides relevant information.

Commencement Information
175. S. 69 in force at 25.7.2003 for specified purposes by S.I. 2003/1900, arts. 1. (2), 2. (1), Sch. 1 (with art. 3) (as amended by S.I. 2003/3142, art. 1. (3))
176. S. 69 in force at 29.12.2003 in so far as not already in force by S.I. 2003/3142, art. 3. (2) (with art. 11)

70. Review of compliance costs

(1) OFCOM may from time to time review the extent (if any) of the financial burden for a particular designated universal service provider of complying in relation to any matter with any one or more of the universal service conditions applied to him.

(2) Where—

(a) regulations under section 66 require the financial burden of so complying to be taken into account in determining whom to designate, and

(b) the regulations provide for a particular method of calculating that burden to be used for the purposes of that determination,

that must be the method of calculation applied on a review under this section.

(3) Where subsection (2) does not apply, the financial burden of so complying is to be taken to be the amount calculated by OFCOM to be the net cost of compliance after allowing for market benefits accruing to the designated universal service provider from—

(a) his designation; and

(b) the application to him of universal service conditions.

(4) After carrying out a review under this section OFCOM must either—

(a) cause the calculations made by them on the review to be audited by a person who appears to them to be independent of designated universal service providers; or

(b) themselves carry out an audit of those calculations.

(5) OFCOM must ensure, in the case of every audit carried out under subsection (4), that a report on the audit—

(a) is prepared; and

(b) if not prepared by OFCOM, is provided to them.

(6) It shall be the duty of OFCOM, in the case of every review under this section, to publish—

(a) their conclusions on the review; and

(b) a summary of the report of the audit which was carried out as respects the calculations made for the purposes of that review.

(7) The publication of anything under subsection (6) must be a publication in such manner as OFCOM consider appropriate for bringing it to the attention of the persons who, in their opinion, are likely to be affected by it.

Commencement Information

I77. S. 70 in force at 25.7.2003 for specified purposes by S.I. 2003/1900, arts. 1. (2), 2. (1), Sch. 1 (with art. 3) (as amended by S.I. 2003/3142, art. 1. (3))

I78. S. 70 in force at 29.12.2003 in so far as not already in force by S.I. 2003/3142, art. 3. (2) (with art. 11)

71. Sharing of burden of universal service obligations

(1) This section applies where OFCOM—

(a) have concluded, on a review under section 70, that complying in relation to any matter with universal service conditions imposes a financial burden on a particular designated universal service provider; and

(b) have published that conclusion in accordance with that section.

(2) OFCOM must determine, in the case of the designated universal service provider, whether they consider it would be unfair for that provider to bear, or to continue to bear, the whole or any part of so much of the burden.

(3) If—

(a) OFCOM determine that it would be unfair for the designated universal service provider to bear, or to continue to bear, the whole or a part of the burden, and

(b) an application for a determination under this subsection is made to OFCOM by that provider,

OFCOM may determine that contributions are to be made by communications providers to whom general conditions are applicable for meeting that burden.

(4) The making of any of the following must be in accordance with regulations made by OFCOM—

(a) a determination by OFCOM of the extent of the financial burden that exists for the designated universal service provider of complying in relation to any matter with universal service conditions;

(b) an application for the purposes of subsection (3)(b);

(c) a determination by OFCOM of whether it is or would be unfair for the designated universal service provider to bear, or to continue to bear, the burden of complying in relation to any matter with universal service conditions;

(d) a determination of the extent (if any) to which that is or would be unfair.

(5) The assessment, collection and distribution of contributions under subsection (3) is not to be carried out except in accordance with a mechanism provided for in a scheme contained in regulations made by OFCOM.

(6) It shall be the duty of OFCOM to exercise their power to make regulations under this section in the manner which they consider will secure that the assessment, collection and distribution of contributions under subsection (3) is carried out—

(a) in an objective and transparent manner;

(b) in a manner that does not involve, or tend to give rise to, any undue discrimination against particular communications providers or particular designated universal service providers, or against a particular description of them; and

(c) in a manner that avoids, or (if that is impracticable) at least minimises, any distortion of competition or of customer demand.

(7) Regulations made by OFCOM under this section may provide for a scheme containing the provision mentioned in subsection (5), and for any fund set up for the purposes of such a scheme,

to be administered either—

(a) by OFCOM; or

(b) by such other person as may be specified in the regulations.

(8) A person other than OFCOM is not to be specified in regulations under this section as the administrator of such a scheme or fund unless he is a person who OFCOM are satisfied is independent of both—

(a) the persons who are designated universal service providers; and

(b) communications providers to whom general conditions are applicable.

(9) Section 403 applies to the powers of OFCOM to make regulations under this section.

Commencement Information

I79. S. 71 in force at 25.7.2003 for specified purposes by S.I. 2003/1900, arts. 1. (2), 2. (1), Sch. 1 (with art. 3) (as amended by S.I. 2003/3142, art. 1. (3))

I80. S. 71 in force at 29.12.2003 in so far as not already in force by S.I. 2003/3142, art. 3. (2) (with art. 11)

72. Report on sharing mechanism

(1) This section applies where regulations under section 71 provide for a scheme for the assessment, collection and distribution of contributions under subsection (3) of that section.

(2) OFCOM must prepare and publish a report setting out, in relation to the period to which it applies—

(a) every determination by OFCOM that has had effect in relation to a time in that period as a determination of the costs of providing anything contained in the universal service order;

(b) the market benefits for each designated universal service provider that have accrued to him during that period from his designation and from the application to him of universal service conditions; and

(c) the contribution made under section 71. (3) by every person who has made a contribution during that period.

(3) The first report under this section must be prepared in relation to the period of twelve months beginning with the coming into force of the first regulations to be made under section 71.

(4) Every subsequent report must be prepared in relation to the period of twelve months beginning with the end of the period to which the previous report applied.

(5) Every report under this section—

(a) must be prepared as soon as practicable after the end of the period to which it is to apply; and

(b) must be published as soon as practicable after its preparation is complete.

(6) OFCOM are not required under this section—

(a) to publish any matter that is confidential in accordance with subsection (7) or (8); or

(b) to publish anything that it would not be reasonably practicable to publish without disclosing such a matter.

(7) A matter is confidential under this subsection if—

(a) it relates specifically to the affairs of a particular body; and

(b) publication of that matter would or might, in OFCOM's opinion, seriously and prejudicially affect the interests of that body.

(8) A matter is confidential under this subsection if—

(a) it relates to the private affairs of an individual; and

(b) publication of that matter would or might, in OFCOM's opinion, seriously and prejudicially affect the interests of that individual.

(9) The publication of a report under this section must be a publication in such manner as OFCOM consider appropriate for bringing it to the attention of the persons who, in their opinion, are affected by the matters to which it relates.

Commencement Information

I81. S. 72 in force at 25.7.2003 for specified purposes by S.I. 2003/1900, arts. 1. (2), 2. (1), Sch. 1 (with art. 3) (as amended by S.I. 2003/3142, art. 1. (3))

I82. S. 72 in force at 29.12.2003 in so far as not already in force by S.I. 2003/3142, art. 3. (2)

Access-related conditions

73. Permitted subject-matter of access-related conditions

(1) The only conditions that may be set under section 45 as access-related conditions are those authorised by this section.

(2) Access-related conditions may include conditions relating to the provision of such network access and service interoperability as appears to OFCOM appropriate for the purpose of securing—

(a) efficiencyF72...;

(b) sustainable competition F73...; F74...

[F75. (ba)efficient investment and innovation; and]

(c) the greatest possible benefit for the end-users of public electronic communications services.

(3) Access-related conditions may include conditions appearing to OFCOM to be appropriate for securing that persons to whom the electronic communications code applies participateF76... in arrangements for—

(a) sharing the use of electronic communications apparatus; and

(b) apportioning and making contributions towards costs incurred in relation to shared electronic communications apparatus.

[F77. (3. A)The power to set access-related conditions falling within subsection (3) is to be exercised for the purpose of—

(a) encouraging efficient investment in infrastructure; and

(b) promoting innovation.]

F78. (4). . . . .

(5) Access-related conditions may include conditions containing any provision required by section 75. (2).

Amendments (Textual)

F72. Words in s. 73. (2)(a) omitted (26.5.2011) by virtue of The Electronic Communications and Wireless Telegraphy Regulations 2011 (S.I. 2011/1210), reg. 1. (2), Sch. 1 para. 38. (a)(i) (with Sch. 3 para. 2)

F73. Words in s. 73. (2)(b) omitted (26.5.2011) by virtue of The Electronic Communications and Wireless Telegraphy Regulations 2011 (S.I. 2011/1210), reg. 1. (2), Sch. 1 para. 38. (a)(ii) (with Sch. 3 para. 2)

F74. Word in s. 73. (2)(b) omitted (26.5.2011) by virtue of The Electronic Communications and Wireless Telegraphy Regulations 2011 (S.I. 2011/1210), reg. 1. (2), Sch. 1 para. 38. (a)(iii) (with Sch. 3 para. 2)

F75. S. 73. (2)(ba) inserted (26.5.2011) by The Electronic Communications and Wireless Telegraphy Regulations 2011 (S.I. 2011/1210), reg. 1. (2), Sch. 1 para. 38. (a)(iii) (with Sch. 3 para. 2)

F76. Words in s. 73. (3) omitted (26.5.2011) by virtue of The Electronic Communications and Wireless Telegraphy Regulations 2011 (S.I. 2011/1210), reg. 1. (2), Sch. 1 para. 38. (b) (with Sch. 3 para. 2)

F77. S. 73. (3. A) inserted (26.5.2011) by The Electronic Communications and Wireless Telegraphy Regulations 2011 (S.I. 2011/1210), reg. 1. (2), Sch. 1 para. 38. (c) (with Sch. 3 para. 2)

F78. S. 73. (4) omitted (26.5.2011) by virtue of The Electronic Communications and Wireless Telegraphy Regulations 2011 (S.I. 2011/1210), reg. 1. (2), Sch. 1 para. 38. (d) (with Sch. 3 para. 2)

Commencement Information

I83. S. 73 in force at 25.7.2003 for specified purposes by S.I. 2003/1900, arts. 1. (2), 2. (1), Sch. 1 (with art. 3) (as amended by S.I. 2003/3142, art. 1. (3))

184. S. 73 in force at 29.12.2003 in so far as not already in force by S.I. 2003/3142, art. 3. (2) (with art. 11)

74. Specific types of access-related conditions

(1) The conditions that may be set by virtue of section 73. (2) include conditions which, for the purpose of securing end-to-end connectivity for the end-users of public electronic communications services provided by means of a series of electronic communications networks—

(a) impose obligations on a person controlling network access to any of those networks; and

(b) require the interconnection of the networks.

[F79. (1. A)The conditions that may be set by virtue of section 73. (2) also include conditions which impose such obligations on a person controlling network access to customers as OFCOM consider necessary for the purpose of securing service interoperability.]

(2) The conditions that may be set by virtue of section 73. (2) also include such conditions imposing obligations on a person providing facilities for the use of application programme interfaces or electronic programme guides as OFCOM consider to be necessary for securing—

(a) that persons are able to have access to such programme services provided in digital form as OFCOM may determine; and

(b) that the facility for using those interfaces or guides is provided on terms which—

(i) are fair and reasonable; and

(ii) do not involve, or tend to give rise to, any undue discrimination against any person or description of persons.

(3) In this section—

"application programme interface" means a facility for allowing software to make use, in connection with any of the matters mentioned in subsection (4), of facilities contained in other software;

"electronic programme guide" means a facility by means of which a person has access to any service which consists of—

- the listing or promotion, or both the listing and the promotion, of some or all of the programmes included in any one or more programme services; and

- a facility for obtaining access, in whole or in part, to the programme service or services listed or promoted in the guide;

"end-to-end connectivity" means the facility—

- for different end-users of the same public electronic communications service to be able to communicate with each other; and

- for the end-users of different such services to be able, each using the service of which he is the end-user, to communicate with each other.

(4) The matters mentioned in subsection (3), in the definition of "application programme interface", are—

(a) allowing a person to have access to programme services;

(b) allowing a person, other than a communications provider or a person who makes associated facilities available, to make use of an electronic communications network by means of which a programme service is broadcast or otherwise transmitted;

(c) allowing a person to become the end-user of a description of public electronic communications service.

(5) This section is not to be construed as restricting the provision that may be made under section 73. (2).

Amendments (Textual)

F79. S. 74. (1. A) inserted (26.5.2011) by The Electronic Communications and Wireless Telegraphy Regulations 2011 (S.I. 2011/1210), reg. 1. (2), Sch. 1 para. 39 (with Sch. 3 para. 2)

Commencement Information

I85. S. 74 in force at 25.7.2003 for specified purposes by S.I. 2003/1900, arts. 1. (2), 2. (1), Sch. 1 (with art. 3) (as amended by S.I. 2003/3142, art. 1. (3))

I86. S. 74 in force at 29.12.2003 in so far as not already in force by S.I. 2003/3142, art. 3. (2) (with art. 11)

75. Conditional access systems and access to digital services

F80. (1). . . . .

(2) It shall be the duty of OFCOM to ensure—

(a) that access-related conditions are applied to every person who provides a conditional access system in relation to a protected programme service; and

(b) that those conditions make all such provision as is required by the provision contained from time to time in Part I of Annex I to the Access Directive (conditions relating to access to digital programme services).

(3) In this section—

"conditional access system" means any system, facility, arrangements or technical measure under or by means of which access to programme services requires—

- a subscription to the service or to a service that includes that service; or

- an authorisation to view it, or to listen to it, on a particular occasion;

"protected programme service" means a programme service the programmes included in which cannot be viewed or listened to in an intelligible form except by the use of a conditional access system.

Amendments (Textual)

F80. S. 75. (1) omitted (26.5.2011) by virtue of The Electronic Communications and Wireless Telegraphy Regulations 2011 (S.I. 2011/1210), reg. 1. (2), Sch. 1 para. 40 (with Sch. 3 para. 2)

Commencement Information

I87. S. 75 in force at 25.7.2003 for specified purposes by S.I. 2003/1900, arts. 1. (2), 2. (1), Sch. 1 (with art. 3) (as amended by S.I. 2003/3142, art. 1. (3))

I88. S. 75 in force at 29.12.2003 in so far as not already in force by S.I. 2003/3142, art. 3. (2) (with art. 11)

76. Modification and revocation of conditions imposed under s. 75.

(1) This section applies in the case of conditions falling within section 75. (2) which have been set by OFCOM in relation to a particular person ("the system provider").

(2) OFCOM must not give effect to a proposal to modify or revoke any of the conditions unless—

(a) they have carried out an analysis for the purpose of determining in accordance with this Chapter whether that person is or remains a person on whom SMP services conditions are capable of being imposed;

(b) they have determined in consequence of that analysis that he is not; and

(c) they are satisfied that the modification or revocation will not have an adverse effect on any or all of the matters mentioned in subsection (3).

(3) Those matters are—

(a) the accessibility to any persons of services that are for the time being included in the list of must-carry services in section 64;

(b) the prospects for effective competition in the market for programme services provided by being broadcast or otherwise transmitted in digital form; and

(c) the prospects for effective competition in the markets for conditional access systems and other associated facilities.

(4) In this section "conditional access system" has the same meaning as in section 75.

Commencement Information

I89. S. 76 in force at 25.7.2003 for specified purposes by S.I. 2003/1900, arts. 1. (2), 2. (1), Sch. 1 (with art. 3) (as amended by S.I. 2003/3142, art. 1. (3))

I90. S. 76 in force at 29.12.2003 in so far as not already in force by S.I. 2003/3142, art. 3. (2) (with art. 11)

[F8176. A.Information about electronic communications apparatus available for shared use

(1) OFCOM may make available to such persons as they consider appropriate information about electronic communications apparatus that in OFCOM's opinion is suitable for shared use.

(2) OFCOM may impose such restrictions as they consider appropriate on the use and further disclosure of information made available under this section.]

Amendments (Textual)

F81. S. 76. A inserted (26.5.2011) by The Electronic Communications and Wireless Telegraphy Regulations 2011 (S.I. 2011/1210), reg. 1. (2), Sch. 1 para. 41 (with Sch. 3 para. 2)

Privileged supplier conditions

77. Imposition of privileged supplier conditions

(1) It shall be the duty of OFCOM to secure that privileged supplier conditions containing all such provision falling within subsection (3) as they consider appropriate are applied to every public communications provider to whom this section applies.

(2) This section applies to every public communications provider who—

(a) enjoys special or exclusive rights in relation to the provision of any non-communications services; and

(b) is not such a provider in respect only of associated facilities.

(3) The provision that may be contained in a condition set under section 45 as a privileged supplier condition is any provision that OFCOM consider appropriate for any one or more of the following purposes—

(a) requiring the provider to whom it applies to keep separate accounts in relation to his public electronic communications network or public electronic communications service and other matters;

(b) requiring that provider to submit the accounts of the different parts of his undertaking, and any financial report relating to a part of that undertaking, to a qualified auditor for auditing;

(c) requiring the accounts of the different parts of his undertaking to be published;

(d) securing, by means other than the keeping of separate accounts, the structural separation of the different parts of his undertaking.

(4) OFCOM are not required under this section to apply a condition to a person where they are satisfied that that person has an annual turnover in relation to all his communications activities that is less than ?50 million.

(5) Where in a case falling within subsection (4) OFCOM are not required to apply a privileged supplier condition to a person, they may apply such a condition to him if they think fit.

(6) The reference in subsection (4) to a person's communications activities is a reference to any activities of his that consist in, or are connected with, either or both of the following—

(a) the provision of any one or more electronic communications networks;

(b) the provision of any one or more electronic communications services.

(7) The making, for the purposes of subsection (4), of—

(a) a determination of the period in respect of which a person's annual turnover in relation to any activities is computed, and

(b) a determination of the amount in Euros of that turnover for any period,

must be in accordance with such rules as OFCOM consider to be reasonable.

(8) OFCOM must publish any rules made by them for the purposes of subsection (7) in such manner as they consider appropriate for bringing them to the attention of the persons who, in their opinion, are likely to be affected by them.

(9) In this section—

"non-communications services", in relation to a person, means services other than those consisting in, or connected with, the provision by him of—

- an electronic communications network; or

- an electronic communications service;

[F82"qualified auditor" means a person who—

- is eligible for appointment as a statutory auditor under Part 42 of the Companies Act 2006, and

- if the appointment to carry out such auditing as is mentioned in subsection (3)(b) were an appointment as a statutory auditor, would not be prohibited from acting by section 1214 of that Act (independence requirement);]

"special or exclusive rights" has the same meaning as in [F83. Article 106 of the Treaty on the Functioning of the European Union] .

Amendments (Textual)

F82. Words in s. 77. (9) substituted (6.4.2008) by The Companies Act 2006 (Consequential Amendments etc) Order 2008 (S.I. 2008/948), art. 2. (2), Sch. 1 para. 30. (3) (with arts. 6, 11, 12)

F83. Words in s. 77. (9) substituted (1.8.2012) by The Treaty of Lisbon (Changes in Terminology or Numbering) Order 2012 (S.I. 2012/1809), art. 2. (1), Sch. Pt. 1 (with art. 2. (2))

Commencement Information

I91. S. 77 in force at 25.7.2003 for specified purposes by S.I. 2003/1900, arts. 1. (2), 2. (1), Sch. 1 (with art. 3) (as amended by S.I. 2003/3142, art. 1. (3))

I92. S. 77 in force at 29.12.2003 in so far as not already in force by S.I. 2003/3142, art. 3. (2) (with art. 11)

SMP conditions: procedure

78. Circumstances required for the setting of SMP conditions

(1) For the purposes of this Chapter a person shall be taken to have significant market power in relation to a market if he enjoys a position which amounts to or is equivalent to dominance of the market.

(2) References in this section to dominance of a market must be construed in accordance with any applicable provisions of Article 14 of the Framework Directive.

(3) A person is to be taken to enjoy a position of dominance of a market if he is one of a number of persons who enjoy such a position in combination with each other.

(4) A person or combination of persons may also be taken to enjoy a position of dominance of a market by reason wholly or partly of his or their position in a closely related market if the links between the two markets allow the market power held in the closely related market to be used in a way that influences the other market so as to strengthen the position in the other market of that person or combination of persons.

(5) The matters that must be taken into account in determining whether a combination of persons enjoys a position of dominance of a services market include, in particular, the matters set out in Annex II to the Framework Directive.

Commencement Information

I93. S. 78 in force at 25.7.2003 for specified purposes by S.I. 2003/1900, arts. 1. (2), 2. (1), Sch. 1 (with art. 3) (as amended by S.I. 2003/3142, art. 1. (3))

I94. S. 78 in force at 29.12.2003 in so far as not already in force by S.I. 2003/3142, art. 3. (2) (with art. 11)

79. Market power determinations

(1) Before making a market power determination, OFCOM must—

(a) identify (by reference, in particular, to area and locality) the markets which in their opinion are the ones which in the circumstances of the United Kingdom are the markets in relation to which it is appropriate to consider whether to make the determination; and

(b) carry out an analysis of the identified markets.

(2) In identifying or analysing any services market for the purposes of this Chapter, OFCOM must take due account of all applicable guidelines and recommendations which—

(a) have been issued or made by the European Commission in pursuance of the provisions of a [F51. EU] instrument; and

(b) relate to market identification and analysis.

(3) In considering whether to make or revise a market power determination in relation to a services market, OFCOM must take due account of all applicable guidelines and recommendations which—

(a) have been issued or made by the European Commission in pursuance of the provisions of a [F51. EU] instrument; and

(b) relate to market analysis or the determination of what constitutes significant market power.

(4) The way in which—

(a) a market is to be identified for the purposes of this section, or

(b) a market power determination is to be made,

is by the publication of a notification containing the identification or determination.

(5) Notifications for the purposes of subsection (4)—

(a) may be given separately;

(b) may be contained in a single notification relating to both the identification of a market and the making of a market determination in relation to that market; or

(c) may be contained in a single notification under section 48. (1) with respect to the setting or modification of an SMP condition and either—

(i) the making of the market power determination by reference to which OFCOM set or modify that condition; or

(ii) the making of that market power determination and the identification of the market in relation to which they make that determination.

(6) The publication of a notification under this section must be in such manner as appears to OFCOM to be appropriate for bringing the contents of the notification to the attention of the persons who, in OFCOM's opinion, are likely to be affected by the matters notified.

(7) References in this section to guidelines and recommendations issued by the European Commission and to a [F51. EU] instrument include references, respectively, to guidelines and recommendations issued after the commencement of this section and to a [F51. EU] instrument made after the commencement of this section.

Amendments (Textual)

F51. Words in Act substituted (22.4.2011) by The Treaty of Lisbon (Changes in Terminology) Order 2011 (S.I. 2011/1043), arts. 2, 3, 6 (with art. 3. (2)(3), 4. (2), 6. (4)(5))

Commencement Information

I95. S. 79 in force at 25.7.2003 for specified purposes by S.I. 2003/1900, arts. 1. (2), 2. (1), Sch. 1 (with art. 3) (as amended by S.I. 2003/3142, art. 1. (3))

I96. S. 79 in force at 29.12.2003 in so far as not already in force by S.I. 2003/3142, art. 3. (2) (with art. 11)

80. Proposals for identifying markets and for market power determinations

[F84. (1)Where section 80. A applies, OFCOM must comply with the applicable requirements of that section and section 80. B before—

(a) identifying a market for the purposes of making a market power determination, or

(b) making a market power determination.

(1. A)Where section 80. A does not apply because of subsection (2) of that section—

(a) any identification of a market or market power determination must be temporary; and

(b) the notification published under section 79. (4) containing the identification or determination must state the period for which the identification or determination is to have effect.

(1. B)Where OFCOM propose to extend or make permanent any such temporary identification or determination—

(a) sections 80. A and 80. B(1) do not apply in relation to the proposal; and

(b) subsections (2) to (8) of section 80. B apply in relation to the proposal as if the words from the beginning of subsection (2) to "appropriate" were omitted.]

(7) The power of OFCOM to [F85identify a market or make a market power determination is subject to section 83] .

Amendments (Textual)

F84. S. 80. (1)(1. A)(1. B) substituted for s. 80. (1)-(6) (26.5.2011) by The Electronic Communications and Wireless Telegraphy Regulations 2011 (S.I. 2011/1210), reg. 1. (2), Sch. 1 para. 42. (a) (with Sch. 3 paras. 2, 11)

F85. Words in s. 80. (7) substituted (26.5.2011) by The Electronic Communications and Wireless Telegraphy Regulations 2011 (S.I. 2011/1210), reg. 1. (2), Sch. 1 para. 42. (b) (with Sch. 3 paras. 2, 11)

Commencement Information

I97. S. 80 in force at 25.7.2003 for specified purposes by S.I. 2003/1900, arts. 1. (2), 2. (1), Sch. 1 (with art. 3) (as amended by S.I. 2003/3142, art. 1. (3))

I98. S. 80 in force at 29.12.2003 in so far as not already in force by S.I. 2003/3142, art. 3. (2) (with art. 11)

[F8680. A.Domestic consultation for market identifications and market power determinations

(1) This section applies where—

(a) OFCOM propose—

(i) to identify a market for the purposes of making a market power determination; or

(ii) to make a market power determination; and

(b) (in the case of a services market) the proposed identification or determination is in OFCOM's opinion likely to result in the setting, modification or revocation of SMP services conditions that will have a significant impact on the market.

(2) But this section does not apply where the proposal is of EU significance and in OFCOM's opinion—

(a) there are exceptional circumstances; and

(b) there is an urgent need to act in order to safeguard competition and to protect the interests of consumers.

(3) OFCOM must publish a notification of what they are proposing to do.

(4) Notifications for the purposes of subsection (3)—

(a) may be given separately;

(b) may be contained in a single notification relating to both the identification of a market and the making of a market power determination in relation to that market; or

(c) may be contained in a single notification under section 48. A(3) with respect to the setting or modification of an SMP condition and either—

(i) the making of the market power determination by reference to which OFCOM are proposing to set or modify that condition; or

(ii) the making of that market power determination and the identification of the market in relation to which they are proposing to make that determination.

(5) A notification under this section relating to a proposal to identify a market or to make a market power determination must—

(a) state that OFCOM are proposing to identify that market or to make that market power determination;

(b) set out the effect of the proposal;

(c) give their reasons for making the proposal; and

(d) specify the period within which representations may be made to OFCOM about their proposal.

(6) That period must be a period of not less than one month after the day of the publication of the notification.

(7) But where OFCOM are satisfied that there are exceptional circumstances justifying the use of a shorter period, the period specified as the period for making representations may be whatever shorter period OFCOM considers reasonable in those circumstances.

(8) The publication of a notification under this section must be in such manner as appears to OFCOM to be appropriate for bringing the contents of the notification to the attention of the persons who, in OFCOM's opinion, are likely to be affected by the matters notified.

(9) OFCOM must—

(a) consider every representation about the proposal made to them during the period specified in the notification; and

(b) have regard to every international obligation of the United Kingdom (if any) which has been notified to them for the purposes of this paragraph by the Secretary of State.

(10) Where the proposal is not of EU significance, OFCOM may then give effect to it, with any modifications that appear to OFCOM to be appropriate.

Amendments (Textual)

F86. Ss. 80. A, 80. B inserted (26.5.2011) by The Electronic Communications and Wireless Telegraphy Regulations 2011 (S.I. 2011/1210), reg. 1. (2), Sch. 1 para. 43 (with Sch. 3 paras. 2, 11)

80. B. EU consultation for market identifications and market power determinations

(1) This section applies where, after complying with section 80. A(9) in relation to a proposal of EU significance, OFCOM wish to proceed with the proposal.

(2) After making any modifications of the proposal that appear to OFCOM to be appropriate, OFCOM must send a copy of the proposal, and of a statement setting out the reasons for it, to—

    (a) the European Commission;

    (b) BEREC; and

    (c) the regulatory authorities in every other member State.

(3) If at the end of the period of one month referred to in paragraph (3) of Article 7 of the Framework Directive no indication has been given to OFCOM by the Commission under paragraph (4) of that Article, OFCOM may give effect to the proposal, with any modifications that appear to them to be appropriate.

(4) Before giving effect to the proposal under subsection (3), OFCOM must consider any comments made by—

    (a) the Commission;

    (b) BEREC; and

    (c) any regulatory authority in any other member State.

(5) Subsections (6) to (8) apply where such an indication is given by the Commission to OFCOM during that period.

(6) If under Article 7. (5)(a) of the Framework Directive the Commission requires OFCOM to withdraw the proposal, OFCOM must amend or withdraw the proposal within 6 months of the date of the Commission's decision.

(7) Where the proposal is amended under subsection (6), section 80 applies in relation to the amended proposal as if it were a new proposal.

(8) OFCOM may give effect to the proposal, with any modifications that appear to them to be appropriate—

    (a) if the Commission takes a decision to lift its reservations in accordance with paragraph (5)(b) of Article 7 of the Framework Directive; or

    (b) if at the end of the period of 2 months referred to in paragraph (4) of that Article the Commission has neither required OFCOM to withdraw the proposal under paragraph (5)(a) nor lifted its reservations under paragraph (5)(b).]

Amendments (Textual)

F86. Ss. 80. A, 80. B inserted (26.5.2011) by The Electronic Communications and Wireless Telegraphy Regulations 2011 (S.I. 2011/1210), reg. 1. (2), Sch. 1 para. 43 (with Sch. 3 paras. 2, 11)

[F8781. Delivery of copies of notifications under sections 79 and 80. A

(1) OFCOM must send to the Secretary of State a copy of every notification published under section 79. (4) or 80. A(3).

(2) OFCOM must send to the European Commission a copy of every notification published under section 79. (4) in relation to a services market.

(3) OFCOM must send to BEREC a copy of every notification published under section 79. (4) where the proposal to identify the market or make a market power determination was a proposal of EU significance.

(4) Where a notification published under section 79. (4) relates to a proposal to which section 80. A did not apply because of subsection (2) of that section, OFCOM must send a copy of a statement setting out the reasons for the proposal and for the urgent need to act to—

    (a) the Commission;

    (b) BEREC; and

    (c) the regulatory authorities in every other member State.]

Amendments (Textual)

F87. S. 81 substituted (26.5.2011) by The Electronic Communications and Wireless Telegraphy Regulations 2011 (S.I. 2011/1210), reg. 1. (2), Sch. 1 para. 44 (with Sch. 3 paras. 2, 11)
Commencement Information
I99. S. 81 in force at 25.7.2003 for specified purposes by S.I. 2003/1900, arts. 1. (2), 2. (1), Sch. 1 (with art. 3) (as amended by S.I. 2003/3142, art. 1. (3))
I100. S. 81 in force at 29.12.2003 in so far as not already in force by S.I. 2003/3142, art. 3. (2) (with art. 11)
F8882. European Commission's powers in respect of proposals
. . . .
Amendments (Textual)
F88. S. 82 omitted (26.5.2011) by virtue of The Electronic Communications and Wireless Telegraphy Regulations 2011 (S.I. 2011/1210), reg. 1. (2), Sch. 1 para. 45 (with Sch. 3 paras. 2, 11)
Commencement Information
I101. S. 82 in force at 25.7.2003 for specified purposes by S.I. 2003/1900, arts. 1. (2), 2. (1), Sch. 1 (with art. 3) (as amended by S.I. 2003/3142, art. 1. (3))
I102. S. 82 in force at 29.12.2003 in so far as not already in force by S.I. 2003/3142, art. 3. (2) (with art. 11)
83. Special rules for transnational markets
(1) This section applies where a services market is for the time being identified by a decision of the European Commission under Article 15. (4) of the Framework Directive as a transnational market.
(2) Where the market area includes the whole or a part of the United Kingdom, OFCOM must enter into and maintain arrangements with the other relevant regulatory authorities about—
    (a) the extent to which the agreement of all the relevant regulatory authorities is required for the doing of any of the things mentioned in subsection (3); and
    (b) the procedures to be followed for securing that agreement where it is required.
(3) Those things are—
    (a) the identification of the whole or a part of the market as a market in relation to which it is appropriate to determine whether a person has significant market power;
    (b) the making of such a determination in relation to the whole or a part of the market;
    (c) the setting of a condition the setting of which requires such a determination to have been made;
    (d) the modification or revocation of such a condition.
(4) OFCOM must not do any of the things mentioned in subsection (3) except in accordance with arrangements maintained under that subsection.
(5) Those arrangements may include arrangements requiring OFCOM, when doing any of those things, to comply with—
    (a) a decision made, by one or more other regulatory authorities; or
    (b) a decision made by a person appointed under the arrangements to act on behalf of some or all of the relevant regulatory authorities.
(6) In this section—
"market area", in relation to a services market identified by the European Commission as a transnational market, means the area identified by that Commission as the area for which the market operates; and
"relevant regulatory authorities", in relation to such a market, means the regulatory authorities for each member State the whole or a part of which is comprised in the market area.
Commencement Information
I103. S. 83 in force at 25.7.2003 for specified purposes by S.I. 2003/1900, arts. 1. (2), 2. (1), Sch. 1 (with art. 3) (as amended by S.I. 2003/3142, art. 1. (3))
I104. S. 83 in force at 29.12.2003 in so far as not already in force by S.I. 2003/3142, art. 3. (2) (with art. 11)
84. Review of services market identifications and determinations

(1) This section applies where OFCOM have identified and analysed a services market for the purposes of making a market power determination.

(2) OFCOM [F89may (and, when required to do so by section 84. A, must)] carry out further analyses of the identified market for one or both of the following purposes—

(a) reviewing market power determinations made on the basis of an earlier analysis;

(b) deciding whether to make proposals for the modification of SMP conditions set by reference to a market power determination made on such a basis.

F90. (3)................................

(4) Where on, or in consequence of, a further analysis under this section, OFCOM determine that a person to whom any SMP conditions apply is no longer a person with significant market power in that market, they must revoke every SMP services condition applied to that person by reference to the market power determination made on the basis of the earlier analysis.

(5) Before carrying out a further analysis under subsection (2), OFCOM may review any decision of theirs identifying the markets which it was appropriate to consider for the purpose of carrying out an earlier analysis.

(6) Where, on such a review, OFCOM conclude that the appropriate markets have changed—

(a) they must identify the markets they now consider to be the appropriate ones; and

(b) those markets shall be the identified markets for the purposes of the further analysis.

(7) Sections 79 to 83 apply—

(a) in relation to the identification of a services market for the purposes of reviewing a market power determination under this section, as they apply in relation to the identification of such a market for the purpose of making a market determination; and

(b) in relation to the review of such a determination, as they apply in relation to the making of such a determination.

Amendments (Textual)

F89. Words in s. 84. (2) substituted (26.5.2011) by The Electronic Communications and Wireless Telegraphy Regulations 2011 (S.I. 2011/1210), reg. 1. (2), Sch. 1 para. 46. (a) (with Sch. 3 paras. 2, 12)

F90. S. 84. (3) omitted (26.5.2011) by virtue of The Electronic Communications and Wireless Telegraphy Regulations 2011 (S.I. 2011/1210), reg. 1. (2), Sch. 1 para. 46. (b) (with Sch. 3 paras. 2, 12)

Commencement Information

I105. S. 84 in force at 25.7.2003 for specified purposes by S.I. 2003/1900, arts. 1. (2), 2. (1), Sch. 1 (with art. 3) (as amended by S.I. 2003/3142, art. 1. (3))

I106. S. 84 in force at 29.12.2003 in so far as not already in force by S.I. 2003/3142, art. 3. (2) (with art. 11)

[F9184. A.Timing of services market identifications and determinations

(1) This section makes provision about the exercise by OFCOM of their powers—

(a) to identify and analyse services markets;

(b) to make and review market power determinations in respect of such markets; and

(c) to set, modify and revoke SMP services conditions by reference to such determinations.

(2) Where under Article 15. (1) of the Framework Directive the European Commission has adopted a revised recommendation identifying a services market not previously notified to the Commission, OFCOM must ensure that within the specified period they have—

(a) carried out any identification and analysis of markets that is necessary in consequence of the recommendation; and

(b) sent the Commission copies of any resulting proposals with respect to market identification, market power determinations and SMP services conditions.

(3) Where, following the identification and analysis of a services market, OFCOM have made a market power determination in relation to it, they must ensure that within the specified period they have—

(a) carried out a further analysis of the market and reviewed the identification and determination made on the basis of the earlier analysis; and

(b) sent the Commission copies of any resulting proposals with respect to market identification, market power determinations and SMP services conditions.

(4) Subsection (3) applies only where the market power determination was made after 25 May 2011.

(5) Where it appears to OFCOM that they are unlikely to be able to comply with the requirements of subsection (2) or (3) within the specified period, they may request assistance from BEREC under Article 16. (7) of the Framework Directive.

(6) Where OFCOM request such assistance—

(a) they must inform the Commission of the request;

(b) subsection (2) or (as the case may be) (3) applies in the case in question as if the words "within the specified period" were omitted; and

(c) within 6 months of the assistance being provided they must send copies of any resulting proposals to the Commission.

(7) In this section "the specified period" means—

(a) in the case of subsection (2), the period of 2 years from the adoption of the recommendation; and

(b) in the case of subsection (3), the period of 3 years from the publication under section 79. (4) of the notification of the market power determination made on the basis of the earlier analysis, subject to any extension of that period under Article 16. (6)(a) of the Framework Directive.]

Amendments (Textual)

F91. S. 84. A inserted (26.5.2011) by The Electronic Communications and Wireless Telegraphy Regulations 2011 (S.I. 2011/1210), reg. 1. (2), Sch. 1 para. 47 (with Sch. 3 para. 2)

85. Review of apparatus market identifications and determinations

(1) This section applies where OFCOM have identified and analysed an apparatus market for the purposes of making a market power determination.

(2) OFCOM must, at such intervals as they consider appropriate, carry out further analyses of the identified market for one or both of the following purposes—

(a) reviewing market power determinations made on the basis of an earlier analysis;

(b) deciding whether to make proposals for the modification of SMP conditions set by reference to any such market power determination.

(3) Where on, or in consequence of, a further analysis under this section, OFCOM determine that a person to whom any SMP conditions apply is no longer a person with significant market power in that market, they shall revoke every SMP apparatus condition applied to that person by reference to the market power determination made on the basis of the earlier analysis.

(4) Before carrying out any further analysis under subsection (2), OFCOM may review any decision of theirs identifying the markets which it was appropriate to consider for the purpose of carrying out any earlier analysis.

(5) Where on such a review OFCOM conclude that the appropriate markets have changed—

(a) they shall identify the markets they now consider to be the appropriate ones; and

(b) those markets shall be the identified markets for the purposes of the further analysis.

(6) Where on such a review OFCOM conclude that there is no person at all with significant market power in relation to the identified market—

(a) they must so inform the Secretary of State; and

(b) the Secretary of State may by order remove or restrict OFCOM's power under this Chapter to set SMP apparatus conditions by reference to that market.

(7) Sections 79, [F9280, 80. A and 81. (1)] apply—

(a) in relation to the identification of a apparatus market for the purposes of reviewing a market power determination under this section, as they apply in relation to the identification of such a market for the purpose of making a market determination; and

(b) in relation to the review of such a determination, as they apply in relation to the making of such a determination.

Amendments (Textual)

F92. Words in s. 85. (7) substituted (26.5.2011) by The Electronic Communications and Wireless

Telegraphy Regulations 2011 (S.I. 2011/1210), reg. 1. (2), Sch. 1 para. 48 (with Sch. 3 paras. 2, 11)

Commencement Information

I107. S. 85 in force at 25.7.2003 for specified purposes by S.I. 2003/1900, arts. 1. (2), 2. (1), Sch. 1 (with art. 3) (as amended by S.I. 2003/3142, art. 1. (3))

I108. S. 85 in force at 29.12.2003 in so far as not already in force by S.I. 2003/3142, art. 3. (2) (with art. 11)

86. Cases where review required

(1) OFCOM must not set an SMP services condition by a notification which does not also make the market power determination by reference to which the condition is set unless—

(a) the condition is set by reference to a market power determination which has been reviewed under section 84 and, in consequence of that review, is confirmed in the notification setting the condition; or

(b) the condition is set by reference to a market power determination made in relation to a market in which OFCOM are satisfied there has been no material change since the determination was made.

(2) OFCOM must not modify or revoke SMP services conditions applying to a person except in a case falling within subsection (3) or (4).

(3) The first case is where, for the purpose of determining whether to make the modification or revocation, OFCOM have—

(a) carried out a further analysis under section 84 of the market in question; and

(b) reviewed the market power determination for the time being in force in that person's case.

(4) The second case is where OFCOM are satisfied that there has not—

(a) in the case of an unmodified condition, since the condition was set, or

(b) in any other case, since the condition was last modified,

been a material change in the market identified or otherwise used for the purposes of the market power determination by reference to which the condition was set or last modified.

(5) OFCOM must not modify SMP apparatus conditions applying to a person except where, for the purpose of determining whether to make the modification or revocation, they have—

(a) carried out a further analysis under section 85 of the market in question; and

(b) reviewed the market power determination for the time being in force in that person's case.

(6) A change is a material change for the purposes of subsection (1) or (4) if it is one that is material to—

(a) the setting of the condition in question; or

(b) the modification or revocation in question.

Commencement Information

I109. S. 86 in force at 25.7.2003 for specified purposes by S.I. 2003/1900, arts. 1. (2), 2. (1), Sch. 1 (with art. 3) (as amended by S.I. 2003/3142, art. 1. (3))

I110. S. 86 in force at 29.12.2003 in so far as not already in force by S.I. 2003/3142, art. 3. (2) (with art. 11)

SMP services conditions: subject-matter

87. Conditions about network access etc.

(1) Where OFCOM have made a determination that a person to whom this section applies ("the dominant provider") has significant market power in an identified services market, they shall—

(a) set such SMP conditions authorised by this section as they consider it appropriate to apply to that person in respect of the relevant network or relevant facilities; and

(b) apply those conditions to that person.

(2) This section applies to—

(a) a person who provides a public electronic communications network; and

(b) a person who makes available facilities that are associated facilities by reference to such a network.

(3) This section authorises SMP conditions requiring the dominant provider to give such entitlements as OFCOM may from time to time direct as respects—

(a) the provision of network access to the relevant network;

(b) the use of the relevant network; and

(c) the availability of the relevant facilities.

(4) In determining what conditions authorised by subsection (3) to set in a particular case, OFCOM must take into account, in particular, the following factors—

(a) the technical and economic viability [F93. (including the viability of other network access products, whether provided by the dominant provider or another person)] , having regard to the state of market development, of installing and using facilities that would make the proposed network access unnecessary;

(b) the feasibility of the provision of the proposed network access;

(c) the investment made by the person initially providing or making available the network or other facility in respect of which an entitlement to network access is proposed [F94. (taking account of any public investment made)] ;

(d) the need to secure effective competition [F95. (including, where it appears to OFCOM to be appropriate, economically efficient infrastructure based competition)] in the long term;

(e) any rights to intellectual property that are relevant to the proposal; and

(f) the desirability of securing that electronic communications services are provided that are available throughout the member States.

(5) The conditions authorised by subsection (3) may include provision—

(a) for securing fairness and reasonableness in the way in which requests for network access are made and responded to; and

(b) for securing that the obligations contained in the conditions are complied with within the periods and at the times required by or under the conditions.

[F96. (5. A)The SMP conditions authorised by this section also include a condition which—

(a) is of a technical or operational nature; and

(b) appears to OFCOM to be appropriate for securing the proper operation of an electronic communications network in compliance with a condition under subsection (3).

(5. B)A condition falling within subsection (5. A) may provide that compliance with the condition is not required unless a person on whom an entitlement is or may be conferred in pursuance of a requirement imposed by a condition under subsection (3) fulfils such technical or operational requirements as may be specified by OFCOM.

(5. C)It shall be the duty of OFCOM, when setting a condition falling within subsection (5. A), to ensure that it contains all such provision as they consider appropriate for the purpose of taking account of the relevant international standards.]

(6) The SMP conditions authorised by this section also include one or more of the following—

(a) a condition requiring the dominant provider not to discriminate unduly against particular persons, or against a particular description of persons, in relation to matters connected with network access to the relevant network or with the availability of the relevant facilities;

(b) a condition requiring the dominant provider to publish, in such manner as OFCOM may from time to time direct, all such information as they may direct for the purpose of securing transparency in relation to such matters;

(c) a condition requiring the dominant provider to publish, in such manner as OFCOM may from time to time direct, the terms and conditions on which he is willing to enter into an access contract;

(d) a condition requiring the terms and conditions on which the dominant provider is willing to enter into an access contract to include such terms and conditions as may be specified or described in the condition;

(e) a condition requiring the dominant provider to make such modifications as OFCOM may direct of any offer by that provider which sets out the terms and conditions on which he is willing to enter into an access contract.

(7) The SMP conditions authorised by this section also include conditions requiring the dominant provider to maintain a separation for accounting purposes between such different matters relating—

(a) to network access to the relevant network, or

(b) to the availability of the relevant facilities,

as OFCOM may from time to time direct.

(8) The SMP conditions authorised by subsection (7) include conditions imposing requirements about the accounting methods to be used in maintaining the separation.

(9) The SMP conditions authorised by this section also include (subject to section 88) conditions imposing on the dominant provider—

(a) such price controls as OFCOM may direct in relation to matters connected with the provision of network access to the relevant network, or with the availability of the relevant facilities;

(b) such rules as they may make in relation to those matters about the recovery of costs and cost orientation;

(c) such rules as they may make for those purposes about the use of cost accounting systems; and

(d) obligations to adjust prices in accordance with such directions given by OFCOM as they may consider appropriate.

(10) The SMP conditions authorised by subsection (9) include conditions requiring the application of presumptions in the fixing and determination of costs and charges for the purposes of the price controls, rules and obligations imposed by virtue of that subsection.

(11) Where OFCOM set a condition authorised by this section which imposes rules on the dominant provider about the use of cost accounting systems, it shall be their duty also to set, and to apply to him, an SMP condition which imposes on him an obligation—

(a) to make arrangements for a description to be made available to the public of the cost accounting system used in pursuance of that condition; and

(b) to include in that description details of—

(i) the main categories under which costs are brought into account for the purposes of that system; and

(ii) the rules applied for the purposes of that system with respect to the allocation of costs.

(12) In this section—

"access contract" means—

- a contract for the provision by a person to whom this section applies to another person of network access to the relevant network; or

- a contract under which the relevant facilities are made available by a person to whom this section applies to another person;

"the relevant facilities", in relation to a person to whom this section applies, means the associated facilities made available by that person in relation to a public electronic communications network; and

"the relevant network", in relation to such a person, means the public electronic communications network provided by him.

Amendments (Textual)

F93. Words in s. 87. (4)(a) inserted (26.5.2011) by The Electronic Communications and Wireless Telegraphy Regulations 2011 (S.I. 2011/1210), reg. 1. (2), Sch. 1 para. 49. (a) (with Sch. 3 para. 2)

F94. Words in s. 87. (4)(c) inserted (26.5.2011) by The Electronic Communications and Wireless Telegraphy Regulations 2011 (S.I. 2011/1210), reg. 1. (2), Sch. 1 para. 49. (b) (with Sch. 3 para. 2)

F95. Words in s. 87. (4)(d) inserted (26.5.2011) by The Electronic Communications and Wireless Telegraphy Regulations 2011 (S.I. 2011/1210), reg. 1. (2), Sch. 1 para. 49. (c) (with Sch. 3 para. 2)

F96. S. 87. (5. A)-(5. C) inserted (26.5.2011) by The Electronic Communications and Wireless

Telegraphy Regulations 2011 (S.I. 2011/1210), reg. 1. (2), Sch. 1 para. 49. (d) (with Sch. 3 para. 2)

Commencement Information
I111. S. 87 in force at 25.7.2003 for specified purposes by S.I. 2003/1900, arts. 1. (2), 2. (1), Sch. 1 (with art. 3) (as amended by S.I. 2003/3142, art. 1. (3))
I112. S. 87 in force at 29.12.2003 in so far as not already in force by S.I. 2003/3142, art. 3. (2) (with art. 11)

88. Conditions about network access pricing etc.

(1) OFCOM are not to set an SMP condition falling within section 87. (9) except where—

(a) it appears to them from the market analysis carried out for the purpose of setting that condition that there is a relevant risk of adverse effects arising from price distortion; and

(b) it also appears to them that the setting of the condition is appropriate for the purposes of—

(i) promoting efficiency;

(ii) promoting sustainable competition; and

(iii) conferring the greatest possible benefits on the end-users of public electronic communications services.

(2) In setting an SMP condition falling within section 87. (9) OFCOM must take account of the extent of the investment in the matters to which the condition relates of the person to whom it is to apply.

(3) For the purposes of this section there is a relevant risk of adverse affects arising from price distortion if the dominant provider might—

(a) so fix and maintain some or all of his prices at an excessively high level, or

(b) so impose a price squeeze,

as to have adverse consequences for end-users of public electronic communications services.

(4) In considering the matters mentioned in subsection (1)(b) OFCOM may—

(a) have regard to the prices at which services are available in comparable competitive markets;

(b) determine what they consider to represent efficiency by using such cost accounting methods as they think fit.

(5) In this section "the dominant provider" has the same meaning as in section 87.

Commencement Information
I113. S. 88 in force at 25.7.2003 for specified purposes by S.I. 2003/1900, arts. 1. (2), 2. (1), Sch. 1 (with art. 3) (as amended by S.I. 2003/3142, art. 1. (3))
I114. S. 88 in force at 29.12.2003 in so far as not already in force by S.I. 2003/3142, art. 3. (2) (with art. 11)

89. Conditions about network access in exceptional cases

(1) This section applies where—

(a) OFCOM have made a determination that a person ("the dominant provider") has significant market power in an identified services market;

(b) that person is the provider of an electronic communications network or a person who makes associated facilities available; and

(c) OFCOM consider that there are exceptional circumstances making it appropriate for conditions with respect to the provision of network access to be applied to the dominant provider in addition to those that are required to be or may be applied to him apart from this section.

(2) OFCOM may set the additional SMP conditions and apply them to the dominant provider if—

(a) they have submitted the additional conditions to the European Commission for approval; and

(b) the Commission has approved the imposition on the dominant provider of the obligations contained in those conditions.

Commencement Information
I115. S. 89 in force at 25.7.2003 for specified purposes by S.I. 2003/1900, arts. 1. (2), 2. (1), Sch. 1 (with art. 3) (as amended by S.I. 2003/3142, art. 1. (3))
I116. S. 89 in force at 29.12.2003 in so far as not already in force by S.I. 2003/3142, art. 3. (2) (with art. 11)

[F9789. A.Functional separation

(1) This section applies where—

(a) OFCOM have made a determination that a person ("the dominant provider") has significant market power in an identified services market;

(b) that person is the provider of a public electronic communications network or a person who makes available facilities that are associated facilities by reference to such a network;

(c) it appears to OFCOM that the setting of conditions applying to the dominant provider under section 87 (and, where OFCOM think it appropriate, section 88) has failed to address competition problems identified by OFCOM in carrying out a market analysis for the purpose of setting or modifying those conditions; and

(d) OFCOM have identified important and persisting competition problems or market failures in relation to the provision of network access.

(2) OFCOM may set an SMP services condition (referred to in this section and section 89. B as a "functional separation condition") requiring the dominant provider to transfer activities relating to the provision of network access to an independently operating business entity which is a part of the dominant provider.

(3) Where a functional separation condition is imposed on the dominant provider, the products or services specified in the condition must be given to the dominant provider and to other persons—

(a) on the same timescales, terms and conditions, including those relating to price and service levels, and

(b) by means of the same systems and processes.

(4) A functional separation condition must, where relevant, specify—

(a) the precise nature and level of separation, specifying in particular the legal status of the entity to which activities are transferred;

(b) an identification of the assets of that entity and the products or services to be supplied by it;

(c) the governance arrangements (including incentive structures) to ensure the independence of the staff employed in that entity;

(d) rules for ensuring compliance with the obligations imposed by the condition;

(e) rules for ensuring transparency of operational procedures, in particular towards persons, other than the dominant provider, who in OFCOM's opinion are likely to be affected by the condition; and

(f) a monitoring programme to ensure compliance, including a requirement for the publication of an annual report.

Amendments (Textual)

F97. Ss. 89. A-89. C inserted (26.5.2011) by The Electronic Communications and Wireless Telegraphy Regulations 2011 (S.I. 2011/1210), reg. 1. (2), Sch. 1 para. 50 (with Sch. 3 para. 2)

89. B.Functional separation conditions: consultation and notification

(1) Where OFCOM propose to apply a functional separation condition to a person, they must submit their proposal, including the draft functional separation condition, to the European Commission.

(2) The proposal must set out—

(a) evidence justifying the conclusions mentioned in section 89. A(1)(c) and (d);

(b) a reasoned assessment that there is little or no prospect of effective and sustainable infrastructure based competition within a reasonable time frame;

(c) an analysis of the expected impact of the condition on—

(i) OFCOM;

(ii) the person on whom the condition is to be imposed;

(iii) the staff of the entity to which activities are to be transferred;

(iv) the electronic communications sector as a whole;

(v) incentives to invest in the electronic communications sector, particularly with regard to the need to ensure social and territorial cohesion;

(vi) competition in the services market affected by the condition; and

(vii) other persons who in OFCOM's opinion are likely to be affected by the condition, including, in particular, consumers; and

(d) an analysis of the reasons why a functional separation condition would be the most effective means of addressing important and persisting competition problems or market failures identified by OFCOM.

(3) OFCOM may set the functional separation condition and apply it to a person if—

(a) the Commission has approved the imposition on the person of the obligations contained in the condition, and

(b) OFCOM have considered the impact that the obligations contained in the condition and approved by the Commission are likely to have on SMP services conditions set in relation to the services markets which, in OFCOM's opinion, will be affected by the proposed condition.

(4) A proposal for a functional separation condition is to be submitted to the European Commission under this section before OFCOM carry out a consultation under section 48. A in relation to the condition.

Amendments (Textual)

F97. Ss. 89. A-89. C inserted (26.5.2011) by The Electronic Communications and Wireless Telegraphy Regulations 2011 (S.I. 2011/1210), reg. 1. (2), Sch. 1 para. 50 (with Sch. 3 para. 2)

89. C.Obligation to notify OFCOM of voluntary separation

(1) This section applies where—

(a) OFCOM have made a determination that a person ("the dominant provider") has significant market power in an identified services market;

(b) the dominant provider is the provider of a public electronic communications network or a person who makes associated facilities available; and

(c) the dominant provider decides to transfer a substantial part or all of the dominant provider's local access network assets to an independently operating business entity (which may be a part of the dominant provider or another person) for the purpose specified in subsection (2).

(2) That purpose is to use the assets to provide products or services to the dominant provider and to other persons—

(a) on the same timescales, terms and conditions, including those relating to price and service levels; and

(b) by means of the same systems and processes.

(3) The dominant provider must notify OFCOM of—

(a) the decision to transfer the assets;

(b) any changes to its intentions; and

(c) the taking effect of the transfer.

(4) Where OFCOM receive a notification under this section, they must, as soon as reasonably practicable, consider the impact that the transfer is likely to have on SMP services conditions set in relation to the services markets which, in OFCOM's opinion, will be affected by the proposed transfer.]

Amendments (Textual)

F97. Ss. 89. A-89. C inserted (26.5.2011) by The Electronic Communications and Wireless Telegraphy Regulations 2011 (S.I. 2011/1210), reg. 1. (2), Sch. 1 para. 50 (with Sch. 3 para. 2)

F9890. Conditions about carrier selection and pre-selection

. . . .

Amendments (Textual)

F98. S. 90 omitted (26.5.2011) by virtue of The Electronic Communications and Wireless Telegraphy Regulations 2011 (S.I. 2011/1210), reg. 1. (2), Sch. 1 para. 51 (with Sch. 3 para. 2)

Commencement Information

I117. S. 90 in force at 25.7.2003 for specified purposes by S.I. 2003/1900, arts. 1. (2), 2. (1), Sch. 1 (with art. 3) (as amended by S.I. 2003/3142, art. 1. (3))

I118. S. 90 in force at 29.12.2003 in so far as not already in force by S.I. 2003/3142, art. 3. (2) (with art. 11)

91. Conditions about regulation of services etc. for end-users

(1) Where—

(a) OFCOM have made a determination that a person ("the dominant provider") has significant market power in an identified services market ("the relevant market"),

(b) the relevant market is one for the end-users of public electronic communications services that are available in that market, and

(c) it appears to OFCOM that the test in subsection (2) is satisfied in the case of that provider, they shall set, and apply to that provider, such SMP conditions authorised by this section as they consider appropriate.

(2) That test is that OFCOM are unable, by the setting of conditions of the sorts specified in subsection (3), to perform, or fully to perform, their duties under section 4 in relation to the market situation in the relevant market.

(3) The sorts of conditions referred to in subsection (2) are—

(a) access-related conditions; and

(b) SMP conditions authorised or required by sections 87 to [F9989] .

(4) The reference in subsection (2) to the market situation in the relevant market is a reference to the situation revealed by such market analyses of that market as may have been carried out for the purposes of this Chapter.

(5) The SMP conditions authorised by this section are conditions imposing on the dominant provider such regulatory controls as OFCOM may from time to time direct in relation to the provision by that provider of any public electronic communications service to the end-users of that service.

(6) Where OFCOM set a condition which is authorised by this section and imposes regulatory control on tariffs or other matters to which costs are relevant, they shall also set, and apply to the dominant provider, an SMP condition which requires him, to the extent that they consider it appropriate—

(a) to use such cost accounting systems as may be determined by them;

(b) to have the use of those systems audited annually by a qualified auditor; and

(c) to publish an annual statement about compliance by the dominant provider with the obligations imposed by virtue of paragraph (a).

F100. (7). . . . .

[F101. (8)In this section "qualified auditor" means a person who—

(a) is eligible for appointment as a statutory auditor under Part 42 of the Companies Act 2006, and

(b) if the appointment to carry out such auditing as is mentioned in subsection (6)(b) were an appointment as a statutory auditor, would not be prohibited from acting by section 1214 of that Act (independence requirement).]

Amendments (Textual)

F99. Word in s. 91. (3)(b) substituted (26.5.2011) by The Electronic Communications and Wireless Telegraphy Regulations 2011 (S.I. 2011/1210), reg. 1. (2), Sch. 1 para. 52. (a) (with Sch. 3 para. 2)

F100. S. 91. (7) omitted (26.5.2011) by virtue of The Electronic Communications and Wireless Telegraphy Regulations 2011 (S.I. 2011/1210), reg. 1. (2), Sch. 1 para. 52. (b) (with Sch. 3 para. 2)

F101. S. 91. (8) substituted (6.4.2008) by The Companies Act 2006 (Consequential Amendments etc) Order 2008 (S.I. 2008/948), art. 2. (2), Sch. 1 para. 30. (4) (with arts. 6, 11, 12)

Commencement Information

I119. S. 91 in force at 25.7.2003 for specified purposes by S.I. 2003/1900, arts. 1. (2), 2. (1), Sch. 1 (with art. 3) (as amended by S.I. 2003/3142, art. 1. (3))

I120. S. 91 in force at 29.12.2003 in so far as not already in force by S.I. 2003/3142, art. 3. (2) (with art. 11)

F10292. Conditions about leased lines

. . . .

Amendments (Textual)

F102. S. 92 omitted (26.5.2011) by virtue of The Electronic Communications and Wireless Telegraphy Regulations 2011 (S.I. 2011/1210), reg. 1. (2), Sch. 1 para. 53 (with Sch. 3 para. 2)

Commencement Information

I121. S. 92 in force at 25.7.2003 for specified purposes by S.I. 2003/1900, arts. 1. (2), 2. (1), Sch. 1 (with art. 3) (as amended by S.I. 2003/3142, art. 1. (3))

I122. S. 92 in force at 29.12.2003 in so far as not already in force by S.I. 2003/3142, art. 3. (2) (with art. 11)

SMP apparatus conditions: subject-matter

93. Conditions about apparatus supply

(1) Where OFCOM have made a determination that a person ("the dominant supplier") has significant market power in an identified apparatus market, they may—

    (a) set such SMP conditions authorised by this section as they consider it appropriate to apply to that person in respect of the supply of electronic communications apparatus; and

    (b) apply those conditions to that person.

(2) This section authorises the setting of SMP conditions of each of the following descriptions—

    (a) conditions requiring the dominant supplier to maintain such a separation for accounting purposes between matters relating to the supply of electronic communications apparatus and other matters as may be described in the conditions;

    (b) conditions imposing requirements about the accounting methods to be used in maintaining the separation; and

    (c) conditions imposing such rules as OFCOM may make, for the purpose of securing the maintenance of the separation, about the use of cost accounting systems.

(3) This section also authorises the setting of SMP conditions imposing price controls in relation to the hiring of telephones which are hardwired to an electronic communications network.

(4) Conditions set under this section must not make provision in relation to the supply of electronic communications apparatus unless the apparatus is of a description of apparatus as respects the supply of which the dominant supplier has been found to have significant market power.

(5) For the purposes of this section a telephone is hardwired to an electronic communications network where, in order for it to be used with that network—

    (a) it has to be physically attached to apparatus comprised in the network; and

    (b) the attachment has to be effected by a process that requires the use of a tool.

Commencement Information

I123. S. 93 in force at 25.7.2003 for specified purposes by S.I. 2003/1900, arts. 1. (2), 2. (1), Sch. 1 (with art. 3) (as amended by S.I. 2003/3142, art. 1. (3))

I124. S. 93 in force at 29.12.2003 in so far as not already in force by S.I. 2003/3142, art. 3. (2) (with art. 11)

Enforcement of conditions

94. Notification of contravention of [F103. SMP apparatus] conditions

(1) Where OFCOM determine that there are reasonable grounds for believing that a person is contravening, or has contravened, [F104an SMP apparatus condition] 5, they may give that person a notification under this section.

(2) A notification under this section is one which—

    (a) sets out the determination made by OFCOM;

    (b) specifies the condition and contravention in respect of which that determination has been made; and

    (c) specifies the period during which the person notified has an opportunity of doing the things specified in subsection (3).

(3) Those things are—

    (a) making representations about the matters notified;

(b) complying with notified conditions of which he remains in contravention; and

(c) remedying the consequences of notified contraventions.

(4) Subject to subsections (5) to (7) and section 98. (3), the period for doing those things must be the period of one month beginning with the day after the one on which the notification was given.

(5) OFCOM may, if they think fit, allow a longer period for doing those things either—

(a) by specifying a longer period in the notification; or

(b) by subsequently, on one or more occasions, extending the specified period.

(6) The person notified shall have a shorter period for doing those things if a shorter period is agreed between OFCOM and the person notified.

(7) The person notified shall also have a shorter period if—

(a) OFCOM have reasonable grounds for believing that the contravention is a repeated contravention;

(b) they have determined that, in those circumstances, a shorter period would be appropriate; and

(c) the shorter period has been specified in the notification.

(8) A notification under this section—

(a) may be given in respect of more than one contravention; and

(b) if it is given in respect of a continuing contravention, may be given in respect of any period during which the contravention has continued.

(9) Where a notification under this section has been given to a person in respect of a contravention of a condition, OFCOM may give a further notification in respect of the same contravention of that condition if, and only if—

(a) the contravention is one occurring after the time of the giving of the earlier notification;

(b) the contravention is a continuing contravention and the subsequent notification is in respect of so much of a period as falls after a period to which the earlier notification relates; or

(c) the earlier notification has been withdrawn without a penalty having been imposed in respect of the notified contravention.

[F105. (10)Before giving a notification under this section, OFCOM must consider whether it would be more appropriate to proceed under the Competition Act 1998.

(10. A)OFCOM must not give a notification under this section if they consider that it would be more appropriate to proceed under the Competition Act 1998.

(10. B)In a case where OFCOM decide that it would be more appropriate to proceed under the Competition Act 1998, they must publish a statement to that effect in such manner as they consider appropriate for bringing their decision to the attention of persons whom they consider are likely to be affected by it.]

(11) For the purposes of this section a contravention is a repeated contravention, in relation to a notification with respect to that contravention, if—

(a) a previous notification under this section has been given in respect of the same contravention or in respect of another contravention of the same condition; and

(b) the subsequent notification is given no more than twelve months after the day of the making by OFCOM of a determination for the purposes of section 95. (2) or 96. (2) that the contravention to which the previous notification related did occur.

Amendments (Textual)

F103. Words in s. 94 heading inserted (26.5.2011) by The Electronic Communications and Wireless Telegraphy Regulations 2011 (S.I. 2011/1210), reg. 1. (2), Sch. 1 para. 54. (b) (with Sch. 3 paras. 2, 13)

F104. Words in s. 94. (1) substituted (26.5.2011) by The Electronic Communications and Wireless Telegraphy Regulations 2011 (S.I. 2011/1210), reg. 1. (2), Sch. 1 para. 54. (a) (with Sch. 3 paras. 2, 13)

F105. S. 94. (10)-(10. B) substituted for s. 94. (10) (1.4.2014) by Enterprise and Regulatory Reform Act 2013 (c. 24), s. 103. (3), Sch. 14 para. 17; S.I. 2014/416, art. 2. (1)(e) (with Sch.)

Modifications etc. (not altering text)

C2. Ss. 94-97 applied (with modifications) by S.I. 2000/730, reg. 18. (5) (as inserted (25.7.2003) by Radio Equipment and Telecommunications Terminal Equipment (Amendment) Regulations 2003 (S.I. 2003/1903), regs. 1. (1), 2. (12)(b))

Commencement Information

I125. S. 94 in force at 25.7.2003 for specified purposes by S.I. 2003/1900, arts. 1. (2), 2. (1), Sch. 1 (with art. 3) (as amended by S.I. 2003/3142, art. 1. (3))

I126. S. 94 in force at 29.12.2003 in so far as not already in force by S.I. 2003/3142, art. 3. (2) (with art. 11)

95. Enforcement notification for contravention of conditions

(1) This section applies where—

(a) a person ("the notified provider") has been given a notification under section 94;

(b) OFCOM have allowed the notified provider an opportunity of making representations about the matters notified; and

(c) the period allowed for the making of the representations has expired.

(2) OFCOM may give the notified provider an enforcement notification if they are satisfied—

(a) that he has, in one or more of the respects notified, been in contravention of a condition specified in the notification under section 94; and

(b) that he has not, during the period allowed under that section, taken all such steps as they consider appropriate—

(i) for complying with that condition; and

(ii) for remedying the consequences of the notified contravention of that condition.

(3) An enforcement notification is a notification which imposes one or both of the following requirements on the notified provider—

(a) a requirement to take such steps for complying with the notified condition as may be specified in the notification;

(b) a requirement to take such steps for remedying the consequences of the notified contravention as may be so specified.

(4) A decision of OFCOM to give an enforcement notification to a person—

(a) must be notified by them to that person, together with the reasons for the decision, no later than one week after the day on which it is taken; and

(b) must fix a reasonable period for the taking of the steps required by the notification.

(5) It shall be the duty of a person to whom an enforcement notification has been given to comply with it.

(6) That duty shall be enforceable in civil proceedings by OFCOM—

(a) for an injunction;

(b) for specific performance of a statutory duty under section 45 of the Court of Session Act 1988 (c. 36); or

(c) for any other appropriate remedy or relief.

Modifications etc. (not altering text)

C2. Ss. 94-97 applied (with modifications) by S.I. 2000/730, reg. 18. (5) (as inserted (25.7.2003) by Radio Equipment and Telecommunications Terminal Equipment (Amendment) Regulations 2003 (S.I. 2003/1903), regs. 1. (1), 2. (12)(b))

Commencement Information

I127. S. 95 in force at 25.7.2003 for specified purposes by S.I. 2003/1900, arts. 1. (2), 2. (1), Sch. 1 (with art. 3) (as amended by S.I. 2003/3142, art. 1. (3))

I128. S. 95 in force at 29.12.2003 in so far as not already in force by S.I. 2003/3142, art. 3. (2) (with art. 11)

96. Penalties for contravention of conditions

(1) This section applies (in addition to section 95) where—

(a) a person ("the notified provider") has been given a notification under section 94;

(b) OFCOM have allowed the notified provider an opportunity of making representations about the matters notified; and

(c) the period allowed for the making of the representations has expired.

(2) OFCOM may impose a penalty on the notified provider if he—

(a) has, in one or more of the respects notified, been in contravention of a condition specified in the notification under section 94; and

(b) has not, during the period allowed under that section, taken the steps OFCOM consider appropriate—

(i) for complying with the notified condition; and

(ii) for remedying the consequences of the notified contravention of that condition.

(3) Where a notification under section 94 relates to more than one contravention, a separate penalty may be imposed in respect of each contravention.

(4) Where such a notification relates to a continuing contravention, no more than one penalty may be imposed in respect of the period of contravention specified in the notification.

(5) OFCOM may also impose a penalty on the notified provider if he has contravened, or is contravening, a requirement of an enforcement notification given under section 95 in respect of the notified contravention.

(6) Where OFCOM impose a penalty on a person under this section, they shall—

(a) within one week of making their decision to impose the penalty, notify that person of that decision and of their reasons for that decision; and

(b) in that notification, fix a reasonable period after it is given as the period within which the penalty is to be paid.

(7) A penalty imposed under this section—

(a) must be paid to OFCOM; and

(b) if not paid within the period fixed by them, is to be recoverable by them accordingly.

Modifications etc. (not altering text)

C2. Ss. 94-97 applied (with modifications) by S.I. 2000/730, reg. 18. (5) (as inserted (25.7.2003) by Radio Equipment and Telecommunications Terminal Equipment (Amendment) Regulations 2003 (S.I. 2003/1903), regs. 1. (1), 2. (12)(b))

Commencement Information

I129. S. 96 in force at 25.7.2003 for specified purposes by S.I. 2003/1900, arts. 1. (2), 2. (1), Sch. 1 (with art. 3) (as amended by S.I. 2003/3142, art. 1. (3))

I130. S. 96 in force at 29.12.2003 in so far as not already in force by S.I. 2003/3142, art. 3. (2) (with art. 11)

[F10696. A.Notification of contravention of condition other than SMP apparatus condition

(1) Where OFCOM determine that there are reasonable grounds for believing that a person is contravening, or has contravened, a condition (other than an SMP apparatus condition) set under section 45, they may give that person a notification under this section.

(2) A notification under this section is one which—

(a) sets out the determination made by OFCOM;

(b) specifies the condition and contravention in respect of which that determination has been made;

(c) specifies the period during which the person notified has an opportunity to make representations;

(d) specifies the steps that OFCOM think should be taken by the person in order to—

(i) comply with the condition;

(ii) remedy the consequences of the contravention;

(e) specifies any penalty which OFCOM are minded to impose in accordance with section 96. B;

(f) where the contravention is serious, specifies any direction which OFCOM are minded to give under section 100; and

(g) where the contravention relates to a condition set under sections 87 to 91, specifies any direction which OFCOM are minded to give under section 100. A.

(3) A notification under this section—

(a) may be given in respect of more than one contravention; and

(b) if it is given in respect of a continuing contravention, may be given in respect of any period during which the contravention has continued.

(4) Where a notification under this section has been given to a person in respect of a contravention of a condition, OFCOM may give a further notification in respect of the same contravention of that condition if, and only if—

(a) the contravention is one occurring after the time of the giving of the earlier notification;

(b) the contravention is a continuing contravention and the subsequent notification is in respect of so much of a period as falls after a period to which the earlier notification relates; or

(c) the earlier notification has been withdrawn without a penalty having been imposed in respect of the notified contravention.

[F107. (5)Before giving a notification under this section, OFCOM must consider whether it would be more appropriate to proceed under the Competition Act 1998.

(6) OFCOM must not give a notification under this section if they consider that it would be more appropriate to proceed under the Competition Act 1998.

(7) In a case where OFCOM decide that it would be more appropriate to proceed under the Competition Act 1998, they must publish a statement to that effect in such manner as they consider appropriate for bringing their decision to the attention of persons whom they consider are likely to be affected by it.]

Amendments (Textual)

F106. Ss. 96. A-96. C inserted (26.5.2011) by The Electronic Communications and Wireless Telegraphy Regulations 2011 (S.I. 2011/1210), reg. 1. (2), Sch. 1 para. 55 (with Sch. 3 paras. 2, 13)

F107. S. 96. A(5)-(7) substituted for s. 96. A(5) (1.4.2014) by Enterprise and Regulatory Reform Act 2013 (c. 24), s. 103. (3), Sch. 14 para. 18; S.I. 2014/416, art. 2. (1)(e) (with Sch.)

96. B.Penalties for contravention of conditions

(1) This section applies where a person is given a notification under section 96. A which specifies a proposed penalty.

(2) Where the notification relates to more than one contravention, a separate penalty may be specified in respect of each contravention.

(3) Where the notification relates to a continuing contravention, no more than one penalty may be specified in respect of the period of contravention specified in the notification.

(4) But, in relation to a continuing contravention, a penalty may be specified in respect of each day on which the contravention continues after—

(a) the giving of a confirmation decision under section 96. C(4)(c) which requires immediate action; or

(b) the expiry of any period specified in the confirmation decision for complying with a requirement so specified.

(5) The amount of a penalty under subsection (4) is to be such amount not exceeding £20,000 per day as OFCOM determine to be—

(a) appropriate; and

(b) proportionate to the contravention in respect of which it is imposed.

Amendments (Textual)

F106. Ss. 96. A-96. C inserted (26.5.2011) by The Electronic Communications and Wireless Telegraphy Regulations 2011 (S.I. 2011/1210), reg. 1. (2), Sch. 1 para. 55 (with Sch. 3 paras. 2, 13)

96. C.Enforcement of notification under section 96. A

(1) This section applies where—

(a) a person has been given a notification under section 96. A;

(b) OFCOM have allowed the person an opportunity to make representations about the matters notified; and

(c) the period allowed for the making of representations has expired.

(2) OFCOM may—

(a) give the person a decision (a "confirmation decision") confirming the imposition of requirements on the person, or the giving of a direction to the person, or both, in accordance with the notification under section 96. A; or

(b) inform the person that they are satisfied with the person's representations and that no further action will be taken.

(3) OFCOM may not give a confirmation decision to a person unless, after considering any representations, they are satisfied that the person has, in one or more of the respects notified, been in contravention of a condition specified in the notification under section 96. A.

(4) A confirmation decision—

(a) must be given to the person without delay;

(b) must include reasons for the decision;

(c) may require immediate action by the person to comply with requirements of a kind mentioned in section 96. A(2)(d), or may specify a period within which the person must comply with those requirements; and

(d) may require the person to pay—

(i) the penalty specified in the notification under section 96. A, or

(ii) such lesser penalty as OFCOM consider appropriate in the light of the person's representations or steps taken by the person to comply with the condition or remedy the consequences of the contravention, and

may specify the period within which the penalty is to be paid.

(5) It is the duty of the person to comply with any requirement imposed by a confirmation decision.

(6) That duty is enforceable in civil proceedings by OFCOM—

(a) for an injunction;

(b) for specific performance of a statutory duty under section 45 of the Court of Session Act 1988; or

(c) for any other appropriate remedy or relief.

(7) A penalty imposed by a confirmation decision—

(a) must be paid to OFCOM; and

(b) if not paid within the period specified by them, is to be recoverable by them accordingly.]

Amendments (Textual)

F106. Ss. 96. A-96. C inserted (26.5.2011) by The Electronic Communications and Wireless Telegraphy Regulations 2011 (S.I. 2011/1210), reg. 1. (2), Sch. 1 para. 55 (with Sch. 3 paras. 2, 13)

97. Amount of penalty under s. 96 [F108or 96. A]

(1) The amount of a penalty imposed under section 96 [F109or notified under section 96. A (other than a penalty falling within section 96. B(4))] is to be such amount not exceeding ten per cent. of the turnover of the [F110person] 's relevant business for the relevant period as OFCOM determine to be—

(a) appropriate; and

(b) proportionate to the contravention in respect of which it is imposed.

(2) In making [F111a determination in relation to a penalty imposed under section 96] OFCOM must have regard to—

(a) any representations made to them by the [F112person] ;

(b) any steps taken by him towards complying with the conditions contraventions of which have been notified to him under section 94; and

(c) any steps taken by him for remedying the consequences of those contraventions.

(3) For the purposes of this section—

(a) the turnover of a person's relevant business for a period shall be calculated in accordance with such rules as may be set out by order made by the Secretary of State; and

(b) provision may also be made by such an order for determining what is to be treated as the network, service, facility or business by reference to which the calculation of that turnover falls to be made.

(4) No order is to be made containing provision authorised by subsection (3) unless a draft of the order has been laid before Parliament and approved by a resolution of each House.

(5) In this section—

"relevant business" means (subject to the provisions of an order under subsection (3) and to subsections (6) and (7)) so much of any business carried on by the [F113person] as consists in any one or more of the following—

- the provision of an electronic communications network;
- the provision of an electronic communications service;
- the making available of associated facilities;
- the supply of directories for use in connection with the use of such a network or service;
- the making available of directory enquiry facilities for use for purposes connected with the use of such a network or service;
- any business not falling within any of the preceding paragraphs which is carried on in association with any business in respect of which any access-related condition is applied to the person carrying it on;

"relevant period", in relation to a contravention by a person of a condition set under section 45, means—

- except in a case falling within paragraph (b) or (c), the period of one year ending with the 31st March next before the time when notification of the contravention was given under section 94 [F114or 96. A] ;
- in the case of a person who at that time has been carrying on that business for a period of less than a year, the period, ending with that time, during which he has been carrying it on; and
- in the case of a person who at that time has ceased to carry on that business, the period of one year ending with the time when he ceased to carry it on.

(6) In the case of a contravention of an SMP apparatus condition the relevant business is so much of any business carried on by the person in respect of whose contravention the penalty is imposed as consists in the supply of electronic communications apparatus.

(7) So much of any business of a person on whom the penalty is imposed as falls within paragraph (f) of the definition of a relevant business shall be disregarded for the purposes of this section except in relation to—

(a) a contravention of an access-related condition imposed in respect of that business; or

(b) a contravention of an enforcement notification given under section 95 [F115or a confirmation decision under section 96. C] relating to such a condition.

F116. (8). . . . .

Amendments (Textual)

F108. Words in s. 97 heading inserted (26.5.2011) by The Electronic Communications and Wireless Telegraphy Regulations 2011 (S.I. 2011/1210), reg. 1. (2), Sch. 1 para. 56. (g) (with Sch. 3 paras. 2, 13)

F109. Words in s. 97. (1) inserted (26.5.2011) by The Electronic Communications and Wireless Telegraphy Regulations 2011 (S.I. 2011/1210), reg. 1. (2), Sch. 1 para. 56. (a) (with Sch. 3 paras. 2, 13)

F110. Word in s. 97. (1) substituted (26.5.2011) by The Electronic Communications and Wireless Telegraphy Regulations 2011 (S.I. 2011/1210), reg. 1. (2), Sch. 1 para. 56. (b) (with Sch. 3 paras. 2, 13)

F111. Words in s. 97. (2) substituted (26.5.2011) by The Electronic Communications and Wireless Telegraphy Regulations 2011 (S.I. 2011/1210), reg. 1. (2), Sch. 1 para. 56. (c) (with Sch. 3 paras. 2, 13)

F112. Word in s. 97. (2)(a) substituted (26.5.2011) by The Electronic Communications and Wireless Telegraphy Regulations 2011 (S.I. 2011/1210), reg. 1. (2), Sch. 1 para. 56. (b) (with Sch. 3 paras. 2, 13)

F113. Word in s. 97. (5) substituted (26.5.2011) by The Electronic Communications and Wireless Telegraphy Regulations 2011 (S.I. 2011/1210), reg. 1. (2), Sch. 1 para. 56. (b) (with Sch. 3 paras. 2, 13)

F114. Words in s. 97. (5) inserted (26.5.2011) by The Electronic Communications and Wireless Telegraphy Regulations 2011 (S.I. 2011/1210), reg. 1. (2), Sch. 1 para. 56. (d) (with Sch. 3 paras. 2, 13)

F115. Words in s. 97. (7) inserted (26.5.2011) by The Electronic Communications and Wireless Telegraphy Regulations 2011 (S.I. 2011/1210), reg. 1. (2), Sch. 1 para. 56. (e) (with Sch. 3 paras. 2, 13)

F116. S. 97. (8) omitted (26.5.2011) by virtue of The Electronic Communications and Wireless Telegraphy Regulations 2011 (S.I. 2011/1210), reg. 1. (2), Sch. 1 para. 56. (f) (with Sch. 3 paras. 2, 13)

Modifications etc. (not altering text)

C2. Ss. 94-97 applied (with modifications) by S.I. 2000/730, reg. 18. (5) (as inserted (25.7.2003) by Radio Equipment and Telecommunications Terminal Equipment (Amendment) Regulations 2003 (S.I. 2003/1903), regs. 1. (1), 2. (12)(b))

Commencement Information

I131. S. 97 in force at 25.7.2003 for specified purposes by S.I. 2003/1900, arts. 1. (2), 2. (1), Sch. 1 (with art. 3) (as amended by S.I. 2003/3142, art. 1. (3))

I132. S. 97 in force at 29.12.2003 in so far as not already in force by S.I. 2003/3142, art. 3. (2) (with art. 11)

98. Power to deal with urgent cases

(1) This section applies where OFCOM determine—

(a) that they are entitled to give a notification under section [F11796. A] with respect to a contravention by a person ("the contravening provider") of a condition set under section 45, F118...;

(b) that there are reasonable grounds for suspecting that the case is an urgent case; and

(c) that the urgency of the case makes it appropriate for OFCOM to take action under this section.

(2) A case is an urgent case for the purposes of this section if the contravention has resulted in, or creates an immediate risk of—

(a) a serious threat to the safety of the public, to public health or to national security;

(b) serious economic or operational problems for persons (other than the contravening provider) who are communications providers or persons who make associated facilities available; or

(c) serious economic or operational problems for persons who make use of electronic communications networks, electronic communications services or associated facilities.

F119. (3). . . . .

(4) OFCOM shall F120... have power to give to the contravening provider—

(a) a direction that his entitlement to provide electronic communications networks or electronic communications services, or to make associated facilities available, is suspended (either generally or in relation to particular networks, services or facilities); or

(b) a direction that that entitlement is restricted in the respects set out in the direction.

(5) A direction under subsection (4)—

(a) must specify the networks, services and facilities to which it relates; and

(b) except so far as it otherwise provides, takes effect for an indefinite period beginning with the time at which it is notified to the person to whom it is given.

(6) A direction under subsection (4)—

(a) in providing for the effect of a suspension or restriction to be postponed, may provide for it to take effect only at a time determined by or in accordance with the terms of the direction; and

(b) in connection with the suspension or restriction contained in the direction or with the postponement of its effect, may impose such conditions on the contravening provider as appear to OFCOM to be appropriate for the purpose of protecting his customers.

(7) Those conditions may include a condition requiring the making of payments—

(a) by way of compensation for loss or damage suffered by the contravening provider's customers as a result of the direction; or

(b) in respect of annoyance, inconvenience or anxiety to which they have been put in consequence of the direction.

(8) OFCOM have power to revoke a direction given under subsection (4)—

(a) with effect from such time as they may direct;

(b) subject to compliance with such requirements as they may specify; and

(c) to such extent and in relation to such networks, services or facilities, or parts of a network, service or facility, as they may determine.

Amendments (Textual)

F117. Word in s. 98. (1)(a) substituted (26.5.2011) by The Electronic Communications and Wireless Telegraphy Regulations 2011 (S.I. 2011/1210), reg. 1. (2), Sch. 1 para. 57. (a) (with Sch. 3 paras. 2, 13)

F118. Words in s. 98. (1)(a) omitted (26.5.2011) by virtue of The Electronic Communications and Wireless Telegraphy Regulations 2011 (S.I. 2011/1210), reg. 1. (2), Sch. 1 para. 57. (a) (with Sch. 3 paras. 2, 13)

F119. S. 98. (3) omitted (26.5.2011) by virtue of The Electronic Communications and Wireless Telegraphy Regulations 2011 (S.I. 2011/1210), reg. 1. (2), Sch. 1 para. 57. (b) (with Sch. 3 paras. 2, 13)

F120. Word in s. 98. (4) omitted (26.5.2011) by virtue of The Electronic Communications and Wireless Telegraphy Regulations 2011 (S.I. 2011/1210), reg. 1. (2), Sch. 1 para. 57. (c) (with Sch. 3 paras. 2, 13)

Commencement Information

I133. S. 98 in force at 25.7.2003 for specified purposes by S.I. 2003/1900, arts. 1. (2), 2. (1), Sch. 1 (with art. 3) (as amended by S.I. 2003/3142, art. 1. (3))

I134. S. 98 in force at 29.12.2003 in so far as not already in force by S.I. 2003/3142, art. 3. (2) (with art. 11)

99. Confirmation of directions under s. 98.

(1) As soon as reasonably practicable after giving a direction under section 98. (4), OFCOM must give the person to whom it is given—

(a) an opportunity of making representations to them about the grounds on which it was given and its effect; and

(b) an opportunity of proposing steps to remedy the situation.

(2) As soon as practicable after the period allowed by OFCOM for making those representations has ended [F121. (and in any event within 3 months beginning with the day on which the direction under section 98. (4) was given)] , they must determine—

(a) whether the contravention providing the grounds for the giving of the direction did occur; and

(b) whether the circumstances made it an urgent case justifying the giving of the direction.

[F122. (2. A)The period of 3 months mentioned in subsection (2) may be extended by up to 3 months if OFCOM—

(a) require additional time to consider representations received; or

(b) decide that it is necessary to obtain additional information from the person in order to make a determination under subsection (2).]

(3) If OFCOM decide that the contravention did occur and that the direction was justified, they may confirm the direction.

(4) If not, they must exercise their power to revoke it.

(5) As soon as reasonably practicable after determining whether to confirm the direction, OFCOM must notify the person to whom it was given of their decision.

(6) Conditions included in a direction by virtue of section 98. (7) have effect only if the direction is confirmed.

Amendments (Textual)

F121. Words in s. 99. (2) inserted (26.5.2011) by The Electronic Communications and Wireless Telegraphy Regulations 2011 (S.I. 2011/1210), reg. 1. (2), Sch. 1 para. 58. (a) (with Sch. 3 paras. 2, 13)

F122. S. 99. (2. A) inserted (26.5.2011) by The Electronic Communications and Wireless Telegraphy Regulations 2011 (S.I. 2011/1210), reg. 1. (2), Sch. 1 para. 58. (b) (with Sch. 3 paras. 2, 13)

Commencement Information

I135. S. 99 in force at 25.7.2003 for specified purposes by S.I. 2003/1900, arts. 1. (2), 2. (1), Sch. 1 (with art. 3) (as amended by S.I. 2003/3142, art. 1. (3))

I136. S. 99 in force at 29.12.2003 in so far as not already in force by S.I. 2003/3142, art. 3. (2) (with art. 11)

100. Suspending service provision for contraventions of conditions

[F123. (1)OFCOM may give a direction under this section to a person where—

(a) either Condition A or Condition B is satisfied in relation to the person; and

(b) the giving of a direction is appropriate and proportionate to the contravention in respect of which it is imposed.

(1. A)Condition A is that—

(a) the person is in serious contravention of a condition set under section 45, other than SMP apparatus conditions; and

(b) the proposed direction has been notified to the person under section 96. A and confirmed by a confirmation decision under section 96. C.

(1. B)Condition B is that—

(a) the person has repeatedly contravened a condition set under section 45, other than SMP apparatus conditions; and

(b) an attempt, by the imposition of penalties or the giving of notifications under section 96. A and confirmation decisions under section 96. C, or both, to secure compliance with the contravened conditions has failed.

(1. C)Where Condition A is satisfied, a direction under this section is given where OFCOM give a confirmation decision under section 96. C to the person in respect of a direction proposed in a notification under section 96. A.

(1. D)Where Condition B is satisfied, a direction under this section is to be given in accordance with the procedure set out in section 102.]

(2) A direction under this section is—

(a) a direction that the entitlement of the [F124person] to provide electronic communications networks or electronic communications services, or to make associated facilities available, is suspended (either generally or in relation to particular networks, services or facilities); or

(b) a direction that that entitlement is restricted in the respects set out in the direction.

(3) A direction under this section—

(a) must specify the networks, services and facilities to which it relates; and

(b) except so far as it otherwise provides, takes effect for an indefinite period beginning with the time at which it is notified to the person to whom it is given.

(4) A direction under this section—

(a) in providing for the effect of a suspension or restriction to be postponed, may provide for it to take effect only at a time determined by or in accordance with the terms of the direction; and

(b) in connection with the suspension or restriction contained in the direction or with the postponement of its effect, may impose such conditions on the [F125person] as appear to OFCOM to be appropriate for the purpose of protecting that provider's customers.

(5) Those conditions may include a condition requiring the making of payments—

(a) by way of compensation for loss or damage suffered by the [F126person] 's customers as a result of the direction; or

(b) in respect of annoyance, inconvenience or anxiety to which they have been put in consequence of the direction.

(6) If OFCOM consider it appropriate to do so (whether or not in consequence of representations or proposals made to them), they may revoke a direction under this section or modify its conditions—

(a) with effect from such time as they may direct;

(b) subject to compliance with such requirements as they may specify; and

(c) to such extent and in relation to such networks, services or facilities, or parts of a network, service or facility, as they may determine.

(7) For the purposes of this section there are repeated contraventions by a person of conditions set

under section 45 to the extent that—

[F127. (a)in the case of a previous notification of a contravention given to that person under section 96. A, OFCOM have given a confirmation decision to that person under section 96. C(2) in respect of the contravention;]

[F128. (b)in the period of 24 months following the giving of that confirmation decision, one or more further confirmation decisions have been given to the person in respect of contraventions of a condition under section 45;]

(c) the previous [F129confirmation decision] and the subsequent ones all relate to contraventions of the same condition (whether the same contravention or different contraventions).

Amendments (Textual)

F123. S. 100. (1)-(1. D) substituted for s. 100. (1) (26.5.2011) by The Electronic Communications and Wireless Telegraphy Regulations 2011 (S.I. 2011/1210), reg. 1. (2), Sch. 1 para. 59. (a) (with Sch. 3 paras. 2, 13, 14)

F124. Word in s. 100. (2)(a) substituted (26.5.2011) by The Electronic Communications and Wireless Telegraphy Regulations 2011 (S.I. 2011/1210), reg. 1. (2), Sch. 1 para. 59. (b) (with Sch. 3 paras. 2, 13)

F125. Word in s. 100. (4)(b) substituted (26.5.2011) by The Electronic Communications and Wireless Telegraphy Regulations 2011 (S.I. 2011/1210), reg. 1. (2), Sch. 1 para. 59. (b) (with Sch. 3 paras. 2, 13)

F126. Word in s. 100. (5)(a) substituted (26.5.2011) by The Electronic Communications and Wireless Telegraphy Regulations 2011 (S.I. 2011/1210), reg. 1. (2), Sch. 1 para. 59. (b) (with Sch. 3 paras. 2, 13)

F127. S. 100. (7)(a) substituted (26.5.2011) by The Electronic Communications and Wireless Telegraphy Regulations 2011 (S.I. 2011/1210), reg. 1. (2), Sch. 1 para. 59. (c)(i) (with Sch. 3 paras. 2, 13)

F128. S. 100. (7)(b) substituted (26.5.2011) by The Electronic Communications and Wireless Telegraphy Regulations 2011 (S.I. 2011/1210), reg. 1. (2), Sch. 1 para. 59. (c)(ii) (with Sch. 3 paras. 2, 13)

F129. Words in s. 100. (7)(c) substituted (26.5.2011) by The Electronic Communications and Wireless Telegraphy Regulations 2011 (S.I. 2011/1210), reg. 1. (2), Sch. 1 para. 59. (c)(iii) (with Sch. 3 paras. 2, 13)

Commencement Information

I137. S. 100 in force at 25.7.2003 for specified purposes by S.I. 2003/1900, arts. 1. (2), 2. (1), Sch. 1 (with art. 3) (as amended by S.I. 2003/3142, art. 1. (3))

I138. S. 100 in force at 29.12.2003 in so far as not already in force by S.I. 2003/3142, art. 3. (2) (with art. 11)

[F130100. A.Suspending service provision for breach of SMP services condition

(1) OFCOM may give a direction under this section to a person who provides a public electronic communications network, or a person who makes available facilities that are associated facilities by reference to such a network, if OFCOM are satisfied that—

(a) the person is or has been in contravention of conditions set under sections 87 to 91; and

(b) the provision of an electronic communications service by the person on that public electronic communications network could result in significant harm to competition.

(2) A direction under this section is given where OFCOM give a confirmation decision under section 96. C to the person in respect of a direction proposed in a notification under section 96. A.

(3) A direction under this section is—

(a) a direction that the entitlement of the person to provide an electronic communications service over the public electronic communications network to which the contravened condition relates is suspended (either generally or in relation to particular services); or

(b) a direction that the person may not begin to provide an electronic communications service over the public electronic communications network to which the contravened provision relates.

(4) A direction under this section—

(a) must specify the electronic communications services to which it relates, and

106

(b) takes effect for an indefinite period beginning with the time at which a confirmation decision relating to the direction is given to the person under section 96. C.

(5) A direction under this section—

(a) may provide for a suspension or prohibition to take effect only at a time determined by or in accordance with the terms of the direction; and

(b) in connection with a suspension or prohibition contained in the direction or with the postponement of its effect, may impose such conditions on the person to whom it is given as appear to OFCOM to be appropriate for the purpose of protecting that person's customers.

(6) Those conditions may include a condition requiring the making of payments—

(a) by way of compensation for loss or damage suffered by the person's customers as a result of the direction; or

(b) in respect of annoyance, inconvenience or anxiety to which they have been put in consequence of the direction.

(7) If OFCOM consider it appropriate to do so (whether or not in consequence of representations or proposals made to them), they may revoke a direction under this section or modify its conditions—

(a) with effect from such time as they may direct;

(b) subject to compliance with such requirements as they may specify; and

(c) to such extent and in relation to such services, or parts of a service, as they may determine.]

Amendments (Textual)

F130 S. 100. A inserted (26.5.2011) by The Electronic Communications and Wireless Telegraphy Regulations 2011 (S.I. 2011/1210), reg. 1. (2), Sch. 1 para. 60 (with Sch. 3 paras. 2, 13, 14)

101. Suspending apparatus supply for contraventions of conditions

(1) OFCOM may give a direction under this section to a person who supplies electronic communications apparatus ("the contravening supplier") if they are satisfied—

(a) that he is or has been in serious and repeated contravention of any SMP apparatus conditions;

(b) that an attempt, by the imposition of penalties or the giving of enforcement notifications under section 95 or both, to secure compliance with the contravened conditions has failed; and

(c) that the giving of the direction is appropriate and proportionate to the seriousness (when repeated as they have been) of the contraventions.

(2) A direction under this section is—

(a) a direction to the contravening supplier to cease to act as a supplier of electronic communications apparatus (either generally or in relation to apparatus of a particular description); or

(b) a direction imposing such restrictions as may be set out in the direction on the supply by that supplier of electronic communications apparatus (either generally or in relation to apparatus of a particular description).

(3) A direction under this section takes effect, except so far as it otherwise provides, for an indefinite period beginning with the time at which it is notified to the person to whom it is given.

(4) A direction under this section—

(a) may provide for a prohibition or restriction to take effect only at a time determined by or in accordance with the terms of the direction; and

(b) in connection with a prohibition or restriction contained in the direction or with the postponement of its effect, may impose such conditions on the contravening supplier as appear to OFCOM to be appropriate for the purpose of protecting that supplier's customers.

(5) Those conditions may include a condition requiring the making of payments—

(a) by way of compensation for loss or damage suffered by the contravening supplier's customers as a result of the direction; or

(b) in respect of annoyance, inconvenience or anxiety to which they have been put in consequence of the direction.

(6) If OFCOM consider it appropriate to do so (whether or not in consequence of representations or proposals made to them), they may at any time revoke a direction under this section or modify

its conditions—

(a) with effect from such time as they may direct;

(b) subject to compliance with such requirements as they may specify; and

(c) to such extent and in relation to such apparatus or descriptions of apparatus as they may determine.

(7) For the purposes of this section there are repeated contraventions by a person of SMP apparatus conditions to the extent that—

(a) in the case of a previous notification given to that person under section 94, OFCOM have determined for the purposes of section 95. (2) or 96. (2) that such a contravention did occur;

(b) in the period of twelve months following the day of the making of that determination, one or more further notifications have been given to that person in respect of contraventions of an SMP apparatus condition; and

(c) the previous notification and the subsequent ones all relate to contraventions of the same condition (whether the same contravention or different contraventions).

Commencement Information

I139. S. 101 in force at 25.7.2003 for specified purposes by S.I. 2003/1900, arts. 1. (2), 2. (1), Sch. 1 (with art. 3) (as amended by S.I. 2003/3142, art. 1. (3))

I140. S. 101 in force at 29.12.2003 in so far as not already in force by S.I. 2003/3142, art. 3. (2) (with art. 11)

102. Procedure for directions under ss. 100 and 101.

(1) Except in an urgent case, [F131or a case where Condition A in section 100 is satisfied,] OFCOM are not to give a direction under section 100 or 101 unless they have—

(a) notified the contravening provider or contravening supplier of the proposed direction and of the conditions (if any) which they are proposing to impose by that direction;

(b) provided him with an opportunity of making representations about the proposals and of proposing steps for remedying the situation; and

(c) considered every representation and proposal made to them during the period allowed by them for the contravening provider or the contravening supplier to take advantage of that opportunity.

[F132. (2)That period must be—

(a) in relation to a direction under section 100, such reasonable period as OFCOM may determine, and

(b) in relation to a direction under section 101, a period ending not less than one month after the day of the giving of the notification.]

(3) As soon as practicable after giving a direction under section 100 or 101 in an urgent case, OFCOM must, provide the contravening provider or contravening supplier with an opportunity of—

(a) making representations about the effect of the direction and of any of its conditions; and

(b) proposing steps for remedying the situation.

[F133. (3. A)In relation to a direction under section 100 in an urgent case, as soon as practicable after the period allowed by OFCOM for making those representations has ended (and in any event within 3 months beginning with the day on which the direction was given), they must determine—

(a) whether the contravention providing the grounds for the giving of the direction did occur; and

(b) whether the circumstances made it an urgent case justifying the giving of the direction.

(3. B)The period of 3 months mentioned in subsection (3. A) may be extended by up to 3 months if OFCOM—

(a) require additional time to consider representations received; or

(b) decide that it is necessary to obtain additional information from the person in order to make a determination under subsection (3. A).]

(4) A case is an urgent case for the purposes of this section if OFCOM—

(a) consider that it would be inappropriate, because the contraventions in question fall within subsection (5), to allow time, before giving a direction under section 100 or 101, for the making and consideration of representations; and

(b) decide for that reason to act in accordance with subsection (3), instead of subsection (1).

(5) The contraventions fall within this subsection if they have resulted in, or create an immediate risk of—

(a) a serious threat to the safety of the public, to public health or to national security;

(b) serious economic or operational problems for persons (apart from the contravening provider or contravening supplier) who are communications providers or persons who make associated facilities available; or

(c) serious economic or operational problems for persons who make use of electronic communications networks, electronic communications services or associated facilities.

(6) In this section—

[F134"contravening provider" means a person who is a communications provider or makes associated facilities available;]

"contravening supplier" has the same meaning as in section 101.

Amendments (Textual)

F131. Words in s. 102. (1) inserted (26.5.2011) by The Electronic Communications and Wireless Telegraphy Regulations 2011 (S.I. 2011/1210), reg. 1. (2), Sch. 1 para. 61. (a) (with Sch. 3 paras. 2, 13)

F132. S. 102. (2) substituted (26.5.2011) by The Electronic Communications and Wireless Telegraphy Regulations 2011 (S.I. 2011/1210), reg. 1. (2), Sch. 1 para. 61. (b) (with Sch. 3 paras. 2, 13)

F133. S. 102. (3. A)(3. B) inserted (26.5.2011) by The Electronic Communications and Wireless Telegraphy Regulations 2011 (S.I. 2011/1210), reg. 1. (2), Sch. 1 para. 61. (c) (with Sch. 3 paras. 2, 13)

F134. Words in s. 102. (6) substituted (26.5.2011) by The Electronic Communications and Wireless Telegraphy Regulations 2011 (S.I. 2011/1210), reg. 1. (2), Sch. 1 para. 61. (d) (with Sch. 3 paras. 2, 13)

Commencement Information

I141. S. 102 in force at 25.7.2003 for specified purposes by S.I. 2003/1900, arts. 1. (2), 2. (1), Sch. 1 (with art. 3) (as amended by S.I. 2003/3142, art. 1. (3))

I142. S. 102 in force at 29.12.2003 in so far as not already in force by S.I. 2003/3142, art. 3. (2) (with art. 11)

103. Enforcement of directions under ss. 98, 100 [F135, 100. A] and 101.

(1) A person is guilty of an offence if he provides an electronic communications network or electronic communications service, or makes available any associated facility—

(a) while his entitlement to do so is suspended by a direction under section [F13698. (4), 100 or 100. A] ; or

(b) in contravention of a restriction contained in such a direction.

(2) A person is guilty of an offence if he supplies electronic communications apparatus—

(a) while prohibited from doing so by a direction under section 101; or

(b) in contravention of a restriction contained in such a direction.

(3) A person guilty of an offence under this section shall be liable—

(a) on summary conviction, to a fine not exceeding the statutory maximum;

(b) on conviction on indictment, to a fine.

[F137. (4)Sections 96. A to 99 apply in relation to a contravention of conditions imposed by a direction under section 98, 100 or 100. A as they apply in relation to a contravention of conditions set under section 45, other than SMP apparatus conditions.

(5) Sections 94 to 96 and 97 to 99 apply in relation to a contravention of conditions imposed by a direction under section 101 as they apply in relation to a contravention of SMP apparatus conditions.]

Amendments (Textual)

F135. Words in s. 103 heading inserted (26.5.2011) by The Electronic Communications and Wireless Telegraphy Regulations 2011 (S.I. 2011/1210), reg. 1. (2), Sch. 1 para. 62. (c) (with Sch.

3 paras. 2, 13)
F136. Words in s. 103. (1)(a) substituted (26.5.2011) by The Electronic Communications and
Wireless Telegraphy Regulations 2011 (S.I. 2011/1210), reg. 1. (2), Sch. 1 para. 62. (a) (with Sch.
3 paras. 2, 13)
F137. S. 103. (4)(5) substituted for s. 103. (4) (26.5.2011) by The Electronic Communications and
Wireless Telegraphy Regulations 2011 (S.I. 2011/1210), reg. 1. (2), Sch. 1 para. 62. (b) (with Sch.
3 paras. 2, 13)
Commencement Information
I143. S. 103 in force at 25.7.2003 for specified purposes by S.I. 2003/1900, arts. 1. (2), 2. (1), Sch.
1 (with art. 3) (as amended by S.I. 2003/3142, art. 1. (3))
I144. S. 103 in force at 29.12.2003 in so far as not already in force by S.I. 2003/3142, art. 3. (2)
(with art. 11)
104. Civil liability for breach of conditions or [F138confirmation decision]
(1) The obligation of a person to comply with—
    (a) the conditions set under section 45 which apply to him,
    (b) requirements imposed on him by an enforcement notification under section 95, F139...
    [F140. (ba)requirements imposed on the person by a notification under section 96. A and a
confirmation decision under section 96. C; and]
    (c) the conditions imposed by a direction under section 98 [F141, 100 or 100. A] ,
shall be a duty owed to every person who may be affected by a contravention of the condition or
requirement.
(2) Where a duty is owed by virtue of this section to a person—
    (a) a breach of the duty that causes that person to sustain loss or damage, and
    (b) an act which—
(i) by inducing a breach of the duty or interfering with its performance, causes that person to
sustain loss or damage, and
(ii) is done wholly or partly for achieving that result,
shall be actionable at the suit or instance of that person.
(3) In proceedings brought against a person by virtue of subsection (2)(a) it shall be a defence for
that person to show that he took all reasonable steps and exercised all due diligence to avoid
contravening the condition or requirement in question.
(4) The consent of OFCOM is required for the bringing of proceedings by virtue of subsection
(1)(a).
(5) Where OFCOM give a consent for the purposes of subsection (4) subject to conditions relating
to the conduct of the proceedings, the proceedings are not to be carried on by that person except in
compliance with those conditions.

Amendments (Textual)
F138. Words in s. 104 heading substituted (26.5.2011) by The Electronic Communications and
Wireless Telegraphy Regulations 2011 (S.I. 2011/1210), reg. 1. (2), Sch. 1 para. 63. (c) (with Sch.
3 paras. 2, 13)
F139. Word in s. 104. (1)(b) omitted (26.5.2011) by virtue of The Electronic Communications and
Wireless Telegraphy Regulations 2011 (S.I. 2011/1210), reg. 1. (2), Sch. 1 para. 63. (a) (with Sch.
3 paras. 2, 13)
F140. S. 104. (1)(ba) inserted (26.5.2011) by The Electronic Communications and Wireless
Telegraphy Regulations 2011 (S.I. 2011/1210), reg. 1. (2), Sch. 1 para. 63. (a) (with Sch. 3 paras.
2, 13)
F141. Words in s. 104. (1)(c) substituted (26.5.2011) by The Electronic Communications and
Wireless Telegraphy Regulations 2011 (S.I. 2011/1210), reg. 1. (2), Sch. 1 para. 63. (b) (with Sch.
3 paras. 2, 13)
Commencement Information
I145. S. 104 in force at 25.7.2003 for specified purposes by S.I. 2003/1900, arts. 1. (2), 2. (1), Sch.
1 (with art. 3) (as amended by S.I. 2003/3142, art. 1. (3))
I146. S. 104 in force at 29.12.2003 in so far as not already in force by S.I. 2003/3142, art. 3. (2)

(with art. 11)

OFCOM's duty to intervene on network access issues

F142105. Consideration and determination of network access questions

. . . .

Amendments (Textual)

F142. S. 105 omitted (26.5.2011) by virtue of The Electronic Communications and Wireless Telegraphy Regulations 2011 (S.I. 2011/1210), reg. 1. (2), Sch. 1 para. 64 (with Sch. 3 para. 2)

Commencement Information

I147. S. 105 in force at 25.7.2003 for specified purposes by S.I. 2003/1900, arts. 1. (2), 2. (1), Sch. 1 (with art. 3) (as amended by S.I. 2003/3142, art. 1. (3))

I148. S. 105 in force at 29.12.2003 in so far as not already in force by S.I. 2003/3142, art. 3. (2) (with art. 11)

[F143. Security of public electronic communications networks and services

Amendments (Textual)

F143. Ss. 105. A-105. D and cross-heading inserted (26.5.2011) by The Electronic Communications and Wireless Telegraphy Regulations 2011 (S.I. 2011/1210), reg. 1. (2), Sch. 1 para. 65 (with Sch. 3 para. 2)

105. A.Requirement to protect security of networks and services

(1) Network providers and service providers must take technical and organisational measures appropriately to manage risks to the security of public electronic communications networks and public electronic communications services.

(2) Measures under subsection (1) must, in particular, include measures to prevent or minimise the impact of security incidents on end-users.

(3) Measures under subsection (1) taken by a network provider must also include measures to prevent or minimise the impact of security incidents on interconnection of public electronic communications networks.

(4) A network provider must also take all appropriate steps to protect, so far as possible, the availability of the provider's public electronic communications network.

(5) In this section and sections 105. B and 105. C—

"network provider" means a provider of a public electronic communications network, and "service provider" means a provider of a public electronic communications service.

105. B.Requirement to notify OFCOM of security breach

(1) A network provider must notify OFCOM—

(a) of a breach of security which has a significant impact on the operation of a public electronic communications network, and

(b) of a reduction in the availability of a public electronic communications network which has a significant impact on the network.

(2) A service provider must notify OFCOM of a breach of security which has a significant impact on the operation of a public electronic communications service.

(3) If OFCOM receive a notification under this section, they must, where they think it appropriate, notify—

(a) the regulatory authorities in other member States, and

(b) the European Network and Information Security Agency ("ENISA").

(4) OFCOM may also inform the public of a notification under this section, or require the network provider or service provider to inform the public, if OFCOM think that it is in the public interest to do so.

(5) OFCOM must prepare an annual report summarising notifications received by them under this section during the year, and any action taken in response to a notification.

(6) A copy of the annual report must be sent to the European Commission and to ENISA.

105. C.Requirement to submit to audit

(1) OFCOM may carry out, or arrange for another person to carry out, an audit of the measures taken by a network provider or a service provider under section 105. A.

(2) A network provider or a service provider must—

(a) co-operate with an audit under subsection (1), and

(b) pay the costs of the audit.

105. D.Enforcement of obligations under sections 105. A to 105. C

(1) Sections 96. A to 96. C, 98 to 100, 102 and 103 apply in relation to a contravention of a requirement under sections 105. A to 105. C as they apply in relation to a contravention of a condition set under section 45, other than an SMP apparatus condition.

(2) The obligation of a person to comply with the requirements of section 105. A to 105. C is a duty owed to every person who may be affected by a contravention of a requirement, and—

(a) section 104 applies in relation to that duty as it applies in relation to the duty set out in subsection (1) of that section, and

(b) section 104. (4) applies in relation to proceedings brought by virtue of this section as it applies in relation to proceedings by virtue of section 104. (1)(a).

(3) The amount of a penalty imposed under sections 96. A to 96. C, as applied by this section, is to be such amount not exceeding £2 million as OFCOM determine to be—

(a) appropriate; and

(b) proportionate to the contravention in respect of which it is imposed.]

Electronic communications code

106. Application of the electronic communications code

(1) In this Chapter "the electronic communications code" means the code set out in Schedule 2 to the Telecommunications Act 1984 (c. 12).

(2) Schedule 3 (which amends Schedule 2 to the Telecommunications Act 1984 (c. 12) for the purpose of translating the telecommunications code into a code applicable in the context of the new regulatory regime established by this Act) shall have effect.

(3) The electronic communications code shall have effect—

(a) in the case of a person to whom it is applied by a direction given by OFCOM; and

(b) in the case of the Secretary of State or any Northern Ireland department where the Secretary of State or that department is providing or proposing to provide an electronic communications network.

(4) The only purposes for which the electronic communications code may be applied in a person's case by a direction under this section are—

(a) the purposes of the provision by him of an electronic communications network; or

(b) the purposes of the provision by him of a system of conduits which he is making available, or proposing to make available, for use by providers of electronic communications networks for the purposes of the provision by them of their networks.

(5) A direction applying the electronic communications code in any person's case may provide for that code to have effect in his case—

(a) in relation only to such places or localities as may be specified or described in the direction;

(b) for the purposes only of the provision of such electronic communications network, or part of an electronic communications network, as may be so specified or described; or

(c) for the purposes only of the provision of such conduit system, or part of a conduit system, as may be so specified or described.

(6) The Secretary of State may by order provide for the electronic communications code to have effect for all purposes with a different amount substituted for the amount for the time being

specified in paragraph 16. (3) of the code (minimum compensation).

(7) In this section "conduit" includes a tunnel, subway, tube or pipe.

Commencement Information

I149. S. 106 in force at 25.7.2003 for specified purposes by S.I. 2003/1900, arts. 1. (2), 2. (1), Sch. 1 (with art. 3) (as amended by S.I. 2003/3142, art. 1. (3))

I150. S. 106 in force at 29.12.2003 in so far as not already in force by S.I. 2003/3142, art. 3. (2) (with art. 11)

107. Procedure for directions applying code

(1) OFCOM are not to give a direction applying the electronic communications code in any person's case except on an application made for the purpose by that person.

[F144. (1. A)Regulation 3 of the Electronic Communications and Wireless Telegraphy Regulations 2011 makes provision about the time within which an application under subsection (1) must be determined.]

(2) If OFCOM publish a notification setting out their requirements with respect to—

   (a) the content of an application for a direction applying the electronic communications code, and

   (b) the manner in which such an application is to be made,

such an application must be made in accordance with the requirements for the time being in force.

(3) OFCOM may—

   (a) from time to time review the requirements for the time being in force for the purposes of subsection (2); and

   (b) on any such review, modify them in such manner as they think fit by giving a notification of the revised requirements.

[F145. (3. A)A modification may not be made under subsection (3) unless the modification is—

   (a) objectively justifiable, and

   (b) proportionate to what it is intended to achieve.

(3. B)Before making a modification under subsection (3), OFCOM must publish a notification of the proposed modification which contains the following—

   (a) a statement of the proposal,

   (b) a statement of their reasons for the proposal, and

   (c) a statement of the period within which representations may be made to them about the proposal.

(3. C)The period specified under subsection (3. B)(c) must end no less than one month after the day of the publication of the notification.]

(4) In considering whether to apply the electronic communications code in any person's case, OFCOM must have regard, in particular, to each of the following matters—

   (a) the benefit to the public of the electronic communications network or conduit system by reference to which the code is to be applied to that person;

   (b) the practicability of the provision of that network or system without the application of the code;

   (c) the need to encourage the sharing of the use of electronic communications apparatus;

   (d) whether the person in whose case it is proposed to apply the code will be able to meet liabilities arising as a consequence of—

(i) the application of the code in his case; and

(ii) any conduct of his in relation to the matters with which the code deals.

(5) For the purposes of subsections (6) and (7) of section 3 OFCOM's duty under subsection (4) ranks equally with their duties under that section.

(6) Before giving a direction under section 106, OFCOM must—

   (a) publish a notification of their proposal to give the direction; and

   (b) consider any representations about that proposal that are made to them within the period specified in the notification.

(7) A notification for the purposes of subsection (6)(a) must contain the following—

   (a) a statement of OFCOM's proposal;

(b) a statement of their reasons for that proposal;

(c) a statement of the period within which representations may be made to them about the proposal.

(8) The statement of OFCOM's proposal must—

(a) contain a statement that they propose to apply the code in the case of the person in question;

(b) set out any proposals of theirs to impose terms under section 106. (5);

but this subsection is subject to sections 113. (7) and 115. (5).

(9) The period specified as the period within which representations may be made must end no less than one month after the day of the publication of the notification.

(10) The publication by OFCOM of a notification for any of the purposes of this section must be a publication in such manner as OFCOM consider appropriate for bringing the notification to the attention of the persons who, in their opinion, are likely to be affected by it.

Amendments (Textual)

F144. S. 107. (1. A) inserted (26.5.2011) by The Electronic Communications and Wireless Telegraphy Regulations 2011 (S.I. 2011/1210), reg. 1. (2), Sch. 1 para. 66. (a) (with Sch. 3 paras. 1, 2)

F145. S. 107. (3. A)-(3. C) inserted (26.5.2011) by The Electronic Communications and Wireless Telegraphy Regulations 2011 (S.I. 2011/1210), reg. 1. (2), Sch. 1 para. 66. (b) (with Sch. 3 para. 2)

Commencement Information

I151. S. 107 in force at 25.7.2003 for specified purposes by S.I. 2003/1900, arts. 1. (2), 2. (1), Sch. 1 (with art. 3) (as amended by S.I. 2003/3142, art. 1. (3))

I152. S. 107 in force at 29.12.2003 in so far as not already in force by S.I. 2003/3142, art. 3. (2) (with art. 11)

108. Register of persons in whose case code applies

(1) It shall be the duty of OFCOM to establish and maintain a register of persons in whose case the electronic communications code applies by virtue of a direction under section 106.

(2) OFCOM must record in the register every direction given under that section.

(3) Information recorded in the register must be recorded in such manner as OFCOM consider appropriate.

(4) It shall be the duty of OFCOM to publish a notification setting out—

(a) the times at which the register is for the time being available for public inspection; and

(b) the fees that must be paid for, or in connection with, an inspection of the register.

(5) The publication of a notification under subsection (4) must be a publication in such manner as OFCOM consider appropriate for bringing it to the attention of the persons who, in their opinion, are likely to be affected by it.

(6) OFCOM must make the register available for public inspection—

(a) during such hours, and

(b) on payment of such fees,

as are set out in the notification for the time being in force under subsection (4).

Commencement Information

I153. S. 108 in force at 25.7.2003 for specified purposes by S.I. 2003/1900, arts. 1. (2), 2. (1), Sch. 1 (with art. 3) (as amended by S.I. 2003/3142, art. 1. (3))

I154. S. 108 in force at 29.12.2003 in so far as not already in force by S.I. 2003/3142, art. 3. (2) (with art. 11)

109. Restrictions and conditions subject to which code applies

(1) Where the electronic communications code is applied in any person's case by a direction given by OFCOM, that code is to have effect in that person's case subject to such restrictions and conditions as may be contained in regulations made by the Secretary of State.

(2) In exercising his power to make regulations under this section it shall be the duty of the Secretary of State to have regard to each of the following—

(a) the duties imposed on OFCOM by sections 3 and 4;

(b) the need to protect the environment and, in particular, to conserve the natural beauty and amenity of the countryside;

[F146. (ba)the need to promote economic growth in the United Kingdom;]

(c) the need to ensure that highways are not damaged or obstructed, and traffic not interfered with, to any greater extent than is reasonably necessary;

(d) the need to encourage the sharing of the use of electronic communications apparatus;

[F147. (da)the need to ensure that restrictions and conditions are objectively justifiable and proportionate to what they are intended to achieve;]

(e) the need to secure that a person in whose case the code is applied will be able to meet liabilities arising as a consequence of—

(i) the application of the code in his case; and

(ii) any conduct of his in relation to the matters with which the code deals.

[F148. (2. A)Subsection (2. B) applies if—

(a) the Secretary of State has complied with subsection (2)(b) in connection with any particular exercise before 6 April 2018 of the power to make regulations under this section, and

(b) the regulations in question are expressed to cease to have effect (other than for transitional purposes) before that date.

(2. B)The Secretary of State is to be treated as also having complied with any duty imposed in connection with that exercise of that power by any of the following—

section 11. A(2) of the National Parks and Access to the Countryside Act 1949;

section 85. (1) of the Countryside and Rights of Way Act 2000;

section 17. A(1) of the Norfolk and Suffolk Broads Act 1988;

section 14 of the National Parks (Scotland) Act 2000 (asp 10);

Article 4. (1) of the Nature Conservation and Amenity Lands (Northern Ireland) Order 1985 (S.I. 1985/170 (N.I. 1)).]

(3) The power of the Secretary of State to provide by regulations for the restrictions and conditions subject to which the electronic communications code has effect includes power to provide for restrictions and conditions which are framed by reference to any one or more of the following—

(a) the making of a determination in accordance with the regulations by a person specified in the regulations;

(b) the giving of an approval or consent by a person so specified; or

(c) the opinion of any person.

(4) Before making any regulations under this section, the Secretary of State must consult—

(a) OFCOM; and

(b) such other persons as he considers appropriate.

Amendments (Textual)

F146. S. 109. (2)(ba) inserted (25.4.2013) by Growth and Infrastructure Act 2013 (c. 27), ss. 9. (1), 35. (2) (with s. 36. (6))

F147. S. 109. (2)(da) inserted (26.5.2011) by The Electronic Communications and Wireless Telegraphy Regulations 2011 (S.I. 2011/1210), reg. 1. (2), Sch. 1 para. 67 (with Sch. 3 para. 2)

F148. S. 109. (2. A)(2. B) inserted (25.4.2013) by Growth and Infrastructure Act 2013 (c. 27), ss. 9. (2), 35. (2)

Modifications etc. (not altering text)

C3. S. 109. (4) modified (25.4.2013) by Growth and Infrastructure Act 2013 (c. 27), ss. 9. (4), 35. (2)

Commencement Information

I155. S. 109 in force at 25.7.2003 for specified purposes by S.I. 2003/1900, arts. 1. (2), 2. (1), Sch. 1 (with art. 3) (as amended by S.I. 2003/3142, art. 1. (3))

I156. S. 109 in force at 29.12.2003 in so far as not already in force by S.I. 2003/3142, art. 3. (2) (with art. 11)

110. Enforcement of restrictions and conditions

(1) Where OFCOM determine that there are reasonable grounds for believing that a person in whose case the electronic communications code applies is contravening, or has contravened, a requirement imposed by virtue of any restrictions or conditions under section 109, they may give

him a notification under this section.

(2) A notification under this section is one which—

(a) sets out the determination made by OFCOM;

(b) specifies the requirement and the contravention in respect of which that determination has been made; F149...

[F150. (c)specifies the period during which the person notified has an opportunity to make representations;

(d) specifies the steps that OFCOM think should be taken by the person in order to—

(i) comply with the requirement;

(ii) remedy the consequences of the contravention;

(e) specifies any penalty which OFCOM are minded to impose in accordance with section 110. A; and

(f) where the contravention is serious, specifies any direction which OFCOM are minded to give under section 113. (4).]

F151. (3). . . . .

F151. (4). . . . .

F151. (5). . . . .

F151. (6). . . . .

F151. (7). . . . .

(8) A notification under this section—

(a) may be given in respect of more than one contravention; and

(b) if it is given in respect of a continuing contravention, may be given in respect of any period during which the contravention has continued.

(9) Where a notification under this section has been given to a person in respect of a contravention of a requirement, OFCOM may give a further notification in respect of the same contravention of that requirement if, and only if—

(a) the contravention is one occurring after the time of the giving of the earlier notification;

(b) the contravention is a continuing contravention and the subsequent notification is in respect of so much of a period as falls after a period to which the earlier notification relates; or

(c) the earlier notification has been withdrawn without a penalty having been imposed in respect of the notified contravention.

F152. (10). . . . .

Amendments (Textual)

F149. Word in s. 110. (2)(b) omitted (26.5.2011) by virtue of The Electronic Communications and Wireless Telegraphy Regulations 2011 (S.I. 2011/1210), reg. 1. (2), Sch. 1 para. 68. (a) (with Sch. 3 paras. 2, 15)

F150. S. 110. (2)(c)-(f) substituted for s. 110. (2)(c) (26.5.2011) by The Electronic Communications and Wireless Telegraphy Regulations 2011 (S.I. 2011/1210), reg. 1. (2), Sch. 1 para. 68. (b) (with Sch. 3 paras. 2, 15)

F151. S. 110. (3)-(7) omitted (26.5.2011) by virtue of The Electronic Communications and Wireless Telegraphy Regulations 2011 (S.I. 2011/1210), reg. 1. (2), Sch. 1 para. 68. (c) (with Sch. 3 paras. 2, 15)

F152. S. 110. (10) omitted (26.5.2011) by virtue of The Electronic Communications and Wireless Telegraphy Regulations 2011 (S.I. 2011/1210), reg. 1. (2), Sch. 1 para. 68. (c) (with Sch. 3 paras. 2, 15)

Commencement Information

I157. S. 110 in force at 25.7.2003 for specified purposes by S.I. 2003/1900, arts. 1. (2), 2. (1), Sch. 1 (with art. 3) (as amended by S.I. 2003/3142, art. 1. (3))

I158. S. 110 in force at 29.12.2003 in so far as not already in force by S.I. 2003/3142, art. 3. (2) (with art. 11)

[F153110. A.Penalties for contravention of code restrictions

(1) This section applies where a person is given a notification under section 110 which specifies a proposed penalty.

(2) Where the notification relates to more than one contravention, a separate penalty may be specified in respect of each contravention.

(3) Where the notification relates to a continuing contravention, no more than one penalty may be specified in respect of the period of contravention specified in the notification.

(4) But, in relation to a continuing contravention, a penalty may be specified in respect of each day on which the contravention continues after—

(a) the giving of a confirmation decision under section 111. (4)(c) which requires immediate action; or

(b) the expiry of any period specified in the confirmation decision for complying with a requirement so specified.

(5) The amount of a penalty under subsection (4) is to be such amount not exceeding £100 per day as OFCOM determine to be—

(a) appropriate; and

(b) proportionate to the contravention in respect of which it is imposed

(6) The amount of any other penalty specified in a notification under section 110 is to be such amount not exceeding £10,000 as OFCOM determine to be—

(a) appropriate, and

(b) proportionate to the contravention in respect of which it is imposed.

(7) The Secretary of State may by order amend this section so as to substitute a different maximum penalty for the maximum penalty for the time being specified in subsection (6).

(8) No order is to be made containing provision authorised by subsection (7) unless a draft of the order has been laid before Parliament and approved by a resolution of each House.]

Amendments (Textual)

F153. S. 110. A inserted (26.5.2011) by The Electronic Communications and Wireless Telegraphy Regulations 2011 (S.I. 2011/1210), reg. 1. (2), Sch. 1 para. 69 (with Sch. 3 paras. 2, 15)

111 [F154. Confirmation decision] for contravention of code restrictions

(1) This section applies where—

(a) a person ("the notified provider") has been given a notification under section 110;

(b) OFCOM have allowed the notified provider an opportunity of making representations about the matters notified; and

(c) the period allowed for the making of the representations has expired.

[F155. (2)OFCOM may—

(a) give the notified provider a decision (a "confirmation decision") confirming the imposition of requirements on the notified provider, or the giving of a direction to the notified provider, or both, in accordance with the notification under section 110; or

(b) notify the notified provider that they are satisfied with the representations and that no further action will be taken.

(3) OFCOM may not give a confirmation decision to the notified provider unless, after considering any representations, they are satisfied that the notified provider has, in one or more of the respects notified, been in contravention of a requirement specified in the notification under section 110.]

[F156. (4)A confirmation decision—

(a) must be given to the person without delay;

(b) must include reasons for the decision;

(c) may require immediate action by the person to comply with requirements of a kind mentioned in section 110. (2)(d), or may specify a period within which the person must comply with those requirements; and

(d) may require the person to pay—

(i) the penalty specified in the notification under section 110. (2)(e), or

(ii) such lesser penalty as OFCOM consider appropriate in the light of the person's representations or steps taken by the person to comply with the condition or remedy the consequences of the contravention, and

may specify the period within which the penalty is to be paid.]

(5) It shall be the duty of a person to whom [F157a confirmation decision] has been given to comply with [F158any requirement imposed by it] .

(6) That duty shall be enforceable in civil proceedings by OFCOM—

　(a) for an injunction;

　(b) for specific performance of a statutory duty under section 45 of the Court of Session Act 1988 (c. 36); or

　(c) for any other appropriate remedy or relief.

[F159. (7)A penalty imposed by a confirmation decision—

　(a) must be paid to OFCOM; and

　(b) if not paid within the period specified by them, is to be recoverable by them accordingly.]

Amendments (Textual)

F154. Words in s. 111 heading substituted (26.5.2011) by The Electronic Communications and Wireless Telegraphy Regulations 2011 (S.I. 2011/1210), reg. 1. (2), Sch. 1 para. 70. (e) (with Sch. 3 paras. 2, 15)

F155. S. 111. (2)(3) substituted (26.5.2011) by The Electronic Communications and Wireless Telegraphy Regulations 2011 (S.I. 2011/1210), reg. 1. (2), Sch. 1 para. 70. (a) (with Sch. 3 paras. 2, 15)

F156. S. 111. (4) substituted (26.5.2011) by The Electronic Communications and Wireless Telegraphy Regulations 2011 (S.I. 2011/1210), reg. 1. (2), Sch. 1 para. 70. (b) (with Sch. 3 paras. 2, 15)

F157. Words in s. 111. (5) substituted (26.5.2011) by The Electronic Communications and Wireless Telegraphy Regulations 2011 (S.I. 2011/1210), reg. 1. (2), Sch. 1 para. 70. (c)(i) (with Sch. 3 paras. 2, 15)

F158. Words in s. 111. (5) substituted (26.5.2011) by The Electronic Communications and Wireless Telegraphy Regulations 2011 (S.I. 2011/1210), reg. 1. (2), Sch. 1 para. 70. (c)(ii) (with Sch. 3 paras. 2, 15)

F159. S. 111. (7) inserted (26.5.2011) by The Electronic Communications and Wireless Telegraphy Regulations 2011 (S.I. 2011/1210), reg. 1. (2), Sch. 1 para. 70. (d) (with Sch. 3 paras. 2, 15)

Commencement Information

I159. S. 111 in force at 25.7.2003 for specified purposes by S.I. 2003/1900, arts. 1. (2), 2. (1), Sch. 1 (with art. 3) (as amended by S.I. 2003/3142, art. 1. (3))

I160. S. 111 in force at 29.12.2003 in so far as not already in force by S.I. 2003/3142, art. 3. (2) (with art. 11)

[F160111. A.Power to deal with urgent cases

(1) This section applies where OFCOM determine—

　(a) that they are entitled to give a notification under section 110 with respect to a contravention by a person ("P") of a requirement imposed by virtue of any restrictions or conditions under section 109;

　(b) that there are reasonable grounds for suspecting that the case is an urgent case; and

　(c) that the urgency of the case makes it appropriate for OFCOM to take action under this section.

(2) A case is an urgent case for the purposes of this section if the contravention has resulted in, or creates an immediate risk of—

　(a) a serious threat to the safety of the public, to public health or to national security;

　(b) serious economic or operational problems for persons (other than P) who are communications providers or persons who make associated facilities available; or

　(c) serious economic or operational problems for persons who make use of electronic communications networks, electronic communications services or associated facilities.

(3) OFCOM may, to the extent specified in subsection (4), give a direction suspending the application in P's case of the electronic communications code if the electronic communications code has been applied to P by a direction under section 106.

(4) The extent of a suspension under subsection (3) must not go beyond the following applications

of the code in that person's case—

(a) its application for the purposes of electronic communications networks, or parts of such a network, which are not yet in existence at the time of the suspension;

(b) its application for the purposes of conduit systems, or parts of such systems, which are not yet in existence or not yet used for the purposes of electronic communications networks; and

(c) its application for other purposes in circumstances in which the provision of an electronic communications network, or part of such a network, would not have to cease if its application for those purposes were suspended.

(5) A direction under subsection (3), except so far as it otherwise provides, shall continue in force until such time (if any) as it is withdrawn by OFCOM.

(6) Subject to subsection (7), where the application of the electronic communications code is suspended in a person's case, the person is not entitled to exercise any right conferred by or by virtue of the code.

(7) The suspension of the application of the electronic communications code in a person's case does not, except so far as otherwise provided by a scheme contained in an order under section 117—

(a) affect (as between the original parties to it) any agreement entered into for the purposes of the code or any agreement having effect in accordance with it;

(b) affect anything done under the code before the suspension of its application; or

(c) require the removal of, or prohibit the use of, any apparatus lawfully installed on, in or over any premises before that suspension.

Amendments (Textual)

F160. Ss. 111. A, 111. B inserted (26.5.2011) by The Electronic Communications and Wireless Telegraphy Regulations 2011 (S.I. 2011/1210), reg. 1. (2), Sch. 1 para. 71 (with Sch. 3 paras. 2, 15)

111. B.Confirmation of direction under section 111. A

(1) As soon as reasonably practicable after giving a direction under section 111. A(3), OFCOM must give the person to whom it is given—

(a) an opportunity to make representations to them about the grounds on which it was given and its effect; and

(b) an opportunity to propose steps to remedy the situation.

(2) As soon as practicable after the period allowed by OFCOM for making those representations has ended (and in any event within 3 months beginning with the day on which the direction was given), they must determine—

(a) whether the contravention providing the grounds for the giving of the direction did occur; and

(b) whether the circumstances made it an urgent case justifying the giving of the direction.

(3) The period of 3 months mentioned in subsection (2) may be extended by up to 3 months if OFCOM—

(a) require additional time to consider representations received; or

(b) decide that it is necessary to obtain additional information from the person in order to make a determination under subsection (2).

(4) If OFCOM decide that the contravention did occur and that the direction was justified, they may confirm the direction.

(5) If not, they must exercise their power to revoke it.

(6) As soon as reasonably practicable after determining whether to confirm the direction, OFCOM must notify the person to whom it was given of their decision.]

Amendments (Textual)

F160. Ss. 111. A, 111. B inserted (26.5.2011) by The Electronic Communications and Wireless Telegraphy Regulations 2011 (S.I. 2011/1210), reg. 1. (2), Sch. 1 para. 71 (with Sch. 3 paras. 2, 15)

F161112. Penalties for contravention of code restrictions

. . . .

Amendments (Textual)

F161. S. 112 omitted (26.5.2011) by virtue of The Electronic Communications and Wireless Telegraphy Regulations 2011 (S.I. 2011/1210), reg. 1. (2), Sch. 1 para. 72 (with Sch. 3 paras. 2, 15)

Commencement Information

I161. S. 112 in force at 25.7.2003 for specified purposes by S.I. 2003/1900, arts. 1. (2), 2. (1), Sch. 1 (with art. 3) (as amended by S.I. 2003/3142, art. 1. (3))

I162. S. 112 in force at 29.12.2003 in so far as not already in force by S.I. 2003/3142, art. 3. (2) (with art. 11)

113. Suspension of application of code

(1) OFCOM may suspend the application of the electronic communications code in any person's case if they are satisfied—

(a) that he is or has been in [F162serious or repeated] contravention of requirements to pay administrative charges fixed under section 38 (whether in respect of the whole or a part of the charges);

[F163. (aa)that, in the case of a single serious contravention, a notification has been given to the contravening provider under section 40 and the period for making representations under that section has expired;]

(b) that [F164, in the case of a repeated contravention] the bringing of proceedings for the recovery of the amounts outstanding has failed to secure complete compliance by the contravening provider with the requirements to pay the charges fixed in his case, or has no reasonable prospect of securing such compliance;

(c) that [F165, in the case of a repeated contravention] an attempt, by the imposition of penalties under section 41, to secure such compliance has failed; and

[F166. (d)that the suspension of the application of the code is appropriate and proportionate to the contravention.]

(2) OFCOM may, to the extent specified in subsection (3), suspend the application in that person's case of the electronic communications code if—

(a) the electronic communications code has been applied by a direction under section 106 in any person's case; and

(b) OFCOM give a direction under section 42, 100 [F167. (including that section as applied by section 105. D)] , 132 or 140 for the suspension or restriction of that person's entitlement to provide an electronic communications network, or a part of such a network.

(3) The extent, in any person's case, of a suspension under subsection (2) must not go beyond the application of the code for the purposes of so much of an electronic communications network as that person is prohibited from providing by virtue of the suspension or restriction of his entitlement to provide such a network, or part of a network.

(4) OFCOM may, to the extent specified in subsection (5), suspend the application in that person's case of the electronic communications code if—

(a) the electronic communications code has been applied by a direction under section 106 in any person's case; and

(b) that person is a person in whose case there have been [F168repeated or serious] contraventions of requirements imposed by virtue of any restrictions or conditions under section 109.

(5) The extent, in any person's case, of a suspension under subsection (4) must not go beyond the following applications of the code in his case—

(a) its application for the purposes of electronic communications networks, or parts of such a network, which are not yet in existence at the time of the suspension;

(b) its application for the purposes of conduit systems, or parts of such systems, which are not yet in existence or not yet used for the purposes of electronic communications networks; and

(c) its application for other purposes in circumstances in which the provision of an electronic communications network, or part of such a network, would not have to cease if its application for those purposes were suspended.

(6) A suspension under this section of the application of the code in any person's case must be by a further direction given to that person by OFCOM under section 106.

(7) The statement required by section 107. (8) to be included, in the case of a direction for the purposes of this section, in the statement of OFCOM's proposal is a statement of their proposal to suspend the application of the code.

(8) A suspension of the application of the electronic communications code in any person's case—

(a) shall cease to have effect if the suspension is under subsection (2) and the network suspension or restriction ceases to have effect; but

(b) subject to that shall continue in force until such time (if any) as it is withdrawn by OFCOM.

(9) In subsection (8) the reference to the network suspension or restriction, in relation to a suspension of the application of the electronic communications code, is a reference to the suspension or restriction of an entitlement to provide an electronic communications network, or part of such a network, which is the suspension or restriction by reference to which the application of the code was suspended under subsection (2).

(10) Subject to subsection (11), where the application of the electronic communications code is suspended in a person's case, he shall not, while it is so suspended, be entitled to exercise any right conferred on him by or by virtue of the code.

(11) The suspension, in a person's case, of the application of the electronic communications code does not, except so far as otherwise provided by a scheme contained in an order under section 117—

(a) affect (as between the original parties to it) any agreement entered into for the purposes of the code or any agreement having effect in accordance with it;

(b) affect anything done under the code before the suspension of its application; or

(c) require the removal of, or prohibit the use of, any apparatus lawfully installed on, in or over any premises before that suspension.

(12) Subsection (9) of section 42 applies for the purposes of subsection (1) as it applies for the purposes of that section.

[F169. (13)For the purposes of subsection (4) there are repeated contraventions by a person of conditions or restrictions under section 109 if—

(a) in the case of a previous notification given to the person under section 110, OFCOM have given a confirmation decision to the person under section 111. (2);

(b) in the period of 24 months following the giving of that confirmation decision, one or more further confirmation decisions have been given to the person in respect of contraventions of a condition or restriction under section 109; and

(c) the previous confirmation decision and the subsequent ones all relate to contraventions of the same condition or restriction (whether the same contravention or different contraventions).]

Amendments (Textual)

F162. Words in s. 113. (1)(a) substituted (26.5.2011) by The Electronic Communications and Wireless Telegraphy Regulations 2011 (S.I. 2011/1210), reg. 1. (2), Sch. 1 para. 73. (a)(i) (with Sch. 3 paras. 2, 15)

F163. S. 113. (1)(aa) inserted (26.5.2011) by The Electronic Communications and Wireless Telegraphy Regulations 2011 (S.I. 2011/1210), reg. 1. (2), Sch. 1 para. 73. (a)(ii) (with Sch. 3 paras. 2, 15)

F164. Words in s. 113. (1)(b) inserted (26.5.2011) by The Electronic Communications and Wireless Telegraphy Regulations 2011 (S.I. 2011/1210), reg. 1. (2), Sch. 1 para. 73. (a)(iii) (with Sch. 3 paras. 2, 15)

F165. Words in s. 113. (1)(c) inserted (26.5.2011) by The Electronic Communications and Wireless Telegraphy Regulations 2011 (S.I. 2011/1210), reg. 1. (2), Sch. 1 para. 73. (a)(iii) (with Sch. 3 paras. 2, 15)

F166. S. 113. (1)(d) substituted (26.5.2011) by The Electronic Communications and Wireless Telegraphy Regulations 2011 (S.I. 2011/1210), reg. 1. (2), Sch. 1 para. 73. (a)(iv) (with Sch. 3 paras. 2, 15)

F167. Words in s. 113. (2)(b) inserted (26.5.2011) by The Electronic Communications and

Wireless Telegraphy Regulations 2011 (S.I. 2011/1210), reg. 1. (2), Sch. 1 para. 73. (b) (with Sch. 3 paras. 2, 15)

F168. Words in s. 113. (4)(b) substituted (26.5.2011) by The Electronic Communications and Wireless Telegraphy Regulations 2011 (S.I. 2011/1210), reg. 1. (2), Sch. 1 para. 73. (c) (with Sch. 3 paras. 2, 15)

F169. S. 113. (13) inserted (26.5.2011) by The Electronic Communications and Wireless Telegraphy Regulations 2011 (S.I. 2011/1210), reg. 1. (2), Sch. 1 para. 73. (d) (with Sch. 3 paras. 2, 15)

Commencement Information

I163. S. 113 in force at 25.7.2003 for specified purposes by S.I. 2003/1900, arts. 1. (2), 2. (1), Sch. 1 (with art. 3) (as amended by S.I. 2003/3142, art. 1. (3))

I164. S. 113 in force at 29.12.2003 in so far as not already in force by S.I. 2003/3142, art. 3. (2) (with art. 11)

114. Procedure for directions under s. 113.

(1) Except in an urgent case [F170, or a case of a single serious contravention,] , OFCOM are not to give a direction under section 113. (4) suspending the application of the electronic communications code in the case of any person ("the operator") unless they have—

  (a) notified the operator of the proposed suspension and of the steps (if any) that they are proposing to take under section 117;

  (b) provided him with an opportunity of making representations about the proposals and of proposing steps for remedying the situation that has given rise to the proposed suspension; and

  (c) considered every representation and proposal made to them during the period allowed by them for the operator to take advantage of that opportunity.

[F171. (2)That period is such reasonable period as OFCOM may specify, beginning with the day on which the notification is given.]

(3) As soon as practicable after giving a direction under section 113 in an urgent case, OFCOM must provide the operator with an opportunity of—

  (a) making representations about the effect of the direction and of any steps taken under section 117 in connection with the suspension; and

  (b) proposing steps for remedying the situation that has given rise to the situation.

[F172. (3. A)As soon as practicable after the period allowed by OFCOM for making those representations has ended (and in any event within 3 months beginning with the day on which the direction was given), they must determine—

  (a) whether the contravention providing the grounds for the giving of the direction did occur; and

  (b) whether the circumstances made it an urgent case justifying the giving of the direction.

(3. B)The period of 3 months mentioned in subsection (3. A) may be extended by up to 3 months if OFCOM—

  (a) require additional time to consider representations received; or

  (b) decide that it is necessary to obtain additional information from the person in order to make a determination under subsection (3. A).

(3. C)If OFCOM decide that the contravention did occur and that the direction was justified, they may confirm the direction.

(3. D)If not, they must revoke it.]

(4) A case is an urgent case for the purposes of this section if OFCOM—

  (a) consider that it would be inappropriate, because the circumstances appearing to OFCOM to require the suspension fall within subsection (5), to allow time, before giving a direction under section 113, for the making and consideration of representations; and

  (b) decide for that reason to act in accordance with subsection (3), instead of subsection (1).

(5) Circumstances fall within this subsection if they have resulted in, or create an immediate risk of—

  (a) a serious threat to the safety of the public, to public health or to national security;

  (b) serious economic or operational problems for persons (apart from the operator) who are communications providers or persons who make associated facilities available; or

(c) serious economic or operational problems for persons who make use of electronic communications networks, electronic communications services or associated facilities.

Amendments (Textual)

F170. Words in s. 114. (1) inserted (26.5.2011) by The Electronic Communications and Wireless Telegraphy Regulations 2011 (S.I. 2011/1210), reg. 1. (2), Sch. 1 para. 74. (a) (with Sch. 3 paras. 2, 15)

F171. S. 114. (2) substituted (26.5.2011) by The Electronic Communications and Wireless Telegraphy Regulations 2011 (S.I. 2011/1210), reg. 1. (2), Sch. 1 para. 74. (b) (with Sch. 3 paras. 2, 15)

F172. S. 114. (3. A)-(3. D) inserted (26.5.2011) by The Electronic Communications and Wireless Telegraphy Regulations 2011 (S.I. 2011/1210), reg. 1. (2), Sch. 1 para. 74. (c) (with Sch. 3 paras. 2, 15)

Commencement Information

I165. S. 114 in force at 25.7.2003 for specified purposes by S.I. 2003/1900, arts. 1. (2), 2. (1), Sch. 1 (with art. 3) (as amended by S.I. 2003/3142, art. 1. (3))

I166. S. 114 in force at 29.12.2003 in so far as not already in force by S.I. 2003/3142, art. 3. (2) (with art. 11)

115. Modification and revocation of application of code

(1) OFCOM may at any time modify the terms on which, by virtue of section 106. (5), the code is applied in a person's case.

(2) OFCOM may revoke a direction applying the electronic communications code in a person's case if an application for the revocation has been made by that person.

(3) If at any time it appears to OFCOM that a person in whose case the electronic communications code has been applied is not the provider of an electronic communications network or conduit system for the purposes of which the code applies, OFCOM may revoke the direction applying the code in his case.

(4) A modification or revocation under this section shall be by a further direction under section 106 to the person in whose case the electronic communications code has been applied by the direction being modified or revoked.

[F173. (4. A)A modification under this section may not be made unless the modification is—

(a) objectively justifiable, and

(b) proportionate to what it is intended to achieve.]

(5) The matters required by section 107. (8) to be included, in the case of a direction for the purposes of this section, in the statement of OFCOM's proposal are whichever of the following is applicable—

(a) a statement of their proposal to modify terms imposed under section 106. (5);

(b) a statement of their proposal to revoke the direction applying the code.

Amendments (Textual)

F173. S. 115. (4. A) inserted (26.5.2011) by The Electronic Communications and Wireless Telegraphy Regulations 2011 (S.I. 2011/1210), reg. 1. (2), Sch. 1 para. 75 (with Sch. 3 para. 2)

Commencement Information

I167. S. 115 in force at 25.7.2003 for specified purposes by S.I. 2003/1900, arts. 1. (2), 2. (1), Sch. 1 (with art. 3) (as amended by S.I. 2003/3142, art. 1. (3))

I168. S. 115 in force at 29.12.2003 in so far as not already in force by S.I. 2003/3142, art. 3. (2) (with art. 11)

116. Notification of cessation by person to whom code applies

(1) This section applies where, by virtue of a direction under section 106, the electronic communications code applies in any person's case for the purposes of the provision by him of—

(a) an electronic communications network which is not of a description designated for the purposes of section 33; or

(b) such a system of conduits as is mentioned in section 106. (4)(b).

(2) If that person ceases to provide that network or conduit system, he must notify OFCOM of that

fact.

(3) A notification under this section must be given within such period and in such manner as may be required by OFCOM.

(4) OFCOM may impose a penalty on a person who fails to comply with a requirement imposed by or under this section.

(5) The amount of a penalty imposed on a person under this section is to be such amount not exceeding £1,000 as OFCOM may determine to be both—

    (a) appropriate; and

    (b) proportionate to the matter in respect of which it is imposed.

(6) Where OFCOM impose a penalty on a person under this section, they shall—

    (a) within one week of making their decision to impose the penalty, notify that person of that decision and of their reasons for that decision; and

    (b) in that notification, fix a reasonable period after it is given as the period within which the penalty is to be paid.

(7) A penalty imposed under this section—

    (a) must be paid to OFCOM; and

    (b) if not paid within the period fixed by them, is to be recoverable by them accordingly.

(8) The Secretary of State may by order amend this section so as to substitute a different maximum penalty for the maximum penalty for the time being specified in subsection (5).

(9) No order is to be made containing provision authorised by subsection (8) unless a draft of the order has been laid before Parliament and approved by a resolution of each House.

Commencement Information

I169. S. 116 in force at 25.7.2003 for specified purposes by S.I. 2003/1900, arts. 1. (2), 2. (1), Sch. 1 (with art. 3) (as amended by S.I. 2003/3142, art. 1. (3))

I170. S. 116 in force at 29.12.2003 in so far as not already in force by S.I. 2003/3142, art. 3. (2) (with art. 11)

117. Transitional schemes on cessation of application of code

(1) Where it appears to OFCOM—

    (a) that the electronic communications code has ceased or is to cease to apply, to any extent, in the case of any person ("the former operator"),

    (b) that it has ceased or will cease so to apply for either of the reasons specified in subsection (2), and

    (c) that it is appropriate for transitional provision to be made in connection with it ceasing to apply in the case of the former operator,

they may by order make a scheme containing any such transitional provision as they think fit in that case.

(2) Those reasons are—

    (a) the suspension under section 113 of the application of the code in the former operator's case;

    (b) the revocation or modification under section 115 of the direction applying the code in his case.

(3) A scheme contained in an order under this section may, in particular—

    (a) impose any one or more obligations falling within subsection (4) on the former operator;

    (b) provide for those obligations to be enforceable in such manner (otherwise than by criminal penalties) and by such persons as may be specified in the scheme;

    (c) authorise the retention of apparatus on any land pending its subsequent use for the purposes of an electronic communications network, electronic communications service or conduit system to be provided by any person;

    (d) provide for the transfer to such persons as may be specified in, or determined in accordance with, the scheme of any rights or liabilities arising out of any agreement or other obligation entered into or incurred in pursuance of the code by the former operator;

    (e) provide, for the purposes of any provision contained in the scheme by virtue of any of the preceding paragraphs, for such questions arising under the scheme as are specified in the scheme, or are of a description so specified, to be referred to, and determined by, OFCOM.

(4) The obligations referred to in subsection (3)(a) are—

(a) an obligation to remove anything installed in pursuance of any right conferred by or in accordance with the code;

(b) an obligation to restore land to its condition before anything was done in pursuance of any such right; or

(c) an obligation to pay the expenses of any such removal or restoration.

(5) Sections 110 to 112 apply in relation to the requirements imposed by virtue of a scheme contained in an order under this section as they apply in relation to a requirement imposed by virtue of restrictions or conditions under section 109.

(6) Section 403 applies to the power of OFCOM to make an order under this section.

Commencement Information

I171. S. 117 in force at 25.7.2003 for specified purposes by S.I. 2003/1900, arts. 1. (2), 2. (1), Sch. 1 (with art. 3) (as amended by S.I. 2003/3142, art. 1. (3))

I172. S. 117 in force at 29.12.2003 in so far as not already in force by S.I. 2003/3142, art. 3. (2) (with art. 11)

118. Compulsory acquisition of land etc.

Schedule 4 (which provides for compulsory acquisition of land by the provider of an electronic communications network in whose case the electronic communications code applies and for entry on land by persons nominated by such a provider) shall have effect.

Commencement Information

I173. S. 118 in force at 25.7.2003 for specified purposes by S.I. 2003/1900, arts. 1. (2), 2. (1), Sch. 1 (with art. 3) (as amended by S.I. 2003/3142, art. 1. (3))

I174. S. 118 in force at 29.12.2003 in so far as not already in force by S.I. 2003/3142, art. 3. (2) (with art. 11)

119. Power to give assistance in relation to certain proceedings

(1) This section applies where any actual or prospective party to any proceedings falling within subsection (2) (other than the operator, within the meaning of the electronic communications code) applies to OFCOM for assistance under this section in relation to those proceedings.

(2) The proceedings falling within this subsection are any actual or prospective proceedings in which there falls to be determined any question arising under, or in connection with—

(a) the electronic communications code as applied in any person's case by a direction under section 106; or

(b) any restriction or condition subject to which that code applies.

(3) OFCOM may grant the application if, on any one or more of the following grounds, they think fit to do so—

(a) on the ground that the case raises a question of principle;

(b) on the ground that it is unreasonable, having regard to the complexity of the case or to any other matter, to expect the applicant to deal with the case without assistance under this section;

(c) by reason of any other special consideration.

(4) Assistance by OFCOM under this section may include—

(a) giving advice or arranging for the giving of advice by a solicitor or counsel;

(b) procuring or attempting to procure the settlement of the matter in dispute;

(c) arranging for the giving of any assistance usually given by a solicitor or counsel—

(i) in the steps preliminary or incidental to proceedings; or

(ii) in arriving at, or giving effect to, a compromise to avoid proceedings or to bring them to an end;

(d) arranging for representation by a solicitor or counsel;

(e) arranging for the giving of any other assistance by a solicitor or counsel;

(f) any other form of assistance which OFCOM consider appropriate.

(5) Nothing in subsection (4)(d) shall be taken to affect the law and practice regulating the descriptions of persons who may appear in, conduct or defend any proceedings, or who may address the court in any proceedings.

(6) In so far as expenses are incurred by OFCOM in providing the applicant with assistance under

this section, the recovery of those expenses (as taxed or assessed in such manner as may be prescribed by rules of court) shall constitute a first charge for the benefit of OFCOM—

(a) on any costs or expenses which (whether by virtue of a judgment or order of a court, or an agreement or otherwise) are payable to the applicant by any other person in respect of the matter in connection with which the assistance is given; and

(b) so far as relates to costs or expenses, on the applicant's rights under a compromise or settlement arrived at in connection with that matter to avoid proceedings, or to bring them to an end.

(7) A charge conferred by subsection (6) is subject to—

(a) any charge imposed by [F174section 25 of the Legal Aid, Sentencing and Punishment of Offenders Act 2012] and any provision made by or under Part 1 of that Act for the payment of any sum to the [F175. Lord Chancellor] ;

(b) any charge or obligation for payment in priority to other debts under the Legal Aid (Scotland) Act 1986 (c. 47); or

(c) any charge under the Legal Aid, Advice and Assistance (Northern Ireland) Order 1981 (S.I. 1981/228 (N.I. 8)).

Amendments (Textual)

F174. Words in s. 119. (7)(a) substituted (1.4.2013) by Legal Aid, Sentencing and Punishment of Offenders Act 2012 (c. 10), s. 151. (1), Sch. 5 para. 61. (a); S.I. 2013/453, art. 3. (h) (with savings and transitional provisions in S.I. 2013/534, art. 6)

F175. Words in s. 119. (7)(a) substituted (1.4.2013) by Legal Aid, Sentencing and Punishment of Offenders Act 2012 (c. 10), s. 151. (1), Sch. 5 para. 61. (b); S.I. 2013/453, art. 3. (h) (with savings and transitional provisions in S.I. 2013/534, art. 6)

Commencement Information

I175. S. 119 in force at 25.7.2003 for specified purposes by S.I. 2003/1900, arts. 1. (2), 2. (1), Sch. 1 (with art. 3) (as amended by S.I. 2003/3142, art. 1. (3))

I176. S. 119 in force at 29.12.2003 in so far as not already in force by S.I. 2003/3142, art. 3. (2) (with art. 11)

Regulation of premium rate services

120. Conditions regulating premium rate services

(1) OFCOM shall have the power, for the purpose of regulating the provision, content, promotion and marketing of premium rate services, to set conditions under this section that bind the persons to whom they are applied.

(2) Conditions under this section may be applied either—

(a) generally to every person who provides a premium rate service; or

(b) to every person who is of a specified description of such persons, or who provides a specified description of such services.

(3) The only provision that may be made by conditions under this section is provision requiring the person to whom the condition applies to comply, to the extent required by the condition, with—

[F176. (za)the provisions of an approved code;]

(a) directions given in accordance with an approved code by the enforcement authority and for the purpose of enforcing its provisions; and

(b) if there is no such code, the provisions of the order for the time being in force under section 122.

(4) The power to set a condition under this section includes power to modify or revoke the conditions for the time being in force under this section.

(5) [F177. Section 47 applies] to the setting, modification and revocation of a condition under this section as [F177it applies] to the setting, modification and revocation of a condition under section 45.

F178. (6). . . . .

(7) A service is a premium rate service for the purposes of this Chapter if—

(a) it is a service falling within subsection (8);

(b) there is a charge for the provision of the service;

(c) the charge is required to be paid to a person providing an electronic communications service by means of which the service in question is provided; and

(d) that charge is imposed in the form of a charge made by that person for the use of the electronic communications service.

(8) A service falls within this subsection if its provision consists in—

(a) the provision of the contents of communications transmitted by means of an electronic communications network; or

(b) allowing the user of an electronic communications service to make use, by the making of a transmission by means of that service, of a facility made available to the users of the electronic communications service.

(9) For the purposes of this Chapter a person provides a premium rate service ("the relevant service") if—

(a) he provides the contents of the relevant service;

(b) he exercises editorial control over the contents of the relevant service;

(c) he is a person who packages together the contents of the relevant service for the purpose of facilitating its provision;

(d) he makes available a facility comprised in the relevant service; or

(e) he falls within subsection (10), (11) or (12).

(10) A person falls within this subsection if—

(a) he is the provider of an electronic communications service used for the provision of the relevant service; and

(b) under arrangements made with a person who is a provider of the relevant service falling within subsection (9)(a) to (d), he is entitled to retain some or all of the charges received by him in respect of the provision of the relevant service or of the use of his electronic communications service for the purposes of the relevant service.

(11) A person falls within this subsection if—

(a) he is the provider of an electronic communications network used for the provision of the relevant service; and

(b) an agreement relating to the use of the network for the provision of that service subsists between the provider of the network and a person who is a provider of the relevant service falling within subsection (9)(a) to (d).

(12) A person falls within this subsection if—

(a) he is the provider of an electronic communications network used for the provision of the relevant service; and

(b) the use of that network for the provision of premium rate services, or of services that include or may include premium rate services, is authorised by an agreement subsisting between that person and either an intermediary service provider or a person who is a provider of the relevant service by virtue of subsection (10) or (11).

(13) Where one or more persons are employed or engaged under the direction of another to do any of the things mentioned in subsection (9)(a) to (d), only that other person shall be a provider of the relevant service for the purposes of this Chapter.

(14) References in this section to a facility include, in particular, references to—

(a) a facility for making a payment for goods or services;

(b) a facility for entering a competition or claiming a prize; and

(c) a facility for registering a vote or recording a preference.

(15) In this section—

"approved code" means a code for the time being approved under section 121;

"enforcement authority", in relation to such a code, means the person who under the code has the function of enforcing it; and "intermediary service provider" means a person who—

- provides an electronic communications service used for the provision of the relevant service or an electronic communications network so used; and

- is a party to an agreement with—

a provider of the relevant service falling within subsection (9)(a) to (d), or

another intermediary service provider,

- which relates to the use of that electronic communications service or network for the provision of premium rate services, or of services that include or may include premium rate services.

Amendments (Textual)

F176. S. 120. (3)(za) inserted (1.10.2015) by Consumer Rights Act 2015 (c. 15), ss. 80. (1), 100. (5); S.I. 2015/1630, art. 3. (e) (with art. 7)

F177. Words in s. 120. (5) substituted (26.5.2011) by The Electronic Communications and Wireless Telegraphy Regulations 2011 (S.I. 2011/1210), reg. 1. (2), Sch. 1 para. 76. (a) (with Sch. 3 paras. 2, 16)

F178. S. 120. (6) omitted (26.5.2011) by virtue of The Electronic Communications and Wireless Telegraphy Regulations 2011 (S.I. 2011/1210), reg. 1. (2), Sch. 1 para. 76. (b) (with Sch. 3 paras. 2, 16)

Commencement Information

I177. S. 120 in force at 29.12.2003 by S.I. 2003/3142, art. 3. (1), Sch. 1 (with art. 11)

[F179120. A.Procedure for setting, modifying and revoking premium rate services conditions

(1) The way in which conditions are to be set or modified under section 120 is by the publication of a notification setting out the conditions or modifications.

(2) The way in which such a condition is to be revoked is by the publication of a notification stating that the condition is revoked.

(3) Before setting such conditions, or modifying or revoking a condition so set, OFCOM must publish a notification—

(a) stating that they are proposing to set, modify or revoke the conditions that are specified in the notification;

(b) setting out the effect of those conditions, modifications or revocations;

(c) giving their reasons for making the proposal; and

(d) specifying the period within which representations may be made to OFCOM about their proposal.

(3) That period must end no less than one month after the day of the publication of the notification.

(4) But where OFCOM are satisfied that there are exceptional circumstances justifying the use of a shorter period, the period specified as the period for making representations may be whatever shorter period OFCOM consider reasonable in those circumstances.

(5) OFCOM may give effect to the proposal, with any modifications that appear to OFCOM to be appropriate, after—

(a) considering every representation about the proposal made to them during the period specified in the notification; and

(b) having regard to every international obligation of the United Kingdom (if any) which has been notified to them for the purposes of this paragraph by the Secretary of State.

(6) The publication of a notification under this section must be in such manner as appears to OFCOM to be appropriate for bringing the contents of the notification to the attention of the persons who, in OFCOM's opinion, are likely to be affected by its contents.

(7) OFCOM must send a copy of every notification published under this section to the Secretary of State.]

Amendments (Textual)

F179. S. 120. A inserted (26.5.2011) by The Electronic Communications and Wireless Telegraphy Regulations 2011 (S.I. 2011/1210), reg. 1. (2), Sch. 1 para. 77 (with Sch. 3 paras. 2, 16)

121. Approval of code for premium rate services

(1) If it appears to OFCOM—

(a) that a code has been made by any person for regulating the provision and contents of premium rate services, and the facilities made available in the provision of such services;

(b) that the code contains provision for regulating, to such extent (if any) as they think fit, the arrangements made by the providers of premium rate services for promoting and marketing those services; and

(c) that it would be appropriate for them to approve that code for the purposes of section 120, they may approve that code for those purposes.

(2) OFCOM are not to approve a code for those purposes unless they are satisfied—

(a) that there is a person who, under the code, has the function of administering and enforcing it; and

(b) that that person is sufficiently independent of the providers of premium rate services;

(c) that adequate arrangements are in force for funding the activities of that person in relation to the code;

(d) that the provisions of the code are objectively justifiable in relation to the services to which it relates;

(e) that those provisions are not such as to discriminate unduly against particular persons or against a particular description of persons;

(f) that those provisions are proportionate to what they are intended to achieve; and

(g) that, in relation to what those provisions are intended to achieve, they are transparent.

(3) OFCOM are not for those purposes to approve so much of a code as imposes an obligation as respects a premium rate service on a person who is a provider of the service by virtue only of section 120. (12) ("the relevant provider") unless they are satisfied that the obligation—

(a) arises only if there is no one who is a provider of the service otherwise than by virtue of section 120. (12) against whom it is practicable to take action;

(b) arises only after a notice identifying the service and setting out respects in which requirements of the code have been contravened in relation to it has been given to the relevant provider by the person responsible for enforcing the code; and

(c) is confined to an obligation to secure that electronic communications networks provided by the relevant provider are not used for making the service available to persons who are in the United Kingdom.

(4) The provision that may be contained in a code and approved under this section includes, in particular, provision about the pricing of premium rate services and provision for the enforcement of the code.

(5) The provision for the enforcement of a code that may be approved under this section includes—

(a) provision for the payment, to a person specified in the code, of a penalty not exceeding the maximum penalty for the time being specified in section 123. (2);

[F180. (aa)provision that applies where there is or has been more than one contravention of the code or directions given in accordance with it by a person and which enables—
(i) a single penalty (which does not exceed that maximum penalty) to be imposed on the person in respect of all of those contraventions, or
(ii) separate penalties (each of which does not exceed that maximum penalty) to be imposed on the person in respect of each of those contraventions,
according to whether the person imposing the penalty determines that a single penalty or separate penalties are appropriate and proportionate to those contraventions;]

(b) provision requiring a provider of a premium rate service to secure that the provision of the service is suspended or otherwise ceases or is restricted in any respect;

(c) provision for the imposition on a person, in respect of a contravention of the code, of a temporary or permanent prohibition or restriction on his working in connection with the provision of premium rate services or, in the case of a body corporate, on its providing such services or on its carrying on other activities in connection with their provision.

(6) OFCOM may, at any time, for the purposes of section 120—

(a) approve modifications that have been made to an approved code; or

(b) withdraw their approval from an approved code.

(7) Where OFCOM give or withdraw an approval for the purposes of section 120, they must give notification of their approval or of its withdrawal.

(8) The notification must be published in such manner as OFCOM consider appropriate for bringing it to the attention of the persons who, in OFCOM's opinion, are likely to be affected by the approval or withdrawal.

Amendments (Textual)

F180. S. 121. (5)(aa) inserted (1.10.2015) by Consumer Rights Act 2015 (c. 15), ss. 80. (2), 100. (5); S.I. 2015/1630, art. 3. (e) (with art. 7)

Commencement Information

I178. S. 121 in force at 29.12.2003 by S.I. 2003/3142, art. 3. (1), Sch. 1 (with art. 11)

122. Orders by OFCOM in the absence of a code under s. 121.

(1) OFCOM may make an order under this section if, at any time, they consider that there is no code in force to which they think it would be appropriate to give, or to continue to give, their approval under section 121.

(2) An order under this section may make such of the following provisions as OFCOM think fit—

(a) provision imposing requirements with respect to the provision and contents of premium rate services, and with respect to the facilities made available in the provision of such services (including provision about pricing);

(b) provision imposing requirements with respect to the arrangements made by the providers of premium rate services for the promotion and marketing of those services;

(c) provision for the enforcement of requirements imposed by virtue of paragraph (a) or (b);

(d) provision making other arrangements for the purposes of those requirements.

(3) The power to make provision by an order under this section includes, in particular—

(a) power to establish a body corporate with the capacity to make its own rules and to establish its own procedures;

(b) power to determine the jurisdiction of a body established by such an order or, for the purposes of the order, of any other person;

(c) power to confer jurisdiction with respect to any matter on OFCOM themselves;

(d) power to provide for a person on whom jurisdiction is conferred by the arrangements to make awards of compensation, to direct the reimbursement of costs or expenses, or to do both;

(e) power to provide for such a person to enforce, or to participate in the enforcement of, any awards or directions made under such an order;

(f) power to make provision falling within section 121. (5)(c) for the enforcement of the provisions of the order; and

(g) power to make such other provision as OFCOM think fit for the enforcement of such awards and directions.

(4) An order under this section may require such providers of premium rate services as may be determined by or under the order to make payments to OFCOM in respect of expenditure incurred by OFCOM in connection with—

(a) the establishment and maintenance, in accordance with such an order, of any body corporate or procedure; or

(b) the making of other arrangements for the purposes of the requirements of such an order.

(5) An order under this section is not to impose an obligation as respects a premium rate service on a person who is a provider of the service by virtue only of section 120. (12) ("the relevant provider") unless the obligation—

(a) arises only if there is no one who is a provider of the service otherwise than by virtue of section 120. (12) against whom it is practicable to take action;

(b) arises only after a notice identifying the service and setting out respects in which requirements of the order have been contravened in relation to it has been given to the relevant provider by OFCOM; and

(c) is confined to an obligation to secure that electronic communications networks provided by the relevant provider are not used for making the service available to persons who are in the

United Kingdom.

(6) The consent of the Secretary of State is required for the making by OFCOM of an order under this section.

(7) Section 403 applies to the power of OFCOM to make an order under this section.

(8) A statutory instrument containing an order made by OFCOM under this section shall be subject to annulment in pursuance of a resolution of either House of Parliament.

Commencement Information

I179. S. 122 in force at 29.12.2003 by S.I. 2003/3142, art. 3. (1), Sch. 1 (with art. 11)

123. Enforcement of s. 120 conditions

(1) Sections 94 to 96 apply in relation to a contravention of conditions set under section 120 as they apply in relation to a contravention of a condition set under section 45.

[F181. (1. A)Subsection (1. B) applies where a notification under section 94 as applied by this section relates to more than one contravention of—

    (a) a code approved under section 121,

    (b) directions given in accordance with such a code, or

    (c) an order under section 122.

(1. B)Section 96. (3) as applied by this section enables OFCOM to impose—

    (a) a single penalty in respect of all of those contraventions, or

    (b) separate penalties in respect of each of those contraventions,

according to whether OFCOM determine that a single penalty or separate penalties are appropriate and proportionate to those contraventions.]

(2) The amount of [F182each penalty] imposed under section 96 as applied by this section is to be such amount not exceeding [F183£250,000] as OFCOM determine to be—

    (a) appropriate; and

    (b) proportionate to the contravention in respect of which it is imposed.

(3) In making that determination OFCOM must have regard to—

    (a) any representations made to them by the notified provider;

    (b) any steps taken by him towards complying with the conditions contraventions of which have been notified to him under section 94 (as applied); and

    (c) any steps taken by him for remedying the consequences of those contraventions.

(4) The Secretary of State may by order amend this section so as to substitute a different maximum penalty for the maximum penalty for the time being specified in subsection (2).

(5) No order is to be made containing provision authorised by subsection (4) unless a draft of the order has been laid before Parliament and approved by a resolution of each House.

Amendments (Textual)

F181. S. 123. (1. A)(1. B) inserted (1.10.2015) by Consumer Rights Act 2015 (c. 15), ss. 80. (4), 100. (5); S.I. 2015/1630, art. 3. (e) (with art. 7)

F182. Words in s. 123. (2) substituted (1.10.2015) by Consumer Rights Act 2015 (c. 15), ss. 80. (5), 100. (5); S.I. 2015/1630, art. 3. (e) (with art. 7)

F183. Word in s. 123. (2) substituted (30.12.2005) by Communications Act 2003 (Maximum Penalty and Disclosure of Information) Order 2005 (S.I. 2005/3469), arts. 1. (1), 2 (with art. 2. (2))

Commencement Information

I180. S. 123 in force at 29.12.2003 by S.I. 2003/3142, art. 3. (1), Sch. 1 (with art. 11)

124. Suspending service provision for contraventions of s. 120 conditions

(1) OFCOM may give a direction under this section to a person who is a communications provider ("the contravening provider") if they are satisfied—

    (a) that he is or has been in serious and repeated contravention of conditions set under section 120;

    (b) that an attempt, by the imposition of penalties or the giving of enforcement notifications under section 95 (as applied by section 123) or both, to secure compliance with the contravened conditions has failed;

    (c) that the giving of the direction is appropriate and proportionate to the seriousness (when repeated as they have been) of the contraventions; and

(d) that the giving of the direction is required for reasons of public policy.

(2) OFCOM may also give a direction under this section to a person who is a communications provider ("the contravening provider") if they are satisfied—

(a) that he is, or has been, in contravention of conditions set under section 120 in respect of a premium rate service;

(b) that the circumstances of the contravention make it appropriate for OFCOM to suspend or restrict the provision of premium rate services provided by the contravening provider without the conditions set out in subsection (1) being satisfied; and

(c) that in those circumstances the giving of the direction is urgently required for reasons of public policy.

(3) A direction under this section is—

(a) a direction to the contravening provider to secure the suspension of the provision of premium rate services provided by him; or

(b) a direction requiring him to secure compliance with restrictions, set out in the direction, on the provision of such services.

(4) A direction under this section—

(a) must specify the services to which it relates; and

(b) except so far as it otherwise provides, takes effect for an indefinite period beginning with the time at which it is notified to the person to whom it is given.

(5) A direction under this section—

(a) in providing for the effect of a suspension or restriction to be postponed, may provide for it to take effect only at a time determined by or in accordance with the terms of the direction; and

(b) in connection with the suspension or restriction contained in the direction or with the postponement of its effect, may impose such conditions on the contravening provider as appear to OFCOM to be appropriate for the purpose of protecting that provider's customers.

(6) Those conditions may include a condition requiring the making of payments—

(a) by way of compensation for loss or damage suffered by the contravening provider's customers as a result of the direction; or

(b) in respect of annoyance, inconvenience or anxiety to which they have been put in consequence of the direction.

(7) If OFCOM consider it appropriate to do so (whether or not in consequence of representations or proposals made to them), they may revoke a direction under this section or modify its conditions—

(a) with effect from such time as they may direct;

(b) subject to compliance with such requirements as they may specify; and

(c) to such extent and in relation to such services as they may determine.

(8) Sections 102 and 103 apply in the case of a direction under this section as they apply in the case of a direction under section 100, but as if references in section 103. (1) to an electronic communications network or electronic communications service were references to a premium rate service.

(9) For the purposes of this section there are repeated contraventions by a person of conditions set under section 120 to the extent that—

(a) in the case of a previous notification given to that person under section section 94 (as applied by section 123), OFCOM have determined for the purposes of section 95. (2) or 96. (2) (as so applied) that such a contravention did occur; and

(b) in the period of twelve months following the day of the making of that determination, one or more further notifications have been given to that person in respect of contraventions of a condition set under section 120.

(10) For the purposes of this section the seriousness of repeated contraventions of conditions set under section 120 has to be determined by reference to the seriousness of the contraventions of the approved code or order by reference to which the conditions have effect.

Commencement Information

I181. S. 124 in force at 29.12.2003 by S.I. 2003/3142, art. 3. (1), Sch. 1 (with art. 11)

[F184. Online infringement of copyright: obligations of internet service providers

Amendments (Textual)
F184. S. 124. A and cross-heading inserted (8.6.2010) by Digital Economy Act 2010 (c. 24), ss. 3, 47. (1)

124. AObligation to notify subscribers of copyright infringement reports

(1) This section applies if it appears to a copyright owner that—

(a) a subscriber to an internet access service has infringed the owner's copyright by means of the service; or

(b) a subscriber to an internet access service has allowed another person to use the service, and that other person has infringed the owner's copyright by means of the service.

(2) The owner may make a copyright infringement report to the internet service provider who provided the internet access service if a code in force under section 124. C or 124. D (an "initial obligations code") allows the owner to do so.

(3) A "copyright infringement report" is a report that—

(a) states that there appears to have been an infringement of the owner's copyright;

(b) includes a description of the apparent infringement;

(c) includes evidence of the apparent infringement that shows the subscriber's IP address and the time at which the evidence was gathered;

(d) is sent to the internet service provider within the period of 1 month beginning with the day on which the evidence was gathered; and

(e) complies with any other requirement of the initial obligations code.

(4) An internet service provider who receives a copyright infringement report must notify the subscriber of the report if the initial obligations code requires the provider to do so.

(5) A notification under subsection (4) must be sent to the subscriber within the period of 1 month beginning with the day on which the provider receives the report.

(6) A notification under subsection (4) must include—

(a) a statement that the notification is sent under this section in response to a copyright infringement report;

(b) the name of the copyright owner who made the report;

(c) a description of the apparent infringement;

(d) evidence of the apparent infringement that shows the subscriber's IP address and the time at which the evidence was gathered;

(e) information about subscriber appeals and the grounds on which they may be made;

(f) information about copyright and its purpose;

(g) advice, or information enabling the subscriber to obtain advice, about how to obtain lawful access to copyright works;

(h) advice, or information enabling the subscriber to obtain advice, about steps that a subscriber can take to protect an internet access service from unauthorised use; and

(i) anything else that the initial obligations code requires the notification to include.

(7) For the purposes of subsection (6)(h) the internet service provider must take into account the suitability of different protection for subscribers in different circumstances.

(8) The things that may be required under subsection (6)(i), whether in general or in a particular case, include in particular—

(a) a statement that information about the apparent infringement may be kept by the internet service provider;

(b) a statement that the copyright owner may require the provider to disclose which copyright infringement reports made by the owner to the provider relate to the subscriber;

(c) a statement that, following such a disclosure, the copyright owner may apply to a court to

133

learn the subscriber's identity and may bring proceedings against the subscriber for copyright infringement; and

(d) where the requirement for the provider to send the notification arises partly because of a report that has already been the subject of a notification under subsection (4), a statement that the number of copyright infringement reports relating to the subscriber may be taken into account for the purposes of any technical measures.

(9) In this section "notify", in relation to a subscriber, means send a notification to the electronic or postal address held by the internet service provider for the subscriber (and sections 394 to 396 do not apply).]

[F185124. BObligation to provide copyright infringement lists to copyright owners

(1) An internet service provider must provide a copyright owner with a copyright infringement list for a period if—

(a) the owner requests the list for that period; and

(b) an initial obligations code requires the internet service provider to provide it.

(2) A "copyright infringement list" is a list that—

(a) sets out, in relation to each relevant subscriber, which of the copyright infringement reports made by the owner to the provider relate to the subscriber, but

(b) does not enable any subscriber to be identified.

(3) A subscriber is a "relevant subscriber" in relation to a copyright owner and an internet service provider if copyright infringement reports made by the owner to the provider in relation to the subscriber have reached the threshold set in the initial obligations code.]

Amendments (Textual)

F185. S. 124. B inserted (8.6.2010) by Digital Economy Act 2010 (c. 24), ss. 4, 47. (1)

[F186124. CApproval of code about the initial obligations

(1) The obligations of internet service providers under sections 124. A and 124. B are the "initial obligations".

(2) If it appears to OFCOM—

(a) that a code has been made by any person for the purpose of regulating the initial obligations; and

(b) that it would be appropriate for them to approve the code for that purpose,

they may by order approve it, with effect from the date given in the order.

(3) The provision that may be contained in a code and approved under this section includes provision that—

(a) specifies conditions that must be met for rights and obligations under the copyright infringement provisions or the code to apply in a particular case;

(b) requires copyright owners or internet service providers to provide any information or assistance that is reasonably required to determine whether a condition under paragraph (a) is met.

(4) The provision mentioned in subsection (3)(a) may, in particular, specify that a right or obligation does not apply in relation to a copyright owner unless the owner has made arrangements with an internet service provider regarding—

(a) the number of copyright infringement reports that the owner may make to the provider within a particular period; and

(b) payment in advance of a contribution towards meeting costs incurred by the provider.

(5) The provision mentioned in subsection (3)(a) may also, in particular, provide that—

(a) except as provided by the code, rights and obligations do not apply in relation to an internet service provider unless the number of copyright infringement reports the provider receives within a particular period reaches a threshold set in the code; and

(b) if the threshold is reached, rights or obligations apply with effect from the date when it is reached or from a later time.

(6) OFCOM must not approve a code under this section unless satisfied that it meets the criteria set out in section 124. E.

(7) Not more than one approved code may have effect at a time.

(8) OFCOM must keep an approved code under review.

(9) OFCOM may by order, at any time, for the purpose mentioned in subsection (2)—

(a) approve modifications that have been made to an approved code; or

(b) withdraw their approval from an approved code,

with effect from the date given in the order, and must do so if the code ceases to meet the criteria set out in section 124. E.

(10) The consent of the Secretary of State is required for the approval of a code or the modification of an approved code.

(11) An order made by OFCOM under this section approving a code or modification must set out the code or modification.

(12) Section 403 applies to the power of OFCOM to make an order under this section.

(13) A statutory instrument containing an order made by OFCOM under this section is subject to annulment in pursuance of a resolution of either House of Parliament.]

Amendments (Textual)

F186. S. 124. C inserted (8.4.2010) by Digital Economy Act 2010 (c. 24), ss. 5, 47. (2)(a)

[F187124. DInitial obligations code by OFCOM in the absence of an approved code

(1) For any period when sections 124. A and 124. B are in force but for which there is no approved initial obligations code under section 124. C, OFCOM must by order make a code for the purpose of regulating the initial obligations.

(2) OFCOM may but need not make a code under subsection (1) for a time before the end of—

(a) the period of six months beginning with the day on which sections 124. A and 124. B come into force, or

(b) such longer period as the Secretary of State may specify by notice to OFCOM.

(3) The Secretary of State may give a notice under subsection (2)(b) only if it appears to the Secretary of State that it is not practicable for OFCOM to make a code with effect from the end of the period mentioned in subsection (2)(a) or any longer period for the time being specified under subsection (2)(b).

(4) A code under this section may do any of the things mentioned in section 124. C(3) to (5).

(5) A code under this section may also—

(a) confer jurisdiction with respect to any matter (other than jurisdiction to determine appeals by subscribers) on OFCOM themselves;

(b) provide for OFCOM, in exercising such jurisdiction, to make awards of compensation, to direct the reimbursement of costs, or to do both;

(c) provide for OFCOM to enforce, or to participate in the enforcement of, any awards or directions made under the code;

(d) make other provision for the enforcement of such awards and directions;

(e) establish a body corporate, with the capacity to make its own rules and establish its own procedures, for the purpose of determining subscriber appeals;

(f) provide for a person with the function of determining subscriber appeals to enforce, or to participate in the enforcement of, any awards or directions made by the person;

(g) make other provision for the enforcement of such awards and directions; and

(h) make other provision for the purpose of regulating the initial obligations.

(6) OFCOM must not make a code under this section unless they are satisfied that it meets the criteria set out in section 124. E.

(7) OFCOM must—

(a) keep a code under this section under review; and

(b) by order make any amendment of it that is necessary to ensure that while it is in force it continues to meet the criteria set out in section 124. E.

(8) The consent of the Secretary of State is required for the making or amendment by OFCOM of a code under this section.

(9) Section 403 applies to the power of OFCOM to make an order under this section.

(10) A statutory instrument containing an order made by OFCOM under this section is subject to annulment in pursuance of a resolution of either House of Parliament.]

Amendments (Textual)

F187. S. 124. D inserted (8.4.2010) by Digital Economy Act 2010 (c. 24), ss. 6, 47. (2)(a)

[F188124. EContents of initial obligations code

(1) The criteria referred to in sections 124. C(6) and 124. D(6) are—

(a) that the code makes the required provision about copyright infringement reports (see subsection (2));

(b) that it makes the required provision about the notification of subscribers (see subsections (3) and (4));

(c) that it sets the threshold applying for the purposes of determining who is a relevant subscriber within the meaning of section 124. B(3) (see subsections (5) and (6));

(d) that it makes provision about how internet service providers are to keep information about subscribers;

(e) that it limits the time for which they may keep that information;

(f) that it makes any provision about contributions towards meeting costs that is required to be included by an order under section 124. M;

(g) that the requirements concerning administration and enforcement are met in relation to the code (see subsections (7) and (8));

(h) that the requirements concerning subscriber appeals are met in relation to the code (see section 124. K);

(i) that the provisions of the code are objectively justifiable in relation to the matters to which it relates;

(j) that those provisions are not such as to discriminate unduly against particular persons or against a particular description of persons;

(k) that those provisions are proportionate to what they are intended to achieve; and

(l) that, in relation to what those provisions are intended to achieve, they are transparent.

(2) The required provision about copyright infringement reports is provision that specifies—

(a) requirements as to the means of obtaining evidence of infringement of copyright for inclusion in a report;

(b) the standard of evidence that must be included; and

(c) the required form of the report.

(3) The required provision about the notification of subscribers is provision that specifies, in relation to a subscriber in relation to whom an internet service provider receives one or more copyright infringement reports—

(a) requirements as to the means by which the provider identifies the subscriber;

(b) which of the reports the provider must notify the subscriber of; and

(c) requirements as to the form, contents and means of the notification in each case.

(4) The provision mentioned in subsection (3) must not permit any copyright infringement report received by an internet service provider more than 12 months before the date of a notification of a subscriber to be taken into account for the purposes of the notification.

(5) The threshold applying in accordance with subsection (1)(c) may, subject to subsection (6), be set by reference to any matter, including in particular one or more of—

(a) the number of copyright infringement reports;

(b) the time within which the reports are made; and

(c) the time of the apparent infringements to which they relate.

(6) The threshold applying in accordance with subsection (1)(c) must operate in such a way that a copyright infringement report received by an internet service provider more than 12 months before a particular date does not affect whether the threshold is met on that date; and a copyright infringement list provided under section 124. B must not take into account any such report.

(7) The requirements concerning administration and enforcement are—

(a) that OFCOM have, under the code, the functions of administering and enforcing it, including the function of resolving owner-provider disputes;

(b) that there are adequate arrangements under the code for OFCOM to obtain any information or assistance from internet service providers or copyright owners that OFCOM reasonably require for the purposes of administering and enforcing the code; and

(c) that there are adequate arrangements under the code for the costs incurred by OFCOM in administering and enforcing the code to be met by internet service providers and copyright owners.

(8) The provision mentioned in subsection (7) may include, in particular—

(a) provision for the payment, to a person specified in the code, of a penalty not exceeding the maximum penalty for the time being specified in section 124. L(2);

(b) provision requiring a copyright owner to indemnify an internet service provider for any loss or damage resulting from the owner's failure to comply with the code or the copyright infringement provisions.

(9) In this section "owner-provider dispute" means a dispute that—

(a) is between persons who are copyright owners or internet service providers; and

(b) relates to an act or omission in relation to an initial obligation or an initial obligations code.]

Amendments (Textual)

F188. S. 124. E inserted (8.4.2010) by Digital Economy Act 2010 (c. 24), ss. 7, 47. (2)(a)

[F189124. FProgress reports

(1) OFCOM must prepare the following reports for the Secretary of State about the infringement of copyright by subscribers to internet access services.

(2) OFCOM must prepare a full report for—

(a) the period of 12 months beginning with the first day on which there is an initial obligations code in force; and

(b) each successive period of 12 months.

(3) OFCOM must prepare an interim report for—

(a) the period of 3 months beginning with the first day on which there is an initial obligations code in force; and

(b) each successive period of 3 months, other than one ending at the same time as a period of 12 months under subsection (2).

But this is subject to any direction by the Secretary of State under subsection (4).

(4) The Secretary of State may direct that subsection (3) no longer applies, with effect from the date given in the direction.

(5) A full report under this section must include—

(a) an assessment of the current level of subscribers' use of internet access services to infringe copyright;

(b) a description of the steps taken by copyright owners to enable subscribers to obtain lawful access to copyright works;

(c) a description of the steps taken by copyright owners to inform, and change the attitude of, members of the public in relation to the infringement of copyright;

(d) an assessment of the extent of the steps mentioned in paragraphs (b) and (c);

(e) an assessment of the extent to which copyright owners have made copyright infringement reports;

(f) an assessment of the extent to which they have brought legal proceedings against subscribers in relation to whom such reports have been made;

(g) an assessment of the extent to which any such proceedings have been against subscribers in relation to whom a substantial number of reports have been made; and

(h) anything else that the Secretary of State directs OFCOM to include in the report.

(6) An interim report under this section must include—

(a) the assessments mentioned in subsection (5)(a), (e) and (f); and

(b) anything else that the Secretary of State directs OFCOM to include in the report.

(7) OFCOM must send a report prepared under this section to the Secretary of State as soon as practicable after the end of the period for which it is prepared.

(8) OFCOM must publish every full report under this section—

(a) as soon as practicable after they send it to the Secretary of State, and

(b) in such manner as they consider appropriate for bringing it to the attention of persons who, in their opinion, are likely to have an interest in it.

(9) OFCOM may exclude information from a report when it is published under subsection (8) if they consider that it is information that they could refuse to disclose in response to a request under the Freedom of Information Act 2000.]

Amendments (Textual)

F189. S. 124. F inserted (8.6.2010) by Digital Economy Act 2010 (c. 24), ss. 8, 47. (1)

[F190124. GObligations to limit internet access: assessment and preparation

(1) The Secretary of State may direct OFCOM to—

   (a) assess whether one or more technical obligations should be imposed on internet service providers;

   (b) take steps to prepare for the obligations;

   (c) provide a report on the assessment or steps to the Secretary of State.

(2) A "technical obligation", in relation to an internet service provider, is an obligation for the provider to take a technical measure against some or all relevant subscribers to its service for the purpose of preventing or reducing infringement of copyright by means of the internet.

(3) A "technical measure" is a measure that—

   (a) limits the speed or other capacity of the service provided to a subscriber;

   (b) prevents a subscriber from using the service to gain access to particular material, or limits such use;

   (c) suspends the service provided to a subscriber; or

   (d) limits the service provided to a subscriber in another way.

(4) A subscriber to an internet access service is "relevant" if the subscriber is a relevant subscriber, within the meaning of section 124. B(3), in relation to the provider of the service and one or more copyright owners.

(5) The assessment and steps that the Secretary of State may direct OFCOM to carry out or take under subsection (1) include, in particular—

   (a) consultation of copyright owners, internet service providers, subscribers or any other person;

   (b) an assessment of the likely efficacy of a technical measure in relation to a particular type of internet access service; and

   (c) steps to prepare a proposed technical obligations code.

(6) Internet service providers and copyright owners must give OFCOM any assistance that OFCOM reasonably require for the purposes of complying with any direction under this section.

(7) The Secretary of State must lay before Parliament any direction under this section.

(8) OFCOM must publish every report under this section—

   (a) as soon as practicable after they send it to the Secretary of State, and

   (b) in such manner as they consider appropriate for bringing it to the attention of persons who, in their opinion, are likely to have an interest in it.

(9) OFCOM may exclude information from a report when it is published under subsection (8) if they consider that it is information that they could refuse to disclose in response to a request under the Freedom of Information Act 2000.]

Amendments (Textual)

F190. S. 124. G inserted (8.6.2010) by Digital Economy Act 2010 (c. 24), ss. 9, 47. (1)

[F191124. HObligations to limit internet access

(1) The Secretary of State may by order impose a technical obligation on internet service providers if—

   (a) OFCOM have assessed whether one or more technical obligations should be imposed on internet service providers; and

   (b) taking into account that assessment, reports prepared by OFCOM under section 124. F, and any other matter that appears to the Secretary of State to be relevant, the Secretary of State considers it appropriate to make the order.

(2) No order may be made under this section within the period of 12 months beginning with the first day on which there is an initial obligations code in force.

(3) An order under this section must specify the date from which the technical obligation is to have effect, or provide for it to be specified.

(4) The order may also specify—

(a) the criteria for taking the technical measure concerned against a subscriber;

(b) the steps to be taken as part of the measure and when they are to be taken.

(5) No order is to be made under this section unless—

(a) the Secretary of State has complied with subsections (6) to (10), and

(b) a draft of the order has been laid before Parliament and approved by a resolution of each House.

(6) If the Secretary of State proposes to make an order under this section, the Secretary of State must lay before Parliament a document that—

(a) explains the proposal, and

(b) sets it out in the form of a draft order.

(7) During the period of 60 days beginning with the day on which the document was laid under subsection (6) ("the 60-day period"), the Secretary of State may not lay before Parliament a draft order to give effect to the proposal (with or without modifications).

(8) In preparing a draft order under this section to give effect to the proposal, the Secretary of State must have regard to any of the following that are made with regard to the draft order during the 60-day period—

(a) any representations, and

(b) any recommendations of a committee of either House of Parliament charged with reporting on the draft order.

(9) When laying before Parliament a draft order to give effect to the proposal (with or without modifications), the Secretary of State must also lay a document that explains any changes made to the proposal contained in the document laid before Parliament under subsection (6).

(10) In calculating the 60-day period, no account is to be taken of any time during which Parliament is dissolved or prorogued or during which either House is adjourned for more than 4 days.]

Amendments (Textual)

F191. S. 124. H inserted (8.6.2010) by Digital Economy Act 2010 (c. 24), ss. 10, 47. (1)

[F192124. ICode by OFCOM about obligations to limit internet access

(1) For any period during which there are one or more technical obligations in force under section 124. H, OFCOM must by order make a technical obligations code for the purpose of regulating those obligations.

(2) The code may be made separately from, or in combination with, any initial obligations code under section 124. D.

(3) A code under this section may—

(a) do any of the things mentioned in section 124. C(3) to (5) or section 124. D(5)(a) to (g); and

(b) make other provision for the purpose of regulating the technical obligations.

(4) OFCOM must not make a code under this section unless they are satisfied that it meets the criteria set out in section 124. J.

(5) OFCOM must—

(a) keep a code under this section under review; and

(b) by order make any amendment of it that is necessary to ensure that while it is in force it continues to meet the criteria set out in section 124. J.

(6) The consent of the Secretary of State is required for the making or amendment by OFCOM of a code under this section.

(7) Section 403 applies to the power of OFCOM to make an order under this section.

(8) A statutory instrument containing an order made by OFCOM under this section is subject to annulment in pursuance of a resolution of either House of Parliament.]

Amendments (Textual)

F192. S. 124. I inserted (8.6.2010) by Digital Economy Act 2010 (c. 24), ss. 11, 47. (1)

[F193124. JContents of code about obligations to limit internet access

(1) The criteria referred to in section 124. I(4) are—

(a) that the requirements concerning enforcement and related matters are met in relation to the code (see subsections (2) and (3));

(b) that the requirements concerning subscriber appeals are met in relation to the code (see section 124. K);

(c) that it makes any provision about contributions towards meeting costs that is required to be included by an order under section 124. M;

(d) that it makes any other provision that the Secretary of State requires it to make;

(e) that the provisions of the code are objectively justifiable in relation to the matters to which it relates;

(f) that those provisions are not such as to discriminate unduly against particular persons or against a particular description of persons;

(g) that those provisions are proportionate to what they are intended to achieve; and

(h) that, in relation to what those provisions are intended to achieve, they are transparent.

(2) The requirements concerning enforcement and related matters are—

(a) that OFCOM have, under the code, the functions of administering and enforcing it, including the function of resolving owner-provider disputes;

(b) that there are adequate arrangements under the code for OFCOM to obtain any information or assistance from internet service providers or copyright owners that OFCOM reasonably require for the purposes of administering and enforcing the code; and

(c) that there are adequate arrangements under the code for the costs incurred by OFCOM in administering and enforcing the code to be met by internet service providers and copyright owners.

(3) The provision made concerning enforcement and related matters may also (unless the Secretary of State requires otherwise) include, in particular—

(a) provision for the payment, to a person specified in the code, of a penalty not exceeding the maximum penalty for the time being specified in section 124. L(2);

(b) provision requiring a copyright owner to indemnify an internet service provider for any loss or damage resulting from the owner's infringement or error in relation to the code or the copyright infringement provisions.

(4) In this section "owner-provider dispute" means a dispute that—

(a) is between persons who are copyright owners or internet service providers; and

(b) relates to an act or omission in relation to a technical obligation or a technical obligations code.]

Amendments (Textual)

F193. S. 124. J inserted (8.6.2010) by Digital Economy Act 2010 (c. 24), ss. 12, 47. (1)

[F194124. KSubscriber appeals

(1) The requirements concerning subscriber appeals are—

(a) for the purposes of section 124. E(1)(h), the requirements of subsections (2) to (8); and

(b) for the purposes of section 124. J(1)(b), the requirements of subsections (2) to (11).

(2) The requirements of this subsection are—

(a) that the code confers on subscribers the right to bring a subscriber appeal and, in the case of a technical obligations code, a further right of appeal to the First-tier Tribunal;

(b) that there is a person who, under the code, has the function of determining subscriber appeals;

(c) that that person is for practical purposes independent (so far as determining subscriber appeals is concerned) of internet service providers, copyright owners and OFCOM; and

(d) that there are adequate arrangements under the code for the costs incurred by that person in determining subscriber appeals to be met by internet service providers, copyright owners and the subscriber concerned.

(3) The code must provide for the grounds of appeal (so far as an appeal relates to, or to anything done by reference to, a copyright infringement report) to include the following—

(a) that the apparent infringement to which the report relates was not an infringement of copyright;

(b) that the report does not relate to the subscriber's IP address at the time of the apparent infringement.

(4) The code must provide for the grounds of appeal to include contravention by the copyright owner or internet service provider of the code or of an obligation regulated by the code.

(5) The code must provide that an appeal on any grounds must be determined in favour of the subscriber unless the copyright owner or internet service provider shows that, as respects any copyright infringement report to which the appeal relates or by reference to which anything to which the appeal relates was done (or, if there is more than one such report, as respects each of them)—

(a) the apparent infringement was an infringement of copyright, and

(b) the report relates to the subscriber's IP address at the time of that infringement.

(6) The code must provide that, where a ground mentioned in subsection (3) is relied on, the appeal must be determined in favour of the subscriber if the subscriber shows that—

(a) the act constituting the apparent infringement to which the report relates was not done by the subscriber, and

(b) the subscriber took reasonable steps to prevent other persons infringing copyright by means of the internet access service.

(7) The powers of the person determining subscriber appeals must include power—

(a) to secure so far as practicable that a subscriber is not prejudiced for the purposes of the copyright infringement provisions by an act or omission in respect of which an appeal is determined in favour of the subscriber;

(b) to make an award of compensation to be paid by a copyright owner or internet service provider to a subscriber affected by such an act or omission; and

(c) where the appeal is determined in favour of the subscriber, to direct the copyright owner or internet service provider to reimburse the reasonable costs of the subscriber.

(8) The code must provide that the power to direct the reimbursement of costs under subsection (7)(c) is to be exercised to award reasonable costs to a subscriber whose appeal is successful, unless the person deciding the appeal is satisfied that it would be unjust to give such a direction having regard to all the circumstances including the conduct of the parties before and during the proceedings.

(9) In the case of a technical obligations code, the powers of the person determining subscriber appeals must include power—

(a) on an appeal in relation to a technical measure or proposed technical measure—

(i) to confirm the measure;

(ii) to require the measure not to be taken or to be withdrawn;

(iii) to substitute any other technical measure that the internet service provider has power to take;

(b) to exercise the power mentioned in paragraph (a)(ii) or (iii) where an appeal is not upheld but the person determining it is satisfied that there are exceptional circumstances that justify the exercise of the power;

(c) to take any steps that OFCOM could take in relation to the act or omission giving rise to the technical measure; and

(d) to remit the decision whether to confirm the technical measure, or any matter relating to that decision, to OFCOM.

(10) In the case of a technical obligations code, the code must make provision—

(a) enabling a determination of a subscriber appeal to be appealed to the First-tier Tribunal, including on grounds that it was based on an error of fact, wrong in law or unreasonable;

(b) giving the First-tier Tribunal, in relation to an appeal to it, the powers mentioned in subsections (7) and (9); and

(c) in relation to recovery of costs awarded by the Tribunal.

(11) In the case of a technical obligations code, the code must include provision to secure that a technical measure is not taken against a subscriber until—

(a) the period for bringing a subscriber appeal, or any further appeal to the First-tier Tribunal, in relation to the proposed measure has ended (or the subscriber has waived the right to appeal); and

(b) any such subscriber appeal or further appeal has been determined, abandoned or otherwise disposed of.]

Amendments (Textual)

F194. S. 124. K inserted (8.6.2010) by Digital Economy Act 2010 (c. 24), ss. 13, 47. (1)

[F195124. LEnforcement of obligations

(1) Sections 94 to 96 apply in relation to a contravention of an initial obligation or a technical obligation, or a contravention of an obligation under section 124. G(6), as they apply in relation to a contravention of a condition set out under section 45.

(2) The amount of the penalty imposed under section 96 as applied by this section is to be such amount not exceeding £250,000 as OFCOM determine to be—

    (a) appropriate; and

    (b) proportionate to the contravention in respect of which it is imposed.

(3) In making that determination OFCOM must have regard to—

    (a) any representations made to them by the internet service provider or copyright owner on whom the penalty is imposed;

    (b) any steps taken by the provider or owner towards complying with the obligations contraventions of which have been notified to the provider or owner under section 94 (as applied); and

    (c) any steps taken by the provider or owner for remedying the consequences of those contraventions.

(4) The Secretary of State may by order amend this section so as to substitute a different maximum penalty for the maximum penalty for the time being specified in subsection (2).

(5) No order is to be made containing provision authorised by subsection (4) unless a draft of the order has been laid before Parliament and approved by a resolution of each House.]

Amendments (Textual)

F195. S. 124. L inserted (8.6.2010) by Digital Economy Act 2010 (c. 24), ss. 14, 47. (1)

[F196124. MSharing of costs

(1) The Secretary of State may by order specify provision that must be included in an initial obligations code or a technical obligations code about payment of contributions towards costs incurred under the copyright infringement provisions.

(2) Any provision specified under subsection (1) must relate to payment of contributions by one or more of the following only—

    (a) copyright owners;

    (b) internet service providers;

    (c) in relation to a subscriber appeal or a further appeal by a subscriber to the First-tier Tribunal, the subscriber.

(3) Provision specified under subsection (1) may relate to, in particular—

    (a) payment by a copyright owner of a contribution towards the costs that an internet service provider incurs;

    (b) payment by a copyright owner or internet service provider of a contribution towards the costs that OFCOM incur.

(4) Provision specified under subsection (1) may include, in particular—

    (a) provision about costs incurred before the provision is included in an initial obligations code or a technical obligations code;

    (b) provision for payment in advance of expected costs (and for reimbursement of overpayments where the costs incurred are less than expected);

    (c) provision about how costs, expected costs or contributions must be calculated;

    (d) other provision about when and how contributions must be paid.

(5) No order is to be made under this section unless a draft of the order has been laid before Parliament and approved by a resolution of each House.]

Amendments (Textual)

F196. S. 124. M inserted (8.4.2010) by virtue of Digital Economy Act 2010 (c. 24), ss. 15, 47. (2)(a)

[F197124. NInterpretation

In sections 124. A to 124. M and this section—

"apparent infringement", in relation to a copyright infringement report, means the infringement of copyright that the report states appears to have taken place;

"copyright infringement list" has the meaning given in section 124. B(2);

"copyright infringement provisions" means sections 124. A to 124. M and this section;

"copyright infringement report" has the meaning given in section 124. A(3);

"copyright owner" means—

   - a copyright owner within the meaning of Part 1 of the Copyright, Designs and Patents Act 1988 (see section 173 of that Act); or

   - someone authorised by that person to act on the person's behalf;

"copyright work" has the same meaning as in Part 1 of the Copyright, Designs and Patents Act 1988 (see section 1. (2) of that Act);

"initial obligations" has the meaning given in section 124. C(1);

"initial obligations code" has the meaning given in section 124. A(2);

"internet access service" means an electronic communications service that—

   - is provided to a subscriber;

   - consists entirely or mainly of the provision of access to the internet; and

   - includes the allocation of an IP address or IP addresses to the subscriber to enable that access;

"internet service provider" means a person who provides an internet access service;

"IP address" means an internet protocol address;

"subscriber", in relation to an internet access service, means a person who—

   - receives the service under an agreement between the person and the provider of the service; and

   - does not receive it as a communications provider;

"subscriber appeal" means—

   - in relation to an initial obligations code, an appeal by a subscriber on grounds specified in the code in relation to—

the making of a copyright infringement report;

notification under section 124. A(4);

the inclusion or proposed inclusion of an entry in a copyright infringement list; or

any other act or omission in relation to an initial obligation or an initial obligations code;

   - in relation to a technical obligations code, an appeal by a subscriber on grounds specified in the code in relation to—

the proposed taking of a technical measure; or

any other act or omission in relation to a technical obligation or a technical obligations code;

"technical measure" has the meaning given in section 124. G(3);

"technical obligation" has the meaning given in section 124. G(2);

"technical obligations code" means a code in force under section 124. I.]

Amendments (Textual)

F197. S. 124. N inserted (8.4.2010) by Digital Economy Act 2010 (c. 24), ss. 16. (1), 47. (2)(a)

Offences relating to networks and services

125. Dishonestly obtaining electronic communications services

(1) A person who—

   (a) dishonestly obtains an electronic communications service, and

   (b) does so with intent to avoid payment of a charge applicable to the provision of that service,

is guilty of an offence.

(2) It is not an offence under this section to obtain a service mentioned in section 297. (1) of the Copyright, Designs and Patents Act 1988 (c. 48) (dishonestly obtaining a broadcasting F198... service provided from a place in the UK).

(3) A person guilty of an offence under this section shall be liable—

(a) on summary conviction, to imprisonment for a term not exceeding six months or to a fine not exceeding the statutory maximum, or to both;

(b) on conviction on indictment, to imprisonment for a term not exceeding five years or to a fine, or to both.

Amendments (Textual)

F198. Words in s. 125. (2) repealed (31.10.2003) by The Copyright and Related Rights Regulations 2003 (S.I. 2003/2498), reg. 1, Sch. 2 (with regs. 31-40)

Commencement Information

I182. S. 125 in force at 25.7.2003 for specified purposes by S.I. 2003/1900, arts. 1. (2), 2. (1), Sch. 1 (with art. 3) (as amended by S.I. 2003/3142, art. 1. (3))

I183. S. 125 in force at 29.12.2003 in so far as not already in force by S.I. 2003/3142, art. 3. (2) (with art. 11)

126. Possession or supply of apparatus etc. for contravening s. 125.

(1) A person is guilty of an offence if, with an intention falling within subsection (3), he has in his possession or under his control anything that may be used—

(a) for obtaining an electronic communications service; or

(b) in connection with obtaining such a service.

(2) A person is guilty of an offence if—

(a) he supplies or offers to supply anything which may be used as mentioned in subsection (1); and

(b) he knows or believes that the intentions in relation to that thing of the person to whom it is supplied or offered fall within subsection (3).

(3) A person's intentions fall within this subsection if he intends—

(a) to use the thing to obtain an electronic communications service dishonestly;

(b) to use the thing for a purpose connected with the dishonest obtaining of such a service;

(c) dishonestly to allow the thing to be used to obtain such a service; or

(d) to allow the thing to be used for a purpose connected with the dishonest obtaining of such a service.

(4) An intention does not fall within subsection (3) if it relates exclusively to the obtaining of a service mentioned in section 297. (1) of the Copyright, Designs and Patents Act 1988 (c. 48).

(5) A person guilty of an offence under this section shall be liable—

(a) on summary conviction, to imprisonment for a term not exceeding six months or to a fine not exceeding the statutory maximum, or to both; and

(b) on conviction on indictment, to imprisonment for a term not exceeding five years or to a fine, or to both.

(6) In this section, references, in the case of a thing used for recording data, to the use of that thing include references to the use of data recorded by it.

Commencement Information

I184. S. 126 in force at 25.7.2003 for specified purposes by S.I. 2003/1900, arts. 1. (2), 2. (1), Sch. 1 (with art. 3) (as amended by S.I. 2003/3142, art. 1. (3))

I185. S. 126 in force at 29.12.2003 in so far as not already in force by S.I. 2003/3142, art. 3. (2) (with art. 11)

127. Improper use of public electronic communications network

(1) A person is guilty of an offence if he—

(a) sends by means of a public electronic communications network a message or other matter that is grossly offensive or of an indecent, obscene or menacing character; or

(b) causes any such message or matter to be so sent.

(2) A person is guilty of an offence if, for the purpose of causing annoyance, inconvenience or needless anxiety to another, he—

(a) sends by means of a public electronic communications network, a message that he knows to be false,

(b) causes such a message to be sent; or

(c) persistently makes use of a public electronic communications network.

(3) A person guilty of an offence under this section shall be liable, on summary conviction, to imprisonment for a term not exceeding six months or to a fine not exceeding level 5 on the standard scale, or to both.

(4) Subsections (1) and (2) do not apply to anything done in the course of providing a programme service (within the meaning of the Broadcasting Act 1990 (c. 42)).

[F199. (5)An information or complaint relating to an offence under this section may be tried by a magistrates' court in England and Wales or Northern Ireland if it is laid or made—

(a) before the end of the period of 3 years beginning with the day on which the offence was committed, and

(b) before the end of the period of 6 months beginning with the day on which evidence comes to the knowledge of the prosecutor which the prosecutor considers sufficient to justify proceedings.

(6) Summary proceedings for an offence under this section may be commenced in Scotland—

(a) before the end of the period of 3 years beginning with the day on which the offence was committed, and

(b) before the end of the period of 6 months beginning with the day on which evidence comes to the knowledge of the prosecutor which the prosecutor considers sufficient to justify proceedings, and section 136. (3) of the Criminal Procedure (Scotland) Act 1995 (date when proceedings deemed to be commenced) applies for the purposes of this subsection as it applies for the purposes of that section.

(7) A certificate of a prosecutor as to the date on which evidence described in subsection (5)(b) or (6)(b) came to his or her knowledge is conclusive evidence of that fact.]

Amendments (Textual)

F199. S. 127. (5)-(7) inserted (13.4.2015) by Criminal Justice and Courts Act 2015 (c. 2), ss. 51. (1), 95. (1) (with s. 51. (2)); S.I. 2015/778, art. 3, Sch. 1 para. 42

Commencement Information

I186. S. 127 in force at 25.7.2003 for specified purposes by S.I. 2003/1900, arts. 1. (2), 2. (1), Sch. 1 (with art. 3) (as amended by S.I. 2003/3142, art. 1. (3))

I187. S. 127 in force at 29.12.2003 in so far as not already in force by S.I. 2003/3142, art. 3. (2) (with art. 11)

Persistent misuse of network or service

128. Notification of misuse of networks and services

(1) Where OFCOM determine that there are reasonable grounds for believing that a person has persistently misused an electronic communications network or electronic communications services, they may give that person a notification under this section.

(2) A notification under this section is one which—

(a) sets out the determination made by OFCOM;

(b) specifies the use that OFCOM consider constitutes persistent misuse; and

(c) specifies the period during which the person notified has an opportunity of making representations about the matters notified.

(3) That period must not be less than the following—

(a) in an urgent case, seven days; and

(b) in any other case, one month.

(4) A case is an urgent case for the purposes of subsection (3) if OFCOM consider—

(a) that the misuse in question is continuing; and

(b) that the harm it causes makes it necessary for it to be stopped as soon as possible.

(5) For the purposes of this Chapter a person misuses an electronic communications network or electronic communications service if—

(a) the effect or likely effect of his use of the network or service is to cause another person unnecessarily to suffer annoyance, inconvenience or anxiety; or

(b) he uses the network or service to engage in conduct the effect or likely effect of which is to cause another person unnecessarily to suffer annoyance, inconvenience or anxiety.

(6) For the purposes of this Chapter the cases in which a person is to be treated as persistently misusing a network or service include any case in which his misuse is repeated on a sufficient number of occasions for it to be clear that the misuse represents—

(a) a pattern of behaviour or practice; or

(b) recklessness as to whether persons suffer annoyance, inconvenience or anxiety.

(7) For the purpose of determining whether misuse on a number of different occasions constitutes persistent misuse for the purposes of this Chapter, each of the following is immaterial—

(a) that the misuse was in relation to a network on some occasions and in relation to a service on others;

(b) that different networks or services were involved on different occasions; and

(c) that the persons who were or were likely to suffer annoyance inconvenience or anxiety were different on different occasions.

(8) If he considers that appropriate alternative means of dealing with it exists, the Secretary of State may by order provide that a use of a description specified in the order is not to be treated for the purposes of this Chapter as a misuse of an electronic communications network or electronic communications service.

Commencement Information

I188. S. 128 in force at 25.7.2003 for specified purposes by S.I. 2003/1900, arts. 1. (2), 2. (1), Sch. 1 (with art. 3) (as amended by S.I. 2003/3142, art. 1. (3))

I189. S. 128 in force at 29.12.2003 in so far as not already in force by S.I. 2003/3142, art. 3. (2) (with art. 11)

129. Enforcement notifications for stopping persistent misuse

(1) This section applies where—

(a) a person ("the notified misuser") has been given a notification under section 128;

(b) OFCOM have allowed the notified misuser an opportunity of making representations about the matters notified; and

(c) the period allowed for the making of the representations has expired.

(2) OFCOM may give the notified misuser an enforcement notification if they are satisfied—

(a) that he has, in one or more of the notified respects, persistently misused an electronic communications network or electronic communications service; and

(b) that he has not, since the giving of the notification, taken all such steps as OFCOM consider appropriate for—

(i) securing that his misuse is brought to an end and is not repeated; and

(ii) remedying the consequences of the notified misuse.

(3) An enforcement notification is a notification which imposes a requirement on the notified misuser to take all such steps for—

(a) securing that his misuse is brought to an end and is not repeated, and

(b) remedying the consequences of the notified misuse,

as may be specified in the notification.

(4) A decision of OFCOM to give an enforcement notification to a person must fix a reasonable period for the taking of the steps required by the notification.

(5) It shall be the duty of a person to whom an enforcement notification has been given to comply with it.

(6) That duty shall be enforceable in civil proceedings by OFCOM—

(a) for an injunction;

(b) for specific performance of a statutory duty under section 45 of the Court of Session Act 1988 (c. 36); or

(c) for any other appropriate remedy or relief.

(7) References in this section to remedying the consequences of misuse include references to paying an amount to a person—

(a) by way of compensation for loss or damage suffered by that person; or

(b) in respect of annoyance, inconvenience or anxiety to which he has been put.

Commencement Information

I190. S. 129 in force at 25.7.2003 for specified purposes by S.I. 2003/1900, arts. 1. (2), 2. (1), Sch. 1 (with art. 3) (as amended by S.I. 2003/3142, art. 1. (3))

I191. S. 129 in force at 29.12.2003 in so far as not already in force by S.I. 2003/3142, art. 3. (2) (with art. 11)

130. Penalties for persistent misuse

(1) This section applies (in addition to section 129) where—

(a) a person ("the notified misuser") has been given a notification under section 128;

(b) OFCOM have allowed the notified misuser an opportunity of making representations about the matters notified; and

(c) the period allowed for the making of the representations has expired.

(2) OFCOM may impose a penalty on the notified misuser if he has, in one or more of the notified respects, persistently misused an electronic communications network or electronic communications service.

(3) OFCOM may also impose a penalty on the notified misuser if he has contravened a requirement of an enforcement notification given in respect of the notified misuse.

(4) The amount of a penalty imposed is to be such amount not exceeding [F200£2,000,000] as OFCOM determine to be—

(a) appropriate; and

(b) proportionate to the misuse in respect of which it is imposed.

(5) In making that determination OFCOM must have regard to—

(a) any representations made to them by the notified misuser;

(b) any steps taken by him for securing that his misuse is brought to an end and is not repeated; and

(c) any steps taken by him for remedying the consequences of the notified misuse.

(6) Where OFCOM impose a penalty on a person under this section, they shall—

(a) notify the person penalised; and

(b) in that notification, fix a reasonable period after it is given as the period within which the penalty is to be paid.

(7) A penalty imposed under this section—

(a) must be paid to OFCOM; and

(b) if not paid within the period fixed by them, is to be recoverable by them accordingly.

(8) It is to be possible for a person to be both liable for an offence under sections 125 to 127 and to have a penalty imposed on him under this section in respect of the same conduct.

(9) The Secretary of State may by order amend this section so as to substitute a different maximum penalty for the maximum penalty for the time being specified in subsection (4).

(10) No order is to be made containing provision authorised by subsection (9) unless a draft of the order has been laid before Parliament and approved by a resolution of each House.

Amendments (Textual)

F200. Word in s. 130. (4) substituted (25.9.2010) by Communications Act 2003 (Maximum Penalty for Persistent Misuse of Network or Service) Order 2010 (S.I. 2010/2291), arts. 1, 2. (1) (with art. 2. (2))

Commencement Information

I192. S. 130 in force at 25.7.2003 for specified purposes by S.I. 2003/1900, arts. 1. (2), 2. (1), Sch. 1 (with art. 3) (as amended by S.I. 2003/3142, art. 1. (3))

I193. S. 130 in force at 29.12.2003 in so far as not already in force by S.I. 2003/3142, art. 3. (2) (with art. 11)

131. Statement of policy on persistent misuse

(1) It shall be the duty of OFCOM to prepare and publish a statement of their general policy with respect to the exercise of their powers under sections 128 to 130.

(2) OFCOM may from time to time revise that statement as they think fit.

(3) Where OFCOM make or revise their statement of policy under this section, they must publish that statement or (as the case may be) the revised statement in such manner as they consider

appropriate for bringing it to the attention of the persons who, in their opinion, are likely to be affected by it.

(4) It shall be the duty of OFCOM, in exercising the powers conferred on them by sections 128 to 130, to have regard to the statement for the time being in force under this section.

Commencement Information

I194. S. 131 in force at 25.7.2003 for specified purposes by S.I. 2003/1900, arts. 1. (2), 2. (1), Sch. 1 (with art. 3) (as amended by S.I. 2003/3142, art. 1. (3))

I195. S. 131 in force at 29.12.2003 in so far as not already in force by S.I. 2003/3142, art. 3. (2) (with art. 11)

Powers to deal with emergencies

132. Powers to require suspension or restriction of a provider's entitlement

(1) If the Secretary of State has reasonable grounds for believing that it is necessary to do so—

    (a) to protect the public from any threat to public safety or public health, or

    (b) in the interests of national security,

he may, by a direction to OFCOM, require them to give a direction under subsection (3) to a person ("the relevant provider") who provides an electronic communications network or electronic communications service or who makes associated facilities available.

(2) OFCOM must comply with a requirement of the Secretary of State under subsection (1) by giving to the relevant provider such direction under subsection (3) as they consider necessary for the purpose of complying with the Secretary of State's direction.

(3) A direction under this section is—

    (a) a direction that the entitlement of the relevant provider to provide electronic communications networks or electronic communications services, or to make associated facilities available, is suspended (either generally or in relation to particular networks, services or facilities); or

    (b) a direction that that entitlement is restricted in the respects set out in the direction.

(4) A direction under subsection (3)—

    (a) must specify the networks, services and facilities to which it relates; and

    (b) except so far as it otherwise provides, takes effect for an indefinite period beginning with the time at which it is notified to the person to whom it is given.

(5) A direction under subsection (3)—

    (a) in providing for the effect of a suspension or restriction to be postponed, may provide for it to take effect only at a time determined by or in accordance with the terms of the direction; and

    (b) in connection with the suspension or restriction contained in the direction or with the postponement of its effect, may impose such conditions on the relevant provider as appear to OFCOM to be appropriate for the purpose of protecting that provider's customers.

(6) Those conditions may include a condition requiring the making of payments—

    (a) by way of compensation for loss or damage suffered by the relevant provider's customers as a result of the direction; or

    (b) in respect of annoyance, inconvenience or anxiety to which they have been put in consequence of the direction.

(7) Where OFCOM give a direction under subsection (3), they shall, as soon as practicable after doing so, provide that person with an opportunity of—

    (a) making representations about the effect of the direction; and

    (b) proposing steps for remedying the situation.

(8) If OFCOM consider it appropriate to do so (whether in consequence of any representations or proposals made to them under subsection (3) or otherwise), they may, without revoking it, at any time modify the terms of a direction under subsection (3) in such manner as they consider appropriate.

(9) If the Secretary of State considers it appropriate to do so, he may, by a direction to OFCOM,

require them to revoke a direction under subsection (3).

(10) Where OFCOM modify or revoke a direction they have given under subsection (3), they may do so—

(a) with effect from such time as they may direct;

(b) subject to compliance with such requirements as they may specify; and

(c) to such extent and in relation to such networks, services or facilities, or parts of a network, service or facility, as they may determine.

(11) It shall be the duty of OFCOM to comply with—

(a) a requirement under subsection (9) to revoke a direction; and

(b) a requirement contained in that direction as to how they should exercise their powers under subsection (10) in the case of the required revocation.

Commencement Information

I196. S. 132 in force at 25.7.2003 for specified purposes by S.I. 2003/1900, arts. 1. (2), 2. (1), Sch. 1 (with art. 3) (as amended by S.I. 2003/3142, art. 1. (3))

I197. S. 132 in force at 29.12.2003 in so far as not already in force by S.I. 2003/3142, art. 3. (2) (with art. 11)

133. Enforcement of directions under s. 132.

(1) A person is guilty of an offence if he provides an electronic communications network or electronic communications service, or makes available any associated facility—

(a) while his entitlement to do so is suspended by a direction under section 132; or

(b) in contravention of a restriction contained in such a direction.

(2) A person guilty of an offence under subsection (1) shall be liable—

(a) on summary conviction, to a fine not exceeding the statutory maximum;

(b) on conviction on indictment, to a fine.

(3) The duty of a person to comply with a condition of a direction under section 132 shall be a duty owed to every person who may be affected by a contravention of the condition.

(4) Where a duty is owed by virtue of subsection (3) to a person—

(a) a breach of the duty that causes that person to sustain loss or damage, and

(b) an act which—

(i) by inducing a breach of the duty or interfering with its performance, causes that person to sustain loss or damage, and

(ii) is done wholly or partly for achieving that result,

shall be actionable at the suit or instance of that person.

(5) In proceedings brought against a person by virtue of subsection (4)(a) it shall be a defence for that person to show that he took all reasonable steps and exercised all due diligence to avoid contravening the condition in question.

(6) Sections [F20196. A] to 99 apply in relation to a contravention of conditions imposed by a direction under section 132 as they apply in relation to a contravention of conditions set under section 45 [F202, other than SMP apparatus conditions] .

Amendments (Textual)

F201. Word in s. 133. (6) substituted (26.5.2011) by The Electronic Communications and Wireless Telegraphy Regulations 2011 (S.I. 2011/1210), reg. 1. (2), Sch. 1 para. 78 (with Sch. 3 paras. 2, 17)

F202. Words in s. 133. (6) inserted (26.5.2011) by The Electronic Communications and Wireless Telegraphy Regulations 2011 (S.I. 2011/1210), reg. 1. (2), Sch. 1 para. 78 (with Sch. 3 paras. 2, 17)

Commencement Information

I198. S. 133 in force at 25.7.2003 for specified purposes by S.I. 2003/1900, arts. 1. (2), 2. (1), Sch. 1 (with art. 3) (as amended by S.I. 2003/3142, art. 1. (3))

I199. S. 133 in force at 29.12.2003 in so far as not already in force by S.I. 2003/3142, art. 3. (2) (with art. 11)

Restrictions in leases and licences

134. Restrictions in leases and licences

(1) This section applies where provision contained in a lease, licence or other agreement relating to premises has the effect of imposing on the occupier a prohibition or restriction under which his choice of—

(a) the person from whom he obtains electronic communications services, or particular electronic communications services, or

(b) the person through whom he arranges to be provided with electronic communications services, or particular electronic communications services,

is confined to a person with an interest in the premises, to a person selected by a person with such an interest or to persons who are one or the other.

(2) This section also applies where—

(a) provision contained in a lease for a year or more has the effect of imposing any other prohibition or restriction on the lessee with respect to an electronic communications matter; or

(b) provision contained in an agreement relating to premises to which a lease for a year or more applies has the effect of imposing a prohibition or restriction on the lessee with respect to such a matter.

(3) A provision falling within subsection (1) shall have effect—

(a) as if the prohibition or restriction applied only where the lessor, licensor or other party to the agreement has not given his consent to a departure from the requirements imposed by the prohibition or restriction; and

(b) as if the lessor, licensor or other party were required not to withhold that consent unreasonably.

(4) A provision falling within subsection (2)(a) or (b) shall have effect—

(a) in relation to things done inside a building occupied by the lessee under the lease, or

(b) for purposes connected with the provision to the lessee of an electronic communications service,

as if the prohibition or restriction applied only where the lessor has not given his consent in relation to the matter in question and as if the lessor were required not to withhold that consent unreasonably.

(5) Where (whether by virtue of this section or otherwise) a provision falling within subsection (1) or (2) imposes a requirement on a lessor, licensor or party to an agreement not unreasonably to withhold his consent—

(a) in relation to an electronic communications matter, or

(b) to the obtaining by the occupier of premises of an electronic communications service from or through a particular person,

the question whether the consent is unreasonably withheld has to be determined having regard to all the circumstances and to the principle that no person should unreasonably be denied access to an electronic communications network or to electronic communications services.

(6) OFCOM may by order provide for this section not to apply in the case of such provisions as may be described in the order.

(7) References in this section to electronic communications matters are references to—

(a) the provision of an electronic communications network or electronic communications service;

(b) the connection of electronic communications apparatus to a relevant electronic communications network or of any such network to another; and

(c) the installation, maintenance, adjustment, repair, alteration or use for purposes connected with the provision of such a network or service of electronic communications apparatus.

(8) In this section—

"alteration" has the same meaning as in the electronic communications code;

"lease" includes—

- a leasehold tenancy (whether in the nature of a head lease, sub-lease or under lease) and an agreement to grant such a tenancy, and

- in Scotland, a sub-lease and an agreement to grant a sub-lease,

and "lessor" and "lessee" are to be construed accordingly;

"relevant electronic communications network" means—

- a public electronic communications network that is specified for the purposes of this section in an order made by the Secretary of State; or

- an electronic communications network that is, or is to be, connected (directly or indirectly) to such a network.

(9) This section applies to provisions contained in leases, licences or agreements granted or entered into before the commencement of this section to the extent only that provision to that effect is contained in an order made by OFCOM.

(10) This section is not to be construed as affecting the operation of paragraph 2. (3) of the electronic communications code (lessees etc. bound by rights granted under code by owners).

(11) The consent of the Secretary of State is required for the making by OFCOM of an order under this section.

(12) Section 403 applies to the powers of OFCOM to make orders under this section.

(13) A statutory instrument containing an order made by OFCOM under this section shall be subject to annulment in pursuance of a resolution of either House of Parliament.

Commencement Information

I200. S. 134 in force at 25.7.2003 for specified purposes by S.I. 2003/1900, arts. 1. (2), 2. (1), Sch. 1 (with art. 3) (as amended by S.I. 2003/3142, art. 1. (3))

I201. S. 134 in force at 29.12.2003 in so far as not already in force by S.I. 2003/3142, art. 3. (2) (with art. 11)

[F203. Reports on infrastructure etc

Amendments (Textual)

F203. Ss. 134. A-134. C and cross-headings inserted (8.6.2010) by Digital Economy Act 2010 (c. 24), ss. 1. (1), 47. (1)

134. A OFCOM reports on infrastructure etc

(1) OFCOM must prepare reports in accordance with subsections (2) and (3) and each report must deal with—

(a) the electronic communications networks matters listed in section 134. B(1), and

(b) the electronic communications services matters listed in section 134. B(2).

(2) The first report must—

(a) relate to the position on a day specified in the report which falls within the period of 12 months beginning with the day on which this section comes into force, and

(b) be sent to the Secretary of State by OFCOM not more than 2 months after the specified day.

(3) A further report must—

(a) be prepared for each relevant period, and

(b) be sent to the Secretary of State by OFCOM as soon as practicable after the end of the relevant period.

(4) "Relevant period" means—

(a) the period of 3 years beginning with the day specified in the first report, and

(b) each subsequent period of 3 years beginning with the end of the previous period.

(5) Where there is a significant change in connection with a matter listed in section 134. B(1) or (2) and OFCOM consider that the change should be brought to the attention of the Secretary of State, OFCOM must—

(a) prepare a report on the change, and

(b) send it to the Secretary of State as soon as practicable.

(6) For the purposes of subsection (5), a change is significant if OFCOM consider that it has, or is

likely to have, a significant adverse impact on—

(a) persons carrying on business in the United Kingdom or a part of the United Kingdom, or

(b) the general public in the United Kingdom or a part of the United Kingdom.

(7) OFCOM must publish every report under this section—

(a) as soon as practicable after they send it to the Secretary of State, and

(b) in such manner as they consider appropriate for bringing it to the attention of persons who, in their opinion, are likely to have an interest in it.

(8) OFCOM may exclude information from a report when it is published under subsection (7) if they consider that it is information that they could refuse to disclose in response to a request under the Freedom of Information Act 2000.

134. BNetworks and services matters

(1) For the purposes of section 134. A, the electronic communications networks matters are—

(a) the different types of electronic communications network provided in the United Kingdom ("UK networks"),

(b) the geographic coverage of the different UK networks,

(c) the proportion of the population covered by the different UK networks,

(d) the extent to which UK networks share infrastructure,

(e) the capacity of the different UK networks,

(f) the extent to which the providers of the different UK networks allow other communications providers to use their networks to provide services,

(g) the amount of time for which the different UK networks are and are not available, including the steps that have been or are to be taken to maintain or improve the level of availability,

(h) the preparations made by providers of UK networks for responding to an emergency, including preparations for restoring normal operation of UK networks disrupted by the emergency, and

(i) the standard of the different UK networks in comparison with electronic communications networks provided in a range of other countries, having regard, in particular, to their coverage and capacity.

(2) For the purposes of section 134. A, the electronic communications services matters are—

(a) the use of the electromagnetic spectrum for wireless telegraphy in the United Kingdom,

(b) the different types of electronic communications service provided in the United Kingdom ("UK services"),

(c) the geographic coverage of the different UK services,

(d) the proportion of the population covered by the different UK services,

(e) the amount of time for which the different UK services are and are not available, including the steps that have been or are to be taken to maintain or improve the level of availability,

(f) the preparations made by providers of UK services for responding to an emergency, including preparations for restoring normal operation of UK services disrupted by the emergency, and

(g) the standard of the different UK services in comparison with electronic communications services provided in a range of other countries.

(3) The preparations referred to in subsections (1)(h) and (2)(f) include—

(a) the steps taken to assess the risks of different types of emergency occurring,

(b) the steps taken to reduce or remove those risks, and

(c) the testing of proposed responses to different types of emergency.

(4) In a report under section 134. A, OFCOM are required to include only information about, and analysis of, such networks, services and providers as they consider appropriate.

(5) In this section "emergency" means an event or situation that seriously disrupts a UK network or UK service.

Reports on internet domain names

134. C OFCOM reports on internet domain names

(1) OFCOM must, if requested to do so by the Secretary of State—

(a) prepare a report on matters specified by the Secretary of State relating to internet domain names, and

(b) send the report to the Secretary of State as soon as practicable.

(2) The specified matters may, in particular, include matters relating to—

(a) the allocation and registration of internet domain names, and

(b) the misuse of internet domain names.

(3) OFCOM must publish every report under this section—

(a) as soon as practicable after they send it to the Secretary of State, and

(b) in such manner as they consider appropriate for bringing it to the attention of persons who, in their opinion, are likely to have an interest in it.

(4) OFCOM may exclude information from a report when it is published under subsection (3) if they consider that it is information that they could refuse to disclose in response to a request under the Freedom of Information Act 2000.]

Information provisions

135. Information required for purposes of Chapter 1 functions

(1) OFCOM may require a person falling within subsection (2) to provide them with all such information as they consider necessary for the purpose of carrying out their functions under this Chapter.

(2) The persons falling within this subsection are—

(a) a communications provider;

(b) a person who has been a communications provider;

(c) a person who makes, or has made, any associated facilities available to others;

(d) a person, other than a communications provider, to whom a universal service condition applies or has applied;

(e) a person who supplies electronic communications apparatus;

(f) a person not falling within the preceding paragraphs who appears to OFCOM to have information required by them for the purpose of carrying out their functions under this Chapter.

(3) The information that may be required by OFCOM under subsection (1) includes, in particular, information that they require for any one or more of the following purposes—

(a) ascertaining whether a contravention of a condition or other requirement set or imposed by or under this Chapter has occurred or is occurring;

(b) ascertaining or verifying the charges payable by a person under section 38;

(c) ascertaining whether a provision of a condition set under section 45 which is for the time being in force continues to be effective for the purpose for which it was made;

(d) ascertaining or verifying amounts payable by virtue of a condition falling within section 51. (1)(d);

(e) making a designation in accordance with regulations made under section 66;

(f) carrying out a review under section 66 or 70;

(g) identifying markets and carrying out market analyses in accordance with, or for the purposes of, any provision of this Chapter;

F204. (h). . . . .

(i) considering a matter in exercise of that duty;

[F205. (ia)preparing a report under section 124. F;

(ib) carrying out an assessment, taking steps or providing a report under section 124. G;]

[F206. (ic)preparing a report under section 134. A;

(id) preparing a report under section 134. C;]

[F207. (ie)assessing the security of a public electronic communications network or a public electronic communications service;

(if) assessing the availability of a public electronic communications network;

(ig) identifying electronic communications apparatus that is suitable for shared use;]

(j) statistical purposes connected with the carrying out of any of OFCOM's functions under this Chapter.

[F208. (3. A)The descriptions of information that a person may be required to provide under subsection (1) include, in particular—

(a) information concerning future developments of an electronic communications network or electronic communications service that could have an impact on the wholesale services made available by the person to competitors, and

(b) if a market power determination made in relation to a wholesale market is in force in the person's case, accounting data relating to any retail market associated with the wholesale market.]

(4) A person required to provide information under this section must provide it in such manner and within such reasonable period as may be specified by OFCOM.

(5) The powers in this section are subject to the limitations in section 137.

Amendments (Textual)

F204. S. 135. (3)(h) omitted (26.5.2011) by virtue of The Electronic Communications and Wireless Telegraphy Regulations 2011 (S.I. 2011/1210), reg. 1. (2), Sch. 1 para. 79. (a)(i) (with Sch. 3 para. 2)

F205. S. 135. (3)(ia)(ib) inserted (8.6.2010) by Digital Economy Act 2010 (c. 24), ss. 16. (2), 47. (1)

F206. S. 135. (3)(ic)(id) inserted (8.6.2010) by Digital Economy Act 2010 (c. 24), ss. 1. (2), 47. (1)

F207. S. 135. (3)(ie)-(ig) inserted (26.5.2011) by The Electronic Communications and Wireless Telegraphy Regulations 2011 (S.I. 2011/1210), reg. 1. (2), Sch. 1 para. 79. (a)(ii) (with Sch. 3 para. 2)

F208. S. 135. (3. A) inserted (26.5.2011) by The Electronic Communications and Wireless Telegraphy Regulations 2011 (S.I. 2011/1210), reg. 1. (2), Sch. 1 para. 79. (b) (with Sch. 3 para. 2)

Commencement Information

I202. S. 135 in force at 25.7.2003 for specified purposes by S.I. 2003/1900, arts. 1. (2), 2. (1), Sch. 1 (with art. 3) (as amended by S.I. 2003/3142, art. 1. (3))

I203. S. 135 in force at 29.12.2003 in so far as not already in force by S.I. 2003/3142, art. 3. (2) (with art. 11)

136. Information required for related purposes

(1) OFCOM may require—

(a) a communications provider, or

(b) a person who makes associated facilities available to others,

to provide OFCOM with all such information as they consider necessary for the purpose specified in subsection (2).

(2) That purpose is the carrying out—

(a) with a view to publication, and

(b) in the interest of the end-users of public electronic communications services,

of comparative overviews of the quality and prices of such services.

(3) OFCOM may also require—

(a) a communications provider, or

(b) a person who makes associated facilities available to others,

to provide them, for use for such statistical purposes as they think fit, with information relating to any electronic communications network, electronic communications service or associated facilities.

(4) A person required to provide information under this section must provide it in such manner and within such reasonable period as may be specified by OFCOM.

(5) The powers in this section are subject to the limitations in section 137.

Commencement Information

I204. S. 136 in force at 25.7.2003 for specified purposes by S.I. 2003/1900, arts. 1. (2), 2. (1), Sch. 1 (with art. 3) (as amended by S.I. 2003/3142, art. 1. (3))

I205. S. 136 in force at 29.12.2003 in so far as not already in force by S.I. 2003/3142, art. 3. (2) (with art. 11)

137. Restrictions on imposing information requirements

(1) This section limits the purposes for which, and manner in which, information may be required under sections 135 and 136.

(2) OFCOM are not to require the provision of information for the purpose of ascertaining whether a contravention of a general condition has occurred, or is occurring, unless—

(a) the requirement is imposed for the purpose of investigating a matter about which OFCOM have received a complaint;

(b) the requirement is imposed for the purposes of an investigation that OFCOM have decided to carry out into whether or not the general condition in question has been complied with;

(c) the condition in question is one which OFCOM have reason to suspect is one that has been or is being contravened; F209...

(d) the condition in question is one falling within section 51. (1)(d)[F210; or

(e) the condition in question is one relating to the effective and efficient use of telephone numbers.]

[F211. (2. A)OFCOM are not to require the provision of information for a purpose specified in section 135. (3)(ie) or (if) unless—

(a) the requirement is imposed for the purpose of investigating a matter about which OFCOM have received a complaint;

(b) the requirement is imposed for the purposes of an investigation that OFCOM have decided to carry out into whether or not an obligation under section 105. A has been complied with; or

(c) OFCOM have reason to suspect that an obligation under section 105. A has been or is being contravened.]

(3) OFCOM are not to require the provision of information under section 135 or 136 except—

(a) by a demand for the information that describes the required information and sets out OFCOM's reasons for requiring it; and

(b) where the making of a demand for the information is proportionate to the use to which the information is to be put in the carrying out of OFCOM's functions.

(4) The reasons for requiring information for statistical purposes under section 135 or 136 must set out the statistical purposes for which the information is required.

(5) Except in the case of a demand made in the manner authorised by subsection (6), a demand for information required under section 135 or 136 must be contained in a notice served on the person from whom the information is required.

(6) In the case of information required by OFCOM for the purpose of ascertaining who is liable to charges under section 38, the demand may—

(a) be made by being published in such manner as OFCOM consider appropriate for bringing it to the attention of the persons who are described in the demand as the persons from whom the information is required; and

(b) take the form of a general demand for a person so described to provide information when specified conditions relevant to his liability to such charges are satisfied in his case.

Amendments (Textual)

F209. Word in s. 137. (2)(c) omitted (26.5.2011) by virtue of The Electronic Communications and Wireless Telegraphy Regulations 2011 (S.I. 2011/1210), reg. 1. (2), Sch. 1 para. 80. (a)(i) (with Sch. 3 para. 2)

F210. S. 137. (2)(e) and word inserted (26.5.2011) by The Electronic Communications and Wireless Telegraphy Regulations 2011 (S.I. 2011/1210), reg. 1. (2), Sch. 1 para. 80. (a)(ii) (with Sch. 3 para. 2)

F211. S. 137. (2. A) inserted (26.5.2011) by The Electronic Communications and Wireless Telegraphy Regulations 2011 (S.I. 2011/1210), reg. 1. (2), Sch. 1 para. 80. (b) (with Sch. 3 para. 2)

Commencement Information

I206. S. 137 in force at 25.7.2003 for specified purposes by S.I. 2003/1900, arts. 1. (2), 2. (1), Sch. 1 (with art. 3) (as amended by S.I. 2003/3142, art. 1. (3))

I207. S. 137 in force at 29.12.2003 in so far as not already in force by S.I. 2003/3142, art. 3. (2) (with art. 11)

138. Notification of contravention of information requirements

(1) Where OFCOM determine that there are reasonable grounds for believing that a person is contravening, or has contravened, a requirement imposed under section 135 or 136, they may give that person a notification under this section.

(2) A notification under this section is one which—

(a) sets out the determination made by OFCOM;

(b) specifies the requirement and contravention in respect of which that determination has been made; F212...

[F213. (c)specifies the period during which the person notified has an opportunity to make representations;

(d) specifies the information to be provided by the person to OFCOM in order to comply with a requirement under section 135 or 136;

(e) specifies any penalty which OFCOM are minded to impose in accordance with section 139; and

(f) where the contravention is serious, specifies any direction which OFCOM are minded to give under section 140.]

F214. (3). . . . .

F214. (4). . . . .

F214. (5). . . . .

F214. (6). . . . .

F214. (7). . . . .

(8) A notification under this section—

(a) may be given in respect of more than one contravention; and

(b) if it is given in respect of a continuing contravention, may be given in respect of any period during which the contravention has continued.

(9) Where a notification under this section has been given to a person in respect of a contravention of a requirement, OFCOM may give a further notification in respect of the same contravention of that requirement if, and only if—

(a) the contravention is one occurring after the time of the giving of the earlier notification;

(b) the contravention is a continuing contravention and the subsequent notification is in respect of so much of a period as falls after a period to which the earlier notification relates; or

(c) the earlier notification has been withdrawn without a penalty having been imposed in respect of the notified contravention.

[F215. (9. A)OFCOM may not give a person a notification under this section in respect of a contravention of a requirement imposed under section 135. (3)(ig) if the information required was previously provided by the person to OFCOM within the period of 6 months ending with the day on which the requirement was imposed.]

F216. (10). . . . .

Amendments (Textual)

F212. Word in s. 138. (2)(b) omitted (26.5.2011) by virtue of The Electronic Communications and Wireless Telegraphy Regulations 2011 (S.I. 2011/1210), reg. 1. (2), Sch. 1 para. 81. (a) (with Sch. 3 paras. 2, 18)

F213. S. 138. (2)(c)-(f) substituted for s. 138. (2)(c) (26.5.2011) by The Electronic Communications and Wireless Telegraphy Regulations 2011 (S.I. 2011/1210), reg. 1. (2), Sch. 1 para. 81. (a) (with Sch. 3 paras. 2, 18)

F214. S. 138. (3)-(7) omitted (26.5.2011) by virtue of The Electronic Communications and Wireless Telegraphy Regulations 2011 (S.I. 2011/1210), reg. 1. (2), Sch. 1 para. 81. (b) (with Sch. 3 paras. 2, 18)

F215. S. 138. (9. A) inserted (26.5.2011) by The Electronic Communications and Wireless Telegraphy Regulations 2011 (S.I. 2011/1210), reg. 1. (2), Sch. 1 para. 81. (c) (with Sch. 3 paras. 2, 18)

F216. S. 138. (10) omitted (26.5.2011) by virtue of The Electronic Communications and Wireless Telegraphy Regulations 2011 (S.I. 2011/1210), reg. 1. (2), Sch. 1 para. 81. (b) (with Sch. 3 paras. 2, 18)

Modifications etc. (not altering text)

C4. Ss. 138-139. A applied (with modifications) (31.7.2016) by The Communications (Access to Infrastructure) Regulations 2016 (S.I. 2016/700), regs. 1, 17. (6), (7)

Commencement Information

I208. S. 138 in force at 25.7.2003 for specified purposes by S.I. 2003/1900, arts. 1. (2), 2. (1), Sch. 1 (with art. 3) (as amended by S.I. 2003/3142, art. 1. (3))

I209. S. 138 in force at 29.12.2003 in so far as not already in force by S.I. 2003/3142, art. 3. (2) (with art. 11)

139. Penalties for contravention of information requirements

[F217. (1)This section applies where a person is given a notification under section 138 which specifies a proposed penalty.]

(2) OFCOM may [F218specify a penalty] if—

    F219. (a)...............................

    F219. (b)...............................

    (c) no proceedings for an offence under section 144 have been brought against the notified person in respect of the contravention.

(3) Where a notification under section 138 relates to more than one contravention, a separate penalty may be [F220specified] in respect of each contravention.

(4) Where such a notification relates to a continuing contravention, no more than one penalty may be [F221specified] in respect of the period of contravention specified in the notification.

[F222. (4. A)But, in relation to a continuing contravention, a penalty may be specified in respect of each day on which the contravention continues after—

    (a) the giving of a confirmation decision under section 139. A(4)(c) which requires immediate action; or

    (b) the expiry of any period specified in the confirmation decision for complying with a requirement so specified.

(4. B)The amount of a penalty under subsection (4. A) is to be such amount not exceeding £500 per day as OFCOM determine to be—

    (a) appropriate; and

    (b) proportionate to the contravention in respect of which it is imposed.]

(5) The amount of [F223any other penalty notified] under this section is to be such amount not exceeding [F224£2,000,000] as OFCOM determine to be both—

    (a) appropriate; and

    (b) proportionate to the contravention in respect of which it is imposed.

F225. (6)...............................

F225. (7)...............................

F225. (8)...............................

(9) The Secretary of State may by order amend this section so as to substitute a different maximum penalty for the maximum penalty for the time being specified in subsection (5).

(10) No order is to be made containing provision authorised by subsection (9) unless a draft of the order has been laid before Parliament and approved by a resolution of each House.

Amendments (Textual)

F217. S. 139. (1) substituted (26.5.2011) by The Electronic Communications and Wireless Telegraphy Regulations 2011 (S.I. 2011/1210), reg. 1. (2), Sch. 1 para. 82. (a) (with Sch. 3 paras. 2, 18)

F218. Words in s. 139. (2) substituted (26.5.2011) by The Electronic Communications and Wireless Telegraphy Regulations 2011 (S.I. 2011/1210), reg. 1. (2), Sch. 1 para. 82. (b) (with Sch.

3 paras. 2, 18)

F219. S. 139. (2)(a)(b) omitted (26.5.2011) by virtue of The Electronic Communications and Wireless Telegraphy Regulations 2011 (S.I. 2011/1210), reg. 1. (2), Sch. 1 para. 82. (c) (with Sch. 3 paras. 2, 18)

F220. Word in s. 139. (3) substituted (26.5.2011) by The Electronic Communications and Wireless Telegraphy Regulations 2011 (S.I. 2011/1210), reg. 1. (2), Sch. 1 para. 82. (d) (with Sch. 3 paras. 2, 18)

F221. Word in s. 139. (4) substituted (26.5.2011) by The Electronic Communications and Wireless Telegraphy Regulations 2011 (S.I. 2011/1210), reg. 1. (2), Sch. 1 para. 82. (d) (with Sch. 3 paras. 2, 18)

F222. S. 139. (4. A)(4. B) inserted (26.5.2011) by The Electronic Communications and Wireless Telegraphy Regulations 2011 (S.I. 2011/1210), reg. 1. (2), Sch. 1 para. 82. (e) (with Sch. 3 paras. 2, 18)

F223. Words in s. 139. (5) substituted (26.5.2011) by The Electronic Communications and Wireless Telegraphy Regulations 2011 (S.I. 2011/1210), reg. 1. (2), Sch. 1 para. 82. (f) (with Sch. 3 paras. 2, 18)

F224. Word in s. 139. (5) substituted (13.7.2011) by The Communications Act 2003 (Maximum Penalty for Contravention of Information Requirements) Order 2011 (S.I. 2011/1773), arts. 1, 2. (1) (with art. 2. (2))

F225. S. 139. (6)-(8) omitted (26.5.2011) by virtue of The Electronic Communications and Wireless Telegraphy Regulations 2011 (S.I. 2011/1210), reg. 1. (2), Sch. 1 para. 82. (g) (with Sch. 3 paras. 2, 18)

Modifications etc. (not altering text)

C4. Ss. 138-139. A applied (with modifications) (31.7.2016) by The Communications (Access to Infrastructure) Regulations 2016 (S.I. 2016/700), regs. 1, 17. (6), (7)

Commencement Information

I210. S. 139 in force at 25.7.2003 for specified purposes by S.I. 2003/1900, arts. 1. (2), 2. (1), Sch. 1 (with art. 3) (as amended by S.I. 2003/3142, art. 1. (3))

I211. S. 139 in force at 29.12.2003 in so far as not already in force by S.I. 2003/3142, art. 3. (2) (with art. 11)

[F226139. A.Enforcement of notification under section 138.

(1) This section applies where—

   (a) a person has been given a notification under section 138;

   (b) OFCOM have allowed the person an opportunity to make representations about the matters notified; and

   (c) the period allowed for the making of representations has expired.

(2) OFCOM may—

   (a) give the person a decision (a "confirmation decision") confirming the imposition of requirements on the person, or the giving of a direction to the person, or both, in accordance with the notification under section 138; or

   (b) inform the person that they are satisfied with the person's representations and that no further action will be taken.

(3) OFCOM may not give a confirmation decision to a person unless, after considering any representations, they are satisfied that the person has, in one or more of the respects notified, been in contravention of a requirement notified under section 138.

(4) A confirmation decision—

   (a) must be given to the person without delay;

   (b) must include reasons for the decision;

   (c) may require immediate action by the person to comply with a requirement notified under section 138. (2)(d), or may specify a period within which the person must comply with the requirement; and

   (d) may require the person to pay—

(i) the penalty specified in the notification under section 138, or

158

(ii) such lesser penalty as OFCOM consider appropriate in the light of the person's representations or steps taken by the person to comply with the condition or remedy the consequences of the contravention,

and may specify the period within which the penalty is to be paid.

(5) It is the duty of the person to comply with any requirement imposed by a confirmation decision.

(6) That duty is enforceable in civil proceedings by OFCOM—

(a) for an injunction;

(b) for specific performance of a statutory duty under section 45 of the Court of Session Act 1988; or

(c) for any other appropriate remedy or relief.

(7) A penalty imposed by a confirmation decision—

(a) must be paid to OFCOM; and

(b) if not paid within the period specified by them, is to be recoverable by them accordingly.

Amendments (Textual)

F226. Ss. 139. A-139. C inserted (26.5.2011) by The Electronic Communications and Wireless Telegraphy Regulations 2011 (S.I. 2011/1210), reg. 1. (2), Sch. 1 para. 83 (with Sch. 3 paras. 2, 18)

Modifications etc. (not altering text)

C4. Ss. 138-139. A applied (with modifications) (31.7.2016) by The Communications (Access to Infrastructure) Regulations 2016 (S.I. 2016/700), regs. 1, 17. (6), (7)

139. B.Power to deal with urgent cases

(1) This section applies where OFCOM determine—

(a) that they are entitled to give a notification under section 138 with respect to a contravention by a person ("P") of a requirement imposed under section 135 or 136;

(b) that there are reasonable grounds for suspecting that the case is an urgent case; and

(c) that the urgency of the case makes it appropriate for OFCOM to take action under this section.

(2) A case is an urgent case for the purposes of this section if the contravention has resulted in, or creates an immediate risk of—

(a) a serious threat to the safety of the public, to public health or to national security;

(b) serious economic or operational problems for persons (other than P) who are communications providers or persons who make associated facilities available; or

(c) serious economic or operational problems for persons who make use of electronic communications networks, electronic communications services or associated facilities.

(3) OFCOM may give P a direction—

(a) that the entitlement of P to provide electronic communications networks or electronic communications services, or to make associated facilities available, is suspended (either generally or in relation to particular networks, services or facilities); or

(b) that that entitlement is restricted in the respects set out in the direction.

(4) Subsections (3) to (6) of section 140 apply in relation to a direction under subsection (3) as they apply in relation to a direction under section 140.

Amendments (Textual)

F226. Ss. 139. A-139. C inserted (26.5.2011) by The Electronic Communications and Wireless Telegraphy Regulations 2011 (S.I. 2011/1210), reg. 1. (2), Sch. 1 para. 83 (with Sch. 3 paras. 2, 18)

139. C.Confirmation of direction under section 139. B

(1) As soon as reasonably practicable after giving a direction under section 139. B(3), OFCOM must give the person to whom it is given—

(a) an opportunity to make representations to them about the grounds on which it was given and its effect; and

(b) an opportunity to propose steps to remedy the situation.

(2) As soon as practicable after the period allowed by OFCOM for making those representations

has ended (and in any event within 3 months beginning with the day on which the direction was given), they must determine—

(a) whether the contravention providing the grounds for the giving of the direction did occur; and

(b) whether the circumstances made it an urgent case justifying the giving of the direction.

(3) The period of 3 months mentioned in subsection (2) may be extended by up to 3 months if OFCOM—

(a) require additional time to consider representations received; or

(b) decide that it is necessary to obtain additional information from the person in order to make a determination under subsection (2).

(4) If OFCOM decide that the contravention did occur and that the direction was justified, they may confirm the direction.

(5) If not, they must exercise their power to revoke it.

(6) As soon as reasonably practicable after deciding whether to confirm the direction, OFCOM must notify the person to whom it was given of their decision.]

Amendments (Textual)

F226. Ss. 139. A-139. C inserted (26.5.2011) by The Electronic Communications and Wireless Telegraphy Regulations 2011 (S.I. 2011/1210), reg. 1. (2), Sch. 1 para. 83 (with Sch. 3 paras. 2, 18)

140. Suspending service provision for information contraventions

(1) OFCOM may give a direction under this section to a person who is a communications provider or who makes associated facilities available ("the contravening provider") if they are satisfied—

(a) that he is or has been in [F227serious or repeated] contravention of requirements imposed under sections 135 and 136, or either of them;

(b) the requirements are not requirements imposed for purposes connected with the carrying out of OFCOM's functions in relation to SMP apparatus conditions;

(c) [F228in the case of a repeated contravention,] that an attempt, by the imposition of penalties [F229or the giving of notifications under section 138 and confirmation decisions under section 139. A, or both,] or the bringing of proceedings for an offence under section 144, to secure compliance with the contravened requirements has failed; and

[F230. (d)that the giving of the direction is appropriate and proportionate to the contravention in respect of which it is given.]

(2) A direction under this section is—

(a) a direction that the entitlement of the contravening provider to provide electronic communications networks or electronic communications services, or to make associated facilities available, is suspended (either generally or in relation to particular networks, services or facilities); or

(b) a direction that that entitlement is restricted in the respects set out in the direction.

(3) A direction under this section—

(a) must specify the networks, services and facilities to which it relates; and

(b) except so far as it otherwise provides, takes effect for an indefinite period beginning with the time at which it is notified to the person to whom it is given.

(4) A direction under this section—

(a) in providing for the effect of a suspension or restriction to be postponed, may provide for it to take effect only at a time determined by or in accordance with the terms of the direction; and

(b) in connection with the suspension or restriction contained in the direction or with the postponement of its effect, may impose such conditions on the contravening provider as appear to OFCOM to be appropriate for the purpose of protecting that provider's customers.

(5) Those conditions may include a condition requiring the making of payments—

(a) by way of compensation for loss or damage suffered by the contravening provider's customers as a result of the direction; or

(b) in respect of annoyance, inconvenience or anxiety to which they have been put in consequence of the direction.

(6) If OFCOM consider it appropriate to do so (whether or not in consequence of any representations or proposals made to them), they may revoke a direction under this section or modify its conditions—

(a) with effect from such time as they may direct;

(b) subject to compliance with such requirements as they may specify; and

(c) to such extent and in relation to such networks, services or facilities, or parts of a network, service or facility, as they may determine.

(7) For the purposes of this section there are repeated contraventions by a person of requirements imposed under sections 135 and 136, or either of them, to the extent that—

[F231. (a)in the case of a previous notification of a contravention given to that person under section 138, OFCOM have given a confirmation decision to that person under section 139. A(2) in respect of the contravention; and

(b) in the period of 24 months following the giving of that confirmation decision, one or more further confirmation decisions have been given to the person in respect of contraventions of numbering conditions;]

and for the purposes of this subsection it shall be immaterial whether the notifications related to the same contravention or to different contraventions of the same or different requirements or of requirements under different sections.

Amendments (Textual)

F227. Words in s. 140. (1)(a) substituted (26.5.2011) by The Electronic Communications and Wireless Telegraphy Regulations 2011 (S.I. 2011/1210), reg. 1. (2), Sch. 1 para. 84. (a)(i) (with Sch. 3 paras. 2, 18, 19)

F228. Words in s. 140. (1)(c) inserted (26.5.2011) by The Electronic Communications and Wireless Telegraphy Regulations 2011 (S.I. 2011/1210), reg. 1. (2), Sch. 1 para. 84. (a)(ii) (with Sch. 3 paras. 2, 18, 19)

F229. Words in s. 140. (1)(c) substituted (26.5.2011) by The Electronic Communications and Wireless Telegraphy Regulations 2011 (S.I. 2011/1210), reg. 1. (2), Sch. 1 para. 84. (a)(ii) (with Sch. 3 paras. 2, 18, 19)

F230. S. 140. (1)(d) substituted (26.5.2011) by The Electronic Communications and Wireless Telegraphy Regulations 2011 (S.I. 2011/1210), reg. 1. (2), Sch. 1 para. 84. (a)(iii) (with Sch. 3 paras. 2, 18, 19)

F231. S. 140. (7)(a)(b) substituted (26.5.2011) by The Electronic Communications and Wireless Telegraphy Regulations 2011 (S.I. 2011/1210), reg. 1. (2), Sch. 1 para. 84. (b) (with Sch. 3 paras. 2, 18, 19)

Commencement Information

I212. S. 140 in force at 25.7.2003 for specified purposes by S.I. 2003/1900, arts. 1. (2), 2. (1), Sch. 1 (with art. 3) (as amended by S.I. 2003/3142, art. 1. (3))

I213. S. 140 in force at 29.12.2003 in so far as not already in force by S.I. 2003/3142, art. 3. (2) (with art. 11)

141. Suspending apparatus supply for information contraventions

(1) OFCOM may give a direction under this section to a person who supplies electronic communications apparatus ("the contravening supplier") if they are satisfied—

(a) that he is or has been in serious and repeated contravention of requirements imposed under section 135;

(b) that an attempt, by the imposition of penalties under section 139 or the bringing of proceedings for an offence under section 144, to secure compliance with the contravened requirements has failed; and

(c) that the giving of the direction is appropriate and proportionate to the seriousness (when repeated as they have been) of the contraventions.

(2) A direction under this section is—

(a) a direction to the contravening supplier to cease to act as a supplier of electronic communications apparatus (either generally or in relation to apparatus of a particular description); or

(b) a direction imposing such restrictions as may be set out in the direction on the supply by that supplier of electronic communications apparatus (either generally or in relation to apparatus of a particular description).

(3) A direction under this section takes effect, except so far as it otherwise provides, for an indefinite period beginning with the time at which it is notified to the person to whom it is given.

(4) A direction under this section—

(a) may provide for a prohibition or restriction to take effect only at a time determined by or in accordance with the terms of the direction; and

(b) in connection with a prohibition or restriction contained in the direction or with the postponement of its effect, may impose such conditions on the contravening supplier as appear to OFCOM to be appropriate for the purpose of protecting that supplier's customers.

(5) Those conditions may include a condition requiring the making of payments—

(a) by way of compensation for loss or damage suffered by the contravening supplier's customers as a result of the direction; or

(b) in respect of annoyance, inconvenience or anxiety to which they have been put in consequence of the direction.

(6) If OFCOM consider it appropriate to do so (whether or not in consequence of representations or proposals made to them), they may revoke a direction under this section or modify its conditions—

(a) with effect from such time as they may direct;

(b) subject to compliance with such requirements as they may specify; and

(c) to such extent and in relation to such apparatus or descriptions of apparatus as they may determine.

(7) For the purposes of this section contraventions by a person of requirements imposed under section 135 are repeated contraventions if—

(a) in the case of a previous notification given to that person under section 138, OFCOM have determined for the purposes of section 139. (2) that such a contravention did occur; and

(b) in the period of twelve months following the day of the making of that determination, one or more further notifications have been given to that person in respect of contraventions of such requirements;

and for the purposes of this subsection it shall be immaterial whether the notifications related to the same contravention or to different contraventions of the same or different requirements.

Commencement Information

I214. S. 141 in force at 25.7.2003 for specified purposes by S.I. 2003/1900, arts. 1. (2), 2. (1), Sch. 1 (with art. 3) (as amended by S.I. 2003/3142, art. 1. (3))

I215. S. 141 in force at 29.12.2003 in so far as not already in force by S.I. 2003/3142, art. 3. (2) (with art. 11)

142. Procedure for directions under ss. 140 and 141.

(1) Except in an urgent case, [F232or a case where a proposed direction has been notified to a person in accordance with section 138. (2)(f)] OFCOM are not to give a direction under section 140 or 141 unless they have—

(a) notified the contravening provider or contravening supplier of the proposed direction and of the conditions (if any) which they are proposing to impose by that direction;

(b) provided him with an opportunity of making representations about the proposals and of proposing steps for remedying the situation; and

(c) considered every representation and proposal made to them during the period allowed by them for the contravening provider or the contravening supplier to take advantage of that opportunity.

[F233. (2. A)That period must be—

(a) in relation to a direction under section 140, such reasonable period as OFCOM may determine, and

(b) in relation to a direction under section 141, a period ending not less than one month after the day of the giving of the notification.]

(3) As soon as practicable after giving a direction under section 140 or 141 in an urgent case, OFCOM must provide the contravening provider or contravening supplier with an opportunity of—

(a) making representations about the effect of the direction and of any of its conditions; and

(b) proposing steps for remedying the situation.

[F234. (3. A)In relation to a direction under section 140 in an urgent case, as soon as practicable after the period allowed by OFCOM for making those representations has ended (and in any event within 3 months beginning with the day on which the direction was given), they must determine—

(a) whether the contravention providing the grounds for the giving of the direction did occur; and

(b) whether the circumstances made it an urgent case justifying the giving of the direction.

(3. B)The period of 3 months mentioned in subsection (3. A) may be extended by up to 3 months if OFCOM—

(a) require additional time to consider representations received; or

(b) decide that it is necessary to obtain additional information from the person in order to make a determination under subsection (3. A).]

(4) A case is an urgent case for the purposes of this section if OFCOM—

(a) consider that it would be inappropriate, because the contraventions in question fall within subsection (5), to allow time, before giving a direction under section 140 or 141, for the making and consideration of representations; and

(b) decide for that reason to act in accordance with subsection (3), instead of subsection (1).

(5) The contraventions fall within this subsection if they have resulted in, or create an immediate risk of—

(a) a serious threat to the safety of the public, to public health or to national security;

(b) serious economic or operational problems for persons (apart from the contravening provider or contravening supplier) who are communications providers or persons who make associated facilities available; or

(c) serious economic or operational problems for persons who make use of electronic communications networks, electronic communications services or associated facilities.

(6) In this section—

"contravening provider" has the same meaning as in section 140; and

"contravening supplier" has the same meaning as in section 141.

Amendments (Textual)

F232. Words in s. 142. (1) inserted (26.5.2011) by The Electronic Communications and Wireless Telegraphy Regulations 2011 (S.I. 2011/1210), reg. 1. (2), Sch. 1 para. 85. (a) (with Sch. 3 paras. 2, 18, 19)

F233. S. 142. (2. A) substituted for s. 142. (2) (26.5.2011) by The Electronic Communications and Wireless Telegraphy Regulations 2011 (S.I. 2011/1210), reg. 1. (2), Sch. 1 para. 85. (b) (with Sch. 3 paras. 2, 18, 19)

F234. S. 142. (3. A)(3. B) inserted (26.5.2011) by The Electronic Communications and Wireless Telegraphy Regulations 2011 (S.I. 2011/1210), reg. 1. (2), Sch. 1 para. 85. (c) (with Sch. 3 paras. 2, 18, 19)

Commencement Information

I216. S. 142 in force at 25.7.2003 for specified purposes by S.I. 2003/1900, arts. 1. (2), 2. (1), Sch. 1 (with art. 3) (as amended by S.I. 2003/3142, art. 1. (3))

I217. S. 142 in force at 29.12.2003 in so far as not already in force by S.I. 2003/3142, art. 3. (2) (with art. 11)

143. Enforcement of directions under ss. 140 and 141.

(1) A person is guilty of an offence if he provides an electronic communications network or electronic communications service, or makes available any associated facility—

(a) while his entitlement to do so is suspended by a direction under section 140; or

(b) in contravention of a restriction contained in such a direction.

(2) A person is guilty of an offence if he supplies electronic communications apparatus—

(a) while prohibited from doing so by a direction under section 141; or

(b) in contravention of a restriction contained in such a direction.

(3) A person guilty of an offence under this section shall be liable—

(a) on summary conviction, to a fine not exceeding the statutory maximum;

(b) on conviction on indictment, to a fine.

[F235. (4)Sections 96. A to 99 apply in relation to a contravention of conditions imposed by a direction under section 139. B or 140 as they apply in relation to a contravention of conditions set under section 45, other than SMP apparatus conditions.

(5) Sections 94 to 96 and 97 to 99 apply in relation to a contravention of conditions imposed by a direction under section 141 as they apply in relation to a contravention of SMP apparatus conditions.]

Amendments (Textual)

F235. S. 143. (4)(5) substituted for s. 143. (4) (26.5.2011) by The Electronic Communications and Wireless Telegraphy Regulations 2011 (S.I. 2011/1210), reg. 1. (2), Sch. 1 para. 86 (with Sch. 3 paras. 2, 18, 19)

Commencement Information

I218. S. 143 in force at 25.7.2003 for specified purposes by S.I. 2003/1900, arts. 1. (2), 2. (1), Sch. 1 (with art. 3) (as amended by S.I. 2003/3142, art. 1. (3))

I219. S. 143 in force at 29.12.2003 in so far as not already in force by S.I. 2003/3142, art. 3. (2) (with art. 11)

144. Offences in connection with information requirements

(1) A person who fails to provide information in accordance with a requirement of OFCOM under section 135 or 136 is guilty of an offence and shall be liable—

(a) on summary conviction, to a fine not exceeding the statutory maximum;

(b) on conviction on indictment, to a fine.

(2) In proceedings against a person for an offence under subsection (1) it shall be a defence for that person to show—

(a) that it was not reasonably practicable for him to comply with the requirement within the period specified by OFCOM; but

(b) that he has taken all reasonable steps to provide the required information after the end of that period.

(3) A person is guilty of an offence if—

(a) in pursuance of any requirement under section 135 or 136, he provides any information that is false in any material particular; and

(b) at the time he provides it, he either knows it to be false or is reckless as to whether or not it is false.

(4) A person guilty of an offence under subsection (3) shall be liable—

(a) on summary conviction, to a fine not exceeding the statutory maximum;

(b) on conviction on indictment, to imprisonment for a term not exceeding two years or to a fine, or to both.

(5) Proceedings for an offence under subsection (1) may be brought in respect of a contravention by a person of a requirement imposed under section 135 or 136 only if—

(a) OFCOM have given the person a notification under section 138 in respect of that contravention;

[F236. (b)the notification required the person to provide information, a confirmation decision has been given under section 139. A in respect of that requirement and the period allowed under that decision has expired without the required information having been provided; and]

(c) OFCOM have not imposed a financial penalty under section 139 in respect of that contravention.

Amendments (Textual)

F236. S. 144. (5)(b) substituted (26.5.2011) by The Electronic Communications and Wireless Telegraphy Regulations 2011 (S.I. 2011/1210), reg. 1. (2), Sch. 1 para. 87 (with Sch. 3 paras. 2, 18, 19)

Commencement Information
I220. S. 144 in force at 25.7.2003 for specified purposes by S.I. 2003/1900, arts. 1. (2), 2. (1), Sch. 1 (with art. 3) (as amended by S.I. 2003/3142, art. 1. (3))
I221. S. 144 in force at 29.12.2003 in so far as not already in force by S.I. 2003/3142, art. 3. (2) (with art. 11)

145. Statement of policy on information gathering

(1) It shall be the duty of OFCOM to prepare and publish a statement of their general policy with respect to—

(a) the exercise of their powers under sections 135 to 136; and

(b) the uses to which they are proposing to put information obtained under those sections.

(2) OFCOM may from time to time revise that statement as they think fit.

(3) Where OFCOM make or revise their statement of policy under this section, they must publish that statement or (as the case may be) the revised statement in such manner as they consider appropriate for bringing it to the attention of the persons who, in their opinion, are likely to be affected by it.

(4) It shall be the duty of OFCOM, in exercising the powers conferred on them by sections 135 to 144 to have regard to the statement for the time being in force under this section.

Commencement Information
I222. S. 145 in force at 25.7.2003 for specified purposes by S.I. 2003/1900, arts. 1. (2), 2. (1), Sch. 1 (with art. 3) (as amended by S.I. 2003/3142, art. 1. (3))
I223. S. 145 in force at 29.12.2003 in so far as not already in force by S.I. 2003/3142, art. 3. (2) (with art. 11)

146. Provision of information by OFCOM

(1) OFCOM must comply with a request made by a person for the purposes of this section—

(a) to notify the person whether or not a notification is required to be submitted by him under section 33;

(b) to notify the person whether a notification submitted by him for the purposes of that section satisfies the requirements of this Chapter;

(c) to provide the person with such information about his rights as may be necessary for the purpose of facilitating the negotiation by him of his right to network access; or

(d) to provide the person with such information as they consider necessary to enable the applicant to apply for a direction under section 106 to be made in his case.

(2) A request for the purposes of this section must be made in such manner as OFCOM may require.

(3) OFCOM are not required to comply with a request under this section if (without having been asked to do so) they have already given that person the notification or information for which he is asking.

(4) Any notification or information which under subsection (1) must be given or provided by OFCOM must be given or provided before the end of the period of one week beginning with the day on which the request for the notification or information was made to OFCOM.

Commencement Information
I224. S. 146 in force at 25.7.2003 for specified purposes by S.I. 2003/1900, arts. 1. (2), 2. (1), Sch. 1 (with art. 3) (as amended by S.I. 2003/3142, art. 1. (3))
I225. S. 146 in force at 29.12.2003 in so far as not already in force by S.I. 2003/3142, art. 3. (2) (with art. 11)

[F237146. A.Rights of third parties to use information without charge

(1) Any person has a right to use, free of charge, information published by a communications provider if the use is for the purpose specified in subsection (2).

(2) That purpose is to sell or make available an interactive guide or other technique for evaluating the cost of alternative usage patterns in relation to electronic communications services.]

Amendments (Textual)
F237. S. 146. A inserted (26.5.2011) by The Electronic Communications and Wireless Telegraphy Regulations 2011 (S.I. 2011/1210), reg. 1. (2), Sch. 1 para. 88 (with Sch. 3 para. 2)

Abolition of telecommunications licensing etc.

147. Repeal of provisions of Telecommunications Act 1984.

The following provisions of the Telecommunications Act 1984 (c. 12) shall cease to have effect—

 (a) sections 5 to 8 (licensing provisions);

 (b) sections 9 to 11 (public telecommunications systems);

 (c) sections 12 to 15 (modification of licences);

 (d) sections 16 to 19 (enforcement of licences); and

 (e) sections 27. A to 27. L (standards of performance of designated public telecommunications operators).

Commencement Information

I226. S. 147 in force at 25.7.2003 for specified purposes by S.I. 2003/1900, arts. 1. (2), 2. (1), Sch. 1 (with art. 3) (as amended by S.I. 2003/3142, art. 1. (3))

I227. S. 147 in force at 29.12.2003 in so far as not already in force by S.I. 2003/3142, art. 3. (2) (with art. 11)

Local authority powers in relation to networks and services

148. Powers of local authorities in connection with networks

(1) A local authority may borrow money for the purpose of providing a public electronic communications network or public electronic communications service.

(2) A local authority may—

 (a) provide a public electronic communications network part of which is outside their area; and

 (b) provide a public electronic communications service even if some of the persons to whom they provide the service are outside their area.

(3) In this section, a "local authority" means—

 (a) in relation to England, a London borough council or a district council;

 (b) in relation to Wales, a county council or a county borough council;

 (c) in Scotland, a council constituted under section 2 of the Local Government etc. (Scotland) Act 1994 (c. 39).

Commencement Information

I228. S. 148 in force at 25.7.2003 for specified purposes by S.I. 2003/1900, arts. 1. (2), 2. (1), Sch. 1 (with art. 3) (as amended by S.I. 2003/3142, art. 1. (3))

I229. S. 148 in force at 29.12.2003 in so far as not already in force by S.I. 2003/3142, art. 3. (2) (with art. 11)

Grants for networks and services in Northern Ireland

149. Grants by Department of Enterprise, Trade and InvestmentN.I.

(1) The Department of Enterprise, Trade and Investment may, in accordance with this section, make payments to persons engaged in, or in commercial activities connected with—

 (a) the provision of electronic communications networks and electronic communications services in Northern Ireland; or

 (b) improving the extent, quality and reliability of such networks or services.

(2) A payment shall not be made under this section unless in the opinion of the Department of Enterprise, Trade and Investment—

 (a) the making of the payment is likely to achieve—

(i) one or more of the purposes set out in subsection (1); and

(ii) any other purposes prescribed by regulations made by that Department with the approval of the Department of Finance and Personnel; and

(b) the amount of the payment is reasonable having regard to all the circumstances.

(3) Payments under this section shall—

(a) be of such amounts, and

(b) be made subject to such conditions (including conditions as to repayment),

as the Department of Enterprise, Trade and Investment may determine.

(4) This section extends only to Northern Ireland.

Commencement Information

I230. S. 149 in force at 25.7.2003 for specified purposes by S.I. 2003/1900, arts. 1. (2), 2. (1), Sch. 1 (with art. 3) (as amended by S.I. 2003/3142, art. 1. (3))

I231. S. 149 in force at 29.12.2003 in so far as not already in force by S.I. 2003/3142, art. 3. (2) (with art. 11)

150. Grants by district councils

(1) This section applies where a district council in Northern Ireland consider that it would be for the benefit of their area—

(a) for a public electronic communications network or electronic communications service to be provided by a particular person;

(b) for facilities to be made available by a particular person for the purposes of, or in connection with, the provision of such a network or service; or

(c) for such a network or service that is being provided by a particular person, or for any such facilities that are being so made available by a particular person, to continue to be provided or made available.

(2) The district council may—

(a) undertake to pay to that person, and

(b) pay him,

whatever sums they think appropriate for, or towards, compensating him for losses sustained in the provision of the network or service or in making the facilities available.

(3) For the purposes of this section it is immaterial—

(a) in the case of a network, whether any part of the network is situated in the council's area; and

(b) in the case of a service or facility, whether any of the persons to whom the service or facility is provided or made available are in that area.

Commencement Information

I232. S. 150 in force at 25.7.2003 for specified purposes by S.I. 2003/1900, arts. 1. (2), 2. (1), Sch. 1 (with art. 3) (as amended by S.I. 2003/3142, art. 1. (3))

I233. S. 150 in force at 29.12.2003 in so far as not already in force by S.I. 2003/3142, art. 3. (2) (with art. 11)

Interpretation of Chapter 1.

[F238150. A.Proposals of EU significance

(1) This section applies in relation to a proposal—

(a) to set, modify or revoke a condition under section 45;

(b) to give a direction, approval or consent for the purposes of such a condition;

(c) to modify or withdraw such a direction, approval or consent;

(d) to identify a market for the purposes of making or reviewing a market power determination; or

(e) to make or review a market power determination.

(2) The proposal is of EU significance for the purposes of this Chapter if—

(a) paragraph (3) of Article 7 of the Framework Directive applies, or would apply but for paragraph (9) of that Article, in relation to it;

(b) (in a case within paragraph (a), (b) or (c) of subsection (1)) the condition is an access-related condition falling within section 73. (2) or an SMP services condition;

167

(c) (in a case within paragraph (d) or (e) of subsection (1)) the market in question is a services market; and

(d) in OFCOM's opinion it would affect trade between member States.]

Amendments (Textual)

F238 S. 150. A inserted (26.5.2011) by The Electronic Communications and Wireless Telegraphy Regulations 2011 (S.I. 2011/1210), reg. 1. (2), Sch. 1 para. 89 (with Sch. 3 para. 2)

151. Interpretation of Chapter 1.

(1) In this Chapter—

"the Access Directive" means Directive 2002/19/EC of the European Parliament and of the Council on access to, and interconnection of, electronic communications networks and associated facilities [F239, as amended by Directive 2009/140/EC of the European Parliament and of the Council] ;

"access-related condition" means a condition set as an access-related condition under section 45;

"allocation" and "adoption", in relation to telephone numbers, and cognate expressions, are to be construed in accordance with section 56;

"apparatus market", in relation to a market power determination, is to be construed in accordance with section 46. (9)(b);

"designated universal service provider" means a person who is for the time being designated in accordance with regulations under section 66 as a person to whom universal service conditions are applicable;

"electronic communications apparatus"—

- in relation to SMP apparatus conditions and in section 141, means apparatus that is designed or adapted for a use which consists of or includes the sending or receiving of communications or other signals (within the meaning of section 32) that are transmitted by means of an electronic communications network; and

- in all other contexts, has the same meaning as in the electronic communications code;

"the electronic communications code" has the meaning given by section 106. (1);

"end-user", in relation to a public electronic communications service, means—

- a person who, otherwise than as a communications provider, is a customer of the provider of that service;

- a person who makes use of the service otherwise than as a communications provider; or

- a person who may be authorised, by a person falling within paragraph (a), so to make use of the service;

"the Framework Directive" means Directive 2002/21/EC of the European Parliament and of the Council on a common regulatory framework for electronic communications networks and services [F240, as amended by Directive 2009/140/EC of the European Parliament and of the Council] ;

"general condition" means a condition set as a general condition under section 45;

"interconnection" is to be construed in accordance with subsection (2);

"market power determination" means—

- a determination, for the purposes of provisions of this Chapter, that a person has significant market power in an identified services market or an identified apparatus market, or

- a confirmation for such purposes of a market power determination reviewed on a further analysis under section 84 or 85;

"misuse", in relation to an electronic communications network or electronic communications service, is to be construed in accordance with section 128. (5) and (8), and cognate expressions are to be construed accordingly;

"network access" is to be construed in accordance with subsection (3);

"persistent" and "persistently", in relation to misuse of an electronic communications network or electronic communications service, are to be construed in accordance with section 128. (6) and (7);

"premium rate service" is to be construed in accordance with section 120. (7);

"privileged supplier condition" means a condition set as a privileged supplier condition under section 45;

"provider", in relation to a premium rate service, is to be construed in accordance with section 120. (9) to (12), and cognate expressions are to be construed accordingly;

"public communications provider" means—

- a provider of a public electronic communications network;

- a provider of a public electronic communications service; or

- a person who makes available facilities that are associated facilities by reference to a public electronic communications network or a public electronic communications service;

"public electronic communications network" means an electronic communications network provided wholly or mainly for the purpose of making electronic communications services available to members of the public;

"public electronic communications service" means any electronic communications service that is provided so as to be available for use by members of the public;

"regulatory authorities" is to be construed in accordance with subsection (5);

"relevant international standards" means—

- any standards or specifications from time to time drawn up and published in accordance with Article 17 of the Framework Directive;

- the standards and specifications from time to time adopted by—

the European Committee for Standardisation,

the European Committee for Electrotechnical Standardisation; or

the European Telecommunications Standards Institute; and

- the international standards and recommendations from time to time adopted by—

the International Telecommunication Union;

the International Organisation for Standardisation; or

the International Electrotechnical Committee;

"service interoperability" means interoperability between different electronic communications services;

"services market", in relation to a market power determination or market identification, is to be construed in accordance with section 46. (8)(a);

"significant market power" is to be construed in accordance with section 78;

"SMP condition" means a condition set as an SMP condition under section 45, and "SMP services condition" and "SMP apparatus condition" are to be construed in accordance with subsections (8) and (9) of that section respectively;

"telephone number" has the meaning given by section 56. (5);

"the Universal Service Directive" means Directive 2002/22/EC of the European Parliament and of the Council on universal service and users' rights relating to electronic communications networks and services [F241, as amended by Directive 2009/136/EC of the European Parliament and of the Council] ;

"universal service condition" means a condition set as a universal service condition under section 45;

"the universal service order" means the order for the time being in force under section 65.

(2) In this Chapter references to interconnection are references to the linking (whether directly or indirectly by physical or logical means, or by a combination of physical and logical means) of one public electronic communications network to another for the purpose of enabling the persons using one of them to be able—

(a) to communicate with users of the other one; or

(b) to make use of services provided by means of the other one (whether by the provider of that network or by another person).

(3) In this Chapter references to network access are references to—

(a) interconnection of public electronic communications networks; or

(b) any services, facilities or arrangements which—

(i) are not comprised in interconnection; but

(ii) are services, facilities or arrangements by means of which [F242a person] is able, for the purposes of the provision of an electronic communications service (whether by him or by another),

to make use of anything mentioned in subsection (4);
and references to providing network access include references to providing any such services, making available any such facilities or entering into any such arrangements.

(4) The things referred to in subsection (3)(b) are—

(a) any electronic communications network or electronic communications service provided by another communications provider;

(b) any apparatus comprised in such a network or used for the purposes of such a network or service;

[F243. (ba)any electronic communications apparatus;]

(c) any facilities made available by another that are associated facilities by reference to any network or service (whether one provided by that provider or by another);

(d) any other services or facilities which are provided or made available by another person and are capable of being used for the provision of an electronic communications service.

[F244. (4. A)In subsections (3)(b)(ii) and (4)(d), the references to an electronic communications service include the conveyance by means of an electronic communications network of signals, including an information society service or content service so conveyed.

(4. B)In subsection (4. A)—

"content service" has the meaning given by section 32. (7), and

"information society service" has the meaning given by Article 2. (a) of Directive 2000/31/EC of the European Parliament and of the Council of 8 June 2000 on certain legal aspects of information society services, in particular electronic commerce, in the Internal Market.]

(5) References in this Chapter to the regulatory authorities of member States are references to such of the authorities of the member States as have been notified to the European Commission as the regulatory authorities of those States for the purposes of the Framework Directive.

(6) For the purposes of this Chapter, where there is a contravention of an obligation that requires a person to do anything within a particular period or before a particular time, that contravention shall be taken to continue after the end of that period, or after that time, until that thing is done.

(7) References in this Chapter to remedying the consequences of a contravention include references to paying an amount to a person—

(a) by way of compensation for loss or damage suffered by that person; or

(b) in respect of annoyance, inconvenience or anxiety to which he has been put.

(8) In determining for the purposes of provisions of this Chapter whether a contravention is a repeated contravention for any purposes, a notification of a contravention under that provision shall be disregarded if it has been withdrawn before the imposition of a penalty in respect of the matters notified.

(9) For the purposes of this section a service is made available to members of the public if members of the public are customers, in respect of that service, of the provider of that service.

Amendments (Textual)

F239. Words in s. 151. (1) inserted (26.5.2011) by The Electronic Communications and Wireless Telegraphy Regulations 2011 (S.I. 2011/1210), reg. 1. (2), Sch. 1 para. 90. (a)(i) (with Sch. 3 para. 2, 20)

F240. Words in s. 151. (1) inserted (26.5.2011) by The Electronic Communications and Wireless Telegraphy Regulations 2011 (S.I. 2011/1210), reg. 1. (2), Sch. 1 para. 90. (a)(ii) (with Sch. 3 para. 2, 20)

F241. Words in s. 151. (1) inserted (26.5.2011) by The Electronic Communications and Wireless Telegraphy Regulations 2011 (S.I. 2011/1210), reg. 1. (2), Sch. 1 para. 90. (a)(iii) (with Sch. 3 para. 2, 20)

F242. Words in s. 151. (3)(b)(ii) substituted (26.5.2011) by The Electronic Communications and Wireless Telegraphy Regulations 2011 (S.I. 2011/1210), reg. 1. (2), Sch. 1 para. 90. (b) (with Sch. 3 para. 2)

F243. S. 151. (4)(ba) inserted (26.5.2011) by The Electronic Communications and Wireless Telegraphy Regulations 2011 (S.I. 2011/1210), reg. 1. (2), Sch. 1 para. 90. (c) (with Sch. 3 para. 2)

F244. S. 151. (4. A)(4. B) inserted (26.5.2011) by The Electronic Communications and Wireless Telegraphy Regulations 2011 (S.I. 2011/1210), reg. 1. (2), Sch. 1 para. 90. (d) (with Sch. 3 para. 2)

Commencement Information

I234. S. 151 in force at 25.7.2003 for specified purposes by S.I. 2003/1900, arts. 1. (2), 2. (1), Sch. 1 (with art. 3) (as amended by S.I. 2003/3142, art. 1. (3))

I235. S. 151 in force at 29.12.2003 in so far as not already in force by S.I. 2003/3142, art. 3. (2) (with art. 11)

Chapter 2. Spectrum use

F245152. General functions of OFCOM in relation to radio spectrum

· ·

Amendments (Textual)

F245. Ss. 152-184 repealed (8.2.2007) by Wireless Telegraphy Act 2006 (c. 36), s. 126. (2), Sch. 9 Pt. 1 (with Sch. 8 Pt. 1)

F245153. United Kingdom Plan for Frequency Authorisation

· ·

Amendments (Textual)

F245. Ss. 152-184 repealed (8.2.2007) by Wireless Telegraphy Act 2006 (c. 36), s. 126. (2), Sch. 9 Pt. 1 (with Sch. 8 Pt. 1)

Commencement Information

I236. S. 153 in force at 25.7.2003 for specified purposes by S.I. 2003/1900, arts. 1. (2), 2. (1), Sch. 1 (with art. 3) (as amended by S.I. 2003/3142, art. 1. (3))

I237. S. 153 in force at 29.12.2003 in so far as not already in force by S.I. 2003/3142, art. 3. (2) (with art. 11)

F245154. Duties of OFCOM when carrying out spectrum functions

· ·

Amendments (Textual)

F245. Ss. 152-184 repealed (8.2.2007) by Wireless Telegraphy Act 2006 (c. 36), s. 126. (2), Sch. 9 Pt. 1 (with Sch. 8 Pt. 1)

Commencement Information

I238. S. 154 in force at 25.7.2003 for specified purposes by S.I. 2003/1900, arts. 1. (2), 2. (1), Sch. 1 (with art. 3) (as amended by S.I. 2003/3142, art. 1. (3))

I239. S. 154 in force at 29.12.2003 in so far as not already in force by S.I. 2003/3142, art. 3. (2) (with art. 11)

F245155. Advisory service in relation to interference

· ·

Amendments (Textual)

F245. Ss. 152-184 repealed (8.2.2007) by Wireless Telegraphy Act 2006 (c. 36), s. 126. (2), Sch. 9 Pt. 1 (with Sch. 8 Pt. 1)

Commencement Information

I240. S. 155 in force at 29.12.2003 by S.I. 2003/3142, art. 3. (1), Sch. 1 (with art. 11)

F245156. Directions with respect to the radio spectrum

· ·

Amendments (Textual)

F245. Ss. 152-184 repealed (8.2.2007) by Wireless Telegraphy Act 2006 (c. 36), s. 126. (2), Sch. 9 Pt. 1 (with Sch. 8 Pt. 1)

Commencement Information

I241. S. 156 in force at 29.12.2003 by S.I. 2003/3142, art. 3. (1), Sch. 1 (with art. 11)

F245157. Procedure for directions under s. 156.

· ·

Reservation of spectrum for multiplex use

F245158. Special duty in relation to television multiplexes

. . . .

Recognised spectrum access

F245159. Grant of recognised spectrum access

. . . .

F245160. Effect of grant of recognised spectrum access

. . . .

F245161. Charges in respect of grants of recognised spectrum access

. . . .

F245162. Conversion into and from wireless telegraphy licences

. . . .

Crown use of the radio spectrum

F245163. Payments for use of radio spectrum by the Crown

. . . .

Limitations and exemptions applied to spectrum use

F245164. Limitations on authorised spectrum use

. . . .

F245165. Terms etc. of wireless telegraphy licences

. . . .

F245166. Exemption from need for wireless telegraphy licence

. . . .

Award and transfer of licences

F245167. Bidding for wireless telegraphy licences

. . . .

F245168. Spectrum trading

Amendments (Textual)
F245. Ss. 152-184 repealed (8.2.2007) by Wireless Telegraphy Act 2006 (c. 36), s. 126. (2), Sch. 9 Pt. 1 (with Sch. 8 Pt. 1)
Commencement Information
I257. S. 168 in force at 29.12.2003 by S.I. 2003/3142, art. 3. (1), Sch. 1 (with art. 11)

Variation and revocation of licences

F245169. Variation and revocation of wireless telegraphy licences

. . . .
Amendments (Textual)
F245. Ss. 152-184 repealed (8.2.2007) by Wireless Telegraphy Act 2006 (c. 36), s. 126. (2), Sch. 9 Pt. 1 (with Sch. 8 Pt. 1)
Commencement Information
I258. S. 169 in force at 25.7.2003 for specified purposes by S.I. 2003/1900, arts. 1. (2), 2. (1), Sch. 1 (with art. 3) (as amended by S.I. 2003/3142, art. 1. (3))
I259. S. 169 in force at 29.12.2003 in so far as not already in force by S.I. 2003/3142, art. 3. (2) (with art. 11)

Wireless telegraphy register

F245170. Wireless telegraphy register

. . . .
Amendments (Textual)
F245. Ss. 152-184 repealed (8.2.2007) by Wireless Telegraphy Act 2006 (c. 36), s. 126. (2), Sch. 9 Pt. 1 (with Sch. 8 Pt. 1)
Commencement Information
I260. S. 170 in force at 29.12.2003 by S.I. 2003/3142, art. 3. (1), Sch. 1 (with art. 11)

Information requirements

F245171. Information requirements in relation to wireless telegraphy licences

. . . .
Amendments (Textual)
F245. Ss. 152-184 repealed (8.2.2007) by Wireless Telegraphy Act 2006 (c. 36), s. 126. (2), Sch. 9 Pt. 1 (with Sch. 8 Pt. 1)
Commencement Information
I261. S. 171 in force at 29.12.2003 by S.I. 2003/3142, art. 3. (1), Sch. 1 (with art. 11)

Criminal proceedings etc.

F245172. Contraventions of conditions for use of wireless telegraphy

. . . .
Amendments (Textual)
F245. Ss. 152-184 repealed (8.2.2007) by Wireless Telegraphy Act 2006 (c. 36), s. 126. (2), Sch. 9 Pt. 1 (with Sch. 8 Pt. 1)
Commencement Information
I262. S. 172 in force at 25.7.2003 for specified purposes by S.I. 2003/1900, arts. 1. (2), 2. (1), Sch. 1 (with art. 3) (as amended by S.I. 2003/3142, art. 1. (3))
I263. S. 172 in force at 29.12.2003 in so far as not already in force by S.I. 2003/3142, art. 3. (2)

(with art. 11)

F245173. Meaning of "repeated contravention" in s. 172.

. . . .

Amendments (Textual)

F245. Ss. 152-184 repealed (8.2.2007) by Wireless Telegraphy Act 2006 (c. 36), s. 126. (2), Sch. 9 Pt. 1 (with Sch. 8 Pt. 1)

Commencement Information

I1264. S. 173 in force at 25.7.2003 for specified purposes by S.I. 2003/1900, arts. 1. (2), 2. (1), Sch. 1 (with art. 3) (as amended by S.I. 2003/3142, art. 1. (3))

I1265. S. 173 in force at 29.12.2003 in so far as not already in force by S.I. 2003/3142, art. 3. (2) (with art. 11)

F245174. Procedure for prosecutions of wireless telegraphy offences

. . . .

Amendments (Textual)

F245. Ss. 152-184 repealed (8.2.2007) by Wireless Telegraphy Act 2006 (c. 36), s. 126. (2), Sch. 9 Pt. 1 (with Sch. 8 Pt. 1)

Commencement Information

I1266. S. 174 in force at 25.7.2003 for specified purposes by S.I. 2003/1900, arts. 1. (2), 2. (1), Sch. 1 (with art. 3) (as amended by S.I. 2003/3142, art. 1. (3))

I1267. S. 174 in force at 29.12.2003 in so far as not already in force by S.I. 2003/3142, art. 3. (2) (with art. 11)

F245175. Special procedure for contraventions by multiplex licence holders

. . . .

Amendments (Textual)

F245. Ss. 152-184 repealed (8.2.2007) by Wireless Telegraphy Act 2006 (c. 36), s. 126. (2), Sch. 9 Pt. 1 (with Sch. 8 Pt. 1)

Commencement Information

I1268. S. 175 in force at 29.12.2003 by S.I. 2003/3142, art. 3. (1), Sch. 1 (with art. 11)

F245176. Amount of penalty under s. 175.

. . . .

Amendments (Textual)

F245. Ss. 152-184 repealed (8.2.2007) by Wireless Telegraphy Act 2006 (c. 36), s. 126. (2), Sch. 9 Pt. 1 (with Sch. 8 Pt. 1)

Commencement Information

I1269. S. 176 in force at 29.12.2003 by S.I. 2003/3142, art. 3. (1), Sch. 1 (with art. 11)

F245177"Relevant amount of gross revenue" for the purposes of s. 176.

. . . .

Amendments (Textual)

F245. Ss. 152-184 repealed (8.2.2007) by Wireless Telegraphy Act 2006 (c. 36), s. 126. (2), Sch. 9 Pt. 1 (with Sch. 8 Pt. 1)

Commencement Information

I1270. S. 177 in force at 29.12.2003 by S.I. 2003/3142, art. 3. (1), Sch. 1 (with art. 11)

F245178. Proceedings for an offence relating to apparatus use

. . . .

Amendments (Textual)

F245. Ss. 152-184 repealed (8.2.2007) by Wireless Telegraphy Act 2006 (c. 36), s. 126. (2), Sch. 9 Pt. 1 (with Sch. 8 Pt. 1)

Commencement Information

I1271. S. 178 in force at 25.7.2003 for specified purposes by S.I. 2003/1900, arts. 1. (2), 2. (1), Sch. 1 (with art. 3) (as amended by S.I. 2003/3142, art. 1. (3))

I1272. S. 178 in force at 29.12.2003 in so far as not already in force by S.I. 2003/3142, art. 3. (2) (with art. 11)

F245179. Modification of penalties for certain wireless telegraphy offences

Amendments (Textual)
F245. Ss. 152-184 repealed (8.2.2007) by Wireless Telegraphy Act 2006 (c. 36), s. 126. (2), Sch. 9 Pt. 1 (with Sch. 8 Pt. 1)
Commencement Information
I273. S. 179 in force at 18.9.2003 by S.I. 2003/1900, art. 2. (2), Sch. 2
Prospective
F245180. Fixed penalties for certain wireless telegraphy offences

. . . .
Amendments (Textual)
F245. Ss. 152-184 repealed (8.2.2007) by Wireless Telegraphy Act 2006 (c. 36), s. 126. (2), Sch. 9 Pt. 1 (with Sch. 8 Pt. 1)
F245181. Power of arrest

. . . .
Amendments (Textual)
F245. Ss. 152-184 repealed (8.2.2007) by Wireless Telegraphy Act 2006 (c. 36), s. 126. (2), Sch. 9 Pt. 1 (with Sch. 8 Pt. 1)
Commencement Information
I274. S. 181 in force at 18.9.2003 by S.I. 2003/1900, art. 2. (2), Sch. 2
F245182. Forfeiture etc. of restricted apparatus

. . . .
Amendments (Textual)
F245. Ss. 152-184 repealed (8.2.2007) by Wireless Telegraphy Act 2006 (c. 36), s. 126. (2), Sch. 9 Pt. 1 (with Sch. 8 Pt. 1)
Commencement Information
I275. S. 182 in force at 29.12.2003 by S.I. 2003/3142, art. 3. (1), Sch. 1 (with art. 11)

Construction of 1949 Act

F245183. Modification of definition of "undue interference"

. . . .
Amendments (Textual)
F245. Ss. 152-184 repealed (8.2.2007) by Wireless Telegraphy Act 2006 (c. 36), s. 126. (2), Sch. 9 Pt. 1 (with Sch. 8 Pt. 1)
Commencement Information
I276. S. 183 in force at 25.7.2003 for specified purposes by S.I. 2003/1900, arts. 1. (2), 2. (1), Sch. 1 (with art. 3) (as amended by S.I. 2003/3142, art. 1. (3))
I277. S. 183 in force at 29.12.2003 in so far as not already in force by S.I. 2003/3142, art. 3. (2) (with art. 11)
F245184. Modification of definition of "wireless telegraphy"

. . . .
Amendments (Textual)
F245. Ss. 152-184 repealed (8.2.2007) by Wireless Telegraphy Act 2006 (c. 36), s. 126. (2), Sch. 9 Pt. 1 (with Sch. 8 Pt. 1)
Commencement Information
I278. S. 184 in force at 18.9.2003 by S.I. 2003/1900, art. 2. (2), Sch. 2

Chapter 3. Disputes and appeals

185. Reference of disputes to OFCOM
(1) This section applies in the case of a dispute relating to the provision of network access if it is—
    (a) a dispute between different communications providers;

(b) a dispute between a communications provider and a person who makes associated facilities available;

(c) a dispute between different persons making such facilities available;

F246. (d). . . . .

F246. (e). . . . .

[F247. (1. A)This section also applies in the case of a dispute relating to the provision of network access if—

(a) it is a dispute between a communications provider and a person who is identified, or is a member of a class identified, in a condition imposed on the communications provider under section 45; and

(b) the dispute relates to entitlements to network access that the communications provider is required to provide to that person by or under that condition.]

(2) This section also applies in the case of any other dispute if—

(a) it relates to rights or obligations conferred or imposed by or under [F248a condition set under section 45, or any of the enactments relating to the management of the radio spectrum] ;

(b) it is a dispute between different communications providers; and

(c) it is not an excluded dispute.

(3) Any one or more of the parties to the dispute may refer it to OFCOM.

(4) A reference made under this section is to be made in such manner as OFCOM may require.

(5) The way in which a requirement under subsection (4)—

(a) is to be imposed, or

(b) may be withdrawn or modified,

is by a notice published in such manner as OFCOM consider appropriate for bringing the requirement, withdrawal or modification to the attention of the persons who, in their opinion, are likely to be affected by it.

(6) Requirements imposed under subsection (4) may make different provision for different cases.

(7) A dispute is an excluded dispute for the purposes of subsection (2) if it is about—

(a) obligations imposed on a communications provider by SMP apparatus conditions;

F249. (b). . . . .

F249. (c). . . . .

F249. (d). . . . .

(8) For the purposes of this section—

(a) the disputes that relate to the provision of network access include disputes as to the terms or conditions on which it is or may be provided in a particular case; and

(b) the disputes that relate to an obligation include disputes as to the terms or conditions on which any transaction is to be entered into for the purpose of complying with that obligation.

Amendments (Textual)

F246. S. 185. (1)(d)(e) omitted (26.5.2011) by virtue of The Electronic Communications and Wireless Telegraphy Regulations 2011 (S.I. 2011/1210), reg. 1. (2), Sch. 1 para. 91. (a) (with Sch. 3 para. 2)

F247. S. 185. (1. A) inserted (26.5.2011) by The Electronic Communications and Wireless Telegraphy Regulations 2011 (S.I. 2011/1210), reg. 1. (2), Sch. 1 para. 91. (b) (with Sch. 3 para. 2)

F248. Words in s. 185. (2)(a) substituted (26.5.2011) by The Electronic Communications and Wireless Telegraphy Regulations 2011 (S.I. 2011/1210), reg. 1. (2), Sch. 1 para. 91. (c) (with Sch. 3 para. 2)

F249. S. 185. (7)(b)-(d) omitted (26.5.2011) by virtue of The Electronic Communications and Wireless Telegraphy Regulations 2011 (S.I. 2011/1210), reg. 1. (2), Sch. 1 para. 91. (d) (with Sch. 3 para. 2)

Commencement Information

I279. S. 185 in force at 25.7.2003 for specified purposes by S.I. 2003/1900, arts. 1. (2), 2. (1), Sch. 1 (with art. 3) (as amended by S.I. 2003/3142, art. 1. (3))

I280. S. 185 in force at 29.12.2003 in so far as not already in force by S.I. 2003/3142, art. 3. (2)

(with art. 11)

[F250185. A.Power of OFCOM to invite parties to refer dispute

OFCOM may invite any one or more of the parties to a dispute falling within section 185. (1) to refer the dispute to OFCOM under section 185. (3).]

Amendments (Textual)

F250. S. 185. A inserted (26.5.2011) by The Electronic Communications and Wireless Telegraphy Regulations 2011 (S.I. 2011/1210), reg. 1. (2), Sch. 1 para. 92 (with Sch. 3 para. 2)

186. Action by OFCOM on dispute reference

(1) This section applies where a dispute is referred to OFCOM under and in accordance with section 185.

(2) OFCOM must decide whether or not it is appropriate for them to handle the dispute.

[F251. (2. A)In relation to a dispute falling within subsection 185. (1), OFCOM may in particular take into account their priorities and available resources in considering whether it is appropriate for them to handle the dispute.]

(3) [F252. In relation to a dispute falling within section 185. (1. A) or (2),] Unless they consider—

  (a) that there are alternative means available for resolving the dispute,

  (b) that a resolution of the dispute by those means would be consistent with [F253. European Union] requirements set out in section 4, and

  (c) that a prompt and satisfactory resolution of the dispute is likely if those alternative means are used for resolving it,

their decision must be a decision that it is appropriate for them to handle the dispute.

(4) As soon as reasonably practicable after OFCOM have decided—

  (a) that it is appropriate for them to handle the dispute, or

  (b) that it is not,

they must inform each of the parties to the dispute of their decision and of their reasons for it.

(5) The notification must state the date of the decision.

(6) [F254. In relation to a dispute falling within section 185. (1. A) or (2),] Where—

  (a) OFCOM decide that it is not appropriate for them to handle the dispute, but

  (b) the dispute is not resolved by other means before the end of the four months after the day of OFCOM's decision,

the dispute may be referred back to OFCOM by one or more of the parties to the dispute.

Amendments (Textual)

F251. S. 186. (2. A) inserted (26.5.2011) by The Electronic Communications and Wireless Telegraphy Regulations 2011 (S.I. 2011/1210), reg. 1. (2), Sch. 1 para. 93. (a) (with Sch. 3 para. 2)

F252. Words in s. 186. (3) inserted (26.5.2011) by The Electronic Communications and Wireless Telegraphy Regulations 2011 (S.I. 2011/1210), reg. 1. (2), Sch. 1 para. 93. (b) (with Sch. 3 para. 2)

F253. Words in Act substituted (22.4.2011) by The Treaty of Lisbon (Changes in Terminology) Order 2011 (S.I. 2011/1043), arts. 2, 3, 4 (with art. 3. (2)(3), 4. (2), 6. (4)(5))

F254. Words in s. 186. (6) inserted (26.5.2011) by The Electronic Communications and Wireless Telegraphy Regulations 2011 (S.I. 2011/1210), reg. 1. (2), Sch. 1 para. 93. (b) (with Sch. 3 para. 2)

Commencement Information

I281. S. 186 in force at 25.7.2003 for specified purposes by S.I. 2003/1900, arts. 1. (2), 2. (1), Sch. 1 (with art. 3) (as amended by S.I. 2003/3142, art. 1. (3))

I282. S. 186 in force at 29.12.2003 in so far as not already in force by S.I. 2003/3142, art. 3. (2) (with art. 11)

187. Legal proceedings about referred disputes

(1) Where a dispute is referred or referred back to OFCOM under this Chapter, the reference is not to prevent—

  (a) the person making it,

  (b) another party to the dispute,

(c) OFCOM, or

(d) any other person,

from bringing, or continuing, any legal proceedings with respect to any of the matters under dispute.

(2) Nor is the reference or reference back to OFCOM under this Chapter of a dispute to prevent OFCOM from—

(a) giving a notification in respect of something that they have reasonable grounds for believing to be a contravention of any obligation imposed by or under any an enactment;

(b) exercising any of their other powers under any enactment in relation to a contravention of such an obligation; or

(c) taking any other step in preparation for or with a view to doing anything mentioned in the preceding paragraphs.

(3) If, in any legal proceedings with respect to a matter to which a dispute relates, the court orders the handling of the dispute by OFCOM to be stayed or sisted—

(a) OFCOM are required to make a determination for resolving the dispute only if the stay or sist is lifted or expires; and

(b) the period during which the stay or sist is in force must be disregarded in determining the period within which OFCOM are required to make such a determination.

(4) Subsection (1) is subject to section 190. (8) and to any agreement to the contrary binding the parties to the dispute.

(5) In this section "legal proceedings" means civil or criminal proceedings in or before a court.

Commencement Information

I283. S. 187 in force at 25.7.2003 for specified purposes by S.I. 2003/1900, arts. 1. (2), 2. (1), Sch. 1 (with art. 3) (as amended by S.I. 2003/3142, art. 1. (3))

I284. S. 187 in force at 29.12.2003 in so far as not already in force by S.I. 2003/3142, art. 3. (2) (with art. 11)

188. Procedure for resolving disputes

(1) This section applies where—

(a) OFCOM have decided under section 186. (2) that it is appropriate for them to handle a dispute; or

(b) a dispute is referred back to OFCOM under section 186. (6).

(2) OFCOM must—

(a) consider the dispute; and

(b) make a determination for resolving it.

(3) The procedure for the consideration and determination of the dispute is to be the procedure that OFCOM consider appropriate.

(4) In the case of a dispute referred back to OFCOM under section 186. (6), that procedure may involve allowing the continuation of a procedure that has already been begun for resolving the dispute by alternative means.

(5) Except in exceptional circumstances and subject to section 187. (3), OFCOM must make their determination no more than four months after the following day—

(a) in a case falling within subsection (1)(a), the day of the decision by OFCOM that it is appropriate for them to handle the dispute; and

(b) in a case falling within subsection (1)(b), the day on which the dispute is referred back to them.

(6) Where it is practicable for OFCOM to make their determination before the end of the four month period, they must make it as soon in that period as practicable.

(7) OFCOM must—

(a) send a copy of their determination, together with a full statement of their reasons for it, to every party to the dispute; and

(b) publish so much of their determination as (having regard, in particular, to the need to preserve commercial confidentiality) they consider it appropriate to publish.

(8) The publication of information under this section must be in such manner as OFCOM consider

appropriate for bringing it to the attention, to the extent that they consider appropriate, of members of the public.

Commencement Information

I285. S. 188 in force at 25.7.2003 for specified purposes by S.I. 2003/1900, arts. 1. (2), 2. (1), Sch. 1 (with art. 3) (as amended by S.I. 2003/3142, art. 1. (3))

I286. S. 188 in force at 29.12.2003 in so far as not already in force by S.I. 2003/3142, art. 3. (2) (with art. 11)

189. Disputes involving other member States

(1) This section applies where it appears to OFCOM that a dispute referred or referred back to them under this Chapter [F255. (other than a dispute falling within section 185. (1))] relates partly to a matter falling within the jurisdiction of the regulatory authorities of another member State.

(2) A dispute relates to matters falling within the jurisdiction of the regulatory authorities of another member State to the extent that—

(a) it relates to the carrying on of activities by one or both of the parties to the dispute in more than one member State or to activities carried on by different parties to the dispute in different member States; and

(b) the activities to which the dispute relates, so far as they are carried on in another member State, are carried on in the member State for which those authorities are the regulatory authorities.

(3) For the purposes of subsection (2) the activities that are carried on in a member State include anything done by means of an electronic communications network, or part of such a network, which is situated in that member State.

(4) Before taking any steps under this Chapter in relation to the reference or the dispute, OFCOM

[F256. (a)must co-ordinate their efforts with the other regulatory authorities within whose jurisdiction the matter falls,

(b) may consult BEREC in order to bring about a consistent resolution of the dispute, and

(c) may request BEREC to adopt an opinion as to the action to be taken to resolve the dispute.]

(5) It shall be the duty of OFCOM to secure that steps taken in relation to the reference or dispute (whether taken by them or by the other regulatory authorities) are, so far as practicable, agreed between OFCOM and those authorities.

[F257. (5. A)Where an opinion is received from BEREC in relation to the reference or dispute, it shall be the duty of OFCOM to secure that steps taken in relation to the reference or dispute take account of the opinion (whether the opinion was requested by OFCOM or by the other regulatory authorities).]

(6) Accordingly, section 188 is to have effect in relation to the reference as if the period for making a determination which is specified in subsection (5) of that section were such period (if any) as may be agreed between—

(a) OFCOM; and

(b) the other regulatory authorities within whose jurisdiction the matter falls.

[F258. (7)OFCOM must—

(a) ensure, so far as practicable, that a period agreed under subsection (6) is long enough for BEREC to provide an opinion, if one has been requested by OFCOM or by the other regulatory authorities, and

(b) agree to any necessary extension of the period if an opinion is requested from BEREC (by OFCOM or by the other regulatory authorities) after the period has been agreed.

(8) Subsection (7) does not apply if the dispute in question has resulted in, or creates an immediate risk of—

(a) a serious threat to the safety of the public, to public health or to national security;

(b) serious economic or operational problems for persons who are communications providers or persons who make associated facilities available; or

(c) serious economic or operational problems for persons who make use of electronic communications networks, electronic communications services or associated facilities, or for other users of the radio spectrum.]

Amendments (Textual)

F255. Words in s. 189. (1) inserted (26.5.2011) by The Electronic Communications and Wireless Telegraphy Regulations 2011 (S.I. 2011/1210), reg. 1. (2), Sch. 1 para. 94. (a) (with Sch. 3 para. 2)

F256. S. 189. (4)(a)(b)(c) substituted for words (26.5.2011) by The Electronic Communications and Wireless Telegraphy Regulations 2011 (S.I. 2011/1210), reg. 1. (2), Sch. 1 para. 94. (b) (with Sch. 3 para. 2)

F257. S. 189. (5. A) inserted (26.5.2011) by The Electronic Communications and Wireless Telegraphy Regulations 2011 (S.I. 2011/1210), reg. 1. (2), Sch. 1 para. 94. (c) (with Sch. 3 para. 2)

F258. S. 189. (7)(8) inserted (26.5.2011) by The Electronic Communications and Wireless Telegraphy Regulations 2011 (S.I. 2011/1210), reg. 1. (2), Sch. 1 para. 94. (d) (with Sch. 3 para. 2)

Commencement Information

I287. S. 189 in force at 25.7.2003 for specified purposes by S.I. 2003/1900, arts. 1. (2), 2. (1), Sch. 1 (with art. 3) (as amended by S.I. 2003/3142, art. 1. (3))

I288. S. 189 in force at 29.12.2003 in so far as not already in force by S.I. 2003/3142, art. 3. (2) (with art. 11)

190. Resolution of referred disputes

(1) Where OFCOM make a determination for resolving a dispute referred to them under this Chapter, their only powers are those conferred by this section.

(2) Their main power (except in the case of a dispute relating to rights and obligations conferred or imposed by or under the enactments relating to the management of the radio spectrum) is to do one or more of the following—

(a) to make a declaration setting out the rights and obligations of the parties to the dispute;

(b) to give a direction fixing the terms or conditions of transactions between the parties to the dispute;

(c) to give a direction imposing an obligation, enforceable by the parties to the dispute, to enter into a transaction between themselves on the terms and conditions fixed by OFCOM; and

(d) for the purpose of giving effect to a determination by OFCOM of the proper amount of a charge in respect of which amounts have been paid by one of the parties of the dispute to the other, to give a direction, enforceable by the party to whom the sums are to be paid, requiring the payment of sums by way of adjustment of an underpayment or overpayment.

[F259. (2. A)In relation to a dispute falling within section 185. (1), OFCOM must exercise their powers under subsection (2) in the way that seems to them most appropriate for the purpose of securing—

(a) efficiency;

(b) sustainable competition;

(c) efficient investment and innovation; and

(d) the greatest possible benefit for the end-users of public electronic communications services.]

(3) Their main power in the excepted case is just to make a declaration setting out the rights and obligations of the parties to the dispute.

(4) Nothing in this section prevents OFCOM from exercising the following powers in consequence of their consideration under this Chapter of any dispute—

(a) their powers under Chapter 1 of this Part to set, modify or revoke general conditions, universal service conditions, access related conditions, privileged supplier conditions or SMP conditions;

(b) their powers to vary, modify or revoke wireless telegraphy licences or grants of recognised spectrum access;

(c) their power to make, amend or revoke [F260regulations under section 8 or 45 of the Wireless Telegraphy Act 2006] .

(5) In the case of a dispute referred back to OFCOM under section 186. (6)—

(a) OFCOM may, in making their determination, take account of decisions already made by others in the course of an attempt to resolve the dispute by alternative means; and

(b) the determination made by OFCOM may include provision ratifying decisions so made.

(6) Where OFCOM make a determination for resolving a dispute, they may require a party to the dispute—

(a) to make payments to another party to the dispute in respect of costs and expenses incurred by that other party in consequence of the reference of the dispute to OFCOM, or in connection with it; and

(b) to make payments to OFCOM in respect of costs and expenses incurred by them in dealing with the dispute.

[F261and may determine the amount of the costs and when the costs are to be paid.]

[F262. (6. A)OFCOM may not, under subsection (6)(a), require a party to the dispute to make payments to another party unless OFCOM have considered—

(a) the conduct of the party before and after the reference to OFCOM (including, in particular, whether any attempt has been made to resolve the dispute), and

(b) whether OFCOM has made a decision in the party's favour in respect of the whole or a part of the dispute.

(6. B)OFCOM may not, under subsection (6)(b), require payments to be made to them by a party to the dispute unless—

(a) the dispute relates to the rights and obligations of the parties to the dispute under the enactments relating to the management of the radio spectrum, or

(b) they have considered the matters referred to in subsection (6. A)(a) and (b).]

F263. (7). . . . .

(8) A determination made by OFCOM for resolving a dispute referred or referred back to them under this Chapter binds all the parties to the dispute.

(9) Subsection (8) is subject to section 192.

Amendments (Textual)

F259. S. 190. (2. A) inserted (26.5.2011) by The Electronic Communications and Wireless Telegraphy Regulations 2011 (S.I. 2011/1210), reg. 1. (2), Sch. 1 para. 95. (a) (with Sch. 3 para. 2)

F260. Words in s. 190. (4)(c) substituted (8.2.2007) by Wireless Telegraphy Act 2006 (c. 36), s. 126. (2), Sch. 7 para. 27

F261. Words in s. 190. (6) inserted (26.5.2011) by The Electronic Communications and Wireless Telegraphy Regulations 2011 (S.I. 2011/1210), reg. 1. (2), Sch. 1 para. 95. (b) (with Sch. 3 para. 2)

F262. S. 190. (6. A)(6. B) inserted (26.5.2011) by The Electronic Communications and Wireless Telegraphy Regulations 2011 (S.I. 2011/1210), reg. 1. (2), Sch. 1 para. 95. (c) (with Sch. 3 para. 2)

F263. S. 190. (7) omitted (26.5.2011) by virtue of The Electronic Communications and Wireless Telegraphy Regulations 2011 (S.I. 2011/1210), reg. 1. (2), Sch. 1 para. 95. (d) (with Sch. 3 para. 2)

Commencement Information

I289. S. 190 in force at 25.7.2003 for specified purposes by S.I. 2003/1900, arts. 1. (2), 2. (1), Sch. 1 (with art. 3) (as amended by S.I. 2003/3142, art. 1. (3))

I290. S. 190 in force at 29.12.2003 in so far as not already in force by S.I. 2003/3142, art. 3. (2) (with art. 11)

191. OFCOM's power to require information in connection with dispute

(1) Where a dispute has been referred or referred back to OFCOM under this Chapter, they may require any person to whom subsection (2) applies to provide them with all such information as they may require for the purpose of—

(a) deciding whether it is appropriate for them to handle the dispute;

(b) determining whether it is necessary for them to consult the regulatory authorities of another member State; or

(c) considering the dispute and making a determination for resolving it.

(2) This subsection applies to—

(a) a party to the dispute; and

(b) a person who is not a party to the dispute but appears to OFCOM to have information that is relevant to the matters mentioned in subsection (1)(a) to (c).

(3) A person required to provide information under this section must provide it in such manner and within such reasonable period as may be specified by OFCOM.

(4) In fixing the period within which information is to be provided in accordance with a requirement under this section OFCOM must have regard, in particular, to—

(a) their obligation to make a determination for resolving the dispute within the period specified in section 188;

(b) the nature of the dispute; and

(c) the information that is required.

(5) Sections 138 to 144 apply for the enforcement of a requirement under this section as they apply for the enforcement of requirements under section 135 or 136.

F264. (6). . . . .

Amendments (Textual)

F264. S. 191. (6) omitted (26.5.2011) by virtue of The Electronic Communications and Wireless Telegraphy Regulations 2011 (S.I. 2011/1210), reg. 1. (2), Sch. 1 para. 96 (with Sch. 3 para. 2)

Commencement Information

I291. S. 191 in force at 25.7.2003 for specified purposes by S.I. 2003/1900, arts. 1. (2), 2. (1), Sch. 1 (with art. 3) (as amended by S.I. 2003/3142, art. 1. (3))

I292. S. 191 in force at 29.12.2003 in so far as not already in force by S.I. 2003/3142, art. 3. (2) (with art. 11)

Appeals

192. Appeals against decisions by OFCOM, the Secretary of State etc.

(1) This section applies to the following decisions—

(a) a decision by OFCOM under this Part [F265or any of Parts 1 to 3 of the Wireless Telegraphy Act 2006] that is not a decision specified in Schedule 8;

(b) a decision (whether by OFCOM or another) to which effect is given by a direction, approval or consent given for the purposes of a provision of a condition set under section 45;

(c) a decision to which effect is given by the modification or withdrawal of such a direction, approval or consent;

(d) a decision by the Secretary of State to which effect is given by one of the following—

(i) a specific direction under section 5 that is not about the making of a decision specified in Schedule 8;

(ii) a restriction or condition set by regulations under section 109;

(iii) a direction to OFCOM under section 132;

(iv) a specific direction under [F266section 5 of the Wireless Telegraphy Act 2006] that is not about the making of a decision specified in Schedule 8.

[F267. (e)a decision by the CMA to which effect is given by an order made under section 193. A.]

(2) A person affected by a decision to which this section applies may appeal against it to the Tribunal.

(3) The means of making an appeal is by sending the Tribunal a notice of appeal in accordance with Tribunal rules.

(4) The notice of appeal must be sent within the period specified, in relation to the decision appealed against, in those rules.

(5) The notice of appeal must set out—

(a) the provision under which the decision appealed against was taken; and

(b) the grounds of appeal.

(6) The grounds of appeal must be set out in sufficient detail to indicate—

(a) to what extent (if any) the appellant contends that the decision appealed against was based on an error of fact or was wrong in law or both; and

(b) to what extent (if any) the appellant is appealing against the exercise of a discretion by OFCOM, by the Secretary of State [F268, by the CMA] or by another person.

(7) In this section and Schedule 8 references to a decision under an enactment—

(a) include references to a decision that is given effect to by the exercise or performance of a power or duty conferred or imposed by or under an enactment; but

(b) include references to a failure to make a decision, and to a failure to exercise a power or to perform a duty, only where the failure constitutes a failure to grant an application or to comply with any other form of request to make the decision, to exercise the power or to perform the duty; and references in the following provisions of this Chapter to a decision appealed against are to be construed accordingly.

(8) For the purposes of this section and the following provisions of this Chapter a decision to which effect is given by the exercise or performance of a power or duty conferred or imposed by or under an enactment shall be treated, except where provision is made for the making of that decision at a different time, as made at the time when the power is exercised or the duty performed.

Amendments (Textual)

F265. Words in s. 192. (1)(a) substituted (8.2.2007) by Wireless Telegraphy Act 2006 (c. 36), s. 126. (2), Sch. 7 para. 28. (a)

F266. Words in s. 192. (1)(d)(iv) substituted (8.2.2007) by Wireless Telegraphy Act 2006 (c. 36), s. 126. (2), Sch. 7 para. 28. (b)

F267. S. 192. (1)(e) inserted (1.4.2014) by Enterprise and Regulatory Reform Act 2013 (c. 24), s. 103. (3), Sch. 15 para. 43. (2); S.I. 2014/416, art. 2. (1)(f) (with Sch.)

F268. Words in s. 192. (6)(b) inserted (1.4.2014) by Enterprise and Regulatory Reform Act 2013 (c. 24), s. 103. (3), Sch. 15 para. 43. (3); S.I. 2014/416, art. 2. (1)(f) (with Sch.)

Commencement Information

I293. S. 192 in force at 25.7.2003 for specified purposes by S.I. 2003/1900, arts. 1. (2), 2. (1), Sch. 1 (with art. 3) (as amended by S.I. 2003/3142, art. 1. (3))

I294. S. 192 in force at 29.12.2003 in so far as not already in force by S.I. 2003/3142, art. 3. (2) (with art. 11)

193. Reference of price control matters to the [F269. CMA]

(1) Tribunal rules must provide in relation to appeals under section 192. (2) relating to price control that the price control matters arising in that appeal, to the extent that they are matters of a description specified in the rules, must be referred by the Tribunal to the [F270. CMA] for determination.

(2) Where a price control matter is referred in accordance with Tribunal rules to the [F271. CMA] for determination, [F272the determination of the matter is to be carried out on behalf of the CMA by a group constituted for the purpose by the chair of the CMA under Schedule 4 to the Enterprise and Regulatory Reform Act 2013, and is to be performed] —

(a) in accordance with the provision made by the rules;

(b) in accordance with directions given to [F273the CMA] by the Tribunal in exercise of powers conferred by the rules; and

(c) subject to the rules and any such directions, using such procedure as the [F274. CMA] consider appropriate.

(3) The provision that may be made by Tribunal rules about the determination of a price control matter referred to the [F275. CMA] in accordance with the rules includes provision about the period within which that matter is to be determined by [F276the CMA] .

(4) Where the [F277. CMA] determines a price control matter in accordance with Tribunal rules, they must notify the Tribunal of the determination they have made.

(5) The notification must be given as soon as practicable after the making of the notified determination.

(6) Where a price control matter arising in an appeal is required to be referred to the [F278. CMA]

under this section, the Tribunal, in deciding the appeal on the merits under section 195, must decide that matter in accordance with the determination of [F279the CMA] .

(7) Subsection (6) does not apply to the extent that the Tribunal decides, applying the principles applicable on an application for judicial review, that the determination of the [F280. CMA] is a determination that would fall to be set aside on such an application.

(8) Section 117 of the Enterprise Act 2002 (c. 40) (offences of supplying false or misleading information) shall have effect in relation to information supplied to the [F280. CMA] in connection with their functions under this section as it has effect in relation to information supplied to them in connection with their functions under Part 3 of that Act.

(9) For the purposes of this section an appeal relates to price control if the matters to which the appeal relates are or include price control matters.

(10) In this section [F281and section 193. A] "price control matter" means a matter relating to the imposition of any form of price control by an SMP condition the setting of which is authorised by—

    (a) section 87. (9);

    (b) section 91; or

    (c) section 93. (3).

Amendments (Textual)

F269. Word in s. 193 heading substituted (1.4.2014) by Enterprise and Regulatory Reform Act 2013 (c. 24), s. 103. (3), Sch. 6 para. 98. (8); S.I. 2014/416, art. 2. (1)(d) (with Sch.)

F270. Word in s. 193. (1) substituted (1.4.2014) by Enterprise and Regulatory Reform Act 2013 (c. 24), s. 103. (3), Sch. 6 para. 98. (2); S.I. 2014/416, art. 2. (1)(d) (with Sch.)

F271. Word in s. 193. (2) substituted (1.4.2014) by Enterprise and Regulatory Reform Act 2013 (c. 24), s. 103. (3), Sch. 6 para. 98. (3)(a); S.I. 2014/416, art. 2. (1)(d) (with Sch.)

F272. Words in s. 193. (2) substituted (1.4.2014) by Enterprise and Regulatory Reform Act 2013 (c. 24), s. 103. (3), Sch. 6 para. 98. (3)(b); S.I. 2014/416, art. 2. (1)(d) (with Sch.)

F273. Words in s. 193. (2)(b) substituted (1.4.2014) by Enterprise and Regulatory Reform Act 2013 (c. 24), s. 103. (3), Sch. 6 para. 98. (3)(c); S.I. 2014/416, art. 2. (1)(d) (with Sch.)

F274. Word in s. 193. (2)(c) substituted (1.4.2014) by Enterprise and Regulatory Reform Act 2013 (c. 24), s. 103. (3), Sch. 6 para. 98. (3)(d); S.I. 2014/416, art. 2. (1)(d) (with Sch.)

F275. Word in s. 193. (3) substituted (1.4.2014) by Enterprise and Regulatory Reform Act 2013 (c. 24), s. 103. (3), Sch. 6 para. 98. (4)(a); S.I. 2014/416, art. 2. (1)(d) (with Sch.)

F276. Words in s. 193. (3) substituted (1.4.2014) by Enterprise and Regulatory Reform Act 2013 (c. 24), s. 103. (3), Sch. 6 para. 98. (4)(b); S.I. 2014/416, art. 2. (1)(d) (with Sch.)

F277. Word in s. 193. (4) substituted (1.4.2014) by Enterprise and Regulatory Reform Act 2013 (c. 24), s. 103. (3), Sch. 6 para. 98. (5); S.I. 2014/416, art. 2. (1)(d) (with Sch.)

F278. Word in s. 193. (6) substituted (1.4.2014) by Enterprise and Regulatory Reform Act 2013 (c. 24), s. 103. (3), Sch. 6 para. 98. (6)(a); S.I. 2014/416, art. 2. (1)(d) (with Sch.)

F279. Words in s. 193. (6) substituted (1.4.2014) by Enterprise and Regulatory Reform Act 2013 (c. 24), s. 103. (3), Sch. 6 para. 98. (6)(b); S.I. 2014/416, art. 2. (1)(d) (with Sch.)

F280. Word in s. 193. (7)(8) substituted (1.4.2014) by Enterprise and Regulatory Reform Act 2013 (c. 24), s. 103. (3), Sch. 6 para. 98. (7); S.I. 2014/416, art. 2. (1)(d) (with Sch.); S.I. 2014/416, art. 2. (1)(d) (with Sch.)

F281. Words in s. 193. (10) inserted (1.4.2014) by Enterprise and Regulatory Reform Act 2013 (c. 24), s. 103. (3), Sch. 15 para. 44; S.I. 2014/416, art. 2. (1)(f) (with Sch.)

Commencement Information

I295. S. 193 in force at 25.7.2003 for specified purposes by S.I. 2003/1900, arts. 1. (2), 2. (1), Sch. 1 (with art. 3) (as amended by S.I. 2003/3142, art. 1. (3))

I296. S. 193 in force at 29.12.2003 in so far as not already in force by S.I. 2003/3142, art. 3. (2) (with art. 11)

[F282193. ARecovery of CMA's costs in respect of price control references

(1) Where a determination is made on a price control matter referred by virtue of section 193, the CMA may make an order in respect of the costs incurred by it in connection with the reference (a

"costs order").

(2) A costs order may require the payment to the CMA of some or all of those costs by such parties to the appeal which gave rise to the reference, other than OFCOM, as the CMA considers appropriate.

(3) A costs order must—

(a) set out the total costs incurred by the CMA in connection with the reference, and

(b) specify the proportion of those costs to be paid by each party to the appeal in respect of whom the order is made.

(4) In deciding on the proportion of costs to be paid by a party to the appeal the CMA must, in particular, consider—

(a) the extent to which the determination on the reference upholds OFCOM's decision in relation to the price control matter in question,

(b) the extent to which the costs were attributable to the involvement in the appeal of the party, and

(c) the conduct of the party.

(5) A costs order—

(a) must be made as soon as reasonably practicable after the making of the determination on the reference, but

(b) does not take effect unless the Tribunal, in deciding the appeal which gave rise to the reference, decides the price control matter which is the subject of the reference in accordance with the determination of the CMA (see section 193. (6)).

(6) In a case where the Tribunal decides the price control matter in question otherwise than as mentioned in subsection (5)(b), the CMA may make an order under this subsection in respect of the costs incurred by it in connection with the reference.

(7) Subsections (2) to (4) apply in relation to an order under subsection (6) as they apply in relation to an order under subsection (1); but for that purpose the reference in subsection (4)(a) to the determination on the reference is to be read as a reference to the decision of the Tribunal mentioned in subsection (6).

(8) An order under subsection (6) must be made as soon as reasonably practicable after the decision of the Tribunal mentioned in that subsection.

(9) An amount payable to the CMA by virtue of an order made under this section is recoverable summarily as a civil debt (but this does not affect any other method of recovery).

(10) The CMA must pay any sums it receives by virtue of this section into the Consolidated Fund.

(11) The functions of the CMA under this section, other than those under subsections (9) and (10), are to be carried out on behalf of the CMA by the group constituted by the chair of the CMA in relation to the reference in question.]

Amendments (Textual)

F282. S. 193. A inserted (1.4.2014) by Enterprise and Regulatory Reform Act 2013 (c. 24), ss. 54, 103. (3); S.I. 2014/416, art. 2. (1)(b) (with Sch.)

F283194. Composition of Competition Commission for price control references

. . . .

Amendments (Textual)

F283. S. 194 omitted (1.4.2014) by virtue of Enterprise and Regulatory Reform Act 2013 (c. 24), s. 103. (3), Sch. 6 para. 99; S.I. 2014/416, art. 2. (1)(d) (with Sch.)

Commencement Information

I297. S. 194 in force at 25.7.2003 for specified purposes by S.I. 2003/1900, arts. 1. (2), 2. (1), Sch. 1 (with art. 3) (as amended by S.I. 2003/3142, art. 1. (3))

I298. S. 194 in force at 29.12.2003 in so far as not already in force by S.I. 2003/3142, art. 3. (2) (with art. 11)

195. Decisions of the Tribunal

(1) The Tribunal shall dispose of an appeal under section 192. (2) in accordance with this section.

(2) The Tribunal shall decide the appeal on the merits and by reference to the grounds of appeal set out in the notice of appeal.

(3) The Tribunal's decision must include a decision as to what (if any) is the appropriate action for the decision-maker to take in relation to the subject-matter of the decision under appeal.

(4) The Tribunal shall then remit the decision under appeal to the decision-maker with such directions (if any) as the Tribunal considers appropriate for giving effect to its decision.

(5) The Tribunal must not direct the decision-maker to take any action which he would not otherwise have power to take in relation to the decision under appeal.

(6) It shall be the duty of the decision-maker to comply with every direction given under subsection (4).

(7) In the case of an appeal against a decision given effect to by a restriction or condition set by regulations under section 109, the Tribunal must take only such steps for disposing of the appeal as it considers are not detrimental to good administration.

(8) In its application to a decision of the Tribunal under this section, paragraph 1. (2)(b) of Schedule 4 to the Enterprise Act 2002 (c. 40) (exclusion of commercial information from documents recording Tribunal decisions) is to have effect as if for the reference to the undertaking to which commercial information relates there were substituted a reference to any person to whom it relates.

(9) In this section "the decision-maker" means—

(a) OFCOM [F284the Secretary of State or the CMA] , according to who took the decision appealed against; or

(b) in the case of an appeal against—

(i) a direction, approval or consent given by a person other than OFCOM [F284the Secretary of State or the CMA] , or

(ii) the modification or withdrawal by such a person of such a direction, approval or consent, that other person.

Amendments (Textual)

F284. Words in s. 195. (9) substituted (1.4.2014) by Enterprise and Regulatory Reform Act 2013 (c. 24), s. 103. (3), Sch. 15 para. 45; S.I. 2014/416, art. 2. (1)(f) (with Sch.)

Commencement Information

I299. S. 195 in force at 25.7.2003 for specified purposes by S.I. 2003/1900, arts. 1. (2), 2. (1), Sch. 1 (with art. 3) (as amended by S.I. 2003/3142, art. 1. (3))

I300. S. 195 in force at 29.12.2003 in so far as not already in force by S.I. 2003/3142, art. 3. (2) (with art. 11)

196. Appeals from the Tribunal

(1) A decision of the Tribunal on an appeal under section 192. (2) may itself be appealed.

(2) An appeal under this section—

(a) lies to the Court of Appeal or to the Court of Session; and

(b) must relate only to a point of law arising from the decision of the Tribunal.

(3) An appeal under this section may be brought by—

(a) a party to the proceedings before the Tribunal; or

(b) any other person who has a sufficient interest in the matter.

(4) An appeal under this section requires the permission of the Tribunal or of the court to which it is to be made.

(5) In this section references to a decision of the Tribunal include references to a direction given by it under section 195. (4).

Commencement Information

I301. S. 196 in force at 25.7.2003 for specified purposes by S.I. 2003/1900, arts. 1. (2), 2. (1), Sch. 1 (with art. 3) (as amended by S.I. 2003/3142, art. 1. (3))

I302. S. 196 in force at 29.12.2003 in so far as not already in force by S.I. 2003/3142, art. 3. (2) (with art. 11)

Interpretation of Chapter 3.

197. Interpretation of Chapter 3.

(1) In this Chapter—

[F285"the CMA" means the Competition and Markets Authority;]

"network access" has the same meaning as in Chapter 1 of this Part;

"the Tribunal" means the Competition Appeal Tribunal; and

"Tribunal rules" means rules made under section 15 of the Enterprise Act 2002.

(2) References in this Chapter, in relation to a dispute, to the regulatory authorities of other member States are references to such of the authorities of the other member States as have been notified under the Framework Directive to the European Commission as the regulatory authorities of those States for the purposes of the matters to which the dispute relates.

(3) In this section "the Framework Directive" has the same meaning as in Chapter 1 of this Part.

Amendments (Textual)

F285. Words in s. 197 inserted (1.4.2014) by Enterprise and Regulatory Reform Act 2013 (c. 24), s. 103. (3), Sch. 6 para. 100; S.I. 2014/416, art. 2. (1)(d) (with Sch.)

Commencement Information

I303. S. 197 in force at 25.7.2003 for specified purposes by S.I. 2003/1900, arts. 1. (2), 2. (1), Sch. 1 (with art. 3) (as amended by S.I. 2003/3142, art. 1. (3))

I304. S. 197 in force at 29.12.2003 in so far as not already in force by S.I. 2003/3142, art. 3. (2) (with art. 11)

Part 3. Television and Radio Services ETC

Part 3. Television and Radio Services [F1. ETC]

Amendments (Textual)

F1. Word in Pt. 3 inserted (8.6.2010) by Digital Economy Act 2010 (c. 24), ss. 22. (4), 47. (1)

Modifications etc. (not altering text)

C1. Pt. 3: amendment to earlier affecting provision S.I. 2012/292, Sch. Pt. 2 (12.7.2012) by The Broadcasting (Local Digital Television Programme Services and Independent Productions) (Amendment) Order 2012 (S.I. 2012/1842), art. 4

C2. Pt. 3 applied (with modifications) (14.2.2012) by The Local Digital Television Programme Services Order 2012 (S.I. 2012/292), arts. 1, 4, Sch. Pt. 2

Chapter 1. The BBC, C4. C the Welsh Authority and the Gaelic media service

198. Functions of OFCOM in relation to the BBC

(1) It shall be a function of OFCOM, to the extent that provision for them to do so is contained in—

    (a) the BBC Charter and Agreement, and

    (b) the provisions of this Act and of Part 5 of the 1996 Act,

to regulate the provision of the BBC's services and the carrying on by the BBC of other activities for purposes connected with the provision of those services.

(2) For the purposes of the carrying out of that function OFCOM—

    (a) are to have such powers and duties as may be conferred on them by or under the BBC Charter and Agreement; and

    (b) are entitled, to the extent that they are authorised to do so by the Secretary of State or under the terms of that Charter and Agreement, to act on his behalf in relation to that Charter and Agreement.

(3) The BBC must pay OFCOM such penalties in respect of contraventions by the BBC of

provision made by or under—

(a) this Part,

[F2. (aa)Part 4. A,] or

(b) the BBC Charter and Agreement,

as are imposed by OFCOM in exercise of powers conferred on them by that Charter and Agreement.

(4) The BBC are also to be liable to pay OFCOM such sums in respect of the carrying out by OFCOM of their functions in relation to the BBC as may be—

(a) agreed from time to time between the BBC and OFCOM; or

(b) (in default of agreement) fixed by the Secretary of State.

(5) The maximum penalty that may be imposed on the BBC on any occasion by OFCOM in exercise of a power conferred by virtue of the BBC Charter and Agreement is £250,000.

(6) The Secretary of State may by order substitute a different sum for the sum for the time being specified in subsection (5).

(7) No order is to be made containing provision authorised by subsection (6) unless a draft of the order has been laid before Parliament and approved by a resolution of each House.

(8) It shall be the duty of OFCOM to have regard to their functions under this section when carrying out their functions under the 1990 Act, the 1996 Act and this Part in relation to services provided by persons other than the BBC.

(9) In this section "the BBC's services" means such of the services provided by the BBC (excluding the services comprised in the World Service) as are of a description of service which, if provided by a BBC company, would fall to be regulated by OFCOM by virtue of section 211 or 245 [F3or by the appropriate regulatory authority by virtue of section 368. C] .

Amendments (Textual)

F2. S. 198. (3)(aa) inserted (19.12.2009) by Audiovisual Media Services Regulations 2009 (S.I. 2009/2979), regs. 1. (1), 3. (1)(a)

F3. Words in s. 198. (9) inserted (19.12.2009) by Audiovisual Media Services Regulations 2009 (S.I. 2009/2979), regs. 1. (1), 3. (1)(b)

Commencement Information

I1. S. 198 in force at 29.12.2003 by S.I. 2003/3142, art. 3. (1), Sch. 1 (with art. 11)

C4. C

[F4198. AC4. C's functions in relation to media content

(1) C4. C must participate in—

(a) the making of a broad range of relevant media content of high quality that, taken as a whole, appeals to the tastes and interests of a culturally diverse society,

(b) the making of high quality films intended to be shown to the general public at the cinema in the United Kingdom, and

(c) the broadcasting and distribution of such content and films.

(2) C4. C must, in particular, participate in—

(a) the making of relevant media content that consists of news and current affairs,

(b) the making of relevant media content that appeals to the tastes and interests of older children and young adults,

(c) the broadcasting or distribution by means of electronic communications networks of feature films that reflect cultural activity in the United Kingdom (including third party films), and

(d) the broadcasting or distribution of relevant media content by means of a range of different types of electronic communications networks.

(3) In performing their duties under subsections (1) and (2) C4. C must—

(a) promote measures intended to secure that people are well-informed and motivated to participate in society in a variety of ways, and

(b) contribute towards the fulfilment of the public service objectives (as defined in section 264.

A).

(4) In performing their duties under subsections (1) to (3) C4. C must—

(a) support the development of people with creative talent, in particular—

(i) people at the beginning of their careers in relevant media content or films, and

(ii) people involved in the making of innovative content and films,

(b) support and stimulate well-informed debate on a wide range of issues, including by providing access to information and views from around the world and by challenging established views,

(c) promote alternative views and new perspectives, and

(d) provide access to material that is intended to inspire people to make changes in their lives.

(5) In performing those duties C4. C must have regard to the desirability of—

(a) working with cultural organisations,

(b) encouraging innovation in the means by which relevant media content is broadcast or distributed, and

(c) promoting access to and awareness of services provided in digital form.

(6) In this section—

"participate in" includes invest in or otherwise procure;

"relevant media content" means material, other than advertisements, which is included in any of the following services that are available to members of the public in all or part of the United Kingdom—

- television programme services, additional television services or digital additional television services,

- on-demand programme services, or

- other services provided by means of the internet where there is a person who exercises editorial control over the material included in the service;

and a film is a "third party film" if C4. C did not participate in making it.

(7) The services that are to be taken for the purposes of this section to be available to members of the public include any service which—

(a) is available for reception by members of the public (within the meaning of section 361); or

(b) is available for use by members of the public (within the meaning of section 368. R(4)).]

Amendments (Textual)

F4. S. 198. A inserted (8.6.2010) by Digital Economy Act 2010 (c. 24), ss. 22. (1), 47. (1)

[F5198. BStatement of media content policy

(1) C4. C must prepare a statement of media content policy—

(a) at the same time as they prepare the first statement of programme policy that is prepared under section 266 after this section comes into force, and

(b) subsequently at annual intervals.

(2) C4. C must monitor their performance in carrying out the proposals contained in their statements of media content policy.

(3) A statement of media content policy must—

(a) set out C4. C's proposals for securing that, during the following year, they will discharge their duties under section 198. A, and

(b) include a report on their performance in carrying out the proposals contained in the previous statement.

(4) In preparing the statement, C4. C must—

(a) have regard to guidance given by OFCOM, and

(b) consult OFCOM.

(5) C4. C must publish each statement of media content policy—

(a) as soon as practicable after its preparation is complete, and

(b) in such manner as they consider appropriate, having regard to any guidance given by OFCOM.

(6) OFCOM must—

(a) from time to time review the guidance for the time being in force for the purposes of this section, and

(b) revise that guidance as they think fit.

Amendments (Textual)

F5. Ss. 198. B-198. D inserted (8.6.2010) by Digital Economy Act 2010 (c. 24), ss. 23. (1), 47. (1)

198. C OFCOM reports on C4. C's media content duties

(1) For each relevant period, OFCOM must—

(a) carry out a review of the extent to which C4. C have discharged their duties under section 198. A, and

(b) prepare a report on the matters found on the review.

(2) OFCOM must publish each report under this section—

(a) as soon as practicable after its preparation is complete, and

(b) in such manner as they consider appropriate.

(3) "Relevant period" means each period selected by OFCOM for the purposes of section 264. (1)(b) that ends after this section comes into force.

Amendments (Textual)

F5. Ss. 198. B-198. D inserted (8.6.2010) by Digital Economy Act 2010 (c. 24), ss. 23. (1), 47. (1)

198. DDirections in relation to C4. C's media content duties

(1) This section applies if OFCOM—

(a) are of the opinion that C4. C have failed to perform one or more of their duties under section 198. A or section 198. B(1), (3) or (5),

(b) are of the opinion that the failure is serious and is not excused by economic or market conditions, and

(c) determine that the situation requires the exercise of their functions under this section.

(2) In making a determination under subsection (1)(c), OFCOM must have regard, in particular, to—

(a) C4. C's statements of media content policy,

(b) C4. C's effectiveness and efficiency in monitoring their own performance, and

(c) general economic and market conditions affecting the provision of relevant media content (as defined in section 198. A).

(3) OFCOM may give directions to C4. C to do one or both of the following—

(a) to revise the latest statement of media content policy in accordance with the direction;

(b) to take such steps for remedying the failure as OFCOM specify in the direction.

(4) A direction given under this section must set out—

(a) a reasonable timetable for complying with it, and

(b) the factors that OFCOM will take into account in determining whether or not a failure has been remedied.

(5) OFCOM must consult C4. C before giving a direction under this section.]

Amendments (Textual)

F5. Ss. 198. B-198. D inserted (8.6.2010) by Digital Economy Act 2010 (c. 24), ss. 23. (1), 47. (1)

199 [F6. Other] Functions of C4. C

(1) The activities that C4. C are able to carry on include any activities which appear to them—

(a) to be activities that it is appropriate for them to carry on in association with the carrying out of their primary functions; and

(b) to be connected, otherwise than merely in financial terms, with activities undertaken by them for the carrying out of those functions.

(2) [F7 In subsection (1) "primary functions" means—

(za) the performance of C4. C's duties under section 198. A;]

(a) securing the continued provision of Channel 4; and

(b) the fulfilment of the public service remit for that Channel under section 265.

(3) Section 24. (5)(b) and (6) of the 1990 Act (power of C4. C to establish, acquire an interest in or assist a qualifying company) shall cease to have effect.

(4) For sub-paragraphs (3) and (4) of paragraph 1 of Schedule 3 to the 1990 Act (power of C4. C to do things incidental or conducive to the carrying out of their functions) there shall be

substituted—

"(3)The Corporation may do anything which appears to them to be incidental or conducive to the carrying out of their functions.

(4) The powers of the Corporation under sub-paragraph (3) include power, to the extent that it appears to them incidental or conducive to the carrying out of their functions to do so—

(a) to borrow money;

(b) to carry on activities (other than those comprised in their duty to carry out their primary functions) through Channel 4 companies; and

(c) to participate with others in the carrying on of any such activities."

(5) Schedule 9 (which makes provision for the approval by OFCOM, and for the enforcement, of arrangements made by C4. C about the carrying on of their activities) shall have effect.

Amendments (Textual)

F6. Word in s. 199 heading inserted (8.6.2010) by Digital Economy Act 2010 (c. 24), ss. 22. (2), 47. (1)

F7. Words in s. 199. (2) substituted (8.6.2010) by Digital Economy Act 2010 (c. 24), ss. 22. (2), 47. (1)

Modifications etc. (not altering text)

C3. S. 199. (2)(b) modified (temp.) (8.12.2003) by The Office of Communications Act 2002 (Commencement No. 3) and Communications Act 2003 (Commencement No. 2) Order 2003 (S.I. 2003/3142), art. 7 (with art. 11)

Commencement Information

I2. S. 199 in force at 29.12.2003 by S.I. 2003/3142, art. 3. (1), Sch. 1 (with art. 11)

200. Removal of members of C4. C

(1) In paragraph 3 of Schedule 3 to the 1990 Act (term of office of members of C4. C), after sub-paragraph (2) there shall be inserted—

"(2. A)OFCOM may at any time, by notice to a member of the Corporation, terminate the appointment of that member.

(2. B)Before terminating a person's appointment under sub-paragraph (2. A), OFCOM must consult the Secretary of State."

(2) This section applies only to a member whose appointment was made, or last renewed, after the coming into force of this section.

Commencement Information

I3. S. 200 in force at 29.12.2003 by S.I. 2003/3142, art. 3. (1), Sch. 1 (with art. 11)

201. Deficits and surpluses of C4. C

(1) Sections 26 and 27 of the 1990 Act (revenue deficits of C4. C to be funded by providers of Channel 3 services and application of excess revenues of C4. C) shall cease to have effect.

(2) This section has effect in relation to a deficit or excess for a year ending after the commencement of this section.

Commencement Information

I4. S. 201 in force at 29.12.2003 by S.I. 2003/3142, art. 3. (1), Sch. 1 (with art. 11)

202. Borrowing limit for C4. C

(1) The Secretary of State may by order provide for a limit on the borrowing that C4. C is allowed to undertake.

(2) The order may fix the limit either—

(a) by specifying the sum which the outstanding borrowing of C4. C must not at any time exceed; or

(b) by providing a method of determining the sum which that borrowing must not exceed.

(3) C4. C are not to borrow money if the effect of the borrowing would be to cause the amount of their outstanding borrowing to be, or to remain, in excess of the limit (if any) that is for the time being in force.

(4) For the purposes of this section the amount of C4. C's outstanding borrowing at any time is the aggregate amount outstanding at that time in respect of the principal of sums borrowed by them, but after allowing sums borrowed to repay existing loans to be applied for that purpose.

(5) Before making an order under this section, the Secretary of State must consult C4. C.

(6) The consent of the Treasury is required for the making of an order under this section.

Commencement Information

I5. S. 202 in force at 29.12.2003 by S.I. 2003/3142, art. 3. (1), Sch. 1 (with art. 11)

The Welsh Authority

203. Function of OFCOM in relation to the Welsh Authority

It shall be a function of OFCOM, to the extent that provision for them to do so is contained in this Act and Part 5 of the 1996 Act, to regulate the services provided by the Welsh Authority.

Commencement Information

I6. S. 203 in force at 29.12.2003 by S.I. 2003/3142, art. 3. (1), Sch. 1 (with art. 11)

204. Welsh Authority's function of providing S4. C and S4. C Digital

(1) The Welsh Authority shall continue in existence with the substitution of the following function for their functions under section 57 of the 1990 Act.

(2) The Welsh Authority shall have the function of providing television programme services of high quality with a view to their being available for reception wholly or mainly by members of the public in Wales.

[F8. (3)The carrying out of that function—

(a) must include the continuing provision of the service provided in digital form and known as S4. C Digital; and

(b) may include the continuing provision of the television broadcasting service known as Sianel Pedwar Cymru ("S4. C").]

[F9. (4)The duty of the Welsh Authority to provide S4. C Digital includes a duty to secure that arrangements are made and remain in force for it to be broadcast in digital form.]

(5) It shall be the duty of the Welsh Authority to secure that S4. C and S4. C Digital each represents a public service for the dissemination of information, education and entertainment.

(6) The Welsh Authority may use part of the signals carrying S4. C to provide—

(a) subtitling in relation to programmes included in the service; and

(b) other services which are ancillary to programmes included in S4. C and which are directly related to their contents.

(7) In providing S4. C Digital the Welsh Authority may also provide—

(a) assistance for disabled people in relation to programmes included in the service; and

(b) any other service (other than one mentioned in paragraph (a)) which is an ancillary service in relation to S4. C Digital.

(8) The Secretary of State may by order modify this Act and such other enactments as he thinks fit for the purpose of—

(a) replacing the requirement of the Welsh Authority to provide S4. C with a requirement to provide a service in digital form;

(b) requiring the Welsh Authority to secure that arrangements are made for that service and S4. C Digital to be merged and provided as one service (also to be known as "S4. C Digital"); and

(c) applying enactments relating to the provision of S4. C or S4. C Digital to the provision of the merged service.

(9) An order under subsection (8) may require the Welsh Authority to ensure that, from the coming into force of a requirement to provide a merged service in digital form until a time determined in the manner described in the order, the whole or a part of the merged service is also to be provided for broadcasting in analogue form.

(10) In this section "programme" does not include an advertisement.

Amendments (Textual)

F8. S. 204. (3) substituted (12.8.2009) by Welsh Authority (Digital Switchover) Order 2009 (S.I. 2009/1968), arts. 1, 2. (2)

F9. S. 204. (4) substituted (12.8.2009) by Welsh Authority (Digital Switchover) Order 2009 (S.I.

2009/1968), arts. 1, 2. (3)

Commencement Information
I7. S. 204 in force at 29.12.2003 by S.I. 2003/3142, art. 3. (1), Sch. 1 (with art. 11)

205. Powers to provide other services

(1) The Welsh Authority are not, in the carrying out of their function under section 204, to provide any television programme service (apart from S4. C and S4. C Digital) unless—

  (a) the service appears to them to satisfy the requirements of subsection (3); and

  (b) the provision by them of the service has been approved by an order made by the Secretary of State.

(2) The functions of the Welsh Authority include the provision of services that are neither television programme services nor sound services but—

  (a) are provided with a view to being made available for reception wholly or mainly by members of the public in Wales or otherwise to be received or used by persons in Wales;

  (b) are services appearing to them to satisfy the requirements of subsection (3); and

  (c) are services the provision of which by the Authority has been approved by an order made by the Secretary of State.

(3) A service provided under this section must be a public service of high quality for the dissemination of information, education or entertainment (or a combination of them) wholly or mainly to members of the public in Wales.

(4) The Welsh Authority are not to provide a television programme service under this section unless it is one the provision of which by them broadens the range of television programme services available for reception by members of the public in Wales.

(5) The Welsh Authority must ensure, in the case of every television programme service provided with the approval of the Secretary of State under this section, that a substantial proportion of the programmes included in the service consists of programmes in Welsh.

(6) An order under this section approving the provision of a service must set out—

  (a) the nature and other characteristics of the service that is approved; and

  (b) in the case of a service that is a television programme service, a public service remit for that service.

(7) In providing a service approved under this section the Welsh Authority may also provide—

  (a) assistance for disabled people in relation to programmes included in the service;

  (b) other services which are ancillary to programmes included in the service and which are directly related to their contents; and

  (c) any other service (other than one mentioned in paragraph (a) or (b)) which is an ancillary service in relation to so much of the service as is provided in digital form.

(8) A television programme service provided under this section in digital form is a qualifying service for the purposes of the 1996 Act.

(9) In this section "sound service" means a service which would fall to be regulated under section 245 if provided by an S4. C company.

Commencement Information
I8. S. 205 in force at 29.12.2003 by S.I. 2003/3142, art. 3. (1), Sch. 1 (with art. 11)

206. Other activities of Welsh Authority

(1) The activities that the Welsh Authority are able to carry on include activities which appear to them—

  (a) to be activities that it is appropriate for them to carry on in association with the carrying out of their function of providing S4. C, S4. C Digital or a service the provision of which is approved under section 205; and

  (b) to be connected, otherwise than merely in financial terms, with activities undertaken by them for the carrying out of that function.

(2) The approval of the Secretary of State is required for the carrying on by the Welsh Authority of activities authorised only by subsection (1).

(3) The approval of the Secretary of State—

  (a) must be contained in an order made by him; and

(b) may be a general approval in relation to a description of activities or a specific approval in relation to particular activities.

(4) The activities capable of being authorised under subsection (1)—

(a) do not include the provision of a licensable service; but

(b) do include activities for securing the provision of such a service by an S4. C company and other activities connected with the provision of such a service by such a company.

(5) The activities referred to in subsection (4)(b) include—

(a) the formation of a company to provide a programme service;

(b) the taking of steps by means of which a company that is providing such a service becomes an S4. C company.

(6) For sub-paragraphs (2) and (3) of paragraph 1 of Schedule 6 to the 1990 Act (power of Welsh Authority to do things incidental or conducive to the carrying out of their functions) there shall be substituted—

"(2)The Authority may do anything which appears to them to be incidental or conducive to the carrying out of their functions.

(3) The powers of the Authority under sub-paragraph (2) include power, to the extent that it appears to them incidental or conducive to the carrying out of their functions to do so—

(a) to carry on activities (other than those comprised in their duty to carry out their functions under section 204 of the Communications Act 2003) through S4. C companies; and

(b) to participate with others in the carrying on of any such activities."

(7) In this section "licensable service" means a service that would fall to be regulated under section 211 or 245 if provided by an S4. C company.

(8) Section 57. (1. A)(b) and (1. B) of the 1990 Act (power of Welsh Authority to establish, acquire an interest in or assist a qualifying company) shall cease to have effect.

Commencement Information

I9. S. 206 in force at 29.12.2003 by S.I. 2003/3142, art. 3. (1), Sch. 1 (with art. 11)

207. Welsh Authority finances

(1) The Welsh Authority must not, whether directly or indirectly, impose charges on persons—

(a) in respect of their reception or use in Wales of any of the Authority's public services;

(b) in respect of their reception in Wales of any service consisting in the provision of assistance for disabled people in relation to programmes included in any one or more of those services; or

(c) in respect of their reception in Wales of any service (other than one mentioned in paragraph (b)) which is an ancillary service in relation to any of the Authority's public services provided in digital form.

(2) It shall be unlawful to impose a charge in contravention of subsection (1).

(3) The power of the Welsh Authority to do anything that appears to them to be conducive or incidental to the carrying out of their functions includes power, subject to subsection (4), to borrow money.

(4) The Welsh Authority are not to borrow money except with the approval of the Secretary of State.

(5) The consent of the Treasury is to be required for the giving of an approval for the purposes of subsection (4).

(6) The Welsh Authority are to be liable to pay OFCOM such sums in respect of the carrying out by OFCOM of their functions in relation to the Authority as may be—

(a) agreed from time to time between the Authority and OFCOM; or

(b) (in default of agreement) fixed by the Secretary of State.

(7) In section 61. (4) of the 1990 Act (power of Secretary of State to increase amount of grant to the Welsh Authority), for "transmitting S4. C and the service referred to in section 57. (1. A)(a), by order" there shall be substituted—

"(a)providing services that are public services of the Authority (within the meaning of section 207 of the Communications Act 2003), and

(b) arranging for the broadcasting or distribution of those services, by order ".

(8) In section 61. A of the 1990 Act (the public service fund)—

    (a) in subsection (2) (application of fund), for "their functions under section 57. (1) or (1. A)(a)" there shall be substituted " their functions in relation to the provision of the services that are public services of the Authority (within the meaning of section 207 of the Communications Act 2003). "; and

    (b) in subsection (4) (programmes to be broadcast first on S4. C or S4. C Digital), for the words from "on S4. C" onwards there shall be substituted " on a television programme service that is one of their public services (within the meaning of section 207 of the Communications Act 2003) ".

(9) In this section references to the Welsh Authority's public services are references to the following—

    (a) S4. C;

    (b) S4. C Digital; and

    (c) the services the provision of which by the Authority is authorised by or under section 205.

Commencement Information

I10. S. 207 in force at 29.12.2003 by S.I. 2003/3142, art. 3. (1), Sch. 1 (with art. 11)

The Gaelic Media Service

208. The Gaelic Media Service

(1) The body established for the purposes of section 183 of the 1990 Act (financing of programmes in Gaelic out of the Gaelic Television Fund) is hereby renamed Seirbheis nam Meadhanan Gàidhlig (the Gaelic Media Service).

(2) References in any instrument or other document to Comataidh Craolaidh Gaidhlig or to the Gaelic Broadcasting Committee are to be construed accordingly.

(3) For subsection (4) of that section there shall be substituted—

"(3. B)The functions of the Service shall be to secure that a wide and diverse range of high quality programmes in Gaelic are broadcast or otherwise transmitted so as to be available to persons in Scotland.

(4) The Service may—

    (a) make grants out of the Fund, or

    (b) otherwise apply it,

for any of the purposes of carrying out their functions or for any purpose connected with the carrying out of those functions.

(4. A)In carrying out their functions, the Service may finance, or engage in, any of the following—

    (a) the making of programmes in Gaelic with a view to those programmes being broadcast or otherwise transmitted so as to be available to persons in Scotland;

    (b) the provision of training for persons employed, or to be employed, in connection with the making of programmes in Gaelic to be so broadcast or otherwise transmitted;

    (c) research into the types of programmes in Gaelic that members of the Gaelic-speaking community would like to be broadcast or otherwise transmitted.

(4. B)But the Service are not to be entitled, for the purpose of carrying out their functions, to provide—

    (a) a Channel 3 service;

    (b) Channel 4;

    (c) Channel 5;

    (d) a national sound broadcasting service;

    (e) a national digital sound programme service; or

    (f) a television multiplex service or a radio multiplex service."

(4) For subsection (9) of that section there shall be substituted—

"(9)In this section, section 183. A and Schedule 19—

"Channel 3 service", "Channel 4" and "Channel 5" each has the same meaning as in Part 1;

"national digital sound programme service" has the same meaning as in Part 2 of the Broadcasting

Act 1996;

"national sound broadcasting service" means a sound broadcasting service within the meaning of Part 3 which, under subsection (4)(a) of section 245 of the Communications Act 2003, is a national service for the purposes of that section;

"Gaelic" means the Gaelic language as spoken in Scotland;

"programme" includes any item included in a programme service;

"radio multiplex service" has the same meaning as in Part 2 of the Broadcasting Act 1996;

"the Service" means the body established under subsection (3) and known as Seirbheis nam Meadhanan Gàidhlig (the Gaelic Media Service);

"television multiplex service" has the meaning given by section 241. (1) of the Communications Act 2003 to a multiplex service within the meaning of Part 1 of the Broadcasting Act 1996; and a reference to being available to persons in Scotland includes a reference to being available both to persons in Scotland and to others."

Commencement Information

I11. S. 208 in force at 29.12.2003 by S.I. 2003/3142, art. 3. (1), Sch. 1 (with art. 11)

209. Membership of the Service

After section 183 of the 1990 Act there shall be inserted—

"183. AMembership of the Gaelic Media Service

(1) The Service shall consist of not more than twelve members.

(2) The members of the Service are to be appointed by OFCOM

(3) OFCOM must appoint one of the members to be the chairman of the Service.

(4) The approval of the Secretary of State is required for the appointment of a person as a member of the Service, and for the appointment of a member as their chairman.

(5) The members of the Service must include—

(a) a member nominated by the BBC;

(b) a member nominated by Highlands and Islands Enterprise; and

(c) a member nominated by Bòrd Gàidhlig na h-Alba (the Gaelic Development Agency).

(6) When appointing members of the Service, OFCOM must have regard to—

(a) the desirability of having members of the Service who are proficient in written and spoken Gaelic; and

(b) any guidance issued by the Secretary of State for the purposes of this section.

(7) OFCOM must secure, so far as practicable, that the membership of the Service is such that the interests of each of the following are adequately represented—

(a) the holders of licences to provide regional Channel 3 services for areas wholly in Scotland;

(b) the holders of licences to provide regional Channel 3 services in respect of which determinations under section 184. (4)(b) are for the time being in force;

(c) the independent television and radio production industries in Scotland;

(d) other persons and bodies concerned with the promotion and use of the Gaelic language, including those concerned with education in Gaelic and in Gaelic culture.

(8) Schedule 19 to this Act shall have effect with respect to the Service.

(9) In this section—

"Bòrd Gàidhlig na h-Alba" means the body of that name formed under section 5 of the National Heritage (Scotland) Act 1985;

"regional Channel 3 service" has the same meaning as in Part 1.

(10) The Secretary of State may by order amend the reference in subsection (5) to Bòrd Gàidhlig na h-Alba (the Gaelic Development Agency)—

(a) by substituting a reference to another body formed under section 5 of the National Heritage (Scotland) Act 1985 with functions relating to the promotion of Gaelic; or

(b) for the purpose of giving effect to a change to the name of the body referred to in that subsection.

(11) An order under this section shall be subject to annulment in pursuance of a resolution of either House of Parliament."

Commencement Information

I12. S. 209 in force at 29.12.2003 by S.I. 2003/3142, art. 3. (1), Sch. 1 (with art. 11)

210. Supplementary provisions about the Service

(1) Schedule 19 to the 1990 Act (supplementary provisions about the Gaelic Broadcasting Committee) shall be amended as follows.

(2) In paragraph 2 (tenure of office and remuneration)—

(a) in sub-paragraph (1), for "sub-paragraph (2)" there shall be substituted " sub-paragraphs (1. A) and (2) ";

(b) after sub-paragraph (1) there shall be inserted—

"(1. A)A person is not to be appointed as a member of the Service for a term of more than four years (but a person so appointed shall be eligible for re-appointment at the end of his term of office)."

(3) In paragraph 7 (employees of the Committee), after sub-paragraph (3) there shall be inserted—

"(4)A person who is an employee of the Service is not to be eligible to be appointed as a member of the Service."

(4) After paragraph 8 (financial provision) there shall be inserted—

"8. A(1)The Service must pay all their receipts to OFCOM.

(2) OFCOM must hold amounts received by them under this paragraph to the credit of the Gaelic Broadcasting Fund (and, accordingly, those amounts are not to be regarded as forming part of OFCOM's revenues)."

(5) In paragraph 12 (annual reports), after sub-paragraph (1) there shall be inserted—

"(1. A)The report must include a statement of how the Service are proposing to carry out their functions during the next financial year."

Commencement Information

I13. S. 210 in force at 29.12.2003 by S.I. 2003/3142, art. 3. (1), Sch. 1 (with art. 11)

Chapter 2. Regulatory Structure for Independent Television Services

211. Regulation of independent television services

(1) It shall be a function of OFCOM to regulate the following services in accordance with this Act, the 1990 Act and the 1996 Act—

(a) services falling within subsection (2) that are provided otherwise than by the BBC or the Welsh Authority; and

(b) services falling within subsection (3) that are provided otherwise than by the BBC.

(2) The services referred to in subsection (1)(a) are—

(a) television broadcasting services that are provided from places in the United Kingdom with a view to their being broadcast otherwise than only from a satellite;

(b) television licensable content services that are provided by persons under the jurisdiction of the United Kingdom for the purposes of the [F12. Audiovisual Media Services Directive] ;

(c) digital television programme services that are provided by persons under the jurisdiction of the United Kingdom for the purposes of that Directive;

(d) restricted television services that are provided from places in the United Kingdom; and

(e) additional television services that are provided from places in the United Kingdom.

(3) The services referred to in subsection (1)(b) are—

(a) television multiplex services that are provided from places in the United Kingdom; and

(b) digital additional television services that are provided by persons under the jurisdiction of the United Kingdom for the purposes of the [F13. Audiovisual Media Services Directive] .

Amendments (Textual)

F12. Words in s. 211. (2)(b) substituted (19.12.2009) by Audiovisual Media Services Regulations 2009 (S.I. 2009/2979), regs. 1. (1), 8. (a)

F13. Words in s. 211. (3)(b) substituted (19.12.2009) by Audiovisual Media Services Regulations 2009 (S.I. 2009/2979), regs. 1. (1), 8. (a)

212. Abolition of function of assigning television frequencies

The Secretary of State shall cease to have any function under the 1990 Act or the 1996 Act of assigning frequencies for the purposes of any of the following—

(a) services falling to be licensed under Part 1 of the 1990 Act;

(b) S4. C; or

(c) television multiplex services falling to be licensed under Part 1 of the 1996 Act.

213. Abolition of licensing for local cable systems

On and after the television transfer date no licence shall be required under Part 2 of the 1990 Act for the provision of a local delivery service.

Channels 3 and 5.

214. Digital Channel 3 and Channel 5 licences

(1) This section applies to the grant by OFCOM, at any time on or after the television transfer date, of a licence under Part 1 of the 1990 Act to provide a Channel 3 service or to provide Channel 5.

(2) The licence must—

(a) be a licence to provide the licensed service with a view to its being broadcast in digital form; and

(b) contain such condition (if any) requiring the provider of the service to ensure that the whole or a part of the service is also provided for broadcasting in analogue form as OFCOM consider appropriate.

(3) The conditions included in a licence by virtue of subsection (2)(b) must be such as to enable effect to be given to any directions given from time to time by the Secretary of State to OFCOM about the continuance of the provision of services in analogue form.

(4) Where the licence contains a condition falling within subsection (2)(b), it must also contain a condition that—

(a) the programmes (apart from the advertisements) that are included in the service provided in analogue form, and

(b) the times at which they are broadcast,

are to be the same as in the case of, or of the specified part of, the service provided for broadcasting in digital form.

(5) The licence—

(a) must be a licence which continues in force, from the time from which it takes effect, until the end of the licensing period beginning or current at that time; and

(b) shall be renewable, on one or more occasions, under section 216.

(6) For the purposes of subsection (5) a licensing period [F16, in relation to a licence,] is—

(a) the period beginning with the commencement of this section and ending with the initial expiry date [F17for that type of licence] ; or

(b) any subsequent period of ten years beginning with the end of the previous licensing period

[F18for that type of licence] .

(7) The licence must contain the conditions that OFCOM consider appropriate for the purpose of performing their duty under section 263.

(8) The conditions of the licence must also include conditions prohibiting the imposition, whether directly or indirectly, of the following—

(a) charges on persons in respect of their reception in the United Kingdom of the licensed service;

(b) charges on persons in respect of their reception in the United Kingdom of any service consisting in the provision of assistance for disabled people in relation to programmes included in the licensed service; and

(c) charges on persons in respect of their reception in the United Kingdom of any service (other than one mentioned in paragraph (b)) which is an ancillary service in relation to so much of the licensed service as is provided in digital form.

(9) It shall be unlawful to impose a charge in contravention of a condition imposed under subsection (8).

Amendments (Textual)

F16. Words in s. 214. (6) inserted (8.6.2010) by Digital Economy Act 2010 (c. 24), ss. 26. (2)(a), 47. (1)

F17. Words in s. 214. (6)(a) inserted (8.6.2010) by Digital Economy Act 2010 (c. 24), ss. 26. (2)(b), 47. (1)

F18. Words in s. 214. (6)(b) inserted (8.6.2010) by Digital Economy Act 2010 (c. 24), ss. 26. (2)(c), 47. (1)

Commencement Information

I17. S. 214 in force at 29.12.2003 by S.I. 2003/3142, art. 3. (1), Sch. 1 (with art. 11)

215. Replacement of existing Channel 3 and Channel 5 licences

(1) It shall be the duty of OFCOM to make an offer under this section to every person who, when the offer is made, is the holder of a licence (an "existing licence")—

(a) to provide a Channel 3 service; or

(b) to provide Channel 5.

(2) The offer made to a person under this section—

(a) must be an offer to exchange his existing licence for a replacement licence; and

(b) must be made as soon as practicable after the television transfer date.

(3) The replacement licence offered must be one granted in accordance with the provisions of—

(a) Part 1 of the 1990 Act; and

(b) section 214 of this Act;

but sections 15 to 17. A of the 1990 Act (award of licences), are not to apply in the case of the replacement licence.

(4) Subject to subsection (5), where OFCOM make an offer under this section to a person, the service which they are proposing to license by the replacement licence must be a service which—

(a) is provided with a view to its being broadcast in digital form; but

(b) subject to that and to any requirements of section 214, appears to OFCOM to be a service that is equivalent in all material respects to the service the provision of which in analogue form was authorised by the existing licence.

(5) An offer under this section may, to such extent as OFCOM think fit, propose the grant of a licence to provide a service for an area or at times which, though substantially the same as in the case of the existing licence, are not identical.

(6) The offer must propose the inclusion in the replacement licence of conditions as to the payment of amounts to OFCOM which require the payment of—

(a) the same amount in respect of each complete calendar year falling wholly or partly within the period for which the replacement licence is in force, and

(b) an amount equal to the same percentage of the qualifying revenue for each accounting period of the licence holder falling within that period,

as would have been payable under the existing licence had that licence continued in force until the end of the period for which the replacement licence is granted.

(7) That offer must also propose the conditions for allowing amounts paid for a period under the existing licence to be set off against liabilities for the same period arising under the replacement licence.

(8) An offer under this section must set out—

(a) the terms of the proposed replacement licence;

(b) the conditions on which OFCOM are proposing to grant the replacement licence;

(c) the period for which the offer is open;

(d) the date on which the proposed replacement licence will be granted if the offer is accepted;

(e) the time as from which it is proposed that that licence will take effect if the offer is accepted; and

(f) the time from which the existing licence will cease to have effect if the offer is not accepted.

(9) The times set out under subsection (8) must—

(a) in the case of the time set out under paragraph (e), be in the period of twelve months beginning with the television transfer date; and

(b) in the case of the time set out under paragraph (f), be in the period of eighteen months after the end of the period set out under paragraph (c) of that subsection.

(10) Where a person to whom an offer has been made under this section elects, by notification to OFCOM, to exchange his licence for the replacement licence offered to him—

(a) he is entitled, on the date set out in the offer, to be granted, in accordance with Part 1 of the 1990 Act and section 214 of this Act, a replacement licence under that Part in the terms, and on the conditions, so set out;

(b) the replacement licence shall come into force, and the existing licence cease to have effect, at the time specified in the offer, or such later time as OFCOM may, with the consent of that person, direct; and

(c) the service which he is authorised to provide by the replacement licence, so far as it is provided in digital form, shall be a qualifying service for the purposes of Part 1 of the 1996 Act.

(11) Where the person to whom an offer has been made under this section—

(a) does not elect, during the period for which the offer is open, to exchange the existing licence for the replacement licence, or

(b) rejects the offer before the end of that period,

the existing licence shall have effect as if the period for which it is to continue in force ended with the time specified in the offer for the purposes of subsection (8)(f).

(12) In this section "qualifying revenue" has the same meaning as in section 19 of the 1990 Act.

Commencement Information

I18. S. 215 in force at 29.12.2003 by S.I. 2003/3142, art. 3. (1), Sch. 1 (with art. 11)

216. Renewal of Channel 3 and 5 licences

(1) The holder of—

(a) a licence to provide a Channel 3 service, or

(b) a licence to provide Channel 5,

may apply to OFCOM for the renewal of his licence for a period of ten years from the end of the licensing period current at the time of the application.

(2) An application for renewal may only be made in the period which—

(a) begins four years before the end of the current licensing period; and

(b) ends three months before the day that OFCOM have determined to be the day by which they would need to publish a tender notice if they were proposing to grant a fresh licence to take effect from the end of that period.

(3) A determination for the purposes of subsection (2)(b)—

(a) must be made at least one year before the day determined; and

(b) must be notified by OFCOM to every person who, at the time of the determination, holds a licence in respect of which there is right to apply for renewal under this section.

[F19. (4)Where OFCOM receive an application under this section for the renewal of a licence they must—

(a) decide whether to renew the licence; and

(b) notify the applicant of their decision.

(4. A)If OFCOM decide to renew the licence they must—

(a) in the case of a licence to provide a Channel 3 service, determine in accordance with section 216. A the area for which the licence will be renewed;

(b) in every case, determine in accordance with section 217 the financial terms on which the licence will be renewed; and

(c) notify the applicant of their determinations.]

(5) Section 17. (5) to (7) of the 1990 Act (suspect sources of funds) apply in relation to an applicant for a renewal under this section as they apply in relation to an applicant mentioned in section 17. (5) of that Act, but as if references to the award of a licence were references to its renewal.

(6) OFCOM may decide not to renew the licence if they are not satisfied that the applicant (if his licence were renewed) would provide a service complying with the requirements imposed under Chapter 4 of this Part by conditions relating to—

(a) the public service remit for the licensed service;

(b) programming quotas;

(c) news and current affairs programmes; and

(d) programme production and regional programming.

[F20. (6. A)OFCOM may also decide not to renew a licence to provide a Channel 3 service if, for the licensing period in question, they have renewed or propose to renew one or more other licences to provide a Channel 3 service for all of the area to which the licence relates.]

(7) OFCOM may also decide not to renew the licence if they propose to grant a fresh licence for a service replacing the licensed service which would differ from the licensed service in—

(a) the area for which it would be provided; or

(b) the times of the day, or days of the week, between or on which it would be provided.

(8) In all cases in which—

(a) the applicant notifies OFCOM that he accepts the terms notified to him under [F21subsection (4. A)(c)] , and

(b) they are not required or allowed by subsections (5) to (7) to refuse a renewal,

they must grant the renewal as soon as reasonably practicable.

(9) But OFCOM must not grant a renewal under this section more than eighteen months before the end of the licensing period from the end of which the renewal will take effect.

(10) Where a licence is renewed under this section, it must be renewed on the same terms and conditions, subject only to such modifications as are required to give effect [F22—

(a) to any determination under subsection (4. A)(a);

(b) in accordance with the determination under subsection (4. A)(b), to the requirements imposed by section 217. (4).]

(11) Nothing in this section requires OFCOM, following the receipt of an application for the renewal of a licence—

(a) to make a decision or determination, or

(b) to take any other step under this section,

at any time after an order under section 230 has come into force preventing the renewal of the licence.

(12) For the purposes of this section a licensing period [F23, in relation to a licence,] is—

(a) the period beginning with the commencement of this section and ending with the initial expiry date [F24for that type of licence] ; or

(b) any subsequent period of ten years beginning with the end of the previous licensing period [F25for that type of licence] .

(13) In this section "tender notice" means a notice under section 15 of the 1990 Act.

Amendments (Textual)

F19. S. 216. (4)(4. A) substituted for s. 216. (4) (8.6.2010) by Digital Economy Act 2010 (c. 24), ss. 24. (3), 47. (1)

F20. S. 216. (6. A) inserted (8.6.2010) by Digital Economy Act 2010 (c. 24), ss. 24. (4), 47. (1)

F21. Words in s. 216. (8)(a) substituted (8.6.2010) by Digital Economy Act 2010 (c. 24), ss. 24. (5), 47. (1)

F22. Words in s. 216. (10) substituted (8.6.2010) by Digital Economy Act 2010 (c. 24), ss. 24. (6), 47. (1)

F23. Words in s. 216. (12) inserted (8.6.2010) by Digital Economy Act 2010 (c. 24), ss. 26. (2)(a), 47. (1)

F24. Words in s. 216. (12)(a) inserted (8.6.2010) by Digital Economy Act 2010 (c. 24), ss. 26. (2)(b), 47. (1)

F25. Words in s. 216. (12)(b) inserted (8.6.2010) by Digital Economy Act 2010 (c. 24), ss. 26. (2)(c), 47. (1)

Commencement Information

I19. S. 216 in force at 29.12.2003 by S.I. 2003/3142, art. 3. (1), Sch. 1 (with art. 11)

[F26216. ARenewal of Channel 3 licences: determination of licence areas

(1) This section applies if OFCOM decide under section 216. (4) to renew a licence to provide a Channel 3 service.

(2) The area determined under section 216. (4. A)(a) for the licence—

(a) must include all or part of the area to which the licence being renewed currently relates, and

(b) may include all or part of another area if the holder of the licence to provide a Channel 3 service for the other area gives (and does not withdraw) consent before the determination is made.]

Amendments (Textual)

F26. S. 216. A inserted (8.6.2010) by Digital Economy Act 2010 (c. 24), ss. 24. (7), 47. (1)

217. Financial terms of licence renewed under s. 216.

(1) The determination under [F27section 216. (4. A)(b)] must comprise—

(a) a determination of the amount which the holder of the renewed licence will be required by the conditions of that licence to pay to OFCOM in respect of the first complete calendar year falling within the renewal period; and

(b) a determination of the percentage of qualifying revenue for each accounting period of the licence holder falling within the renewal period which the holder of that licence will be required by those conditions to pay to OFCOM.

(2) The amount determined under subsection (1)(a) must be equal to the amount which, in OFCOM's opinion, would have been the cash bid of the licence holder were the licence (instead of being renewed) to be granted for the period of the renewal on an application made in accordance with section 15 of the 1990 Act.

(3) For the purposes of subsection (1)(b)—

(a) different percentages may be determined for different accounting periods; and

(b) the percentages that may be determined for an accounting period include a nil percentage.

(4) The renewed licence is required, as renewed, to include conditions requiring the licence holder to pay to OFCOM—

(a) in addition to any fees required to be paid by virtue of section 4. (1)(b) of the 1990 Act, but

(b) instead of the amounts payable under the corresponding provision applicable under the conditions of the licence to the period before the renewal takes effect,

the amounts specified in subsection (5).

(5) Those amounts are—

(a) in respect of the first complete calendar year falling within the renewal period, the amount determined under subsection (1)(a);

(b) in respect of each subsequent year falling wholly or partly within the renewal period, that amount increased by the appropriate percentage; and

(c) in respect of each accounting period of the licence holder falling within the renewal period, an amount representing a specified percentage of qualifying revenue for that accounting period.

(6) The percentage specified for the purposes of subsection (5)(c) in respect of an accounting period must be the amount determined for that period under subsection (1)(b).

(7) In this section—

"the appropriate percentage" and "qualifying revenue" each has the same meaning as in section 19 of the 1990 Act; and

"renewal period", in relation to a licence, means the period for which the licence is in force by reason of its renewal.

Amendments (Textual)

F27. Words in s. 217. (1) substituted (8.6.2010) by Digital Economy Act 2010 (c. 24), ss. 24. (8), 47. (1)

Commencement Information

I20. S. 217 in force at 29.12.2003 by S.I. 2003/3142, art. 3. (1), Sch. 1 (with art. 11)

The public teletext service

218. Duty to secure the provision of a public teletext service

(1) OFCOM must do all that they can to secure the provision, in accordance with this Chapter and Part 1 of the 1996 Act, of a teletext service that is available nationwide.

(2) The service must consist of—

(a) a single teletext service provided in digital form with a view to its being broadcast by means of a television multiplex service; and

(b) for so long as Channel 4, S4. C and one or more Channel 3 services are broadcast in analogue form, an analogue teletext service.

(3) The service, if licensed to do so in accordance with section 219, may continue to include an analogue teletext service after it is no longer required under subsection (2)(b) to include such a service.

(4) The analogue teletext service that must be or may be comprised in the public teletext service is a single additional television service that uses the combined spare capacity available for the provision of additional television services on the frequencies on which Channel 3 services, Channel 4 and S4. C (or any of them) are broadcast in analogue form.

(5) For so long as the public teletext service must consist of both a teletext service provided in digital form and an analogue teletext service, OFCOM must secure that both services are provided by the same person.

(6) But nothing in this section—

(a) requires the contents of the two services comprised in the public teletext service to be the same;

(b) prevents the service from including different items for different parts of the United Kingdom or prevents the different items from being made available only in the parts of the United Kingdom for which they are included; or

(c) prevents the licence holder from making arrangements authorised by virtue of section 220 for the provision of the whole or a part of the public teletext service by another.

(7) OFCOM must exercise their powers—

(a) to make frequencies available for the purposes of Channel 3 services, Channel 4 and S4. C; and

(b) to make determinations for the purposes of section 48. (2)(b) of the 1990 Act (determinations of spare capacity),

in a manner that takes account of their duty under this section.

Commencement Information

I21. S. 218 in force at 29.12.2003 by S.I. 2003/3142, art. 3. (1), Sch. 1 (with art. 11)

[F28218. ADuty to report on public teletext service

(1) OFCOM must—

(a) prepare a report on the public teletext service, and

(b) send it to the Secretary of State as soon as practicable after this section comes into force.

(2) OFCOM must prepare and send to the Secretary of State further reports on the public teletext service when asked to do so by the Secretary of State.

(3) Each report must include, in particular—

(a) an assessment of the advantages and disadvantages for members of the public of the public teletext service being provided, and

(b) an assessment of whether the public teletext service can be provided at a cost to the licence holder that is commercially sustainable.

(4) An assessment under subsection (3)(a) must take account of alternative uses for the capacity that would be available if the public teletext service were not provided.

(5) OFCOM must publish every report under this section—

(a) as soon as practicable after they send it to the Secretary of State, and

(b) in such manner as they consider appropriate.

(6) "Capacity" means capacity on the frequencies on which Channel 3 services, Channel 4, S4. C and television multiplex services are broadcast.]

Amendments (Textual)

F28. S. 218. A inserted (8.6.2010) by Digital Economy Act 2010 (c. 24), ss. 27, 47. (1)

219. Licensing of the public teletext service

(1) The licence that is required for the purposes of section 13 of the 1990 Act in respect of the public teletext service is a licence under Part 1 of that Act complying with this section.

(2) The licence—

(a) must be a licence which continues in force, from the time from which it takes effect, until the end of the licensing period beginning or current at that time; and

(b) shall be renewable, on one or more occasions, under section 222.

(3) For the purposes of subsection (2) a licensing period is—

(a) the period beginning with the commencement of this section and ending with the initial expiry date [F29for the licence to provide the public teletext service] ; or

(b) any subsequent period of ten years beginning with the end of the previous licensing period [F30for that type of licence] .

(4) The licence must contain the conditions that OFCOM consider appropriate for the purpose of performing their duty under section 263.

(5) The conditions of the licence must also include conditions prohibiting the imposition, whether directly or indirectly, of any charges on persons in respect of their reception in the United Kingdom of the licensed service.

(6) It shall be unlawful to impose a charge in contravention of a condition imposed under subsection (5).

(7) The service authorised by a licence under this section, so far as it comprises a service provided in digital form, is a qualifying service for the purposes of Part 1 of the 1996 Act.

(8) Schedule 10 (which makes further provision about the award and grant of the licence for the public teletext service and about the conditions and enforcement of that licence) shall have effect.

Amendments (Textual)

F29. Words in s. 219. (3)(a) inserted (8.6.2010) by Digital Economy Act 2010 (c. 24), ss. 26. (3)(a), 47. (1)

F30. Words in s. 219. (3)(b) inserted (8.6.2010) by Digital Economy Act 2010 (c. 24), ss. 26. (3)(b), 47. (1)

Modifications etc. (not altering text)

C4. S. 219 excluded (8.12.2003) by The Office of Communications Act 2002 (Commencement No. 3) and Communications Act 2003 (Commencement No. 2) Order 2003 (S.I. 2003/3142), art. 8. (1) (with art. 11)

Commencement Information

I22. S. 219 in force at 29.12.2003 by S.I. 2003/3142, art. 3. (1), Sch. 1 (with art. 11)

220. Delegation of provision of public teletext service

(1) The licence for the provision of the public teletext service may—

(a) include provision enabling the licence holder to authorise an eligible person to provide the whole or a part of the public teletext service on his behalf; and

(b) impose conditions subject to and in accordance with which the whole or a part of that service may be provided by a person authorised by the licence holder.

(2) The conditions of the licence to provide the public teletext service apply in relation to its provision by a person authorised to do so on the licence holder's behalf as they apply to its provision by the licence holder.

(3) A contravention of those conditions by a person so authorised shall be treated for the purposes of this Chapter and the 1990 Act as a contravention on the part of the licence holder.

(4) In this section "eligible person" means a person who is not a disqualified person under Part 2 of Schedule 2 to the 1990 Act in relation to the licence for the public teletext service.

Modifications etc. (not altering text)

C5. S. 220 excluded (8.12.2003) by The Office of Communications Act 2002 (Commencement No. 3) and Communications Act 2003 (Commencement No. 2) Order 2003 (S.I. 2003/3142), art. 8. (1) (with art. 11)

Commencement Information

I23. S. 220 in force at 29.12.2003 by S.I. 2003/3142, art. 3. (1), Sch. 1 (with art. 11)

221. Replacement of existing public teletext provider's licence

(1) It shall be the duty of OFCOM to make an offer under this section to the person who, when the offer is made, is the holder of the licence to provide the existing service (the "existing licence").

(2) The offer made to a person under this section—

(a) must be an offer to exchange his existing licence for a replacement licence; and

(b) must be made as soon as practicable after the television transfer date.

(3) The replacement licence is to be one which is granted—

(a) for the purposes of section 218 of this Act; and

(b) in accordance with section 219 of this Act and the provisions of Part 1 of the 1990 Act; but Part 1 of Schedule 10 to this Act is not to apply in the case of the replacement licence.

(4) Where OFCOM make an offer under this section, the service which they are proposing to license by or under the replacement licence must be a service which comprises both—

(a) a service that appears to OFCOM to be equivalent in all material respects to the existing service; and

(b) a service that appears to them to be equivalent in all material respects to the teletext service in digital form which that person is required to provide by virtue of section 30 of the 1996 Act.

(5) The offer must propose the inclusion in the replacement licence of conditions as to the payment of amounts to OFCOM which require the payment of—

(a) the same amount in respect of each complete calendar year falling wholly or partly within the period for which the replacement licence is in force, and

(b) an amount equal to the same percentage of the qualifying revenue for each accounting period of the licence holder falling within that period, as would have been payable under the existing licence had that licence continued in force until the end of the period for which the replacement licence is granted.

(6) That offer must also propose conditions allowing amounts paid for a period under the existing licence to be set off against liabilities for the same period arising under the replacement licence.

(7) An offer under this section must set out—

(a) the terms of the proposed replacement licence;

(b) the conditions on which OFCOM are proposing to grant the replacement licence;

(c) the period for which the offer is open;

(d) the time as from which it is proposed the replacement licence will take effect if the offer is accepted; and

(e) the time from which the existing licence will cease to have effect if the offer is not accepted.

(8) The times set out under subsection (7) must—

(a) in the case of the time set out under paragraph (d), be in the period of twelve months beginning with the television transfer date; and

(b) in the case of the time set out under paragraph (e), be in the period of eighteen months after the end of the period set out under paragraph (c) of that subsection.

(9) Where the person to whom an offer has been made under this section elects, by notification to

OFCOM, to exchange his licence for the replacement licence offered to him—

(a) he is entitled to be granted the replacement licence in the terms, and on the conditions, set out in the offer; and

(b) the replacement licence shall come into force, and the existing licence cease to have effect, at the time specified in the offer, or such later time as OFCOM may, with the consent of that person, direct.

(10) Where the person to whom an offer has been made under this section—

(a) does not elect, during the period for which the offer is open, to exchange the existing licence for the replacement licence, or

(b) rejects the offer before the end of that period,

the existing licence shall have effect as if the period for which it is to continue in force ended with the time specified in the offer for the purposes of subsection (7)(e).

(11) In this section "the existing service" means the teletext service which—

(a) is being provided immediately before the television transfer date on the combined spare capacity available for the provision of additional television services on frequencies on which Channel 3 services and Channel 4 are provided; and

(b) is the service by reference to which the Independent Television Commission have discharged their duty under section 49. (2) of the 1990 Act.

(12) In this section "qualifying revenue" means the revenue which would be qualifying revenue (within the meaning of section 52 of the 1990 Act) in relation to the holder of a licence to provide the analogue teletext service comprised in the public teletext service.

Commencement Information

I24. S. 221 in force at 29.12.2003 by S.I. 2003/3142, art. 3. (1), Sch. 1 (with art. 11)

222. Renewal of public teletext licence

(1) The holder of the licence to provide the public teletext service may apply to OFCOM for the renewal of his licence for a period of ten years from the end of the licensing period current at the time of the application.

(2) An application for renewal may only be made in the period which—

(a) begins four years before the end of the current licensing period; and

(b) ends three months before the day that OFCOM have determined to be the day by which they would need to publish a tender notice if they were proposing to grant a fresh licence to take effect from the end of that period.

(3) A determination for the purposes of subsection (2)(b)—

(a) must be made at least one year before the day determined; and

(b) must be notified by OFCOM to the holder, at the time of the determination, of the licence to provide the public teletext service.

(4) Where OFCOM receive an application under this section for the renewal of a licence, they must—

(a) decide whether they will be renewing the licence;

(b) if they decide that they will be, determine in accordance with section 223 the financial terms on which the licence will be renewed; and

(c) notify the applicant of their decision and determination.

(5) Section 17. (5) to (7) of the 1990 Act (suspect sources of funds) apply in relation to an applicant for a renewal under this section as they apply in relation to an applicant mentioned in section 17. (5) of that Act, but as if—

(a) references to the award of a licence were references to its renewal; and

(b) the reference in subsection (7)(a) to section 19. (1) of that Act were a reference to paragraph 7 of Schedule 10.

(6) OFCOM may decide not to renew the licence if they are not satisfied that the applicant (if his licence were renewed) would provide a service complying with the requirements imposed under Chapter 4 of this Part by conditions relating to—

(a) the public service remit for the public teletext service;

(b) news; and

(c) regional matters.

(7) OFCOM may also decide not to renew the licence if they propose to grant a fresh licence for the public teletext service which would differ in any material respect from the licensed service.

(8) In all cases in which—

(a) the applicant notifies OFCOM that he accepts the terms notified to him under subsection (4)(c), and

(b) they are not required or allowed by subsections (5) to (7) to refuse a renewal,

they must grant the renewal as soon as reasonably practicable.

(9) But OFCOM must not grant a renewal under this section more than eighteen months before the end of the licensing period from the end of which the renewal will take effect.

(10) Where a licence is renewed under this section, it must be renewed on the same terms and conditions subject only to such modifications as are required to give effect, in accordance with the determination under subsection (4)(b), to paragraph 7 of Schedule 10.

(11) Nothing in this section requires OFCOM, following the receipt of an application for the renewal of a licence—

(a) to make a decision or determination, or

(b) to take any other step under this section,

at any time after an order under section 230 has come into force preventing the renewal of the licence.

(12) For the purposes of this section a licensing period is—

(a) the period beginning with the commencement of this section and ending with the initial expiry date [F31for the licence to provide the public teletext service] ; or

(b) any subsequent period of ten years beginning with the end of the previous licensing period [F32for that type of licence] .

(13) In this section "tender notice" means a notice under paragraph 1 of Schedule 10.

Amendments (Textual)

F31. Words in s. 222. (12)(a) inserted (8.6.2010) by Digital Economy Act 2010 (c. 24), ss. 26. (3)(a), 47. (1)

F32. Words in s. 222. (12)(b) inserted (8.6.2010) by Digital Economy Act 2010 (c. 24), ss. 26. (3)(b), 47. (1)

Commencement Information

I25. S. 222 in force at 29.12.2003 by S.I. 2003/3142, art. 3. (1), Sch. 1 (with art. 11)

223. Financial terms of licence renewed under s. 222.

(1) The determination under section 222. (4)(b) must comprise—

(a) a determination of the amount which the holder of the renewed licence will be required by the conditions of that licence to pay to OFCOM in respect of the first complete calendar year falling within the renewal period;

(b) a determination of the percentage of qualifying revenue for each accounting period of the licence holder falling within the renewal period which he will be required by those conditions to pay to OFCOM.

(2) The amount determined under subsection (1)(a) must be equal to the amount which, in OFCOM's opinion, would have been the cash bid of the licence holder were the licence (instead of being renewed) to be granted for the period of the renewal on an application made in accordance with Part 1 of Schedule 10.

(3) For the purposes of subsection (1)(b)—

(a) different percentages may be determined for different accounting periods; and

(b) the percentages that may be determined for an accounting period include a nil percentage.

(4) In this section "renewal period", in relation to a licence, means the period for which the licence is in force by reason of its renewal.

(5) Part 3 of Schedule 10 applies for construing this section as it applies for construing that Schedule.

Commencement Information

I26. S. 223 in force at 29.12.2003 by S.I. 2003/3142, art. 3. (1), Sch. 1 (with art. 11)

Meaning of initial expiry date

224. Meaning of "initial expiry date"
[F33. (1)Subject to any postponement under this section, for the purposes of this Part the initial expiry date for the following types of licence is 31 December 2014—

    (a) a licence to provide a Channel 3 service;

    (b) a licence to provide Channel 5;

    (c) the licence to provide the public teletext service.]

(2) The Secretary of State may (on one or more occasions) by order postpone the initial expiry date [F34for one or more of the types of licence mentioned in subsection (1)] .

F35. (3). . . . .

(4) Where the Secretary of State makes an order under this section at a time after he has fixed a date for digital switchover, the date to which the initial expiry date is postponed must be a date not less than eighteen months after the date for digital switchover.

(5) The Secretary of State must exercise his power to postpone the initial expiry date if it at any time appears to him that that date would otherwise fall within the period of eighteen months immediately following the date fixed for digital switchover.

(6) Where an order under this section extends a licensing period for which a licence has been granted in accordance with section 214 or 219, the 1990 Act and this Part shall have effect (subject to subsection (7)) as if the licence had originally been granted for the extended period.

(7) Where an order under this section extends the period for which a licence is to continue in force—

    (a) that order shall not affect the earliest time at which an application for the renewal of that licence may be made in accordance with section 216. (2)(a) or 222. (2)(a);

    (b) as soon as reasonably practicable after making the order, OFCOM must make such modification of any determination made by them in the case of that licence for the purposes of section 216. (2)(b) or 222. (2)(b) as they consider appropriate in consequence of the extension; and

    (c) neither section 216. (3)(a) nor section 222. (3)(a) applies to the making of that modification.

(8) In this section a reference to the date for digital switchover is a reference to the date fixed by the Secretary of State for the purposes of this section as the date which appears to him, in consequence of directions given by him for the purposes of the conditions of the licences for the relevant public broadcasting services, to be the date after which none of those services will be broadcast to any significant extent in analogue form.

(9) In this section "the relevant public broadcasting service" means any of the following—

    (a) the services comprised in Channel 3; and

    (b) Channel 5.

Amendments (Textual)

F33. S. 224. (1) substituted (8.6.2010) by Digital Economy Act 2010 (c. 24), ss. 25. (2), 47. (1)

F34. Words in s. 224. (2) inserted (8.6.2010) by Digital Economy Act 2010 (c. 24), ss. 25. (3), 47. (1)

F35. S. 224. (3) repealed (8.6.2010) by Digital Economy Act 2010 (c. 24), ss. 25. (4), 47. (1), Sch. 2

Commencement Information

I27. S. 224 in force at 29.12.2003 by S.I. 2003/3142, art. 3. (1), Sch. 1 (with art. 11)

Reviews relating to licensing of Channels 3 & 5 and teletext

225. Application for review of financial terms of replacement licences

(1) The holder of a replacement licence granted under section 215 or 221 may apply to OFCOM, at any time in the first or any subsequent review period, for a review of the financial terms on which that licence is held.

(2) For the purposes of this section the first review period is the period which—

(a) begins four years before the first notional expiry date; and

(b) ends with the day before the day that OFCOM have determined to be the one by which they would need to publish a tender notice if they were proposing to grant a fresh licence to take effect from the first notional expiry date.

(3) For the purposes of this section a subsequent review period in the case of a replacement licence is so much (if any) of the following period as falls before the end of the initial expiry date [F36for that type of licence] , namely, the period which—

(a) begins four years before a subsequent notional expiry date; and

(b) ends with the day before the day that OFCOM have determined to be the one by which they would need to publish a tender notice if they were proposing to grant a fresh licence to take effect from that notional expiry date.

(4) A determination for the purposes of subsection (2)(b) or (3)(b) in respect of a replacement licence—

(a) must be made at least one year before the day determined; and

(b) must be notified by OFCOM to the person who, at the time of the determination, holds the licence in question.

(5) No application under this section for a review of the financial terms on which a replacement licence is held is to be made—

(a) at any time when an application under section 226 for a review of those terms is pending; or

(b) at any time in the period of twelve months following the day on which a determination by OFCOM on such an application is notified to the licence holder.

(6) For the purposes of this section an application for a review under section 226 is pending from the time when the application is made until the end of the day on which OFCOM's determination on the review is notified to the licence holder.

(7) In this section—

"the first notional expiry date", in relation to a replacement licence, means the date with which (apart from this Act) the existing licence would have expired if not renewed;

"subsequent notional expiry date", in relation to a replacement licence, means—

- in a case in which an application by the licence holder for a review under this section was made during the review period beginning four years before the last notional expiry date, the tenth anniversary of the date on which OFCOM's determination on that review was notified to the licence holder; and

- in any other case, the tenth anniversary of the last notional expiry date;

"tender notice" means a notice under section 15. (1) of the 1990 Act or (as the case may be) paragraph 1 of Schedule 10.

(8) In subsection (7) "existing licence" has the same meaning as in section 215 or (as the case may be) 221.

Amendments (Textual)

F36. Words in s. 225. (3) inserted (8.6.2010) by Digital Economy Act 2010 (c. 24), ss. 26. (4), 47. (1)

Commencement Information

I28. S. 225 in force at 29.12.2003 by S.I. 2003/3142, art. 3. (1), Sch. 1 (with art. 11)

226. Application for review of financial terms in consequence of new obligations

(1) This section applies where an order is made under section 411 that brings section 272, 273 or 274 (or any two or more of them) into force for the purpose of including conditions in the regulatory regime for—

(a) a Channel 3 service;

(b) Channel 5; or

(c) the public teletext service.

(2) The holder of a licence in which conditions mentioned in section 272, 273 or 274 will fall to be included when the order comes into force may apply to OFCOM, at any time in the review period, for a review of the financial terms on which the licence is held.

(3) For the purposes of this section the review period in the case of an order under section 411 is the period which—

(a) begins with the day on which the order is made; and

(b) ends with the time at which, by virtue of the order, one or more of sections 272, 273 and 274 come into force in the case of the licence in question.

(4) If in the case of the same order there is more than one time falling within subsection (3)(b), the review period ends with the later or latest of them.

Commencement Information

I29. S. 226 in force at 29.12.2003 by S.I. 2003/3142, art. 3. (1), Sch. 1 (with art. 11)

227. Reviews under ss. 225 and 226.

(1) This section applies where an application is made under section 225 or 226 for a review of the financial terms on which a licence is held.

(2) As soon as reasonably practicable after receiving the application, OFCOM must—

(a) determine the amount to be paid to them under the conditions of the licence for the first calendar year falling wholly or partly within the period under review to begin after the application date; and

(b) determine the percentage to be used for computing the payments to be made to them under those conditions in respect of each accounting period falling within the period under review to begin after that date.

(3) The amount determined under subsection (2)(a) must be equal to the amount which, in OFCOM's opinion, would have been the cash bid of the licence holder were the licence being granted afresh on an application made in accordance with—

(a) section 15 of the 1990 Act (licences for Channel 3 service or Channel 5); or

(b) paragraph 3 of Schedule 10 to this Act.

(4) The determination required by subsection (2)(b) is a determination of the percentage of qualifying revenue for each accounting period that is to be paid to OFCOM.

(5) For the purposes of subsection (2)(b)—

(a) different percentages may be determined for different accounting periods; and

(b) the percentages that may be determined for an accounting period include a nil percentage.

(6) In making their determinations on an application under section 226 OFCOM are to have regard, in particular, to any additional costs that are likely to be incurred by the licence holder in consequence of the commencement of so much of section 272, 273 or 274 (or any two or more of them) as is brought into force by the commencement order in question.

(7) References in this section to qualifying revenue for an accounting period are to be construed—

(a) in the case of the holder of a licence to provide a Channel 3 service or Channel 5, in accordance with section 19 of and Part 1 of Schedule 7 to the 1990 Act; and

(b) in the case of the holder of the licence to provide the public teletext service, in accordance with Part 3 of Schedule 10 to this Act.

(8) In this section—

"the application date", in relation to a review, means the date of the making under section 225 or 226 of the application for the review; and

"the period under review", in relation to a review of the financial terms of a licence, means so much of the period for which the licence will (if not renewed) continue in force after the application date.

Commencement Information

I30. S. 227 in force at 29.12.2003 by S.I. 2003/3142, art. 3. (1), Sch. 1 (with art. 11)

228. Giving effect to reviews under ss. 225 and 226.

(1) As soon as reasonably practicable after making a determination under section 227 on an application under section 225 or 226, OFCOM must give a notification of their determination to the applicant.

(2) The notification must set out—

(a) the determination made by OFCOM;

(b) the modifications of the applicant's licence that are required to give effect to the determination;

(c) a date by which the applicant must notify OFCOM whether or not he accepts the determination and modifications; and

(d) a subsequent date by which the applicant's licence will cease to have effect if he does not.

(3) The modifications set out in accordance with subsection (2)(b) must secure that the amount falling to be paid under the conditions of the applicant's licence for each calendar year subsequent to that for which an amount has been determined in accordance with section 227. (2)(a) is the amount so determined as increased by the appropriate percentage.

(4) In the case of a determination on an application under section 225, the date specified in accordance with subsection (2)(d) must not fall before whichever is the earlier of —

(a) the next notional expiry date after the application for the review; and

(b) the end of the licensing period in which that application was made.

(5) Where the applicant notifies OFCOM that he accepts the determination—

(a) his licence is to have effect with the modifications set out in OFCOM's notification; and

(b) all such adjustments by way of payment or repayment as may be necessary for giving effect to the modifications are to be made in respect of any payments already made for years or periods affected by the modifications.

(6) Where the applicant does not, before the date specified in accordance with paragraph (c) of subsection (2), notify OFCOM that he accepts the determination, his licence shall have effect as if the period for which it is to continue in force ended with the time specified in accordance with paragraph (d) of that subsection.

(7) Where the time at which a licence would cease to have effect in accordance with subsection (6) is the end of a licensing period, that subsection does not affect any rights of the licence holder with respect to the renewal of his licence from the end of that period.

(8) In this section—

"the appropriate percentage" has the same meaning as in section 19 of the 1990 Act;

"licensing period" [F37, in relation to a licence,] means—

- the period beginning with the commencement of this section and ending with the initial expiry date [F38for that type of licence] ; or

- any subsequent period of ten years beginning with the end of the previous licensing period [F39for that type of licence] ;

"notional expiry date" means a first or subsequent notional expiry date within the meaning of section 225.

Amendments (Textual)

F37. Words in s. 228. (8) inserted (8.6.2010) by Digital Economy Act 2010 (c. 24), ss. 26. (5)(a), 47. (1)

F38. Words in s. 228. (8) inserted (8.6.2010) by Digital Economy Act 2010 (c. 24), ss. 26. (5)(b), 47. (1)

F39. Words in s. 228. (8) inserted (8.6.2010) by Digital Economy Act 2010 (c. 24), ss. 26. (5)(c), 47. (1)

Commencement Information

I31. S. 228 in force at 29.12.2003 by S.I. 2003/3142, art. 3. (1), Sch. 1 (with art. 11)

229. Report in anticipation of new licensing round

(1) OFCOM must, in anticipation of the end of each licensing period [F40for a type of relevant licence] —

(a) prepare a report under this section; and

(b) submit it to the Secretary of State no later than thirty months before the end of that period.

(2) A report under this section must set out OFCOM's opinion on the effect of each of the matters mentioned in subsection (3) on the capacity of the [F41holder or holders of that type of licence] to contribute, in the next licensing period, to the fulfilment of the purposes of public service television broadcasting in the United Kingdom at a cost to the [F42licence holder or holders] that is commercially sustainable.

(3) Those matters are—

(a) the arrangements that (but for an order under section 230) would allow for the renewal of [F43that type of licence] from the end of the current licensing period; and

(b) the conditions included in the regulatory regimes for the services provided under [F44that type of licence] .

(4) A report under this section must also include the recommendations (if any) which OFCOM consider, in the light of the opinion set out in the report, should be made to the Secretary of State for the exercise by him of—

(a) his power under section 230; or

(b) any of the powers to make statutory instruments that are conferred on him by Chapter 4 of this Part.

[F45. (4. A)Subsection (5) applies where the Secretary of State—

(a) receives a report under this section in anticipation of the end of a licensing period for a type of relevant licence, and

(b) subsequently makes an order under section 224 extending the licensing period for that type of licence.]

(5) [F46. Where this subsection applies—]

(a) [F47the Secretary of State] may require OFCOM to prepare a supplementary report in the light of the postponement of the beginning of the next licensing period [F48for that type of licence] ; and

(b) it shall be the duty of OFCOM, within such period as may be specified by the Secretary of State, to prepare the required supplementary report and to submit it to him.

(6) In this section—

"licensing period" [F49, in relation to a licence,] means—

- the period beginning with the commencement of this section and ending with the initial expiry date [F50for that type of licence] ; or

- any subsequent period of ten years beginning with the end of the previous licensing period [F51for that type of licence] ;

"relevant licence" means—

- a licence to provide a Channel 3 service;

- a licence to provide Channel 5; or

- the licence to provide the public teletext service.

Amendments (Textual)

F40. Words in s. 229. (1) inserted (8.6.2010) by Digital Economy Act 2010 (c. 24), ss. 26. (7), 47. (1)

F41. Words in s. 229. (2) substituted (8.6.2010) by Digital Economy Act 2010 (c. 24), ss. 26. (8)(a), 47. (1)

F42. Words in s. 229. (2) substituted (8.6.2010) by Digital Economy Act 2010 (c. 24), ss. 26. (8)(b), 47. (1)

F43. Words in s. 229. (3)(a) substituted (8.6.2010) by Digital Economy Act 2010 (c. 24), ss. 26. (9), 47. (1)

F44. Words in s. 229. (3)(b) substituted (8.6.2010) by Digital Economy Act 2010 (c. 24), ss. 26. (9), 47. (1)

F45. S. 229. (4. A) inserted (8.6.2010) by Digital Economy Act 2010 (c. 24), ss. 26. (10), 47. (1)

F46. Words in s. 229. (5) substituted (8.6.2010) by Digital Economy Act 2010 (c. 24), ss. 26. (11)(a), 47. (1)

F47. Word in s. 229. (5)(a) substituted (8.6.2010) by Digital Economy Act 2010 (c. 24), ss. 26. (11)(b), 47. (1)

F48. Words in s. 229. (5)(a) inserted (8.6.2010) by Digital Economy Act 2010 (c. 24), ss. 26. (11)(b), 47. (1)

F49. Words in s. 229. (6) inserted (8.6.2010) by Digital Economy Act 2010 (c. 24), ss. 26. (12)(a), 47. (1)

F50. Words in s. 229. (6) inserted (8.6.2010) by Digital Economy Act 2010 (c. 24), ss. 26. (12)(b), 47. (1)

F51. Words in s. 229. (6) inserted (8.6.2010) by Digital Economy Act 2010 (c. 24), ss. 26. (12)(c), 47. (1)

Commencement Information

I32. S. 229 in force at 29.12.2003 by S.I. 2003/3142, art. 3. (1), Sch. 1 (with art. 11)

230. Orders suspending rights of renewal

(1) This section applies where the Secretary of State has received and considered a report submitted to him by OFCOM under section 229.

(2) If—

(a) the report contains a recommendation by OFCOM for the making of an order under this section, or

(b) the Secretary of State considers, notwithstanding the absence of such a recommendation, that it would be appropriate to do so,

he may by order provide that [F52a licence for the time being in force that is of a description specified in the order is] not to be renewable under section 216 or 222 from the end of the licensing period in which he received the report [F53. (but see subsection (7))] .

(3) An order under this section preventing the renewal of [F54a licence] from the end of a licensing period must be made at least eighteen months before the end of that period.

(4) The Secretary of State is not to make an order under this section preventing the renewal of [F55a licence] from the end of the initial licensing period unless he has fixed a date before the end of that period as the date for digital switchover.

(5) Where the Secretary of State postpones the date for digital switchover after making an order under this section preventing the renewal of [F56a licence] from the end of the initial licensing period, the order shall have effect only if the date to which digital switchover is postponed falls before the end of that period.

(6) Subsection (5) does not affect the power of the Secretary of State to make another order under this section after postponing the date for digital switchover.

(7) An order under this section with respect to [F57a Channel 3 licence] must be an order of one of the following descriptions—

(a) an order applying to every licence to provide a Channel 3 service;

(b) an order applying to every licence to provide a national Channel 3 service; or

(c) an order applying to every licence to provide a regional Channel 3 service.

(8) An order under this section does not affect—

(a) the person to whom a licence may be granted on an application made under section 15 of the 1990 Act or under paragraph 3 of Schedule 10 to this Act; or

(b) rights of renewal in respect of [F58a licence] first granted so as to take effect from the beginning of a licensing period beginning after the making of the order, or from a subsequent time.

(9) No order is to be made containing provision authorised by this section unless a draft of the order has been laid before Parliament and approved by a resolution of each House.

(10) Subsection (8) of section 224 applies for construing references in this section to the date for digital switchover as it applies for the purposes of that section.

(11) In this section—

"initial licensing period" [F59, in relation to a licence,] means the licensing period ending with the initial expiry date [F60for that type of licence] ; and

"licensing period" has the same meaning as in section 229.

Amendments (Textual)

F52. Words in s. 230. (2) substituted (8.6.2010) by Digital Economy Act 2010 (c. 24), ss. 26. (14), 47. (1)

F53. Words in s. 230. (2) inserted (8.6.2010) by Digital Economy Act 2010 (c. 24), ss. 26. (15), 47. (1)

F54. Word in s. 230. (3) substituted (8.6.2010) by Digital Economy Act 2010 (c. 24), ss. 26. (16), 47. (1)

F55. Word in s. 230. (4) substituted (8.6.2010) by Digital Economy Act 2010 (c. 24), ss. 26. (16),

47. (1)

F56. Word in s. 230. (5) substituted (8.6.2010) by Digital Economy Act 2010 (c. 24), ss. 26. (16), 47. (1)

F57. Words in s. 230. (7) substituted (8.6.2010) by Digital Economy Act 2010 (c. 24), ss. 26. (17), 47. (1)

F58. Word in s. 230. (8)(b) substituted (8.6.2010) by Digital Economy Act 2010 (c. 24), ss. 26. (16), 47. (1)

F59. Words in s. 230. (11) inserted (8.6.2010) by Digital Economy Act 2010 (c. 24), ss. 26. (18)(a), 47. (1)

F60. Words in s. 230. (11) inserted (8.6.2010) by Digital Economy Act 2010 (c. 24), ss. 26. (18)(b), 47. (1)

Commencement Information

I33. S. 230 in force at 29.12.2003 by S.I. 2003/3142, art. 3. (1), Sch. 1 (with art. 11)

Replacement of Channel 4 licence

231. Replacement of Channel 4 licence

(1) On the commencement of this subsection—

(a) Channel 4 shall cease to be licensed under the licence in force for the purposes of section 24. (3) of the 1990 Act immediately before the commencement of this subsection; and

(b) a licence granted for those purposes in accordance with the following provisions of this section shall come into force as the licence under which Channel 4 is licensed.

(2) It shall be the duty of OFCOM, as soon as practicable after the television transfer date—

(a) to prepare a draft of a licence under Part 1 of the 1990 Act to replace the licence that is likely to be in force for the purposes of section 24. (3) of the 1990 Act when subsection (1) of this section comes into force;

(b) to notify C4. C of the terms and conditions of the replacement licence they propose; and

(c) after considering any representations made by C4. C, to grant such a replacement licence to C4. C so that it takes effect in accordance with paragraph (b) of subsection (1) of this section.

(3) A replacement licence proposed or granted under this section—

(a) must be a licence to provide a service with a view to its being broadcast in digital form; and

(b) must contain such conditions (if any) requiring C4. C to ensure that the whole or a part of Channel 4 is also provided for broadcasting in analogue form as OFCOM consider appropriate.

(4) The conditions included in a licence by virtue of subsection (3)(b) must be such as to enable effect to be given to any directions given from time to time by the Secretary of State to OFCOM about the continuance of the provision of services in analogue form.

(5) Where a replacement licence proposed or granted under this section contains a condition falling within subsection (3)(b), it must also contain a condition that—

(a) the programmes (apart from the advertisements) that are included in the service provided in analogue form, and

(b) the times at which they are broadcast,

are to be the same as in the case of, or of the specified part of, the service provided for broadcasting in digital form.

(6) The terms of a replacement licence proposed or granted under this section must provide for it to continue in force until the end of 2014.

(7) But—

(a) such a licence may be renewed, on one or more occasions, for such period as OFCOM may think fit in relation to the occasion in question; and

(b) the provisions of this section (apart from subsections (1), (2) and (6)) are to apply in the case of a licence granted by way of a renewal of a licence granted under this section as they apply in the case of the replacement licence.

(8) The conditions of a replacement licence proposed or granted under this section must include

the conditions that OFCOM consider appropriate for the purpose of performing their duty under section 263.

(9) The conditions of such a licence must also include a condition prohibiting the imposition, whether directly or indirectly, of the following—

(a) charges on persons in respect of their reception in the United Kingdom of Channel 4;

(b) charges on persons in respect of their reception in the United Kingdom of any service consisting in the provision of assistance for disabled people in relation to programmes included in Channel 4; and

(c) charges on persons in respect of their reception in the United Kingdom of any service (other than one mentioned in paragraph (b)) which is an ancillary service in relation to so much of Channel 4 as is provided in digital form.

(10) It shall be unlawful to impose a charge in contravention of a condition falling within subsection (9).

Commencement Information

I34. S. 231. (1) in force at 28.12.2004 by S.I. 2004/3309, art. 3

I35. S. 231. (2)(a) (b) (3)-(10) in force at 29.12.2003 by S.I. 2003/3142, art. 3. (1), Sch. 1 (with art. 11)

I36. S. 231. (2)(c) in force at 10.12.2004 by S.I. 2004/3309, art. 2

Television licensable content services

232. Meaning of "television licensable content service"

(1) In this Part "television licensable content service" means (subject to section 233) any service falling within subsection (2) in so far as it is provided with a view to its availability for reception by members of the public being secured by one or [F61more] of the following means—

(a) the broadcasting of the service (whether by the person providing it or by another) from a satellite; F62...

[F63. (aa)the broadcasting of the service (whether by that person or by another) by means of a radio multiplex service; or]

(b) the distribution of the service (whether by that person or by another) by any means involving the use of an electronic communications network.

(2) A service falls within this subsection if it—

(a) is provided (whether in digital or in analogue form) as a service that is to be made available for reception by members of the public; and

(b) consists of [F64 or has as its principal purpose the provision of] television programmes or electronic programme guides, or both.

(3) Where—

(a) a service consisting of television programmes, an electronic programme guide or both ("the main service") is provided by a person as a service to be made available for reception by members of the public, and

(b) that person provides the main service with other services or facilities that are ancillary to, or otherwise relate to, the main service and are also provided so as to be so available or in order to make a service so available,

subsection (1) has effect as if the main service and such of the other services or facilities as are relevant ancillary services and are not two-way services constituted a single service falling within subsection (2).

(4) Where a person providing the main service provides it with a facility giving access to another service, the other service shall also be taken for the purposes of this section as provided by that person with the main service only if what is comprised in the other service is something over which that person has general control.

(5) A service is a two-way service for the purposes of this section if it is provided by means of an electronic communications network and an essential feature of the service is that the purposes for

which it is provided involve the use of that network, or a part of it, both—

(a) for the transmission of visual images or sounds (or both) by the person providing the service to users of the service; and

(b) for the transmission of visual images or sounds (or both) by those users for reception by the person providing the service or by other users of the service.

(6) In this section—

"electronic programme guide" means a service which consists of—

- the listing or promotion, or both the listing and the promotion, of some or all of the programmes included in any one or more programme services the providers of which are or include persons other than the provider of the guide; and

- a facility for obtaining access, in whole or in part, to the programme service or services listed or promoted in the guide;

"relevant ancillary service", in relation to the main service, means a service or facility provided or made available by the provider of the main service that consists of or gives access to—

- assistance for disabled people in relation to some or all of the programmes included in the main service;

- a service (apart from advertising) which is not an electronic programme guide but relates to the promotion or listing of programmes so included; or

- any other service (apart from advertising) which is ancillary to one or more programmes so included and relates directly to their contents.

Amendments (Textual)

F61. Word in s. 232. (1) substituted (25.7.2006) by Television Licensable Content Services Order 2006 (S.I. 2006/2131), arts. 1. (1), 2. (1)(a)

F62. Word in s. 232. (1)(a) omitted (25.7.2006) by virtue of Television Licensable Content Services Order 2006 (S.I. 2006/2131), arts. 1. (1), 2. (1)(b)

F63. S. 232. (1)(aa) inserted (25.7.2006) by Television Licensable Content Services Order 2006 (S.I. 2006/2131), arts. 1. (1), 2. (1)(c)

F64. Words in s. 232. (2)(b) inserted (19.12.2009) by Audiovisual Media Services Regulations 2009 (S.I. 2009/2979), regs. 1. (1), 6. (1)

Commencement Information

I37. S. 232 in force at 29.12.2003 by S.I. 2003/3142, art. 3. (1), Sch. 1 (with art. 11)

233. Services that are not television licensable content services

(1) A service is not a television licensable content service to the extent that it is provided with a view to its being broadcast by means of a [F65television multiplex service or a general multiplex service] .

(2) A service is not a television licensable content service to the extent that it consists of a service the provision of which is authorised by—

(a) a licence to provide a television broadcasting service;

(b) the licence to provide the public teletext service; or

(c) a licence to provide additional television services.

F66. (3). . . . .

(4) A service is not a television licensable content service if it is a two-way service (within the meaning of section 232).

(5) A service is not a television licensable content service if—

(a) it is distributed by means of an electronic communications network only to persons all of whom are on a single set of premises; and

(b) that network is wholly within those premises and is not connected to an electronic communications network any part of which is outside those premises.

(6) For the purposes of subsection (5)—

(a) a set of premises is a single set of premises if, and only if, the same person is the occupier of all the premises; and

(b) two or more vehicles are capable of constituting a single set of premises if, and only if, they are coupled together.

(7) A service is not a television licensable content service if it is provided for the purpose only of being received by persons who have qualified as users of the service by reason of being—

(a) persons who have a business interest in the programmes included in the service; or

(b) persons who are to receive the programmes for the purpose only of showing them to persons falling within sub-paragraph (a) or to persons all of whom are on the business premises of the person receiving them.

(8) For the purposes of subsection (7) a person has a business interest in programmes if he has an interest in receiving or watching them—

(a) for the purposes of a business carried on by him; or

(b) for the purposes of his employment.

(9) In this section—

"business premises", in relation to a person, means premises at or from which any business of that person is carried on;

F67...

"premises" includes a vehicle;

"vehicle" includes a vessel, aircraft or hovercraft.

(10) References in this section, in relation to a person, to a business include references to—

(a) any business or other activities carried on by a body of which he is a member and the affairs of which are managed by its members; and

(b) the carrying out of any functions conferred on that person, or on any such body, by or under any enactment.

Amendments (Textual)

F65. Words in s. 233. (1) substituted (25.7.2006) by Television Licensable Content Services Order 2006 (S.I. 2006/2131), arts. 1. (1), 2. (2)(a)

F66. S. 233. (3) omitted (19.12.2009) by virtue of Audiovisual Media Services Regulations 2009 (S.I. 2009/2979), regs. 1. (1), 6. (2)

F67. Words in s. 233. (9) omitted (25.7.2006) by virtue of Television Licensable Content Services Order 2006 (S.I. 2006/2131), arts. 1. (1), 2. (2)(b)

Commencement Information

I38. S. 233 in force at 29.12.2003 by S.I. 2003/3142, art. 3. (1), Sch. 1 (with art. 11)

234. Modification of ss. 232 and 233.

(1) The Secretary of State may by order modify any of the provisions of section 232 or 233 if it appears to him appropriate to do so having regard to any one or more of the following—

(a) the protection which, taking account of the means by which the programmes and services are received or may be accessed, is expected by members of the public as respects the contents of television programmes;

(b) the extent to which members of the public are able, before television programmes are watched or accessed, to make use of facilities for exercising control, by reference to the contents of the programmes, over what is watched or accessed;

(c) the practicability of applying different levels of regulation in relation to different services;

(d) the financial impact for providers of particular services of any modification of the provisions of that section; and

(e) technological developments that have occurred or are likely to occur.

(2) The Secretary of State may also by order provide, in cases where it otherwise appears to him appropriate to do so, that a description of service specified in the order is not to be treated as a television licensable content service for the purposes of the provisions of this Act that are so specified.

(3) No order is to be made containing provision authorised by this section unless a draft of the order has been laid before Parliament and approved by a resolution of each House.

Commencement Information

I39. S. 234 in force at 29.12.2003 by S.I. 2003/3142, art. 3. (1), Sch. 1 (with art. 11)

235. Licensing of television licensable content services

(1) The licence that is required for the purposes of section 13 of the 1990 Act in respect of a

television licensable content service is a licence granted under Part 1 of that Act on an application complying with this section.

(2) An application for a licence to provide a television licensable content service—

(a) must be made in such manner,

(b) must contain such information about the applicant, his business and the service he proposes to provide, and

(c) must be accompanied by such fee (if any),

as OFCOM may determine.

(3) Where an application is made to OFCOM in accordance with subsection (2) for a licence to provide a television licensable content service, OFCOM are entitled to refuse the application only if—

(a) they are required to do so by section 3. (3) of the 1990 Act (licences to be held only by fit and proper persons);

(b) they are required to do so by section 5 of the 1990 Act (restrictions on the holding of licences); or

(c) they are satisfied that, if the application were to be granted, the provision of the service would be likely to involve contraventions of—

(i) standards set under section 319 of this Act; or

(ii) the provisions of a code of practice in force under Part 5 of the 1996 Act (fairness).

(4) The provision of more than one television licensable content service shall require a separate licence under Part 1 of the 1990 Act to be granted and held in respect of each service.

(5) A single licence to provide a television licensable content service may authorise the provision of a service which consists (to any extent) of different programmes to be broadcast simultaneously, or virtually so.

(6) A licence to provide a television licensable content service shall continue in force until such time as it is surrendered or is revoked in accordance with any of the provisions of this Chapter or of the 1990 Act.

[F68. (7)A licence to provide a television licensable content service must contain such conditions as OFCOM consider appropriate for requiring the licence holder—

(a) on entering into any agreement with the provider of a radio multiplex service for the provision of a television licensable content service to be broadcast by means of that multiplex service, to notify OFCOM—

(i) of the identity of the radio multiplex service;

(ii) of the period during which the service will be provided; and

(iii) where under the agreement he will be entitled to the use of a specified amount of digital capacity, of that amount;

(b) when any such agreement is varied so far as it relates to any of the matters mentioned in paragraph (a)(i), (ii) or (iii), to notify OFCOM of the variation so far as relating to those matters; and

(c) where he is providing a television licensable content service to the provider of a radio multiplex service in accordance with such an agreement as is mentioned in paragraph (a) but intends to cease doing so, to notify OFCOM of that fact.]

Amendments (Textual)

F68. S. 235. (7) inserted (25.7.2006) by Television Licensable Content Services Order 2006 (S.I. 2006/2131), arts. 1. (1), 3

Commencement Information

I40. S. 235 in force at 29.12.2003 by S.I. 2003/3142, art. 3. (1), Sch. 1 (with art. 11)

236. Direction to licensee to take remedial action

(1) This section applies if OFCOM are satisfied—

(a) that the holder of a licence to provide a television licensable content service has contravened a condition of the licence; and

(b) that the contravention can be appropriately remedied by the inclusion in the licensed service of a correction or a statement of findings (or both).

(2) OFCOM may direct the licence holder to include a correction or a statement of findings (or both) in the licensed service.

(3) A direction may require the correction or statement of findings to be in such form, and to be included in programmes at such time or times, as OFCOM may determine.

(4) OFCOM are not to give a person a direction under this section unless they have given him a reasonable opportunity of making representations to them about the matters appearing to them to provide grounds for the giving of the direction.

(5) Where the holder of a licence includes a correction or a statement of findings in the licensed service in pursuance of a direction under this section, he may announce that he is doing so in pursuance of such a direction.

(6) If OFCOM are satisfied that the inclusion of a programme in a television licensable content service involved a contravention of a condition of the licence to provide that service, they may direct the holder of the licence not to include that programme in that service on any future occasion.

(7) Where OFCOM—

    (a) give a direction to a BBC company under subsection (2), or

    (b) receive representations from a BBC company by virtue of subsection (4),

they must send a copy of the direction or representations to the Secretary of State.

(8) For the purposes of this section a statement of findings, in relation to a case in which OFCOM are satisfied that the holder of a licence has contravened the conditions of his licence, is a statement of OFCOM's findings in relation to that contravention.

Modifications etc. (not altering text)

C6. S. 236. (2) modified (20.7.2004) by Contracting Out (Functions relating to Broadcast Advertising) and Specification of Relevant Functions Order 2004 (S.I. 2004/1975), art. 1, Sch. para. 2. (c) (with art. 5)

Commencement Information

I41. S. 236 in force at 29.12.2003 by S.I. 2003/3142, art. 3. (1), Sch. 1 (with art. 11)

237. Penalties for contravention of licence condition or direction

(1) If OFCOM are satisfied that the holder of a licence to provide a television licensable content service—

    (a) has contravened a condition of the licence, or

    (b) has failed to comply with a direction given by OFCOM under or by virtue of a provision of this Part, Part 1 of the 1990 Act or Part 5 of the 1996 Act,

they may serve on him a notice requiring him to pay them, within a specified period, a specified penalty.

(2) The amount of the penalty under this section must not exceed the maximum penalty given by subsection (3).

(3) The maximum penalty is whichever is the greater of—

    (a) £250,000; and

    (b) 5 per cent. of the qualifying revenue for the licence holder's last complete accounting period falling within the period for which his licence has been in force ("the relevant period").

(4) In relation to a person whose first complete accounting period falling within the relevant period has not ended when the penalty is imposed, subsection (3) is to be construed as referring to 5 per cent of the amount which OFCOM estimate will be the qualifying revenue for that accounting period.

(5) Section 19. (2) to (6) of the 1990 Act and Part 1 of Schedule 7 to that Act (calculation of qualifying revenue), with any necessary modifications, are to apply for the purposes of subsection (3) as they apply for the purposes of Part 1 of that Act.

(6) OFCOM are not to serve a notice on a person under subsection (1) unless they have given him a reasonable opportunity of making representations to them about the matters appearing to them to provide grounds for the service of the notice.

(7) Where OFCOM—

    (a) serve a notice on a BBC company under subsection (1), or

(b) receive representations from a BBC company by virtue of subsection (6),
they must send a copy of the notice or representations to the Secretary of State.

(8) An exercise by OFCOM of their powers under subsection (1) does not preclude any exercise by them of their powers under section 236 in respect of the same contravention.

(9) The Secretary of State may by order substitute a different sum for the sum for the time being specified in subsection (3)(a).

(10) No order is to be made containing provision authorised by subsection (9) unless a draft of the order has been laid before Parliament and approved by a resolution of each House.

Modifications etc. (not altering text)

C7. S. 237 restricted (8.12.2003) by The Office of Communications Act 2002 (Commencement No. 3) and Communications Act 2003 (Commencement No. 2) Order 2003 (S.I. 2003/3142), art. 9 (with art. 11)

Commencement Information

I42. S. 237 in force at 29.12.2003 by S.I. 2003/3142, art. 3. (1), Sch. 1 (with art. 11)

238. Revocation of television licensable content service licence

(1) OFCOM must serve a notice under subsection (2) on the holder of a licence to provide a television licensable content service if they are satisfied—

(a) that the holder of the licence is in contravention of a condition of the licence or is failing to comply with a direction given by them under or by virtue of any provision of this Part, Part 1 of the 1990 Act or Part 5 of the 1996 Act; and

(b) that the contravention or failure, if not remedied, would justify the revocation of the licence.

(2) A notice under this subsection must—

(a) state that OFCOM are satisfied as mentioned in subsection (1);

(b) specify the respects in which, in their opinion, the licence holder is contravening the condition or failing to comply with the direction; and

(c) state that OFCOM will revoke the licence unless the licence holder takes, within such period as is specified in the notice, such steps to remedy the failure as are so specified.

(3) If, at the end of the period specified in a notice under subsection (2), OFCOM are satisfied—

(a) that the person on whom the notice was served has failed to take the steps specified in it, and

(b) that it is necessary in the public interest to revoke his licence,
they shall serve a notice on him revoking his licence.

(4) If OFCOM are satisfied in the case of a licence to provide a television licensable content service—

(a) that the holder of the licence has ceased to provide the licensed service, and

(b) that it is appropriate for them to do so,
they shall serve a notice on him revoking his licence.

(5) If OFCOM are satisfied—

(a) that the holder of a licence to provide a television licensable content service has provided them, in connection with his application for the licence, with information which was false in a material particular, or

(b) that, in connection with his application for the licence, the holder of such a licence withheld any material information with the intention of causing them to be misled,
they may serve a notice on him revoking his licence.

(6) A notice under this section revoking a licence to provide a television licensable content service takes effect as from the time when it is served on the licence holder.

(7) OFCOM are not to serve a notice on a person under this section unless they have given him a reasonable opportunity of making representations to them about the matters in respect of which it is served.

(8) Where OFCOM—

(a) serve a notice on a BBC company under this section, or

(b) receive representations from a BBC company by virtue of subsection (7),
they must send a copy of the notice or representations to the Secretary of State.

(9) Nothing in this section applies to the revocation of a licence in exercise of the power conferred

by section 239.

Commencement Information

I43. S. 238 in force at 29.12.2003 by S.I. 2003/3142, art. 3. (1), Sch. 1 (with art. 11)

239. Action against licence holders who incite crime or disorder

(1) OFCOM must serve a notice under subsection (2) on the holder of a licence to provide a television licensable content service if they are satisfied—

    (a) that the holder of the licence has included in the service one or more programmes containing material likely to encourage or to incite the commission of crime, or to lead to disorder;

    (b) that, in doing so, he has contravened conditions contained by virtue of Chapter 4 of this Part in the licence to provide that service; and

    (c) that the contravention is such as to justify the revocation of the licence.

(2) A notice under this subsection must—

    (a) state that OFCOM are satisfied as mentioned in subsection (1);

    (b) specify the respects in which, in their opinion, the licence holder has contravened the condition mentioned in paragraph (b) of that subsection;

    (c) state that OFCOM may revoke the licence after the end of the period of twenty-one days beginning with the day on which the notice is served on the licence holder; and

    (d) inform the licence holder of his right to make representations to OFCOM within that period about the matters appearing to OFCOM to provide grounds for revoking the licence.

(3) The effect of a notice under subsection (2) shall be to suspend the licence as from the time when the notice is served on the licence holder until either—

    (a) the revocation of the licence takes effect; or

    (b) OFCOM decide not to revoke the licence.

(4) If, after considering any representations made to them by the licence holder within the period specified for the purposes of subsection (2)(c), OFCOM are satisfied that it is necessary in the public interest to revoke the licence, they shall serve a notice of revocation on the licence holder.

(5) The revocation of a licence by a notice under subsection (4) takes effect from such time as may be specified in the notice.

(6) A notice of revocation under subsection (4) must not specify a time for it to take effect that falls before the end of the period of twenty-eight days beginning with the day on which the notice is served on the licence holder.

Commencement Information

I44. S. 239 in force at 29.12.2003 by S.I. 2003/3142, art. 3. (1), Sch. 1 (with art. 11)

240. Abolition of separate licences for certain television services

(1) The authorisations that are to be capable of being granted on or after the television transfer date by or under a licence under Part 1 of the 1990 Act do not include the authorisation of the provision, as such, of—

    (a) any satellite television service (as defined, disregarding its repeal by this Act, in section 43. (1) of the 1990 Act); or

    (b) any licensable programme service (as defined, disregarding its repeal by this Act, in section 46. (1) of that Act).

(2) Subsection (1) does not affect OFCOM's power, by means of a licence authorising the provision of a service falling within section 211. (1), to authorise the provision of so much of any formerly regulated television service as is comprised in the licensed service.

(3) So much of any relevant existing licence as authorises the provision of a service which consists in or includes a television licensable content service—

    (a) shall have effect, on and after the television transfer date, as a licence under Part 1 of the 1990 Act authorising the provision of the television licensable content service comprised in the licensed service;

    (b) shall so have effect as a licence which, notwithstanding its terms and conditions, is to continue in force until such time as it is surrendered or is revoked in accordance with provisions of this Chapter or of the 1990 Act; and

    (c) shall otherwise have effect as a licence on the same terms and conditions as those on which it had effect immediately before the television transfer date.

(4) It shall be the duty of OFCOM to exercise their power under section 3 of the 1990 Act to make such variations of any licence having effect in accordance with subsection (3) of this section as (after complying with subsection (4)(b) of that section) they consider appropriate for the purpose of performing their duty under section 263 of this Act.

(5) In this section—

"formerly regulated television service" means a service mentioned in subsection (1); and "relevant existing licence", means any licence which—

- was granted by the Independent Television Commission under Part 1 of the 1990 Act before the television transfer date; and

- is in force immediately before the television transfer date as a licence authorising the provision of a formerly regulated service.

Commencement Information

I45. S. 240 in force at 29.12.2003 by S.I. 2003/3142, art. 3. (1), Sch. 1 (with art. 11)

Television multiplex services

241. Television multiplex services

(1) Subject to the following provisions of this section, references in Part 1 of the 1996 Act to a multiplex service, other than those comprised in express references to a general multiplex service, shall have effect as references to any service ("a television multiplex service") which—

(a) falls within subsection (2); and

(b) is provided for broadcasting for general reception but otherwise than from a satellite.

(2) A service falls within this subsection if—

(a) it consists in the packaging together of two or more services which include at least one relevant television service and are provided for inclusion together in the service by a combination of the relevant information in digital form; or

(b) it is a service provided with a view to its being a service falling within paragraph (a) but is one in the case of which only one service is for the time being comprised in digital form in what is provided.

(3) The provision, at a time after the commencement of this section, of a television multiplex service the provision of which is not authorised by or under a licence under Part 1 of the 1996 Act is not to be an offence under section 13 of the 1990 Act.

(4) Accordingly, after the commencement of this section, a licence under Part 1 of the 1996 Act shall be required for the provision of a television multiplex service only in so far as it is required for the purposes of a limitation falling within subsection (5) that is contained in a wireless telegraphy licence, or is deemed to be so contained.

(5) A limitation falls within this subsection, in relation to a wireless telegraphy licence, if it provides that the only television multiplex services that are authorised to be broadcast using the station or apparatus to which the licence relates are those that are licensed under Part 1 of the 1996 Act.

(6) Where immediately before the coming into force of this section—

(a) a television multiplex service is licensed under Part 1 of the 1996 Act; and

(b) that service is one broadcast using a station or apparatus the use of which is authorised by a wireless telegraphy licence,

that wireless telegraphy licence shall be deemed to contain a limitation falling within subsection (5).

(7) In any case where a wireless telegraphy licence is deemed by virtue of subsection (6) to contain a limitation falling within subsection (5) and the person providing the television multiplex service in question—

(a) ceases to be licensed under Part 1 of the 1996 Act in respect of that service, or

(b) ceases to exist,

OFCOM may revoke the wireless telegraphy licence.

(8) Subsection (7) is not to be construed as restricting the powers of revocation exercisable apart from this section.

(9) In subsection (2) "relevant television service" means any of the following—

(a) any Channel 3 service in digital form;

(b) Channel 4 in digital form;

(c) Channel 5 in digital form;

(d) S4. C Digital;

(e) any digital television programme service;

(f) the digital public teletext service.

Commencement Information

I46. S. 241 in force at 29.12.2003 by S.I. 2003/3142, art. 3. (1), Sch. 1 (with art. 11)

242. Composition of services in television multiplexes

(1) In subsection (1) of section 12 of the 1996 Act—

(a) in paragraph (c), (digital programmes services included in multiplex must be provided by a licence holder or EEA broadcaster), after "section 18" there shall be inserted " , by the BBC ";

(b) in paragraph (d), (digital additional services included in multiplex must be provided by a licence holder or EEA broadcaster), after "section 25" there shall be inserted " , by the BBC ";

(c) after that paragraph there shall be inserted—

"(da)that the only digital sound programme services broadcast under the licence are services provided by the holder of a national digital sound programme licence (within the meaning of section 60) or by the BBC;"

(d) in paragraph (e), after "digital programme services" there shall be inserted " , digital sound programme services ";

(e) in paragraph (f), after "digital programme service" there shall be inserted " , a digital sound programme service "; and

(f) for paragraph (h) (conditions as to composition of multiplex service), there shall be substituted—

"(h)that, while the licence is in force, at least the required percentage of the digital capacity on the frequency or frequencies on which the service is broadcast is used, or left available to be used, for the broadcasting of services falling within subsection (1. A)."

(2) After that subsection there shall be inserted—

"(1. A)The services falling within this subsection are—

(a) qualifying services;

(b) digital programme services licensed under this Part or provided by the BBC;

(c) digital sound programme services provided by the BBC;

(d) programme-related services; and

(e) relevant technical services."

(3) In subsection (3) of that section—

(a) after the words "digital programme services", in the first place where they occur, there shall be inserted " or digital sound programme services "; and

(b) for "digital programme services broadcast under the licence" there shall be substituted " so much of what is broadcast under the licence as consists of digital programme services, or of such services together with digital sound programme services, ".

(4) In subsection (4) of that section (interpretation of subsection (1)(h))—

(a) for "(1)(h)" there shall be substituted " (1. A) ";

(b) in paragraph (a), for "the qualifying teletext service" there shall be substituted " the digital public teletext service ";

(c) in paragraph (b)(i), after "the 1990 Act)" there shall be inserted " , or in one or more digital sound programme services provided by the BBC, "

(d) in paragraph (c), for "digital programme services" there shall be substituted " services falling within subsection (1. A) which are comprised in the multiplex in question ".

(5) After that subsection there shall be inserted—

"(4. A)In subsection (1)(h), the reference to the required percentage is a reference to such percentage equal to or more than 90 per cent. as OFCOM—

(a) consider appropriate; and

(b) specify in the condition."

(6) In subsection (5) of that section (power to change percentage in subsection (1)(h)), for "(1)(h)" there shall be substituted " (4. A) ".

Commencement Information

I47. S. 242 in force at 29.12.2003 by S.I. 2003/3142, art. 3. (1), Sch. 1 (with art. 11)

243. Powers where frequencies reserved for qualifying services

(1) The Secretary of State may by order provide, in relation to the matters mentioned in subsection (2)—

(a) for any or all of the provisions of sections 7 to 16 and of sections 18 and 19 of the 1996 Act to have effect with the modifications specified in the order; and

(b) for provision made by the order to have effect in place of any or all of those provisions.

(2) Those matters are—

(a) licences under Part 1 of the 1996 Act, and

(b) the awarding and grant of such licences,

in a case in which the licence is, or is to be, a licence to provide a service for broadcasting on any one or more reserved frequencies.

(3) An order under this section may require OFCOM to include conditions falling within subsection (4) in any Broadcasting Act licence to provide a television multiplex service to be broadcast on a reserved frequency.

(4) Conditions falling within this subsection are conditions that OFCOM consider appropriate for securing that, in consideration for the making by any relevant public service broadcaster of such payments as are from time to time—

(a) agreed between the broadcaster and the holder of the licence to provide the television multiplex service, or

(b) in default of agreement, determined by OFCOM in accordance with the order,

the holder of that licence will use digital capacity reserved in accordance with conditions imposed under section 12 of the 1996 Act or any order under this section for the broadcasting of services provided by that broadcaster.

(5) Subsection (3) is not to be construed as restricting the provision that may be made under subsection (1).

(6) A frequency is a reserved frequency for the purposes of this section if it is one as respects which OFCOM have made a determination, in exercise of their functions under the enactments relating to the management of the radio spectrum, that the frequency should be reserved for the broadcasting of television multiplex services.

(7) In this section "relevant public service broadcaster" means any of the following—

(a) the holder of a licence to provide a Channel 3 service;

(b) C4. C;

(c) the holder of a licence to provide Channel 5;

(d) the Welsh Authority;

(e) the public teletext provider.

Commencement Information

I48. S. 243 in force at 29.12.2003 by S.I. 2003/3142, art. 3. (1), Sch. 1 (with art. 11)

Local digital television services

244. Local digital television services

(1) The Secretary of State may by order provide for—

(a) any of the provisions of this Part (apart from this section and the provisions relating exclusively to sound services), or

(b) any provision of Part 1 of the 1990 Act or of Part 1 of the 1996 Act (regulation of television services),

to have effect, in relation to services of such descriptions as may be set out in an order under this section, with such modifications as he considers necessary or appropriate for services of that description.

(2) The Secretary of State is not to make an order under this section in relation to a description of services except where—

(a) the description is of services to be provided in digital form with a view to their being included in a television multiplex service;

(b) the description is confined to services falling within one or both of subsections (3) and (4); and

(c) the Secretary of State is satisfied that the making of an order under this section in relation to that description of services will make possible, facilitate or encourage the provision of services so falling.

(3) Services fall within this subsection if they are—

(a) intended for reception only at a particular establishment or otherwise on particular premises; or

(b) provided for the purposes only of a particular event.

(4) Services fall within this subsection if the Secretary of State considers that they are services in relation to which all the following conditions are satisfied—

(a) they are intended for reception only within a particular area or locality;

(b) their provision meets, or would meet, the needs of the area or locality where they are received;

(c) their provision is or would be likely to broaden the range of television programmes available for viewing by persons living or working in that area or locality; and

(d) their provision is or would be likely to increase the number and range of the programmes about that area or locality that are available for such viewing, or to increase the number of programmes made in that area or locality that would be so available.

(5) Services shall be taken for the purposes of subsection (4) to meet the needs of an area or locality if, and only if—

(a) their provision brings social or economic benefits to the area or locality, or to different categories of persons living or working in that area or locality; or

(b) they cater for the tastes, interests and needs of some or all of the different descriptions of people living or working in the area or locality (including, in particular, tastes, interests and needs that are of special relevance in the light of the descriptions of people who do so live and work).

(6) In subsections (4) and (5), the references to persons living or working in an area or locality include references to persons undergoing education or training in that area or locality.

(7) An order under this section in relation to a description of services may, in particular, impose prohibitions or limitations on the inclusion of advertisements in services of that description and on the sponsorship of programmes included in the services.

(8) The power, by an order under this section, to make incidental, supplemental or consequential provision in connection with provision authorised by subsection (1) includes power to make incidental, supplemental or consequential provision modifying provisions of the 1990 Act, the 1996 Act or this Act that are not mentioned in that subsection.

(9) No order is to be made containing provision authorised by this section unless a draft of the order has been laid before Parliament and approved by a resolution of each House.

Commencement Information

I49. S. 244 in force at 29.12.2003 by S.I. 2003/3142, art. 3. (1), Sch. 1 (with art. 11)

Chapter 3. Regulatory Structure for Independent Radio Services

245. Regulation of independent radio services

(1) It shall be a function of OFCOM to regulate the following services in accordance with this Act, the 1990 Act and the 1996 Act—

(a) services specified in subsection (2) that are provided from places in the United Kingdom and otherwise than by the BBC;

(b) services so specified that do not fall within paragraph (a) but are provided by a person, other than the BBC, whose principal place of business is in the United Kingdom.

(2) The services referred to in subsection (1)(a) are—

(a) sound broadcasting services to which subsection (3) applies;

(b) radio licensable content services;

(c) additional radio services;

(d) radio multiplex services;

(e) digital sound programme services;

(f) digital additional sound services.

(3) This subsection applies to a sound broadcasting service which—

(a) is provided with a view to its being broadcast otherwise than only from a satellite; and

(b) is a national service, local service or restricted service.

(4) For the purposes of this section—

(a) a service is a national service if it is a sound broadcasting service provided as mentioned in subsection (3)(a) with a view to its being broadcast for reception in any such minimum area of the United Kingdom as may be determined in accordance with section 98. (2) of the 1990 Act;

(b) a service is a local service if it is a sound broadcasting service which (without being a national service) is provided as mentioned in subsection (3)(a) with a view to its being broadcast for reception in a particular area or locality in the United Kingdom; and

(c) a service is a restricted service if it is a sound broadcasting service provided as mentioned in subsection (3)(a) with a view to its being broadcast for reception—

(i) within a particular establishment in the United Kingdom or at another defined location in the United Kingdom; or

(ii) for the purposes of a particular event taking place within the United Kingdom.

(5) The services that are to be treated for the purposes of this section as provided from places in the United Kingdom include every radio licensable content service which would not fall to be so treated apart from this subsection but which—

(a) is provided with a view to its being broadcast from a satellite;

(b) is a service the broadcasting of which involves its transmission to the satellite by means of an electronic communications network from a place in the United Kingdom; and

(c) is not a service the provision of which is licensed or otherwise authorised under the laws of another EEA State.

(6) The services that are to be treated as so provided also include every service provided by a BBC company, a C4 company or an S4. C company.

(7) A reference in subsection (4)(b) to an area of the United Kingdom does not include an area which comprises or includes the whole of England.

Commencement Information

I50. S. 245 in force at 29.12.2003 by S.I. 2003/3142, art. 3. (1), Sch. 1 (with art. 11)

246. Abolition of function of assigning radio frequencies

The Secretary of State shall cease to have any function under the 1990 Act or the 1996 Act of assigning frequencies—

(a) for any of the purposes of Part 3 of the 1990 Act (regulation of radio services); or

(b) for the purposes of the provision of any radio multiplex services.

Commencement Information

I51. S. 246 in force at 29.12.2003 by S.I. 2003/3142, art. 3. (1), Sch. 1 (with art. 11)

Radio licensable content services

247. Meaning of "radio licensable content services"

(1) In this Part "radio licensable content service" means (subject to section 248) any service falling within subsection (2) in so far as it is provided with a view to its availability for reception by members of the public being secured by one or both of the following means—

(a) the broadcasting of the service (whether by the person providing it or by another) from a satellite; or

(b) the distribution of the service (whether by that person or by another) by any means involving the use of an electronic communications network.

(2) A service falls within this subsection if it—

(a) consists of sound programmes; and

(b) is provided (whether in digital or in analogue form) as a service that is to be made available for reception by members of the public.

Commencement Information

I52. S. 247 in force at 29.12.2003 by S.I. 2003/3142, art. 3. (1), Sch. 1 (with art. 11)

248. Services that are not radio licensable content services

(1) A service is not a radio licensable content service to the extent that—

(a) it is provided with a view to its being broadcast by means of a multiplex service;

(b) it is a sound broadcasting service to which subsection (3) of section 245 applies; or

(c) it is comprised in a television licensable content service.

(2) A service is not a radio licensable content service to the extent that it is provided by means of an electronic communications service if—

(a) it forms part only of a service provided by means of that electronic communications service or is one of a number of services access to which is made available by means of a service so provided; and

(b) the service of which it forms part, or by which it may be accessed, is provided for purposes that do not consist wholly or mainly in making available services of radio programmes or television programmes (or both) for reception by members of the public.

(3) A service is not a radio licensable content service if it is a two-way service.

(4) A service is a two-way service for the purposes of subsection (3) if it is provided by means of an electronic communications network and an essential feature of the service is that the purposes for which it is provided involve the use of that network, or a part of it, both—

(a) for the transmission of sounds by the person providing the service to users of the service; and

(b) for the transmission of sounds by those users for reception by the person providing the service or by other users of the service.

(5) A service is not a radio licensable content service if—

(a) it is distributed by means of an electronic communications network only to persons all of whom are on a single set of premises; and

(b) that network is wholly within those premises and is not connected to an electronic communications network any part of which is outside those premises.

(6) For the purposes of subsection (5)—

(a) a set of premises is a single set of premises if, and only if, the same person is the occupier of all the premises; and

(b) two or more vehicles are capable of constituting a single set of premises if, and only if, they are coupled together.

(7) A service is not a radio licensable content service if it is provided for the purpose only of being received by persons who have qualified as users of the service by reason of being—

(a) persons who have a business interest in the programmes included in the service; or

(b) persons who are to receive the programmes for the purpose only of allowing them to be listened to by persons falling within sub-paragraph (a) or by persons all of whom are on the business premises of the person receiving them.

(8) For the purposes of subsection (7) a person has a business interest in programmes if he has an interest in receiving or listening to them—

(a) for the purposes of a business carried on by him; or

(b) for the purposes of his employment.

(9) In this section—

"business premises", in relation to a person, means premises at or from which any business of that person is carried on;

"multiplex service" means a television multiplex service, a radio multiplex service or a general multiplex service;

"premises" includes a vehicle;

"vehicle" includes a vessel, aircraft or hovercraft.

(10) References in this section, in relation to a person, to a business include references to—

(a) any business or other activities carried on by a body of which he is a member and the affairs of which are managed by its members; and

(b) the carrying out of any functions conferred on that person, or on any such body, by or under any enactment.

Commencement Information

I53. S. 248 in force at 29.12.2003 by S.I. 2003/3142, art. 3. (1), Sch. 1 (with art. 11)

249. Modification of ss. 247 and 248.

(1) The Secretary of State may by order modify any of the provisions of section 247 or 248 if it appears to him appropriate to do so having regard to any one or more of the following—

(a) the protection which is expected by members of the public as respects the contents of sound programmes;

(b) the practicability of applying different levels of regulation in relation to different services;

(c) the financial impact for providers of particular services of any modification of the provisions of that section; and

(d) technological developments that have occurred or are likely to occur.

(2) The Secretary of State may also by order provide, in cases where it otherwise appears to him appropriate to do so, that a description of service specified in the order is not to be treated as a radio licensable content service for the purposes of the provisions of this Act that are so specified.

(3) No order is to be made containing provision authorised by this section unless a draft of the order has been laid before Parliament and approved by a resolution of each House.

Commencement Information

I54. S. 249 in force at 29.12.2003 by S.I. 2003/3142, art. 3. (1), Sch. 1 (with art. 11)

250. Licensing of radio licensable content services

(1) The licence that is required for the purposes of section 97 of the 1990 Act in respect of a radio licensable content service is a licence granted under Part 3 of that Act on an application complying with this section.

(2) An application for a licence under Part 3 of the 1990 Act to provide a radio licensable content service—

(a) must be made in such manner,

(b) must contain such information about the applicant, his business and the service he proposes to provide, and

(c) must be accompanied by such fee (if any),

as OFCOM may determine.

(3) Sections 109 to 111. A of the 1990 Act (enforcement of licences) apply in relation to licences for radio licensable content services as they apply in relation to licences under Chapter 2 of Part 3 of the 1990 Act but with—

(a) the substitution of the word " or " for paragraph (b) of subsection (1) of section 110 (power to shorten licence period); and

(b) the omission of "(b)" in subsection (4) of that section and of subsection (5) of that section (which refer to the power disapplied by paragraph (a) of this subsection).

Commencement Information

I55. S. 250 in force at 29.12.2003 by S.I. 2003/3142, art. 3. (1), Sch. 1 (with art. 11)

251. Abolition of separate licences for certain sound services

(1) The authorisations that are to be capable of being granted on or after the radio transfer date by or under a licence under Part 3 of the 1990 Act do not include the authorisation of the provision, as such, of—

(a) any satellite service (as defined, disregarding its repeal by this Act, in section 84. (2)(b) of the 1990 Act); or

(b) any licensable sound programme service (as defined, disregarding its repeal by this Act, in section 112. (1) of that Act).

(2) Subsection (1) does not affect OFCOM's power, by means of a licence authorising the provision of a service falling within section 245. (1), to authorise the provision of so much of any formerly regulated radio service as is comprised in the licensed service.

(3) So much of any relevant existing licence as authorises the provision of a service which consists in or includes a radio licensable content service—

(a) shall have effect, on and after the radio transfer date, as a licence under Part 3 of the 1990 Act authorising the provision of the radio licensable content service comprised in the licensed service;

(b) shall so have effect as a licence which, notwithstanding its terms and conditions, is to continue in force until such time as it is surrendered or is revoked in accordance with provisions of the 1990 Act; and

(c) shall otherwise have effect as a licence on the same terms and conditions as those on which it had effect immediately before the radio transfer date.

(4) It shall be the duty of OFCOM to exercise their power under section 86 of the 1990 Act to make such variations of any licence having effect in accordance with subsection (3) of this section as (after complying with subsection (5)(b) of that section) they consider appropriate for the purpose of performing their duty under section 263 of this Act.

(5) In this section—

"formerly regulated radio service" means a service mentioned in subsection (1); and

"relevant existing licence" means any licence which—

- was granted by the Radio Authority under Part 3 of the 1990 Act before the radio transfer date; and

- is in force immediately before the radio transfer date as a licence authorising the provision of a formerly regulated service.

Commencement Information

I56. S. 251 in force at 29.12.2003 by S.I. 2003/3142, art. 3. (1), Sch. 1 (with art. 11)

Licence periods etc.

252. Extension of licence periods

(1) In subsection (1) of section 86 of the 1990 Act (period of licences), for the words from "for such period" onwards there shall be substituted "(subject to a suspension of the licence under section 111. B)—

(a) in the case of a licence to provide radio licensable content services, until such time as it is surrendered or is revoked in accordance with any of the following provisions of this Part; and

(b) in any other case, until whichever is the earlier of any such time or the end of the period specified in the licence."

(2) For subsection (3) of that section there shall be substituted—

"(3) A licence to provide a local or national service or to provide an additional service must specify a period of no more than twelve years as the period for which it is to be in force."

Commencement Information

I57. S. 252 in force at 29.12.2003 by S.I. 2003/3142, art. 3. (1), Sch. 1 (with art. 11)

253. Extension and modification of existing licences

(1) A person who immediately before the radio transfer date holds a pre-transfer national licence or a pre-transfer local licence is entitled, in accordance with the following provisions of this

section, to apply to OFCOM for an extension of the licence.

(2) The period for which a licence may be extended on such an application is a period ending not more than four years after the end of the period for which it was granted originally or (if it has been renewed) for which it was last renewed.

(3) An application under subsection (1) may only be made in the period which—

(a) begins three years before the date on which the licence would otherwise expire; and

(b) ends three months before the day that OFCOM have determined to be the day by which they would need to publish a notice under section 98. (1) or 104. (1) of the 1990 Act if they were proposing to grant a fresh licence to take effect from that date.

(4) A determination for the purposes of subsection (3)(b)—

(a) must be made at least one year before the day determined; and

(b) must be notified by OFCOM to the person who holds the licence in question.

(5) An application under subsection (1)—

(a) must be made in such manner,

(b) must contain such information about the applicant, his business and the service he proposes to provide, and

(c) must be accompanied by such fee (if any),

as OFCOM may determine.

(6) If, on an application for an extension under subsection (1), OFCOM are satisfied as to the matters mentioned in subsection (7), they shall—

(a) modify the licence by extending the period for which the licence is to be in force by such period authorised by subsection (2) as they think fit; and

(b) make such other modifications as appear to them to be necessary for the purpose of securing that the provisions of the licence correspond to those that would be contained in a national sound broadcasting licence or (as the case may be) a local sound broadcasting licence granted after the radio transfer date.

(7) Those matters are—

(a) the ability of the licence holder to maintain the service for the period of the extension; and

(b) the likelihood of a contravention by the licence holder of a requirement imposed by—

(i) a condition included in the licence by virtue of section 106 of the 1990 Act; or

(ii) a condition of the licence varied in accordance with subsection (8).

(8) For the purposes of the modification under this section of a national licence, OFCOM—

(a) shall determine an amount which is to be payable to OFCOM by the licence holder in respect of the first complete calendar year falling within the period for which the licence is extended; and

(b) may, in relation to any accounting period of the licence holder during the period of the extension, modify a condition included in the licence in pursuance of section 102. (1)(c) of the 1990 Act (additional payments to be made in respect of national licences) by specifying a different percentage of the qualifying revenue for that accounting period from that which was previously specified in the condition.

(9) The amount determined by OFCOM under subsection (8)(a) must be the amount which, in OFCOM's opinion, would have been the cash bid of the licence holder were the licence (instead of being extended) being granted afresh on an application made in accordance with section 98 of the 1990 Act.

(10) For the purposes of subsection (8)(b)—

(a) different percentages may be specified for different accounting periods; and

(b) the percentages that may be specified for an accounting period include a nil percentage.

(11) The modifications set out in accordance with subsection (6)(b) must secure—

(a) that the amount falling to be paid under the conditions of the licence for each calendar year subsequent to that for which an amount has been determined in accordance with subsection (8)(a) is the amount so determined as increased by the appropriate percentage; and

(b) that such adjustments as are appropriate are made as respects sums already paid in respect of any year or accounting period to which a modification under subsection (8) applies.

(12) Where OFCOM have granted a person's application under this section, the extensions and modifications take effect only if that person—

(a) has been notified by OFCOM of their proposals for modifications by virtue of subsection (6)(b) or (8)(b), and for the making of a determination under subsection (8)(a); and

(b) has consented to the extension on the terms proposed.

(13) In this section—

"the appropriate percentage" has the same meaning as in section 102 of the 1990 Act;

"national sound broadcasting licence" means a licence under Part 3 of the 1990 Act to provide a sound broadcasting service which, under subsection (4)(a) of section 245 is a national service for the purposes of that section;

"pre-transfer licence" means a licence which was granted under Part 3 of the 1990 Act before the radio transfer date and has not been modified under this section or renewed at any time on or after that date;

"pre-transfer local licence" means a pre-transfer licence which was granted as a local licence (within the meaning of Part 3 of the 1990 Act, as it had effect without the amendments made by this Act);

"pre-transfer national licence" means a pre-transfer licence granted or last renewed as a national licence (within the meaning of Part 3 of the 1990 Act, as it had effect without the amendments made by this Act).

Commencement Information

I58. S. 253 in force at 2.1.2004 by S.I. 2003/3142, art. 4. (1) (with art. 11)

254. Renewal of local licences

In section 104. A(5) of the 1990 Act (conditions of renewal of local licence), after paragraph (b) there shall be inserted—

"(c)they are satisfied that the period for which the nominated local digital sound programme service will be available for reception and the times at which it will be available will not be significantly different, week by week, from those for which and at which the licensed local service will be broadcast;".

Commencement Information

I59. S. 254 in force at 29.12.2003 by S.I. 2003/3142, art. 3. (1), Sch. 1 (with art. 11)

255. Extension of special application procedure for local licences

In section 104. B(1) of the 1990 Act (special application procedure for local licences for areas with 4.5 million residents or fewer)—

(a) the word " and " shall be inserted at the end of paragraph (a); and

(b) paragraph (b) (which excludes areas with more than 4.5 million residents) shall cease to have effect.

Commencement Information

I60. S. 255 in force at 29.12.2003 by S.I. 2003/3142, art. 3. (1), Sch. 1 (with art. 11)

Provision of simulcast radio services

256. Definition of simulcast radio services

(1) In section 41 of the 1996 Act (meaning of simulcast radio service), for subsection (2) there shall be substituted—

"(2)In this Part, a "simulcast radio service" means a service provided by a person for broadcasting in digital form and corresponding to a service which is a national service within the meaning of Part 3 of the 1990 Act and is provided by that person."

(2) In subsection (1) of section 126 of the 1990 Act (interpretation of Part 3), before the definition of "sound broadcasting service" there shall be inserted—

""simulcast radio service" means a simulcast radio service within the meaning given by section 41. (2) of the Broadcasting Act 1996 for the purposes of Part 2 of that Act;".

(3) After that subsection there shall be inserted—

"(1. A)For the purposes of this Part a simulcast radio service corresponds to a national service if, in accordance with section 41. (3) of the Broadcasting Act 1996, it falls to be treated as so corresponding for the purposes of Part 2 of that Act."

Commencement Information

I61. S. 256 in force at 29.12.2003 by S.I. 2003/3142, art. 3. (1), Sch. 1 (with art. 11)

257. Promotion of simulcast radio services

(1) Chapter 2 of Part 3 of the 1990 Act (sound broadcasting services) shall be amended as follows.

(2) In section 98. (1) (notices of proposals to grant national licences), after paragraph (b)(ii) there shall be inserted—

"(iia)the digital capacity that is likely, in their opinion, to be available from the holders of national radio multiplex licences for the broadcasting of a simulcast radio service corresponding to the service;".

(3) In section 98. (3) (applications for national licences), after paragraph (a) there shall be inserted—

"(aa)the applicant's proposals (if any) for providing a simulcast radio service corresponding to the service;".

(4) In section 98. (7) (construction of section), after "this section" there shall be inserted—

""national radio multiplex licence" has the same meaning as in Part 2 of the Broadcasting Act 1996; and".

(5) In section 100 (award of national licence to person submitting highest cash bid), for subsection (2) there shall be substituted—

"(1. A)If, in a case in which one or more of the applicants has made a proposal to provide a simulcast radio service corresponding to the service to be licensed (a "simulcast applicant"), the highest cash bid is made by an applicant who is not a simulcast applicant, OFCOM may—

(a) disregard the requirement imposed by subsection (1); and

(b) award the licence to the simulcast applicant whose cash bid is the highest of the bids submitted by simulcast applicants.

(2) Where—

(a) two or more applicants for a licence have submitted cash bids specifying an identical amount and that amount is higher than the amount of every other bid, or

(b) two or more simulcast applicants have submitted cash bids specifying an identical amount and that amount is higher than the amount of every other bid submitted by a simulcast applicant, OFCOM must invite those applicants and (in a case falling within paragraph (b)) every applicant who has made a higher bid to submit further cash bids in respect of that licence.

(2. A)OFCOM may decide not to invite an applicant to submit a further cash bid under subsection (2) if—

(a) the applicant is not a simulcast applicant and they propose to exercise their power under subsection (1. A); or

(b) they propose to exercise their power under subsection (3).

(2. B)Subsection (2. A) is not to be construed as preventing OFCOM from making a decision to exercise their power under subsection (1. A) or (3) after they have received further bids in response to invitations under subsection (2).

(2. C)In this Part references to a person's cash bid, in relation to a person who has submitted a further cash bid in pursuance of subsection (2), have effect as references to his further bid."

(6) After section 100 there shall be inserted—

"100. ALicence conditions relating to simulcast radio services

Where OFCOM award a national licence to a person whose application for that licence included proposals to provide a simulcast radio service, that licence must include a condition requiring the licence holder—

(a) to provide, from a date specified in the licence, a simulcast radio service corresponding to the licensed service; and

(b) to do all that he can to secure the broadcasting of that service."

Commencement Information

162. S. 257 in force at 29.12.2003 by S.I. 2003/3142, art. 3. (1), Sch. 1 (with art. 11)

Multiplexes broadcasting sound programmes

258. Radio multiplex services

(1) Subject to the following provisions of this section, references in Part 2 of the 1996 Act to a radio multiplex service shall have effect as references to any service which—

(a) falls within subsection (2);

(b) is provided for broadcasting for general reception but otherwise than from a satellite; and

(c) is not a television multiplex service.

(2) A service falls within this subsection if—

(a) it consists in the packaging together (with or without other services) of two or more relevant sound services which are provided for inclusion together in that service by a combination of the relevant information in digital form; or

(b) it is a service provided with a view to its being a service falling within paragraph (a) but is one in the case of which only one relevant sound service is for the time being comprised in digital form in what is provided.

(3) The provision, at a time after the commencement of this section, of a radio multiplex service the provision of which is not authorised by or under a licence under Part 2 of the 1996 Act is not to be an offence under section 97 of the 1990 Act.

(4) Accordingly, after the commencement of this section, a licence under Part 2 of the 1996 Act shall be required for the provision of a radio multiplex service only in so far as it is required for the purposes of a limitation falling within subsection (5) which is contained in a wireless telegraphy licence, or is deemed to be so contained.

(5) A limitation falls within this subsection, in relation to a wireless telegraphy licence, if it provides that the only radio multiplex services that are authorised to be broadcast using the station or apparatus to which the licence relates are those that are licensed under Part 2 of the 1996 Act.

(6) Where immediately before the coming into force of this section—

(a) a radio multiplex service is licensed under Part 2 of the 1996 Act; and

(b) that service is one broadcast using a station or apparatus the use of which is authorised by a wireless telegraphy licence,

that wireless telegraphy licence shall be deemed to contain a limitation falling within subsection (5).

(7) In any case where a wireless telegraphy licence is deemed by virtue of subsection (6) to contain a limitation falling within subsection (5) and the person providing the radio multiplex service in question—

(a) ceases to be licensed under Part 2 of the 1996 Act in respect of that service, or

(b) ceases to exist,

OFCOM may revoke the wireless telegraphy licence.

(8) Subsection (7) is not to be construed as restricting the powers of revocation exercisable apart from this section.

(9) In subsection (2) "relevant sound service" means any of the following—

(a) a digital sound programme service;

(b) a simulcast radio service; and

(c) a digital additional sound service.

Commencement Information

163. S. 258 in force at 29.12.2003 by S.I. 2003/3142, art. 3. (1), Sch. 1 (with art. 11)

259. Composition of services in radio multiplexes

(1) Section 54 of the 1996 Act (conditions attached to radio multiplex licences) shall be amended as follows.

(2) For paragraph (h) of subsection (1) (conditions as to composition of service) there shall be substituted—

"(h)that, while the licence is in force, at least the required percentage of the digital capacity on the frequency or frequencies on which the service is broadcast is used, or left available to be used, for the broadcasting of services falling within subsection (1. A)."

(3) After that subsection there shall be inserted—

"(1. A)The services falling within this subsection are—

(a) digital sound programme services;

(b) simulcast radio services;

(c) programme-related services; and

(d) relevant technical services."

(4) In subsection (2) (meaning of services referred to in paragraph (h) of subsection (1))—

(a) for "paragraph (1)(h)" there shall be substituted " subsection (1. A) "; and

(b) in sub-paragraph (i), for the words from "(within" to "1990 Act" there shall be substituted " (within the meaning of section 245 of the Communications Act 2003) ".

(5) After that subsection there shall be inserted—

"(2. A)In subsection (1)(h), the reference to the required percentage is a reference to such percentage equal to or more than 80 per cent. as OFCOM—

(a) consider appropriate; and

(b) specify in the condition."

(6) In subsection (3) (power to vary percentage in subsection (1)(h))—

(a) for "subsection (1)" there shall be substituted " subsection (2. A) "; and

(b) for "paragraph (h) of that subsection" there shall be substituted " that subsection ".

Commencement Information

I64. S. 259 in force at 29.12.2003 by S.I. 2003/3142, art. 3. (1), Sch. 1 (with art. 11)

260. Digital sound services for inclusion in non-radio multiplexes

(1) In section 60. (1)(a) of the 1996 Act (national digital sound programme services defined as services broadcast with a view to being broadcast by means of a national radio multiplex service), after "national radio multiplex service" there shall be inserted " , by means of a television multiplex service or by means of a general multiplex service ".

(2) In section 63. (1) of the 1996 Act (meaning of digital additional sound service), for paragraph (a) there shall be substituted—

"(a)is provided by a person with a view to its being broadcast in digital form (whether by him or some other person) so as to be available for reception by members of the public;

(aa) is so provided with a view to the broadcasting being by means of a radio multiplex service or by means of a general multiplex service; and".

(3) After subsection (3) of section 63 of the 1996 Act there shall be inserted—

"(3. A)In this section "available for reception by members of the public" shall be construed in accordance with section 361 of the Communications Act 2003."

(4) In section 72. (1) of the 1996 Act (interpretation of Part 2)—

(a) after the definitions of "digital sound programme service" and "digital sound programme licence" there shall be inserted—

""general multiplex service" has the same meaning as in Part 3 of the Communications Act 2003;"

(b) after the definition of "technical service" there shall be inserted—

""television multiplex service" has the meaning given by section 241 of the Communications Act 2003."

Commencement Information

I65. S. 260 in force at 29.12.2003 by S.I. 2003/3142, art. 3. (1), Sch. 1 (with art. 11)

261. Renewal of radio multiplex licences

In section 58. (2) of the 1996 Act (renewal for twelve years of radio multiplex licences granted within six years of commencement)—

(a) for "which is granted within six years" there shall be substituted " granted within ten years "; and

(b) for the words from "for a period" onwards there shall be substituted—

"(a)in the case of a licence granted within six years of that commencement, for a period of twelve years beginning with the date on which it would otherwise expire; and

(b) in any other case, for a period of eight years beginning with that date."

Commencement Information

I66. S. 261 in force at 29.12.2003 by S.I. 2003/3142, art. 3. (1), Sch. 1 (with art. 11)

Community radio

262. Community radio

(1) The Secretary of State may by order provide for—

(a) any of the provisions of this Part (apart from this section and the provisions relating exclusively to television), or

(b) any provision of Part 3 of the 1990 Act or of Part 2 of the 1996 Act (regulation of radio services),

to have effect, in relation to services of such descriptions as may be set out in an order under this section, with such modifications as he considers necessary or appropriate for services of that description.

(2) The Secretary of State is not to make an order under this section in relation to a description of services unless—

(a) the description is of services to be provided primarily for the good of members of the public or of a particular community, rather than for commercial reasons; and

(b) he considers that the provision of services of that description confer, or would confer, significant benefits on the public or on the communities for which they are provided.

(3) An order under this section in relation to a description of services may, in particular, impose prohibitions or limitations on the inclusion of advertisements in services of that description and on the sponsorship of programmes included in the services.

(4) The power, by an order under this section, to make incidental, supplemental or consequential provision in connection with provision authorised by subsection (1) includes power to make incidental, supplemental or consequential provision modifying provisions of the 1990 Act, the 1996 Act or this Act that are not mentioned in that subsection.

(5) No order is to be made containing provision authorised by this section unless a draft of the order has been laid before Parliament and approved by a resolution of each House.

Commencement Information

I67. S. 262 in force at 29.12.2003 by S.I. 2003/3142, art. 3. (1), Sch. 1 (with art. 11)

Chapter 4. Regulatory provisions

263. Application of regulatory regimes

(1) It shall be the duty of OFCOM, by exercising—

(a) their powers under the 1990 Act and the 1996 Act, and

(b) their powers under this Part,

to secure that the holder of every Broadcasting Act licence at all times holds his licence on the conditions which are for the time being included, under this Chapter and Chapter 5 of this Part, in the regulatory regime for the licensed service.

(2) It shall also be the duty of OFCOM to do all that they can to secure that the holder of every such licence complies, in relation to the licensed service, with the conditions so included in the regulatory regime for that service.

(3) Where—

(a) the licence for a Channel 3 service, for Channel 4, for Channel 5 or for the public teletext service ("the main service") authorises or requires a corresponding or additional service to be provided in analogue form, and

(b) the regulatory regime for the main service imposes obligations in relation to programmes and other items included in that service, those obligations are to apply equally to programmes that are included in the analogue service without being included in the main service.

[F71. (4)The Secretary of State may by order provide for—

(a) a condition included by virtue of this Act in a regulatory regime to be excluded from the regime;

(b) a condition excluded from a regulatory regime by an order under this subsection to be included in the regime again.

(4. A)An order under subsection (4) may, in particular, provide for a condition to be included or excluded for a period specified in the order.]

(5) No order is to be made containing provision authorised by subsection (4) unless a draft of the order has been laid before Parliament and approved by a resolution of each House.

(6) This section does not restrict OFCOM's powers and duties apart from this section to impose obligations by means of the inclusion of conditions in a Broadcasting Act licence.

Amendments (Textual)

F71. S. 263. (4)(4. A) substituted for s. 263. (4) (8.6.2010) by Digital Economy Act 2010 (c. 24), ss. 37, 47. (1)

Commencement Information

I68. S. 263 in force at 29.12.2003 by S.I. 2003/3142, art. 3. (1), Sch. 1 (with art. 11)

The public service remit for television

264. OFCOM reports on the fulfilment of the public service remit

(1) It shall be the duty of OFCOM—

(a) as soon as practicable after the end of the period of twelve months beginning with the commencement of this section, and

(b) as soon as practicable after the end of each such subsequent period as may be selected by OFCOM for the purposes of this section,

to satisfy, for that period, the review and reporting obligations of subsection (3).

(2) The period selected by OFCOM for the purposes of subsection (1)(b) must be a period of not more than five years beginning with the end of the previous period for which OFCOM have satisfied those review and reporting obligations.

(3) The review and reporting obligations for a period are—

(a) an obligation to carry out a review of the extent to which the public service broadcasters have, during that period, provided relevant television services which (taking them all together over the period as a whole) fulfil the purposes of public service television broadcasting in the United Kingdom; and

(b) an obligation, with a view to maintaining and strengthening the quality of public service television broadcasting in the United Kingdom, to prepare a report on the matters found on the review.

(4) The purposes of public service television broadcasting in the United Kingdom are—

(a) the provision of relevant television services which secure that programmes dealing with a wide range of subject-matters are made available for viewing;

(b) the provision of relevant television services in a manner which (having regard to the days on which they are shown and the times of day at which they are shown) is likely to meet the needs and satisfy the interests of as many different audiences as practicable;

(c) the provision of relevant television services which (taken together and having regard to the same matters) are properly balanced, so far as their nature and subject-matters are concerned, for meeting the needs and satisfying the interests of the available audiences; and

(d) the provision of relevant television services which (taken together) maintain high general standards with respect to the programmes included in them, and, in particular with respect to—

(i) the contents of the programmes;

(ii) the quality of the programme making; and

(iii) the professional skill and editorial integrity applied in the making of the programmes.

(5) When—

(a) determining the extent to which any of the purposes of public service television broadcasting in the United Kingdom are fulfilled, and

(b) reviewing and reporting on that matter,

OFCOM must have regard to the desirability of those purposes being fulfilled in a manner that is compatible with subsection (6).

(6) A manner of fulfilling the purposes of public service television broadcasting in the United Kingdom is compatible with this subsection if it ensures—

(a) that the relevant television services (taken together) comprise a public service for the dissemination of information and for the provision of education and entertainment;

(b) that cultural activity in the United Kingdom, and its diversity, are reflected, supported and stimulated by the representation in those services (taken together) of drama, comedy and music, by the inclusion of feature films in those services and by the treatment of other visual and performing arts;

(c) that those services (taken together) provide, to the extent that is appropriate for facilitating civic understanding and fair and well-informed debate on news and current affairs, a comprehensive and authoritative coverage of news and current affairs in, and in the different parts of, the United Kingdom and from around the world;

(d) that those services (taken together) satisfy a wide range of different sporting and other leisure interests;

(e) that those services (taken together) include what appears to OFCOM to be a suitable quantity and range of programmes on educational matters, of programmes of an educational nature and of other programmes of educative value;

(f) that those services (taken together) include what appears to OFCOM to be a suitable quantity and range of programmes dealing with each of the following, science, religion and other beliefs, social issues, matters of international significance or interest and matters of specialist interest;

(g) that the programmes included in those services that deal with religion and other beliefs include—

(i) programmes providing news and other information about different religions and other beliefs;

(ii) programmes about the history of different religions and other beliefs; and

(iii) programmes showing acts of worship and other ceremonies and practices (including some showing acts of worship and other ceremonies in their entirety);

(h) that those services (taken together) include what appears to OFCOM to be a suitable quantity and range of high quality and original programmes for children and young people;

(i) that those services (taken together) include what appears to OFCOM to be a sufficient quantity of programmes that reflect the lives and concerns of different communities and cultural interests and traditions within the United Kingdom, and locally in different parts of the United Kingdom;

(j) that those services (taken together), so far as they include programmes made in the United Kingdom, include what appears to OFCOM to be an appropriate range and proportion of programmes made outside the M25 area.

(7) In carrying out a review under this section OFCOM must consider—

(a) the costs to persons providing relevant television services of the fulfilment of the purposes of public service television broadcasting in a manner compatible with subsection (6); and

(b) the sources of income available to each of them for meeting those costs.

(8) Every report under this section must—

(a) specify, and comment on, whatever changes appear to OFCOM to have occurred, during the period to which the report relates, in the extent to which the purposes of public service television broadcasting in the United Kingdom have been satisfied;

(b) specify, and comment on, whatever changes appear to OFCOM to have occurred, during that period, in the manner in which those purposes are fulfilled;

(c) set out the findings of OFCOM on their consideration of the matters mentioned in subsection

(7) and any conclusions they have arrived at in relation to those findings; and

(d) set out OFCOM's conclusions on the current state of public service television broadcasting in the United Kingdom.

(9) In performing their duties under this section, OFCOM must have regard, in particular, to—

(a) every statement of programme or service policy which has been made by virtue of this Chapter by a public service broadcaster, or which is treated as such a statement;

(b) every equivalent statement of policy made by the BBC in pursuance of the BBC Charter and Agreement; and

(c) such matters arising at times before the coming into force of this section as OFCOM consider material.

(10) Every report prepared by OFCOM under this section must be published by them—

(a) as soon as practicable after its preparation is complete; and

(b) in such manner as they consider appropriate.

(11) The following are relevant television services for the purposes of this section—

(a) the television broadcasting services provided by the BBC;

(b) the television programme services that are public services of the Welsh Authority (within the meaning of section 207);

(c) every Channel 3 service;

(d) Channel 4;

(e) Channel 5;

(f) the public teletext service.

(12) The following are public service broadcasters for the purposes of this section—

(a) the BBC;

(b) the Welsh Authority;

(c) the providers of the licensed public service channels; and

(d) the public teletext provider.

(13) In this section—

"belief" means a collective belief in, or other adherence to, a systemised set of ethical or philosophical principles or of mystical or transcendental doctrines; and

"drama" includes contemporary and other drama in a variety of different formats.

Commencement Information

I69. S. 264 in force at 25.7.2003 by S.I. 2003/1900, art. 2. (1), Sch. 1 (with art. 4)

[F72264. A OFCOM reports: wider review and reporting obligations

(1) When carrying out a review under section 264 for a period, OFCOM must also carry out a review of the extent to which material included in media services during that period (taken together over the period as a whole) contributed towards the fulfilment of the public service objectives.

(2) Every report under section 264 must—

(a) include a report on the matters found on the review under this section,

(b) specify, and comment on, whatever changes appear to OFCOM to have occurred, during the period to which the report relates, in the extent to which the public service objectives have been fulfilled,

(c) specify, and comment on, whatever changes appear to OFCOM to have occurred, during that period, in the manner in which those objectives are fulfilled, and

(d) set out OFCOM's conclusions on the current state of material included in media services.

(3) "The public service objectives" are the objectives set out in paragraphs (b) to (j) of section 264. (6) (as modified by subsection (4)).

(4) Paragraphs (b) to (j) of section 264. (6) have effect for the purposes of subsection (3) as if—

(a) references to the relevant television services were to media services, and

(b) references to programmes were to material included in such services.

(5) In this section—

"material" does not include advertisements;

"media services" means any of the following services that are available to members of the public

239

in all or part of the United Kingdom—
- television and radio services,
- on-demand programme services, and
- other services provided by means of the internet where there is a person who exercises editorial control over the material included in the service.
(6) The services that are to be taken for the purposes of this section to be available to members of the public include any service which—
(a) is available for reception by members of the public (within the meaning of section 361); or
(b) is available for use by members of the public (within the meaning of section 368. R(4)).]
Amendments (Textual)
F72. S. 264. A inserted (8.6.2010) by Digital Economy Act 2010 (c. 24), ss. 2, 47. (1)
265. Public service remits of licensed providers
(1) The regulatory regime for every licensed public service channel, and for the public teletext service, includes a condition requiring the provider of the channel or service to fulfil the public service remit for that channel or service.
(2) The public service remit—
(a) for every Channel 3 service, and
(b) for Channel 5,
is the provision of a range of high quality and diverse programming.
(3) The public service remit for Channel 4 is the provision of a broad range of high quality and diverse programming which, in particular—
(a) demonstrates innovation, experiment and creativity in the form and content of programmes;
(b) appeals to the tastes and interests of a culturally diverse society;
(c) makes a significant contribution to meeting the need for the licensed public service channels to include programmes of an educational nature and other programmes of educative value; and
(d) exhibits a distinctive character.
(4) The public service remit for the public teletext service is the provision of a range of high quality and diverse text material.
(5) For so long as the public teletext service comprises both—
(a) an analogue teletext service, and
(b) a teletext service provided in digital form,
the conditions imposed under this section must require the public service remit of the public teletext service to be fulfilled separately in the case of each of those services.
Commencement Information
I70. S. 265 in force at 28.12.2004 by S.I. 2004/3309, art. 3
266. Statements of programme policy
(1) The regulatory regime for every licensed public service channel includes a condition requiring the provider of the channel—
(a) as soon as practicable after the coming into force of this section and subsequently at annual intervals, to prepare a statement of programme policy; and
(b) to monitor his own performance in the carrying out of the proposals contained in the statements made in pursuance of the condition.
(2) The condition must require every statement of programme policy prepared in accordance with the condition to set out the proposals of the provider of the channel for securing that, during the following year—
(a) the public service remit for the channel will be fulfilled; and
(b) the duties imposed on the provider by virtue of sections 277 to 296 will be performed.
(3) The condition must also require every such statement to contain a report on the performance of the provider of the channel in the carrying out, during the period since the previous statement, of the proposals contained in that statement.
(4) The condition must also provide that every such statement—
(a) must be prepared having regard to guidance given by OFCOM;
(b) must be prepared taking account of the reports previously published by OFCOM under

sections 264 and 358;

(c) must take special account of the most recent such reports;

(d) must be published by the provider of the channel in question as soon as practicable after its preparation is complete; and

(e) must be published in such manner as, having regard to any guidance given by OFCOM, the provider considers appropriate.

(5) In preparing guidance about the preparation of such a statement, OFCOM must have regard, in particular, to the matters which, in the light of the provisions of section 264. (4) and (6), they consider should be included in statements of programme policy.

(6) It shall be the duty of OFCOM—

(a) from time to time to review the guidance for the time being in force for the purposes of this section; and

(b) to make such revisions of that guidance as they think fit.

(7) The conditions of a licence to provide a licensed public service channel may provide that a previous statement of policy made by the provider of the channel is to be treated for the purposes of this Part—

(a) as if it were a statement made in relation to such period as may be so specified; and

(b) were a statement of programme policy for the purposes of a condition imposed under this section.

(8) The reference in subsection (7) to a previous statement of policy is a reference to any statement made by the provider of the channel—

(a) whether before or after the commencement of this section, for the purposes of his application for a Broadcasting Act licence for the channel; or

(b) at any time before the commencement of this section, for any other purpose.

(9) A condition under subsection (7) cannot contain provision the effect of which is to postpone the time at which a licence holder is required to make the first statement of programme policy which (apart from that subsection) he is required to make in pursuance of a condition imposed under this section.

Commencement Information

I71. S. 266 in force at 28.12.2004 by S.I. 2004/3309, art. 3

267. Changes of programme policy

(1) The regulatory regime for every licensed public service channel includes a condition requiring compliance with subsection (2) in the case of a statement of programme policy containing proposals for a significant change.

(2) This subsection requires the provider of the channel—

(a) to consult OFCOM before preparing the statement; and

(b) to take account, in the preparation of the statement, of any opinions expressed to the provider of the channel by OFCOM.

(3) A condition imposed under this section must further provide that, if it appears to OFCOM that a statement of programme policy has been prepared by the provider of the channel in contravention of a condition imposed under subsection (1), the provider is—

(a) to revise that statement in accordance with any directions given to him by OFCOM; and

(b) to publish a revision of the statement in accordance with any such directions only after the revision has been approved by OFCOM.

(4) A change is a significant change for the purposes of this section if it is a change as a result of which the channel would in any year be materially different in character from in previous years.

(5) In determining for the purposes of any condition under this section whether a change is a significant change—

(a) regard must be had to any guidance issued by OFCOM;

(b) the changes to be considered include any changes that, together with any proposed change for a particular year, would constitute a change occurring gradually over a period of not more than three years; and

(c) the previous years with which a comparison is to be made must be those immediately preceding the year in which the change is made, or in which the changes comprised in it began to occur.

(6) It shall be the duty of OFCOM—

(a) from time to time to review the guidance for the time being in force for the purposes of this section; and

(b) to make such revisions of that guidance as they think fit.

Commencement Information

I72. S. 267 in force at 28.12.2004 by S.I. 2004/3309, art. 3

268. Statements of service policy by the public teletext provider

(1) The regulatory regime for the public teletext service includes a condition requiring the public teletext provider—

(a) as soon as practicable after the coming into force of this section and subsequently at annual intervals, to prepare a statement of service policy; and

(b) to monitor his own performance in the carrying out of the proposals contained in statements made in pursuance of the condition.

(2) The condition must require every statement of service policy prepared in accordance with the condition to set out the proposals of the public teletext provider for securing that, during the following year, the public service remit for the public teletext service will be fulfilled.

(3) The condition must also require every such statement to contain a report on the performance of the public teletext provider in the carrying out, during the period since the previous statement, of the proposals contained in that statement.

(4) The condition must provide that the proposals or report for a period in the course of which the public teletext service will comprise or has comprised both—

(a) an analogue teletext service, and

(b) a teletext service provided in digital form,

must deal separately with each of those services.

(5) The condition must also provide that every statement in pursuance of the condition—

(a) must be prepared having regard to guidance given by OFCOM;

(b) must be prepared taking account of the reports previously published by OFCOM under sections 264 and 358;

(c) must take special account of the most recent such reports;

(d) must be published by the public teletext provider as soon as practicable after its preparation is complete; and

(e) must be published in such manner as, having regard to any guidance given by OFCOM, that provider considers appropriate.

(6) In preparing guidance about the preparation of such a statement, OFCOM must have regard, in particular, to the matters which, in the light of the provisions of section 264. (4) and (6), they consider should be included in statements of service policy by the public teletext provider.

(7) It shall be the duty of OFCOM—

(a) from time to time to review the guidance for the time being in force for the purposes of this section; and

(b) to make such revisions of that guidance as they think fit.

(8) The conditions of the licence to provide the public teletext service may provide that a previous statement of policy made by the public teletext provider is to be treated for the purposes of this Part—

(a) as if it were a statement made in relation to such period as may be so specified; and

(b) were a statement of service policy for the purposes of a condition imposed under this section.

(9) The reference in subsection (8) to a previous statement of policy is a reference to any statement made by the public teletext provider—

(a) whether before or after the commencement of this section, for the purposes of his application for a Broadcasting Act licence for the public teletext service or for the existing service (within the meaning of section 221); or

(b) at any time before the commencement of this section, for any other purpose.

(10) A condition under subsection (8) cannot contain provision the effect of which is to postpone the time at which a licence holder is required to make the first statement of service policy which (apart from that subsection) he is required to make in pursuance of a condition imposed under this section.

Commencement Information

I73. S. 268 in force at 28.12.2004 by S.I. 2004/3309, art. 3

269. Changes of service policy

(1) The regulatory regime for the public teletext service includes a condition requiring compliance with subsection (2) in the case of a statement of service policy containing proposals for a significant change.

(2) This subsection requires the provider of the service—

(a) to consult OFCOM before preparing the statement; and

(b) to take account, in the preparation of the statement, of any opinions expressed to the provider of the service by OFCOM.

(3) A condition imposed under this section must further provide that, if it appears to OFCOM that a statement of service policy has been prepared by the public teletext provider in contravention of a condition imposed under subsection (1), that provider is—

(a) to revise that statement in accordance with any directions given to him by OFCOM; and

(b) to publish a revision of the statement in accordance with any such directions only after the revision has been approved by OFCOM.

(4) A change is a significant change for the purposes of this section if it is a change as a result of which the service would in any year be materially different in character from in previous years.

(5) In determining for the purposes of any condition under this section whether a change is a significant change—

(a) regard must be had to any guidance issued by OFCOM;

(b) the changes to be considered include any changes that, together with any proposed change for a particular year, would constitute a change occurring gradually over a period of not more than three years;

(c) the previous years with which a comparison is to be made must be those immediately preceding the year in which the change is made, or in which the changes comprised in it began to occur; and

(d) any change that is a significant change in relation to so much of the public teletext service as is provided in digital form or in relation to so much of it as is provided in analogue form is to be regarded as a significant change in relation to the whole service.

(6) It shall be the duty of OFCOM—

(a) from time to time to review the guidance for the time being in force for the purposes of this section; and

(b) to make such revisions of that guidance as they think fit.

Commencement Information

I74. S. 269 in force at 28.12.2004 by S.I. 2004/3309, art. 3

270. Enforcement of public service remits

(1) This section applies if OFCOM are of the opinion that the provider of a licensed public service channel or the public teletext provider—

(a) has failed to fulfil the public service remit for that channel or the public teletext service; or

(b) has failed, in any respect, to make an adequate contribution towards the fulfilment of the purposes of public service television broadcasting in the United Kingdom.

(2) This section does not apply unless—

(a) OFCOM are of the opinion that the failure of the provider is serious and is not excused by economic or market conditions; and

(b) OFCOM determine that the situation requires the exercise of their powers under this section.

(3) In making a determination under subsection (2)(b), OFCOM must have regard, in particular, to—

(a) the public service remit of that provider;

(b) the statements of programme policy or statements of service policy made (or treated as made) by the provider under section 266 or 268;

(c) the record generally of the provider in relation to the carrying out of obligations imposed by conditions of licences under the 1990 Act and the 1996 Act (including past obligations);

(d) the effectiveness and efficiency of the provider in monitoring his own performance; and

(e) general economic and market conditions affecting generally the providers of television programme services or the providers of television multiplex services, or both of them.

(4) OFCOM shall have power to give directions to the provider to do one or both of the following—

(a) to revise the provider's latest statement of programme policy, or statement of service policy, in accordance with the directions; and

(b) to take such steps for remedying the provider's failure as OFCOM may specify in the direction as necessary for that purpose.

(5) A direction given under this section must set out—

(a) a reasonable timetable for complying with it; and

(b) the factors that will be taken into account by OFCOM in determining—

(i) whether or not a failure of the provider has been remedied; and

(ii) whether or not to exercise their powers under subsection (6).

(6) If OFCOM are satisfied—

(a) that the provider of a public service channel or the public teletext provider has failed to comply with a direction under this section,

(b) that that provider is still failing to fulfil the public service remit for that channel or service or adequately to contribute to the fulfilment of the purposes of public service television broadcasting in the United Kingdom, and

(c) that it would be both reasonable and proportionate to the seriousness of that failure to vary the provider's licence in accordance with this subsection,

OFCOM may, by notice to the provider, vary that licence so as to replace self-regulation with detailed regulation.

(7) For the purposes of subsection (6) a variation replacing self-regulation with detailed regulation is a variation which—

(a) omits the conditions imposed by virtue of sections 265 to 269; and

(b) replaces those conditions with such specific conditions as OFCOM consider appropriate for securing that the provider—

(i) fulfils the public service remit for his service; and

(ii) makes an adequate contribution towards the fulfilment of the purposes of public service television broadcasting in the United Kingdom.

(8) If, at any time following a variation in accordance with subsection (6) of a provider's licence, OFCOM consider that detailed regulation is no longer necessary, they may again vary the licence so as, with effect from such time as they may determine—

(a) to provide for the conditions required by virtue of sections 265 to 269 again to be included in the regulatory regime for the service provided by that provider; and

(b) to remove or modify some or all of the specific conditions inserted under that subsection.

(9) Before giving a direction under this section to a provider or exercising their power under this section to vary a provider's licence, OFCOM must consult that provider.

(10) In accordance with section 265. (5), the reference in subsection (1) to a failure to fulfil the public service remit for the public teletext service includes a failure to fulfil that remit as respects only one of the services comprised in that service.

Commencement Information

175. S. 270 in force at 28.12.2004 by S.I. 2004/3309, art. 3

271. Power to amend public service remits

(1) The Secretary of State may by order modify any one or more of the following—

(a) the public service remit for any licensed public service channel or for the public teletext service;

(b) the purposes of public service television broadcasting in the United Kingdom (within the meaning given by subsection (4) of section 264);

(c) the matters to which OFCOM are to have regard under subsections (5) and (6) of that section.

(2) The Secretary of State is not to make an order under this section except where—

(a) OFCOM have made a recommendation for the making of such an order in their most recent report under section 229 or 264; or

(b) subsection (3) applies to the order.

(3) This subsection applies to an order if—

(a) it is made by the Secretary of State less than twelve months after the date on which he has received a report under section 229;

(b) he has considered that report; and

(c) he is satisfied that the making of the order is required, notwithstanding the absence of a recommendation by OFCOM, by circumstances or other matters which are dealt with in that report or which (in his opinion) should have been.

(4) Before including a recommendation for the making of an order under this section in a report under section 229 or 264, OFCOM must consult—

(a) members of the public in the United Kingdom;

(b) such public service broadcasters as they consider are likely to be affected if the Secretary of State gives effect to the recommendation they are proposing to make; and

(c) such of the other persons providing television and radio services as OFCOM consider appropriate.

(5) Before making an order under this section, the Secretary of State must consult the persons mentioned in subsection (6) about its terms (even if the order is the one recommended by OFCOM).

(6) Those persons are—

(a) OFCOM;

(b) such public service broadcasters as they consider are likely to be affected by the order; and

(c) such of the other persons providing television and radio services as he considers appropriate.

(7) No order is to be made containing provision authorised by this section unless a draft of the order has been laid before Parliament and approved by a resolution of each House.

(8) In this section "public service broadcaster" means any of the persons who are public service broadcasters for the purposes of section 264.

Commencement Information

I76. S. 271 in force at 29.12.2003 by S.I. 2003/3142, art. 3. (1), Sch. 1 (with art. 11)

[F73271. ARemedying failure by C4. C to perform media content duties

(1) This section applies if OFCOM are satisfied—

(a) that C4. C have failed to comply with a direction under section 198. D in respect of a failure to perform one or more of their duties under section 198. A,

(b) that C4. C are still failing to perform that duty or those duties, and

(c) that it would be both reasonable and proportionate to the seriousness of the failure to vary the licence under which Channel 4 is licensed ("the Channel 4 licence") in accordance with this section.

(2) OFCOM may, by notice to C4. C, vary the Channel 4 licence by adding such conditions, or making such modifications of conditions, as OFCOM consider appropriate for remedying (entirely or partly) C4. C's failure to perform the duty or duties under section 198. A.

(3) If, at any time following such a variation, OFCOM consider that any of the additional conditions or modifications is no longer necessary, they may again vary the licence with effect from such time as they may determine.

(4) OFCOM must consult C4. C before exercising their power under this section to vary the Channel 4 licence.]

Amendments (Textual)

F73. S. 271. A inserted (8.6.2010) by Digital Economy Act 2010 (c. 24), ss. 23. (2), 47. (1)

Must-offer obligations etc. affecting public service television

272. Must-offer obligations in relation to networks

(1) The regulatory regime for—

  (a) every licensed public service channel,

  (b) the public teletext service, and

  (c) every licensed television service added by order under section 64 to the list of must-carry services,

includes the conditions that OFCOM consider appropriate for securing the three objectives set out in this section (so far as they are not secured by provision made under section 243).

(2) The first objective is that the channel or other service, so far as it is provided in digital form, is at all times offered as available (subject to the need to agree terms) to be broadcast or distributed by means of every appropriate network.

(3) The second objective is that the person providing the channel or other service does his best to secure that arrangements are entered into, and kept in force, that ensure—

  (a) that the channel or other service, so far as it is provided in digital form, is broadcast or distributed on appropriate networks; and

  (b) that the broadcasting and distribution of the channel or other service, in accordance with those arrangements, result in its being available for reception, by means of appropriate networks, by as many members of its intended audience as practicable.

(4) The third objective is that the arrangements entered into and kept in force for the purpose of securing the second objective prohibit the imposition, for or in connection with the provision of an appropriate network, of any charge that is attributable (whether directly or indirectly) to the conferring of an entitlement to receive the channel or other service in question in an intelligible form by means of that network.

(5) The three objectives apply only in relation to times when the channel or other service in its digital form is included in the list of must-carry services in section 64.

(6) Conditions imposed under this section in relation to a channel or other service must, to such extent as OFCOM consider appropriate—

  (a) require arrangements made or kept in force for the purpose of securing the second objective to apply in the case of every service which is an ancillary service by reference to the channel or other service in question as they apply to the channel or other service itself; and

  (b) provide for the channel or other service to which the conditions apply to be treated, in relation to particular appropriate networks, as constituting such services comprised in or provided with that channel or other service as may be determined by OFCOM.

(7) In this section—

"appropriate network" means (subject to subsection (8)) an electronic communications network by means of which public electronic communications services are provided that are used by a significant number of end-users as their principal means of receiving television programmes;

"intended audience", in relation to a channel or other service, means—

  - if the channel or other service is one provided only for a particular area or locality of the United Kingdom, members of the public in that area or locality;

  - if the channel or other service is one provided for members of a particular community, members of that community; and

  - in any other case, members of the public in the United Kingdom;

"licensed television service" means a service falling to be licensed under Part 1 of the 1990 Act or Part 1 of the 1996 Act.

(8) For the purposes of this section an electronic communications network is not an appropriate network in relation to so much of a channel or other service as is provided only for a particular area or locality of the United Kingdom unless it is a network by means of which electronic

communications services are provided to persons in that area or locality

(9) In subsection (7) "public electronic communications service" and "end-user" each has the same meaning as in Part 2.

(10) An order under section 411 must not appoint a day for provisions of this section to come into force that falls less than six months after the day on which the order is made.

Commencement Information

I77. S. 272 in force at 31.1.2010 by S.I. 2009/2130, art. 2

273. Must-offer obligations in relation to satellite services

(1) The regulatory regime for—

(a) every licensed public service channel,

(b) the public teletext service, and

(c) every other licensed television service specified for the purposes of this section in an order made by the Secretary of State,

includes the conditions that OFCOM consider appropriate for securing the three objectives set out in this section (so far as they are not secured by conditions imposed under section 272).

(2) The first objective is that the channel or other service, so far as it is provided in digital form, is at all times offered as available (subject to the need to agree terms) to be broadcast by means of every satellite television service that is available for reception by members of the public in the whole or a part of the United Kingdom.

(3) The second objective is that the person providing the channel or other service does his best to secure that arrangements are entered into, and kept in force, that ensure—

(a) that the channel or other service, so far as it is provided in digital form, is broadcast by means of satellite television services that are broadcast so as to be available for reception by members of the public in the United Kingdom; and

(b) that the broadcasting, in accordance with those arrangements, of the channel or other service by means of those satellite television services results in its being available for reception in an intelligible form and by means of those services by as many members of its intended audience as practicable.

(4) The third objective is that the arrangements entered into and kept in force for the purpose of securing the second objective prohibit the imposition, for or in connection with the provision of a satellite television service, of any charge that is attributable (whether directly or indirectly) to the conferring of an entitlement to receive the channel or other service in question in an intelligible form by means of that service.

(5) The three objectives apply only in relation to a time when the channel or service is included, in its digital form, in the list of services that are must-provide services for the purposes of section 274.

(6) Conditions imposed under this section in relation to a channel or other service must, to such extent as OFCOM consider appropriate—

(a) require arrangements made or kept in force for the purpose of securing the second objective to apply in the case of every service which is an ancillary service by reference to the channel or other service in question as they apply to the channel or other service itself; and

(b) provide for the channel or other service to which the conditions apply to be treated, in relation to particular satellite television services, as constituting such services comprised in or provided with the channel or other service as may be determined by OFCOM.

(7) In this section—

"intended audience", in relation to a channel or other service, means—

- if the channel or other service is one provided only for a particular area or locality of the United Kingdom, members of the public in that area or locality;

- if the channel or other service is one provided for members of a particular community, members of that community; and

- in any other case, members of the public in the United Kingdom;

"licensed television service" means a service falling to be licensed under Part 1 of the 1990 Act or Part 1 of the 1996 Act; and

247

"satellite television service" means a service which—
- consists in or involves the broadcasting of television programme services from a satellite; and
- is used by a significant number of the persons by whom the broadcasts are received in an intelligible form as their principal means of receiving television programmes.

(8) An order under section 411 must not appoint a day for provisions of this section to come into force that falls less than six months after the day on which the order is made.

Commencement Information

I78. S. 273 in force at 31.1.2010 by S.I. 2009/2130, art. 2

Prospective

274. Securing reception of must-provide services in certain areas

(1) The regulatory regime for—

(a) every licensed public service channel,

(b) the public teletext service, and

(c) every licensed television service added by order under section 275 to the list of must-provide services,

includes the conditions that OFCOM consider appropriate for securing that arrangements satisfying the requirements of this section are entered into and maintained by all the persons who provide must-provide services.

(2) The conditions imposed on a person under this section may include the conditions that OFCOM consider appropriate for securing, in a case where—

(a) the persons providing must-provide services fail to enter into or maintain arrangements satisfying the requirements of this section, and

(b) OFCOM make and impose arrangements of their own instead,

that the person bound by the conditions is required to act in accordance with arrangements imposed by OFCOM.

(3) The arrangements that are to be entered into, or may be imposed, are arrangements that secure—

(a) that a facility for receiving each must-provide service is made available to every member of the intended audience for that service who is unable, without the use of that facility, to receive it in an intelligible form and free of charge;

(b) that the facility is one under which every such member of the intended audience for a must-provide service is entitled, free of charge, to receive in an intelligible form so much of a service broadcast from a satellite as includes that must-provide service;

(c) that the cost of making that facility available is shared, in appropriate proportions, by all the persons providing must-provide services;

(d) that procedures are established and maintained for dealing with complaints from persons claiming to be entitled, in accordance with the arrangements, to receive a service free of charge, and for resolving disputes about the existence or extent of such an entitlement;

(e) that the availability of those procedures is adequately publicised in accordance with guidance given from time to time by OFCOM.

(4) Arrangements entered into by the providers of must-provide services for the purposes of subsection (3), and any modifications of such arrangements made by the parties to them, are to have effect only if approved by OFCOM.

(5) Before imposing any arrangements for the purposes of a condition under subsection (2), OFCOM must consult all the persons who provide must-provide services.

(6) For the purposes of this section the reception of a service is not free of charge—

(a) if reception of the service is made conditional on the acceptance of an entitlement to receive another service in relation to which a charge is imposed (whether directly or indirectly);

(b) if a charge is made for or in connection with the provision of a service which is an ancillary service in relation to the service in question;

(c) if any consideration is required from the persons to whom it is made available for the provision of assistance for disabled people in respect of programmes included in the service; or

(d) if any other consideration is required to be given, by the person entitled to receive it, for or in connection with its provision or availability.

(7) A service is not prevented from being free of charge by a requirement to pay sums in accordance with regulations under section 365.

(8) The quality of reception that is required before someone is to be treated for the purposes of any conditions imposed under this section as able to receive a service in an intelligible form is to be determined by OFCOM.

(9) References in this section to a facility for receiving a must-provide service include references to—

   (a) software to be used in giving effect to the entitlement to receive a must-provide service in an intelligible form, and

   (b) apparatus to be used in associating apparatus capable of being used for receiving such a service, or for putting it into an intelligible form, with a person having such an entitlement,
but do not otherwise include references to apparatus.

(10) In this section—
"intended audience", in relation to a must-provide service, means—
   - if the service is one provided only for a particular area or locality of the United Kingdom, members of the public in that area or locality;
   - if the service is one provided for members of a particular community, members of that community; and
   - in any other case, members of the public in the United Kingdom;
"licensed television service" means a service falling to be licensed under Part 1 of the 1990 Act or Part 1 of the 1996 Act;
"must-provide service" means a service for the time being included in the list of must-provide services in section 275.

(11) An order under section 411 must not appoint a day for provisions of this section to come into force that falls less than six months after the day on which the order is made.

275. Must-provide services for the purposes of s. 274.

(1) For the purposes of section 274 the list of must-provide services is as follows—

   (a) every service of television programmes provided by the BBC so far as it is provided in digital form and is a service in relation to which OFCOM have functions;

   (b) the Channel 3 services so far as provided in digital form;

   (c) Channel 4 so far as provided in digital form;

   (d) Channel 5 so far as provided in digital form;

   (e) S4. C Digital;

   (f) the digital public teletext service.

(2) The Secretary of State may by order modify the list of must-provide services in subsection (1).

(3) In determining whether it is appropriate, by an order under subsection (2), to add a service to the list of must-provide services or to remove a service from that list, the Secretary of State must have regard, in particular, to—

   (a) the public benefit to be secured by the addition of the service to the list, or by its retention in the list;

   (b) the likely effect of the proposed modification as respects the costs to be borne, under arrangements entered into or imposed under section 274, by the persons who, after the coming into force of the modification, would have to be parties to those arrangements; and

   (c) the extent to which that effect is proportionate to the benefit mentioned in paragraph (a).

Commencement Information

I79. S. 275 in force at 29.12.2003 by S.I. 2003/3142, art. 3. (1), Sch. 1 (with art. 11)

276. Co-operation with the public teletext provider

(1) The regulatory regime for every Channel 3 service and for Channel 4 includes the conditions that OFCOM consider appropriate for securing that the provider of the service or channel grants access to the facilities mentioned in subsection (2)—

   (a) to the public teletext provider; and

   (b) to any person authorised by virtue of section 220 to provide the whole or a part of the public teletext service on his behalf.

(2) Those facilities are the facilities that are reasonably required by the public teletext provider or the authorised person for the purposes of, or in connection with, the provision of the public teletext service.

(3) A licence holder granting access to facilities in pursuance of a condition imposed under this section may require the public teletext provider or authorised person to pay a reasonable charge in respect of the facilities.

(4) In the event of a dispute, the amount of the charge is to be determined by OFCOM.

Modifications etc. (not altering text)

C8. S. 276 excluded (8.12.2003) by The Office of Communications Act 2002 (Commencement No. 3) and Communications Act 2003 (Commencement No. 2) Order 2003 (S.I. 2003/3142), art. 8. (2) (with art. 11)

Commencement Information

180. S. 276 in force at 29.12.2003 by S.I. 2003/3142, art. 3. (1), Sch. 1 (with art. 11)

Programming quotas for public service television

277. Programming quotas for independent productions

(1) The regulatory regime for every licensed public service channel includes the conditions that OFCOM consider appropriate for securing that, in each year, not less than 25 per cent. of the total amount of time allocated to the broadcasting of qualifying programmes included in the channel is allocated to the broadcasting of a range and diversity of independent productions.

(2) In this section—

(a) a reference to qualifying programmes is a reference to programmes of such description as the Secretary of State may by order specify as describing the programmes that are to be qualifying programmes for the purposes of this section;

(b) a reference to independent productions is a reference to programmes of such description as the Secretary of State may by order specify as describing the programmes that are to be independent productions for the purposes of this section; and

(c) a reference to a range of independent productions is a reference to a range of such productions in terms of cost of acquisition as well as in terms of the types of programme involved.

(3) The Secretary of State may by order amend subsection (1) by substituting a different percentage for the percentage for the time being specified in that subsection.

(4) The Secretary of State may also by order provide for the regulatory regime for every licensed public service channel to include conditions falling within subsection (5), either instead of or as well as those falling within subsection (1).

(5) The conditions falling within this subsection are those that OFCOM consider appropriate for securing that, in each year, not less than the percentage specified in the order of the programming budget for that year for that channel is applied in the acquisition of independent productions.

(6) The power to make an order under subsection (4) includes power to provide that conditions that have previously ceased under such an order to be included in the regulatory regime for every licensed public service channel are again so included, in addition to or instead of the conditions already so included (apart from the exercise of that power) by virtue of this section.

(7) The Secretary of State is not to make an order for the regulatory regime of every licensed public service channel to include or exclude conditions falling within subsection (1) or conditions falling within subsection (5) unless—

(a) OFCOM have made a recommendation to him for those conditions to be included or excluded; and

(b) the order gives effect to that recommendation.

(8) The regulatory regime for every licensed public service channel also includes a condition requiring the provider of the channel to comply with directions given to him by OFCOM for the purpose of—

(a) carrying forward to one or more subsequent years determined in accordance with the direction any shortfall for any year in his compliance with the requirements of conditions imposed by virtue of subsection (1) or (4); and

(b) thereby increasing the percentage applicable for the purposes of those conditions to the subsequent year or years.

(9) For the purposes of conditions imposed by virtue of this section—

(a) the amount of the programming budget for a licensed public service channel for a year, and

(b) the means of determining the amount of that budget that is applied for any purpose,

are to be computed in accordance with such provision as may be set out in an order made by the Secretary of State, or as may be determined by OFCOM in accordance with such an order.

(10) The powers of the Secretary of State to make orders under this section do not include—

(a) power to specify different percentages for the purposes of subsection (1), or of a condition falling within subsection (5), for different regional Channel 3 services or for different national Channel 3 services; or

(b) power to make different provision for different licensed public service channels as to whether conditions falling within subsection (1) or conditions falling within subsection (5), or both, are included in the regulatory regimes for those services.

(11) Before making an order under this section the Secretary of State must consult OFCOM, the BBC and the Welsh Authority.

(12) No order is to be made containing provision authorised by this section unless a draft of the order has been laid before Parliament and approved by a resolution of each House.

(13) In this section—

"acquisition", in relation to a programme, includes commissioning and the acquisition of a right to include it in a service or to have it broadcast;

"programme" does not include an advertisement; and

"programming budget" means the budget for the production and acquisition of qualifying programmes.

Commencement Information

I81. S. 277 in force at 29.12.2003 by S.I. 2003/3142, art. 3. (1), Sch. 1 (with art. 11)

278. Programming quotas for original productions

(1) The regulatory regime for every licensed public service channel includes the conditions that OFCOM consider appropriate for securing—

(a) that the time allocated, in each year, to the broadcasting of original productions included in that channel is no less than what appears to them to be an appropriate proportion of the total amount of time allocated to the broadcasting of all the programmes included in the channel; and

(b) that the time allocated to the broadcasting of original productions is split in what appears to them to be an appropriate manner between peak viewing times and other times.

(2) The proportion determined by OFCOM for the purposes of subsection (1)—

(a) must, in the case of each licensed public service channel, be such proportion as OFCOM consider appropriate for ensuring that the channel is consistently of a high quality; and

(b) may, for the purposes of paragraph (b) of that subsection, be expressed as the cumulative effect of two different minimum proportions, one applying to peak viewing times and the other to other times.

(3) A condition contained in a licence by virtue of this section may provide—

(a) that specified descriptions of programmes are to be excluded in determining the programmes a proportion of which is to consist of original productions;

(b) that, in determining for the purposes of the condition whether a programme is of a description of programmes excluded by virtue of paragraph (a), regard is to be had to any guidance prepared and published, and from to time revised, by OFCOM.

(4) Before imposing a condition under this section, OFCOM must consult the person on whom it is to be imposed.

(5) The requirement to consult is satisfied, in the case of the imposition of a condition by way of a variation of a licence, by compliance with section 3. (4)(b) of the 1990 Act (obligation to give

opportunity to make representations about variation).

(6) References in this section, in relation to a licensed public service channel, to original productions are references to programmes of such description as the Secretary of State may by order specify as describing the programmes that are to be original productions for the purposes of this section.

(7) The power to specify descriptions of programmes by order under subsection (6) includes power to confer such discretions on OFCOM as the Secretary of State thinks fit.

(8) Before making an order under this section the Secretary of State must consult OFCOM, the BBC and the Welsh Authority.

(9) No order is to be made containing provision authorised by this section unless a draft of the order has been laid before Parliament and approved by a resolution of each House.

(10) In this section—

"peak viewing time", in relation to a licensed public service channel, means a time that appears to OFCOM to be, or to be likely to be, a peak viewing time for that channel; and

"programme" does not include an advertisement.

(11) Before determining for the purposes of this section what constitutes a peak viewing time for a channel, OFCOM must consult the provider of the channel.

Commencement Information

I82. S. 278 in force at 1.7.2004 by S.I. 2003/3142, art. 4. (4)(a) (with art. 11) (as amended (4.3.2004) by S.I. 2004/545, art. 2. (2)(3)(b))

News provision etc. on public service television

279. News and current affairs programmes

(1) The regulatory regime for every licensed public service channel includes the conditions that OFCOM consider appropriate for securing—

   (a) that the programmes included in the channel include news programmes and current affairs programmes;

   (b) that the news programmes and current affairs programmes included in the service are of high quality and deal with both national and international matters; and

   (c) that the news programmes so included are broadcast for viewing at intervals throughout the period for which the channel is provided.

(2) That regime also includes the conditions that OFCOM consider appropriate for securing that, in each year—

   (a) the time allocated to the broadcasting of news programmes included in the service, and

   (b) the time allocated to the broadcasting of current affairs programmes so included,

each constitutes no less than what appears to OFCOM to be an appropriate proportion of the time allocated to the broadcasting of all the programmes included in the channel.

(3) It further includes the conditions that OFCOM consider appropriate for securing that the time allocated—

   (a) to the broadcasting of news programmes included in the service, and

   (b) to the broadcasting of current affairs programmes so included,

is, in each case, split in what appears to OFCOM to be an appropriate manner between peak viewing times and other times.

(4) The proportion determined by OFCOM for the purposes of subsection (2) may, for the purposes of subsection (3), be expressed as the cumulative effect of two different minimum proportions, one applying to peak viewing times and the other to other times.

(5) In this section "peak viewing time", in relation to a licensed public service channel, means a time determined by OFCOM to be, or to be likely to be, a peak viewing time for that channel.

(6) Before determining for the purposes of this section—

   (a) the proportion of time to be allocated to the broadcasting of news programmes or current affairs programmes; or

(b) what constitutes a peak viewing time for a channel,
OFCOM must consult the provider of the channel or (as the case may be) the person who is proposing to provide it.

(7) The requirement to consult is satisfied, in the case of the imposition of a condition by way of a variation of a licence, by compliance with section 3. (4)(b) of the 1990 Act (obligation to give opportunity to make representations about variation).

Commencement Information

I83. S. 279 in force at 29.12.2003 by S.I. 2003/3142, art. 3. (1), Sch. 1 (with art. 11)

280. Appointed news providers for Channel 3.

(1) The regulatory regime for every regional Channel 3 service includes the conditions that OFCOM consider appropriate for securing the nationwide broadcasting, on the regional Channel 3 services (taken together), of news programmes that are able to compete effectively with other television news programmes broadcast nationwide in the United Kingdom.

(2) The conditions imposed under this section must include a condition requiring the holder of a regional Channel 3 licence to do all that he can to ensure—

(a) that arrangements for the appointment of a single body corporate as the appointed news provider are maintained between all the holders of regional Channel 3 licences; and

(b) that, at all times while he is providing a regional Channel 3 service, there is in force an appointment made in accordance with those arrangements.

(3) The arrangements that are required to be maintained by virtue of conditions imposed under subsection (2) must provide—

(a) for the terms on which a body is appointed as the appointed news provider to include the terms appearing to OFCOM to be appropriate for securing that the body's finances are adequate, throughout the period of its appointment, to ensure that the Channel 3 news obligations are capable of being met; and

(b) for the approval of OFCOM to be required for the purposes of paragraph (a) to the terms on which an appointment is made.

(4) The conditions imposed under this section must include the conditions that OFCOM consider appropriate for securing that arrangements maintained between—

(a) the holders of regional Channel 3 licences, and

(b) the body which is the appointed news provider,

ensure that that body is subject to an obligation, enforceable by OFCOM, to provide OFCOM with all such information as they may require for the purpose of carrying out their functions.

(5) The conditions imposed under this section must include a condition requiring the news programmes included in a regional Channel 3 service—

(a) to be programmes provided by the body which is for the time being the appointed news provider for the purposes of this section; and

(b) to be so included in that service as to be broadcast simultaneously with the broadcasting of news programmes included, in accordance with conditions imposed under this subsection, in other regional Channel 3 services.

(6) Those conditions must also require the news programmes provided by the appointed news provider which, in accordance with a condition imposed under subsection (5), are included in a regional Channel 3 service to be programmes that are presented live.

(7) OFCOM—

(a) may issue guidance as to the terms that will satisfy requirements imposed by virtue of subsection (3)(a); and

(b) must have regard to guidance for the time being in force under this subsection when considering whether to give an approval for the purposes of provision made by virtue of subsection (3)(b).

(8) For the purposes of this section the Channel 3 news obligations are—

(a) the requirements of any conditions imposed in relation to regional Channel 3 services under section 279; and

(b) the nationwide broadcasting on the regional Channel 3 services (taken together) of news programmes that are able to compete effectively with other television news programmes broadcast nationwide in the United Kingdom.

(9) Conditions imposed under this section are not to require arrangements to make provision falling within subsection (3)(a) or (b) or (4) in relation to appointments made before the commencement of this section.

(10) Section 32 of the 1990 Act (nomination of bodies eligible for appointment as news providers) shall cease to have effect.

Commencement Information

I84. S. 280 in force at 29.12.2003 by S.I. 2003/3142, art. 3. (1), Sch. 1 (with art. 11)

281. Disqualification from appointment as news provider

(1) The regulatory regime for every regional Channel 3 service includes the conditions that OFCOM consider appropriate for securing—

(a) that a body is not appointed as the appointed news provider if it falls within subsection (2); and

(b) that the appointment of a body as the appointed news provider ceases to have effect if it becomes a body falling within that subsection.

(2) A body falls within this subsection if—

(a) it is a disqualified person under Part 2 of Schedule 2 to the 1990 Act in relation to a Channel 3 licence; or

(b) there would be a contravention of Part 1 of Schedule 14 to this Act (whether by that body or by another person) if that body held a licence to provide a Channel 3 service, or held a licence to provide such a service for a particular area for which such a service is provided.

[F74. (3)The reference in subsection (2)(a) to a body which is a disqualified person under Part 2 of Schedule 2 to the 1990 Act in relation to a Channel 3 licence includes a reference to a person who is disqualified by virtue of a disqualification order under section 145 of the 1996 Act.]

Amendments (Textual)

F74. S. 281. (3) added (29.12.2003) by Media Ownership (Local Radio and Appointed News Provider) Order 2003 (S.I. 2003/3299), arts. 1. (2), 13. (1)

Commencement Information

I85. S. 281 in force at 29.12.2003 by S.I. 2003/3142, art. 3. (1), Sch. 1 (with art. 11)

282. Power to repeal or modify Channel 3 news provider provisions

(1) If it appears to the Secretary of State appropriate to do so, he may by order repeal or otherwise modify any of the provisions of section 280 or 281.

(2) Except in a case to which subsection (3) applies, the Secretary of State must consult OFCOM before making an order under this section.

(3) Consultation with OFCOM is not required if the order is confined to giving effect to recommendations by OFCOM that are contained in a report of a review under section 391.

(4) No order is to be made containing provision authorised by this section unless a draft of the order has been laid before Parliament and approved by a resolution of each House.

Commencement Information

I86. S. 282 in force at 12.12.2003 by S.I. 2003/3142, art. 2 (with art. 11)

283. News providers for Channel 5.

(1) If it appears to the Secretary of State appropriate to do so, he may by order make provision requiring news programmes included in Channel 5 to be provided by a person appointed as a news provider in accordance with the order.

(2) An order under this section may make provision in relation to Channel 5 that corresponds, with such modifications as the Secretary of State thinks fit, to any provision made in relation to regional Channel 3 services by section 280 or 281.

(3) Subsection (2) applies irrespective of any repeal or other modification by an order under this Act of section 280 or 281.

(4) An order under this section may include provision for section 194. A of the 1990 Act (application of Competition Act 1998 to Channel 3 news provision) to have effect (with such modifications as may be specified in the order) in relation to the appointment of a person as a

news provider for Channel 5 as it has effect in relation to the appointment of a body as a news provider for Channel 3.

(5) The Secretary of State is not to make an order under this section for the imposition of obligations in relation to Channel 5 unless he is satisfied that Channel 5's share of the audience for television broadcasting services is broadly equivalent to that of the services comprising Channel 3.

(6) An order under this section must require a licence holder to have a reasonable opportunity of making representations to OFCOM before his licence is varied in pursuance of the order.

(7) Except in a case to which subsection (8) applies, the Secretary of State must consult OFCOM before making an order under this section.

(8) Consultation with OFCOM is not required if the order is confined to giving effect to recommendations by OFCOM that are contained in a report of a review under section 391.

(9) No order is to be made containing provision authorised by this section unless a draft of the order has been laid before Parliament and approved by a resolution of each House.

Commencement Information

I87. S. 283 in force at 29.12.2003 by S.I. 2003/3142, art. 3. (1), Sch. 1 (with art. 11)

284. News provision on the public teletext service

(1) The regulatory regime for the public teletext service includes the conditions that OFCOM consider appropriate for securing—

(a) that the service includes what appears to OFCOM to be a suitable quantity and variety of news items; and

(b) that the news items included in the service are up to date and regularly revised.

(2) Conditions imposed under this section in relation to a time when the public teletext service comprises both—

(a) an analogue teletext service, and

(b) a teletext service provided in digital form,

must apply to both services but may make different provision for each of them.

Commencement Information

I88. S. 284 in force at 29.12.2003 by S.I. 2003/3142, art. 3. (1), Sch. 1 (with art. 11)

Independent and regional productions and programmes for public service television

285. Code relating to programme commissioning

(1) The regulatory regime for every licensed public service channel includes the conditions that OFCOM consider appropriate for securing that the provider of the channel draws up and from time to time revises a code of practice setting out the principles he will apply when agreeing terms for the commissioning of independent productions.

(2) That regime also includes the conditions that OFCOM consider appropriate for securing that the provider of every licensed public service channel—

(a) at all times complies with a code of practice which has been drawn up by him by virtue of this section and is for the time being in force; and

(b) exercises his power to revise his code to take account of revisions from time to time of the guidance issued by OFCOM for the purposes of this section.

(3) The conditions imposed under this section must ensure that the code for the time being in force in the case of every licensed public service channel secures, in the manner described in guidance issued by OFCOM—

(a) that a reasonable timetable is applied to negotiations for the commissioning of an independent production and for the conclusion of a binding agreement;

(b) that there is what appears to OFCOM to be sufficient clarity, when an independent production is commissioned, about the different categories of rights to broadcast or otherwise to make use of or exploit the commissioned production that are being disposed of;

(c) that there is what appears to OFCOM to be sufficient transparency about the amounts to be paid in respect of each category of rights;

(d) that what appear to OFCOM to be satisfactory arrangements are made about the duration and exclusivity of those rights;

(e) that procedures exist for reviewing the arrangements adopted in accordance with the code and for demonstrating compliance with it;

(f) that those procedures include requirements for the monitoring of the application of the code and for the making of reports to OFCOM;

(g) that provision is made for resolving disputes arising in respect of the provisions of the code (by independent arbitration or otherwise) in a manner that appears to OFCOM to be appropriate.

(4) The conditions imposed under this section must also ensure that the drawing up or revision of a code by virtue of this section is in accordance with guidance issued by OFCOM as to—

(a) the times when the code is to be drawn up or reviewed with a view to revision;

(b) the consultation to be undertaken before a code is drawn up or revised; and

(c) the publication of every code or revised code.

(5) The provision that may be included in a condition imposed under this section includes—

(a) provision requiring a draft of a code or of any revision of a code to be submitted to OFCOM for approval;

(b) provision for the code or revision to have effect only if approved by OFCOM; and

(c) provision for a code or revision that is approved by OFCOM subject to modifications to have effect with those modifications.

(6) OFCOM—

(a) must issue and may from time to time revise guidance for the purposes of this section;

(b) must ensure that there is always guidance for those purposes in force;

(c) must, before issuing their guidance or revised guidance, consult the providers of licensed public service channels, persons who make independent productions (or persons appearing to OFCOM to represent them), the BBC and the Welsh Authority; and

(d) must publish their guidance or revised guidance in such manner as they think appropriate.

(7) Guidance issued by OFCOM for the purposes of this section must be general guidance and is not to specify particular terms to be included in agreements to which the guidance relates.

(8) Conditions imposed under this section requiring a code to be drawn up or approved may include transitional provision for treating a code drawn up before the imposition of the condition

—

(a) as satisfying the requirements of that condition; and

(b) as a code approved by OFCOM for the purposes of conditions so imposed.

(9) In this section "independent production" has the same meaning as in section 277.

Commencement Information

I89. S. 285 in force at 29.12.2003 by S.I. 2003/3142, art. 3. (1), Sch. 1 (with art. 11)

286. Regional programme-making for Channels 3 and 5.

(1) The regulatory regime for every Channel 3 service includes the conditions (if any) that OFCOM consider appropriate in the case of that service for securing—

(a) that what appears to OFCOM to be a suitable proportion of Channel 3 programmes made in the United Kingdom are programmes made in the United Kingdom outside the M25 area;

(b) that the Channel 3 programmes that are made in the United Kingdom outside the M25 area (taken together) constitute what appears to OFCOM to be a suitable range of programmes;

(c) that what appears to OFCOM to be a suitable proportion of the expenditure of the providers of Channel 3 services on Channel 3 programmes made in the United Kingdom is referable to programme production at different production centres outside the M25 area; and

(d) that the different programme production centres to which that expenditure is referable constitute what appears to OFCOM to be a suitable range of such production centres.

(2) In the case of a national Channel 3 service, subsection (1) requires the inclusion of conditions in the licence for the service only where OFCOM consider, having regard to the nature of the service, that it would be appropriate for conditions falling within that subsection to be so included.

(3) The regulatory regime for Channel 5 includes the conditions that OFCOM consider appropriate

for securing—

(a) that what appears to OFCOM to be a suitable proportion of the programmes made in the United Kingdom for viewing on that Channel are programmes made in the United Kingdom outside the M25 area;

(b) that the programmes for such viewing that are made in the United Kingdom outside the M25 area (taken together) constitute what appears to OFCOM to be a suitable range of programmes;

(c) that what appears to OFCOM to be a suitable proportion of the expenditure of the provider of Channel 5 on programmes made in the United Kingdom for viewing on that Channel is referable to programme production at different production centres outside the M25 area; and

(d) that the different programme production centres to which that expenditure is referable constitute what appears to OFCOM to be a suitable range of such production centres.

(4) Before imposing a condition under this section, OFCOM must consult the person on whom it is to be imposed.

(5) The requirement to consult is satisfied, in the case of the imposition of a condition by way of a variation of a licence, by compliance with section 3. (4)(b) of the 1990 Act (obligation to give opportunity to make representations about variation).

(6) A proportion is not to be regarded by OFCOM as suitable for the purposes of a provision of this section if it constitutes less than a significant proportion of the programmes or expenditure in question.

(7) In this section—

"Channel 3 programmes" means programmes made for viewing on Channel 3 in more than one area for which regional Channel 3 services are provided, including any programme made for viewing on a national Channel 3 service other than a regional programme;

"expenditure", in relation to a programme, means—

- expenditure which constitutes an investment in or is otherwise attributable to the making of the programme; or

- expenditure on the commissioning or other acquisition of the programme or on the acquisition of a right to include it in a service or to have it broadcast;

"programme" does not include an advertisement; and

"regional programme" means a programme made with a view to its inclusion in a national Channel 3 service as a programme of particular interest to persons living within a particular area of the United Kingdom.

Commencement Information

I90. S. 286 in force at 29.12.2003 by S.I. 2003/3142, art. 3. (1), Sch. 1 (with art. 11)

287. Regional programmes on Channel 3.

(1) The regulatory regime for every regional Channel 3 service includes the conditions that OFCOM consider appropriate for securing—

(a) that what appears to OFCOM, in the case of that service, to be a sufficient amount of time is given in the programmes included in the service to what appears to them to be a suitable range of programmes (including regional news programmes) which are of particular interest to persons living within the area for which the service is provided;

(b) that the regional programmes included in the service are of high quality;

(c) that what appears to OFCOM, in the case of that service, to be a suitable proportion of the regional programmes included in the service consists of programmes made in that area;

(d) that the regional news programmes included in the service are broadcast for viewing at intervals throughout the period for which the service is provided and, in particular, at peak viewing times;

(e) that what appears to OFCOM, in the case of that service, to be a suitable proportion of the other regional programmes that are included in the service consists of programmes broadcast for viewing—

(i) at peak viewing times; and

(ii) at times immediately preceding or following those times.

(2) The regulatory regime for every local Channel 3 service includes the conditions that OFCOM

consider appropriate for securing—

(a) that what appears to OFCOM, in the case of that service, to be a sufficient amount of time is given in the programmes included in the service to what appears to them to be a suitable range of local programmes;

(b) that, in the case of each part of an area or each community for which the service is provided, the range of local programmes is a range of programmes (including news programmes) which are of particular interest to persons living within that part of that area or to that community;

(c) that the local programmes included in the service are of high quality;

(d) that what appears to OFCOM, in the case of that service, to be a suitable proportion of the local programmes included in the service consists of programmes made in the area for which the service is provided;

(e) that the local news programmes included in the service are broadcast for viewing at intervals throughout the period for which the service is provided and, in particular, at peak viewing times;

(f) that what appears to OFCOM, in the case of that service, to be a suitable proportion of the other local programmes that are included in the service consists of programmes broadcast for viewing—

(i) at peak viewing times; and

(ii) at times immediately preceding or following those times.

(3) In the case of a local Channel 3 service, the conditions included in the regulatory regime for the service include conditions falling within subsection (1) to the extent only that it appears to OFCOM that the requirements of subsection (1) are not adequately met by conditions falling within subsection (2).

(4) In the case of a national Channel 3 service in the case of which OFCOM consider that it would be appropriate to impose conditions under this subsection, the regulatory regime for the service includes the conditions that OFCOM consider appropriate for securing—

(a) that what appears to OFCOM, in the case of that service, to be a sufficient amount of time is given in the programmes included in the service to what appears to them to be a suitable range of programmes (including regional news programmes) which are of particular interest to persons living within particular areas of the United Kingdom;

(b) that the regional programmes included in the service are of high quality;

(c) that what appears to OFCOM, in the case of that service, to be a suitable proportion of the regional programmes included in the service consists of programmes made in the area by reference to which they are regional programmes;

(d) that the regional news programmes included in the service are broadcast for viewing at intervals throughout the period for which the service is provided and, in particular, at peak viewing times;

(e) that what appears to OFCOM, in the case of that service, to be a suitable proportion of the other regional programmes that are included in the service consists of programmes broadcast for viewing—

(i) at peak viewing times; and

(ii) at times immediately preceding or following those times.

(5) Before imposing a condition under this section, OFCOM must consult the person on whom it is to be imposed.

(6) The requirement to consult is satisfied, in the case of the imposition of a condition by way of a variation of a licence, by compliance with section 3. (4)(b) of the 1990 Act (obligation to give opportunity to make representations about variation).

(7) A proportion is not to be regarded by OFCOM as suitable for the purposes of a provision of this section if it constitutes less than a significant proportion of the programmes in question.

(8) In this section—

"local Channel 3 service" means a regional Channel 3 service the provision of which includes the provision (in pursuance of a determination under section 14. (3) of the 1990 Act) of different programmes for different parts of an area or for different communities living within an area;

"local programme", in relation to a service provided for different parts of an area or for different communities, means a programme included in that service for any of the parts of that area or for any of those communities, and "local news programme" is to be construed accordingly;

"peak viewing time", in relation to a service, means a time determined by OFCOM to be, or to be likely to be, a peak viewing time for that service;

"programme" does not include an advertisement;

"regional programme"—

- in relation to a regional Channel 3 service, means a programme included in that service with a view to its being of particular interest to persons living within the area for which the service is provided;

- in relation to a national Channel 3 service, means a programme included in that service with a view to its being of particular interest to persons living within a particular area of the United Kingdom;

and "regional news programme" is to be construed accordingly.

Commencement Information

I91. S. 287 in force at 29.12.2003 by S.I. 2003/3142, art. 3. (1), Sch. 1 (with art. 11)

288. Regional programme-making for Channel 4.

(1) The regulatory regime for Channel 4 includes the conditions that OFCOM consider appropriate for securing—

(a) that what appears to OFCOM to be a suitable proportion of programmes made in the United Kingdom for viewing on Channel 4 are programmes made in the United Kingdom outside the M25 area;

(b) that the programmes for such viewing that are made in the United Kingdom outside the M25 area (taken together) constitute what appears to OFCOM to be a suitable range of programmes;

(c) that what appears to OFCOM to be a suitable proportion of the expenditure of C4. C on programmes made in the United Kingdom for viewing on Channel 4 is referable to programme production at different production centres outside the M25 area; and

(d) that the different programme production centres to which that expenditure is referable constitute what appears to OFCOM to be a suitable range of such production centres.

(2) Before imposing a condition under this section, OFCOM must consult C4. C.

(3) The requirement to consult is satisfied, in the case of the imposition of a condition by way of a variation of a licence, by compliance with section 3. (4)(b) of the 1990 Act (obligation to give opportunity to make representations about variation).

(4) A proportion is not to be regarded by OFCOM as suitable for the purposes of a provision of this section if it constitutes less than a significant proportion of the programmes or expenditure in question.

(5) In this section—

"expenditure", in relation to a programme, means—

- expenditure which constitutes an investment in or is otherwise attributable to the making of the programme; or

- expenditure on the commissioning or other acquisition of the programme or on the acquisition of a right to include it in a service or to have it broadcast; and

"programme" does not include an advertisement.

Commencement Information

I92. S. 288 in force at 29.12.2003 by S.I. 2003/3142, art. 3. (1), Sch. 1 (with art. 11)

289. Regional matters in the public teletext service

(1) The regulatory regime for the public teletext service includes the conditions that OFCOM consider appropriate for securing that the service includes what appears to them to be an appropriate proportion of material that is of particular interest to persons living in different parts of the United Kingdom.

(2) Conditions imposed under this section in relation to a time when the public teletext service comprises both—

(a) an analogue teletext service, and

(b) a teletext service provided in digital form,

must apply to both services but may make different provision for each of them.

Commencement Information

I93. S. 289 in force at 29.12.2003 by S.I. 2003/3142, art. 3. (1), Sch. 1 (with art. 11)

Networking arrangements for Channel 3.

290. Proposals for arrangements

(1) An application for a regional Channel 3 licence, in addition to being accompanied by the proposals mentioned in section 15. (3)(b) of the 1990 Act, must be accompanied by the applicant's proposals for participating in networking arrangements.

(2) OFCOM may publish general guidance to applicants for regional Channel 3 licences as to the kinds of proposals which they are likely to consider satisfactory.

(3) The publication of guidance under subsection (2) is to be in such manner as OFCOM consider appropriate.

(4) Arrangements are networking arrangements for the purposes of this Part if they—

(a) apply to all the holders of regional Channel 3 licences;

(b) provide for programmes made, commissioned or acquired by or on behalf of one or more of the holders of such licences to be available for broadcasting in all regional Channel 3 services; and

(c) are made for the purpose of enabling regional Channel 3 services (taken as a whole) to be a nationwide system of services which is able to compete effectively with other television programme services provided in the United Kingdom.

Commencement Information

I94. S. 290 in force at 29.12.2003 by S.I. 2003/3142, art. 3. (1), Sch. 1 (with art. 11)

291. Obligation as to making and continuance of approved arrangements

(1) The regulatory regime for every regional Channel 3 service includes the conditions that OFCOM consider appropriate for securing that the licence holder does all that he can to ensure that approved networking arrangements are in force whenever—

(a) the licence holder is providing the licensed service; and

(b) no networking arrangements imposed by OFCOM under section 292 are in force.

(2) In this section "approved networking arrangements" means networking arrangements which are for the time being approved by OFCOM in accordance with Schedule 11.

(3) In paragraph 5 of Schedule 2 to the Competition Act 1998 (c. 41) (exclusion of networking arrangements from Chapter I prohibition), for sub-paragraph (1) there shall be substituted—

"(1)The Chapter I prohibition does not apply in respect of any networking arrangements to the extent that they—

(a) have been approved for the purposes of licence conditions imposed under section 291 of the Communications Act 2003; or

(b) are arrangements that have been considered under Schedule 4 to the Broadcasting Act 1990 and fall to be treated as so approved;

nor does that prohibition apply in respect of things done with a view to arrangements being entered into or approved to the extent that those things have effect for purposes that are directly related to, and necessary for compliance with, conditions so imposed."

(4) For sub-paragraph (4) of that paragraph there shall be substituted—

"(4)In this paragraph "networking arrangements" has the same meaning as in Part 3 of the Communications Act 2003."

Commencement Information

I95. S. 291 in force at 29.12.2003 by S.I. 2003/3142, art. 3. (1), Sch. 1 (with art. 11)

292. OFCOM's power to impose arrangements

(1) This section applies on each occasion on which OFCOM—

(a) are proposing to award one or more regional Channel 3 licences; and

(b) for that purpose publish a notice under section 15. (1) of the 1990 Act.

(2) OFCOM must—

(a) determine the date by which the holders of the licences awarded and all other regional Channel 3 providers (if any) must have entered into networking arrangements (the "networking date"); and

(b) set out that date in that notice.

(3) The networking date must be the date by which, in OFCOM's opinion, the networking arrangements must have been entered into if approved networking arrangements are to be fully in force before the persons awarded licences begin to provide their licensed services.

(4) If—

(a) no suitable networking arrangements exist by the networking date, or

(b) the suitable networking arrangements that exist at that date cease to apply to all regional Channel 3 providers on or after that date,

OFCOM may impose on all regional Channel 3 providers the networking arrangements that OFCOM consider appropriate.

(5) For the purposes of subsection (4) arrangements are suitable networking arrangements if it appears to OFCOM that they—

(a) have been submitted to them for approval or have been approved by them; and

(b) will be in force as approved networking arrangements when the persons awarded licences begin to provide their licensed services.

(6) Arrangements imposed under this section come into force on the date determined by OFCOM.

(7) The regulatory regime for every regional Channel 3 service includes the conditions that OFCOM consider appropriate for securing that the licence holder complies with the provisions of any networking arrangements imposed under this section.

(8) Where—

(a) networking arrangements are imposed under this section,

(b) other networking arrangements are entered into between the licence holders bound by the imposed arrangements, and

(c) the other arrangements entered into are approved by OFCOM,

the imposed arrangements shall cease to have effect on the coming into force of the other arrangements as approved networking arrangements.

(9) In this section—

"approved networking arrangements" has the same meaning as in section 291; and

"regional Channel 3 providers" means persons who will be licensed to provide regional Channel 3 services and will be providing such services when the licences to be awarded come into force.

Commencement Information

I96. S. 292 in force at 29.12.2003 by S.I. 2003/3142, art. 3. (1), Sch. 1 (with art. 11)

293. Review of approved networking arrangements etc.

(1) It shall be the duty of OFCOM from time to time to carry out general reviews of the networking arrangements (whether approved or imposed by OFCOM) that are in force.

(2) The first such review must be carried out no later than six months after the date on which the offers made under section 215. (1) close or (if those offers close on different dates) the latest of those dates.

(3) Every subsequent review must be carried out no more than one year after the previous one.

(4) OFCOM may also, at any other time, carry out a review of whether those arrangements continue to satisfy one of the two competition tests set out in paragraph 6 of Schedule 11.

(5) If, on a review under this section, OFCOM are satisfied that modifications are required of the networking arrangements for the time being in force, they may—

(a) require the holders of regional Channel 3 licences to give effect to the modifications proposed by OFCOM; or

(b) in the case of arrangements imposed by OFCOM, make those modifications themselves.

(6) OFCOM must not exercise any of their powers under this Act or the 1990 Act so as to modify the requirements imposed on the holder of a regional Channel 3 licence by approved networking arrangements that are already in force except—

(a) following a review under this section; or

(b) with the consent of the licence holder.

(7) The regulatory regime for every Channel 3 service includes the conditions that OFCOM consider appropriate for securing that the licence holder does all that he can to ensure that modifications proposed by OFCOM under this section are given effect to.

(8) In this section "approved networking arrangements" has the same meaning as in section 291.

Commencement Information

I97. S. 293 in force at 29.12.2003 by S.I. 2003/3142, art. 3. (1), Sch. 1 (with art. 11)

294. Supplemental provision about networking arrangements

(1) Schedule 11 (which makes provision about the approval of networking arrangements and the imposition or modification of such arrangements) shall have effect.

(2) The obligations arising under conditions imposed in accordance with sections 291 to 293 are subject to the rights of appeal conferred by that Schedule.

Commencement Information

I98. S. 294 in force at 29.12.2003 by S.I. 2003/3142, art. 3. (1), Sch. 1 (with art. 11)

Special obligations for Channel 4.

295. Involvement of C4 Corporation in programme-making

(1) The regulatory regime for Channel 4 includes a condition requiring C4. C not to be involved, except to such extent as OFCOM may allow, in the making of programmes to be broadcast on Channel 4.

(2) In this section "programme" does not include an advertisement.

Commencement Information

I99. S. 295 in force at 29.12.2003 by S.I. 2003/3142, art. 3. (1), Sch. 1 (with art. 11)

296. Schools programmes on Channel 4.

(1) The regulatory regime for Channel 4 includes the conditions that OFCOM consider appropriate for securing that what appears to them to be a suitable proportion of the programmes which are included in Channel 4 are schools programmes.

(2) A licence under the 1990 Act to provide Channel 4 may also include conditions authorised by the following provisions of this section.

(3) The conditions authorised by this section include conditions requiring C4. C—

(a) to finance the production of schools programmes; and

(b) to acquire schools programmes provided by other persons.

(4) The conditions authorised by this section include conditions requiring C4. C to ensure that schools programmes on Channel 4—

(a) are of high quality; and

(b) are suitable to meet the needs of schools throughout the United Kingdom.

(5) The conditions authorised by this section include conditions specifying the minimum number of hours in term time, or within normal school hours, that are to be allocated to the broadcasting of schools programmes on Channel 4.

(6) The conditions authorised by this section include conditions requiring C4. C to provide such material for use in connection with the schools programmes broadcast by them as may be necessary to secure that effective use is made of those programmes in schools.

(7) The conditions authorised by this section include conditions requiring C4. C from time to time to consult such persons who—

(a) are concerned with schools or with the production of schools programmes, or

(b) have an interest in schools or in the production of schools programmes,

as OFCOM think fit.

(8) Before imposing a condition under this section, OFCOM must consult C4. C.

(9) The requirement to consult is satisfied, in the case of the imposition of a condition by way of a variation of a licence, by compliance with section 3. (4)(b) of the 1990 Act (obligation to give opportunity to make representations about variation).

(10) In determining for the purposes of subsection (1) what proportion of the programmes included in Channel 4 should be schools programmes, OFCOM must take into account services, facilities and materials which C4. C provide to schools, or make available for schools, otherwise than by the inclusion of programmes in Channel 4.

(11) Section 34 of the 1990 Act (requirement as to schools programmes in relation to all licensed public service channels taken together) shall cease to have effect.

(12) In this section "schools programmes" means programmes which are intended for use in schools.

Commencement Information

I100. S. 296 in force at 29.12.2003 by S.I. 2003/3142, art. 3. (1), Sch. 1 (with art. 11)

297. Channel 4 contribution towards national television archive

(1) Section 185 of the 1990 Act (contributions towards maintenance of the national television archive) shall be amended as follows.

(2) In subsections (1) and (3), after "Channel 3" there shall be inserted " , Channel 4 ".

(3) In subsection (5), at the end there shall be inserted—

""Channel 4 licence" means—

(a) the licence referred to in section 231. (1)(b) of the Communications Act 2003; and

(b) a licence renewing that licence on the first or any subsequent occasion."

(4) This section has effect in relation only to financial years beginning after the television transfer date.

Commencement Information

I101. S. 297 in force at 29.12.2003 by S.I. 2003/3142, art. 3. (1), Sch. 1 (with art. 11)

Special obligation for the public teletext provider

298. Conditions prohibiting interference with other services

The regulatory regime for the public teletext service includes the conditions that OFCOM consider appropriate for securing that the provision of so much of the public teletext service as is provided in analogue form does not cause interference with—

(a) the television broadcasting service or services on whose frequency or frequencies it is provided; or

(b) any other wireless telegraphy transmissions.

Modifications etc. (not altering text)

C9. S. 298 excluded (8.12.2003) by The Office of Communications Act 2002 (Commencement No. 3) and Communications Act 2003 (Commencement No. 2) Order 2003 (S.I. 2003/3142), art. 8. (1) (with art. 11)

Commencement Information

I102. S. 298 in force at 29.12.2003 by S.I. 2003/3142, art. 3. (1), Sch. 1 (with art. 11)

Sporting and other events of national interest

299. Categorisation of listed events

(1) For subsections (1) and (2) of section 97 of the 1996 Act (listed events), there shall be substituted—

"(1)The Secretary of State may, for the purposes of this Part, maintain a list of sporting and other events of national interest, and an event for the time being included in the list is referred to in this Part as a "listed event".

(1. A)A list maintained under subsection (1) must be divided into two categories, and those categories are referred to in this Part as "Group A" and "Group B".

(1. B)Each listed event must be allocated either to Group A or to Group B.

(2) Before drawing up such a list, or revising or ceasing to maintain it, the Secretary of State must consult—

(a) OFCOM,

(b) the BBC,

(c) the Welsh Authority, and

(d) in relation to a relevant event, the person from whom the rights to televise that event may be acquired.

(2. A)For the purposes of subsection (2)(d), a relevant event is an event which the Secretary of State proposes—

(a) to include in a list maintained under subsection (1),

(b) to omit from such a list, or

(c) to move from one category in such a list to the other."

(2) In subsection (3)(b) of that section, the words "by the Commission" and "by them" shall be omitted.

(3) In subsection (5) of that section—

(a) for the words "addition of any relevant event to" there shall be substituted " inclusion of any event in "; and

(b) in paragraph (a), for "addition" there shall be substituted " inclusion ".

(4) After that subsection, there shall be inserted—

"(5. A)The allocation or transfer of an event to group A does not affect the validity of a contract entered into before the day on which the Secretary of State consulted the persons mentioned in subsection (2) in relation to the proposed allocation or transfer.

(5. B)The Secretary of State may direct that, for the transitional purposes set out in the direction, the transfer of a Group B event to Group A is not to affect the application to that event of provisions of this Part relating to a Group B event."

Commencement Information

I103. S. 299. (1)(3)(4) in force at 30.6.2004 by S.I. 2003/3142, art. 4. (3) (with art. 11)

I104. S. 299. (2) in force at 29.12.2003 by S.I. 2003/3142, art. 3. (1), Sch. 1 (with art. 11)

300. Effects of categorisation of listed events

(1) In section 99. (1) of the 1996 Act (avoidance of contracts for exclusive rights to televise listed events), for "listed event" there shall be substituted " Group A listed event ".

(2) In section 101 of that Act (restriction on televising of listed events), for subsection (1) there shall be substituted—

"(1)A television programme provider who—

(a) is providing a service ("the first service") falling within either category, and

(b) is providing it with a view to its being available (within the meaning of Part 3 of the Communications Act 2003) for reception by members of the public in the United Kingdom, or in any area of the United Kingdom,

must not include live coverage of a listed event in that service unless it is authorised by subsection (1. A), (1. B) or (1. C).

(1. A)Live coverage of a listed event is authorised by this subsection if—

(a) a television programme provider (other than the provider of the first service) has acquired the right to include live coverage of the event in his service ("the second service"); and

(b) the second service—

(i) falls into a different category from the first service, and

(ii) is provided for an area that consists of or includes all or almost all of the area for which the first service is provided.

(1. B)Live coverage of a listed event is authorised by this subsection if OFCOM have consented in advance to inclusion of that coverage in the first service.

(1. C)Live coverage of a listed event is authorised by this subsection if—

(a) the listed event is a Group B event,

(b) rights to provide coverage of the event have been acquired by one or more persons in addition to the provider of the first service,

(c) that additional coverage constitutes adequate alternative coverage of the event, and

(d) the person or persons who have acquired rights to provide the additional coverage satisfy the requirements in relation to that coverage of any regulations made under section 104. ZA for the purposes of this paragraph.

(1. D)Subsections (1) to (1. C) apply to the coverage of a part of a listed event as they apply to the coverage of the whole of that event."

(3) In subsection (2) of that section, for "under subsection (1)" there shall be substituted " for the purposes of subsection (1. B). "

(4) After subsection (4) of that section there shall be inserted—

"(5)References in this section to a category of service are references to a category of service set out in section 98. (1)."

(5) In section 102. (2) of that Act (penalties), for "under subsection (1) of section 101" there shall be substituted " for the purposes of section 101. (1. B) ".

(6) In section 103. (2) of that Act (reports to the Secretary of State), for "under subsection (1) of section 101" there shall be substituted " for the purposes of section 101. (1. B) ".

Commencement Information

I105. S. 300 in force at 30.6.2004 by S.I. 2003/3142, art. 4. (3) (with art. 11)

301. Code relating to listed events

(1) For subsection (1) of section 104 of the 1996 Act (code in relation to listed events) there shall be substituted—

"(1)OFCOM shall draw up, and may from time to time revise, a code giving guidance—

   (a) as to the matters which they will take into account in determining whether to give or to revoke their consent for the purposes of section 101. (1. B) or section 101. B(1); and

   (b) as to the matters which they will take into account in determining for the purposes of section 102. (1) or 103. (1), whether in all the circumstances it is unreasonable to expect a television programme provider to comply with section 101. (1) or section 101. B(1)."

(2) Where OFCOM are required to draw up a code by virtue of this section—

   (a) they shall do so as soon as practicable after the commencement of this section; but

   (b) the code shall have no effect in relation to any time before the commencement of section 300 of this Act.

Commencement Information

I106. S. 301 in force at 29.12.2003 by S.I. 2003/3142, art. 3. (1), Sch. 1 (with art. 11)

302. Regulations about coverage of listed events

(1) After section 104 of the 1996 Act there shall be inserted—

"104. ZARegulations about coverage of listed events

(1) OFCOM may make regulations for determining for the purposes of this Part—

   (a) the circumstances in which the televising of listed events generally, or of a particular listed event, is or is not to be treated as live;

   (b) what (whether generally or in relation to particular circumstances) is to be taken to represent the provision of adequate alternative coverage; and

   (c) the requirements that must be satisfied for the purposes of section 101. (1. C)(d) by persons who have acquired rights to provide adequate alternative coverage.

(2) The power conferred by subsection (1)(a) does not include power to define "live" for the purposes of section 101. B.

(3) Section 403 of the Communications Act 2003 (procedure for regulations and orders made by OFCOM) applies to the power of OFCOM to make regulations under this section."

(2) In section 105. (1) (interpretation of Part 4), before the definition of "Channel 4" there shall be inserted—

""adequate alternative coverage" and "live" are to be construed in accordance with any regulations under section 104. ZA;".

Commencement Information

I107. S. 302 in force at 29.12.2003 by S.I. 2003/3142, art. 3. (1), Sch. 1 (with art. 11)

Television services for the deaf and visually impaired

303. Code relating to provision for the deaf and visually impaired

(1) It shall be the duty of OFCOM to draw up, and from time to time to review and revise, a code giving guidance as to—

(a) the extent to which the services to which this section applies should promote the understanding and enjoyment by—

(i) persons who are deaf or hard of hearing,

(ii) persons who are blind or partially-sighted, and

(iii) persons with a dual sensory impairment,

of the programmes to be included in such services; and

(b) the means by which such understanding and enjoyment should be promoted.

(2) The code must include provision for securing that every provider of a service to which this section applies ensures that adequate information about the assistance for disabled people that is provided in relation to that service is made available to those who are likely to want to make use of it.

(3) The code must also require that, from the fifth and tenth anniversaries of the relevant date, the obligations in subsections (4) and (5), respectively, must be fulfilled by reference to averages computed over each of the following—

(a) the twelve month period beginning with the anniversary in question; and

(b) every twelve month period ending one week after the end of the previous period for which an average fell to be computed.

(4) The obligation to be fulfilled from the fifth anniversary of the relevant date is that at least 60 per cent. of so much of every service which—

(a) is a service to which this section applies, and

(b) has a relevant date after the passing of this Act,

as consists of programmes that are not excluded programmes must be accompanied by subtitling.

(5) The obligations to be fulfilled from the tenth anniversary of the relevant date are—

(a) that at least 90 per cent. of so much of a Channel 3 service or of Channel 4 as consists of programmes that are not excluded programmes must be accompanied by subtitling;

(b) that at least 80 per cent. of so much of every other service to which this section applies as consists of programmes that are not excluded programmes must be accompanied by subtitling;

(c) that at least 10 per cent. of so much of every service to which this section applies as consists of programmes that are not excluded programmes must be accompanied by audio-description for the blind; and

(d) that at least 5 per cent. of so much of every service to which this section applies as consists of programmes that are not excluded programmes must be presented in, or translated into, sign language.

(6) A reference in subsection (4) or in any paragraph of subsection (5) to excluded programmes is a reference to programmes of the description for the time being set out under subsection (7) in relation to that subsection or paragraph and also in relation to the service in question.

(7) The code must set out, in relation to subsection (4) and each of the paragraphs of subsection (5), the descriptions of programmes that OFCOM consider should be excluded programmes for the purposes of the requirement contained in that subsection or paragraph.

(8) In complying with subsection (7), OFCOM must have regard, in particular, to—

(a) the extent of the benefit which would be conferred by the provision of assistance for disabled people in relation to the programmes;

(b) the size of the intended audience for the programmes;

(c) the number of persons who would be likely to benefit from the assistance and the extent of the likely benefit in each case;

(d) the extent to which members of the intended audience for the programmes are resident in places outside the United Kingdom;

(e) the technical difficulty of providing the assistance; and

(f) the cost, in the context of the matters mentioned in paragraphs (a) to (e), of providing the assistance.

(9) The exclusions that may be set out in the code under subsection (7)—

(a) may include different descriptions of programmes in relation to different services to which this section applies; and

(b) in the case of a service which OFCOM are satisfied (having regard to the matters mentioned in subsection (8)) is a special case, may include all the programmes included in the service.

(10) The requirements that may be imposed by the code include, in particular—

(a) requirements on persons providing services to which this section applies to meet interim targets falling within subsection (11), from dates falling before an anniversary mentioned in subsection (3);

(b) requirements on persons providing such services to meet further targets from dates falling after the anniversary mentioned in subsection (5); and

(c) requirements with respect to the provision of assistance for disabled people in relation to excluded programmes, or in relation to a particular description of them.

(11) The interim targets mentioned in subsection (10)(a) are the targets with respect to the provision of assistance for disabled people which OFCOM consider it appropriate to impose as targets on the way to meeting the targets imposed in pursuance of subsection (3).

(12) This section applies to the following services—

(a) S4. C Digital or any other television programme service provided by the Welsh Authority for broadcasting in digital form so as to be available for reception by members of the public;

(b) any licensed public service channel;

(c) a digital television programme service but not an electronic programme guide;

(d) a television licensable content service but not an electronic programme guide;

(e) a restricted television service.

(13) In this section—

"electronic programme guide" means a service which—

- is or is included in a television licensable content service or a digital television programme service; and

- consists of—

the listing or promotion, or both the listing and the promotion, of some or all of the programmes included in any one or more programme services the providers of which are or include persons other than the provider of the guide; and

a facility for obtaining access, in whole or in part, to the programme service or services listed or promoted in the guide;

"programme" does not include an advertisement.

Commencement Information

I108. S. 303 in force at 29.12.2003 by S.I. 2003/3142, art. 3. (1), Sch. 1 (with art. 11)

304. Procedure for issuing and revising code under s. 303.

(1) Before drawing up a code under section 303 or reviewing or revising it in pursuance of that section, OFCOM must consult—

(a) such persons appearing to them to represent the interests of persons falling within subsection (1)(a)(i), (ii) or (iii) of that section as OFCOM think fit; and

(b) such persons providing services to which that section applies as OFCOM think fit.

(2) OFCOM must publish the code drawn up under section 303, and every revision of it, in such manner as, having regard to the need to make the code or revision accessible to—

(a) persons who are deaf or hard of hearing,

(b) persons who are blind or partially sighted, and

(c) persons with a dual sensory impairment,

they consider appropriate.

Commencement Information

I109. S. 304 in force at 29.12.2003 by S.I. 2003/3142, art. 3. (1), Sch. 1 (with art. 11)

305. Meaning of "relevant date" in s. 303.

(1) In relation to a service, the relevant date for the purposes of section 303 is—

(a) in a case to which any of subsections (2) to (4) applies, the date given by that subsection; and

(b) in any other case, the date (whether before or after the passing of this Act) when the provision of that service began or begins.

(2) In the case of a service the provision of which began before the television transfer date but which is not—

(a) a service provided by the Welsh Authority,

(b) a licensed public service channel, or

(c) a digital television programme service,

the relevant date is the date of the coming into force of this section.

(3) In the case of—

(a) a Channel 3 service the provision of which began before the date of the passing of this Act, and

(b) Channel 4 and S4. C Digital,

the relevant date is 1st January 2000.

(4) In the case of Channel 5, so far as it consists of a service the provision of which began before the date of the passing of this Act, the relevant date is 1st January 1998.

(5) OFCOM may determine that a service provided by a person is to be treated for the purposes of section 303 and this section as a continuation of a service previously provided by him.

Commencement Information

I110. S. 305 in force at 29.12.2003 by S.I. 2003/3142, art. 3. (1), Sch. 1 (with art. 11)

306. Power to modify targets in s. 303.

(1) Where it appears to the Secretary of State, in the case of services of a particular description, that the obligation specified in section 303. (4) has been or is likely to be fulfilled in their case before the anniversary so specified, he may by order modify section 303 so as to do one or both of the following—

(a) increase the percentage so specified in relation to services of that description;

(b) substitute a different anniversary for the anniversary by which that obligation must be fulfilled in the case of such services.

(2) The Secretary of State may by order modify section 303 so as to do one or both of the following—

(a) substitute a later anniversary for the anniversary by which the obligations specified in subsection (5) of that section must be fulfilled;

(b) substitute a higher percentage for the percentage for the time being specified in any paragraph of that subsection.

(3) The provision that may be made by an order under this section includes—

(a) modifications for requiring the code to set out additional obligations to be fulfilled once the obligations previously required to be set out in the code have been fulfilled; and

(b) savings for the obligations previously set out in the code.

(4) Before making an order under this section the Secretary of State must consult OFCOM.

(5) No order is to be made containing provision authorised by this section unless a draft of the order has been laid before Parliament and approved by a resolution of each House.

Commencement Information

I111. S. 306 in force at 29.12.2003 by S.I. 2003/3142, art. 3. (1), Sch. 1 (with art. 11)

307. Observance of code under s. 303.

(1) The regulatory regime for every service to which this section applies includes the conditions that OFCOM consider appropriate for securing that the code maintained by them under section 303 is observed in the provision of those services.

(2) This section applies to every service to which section 303 applies which is licensed by a Broadcasting Act licence.

Commencement Information

I112. S. 307 in force at 29.12.2003 by S.I. 2003/3142, art. 3. (1), Sch. 1 (with art. 11)

308. Assistance for the visually impaired with the public teletext service

The regulatory regime for the public teletext service includes the conditions that OFCOM consider appropriate for securing, so far as it is reasonable and practicable, by the inclusion of features in that service, to do so, that persons with disabilities affecting their sight are able to make use of the service.

Modifications etc. (not altering text)

C10. S. 308 excluded (8.12.2003) by The Office of Communications Act 2002 (Commencement No. 3) and Communications Act 2003 (Commencement No. 2) Order 2003 (S.I. 2003/3142), art. 8. (2) (with art. 11)

Commencement Information

I113. S. 308 in force at 29.12.2003 by S.I. 2003/3142, art. 3. (1), Sch. 1 (with art. 11)

Programming quotas for digital television programme services

309. Quotas for independent programmes

(1) The regulatory regime for every digital television programme service that is not comprised in a licensed public service channel includes the conditions that OFCOM consider appropriate for securing that, in each year, not less than 10 per cent. of the total amount of time allocated to the broadcasting of qualifying programmes included in the service is allocated to the broadcasting of a range and diversity of independent productions.

(2) In subsection (1)—

   (a) the reference to qualifying programmes is a reference to programmes of such description as the Secretary of State may by order specify as describing the programmes that are to be qualifying programmes for the purposes of that subsection;

   (b) the reference to independent productions is a reference to programmes of such description as the Secretary of State may by order specify as describing the programmes that are to be independent productions for the purposes of that subsection; and

   (c) the reference to a range of independent productions is a reference to a range of such productions in terms of cost of acquisition as well as in terms of the types of programme involved.

(3) The Secretary of State may by order amend subsection (1) by substituting a different percentage for the percentage for the time being specified in that subsection.

(4) Before making an order under this section the Secretary of State must consult OFCOM.

(5) No order is to be made containing provision authorised by this section unless a draft of the order has been laid before Parliament and approved by a resolution of each House.

(6) In this section "programme" does not include an advertisement.

Commencement Information

I114. S. 309 in force at 29.12.2003 by S.I. 2003/3142, art. 3. (1), Sch. 1 (with art. 11)

Regulation of electronic programme guides

310. Code of practice for electronic programme guides

(1) It shall be the duty of OFCOM to draw up, and from time to time to review and revise, a code giving guidance as to the practices to be followed in the provision of electronic programme guides.

(2) The practices required by the code must include the giving, in the manner provided for in the code, of such degree of prominence as OFCOM consider appropriate to—

   (a) the listing or promotion, or both the listing and promotion, for members of its intended audience, of the programmes included in each public service channel; and

   (b) the facilities, in the case of each such channel, for members of its intended audience to select or access the programmes included in it.

(3) The practices required by the code must also include the incorporation of such features in electronic programme guides as OFCOM consider appropriate for securing that persons with disabilities affecting their sight or hearing or both —

   (a) are able, so far as practicable, to make use of such guides for all the same purposes as persons without such disabilities; and

(b) are informed about, and are able to make use of, whatever assistance for disabled people is provided in relation to the programmes listed or promoted.

(4) Subject to subsection (5), in subsection (2) the reference to the public service channels is a reference to any of the following—

(a) any service of television programmes provided by the BBC in digital form so as to be available for reception by members of the public;

(b) any Channel 3 service in digital form;

(c) Channel 4 in digital form;

(d) Channel 5 in digital form;

(e) S4. C Digital;

(f) the digital public teletext service.

[F75. (g)a local digital television programme service;

(h) a simulcast local service.]

(5) The Secretary of State may by order—

(a) add any programme service to the services for the time being specified in subsection (4) as public service channels; or

(b) delete a service from that subsection.

(6) Before making an order under subsection (5) the Secretary of State must consult OFCOM.

(7) In this section "intended audience", in relation to a service of any description, means—

(a) if the service is provided only for a particular area or locality of the United Kingdom, members of the public in that area or locality;

(b) if it is provided for members of a particular community, members of that community; and

(c) in any other case, members of the public in the United Kingdom.

(8) In this section "electronic programme guide" means a service which consists of—

(a) the listing or promotion, or both the listing and the promotion, of some or all of the programmes included in any one or more programme services the providers of which are or include persons other than the provider of the guide; and

(b) a facility for obtaining access, in whole or in part, to the programme service or services listed or promoted in the guide.

[F76. (9)In this section "local digital television programme service" means any service which falls within a description of service in relation to which provision is for the time being made under section 244 (local digital television services).

(10) In this section "simulcast local service" means a service provided in digital form and corresponding to a local digital television programme service.

(11) For the purposes of subsection (10), a service corresponds to a local digital television programme service ("the relevant service") if all of the programmes included in the relevant service are provided at the same time on both services.]

Amendments (Textual)

F75. S. 310. (4)(g)(h) inserted (31.1.2012) by The Code of Practice for Electronic Programme Guides (Addition of Programme Services) Order 2011 (S.I. 2011/3003), arts. 1, 2. (a)

F76. S. 310. (9)-(11) inserted (31.1.2012) by The Code of Practice for Electronic Programme Guides (Addition of Programme Services) Order 2011 (S.I. 2011/3003), arts. 1, 2. (b)

Commencement Information

I115. S. 310 in force at 29.12.2003 by S.I. 2003/3142, art. 3. (1), Sch. 1 (with art. 11)

311. Conditions to comply with code under s. 310.

(1) The regulatory regime for every service consisting in or including an electronic programme guide includes whatever conditions (if any) OFCOM consider appropriate for securing that the code maintained by them under section 310 is observed in the provision of those services.

(2) In this section "electronic programme guide" has the same meaning as in section 310.

Commencement Information

I116. S. 311 in force at 29.12.2003 by S.I. 2003/3142, art. 3. (1), Sch. 1 (with art. 11)

Character and coverage of radio services

312. Character and coverage of sound broadcasting services

(1) Section 106 of the 1990 Act (requirements as to character and coverage of local and national radio services) shall be amended as follows.

(2) In subsection (1), the words from "except" onwards shall be omitted.

(3) After subsection (1) (duty to ensure character preserved subject to departures that do not restrict service) there shall be inserted—

"(1. A)Conditions included in a licence for the purposes of subsection (1) may provide that OFCOM may consent to a departure from the character of the licensed service if, and only if, they are satisfied—

  (a) that the departure would not substantially alter the character of the service;

  (b) that the departure would not narrow the range of programmes available by way of relevant independent radio services to persons living in the area or locality for which the service is licensed to be provided;

  (c) that, in the case of a local licence, the departure would be conducive to the maintenance or promotion of fair and effective competition in that area or locality; or

  (d) that, in the case of a local licence, there is evidence that, amongst persons living in that area or locality, there is a significant demand for, or significant support for, the change that would result from the departure.

(1. B)The matters to which OFCOM must have regard in determining for the purposes of this section the character of a service provided under a local licence include, in particular, the selection of spoken material and music in programmes included in the service."

(4) For subsection (5) (restriction on power to extend licence to new area or locality) there shall be substituted—

"(5)OFCOM shall only exercise the power conferred on them by subsection (4) if it appears to them—

  (a) that to do so would not result in a significant increase of the area or locality for which the service in question is licensed to be provided; or

  (b) that the increase that would result is justifiable in the exceptional circumstances of the case."

(5) After subsection (6) of that section there shall be inserted—

"(7)In this section "relevant independent radio services" means the following services so far as they are services falling to be regulated under section 245 of the Communications Act 2003—

  (a) sound broadcasting services;

  (b) radio licensable content services;

  (c) additional services;

but, in relation to a departure from the character of a service provided under a local licence, does not include a service that is provided otherwise than wholly or mainly for reception by persons living and working in the area or locality in question."

Commencement Information

I117. S. 312 in force at 29.12.2003 by S.I. 2003/3142, art. 3. (1), Sch. 1 (with art. 11)

313. Consultation about change of character of local services

After section 106 of the 1990 Act there shall be inserted—

"106. ZAConsultation about change of character of local services

(1) Before deciding for the purposes of a condition imposed under subsection (1. A) of section 106 whether to consent to a departure from the character of a service provided under a local licence on any of the grounds mentioned in paragraphs (b) to (d) of that subsection, OFCOM must publish a notice specifying—

  (a) the proposed departure; and

  (b) the period in which representations may be made to OFCOM about the proposal.

(2) That period must end not less than 28 days after the date of publication of the notice.

(3) The notice must be published in such manner as appears to OFCOM to be appropriate for

bringing it to the attention of the persons who, in OFCOM's opinion, are likely to be affected by the departure.

(4) OFCOM—

(a) are not required to publish a notice under this section, and

(b) may specify a period of less than 28 days in such a notice as the period for representations, if they consider that the publication of the notice, or allowing a longer period for representations, would result in a delay that would be likely prejudicially to affect the interests of the licence holder.

(5) OFCOM are not required under this section—

(a) to publish any matter that is confidential in accordance with subsection (6) or (7); or

(b) to publish anything that it would not be reasonably practicable to publish without disclosing such a matter.

(6) A matter is confidential under this subsection if—

(a) it relates specifically to the affairs of a particular body; and

(b) its publication would or might, in OFCOM's opinion, seriously and prejudicially affect the interests of that body.

(7) A matter is confidential under this subsection if—

(a) it relates specifically to the private affairs of an individual; and

(b) its publication would or might, in OFCOM's opinion, seriously and prejudicially affect the interests of that individual."

Commencement Information

I118. S. 313 in force at 29.12.2003 by S.I. 2003/3142, art. 3. (1), Sch. 1 (with art. 11)

314. Local content and character of local sound broadcasting services

(1) It shall be the duty of OFCOM to carry out their functions in relation to local sound broadcasting services in the manner that they consider is best calculated to secure—

(a) that programmes consisting of or including local material are included in such services F77...; and

(b) that, where such programmes are included in such a service, what appears to OFCOM to be a suitable proportion of them consists of locally-made programmes.

[F78. (1. A)Paragraphs (a) and (b) of subsection (1) apply in the case of each local sound broadcasting service only if and to the extent (if any) that OFCOM consider it appropriate in that case.]

(2) OFCOM must—

(a) draw up guidance as to how they consider the requirements of subsection (1)(a) and (b) should be satisfied; and

(b) have regard to that guidance in carrying out their functions in relation to local sound broadcasting services.

(3) The guidance may be different for different descriptions of services.

(4) OFCOM may revise the guidance from time to time.

(5) Before drawing up or revising the guidance, OFCOM must consult—

(a) such persons as appear to them to represent the interests of persons for whom local sound broadcasting services are or would be provided;

(b) persons holding licences to provide local sound broadcasting services or persons appearing to represent such persons, or both; and

(c) such other persons as they consider appropriate.

(6) OFCOM must publish the guidance and every revision of it in such manner as they consider appropriate.

(7) In this section—

[F79"approved area", in relation to programmes included in a local sound broadcasting service, means an area approved by OFCOM for the purposes of this section that includes the area or locality for which the service is provided;]

" local material", in relation to a local sound broadcasting service, means material which is of particular interest—

- to persons living or working within the area or locality for which the service is provided;
- to persons living or working within a part of that area or locality; or
- to particular communities living or working within that area or locality or a part of it;

"locally-made", in relation to programmes included in a local sound broadcasting service, means made wholly or partly at premises in the area or locality for which that service is provided [F80or, if there is an approved area for the programmes, that area] ;

"material" includes news, information and other spoken material and music; and

"programme" does not include an advertisement.

(8) References in this section to persons living or working within an area or locality include references to persons undergoing education or training in that area or locality.

[F81. (9)Before approving an area for the purposes of this section, OFCOM must publish a document specifying—

(a) the area that they propose to approve, and

(b) a period in which representations may be made to OFCOM about the proposals.

(10) OFCOM may withdraw their approval of all or part of an area at any time if the holder of the licence to provide the local sound broadcasting service concerned consents.

(11) Where OFCOM approve an area or withdraw their approval of an area, they must publish, in such manner as they consider appropriate, a notice giving details of the area.]

Amendments (Textual)

F77. Words in s. 314. (1)(a) repealed (8.6.2010) by Digital Economy Act 2010 (c. 24), ss. 34. (3), 47. (1), Sch. 2

F78. S. 314. (1. A) inserted (8.6.2010) by Digital Economy Act 2010 (c. 24), ss. 34. (4), 47. (1)

F79. Words in s. 314. (7) inserted (8.6.2010) by Digital Economy Act 2010 (c. 24), ss. 34. (5)(a), 47. (1)

F80. Words in s. 314. (7) inserted (8.6.2010) by Digital Economy Act 2010 (c. 24), ss. 34. (5)(b), 47. (1)

F81. S. 314. (9)-(11) inserted (8.6.2010) by Digital Economy Act 2010 (c. 24), ss. 34. (6), 47. (1) (with s. 34. (7))

Commencement Information

I119. S. 314 in force at 29.12.2003 by S.I. 2003/3142, art. 3. (1), Sch. 1 (with art. 11)

315. Variations of radio multiplex licences affecting service characteristics

For subsection (6) of section 54 of the 1996 Act (variations of radio multiplex licence affecting service characteristics) there shall be substituted—

"(6)Where the licence holder applies to OFCOM for the variation of a condition which—

(a) was imposed under subsection (1)(b), and

(b) relates to the characteristics of digital sound programme services to be broadcast under the licence,

then (subject to subsections (6. A) and (6. B)) OFCOM must vary the condition in accordance with the application.

(6. A)OFCOM are not to vary a national radio multiplex licence in accordance with an application under subsection (6) if it appears to them that, if the application were granted, the capacity of the digital sound programme services broadcast under the licence to appeal to a variety of tastes and interests would be unacceptably diminished.

(6. B)OFCOM are to vary a local radio multiplex licence in accordance with such an application only if they are satisfied—

(a) that the variation would not unacceptably narrow the range of programmes available by way of local digital sound programme services to persons living in the area or locality for which the licensed multiplex service is provided;

(b) that the variation would be conducive to the maintenance or promotion of fair and effective competition in that area or locality; or

(c) that there is evidence that, amongst persons living in that area or locality, there is a significant demand for, or significant support for, the change that would result from the variation."

Commencement Information

I120. S. 315 in force at 29.12.2003 by S.I. 2003/3142, art. 3. (1), Sch. 1 (with art. 11)

Competition between licensed providers etc.

316. Conditions relating to competition matters

(1) The regulatory regime for every licensed service includes the conditions (if any) that OFCOM consider appropriate for ensuring fair and effective competition in the provision of licensed services or of connected services.

(2) Those conditions must include the conditions (if any) that OFCOM consider appropriate for securing that the provider of the service does not—

(a) enter into or maintain any arrangements, or

(b) engage in any practice,

which OFCOM consider, or would consider, to be prejudicial to fair and effective competition in the provision of licensed services or of connected services.

(3) A condition imposed under this section may require a licence holder to comply with one or both of the following—

(a) a code for the time being approved by OFCOM for the purposes of the conditions; and

(b) directions given to him by OFCOM for those purposes.

(4) In this section—

"connected services", in relation to licensed services, means the provision of programmes for inclusion in licensed services and any other services provided for purposes connected with, or with the provision of, licensed services; and

"licensed service" means a service licensed by a Broadcasting Act licence.

Commencement Information

I121. S. 316 in force at 29.12.2003 by S.I. 2003/3142, art. 3. (1), Sch. 1 (with art. 11)

317. Exercise of Broadcasting Act powers for a competition purpose

(1) This section applies to the following powers of OFCOM (their "Broadcasting Act powers")—

(a) their powers under this Part of this Act and under the 1990 Act and the 1996 Act to impose or vary the conditions of a Broadcasting Act licence;

(b) every power of theirs to give an approval for the purposes of provision contained in the conditions of such a licence;

(c) every power of theirs to give a direction to a person who is required to comply with it by the conditions of such a licence; and

(d) every power of theirs that is exercisable for the purpose of enforcing an obligation imposed by the conditions of such a licence.

(2) Before exercising any of their Broadcasting Act powers for a competition purpose, OFCOM must consider whether a more appropriate way of proceeding in relation to some or all of the matters in question would be under the Competition Act 1998 (c. 41).

(3) If OFCOM decide that a more appropriate way of proceeding in relation to a matter would be under the Competition Act 1998, they are not, to the extent of that decision, to exercise their Broadcasting Act powers in relation to that matter.

(4) If OFCOM have decided to exercise any of their Broadcasting Act powers for a competition purpose, they must, on or before doing so, give a notification of their decision.

(5) A notification under subsection (4) must—

(a) be given to such persons, or published in such manner, as appears to OFCOM to be appropriate for bringing it to the attention of the persons who, in OFCOM's opinion, are likely to be affected by their decision; and

(b) must describe the rights conferred by subsection (6) on the persons affected by that decision.

(6) A person affected by a decision by OFCOM to exercise any of their Broadcasting Act powers for a competition purpose may appeal to the Competition Appeal Tribunal against so much of that decision as relates to the exercise of that power for that purpose.

(7) Sections 192. (3) to (8), 195 and 196 apply in the case of an appeal under subsection (6) as

they apply in the case of an appeal under section 192. (2).

(8) The jurisdiction of the Competition Appeal Tribunal on an appeal under subsection (6) excludes—

(a) whether OFCOM have complied with subsection (2); and

(b) whether any of OFCOM's Broadcasting Act powers have been exercised in contravention of subsection (3);

and, accordingly, those decisions by OFCOM on those matters fall to be questioned only in proceedings for judicial review.

(9) For the purposes of this section a power is exercised by OFCOM for a competition purpose if the only or main reason for exercising it is to secure that the holder of a Broadcasting Act licence does not—

(a) enter into or maintain arrangements, or

(b) engage in a practice,

which OFCOM consider, or would consider, to be prejudicial to fair and effective competition in the provision of licensed services or of connected services.

(10) Nothing in this section applies to—

(a) the exercise by OFCOM of any of their powers under sections 290 to 294 or Schedule 11;

(b) the exercise by them of any power for the purposes of any provision of a condition included in a licence in accordance with any of those sections;

(c) the exercise by them of any power for the purpose of enforcing such a condition.

(11) In subsection (9) "connected services" and "licensed service" each has the same meaning as in section 316.

(12) References in this section to the exercise of a power include references to an exercise of a power in pursuance of a duty imposed on OFCOM by or under an enactment.

Commencement Information

I122. S. 317 in force at 29.12.2003 by S.I. 2003/3142, art. 3. (1), Sch. 1 (with art. 11)

318. Review of powers exercised for competition purposes

(1) It shall be the duty of OFCOM, at such intervals as they consider appropriate, to carry out a review of so much of each of the following as has effect for a competition purpose—

(a) every code made or approved by them under or for the purposes of a broadcasting provision;

(b) the guidance issued by them under or for the purposes of broadcasting provisions; and

(c) every direction given by them under or for the purposes of a broadcasting provision.

(2) Before modifying or revoking, or withdrawing their approval from, anything which is subject to periodic review under this section, OFCOM must consult such persons as they consider appropriate.

(3) Subsection (2) applies irrespective or whether the modification, revocation or withdrawal is in consequence of a review under this section.

(4) For the purposes of this section a provision has effect for a competition purpose to the extent that its only or main purpose is to secure that the holder of a Broadcasting Act licence does not—

(a) enter into or maintain arrangements, or

(b) engage in a practice,

which OFCOM consider, or would consider, to be prejudicial to fair and effective competition in the provision of licensed services or of connected services.

(5) In this section "broadcasting provision" means—

(a) a provision of this Part of this Act, of the 1990 Act or of the 1996 Act, or

(b) any provision of a Broadcasting Act licence,

other than provision contained in any of sections 290 to 294 of this Act or Schedule 11 to this Act.

Commencement Information

I123. S. 318 in force at 29.12.2003 by S.I. 2003/3142, art. 3. (1), Sch. 1 (with art. 11)

Programme and fairness standards for television and radio

319. OFCOM's standards code

(1) It shall be the duty of OFCOM to set, and from time to time to review and revise, such standards for the content of programmes to be included in television and radio services as appear to them best calculated to secure the standards objectives.

(2) The standards objectives are—

(a) that persons under the age of eighteen are protected;

(b) that material likely to encourage or to incite the commission of crime or to lead to disorder is not included in television and radio services;

(c) that news included in television and radio services is presented with due impartiality and that the impartiality requirements of section 320 are complied with;

(d) that news included in television and radio services is reported with due accuracy;

(e) that the proper degree of responsibility is exercised with respect to the content of programmes which are religious programmes;

(f) that generally accepted standards are applied to the contents of television and radio services so as to provide adequate protection for members of the public from the inclusion in such services of offensive and harmful material;

[F82. (fa)that the product placement requirements referred to in section 321. (3. A) are met in relation to programmes included in a television programme service (other than advertisements);]

(g) that advertising that contravenes the prohibition on political advertising set out in section 321. (2) is not included in television or radio services;

(h) that the inclusion of advertising which may be misleading, harmful or offensive in television and radio services is prevented;

(i) that the international obligations of the United Kingdom with respect to advertising included in television and radio services are complied with;

(j) that the unsuitable sponsorship of programmes included in television and radio services is prevented;

(k) that there is no undue discrimination between advertisers who seek to have advertisements included in television and radio services; and

(l) that there is no use of techniques which exploit the possibility of conveying a message to viewers or listeners, or of otherwise influencing their minds, without their being aware, or fully aware, of what has occurred.

(3) The standards set by OFCOM under this section must be contained in one or more codes.

(4) In setting or revising any standards under this section, OFCOM must have regard, in particular and to such extent as appears to them to be relevant to the securing of the standards objectives, to each of the following matters—

(a) the degree of harm or offence likely to be caused by the inclusion of any particular sort of material in programmes generally, or in programmes of a particular description;

(b) the likely size and composition of the potential audience for programmes included in television and radio services generally, or in television and radio services of a particular description;

(c) the likely expectation of the audience as to the nature of a programme's content and the extent to which the nature of a programme's content can be brought to the attention of potential members of the audience;

(d) the likelihood of persons who are unaware of the nature of a programme's content being unintentionally exposed, by their own actions, to that content;

(e) the desirability of securing that the content of services identifies when there is a change affecting the nature of a service that is being watched or listened to and, in particular, a change that is relevant to the application of the standards set under this section; and

(f) the desirability of maintaining the independence of editorial control over programme content.

(5) OFCOM must ensure that the standards from time to time in force under this section include—

(a) minimum standards applicable to all programmes included in television and radio services; and

(b) such other standards applicable to particular descriptions of programmes, or of television and radio services, as appear to them appropriate for securing the standards objectives.

(6) Standards set to secure the standards objective specified in subsection (2)(e) shall, in particular, contain provision designed to secure that religious programmes do not involve—

(a) any improper exploitation of any susceptibilities of the audience for such a programme; or

(b) any abusive treatment of the religious views and beliefs of those belonging to a particular religion or religious denomination.

(7) In setting standards under this section, OFCOM must take account of such of the international obligations of the United Kingdom as the Secretary of State may notify to them for the purposes of this section.

(8) In this section "news" means news in whatever form it is included in a service.

[F83. (9)[F84. Subject to subsection (10),] Subsection (2)(fa) applies only in relation to programmes the production of which begins after 19th December 2009.]

[F85. (10)So far as relating to product placement falling within paragraph 4. (ba) of Schedule 11. A (electronic cigarettes and electronic cigarette refill containers), subsection (2)(fa) applies only in relation to programmes the production of which begins after 19th May 2016.]

Amendments (Textual)

F82. S. 319. (2)(fa) inserted (16.4.2010) by The Audiovisual Media Services (Product Placement) Regulations 2010 (S.I. 2010/831), regs. 1. (1), 2. (2)

F83. S. 319. (9) inserted (16.4.2010) by The Audiovisual Media Services (Product Placement) Regulations 2010 (S.I. 2010/831), regs. 1. (1), 2. (3)

F84. Words in s. 319. (9) inserted (20.5.2016) by The Tobacco and Related Products Regulations 2016 (S.I. 2016/507), regs. 1. (2), 45. (1)(a) (with reg. 57)

F85. S. 319. (10) inserted (20.5.2016) by The Tobacco and Related Products Regulations 2016 (S.I. 2016/507), regs. 1. (2), 45. (1)(b) (with reg. 57)

Modifications etc. (not altering text)

C11. S. 319. (1) modified (20.7.2004) by Contracting Out (Functions relating to Broadcast Advertising) and Specification of Relevant Functions Order 2004 (S.I. 2004/1975), art. 1, Sch. para. 1. (a) (with art. 5)

Commencement Information

I124. S. 319 in force at 29.12.2003 by S.I. 2003/3142, art. 3. (1), Sch. 1 (with art. 11)

320. Special impartiality requirements

(1) The requirements of this section are—

(a) the exclusion, in the case of television and radio services (other than a restricted service within the meaning of section 245), from programmes included in any of those services of all expressions of the views or opinions of the person providing the service on any of the matters mentioned in subsection (2);

(b) the preservation, in the case of every television programme service, teletext service, national radio service and national digital sound programme service, of due impartiality, on the part of the person providing the service, as respects all of those matters;

(c) the prevention, in the case of every local radio service, local digital sound programme service or radio licensable content service, of the giving of undue prominence in the programmes included in the service to the views and opinions of particular persons or bodies on any of those matters.

(2) Those matters are—

(a) matters of political or industrial controversy; and

(b) matters relating to current public policy.

(3) Subsection (1)(a) does not require—

(a) the exclusion from television programmes of views or opinions relating to the provision of programme services; or

(b) the exclusion from radio programmes of views or opinions relating to the provision of programme services.

(4) For the purposes of this section—

(a) the requirement specified in subsection (1)(b) is one that (subject to any rules under subsection (5)) may be satisfied by being satisfied in relation to a series of programmes taken as a whole;

(b) the requirement specified in subsection (1)(c) is one that needs to be satisfied only in relation to all the programmes included in the service in question, taken as a whole.

(5) OFCOM's standards code shall contain provision setting out the rules to be observed in connection with the following matters—

(a) the application of the requirement specified in subsection (1)(b);

(b) the determination of what, in relation to that requirement, constitutes a series of programmes for the purposes of subsection (4)(a);

(c) the application of the requirement in subsection (1)(c).

(6) Any provision made for the purposes of subsection (5)(a) must, in particular, take account of the need to ensure the preservation of impartiality in relation to the following matters (taking each matter separately)—

(a) matters of major political or industrial controversy, and

(b) major matters relating to current public policy,

as well as of the need to ensure that the requirement specified in subsection (1)(b) is satisfied generally in relation to a series of programmes taken as a whole.

(7) In this section "national radio service" and "local radio service" mean, respectively, a sound broadcasting service which is a national service within the meaning of section 245 and a sound broadcasting service which is a local service within the meaning of that section.

Commencement Information

I125. S. 320 in force at 29.12.2003 by S.I. 2003/3142, art. 3. (1), Sch. 1 (with art. 11)

321[F86. Objectives for advertisements, sponsorship and product placement]

(1) Standards set by OFCOM to secure the objectives mentioned in section 319. (2)(a) and [F87. (fa)] to (j)—

(a) must include general provision governing standards and practice in advertising and in the sponsoring of programmes [F88and, in relation to television programme services, general provision governing standards and practice in product placement] ; F89...

(b) may include provision prohibiting advertisements and forms and methods of advertising or sponsorship (whether generally or in particular circumstances)[F90; and

(c) in relation to television programme services, may include provision prohibiting forms and methods of product placement (including product placement of products, services or trade marks of any description) (whether generally or in particular circumstances).]

(2) For the purposes of section 319. (2)(g) an advertisement contravenes the prohibition on political advertising if it is—

(a) an advertisement which is inserted by or on behalf of a body whose objects are wholly or mainly of a political nature;

(b) an advertisement which is directed towards a political end; or

(c) an advertisement which has a connection with an industrial dispute.

(3) For the purposes of this section objects of a political nature and political ends include each of the following—

(a) influencing the outcome of elections or referendums, whether in the United Kingdom or elsewhere;

(b) bringing about changes of the law in the whole or a part of the United Kingdom or elsewhere, or otherwise influencing the legislative process in any country or territory;

(c) influencing the policies or decisions of local, regional or national governments, whether in the United Kingdom or elsewhere;

(d) influencing the policies or decisions of persons on whom public functions are conferred by or under the law of the United Kingdom or of a country or territory outside the United Kingdom;

(e) influencing the policies or decisions of persons on whom functions are conferred by or under international agreements;

(f) influencing public opinion on a matter which, in the United Kingdom, is a matter of public controversy;

(g) promoting the interests of a party or other group of persons organised, in the United Kingdom or elsewhere, for political ends.

[F91. (3. A)For the purposes of section 319. (2)(fa) the product placement requirements are the requirements set out in Schedule 11. A.]

(4) OFCOM—

(a) [F92shall—

(i)]in relation to programme services, have a general responsibility with respect to advertisements and methods of advertising and sponsorship; and

[F93. (ii)in relation to television programme services, have a general responsibility with respect to methods of product placement; and]

(b) in the discharge of that responsibility may include conditions in any licence which is granted by them for any such service that enable OFCOM to impose requirements with respect to any of those matters that go beyond the provisions of OFCOM's standards code.

(5) OFCOM must, from time to time, consult the Secretary of State about—

(a) the descriptions of advertisements that should not be included in programme services; F94...

(b) the forms and methods of advertising and sponsorship that should not be employed in, or in connection with, the provision of such services[F95; and

(c) the forms and methods of product placement that should not be employed in the provision of a television programme service (including the descriptions of products, services or trade marks for which product placement should not be employed).]

(6) The Secretary of State may give OFCOM directions as to the matters mentioned in subsection (5); and it shall be the duty of OFCOM to comply with any such direction.

(7) Provision included by virtue of this section in standards set under section 319 is not to apply to, or to be construed as prohibiting the inclusion in a programme service of—

(a) an advertisement of a public service nature inserted by, or on behalf of, a government department; or

(b) a party political or referendum campaign broadcast the inclusion of which is required by a condition imposed under section 333 or by paragraph 18 of Schedule 12 to this Act.

(8) In this section "programme service" does not include a service provided by the BBC [F96. (except in the expression "television programme service")] .

Amendments (Textual)

F86. S. 321 heading substituted (16.4.2010) by The Audiovisual Media Services (Product Placement) Regulations 2010 (S.I. 2010/831), regs. 1. (1), 3. (2)

F87. Word in s. 321. (1) substituted (16.4.2010) by The Audiovisual Media Services (Product Placement) Regulations 2010 (S.I. 2010/831), regs. 1. (1), 3. (3)(a)

F88. Words in s. 321. (1)(a) inserted (16.4.2010) by The Audiovisual Media Services (Product Placement) Regulations 2010 (S.I. 2010/831), regs. 1. (1), 3. (3)(b)

F89. Word in s. 321. (1)(a) omitted (16.4.2010) by virtue of The Audiovisual Media Services (Product Placement) Regulations 2010 (S.I. 2010/831), regs. 1. (1), 3. (3)(c)

F90. S. 321. (1)(c) and word inserted (16.4.2010) by The Audiovisual Media Services (Product Placement) Regulations 2010 (S.I. 2010/831), regs. 1. (1), 3. (3)(d)

F91. S. 321. (3. A) inserted (16.4.2010) by The Audiovisual Media Services (Product Placement) Regulations 2010 (S.I. 2010/831), regs. 1. (1), 3. (4)

F92. Words in s. 321. (4)(a) substituted (16.4.2010) by The Audiovisual Media Services (Product Placement) Regulations 2010 (S.I. 2010/831), regs. 1. (1), 3. (5)(a)

F93. S. 321. (4)(a)(ii) inserted (16.4.2010) by The Audiovisual Media Services (Product Placement) Regulations 2010 (S.I. 2010/831), regs. 1. (1), 3. (5)(b)

F94. Word in s. 321. (5)(a) omitted (16.4.2010) by virtue of The Audiovisual Media Services (Product Placement) Regulations 2010 (S.I. 2010/831), regs. 1. (1), 3. (6)(a)

F95. S. 321. (5)(c) and word inserted (16.4.2010) by The Audiovisual Media Services (Product Placement) Regulations 2010 (S.I. 2010/831), regs. 1. (1), 3. (6)(b)

F96. Words in s. 321. (8) inserted (16.4.2010) by The Audiovisual Media Services (Product

Placement) Regulations 2010 (S.I. 2010/831), regs. 1. (1), 3. (7)

Commencement Information

I126. S. 321 in force at 29.12.2003 by S.I. 2003/3142, art. 3. (1), Sch. 1 (with art. 11)

322. Supplementary powers relating to advertising

(1) The regulatory regime for each of the following—

(a) every television programme service licensed by a Broadcasting Act licence,

(b) the public teletext service, and

(c) every other teletext service so licensed that consists in an additional television service or a digital additional television service,

includes a condition requiring the person providing the service to comply with every direction given to him by OFCOM with respect to any of the matters mentioned in subsection (2).

(2) Those matters are—

(a) the maximum amount of time to be given to advertisements in any hour or other period;

(b) the minimum interval which must elapse between any two periods given over to advertisements;

(c) the number of such periods to be allowed in any programme or in any hour or day; and

(d) the exclusion of advertisements from a specified part of a licensed service.

(3) Directions under this section—

(a) may be either general or specific;

(b) may be qualified or unqualified; and

(c) may make different provision for different parts of the day, different days of the week, different types of programmes or for other differing circumstances.

(4) In giving a direction under this section, OFCOM must take account of such of the international obligations of the United Kingdom as the Secretary of State may notify to them for the purposes of this section.

Commencement Information

I127. S. 322 in force at 29.12.2003 by S.I. 2003/3142, art. 3. (1), Sch. 1 (with art. 11)

323. Modification of matters to be taken into account under s. 319.

(1) The Secretary of State may by order modify the list of matters in section 319. (4) to which OFCOM are to have regard when setting or revising standards.

(2) Before making an order under this section, the Secretary of State must consult OFCOM.

(3) No order is to be made containing provision authorised by subsection (1) unless a draft of the order has been laid before Parliament and approved by a resolution of each House.

Commencement Information

I128. S. 323 in force at 29.12.2003 by S.I. 2003/3142, art. 3. (1), Sch. 1 (with art. 11)

324. Setting and publication of standards

(1) Before setting standards under section 319, OFCOM must publish, in such manner as they think fit, a draft of the proposed code containing those standards.

(2) After publishing the draft code and before setting the standards, OFCOM must consult every person who holds a relevant licence and such of the following as they think fit—

(a) persons appearing to OFCOM to represent the interests of those who watch television programmes;

(b) persons appearing to OFCOM to represent the interests of those who make use of teletext services; and

(c) persons appearing to OFCOM to represent the interests of those who listen to sound programmes.

(3) After publishing the draft code and before setting the standards, OFCOM must also consult—

(a) the Welsh Authority, about so much of the draft code as relates to television programme services;

(b) the BBC, about so much of the draft code as contains standards other than those for advertising or sponsorship; and

(c) such of the persons mentioned in subsection (4) as OFCOM think fit, about so much of the draft code as contains standards for advertising or sponsorship [F97or for product placement] .

(4) Those persons are—

(a) persons appearing to OFCOM to represent the interests of those who will have to take account of the contents of the proposed standards for advertising or sponsorship [F98or for product placement] ;

(b) bodies and associations appearing to OFCOM to be concerned with the application of standards of conduct in advertising; and

(c) professional organisations appearing to OFCOM to be qualified to give relevant advice in relation to the advertising of particular products.

(5) If it appears to OFCOM that a body exists which represents the interests of a number of the persons who hold relevant licences, they may perform their duty under subsection (2) of consulting such persons, so far as it relates to the persons whose interests are so represented, by consulting that body.

(6) OFCOM may set standards under section 319 either—

(a) in the terms proposed in a draft code published under subsection (1); or

(b) with such modifications as OFCOM consider appropriate in the light of the consultation carried out as a result of subsections (2) to (5).

(7) Subsections (1) to (6) apply to a proposal by OFCOM to revise standards set under section 319 as they apply to a proposal to set such standards.

(8) Where OFCOM set standards under section 319, they must publish the code containing the standards in such manner as they consider appropriate for bringing it to the attention of the persons who, in their opinion, are likely to be affected by the standards.

(9) Where OFCOM revise standards set under section 319, they shall so publish the code containing the standards as revised.

(10) Where OFCOM publish a code under subsection (8) or (9), they shall send a copy of it—

(a) to the Secretary of State;

(b) except in the case of a code containing standards for advertising or sponsorship, to the BBC; and

(c) if the code relates to television programme services, to the Welsh Authority.

(11) A code (or draft code) contains standards for advertising or sponsorship for the purposes of this section to the extent that it sets standards under section 319 for securing any of the objectives mentioned in any of paragraphs (g) to (k) of subsection (2) of that section.

[F99. (11. A)A code (or draft code) contains standards for product placement for the purposes of this section to the extent that it sets standards under section 319 for securing the objective mentioned in paragraph (fa) of subsection (2) of that section.]

(12) In this section "relevant licence", in relation to a draft code, means—

(a) to the extent that the draft code relates to

(i) television programme services,

(ii) the public teletext service, or

(iii) an additional television service,

a licence under Part 1 of the 1990 Act (independent television services), under section 18 of the 1996 Act (digital television programme services) under section 25 of that Act (digital additional television services) or under section 219 of this Act; and

(b) to the extent that the draft code relates to radio programme services, any licence under Part 3 of the 1990 Act (independent radio services), under section 60 of the 1996 Act (digital sound programme service) or under section 64 of that Act (digital additional services).

Amendments (Textual)

F97. Words in s. 324. (3)(c) inserted (16.4.2010) by The Audiovisual Media Services (Product Placement) Regulations 2010 (S.I. 2010/831), regs. 1. (1), 4. (2)

F98. Words in s. 324. (4)(a) inserted (16.4.2010) by The Audiovisual Media Services (Product Placement) Regulations 2010 (S.I. 2010/831), regs. 1. (1), 4. (2)

F99. S. 324. (11. A) inserted (16.4.2010) by The Audiovisual Media Services (Product Placement) Regulations 2010 (S.I. 2010/831), regs. 1. (1), 4. (3)

Commencement Information

I129. S. 324 in force at 29.12.2003 by S.I. 2003/3142, art. 3. (1), Sch. 1 (with art. 11)

325. Observance of standards code

(1) The regulatory regime for every programme service licensed by a Broadcasting Act licence includes conditions for securing—

(a) that standards set under section 319 are observed in the provision of that service; and

(b) that procedures for the handling and resolution of complaints about the observance of those standards are established and maintained.

(2) It shall be the duty of OFCOM themselves to establish procedures for the handling and resolution of complaints about the observance of standards set under section 319.

(3) OFCOM may from time to time make a report to the Secretary of State on any issues with respect to OFCOM's standards code which—

(a) have been identified by them in the course of carrying out their functions; and

(b) appear to them to raise questions of general broadcasting policy.

(4) The conditions of a licence which is granted by OFCOM for a programme service must, for the purpose of securing compliance—

(a) with OFCOM's standards code, so far as it relates to advertising [F100, the sponsorship of programmes and product placement] , and

(b) with any such requirements as are mentioned in section 321. (4) which relate to advertising [F101, sponsorship and product placement] but go beyond that code,

include a condition requiring the licence holder to comply with every direction given to him by OFCOM with respect to any of the matters mentioned in subsection (5).

(5) Those matters are—

(a) the exclusion from the service of a particular advertisement, or its exclusion in particular circumstances;

(b) the descriptions of advertisements and methods of advertising to be excluded from the service (whether generally or in particular circumstances); F102...

(c) the forms and methods of sponsorship to be excluded from the service (whether generally or in particular circumstances)[F103; and

(d) in the case of a television programme service, the forms and methods of product placement to be excluded from the service (including descriptions of products, services or trade marks product placement of which is to be excluded) (whether generally or in particular circumstances).]

(6) OFCOM's powers and duties under this section are not to be construed as restricting any power of theirs, apart from this section—

(a) to include conditions with respect to the content of programmes included in any service in the licence to provide that service; or

(b) to include conditions in a licence requiring the holder of a licence to comply with directions given by OFCOM or by any other person.

Amendments (Textual)

F100. Words in s. 325. (4)(a) substituted (16.4.2010) by The Audiovisual Media Services (Product Placement) Regulations 2010 (S.I. 2010/831), regs. 1. (1), 5. (2)(a)

F101. Words in s. 325. (4)(b) substituted (16.4.2010) by The Audiovisual Media Services (Product Placement) Regulations 2010 (S.I. 2010/831), regs. 1. (1), 5. (2)(b)

F102. Word in s. 325. (5)(b) omitted (16.4.2010) by virtue of The Audiovisual Media Services (Product Placement) Regulations 2010 (S.I. 2010/831), regs. 1. (1), 5. (3)(a)

F103. S. 325. (5)(d) and word inserted (16.4.2010) by The Audiovisual Media Services (Product Placement) Regulations 2010 (S.I. 2010/831), regs. 1. (1), 5. (3)(b)

Modifications etc. (not altering text)

C12. S. 325. (2) modified (20.7.2004) by Contracting Out (Functions relating to Broadcast Advertising) and Specification of Relevant Functions Order 2004 (S.I. 2004/1975), art. 1, Sch. para. 1. (b) (with art. 5)

C13. S. 325. (4) modified (20.7.2004) by Contracting Out (Functions relating to Broadcast Advertising) and Specification of Relevant Functions Order 2004 (S.I. 2004/1975), art. 1, Sch. para. 1. (c) (with art. 5)

Commencement Information

I130. S. 325 in force at 29.12.2003 by S.I. 2003/3142, art. 3. (1), Sch. 1 (with art. 11)

326. Duty to observe fairness code

The regulatory regime for every programme service licensed by a Broadcasting Act licence includes the conditions that OFCOM consider appropriate for securing observance—

(a) in connection with the provision of that service, and

(b) in relation to the programmes included in that service,

of the code for the time being in force under section 107 of the 1996 Act (the fairness code).

Commencement Information

I131. S. 326 in force at 29.12.2003 by S.I. 2003/3142, art. 3. (1), Sch. 1 (with art. 11)

327. Standards with respect to fairness

(1) Part 5 of the 1996 Act (functions of the Broadcasting Standards Commission which are transferred to OFCOM so far as they relate to codes of practice and complaints with respect to fairness and privacy) shall be amended as follows.

(2) No person shall be entitled to make a standards complaint under that Part at any time after the coming into force of this section, and no person shall be required to entertain any such complaint that is so made.

(3) In section 115 (consideration of fairness complaint)—

(a) in subsection (4) (matters to be provided in response to a fairness complaint), after paragraph (d) there shall be inserted—

"(da)to provide OFCOM with such other things appearing to OFCOM to be relevant to their consideration of the complaint, and to be in the possession of the relevant person, as may be specified or described by OFCOM;"

(b) in subsection (7) (requests in relation to which the relevant person is required to secure the compliance of another), after paragraph (c) there shall be inserted—

"(ca)a request to provide OFCOM with such other things appearing to OFCOM to be relevant to their consideration of the complaint, and to be in the possession of the person requested, as may be specified or described by OFCOM;".

(4) For subsection (7) of section 119 (directions on determination of fairness complaint) there shall be substituted—

"(7)The regulatory regime for every licensed service includes the conditions that OFCOM consider appropriate for securing that the licence holder complies with every direction given to him under this section.

(7. A)Section 263 of the Communications Act 2003 applies in relation to conditions included by virtue of subsection (7) in the regulatory regime for a licensed service as it applies in relation to conditions which are so included by virtue of a provision of Chapter 4 of Part 3 of that Act.

(7. B)It is hereby declared that, where—

(a) OFCOM exercise their powers under this Part to adjudicate upon a fairness complaint or to give a direction under subsection (1), and

(b) it appears to them that the matters to which the complaint in question relates consist in or include a contravention of the conditions of the licence for a licensed service,

the exercise by OFCOM of their powers under this Part is not to preclude the exercise by them of their powers under any other enactment in respect of the contravention.

(7. C)Where OFCOM are proposing to exercise any of their powers in respect of a contravention of a licence condition in a case in which the contravention relates to matters that have been the subject-matter of a fairness complaint—

(a) OFCOM may have regard, in the exercise of those powers, to any matters considered or steps taken by them for the purpose of adjudicating upon that complaint and to any direction given by them under this section; but

(b) steps taken for the purposes of this Part do not satisfy a requirement to give the licence holder in relation to whom those powers are to be exercised a reasonable opportunity, before they are exercised, of making representations to OFCOM."

(5) For subsection (2) of section 120 of that Act (reports on supplementary action taken in

response to findings on fairness complaint) there shall be substituted—

"(2)Where the relevant programme was included in a licensed service, the licence holder shall send to OFCOM a report of any supplementary action taken by him or by any other person responsible for the making or provision of the relevant programme."

Commencement Information

I132. S. 327 in force at 29.12.2003 by S.I. 2003/3142, art. 3. (1), Sch. 1 (with art. 11)

328. Duty to publicise OFCOM's functions in relation to complaints

(1) The regulatory regime for every programme service licensed by a Broadcasting Act licence includes the conditions that OFCOM consider appropriate for securing that—

(a) the procedures which, by virtue of section 325, are established and maintained for handling and resolving complaints about the observance of standards set under section 319, and

(b) their functions under Part 5 of the 1996 Act in relation to that service,

are brought to the attention of the public (whether by means of broadcasts or otherwise).

(2) Conditions included in a licence by virtue of subsection (1) may require the holder of the licence to comply with every direction given to him by OFCOM for the purpose mentioned in that subsection.

Commencement Information

I133. S. 328 in force at 29.12.2003 by S.I. 2003/3142, art. 3. (1), Sch. 1 (with art. 11)

Power to proscribe unacceptable foreign television and radio services

329. Proscription orders

(1) Where—

(a) a foreign service to which this section applies comes to OFCOM's attention, and

(b) they consider that the service is unacceptable and should be the subject of an order under this section,

they must send a notification to the Secretary of State giving details of the service and their reasons for considering that an order should be made.

(2) A service is not to be considered unacceptable by OFCOM unless they are satisfied that—

(a) programmes containing objectionable matter are included in the service; and

(b) that the inclusion of objectionable matter in programmes so included is occurring repeatedly.

(3) Matter is objectionable for the purposes of subsection (2) only if—

(a) it offends against taste or decency;

(b) it is likely to encourage or to incite the commission of crime;

(c) it is likely to lead to disorder; or

(d) it is likely to be offensive to public feeling.

(4) Where the Secretary of State has received a notification under this section in the case of a service, he may make an order—

(a) identifying the service in such manner as he thinks fit; and

(b) proscribing it.

(5) The Secretary of State is not to make an order proscribing a service unless he is satisfied that the making of the order is—

(a) in the public interest; and

(b) compatible with the international obligations of the United Kingdom.

(6) The television and sound services to which this section applies are—

(a) television licensable content services provided otherwise than by broadcasting from a satellite;

(b) digital television programme services;

(c) digital additional television services;

(d) radio licensable sound services provided otherwise than by being broadcast from a satellite;

(e) digital sound programme services; and

(f) digital additional sound services.

(7) A service to which this section applies is a foreign service if it—

(a) is a service capable of being received in the United Kingdom for the provision of which no Broadcasting Act licence is either in force or required to be in force; but

(b) is also a service for the provision of which such a licence would be required—

(i) in the case of a service falling within subsection (6)(a) to (c), if the person providing it were under the jurisdiction of the United Kingdom for the purposes of the [F104. Audiovisual Media Services Directive] ; and

(ii) in any other case, if the person providing it provided it from a place in the United Kingdom or were a person whose principal place of business is in the United Kingdom.

Amendments (Textual)

F104. Words in s. 329. (7)(b)(i) substituted (19.12.2009) by Audiovisual Media Services Regulations 2009 (S.I. 2009/2979), regs. 1. (1), 8. (b)

Commencement Information

I134. S. 329 in force at 29.12.2003 by S.I. 2003/3142, art. 3. (1), Sch. 1 (with art. 11)

330. Effect of proscription order

(1) This section applies where a service is for the time being proscribed by an order under section 329.

(2) The proscribed service is not to be included in—

(a) a multiplex service; or

(b) a cable package.

(3) In this section "multiplex service" means a television multiplex service, a radio multiplex service or a general multiplex service.

(4) In this section "cable package" means (subject to subsection (5)) a service by means of which programme services are packaged together with a view to their being distributed—

(a) by means of an electronic communications service;

(b) so as to be available for reception by members of the public in the United Kingdom; and

(c) without the final delivery of the programme services to the persons to whom they are distributed being by wireless telegraphy.

(5) Programme services distributed by means of an electronic communications service do not form part of a cable package if—

(a) the distribution of those services forms only part of a service provided by means of that electronic communications service; and

(b) the purposes for which the service of which it forms a part is provided do not consist wholly or mainly in making available television programmes or radio programmes (or both) for reception by members of the public.

Commencement Information

I135. S. 330 in force at 29.12.2003 by S.I. 2003/3142, art. 3. (1), Sch. 1 (with art. 11)

331. Notification for enforcing proscription

(1) Where OFCOM determine that there are reasonable grounds for believing that there has been a contravention of section 330 in relation to a multiplex service or a cable package, they may give a notification under this section to—

(a) the provider of that multiplex service; or

(b) the person providing the cable package.

(2) A notification under this section is one which—

(a) sets out the determination made by OFCOM; and

(b) requires the person to whom it is given to secure that the proscribed service (so long as it remains proscribed) is not—

(i) included in the notified person's multiplex service, or

(ii) distributed as part of his cable package,

at any time more than seven days after the day of the giving of the notification.

(3) If it is reasonably practicable for a person to whom a notification is given under this section to secure that the proscribed service ceases to be included in that person's multiplex service, or to be

distributed as part of his cable package, before the end of that seven days, then he must do so.

(4) It shall be the duty of a person to whom a notification is given under this section to comply with the requirements imposed by the notification and by subsection (3).

(5) That duty shall be enforceable in civil proceedings by OFCOM—

(a) for an injunction;

(b) for specific performance of a statutory duty under section 45 of the Court of Session Act 1988 (c. 36); or

(c) for any other appropriate remedy or relief.

(6) In this section "cable package" and "multiplex service" each has the same meaning as in section 330.

Commencement Information

I136. S. 331 in force at 29.12.2003 by S.I. 2003/3142, art. 3. (1), Sch. 1 (with art. 11)

332. Penalties for contravention of notification under s. 331.

(1) OFCOM may impose a penalty on a person who contravenes a requirement imposed on him by or under section 331.

(2) Before imposing a penalty on a person under this section OFCOM must give him a reasonable opportunity of making representations to them about their proposal to impose the penalty.

(3) The amount of the penalty imposed on a person is to be such amount not exceeding £5,000 as OFCOM determine to be—

(a) appropriate; and

(b) proportionate to the contravention in respect of which it is imposed.

(4) In making that determination OFCOM must have regard to—

(a) any representations made to them by the person notified under section 331; and

(b) any steps taken by him for complying with the requirements imposed on him under that section.

(5) Where OFCOM impose a penalty on a person under this section, they shall—

(a) notify the person penalised; and

(b) in that notification, fix a reasonable period after it is given as the period within which the penalty is to be paid.

(6) A penalty imposed under this section must be paid to OFCOM within the period fixed by them.

(7) The Secretary of State may by order amend this section so as to substitute a different maximum penalty for the maximum penalty for the time being specified in subsection (3).

(8) No order is to be made containing provision authorised by subsection (7) unless a draft of the order has been laid before Parliament and approved by a resolution of each House.

(9) For the purposes of this section there is a separate contravention in respect of every day on which the proscribed service is at any time included in a person's multiplex service or distributed as part of his cable package.

(10) In this section "multiplex service" and "cable package" each has the same meaning as in section 330.

Commencement Information

I137. S. 332 in force at 29.12.2003 by S.I. 2003/3142, art. 3. (1), Sch. 1 (with art. 11)

Party political broadcasts on television and radio

333. Party political broadcasts

(1) The regulatory regime for every licensed public service channel, and the regulatory regime for every national radio service, includes—

(a) conditions requiring the inclusion in that channel or service of party political broadcasts and of referendum campaign broadcasts; and

(b) conditions requiring that licence holder to observe such rules with respect to party political broadcasts and referendum campaign broadcasts as may be made by OFCOM.

(2) The rules made by OFCOM for the purposes of this section may, in particular, include provision for determining—

(a) the political parties on whose behalf party political broadcasts may be made;

(b) in relation to each political party on whose behalf such broadcasts may be made, the length and frequency of the broadcasts; and

(c) in relation to each designated organisation on whose behalf referendum campaign broadcasts are required to be broadcast, the length and frequency of such broadcasts.

(3) Those rules are to have effect subject to sections 37 and 127 of the Political Parties, Elections and Referendums Act 2000 (c. 41) (only registered parties and designated organisations to be entitled to party political broadcasts or referendum campaign broadcasts).

(4) Rules made by OFCOM for the purposes of this section may make different provision for different cases.

(5) Before making any rules for the purposes of this section, OFCOM must have regard to any views expressed by the Electoral Commission.

(6) In this section—

"designated organisation", in relation to a referendum, means a person or body designated by the Electoral Commission under section 108 of the Political Parties, Elections and Referendums Act 2000 (c. 41) in respect of that referendum;

"national radio service" means a national service within the meaning of section 245 of this Act; and

"referendum campaign broadcast" has the meaning given by section 127 of that Act.

Commencement Information

I138. S. 333 in force at 29.12.2003 by S.I. 2003/3142, art. 3. (1), Sch. 1 (with art. 11)

Monitoring of programmes

334. Retention and production of recordings

(1) The regulatory regime for every programme service licensed by a Broadcasting Act licence includes conditions imposing on the provider of the service—

(a) a requirement in respect of every programme included in the service to retain a recording of the programme in a specified form and for a specified period after its inclusion;

(b) a requirement to comply with any request by OFCOM to produce to them for examination or reproduction a recording retained in pursuance of the conditions in the licence; and

(c) a requirement, if the provider is able to do so, to comply with any request by OFCOM to produce to them a script or transcript of a programme included in the programme service.

(2) The period specified for the purposes of a condition under subsection (1)(a) must be—

(a) in the case of a programme included in a television programme service, a period not exceeding ninety days; and

(b) in the case of a programme included in a radio programme service, a period not exceeding forty-two days.

(3) For the purpose of maintaining supervision of the programmes included in programme services, OFCOM may themselves make and use recordings of those programmes or any part of them.

(4) Nothing in this Part is to be construed as requiring OFCOM, in the carrying out of their functions under this Part as respects programme services and the programmes included in them, to view or listen to programmes in advance of their being included in such services.

Commencement Information

I139. S. 334 in force at 29.12.2003 by S.I. 2003/3142, art. 3. (1), Sch. 1 (with art. 11)

International obligations

335. Conditions securing compliance with international obligations

(1) The regulatory regime for every service to which this section applies includes the conditions that OFCOM consider appropriate for securing that the relevant international obligations of the United Kingdom are complied with.

(2) In this section "relevant international obligations of the United Kingdom" means the international obligations of the United Kingdom which have been notified to OFCOM by the Secretary of State for the purposes of this section.

(3) This section applies to the following services—

    (a) any Channel 3 service;

    (b) Channel 4;

    (c) Channel 5;

    (d) the public teletext service;

    (e) any television licensable content service;

    (f) any digital television programme service;

    (g) any additional television service;

    (h) any digital additional television service;

    (i) any restricted television service.

(4) The conditions included in any licence in accordance with the other provisions of this Chapter are in addition to any conditions included in that licence in pursuance of this section and have effect subject to them.

Commencement Information

I140. S. 335 in force at 29.12.2003 by S.I. 2003/3142, art. 3. (1), Sch. 1 (with art. 11)

[F105. Co-operation with other Member States

Amendments (Textual)

F105 S. 335. A and cross-heading inserted (19.12.2009) by Audiovisual Media Services Regulations 2009 (S.I. 2009/2979), regs. 1. (1), 7

335. ACo-operation with other Member States

(1) Where OFCOM—

    (a) receive under Article [F1064] of the Audiovisual Media Services Directive a request from another member State relating to a relevant broadcaster, and

    (b) consider that the request is substantiated, they must ask the broadcaster to comply with the rule identified in that request.

(2) In this section "relevant broadcaster" means—

    (a) the BBC;

    (b) C4. C;

    (c) the Welsh Authority; or

    (d) the holder of—

(i) a Channel 3 licence;

(ii) a Channel 5 licence; or

(iii) a licence to provide any relevant regulated television service within the meaning of section 13. (1) of the Broadcasting Act 1990.]

Amendments (Textual)

F106. Word in s. 335. A(1)(a) substituted (18.8.2010) by The Audiovisual Media Services (Codification) Regulations 2010 (S.I. 2010/1883), regs. 1, 4

Government requirements for licensed services

336. Government requirements for licensed services

(1) If it appears to the Secretary of State or any other Minister of the Crown to be appropriate to do so in connection with any of his functions, the Secretary of State or that Minister may at any time by notice require OFCOM to give a direction under subsection (2).

(2) A direction under this subsection is a direction to the holders of the Broadcasting Act licences specified in the notice under subsection (1) to include an announcement so specified in their licensed services.

(3) The direction may specify the times at which the announcement is to be broadcast or otherwise transmitted.

(4) Where the holder of a Broadcasting Act licence includes an announcement in his licensed service in pursuance of a direction under this section, he may announce that he is doing so in pursuance of such a direction.

(5) The Secretary of State may, at any time, by notice require OFCOM to direct the holders of the Broadcasting Act licences specified in the notice to refrain from including in their licensed services any matter, or description of matter, specified in the notice.

(6) Where—

(a) OFCOM have given the holder of a Broadcasting Act licence a direction in accordance with a notice under subsection (5),

(b) in consequence of the revocation by the Secretary of State of such a notice, OFCOM have revoked such a direction, or

(c) such a notice has expired,

the holder of the licence in question may include in the licensed service an announcement of the giving or revocation of the direction or of the expiration of the notice, as the case may be.

(7) OFCOM must comply with every requirement contained in a notice under this section.

(8) The powers conferred by this section are in addition to any powers specifically conferred on the Secretary of State by or under this Act or any other enactment.

(9) In this section "Minister of the Crown" includes the Treasury.

Commencement Information

I141. S. 336 in force at 29.12.2003 by S.I. 2003/3142, art. 3. (1), Sch. 1 (with art. 11)

Equal opportunities and training

337. Promotion of equal opportunities and training

(1) The regulatory regime for every service to which this section applies includes the conditions that OFCOM consider appropriate for requiring the licence holder to make arrangements for promoting, in relation to employment with the licence holder, equality of opportunity—

(a) between men and women; and

(b) between persons of different racial groups.

(2) That regime includes conditions requiring the licence holder to make arrangements for promoting, in relation to employment with the licence holder, the equalisation of opportunities for disabled persons.

(3) The regulatory regime for every service to which this section applies includes the conditions that OFCOM consider appropriate for requiring the licence holder to make arrangements for the training and retraining of persons whom he employs, in or in connection with—

(a) the provision of the licensed service; or

(b) the making of programmes to be included in that service.

(4) The conditions imposed by virtue of subsections (1) to (3) must contain provision, in relation to the arrangements made in pursuance of those conditions, requiring the person providing the service in question—

(a) to take appropriate steps to make those affected by the arrangements aware of them (including such publication of the arrangements as may be required in accordance with the conditions);

(b) from time to time, to review the arrangements; and

(c) from time to time (and at least annually) to publish, in such manner as he considers appropriate, his observations on the current operation and effectiveness of the arrangements.

(5) The conditions imposed by virtue of this section may include provision for treating obligations

to make the arrangements mentioned in subsections (1) to (3), or to do anything mentioned in subsection (4), as discharged where a member of a group of companies to which the licence holder belongs—

(a) has made the required arrangements in relation to employment with the licence holder; or

(b) has done anything required by subsection (4) in relation to those arrangements.

(6) This section applies to a service if—

(a) it is a service the provision of which is authorised by a Broadcasting Act licence; and

(b) the requirements of both subsections (7) and (8) are satisfied in the case of that service.

(7) The requirements of this subsection are satisfied in the case of a service provided by a person if—

(a) that person employs, or is likely to employ, more than the threshold number of individuals in connection with the provision of licensed services; or

(b) the threshold number is exceeded by the aggregate number of individuals who are, or are likely to be, employed in that connection by members of a group of companies comprising that person and one or more other bodies corporate.

(8) The requirements of this subsection are satisfied in the case of a service if the licence authorising the provision of that service authorises either that service or another service authorised by that licence to be provided on a number of days in any year which exceeds the threshold number of days (whether or not the service is in fact provided on those days).

(9) In this section—

"disabled" has the same meaning as in [F107the Equality Act 2010 or, in Northern Ireland,] the Disability Discrimination Act 1995 (c. 50);

"licensed service", in relation to an employee or likely employee of a person, means a service the provision of which—

- by that person, or

- by a body corporate which is a member of the same group of companies as that person,

is authorised by a Broadcasting Act licence;

"racial group" has the same meaning as in the [F108. Race Relations Act 1976 (c. 74)] [F108. Equality Act 2010] or, in Northern Ireland, the Race Relations (Northern Ireland) Order 1997 (S.I. 1997/869 (N.I. 6));

"the threshold number" means—

- in relation to individuals, twenty; and

- in relation to days, thirty-one.

(10) For the purposes of this section a person is a member of a group of companies to which a person licensed to provide a service belongs if, and only if, both of them are bodies corporate and either—

(a) one of them is controlled by the other; or

(b) both of them are controlled by the same person.

(11) In subsection (10) "controlled" has the same meaning as in Part 1 of Schedule 2 to the 1990 Act.

(12) The Secretary of State may, by order—

(a) amend subsection (1) by adding any other form of equality of opportunity that he considers appropriate;

(b) amend the definition of "the threshold number" in subsection (9).

(13) No order is to be made containing provision authorised by subsection (12) unless a draft of the order has been laid before Parliament and approved by a resolution of each House.

Amendments (Textual)

F107. Words in s. 337. (9) inserted by 2010 c. 15, Sch. 26 Pt. 1 para. 55. (a) (as inserted (E.W.S.) (1.10.2010) by The Equality Act 2010 (Consequential Amendments, Saving and Supplementary Provisions) Order 2010 (S.I. 2010/2279), art. 1. (2), Sch. 1 para. 5) (see S.I. 2010/2317, art. 2)

F108. Words in s. 337. (9) substituted by 2010 c. 15, Sch. 26 Pt. 1 para. 55. (b) (as inserted (E.W.S.) (1.10.2010) by The Equality Act 2010 (Consequential Amendments, Saving and Supplementary Provisions) Order 2010 (S.I. 2010/2279), art. 1. (2), Sch. 1 para. 5) (see S.I.

2010/2317, art. 2)
Commencement Information
I142. S. 337 in force at 29.12.2003 by S.I. 2003/3142, art. 3. (1), Sch. 1 (with art. 11)

Corresponding rules for the BBC and Welsh Authority

338. Corresponding rules for the BBC and the Welsh Authority
Schedule 12 (which provides for the imposition on the BBC and the Welsh Authority of obligations corresponding to obligations included in the regulatory regime for licensed providers) shall have effect.
Commencement Information
I143. S. 338 in force at 29.12.2003 for specified purposes by S.I. 2003/3142, art. 3. (1), Sch. 1 (with art. 11)

Enforcement against the Welsh Authority

339. Review of fulfilment by Welsh Authority of public service remits
(1) The Secretary of State may carry out a review of the performance by the Welsh Authority of their duty to secure that each of the following public service remits—
    (a) that for S4. C;
    (b) that for S4. C Digital; and
    (c) that for each of the television programme services provided by them with the approval of the Secretary of State under section 205,
is fulfilled in relation the services to which it applies.
(2) The first review carried out under this section—
    (a) shall be a review relating to the period since the passing of this Act; and
    (b) must not be carried out before the end of the period of five years beginning with the day of the passing of this Act.
(3) A subsequent review—
    (a) shall be a review relating to the period since the end of the period to which the previous review related; and
    (b) must not be carried out less than five years after the day of the publication of the report of the previous review.
(4) On a review under this section the Secretary of State—
    (a) shall consult the National Assembly for Wales and the Welsh Authority on the matters under review; and
    (b) shall have regard to their opinions when reaching his conclusions.
(5) The Secretary of State shall also consult such other persons as he considers are likely to be affected by whether, and in what manner, the Welsh Authority perform the duty mentioned in subsection (1).
(6) As soon as practicable after the conclusion of a review under this section the Secretary of State must publish a report of his conclusions.
Commencement Information
I144. S. 339 in force at 29.12.2003 by S.I. 2003/3142, art. 3. (1), Sch. 1 (with art. 11)
340. Directions to Welsh Authority to take remedial action
(1) This section applies if the Secretary of State's conclusions on a review under section 339 include a finding—
    (a) that the Welsh Authority has failed in any respect to perform their duty to secure that the public service remit for a service mentioned in that section is fulfilled; and
    (b) that there is no reasonable excuse for the failure.
(2) The Secretary of State may give the Welsh Authority general or specific directions requiring them to take the steps that he considers will ensure that the Authority perform their duty properly

in future.

(3) The Secretary of State is not to give a direction under this section unless a draft of the proposed direction has been laid before Parliament and approved by a resolution of each House.

(4) Before laying a proposed direction before Parliament, the Secretary of State must consult the Welsh Authority.

(5) It shall be the duty of the Welsh Authority to comply with every direction under this section.

Commencement Information

1145. S. 340 in force at 29.12.2003 by S.I. 2003/3142, art. 3. (1), Sch. 1 (with art. 11)

341. Imposition of penalties on the Welsh Authority

(1) This section applies to the following requirements so far as they are imposed on the Welsh Authority in relation to services provided by them—

(a) the requirements imposed by or under paragraphs 7 and 8 of Schedule 12 (programme quotas);

(b) the requirements imposed by paragraph 9. (1) and (3) of that Schedule (news and current affairs);

(c) the requirements imposed by paragraph 10 of that Schedule (code relating to programme commissioning) or by a direction under sub-paragraph (3)(d) of that paragraph;

(d) the requirement imposed by virtue of paragraph 12 of that Schedule to comply with standards set under section 319, so far as that requirement relates to standards set otherwise than for the purpose of securing the objectives set out in subsection (2)(c) or (d) of that section;

(e) the requirements imposed by paragraphs 14 and 16 of that Schedule (advertising or sponsorship) to comply with a direction under those paragraphs;

(f) the requirement imposed by paragraph 17 of that Schedule (observance of the fairness code);

(g) the requirement imposed by paragraph 19 of that Schedule (publicising complaints procedure);

(h) the requirement imposed by paragraph 20 of that Schedule (monitoring of programmes);

(i) the requirement imposed by paragraph 21 of that Schedule (international obligations) to comply with a direction under that paragraph;

(j) the requirement under paragraph 22 of that Schedule (assistance for disabled people) to comply with the code for the time being in force under section 303;

[F109. (ja)the requirement imposed by paragraph 23. A of that Schedule (complaints procedures for on-demand programme services) to comply with a direction under that paragraph;

(jb) the requirements imposed by section 368. D and section 368. Q(3) (on-demand programme services), except the requirement imposed by section 368. D(1) so far as it relates to advertising [F110and the requirement imposed by section 368. D(3)(za)] .]

(k) the requirement to comply with a direction under section 119. (1) of the 1996 Act (directions in respect of fairness matters).

(2) If OFCOM are satisfied that there has been a contravention of a requirement to which this section applies, they may serve on the Welsh Authority a notice requiring the Authority, within the specified period, to pay OFCOM a specified penalty.

(3) The amount of the penalty must not exceed £250,000.

(4) OFCOM are not to serve a notice on the Welsh Authority under this section unless they have given them a reasonable opportunity of making representations to OFCOM about the matters appearing to OFCOM to provide grounds for the service of the notice.

(5) An exercise by OFCOM of their powers under this section does not preclude any exercise by them of their powers under paragraph 15 of Schedule 12 in respect of the same contravention.

(6) The Secretary of State may by order substitute a different sum for the sum for the time being specified in subsection (3).

(7) No order is to be made containing provision authorised by subsection (6) unless a draft of the order has been laid before Parliament and approved by a resolution of each House.

Amendments (Textual)

F109. S. 341. (1)(ja)(jb) inserted (19.12.2009) by Audiovisual Media Services Regulations 2009 (S.I. 2009/2979), regs. 1. (1), 5

F110. Words in s. 341. (1)(jb) inserted (18.3.2010) by The Audiovisual Media Services Regulations 2010 (S.I. 2010/419), regs. 1. (1), 14. (7)

Modifications etc. (not altering text)

C14. S. 341. (2) modified (20.7.2004) by Contracting Out (Functions relating to Broadcast Advertising) and Specification of Relevant Functions Order 2004 (S.I. 2004/1975), art. 1, Sch. para. 5 (with art. 5)

Commencement Information

I146. S. 341 in force at 29.12.2003 by S.I. 2003/3142, art. 3. (1), Sch. 1 (with art. 11)

342. Contraventions recorded in Welsh Authority's annual report

In paragraph 13 of Schedule 6 to the 1990 Act (annual report of the Welsh Authority)—

(a) in sub-paragraph (2), the words from "and shall include" onwards shall be omitted; and

(b) after that sub-paragraph there shall be inserted—

"(3)The report shall also—

(a) set out every contravention notification given by OFCOM to the Authority during the year; and

(b) include such other information (including information relating to the Authority's financial position) as the Secretary of State may from time to time direct.

(4) In sub-paragraph (3), "contravention notification" means a notification of a determination by OFCOM of a contravention by the Authority of any obligation imposed by or under this Act, the 1996 Act or Part 3 of the Communications Act 2003."

Commencement Information

I147. S. 342 in force at 29.12.2003 by S.I. 2003/3142, art. 3. (1), Sch. 1 (with art. 11)

343. Provision of information by Welsh Authority

(1) It shall be the duty of the Welsh Authority to comply with every direction given to them by OFCOM to provide OFCOM with information falling within subsection (2).

(2) The information that the Welsh Authority may be directed to provide is any information which OFCOM may reasonably require for the purposes of carrying out their functions in relation to the Welsh Authority under this Act, the 1990 Act or the 1996 Act.

(3) Information that is required to be provided by a direction under this section must be provided in such manner and at such times as may be required by the direction.

Modifications etc. (not altering text)

C15. S. 343 modified (20.7.2004) by Contracting Out (Functions relating to Broadcast Advertising) and Specification of Relevant Functions Order 2004 (S.I. 2004/1975), arts. 1, 10. (1)(b) (with art. 5)

Commencement Information

I148. S. 343 in force at 29.12.2003 by S.I. 2003/3142, art. 3. (1), Sch. 1 (with art. 11)

Enforcement of licence conditions

344. Transmission of statement of findings

(1) Sections 40 and 109 of the 1990 Act (power to direct licensee to broadcast correction or apology) shall be amended as follows.

(2) For "apology", wherever occurring, there shall be substituted " a statement of findings ".

(3) After subsection (5), there shall be inserted—

"(6)For the purposes of this section a statement of findings, in relation to a case in which OFCOM are satisfied that the holder of a licence has contravened the conditions of his licence, is a statement of OFCOM's findings in relation to that contravention."

Commencement Information

I149. S. 344 in force at 29.12.2003 by S.I. 2003/3142, art. 3. (1), Sch. 1 (with art. 11)

345. Financial penalties imposable on licence holders

Schedule 13 (which modifies the maximum penalties that may be imposed on the holders of Broadcasting Act licences) shall have effect.

Commencement Information
I150. S. 345 in force at 29.12.2003 by S.I. 2003/3142, art. 3. (1), Sch. 1 (with art. 11)

346. Recovery of fees and penalties

(1) This section applies to the following amounts—

(a) any amount payable to OFCOM under a Broadcasting Act licence;

(b) the amount of a penalty imposed by OFCOM under Part 1 or 3 of the 1990 Act, Part 1 or 2 of the 1996 Act or this Part of this Act.

(2) Every amount to which this section applies shall be recoverable by OFCOM as a debt due to them from the person obliged to pay it.

(3) The following liabilities—

(a) a person's liability to have a penalty imposed on him under Part 1 or 3 of the 1990 Act, Part 1 or 2 of the 1996 Act or this Part in respect of acts or omissions of his occurring while he was the holder of a Broadcasting Act licence, and

(b) a liability of a person as the holder of such a licence to pay an amount to which this section applies,

are not affected by that person's Broadcasting Act licence having ceased (for any reason) to be in force before the imposition of the penalty or the payment of that amount.

Commencement Information
I151. S. 346 in force at 29.12.2003 by S.I. 2003/3142, art. 3. (1), Sch. 1 (with art. 11)

Broadcasting Act licence fees

347. Statement of charging principles

(1) OFCOM are not to fix a tariff under section 4. (3) or 87. (3) of the 1990 Act or under section 4. (3) or 43. (3) of the 1996 Act (tariffs for fees payable under Broadcasting Act licences for recovering OFCOM's costs) unless—

(a) at the time they do so, there is in force a statement of the principles that OFCOM are proposing to apply in fixing that tariff; and

(b) the tariff is fixed in accordance with those principles.

(2) Those principles must be such as appear to OFCOM to be likely to secure, on the basis of such estimates of the likely costs that it is practicable for them to make—

(a) that the aggregate amount of the Broadcasting Act licence fees that are required to be paid to OFCOM during a financial year is sufficient to enable them to meet, but does not exceed, the cost to them of the carrying out during that year of their functions relating to the regulation of broadcasting;

(b) that the requirement imposed by virtue of paragraph (a) is satisfied by the application to such fees of tariffs that are justifiable and proportionate to the matters in respect of which they are imposed; and

(c) that the relationship between meeting the cost of carrying out those functions and the tariffs applied to such fees is transparent.

(3) Before making or revising a statement of principles OFCOM must consult such of the persons who, in OFCOM's opinion, are likely to be affected by those principles as they think fit.

(4) The making or revision of a statement of principles for the purposes of this section has to be by the publication of the statement, or revised statement, in such manner as OFCOM consider appropriate for bringing it to the attention of the persons who, in their opinion, are likely to be affected by it.

(5) As soon as reasonably practicable after the end of each financial year, OFCOM must publish a statement setting out, for that year—

(a) the aggregate amount received by them during that year in respect of Broadcasting Act licence fees required to be paid during that year;

(b) the aggregate amount outstanding and likely to be paid or recovered in respect of Broadcasting Act licence fees that are required to be so paid; and

(c) the cost to OFCOM of the carrying out during that year of their functions relating to the regulation of broadcasting.

(6) Any deficit or surplus shown (after applying this subsection for all previous years) by a statement under subsection (5) shall be—

(a) carried forward; and

(b) taken into account in determining what is required to satisfy the requirement imposed by virtue of subsection (2)(a) in relation to the following year.

(7) References in this section to OFCOM's functions relating to the regulation of broadcasting do not include references to any of their functions in relation to the BBC or the Welsh Authority.

(8) In this section—

"Broadcasting Act licence fee" means a fee required to be paid to OFCOM in pursuance of conditions included in a Broadcasting Act licence under any of the following provisions—

- section 4. (1)(b) or 87. (1)(c) of the 1990 Act; or

- section 4. (1)(b) or 43. (1)(c) of the 1996 Act;

"financial year" means a period of twelve months ending with 31st March.

Commencement Information

I152. S. 347 in force at 29.12.2003 by S.I. 2003/3142, art. 3. (1), Sch. 1 (with art. 11)

Chapter 5. Media ownership and control

348. Modification of disqualification provisions

(1) In Part 2 of Schedule 2 to the 1990 Act (disqualification from holding licences), paragraphs (a) and (b) of paragraph 1. (1) (individuals and bodies from outside the member States) shall cease to have effect.

(2) In sub-paragraph (1) of paragraph 2 of that Part (disqualification of religious bodies etc.), for the words before paragraph (a) there shall be substituted—

"2. (1)The following persons are disqualified persons in relation only to licences falling within sub-paragraph (1. A)—".

(3) For sub-paragraphs (2) and (3) of that paragraph there shall be substituted—

"(1. A)A licence falls within this sub-paragraph if it is—

(a) a Channel 3 licence;

(b) a Channel 5 licence;

(c) a national sound broadcasting licence;

(d) a public teletext licence;

(e) an additional television service licence;

(f) a television multiplex licence; or

(g) a radio multiplex licence.

(1. B)In this paragraph—

"additional television service licence" means a licence under Part 1 of this Act to provide an additional television service within the meaning of Part 3 of the Communications Act 2003;

"Channel 3 licence" and "Channel 5 licence" each has the same meaning as in Part 1 of this Act;

"national sound broadcasting licence" means a licence to provide a sound broadcasting service (within the meaning of Part 3 of this Act) which is a national service (within the meaning of that Part);

"public teletext licence" means a licence to provide the public teletext service (within the meaning of Part 3 of the Communications Act 2003);

"radio multiplex licence" means a licence under Part 2 of the Broadcasting Act 1996 to provide a radio multiplex service within the meaning of that Part; and

"television multiplex licence" means a licence under Part 1 of the Broadcasting Act 1996 to provide a multiplex service within the meaning of that Part."

(4) In paragraph 4. (2)(b) of that Part (bodies that are relevant bodies for the purposes of general disqualification on grounds of undue influence) for "as mentioned in paragraph (a)(i) or (ii)

above" there shall be substituted—

"(i)by a person falling within paragraph 1. (1)(c) to (g) above;

(ii) by a person falling within paragraph 3 above; or

(iii) by two or more persons taken together each of whom falls within sub-paragraph (i) or (ii) (whether or not they all fall within the same sub-paragraph)."

(5) The Secretary of State may by order make provision—

(a) for repealing paragraph 2 of Part 2 of Schedule 2 to the 1990 Act; or

(b) for making such other modifications of that paragraph and any enactment referring to it as he thinks fit.

(6) Before making an order under subsection (5) (other than one that is confined to giving effect to recommendations made by OFCOM in a report of a review under section 391), the Secretary of State must consult OFCOM.

(7) No order is to be made containing provision authorised by subsection (5) unless a draft of the order has been laid before Parliament and approved by a resolution of each House.

Commencement Information

I153. S. 348 in force at 29.12.2003 by S.I. 2003/3142, art. 3. (1), Sch. 1 (with art. 11)

I154. S. 348. (2) (3) (5)-(7) in force at 18.9.2003 by S.I. 2003/1900, art. 2. (2), Sch. 2 (with art. 5)

349. Licence holding by local authorities

(1) In Part 2 of Schedule 2 to the 1990 Act (disqualification from holding licences), in paragraph 1 (which includes a disqualification for local authorities)—

(a) in sub-paragraph (1), for "sub-paragraph (2)" there shall be substituted " sub-paragraph (1. A) "; and

(b) after that sub-paragraph there shall be inserted—

"(1. A)Where a service is provided exclusively for the purposes of the carrying out of the functions of a local authority under section 142 of the Local Government Act 1972 (provision by local authorities of information relating to their activities), a person is disqualified by virtue of sub-paragraph (1) in relation to a licence to provide that service only if he would be so disqualified disregarding paragraph (c) of that sub-paragraph."

(2) In section 142 of the Local Government Act 1972 (c. 70) (provision by local authorities of information relating to their activities), after subsection (1. A) there shall be inserted—

"(1. AA)A local authority may—

(a) for the purpose of broadcasting or distributing information falling within subsection (1. AB), provide an electronic communications network or electronic communications service, or

(b) arrange with the provider of such a network or service for the broadcasting or distribution of such information by means of the network or service.

(1. AB)Information falls within this subsection, in relation to a local authority, if it is one or both of the following—

(a) information concerning the services within the area of the authority that are provided either by the authority themselves or by other authorities mentioned in subsection (1. B) below;

(b) information relating to the functions of the authority.

(1. AC)Nothing in subsection (1. AA) entitles a local authority to do anything in contravention of a requirement or restriction imposed by or under—

(a) the Wireless Telegraphy Act 1949,

(b) the Broadcasting Act 1990,

(c) the Broadcasting Act 1996, or

(d) the Communications Act 2003,

and in that subsection "electronic communications network" and "electronic communications service" each has the same meaning as in the Communications Act 2003."

(3) In section 2. (1) of the Local Government Act 1986 (c. 10) (restriction on publication by a local authority of material designed to affect support for a political party), after "publish" there shall be inserted " , or arrange for the publication of, ".

Commencement Information

I155. S. 349 in force at 29.12.2003 by S.I. 2003/3142, art. 3. (1), Sch. 1 (with art. 11)

350. Relaxation of licence-holding restrictions

(1) Parts 3 to 5 of Schedule 2 to the 1990 Act (restrictions on accumulations of interests and on licence holding by newspaper proprietors and public telecommunications providers) shall cease to have effect.

(2) In each of sections 5 and 88 of the 1990 Act and of sections 5 and 44 of the 1996 Act (under which the provisions of Schedule 2 to the 1990 Act are given effect), for paragraph (b) of subsection (1) there shall be substituted—

"(b)that a person does not become the holder of a licence if requirements imposed by or under Schedule 14 to the Communications Act 2003 would be contravened were he to do so; and

(c) that those requirements are not contravened in the case of a person who already holds a licence."

(3) Schedule 14 (which provides for the imposition of requirements which, in the case of Channel 3 services and certain radio services, replace those imposed by or under Parts 3 and 4 of Schedule 2 to the 1990 Act and requires approval for the holding of certain licences by religious bodies etc.) shall have effect.

(4) The Secretary of State must not by order under section 411 appoint a day falling before the commencement day for paragraph 11 of Schedule 14 as the day for the coming into force of the repeal by this Act of any of the provisions of Parts 3 and 4 of Schedule 2 to the 1990 Act so far as they relate to the holding of licences for the provision of any local services (within the meaning of Part 3 of that Act).

(5) The Secretary of State must not by order under section 411 appoint a day falling before the commencement day for paragraph 12 of Schedule 14 as the day for the coming into force of the repeal by this Act of any of the provisions of Parts 3 and 4 of Schedule 2 to the 1990 Act so far as they relate to the holding of local digital sound programme licences or the provision of local digital sound programme services.

(6) In this section "the commencement day", in relation paragraph 11 or 12 of Schedule 14, means the day on which the first order to be made under that paragraph comes into force.

Commencement Information

I156. S. 350. (1) (2) (4)-(6) in force at 29.12.2003 by S.I. 2003/3142, art. 3. (1), Sch. 1 (with art. 11)

I157. S. 350. (3) in force at 18.9.2003 for specified purposes by S.I. 2003/1900, art. 2. (2), Sch. 2

I158. S. 350. (3) in force at 29.12.2003 in so far as not already in force by S.I. 2003/3142, art. 3. (1), Sch. 1 (with art. 11)

Changes of control

351. Changes of control of Channel 3 services

(1) The regulatory regime for every Channel 3 service provided by a body corporate includes—

(a) a condition requiring the licence holder to give OFCOM advance notification of any proposals known to the body that may give rise to a relevant change of control; and

(b) a condition requiring the licence holder to provide OFCOM, in such manner and at such times as they may reasonably require, with such information as they consider necessary for the purposes of exercising their functions under this section and section 352.

(2) OFCOM must carry out a review where—

(a) they receive notification, in accordance with a condition of a Channel 3 licence, of proposals that may give rise to a relevant change of control; or

(b) a relevant change of control takes place (whether or not that change has been previously notified to OFCOM).

(3) The review shall be a review of the effects or likely effects, in relation to the matters mentioned in subsections (4) to (7), of—

(a) the change to which the proposals may give rise; or

(b) the change that has taken place.

(4) The matters mentioned in this subsection are—

(a) the extent to which time available for broadcasting programmes included in the service is allocated to programmes of each of the following descriptions—

(i) original productions;

(ii) news programmes; and

(iii) current affairs programmes;

(b) the extent to which programmes of each of those descriptions that are included in the service are broadcast at peak viewing times.

(5) The matters mentioned in this subsection are—

(a) the extent to which Channel 3 programmes made in the United Kingdom that are included in the service are programmes made outside the M25 area;

(b) the range of Channel 3 programmes made in the United Kingdom outside that area that are included in the service;

(c) the extent to which the expenditure of the provider of the service on Channel 3 programmes is referable to programme production at different production centres outside the M25 area;

(d) the range of different such production centres to which that expenditure is referable.

(6) The matters mentioned in this subsection are—

(a) the quality and range of regional programmes included in the service;

(b) the quality and range of other programmes included in the service which contribute to the regional character of the service;

(c) the quality and range of the programmes made available by the licence holder for the purposes of inclusion in the nationwide system of services referred to in section 14. (1) of the 1990 Act (nationwide Channel 3 service).

(7) The matters mentioned in this subsection are—

(a) the amount of time given, in the programmes included in the service—

(i) to regional programmes; and

(ii) to programmes included in the service which contribute to the regional character of the service;

(b) the proportion of regional programmes included in the service which are made within the area for which the service is provided;

(c) the extent of the use, in connection with the service, of the services of persons employed (whether by the licence holder or any other person) within that area;

(d) the extent to which managerial or editorial decisions relating to programmes to be included in the service are taken by persons so employed within that area.

(8) In relation to a national Channel 3 service, subsections (3) to (7) have effect as if—

(a) subsection (5) applied only where the service is subject to conditions imposed by virtue of a decision of OFCOM under section 286. (2) or OFCOM otherwise consider, having regard to the nature of the service, that it is appropriate to consider the matters mentioned in that subsection;

(b) references to regional programmes were references to programmes which are regional programmes (within the meaning of section 287) in relation to that service and are included in it in accordance with a condition imposed under subsection (4)(a) of that section;

(c) references to the regional character of the service were references to the regional character of parts of the service;

(d) subsection (6)(c) of this section were omitted; and

(e) references, in relation to programmes such as are mentioned in paragraph (b), to the area for which the service is provided were references to the part of that area where the people are living to whom those programmes are likely to be of particular interest.

(9) Where OFCOM carry out a review under subsection (2), they must publish a report of that review—

(a) setting out their conclusions; and

(b) specifying any steps which they propose to take under section 352.

(10) In this section—

"Channel 3 programmes" and "expenditure" each has the same meaning as in section 286;

"original production" has the same meaning as in section 278;
"peak viewing time"—
    - in relation to original productions, means a time determined by OFCOM for the purposes of section 278 to be a peak viewing time for the service in question; and
    - in relation to news programmes or current affairs programmes, means a time so determined for the purposes of section 279;
"regional programme", in relation to a Channel 3 service, means (subject to subsection (8)) a programme (including a news programme) which is of particular interest—
    - to persons living within the area for which the service is provided;
    - to persons living within a part of that area; or
    - to particular communities living within that area;
"relevant change of control" means a change in the persons having control over—
    - a body holding the licence to provide a Channel 3 service; or
    - any body which—
is connected with a body holding such a licence; and
is involved, to a substantial extent, in the provision of the programmes included in the service provided under that licence, or is likely to become so involved.
(11) Expressions used in this section and in Part 1 of Schedule 2 to the 1990 Act (restrictions on licence holders) have the same meanings in this section as in that Part.
Commencement Information
I159. S. 351. (1)-(3) (4)(a)(ii) (iii) (b) (5)-(9) (11) in force at 29.12.2003 by S.I. 2003/3142, art. 3. (1), Sch. 1 (with art. 11)
I160. S. 351. (4)(a)(i) in force at 1.7.2004 by S.I. 2003/3142, art. 4. (4)(b) (with art. 11) (as amended (4.3.2004) by S.I. 2004/545, art. 2. (2)(3)(a))
I161. S. 351. (10) in force at 29.12.2003 for specified purposes by S.I. 2003/3142, art. 3. (1), Sch. 1 (with art. 11)
I162. S. 351. (10) in force at 1.7.2004 in so far as not already in force by S.I. 2003/3142, art. 4. (4)(b) (with art. 11) (as amended (4.3.2004) by S.I. 2004/545, art. 2. (2)(3)(a))
352. Action following review under s. 351.
(1) If, on a review under subsection (2) of section 351, it appears to OFCOM that the relevant change of control is or would be prejudicial to one or more of the matters mentioned in subsections (4) to (6) of that section, they shall vary the licence in accordance with subsection (2).
(2) The variation—
    (a) must be made with a view to ensuring that the relevant change of control is not prejudicial to any of the matters so mentioned; and
    (b) must be a variation for the inclusion in the licence of such conditions relating to any of those matters as they consider appropriate.
(3) If it appears to OFCOM, having regard to the matters mentioned in subsection (7) of section 351—
    (a) that the proposed change of control would be prejudicial to the regional character of the service or (as the case may be) of any parts of it, or
    (b) that the actual change of control is so prejudicial,
they may vary the licence so as to include in it such conditions relating to any of those matters as they consider appropriate.
(4) Subject to subsection (5), any new or varied condition imposed under this section in relation to any matter may be more onerous than the conditions relating to that matter having effect before the relevant change of control.
(5) A variation under this section must not provide for the inclusion of a new or varied condition in a licence unless the new condition, or the condition as varied, is one which (with any necessary modifications) would have been satisfied by the licence holder throughout the twelve months immediately before the relevant date.
(6) In subsection (5) "the relevant date" is the date of the relevant change of control or, if earlier, the date on which OFCOM exercise their powers under this section.

(7) A variation of a licence under this section shall be effected by the service of a notice of the variation on the licence holder.

(8) OFCOM are not to serve a notice of a variation under this section unless they have given the body on whom it is served a reasonable opportunity, after the publication of the report of the review under section 351, of making representations to them about the variation.

(9) Where, in a case of a proposed change of control, a notice varying a licence under this section is served before the change to which it relates takes place, the variation is not to take effect until the change takes place.

(10) A condition included in a licence by a variation under this section may be further varied by OFCOM either—

(a) with the consent of the licence holder; or

(b) in any other case, after complying with the requirements of section 3. (4)(b) of the 1990 Act (variation after giving opportunity for representations by the licence holder).

(11) Expressions used in this section and section 351 have the same meanings in this section as in that.

Commencement Information

I163. S. 352 in force at 29.12.2003 by S.I. 2003/3142, art. 3. (1), Sch. 1 (with art. 11)

353. Changes of control of Channel 5.

(1) The regulatory regime for Channel 5 includes, in every case where it is provided by a body corporate—

(a) a condition requiring the licence holder to give OFCOM advance notification of any proposals known to the body that may give rise to a relevant change of control; and

(b) a condition requiring the licence holder to provide OFCOM, in such manner and at such times as they may reasonably require, with such information as they consider necessary for the purposes of exercising their functions under this section and section 354.

(2) OFCOM must carry out a review where—

(a) they receive notification, in accordance with a condition of the licence to provide Channel 5, of proposals that may give rise to a relevant change of control; or

(b) a relevant change of control takes place (whether or not that change has been previously notified to OFCOM).

(3) The review shall be a review of the effects or likely effects, in relation to the matters mentioned in subsections (4) and (5), of—

(a) the change to which the proposals may give rise; or

(b) the change that has taken place.

(4) The matters mentioned in this subsection are—

(a) the extent to which time available for broadcasting programmes included in Channel 5 is allocated to programmes of each of the following descriptions—

(i) original productions;

(ii) news programmes; and

(iii) current affairs programmes;

(b) the extent to which programmes of each of those descriptions that are included in that Channel are broadcast at peak viewing times.

(5) The matters mentioned in this subsection are—

(a) the extent to which programmes made in the United Kingdom that are included in the service are programmes made outside the M25 area;

(b) the range of programmes made in the United Kingdom outside that area that are included in Channel 5;

(c) the extent to which the expenditure of the provider of Channel 5 on programmes made in the United Kingdom is referable to programme production at different production centres outside the M25 area;

(d) the range of different such production centres to which that expenditure is referable.

(6) Where OFCOM carry out a review under subsection (2), they must publish a report of that review—

(a) setting out their conclusions; and

(b) specifying any steps which they propose to take under section 354.

(7) In this section—

"expenditure", in relation to a programme, means—

- expenditure which constitutes an investment in or is otherwise attributable to the making of the programme; or

- expenditure on the commissioning or other acquisition of the programme or on the acquisition of a right to include it in a service or to have it broadcast;

"original production" has the same meaning as in section 278;

"peak viewing time"—

- in relation to original productions, means a time determined by OFCOM for the purposes of section 278 to be a peak viewing time for Channel 5; and

- in relation to news programmes or current affairs programmes, means a time so determined for the purposes of section 279;

"relevant change of control" means a change in the persons having control over—

- a body holding a licence to provide Channel 5; or

- any body which—

is connected with a body holding such a licence; and

is involved, to a substantial extent, in the provision of the programmes included in that channel, or is likely to become so involved.

(8) Expressions used in this section and in Part 1 of Schedule 2 to the 1990 Act (restrictions on licence holders) have the same meanings in this section as in that Part.

Commencement Information

I164. S. 353. (1)-(3) (4)(a)(ii) (iii) (b) (5) (6) (8) in force at 29.12.2003 by S.I. 2003/3142, art. 3. (1), Sch. 1 (with art. 11)

I165. S. 353. (4)(a)(i) in force at 1.7.2004 by S.I. 2003/3142, art. 4. (4)(b) (with art. 11) (as amended (4.3.2004) by S.I. 2004/545, art. 2. (2)(3)(a))

I166. S. 353. (7) in force at 29.12.2003 for specified purposes by S.I. 2003/3142, art. 3. (1), Sch. 1 (with art. 11)

I167. S. 353. (7) in force at 1.7.2004 in so far as not already in force by S.I. 2003/3142, art. 4. (4)(b) (with art. 11) (as amended (4.3.2004) by S.I. 2004/545, art. 2. (2)(3)(a))

354. Action following review under s. 353.

(1) If, on a review under subsection (2) of section 353, it appears to OFCOM that the relevant change of control is or would be prejudicial to one or more of the matters mentioned in subsections (4) and (5) of that section, they shall vary the licence in accordance with subsection (2).

(2) The variation—

(a) must be made with a view to ensuring that the relevant change of control is not prejudicial to any of the matters so mentioned; and

(b) must be a variation for the inclusion in the licence of such conditions relating to any of those matters as they consider appropriate.

(3) Subject to subsection (4), any new or varied condition imposed under this section in relation to any matter may be more onerous than the conditions relating to that matter having effect before the relevant change of control.

(4) A variation under this section must not provide for the inclusion of a new or varied condition in a licence unless the new condition, or the condition as varied, is one which (with any necessary modifications) would have been satisfied by the licence holder throughout the twelve months immediately before the relevant date.

(5) In subsection (4) "the relevant date" is the date of the relevant change of control or, if earlier, the date on which OFCOM exercise their powers under this section.

(6) A variation of a licence under this section shall be effected by the service of a notice of the variation on the licence holder.

(7) OFCOM are not to serve a notice of a variation under this section unless they have given the

body on whom it is served a reasonable opportunity, after the publication of the report of the review under section 353, of making representations to them about the variation.

(8) Where, in a case of a proposed change of control, a notice varying a licence under this section is served before the change to which it relates takes place, the variation is not to take effect until the change takes place.

(9) A condition included in a licence by a variation under this section may be further varied by OFCOM either—

(a) with the consent of the licence holder; or

(b) in any other case, after complying with the requirements of section 3. (4)(b) of the 1990 Act (variation after giving opportunity for representations by the licence holder).

(10) Expressions used in this section and section 353 have the same meanings in this section as in that.

Commencement Information

I168. S. 354 in force at 29.12.2003 by S.I. 2003/3142, art. 3. (1), Sch. 1 (with art. 11)

355. Variation of local licence following change of control

(1) The regulatory regime for every local sound broadcasting service provided by a body corporate includes—

(a) a condition requiring the licence holder to give OFCOM advance notification of any proposals known to it that may give rise to a relevant change of control; and

(b) a condition requiring the licence holder to provide OFCOM, in such manner and at such times as they may reasonably require, with such information as they consider necessary for the purposes of exercising their functions under this section and section 356.

(2) OFCOM must carry out a review where—

(a) they receive notification, in accordance with a condition of a local sound broadcasting licence, of proposals that may give rise to a relevant change of control; or

(b) a relevant change of control takes place (whether or not that change has been previously notified to OFCOM).

(3) The review shall be a review of the effects or likely effects, in relation to the matters mentioned in subsection (4), of—

(a) the change to which the proposals may give rise; or

(b) the change that has taken place.

(4) Those matters are—

(a) the quality and range of programmes included in the service;

(b) the character of the service;

(c) the extent to which OFCOM's duty under section 314 is performed in relation to the service.

(5) The matters to which OFCOM must have regard in determining for the purposes of this section the character of a local sound broadcasting service, include, in particular, the selection of spoken material and music in programmes included in the service.

(6) Where OFCOM carry out a review under subsection (2), they must publish a report of that review—

(a) setting out their conclusions; and

(b) specifying any steps which they propose to take under section 356.

(7) In this section "relevant change of control" means a change in the persons having control over—

(a) a body holding the licence to provide a local sound broadcasting service; or

(b) any body which—

(i) is connected with a body holding such a licence; and

(ii) is involved, to a substantial extent, in the provision of the programmes included in the service provided under that licence, or is likely to become so involved.

(8) Expressions used in this section and in Schedule 2 to the 1990 Act (restrictions on licence holders) have the same meanings in this section as in that Schedule.

Commencement Information

I169. S. 355 in force at 29.12.2003 by S.I. 2003/3142, art. 3. (1), Sch. 1 (with art. 11)

356. Action following review under s. 355.

(1) If, on a review under section 355, it appears to OFCOM that the relevant change of control is or would be prejudicial to one or more of the matters mentioned in subsection (4) of that section, they must vary the local licence in accordance with subsection (2).

(2) The variation—

(a) must be made with a view to ensuring that the relevant change of control is not prejudicial to any of the matters so mentioned; and

(b) must be a variation for the inclusion in the licence of such conditions relating to any of those matters as they consider appropriate.

(3) Subject to subsection (4), any new or varied condition imposed under this section in relation to any matter may be more onerous than the conditions relating to that matter having effect before the relevant change of control.

(4) A variation under this section must not provide for the inclusion of any new or varied condition in a licence unless the new condition, or the condition as varied, is one which (with any necessary modifications) would have been satisfied by the licence holder throughout—

(a) the three months immediately before the relevant date; or

(b) such other three month period as has been notified under subsection (5).

(5) If OFCOM consider that the performance of the licence holder during the three month period immediately preceding the relevant date is not typical of his performance during the twelve months before the relevant date they—

(a) may determine that subsection (4) is to apply by reference to such other three month period falling within those twelve months as they may determine; and

(b) must notify any determination under this subsection to the licence holder.

(6) In subsection (4) "the relevant date" is the date of the relevant change of control or, if earlier, the date on which OFCOM exercise their powers under this section.

(7) A variation of a licence under this section shall be effected by the service of a notice of the variation on the licence holder.

(8) OFCOM are not to serve a notice of a variation under this section unless they have given the body on whom it is served a reasonable opportunity, after the publication of the report of the review under section 355, of making representations to them about the variation.

(9) Where, in a case of a proposed change of control, a notice varying a licence under this section is served before the change to which it relates takes place, the variation is not to take effect until that change takes place.

(10) A condition included in a licence by a variation under this section may be further varied by OFCOM either—

(a) with the consent of the licence holder; or

(b) in any other case, after complying with the requirements of section 86. (5)(b) of the 1990 Act (variation after giving opportunity for representations by the licence holder).

(11) Expressions used in this section and section 355 have the same meanings in this section as in that.

Commencement Information

I170. S. 356 in force at 29.12.2003 by S.I. 2003/3142, art. 3. (1), Sch. 1 (with art. 11)

Meaning of control

357. Meaning of "control"

(1) In paragraph 1. (3)(b) of Part 1 of Schedule 2 to the 1990 Act (control where a person will be able, without having at least a 50 per cent. interest in it, to have the affairs of a body conducted in accordance with his wishes)—

(a) for "will be able" there shall be substituted " would (if he chose to) be able in most cases or in significant respects "; and

(b) for "the affairs" there shall be substituted " affairs ".

(2) It shall be the duty of OFCOM to publish guidance setting out their intentions concerning the inclusion of particular matters in the matters that they will take into account when determining whether a person has control of a body, within the meaning of paragraph 1. (3)(b) of Part 1 of Schedule 2 to the 1990 Act.

(3) OFCOM may from time to time revise the guidance issued by them under this section.

(4) OFCOM must publish the guidance and, where they revise it, the revised guidance in such manner as they consider appropriate for bringing it to the attention of the persons who, in their opinion, are likely to be affected by it.

Commencement Information

I171. S. 357 in force at 29.12.2003 by S.I. 2003/3142, art. 3. (1), Sch. 1 (with art. 11)

Chapter 6. Other provisions about television and radio services

358. Annual factual and statistical report

(1) It shall be the duty of OFCOM—

(a) as soon as practicable after the end of the period of twelve months beginning with the commencement of this section, and

(b) as soon as practicable after the end of every subsequent period of twelve months, to satisfy for that period the review and reporting requirements of this section.

(2) For any period those obligations are—

(a) to carry out a review of the provision of the television and radio services available for reception by members of the public in the United Kingdom during that period; and

(b) to prepare a factual and statistical report for that period on the provision of those services and on the state of the market in which they are provided.

(3) In carrying out a review for any period under this section, OFCOM must consider, in particular, each of the following—

(a) the extent to which programmes included during that period in television and radio services are representative of what OFCOM consider to be the principal genres for such programmes;

(b) the extent to which codes made by OFCOM under this Part or Part 4 or 5 of the 1996 Act (listed events and fairness) have been complied with during that period;

(c) the extent to which any guidance given by OFCOM under section 314 has been followed during that period;

(d) any trends appearing or operating during that period in the size and behaviour of the audience for radio and television services;

(e) the financial condition during that period of the market in which those services are provided and of the market in which programmes for such services are produced;

(f) what it is appropriate to achieve by conditions and duties under section 277 and paragraphs 1 and 7 of Schedule 12 and the effectiveness for that purpose of the conditions and duties for the time being in force;

(g) whether it would be appropriate to recommend to the Secretary of State that he exercises any of his powers under that section or those paragraphs;

(h) the extent to which work on independent productions (within the meaning of that section and those paragraphs) that are produced in the United Kingdom is done in a range of production centres outside the M25 area;

(i) any issues relating to intellectual property in programmes that have arisen or been of significance during that period;

(j) developments in technology that have occurred or become important during that period and are relevant to the provision, broadcasting or distribution of television and radio programmes;

(k) the availability during that period of persons with skills that are used or likely to be useful in connection with the provision of television and radio services and the production of programmes for inclusion in such services;

(l) the availability during that period of facilities for the provision of training in such skills.

(4) Every report under this section must set out OFCOM's findings on their consideration of the matters mentioned in subsection (3).

(5) Every report prepared by OFCOM under this section must be published by them—

    (a) as soon as practicable after its preparation is complete; and

    (b) in such manner as they consider appropriate.

(6) OFCOM's duties under this section are in addition to their duties under section 264.

Commencement Information

I172. S. 358 in force at 29.12.2003 by S.I. 2003/3142, art. 3. (1), Sch. 1 (with art. 11)

Community radio and local digital television

359. Grants to providers

(1) OFCOM may make such grants as they consider appropriate to the provider of any service of a description of service in relation to which provision is for the time being in force under section 262.

(2) The Secretary of State may by order provide that OFCOM may also make such grants as they consider appropriate to the provider of any service of a description of service in relation to which provision is for the time being in force under section 244.

(3) A grant made by virtue of this section may be made on such terms and conditions, and shall become repayable to OFCOM in such circumstances, as may be specified by OFCOM when making the grant.

(4) A person is not—

    (a) by reason of the making to him of a grant by virtue of this section, or

    (b) by reason of any terms or conditions (including any provisions for repayment) subject to which such a grant is or has been made to him,

to be a disqualified person by virtue of any provision of Schedule 2 to the 1990 Act in relation to a licence mentioned in subsection (5).

(5) Those licences are—

    (a) a licence under Part 1 of the 1990 Act, or under Part 1 of the 1996 Act, which is granted in accordance with any provision made by an order under section 244 of this Act; and

    (b) a licence under Part 3 of the 1990 Act, or under Part 2 of the 1996 Act, which is granted in accordance with any provision made by an order under section 262 of this Act.

(6) No order is to be made containing provision authorised by this section unless a draft of the order has been laid before Parliament and approved by a resolution of each House.

Commencement Information

I173. S. 359 in force at 29.12.2003 by S.I. 2003/3142, art. 3. (1), Sch. 1 (with art. 11)

Supplemental provisions of Part 3.

360. Amendments of the 1990 and 1996 Acts

(1) In section 201 of the 1990 Act (programme services), in subsection (1)—

    (a) for paragraphs (a) to (bb) there shall be substituted—

"(aa)any service which is a programme service within the meaning of the Communications Act 2003;"

    (b) in paragraph (c), for "a telecommunication system" there shall be substituted " an electronic communications network (within the meaning of the Communications Act 2003) ".

(2) For subsection (2) of that section there shall be substituted—

"(2. A)Subsection (1)(c) does not apply to so much of a service consisting only of sound programmes as—

    (a) is a two-way service (within the meaning of section 248. (4) of the Communications Act 2003);

    (b) satisfies the conditions in section 248. (5) of that Act; or

(c) is provided for the purpose only of being received by persons who have qualified as users of the service by reason of being persons who fall within paragraph (a) or (b) of section 248. (7) of that Act.

(2. B)Subsection (1)(c) does not apply to so much of a service not consisting only of sound programmes as—

(a) is a two-way service (within the meaning of section 232 of the Communications Act 2003);

(b) satisfies the conditions in section 233. (5) of that Act; or

(c) is provided for the purpose only of being received by persons who have qualified as users of the service by reason of being persons who fall within paragraph (a) or (b) of section 233. (7) of that Act."

(3) Schedule 15 (which makes minor and consequential amendments of the 1990 Act and the 1996 Act for purposes connected with the other provisions of this Chapter) shall have effect.

Commencement Information

I174. S. 360. (1)(2) in force at 29.12.2003 by S.I. 2003/3142, art. 3. (1), Sch. 1 (with art. 11)

I175. S. 360. (3) in force at 25.7.2003 for specified purposes by S.I. 2003/1900, art. 2. (1), Sch. 1

I176. S. 360. (3) in force at 18.9.2003 for specified purposes by S.I. 2003/1900, art. 2. (2), Sch. 2

I177. S. 360. (3) in force at 29.12.2003 in so far as not already in force by S.I. 2003/3142, art. 3. (1), Sch. 1 (with art. 11)

361. Meaning of "available for reception by members of the public"

(1) The services that are to be taken for the purposes of this Part to be available for reception by members of the public include (subject to subsection (2)) any service which—

(a) is made available for reception, or is made available for reception in an intelligible form, only to persons who subscribe to the service (whether for a period or in relation to a particular occasion) or who otherwise request its provision; but

(b) is a service the facility of subscribing to which, or of otherwise requesting its provision, is offered or made available to members of the public.

[F111. (2)A service is not to be treated as available for reception by members of the public if it is an on-demand programme service.]

(6) References in this section to members of the public are references to members of the public in, or in any area of, any one or more countries or territories (which may or may not include the United Kingdom).

(7) The Secretary of State may by order modify any of the provisions of this section if it appears to him appropriate to do so having regard to any one or more of the following—

(a) the protection which, taking account of the means by which the programmes and services are received or may be accessed, is expected by members of the public as respects the contents of television programmes or sound programmes;

(b) the extent to which members of the public are able, before television programmes are watched or accessed, to make use of facilities for exercising control, by reference to the contents of the programmes, over what is watched or accessed;

(c) the practicability of applying different levels of regulation in relation to different services;

(d) the financial impact for providers of particular services of any modification of the provisions of that section; and

(e) technological developments that have occurred or are likely to occur.

(8) No order is to be made containing provision authorised by subsection (7) unless a draft of the order has been laid before Parliament and approved by a resolution of each House.

F112. (9). . . . .

Amendments (Textual)

F111. S. 361. (2) substituted for s. 361. (2)-(5) (19.12.2009) by Audiovisual Media Services Regulations 2009 (S.I. 2009/2979), regs. 1. (1), 9. (a)

F112. S. 361. (9) omitted (19.12.2009) by virtue of Audiovisual Media Services Regulations 2009 (S.I. 2009/2979), regs. 1. (1), 9. (b)

Commencement Information

I178. S. 361 in force at 25.7.2003 by S.I. 2003/1900, art. 2. (1), Sch. 1

362. Interpretation of Part 3.

(1) In this Part—

"additional radio service" means an additional service within the meaning given by section 114. (1) of the 1990 Act for the purposes of Part 3 of that Act;

"additional television service" (except in the expression "digital additional television service") means an additional service within the meaning given by section 48 of the 1990 Act for the purposes of Part 1 of the 1990 Act;

"analogue teletext service" is to be construed in accordance with section 218. (4);

"ancillary service" has the same meaning as it has, by virtue of section 24. (2) of the 1996 Act, in Part 1 of that Act;

"assistance for disabled people" means any of the following—

- subtitling;
- audio-description for the blind and partially sighted; and
- presentation in, or translation into, sign language;

"available for reception by members of the public" is to be construed in accordance with section 361;

"the BBC Charter and Agreement" means the following documents, or any one or more of them, so far as they are for the time being in force—

- a Royal Charter for the continuance of the BBC;
- supplemental Charters obtained by the BBC under such a Royal Charter;
- an agreement between the BBC and the Secretary of State entered into (whether before or after the passing of this Act) for purposes that include the regulation of activities carried on by the BBC;

"BBC company" means—

- a body corporate which is controlled by the BBC; or
- a body corporate in which the BBC or a body corporate controlled by the BBC is (to any extent) a participant;

"C4 company" means—

- a body corporate which is controlled by C4. C; or
- a body corporate in which C4. C or a body corporate controlled by C4. C is (to any extent) a participant;

"Channel 3", "Channel 4" and "Channel 5" each has the same meaning as in Part 1 of the 1990 Act (see section 71 of that Act);

"Channel 3 licence" means a licence to provide a Channel 3 service;

"a Channel 3 service" means a television broadcasting service comprised in Channel 3;

"digital additional sound service" means a digital additional service within the meaning given by section 63 of the 1996 Act for the purposes of Part 2 of that Act;

"digital additional television service" means a digital additional service within the meaning given by section 24. (1) of the 1996 Act for the purposes of Part 1 of that Act;

"the digital public teletext service" means so much of the public teletext service as consists of a service provided in digital form;

"digital sound programme licence" and "digital sound programme service" each has the same meaning as in Part 2 of the 1996 Act (see sections 40 and 72 of that Act);

"digital television programme service" means a digital programme service within the meaning given by section 1. (4) of the 1996 Act for the purposes of Part 1 of that Act;

[F113"EEA State" has the meaning given by Schedule 1 to the Interpretation Act 1978, and "another EEA State" means an EEA State other than the United Kingdom;]

"general multiplex service" means a multiplex service within the meaning of section 175 which is neither a television multiplex service nor a radio multiplex service;

"initial expiry date" has the meaning given by section 224;

"licensed public service channel" means any of the following services (whether provided for broadcasting in digital or in analogue form)—

- any Channel 3 service;

- Channel 4;
- Channel 5;
"local digital sound programme licence" and "local digital sound programme service" each has the same meaning as in Part 2 of the 1996 Act (see sections 60 and 72 of that Act);
"local radio multiplex licence" and "local radio multiplex service" each has the same meaning as in Part 2 of the 1996 Act (see sections 40 and 72 of that Act);
"local sound broadcasting licence" means a licence under Part 3 of the 1990 Act to provide a local sound broadcasting service;
"local sound broadcasting service" means a sound broadcasting service which, under subsection (4)(b) of section 245, is a local service for the purposes of that section;
"the M25 area" means the area the outer boundary of which is represented by the London Orbital Motorway (M25);
"national Channel 3 service" means a Channel 3 service provided between particular times of the day for more than one area for which regional Channel 3 services are provided;
"national digital sound programme service" has the same meaning as in Part 2 of the 1996 Act;
"national radio multiplex licence" and "national radio multiplex service" each has the same meaning as in Part 2 of the 1996 Act (see sections 40 and 72 of that Act);
"networking arrangements" has the meaning given by section 290;
"OFCOM's standards code" means any code or codes for the time being in force containing standards set by OFCOM under section 319 (whether originally or by way of any revision of any standards previously so set);
[F114"product placement" has the meaning given by paragraph 1 of Schedule 11. A;]
"provision", in relation to a service, is to be construed (subject to subsection (3)) in accordance with subsection (2), and cognate expressions are to be construed accordingly;
"the public teletext provider" means—
- subject to paragraph (b), the person holding the licence under section 219 to provide the public teletext service; and
- in relation to a time before the grant of the first licence to be granted under that section, the person holding the Broadcasting Act licence to provide the existing service (within the meaning of section 221);
"the public teletext service" means the service the provision of which is required to be secured in accordance with section 218;
"qualifying service" has the same meaning as in Part 1 of the 1996 Act (see section 2. (2) of that Act);
"radio licensable content service" has the meaning given by section 247;
"radio multiplex service" has the same meaning as (by virtue of section 258 of this Act) it has in Part 2 of the 1996 Act;
"radio programme service" means any of the following—
- a service the provision of which is licensed under Part 3 of the 1990 Act;
- a digital sound programme service the provision of which is licensed under Part 2 of the 1996 Act;
- a digital additional sound service the provision of which is licensed under section 64 of the 1996 Act;
"regional Channel 3 licence" means a licence under Part 1 of the 1990 Act to provide a regional Channel 3 service;
"regional Channel 3 service" means a Channel 3 service provided for a particular area determined under section 14. (2) of the 1990 Act;
"restricted television service" means any restricted service within the meaning given by section 42. A of the 1990 Act for the purposes of Part 1 of that Act;
"S4. C" and "S4. C Digital" means the services so described in section 204. (3);
"S4. C company" means—
- a body corporate which is controlled by the Welsh Authority; or
- a body corporate in which that Authority or a body corporate controlled by that Authority is

(to any extent) a participant;

"simulcast radio service" means any simulcast radio service within the meaning given by section 41. (2) of the 1996 Act for the purposes of Part 2 of that Act;

"sound broadcasting service" has the same meaning as in Part 3 of the 1990 Act (see section 126 of that Act);

"standards objectives" has the meaning given by section 319. (2);

"subtitling" means subtitling for the deaf or hard of hearing, whether provided by means of a teletext service or otherwise;

"television broadcasting service" means (subject to subsection (4)) a service which—

- consists in a service of television programmes provided with a view to its being broadcast (whether in digital or in analogue form);

- is provided so as to be available for reception by members of the public; and

- is not—

a restricted television service;

a television multiplex service;

a service provided under the authority of a licence under Part 1 of the 1990 Act to provide a television licensable content service; or

a service provided under the authority of a licence under Part 1 of the 1996 Act to provide a digital television programme service;

"television licensable content service" has the meaning given by section 232 of this Act;

"television multiplex service" has meaning given by section 241. (1) of this Act to a multiplex service within the meaning of Part 1 of the 1996 Act;

"television programme service" means any of the following—

- a television broadcasting service;

- a television licensable content service;

- a digital television programme service;

- a restricted television service;

F115...

"text service" means any teletext service or other service in the case of which the visual images broadcast or distributed by means of the service consist wholly or mainly of non-representational images.

(2) In the case of any of the following services—

(a) a television broadcasting service or sound broadcasting service,

(b) the public teletext service;

(c) a television licensable content service or radio licensable content service,

(d) a digital television programme service or digital sound programme service,

(e) a restricted television service,

(f) an additional television service or additional radio service,

(g) a digital additional television service or a digital additional sound service,

the person, and the only person, who is to be treated for the purposes of this Part as providing the service is the person with general control over which programmes and other services and facilities are comprised in the service (whether or not he has control of the content of individual programmes or of the broadcasting or distribution of the service).

(3) For the purposes of this Part—

(a) the provision of a service by the BBC does not include its provision by a BBC company;

(b) the provision of a service by C4. C does not include its provision by a C4 company;

(c) the provision of a service by the Welsh Authority does not include its provision by an S4. C company;

and, accordingly, control that is or is capable of being exercised by the BBC, C4. C or the Welsh Authority over decisions by a BBC company, C4 company or S4. C company about what is to be comprised in a service shall be disregarded for the purposes of subsection (2).

(4) References in this Part to a television broadcasting service do not include references to any text service.

(5) References in this Part to imposing a charge on a person in respect of his reception of a service in, or in a part of, the United Kingdom include references to imposing charges—

(a) for his use of the service at a place in the United Kingdom or in that part of it;

(b) for an entitlement of his to receive it at such place;

(c) for the use of a facility by means of which he exercises such an entitlement; or

(d) for the service's being made available for reception by him at such a place.

(6) In subsection (1) "controlled" and "participant" each has the same meaning as in Schedule 2 to the 1990 Act.

(7) In this section "non-representational images" means visual images which are neither still pictures nor comprised within sequences of visual images capable of being seen as moving pictures.

Amendments (Textual)

F113. Words in s. 362. (1) substituted (1.10.2013) by The Broadcasting and Communications (Amendment) Regulations 2013 (S.I. 2013/2217), regs. 1, 7

F114. Words in s. 362. (1) inserted (16.4.2010) by The Audiovisual Media Services (Product Placement) Regulations 2010 (S.I. 2010/831), regs. 1. (1), 6

F115. Words in s. 362. (1) omitted (19.12.2009) by virtue of Audiovisual Media Services Regulations 2009 (S.I. 2009/2979), regs. 1. (1), 10

Modifications etc. (not altering text)

C16. S. 362. (2)(3) applied by 1990 c. 42, s. 202. (6. A) (as inserted (29.12.2003) by Communications Act 2003 (c. 21), s. 411. (2), Sch. 15 para. 68. (3) (with Sch. 18); S.I. 2003/3142, art. 3. (1), Sch. 1 (with art. 11))

Commencement Information

I179. S. 362 in force at 25.7.2003 by S.I. 2003/1900, art. 2. (1), Sch. 1 (with art. 6)

Supplemental provisions of Part 3

360. Amendments of the 1990 and 1996 Acts

(1) In section 201 of the 1990 Act (programme services), in subsection (1)—

(a) for paragraphs (a) to (bb) there shall be substituted—

"(aa)any service which is a programme service within the meaning of the Communications Act 2003;"

(b) in paragraph (c), for "a telecommunication system" there shall be substituted " an electronic communications network (within the meaning of the Communications Act 2003) ".

(2) For subsection (2) of that section there shall be substituted—

"(2. A)Subsection (1)(c) does not apply to so much of a service consisting only of sound programmes as—

(a) is a two-way service (within the meaning of section 248. (4) of the Communications Act 2003);

(b) satisfies the conditions in section 248. (5) of that Act; or

(c) is provided for the purpose only of being received by persons who have qualified as users of the service by reason of being persons who fall within paragraph (a) or (b) of section 248. (7) of that Act.

(2. B)Subsection (1)(c) does not apply to so much of a service not consisting only of sound programmes as—

(a) is a two-way service (within the meaning of section 232 of the Communications Act 2003);

(b) satisfies the conditions in section 233. (5) of that Act; or

(c) is provided for the purpose only of being received by persons who have qualified as users of the service by reason of being persons who fall within paragraph (a) or (b) of section 233. (7) of that Act."

(3) Schedule 15 (which makes minor and consequential amendments of the 1990 Act and the 1996 Act for purposes connected with the other provisions of this Chapter) shall have effect.

Commencement Information

I1. S. 360. (1)(2) in force at 29.12.2003 by S.I. 2003/3142, art. 3. (1), Sch. 1 (with art. 11)

I2. S. 360. (3) in force at 25.7.2003 for specified purposes by S.I. 2003/1900, art. 2. (1), Sch. 1

I3. S. 360. (3) in force at 18.9.2003 for specified purposes by S.I. 2003/1900, art. 2. (2), Sch. 2

I4. S. 360. (3) in force at 29.12.2003 in so far as not already in force by S.I. 2003/3142, art. 3. (1), Sch. 1 (with art. 11)

361. Meaning of "available for reception by members of the public"

(1) The services that are to be taken for the purposes of this Part to be available for reception by members of the public include (subject to subsection (2)) any service which—

(a) is made available for reception, or is made available for reception in an intelligible form, only to persons who subscribe to the service (whether for a period or in relation to a particular occasion) or who otherwise request its provision; but

(b) is a service the facility of subscribing to which, or of otherwise requesting its provision, is offered or made available to members of the public.

[F1. (2)A service is not to be treated as available for reception by members of the public if it is an on-demand programme service.]

(6) References in this section to members of the public are references to members of the public in, or in any area of, any one or more countries or territories (which may or may not include the United Kingdom).

(7) The Secretary of State may by order modify any of the provisions of this section if it appears to him appropriate to do so having regard to any one or more of the following—

(a) the protection which, taking account of the means by which the programmes and services are received or may be accessed, is expected by members of the public as respects the contents of television programmes or sound programmes;

(b) the extent to which members of the public are able, before television programmes are watched or accessed, to make use of facilities for exercising control, by reference to the contents of the programmes, over what is watched or accessed;

(c) the practicability of applying different levels of regulation in relation to different services;

(d) the financial impact for providers of particular services of any modification of the provisions of that section; and

(e) technological developments that have occurred or are likely to occur.

(8) No order is to be made containing provision authorised by subsection (7) unless a draft of the order has been laid before Parliament and approved by a resolution of each House.

F2. (9). . . . .

Amendments (Textual)

F1. S. 361. (2) substituted for s. 361. (2)-(5) (19.12.2009) by Audiovisual Media Services Regulations 2009 (S.I. 2009/2979), regs. 1. (1), 9. (a)

F2. S. 361. (9) omitted (19.12.2009) by virtue of Audiovisual Media Services Regulations 2009 (S.I. 2009/2979), regs. 1. (1), 9. (b)

Commencement Information

I5. S. 361 in force at 25.7.2003 by S.I. 2003/1900, art. 2. (1), Sch. 1

362. Interpretation of Part 3.

(1) In this Part—

"additional radio service" means an additional service within the meaning given by section 114. (1) of the 1990 Act for the purposes of Part 3 of that Act;

"additional television service" (except in the expression "digital additional television service") means an additional service within the meaning given by section 48 of the 1990 Act for the purposes of Part 1 of the 1990 Act;

"analogue teletext service" is to be construed in accordance with section 218. (4);

"ancillary service" has the same meaning as it has, by virtue of section 24. (2) of the 1996 Act, in Part 1 of that Act;

"assistance for disabled people" means any of the following—

- subtitling;

- audio-description for the blind and partially sighted; and
- presentation in, or translation into, sign language;

"available for reception by members of the public" is to be construed in accordance with section 361;

"the BBC Charter and Agreement" means the following documents, or any one or more of them, so far as they are for the time being in force—
- a Royal Charter for the continuance of the BBC;
- supplemental Charters obtained by the BBC under such a Royal Charter;
- an agreement between the BBC and the Secretary of State entered into (whether before or after the passing of this Act) for purposes that include the regulation of activities carried on by the BBC;

"BBC company" means—
- a body corporate which is controlled by the BBC; or
- a body corporate in which the BBC or a body corporate controlled by the BBC is (to any extent) a participant;

"C4 company" means—
- a body corporate which is controlled by C4. C; or
- a body corporate in which C4. C or a body corporate controlled by C4. C is (to any extent) a participant;

"Channel 3", "Channel 4" and "Channel 5" each has the same meaning as in Part 1 of the 1990 Act (see section 71 of that Act);

"Channel 3 licence" means a licence to provide a Channel 3 service;

"a Channel 3 service" means a television broadcasting service comprised in Channel 3;

"digital additional sound service" means a digital additional service within the meaning given by section 63 of the 1996 Act for the purposes of Part 2 of that Act;

"digital additional television service" means a digital additional service within the meaning given by section 24. (1) of the 1996 Act for the purposes of Part 1 of that Act;

"the digital public teletext service" means so much of the public teletext service as consists of a service provided in digital form;

"digital sound programme licence" and "digital sound programme service" each has the same meaning as in Part 2 of the 1996 Act (see sections 40 and 72 of that Act);

"digital television programme service" means a digital programme service within the meaning given by section 1. (4) of the 1996 Act for the purposes of Part 1 of that Act;

[F3"EEA State" has the meaning given by Schedule 1 to the Interpretation Act 1978, and "another EEA State" means an EEA State other than the United Kingdom;]

"general multiplex service" means a multiplex service within the meaning of section 175 which is neither a television multiplex service nor a radio multiplex service;

"initial expiry date" has the meaning given by section 224;

"licensed public service channel" means any of the following services (whether provided for broadcasting in digital or in analogue form)—
- any Channel 3 service;
- Channel 4;
- Channel 5;

"local digital sound programme licence" and "local digital sound programme service" each has the same meaning as in Part 2 of the 1996 Act (see sections 60 and 72 of that Act);

"local radio multiplex licence" and "local radio multiplex service" each has the same meaning as in Part 2 of the 1996 Act (see sections 40 and 72 of that Act);

"local sound broadcasting licence" means a licence under Part 3 of the 1990 Act to provide a local sound broadcasting service;

"local sound broadcasting service" means a sound broadcasting service which, under subsection (4)(b) of section 245, is a local service for the purposes of that section;

"the M25 area" means the area the outer boundary of which is represented by the London Orbital Motorway (M25);

"national Channel 3 service" means a Channel 3 service provided between particular times of the day for more than one area for which regional Channel 3 services are provided;

"national digital sound programme service" has the same meaning as in Part 2 of the 1996 Act;

"national radio multiplex licence" and "national radio multiplex service" each has the same meaning as in Part 2 of the 1996 Act (see sections 40 and 72 of that Act);

"networking arrangements" has the meaning given by section 290;

"OFCOM's standards code" means any code or codes for the time being in force containing standards set by OFCOM under section 319 (whether originally or by way of any revision of any standards previously so set);

[F4"product placement" has the meaning given by paragraph 1 of Schedule 11. A;]

"provision", in relation to a service, is to be construed (subject to subsection (3)) in accordance with subsection (2), and cognate expressions are to be construed accordingly;

"the public teletext provider" means—

- subject to paragraph (b), the person holding the licence under section 219 to provide the public teletext service; and

- in relation to a time before the grant of the first licence to be granted under that section, the person holding the Broadcasting Act licence to provide the existing service (within the meaning of section 221);

"the public teletext service" means the service the provision of which is required to be secured in accordance with section 218;

"qualifying service" has the same meaning as in Part 1 of the 1996 Act (see section 2. (2) of that Act);

"radio licensable content service" has the meaning given by section 247;

"radio multiplex service" has the same meaning as (by virtue of section 258 of this Act) it has in Part 2 of the 1996 Act;

"radio programme service" means any of the following—

- a service the provision of which is licensed under Part 3 of the 1990 Act;

- a digital sound programme service the provision of which is licensed under Part 2 of the 1996 Act;

- a digital additional sound service the provision of which is licensed under section 64 of the 1996 Act;

"regional Channel 3 licence" means a licence under Part 1 of the 1990 Act to provide a regional Channel 3 service;

"regional Channel 3 service" means a Channel 3 service provided for a particular area determined under section 14. (2) of the 1990 Act;

"restricted television service" means any restricted service within the meaning given by section 42. A of the 1990 Act for the purposes of Part 1 of that Act;

"S4. C" and "S4. C Digital" means the services so described in section 204. (3);

"S4. C company" means—

- a body corporate which is controlled by the Welsh Authority; or

- a body corporate in which that Authority or a body corporate controlled by that Authority is (to any extent) a participant;

"simulcast radio service" means any simulcast radio service within the meaning given by section 41. (2) of the 1996 Act for the purposes of Part 2 of that Act;

"sound broadcasting service" has the same meaning as in Part 3 of the 1990 Act (see section 126 of that Act);

"standards objectives" has the meaning given by section 319. (2);

"subtitling" means subtitling for the deaf or hard of hearing, whether provided by means of a teletext service or otherwise;

"television broadcasting service" means (subject to subsection (4)) a service which—

- consists in a service of television programmes provided with a view to its being broadcast (whether in digital or in analogue form);

- is provided so as to be available for reception by members of the public; and

- is not—

a restricted television service;

a television multiplex service;

a service provided under the authority of a licence under Part 1 of the 1990 Act to provide a television licensable content service; or

a service provided under the authority of a licence under Part 1 of the 1996 Act to provide a digital television programme service;

"television licensable content service" has the meaning given by section 232 of this Act;

"television multiplex service" has meaning given by section 241. (1) of this Act to a multiplex service within the meaning of Part 1 of the 1996 Act;

"television programme service" means any of the following—

- a television broadcasting service;
- a television licensable content service;
- a digital television programme service;
- a restricted television service;

F5...

"text service" means any teletext service or other service in the case of which the visual images broadcast or distributed by means of the service consist wholly or mainly of non-representational images.

(2) In the case of any of the following services—

(a) a television broadcasting service or sound broadcasting service,

(b) the public teletext service;

(c) a television licensable content service or radio licensable content service,

(d) a digital television programme service or digital sound programme service,

(e) a restricted television service,

(f) an additional television service or additional radio service,

(g) a digital additional television service or a digital additional sound service,

the person, and the only person, who is to be treated for the purposes of this Part as providing the service is the person with general control over which programmes and other services and facilities are comprised in the service (whether or not he has control of the content of individual programmes or of the broadcasting or distribution of the service).

(3) For the purposes of this Part—

(a) the provision of a service by the BBC does not include its provision by a BBC company;

(b) the provision of a service by C4. C does not include its provision by a C4 company;

(c) the provision of a service by the Welsh Authority does not include its provision by an S4. C company;

and, accordingly, control that is or is capable of being exercised by the BBC, C4. C or the Welsh Authority over decisions by a BBC company, C4 company or S4. C company about what is to be comprised in a service shall be disregarded for the purposes of subsection (2).

(4) References in this Part to a television broadcasting service do not include references to any text service.

(5) References in this Part to imposing a charge on a person in respect of his reception of a service in, or in a part of, the United Kingdom include references to imposing charges—

(a) for his use of the service at a place in the United Kingdom or in that part of it;

(b) for an entitlement of his to receive it at such place;

(c) for the use of a facility by means of which he exercises such an entitlement; or

(d) for the service's being made available for reception by him at such a place.

(6) In subsection (1) "controlled" and "participant" each has the same meaning as in Schedule 2 to the 1990 Act.

(7) In this section "non-representational images" means visual images which are neither still pictures nor comprised within sequences of visual images capable of being seen as moving pictures.

Amendments (Textual)

F3. Words in s. 362. (1) substituted (1.10.2013) by The Broadcasting and Communications (Amendment) Regulations 2013 (S.I. 2013/2217), regs. 1, 7

F4. Words in s. 362. (1) inserted (16.4.2010) by The Audiovisual Media Services (Product Placement) Regulations 2010 (S.I. 2010/831), regs. 1. (1), 6

F5. Words in s. 362. (1) omitted (19.12.2009) by virtue of Audiovisual Media Services Regulations 2009 (S.I. 2009/2979), regs. 1. (1), 10

Modifications etc. (not altering text)

C1. S. 362. (2)(3) applied by 1990 c. 42, s. 202. (6. A) (as inserted (29.12.2003) by Communications Act 2003 (c. 21), s. 411. (2), Sch. 15 para. 68. (3) (with Sch. 18); S.I. 2003/3142, art. 3. (1), Sch. 1 (with art. 11))

Commencement Information

I6. S. 362 in force at 25.7.2003 by S.I. 2003/1900, art. 2. (1), Sch. 1 (with art. 6)

Interpretation of Part 3

362. Interpretation of Part 3.

(1) In this Part—

"additional radio service" means an additional service within the meaning given by section 114. (1) of the 1990 Act for the purposes of Part 3 of that Act;

"additional television service" (except in the expression "digital additional television service") means an additional service within the meaning given by section 48 of the 1990 Act for the purposes of Part 1 of the 1990 Act;

"analogue teletext service" is to be construed in accordance with section 218. (4);

"ancillary service" has the same meaning as it has, by virtue of section 24. (2) of the 1996 Act, in Part 1 of that Act;

"assistance for disabled people" means any of the following—

- subtitling;
- audio-description for the blind and partially sighted; and
- presentation in, or translation into, sign language;

"available for reception by members of the public" is to be construed in accordance with section 361;

"the BBC Charter and Agreement" means the following documents, or any one or more of them, so far as they are for the time being in force—

- a Royal Charter for the continuance of the BBC;
- supplemental Charters obtained by the BBC under such a Royal Charter;
- an agreement between the BBC and the Secretary of State entered into (whether before or after the passing of this Act) for purposes that include the regulation of activities carried on by the BBC;

"BBC company" means—

- a body corporate which is controlled by the BBC; or
- a body corporate in which the BBC or a body corporate controlled by the BBC is (to any extent) a participant;

"C4 company" means—

- a body corporate which is controlled by C4. C; or
- a body corporate in which C4. C or a body corporate controlled by C4. C is (to any extent) a participant;

"Channel 3", "Channel 4" and "Channel 5" each has the same meaning as in Part 1 of the 1990 Act (see section 71 of that Act);

"Channel 3 licence" means a licence to provide a Channel 3 service;

"a Channel 3 service" means a television broadcasting service comprised in Channel 3;

"digital additional sound service" means a digital additional service within the meaning given by section 63 of the 1996 Act for the purposes of Part 2 of that Act;

"digital additional television service" means a digital additional service within the meaning given by section 24. (1) of the 1996 Act for the purposes of Part 1 of that Act;

"the digital public teletext service" means so much of the public teletext service as consists of a service provided in digital form;

"digital sound programme licence" and "digital sound programme service" each has the same meaning as in Part 2 of the 1996 Act (see sections 40 and 72 of that Act);

"digital television programme service" means a digital programme service within the meaning given by section 1. (4) of the 1996 Act for the purposes of Part 1 of that Act;

[F1"EEA State" has the meaning given by Schedule 1 to the Interpretation Act 1978, and "another EEA State" means an EEA State other than the United Kingdom;]

"general multiplex service" means a multiplex service within the meaning of section 175 which is neither a television multiplex service nor a radio multiplex service;

"initial expiry date" has the meaning given by section 224;

"licensed public service channel" means any of the following services (whether provided for broadcasting in digital or in analogue form)—
    - any Channel 3 service;
    - Channel 4;
    - Channel 5;

"local digital sound programme licence" and "local digital sound programme service" each has the same meaning as in Part 2 of the 1996 Act (see sections 60 and 72 of that Act);

"local radio multiplex licence" and "local radio multiplex service" each has the same meaning as in Part 2 of the 1996 Act (see sections 40 and 72 of that Act);

"local sound broadcasting licence" means a licence under Part 3 of the 1990 Act to provide a local sound broadcasting service;

"local sound broadcasting service" means a sound broadcasting service which, under subsection (4)(b) of section 245, is a local service for the purposes of that section;

"the M25 area" means the area the outer boundary of which is represented by the London Orbital Motorway (M25);

"national Channel 3 service" means a Channel 3 service provided between particular times of the day for more than one area for which regional Channel 3 services are provided;

"national digital sound programme service" has the same meaning as in Part 2 of the 1996 Act;

"national radio multiplex licence" and "national radio multiplex service" each has the same meaning as in Part 2 of the 1996 Act (see sections 40 and 72 of that Act);

"networking arrangements" has the meaning given by section 290;

"OFCOM's standards code" means any code or codes for the time being in force containing standards set by OFCOM under section 319 (whether originally or by way of any revision of any standards previously so set);

[F2"product placement" has the meaning given by paragraph 1 of Schedule 11. A;]

"provision", in relation to a service, is to be construed (subject to subsection (3)) in accordance with subsection (2), and cognate expressions are to be construed accordingly;

"the public teletext provider" means—
    - subject to paragraph (b), the person holding the licence under section 219 to provide the public teletext service; and
    - in relation to a time before the grant of the first licence to be granted under that section, the person holding the Broadcasting Act licence to provide the existing service (within the meaning of section 221);

"the public teletext service" means the service the provision of which is required to be secured in accordance with section 218;

"qualifying service" has the same meaning as in Part 1 of the 1996 Act (see section 2. (2) of that Act);

"radio licensable content service" has the meaning given by section 247;

"radio multiplex service" has the same meaning as (by virtue of section 258 of this Act) it has in Part 2 of the 1996 Act;

"radio programme service" means any of the following—
- a service the provision of which is licensed under Part 3 of the 1990 Act;
- a digital sound programme service the provision of which is licensed under Part 2 of the 1996 Act;
- a digital additional sound service the provision of which is licensed under section 64 of the 1996 Act;

"regional Channel 3 licence" means a licence under Part 1 of the 1990 Act to provide a regional Channel 3 service;

"regional Channel 3 service" means a Channel 3 service provided for a particular area determined under section 14. (2) of the 1990 Act;

"restricted television service" means any restricted service within the meaning given by section 42. A of the 1990 Act for the purposes of Part 1 of that Act;

"S4. C" and "S4. C Digital" means the services so described in section 204. (3);

"S4. C company" means—
- a body corporate which is controlled by the Welsh Authority; or
- a body corporate in which that Authority or a body corporate controlled by that Authority is (to any extent) a participant;

"simulcast radio service" means any simulcast radio service within the meaning given by section 41. (2) of the 1996 Act for the purposes of Part 2 of that Act;

"sound broadcasting service" has the same meaning as in Part 3 of the 1990 Act (see section 126 of that Act);

"standards objectives" has the meaning given by section 319. (2);

"subtitling" means subtitling for the deaf or hard of hearing, whether provided by means of a teletext service or otherwise;

"television broadcasting service" means (subject to subsection (4)) a service which—
- consists in a service of television programmes provided with a view to its being broadcast (whether in digital or in analogue form);
- is provided so as to be available for reception by members of the public; and
- is not—

a restricted television service;

a television multiplex service;

a service provided under the authority of a licence under Part 1 of the 1990 Act to provide a television licensable content service; or

a service provided under the authority of a licence under Part 1 of the 1996 Act to provide a digital television programme service;

"television licensable content service" has the meaning given by section 232 of this Act;

"television multiplex service" has meaning given by section 241. (1) of this Act to a multiplex service within the meaning of Part 1 of the 1996 Act;

"television programme service" means any of the following—
- a television broadcasting service;
- a television licensable content service;
- a digital television programme service;
- a restricted television service;

F3...

"text service" means any teletext service or other service in the case of which the visual images broadcast or distributed by means of the service consist wholly or mainly of non-representational images.

(2) In the case of any of the following services—
(a) a television broadcasting service or sound broadcasting service,
(b) the public teletext service;
(c) a television licensable content service or radio licensable content service,
(d) a digital television programme service or digital sound programme service,
(e) a restricted television service,

(f) an additional television service or additional radio service,

(g) a digital additional television service or a digital additional sound service,

the person, and the only person, who is to be treated for the purposes of this Part as providing the service is the person with general control over which programmes and other services and facilities are comprised in the service (whether or not he has control of the content of individual programmes or of the broadcasting or distribution of the service).

(3) For the purposes of this Part—

(a) the provision of a service by the BBC does not include its provision by a BBC company;

(b) the provision of a service by C4. C does not include its provision by a C4 company;

(c) the provision of a service by the Welsh Authority does not include its provision by an S4. C company;

and, accordingly, control that is or is capable of being exercised by the BBC, C4. C or the Welsh Authority over decisions by a BBC company, C4 company or S4. C company about what is to be comprised in a service shall be disregarded for the purposes of subsection (2).

(4) References in this Part to a television broadcasting service do not include references to any text service.

(5) References in this Part to imposing a charge on a person in respect of his reception of a service in, or in a part of, the United Kingdom include references to imposing charges—

(a) for his use of the service at a place in the United Kingdom or in that part of it;

(b) for an entitlement of his to receive it at such place;

(c) for the use of a facility by means of which he exercises such an entitlement; or

(d) for the service's being made available for reception by him at such a place.

(6) In subsection (1) "controlled" and "participant" each has the same meaning as in Schedule 2 to the 1990 Act.

(7) In this section "non-representational images" means visual images which are neither still pictures nor comprised within sequences of visual images capable of being seen as moving pictures.

Amendments (Textual)

F1. Words in s. 362. (1) substituted (1.10.2013) by The Broadcasting and Communications (Amendment) Regulations 2013 (S.I. 2013/2217), regs. 1, 7

F2. Words in s. 362. (1) inserted (16.4.2010) by The Audiovisual Media Services (Product Placement) Regulations 2010 (S.I. 2010/831), regs. 1. (1), 6

F3. Words in s. 362. (1) omitted (19.12.2009) by virtue of Audiovisual Media Services Regulations 2009 (S.I. 2009/2979), regs. 1. (1), 10

Modifications etc. (not altering text)

C1. S. 362. (2)(3) applied by 1990 c. 42, s. 202. (6. A) (as inserted (29.12.2003) by Communications Act 2003 (c. 21), s. 411. (2), Sch. 15 para. 68. (3) (with Sch. 18); S.I. 2003/3142, art. 3. (1), Sch. 1 (with art. 11))

Commencement Information

I1. S. 362 in force at 25.7.2003 by S.I. 2003/1900, art. 2. (1), Sch. 1 (with art. 6)

Part 4. Licensing of TV reception

Part 4. Licensing of TV reception

363. Licence required for use of TV receiver

(1) A television receiver must not be installed or used unless the installation and use of the receiver is authorised by a licence under this Part.

(2) A person who installs or uses a television receiver in contravention of subsection (1) is guilty of an offence.

(3) A person with a television receiver in his possession or under his control who—

(a) intends to install or use it in contravention of subsection (1), or

(b) knows, or has reasonable grounds for believing, that another person intends to install or use it in contravention of that subsection,

is guilty of an offence.

(4) A person guilty of an offence under this section shall be liable, on summary conviction, to a fine not exceeding level 3 on the standard scale.

(5) Subsection (1) is not contravened by anything done in the course of the business of a dealer in television receivers solely for one or more of the following purposes—

(a) installing a television receiver on delivery;

(b) demonstrating, testing or repairing a television receiver.

(6) The Secretary of State may by regulations exempt from the requirement of a licence under subsection (1) the installation or use of television receivers—

(a) of such descriptions,

(b) by such persons,

(c) in such circumstances, and

(d) for such purposes,

as may be provided for in the regulations.

(7) Regulations under subsection (6) may make any exemption for which such regulations provide subject to compliance with such conditions as may be specified in the regulations.

Commencement Information

11. S. 363 in force at 1.4.2004 by S.I. 2003/3142, art. 4. (2), Sch. 2 (with art. 11) (as amended (8.3.2004) by S.I. 2004/697, art. 2. (3))

364. TV licences

(1) A licence for the purposes of section 363 ("a TV licence")—

(a) may be issued by the BBC subject to such restrictions and conditions as the BBC think fit; and

(b) must be issued subject to such restrictions and conditions as the Secretary of State may require by a direction to the BBC.

(2) The matters to which the restrictions and conditions subject to which a TV licence may be issued may relate include, in particular—

(a) the description of television receivers that may be installed and used under the licence;

(b) the persons authorised by the licence to install and use a television receiver;

(c) the places where the installation and use of the television receiver is authorised by the licence;

(d) the circumstances in which the installation and use of such a receiver is so authorised;

(e) the purposes for which the installation and use of such a receiver is so authorised;

(f) the use of such receiver in a manner that causes, or may cause, interference (within the meaning of [F1the Wireless Telegraphy Act 2006]) with wireless telegraphy.

(3) The restrictions and conditions subject to which a TV licence may be issued do not include—

(a) a provision conferring a power of entry to any premises; or

(b) a provision prohibited by a direction to the BBC by the Secretary of State.

(4) A TV licence shall continue in force, unless previously revoked by the BBC, for such period as may be specified in the licence.

(5) The BBC may revoke or modify a TV licence, or the restrictions or conditions of such a licence—

(a) by a notice to the holder of the licence; or

(b) by a general notice published in such manner as may be specified in the licence.

(6) It shall be the duty of the BBC to exercise their power under subsection (5) to revoke or modify a TV licence, or any of its restrictions or conditions, if they are directed to do so by the Secretary of State.

(7) A direction by the Secretary of State under this section may be given either generally in relation to all TV licences (or all TV licences of a particular description) or in relation to a particular licence.

(8) A notice under subsection (5)(a) must be given—

(a) in the manner specified in the licence; or

(b) if no manner of service is so specified, in the manner authorised by section 394.

(9) For the purposes of the application, in relation to the giving of such a notice, of—

(a) section 394; and

(b) section 7 of the Interpretation Act 1978 (c. 30) (service by post) in its application for the purposes of that section,

a person's proper address is any address where he is authorised by a TV licence to install or use a TV receiver or, if there is no such address, his last known address.

Amendments (Textual)

F1. Words in s. 364. (2)(f) substituted (8.2.2007) by Wireless Telegraphy Act 2006 (c. 36), s. 126. (2), Sch. 7 para. 29

Commencement Information

I2. S. 364 in force at 1.4.2004 by S.I. 2003/3142, art. 4. (2), Sch. 2 (with art. 11) (as amended (8.3.2004) by S.I. 2004/697, art. 2. (3))

365. TV licence fees

(1) A person to whom a TV licence is issued shall be liable to pay—

(a) on the issue of the licence (whether initially or by way of renewal), and

(b) in such other circumstances as regulations made by the Secretary of State may provide,

such sum (if any) as may be provided for by any such regulations.

(2) Sums which a person is liable to pay by virtue of regulations under subsection (1) must be paid to the BBC and are to be recoverable by them accordingly.

(3) The BBC are entitled, in such cases as they may determine, to make refunds of sums received by them by virtue of regulations under this section.

(4) Regulations under this section may include provision—

(a) for the means by which an entitlement to a concession must be established; and

(b) for the payment of sums by means of an instalment scheme set out in the regulations.

(5) The reference to a concession in subsection (4) is a reference to any concession under which a person is, on the satisfaction of specified requirements—

(a) exempted from the liability to pay a sum in respect of a TV licence; or

(b) required to pay only a reduced sum in respect of such a licence.

(6) The consent of the Treasury shall be required for the making of any regulations under this section by the Secretary of State.

(7) Subject to subsection (8), sums received by the BBC by virtue of any regulations under this section must be paid into the Consolidated Fund.

(8) The BBC may retain, out of the sums received by them by virtue of regulations under this section, any sums they require for making refunds of sums so received.

Commencement Information

I3. S. 365 in force at 1.4.2004 by S.I. 2003/3142, art. 4. (2), Sch. 2 (with art. 11) (as amended (8.3.2004) by S.I. 2004/697, art. 2. (3))

366. Powers to enforce TV licensing

(1) If a justice of the peace, a sheriff in Scotland or a lay magistrate in Northern Ireland is satisfied

by information on oath that there are reasonable grounds for believing—

(a) that an offence under section 363 has been or is being committed,

(b) that evidence of the commission of the offence is likely to be on premises specified in the information, or in a vehicle so specified, and

(c) that one or more of the conditions set out in subsection (3) is satisfied,

he may grant a warrant under this section.

(2) A warrant under this section is a warrant authorising any one or more persons authorised for the purpose by the BBC or by OFCOM—

(a) to enter the premises or vehicle at any time (either alone or in the company of one or more constables); and

(b) to search the premises or vehicle and examine and test any television receiver found there.

(3) Those conditions are—

(a) that there is no person entitled to grant entry to the premises or vehicle with whom it is practicable to communicate;

(b) that there is no person entitled to grant access to the evidence with whom it is practicable to communicate;

(c) that entry to the premises or vehicle will not be granted unless a warrant is produced;

(d) that the purpose of the search may be frustrated or seriously prejudiced unless the search is carried out by a person who secures entry immediately upon arriving at the premises or vehicle.

(4) A person is not to enter premises or a vehicle in pursuance of a warrant under this section at any time more than one month after the day on which the warrant was granted.

(5) The powers conferred by a warrant under this section on a person authorised by OFCOM are exercisable in relation only to a contravention or suspected contravention of a condition of a TV licence relating to interference with wireless telegraphy.

(6) A person authorised by the BBC, or by OFCOM, to exercise a power conferred by a warrant under this section may (if necessary) use such force as may be reasonable in the exercise of that power.

(7) Where a person has the power by virtue of a warrant under this section to examine or test any television receiver found on any premises, or in any vehicle, it shall be the duty—

(a) of a person who is on the premises or in the vehicle, and

(b) in the case of a vehicle, of a person who has charge of it or is present when it is searched,

to give the person carrying out the examination or test all such assistance as that person may reasonably require for carrying it out.

(8) A person is guilty of an offence if he—

(a) intentionally obstructs a person in the exercise of any power conferred on that person by virtue of a warrant under this section; or

(b) without reasonable excuse, fails to give any assistance that he is under a duty to give by virtue of subsection (7).

(9) A person guilty of an offence under subsection (8) shall be liable, on summary conviction, to a fine not exceeding level 5 on the standard scale.

(10) In this section—

"interference", in relation to wireless telegraphy, has the same meaning as in [F2the Wireless Telegraphy Act 2006] ; and

"vehicle" includes vessel, aircraft or hovercraft.

(11) In the application of this section to Scotland, the reference in subsection (1) to information on oath shall have effect as a reference to evidence on oath.

(12) In the application of this section to Northern Ireland, the reference in subsection (1) to a lay magistrate shall have effect, in relation to times before the coming into force of sections 9 and 10 of the Justice (Northern Ireland) Act 2002 (c. 26), as a reference to a justice of the peace.

Amendments (Textual)

F2. Words in s. 366. (10) substituted (8.2.2007) by Wireless Telegraphy Act 2006 (c. 36), s. 126. (2), Sch. 7 para. 30

Commencement Information

F3367. Interpretation of provisions about dealer notification

. . . .
Amendments (Textual)
F3. S. 367 repealed (25.6.2013) by Enterprise and Regulatory Reform Act 2013 (c. 24), s. 103. (2), Sch. 21 para. 2
Commencement Information
I5. S. 367 in force at 9.3.2004 for specified purposes by S.I. 2003/3142, art. 4. (1. A) (with art. 11) (as inserted (8.3.2004) by S.I. 2004/697, art. 2. (2))
I6. S. 367 in force at 1.4.2004 in so far as not already in force by S.I. 2003/3142, art. 4. (2), Sch. 2 (with art. 11) (as amended (8.3.2004) by S.I. 2004/697, art. 2. (3))

368. Meanings of "television receiver" and "use"

(1) In this Part "television receiver" means any apparatus of a description specified in regulations made by the Secretary of State setting out the descriptions of apparatus that are to be television receivers for the purposes of this Part.
(2) Regulations under this section defining a television receiver may provide for references to such a receiver to include references to software used in association with apparatus.
[F4. (3)References in this Part to using a television receiver are references to using it for—
    (a) receiving all or any part of any television programme, or
    (b) receiving all or any part of a programme included in an on-demand programme service which is provided by the BBC,
and that reference to the provision of an on-demand programme service by the BBC is to be read in accordance with section 368. R(5) and (6).]
(4) The power to make regulations under this section defining a television receiver includes power to modify subsection (3).
Amendments (Textual)
F4. S. 368. (3) substituted (1.9.2016) by The Communications (Television Licensing) (Amendment) Regulations 2016 (S.I. 2016/704), regs. 1. (1), 9. (1) (with reg. 9. (2))
Commencement Information
I7. S. 368 in force at 1.4.2004 by S.I. 2003/3142, art. 4. (2), Sch. 2 (with art. 11) (as amended (8.3.2004) by S.I. 2004/697, art. 2. (3))

PART 4A ON-DEMAND PROGRAMME SERVICES

[F1. PART 4. AON-DEMAND PROGRAMME SERVICES

Amendments (Textual)
F1. Pt. 4. A inserted (19.12.2009) by Audiovisual Media Services Regulations 2009 (S.I. 2009/2979), regs. 1. (1), 2

368. AMeaning of "on-demand programme service"

(1) For the purposes of this Act, a service is an "on-demand programme service" if—

(a) its principal purpose is the provision of programmes the form and content of which are comparable to the form and content of programmes normally included in television programme services;

(b) access to it is on-demand;

(c) there is a person who has editorial responsibility for it;

(d) it is made available by that person for use by members of the public; and

(e) that person is under the jurisdiction of the United Kingdom for the purposes of the Audiovisual Media Services Directive.

(2) Access to a service is on-demand if—

(a) the service enables the user to view, at a time chosen by the user, programmes selected by the user from among the programmes included in the service; and

(b) the programmes viewed by the user are received by the user by means of an electronic communications network (whether before or after the user has selected which programmes to view).

(3) For the purposes of subsection (2)(a), the fact that a programme may be viewed only within a period specified by the provider of the service does not prevent the time at which it is viewed being one chosen by the user.

(4) A person has editorial responsibility for a service if that person has general control—

(a) over what programmes are included in the range of programmes offered to users; and

(b) over the manner in which the programmes are organised in that range;

and the person need not have control of the content of individual programmes or of the broadcasting or distribution of the service (and see section 368. R(6)).

(5) If an on-demand programme service ("the main service") offers users access to a relevant ancillary service, the relevant ancillary service is to be treated for the purposes of this Part as a part of the main service.

(6) In subsection (5), "relevant ancillary service" means a service or facility that consists of or gives access to assistance for disabled people in relation to some or all of the programmes included in the main service.

(7) In this section "assistance for disabled people" has the same meaning as in Part 3.

368. BThe appropriate regulatory authority

(1) OFCOM may designate any body corporate to be, to the extent provided by the designation, the appropriate regulatory authority for the purposes of any provision of this Part, subject to subsection (9).

(2) To the extent that no body is designated for a purpose, OFCOM is the appropriate regulatory authority for that purpose.

(3) Where a body is designated for a purpose, OFCOM may act as the appropriate regulatory authority for that purpose concurrently with or in place of that body.

(4) OFCOM may provide a designated body with assistance in connection with any of the functions of the body under this Part.

(5) A designation may in particular—

(a) provide for a body to be the appropriate regulatory authority in relation to on-demand programme services of a specified description;

(b) provide that a function of the appropriate regulatory authority is exercisable by the designated body—

(i) to such extent as may be specified;

(ii) either generally or in such circumstances as may be specified; and

(iii) either unconditionally or subject to such conditions as may be specified.

(6) The conditions that may be specified pursuant to subsection (5)(b)(iii) include a condition to the effect that a function may, generally or in specified circumstances, be exercised by the body

only with the agreement of OFCOM.

(7) A designation has effect for such period as may be specified and may be revoked by OFCOM at any time.

(8) OFCOM must publish any designation in such manner as they consider appropriate for bringing it to the attention of persons who, in their opinion, are likely to be affected by it.

(9) OFCOM may not designate a body unless, as respects that designation, they are satisfied that the body—

    (a) is a fit and proper body to be designated;

    (b) has consented to being designated;

    (c) has access to financial resources that are adequate to ensure the effective performance of its functions as the appropriate regulatory authority;

    (d) is sufficiently independent of providers of on-demand programme services; and

    (e) will, in performing any function to which the designation relates, have regard in all cases—

(i) to the principles under which regulatory activities should be transparent, accountable, proportionate, consistent and targeted only at cases in which action is needed; and

(ii) to such of the matters mentioned in section 3. (4) as appear to the body to be relevant in the circumstances.

(10) Subject to any enactment or rule of law restricting the disclosure or use of information by OFCOM or by a designated body—

    (a) a designated body may supply information to another designated body for use by that other body in connection with any of its functions as the appropriate regulatory authority;

    (b) a designated body may supply information to OFCOM for use by OFCOM in connection with any of their functions under this Part;

    (c) OFCOM may supply information to a designated body for use by that body in connection with any of its functions as the appropriate regulatory authority.

    [F2. (d)OFCOM may supply information to the video works authority, within the meaning of section 368. E, for use by the video works authority in connection with functions of OFCOM as the appropriate regulatory authority;

    (e) a designated body may supply information to the video works authority, within the meaning of section 368. E, for use by the video works authority in connection with functions of the designated body as the appropriate regulatory authority.]

(11) In carrying out their functions as the appropriate regulatory authority, a designated body may carry out, commission or support (financially or otherwise) research.

(12) In this section—

"designation" means a designation under this section and cognate expressions are to be construed accordingly;

"specified" means specified in a designation.

Amendments (Textual)

F2. S. 368. B(10)(d)(e) inserted (1.12.2014) by The Audiovisual Media Services Regulations 2014 (S.I. 2014/2916), regs. 1. (1), 3

[F3. Notification by providers

Amendments (Textual)

F3. Ss. 368. BA, 368. BB and cross-heading inserted (18.3.2010) by The Audiovisual Media Services Regulations 2010 (S.I. 2010/419), regs. 1. (1), 4

368. BAAdvance notification to appropriate regulatory authority

(1) A person must not provide an on-demand programme service unless, before beginning to provide it, that person has given a notification to the appropriate regulatory authority of the person's intention to provide that service.

(2) A person who has given a notification for the purposes of subsection (1) must, before—
   (a) providing the notified service with any significant differences; or
   (b) ceasing to provide it,
give a notification to the appropriate regulatory authority of the differences or (as the case may be) of an intention to cease to provide the service.
(3) A notification for the purposes of this section must—
   (a) be sent to the appropriate regulatory authority in such manner as the authority may require; and
   (b) contain all such information as the authority may require.

368. BBEnforcement of section 368. BA

(1) Where the appropriate regulatory authority determine that the provider of an on-demand programme service has contravened section 368. BA, they may do one or both of the following—
   (a) give the provider an enforcement notification under this section;
   (b) impose a penalty on the provider in accordance with section 368. J.
(2) The appropriate regulatory authority must not make a determination as mentioned in subsection (1) unless there are reasonable grounds for believing that a contravention of section 368. BA has occurred and they have allowed the provider an opportunity to make representations about that apparent contravention.
(3) An enforcement notification under this section is a notification which specifies the determination made as mentioned in subsection (1) and imposes a requirement on the provider to take all such steps for remedying the contravention of section 368. BA as may be specified in the notification.
(4) An enforcement notification must—
   (a) include reasons for the appropriate regulatory authority's decision to give the enforcement notification, and
   (b) fix a reasonable period for taking the steps required by the notification.
(5) It is the duty of a person to whom an enforcement notification has been given to comply with it.
(6) That duty is enforceable in civil proceedings by the appropriate regulatory authority—
   (a) for an injunction;
   (b) for specific performance of a statutory duty under section 45 of the Court of Session Act 1988; or
   (c) for any other appropriate remedy or relief.]

Duties of the appropriate regulatory authority

368. CDuties of the appropriate regulatory authority

(1) It is the duty of the appropriate regulatory authority to take such steps as appear to them best calculated to secure that every provider of an on-demand programme service complies with the requirements of section 368. D.
(2) The appropriate regulatory authority must encourage providers of on-demand programme services to ensure that their services are progressively made more accessible to people with disabilities affecting their sight or hearing or both.
(3) The appropriate regulatory authority must ensure that providers of on-demand programme services promote, where practicable and by appropriate means, production of and access to European works (within the meaning given in Article 1. (n) of the Audiovisual Media Services Directive).

(4) The appropriate regulatory authority must encourage providers of on-demand programme services to develop codes of conduct regarding standards concerning the appropriate promotion of food or beverages by sponsorship of, or in advertising which accompanies or is included in, children's programmes.

Duties of service providers

368. DDuties of service providers

(1) The provider of an on-demand programme service must ensure that the service complies with the requirements of sections 368. E to 368. H.

(2) The provider of an on-demand programme service ("P") must supply the following information to users of the service—

(a) P's name;

(b) P's address;

(c) P's electronic address;

(d) the name, address and electronic address of any body which is the appropriate regulatory authority for any purpose in relation to P or the service that P provides.

(3) The provider of an on-demand programme service must—

[F4. (za)pay to the appropriate regulatory authority such fee as that authority may require under section 368. NA;

(zb) retain a copy of every programme included in the service for at least forty-two days after the day on which the programme ceases to be available for viewing;]

(a) comply with any requirement under section 368. O (provision of information);

(b) co-operate fully with the appropriate authority for any purpose within section 368. O(2) or (3).

[F5. (3. A)A copy of a programme retained for the purposes of subsection (3)(zb) must be of a standard and in a format which allows the programme to be viewed as it was made available for viewing.]

(4) In this section "electronic address" means an electronic address to which users may send electronic communications, and includes any number or address used for the purposes of receiving such communications.

Amendments (Textual)

F4. S. 368. D(3)(za)(zb) inserted (18.3.2010) by The Audiovisual Media Services Regulations 2010 (S.I. 2010/419), regs. 1. (1), 5. (1)

F5. S. 368. D(3. A) inserted (18.3.2010) by The Audiovisual Media Services Regulations 2010 (S.I. 2010/419), regs. 1. (1), 5. (2)

368. EHarmful material

(1) An on-demand programme service must not contain any material likely to incite hatred based on race, sex, religion or nationality.

[F6. (2)An on-demand programme service must not contain any prohibited material.

(3) "Prohibited material" means—

(a) a video work which the video works authority has determined for the purposes of the 1984 Act not to be suitable for a classification certificate to be issued in respect of it, or

(b) material whose nature is such that it is reasonable to expect that, if the material were contained in a video work submitted to the video works authority for a classification certificate, the video works authority would determine for those purposes that the video work was not suitable for a classification certificate to be issued in respect of it.

(4) An on-demand programme service must not contain any specially restricted material unless the material is made available in a manner which secures that persons under the age of 18 will not normally see or hear it.

(5) "Specially restricted material" means—

(a) a video work in respect of which the video works authority has issued a R18 classification certificate,

(b) material whose nature is such that it is reasonable to expect that, if the material were contained in a video work submitted to the video works authority for a classification certificate, the video works authority would issue a R18 classification certificate, or

(c) other material that might seriously impair the physical, mental or moral development of persons under the age of 18.

(6) In determining whether any material falls within subsection (3)(b) or (5)(b), regard must be had to any guidelines issued by the video works authority as to its policy in relation to the issue of classification certificates.

(7) In this section—

"the 1984 Act" means the Video Recordings Act 1984;

"classification certificate" has the same meaning as in the 1984 Act (see section 7 of that Act);

"R18 classification certificate" means a classification certificate containing the statement mentioned in section 7. (2)(c) of the 1984 Act that no video recording containing the video work is to be supplied other than in a licensed sex shop;

"the video works authority" means the person or persons designated under section 4. (1) of the 1984 Act as the authority responsible for making arrangements in respect of video works other than video games;

"video work" has the same meaning as in the 1984 Act (see section 1. (2) of that Act).]

Amendments (Textual)

F6. Ss. 368. E(2)-(7) substituted for s. 368. E(2) (1.12.2014) by The Audiovisual Media Services Regulations 2014 (S.I. 2014/2916), regs. 1. (1), 2

368. FAdvertising

(1) Advertising of the following products is prohibited in on-demand programme services—

(a) cigarettes or other tobacco products;

[F7. (aa)electronic cigarettes or electronic cigarette refill containers;]

(b) any prescription-only medicine.

(2) Advertising of alcoholic drinks is prohibited in on-demand programme services unless—

(a) it is not aimed at persons under the age of eighteen, and

(b) it does not encourage excessive consumption of such drinks.

(3) Advertising included in an on-demand programme service—

(a) must be readily recognisable as such, and

(b) must not use techniques which exploit the possibility of conveying a message subliminally or surreptitiously.

(4) Advertising included in an on-demand programme service must not—

(a) prejudice respect for human dignity;

(b) include or promote discrimination based on sex, racial or ethnic origin, nationality, religion or belief, disability, age or sexual orientation;

(c) encourage behaviour prejudicial to health or safety;

(d) encourage behaviour grossly prejudicial to the protection of the environment;

(e) cause physical or moral detriment to persons under the age of eighteen;

(f) directly exhort such persons to purchase or rent goods or services in a manner which exploits their inexperience or credulity;

(g) directly encourage such persons to persuade their parents or others to purchase or rent goods or services;

(h) exploit the trust of such persons in parents, teachers or others; or

(i) unreasonably show such persons in dangerous situations.

Amendments (Textual)

F7. S. 368. F(1)(aa) inserted (20.5.2016) by The Tobacco and Related Products Regulations 2016 (S.I. 2016/507), regs. 1. (2), 46. (2)

368. GSponsorship

(1) An on-demand programme service or a programme included in an on-demand programme service must not be sponsored—

(a) for the purpose of promoting cigarettes or other tobacco products, or

(b) by an undertaking whose principal activity is the manufacture or sale of cigarettes or other tobacco products.

[F8. (1. A)An on-demand programme service or a programme included in an on-demand programme service must not be sponsored for the purpose of promoting electronic cigarettes or electronic cigarette refill containers.]

(2) An on-demand programme service or a programme included in an on-demand programme service must not be sponsored for the purpose of promoting a prescription-only medicine.

(3) An on-demand programme service may not include a news programme or current affairs programme that is sponsored.

(4) Subsections (5) to (11) apply to an on-demand programme service that is sponsored or that includes any programme that is sponsored.

(5) The sponsoring of a service or programme must not influence the content of that service or programme in a way that affects the editorial independence of the provider of the service.

(6) Where a service or programme is sponsored for the purpose of promoting goods or services, the sponsored service or programme and sponsorship announcements relating to it must not directly encourage the purchase or rental of the goods or services, whether by making promotional reference to them or otherwise.

(7) Where a service or programme is sponsored for the purpose of promoting an alcoholic drink, the service or programme and sponsorship announcements relating to it must not—

(a) be aimed specifically at persons under the age of eighteen; or

(b) encourage the immoderate consumption of such drinks.

(8) A sponsored service must clearly inform users of the existence of a sponsorship agreement.

(9) The name of the sponsor and the logo or other symbol (if any) of the sponsor must be displayed at the beginning or end of a sponsored programme.

(10) Techniques which exploit the possibility of conveying a message subliminally or surreptitiously must not be used in a sponsorship announcement.

(11) A sponsorship announcement must not—

(a) prejudice respect for human dignity;

(b) include or promote discrimination based on sex, racial or ethnic origin, nationality, religion or belief, disability, age or sexual orientation;

(c) encourage behaviour prejudicial to health or safety;

(d) encourage behaviour grossly prejudicial to the protection of the environment;

(e) cause physical or moral detriment to persons under the age of eighteen;

(f) directly encourage such persons to persuade their parents or others to purchase or rent goods or services;

(g) exploit the trust of such persons in parents, teachers or others; or

(h) unreasonably show such persons in dangerous situations.

(12) For the purposes of this Part a programme included in an on-demand programme service is "sponsored" if a person ("the sponsor") other than—

(a) the provider of that service, or

(b) the producer of that programme,

has met some or all of the costs of the programme for the purpose of promoting the name, trademark, image, activities, services or products of the sponsor or of another person.

(13) But a programme is not sponsored if it falls within this section only by virtue of the inclusion of product placement (see section 368. H(1)) or prop placement (see section 368. H(2)).

(14) For the purposes of subsection (12) a person meets some or all of the costs of a programme included in a service only if that person makes a payment or provides other resources for the purpose of meeting or saving some or all of the costs of—

(a) producing that programme;

(b) transmitting that programme; or

(c) making that programme available as part of the service.

(15) For the purposes of this Part an on-demand programme service is "sponsored" if a person ("the sponsor") other than the provider of the service has met some or all of the costs of providing the service for the purpose of promoting the name, trademark, image, activities, services or products of the sponsor or another person.

(16) For the purposes of subsection (15) a person is not to be taken to have met some or all of the costs of providing a service only because a programme included in the service is sponsored by that person.

(17) In this section a "sponsorship announcement" means—

(a) anything included for the purpose of complying with subsection (8) or (9), and

(b) anything included at the same time as or otherwise in conjunction with anything within paragraph (a).

Amendments (Textual)

F8. S. 368. G(1. A) inserted (20.5.2016) by The Tobacco and Related Products Regulations 2016 (S.I. 2016/507), regs. 1. (2), 46. (3)

368. HProhibition of product placement and exceptions

(1) "Product placement", in relation to a programme included in an on-demand programme service, means the inclusion in the programme of, or of a reference to, a product, service or trade mark, where the inclusion—

(a) is for a commercial purpose,

(b) is in return for the making of any payment, or the giving of other valuable consideration, to any relevant provider or any connected person, and

(c) is not prop placement.

(2) "Prop placement", in relation to a programme included in an on-demand programme service, means the inclusion in the programme of, or of a reference to, a product, service or trade mark where—

(a) the provision of the product, service or trade mark has no significant value; and

(b) no relevant provider, or person connected with a relevant provider, has received any payment or other valuable consideration in relation to its inclusion in, or the reference to it in, the programme, disregarding the costs saved by including the product, service or trademark, or a reference to it, in the programme.

(3) Product placement is prohibited in children's programmes included in on-demand programme services.

(4) Product placement is prohibited in on-demand programme services if—

(a) it is of cigarettes or other tobacco products,

(b) it is by or on behalf of an undertaking whose principal activity is the manufacture or sale of cigarettes or other tobacco products, F9...

[F10. (ba)it is of electronic cigarettes or electronic cigarette refill containers, or]

(c) it is of prescription-only medicines.

(5) Product placement of alcoholic drinks must not —

(a) be aimed specifically at persons under the age of eighteen;

(b) encourage immoderate consumption of such drinks.

(6) Product placement is otherwise permitted in programmes included in on-demand programme services provided that—

(a) conditions A to F are met, and

(b) if subsection (14) applies, condition G is also met.

(7) Condition A is that the programme in which the product, service or trademark, or the reference to it, is included is—

(a) a film made for cinema;

(b) a film or series made for a television programme service or for an on-demand programme service;

(c) a sports programme; or

(d) a light entertainment programme.

(8) Condition B is that the product placement has not influenced the content of the programme in a way that affects the editorial independence of the provider of the service.

(9) Condition C is that the product placement does not directly encourage the purchase or rental of goods or services, whether by making promotional reference to those goods or services or otherwise.

(10) Condition D is that the programme does not give undue prominence to the products, services or trade marks concerned.

(11) Condition E is that the product placement does not use techniques which exploit the possibility of conveying a message subliminally or surreptitiously.

(12) Condition F is that the way in which the product, service or trade mark, or the reference to it, is included in the programme by way of product placement does not—

(a) prejudice respect for human dignity;

(b) promote discrimination based on sex, racial or ethnic origin, nationality, religion or belief, disability, age or sexual orientation;

(c) encourage behaviour prejudicial to health or safety;

(d) encourage behaviour grossly prejudicial to the protection of the environment;

(e) cause physical or moral detriment to persons under the age of eighteen;

(f) directly encourage such persons to persuade their parents or others to purchase or rent goods or services;

(g) exploit the trust of such persons in parents, teachers or others; or

(h) unreasonably show such persons in dangerous situations.

(13) Condition G is that the on-demand programme service in question signals appropriately the fact that product placement is contained in a programme, no less frequently than—

(a) at the start and end of such a programme, and

(b) in the case of an on-demand programme service which includes advertising breaks within it, at the recommencement of the programme after each such advertising break.

(14) This subsection applies where the programme featuring the product placement has been produced or commissioned by the provider of the service or any connected person.

(15) [F11. Subject to subsection (15. A),] This section applies only in relation to programmes the production of which begins after 19th December 2009.

[F12. (15. A)Subsection (4)(ba) applies only in relation to programmes the production of which begins after 19th May 2016.]

(16) In this section—

"connected" has the same meaning as it has in the Broadcasting Act 1990 by virtue of section 202 of that Act;

"film made for cinema" means a film made with a view to its being shown to the general public first in a cinema;

"producer", in relation to a programme, means the person by whom the arrangements necessary for the making of the programme are undertaken;

[F13"programme" does not include an advertisement;]

"relevant provider", in relation to a programme, means—

- the provider of the on-demand programme service in which the programme is included; and
- the producer of the programme;

"residual value" means any monetary or other economic value in the hands of the relevant provider other than the cost saving of including the product, service or trademark, or a reference to it, in a programme;

"significant value" means a residual value that is more than trivial; and

"trade mark", in relation to a business, includes any image (such as a logo) or sound commonly associated with that business or its products or services.

Amendments (Textual)

F9. Word in s. 368. H(4)(b) omitted (20.5.2016) by virtue of The Tobacco and Related Products Regulations 2016 (S.I. 2016/507), regs. 1. (2), 46. (4)(a)

F10. S. 368. H(4)(ba) inserted (20.5.2016) by The Tobacco and Related Products Regulations 2016 (S.I. 2016/507), regs. 1. (2), 46. (4)(b)

F11. Words in s. 368. H(15) inserted (20.5.2016) by The Tobacco and Related Products Regulations 2016 (S.I. 2016/507), regs. 1. (2), 46. (4)(c)

F12. S. 368. H(15. A) inserted (20.5.2016) by The Tobacco and Related Products Regulations 2016 (S.I. 2016/507), regs. 1. (2), 46. (4)(d)

F13. Words in s. 368. H(16) inserted (16.4.2010) by The Audiovisual Media Services (Product Placement) Regulations 2010 (S.I. 2010/831), regs. 1. (1), 7

368. IEnforcement of section 368. D

(1) Where the appropriate regulatory authority determine that a provider of an on-demand programme service is contravening or has contravened section 368. D they may do one or both of the following—

 (a) give the provider an enforcement notification under this section;

 (b) impose a financial penalty on the provider in accordance with section 368. J.

(2) The appropriate regulatory authority must not make a determination as mentioned in subsection (1) unless there are reasonable grounds for believing that a contravention of section 368. D is occurring or has occurred and they have allowed the provider an opportunity to make representations about that apparent contravention.

(3) An enforcement notification under this section is a notification which specifies the determination made as mentioned in subsection (1) and imposes requirements on the provider to take such steps for complying with section 368. D and for remedying the consequences of the contravention of that section as may be specified in the notification.

(4) The requirements specified in an enforcement notification may in particular include requirements to do one or more of the following—

 (a) cease providing or restrict access to–

(i) a specified programme, or

(ii) programmes of a specified description;

 (b) cease showing or restrict access to–

(i) a specified advertisement, or

(ii) advertisements of a specified description;

 (c) provide additional information to users of the service prior to the selection of a specified programme by the user for viewing;

 (d) show an advertisement only with specified modifications;

 (e) publish a correction in the form and place and at the time specified; or

 (f) publish a statement of the findings of the appropriate regulatory authority in the form and place and at the time specified.

(5) An enforcement notification must—

 (a) include reasons for the appropriate regulatory authority's decision to give the enforcement notification, and

(b) fix a reasonable period for the taking of the steps required by the notification.

(6) Where a provider is required by an enforcement notification to publish a correction or a statement of findings, the provider may publish with the correction or statement of findings a statement that it is published in pursuance of the enforcement notification.

(7) It is the duty of a provider to whom an enforcement notification has been given to comply with it.

(8) That duty is enforceable in civil proceedings by the appropriate regulatory authority—

(a) for an injunction;

(b) for specific performance of a statutory duty under section 45 of the Court of Session Act 1988; or

(c) for any other appropriate remedy or relief.

(9) If a provider to whom an enforcement notification has been given does not comply with it within the period fixed by the appropriate regulatory authority in that enforcement notification the appropriate regulatory authority may impose a financial penalty on that provider in accordance with section 368. J.

Financial penalties

368. JFinancial penalties

(1) The amount of a penalty imposed on a provider under section [F14368. BB or] 368. I is to be such amount not exceeding 5 per cent. of the provider's applicable qualifying revenue or £250,000 whichever is the greater amount, as the appropriate regulatory authority determine to be—

(a) appropriate; and

(b) proportionate to the contravention in respect of which it is imposed.

(2) In determining the amount of a penalty under subsection (1) the appropriate regulatory authority must have regard to any statement published by OFCOM under section 392 (guidelines to be followed in determining amount of penalties).

(3) The "applicable qualifying revenue", in relation to a provider, means—

(a) the qualifying revenue for the provider's last complete accounting period falling within the period during which the provider has been providing the service to which the contravention relates; or

(b) in relation to a person whose first complete accounting period falling within that period has not ended when the penalty is imposed, the amount that the appropriate regulatory authority estimate to be the qualifying revenue for that period.

(4) For the purposes of subsection (3) the "qualifying revenue" for an accounting period consists of the aggregate of all the amounts received or to be received by the provider of the service to which the contravention relates or by any connected person in the accounting period —

(a) for the inclusion in that service of advertisements, product placement and sponsorship; and

(b) in respect of charges made in that period for the provision of programmes included in that service.

(5) For the purposes of subsection (4), "connected" has the same meaning as it has in the Broadcasting Act 1990 by virtue of section 202 of that Act.

(6) A financial penalty imposed under this section—

(a) must be paid into the appropriate Consolidated Fund; and

(b) if not paid within the period fixed by the appropriate regulatory authority, is to be recoverable by the appropriate regulatory authority as a debt due to them from the person obliged to pay it.

(7) For the purposes of subsections (3) and (6)—

(a) the amount of a person's qualifying revenue for an accounting period, or

(b) the amount of any payment to be made into the appropriate Consolidated Fund by any person in respect of any such revenue,

is, in the event of a disagreement between the appropriate regulatory authority and that person, the amount determined by the appropriate regulatory authority.

(8) The references in this section to the payment of an amount into the appropriate Consolidated Fund—

(a) in the case of an amount received in respect of matters appearing to OFCOM to have no connection with Northern Ireland, is a reference to the payment of the amount into the Consolidated Fund of the United Kingdom;

(b) in the case of an amount received in respect of matters appearing to OFCOM to have a connection with Northern Ireland but no connection with the rest of the United Kingdom, is a reference to the payment of the amount into the Consolidated Fund of Northern Ireland; and

(c) in any other case, is a reference to the payment of the amount, in such proportions as OFCOM consider appropriate, into each of those Funds.

Amendments (Textual)

F14. Words in s. 368. J(1) inserted (18.3.2010) by The Audiovisual Media Services Regulations 2010 (S.I. 2010/419), regs. 1. (1), 7

Suspension or restriction of service

368. KSuspension or restriction of service for contraventions

(1) The appropriate regulatory authority must serve a notice under subsection (2) on a provider of an on-demand programme service if they are satisfied—

(a) that the provider is in contravention of section [F15368. BA or] 368. D;

(b) that an attempt to secure compliance with section [F16368. BA or] 368. D [F17 (as the case may be)] by the imposition of one or more financial penalties or enforcement notifications under section [F18368. BB or] 368. I has failed; and

(c) that the giving of a direction under this section would be appropriate and proportionate to the seriousness of the contravention.

(2) A notice under this subsection must—

(a) state that the appropriate regulatory authority are satisfied as mentioned in subsection (1);

(b) state the reasons why they are satisfied as mentioned in subsection (1);

(c) state that the appropriate regulatory authority will give a direction under this section unless the provider takes, within a period specified in the notice, such steps to remedy the contravention within subsection (1)(a) as are so specified;

(d) specify any conditions that the appropriate regulatory authority propose to impose in the direction under section 368. M(5)(b); and

(e) inform the provider that the provider has the right to make representations to the appropriate regulatory authority about the matters appearing to the authority to provide grounds for giving the proposed direction within the period specified for the purposes of paragraph (c).

(3) If, after considering any representations made to them by the provider within that period, the appropriate regulatory authority are satisfied that the provider has failed to take the steps specified in the notice for remedying the contravention and that it is necessary in the public interest to give a direction under this section, the appropriate regulatory authority must give such of the following as appears to them appropriate and proportionate as mentioned in subsection (1)(c)—

(a) a direction that the entitlement of the provider to provide an on-demand programme service is suspended (either generally or in relation to a particular service);

(b) a direction that that entitlement is restricted in the respects set out in the direction.

Amendments (Textual)

F15. Words in s. 368. K(1)(a) inserted (18.3.2010) by The Audiovisual Media Services Regulations 2010 (S.I. 2010/419), regs. 1. (1), 8. (2)

F16. Words in s. 368. K(1)(b) inserted (18.3.2010) by The Audiovisual Media Services Regulations 2010 (S.I. 2010/419), regs. 1. (1), 8. (3)(a)

F17. Words in s. 368. K(1)(b) inserted (18.3.2010) by The Audiovisual Media Services Regulations 2010 (S.I. 2010/419), regs. 1. (1), 8. (3)(b)

F18. Words in s. 368. K(1)(b) inserted (18.3.2010) by The Audiovisual Media Services Regulations 2010 (S.I. 2010/419), regs. 1. (1), 8. (3)(c)

368. LSuspension or restriction of service for inciting crime or disorder

(1) The appropriate regulatory authority must serve a notice under subsection (2) on a provider of an on-demand programme service if they are satisfied—

(a) that the service has failed to comply with any requirement of section 368. E to 368. H and that accordingly the provider has contravened section 368. D(1);

(b) that the failure is due to the inclusion in the service of material likely to encourage or to incite the commission of crime, or to lead to disorder; and

(c) that the contravention is such as to justify the giving of a direction under this section.

(2) A notice under this subsection must—

(a) state that the appropriate regulatory authority are satisfied as mentioned in subsection (1);

(b) specify the respects in which, in their opinion, the provider has contravened section 368. D;

(c) specify the effect of the notice in accordance with subsection (3);

(d) state that the appropriate regulatory authority may give a direction under this section after the end of the period of twenty-one days beginning with the day on which the notice is served on the provider; and

(e) inform the provider of the provider's right to make representations to the appropriate regulatory authority within that period about the matters appearing to the appropriate regulatory authority to provide grounds for giving a direction under this section.

(3) A notice under subsection (2) has the effect specified under subsection (2)(c), which may be either—

(a) that the entitlement of the provider to provide an on-demand programme service is suspended (either generally or in relation to a particular service), or

(b) that that entitlement is restricted in the respects set out in the notice.

(4) The suspension or restriction has effect as from the time when the notice is served on the provider until either—

(a) a direction given under this section takes effect; or

(b) the appropriate regulatory authority decide not to give such a direction.

(5) If, after considering any representations made to them by the provider within the period mentioned in subsection (2)(d), the appropriate regulatory authority are satisfied that it is necessary in the public interest to give a direction under this section, they must give such of the following as appears to them justified as mentioned in subsection (1)(c)—

(a) a direction that the entitlement of the provider to provide an on-demand programme service is suspended (either generally or in relation to a particular service);

(b) a direction that that entitlement is restricted in the respects set out in the direction.

368. MSupplementary provision about directions

(1) This section applies to a direction given to a provider under section 368. K or 368. L.

(2) A direction must specify the service to which it relates or specify that it relates to any on-demand programme service provided or to be provided by the provider.

(3) A direction, except so far as it otherwise provides, takes effect for an indefinite period beginning with the time at which it is notified to the provider.

(4) A direction under section 368. L must specify a time for it to take effect, and that time must not fall before the end of twenty-eight days beginning with the day on which the direction is notified to the provider.

(5) A direction—

(a) may provide for the effect of a suspension or restriction to be postponed by specifying that it takes effect only at a time determined by or in accordance with the terms of the direction; and

(b) in connection with the suspension or restriction contained in the direction or with the postponement of its effect, may impose such conditions on the provider as appear to the appropriate regulatory authority to be appropriate for the purpose of protecting that provider's customers.

(6) If the appropriate regulatory authority consider it appropriate to do so (whether or not in consequence of representations or proposals made to them), they may revoke a direction or modify its conditions—

(a) with effect from such time as they may direct;

(b) subject to compliance with such requirements as they may specify; and

(c) to such extent and in relation to such services as they may determine.

368. NEnforcement of directions under section 368. K or 368. L

(1) A person ("P") is guilty of an offence if P provides an on-demand programme service—

(a) while P's entitlement to do so is suspended by a direction under section 368. K or 368. L, or

(b) in contravention of a restriction contained in such a direction.

(2) A person guilty of an offence under this section is liable—

(a) on summary conviction, to a fine not exceeding the statutory maximum;

(b) on conviction on indictment, to a fine.

[F19. Fees

Amendments (Textual)

F19 S. 368. NA and cross-heading inserted (18.3.2010) by The Audiovisual Media Services Regulations 2010 (S.I. 2010/419), regs. 1. (1), 9 (with reg. 13)

368. NAFees

(1) In this section "the authority" means each of these—

(a) the appropriate regulatory authority;

(b) (where they are not the appropriate regulatory authority) OFCOM.

(2) The authority may require a provider of an on-demand programme service to pay them a fee.

(3) The authority must be satisfied that the amount of any fee required under subsection (2)—

(a) represents the appropriate contribution of the provider towards meeting the likely costs described in subsection (5)(a), and

(b) is justifiable and proportionate having regard to the provider who will be required to pay it and the functions in respect of which it is imposed.

(4) A different fee may be required in relation to different cases or circumstances.

(5) The authority must, for each financial year—

(a) prepare such estimate as it is practicable for them to make of the likely costs of carrying out the relevant functions during that year;

(b) ensure that the aggregate amount of the fees that are required to be paid to them under subsection (2) during that year is sufficient to enable them to meet, but not exceed, the costs estimated under paragraph (a);

(c) consult in such manner as they consider appropriate the providers likely to be required to pay them a fee under subsection (2) during that year;

(d) publish in such manner as they consider appropriate the amount of the fees they will require providers to pay to them under subsection (2) during that year.

(6) As soon as reasonably practicable after the end of the financial year, the authority must publish a statement setting out, for that year—

(a) the aggregate amount received by them during that year in respect of fees required to be paid under subsection (2);

(b) the aggregate amount outstanding and likely to be paid or recovered in respect of fees that were required to be so paid under subsection (2); and

(c) the costs to them of carrying out the relevant functions during that year.

(7) Any deficit or surplus shown (after applying this subsection for all previous years) by a statement under subsection (6) is to be—

(a) carried forward; and

(b) taken into account in determining what is required to satisfy the requirement imposed by virtue of subsection (5)(b) in relation to the following year.

(8) The authority may repay to a person some or all of a fee paid to them by a person under subsection (2) if—

(a) that person has ceased to provide an on-demand programme service at some time during the period to which the fee relates;

(b) before ceasing to provide that service, that person gave the appropriate regulatory authority a notification under section 368. BA(2); and

(c) that person did not cease to provide the service following a direction given by the appropriate regulatory authority under section 368. K or 368. L.

(9) The authority may make arrangements with any body designated under section 368. B for that body to provide the authority with assistance in connection with the collection or repayment of fees required by them under this section.

(10) For the purposes of this section—

(a) the authority's costs of carrying out the relevant functions during a financial year include their costs of preparing to carry out the relevant functions incurred during that year; and

(b) the authority's costs of preparing to carry out the relevant functions incurred after 19 December 2009 but before the financial year in which those functions were first carried out by them are to be treated as if they were incurred during that year.

(11) In this section "relevant functions" means—

(a) in relation to the appropriate regulatory authority, their functions as the appropriate regulatory authority;

(b) in relation to OFCOM (where they are not the appropriate regulatory authority), their other functions under this Part.

(12) In this section "financial year" means a period of 12 months ending with 31 March.]

Information

368. OPower to demand information

(1) The appropriate regulatory authority may require a person who appears to them to be or to have been a provider of an on-demand programme service and to have information that they require for a purpose within subsection (2) to provide them with all such information as they consider necessary for that purpose.

(2) The following are within this subsection—

(a) the purposes of an investigation which the appropriate regulatory authority are carrying out in order for it to be determined whether a contravention of section [F20368. BA or section] 368. D has occurred or is occurring, where—

(i) the investigation relates to a matter about which they have received a complaint, or

(ii) they otherwise have reason to suspect that there has been a contravention of that section;

   (b) the purpose of ascertaining or calculating applicable qualifying revenue under section 368. J.

(3) The appropriate regulatory authority may require a person who appears to them to be or to have been a provider of an on-demand programme service and to have information that they require for the purpose of securing compliance with the obligations of the United Kingdom under the Audiovisual Media Services Directive to provide them with all such information as they consider necessary for that purpose.

(4) The appropriate regulatory authority may not require the provision of information under this section unless they have given the person from whom it is required an opportunity of making representations to them about the matters appearing to them to provide grounds for making the request.

(5) The appropriate regulatory authority must not require the provision of information under this section except by a demand for the information contained in a notice served on the person from whom the information is required that describes the required information and sets out the appropriate regulatory authority's reasons for requiring it.

(6) A person who is required to provide information under this section must provide it in such manner and within such reasonable period as may be specified by the appropriate regulatory authority in the demand for information.

(7) Sections 368. I and 368. K apply in relation to a failure to comply with a demand for information imposed under this section as if that failure were a contravention of a requirement of section 368. D.

(8) In this section "information" includes copies of programmes.

Amendments (Textual)

F20. Words in s. 368. O(2)(a) inserted (18.3.2010) by The Audiovisual Media Services Regulations 2010 (S.I. 2010/419), regs. 1. (1), 10

Application and interpretation of Part 4. A

368. PApplication of Part 4. A in relation to the BBC

[F21. (A1)Section 368. BA (advance notification) does not apply in relation to an on-demand programme service provided or to be provided by the BBC.]

[F22. (1)The following provisions do not apply to the BBC—

   (a) section 368. D(3) (duties of providers of on-demand programme services);

   (b) section 368. F (advertising);

   (c) section 368. G (sponsorship);

   (d) section 368. NA (fees).]

(2) In the following provisions references to a provider of an on-demand programme service do not include references to the BBC—

   (a) section 368. C (duties of appropriate regulatory authority);

   F23. (b). . . . .

   F23. (c). . . . .

   (d) section 368. I (enforcement by appropriate regulatory authority);

   (e) section 368. K (suspension or restriction of service for contraventions);

   (f) section 368. L (suspension or restriction of service for inciting crime or disorder);

   (g) section 368. O (power to demand information).

(3) Paragraph 2. (2)(b) of Schedule 12 includes provision imposing obligations on the BBC in relation to on-demand programme services.

Amendments (Textual)

F21. S. 368. P(A1) inserted (18.3.2010) by The Audiovisual Media Services Regulations 2010

(S.I. 2010/419), regs. 1. (1), 11. (a)

F22. S. 368. P(1) substituted (18.3.2010) by The Audiovisual Media Services Regulations 2010 (S.I. 2010/419), regs. 1. (1), 11. (b)

F23. S. 368. P(2)(b)(c) omitted (18.3.2010) by virtue of The Audiovisual Media Services Regulations 2010 (S.I. 2010/419), regs. 1. (1), 11. (c)

368. QApplication of Part 4. A in relation to the Welsh Authority

[F24. (A1)Section 368. BA (advance notification) does not apply in relation to an on-demand programme service provided or to be provided by the Welsh Authority, other than a service that includes advertising.]

(1) In section 368. C (duties of appropriate regulatory authority) references to a provider of an on-demand programme service do not include references to the Welsh Authority.

(2) It is the duty of the appropriate regulatory authority—

(a) to take such steps as appear to them best calculated to secure that the requirements of sections 368. E and 368. F are complied with by the Welsh Authority in relation to advertising, and

(b) to encourage the Welsh Authority to develop the codes of conduct referred to in section 368. C(4) so far as it relates to advertising.

(3) It is the duty of the Welsh Authority in the provision of any on-demand programme service to promote, where practicable and by appropriate means, production of and access to European works (within the meaning given in Article 1. (n) of the Audiovisual Media Services Directive).

(4) Section 368. D(3) [F25. (zb), (a), and (b) (duties of providers of on-demand programme services) do] not apply to the Welsh Authority except in relation to advertising or in relation to the inclusion of advertising in on-demand programme services provided by the Welsh Authority.

(5) Section 368. I (enforcement by appropriate regulatory authority), section 368. K (suspension or restriction of service for contraventions) and section 368. L (suspension or restriction of service for inciting crime or disorder) do not apply in relation to the contravention of section 368. D by the Welsh Authority except in the case of a contravention of section 368. E or 368. F that relates to advertising [F26or in the case of a contravention of section 368. D(3)(za)] .

(6) Section 368. O does not apply in relation to information held by the Welsh Authority except where that information is required by the appropriate regulatory authority for the purposes of—

(a) an investigation which the appropriate regulatory authority are carrying out (whether or not following receipt by them of a complaint) into a matter relating to compliance by the Welsh Authority with section 368. E or 368. F in relation to advertising; or

(b) securing compliance with the international obligations of the United Kingdom under the Audiovisual Media Services Directive in relation to advertising.

(7) Part 2 of Schedule 12 includes provision imposing obligations on the Welsh Authority in relation to on-demand programme services.

Amendments (Textual)

F24. S. 368. Q(A1) inserted (18.3.2010) by The Audiovisual Media Services Regulations 2010 (S.I. 2010/419), regs. 1. (1), 12. (1)

F25. Words in s. 368. Q(4) substituted (18.3.2010) by The Audiovisual Media Services Regulations 2010 (S.I. 2010/419), regs. 1. (1), 12. (2)

F26. Words in s. 368. Q(5) inserted (18.3.2010) by The Audiovisual Media Services Regulations 2010 (S.I. 2010/419), regs. 1. (1), 12. (3)

368. RInterpretation of Part 4. A

(1) In this Part—

"appropriate regulatory authority" is to be construed in accordance with 368. B;

[F27"children's programme" means a programme made—

- for a television programme service or for an on-demand programme service, and
- for viewing primarily by persons under the age of sixteen;]

[F28"electronic cigarette" means a product that—
- can be used for the consumption of nicotine-containing vapour via a mouth piece, or any component of that product, including a cartridge, a tank and the device without cartridge or tank (regardless of whether the product is disposable or refillable by means of a refill container and a tank, or rechargeable with single use cartridges), and
- is not a medicinal product within the meaning of regulation 2 of the Human Medicines Regulations 2012 (S.I. 2012/1916) or a medical device within the meaning of regulation 2 of the Medical Devices Regulations 2002 (S.I. 2002/618);

"electronic cigarette refill container" means a receptacle that—
- contains a nicotine-containing liquid, which can be used to refill an electronic cigarette, and
- is not a medicinal product within the meaning of regulation 2 of the Human Medicines Regulations 2012 or a medical device within the meaning of regulation 2 of the Medical Devices Regulations 2002;]

[F29"prescription-only medicine" means a prescription only medicine within the meaning of regulation 5. (3) of the Human Medicines Regulations 2012;]

"product placement" has the meaning given by section 368. H(1);

"sponsorship" is to be construed in accordance with section 368. G;

"tobacco product" has the meaning given in section 1 of the Tobacco Advertising and Promotion Act 2002.

(2) For the purposes of this Part, a programme is included in an on-demand programme service if it is included in the range of programmes the service offers to users.

(3) For the purposes of this Part, advertising is included in an on-demand programme service if it can be viewed by a user of the service as a result of the user selecting a programme to view.

(4) The services that are to be taken for the purposes of this Part to be available for use by members of the public include any service which—

   (a) is made available for use only to persons who subscribe to the service (whether for a period or in relation to a particular occasion) or who otherwise request its provision; but

   (b) is a service the facility of subscribing to which, or of otherwise requesting its provision, is offered or made available to members of the public.

(5) The person, and the only person, who is to be treated for the purposes of this Part as providing an on-demand programme service is the person who has editorial responsibility for the service (see section 368. A(4)).

(6) For the purposes of this Part—

   (a) the provision of a service by the BBC does not include its provision by a BBC company;

   (b) the provision of a service by the Welsh Authority does not include its provision by an S4. C company;

and, accordingly, control that is or is capable of being exercised by the BBC or the Welsh Authority over decisions by a BBC company or an S4. C company about what is to be comprised in a service is to be disregarded for the purposes of determining who has editorial responsibility for the service.]

Amendments (Textual)

F27. Words in s. 368. R(1) substituted (16.4.2010) by The Audiovisual Media Services (Product Placement) Regulations 2010 (S.I. 2010/831), regs. 1. (1), 8

F28. Words in s. 368. R(1) inserted (20.5.2016) by The Tobacco and Related Products Regulations 2016 (S.I. 2016/507), regs. 1. (2), 46. (5)

F29. Words in s. 368. R(1) substituted (14.8.2012) by The Human Medicines Regulations 2012 (S.I. 2012/1916), reg. 1. (2), Sch. 34 para. 44 (with Sch. 32)

Application and interpretation of Part 4A

Amendments (Textual)
F1. Pt. 4. A inserted (19.12.2009) by Audiovisual Media Services Regulations 2009 (S.I. 2009/2979), regs. 1. (1), 2

368. PApplication of Part 4. A in relation to the BBC

[F2. (A1)Section 368. BA (advance notification) does not apply in relation to an on-demand programme service provided or to be provided by the BBC.]
[F3. (1)The following provisions do not apply to the BBC—
  (a) section 368. D(3) (duties of providers of on-demand programme services);
  (b) section 368. F (advertising);
  (c) section 368. G (sponsorship);
  (d) section 368. NA (fees).]
(2) In the following provisions references to a provider of an on-demand programme service do not include references to the BBC—
  (a) section 368. C (duties of appropriate regulatory authority);
  F4. (b). . . . .
  F4. (c). . . . .
  (d) section 368. I (enforcement by appropriate regulatory authority);
  (e) section 368. K (suspension or restriction of service for contraventions);
  (f) section 368. L (suspension or restriction of service for inciting crime or disorder);
  (g) section 368. O (power to demand information).
(3) Paragraph 2. (2)(b) of Schedule 12 includes provision imposing obligations on the BBC in relation to on-demand programme services.
Amendments (Textual)
F2. S. 368. P(A1) inserted (18.3.2010) by The Audiovisual Media Services Regulations 2010 (S.I. 2010/419), regs. 1. (1), 11. (a)
F3. S. 368. P(1) substituted (18.3.2010) by The Audiovisual Media Services Regulations 2010 (S.I. 2010/419), regs. 1. (1), 11. (b)
F4. S. 368. P(2)(b)(c) omitted (18.3.2010) by virtue of The Audiovisual Media Services Regulations 2010 (S.I. 2010/419), regs. 1. (1), 11. (c)

368. QApplication of Part 4. A in relation to the Welsh Authority

[F5. (A1)Section 368. BA (advance notification) does not apply in relation to an on-demand programme service provided or to be provided by the Welsh Authority, other than a service that includes advertising.]
(1) In section 368. C (duties of appropriate regulatory authority) references to a provider of an on-demand programme service do not include references to the Welsh Authority.
(2) It is the duty of the appropriate regulatory authority—
  (a) to take such steps as appear to them best calculated to secure that the requirements of sections 368. E and 368. F are complied with by the Welsh Authority in relation to advertising, and
  (b) to encourage the Welsh Authority to develop the codes of conduct referred to in section 368. C(4) so far as it relates to advertising.
(3) It is the duty of the Welsh Authority in the provision of any on-demand programme service to promote, where practicable and by appropriate means, production of and access to European works (within the meaning given in Article 1. (n) of the Audiovisual Media Services Directive).
(4) Section 368. D(3) [F6. (zb), (a), and (b) (duties of providers of on-demand programme services) do] not apply to the Welsh Authority except in relation to advertising or in relation to the inclusion of advertising in on-demand programme services provided by the Welsh Authority.
(5) Section 368. I (enforcement by appropriate regulatory authority), section 368. K (suspension or

restriction of service for contraventions) and section 368. L (suspension or restriction of service for inciting crime or disorder) do not apply in relation to the contravention of section 368. D by the Welsh Authority except in the case of a contravention of section 368. E or 368. F that relates to advertising [F7or in the case of a contravention of section 368. D(3)(za)] .

(6) Section 368. O does not apply in relation to information held by the Welsh Authority except where that information is required by the appropriate regulatory authority for the purposes of—

(a) an investigation which the appropriate regulatory authority are carrying out (whether or not following receipt by them of a complaint) into a matter relating to compliance by the Welsh Authority with section 368. E or 368. F in relation to advertising; or

(b) securing compliance with the international obligations of the United Kingdom under the Audiovisual Media Services Directive in relation to advertising.

(7) Part 2 of Schedule 12 includes provision imposing obligations on the Welsh Authority in relation to on-demand programme services.

Amendments (Textual)

F5. S. 368. Q(A1) inserted (18.3.2010) by The Audiovisual Media Services Regulations 2010 (S.I. 2010/419), regs. 1. (1), 12. (1)

F6. Words in s. 368. Q(4) substituted (18.3.2010) by The Audiovisual Media Services Regulations 2010 (S.I. 2010/419), regs. 1. (1), 12. (2)

F7. Words in s. 368. Q(5) inserted (18.3.2010) by The Audiovisual Media Services Regulations 2010 (S.I. 2010/419), regs. 1. (1), 12. (3)

368. RInterpretation of Part 4. A

(1) In this Part—

"appropriate regulatory authority" is to be construed in accordance with 368. B;

[F8"children's programme" means a programme made—

- for a television programme service or for an on-demand programme service, and
- for viewing primarily by persons under the age of sixteen;]

[F9"electronic cigarette" means a product that—

- can be used for the consumption of nicotine-containing vapour via a mouth piece, or any component of that product, including a cartridge, a tank and the device without cartridge or tank (regardless of whether the product is disposable or refillable by means of a refill container and a tank, or rechargeable with single use cartridges), and
- is not a medicinal product within the meaning of regulation 2 of the Human Medicines Regulations 2012 (S.I. 2012/1916) or a medical device within the meaning of regulation 2 of the Medical Devices Regulations 2002 (S.I. 2002/618);

"electronic cigarette refill container" means a receptacle that—

- contains a nicotine-containing liquid, which can be used to refill an electronic cigarette, and
- is not a medicinal product within the meaning of regulation 2 of the Human Medicines Regulations 2012 or a medical device within the meaning of regulation 2 of the Medical Devices Regulations 2002;]

[F10"prescription-only medicine" means a prescription only medicine within the meaning of regulation 5. (3) of the Human Medicines Regulations 2012;]

"product placement" has the meaning given by section 368. H(1);

"sponsorship" is to be construed in accordance with section 368. G;

"tobacco product" has the meaning given in section 1 of the Tobacco Advertising and Promotion Act 2002.

(2) For the purposes of this Part, a programme is included in an on-demand programme service if it is included in the range of programmes the service offers to users.

(3) For the purposes of this Part, advertising is included in an on-demand programme service if it can be viewed by a user of the service as a result of the user selecting a programme to view.

(4) The services that are to be taken for the purposes of this Part to be available for use by

members of the public include any service which—

    (a) is made available for use only to persons who subscribe to the service (whether for a period or in relation to a particular occasion) or who otherwise request its provision; but

    (b) is a service the facility of subscribing to which, or of otherwise requesting its provision, is offered or made available to members of the public.

(5) The person, and the only person, who is to be treated for the purposes of this Part as providing an on-demand programme service is the person who has editorial responsibility for the service (see section 368. A(4)).

(6) For the purposes of this Part—

    (a) the provision of a service by the BBC does not include its provision by a BBC company;

    (b) the provision of a service by the Welsh Authority does not include its provision by an S4. C company;

and, accordingly, control that is or is capable of being exercised by the BBC or the Welsh Authority over decisions by a BBC company or an S4. C company about what is to be comprised in a service is to be disregarded for the purposes of determining who has editorial responsibility for the service.]

Amendments (Textual)

F8. Words in s. 368. R(1) substituted (16.4.2010) by The Audiovisual Media Services (Product Placement) Regulations 2010 (S.I. 2010/831), regs. 1. (1), 8

F9. Words in s. 368. R(1) inserted (20.5.2016) by The Tobacco and Related Products Regulations 2016 (S.I. 2016/507), regs. 1. (2), 46. (5)

F10. Words in s. 368. R(1) substituted (14.8.2012) by The Human Medicines Regulations 2012 (S.I. 2012/1916), reg. 1. (2), Sch. 34 para. 44 (with Sch. 32)

Application of Part 4A in relation to the BBC

[F1368. PApplication of Part 4. A in relation to the BBC

[F2. (A1)Section 368. BA (advance notification) does not apply in relation to an on-demand programme service provided or to be provided by the BBC.]

[F3. (1)The following provisions do not apply to the BBC—

    (a) section 368. D(3) (duties of providers of on-demand programme services);

    (b) section 368. F (advertising);

    (c) section 368. G (sponsorship);

    (d) section 368. NA (fees).]

(2) In the following provisions references to a provider of an on-demand programme service do not include references to the BBC—

    (a) section 368. C (duties of appropriate regulatory authority);

    F4. (b). . . . .

    F4. (c). . . . .

    (d) section 368. I (enforcement by appropriate regulatory authority);

    (e) section 368. K (suspension or restriction of service for contraventions);

    (f) section 368. L (suspension or restriction of service for inciting crime or disorder);

    (g) section 368. O (power to demand information).

(3) Paragraph 2. (2)(b) of Schedule 12 includes provision imposing obligations on the BBC in relation to on-demand programme services.]

Amendments (Textual)

F1. Pt. 4. A inserted (19.12.2009) by Audiovisual Media Services Regulations 2009 (S.I. 2009/2979), regs. 1. (1), 2

F2. S. 368. P(A1) inserted (18.3.2010) by The Audiovisual Media Services Regulations 2010 (S.I.

2010/419), regs. 1. (1), 11. (a)

F3. S. 368. P(1) substituted (18.3.2010) by The Audiovisual Media Services Regulations 2010 (S.I. 2010/419), regs. 1. (1), 11. (b)

F4. S. 368. P(2)(b)(c) omitted (18.3.2010) by virtue of The Audiovisual Media Services Regulations 2010 (S.I. 2010/419), regs. 1. (1), 11. (c)

Application of Part 4A in relation to the Welsh Authority

[F1368. QApplication of Part 4. A in relation to the Welsh Authority

[F2. (A1)Section 368. BA (advance notification) does not apply in relation to an on-demand programme service provided or to be provided by the Welsh Authority, other than a service that includes advertising.]

(1) In section 368. C (duties of appropriate regulatory authority) references to a provider of an on-demand programme service do not include references to the Welsh Authority.

(2) It is the duty of the appropriate regulatory authority—

(a) to take such steps as appear to them best calculated to secure that the requirements of sections 368. E and 368. F are complied with by the Welsh Authority in relation to advertising, and

(b) to encourage the Welsh Authority to develop the codes of conduct referred to in section 368. C(4) so far as it relates to advertising.

(3) It is the duty of the Welsh Authority in the provision of any on-demand programme service to promote, where practicable and by appropriate means, production of and access to European works (within the meaning given in Article 1. (n) of the Audiovisual Media Services Directive).

(4) Section 368. D(3) [F3. (zb), (a), and (b) (duties of providers of on-demand programme services) do] not apply to the Welsh Authority except in relation to advertising or in relation to the inclusion of advertising in on-demand programme services provided by the Welsh Authority.

(5) Section 368. I (enforcement by appropriate regulatory authority), section 368. K (suspension or restriction of service for contraventions) and section 368. L (suspension or restriction of service for inciting crime or disorder) do not apply in relation to the contravention of section 368. D by the Welsh Authority except in the case of a contravention of section 368. E or 368. F that relates to advertising [F4or in the case of a contravention of section 368. D(3)(za)] .

(6) Section 368. O does not apply in relation to information held by the Welsh Authority except where that information is required by the appropriate regulatory authority for the purposes of—

(a) an investigation which the appropriate regulatory authority are carrying out (whether or not following receipt by them of a complaint) into a matter relating to compliance by the Welsh Authority with section 368. E or 368. F in relation to advertising; or

(b) securing compliance with the international obligations of the United Kingdom under the Audiovisual Media Services Directive in relation to advertising.

(7) Part 2 of Schedule 12 includes provision imposing obligations on the Welsh Authority in relation to on-demand programme services.]

Amendments (Textual)

F1. Pt. 4. A inserted (19.12.2009) by Audiovisual Media Services Regulations 2009 (S.I. 2009/2979), regs. 1. (1), 2

F2. S. 368. Q(A1) inserted (18.3.2010) by The Audiovisual Media Services Regulations 2010 (S.I. 2010/419), regs. 1. (1), 12. (1)

F3. Words in s. 368. Q(4) substituted (18.3.2010) by The Audiovisual Media Services Regulations

2010 (S.I. 2010/419), regs. 1. (1), 12. (2)
F4. Words in s. 368. Q(5) inserted (18.3.2010) by The Audiovisual Media Services Regulations
2010 (S.I. 2010/419), regs. 1. (1), 12. (3)

Interpretation of Part 4A

[F1368. RInterpretation of Part 4. A

(1) In this Part—

"appropriate regulatory authority" is to be construed in accordance with 368. B;

[F2"children's programme" means a programme made—

- for a television programme service or for an on-demand programme service, and

- for viewing primarily by persons under the age of sixteen;]

[F3"electronic cigarette" means a product that—

- can be used for the consumption of nicotine containing vapour via a mouth piccc, or any component of that product, including a cartridge, a tank and the device without cartridge or tank (regardless of whether the product is disposable or refillable by means of a refill container and a tank, or rechargeable with single use cartridges), and

- is not a medicinal product within the meaning of regulation 2 of the Human Medicines Regulations 2012 (S.I. 2012/1916) or a medical device within the meaning of regulation 2 of the Medical Devices Regulations 2002 (S.I. 2002/618);

"electronic cigarette refill container" means a receptacle that—

- contains a nicotine-containing liquid, which can be used to refill an electronic cigarette, and

- is not a medicinal product within the meaning of regulation 2 of the Human Medicines Regulations 2012 or a medical device within the meaning of regulation 2 of the Medical Devices Regulations 2002;]

[F4"prescription-only medicine" means a prescription only medicine within the meaning of regulation 5. (3) of the Human Medicines Regulations 2012;]

"product placement" has the meaning given by section 368. H(1);

"sponsorship" is to be construed in accordance with section 368. G;

"tobacco product" has the meaning given in section 1 of the Tobacco Advertising and Promotion Act 2002.

(2) For the purposes of this Part, a programme is included in an on-demand programme service if it is included in the range of programmes the service offers to users.

(3) For the purposes of this Part, advertising is included in an on-demand programme service if it can be viewed by a user of the service as a result of the user selecting a programme to view.

(4) The services that are to be taken for the purposes of this Part to be available for use by members of the public include any service which—

   (a) is made available for use only to persons who subscribe to the service (whether for a period or in relation to a particular occasion) or who otherwise request its provision; but

   (b) is a service the facility of subscribing to which, or of otherwise requesting its provision, is offered or made available to members of the public.

(5) The person, and the only person, who is to be treated for the purposes of this Part as providing an on-demand programme service is the person who has editorial responsibility for the service (see section 368. A(4)).

(6) For the purposes of this Part—

   (a) the provision of a service by the BBC does not include its provision by a BBC company;

   (b) the provision of a service by the Welsh Authority does not include its provision by an S4. C company;

and, accordingly, control that is or is capable of being exercised by the BBC or the Welsh

Authority over decisions by a BBC company or an S4. C compar
in a service is to be disregarded for the purposes of determining
for the service.]
Amendments (Textual)
F1. Pt. 4. A inserted (19.12.2009) by Audiovisual Media Service
2009/2979), regs. 1. (1), 2
F2. Words in s. 368. R(1) substituted (16.4.2010) by The Audio
Placement) Regulations 2010 (S.I. 2010/831), regs. 1. (1), 8
F3. Words in s. 368. R(1) inserted (20.5.2016) by The Tobacco
2016 (S.I. 2016/507), regs. 1. (2), 46. (5)
F4. Words in s. 368. R(1) substituted (14.8.2012) by The Huma.. .....
(S.I. 2012/1916), reg. 1. (2), Sch. 34 para. 44 (with Sch. 32)

Part 5. Competition in communications markets

Part 5. Competition in communications markets

Chapter 1. Functions of OFCOM under competition legislation

369. Matters in relation to which OFCOM have competition functions

(1) In this Chapter references to communications matters are references to any one or more of the following—

   (a) the provision of electronic communications networks;

   (b) the provision of electronic communications services;

   (c) the provision or making available of services or facilities which are provided or made available—

(i) by means of, or in association with the provision (by the same person or another) of, an electronic communications network or electronic communications service; or

(ii) for the purpose of facilitating the use of any such network or service (whether provided by the same person or another);

   (d) apparatus used for providing or making available anything mentioned in the preceding paragraphs;

   (e) broadcasting and related matters.

   [F1. (f)the provision of postal services.]

(2) The Secretary of State may by order make such amendments of subsection (1) as he may consider appropriate for the purpose of modifying the description of activities in respect of which any of the provisions of this Part—

   (a) confer functions on OFCOM under Part 1 of the Competition Act 1998 (c. 41) or relate to the carrying out by OFCOM of those functions; or

   (b) confer functions on OFCOM under Part 4 of the Enterprise Act 2002 (c. 40) or relate to the carrying out by OFCOM of those functions.

(3) No order is to be made containing provision authorised by this section unless a draft of the order has been laid before Parliament and approved by a resolution of each House.

Amendments (Textual)

F1. S. 369. (1)(f) inserted (1.10.2011) by Postal Services Act 2011 (c. 5), s. 93. (2)(3), Sch. 12

2329, art. 3

Information

(a)-(d)(2)(3) in force at 25.7.2003 for specified purposes by S.I. 2003/1900, arts. 1. Sch. 1 (with art. 3) (as amended by S.I. 2003/3142, art. 1. (3))

. (1)(a)-(d) (2) (3) in force at 29.12.2003 in so far as not already in force by S.I. 142, art. 3. (1), Sch. 1 (with art. 11)

S. 369. (1)(e) in force at 29.12.2003 by S.I. 2003/3142, art. 3. (1), Sch. 1 (with art. 11)

370. OFCOM's functions under Part 4 of the Enterprise Act 2002.

(1) The functions to which subsection (2) applies shall be concurrent functions of OFCOM and the [F2. Competition and Markets Authority (referred to in this Part as "the CMA")] .

(2) This subsection applies to the functions of the [F3. CMA] under Part 4 of the Enterprise Act 2002 (market investigations) (other than sections 166 [F4, 171 and 174. E]) so far as [F5those functions—

(a) are exercisable by the CMA Board (within the meaning of Schedule 4 to the Enterprise and Regulatory Reform Act 2013), and

(b) relate to] commercial activities connected with communications matters.

(3) So far as necessary for the purposes of, or in connection with, subsections [F6. (1) and (2)—

(a) references] in Part 4 of the Enterprise Act 2002 to the [F7. CMA] (including references in provisions of that Act applied by that Part) shall be construed as including references to OFCOM [F8. (except in sections 166, 171 and 174. E and where the context otherwise requires);

(b) references in that Part to the CMA carrying out functions under section 5 of the Enterprise Act 2002 are to be construed as including references to OFCOM exercising powers under section 1. (3) of this Act to obtain, compile and keep under review information about matters relating to the carrying out of its functions.]

[F9. (3. A)Section 130. A of the Enterprise Act 2002 is to have effect in its application in relation to OFCOM by virtue of subsections (1) and (2)—

(a) as if for subsection (1) of that section there were substituted—

"(1)Where the Office of Communications—

(a) is proposing to fulfil its duties under section 3. (1) of the Communications Act 2003 by obtaining, compiling and keeping under review information in relation to a matter for the purposes mentioned in subsection (2), and

(b) considers that the matter is one in respect of which it would be appropriate for it to exercise its powers under section 174 (investigation) in connection with deciding whether to make a reference under section 131,

the Office of Communications must publish a notice under this section (referred to in this Part as a "market study notice").", and

(b) as if in subsection (2)(a) of that section, for "the acquisition or supply of goods or services of one or more than one description in the United Kingdom" there were substituted "commercial activities connected with communications matters (within the meaning given by section 369. (1) of the Communications Act 2003)".]

(4) In [F10subsections (2) and (3. A) the references] to activities connected with communications matters, so far as [F11they are references] to activities connected with any apparatus falling within paragraph (d) of section 369. (1), [F12include] a reference to—

(a) the supply and export of any such apparatus; and

(b) the production or acquisition of any such apparatus for supply or export.

(5) Before the [F13. CMA] or OFCOM first exercises in relation to any matter functions which are exercisable concurrently by virtue of this section, that person shall consult the other.

(6) Neither the [F13. CMA] nor OFCOM shall exercise in relation to any matter functions which are exercisable concurrently by virtue of this section if functions which are so exercisable have been exercised in relation to that matter by the other.

(7) It shall be the duty of OFCOM, for the purpose of assisting [F14a CMA group] in carrying out an investigation on a [F15market investigation reference made by OFCOM (under section 131 of the Enterprise Act 2002)] by virtue of subsection (1), to give to the [F16group] —

(a) any information which is in OFCOM's possession and relates to matters falling within the scope of the investigation and—
(i) is requested by the [F16group] for that purpose, or
(ii) is information which, in OFCOM's opinion, it would be appropriate for that purpose to give to the [F16group] without any such request;
and

(b) any other assistance which the [F16group] may require, and which it is within OFCOM's power to give, in relation to any such matters,
and the [F16group] , for the purposes of carrying out any such investigation, shall take into account any information given to it for that purpose under this subsection.
[F17. (7. A)In subsection (7) "CMA group" has the same meaning as in Schedule 4 to the Enterprise and Regulatory Reform Act 2013.]
(8) If any question arises as to whether, by virtue of this section, any functions fall to be, or are capable of being, carried out by OFCOM in relation to any particular case, that question shall be referred to and determined by the Secretary of State.
(9) No objection shall be taken to anything done under Part 4 of the Enterprise Act 2002 (c. 40) by or in relation to OFCOM on the ground that it should have been done by or in relation to the [F18. CMA] .
(10) Section 117 of the Enterprise Act 2002 (offences of supplying false or misleading information) as applied by section 180 of that Act shall have effect so far as relating to functions exercisable by OFCOM by virtue of this section as if the references in section 117. (1)(a) and (2) to the [F18. CMA] included references to OFCOM.
(11) Subject to subsection (12), [F19section 3 of this Act (general duties) and section 29 of the Postal Services Act 2011 (duty to secure provision of universal postal service) do not] apply in relation to anything done by OFCOM in the carrying out of their functions by virtue of this section.
(12) In the carrying out of any functions by virtue of this section OFCOM may nevertheless have regard to any of the matters in respect of which a duty is imposed by [F20section 3. (1) to (4) of this Act or section 29 of the Postal Services Act 2011] if it is a matter to which the [F21. CMA] is entitled to have regard in the carrying out of those functions.
Amendments (Textual)
F2. Words in s. 370. (1) substituted (1.4.2014) by The Enterprise and Regulatory Reform Act 2013 (Competition) (Consequential, Transitional and Saving Provisions) Order 2014 (S.I. 2014/892), art. 1. (1), Sch. 1 para. 161. (2) (with art. 3)
F3. Word in s. 370. (2) substituted (1.4.2014) by The Enterprise and Regulatory Reform Act 2013 (Competition) (Consequential, Transitional and Saving Provisions) Order 2014 (S.I. 2014/892), art. 1. (1), Sch. 1 para. 161. (3)(b) (with art. 3)
F4. Words in s. 370. (2) substituted (1.4.2014) by The Enterprise and Regulatory Reform Act 2013 (Competition) (Consequential, Transitional and Saving Provisions) Order 2014 (S.I. 2014/892), art. 1. (1), Sch. 1 para. 161. (3)(a) (with art. 3)
F5. Words in s. 370. (2) substituted (1.4.2014) by The Enterprise and Regulatory Reform Act 2013 (Competition) (Consequential, Transitional and Saving Provisions) Order 2014 (S.I. 2014/892), art. 1. (1), Sch. 1 para. 161. (3)(c) (with art. 3)
F6. Words in s. 370. (3) substituted (1.4.2014) by The Enterprise and Regulatory Reform Act 2013 (Competition) (Consequential, Transitional and Saving Provisions) Order 2014 (S.I. 2014/892), art. 1. (1), Sch. 1 para. 161. (4)(a) (with art. 3)
F7. Word in s. 370. (3)(a) substituted (1.4.2014) by The Enterprise and Regulatory Reform Act 2013 (Competition) (Consequential, Transitional and Saving Provisions) Order 2014 (S.I. 2014/892), art. 1. (1), Sch. 1 para. 161. (4)(b) (with art. 3)
F8. Words in s. 370. (3) substituted (1.4.2014) by The Enterprise and Regulatory Reform Act

2013 (Competition) (Consequential, Transitional and Saving Provisions) Order 2014 (S.I. 2014/892), art. 1. (1), Sch. 1 para. 161. (4)(c) (with art. 3)

F9. S. 370. (3. A) inserted (1.4.2014) by The Enterprise and Regulatory Reform Act 2013 (Competition) (Consequential, Transitional and Saving Provisions) Order 2014 (S.I. 2014/892), art. 1. (1), Sch. 1 para. 161. (5) (with art. 3)

F10. Words in s. 370. (4) substituted (1.4.2014) by The Enterprise and Regulatory Reform Act 2013 (Competition) (Consequential, Transitional and Saving Provisions) Order 2014 (S.I. 2014/892), art. 1. (1), Sch. 1 para. 161. (6)(a) (with art. 3)

F11. Words in s. 370. (4) substituted (1.4.2014) by The Enterprise and Regulatory Reform Act 2013 (Competition) (Consequential, Transitional and Saving Provisions) Order 2014 (S.I. 2014/892), art. 1. (1), Sch. 1 para. 161. (6)(b) (with art. 3)

F12. Word in s. 370. (4) substituted (1.4.2014) by The Enterprise and Regulatory Reform Act 2013 (Competition) (Consequential, Transitional and Saving Provisions) Order 2014 (S.I. 2014/892), art. 1. (1), Sch. 1 para. 161. (6)(c) (with art. 3)

F13. Word in s. 370. (5)(6) substituted (1.4.2014) by The Enterprise and Regulatory Reform Act 2013 (Competition) (Consequential, Transitional and Saving Provisions) Order 2014 (S.I. 2014/892), art. 1. (1), Sch. 1 para. 161. (7) (with art. 3)

F14. Words in s. 370. (7) substituted (1.4.2014) by The Enterprise and Regulatory Reform Act 2013 (Competition) (Consequential, Transitional and Saving Provisions) Order 2014 (S.I. 2014/892), art. 1. (1), Sch. 1 para. 161. (8)(a) (with art. 3)

F15. Words in s. 370. (7) substituted (1.4.2014) by The Enterprise and Regulatory Reform Act 2013 (Competition) (Consequential, Transitional and Saving Provisions) Order 2014 (S.I. 2014/892), art. 1. (1), Sch. 1 para. 161. (8)(b) (with art. 3)

F16. Word in s. 370. (7) substituted (1.4.2014) by The Enterprise and Regulatory Reform Act 2013 (Competition) (Consequential, Transitional and Saving Provisions) Order 2014 (S.I. 2014/892), art. 1. (1), Sch. 1 para. 161. (8)(c) (with art. 3)

F17. S. 370. (7. A) inserted (1.4.2014) by The Enterprise and Regulatory Reform Act 2013 (Competition) (Consequential, Transitional and Saving Provisions) Order 2014 (S.I. 2014/892), art. 1. (1), Sch. 1 para. 161. (9) (with art. 3)

F18. Word in s. 370. (9)(10) substituted (1.4.2014) by The Enterprise and Regulatory Reform Act 2013 (Competition) (Consequential, Transitional and Saving Provisions) Order 2014 (S.I. 2014/892), art. 1. (1), Sch. 1 para. 161. (10) (with art. 3)

F19. Words in s. 370. (11) substituted (1.10.2011) by Postal Services Act 2011 (c. 5), s. 93. (2)(3), Sch. 12 para. 63. (2); S.I. 2011/2329, art. 3

F20. Words in s. 370. (12) substituted (1.10.2011) by Postal Services Act 2011 (c. 5), s. 93. (2)(3), Sch. 12 para. 63. (3); S.I. 2011/2329, art. 3

F21. Word in s. 370. (12) substituted (1.4.2014) by The Enterprise and Regulatory Reform Act 2013 (Competition) (Consequential, Transitional and Saving Provisions) Order 2014 (S.I. 2014/892), art. 1. (1), Sch. 1 para. 161. (10) (with art. 3)

Commencement Information

I4. S. 370 in force at 25.7.2003 for specified purposes by S.I. 2003/1900, arts. 1. (2), 2. (1), Sch. 1 (with art. 3) (as amended by S.I. 2003/3142, art. 1. (3))

I5. S. 370 in force at 29.12.2003 in so far as not already in force by S.I. 2003/3142, art. 3. (2) (with art. 11)

371. OFCOM's functions under the Competition Act 1998.

(1) The functions to which subsection (2) applies shall be concurrent functions of OFCOM and the [F22. CMA] .

[F23. (2)This subsection applies to the functions of the [F22. CMA] under the provisions of Part 1 of the Competition Act 1998 (other than sections 31. D(1) to (6), 38. (1) to (6) [F24, 40. B(1) to (4)] and 51), so far as relating to—

(a) agreements, decisions or concerted practices of the kind mentioned in section 2. (1) of that Act,

(b) conduct of the kind mentioned in section 18. (1) of that Act,

(c) agreements, decisions or concerted practices of the kind mentioned in [F25. Article 101. (1) of the Treaty on the Functioning of the European Union] , or

(d) conduct which amounts to abuse of the kind mentioned in [F26. Article 102 of the Treaty on the Functioning of the European Union] ,

which relate to activities connected with communications matters.]

(3) So far as necessary for the purposes of, or in connection with, the provisions of subsections (1) and (2), references to the [F22. CMA] in Part 1 of the Competition Act 1998 are to be read as including references to OFCOM, except—

(a) [F27in sections 31. D(1) to (6), 38. (1) to (6)] [F28, 40. B(1) to (4)] , 51, 52. (6) and (8) and 54, and

(b) where the context otherwise requires.

(4) In subsection (2), the reference to activities connected with communications matters, so far as it is a reference to activities connected with any apparatus falling within paragraph (d) of section 369. (1), includes a reference to—

(a) the supply and export of any such apparatus; and

(b) the production or acquisition of any such apparatus for supply or export.

(5) In section 54 of the Competition Act 1998—

(a) in subsection (1) (definition of "regulator" for the purposes of Part 1 of that Act), for paragraph (a) there shall be substituted—

"(a)the Office of Communications;"

(b) in subsection (4) (power to make regulations about concurrent functions of the [F22. CMA] and sectoral regulators), "or by Chapter V of Part I of the Transport Act 2000" there shall be inserted " to this Act, by Chapter 5 of Part 1 of the Transport Act 2000 or by section 371 of the Communications Act 2003 ".

(6) In paragraph 5 of Schedule 2 to the Competition Act 1998 (publication of list of networking arrangements under the 1990 Act excluded from the Chapter 1 prohibition)—

(a) in sub-paragraph (2), for "The Independent Television Commission ("ITC")" there shall be substituted " OFCOM "; and

(b) in sub-paragraph (3), for "The ITC" there shall be substituted " OFCOM ".

(7) In section 59. (1) of the Competition Act 1998 (interpretation of Part 1), after the definition of "Minister of the Crown" there shall be inserted—

""OFCOM" means the Office of Communications;".

(8) OFCOM may carry out, in respect of activities connected with communications matters and concurrently with the [F22. CMA] , the functions of the [F22. CMA] under any of paragraphs 3, 7, 19. (3) and 36 to 39 of Schedule 13 to the Competition Act 1998 (transitional provisions).

(9) If any question arises as to whether, by virtue of this section, any functions fall to be, or are capable of being, carried out by OFCOM in relation to a particular case, that question shall be referred to and determined by the Secretary of State.

(10) No objection shall be taken to anything done under by or in relation to OFCOM under the Competition Act 1998 (c. 41) on the ground that it should have been done by or in relation to the [F22. CMA] .

(11) Subject to subsection (12), [F29section 3 of this Act (general duties) and section 29 of the Postal Services Act 2011 (duty to secure provision of universal postal service) do not] apply in relation to anything done by OFCOM in the carrying out of their functions by virtue of this section.

(12) In the carrying out of any functions by virtue of this section OFCOM may nevertheless have regard to any of the matters in respect of which a duty is imposed by [F30section 3. (1) to (4) of this Act or section 29 of the Postal Services Act 2011] if it is a matter to which the [F22. CMA] is entitled to have regard in the carrying out of those functions.

Amendments (Textual)

F22. Word in s. 371 substituted (1.4.2014) by The Enterprise and Regulatory Reform Act 2013 (Competition) (Consequential, Transitional and Saving Provisions) Order 2014 (S.I. 2014/892), art. 1. (1), Sch. 1 para. 162 (with art. 3)

F23. S. 371. (2) substituted (1.5.2004) by The Competition Act 1998 and Other Enactments (Amendment) Regulations 2004 (S.I. 2004/1261), reg. 1. (a), Sch. 2 para. 11. (2)(a)

F24. Words in s. 371. (2) inserted (1.4.2014) by Enterprise and Regulatory Reform Act 2013 (c. 24), s. 103. (3), Sch. 15 para. 46; S.I. 2014/416, art. 2. (1)(f) (with Sch.)

F25. Words in s. 371. (2)(c) substituted (1.8.2012) by The Treaty of Lisbon (Changes in Terminology or Numbering) Order 2012 (S.I. 2012/1809), art. 2. (1), Sch. Pt. 1 (with art. 2. (2))

F26. Words in s. 371. (2)(d) substituted (1.8.2012) by The Treaty of Lisbon (Changes in Terminology or Numbering) Order 2012 (S.I. 2012/1809), art. 2. (1), Sch. Pt. 1 (with art. 2. (2))

F27. Words in s. 371. (3)(a) substituted (1.5.2004) by The Competition Act 1998 and Other Enactments (Amendment) Regulations 2004 (S.I. 2004/1261), reg. 1. (a), Sch. 2 para. 11. (2)(b)

F28. Words in s. 371. (3)(a) inserted (1.4.2014) by Enterprise and Regulatory Reform Act 2013 (c. 24), Sch. 15 para. 46; S.I. 2014/416, art. 2. (1)(f) (with Sch.)

F29. Words in s. 371. (11) substituted (1.10.2011) by Postal Services Act 2011 (c. 5), s. 93. (2)(3), Sch. 12 para. 64. (2); S.I. 2011/2329, art. 3

F30. Words in s. 371. (12) substituted (1.10.2011) by Postal Services Act 2011 (c. 5), s. 93. (2)(3), Sch. 12 para. 64. (3); S.I. 2011/2329, art. 3

Commencement Information

I6. S. 371 in force at 25.7.2003 for specified purposes by S.I. 2003/1900, arts. 1. (2), 2. (1), Sch. 1 (with art. 3) (as amended by S.I. 2003/3142, art. 1. (3))

I7. S. 371 in force at 29.12.2003 in so far as not already in force by S.I. 2003/3142, art. 3. (2) (with art. 11)

372. Application of the Competition Act 1998 to news provision

(1) Section 194. A of the 1990 Act (which modifies the Competition Act 1998 in relation to agreements relating to Channel 3 news provision) shall be amended as follows.

(2) In subsection (1) (meaning of "relevant agreement")—

   (a) for "section 31. A(a)" there shall be substituted " section 280 of the Communications Act 2003 "; and

   (b) for "section 31. (2)" (in both places) there shall be substituted " that section ".

(3) In subsections (2), (6) and (7)(b)(i) (consultations with and notifications to the Office of Fair Trading), after the words "the OFT", in each place where they occur, there shall be inserted " and OFCOM ".

(4) In subsection (3)(b)—

   (a) for "section 31. (2)" there shall be substituted " section 280 of the Communications Act 2003 "; and

   (b) for "section 31. (1) and (2)" there shall be substituted " that section of that Act of 2003 ".

(5) In subsection (5)(c) (declaration without notification), after "the OFT" there shall be inserted " or OFCOM or both of them ".

(6) In subsection (7) (restriction on exercise by Office of Fair Trading of Chapter III powers)—

   (a) for "The OFT may not" there shall be substituted " Neither the OFT nor OFCOM may "; and

   (b) for paragraph (a) there shall be substituted—

"(a)the Secretary of State has been notified by the OFT or (as the case may be) by OFCOM of its or their intention to do so; and".

(7) In subsection (8) (notice by Office of Fair Trading to the Secretary of State), for the words from the beginning to "assist" in paragraph (a) there shall be substituted—

"(8)Where the OFT or OFCOM is or are proposing to exercise any Chapter III powers in respect of a relevant agreement, it or they must give the Secretary of State particulars of the agreement and such other information—

(a) it considers or (as the case may be) they consider will assist".

(8) In subsection (9), in the definition of "Chapter III powers", for "given to the OFT by" there shall be substituted " of the OFT and of OFCOM under ".

Commencement Information

I8. S. 372 in force at 29.12.2003 by S.I. 2003/3142, art. 3. (1), Sch. 1 (with art. 11)

Chapter 2. Media mergers

373. Repeal of existing newspaper merger regime

Sections 57 to 62 of the Fair Trading Act 1973 (c. 41) (newspaper merger references) shall cease to have effect.

Commencement Information

I9. S. 373 in force at 29.12.2003 by S.I. 2003/3142, art. 3. (1), Sch. 1 (with art. 11)

374. Repeal of exclusion for newspaper mergers from general merger controls

Section 69 of the Enterprise Act 2002 (c. 40) (exclusion of newspaper mergers from references under Part 3 of that Act) shall cease to have effect.

Commencement Information

I10. S. 374 in force at 29.12.2003 by S.I. 2003/3142, art. 3. (1), Sch. 1 (with art. 11)

Adaptation for media mergers of main merger regime

375. Media public interest considerations

(1) After subsection (2) of section 58 of the Enterprise Act 2002 (considerations specified as public interest considerations for the purpose of the main merger regime) there shall be inserted—

"(2. A)The need for—

(a) accurate presentation of news; and

(b) free expression of opinion;

in newspapers is specified in this section.

(2. B)The need for, to the extent that it is reasonable and practicable, a sufficient plurality of views in newspapers in each market for newspapers in the United Kingdom or a part of the United Kingdom is specified in this section.

(2. C)The following are specified in this section—

(a) the need, in relation to every different audience in the United Kingdom or in a particular area or locality of the United Kingdom, for there to be a sufficient plurality of persons with control of the media enterprises serving that audience;

(b) the need for the availability throughout the United Kingdom of a wide range of broadcasting which (taken as a whole) is both of high quality and calculated to appeal to a wide variety of tastes and interests; and

(c) the need for persons carrying on media enterprises, and for those with control of such enterprises, to have a genuine commitment to the attainment in relation to broadcasting of the standards objectives set out in section 319 of the Communications Act 2003."

(2) After that section there shall be inserted, in Chapter 2 of Part 3—

"58. AConstruction of consideration specified in section 58. (2. C)

(1) For the purposes of section 58 and this section an enterprise is a media enterprise if it consists in or involves broadcasting.

(2) In the case of a merger situation in which at least one of the enterprises ceasing to be distinct consists in or involves broadcasting, the references in section 58. (2. C)(a) or this section to media enterprises include references to newspaper enterprises.

(3) In this Part "newspaper enterprise" means an enterprise consisting in or involving the supply of newspapers.

(4) Wherever in a merger situation two media enterprises serving the same audience cease to be

351

distinct, the number of such enterprises serving that audience shall be assumed to be more immediately before they cease to be distinct than it is afterwards.

(5) For the purposes of section 58, where two or more media enterprises—

(a) would fall to be treated as under common ownership or common control for the purposes of section 26, or

(b) are otherwise in the same ownership or under the same control,

they shall be treated (subject to subsection (4)) as all under the control of only one person.

(6) A reference in section 58 or this section to an audience shall be construed in relation to a media enterprise in whichever of the following ways the decision-making authority considers appropriate—

(a) as a reference to any one of the audiences served by that enterprise, taking them separately;

(b) as a reference to all the audiences served by that enterprise, taking them together;

(c) as a reference to a number of those audiences taken together in such group as the decision-making authority considers appropriate; or

(d) as a reference to a part of anything that could be taken to be an audience under any of paragraphs (a) to (c) above.

(7) The criteria for deciding who can be treated for the purposes of this section as comprised in an audience, or as comprised in an audience served by a particular service—

(a) shall be such as the decision-making authority considers appropriate in the circumstances of the case; and

(b) may allow for persons to be treated as members of an audience if they are only potentially members of it.

(8) In this section "audience" includes readership.

(9) The power under subsection (3) of section 58 to modify that section includes power to modify this section."

(3) In section 127. (1) of that Act (associated persons to be treated as one person), for the word "and" at the end of paragraph (a) there shall be substituted—

"(aa)for the purposes of section 58. (2. C); and".

Commencement Information

I11. S. 375 in force at 29.12.2003 by S.I. 2003/3142, art. 3. (1), Sch. 1 (with art. 11)

376. Adaptation of role of OFT in initial investigations and reports

(1) In section 44. (3)(b) of the Enterprise Act 2002 (c. 40) (initial report by OFT in public interest cases must include summary of representations about public interest considerations) after the word "concerned" there shall be inserted " (other than a media public interest consideration) ".

(2) After section 44. (5) of that Act there shall be inserted—

"(5. A)The report may, in particular, contain a summary of any representations about the case which have been received by the OFT and which relate to any media public interest consideration mentioned in the intervention notice concerned and which is or may be relevant to the Secretary of State's decision as to whether to make a reference under section 45."

(3) After section 44. (7) of that Act there shall be inserted—

"(8)In this Part "media public interest consideration" means any consideration which, at the time of the giving of the intervention notice concerned—

(a) is specified in section 58. (2. A) to (2. C); or

(b) in the opinion of the Secretary of State, is concerned with broadcasting or newspapers and ought to be specified in section 58.

(9) In this Part "broadcasting" means the provision of services the provision of which—

(a) is required to be licensed under Part 1 or 3 of the Broadcasting Act 1990 or Part 1 or 2 of the Broadcasting Act 1996; or

(b) would be required to be so licensed if provided by a person subject to licensing under the Part in question.

(10) In this Part "newspaper" means a daily, Sunday or local (other than daily or Sunday) newspaper circulating wholly or mainly in the United Kingdom or in a part of the United Kingdom.

(11) The Secretary of State may by order amend subsections (9) and (10)."

Commencement Information

I12. S. 376 in force at 29.12.2003 by S.I. 2003/3142, art. 3. (1), Sch. 1 (with art. 11)

377. Additional investigation and report by OFCOM

After section 44 of the Enterprise Act 2002 (investigation and report by OFT in public interest cases) there shall be inserted—

"44. AAdditional investigation and report by OFCOM: media mergers

(1) Subsection (2) applies where—

(a) the Secretary of State has given an intervention notice in relation to a relevant merger situation; and

(b) the intervention notice mentions any media public interest consideration.

(2) OFCOM shall, within such period as the Secretary of State may require, give a report to the Secretary of State on the effect of the consideration or considerations concerned on the case.

(3) The report shall contain—

(a) advice and recommendations on any media public interest consideration mentioned in the intervention notice concerned and which is or may be relevant to the Secretary of State's decision as to whether to make a reference under section 45; and

(b) a summary of any representations about the case which have been received by OFCOM and which relate to any such consideration.

(4) OFCOM shall carry out such investigations as they consider appropriate for the purposes of producing a report under this section."

Commencement Information

I13. S. 377 in force at 29.12.2003 by S.I. 2003/3142, art. 3. (1), Sch. 1 (with art. 11)

Extension of special public interest regime

378. Extension of special public interest regime for certain media mergers

(1) In section 59 of the Enterprise Act 2002 (c. 40) (intervention by Secretary of State in special public interest cases), for subsections (3) and (4) (definition of "special merger situation") there shall be substituted—

"(3)For the purposes of this Part a special merger situation has been created if—

(a) the condition mentioned in subsection (3. A) is satisfied; and

(b) immediately before the enterprises concerned ceased to be distinct—

(i) the conditions mentioned in subsection (3. B) were satisfied;

(ii) the condition mentioned in subsection (3. C) was satisfied; or

(iii) the condition mentioned in subsection (3. D) was satisfied.

(3. A)The condition mentioned in this subsection is that—

(a) no relevant merger situation has been created because of section 23. (1)(b) and (2)(b); but

(b) a relevant merger situation would have been created if those enactments were disregarded.

(3. B)The conditions mentioned in this subsection are that—

(a) at least one of the enterprises concerned was carried on in the United Kingdom or by or under the control of a body corporate incorporated in the United Kingdom; and

(b) a person carrying on one or more of the enterprises concerned was a relevant government contractor.

(3. C)The condition mentioned in this subsection is that, in relation to the supply of newspapers of any description, at least one-quarter of all the newspapers of that description which were supplied in the United Kingdom, or in a substantial part of the United Kingdom, were supplied by the person or persons by whom one of the enterprises concerned was carried on.

(3. D)The condition mentioned in this subsection is that, in relation to the provision of broadcasting of any description, at least one-quarter of all broadcasting of that description provided in the United Kingdom, or in a substantial part of the United Kingdom, was provided by the person or persons by whom one of the enterprises concerned was carried on."

(2) After subsection (6) of that section there shall be inserted—

"(6. A)The Secretary of State may by order amend the conditions mentioned in subsection (3)(b)(ii) and (iii)."

(3) After that section there shall be inserted—

"59. AConstruction of conditions in section 59. (3. C) and (3. D)

(1) For the purpose of deciding whether the proportion of one-quarter mentioned in section 59. (3. C) or (3. D) is fulfilled with respect to—

    (a) newspapers of any description, or

    (b) broadcasting of any description,

the decision-making authority shall apply such criterion (whether value, cost, price, quantity, capacity, number of workers employed or some other criterion, of whatever nature), or such combination of criteria, as the decision-making authority considers appropriate.

(2) References in section 59. (3. C) to the supply of newspapers shall, in relation to newspapers of any description which are the subject of different forms of supply, be construed in whichever of the following ways the decision-making authority considers appropriate—

    (a) as references to any of those forms of supply taken separately;

    (b) as references to all those forms of supply taken together; or

    (c) as references to any of those forms of supply taken in groups.

(3) For the purposes of subsection (2) the decision-making authority may treat newspapers as being the subject of different forms of supply whenever—

    (a) the transactions concerned differ as to their nature, their parties, their terms or their surrounding circumstances; and

    (b) the difference is one which, in the opinion of the decision-making authority, ought for the purposes of that subsection to be treated as a material difference.

(4) References in section 59. (3. D) to the provision of broadcasting shall, in relation to broadcasting of any description which is the subject of different forms of provision, be construed in whichever of the following ways the decision-making authority considers appropriate—

    (a) as references to any of those forms of provision taken separately;

    (b) as references to all those forms of provision taken together; or

    (c) as references to any of those forms of provision taken in groups.

(5) For the purposes of subsection (4) the decision-making authority may treat broadcasting as being the subject of different forms of provision whenever—

    (a) the transactions concerned differ as to their nature, their parties, their terms or their surrounding circumstances; and

    (b) the difference is one which, in the opinion of the decision-making authority, ought for the purposes of that subsection to be treated as a material difference.

(6) The criteria for deciding when newspapers or broadcasting can be treated, for the purposes of section 59, as newspapers or broadcasting of a separate description shall be such as in any particular case the decision-making authority considers appropriate in the circumstances of that case.

(7) In section 59 and this section "provision" and cognate expressions have the same meaning in relation to broadcasting as in Part 3 of the Communications Act 2003; but this subsection is subject to subsections (4) and (5) of this section."

Commencement Information

I14. S. 378 in force at 29.12.2003 by S.I. 2003/3142, art. 3. (1), Sch. 1 (with art. 11)

379. Adaptation of role of OFT in special public interest regime

(1) Section 61 of the Enterprise Act 2002 (c. 40) (initial investigation and report by OFT in special public interest cases) shall be amended as follows.

(2) In subsection (3)(b) (report must include summary of representations about considerations specified in section 58) after the word "concerned" there shall be inserted " (other than a consideration which, at the time of the giving of the notice, was specified in section 58. (2. A) to (2. C)) ".

(3) In subsection (4) for the words "59. (4)(b)" there shall be substituted " 59. (3. B)(b) ".

(4) After subsection (4) there shall be inserted—

"(4. A)The report may, in particular, contain a summary of any representations about the case which have been received by the OFT and which relate to any consideration which—

(a) is mentioned in the special intervention notice concerned and, at the time of the giving of that notice, was specified in section 58. (2. A) to (2. C); and

(b) is or may be relevant to the Secretary of State's decision as to whether to make a reference under section 62."

Commencement Information

I15. S. 379 in force at 29.12.2003 by S.I. 2003/3142, art. 3. (1), Sch. 1 (with art. 11)

380. Additional investigation and report by OFCOM: special public interest cases

After section 61 of the Enterprise Act 2002 (initial investigation and report by OFT in special public interest cases) there shall be inserted—

"61. AAdditional investigation and report by OFCOM: certain media mergers

(1) Subsection (2) applies where—

(a) the Secretary of State has given a special intervention notice in relation to a special merger situation; and

(b) the special intervention notice mentions any consideration which, at the time of the giving of the notice, was specified in section 58. (2. A) to (2. C).

(2) OFCOM shall, within such period as the Secretary of State may require, give a report to the Secretary of State on the effect of the consideration or considerations concerned on the case.

(3) The report shall contain—

(a) advice and recommendations on any consideration which—

(i) is mentioned in the special intervention notice concerned and, at the time of the giving of that notice, was specified in section 58. (2. A) to (2. C); and

(ii) is or may be relevant to the Secretary of State's decision as to whether to make a reference under section 62; and

(b) a summary of any representations about the case which have been received by OFCOM and which relate to any such consideration.

(4) OFCOM shall carry out such investigations as they consider appropriate for the purposes of producing a report under this section."

Commencement Information

I16. S. 380 in force at 29.12.2003 by S.I. 2003/3142, art. 3. (1), Sch. 1 (with art. 11)

New general functions in relation to media mergers

381. Public consultation in relation to media mergers

After section 104 of the Enterprise Act 2002 (c. 40) there shall be inserted—

"104. APublic consultation in relation to media mergers

(1) Subsection (2) applies where the Commission—

(a) is preparing—

(i) a report under section 50 on a reference which specifies a media public interest consideration; or

(ii) a report under section 65 on a reference which specifies a consideration specified in section 58. (2. A) to (2. C); and

(b) is not under a duty to disregard the consideration concerned.

(2) The Commission shall have regard (among other things) to the need to consult the public so far as they might be affected by the creation of the relevant merger situation or special merger situation concerned and so far as such consultation is practicable.

(3) Any consultation of the kind mentioned in subsection (2) may be undertaken by the Commission by consulting such representative sample of the public or section of the public concerned as the Commission considers appropriate."

Commencement Information

I17. S. 381 in force at 29.12.2003 by S.I. 2003/3142, art. 3. (1), Sch. 1 (with art. 11)

382. General information duties in relation to media mergers

(1) Section 105 of the Enterprise Act 2002 (general information duties of OFT and Competition Commission) shall be amended as follows.

(2) After subsection (1) there shall be inserted—

"(1. A)Where OFCOM decide to investigate a matter so as to make a report under section 44. A or 61. A, they shall, so far as practicable, take such action as they consider appropriate to bring information about the investigation to the attention of those who they consider might be affected by the creation of the relevant merger situation concerned or (as the case may be) the special merger situation concerned."

(3) In subsection (2) (exclusion for merger notices) for the words "Subsection (1) does" there shall be substituted " Subsections (1) and (1. A) do ".

(4) In subsection (3) (duty of OFT to give requested assistance to Competition Commission)—

    (a) after the word "Commission", where it occurs for the first time, there shall be inserted " or OFCOM "; and

    (b) after the word "Commission", where it occurs for the second, third and fourth time, there shall be inserted " or (as the case may be) OFCOM ".

(5) After subsection (3) there shall be inserted—

"(3. A)OFCOM shall give the Commission or the OFT—

    (a) such information in their possession as the Commission or (as the case may be) the OFT may reasonably require to enable the Commission or (as the case may be) the OFT to carry out its functions under this Part; and

    (b) any other assistance which the Commission or (as the case may be) the OFT may reasonably require for the purpose of assisting it in carrying out its functions under this Part and which it is within the power of OFCOM to give."

(6) In subsection (4) (duty of OFT to give unrequested information to Competition Commission)—

    (a) after the word "Commission", where it occurs for the first time, there shall be inserted " or OFCOM "; and

    (b) after the word "Commission", where it occurs for the second and third time, there shall be inserted " or (as the case may be) OFCOM ".

(7) After subsection (4) there shall be inserted—

"(4. A)OFCOM shall give the Commission or the OFT any information in their possession which has not been requested by the Commission or (as the case may be) the OFT but which, in the opinion of OFCOM, would be appropriate to give to the Commission or (as the case may be) the OFT for the purpose of assisting it in carrying out its functions under this Part."

(8) In subsection (5) (duty of OFT and Competition Commission to give requested assistance to the Secretary of State) after the word "OFT", in both places where it occurs, there shall be inserted " , OFCOM ".

(9) In subsection (6) (duty of OFT to give unrequested information to Secretary of State)—

    (a) after the word "OFT", where it occurs for the first time, there shall be inserted " and OFCOM ";

    (b) for the word "its" there shall be substituted " their "; and

    (c) after the word "OFT", where it occurs for the second time, there shall be inserted " or (as the case may be) OFCOM ".

(10) In subsection (7) (duty to have regard to information given) for the words "or (4)" there shall be substituted " , (3. A), (4) or (4. A) ".

(11) After subsection (7) there shall be inserted—

"(7. A)OFCOM shall have regard to any information given to them under subsection (3) or (4); and the OFT shall have regard to any information given to it under subsection (3. A) or (4. A)."

Commencement Information

I18. S. 382 in force at 29.12.2003 by S.I. 2003/3142, art. 3. (1), Sch. 1 (with art. 11)

383. Advice and information in relation to media mergers

After section 106 of the Enterprise Act 2002 (c. 40) there shall be inserted—

"106. AAdvice and information in relation to media mergers

(1) The Secretary of State may prepare and publish general advice and information about the considerations specified in section 58. (2. A) to (2. C).

(2) The Secretary of State may at any time publish revised, or new, advice or information.

(3) Advice or information published under this section shall be prepared with a view to—

(a) explaining the considerations specified in section 58. (2. A) to (2. C) to persons who are likely to be affected by them; and

(b) indicating how the Secretary of State expects this Part to operate in relation to such considerations.

(4) Any advice or information published by the Secretary of State under this section shall be published in such manner as the Secretary of State considers appropriate.

(5) In preparing any advice or information under this section, the Secretary of State shall consult the OFT, OFCOM, the Commission and such other persons as he considers appropriate."

Commencement Information

I19. S. 383 in force at 29.12.2003 by S.I. 2003/3142, art. 3. (1), Sch. 1 (with art. 11)

384. General advisory functions of OFCOM in relation to media mergers

After section 106. A of the Enterprise Act 2002 there shall be inserted—

"106. BGeneral advisory functions of OFCOM

(1) OFCOM may, in connection with any case on which they are required to give a report by virtue of section 44. A or 61. A, give such advice as they consider appropriate to the Secretary of State in relation to—

(a) any report made in such a case by the Commission under section 50 or 65; and

(b) the taking by the Secretary of State of enforcement action under Schedule 7.

(2) OFCOM may, if requested to do so by the Secretary of State, give such other advice as they consider appropriate to the Secretary of State in connection with any case on which they are required to give a report by virtue of section 44. A or 61. A.

(3) OFCOM shall publish any advice given by them under this section but advice given by them in relation to a report of the Commission under section 50 or 65 or related enforcement action shall not be published before the report itself is published."

Commencement Information

I20. S. 384 in force at 29.12.2003 by S.I. 2003/3142, art. 3. (1), Sch. 1 (with art. 11)

385. Other general functions of OFCOM in relation to media mergers

After section 119 of the Enterprise Act 2002 (c. 40) there shall be inserted—

"Further provision about media mergers

119. AOther general functions of OFCOM in relation to this Part

(1) OFCOM have the function of obtaining, compiling and keeping under review information about matters relating to the carrying out of their functions under this Part.

(2) That function is to be carried out with a view to (among other things) ensuring that OFCOM have sufficient information to take informed decisions and to carry out their other functions effectively.

(3) In carrying out that function OFCOM may carry out, commission or support (financially or otherwise) research.

(4) Section 3 of the Communications Act 2003 (general duties of OFCOM) shall not apply in relation to functions of OFCOM under this Part."

Commencement Information

I21. S. 385 in force at 29.12.2003 by S.I. 2003/3142, art. 3. (1), Sch. 1 (with art. 11)

386. Monitoring role for OFT in relation to media mergers

After section 119. A of the Enterprise Act 2002 there shall be inserted—

"119. BMonitoring role for OFT in relation to media mergers

(1) The OFT has the function of obtaining, compiling and keeping under review information about matters which may be relevant to the Secretary of State in deciding whether to give a special intervention notice mentioning a consideration specified in section 58. (2. A) to (2. C).

(2) That function is to be carried out with a view to (among other things) ensuring that the Secretary of State is aware of cases where, in the opinion of the OFT, he might wish to consider giving such a notice.

(3) That function does not extend to obtaining, compiling or keeping under review information with a view to carrying out a detailed analysis in each case of the operation in relation to that case of the consideration specified in section 58. (2. A) to (2. C)."

Commencement Information
I22. S. 386 in force at 29.12.2003 by S.I. 2003/3142, art. 3. (1), Sch. 1 (with art. 11)

Supplemental provisions of Chapter 2.

387. Enforcement powers in relation to newspaper and other media mergers

In Schedule 8 to the Enterprise Act 2002 (provision that may be contained in certain enforcement orders) after paragraph 20 there shall be inserted—

20. A(1)This paragraph applies in relation to any order—

(a) which is to be made following the giving of—

(i) an intervention notice which mentions a newspaper public interest consideration;

(ii) an intervention notice which mentions any other media public interest consideration in relation to a relevant merger situation in which one of the enterprises ceasing to be distinct is a newspaper enterprise;

(iii) a special intervention notice which mentions a consideration specified in section 58. (2. A) or (2. B); or

(iv) a special intervention notice which, in relation to a special merger situation in which one of the enterprises ceasing to be distinct is a newspaper enterprise, mentions a consideration specified in section 58. (2. C); and

(b) to which the consideration concerned is still relevant.

(2) The order may make such provision as the person making the order considers to be appropriate in all circumstances of the case.

(3) Such provision may, in particular, include provision requiring a person to do, or not to do, particular things.

(4) Provision made by virtue of this paragraph may, in particular, include provision—

(a) altering the constitution of a body corporate (whether in connection with the appointment of directors, the establishment of an editorial board or otherwise);

(b) requiring the agreement of the relevant authority or another person before the taking of particular action (including the appointment or dismissal of an editor, journalists or directors or acting as a shadow director);

(c) attaching conditions to the operation of a newspaper;

(d) prohibiting consultation or co-operation between subsidiaries.

(5) In this paragraph "newspaper public interest consideration" means a media public interest consideration other than one which is such a consideration—

(a) by virtue of section 58. (2. C); or

(b) by virtue of having been, in the opinion of the Secretary of State, concerned with broadcasting and a consideration that ought to have been specified in section 58.

(6) This paragraph is without prejudice to the operation of the other paragraphs of this Schedule in relation to the order concerned."

Commencement Information
I23. S. 387 in force at 29.12.2003 by S.I. 2003/3142, art. 3. (1), Sch. 1 (with art. 11)

F31388. Alterations concerning newspaper panel of Competition Commission

. . . .

Amendments (Textual)
F31. S. 388 omitted (1.4.2014) by virtue of The Enterprise and Regulatory Reform Act 2013 (Competition) (Consequential, Transitional and Saving Provisions) Order 2014 (S.I. 2014/892),

art. 1. (1), Sch. 1 para. 163 (with art. 3)
Commencement Information
I24. S. 388 in force at 29.12.2003 by S.I. 2003/3142, art. 3. (1), Sch. 1 (with art. 11)
389. Further provision in connection with media mergers
(1) Schedule 16 (which contains further amendments in connection with media mergers) shall have effect.
(2) Sections 276. (2) and (3) and 277 of the Enterprise Act 2002 (c. 40) (power to make transitional and consequential amendments etc.) shall apply in relation to this Chapter of this Part of this Act and its related repeals as they apply in relation to that Act.
(3) For the avoidance of doubt, the power conferred by virtue of subsection (2) by applying section 277 of the Act of 2002 includes the power to modify that Act.
(4) Section 402 shall not apply in relation to any power to make an order which is exercisable by the Secretary of State by virtue of subsection (2).
Commencement Information
I25. S. 389 in force at 29.12.2003 by S.I. 2003/3142, art. 3. (1), Sch. 1 (with art. 11)

OFCOM's functions under Part 4. of the Enterprise Act 2002

370. OFCOM's functions under Part 4 of the Enterprise Act 2002.

(1) The functions to which subsection (2) applies shall be concurrent functions of OFCOM and the [F1. Competition and Markets Authority (referred to in this Part as "the CMA")] .
(2) This subsection applies to the functions of the [F2. CMA] under Part 4 of the Enterprise Act 2002 (market investigations) (other than sections 166 [F3, 171 and 174. E]) so far as [F4those functions—
  (a) are exercisable by the CMA Board (within the meaning of Schedule 4 to the Enterprise and Regulatory Reform Act 2013), and
  (b) relate to] commercial activities connected with communications matters.
(3) So far as necessary for the purposes of, or in connection with, subsections [F5. (1) and (2)—
  (a) references] in Part 4 of the Enterprise Act 2002 to the [F6. CMA] (including references in provisions of that Act applied by that Part) shall be construed as including references to OFCOM [F7. (except in sections 166, 171 and 174. E and where the context otherwise requires);
  (b) references in that Part to the CMA carrying out functions under section 5 of the Enterprise Act 2002 are to be construed as including references to OFCOM exercising powers under section 1. (3) of this Act to obtain, compile and keep under review information about matters relating to the carrying out of its functions.]
[F8. (3. A)Section 130. A of the Enterprise Act 2002 is to have effect in its application in relation to OFCOM by virtue of subsections (1) and (2)—
  (a) as if for subsection (1) of that section there were substituted—
"(1)Where the Office of Communications—
  (a) is proposing to fulfil its duties under section 3. (1) of the Communications Act 2003 by obtaining, compiling and keeping under review information in relation to a matter for the purposes mentioned in subsection (2), and
  (b) considers that the matter is one in respect of which it would be appropriate for it to exercise its powers under section 174 (investigation) in connection with deciding whether to make a reference under section 131,
the Office of Communications must publish a notice under this section (referred to in this Part as a "market study notice").", and
  (b) as if in subsection (2)(a) of that section, for "the acquisition or supply of goods or services

of one or more than one description in the United Kingdom" there were substituted "commercial activities connected with communications matters (within the meaning given by section 369. (1) of the Communications Act 2003)".]

(4) In [F9subsections (2) and (3. A) the references] to activities connected with communications matters, so far as [F10they are references] to activities connected with any apparatus falling within paragraph (d) of section 369. (1), [F11include] a reference to—

(a) the supply and export of any such apparatus; and

(b) the production or acquisition of any such apparatus for supply or export.

(5) Before the [F12. CMA] or OFCOM first exercises in relation to any matter functions which are exercisable concurrently by virtue of this section, that person shall consult the other.

(6) Neither the [F12. CMA] nor OFCOM shall exercise in relation to any matter functions which are exercisable concurrently by virtue of this section if functions which are so exercisable have been exercised in relation to that matter by the other.

(7) It shall be the duty of OFCOM, for the purpose of assisting [F13a CMA group] in carrying out an investigation on a [F14market investigation reference made by OFCOM (under section 131 of the Enterprise Act 2002)] by virtue of subsection (1), to give to the [F15group] —

(a) any information which is in OFCOM's possession and relates to matters falling within the scope of the investigation and—

(i) is requested by the [F15group] for that purpose, or

(ii) is information which, in OFCOM's opinion, it would be appropriate for that purpose to give to the [F15group] without any such request;

and

(b) any other assistance which the [F15group] may require, and which it is within OFCOM's power to give, in relation to any such matters,

and the [F15group] , for the purposes of carrying out any such investigation, shall take into account any information given to it for that purpose under this subsection.

[F16. (7. A)In subsection (7) "CMA group" has the same meaning as in Schedule 4 to the Enterprise and Regulatory Reform Act 2013.]

(8) If any question arises as to whether, by virtue of this section, any functions fall to be, or are capable of being, carried out by OFCOM in relation to any particular case, that question shall be referred to and determined by the Secretary of State.

(9) No objection shall be taken to anything done under Part 4 of the Enterprise Act 2002 (c. 40) by or in relation to OFCOM on the ground that it should have been done by or in relation to the [F17. CMA] .

(10) Section 117 of the Enterprise Act 2002 (offences of supplying false or misleading information) as applied by section 180 of that Act shall have effect so far as relating to functions exercisable by OFCOM by virtue of this section as if the references in section 117. (1)(a) and (2) to the [F17. CMA] included references to OFCOM.

(11) Subject to subsection (12), [F18section 3 of this Act (general duties) and section 29 of the Postal Services Act 2011 (duty to secure provision of universal postal service) do not] apply in relation to anything done by OFCOM in the carrying out of their functions by virtue of this section.

(12) In the carrying out of any functions by virtue of this section OFCOM may nevertheless have regard to any of the matters in respect of which a duty is imposed by [F19section 3. (1) to (4) of this Act or section 29 of the Postal Services Act 2011] if it is a matter to which the [F20. CMA] is entitled to have regard in the carrying out of those functions.

Amendments (Textual)

F1. Words in s. 370. (1) substituted (1.4.2014) by The Enterprise and Regulatory Reform Act 2013 (Competition) (Consequential, Transitional and Saving Provisions) Order 2014 (S.I. 2014/892), art. 1. (1), Sch. 1 para. 161. (2) (with art. 3)

F2. Word in s. 370. (2) substituted (1.4.2014) by The Enterprise and Regulatory Reform Act 2013 (Competition) (Consequential, Transitional and Saving Provisions) Order 2014 (S.I. 2014/892), art. 1. (1), Sch. 1 para. 161. (3)(b) (with art. 3)

F3. Words in s. 370. (2) substituted (1.4.2014) by The Enterprise and Regulatory Reform Act 2013 (Competition) (Consequential, Transitional and Saving Provisions) Order 2014 (S.I. 2014/892), art. 1. (1), Sch. 1 para. 161. (3)(a) (with art. 3)

F4. Words in s. 370. (2) substituted (1.4.2014) by The Enterprise and Regulatory Reform Act 2013 (Competition) (Consequential, Transitional and Saving Provisions) Order 2014 (S.I. 2014/892), art. 1. (1), Sch. 1 para. 161. (3)(c) (with art. 3)

F5. Words in s. 370. (3) substituted (1.4.2014) by The Enterprise and Regulatory Reform Act 2013 (Competition) (Consequential, Transitional and Saving Provisions) Order 2014 (S.I. 2014/892), art. 1. (1), Sch. 1 para. 161. (4)(a) (with art. 3)

F6. Word in s. 370. (3)(a) substituted (1.4.2014) by The Enterprise and Regulatory Reform Act 2013 (Competition) (Consequential, Transitional and Saving Provisions) Order 2014 (S.I. 2014/892), art. 1. (1), Sch. 1 para. 161. (4)(b) (with art. 3)

F7. Words in s. 370. (3) substituted (1.4.2014) by The Enterprise and Regulatory Reform Act 2013 (Competition) (Consequential, Transitional and Saving Provisions) Order 2014 (S.I. 2014/892), art. 1. (1), Sch. 1 para. 161. (4)(c) (with art. 3)

F8. S. 370. (3. A) inserted (1.4.2014) by The Enterprise and Regulatory Reform Act 2013 (Competition) (Consequential, Transitional and Saving Provisions) Order 2014 (S.I. 2014/892), art. 1. (1), Sch. 1 para. 161. (5) (with art. 3)

F9. Words in s. 370. (4) substituted (1.4.2014) by The Enterprise and Regulatory Reform Act 2013 (Competition) (Consequential, Transitional and Saving Provisions) Order 2014 (S.I. 2014/892), art. 1. (1), Sch. 1 para. 161. (6)(a) (with art. 3)

F10. Words in s. 370. (4) substituted (1.4.2014) by The Enterprise and Regulatory Reform Act 2013 (Competition) (Consequential, Transitional and Saving Provisions) Order 2014 (S.I. 2014/892), art. 1. (1), Sch. 1 para. 161. (6)(b) (with art. 3)

F11. Word in s. 370. (4) substituted (1.4.2014) by The Enterprise and Regulatory Reform Act 2013 (Competition) (Consequential, Transitional and Saving Provisions) Order 2014 (S.I. 2014/892), art. 1. (1), Sch. 1 para. 161. (6)(c) (with art. 3)

F12. Word in s. 370. (5)(6) substituted (1.4.2014) by The Enterprise and Regulatory Reform Act 2013 (Competition) (Consequential, Transitional and Saving Provisions) Order 2014 (S.I. 2014/892), art. 1. (1), Sch. 1 para. 161. (7) (with art. 3)

F13. Words in s. 370. (7) substituted (1.4.2014) by The Enterprise and Regulatory Reform Act 2013 (Competition) (Consequential, Transitional and Saving Provisions) Order 2014 (S.I. 2014/892), art. 1. (1), Sch. 1 para. 161. (8)(a) (with art. 3)

F14. Words in s. 370. (7) substituted (1.4.2014) by The Enterprise and Regulatory Reform Act 2013 (Competition) (Consequential, Transitional and Saving Provisions) Order 2014 (S.I. 2014/892), art. 1. (1), Sch. 1 para. 161. (8)(b) (with art. 3)

F15. Word in s. 370. (7) substituted (1.4.2014) by The Enterprise and Regulatory Reform Act 2013 (Competition) (Consequential, Transitional and Saving Provisions) Order 2014 (S.I. 2014/892), art. 1. (1), Sch. 1 para. 161. (8)(c) (with art. 3)

F16. S. 370. (7. A) inserted (1.4.2014) by The Enterprise and Regulatory Reform Act 2013 (Competition) (Consequential, Transitional and Saving Provisions) Order 2014 (S.I. 2014/892), art. 1. (1), Sch. 1 para. 161. (9) (with art. 3)

F17. Word in s. 370. (9)(10) substituted (1.4.2014) by The Enterprise and Regulatory Reform Act 2013 (Competition) (Consequential, Transitional and Saving Provisions) Order 2014 (S.I. 2014/892), art. 1. (1), Sch. 1 para. 161. (10) (with art. 3)

F18. Words in s. 370. (11) substituted (1.10.2011) by Postal Services Act 2011 (c. 5), s. 93. (2)(3), Sch. 12 para. 63. (2); S.I. 2011/2329, art. 3

F19. Words in s. 370. (12) substituted (1.10.2011) by Postal Services Act 2011 (c. 5), s. 93. (2)(3), Sch. 12 para. 63. (3); S.I. 2011/2329, art. 3

F20. Word in s. 370. (12) substituted (1.4.2014) by The Enterprise and Regulatory Reform Act 2013 (Competition) (Consequential, Transitional and Saving Provisions) Order 2014 (S.I. 2014/892), art. 1. (1), Sch. 1 para. 161. (10) (with art. 3)

Commencement Information

11. S. 370 in force at 25.7.2003 for specified purposes by S.I. 2003/1900, arts. 1. (2), 2. (1), Sch. 1 (with art. 3) (as amended by S.I. 2003/3142, art. 1. (3))
12. S. 370 in force at 29.12.2003 in so far as not already in force by S.I. 2003/3142, art. 3. (2) (with art. 11)

Part 6. Miscellaneous and Supplemental

Part 6. Miscellaneous and Supplemental

390. Annual report on the Secretary of State's functions

(1) The Secretary of State must prepare and lay before Parliament regular reports on the carrying out by him of the functions to which this section applies.
(2) This section applies to the Secretary of State's functions under the following enactments—
    (a) this Act;
    (b) the Office of Communications Act 2002 (c. 11);
    (c) the enactments relating to the management of the radio spectrum so far as not comprised in this Act;
    (d) the 1990 Act;
    (e) the 1996 Act.
(3) The first report under this section must relate to the period which—
    (a) begins with 19th March 2002 (the date of the passing of the Office of Communications Act 2002); and
    (b) ends with the period of twelve months beginning with the first date to be appointed for the purposes of section 2 of this Act.
(4) Every subsequent report must relate to the period of twelve months beginning with the end of the period to which the previous report related.
(5) The obligation under this section to prepare and lay a report before Parliament is an obligation to do that as soon as reasonably practicable after the end of the period to which the report relates.
(6) Where a report for the purposes of this section relates to a period the whole or a part of which falls before the time when the whole of this Act is in force, the functions referred to in subsection (2) are to be taken as excluding all functions under the specified enactments that will have ceased to be functions of the Secretary of State when the whole of this Act is in force.
Commencement Information
11. S. 390 in force at 29.12.2003 by S.I. 2003/3142, art. 3. (1), Sch. 1 (with art. 11)

Review of media ownership

391. Review of media ownership

(1) It shall be the duty of OFCOM—
    (a) to carry out regular reviews of the operation, taken together, of all the provisions to which this section applies; and
    (b) to send a report on every such review to the Secretary of State.
(2) This section applies to—
    (a) the provisions of Schedule 2 to the 1990 Act;
    (b) the provision made by or under Schedule 14 to this Act;

(c) the provisions of sections 280 and 281 of this Act;

(d) whatever provision (if any) has been made under section 283 of this Act; and

(e) the provisions of Part 3 of the Enterprise Act 2002 (c. 40) so far as they relate to intervention by the Secretary of State in connection with newspapers or other media enterprises.

(3) The first review must be carried out no more than three years after the commencement of this section, and subsequent reviews must be carried out at intervals of no more than three years.

(4) The report to the Secretary of State on a review must set out OFCOM's recommendations, in consequence of their conclusions on the review, for the exercise by the Secretary of State of—

(a) his power to make an order under section 348. (5);

(b) his powers to make orders under Schedule 14;

(c) his powers under sections 282 and 283; and

(d) his powers under sections 44. (11), 58. (3) and 59. (6. A) of the Enterprise Act 2002 (media mergers).

(5) OFCOM must publish every report sent by them to the Secretary of State under this section in such manner as they consider appropriate for bringing it to the attention of persons who, in their opinion, are likely to be affected by it.

Commencement Information

I2. S. 391 in force at 29.12.2003 by S.I. 2003/3142, art. 3. (1), Sch. 1 (with art. 11)

Guidelines as to penalties

392. Penalties imposed by OFCOM

(1) It shall be the duty of OFCOM to prepare and publish a statement containing the guidelines they propose to follow in determining the amount of penalties imposed by them under provisions contained in this Act or any other enactment apart from the Competition Act 1998 (c. 41).

(2) OFCOM may from time to time revise that statement as they think fit.

(3) Where OFCOM make or revise their statement under this section, they must publish the statement or (as the case may be) the revised statement in such manner as they consider appropriate for bringing it to the attention of the persons who, in their opinion, are likely to be affected by it.

(4) Before publishing a statement or revised statement under this section OFCOM must consult both—

(a) the Secretary of State, and

(b) such other persons as they consider appropriate,

about the guidelines they are proposing to include in the statement.

(5) Before determining how to publish a statement or revised statement under this section OFCOM must consult the Secretary of State.

(6) It shall be the duty of OFCOM, in determining the amount of any penalty to be imposed by them under this Act or any other enactment (apart from the Competition Act 1998 (c. 41)) to have regard to the guidelines contained in the statement for the time being in force under this section.

(7) References in this section to penalties imposed by OFCOM under provisions contained in this Act include references to penalties which the BBC is liable to pay to OFCOM by virtue of section 198. (3).

Commencement Information

I3. S. 392 in force at 29.12.2003 by S.I. 2003/3142, art. 3. (1), Sch. 1 (with art. 11)

Disclosure of information

393. General restrictions on disclosure of information

(1) Subject to the following provisions of this section, information with respect to a particular business which has been obtained in exercise of a power conferred by—

(a) this Act,

F1. (b). . . . .

(c) the 1990 Act, or

(d) the 1996 Act,

is not, so long as that business continues to be carried on, to be disclosed without the consent of the person for the time being carrying on that business.

(2) Subsection (1) does not apply to any disclosure of information which is made—

(a) for the purpose of facilitating the carrying out by OFCOM of any of their functions;

(b) for the purpose of facilitating the carrying out by any relevant person of any relevant function;

(c) for the purpose of facilitating the carrying out by the Comptroller and Auditor General of any of his functions;

(d) for any of the purposes specified in section 17. (2)(a) to (d) of the Anti-terrorism, Crime and Security Act 2001 (c. 24) (criminal proceedings and investigations);

(e) for the purpose of any civil proceedings brought under or by virtue of this Act or any of the enactments or instruments mentioned in subsection (5); or

(f) for the purpose of securing compliance with an international obligation of the United Kingdom.

(3) Each of the following is a relevant person for the purposes of this section—

(a) a Minister of the Crown and the Treasury;

(b) the Scottish Executive;

(c) a Northern Ireland department;

(d) the [F2. Competition and Markets Authority] ;

F3. (e). . . . .

(f) the Consumer Panel;

(g) the Welsh Authority;

(h) a local weights and measures authority in Great Britain;

(i) any other person specified for the purposes of this subsection in an order made by the Secretary of State.

(4) The following are relevant functions for the purposes of this section—

(a) any function conferred by or under this Act;

(b) any function conferred by or under any enactment or instrument mentioned in subsection (5);

(c) any other function specified for the purposes of this subsection in an order made by the Secretary of State.

(5) The enactments and instruments referred to in subsections (2) and (4) are—

F4. (a). . . . .

F4. (b). . . . .

F5. (c). . . . .

(d) the Trade Descriptions Act 1968 (c. 29);

(e) the Fair Trading Act 1973 (c. 41);

(f) the Consumer Credit Act 1974 (c. 39);

(g) the Competition Act 1980 (c. 21);

(h) the Telecommunications Act 1984 (c. 12);

(i) the Consumer Protection Act 1987 (c. 43);

(j) the 1990 Act;

(k) the 1996 Act;

F6. (l). . . . .

(m) the Competition Act 1998 (c. 41);

(n) the Enterprise Act 2002 (c. 40);

[F7. (na)the Wireless Telegraphy Act 2006;]

(o) the Consumer Protection (Northern Ireland) Order 1987 (S.I. 1987/2049 (N.I. 20));

[F8. (p)the Business Protection from Misleading Marketing Regulations 2008;

(q) the Consumer Protection from Unfair Trading Regulations 2008.]

[F9. (r)Parts 3 and 4 of the Enterprise and Regulatory Reform Act 2013.]

(6) Nothing in this section—

(a) limits the matters that may be published under section 15, 26 or 390;

[F10. (aa)limits the information that may be made available under section 76. A;]

(b) limits the matters that may be included in, or made public as part of, a report made by OFCOM by virtue of a provision of this Act or the Office of Communications Act 2002 (c. 11);

(c) prevents the disclosure of anything for the purposes of a report of legal proceedings in which it has been publicly disclosed;

(d) applies to information that has been published [F11, made public or made available] as mentioned in paragraphs (a) to (c).

(7) Nothing in this section applies to information obtained in exercise of the powers conferred by section 196 of the 1990 Act (powers of entry and search).

(8) Information obtained by OFCOM in exercise of functions which are exercisable by them concurrently with the [F12. Competition and Markets Authority] under Part 1 of the Competition Act 1998 is subject to Part 9 of the Enterprise Act 2002, and not to the preceding provisions of this section.

(9) Section 18 of the Anti-terrorism, Crime and Security Act 2001 (c. 24) (restriction on disclosure of information for overseas purposes) shall have effect in relation to a disclosure by virtue of subsection (2)(d) as it applies in relation to a disclosure in exercise of a power to which section 17 of that Act applies.

(10) A person who discloses information in contravention of this section is guilty of an offence and shall be liable—

(a) on summary conviction, to a fine not exceeding the statutory maximum;

(b) on conviction on indictment, to imprisonment for a term not exceeding two years or to a fine, or to both.

(11) No order is to be made containing provision authorised by subsection (3) or (4) unless a draft of the order has been laid before Parliament and approved by a resolution of each House.

(12) In this section "legal proceedings" means civil or criminal proceedings in or before any court, or proceedings before any tribunal established by or under any enactment.

Amendments (Textual)

F1. S. 393. (1)(b) repealed (8.2.2007) by Wireless Telegraphy Act 2006 (c. 36), s. 126. (2), Sch. 9 Pt. 1 (with Sch. 8 Pt. 1)

F2. Words in s. 393. (3)(d) substituted (1.4.2014) by The Enterprise and Regulatory Reform Act 2013 (Competition) (Consequential, Transitional and Saving Provisions) Order 2014 (S.I. 2014/892), art. 1. (1), Sch. 1 para. 164. (1)(a)(i) (with art. 3)

F3. S. 393. (3)(e) omitted (1.4.2014) by virtue of The Enterprise and Regulatory Reform Act 2013 (Competition) (Consequential, Transitional and Saving Provisions) Order 2014 (S.I. 2014/892), art. 1. (1), Sch. 1 para. 164. (1)(a)(ii) (with art. 3)

F4. S. 393. (5)(a)(b) repealed (8.2.2007) by Wireless Telegraphy Act 2006 (c. 36), s. 126. (2), Sch. 9 Pt. 1 (with Sch. 8 Pt. 1)

F5. S. 393. (5)(c) repealed (25.6.2013) by Enterprise and Regulatory Reform Act 2013 (c. 24), s. 103. (2), Sch. 21 para. 2

F6. S. 393. (5)(l) repealed (8.2.2007) by Wireless Telegraphy Act 2006 (c. 36), s. 126. (2), Sch. 9 Pt. 1 (with Sch. 8 Pt. 1)

F7. S. 393. (5)(na) inserted (8.2.2007) by Wireless Telegraphy Act 2006 (c. 36), s. 126. (2), Sch. 7 para. 31

F8. S. 393. (5)(p)(q) substituted for s. 393. (5)(p) (26.5.2008) by The Consumer Protection from

Unfair Trading Regulations 2008 (S.I. 2008/1277), reg. 1, Sch. 2 para. 72 (with reg. 28. (2)(3))
F9. S. 393. (5)(r) inserted (1.4.2014) by The Enterprise and Regulatory Reform Act 2013 (Competition) (Consequential, Transitional and Saving Provisions) Order 2014 (S.I. 2014/892), art. 1. (1), Sch. 1 para. 164. (1)(b) (with art. 3)
F10. S. 393. (6)(aa) inserted (26.5.2011) by The Electronic Communications and Wireless Telegraphy Regulations 2011 (S.I. 2011/1210), reg. 1. (2), Sch. 1 para. 97. (a) (with Sch. 3 para. 2)
F11. Words in s. 393. (6)(d) substituted (26.5.2011) by The Electronic Communications and Wireless Telegraphy Regulations 2011 (S.I. 2011/1210), reg. 1. (2), Sch. 1 para. 97. (b) (with Sch. 3 para. 2)
F12. Words in s. 393. (8) substituted (1.4.2014) by The Enterprise and Regulatory Reform Act 2013 (Competition) (Consequential, Transitional and Saving Provisions) Order 2014 (S.I. 2014/892), art. 1. (1), Sch. 1 para. 164. (1)(c) (with art. 3)
Modifications etc. (not altering text)
C1. S. 393 applied (20.7.2004) by Contracting Out (Functions relating to Broadcast Advertising) and Specification of Relevant Functions Order 2004 (S.I. 2004/1975), arts. 1, 11. (1) (with art. 5)
Commencement Information
I4. S. 393. (1)(a)(b)(2)-(4)(5)(a)-(i)(l)-(p)(6)(b)-(d)(8)-(12) in force at 25.7.2003 for specified purposes by S.I. 2003/1900, arts. 1. (2), 2. (1), Sch. 1 (with art. 3) (as amended by S.I. 2003/3142, art. 1. (3))
I5. S. 393. (1)(a) (b) (2)-(4) (5)(a)-(i) (l)-(p) (6)(b)-(d) (8)-(12) in force at 29.12.2003 in so far as not already in force by S.I. 2003/3142, art. 3. (1), Sch. 1 (with art. 11)
I6. S. 393. (1)(c)(d)(5)(j)(k)(7) in force at 29.12.2003 by S.I. 2003/3142, art. 3. (1), Sch. 1 (with art. 11)
I7. S. 393. (6)(a) in force at 25.7.2003 for specified purposes by S.I. 2003/1900, arts. 1. (2), 2. (1), Sch. 1 (with art. 3) (as amended by S.I. 2003/3142, art. 1. (3))
I8. S. 393. (6)(a) in force at 29.12.2003 in so far as not already in force by S.I. 2003/3142, art. 3. (1), Sch. 2 (with art. 11)

Notifications etc. and electronic working

394. Service of notifications and other documents

(1) This section applies where provision made (in whatever terms) by or under an enactment specified in subsection (2) authorises or requires—
(a) a notification to be given to any person; or
(b) a document of any other description (including a copy of a document) to be sent to any person.
(2) Those enactments are—
(a) this Act;
(b) the Office of Communications Act 2002 (c. 11);
F13. (c). . . . .
(d) Schedule 2 to the Telecommunications Act 1984 (c. 12);
(e) the 1990 Act; F14...
(f) the 1996 Act.
[F15. (g)Part 3 of the Postal Services Act 2011.]
(3) The notification or document may be given or sent to the person in question—
(a) by delivering it to him;
(b) by leaving it at his proper address; or
(c) by sending it by post to him at that address.
(4) The notification or document may be given or sent to a body corporate by being given or sent

to the secretary or clerk of that body.

(5) The notification or document may be given or sent to a firm by being given or sent to—

(a) a partner in the firm; or

(b) a person having the control or management of the partnership business.

(6) The notification or document may be given or sent to an unincorporated body or association by being given or sent to a member of the governing body of the body or association.

(7) For the purposes of this section and section 7 of the Interpretation Act 1978 (c. 30) (service of documents by post) in its application to this section, the proper address of a person is—

(a) in the case of body corporate, the address of the registered or principal office of the body;

(b) in the case of a firm, unincorporated body or association, the address of the principal office of the partnership, body or association;

(c) in the case of a person to whom the notification or other document is given or sent in reliance on any of subsections (4) to (6), the proper address of the body corporate, firm or (as the case may be) other body or association in question; and

(d) in any other case, the last known address of the person in question.

(8) In the case of—

(a) a company registered outside the United Kingdom,

(b) a firm carrying on business outside the United Kingdom, or

(c) an unincorporated body or association with offices outside the United Kingdom,

the references in subsection (7) to its principal office include references to its principal office within the United Kingdom (if any).

(9) In this section—

"document" includes anything in writing; and

"notification" includes notice;

and references in this section to giving or sending a notification or other document to a person include references to transmitting it to him and to serving it on him.

(10) This section has effect subject to section 395.

Amendments (Textual)

F13. S. 394. (2)(c) repealed (8.2.2007) by Wireless Telegraphy Act 2006 (c. 36), s. 126. (2), Sch. 9 Pt. 1 (with Sch. 8 Pt. 1)

F14. Word in s. 394. (2)(e) omitted (1.10.2011) by virtue of Postal Services Act 2011 (c. 5), s. 93. (2)(3), Sch. 12 para. 65. (a); S.I. 2011/2329, art. 3

F15. S. 394. (2)(g) inserted (1.10.2011) by Postal Services Act 2011 (c. 5), s. 93. (2)(3), Sch. 12 para. 65. (b); S.I. 2011/2329, art. 3

Modifications etc. (not altering text)

C2. Ss. 394, 395 applied (31.7.2016) by The Communications (Access to Infrastructure) Regulations 2016 (S.I. 2016/700), regs. 1, 23

C3. S. 394. (2)(c) modified (temp.) (8.12.2003) by The Office of Communications Act 2002 (Commencement No. 3) and Communications Act 2003 (Commencement No. 2) Order 2003 (S.I. 2003/3142), art. 3. (3)(c) (with art. 11)

Commencement Information

I9. S. 394. (1)(2)(a)-(d)(3)-(10) in force at 25.7.2003 for specified purposes by S.I. 2003/1900, arts. 1. (2), 2. (1), Sch. 1 (with art. 3) (as amended by S.I. 2003/3142, art. 1. (3))

I10. S. 394. (1) (2)(a)-(d) (3)-(10) in force at 29.12.2003 in so far as not already in force by S.I. 2003/3142, art. 3. (1), Sch. 1 (with art. 11)

I11. S. 394. (2)(e)(f) in force at 29.12.2003 by S.I. 2003/3142, art. 3. (1), Sch. 1 (with art. 11)

395. Notifications and documents in electronic form

(1) This section applies where—

(a) section 394 authorises the giving or sending of a notification or other document by its delivery to a particular person ("the recipient"); and

(b) the notification or other document is transmitted to the recipient—

(i) by means of an electronic communications network; or

(ii) by other means but in a form that nevertheless requires the use of apparatus by the recipient to render it intelligible.

(2) The transmission has effect for the purposes of the enactments specified in section 394. (2) as a delivery of the notification or other document to the recipient, but only if the requirements imposed by or under this section are complied with.

(3) Where the recipient is OFCOM—

(a) they must have indicated their willingness to receive the notification or other document in a manner mentioned in subsection (1)(b);

(b) the transmission must be made in such manner and satisfy such other conditions as they may require; and

(c) the notification or other document must take such form as they may require.

(4) Where the person making the transmission is OFCOM, they may (subject to subsection (5)) determine—

(a) the manner in which the transmission is made; and

(b) the form in which the notification or other document is transmitted.

(5) Where the recipient is a person other than OFCOM—

(a) the recipient, or

(b) the person on whose behalf the recipient receives the notification or other document,

must have indicated to the person making the transmission the recipient's willingness to receive notifications or documents transmitted in the form and manner used.

(6) An indication to any person for the purposes of subsection (5)—

(a) must be given to that person in such manner as he may require;

(b) may be a general indication or one that is limited to notifications or documents of a particular description;

(c) must state the address to be used and must be accompanied by such other information as that person requires for the making of the transmission; and

(d) may be modified or withdrawn at any time by a notice given to that person in such manner as he may require.

[F16. (6. A)Subsections (5) and (6) do not apply in relation to a notification or other document given by OFCOM under Part 1 or Chapter 1 of Part 2 to the European Commission, BEREC or the regulatory authorities of member States (within the meaning of that Chapter).]

(7) An indication, requirement or determination given, imposed or made by OFCOM for the purposes of this section is to be given, imposed or made by being published in such manner as they consider appropriate for bringing it to the attention of the persons who, in their opinion, are likely to be affected by it.

(8) Subsection (9) of section 394 applies for the purposes of this section as it applies for the purposes of that section.

Amendments (Textual)

F16. S. 395. (6. A) inserted (26.5.2011) by The Electronic Communications and Wireless Telegraphy Regulations 2011 (S.I. 2011/1210), reg. 1. (2), Sch. 1 para. 98 (with Sch. 3 para. 2)

Modifications etc. (not altering text)

C2. Ss. 394, 395 applied (31.7.2016) by The Communications (Access to Infrastructure) Regulations 2016 (S.I. 2016/700), regs. 1, 23

Commencement Information

I12. S. 395 in force at 25.7.2003 for specified purposes by S.I. 2003/1900, arts. 1. (2), 2. (1), Sch. 1 (with art. 3) (as amended by S.I. 2003/3142, art. 1. (3))

I13. S. 395 in force at 29.12.2003 in so far as not already in force by S.I. 2003/3142, art. 3. (2) (with art. 11)

396. Timing and location of things done electronically

(1) The Secretary of State may by order make provision specifying, for the purposes of the enactments specified in section 394. (2), the manner of determining—

(a) the times at which things done under those enactments by means of electronic communications networks are done; and

(b) the places at which such things are so done, and at which things transmitted by means of such networks are received.

(2) The provision made by subsection (1) may include provision as to the country or territory in which an electronic address is to be treated as located.

(3) An order made by the Secretary of State may also make provision about the manner of proving in any legal proceedings—

(a) that something done by means of an electronic communications network satisfies the requirements of the enactments specified in section 394. (2) for the doing of that thing; and

(b) the matters mentioned in subsection (1)(a) and (b).

(4) An order under this section may provide for such presumptions to apply (whether conclusive or not) as the Secretary of State considers appropriate.

Commencement Information

I14. S. 396 in force at 25.7.2003 for specified purposes by S.I. 2003/1900, arts. 1. (2), 2. (1), Sch. 1 (with art. 3) (as amended by S.I. 2003/3142, art. 1. (3))

I15. S. 396 in force at 29.12.2003 in so far as not already in force by S.I. 2003/3142, art. 3. (2) (with art. 11)

Other miscellaneous provisions

397. Purchase of Duchy of Lancaster land

(1) The Chancellor and Council of the Duchy of Lancaster may, if they think fit, agree with a person who provides a public electronic communications network for the sale, and absolutely make sale, for such sum of money as appears to them sufficient consideration for the same, of any land which—

(a) belongs to Her Majesty in right of the Duchy of Lancaster; and

(b) is land which that person seeks to acquire for, or in connection with, the provision of his network.

(2) In this section "public electronic communications network" has the same meaning as in Chapter 1 of Part 2.

Commencement Information

I16. S. 397 in force at 25.7.2003 for specified purposes by S.I. 2003/1900, arts. 1. (2), 2. (1), Sch. 1 (with art. 3) (as amended by S.I. 2003/3142, art. 1. (3))

I17. S. 397 in force at 29.12.2003 in so far as not already in force by S.I. 2003/3142, art. 3. (2) (with art. 11)

398. Repeal of certain provisions of the Telecommunications Act 1984.

(1) The Telecommunications Act 1984 (c. 12) shall be amended as follows.

(2) In Part 5 (transfer of undertakings of British Telecommunications), the following provisions (which include spent provisions) shall cease to have effect—

(a) section 60;

(b) section 61. (1) to (6);

(c) section 62;

(d) section 63. (1) to (4);

(e) sections 64 to 67;

(f) section 69 to 71;

(g) sections 72. (2), (4) and (5); and

(h) section 73.

(3) In section 68. (2) (liability of Secretary of State on winding up), after "any outstanding liability of the successor company" there shall be inserted " for the payment of pensions ".

(4) In Part 7 (miscellaneous and supplemental) the following provisions shall cease to have effect—

(a) section 93 (grants to promote interests of disabled persons); and

(b) section 97 (contributions by local authorities towards the provision of telecommunications facilities).

Commencement Information

I18. S. 398 in force at 25.7.2003 for specified purposes by S.I. 2003/1900, arts. 1. (2), 2. (1), Sch. 1 (with art. 3) (as amended by S.I. 2003/3142, art. 1. (3))

I19. S. 398 in force at 29.12.2003 in so far as not already in force by S.I. 2003/3142, art. 3. (2) (with art. 11)

Supplemental

399. Expenses

There shall be paid out of money provided by Parliament—

(a) any expenditure incurred by the Secretary of State for or in connection with the carrying out of any of his functions under this Act; and

(b) any increase attributable to this Act in the sums which are payable out of money so provided under any other Act.

Commencement Information

I20. S. 399 in force at 25.7.2003 for specified purposes by S.I. 2003/1900, arts. 1. (2), 2. (1), Sch. 1 (with art. 3) (as amended by S.I. 2003/3142, art. 1. (3))

I21. S. 399 in force at 29.12.2003 in so far as not already in force by S.I. 2003/3142, art. 3. (2) (with art. 11)

400. Destination of licence fees and penalties

(1) This section applies (subject to section 401) to the following amounts—

(a) an amount paid to OFCOM in respect of a penalty imposed by them under Chapter 1 of Part 2 (including a penalty imposed by virtue of section 191. (5));

(b) so much of an amount paid to OFCOM under numbering conditions in respect of an allocation of telephone numbers as is an amount determined by reference to an indication given in response to an invitation such as is mentioned in section 58. (5)(a);

(c) an amount paid to OFCOM in pursuance of an obligation imposed by or under [F17. Chapter 1 or 2 of Part 2 of the Wireless Telegraphy Act 2006] ;

(d) an amount paid to OFCOM in respect of a penalty imposed by them under [F18section 42 [F19or 43. A] of that Act] ;

(e) a cash bid amount paid to OFCOM under a Broadcasting Act licence for the first year falling within the period for which the licence is in force;

(f) an amount paid to OFCOM under such a licence for a subsequent year as the amount equal to a cash bid amount increased by the appropriate percentage;

(g) an amount paid to OFCOM under such a licence as an amount representing a percentage of relevant revenue for an accounting period;

(h) an amount paid to OFCOM in respect of a penalty imposed by them under Part 1 or 3 of the 1990 Act, Part 1 or 2 of the 1996 Act or Part 3 of this Act.

[F20. (i)an amount paid to OFCOM in respect of a penalty imposed by them under Part 3 of the Postal Services Act 2011.]

(2) Where OFCOM receive an amount to which this section applies, it must be paid into the appropriate Consolidated Fund; but this subsection does not apply to an amount which is required by OFCOM for making an adjustment in respect of an overpayment.

(3) The reference in subsection (2) to the payment of an amount into the appropriate Consolidated Fund—

(a) in the case of an amount received in respect of matters appearing to OFCOM to have no connection with Northern Ireland, is a reference to the payment of the amount into the Consolidated Fund of the United Kingdom;

(b) in the case of an amount received in respect of matters appearing to OFCOM to have a connection with Northern Ireland but no connection with the rest of the United Kingdom, is a reference to the payment of the amount into the Consolidated Fund of Northern Ireland; and

(c) in any other case, is a reference to the payment of the amount, in such proportions as OFCOM consider appropriate, into each of those Funds.

(4) OFCOM must, in respect of each financial year, prepare an account showing—

(a) the amounts to which this section applies that have been received by them during that year;

(b) the sums paid into the Consolidated Funds of the United Kingdom and Northern Ireland respectively under this section in respect of those amounts;

(c) the aggregate amount of the sums received by them during that year that is retained in accordance with a statement of principles under section 401 for meeting the costs of carrying out functions mentioned in subsection (4) of that section during that year;

(d) the aggregate amount that they estimate will fall to be so retained out of amounts due to them and likely to be paid or recovered; and

(e) the cost to OFCOM of carrying out during that year the functions in respect of which amounts are or are to be retained in accordance with such a statement.

(5) OFCOM must send that account to the Comptroller and Auditor General not later than the end of the month of November following the financial year to which it relates.

(6) The Comptroller and Auditor General must examine, certify and report on the account and lay copies of it, together with his report, before each House of Parliament.

(7) References in this section to penalties imposed by OFCOM under Part 3 of this Act include references to penalties which the BBC is liable to pay to OFCOM by virtue of section 198. (3).

(8) In this section—

"the appropriate percentage" has the same meaning as in section 19 of the 1990 Act;

"cash bid amount" means an amount specified in a cash bid for a Broadcasting Act licence or the amount determined by OFCOM for the purposes of any provision of the 1990 Act or this Part to be what would have been the amount of a cash bid for a licence;

"financial year" has the same meaning as in the Schedule to the Office of Communications Act 2002 (c. 11);

"numbering conditions" means conditions the setting of which is authorised by section 58 or 59; and

"relevant revenue" means any of the following—

- the amount which for the purposes of section 19, 52. (1), 102. (1) or 118 (1) of the 1990 Act is the amount of qualifying revenue for an accounting period;

- the amount which for the purposes of section 13. (1) or 55. (1) of the 1996 Act is the amount of multiplex revenue for an accounting period; or

- an amount which for the purposes of paragraph 7 of Schedule 10 to this Act is the amount of qualifying revenue for an accounting period.

Amendments (Textual)

F17. Words in s. 400. (1)(c) substituted (8.2.2007) by Wireless Telegraphy Act 2006 (c. 36), s.

126. (2), Sch. 7 para. 32. (a)

F18. Words in s. 400. (1)(d) substituted (8.2.2007) by Wireless Telegraphy Act 2006 (c. 36), s. 126. (2), Sch. 7 para. 32. (b)

F19. Words in s. 400. (1)(d) inserted (8.6.2010) by Digital Economy Act 2010 (c. 24), ss. 39. (3), 47. (1)

F20. S. 400. (1)(i) inserted (1.10.2011) by Postal Services Act 2011 (c. 5), s. 93. (2)(3), Sch. 12 para. 66; S.I. 2011/2329, art. 3

Commencement Information

122. S. 400 in force at 29.12.2003 by S.I. 2003/3142, art. 3. (1), Sch. 1 (with art. 11)

Prospective

401. Power of OFCOM to retain costs of carrying out spectrum functions

(1) OFCOM have power to make a statement of the principles under which they may retain any or all of the amounts paid to them in pursuance of obligations imposed by or under [F21. Chapter 1 or 2 of Part 2 of the Wireless Telegraphy Act 2006] .

(2) Where such a statement of principles authorises the retention of an amount, OFCOM are not required to pay it into the appropriate Consolidated Fund in accordance with section 400.

(3) Principles contained in a statement made by OFCOM under this section must be such as appear to them to be likely to secure, on the basis of such estimates of the likely costs as it is practicable to make—

(a) that, on a year by year basis, the aggregate amount of the amounts retained by OFCOM does not exceed the amount required by OFCOM for meeting the annual cost to OFCOM of carrying out the functions mentioned in subsection (4);

(b) that the amounts retained by OFCOM are objectively justifiable and proportionate to the costs in respect of which they are retained; and

(c) that the relationship between meeting the cost of carrying out those functions and the amounts retained is transparent.

(4) Those functions are—

(a) OFCOM's functions under the enactments relating to the management of the radio spectrum except those specified in subsection (5); and

(b) the function of taking any steps that OFCOM consider it necessary to take—

(i) in preparation for the carrying out of any of the functions mentioned in paragraph (a) of this subsection; or

(ii) for the purpose of facilitating the carrying out of those functions or otherwise in connection with carrying them out.

(5) The excepted functions of OFCOM are—

(a) their functions under section 22. (2);

[F22. (b)their functions under section 1. (1) and (2) of the Wireless Telegraphy Act 2006 so far as carried out in relation to the use of the electromagnetic spectrum at places outside the United Kingdom, and their functions under section 1. (5);

(c) their functions under section 4 of that Act;

(d) their functions under section 7 of that Act;

(e) their functions under section 30 of that Act;

(f) their functions under sections 42 to 44 of that Act;

(g) any functions conferred on them under sections 47 to 49 of that Act; and]

(h) any function not falling within the preceding paragraphs in so far as the costs of carrying it out are met from payments made to OFCOM by virtue of section 28 [F23of this Act or section 1. (8) of the Wireless Telegraphy Act 2006].

(6) A statement under this section may include provision which, for the purposes of the principles contained in the statement and of the preparation of accounts in accordance with section 400. (4),

requires an amount actually received in one year—

(a) to be treated as referable to costs incurred in that year and in one or more subsequent years; and

(b) to be brought into account, in each of those years, in accordance with an apportionment for which provision is made in the statement.

(7) A deficit or surplus shown (after applying this subsection for all previous years) by an account prepared under section 400. (4) is to be carried forward and taken into account in determining what is required by OFCOM in relation to the following year for meeting the costs of carrying out the functions mentioned in subsection (4) of this section.

(8) A statement of principles under this section—

(a) if it is expressed to apply for a limited period, does not apply to any amounts paid to OFCOM after the end of that period; and

(b) in any event, does not apply to amounts paid to them after a withdrawal of the statement takes effect.

(9) OFCOM may revise a statement made under this section.

(10) The consent of the Treasury is required for the making, revision or withdrawal of a statement under this section.

(11) Where OFCOM make or revise a statement of this section they must publish so much of the statement or revised statement as appears to them necessary for demonstrating that the statement or revision complies with subsection (3).

Amendments (Textual)

F21. Words in s. 401. (1) substituted (8.2.2007) by Wireless Telegraphy Act 2006 (c. 36), s. 126. (2), Sch. 7 para. 33. (2)

F22. S. 401. (5)(b)-(g) substituted (8.2.2007) by Wireless Telegraphy Act 2006 (c. 36), s. 126. (2), Sch. 7 para. 33. (3)

F23. Words in s. 401. (5)(h) substituted (8.2.2007) by Wireless Telegraphy Act 2006 (c. 36), s. 126. (2), Sch. 7 para. 33. (4)

402. Power of Secretary of State to make orders and regulations

(1) Every power conferred by this Act on the Secretary of State to make orders or regulations, other than the powers conferred by Schedule 4, is a power exercisable by statutory instrument.

(2) A statutory instrument containing an order or regulations made in exercise of any such power, other than—

(a) an order under section 31 or 411,

F24. (b). . . . .

(c) any order that is required, by any provision of this Act, to be laid before Parliament and approved in draft,

shall be subject to annulment in pursuance of a resolution of either House of Parliament.

(3) Every power of the Secretary of State to make an order or regulations under this Act, other than an order under section 31 or 411 or an order made in exercise of a power conferred by Schedule 4, includes power—

(a) to make different provision for different cases (including different provision in respect of different areas);

(b) to make provision subject to such exemptions and exceptions as the Secretary of State thinks fit; and

(c) to make such incidental, supplemental, consequential and transitional provision as the Secretary of State thinks fit.

Amendments (Textual)

F24. S. 402. (2)(b) repealed (8.2.2007) by Wireless Telegraphy Act 2006 (c. 36), s. 126. (2), Sch. 9 Pt. 1 (with Sch. 8 Pt. 1)

Commencement Information

123. S. 402 in force at 25.7.2003 for specified purposes by S.I. 2003/1900, arts. 1. (2), 2. (1), Sch. 1 (with art. 3) (as amended by S.I. 2003/3142, art. 1. (3))

124. S. 402 in force at 29.12.2003 in so far as not already in force by S.I. 2003/3142, art. 3. (2) (with art. 11)

403. Regulations and orders made by OFCOM

(1) This section applies to any power of OFCOM to make regulations or to make an order or scheme if that power is one to which this section is expressly applied.

(2) The powers to which this section applies shall be exercisable by statutory instrument, and the Statutory Instruments Act 1946 (c. 36) is to apply in relation to those powers as if OFCOM were a Minister of the Crown.

(3) Where an instrument made under a power to which this section applies falls to be laid before Parliament, OFCOM must, immediately after it is made, send it to the Secretary of State for laying by him.

(4) Before making any regulations or order under a power to which this section applies, OFCOM must—

(a) give a notice of their proposal to do so to such persons representative of the persons appearing to OFCOM to be likely to be affected by the implementation of the proposal as OFCOM think fit;

(b) publish notice of their proposal in such manner as they consider appropriate for bringing it to the attention of the persons who, in their opinion, are likely to be affected by it and are not given notice by virtue of paragraph (a); and

(c) consider any representations that are made to OFCOM, before the time specified in the notice.

(5) A notice for the purposes of subsection (4) must—

(a) state that OFCOM propose to make the regulations or order in question;

(b) set out the general effect of the regulations or order;

(c) specify an address from which a copy of the proposed regulations or order may be obtained; and

(d) specify a time before which any representations with respect to the proposal must be made to OFCOM.

(6) The time specified for the purposes of subsection (5)(d) must be no earlier than the end of the period of one month beginning with the day after the latest day on which the notice is given or published for the purposes of subsection (4).

(7) Every power of OFCOM to which this section applies includes power—

(a) to make different provision for different cases (including different provision in respect of different areas);

(b) to make provision subject to such exemptions and exceptions as OFCOM think fit; and

(c) to make such incidental, supplemental, consequential and transitional provision as OFCOM think fit.

(8) The Documentary Evidence Act 1868 (c. 37) (proof of orders and regulations etc.) shall have effect as if—

(a) OFCOM were included in the first column of the Schedule to that Act;

(b) OFCOM and persons authorised to act on their behalf were mentioned in the second column of that Schedule.

Modifications etc. (not altering text)

C4. S. 403 applied by 1998 c. 6, s. 6 (as substituted (25.7.2003 for specified purposes, 29.12.2003 in so far as not already in force) by Communications Act 2003 (c. 21), s. 411. (2), Sch. 17 para. 150 (with Sch. 18); S.I. 2003/1900, arts. 1. (2), 2. (1), Sch. 1 (with art. 3) (as amended by S.I. 2003/3142, art. 1. (3)); S.I. 2003/3142, art. 3. (1), Sch. 1 (with art. 11))

C5. S. 403 applied by 1996 c. 55, s. 104. ZA(3) (as inserted (29.12.2003) by Communications Act

2003 (c. 21), ss. 302. (1), 411. (2) (with Sch. 18 para. 51. (3)); S.I. 2003/3142, art. 3. (1), Sch. 1 (with art. 11))
C6. S. 403 applied (1.10.2011) by Postal Services Act 2011 (c. 5), ss. 63, 93. (2), (3); S.I. 2011/2329, art. 3
Commencement Information
I25. S. 403 in force at 25.7.2003 for specified purposes by S.I. 2003/1900, arts. 1. (2), 2. (1), Sch. 1 (with art. 3) (as amended by S.I. 2003/3142, art. 1. (3))
I26. S. 403 in force at 29.12.2003 in so far as not already in force by S.I. 2003/3142, art. 3. (2) (with art. 11)

404. Criminal liability of company directors etc.

(1) Where an offence under any enactment to which this section applies is committed by a body corporate and is proved to have been committed with the consent or connivance of, or to be attributable to any neglect on the part of—
(a) a director, manager, secretary or other similar officer of the body corporate, or
(b) a person who was purporting to act in any such capacity,
he (as well as the body corporate) is guilty of that offence and shall be liable to be proceeded against and punished accordingly.
(2) Where an offence under any enactment to which this section applies—
(a) is committed by a Scottish firm, and
(b) is proved to have been committed with the consent or connivance of, or to be attributable to any neglect on the part of a partner of the firm,
he (as well as the firm) is guilty of that offence and shall be liable to be proceeded against and punished accordingly.
(3) In this section "director", in relation to a body corporate whose affairs are managed by its members, means a member of the body corporate.
(4) The enactments to which this section applies are every enactment contained in—
(a) this Act;
F25. (b). . . . .
F25. (c). . . . .
F26. (d). . . . .
(e) the Telecommunications Act 1984 (c. 12)[F27; or
(f) Part 3 of the Postal Services Act 2011.]
F28. (5). . . . .
Amendments (Textual)
F25. S. 404. (4)(b)(c) repealed (8.2.2007) by Wireless Telegraphy Act 2006 (c. 36), s. 126. (2), Sch. 9 Pt. 1 (with Sch. 8 Pt. 1)
F26. S. 404. (4)(d) repealed (25.6.2013) by Enterprise and Regulatory Reform Act 2013 (c. 24), s. 103. (2), Sch. 21 para. 2
F27. S. 404. (4)(f) and word inserted (1.10.2011) by Postal Services Act 2011 (c. 5), s. 93. (2)(3), Sch. 12 para. 67. (b); S.I. 2011/2329, art. 3
F28. S. 404. (5) repealed (8.2.2007) by Wireless Telegraphy Act 2006 (c. 36), s. 126. (2), Sch. 9 Pt. 1 (with Sch. 8 Pt. 1)
Commencement Information
I27. S. 404 in force at 25.7.2003 for specified purposes by S.I. 2003/1900, arts. 1. (2), 2. (1), Sch. 1 (with art. 3) (as amended by S.I. 2003/3142, art. 1. (3))
I28. S. 404 in force at 29.12.2003 in so far as not already in force by S.I. 2003/3142, art. 3. (2) (with art. 11)

405. General interpretation

(1) In this Act, except in so far as the context otherwise requires—

"the 1990 Act" means the Broadcasting Act 1990 (c. 42);

"the 1996 Act" means the Broadcasting Act 1996 (c. 55);

"access" is to be construed in accordance with subsection (4);

"apparatus" includes any equipment, machinery or device and any wire or cable and the casing or coating for any wire or cable;

"associated facility" has the meaning given by section 32;

[F29"the Audiovisual Media Services Directive" means Directive 2010/13/EU of the European Parliament and of the Council on the coordination of certain provisions laid down by law, regulation or administrative action in Member States concerning the provision of audiovisual media services]

   - Directive 97/36/EC of the European Parliament and of the Council; and

   - Directive 2007/65 EC of the European Parliament and of the Council;

"the BBC" means the British Broadcasting Corporation;

[F30"BEREC" means the Body of European Regulators for Electronic Communications;]

"body" (without more) means any body or association of persons, whether corporate or unincorporate, including a firm;

"broadcast" means broadcast by wireless telegraphy, and cognate expressions are to be construed accordingly;

"Broadcasting Act licence" means a licence under Part 1 or 3 of the 1990 Act or under Part 1 or 2 of the 1996 Act;

"business" includes any trade or profession;

"C4. C" means the Channel Four Television Corporation;

"communications provider" means a person who (within the meaning of section 32. (4)) provides an electronic communications network or an electronic communications service;

"the Consumer Panel" means the panel established under section 16;

"consumers" has the meaning given by subsection (5);

"Content Board" means the committee of OFCOM established and maintained under section 12;

"contravention" includes a failure to comply, and cognate expressions are to be construed accordingly;

"customers", in relation to a communications provider or a person who makes an associated facility available, means the following (including any of them whose use or potential use of the network, service or facility is for the purposes of, or in connection with, a business)—

   - the persons to whom the network, service or facility is provided or made available in the course of any business carried on as such by the provider or person who makes it available;

   - the persons to whom the communications provider or person making the facility available is seeking to secure that the network, service or facility is so provided or made available;

   - the persons who wish to be so provided with the network or service, or to have the facility so made available, or who are likely to seek to become persons to whom the network, service or facility is so provided or made available;

"distribute", in relation to a service, does not include broadcast, and cognate expressions shall be construed accordingly;

"electronic communications network" and "electronic communications service" have the meanings given by section 32;

"enactment" includes any enactment comprised in an Act of the Scottish Parliament or in any Northern Ireland legislation;

"the enactments relating to the management of the radio spectrum" means—

   - [F31the Wireless Telegraphy Act 2006; and]

   - [F32the provisions of this Act so far as relating to that Act;]

"frequency" includes frequency band;

"holder", in relation to a Broadcasting Act licence, is to be construed in accordance with subsection (7), and cognate expressions are to be construed accordingly;

"information" includes accounts, estimates and projections and any document;

"intelligible" is to be construed in accordance with subsection (9);

"international obligation of the United Kingdom" includes any [F33. EU] obligation and any obligation which will or may arise under any international agreement or arrangements to which the United Kingdom is a party;

"modification" includes omissions, alterations and additions, and cognate expressions are to be construed accordingly;

"OFCOM" means the Office of Communications;

[F34"on-demand programme service" has the meaning given by section 368. A(1);]

"other member State" means a member State other than the United Kingdom;

[F35"postal services" has the meaning given by section 27 of the Postal Services Act 2011;]

"pre-commencement regulator" means any of the following—
   - the Broadcasting Standards Commission;
   - the Director General of Telecommunications;
   - the Independent Television Commission;
   - the Radio Authority;

"programme" includes an advertisement and, in relation to a service, anything included in that service;

"programme service" means—
   - a television programme service;
   - the public teletext service;
   - an additional television service;
   - a digital additional television service;
   - a radio programme service; or
   - a sound service provided by the BBC;

and expressions used in this definition and in Part 3 have the same meanings in this definition as in that Part;

"provide" and cognate expressions, in relation to an electronic communications network, electronic communications service or associated facilities, are to be construed in accordance with section 32. (4);

"purposes of public service television broadcasting in the United Kingdom" shall be construed in accordance with subsection (4) of section 264 and subsections (5) and (6) of that section shall apply for the purposes of any provision of this Act referring to such purposes as they apply for the purposes of a report under that section;

"the radio transfer date" means the date on which the Radio Authority's functions under Part 3 of the 1990 Act and Part 2 of the 1996 Act are transferred under this Act to OFCOM;

"representation", in relation to a proposal or the contents of any notice or notification, includes an objection to the proposal or (as the case may be) to the whole or any part of those contents;

"subordinate legislation" means—
   - any subordinate legislation, within the meaning of the Interpretation Act 1978 (c. 30); or
   - any statutory rules (within the meaning of the Statutory Rules (Northern Ireland) Order 1979 (S.I. 1979/1573 (N.I. 12));

"television and radio services" means—
   - programme services apart from those provided by the BBC; and
   - services provided by the BBC in relation to which OFCOM have functions;

"television programme" means any programme (with or without sounds) which—
   - is produced wholly or partly to be seen on television; and
   - consists of moving or still images or of legible text or of a combination of those things;

"the television transfer date" means the date on which the Independent Television Commission's functions under Part 1 of the 1990 Act and Part 1 of the 1996 Act are transferred under this Act to OFCOM;

"TV licence" means a licence for the purposes of section 363;

"the Welsh Authority" means the authority whose name is, by virtue of section 56. (1) of the 1990 Act, Sianel Pedwar Cymru;

[F36"wireless telegraphy" has the same meaning as in the Wireless Telegraphy Act 2006;]
[F37"wireless telegraphy licence" means a licence granted under section 8 of the Wireless Telegraphy Act 2006.]

(2) Any power under this Act to provide for the manner in which anything is to be done includes power to provide for the form in which it is to be done.

(3) References in this Act to OFCOM's functions under an enactment include references to their power to do anything which appears to them to be incidental or conducive to the carrying out of their functions under that enactment.

(4) References in this Act to access—

(a) in relation to an electronic communications network or electronic communications service, are references to the opportunity of making use of the network or service; and

(b) in relation to a programme service, are references to the opportunity of viewing in an intelligible form the programmes included in the service or (as the case may be) of listening to them in such a form.

(5) For the purposes of this Act persons are consumers in a market for a service, facility or apparatus, if they are—

(a) persons to whom the service, facility or apparatus is provided, made available or supplied (whether in their personal capacity or for the purposes of, or in connection with, their businesses);

(b) persons for whose benefit the service, facility or apparatus is provided, made available or supplied or for whose benefit persons falling within paragraph (a) arrange for it to be provided, made available or supplied;

(c) persons whom the person providing the service or making the facility available, or the supplier of the apparatus, is seeking to make into persons falling within paragraph (a) or (b); or

(d) persons who wish to become persons falling within paragraph (a) or (b) or who are likely to seek to become persons falling within one or both of those paragraphs.

[F38. (5. A)References in this Act to consumers in a market for a service include, where the service is a postal service, addressees.]

(6) References in this Act to services in relation to which OFCOM have functions include references to any services in relation to which OFCOM are required to set standards under section 319.

(7) In this Act references, in relation to a time or a period, to the holder of a Broadcasting Act licence or of a particular description of such licence are references to the person who held that licence at that time or (as the case may be) to every person who held that licence for the whole or a part of that period.

(8) For the purposes of this Act the fact that a service is not in an intelligible form shall be disregarded, except where express provision is made to the contrary, in determining whether it has been provided—

(a) for general reception;

(b) for reception by particular persons; or

(c) for reception at a particular place or in a particular area.

(9) For the purposes of this Act something is not to be regarded as in an intelligible form if it cannot readily be understood without being decrypted or having some comparable process applied to it.

Amendments (Textual)

F29. Words in s. 405. (1) substituted (18.8.2010) by The Audiovisual Media Services (Codification) Regulations 2010 (S.I. 2010/1883), regs. 1, 5

F30. Words in s. 405. (1) inserted (26.5.2011) by The Electronic Communications and Wireless Telegraphy Regulations 2011 (S.I. 2011/1210), reg. 1. (2), Sch. 1 para. 99 (with Sch. 3 para. 2)

F31. Words in s. 405. (1) substituted (8.2.2007) by Wireless Telegraphy Act 2006 (c. 36), s. 126. (2), Sch. 7 para. 34. (2)(a)

F32. Words in s. 405. (1) substituted (8.2.2007) by Wireless Telegraphy Act 2006 (c. 36), s. 126. (2), Sch. 7 para. 34. (2)(b)

F33. Words in Act substituted (22.4.2011) by The Treaty of Lisbon (Changes in Terminology)

Order 2011 (S.I. 2011/1043), arts. 2, 3, 6 (with art. 3. (2)(3), 4. (2), 6. (4)(5))

F34. Words in s. 405. (1) inserted (19.12.2009) by Audiovisual Media Services Regulations 2009 (S.I. 2009/2979), regs. 1. (1), 11. (b)

F35. Words in s. 405. (1) inserted (1.10.2011) by Postal Services Act 2011 (c. 5), s. 93. (2)(3), Sch. 12 para. 68. (2); S.I. 2011/2329, art. 3

F36. Words in s. 405. (1) substituted (8.2.2007) by Wireless Telegraphy Act 2006 (c. 36), s. 126. (2), Sch. 7 para. 34. (3)

F37. Words in s. 405. (1) substituted (8.2.2007) by Wireless Telegraphy Act 2006 (c. 36), s. 126. (2), Sch. 7 para. 34. (4)

F38. S. 405. (5. A) inserted (1.10.2011) by Postal Services Act 2011 (c. 5), s. 93. (2)(3), Sch. 12 para. 68. (3); S.I. 2011/2329, art. 3

406. Minor and consequential amendments, transitionals and repeals

(1) Schedule 17 (which provides for minor and consequential amendments in connection with the other provision made by this Act) shall have effect.

(2) The Secretary of State may by order make such consequential modifications of any enactment as—

  (a) correspond to amendments of any other enactment that are made by Schedule 17; and

  (b) appear to him to be appropriate in consequence of that provision of this Act.

(3) The Secretary of State may by order make any provision that he thinks fit for substituting a reference in any enactment or subordinate legislation to something defined for the purposes of this Act, or of any provisions contained in this Act, for a reference to something equivalent or similar that was defined for the purposes of the Telecommunications Act 1984 (c. 12), or of provisions contained in that Act.

(4) The Secretary of State may by order make such further consequential modifications of—

  (a) an enactment extending only to Scotland,

  (b) an enactment extending only to Northern Ireland,

  (c) a local enactment, or

  (d) the provision of any subordinate legislation,

as appear to him to be appropriate in consequence of any provision of this Act.

(5) If it appears to the Secretary of State that a local enactment contains a provision which corresponds to a provision the effect of which is modified by an amendment in Schedule 17 of this Act of a listed provision, it shall be his duty to exercise his powers under this section to secure that a modification corresponding to that effected by that amendment is made to the local enactment.

(6) Schedule 18 (which contains transitional provisions in connection with the other provision made by this Act) shall have effect.

(7) Subject to the provisions of Schedule 18 and to the savings and commencement provisions set out in the notes to Schedule 19, the enactments and instruments specified in Schedule 19 (which include provisions that are spent or have ceased to be of any practical utility) are hereby repealed or revoked to the extent specified in the second column of that Schedule.

(8) In this section "local enactment" means—

  (a) a local or personal Act;

  (b) a public general Act relating only to London;

  (c) an order or scheme made under an Act which has been confirmed by Parliament or brought into operation in accordance with special Parliamentary procedure;

  (d) an enactment in a public general Act but amending a local enactment.

(9) In subsection (5) "listed provision" means the provisions of the following enactments—

  (a) sections 11 and 14 of the London Overground Wires, etc. Act 1933 (c. xliv);

  (b) section 7. (6) of the London County Council (General Powers) Act 1949 (c. lv);

  (c) section 17. (2) of the Lough Neagh and Lower Bann Drainage and Navigation Act (Northern

Ireland) 1955 (c. 15 (N.I.));

(d) section 17. (4)(a) of the London County Council (General Powers) Act 1963 (c. xvii);

(e) section 7. (6) of the Greater London Council (General Powers) Act 1969 (c. lii);

(f) section 20. (1)(a) of the Thames Barrier and Flood Prevention Act 1972 (c. xlv);

(g) section 32 of and paragraph 3. (2)(b) of Schedule 2 and Part 10 of Schedule 7 to the Channel Tunnel Act 1987 (c. 53);

(h) section 25. (1) of the Norfolk and Suffolk Broads Act 1988 (c. 4);

(i) section 5 of the London Local Authorities (No. 2) Act 1990 (c. xxx);

(j) paragraphs 1. (c) and 16 of Schedule 2, paragraph 3. (2)(c) of Schedule 4 and paragraph 21 of Schedule 7 to the Cardiff Bay Barrage Act 1993 (c. 42);

(k) section 3. (1) of the British Waterways Act 1995 (c. i);

(l) paragraphs 6. (4) and 15. (4) of Schedule 6 and Part 4 of Schedule 15 to the Channel Tunnel Rail Link Act 1996 (c. 61).

(10) This section has effect subject to section 408.

Commencement Information

I29. S. 406 in force at 25.7.2003 for specified purposes by S.I. 2003/1900, arts. 1. (2), 2. (1), Sch. 1 (with art. 3) (as amended by S.I. 2003/3142, art. 1. (3))

I30. S. 406. (1)(6)(7) in force at 18.9.2003 for specified purposes by S.I. 2003/1900, art. 2. (2), Sch. 2

I31. S. 406. (1)(6)(7) in force at 29.12.2003 for specified purposes by S.I. 2003/3142, art. 3. (1), Sch. 1 (with art. 11)

I32. S. 406. (1)(7) in force at 1.4.2004 for specified purposes by S.I. 2003/3142, art. 4. (2), Sch. 2 (with art. 11)

I33. S. 406. (2)-(5) (8)-(10) in force at 29.12.2003 in so far as not already in force by S.I. 2003/3142, art. 3. (2) (with art. 11)

I34. S. 406. (6) in force at 1.4.2004 in so far as not already in force by S.I. 2003/3142, art. 4. (2), Sch. 2 (with art. 11)

407. Pre-consolidation amendments

(1) The Secretary of State may by order make such modifications of—

F39. (a). . . . .

(b) the enactments relating to broadcasting, and

(c) enactments referring to enactments falling within paragraph F40... (b),

as in his opinion facilitate, or are otherwise desirable in connection with, the consolidation of those enactments or any of them.

(2) No order is to be made under this section unless a Bill for repealing and re-enacting—

(a) the enactments modified by the order, or

(b) enactments relating to matters connected with the matters to which enactments modified by the order relate,

has been presented to either House of Parliament.

(3) An order under this section is not to come into force until immediately before the commencement of the Act resulting from that Bill.

(4) No order is to be made containing provision authorised by this section unless a draft of the order has been laid before Parliament and approved by a resolution of each House.

(5) In this section "the enactments relating to broadcasting" means—

(a) the 1990 Act;

(b) the 1996 Act;

(c) Part 3 of this Act; and

(d) the other provisions of this Act so far as relating to the 1990 Act, the 1996 Act or that Part.

Amendments (Textual)

F39. S. 407. (1)(a) repealed (8.2.2007) by Wireless Telegraphy Act 2006 (c. 36), s. 126. (2), Sch.

9 Pt. 1 (with Sch. 8 Pt. 1)
F40. Words in s. 407. (1)(c) repealed (8.2.2007) by Wireless Telegraphy Act 2006 (c. 36), s. 126. (2), Sch. 9 Pt. 1 (with Sch. 8 Pt. 1)
Commencement Information
I35. S. 407 in force at 18.9.2003 by S.I. 2003/1900, art. 2. (2), Sch. 2

408. Transitional provision for anticipatory carrying out of functions

(1) This section applies where an order under section 411 bringing into force—
  (a) a provision of Part 1, 2 or 6, or
  (b) a provision of Chapter 1 of Part 5,
states that that provision is brought into force at a particular time for the purpose only of enabling specified networks and services functions, or specified spectrum functions, to be carried out during the transitional period by the Director General of Telecommunications or the Secretary of State.

(2) In relation to times falling in the transitional period, that provision is to have effect as if—
  (a) references in that provision to OFCOM, and
  (b) references to OFCOM inserted by that provision in any other enactment,
were references, in accordance with subsection (3), to the Director General of Telecommunications or to the Secretary of State.

(3) The references have effect—
  (a) as references to the Director General of Telecommunications to the extent that the provision is brought into force for the purpose of enabling specified networks and services functions to be carried out; and
  (b) as references to the Secretary of State, to the extent that the provision is brought into force for the purpose of enabling specified spectrum functions to be carried out.

(4) An order bringing a provision into force as mentioned in subsection (1) may include provision specifying the extent to which it is to be taken, for the purposes of subsection (3), to have been brought into force for the purpose of enabling particular functions to be carried out.

(5) In relation to times after the end of the transitional period for a provision which has been brought into force for enabling specified functions to be carried out by the Director General of Telecommunications or the Secretary of State, anything which—
  (a) was done, during that period, by or in relation to that Director or the Secretary of State, and
  (b) was so done for the purposes of, or in connection with, the carrying out of those functions,
is to have effect as if had been done by or in relation to OFCOM.

(6) In this section "the transitional period", in relation to a provision brought into force as mentioned in subsection (1) by an order under section 411, means the period which—
  (a) begins with the time when it is so brought into force; and
  (b) ends with the time from which that order, or a subsequent order under that section, brings the provision into force for the purpose of conferring on OFCOM the functions in question.

(7) In this section "networks and services functions" means any of the following functions of OFCOM under this Act—
  (a) their functions under sections 24 and 25;
  (b) their functions under Chapter 1 of Part 2;
  (c) their functions under Chapter 3 of Part 2, except to the extent that those functions relate to—
(i) disputes relating to rights or obligations conferred or imposed by or under the enactments relating to the management of the radio spectrum; or
(ii) decisions made under those enactments;
  (d) their functions under Chapter 1 of Part 5, except to the extent that those functions relate to broadcasting or related matters;
  (e) their functions under Schedule 18 to this Act in relation to the abolition of licensing (within

the meaning of that Schedule).

(8) In this section "spectrum functions" means—

(a) the functions under the enactments relating to the management of the radio spectrum which by virtue of this Act are conferred on OFCOM; and

(b) the functions conferred on OFCOM by so much of Chapter 3 of Part 2 as relates to the disputes and decisions mentioned in subsection (7)(c).

Subordinate Legislation Made

P1. S. 408. (1)(4) power partly exercised: 25.7.2003 and 18.9.2003 appointed for specified provisions and purposes by {S.I. 2003/1900}, art. 2

Commencement Information

I36. S. 408 in force at 25.7.2003 for specified purposes by S.I. 2003/1900, arts. 1. (2), 2. (1), Sch. 1 (with art. 3) (as amended by S.I. 2003/3142, art. 1. (3))

I37. S. 408 in force at 29.12.2003 in so far as not already in force by S.I. 2003/3142, art. 3. (2) (with art. 11)

Prospective

409. Modifications consequential on regulations implementing Directives

(1) This section applies if it appears to the Secretary of State that regulations under section 2 of the European Communities Act 1972 (c. 68) for giving effect to [F33. EU] obligations imposed by the Communications Directives have come into force before the passing of this Act.

(2) The Secretary of State may by order—

(a) repeal any relevant provision of this Act which appears to him to be unnecessary, or to have become spent, in consequence of the regulations;

(b) make such other modifications of the relevant provisions of this Act as he considers appropriate in consequence of the regulations;

(c) revoke provision made by the regulations; and

(d) make transitory or transitional provision in relation to anything done by or under the regulations.

(3) The Secretary of State's power under this section includes power to make consequential amendments of enactments not contained in this Act.

(4) In this section—

"the Communications Directives" means—

- the Access Directive, that is to say, Directive 2002/19/EC of the European Parliament and of the Council on access to, and interconnection of, electronic communications networks and associated facilities;

- the Authorisation Directive, that is to say, Directive 2002/20/EC of the European Parliament and of the Council on the authorisation of electronic communications networks and services;

- the Framework Directive, that is to say, Directive 2002/21/EC of the European Parliament and of the Council on a common regulatory framework for electronic communications networks and services;

- the Universal Service Directive, that is to say, Directive 2002/22/EC of the European Parliament and of the Council on universal service and users' rights relating to electronic communications networks and services;

"relevant provision of this Act" means a provision contained in—

- Part 1, 2 or 6; or

- Chapter 1 of Part 5.

(5) No order is to be made containing provision authorised by this section unless a draft of the order has been laid before Parliament and approved by a resolution of each House.

Amendments (Textual)

F33. Words in Act substituted (22.4.2011) by The Treaty of Lisbon (Changes in Terminology)

410. Application of enactments to territorial sea and other waters

(1) This section applies to—

   (a) provision made by or under Part 2 of this Act;

   (b) any provision of the enactments relating to the management of the radio spectrum that are not contained in that Part [F41or the Wireless Telegraphy Act 2006] ; and

   (c) any provision of Chapter 1 of Part 5 of this Act so far as it relates to a matter as respects which provision falling within paragraph (a) or (b) is made [F42or a matter as respects which the Wireless Telegraphy Act 2006 makes provision] .

(2) Her Majesty may by Order in Council provide—

   (a) for an area of the territorial sea to be treated, for the purposes of any provision to which this section applies, as if it were situated in such part of the United Kingdom as may be specified in the Order; and

   (b) for jurisdiction with respect to questions arising in relation to the territorial sea under any such provision to be conferred on courts in a part of the United Kingdom so specified.

(3) An Order in Council under section 11 of the Petroleum Act 1998 (c. 17) [F43or section 87 of the Energy Act 2004] (application of civil law to offshore installations etc.) may make provision for treating—

   (a) an installation with respect to which provision is made under that section and which is outside the territorial sea but in waters to which that section applies, and

   (b) waters within 500 metres of the installation,

as if for the purposes of provisions to which this section applies, they were situated in such part of the United Kingdom as is specified in the Order.

(4) The jurisdiction conferred on a court by an Order in Council under this section is in addition to any jurisdiction exercisable apart from this section by that or any other court.

(5) Subsection (3) of section 402 applies to the power to make an Order in Council under this section as it applies to any power of the Secretary of State to make an order under this Act, but as if references in that subsection to the Secretary of State were references to Her Majesty in Council.

(6) A statutory instrument containing an Order in Council under this section shall be subject to annulment in pursuance of a resolution of either House of Parliament.

(7) In this section—

"installation" includes any floating structure or device maintained on a station by whatever means, and installations in transit;

"the territorial sea" means the territorial sea adjacent to the United Kingdom.

Amendments (Textual)

F41. Words in s. 410. (1)(b) inserted (8.2.2007) by Wireless Telegraphy Act 2006 (c. 36), s. 126. (2), Sch. 7 para. 35. (a)

F42. Words in s. 410. (1)(c) inserted (8.2.2007) by Wireless Telegraphy Act 2006 (c. 36), s. 126. (2), Sch. 7 para. 35. (b)

F43. Words in s. 410. (3) inserted (5.10.2004) by virtue of Energy Act 2004 (c. 20), ss. 87. (5), 198. (2); S.I. 2004/2575, art. 2. (1), Sch. 1

Commencement Information

I38. S. 410 in force at 25.7.2003 for specified purposes by S.I. 2003/1900, arts. 1. (2), 2. (1), Sch. 1 (with art. 3) (as amended by S.I. 2003/3142, art. 1. (3))

I39. S. 410 in force at 29.12.2003 in so far as not already in force by S.I. 2003/3142, art. 3. (2) (with art. 11)

411. Short title, commencement and extent

(1) This Act may be cited as the Communications Act 2003.

(2) This Act (except the provisions listed in subsection (3), which come into force on the passing of this Act) shall come into force on such day as the Secretary of State may by order appoint; and different days may be appointed under this subsection for different purposes.

(3) Those provisions are sections 31. (1) to (4) and (6) and 405 and this section.

(4) An order under subsection (2) may include provision making such transitional or transitory provision, in addition to that made by Schedule 18, as the Secretary of State considers appropriate in connection with the bringing into force of any provisions of this Act; and the power to make transitional or transitory provision includes power to make—

   (a) different provision for different cases (including different provision in respect of different areas);

   (b) provision subject to such exemptions and exceptions as the Secretary of State thinks fit; and

   (c) such incidental, supplemental and consequential provision as he thinks fit.

(5) This Act extends to Northern Ireland.

(6) Subject to subsection (7), Her Majesty may by Order in Council extend the provisions of this Act, with such modifications as appear to Her Majesty in Council to be appropriate, to any of the Channel Islands or to the Isle of Man.

(7) Subsection (6) does not authorise the extension to any place of a provision of this Act so far as it gives effect to an amendment of an enactment that is not itself capable of being extended there in exercise of a power conferred on Her Majesty in Council.

(8) Subsection (3) of section 402 applies to the power to make an Order in Council under this section as it applies to any power of the Secretary of State to make an order under this Act, but as if references in that subsection to the Secretary of State were references to Her Majesty in Council.
Subordinate Legislation Made
P2. S. 411. (2)(4) power partly exercised: 25.7.2003 and 18.9.2003 appointed for specified provisions and purposes by {S.I. 2003/1900}, art. 2; different dates appointed for further specified provisions and purposes by {S.I. 2003/3142}, arts. 2, 3, 4

Schedules

Schedule 1. Functions transferred to OFCOM

Section 2

Wireless telegraphy functions

F11. . . . .
Amendments (Textual)
F1. Sch. 1 para. 1 repealed (8.2.2007) by Wireless Telegraphy Act 2006 (c. 36), s. 126. (2), Sch. 9 Pt. 1 (with Sch. 8 Pt. 1)
F22. . . . .
Amendments (Textual)
F2. Sch. 1 para. 2 repealed (8.2.2007) by Wireless Telegraphy Act 2006 (c. 36), s. 126. (2), Sch. 9 Pt. 1 (with Sch. 8 Pt. 1)
Commencement Information
I1. Sch. 1 para. 2 in force at 29.12.2003 by S.I. 2003/3142, art. 3. (1), Sch. 1 (with art. 11)

Functions in relation to the licensing etc. of television services

3. The following functions of the Independent Television Commission are transferred to OFCOM—

(a) the function of granting or awarding licences under Part 1 of the 1990 Act (independent television services) and Part 1 of the 1996 Act (digital television broadcasting);

(b) the Commission's functions under those Parts in relation to, and to applications for, licences under either of those Parts;

(c) the function of securing the provision of a nationwide system of television broadcasting services known as Channel 3;

(d) the function of securing the provision of the television broadcasting service known as Channel 5.

Commencement Information

I2. Sch. 1 para. 3 in force at 29.12.2003 by S.I. 2003/3142, art. 3. (1), Sch. 1 (with art. 11)

Functions in relation to C4. C

4. The functions conferred on the Independent Television Commission by or under section 23 of the 1990 Act and under Schedule 3 to that Act (appointment of members of C4. C and related administrative functions) are transferred to OFCOM.

Commencement Information

I3. Sch. 1 para. 4 in force at 29.12.2003 by S.I. 2003/3142, art. 3. (1), Sch. 1 (with art. 11)

Functions in relation to the licensing of radio services

5. The following functions of the Radio Authority are transferred to OFCOM—

(a) the function of granting or awarding licences under Part 3 of the 1990 Act (independent radio services) and Part 2 of the 1996 Act (digital sound broadcasting); and

(b) the Authority's functions under those Parts in relation to licences granted or awarded under those Parts.

Commencement Information

I4. Sch. 1 para. 5 in force at 29.12.2003 by S.I. 2003/3142, art. 3. (1), Sch. 1 (with art. 11)

Functions in relation to the proscription of foreign satellite services

6. The functions of the Independent Television Commission and of the Radio Authority under section 177 of the 1990 Act (proscription of foreign satellite services) are transferred to OFCOM.

Commencement Information

I5. Sch. 1 para. 6 in force at 29.12.2003 by S.I. 2003/3142, art. 3. (1), Sch. 1 (with art. 11)

Functions in relation to Gaelic broadcasting

7. The functions of the Independent Television Commission under sections 183 and 184 of the 1990 Act and the functions of that Commission and of the Radio Authority under Schedule 19 to that Act (Gaelic broadcasting) are transferred to OFCOM.

Commencement Information

I6. Sch. 1 para. 7 in force at 29.12.2003 by S.I. 2003/3142, art. 3. (1), Sch. 1 (with art. 11)

Functions in relation to the national television archive

8. The functions of the Independent Television Commission under section 185 of the 1990 Act

(maintenance of the national television archive) are transferred to OFCOM.
Commencement Information
I7. Sch. 1 para. 8 in force at 29.12.2003 by S.I. 2003/3142, art. 3. (1), Sch. 1 (with art. 11)

Warrants to enter and search premises to enforce broadcasting licences provisions

9. The functions of the Independent Television Commission and of the Radio Authority under section 196. (1) of the 1990 Act (entry and search for the purposes of enforcing licensing provisions of the 1990 and 1996 Acts) are transferred to OFCOM.
Commencement Information
I8. Sch. 1 para. 9 in force at 29.12.2003 by S.I. 2003/3142, art. 3. (1), Sch. 1 (with art. 11)

Variation of existing Channel 3 and Channel 5 licences

10. Any power to vary licences which is conferred on the Independent Television Commission by an order under section 28 of the 1996 Act is transferred to OFCOM.
Commencement Information
I9. Sch. 1 para. 10 in force at 29.12.2003 by S.I. 2003/3142, art. 3. (1), Sch. 1 (with art. 11)

Reports for the purposes of the review of digital broadcasting

11. The functions of the Independent Television Commission and of the Radio Authority under sections 33 and 67 of the 1996 Act (reports to the Secretary of State for the purposes of his review of digital broadcasting) are transferred to OFCOM.
Commencement Information
I10. Sch. 1 para. 11 in force at 29.12.2003 by S.I. 2003/3142, art. 3. (1), Sch. 1 (with art. 11)

Functions in relation to reservation of digital capacity to the BBC

12. The function of the Secretary of State under section 49. (4) of the 1996 Act (reserving digital capacity on a local radio multiplex service for the BBC) is transferred to OFCOM.
Commencement Information
I11. Sch. 1 para. 12 in force at 29.12.2003 by S.I. 2003/3142, art. 3. (1), Sch. 1 (with art. 11)

Functions in relation to listed events

13. The functions of the Independent Television Commission under Part 4 of the 1996 Act (functions in connection with listed events) are transferred to OFCOM.
Commencement Information
I12. Sch. 1 para. 13 in force at 29.12.2003 by S.I. 2003/3142, art. 3. (1), Sch. 1 (with art. 11)

Functions relating to fairness and privacy in broadcasting

14. The following functions of the Broadcasting Standards Commission under Part 5 of the 1996 Act are transferred to OFCOM—
(a) the Commission's function of drawing up and from time to time revising a code of practice under section 107 of that Act (codes of practice relation to fairness and privacy); and
(b) their functions in relation to fairness complaints under that Part.
Commencement Information

Schedule 2. Transfer schemes

Section 30

Contents of transfer scheme

1. (1)A transfer scheme—
(a) shall set out the property, rights and liabilities to be transferred by the scheme; and
(b) may make incidental, supplemental, consequential and transitional provision in connection with the transfer of that property and of those rights and liabilities.
(2) The provisions of the scheme setting out the property, rights and liabilities to be transferred may do so in either or both of the following ways—
(a) by specifying them or describing them in particular; or
(b) by identifying them generally by reference to, or to a specific part of, an undertaking from which they are to be transferred.
(3) The property, rights and liabilities that are to be capable of being transferred by a transfer scheme include—
(a) property, rights and liabilities that would not otherwise be capable of being transferred or assigned by the person from whom they are transferred;
(b) property acquired and rights and liabilities arising in the period after the making of the scheme and before it comes into force;
(c) rights and liabilities arising subsequently in respect of matters occurring in that period;
(d) property situated anywhere in the United Kingdom or elsewhere and rights and liabilities under the law of any part of the United Kingdom or of any place outside the United Kingdom; and
(e) rights and liabilities under an enactment.
(4) The provision that may be made under sub-paragraph (1)(b) includes provision for the creation in favour of a pre-commencement regulator, the Secretary of State or OFCOM of rights or liabilities over or in respect of property transferred to OFCOM or property retained by a pre-commencement regulator or the Secretary of State.
(5) The transfers to which effect may be given by a transfer scheme, and the rights that may be created by means of such a scheme, include transfers that are to take effect, and rights that are to arise, in accordance with the scheme as if there were—
(a) no such requirement to obtain a person's consent or concurrence,
(b) no such liability in respect of any contravention of any other requirement, and
(c) no such interference with any interest or right,
as there would be, in the case of a transaction apart from this Act (whether under any enactment or agreement or otherwise), by reason of any provision having effect in relation to the terms on which a pre-commencement regulator or the Secretary of State is entitled or subject to any property, right or liability.
Commencement Information
I1. Sch. 2 para. 1 in force at 18.9.2003 by S.I. 2003/1900, art. 2. (2), Sch. 2

Effect of transfer scheme

2. (1)Property transferred by a transfer scheme shall, on the coming into force of the scheme, vest in OFCOM without further assurance.
(2) Where any transfer scheme comes into force, any agreement made, transaction effected or other thing done by or in relation to the person from whom any transfers for which the scheme

provides are made shall have effect, so far as necessary for the purposes of those transfers, as if—

(a) it had been made, effected or done by or in relation to OFCOM; and

(b) OFCOM were the same person in law as the person from whom the transfer is made.

(3) Accordingly, references in any agreement, document, process or instrument of any description to the person from whom anything is transferred by means of a transfer scheme shall have effect, so far as necessary for the purpose of giving effect to the transfer from the coming into force of the scheme, as references to OFCOM.

(4) Where any agreement, document, process or instrument of any description has effect, in relation to anything transferred by means of a transfer scheme, as referring (whether expressly or by implication)—

(a) to a member or to an officer of a pre-commencement regulator, or

(b) to an officer of the Secretary of State,

that agreement, document, process or instrument shall have effect so far as necessary for the purposes of the transfers effected by the scheme and in consequence of them, as referring instead to the person mentioned in sub-paragraph (5).

(5) That person is—

(a) the person nominated for the purposes of the transfer by OFCOM; or

(b) in default of a nomination, the member or employee of OFCOM who most closely corresponds to the member or officer originally referred to.

(6) Nothing in sub-paragraph (3) or (4) is to apply in relation to any reference in an enactment or in subordinate legislation.

Commencement Information

I2. Sch. 2 para. 2 in force at 18.9.2003 by S.I. 2003/1900, art. 2. (2), Sch. 2

Retrospective modification of a transfer scheme

3. (1)If at any time after the coming into force of a transfer scheme it appears to the Secretary of State that it is appropriate to do so, he may by order provide for the scheme to be deemed to have come into force with such modifications (including modifications retrospective to the time of the coming into force of the scheme) as may be provided for in the order.

(2) The power under this paragraph to provide by order for the modification of a transfer scheme shall be exercisable for the purpose only of making provision that could have been made by the scheme.

(3) Before making an order under this paragraph the Secretary of State must consult OFCOM.

Commencement Information

I3. Sch. 2 para. 3 in force at 18.9.2003 by S.I. 2003/1900, art. 2. (2), Sch. 2

Compensation

4. (1)Where, in consequence of any provision included in a transfer scheme, the interests, rights or liabilities of a third party are modified as mentioned in sub-paragraph (2), the third party is to be entitled to such compensation as may be just in respect of—

(a) any diminution in the value of any of his interests or rights, or

(b) any increase in the burden of his liabilities,

which is attributable to that modification.

(2) The modifications mentioned in sub-paragraph (1) are modifications by virtue of which—

(a) an interest of the third party in any property is transformed into, or replaced by—

(i) an interest in only part of that property; or

(ii) separate interests in different parts of that property;

(b) a right of the third party against any of the pre-commencement regulators or against the Secretary of State is transformed into, or replaced by, two or more rights which do not include a right which, on its own, is equivalent (disregarding the person against whom it is enforceable) to the right against that regulator or (as the case may be) against the Secretary of State; or

(c) a liability of the third party to any of the pre-commencement regulators or to the Secretary of State is transformed into, or replaced by, two or more separate liabilities at least one of which is a liability enforceable by a person other than the person by whom it was enforceable before being so transformed.

(3) Where—

(a) a third party would, apart from any provision of a transfer scheme, have become entitled to, or to exercise, any interest or right arising or exercisable in respect of the transfer or creation in accordance with such a scheme of any property, rights or liabilities, and

(b) the provisions of that scheme have the effect of preventing that person's entitlement to, or to exercise, that interest or right from arising on any occasion in respect of anything mentioned in paragraph (a), and

(c) provision is not made by a transfer scheme for securing that an entitlement to, or to exercise, that interest or right or an equivalent interest or right, is preserved or created so as to arise in respect of the first occasion when corresponding circumstances next occur after the coming into force of the transfers for which the scheme provides,

the third party is to be entitled to such compensation as may be just in respect of the extinguishment of the interest or right.

(4) A liability to pay compensation under this paragraph shall fall on the persons mentioned in sub-paragraph (5) who (as the case may be)—

(a) have interests in the whole or any part of the property affected by the modification in question,

(b) are subject to the rights of the person to be compensated which are affected by the modification in question,

(c) are entitled to enforce the liabilities of the person to be compensated which are affected by that modification, or

(d) benefit from the extinguishment of the entitlement mentioned in sub-paragraph (3),

and that liability shall be apportioned between those persons in such manner as may be appropriate having regard to the extent of their respective interests, rights or liabilities or the extent of the benefit they respectively obtain from the extinguishment.

(5) Those persons are the pre-commencement regulators and the Secretary of State.

(6) Sub-paragraph (4) shall have effect subject to so much of any transfer scheme (including the one that gives rise to the liability) as makes provision for the transfer of any liability under that sub-paragraph to OFCOM.

(7) Any dispute as to whether, or as to the person by whom, any compensation is to be paid under this paragraph, and any dispute as to the amount of compensation to be paid by a person, shall be referred to and determined—

(a) where the claimant requires the matter to be determined in England and Wales or in Northern Ireland, by an arbitrator appointed by the Lord Chancellor, or

(b) where the claimant requires the matter to be determined in Scotland, by an arbiter appointed by the Lord President of the Court of Session.

(8) In this paragraph "third party", in relation to provisions capable of giving rise to compensation under this paragraph, means any person other than—

(a) a pre-commencement regulator; and

(b) the Secretary of State.

Commencement Information

I4. Sch. 2 para. 4 in force at 18.9.2003 by S.I. 2003/1900, art. 2. (2), Sch. 2

Stamp duty

5. (1)Stamp duty is not to be chargeable—

(a) on a transfer scheme; or

(b) on an instrument or agreement certified by the Secretary of State to the Commissioners of

Inland Revenue as made for the purposes of a transfer scheme, or as made for purposes connected with such a scheme.

(2) But a transfer scheme, or an instrument or agreement so certified, is to be treated as duly stamped only if—

(a) in accordance with section 12 of the Stamp Act 1891 (c. 39) it has been stamped with a stamp denoting either that it is not chargeable to duty or that it has been duly stamped; or

(b) it is stamped with the duty to which it would be chargeable apart from this paragraph.

Commencement Information

I5. Sch. 2 para. 5 in force at 18.9.2003 by S.I. 2003/1900, art. 2. (2), Sch. 2

Stamp duty land tax

[F15. A.(1)For the purposes of stamp duty land tax, a land transaction effected by, or for the purposes of, or for purposes connected with, a transfer scheme is exempt from charge.

(2) Relief under this paragraph must be claimed in a land transaction return or an amendment of such a return.

(3) In this paragraph—

"land transaction" has the meaning given by section 43. (1) of the Finance Act 2003;

"land transaction return" has the meaning given by section 76. (1) of that Act.]

Amendments (Textual)

F1 Sch. 2 para. 5. A inserted (1.12.2003) by The Stamp Duty Land Tax (Consequential Amendment of Enactments) Regulations 2003 (S.I. 2003/2867), reg. 1, Sch. para. 33

Interpretation of Schedule

6. In this Schedule "transfer scheme" means a scheme made by a pre-commencement regulator or by the Secretary of State under section 30.

Commencement Information

I6. Sch. 2 para. 6 in force at 18.9.2003 by S.I. 2003/1900, art. 2. (2), Sch. 2

Schedule 3. Amendments of Schedule 2 to the Telecommunications Act 1984

Section 106

Introductory

1. Schedule 2 to the Telecommunications Act 1984 (c. 12) (the telecommunications code) shall be amended as follows.

Commencement Information

I1. Sch. 3 para. 1 in force at 25.7.2003 for specified purposes by S.I. 2003/1900, arts. 1. (2), 2. (1), Sch. 1 (with art. 3) (as amended by S.I. 2003/3142, art. 1. (3))

I2. Sch. 3 para. 1 in force at 29.12.2003 in so far as not already in force by S.I. 2003/3142, art. 3. (2) (with art. 11)

Meaning of conduit system and electronic communications apparatus, network or service

2. (1)In sub-paragraph (1) of paragraph 1 (interpretation of the code), after the definitions of "bridleway" and "footpath" there shall be inserted—

""conduit" includes a tunnel, subway, tube or pipe;

"conduit system" means a system of conduits provided so as to be available for use by providers of electronic communications networks for the purposes of the provision by them of their networks;".

(2) In that sub-paragraph, after the definition of "the court" there shall be inserted—

""electronic communications apparatus" means—

(a) any apparatus (within the meaning of the Communications Act 2003) which is designed or adapted for use in connection with the provision of an electronic communications network;

(b) any apparatus (within the meaning of that Act) that is designed or adapted for a use which consists of or includes the sending or receiving of communications or other signals that are transmitted by means of an electronic communications network;

(c) any line;

(d) any conduit, structure, pole or other thing in, on, by or from which any electronic communications apparatus is or may be installed, supported, carried or suspended;

and references to the installation of electronic communications apparatus are to be construed accordingly;

"electronic communications network" has the same meaning as in the Communications Act 2003, and references to the provision of such a network are to be construed in accordance with the provisions of that Act;

"electronic communications service" has the same meaning as in the Communications Act 2003, and references to the provision of such a service are to be construed in accordance with the provisions of that Act;".

(3) In that sub-paragraph, for the definition of "line" there shall be substituted—

""line" means any wire, cable, tube, pipe or similar thing (including its casing or coating) which is designed or adapted for use in connection with the provision of any electronic communications network or electronic communications service;".

(4) In that sub-paragraph, after the definition of "road" there shall be inserted—

""signal" has the same meaning as in section 32 of the Communications Act 2003;".

Commencement Information

I3. Sch. 3 para. 2 in force at 25.7.2003 for specified purposes by S.I. 2003/1900, arts. 1. (2), 2. (1), Sch. 1 (with art. 3) (as amended by S.I. 2003/3142, art. 1. (3))

I4. Sch. 3 para. 2 in force at 29.12.2003 in so far as not already in force by S.I. 2003/3142, art. 3. (2) (with art. 11)

Meaning of operator and operator's system

3. (1)In sub-paragraph (1) of paragraph 1 for the definitions of "the operator" and "the operator's system" there shall be substituted—

""the operator" means—

(a) where the code is applied in any person's case by a direction under section 106 of the Communications Act 2003, that person; and

(b) where it applies by virtue of section 106. (3)(b) of that Act, the Secretary of State or (as the case may be) the Northern Ireland department in question;

"the operator's network" means—

(a) in relation to an operator falling within paragraph (a) of the definition of "operator", so much of any electronic communications network or conduit system provided by that operator as is not excluded from the application of the code under section 106. (5) of the Communications Act 2003; and

(b) in relation to an operator falling within paragraph (b) of that definition, the electronic communications network which the Secretary of State or the Northern Ireland department is providing or proposing to provide;".

(2) In that sub-paragraph—

(a) in the definition of "emergency works", in paragraph (b), for "the operator's system" there shall be substituted " the operator's network "; and

(b) in the definition of "the statutory purposes" for "establishing and running the operator's system" there shall be substituted " the provision of the operator's network ".

Commencement Information

I5. Sch. 3 para. 3 in force at 25.7.2003 for specified purposes by S.I. 2003/1900, arts. 1. (2), 2. (1), Sch. 1 (with art. 3) (as amended by S.I. 2003/3142, art. 1. (3))

I6. Sch. 3 para. 3 in force at 29.12.2003 in so far as not already in force by S.I. 2003/3142, art. 3. (2) (with art. 11)

Provision of a conduit system

4. After sub-paragraph (3) of paragraph 1 there shall be inserted—

"(3. A)References in this code to the provision of a conduit system include references to establishing or maintaining such a system."

Commencement Information

I7. Sch. 3 para. 4 in force at 25.7.2003 for specified purposes by S.I. 2003/1900, arts. 1. (2), 2. (1), Sch. 1 (with art. 3) (as amended by S.I. 2003/3142, art. 1. (3))

I8. Sch. 3 para. 4 in force at 29.12.2003 in so far as not already in force by S.I. 2003/3142, art. 3. (2) (with art. 11)

General amendments

5. In paragraphs 2 to 28—

(a) for the words "telecommunication apparatus", wherever occurring, there shall be substituted " electronic communications apparatus ";

(b) for the words "telecommunication services", wherever occurring, there shall be substituted " electronic communications services ";

(c) for the words "a telecommunication system", wherever occurring, there shall be substituted " an electronic communications network or to electronic communications services "; and

(d) for the word "system", wherever occurring (otherwise than in the expression "telecommunication system"), there shall be substituted " network ".

Commencement Information

I9. Sch. 3 para. 5 in force at 25.7.2003 for specified purposes by S.I. 2003/1900, arts. 1. (2), 2. (1), Sch. 1 (with art. 3) (as amended by S.I. 2003/3142, art. 1. (3))

I10. Sch. 3 para. 5 in force at 29.12.2003 in so far as not already in force by S.I. 2003/3142, art. 3. (2) (with art. 11)

Power to fly lines

6. In paragraph 10 (power to fly lines), after sub-paragraph (2) there shall be inserted—

"(3)In this paragraph "business" includes a trade, profession or employment and includes any activity carried on by a body of persons (whether corporate or unincorporate)."

Commencement Information

I11. Sch. 3 para. 6 in force at 25.7.2003 for specified purposes by S.I. 2003/1900, arts. 1. (2), 2. (1), Sch. 1 (with art. 3) (as amended by S.I. 2003/3142, art. 1. (3))

I12. Sch. 3 para. 6 in force at 29.12.2003 in so far as not already in force by S.I. 2003/3142, art. 3. (2) (with art. 11)

Power to require alteration of apparatus

7. In paragraph 20. (4)(b) (alteration not to interfere with service provided by the operator's network), for "provided by" there shall be substituted " which is or is likely to be provided using ".

Commencement Information

I13. Sch. 3 para. 7 in force at 25.7.2003 for specified purposes by S.I. 2003/1900, arts. 1. (2), 2. (1), Sch. 1 (with art. 3) (as amended by S.I. 2003/3142, art. 1. (3))

I14. Sch. 3 para. 7 in force at 29.12.2003 in so far as not already in force by S.I. 2003/3142, art. 3. (2) (with art. 11)

Undertaker's works

8. In paragraph 23. (10) (interpretation of provisions relating to undertakers' works), in paragraph (b) of the definition of "relevant undertaker", for the words "by a licence under section 7 of this Act" there shall be substituted " by a direction under section 106 of the Communications Act 2003 ".

Commencement Information

I15. Sch. 3 para. 8 in force at 25.7.2003 for specified purposes by S.I. 2003/1900, arts. 1. (2), 2. (1), Sch. 1 (with art. 3) (as amended by S.I. 2003/3142, art. 1. (3))

I16. Sch. 3 para. 8 in force at 29.12.2003 in so far as not already in force by S.I. 2003/3142, art. 3. (2) (with art. 11)

Notices under the code

9. (1)In sub-paragraph (1) of paragraph 24 (notices in a form approved by the Director), for "the Director" there shall be substituted " OFCOM ".

(2) For sub-paragraphs (2) to (4) of that paragraph there shall be substituted—

"(2)A notice required to be given to any person for the purposes of any provision of this code is not to be sent to him by post unless it is sent by a registered post service or by recorded delivery.

(2. A)For the purposes, in the case of such a notice, of section 394 of the Communications Act 2003 and the application of section 7 of the Interpretation Act 1978 in relation to that section, the proper address of a person is—

(a) if the person to whom the notice is to be given has furnished the person giving the notice with an address for service under this code, that address; and

(b) only if he has not, the address given by that section of the Act of 2003."

(3) In sub-paragraph (6) of that paragraph—

(a) for "purporting to be signed by the Director" there shall be substituted " issued by OFCOM "; and

(b) for "him" there shall be substituted " them ".

Commencement Information

I17. Sch. 3 para. 9 in force at 25.7.2003 for specified purposes by S.I. 2003/1900, arts. 1. (2), 2. (1), Sch. 1 (with art. 3) (as amended by S.I. 2003/3142, art. 1. (3))

I18. Sch. 3 para. 9 in force at 29.12.2003 in so far as not already in force by S.I. 2003/3142, art. 3. (2) (with art. 11)

Application of code to the Crown

10. In paragraph 26. (4) (Crown application provision not to apply where the telecommunication system is being provided or is to be provided by the Secretary of State or a Northern Ireland department), for "has effect by virtue of section 10. (1)(b) of this Act" there shall be substituted "

applies in the case of the Secretary of State or a Northern Ireland department by virtue of section 106. (3)(b) of the Communications Act 2003 ".

Commencement Information

119. Sch. 3 para. 10 in force at 25.7.2003 for specified purposes by S.I. 2003/1900, arts. 1. (2), 2. (1), Sch. 1 (with art. 3) (as amended by S.I. 2003/3142, art. 1. (3))

120. Sch. 3 para. 10 in force at 29.12.2003 in so far as not already in force by S.I. 2003/3142, art. 3. (2) (with art. 11)

Effect of agreements concerning sharing of apparatus

11. After paragraph 28, there shall be inserted—

29. (1)This paragraph applies where—

(a) this code has been applied by a direction under section 106 of the Communications Act 2003 in a person's case;

(b) this code expressly or impliedly imposes a limitation on the use to which electronic communications apparatus installed by that person may be put or on the purposes for which it may be used; and

(c) that person is a party to a relevant agreement or becomes a party to an agreement which (after he has become a party to it) is a relevant agreement.

(2) The limitation is not to preclude—

(a) the doing of anything in relation to that apparatus, or

(b) its use for particular purposes,

to the extent that the doing of that thing, or the use of the apparatus for those purposes, is in pursuance of the agreement.

(3) This paragraph is not to be construed, in relation to a person who is entitled or authorised by or under a relevant agreement to share the use of apparatus installed by another party to the agreement, as affecting any consent requirement imposed (whether by a statutory provision or otherwise) on that person.

(4) In this paragraph—

"consent requirement", in relation to a person, means a requirement for him to obtain consent or permission to or in connection with—

    - the installation by him of apparatus; or

    - the doing by him of any other thing in relation to apparatus the use of which he is entitled or authorised to share;

"relevant agreement" means an agreement in relation to electronic communications apparatus which—

    - relates to the sharing by different parties to the agreement of the use of that apparatus; and

    - is an agreement that satisfies the requirements of sub-paragraph (5);

"statutory provision" means a provision of an enactment or of an instrument having effect under an enactment.

(5) An agreement satisfies the requirements of this sub-paragraph if—

(a) every party to the agreement is a person in whose case this code applies by virtue of a direction under section 106 of the Communications Act 2003; or

(b) one or more of the parties to the agreement is a person in whose case this code so applies and every other party to the agreement is a qualifying person.

(6) A person is a qualifying person for the purposes of sub-paragraph (5) if he is either—

(a) a person who provides an electronic communications network without being a person in whose case this code applies; or

(b) a designated provider of an electronic communications service consisting in the distribution of a programme service by means of an electronic communications network.

(7) In sub-paragraph (6)—

"designated" means designated by an order made by the Secretary of State;

"programme service" has the same meaning as in the Broadcasting Act 1990."

Commencement Information

I21. Sch. 3 para. 11 in force at 25.7.2003 for specified purposes by S.I. 2003/1900, arts. 1. (2), 2. (1), Sch. 1 (with art. 3) (as amended by S.I. 2003/3142, art. 1. (3))

I22. Sch. 3 para. 11 in force at 29.12.2003 in so far as not already in force by S.I. 2003/3142, art. 3. (2) (with art. 11)

Schedule 4. Compulsory purchase and entry for exploratory purposes

Section 118

Interpretation

1. In this Schedule—

"code operator" means a provider of an electronic communications network in whose case the electronic communications code is applied by a direction under section 106; and

"the operator's network", in relation to a code operator, means so much of the electronic communications network provided by the operator as is not excluded from the application of the electronic communications code under section 106. (5).

Commencement Information

I1. Sch. 4 para. 1 in force at 25.7.2003 for specified purposes by S.I. 2003/1900, arts. 1. (2), 2. (1), Sch. 1 (with art. 3) (as amended by S.I. 2003/3142, art. 1. (3))

I2. Sch. 4 para. 1 in force at 29.12.2003 in so far as not already in force by S.I. 2003/3142, art. 3. (2) (with art. 11)

General duties with respect to powers under Schedule

2. In exercising his powers under this Schedule it shall be the duty of the Secretary of State to have regard, in particular, to each of the following—

(a) the duties imposed on OFCOM by sections 3 and 4;

(b) the need to protect the environment and, in particular, to conserve the natural beauty and amenity of the countryside;

(c) the need to ensure that highways are not damaged or obstructed, and traffic not interfered with, to any greater extent than is reasonably necessary;

(d) the need to encourage the sharing of the use of electronic communications apparatus.

Commencement Information

I3. Sch. 4 para. 2 in force at 25.7.2003 for specified purposes by S.I. 2003/1900, arts. 1. (2), 2. (1), Sch. 1 (with art. 3) (as amended by S.I. 2003/3142, art. 1. (3))

I4. Sch. 4 para. 2 in force at 29.12.2003 in so far as not already in force by S.I. 2003/3142, art. 3. (2) (with art. 11)

Compulsory purchase of land: England and Wales

3. (1)Subject to sub-paragraph (2), the Secretary of State may authorise a code operator to purchase compulsorily any land in England and Wales which is required by the operator—

(a) for, or in connection with, the establishment or running of the operator's network; or

(b) as to which it can reasonably be foreseen that it will be so required.

(2) No order is to be made authorising a compulsory purchase under this paragraph by a code

operator except with OFCOM's consent.

(3) This power to purchase land compulsorily includes power to acquire an easement or other right over land by the creation of a new right.

(4) The Acquisition of Land Act 1981 (c. 67) is to apply to any compulsory purchase under this paragraph as if the code operator were a local authority within the meaning of that Act.

(5) The provisions of the Town and Country Planning Act 1990 (c. 8) specified in sub-paragraph (6) have effect in relation to land acquired compulsorily by a code operator under this paragraph as they have effect in relation to land acquired compulsorily by statutory undertakers.

(6) Those provisions are—

(a) sections 238 to 240 (use and development of consecrated land and burial ground);

(b) section 241 (use and development of land for open spaces); and

(c) sections 271 to 274. (extinguishment of rights of way, and rights as to apparatus, of statutory undertakers).

(7) Where a code operator has acquired land under this paragraph, he must not dispose of that land, or of an interest or right in or over it, except with OFCOM's consent.

Commencement Information

15. Sch. 4 para. 3 in force at 25.7.2003 for specified purposes by S.I. 2003/1900, arts. 1. (2), 2. (1), Sch. 1 (with art. 3) (as amended by S.I. 2003/3142, art. 1. (3))

16. Sch. 4 para. 3 in force at 29.12.2003 in so far as not already in force by S.I. 2003/3142, art. 3. (2) (with art. 11)

Compulsory purchase of land: Scotland

4. (1)Subject to sub-paragraph (2), the Secretary of State may authorise a code operator to purchase compulsorily any land in Scotland which is required by the operator—

(a) for, or in connection with, the establishment or running of the operator's network; or

(b) as to which it can reasonably be foreseen that it will be so required.

(2) No order is to be made authorising a compulsory purchase under this paragraph except with OFCOM's consent.

(3) This power to purchase land compulsorily includes power to acquire a servitude or other right over land by the creation of a new right.

(4) The Acquisition of Land (Authorisation Procedure) (Scotland) Act 1947 (c. 42) applies to any compulsory purchase under this paragraph as if—

(a) the code operator were a local authority within the meaning of that Act; and

(b) this paragraph had been in force immediately before the commencement of that Act.

(5) The provisions of the Town and Country Planning (Scotland) Act 1997 (c. 8) specified in sub-paragraph (6) have effect in relation to land acquired compulsorily by a code operator under this paragraph as they have effect in relation to land acquired compulsorily by statutory undertakers.

(6) Those provisions are—

(a) section 197 (provisions as to churches and burial grounds);

(b) section 198 (use and development of land for open spaces); and

(c) sections 224 to 227 (extinguishment of rights of way, and rights as to apparatus, of statutory undertakers).

(7) Where a code operator has acquired land under this paragraph, he must not dispose of that land, or of any interest or right in or over it, except with OFCOM's consent.

Commencement Information

17. Sch. 4 para. 4 in force at 25.7.2003 for specified purposes by S.I. 2003/1900, arts. 1. (2), 2. (1), Sch. 1 (with art. 3) (as amended by S.I. 2003/3142, art. 1. (3))

18. Sch. 4 para. 4 in force at 29.12.2003 in so far as not already in force by S.I. 2003/3142, art. 3. (2) (with art. 11)

Compulsory purchase of land: Northern Ireland

5. (1)Where a code operator proposes to acquire, otherwise than by agreement, any land in Northern Ireland required by him—

(a) for, or in connection with, the establishment or running of the operator's network, or

(b) as to which it can reasonably be foreseen that it will be so required,

he may, with OFCOM's consent, apply to the Secretary of State for an order vesting that land in him.

(2) On such an application the Secretary of State is to have power to make such an order.

(3) This power to acquire land compulsorily includes power to acquire an easement or other right over land by the creation of a new right.

(4) Where a code operator has acquired land under this paragraph, he must not dispose of that land, or of any interest or right in or over it, except with OFCOM's consent.

(5) The following provisions—

(a) Schedule 6 to the Local Government Act (Northern Ireland) 1972 (c. 9 (N.I.)) (acquisition of land by vesting order), and

(b) Schedule 8 to the Health and Personal Social Services (Northern Ireland) Order 1972 (S.I. 1972/1265 (N.I. 14)) (provisions as to inquiries),

have effect for the purposes of the acquisition of land by means of a vesting order under this paragraph as they have effect for the purposes of that Act and that Order but subject to the modifications set out in sub-paragraph (6).

(6) Those modifications are—

(a) for any reference to the Department substitute a reference to the Secretary of State;

(b) for any reference to the Act or Order in question substitute a reference to this Act;

(c) for any reference in Schedule 6 to the Local Government Act (Northern Ireland) 1972 to a council substitute a reference to the code operator;

(d) in paragraph 6. (2) of that Schedule, for the words from "the fund" onwards substitute " funds of the code operator (in this Schedule referred to as "the compensation fund") and shall be discharged by payments made by the code operator "; and

(e) in paragraph 12. (2) of that Schedule for "the clerk of the council" substitute " such person as may be designated for the purposes of this Schedule by the code operator ".

(7) The enactments for the time being in force relating to the assessment of compensation in respect of land vested in a district council by an order made under Schedule 6 to the Local Government Act (Northern Ireland) 1972 are to apply, subject to any necessary modifications, in relation to land vested in a code operator by an order made under this paragraph.

(8) In this paragraph, "land" has the meaning assigned to it by section 45. (1)(a) of the Interpretation Act (Northern Ireland) 1954 (c. 33 (N.I.)).

Commencement Information

I9. Sch. 4 para. 5 in force at 25.7.2003 for specified purposes by S.I. 2003/1900, arts. 1. (2), 2. (1), Sch. 1 (with art. 3) (as amended by S.I. 2003/3142, art. 1. (3))

I10. Sch. 4 para. 5 in force at 29.12.2003 in so far as not already in force by S.I. 2003/3142, art. 3. (2) (with art. 11)

Entry on land for exploratory purposes: England and Wales

6. (1)A person—

(a) nominated by a code operator, and

(b) duly authorised in writing by the Secretary of State,

may, at any reasonable time, enter upon and survey land in England and Wales for the purpose of ascertaining whether the land would be suitable for use by the code operator for, or in connection with, the establishment or running of the operator's network.

(2) This paragraph does not apply in relation to land covered by buildings or used as a garden or pleasure ground.

(3) Sections 324. (8) and 325. (1) to (5), (8) and (9) of the Town and Country Planning Act 1990 (c. 8) (supplementary provisions relating to powers of entry) have effect in relation to the power conferred by this paragraph—

(a) as they have effect in relation to the powers conferred by section 324 of that Act; but

(b) subject to the modifications set out in sub-paragraph (4).

(4) Those modifications are—

(a) in section 324. (8) (power to search and bore for the purpose of ascertaining the nature of the subsoil or the presence of minerals) omit "or the presence of minerals therein"; and

(b) in section 325. (1) (24 hours' notice to be given of an intended entry upon occupied land) for "24 hours" substitute " 28 days ".

(5) Where, in an exercise of the power conferred by this paragraph, any damage is caused to land or to chattels, the code operator must—

(a) make good the damage; or

(b) pay compensation in respect of the damage to every person interested in the land or chattels.

(6) Where, in consequence of an exercise of the power conferred by this paragraph, a person is disturbed in his enjoyment of land or chattels, the code operator must pay that person compensation in respect of the disturbance.

(7) Section 118 of the Town and Country Planning Act 1990 (c. 8) (determination of disputes as to compensation) applies to any question of disputed compensation under this paragraph as it applies to such questions under Part 4 of that Act.

Commencement Information

I11. Sch. 4 para. 6 in force at 25.7.2003 for specified purposes by S.I. 2003/1900, arts. 1. (2), 2. (1), Sch. 1 (with art. 3) (as amended by S.I. 2003/3142, art. 1. (3))

I12. Sch. 4 para. 6 in force at 29.12.2003 in so far as not already in force by S.I. 2003/3142, art. 3. (2) (with art. 11)

Entry on land for exploratory purposes: Scotland

7. (1)A person—

(a) nominated by a code operator, and

(b) duly authorised in writing by the Secretary of State,

may, at any reasonable time, enter upon and survey any land in Scotland for the purpose of ascertaining whether the land would be suitable for use by the code operator for, or in connection with, the establishment or running of the operator's network.

(2) This paragraph does not apply in relation to land covered by buildings or used as a garden or pleasure ground.

(3) Sections 269. (6) and 270. (1) to (5), (8) and (9) of the Town and Country Planning (Scotland) Act 1997 (c. 8) (supplementary provisions relating to powers of entry) have effect in relation to the power conferred by this paragraph—

(a) as they have effect in relation to the powers conferred by section 269 of that Act; but

(b) subject to the modifications set out in sub-paragraph (4).

(4) Those modifications are—

(a) in section 269. (6) (power to search and bore for the purpose of ascertaining the nature of the subsoil or the presence of minerals), omit "or the presence of minerals therein"; and

(b) in section 270. (1) (24 hours' notice to be given of an intended entry upon occupied land) for "24 hours" substitute " 28 days ".

(5) Where, in an exercise of the power conferred by this paragraph, damage is caused to land or to corporeal moveables, the code operator must—

(a) make good the damage; or

(b) pay compensation in respect of the damage to every person interested in the land or corporeal moveables.

(6) Where, in consequence of an exercise of the power conferred by this paragraph, a person is

disturbed in his enjoyment of any land or corporeal moveables, the code operator must pay that person compensation in respect of the disturbance.

(7) A dispute arising under this paragraph—

(a) as to the effect of damage, or

(b) as to the amount of compensation,

must be determined by arbitration by a single arbiter appointed by agreement between the parties or, in default of an agreement, by the Secretary of State.

Commencement Information

I13. Sch. 4 para. 7 in force at 25.7.2003 for specified purposes by S.I. 2003/1900, arts. 1. (2), 2. (1), Sch. 1 (with art. 3) (as amended by S.I. 2003/3142, art. 1. (3))

I14. Sch. 4 para. 7 in force at 29.12.2003 in so far as not already in force by S.I. 2003/3142, art. 3. (2) (with art. 11)

Entry on land for exploratory purposes: Northern Ireland

8. (1)A person—

(a) nominated by a code operator, and

(b) duly authorised in writing by the Secretary of State,

may, at any reasonable time, enter upon and survey any land in Northern Ireland for the purpose of ascertaining whether the land would be suitable for use by the code operator for, or in connection with, the establishment or running of the operator's network.

(2) This paragraph does not apply in relation to land covered by buildings or used as a garden or pleasure ground.

(3) Subsections (2) to (5) and (8) of section 40 of the Land Development Values (Compensation) Act (Northern Ireland) 1965 (c. 23 (N.I.)) (supplementary provisions relating to powers of entry) have effect in relation to the power of entry conferred by this paragraph—

(a) as they have effect in relation to the power conferred by that section; but

(b) subject to the modifications set out in sub-paragraph (4).

(4) Those modifications are—

(a) in section 40. (2) (power to search and bore for the purpose of ascertaining the nature of the subsoil or the presence of minerals) omit "or the presence of minerals therein"; and

(b) in section 40. (3)(b) (three days' notice to be given of an intended entry upon occupied land) for the word "three" substitute " twenty eight ".

(5) Where, in an exercise of the power conferred by this paragraph, damage is caused to land or to chattels, the code operator must—

(a) make good the damage; or

(b) pay compensation in respect of the damage to every person interested in the land or chattels.

(6) Where, in consequence of an exercise of the power conferred by this paragraph, a person is disturbed in his enjoyment of any land or chattels, the code operator must pay that person compensation in respect of the disturbance.

(7) Section 31 of the Land Development Values (Compensation) Act (Northern Ireland) 1965 (determination of disputes as to compensation) applies to any question of disputed compensation under this paragraph as it applies to such questions under Part 3 of that Act.

Commencement Information

I15. Sch. 4 para. 8 in force at 25.7.2003 for specified purposes by S.I. 2003/1900, arts. 1. (2), 2. (1), Sch. 1 (with art. 3) (as amended by S.I. 2003/3142, art. 1. (3))

I16. Sch. 4 para. 8 in force at 29.12.2003 in so far as not already in force by S.I. 2003/3142, art. 3. (2) (with art. 11)

Acquisition of land by agreement

9. (1)For the purpose of the acquisition by agreement by a code operator of land in England and

Wales, the provisions of Part 1 of the Compulsory Purchase Act 1965 (c. 56) (so far as applicable), other than sections 4 to 8 (time limits, notices to treat etc.) and section 31 (ecclesiastical property), apply as they apply for the purposes of that Act.

(2) For the purpose of the acquisition by agreement by a code operator of land in Scotland, section 109. (2) of the Town and Country Planning (Scotland) Act 1972 (c. 52) (incorporation of Lands Clauses Acts) applies, with any necessary modifications, for the purposes of this Act as it applies for the purposes of that Act.

(3) For the purpose of the acquisition by agreement by a code operator of land in Northern Ireland, the Lands Clauses Acts, except for sections 127 to 132 (sale of superfluous land) and sections 150 and 151 (access to the special Act) of the Lands Clauses Consolidation Act 1845 (c. 18), apply as they apply for the purposes of those Acts.

Commencement Information

I17. Sch. 4 para. 9 in force at 25.7.2003 for specified purposes by S.I. 2003/1900, arts. 1. (2), 2. (1), Sch. 1 (with art. 3) (as amended by S.I. 2003/3142, art. 1. (3))

I18. Sch. 4 para. 9 in force at 29.12.2003 in so far as not already in force by S.I. 2003/3142, art. 3. (2) (with art. 11)

Schedule 5. Procedure for grants of recognised spectrum access

Section 159

. . . .

Amendments (Textual)

F1. Schs. 5-7 repealed (8.2.2007) by Wireless Telegraphy Act 2006 (c. 36), s. 126. (2), Sch. 9 Pt. 1 (with Sch. 8 Pt. 1)

Schedule 6. Fixed penalties for wireless telegraphy offences

Prospective
Section 180

. . . .

Amendments (Textual)

F1. Schs. 5-7 repealed (8.2.2007) by Wireless Telegraphy Act 2006 (c. 36), s. 126. (2), Sch. 9 Pt. 1 (with Sch. 8 Pt. 1)

Schedule 7. Seizure and forfeiture of apparatus

Section 182

. . . .

Amendments (Textual)

F1. Schs. 5-7 repealed (8.2.2007) by Wireless Telegraphy Act 2006 (c. 36), s. 126. (2), Sch. 9 Pt. 1 (with Sch. 8 Pt. 1)

Schedule 8. Decisions not subject to appeal

Section 192

Prosecutions and civil proceedings

1. A decision to institute, bring or carry on any criminal or civil proceedings.
Commencement Information
I1. Sch. 8 para. 1 in force at 25.7.2003 for specified purposes by S.I. 2003/1900, arts. 1. (2), 2. (1),
Sch. 1 (with art. 3) (as amended by S.I. 2003/3142, art. 1. (3))
I2. Sch. 8 para. 1 in force at 29.12.2003 in so far as not already in force by S.I. 2003/3142, art. 3.
(2) (with art. 11)
2. A decision (other than one under section 119) to take preliminary steps for the purpose of
enabling any such proceedings to be instituted.
Commencement Information
I3. Sch. 8 para. 2 in force at 25.7.2003 for specified purposes by S.I. 2003/1900, arts. 1. (2), 2. (1),
Sch. 1 (with art. 3) (as amended by S.I. 2003/3142, art. 1. (3))
I4. Sch. 8 para. 2 in force at 29.12.2003 in so far as not already in force by S.I. 2003/3142, art. 3.
(2) (with art. 11)

This Act

3. A decision relating to the making or revision of a statement under section 38.
Commencement Information
I5. Sch. 8 para. 3 in force at 25.7.2003 for specified purposes by S.I. 2003/1900, arts. 1. (2), 2. (1),
Sch. 1 (with art. 3) (as amended by S.I. 2003/3142, art. 1. (3))
I6. Sch. 8 para. 3 in force at 29.12.2003 in so far as not already in force by S.I. 2003/3142, art. 3.
(2) (with art. 11)
4. A decision required to be published in a notification under section 44. (4).
Commencement Information
I7. Sch. 8 para. 4 in force at 25.7.2003 for specified purposes by S.I. 2003/1900, arts. 1. (2), 2. (1),
Sch. 1 (with art. 3) (as amended by S.I. 2003/3142, art. 1. (3))
I8. Sch. 8 para. 4 in force at 29.12.2003 in so far as not already in force by S.I. 2003/3142, art. 3.
(2) (with art. 11)
5. A decision given effect to by an order under section 55.
Commencement Information
I9. Sch. 8 para. 5 in force at 25.7.2003 for specified purposes by S.I. 2003/1900, arts. 1. (2), 2. (1),
Sch. 1 (with art. 3) (as amended by S.I. 2003/3142, art. 1. (3))
I10. Sch. 8 para. 5 in force at 29.12.2003 in so far as not already in force by S.I. 2003/3142, art. 3.
(2) (with art. 11)
6. A decision given effect to by regulations under section 66.
Commencement Information
I11. Sch. 8 para. 6 in force at 25.7.2003 for specified purposes by S.I. 2003/1900, arts. 1. (2), 2.
(1), Sch. 1 (with art. 3) (as amended by S.I. 2003/3142, art. 1. (3))
I12. Sch. 8 para. 6 in force at 29.12.2003 in so far as not already in force by S.I. 2003/3142, art. 3.
(2) (with art. 11)
7. A decision given effect to by regulations under section 71.
Commencement Information
I13. Sch. 8 para. 7 in force at 25.7.2003 for specified purposes by S.I. 2003/1900, arts. 1. (2), 2.
(1), Sch. 1 (with art. 3) (as amended by S.I. 2003/3142, art. 1. (3))
I14. Sch. 8 para. 7 in force at 29.12.2003 in so far as not already in force by S.I. 2003/3142, art. 3.

(2) (with art. 11)

8. A decision required to be published in a notification under section 108. (4).

Commencement Information

I15. Sch. 8 para. 8 in force at 25.7.2003 for specified purposes by S.I. 2003/1900, arts. 1. (2), 2. (1), Sch. 1 (with art. 3) (as amended by S.I. 2003/3142, art. 1. (3))

I16. Sch. 8 para. 8 in force at 29.12.2003 in so far as not already in force by S.I. 2003/3142, art. 3. (2) (with art. 11)

9. A decision given effect to by an order under section 122.

Commencement Information

I17. Sch. 8 para. 9 in force at 25.7.2003 for specified purposes by S.I. 2003/1900, arts. 1. (2), 2. (1), Sch. 1 (with art. 3) (as amended by S.I. 2003/3142, art. 1. (3))

I18. Sch. 8 para. 9 in force at 29.12.2003 in so far as not already in force by S.I. 2003/3142, art. 3. (2) (with art. 11)

[F19. AA decision relating to any of sections 124. A to 124. N or to anything done under them.]

Amendments (Textual)

F1. Sch. 8 para. 9. A inserted (8.6.2010) by Digital Economy Act 2010 (c. 24), ss. 16. (3), 47. (1)

10. A decision relating to the making or revision of a statement under section 131.

Commencement Information

I19. Sch. 8 para. 10 in force at 25.7.2003 for specified purposes by S.I. 2003/1900, arts. 1. (2), 2. (1), Sch. 1 (with art. 3) (as amended by S.I. 2003/3142, art. 1. (3))

I20. Sch. 8 para. 10 in force at 29.12.2003 in so far as not already in force by S.I. 2003/3142, art. 3. (2) (with art. 11)

11. A decision given effect to by an order under section 134. (6).

Commencement Information

I21. Sch. 8 para. 11 in force at 25.7.2003 for specified purposes by S.I. 2003/1900, arts. 1. (2), 2. (1), Sch. 1 (with art. 3) (as amended by S.I. 2003/3142, art. 1. (3))

I22. Sch. 8 para. 11 in force at 29.12.2003 in so far as not already in force by S.I. 2003/3142, art. 3. (2) (with art. 11)

12. A decision relating to the making or revision of a statement under section 145.

Commencement Information

I23. Sch. 8 para. 12 in force at 25.7.2003 for specified purposes by S.I. 2003/1900, arts. 1. (2), 2. (1), Sch. 1 (with art. 3) (as amended by S.I. 2003/3142, art. 1. (3))

I24. Sch. 8 para. 12 in force at 29.12.2003 in so far as not already in force by S.I. 2003/3142, art. 3. (2) (with art. 11)

F213. . . . .

Amendments (Textual)

F2. Sch. 8 paras. 13-36 repealed (8.2.2007) by Wireless Telegraphy Act 2006 (c. 36), s. 126. (2), Sch. 7 para. 36, Sch. 9 Pt. 1 (with Sch. 8 Pt. 1)

F214. . . . .

Amendments (Textual)

F2. Sch. 8 paras. 13-36 repealed (8.2.2007) by Wireless Telegraphy Act 2006 (c. 36), s. 126. (2), Sch. 7 para. 36, Sch. 9 Pt. 1 (with Sch. 8 Pt. 1)

F215. . . . .

Amendments (Textual)

F2. Sch. 8 paras. 13-36 repealed (8.2.2007) by Wireless Telegraphy Act 2006 (c. 36), s. 126. (2), Sch. 7 para. 36, Sch. 9 Pt. 1 (with Sch. 8 Pt. 1)

F216. . . . .

Amendments (Textual)

F2. Sch. 8 paras. 13-36 repealed (8.2.2007) by Wireless Telegraphy Act 2006 (c. 36), s. 126. (2), Sch. 7 para. 36, Sch. 9 Pt. 1 (with Sch. 8 Pt. 1)

F217. . . . .

Amendments (Textual)

F2. Sch. 8 paras. 13-36 repealed (8.2.2007) by Wireless Telegraphy Act 2006 (c. 36), s. 126. (2),

Sch. 7 para. 36, Sch. 9 Pt. 1 (with Sch. 8 Pt. 1)

F218. . . . .

Amendments (Textual)

F2. Sch. 8 paras. 13-36 repealed (8.2.2007) by Wireless Telegraphy Act 2006 (c. 36), s. 126. (2), Sch. 7 para. 36, Sch. 9 Pt. 1 (with Sch. 8 Pt. 1)

F219. . . . .

Amendments (Textual)

F2. Sch. 8 paras. 13-36 repealed (8.2.2007) by Wireless Telegraphy Act 2006 (c. 36), s. 126. (2), Sch. 7 para. 36, Sch. 9 Pt. 1 (with Sch. 8 Pt. 1)

F220. . . . .

Amendments (Textual)

F2. Sch. 8 paras. 13-36 repealed (8.2.2007) by Wireless Telegraphy Act 2006 (c. 36), s. 126. (2), Sch. 7 para. 36, Sch. 9 Pt. 1 (with Sch. 8 Pt. 1)

F221. . . . .

Amendments (Textual)

F2. Sch. 8 paras. 13-36 repealed (8.2.2007) by Wireless Telegraphy Act 2006 (c. 36), s. 126. (2), Sch. 7 para. 36, Sch. 9 Pt. 1 (with Sch. 8 Pt. 1)

F222. . . . .

Amendments (Textual)

F2. Sch. 8 paras. 13-36 repealed (8.2.2007) by Wireless Telegraphy Act 2006 (c. 36), s. 126. (2), Sch. 7 para. 36, Sch. 9 Pt. 1 (with Sch. 8 Pt. 1)

F223. . . . .

Amendments (Textual)

F2. Sch. 8 paras. 13-36 repealed (8.2.2007) by Wireless Telegraphy Act 2006 (c. 36), s. 126. (2), Sch. 7 para. 36, Sch. 9 Pt. 1 (with Sch. 8 Pt. 1)

F224. . . . .

Amendments (Textual)

F2. Sch. 8 paras. 13-36 repealed (8.2.2007) by Wireless Telegraphy Act 2006 (c. 36), s. 126. (2), Sch. 7 para. 36, Sch. 9 Pt. 1 (with Sch. 8 Pt. 1)

F225. . . . .

Amendments (Textual)

F2. Sch. 8 paras. 13-36 repealed (8.2.2007) by Wireless Telegraphy Act 2006 (c. 36), s. 126. (2), Sch. 7 para. 36, Sch. 9 Pt. 1 (with Sch. 8 Pt. 1)

F226. . . . .

Amendments (Textual)

F2. Sch. 8 paras. 13-36 repealed (8.2.2007) by Wireless Telegraphy Act 2006 (c. 36), s. 126. (2), Sch. 7 para. 36, Sch. 9 Pt. 1 (with Sch. 8 Pt. 1)

Wireless Telegraphy Act 1949.

F227. . . . .

F228. . . . .

Amendments (Textual)

F2. Sch. 8 paras. 13-36 repealed (8.2.2007) by Wireless Telegraphy Act 2006 (c. 36), s. 126. (2), Sch. 7 para. 36, Sch. 9 Pt. 1 (with Sch. 8 Pt. 1)

F229. . . . .

Amendments (Textual)

F2. Sch. 8 paras. 13-36 repealed (8.2.2007) by Wireless Telegraphy Act 2006 (c. 36), s. 126. (2), Sch. 7 para. 36, Sch. 9 Pt. 1 (with Sch. 8 Pt. 1)

F230. . . . .

Amendments (Textual)

F2. Sch. 8 paras. 13-36 repealed (8.2.2007) by Wireless Telegraphy Act 2006 (c. 36), s. 126. (2),

Sch. 7 para. 36, Sch. 9 Pt. 1 (with Sch. 8 Pt. 1)

F231. . . . .

Amendments (Textual)

F2. Sch. 8 paras. 13-36 repealed (8.2.2007) by Wireless Telegraphy Act 2006 (c. 36), s. 126. (2), Sch. 7 para. 36, Sch. 9 Pt. 1 (with Sch. 8 Pt. 1)

F232. . . . .

Amendments (Textual)

F2. Sch. 8 paras. 13-36 repealed (8.2.2007) by Wireless Telegraphy Act 2006 (c. 36), s. 126. (2), Sch. 7 para. 36, Sch. 9 Pt. 1 (with Sch. 8 Pt. 1)

Wireless Telegraphy Act 1998.

F233. . . . .

F234. . . . .

Amendments (Textual)

F2. Sch. 8 paras. 13-36 repealed (8.2.2007) by Wireless Telegraphy Act 2006 (c. 36), s. 126. (2), Sch. 7 para. 36, Sch. 9 Pt. 1 (with Sch. 8 Pt. 1)

F235. . . . .

Amendments (Textual)

F2. Sch. 8 paras. 13-36 repealed (8.2.2007) by Wireless Telegraphy Act 2006 (c. 36), s. 126. (2), Sch. 7 para. 36, Sch. 9 Pt. 1 (with Sch. 8 Pt. 1)

F236. . . . .

Amendments (Textual)

F2. Sch. 8 paras. 13-36 repealed (8.2.2007) by Wireless Telegraphy Act 2006 (c. 36), s. 126. (2), Sch. 7 para. 36, Sch. 9 Pt. 1 (with Sch. 8 Pt. 1)

[F3. Wireless Telegraphy Act 2006.

Amendments (Textual)

F3. Sch. 8 paras. 37-46 and cross-heading inserted (8.2.2007) by Wireless Telegraphy Act 2006 (c. 36), s. 126. (2), Sch. 7 para. 36

37. A decision relating to the publication of the United Kingdom Plan for Frequency Authorisation.

38. A decision in exercise of the functions conferred on OFCOM by section 1 as to—

(a) the services, records and advice to be provided, maintained or given by them;

(b) the research to be carried out or the arrangements made for carrying it out; or

(c) the making or terms of any grant.

39. A decision under section 4 or 7.

40. A decision given effect to—

(a) by regulations under section 8. (3), 12, 14, 18, 21, 23, 27, 30, 45 or 54 or paragraph 1 of Schedule 1 or paragraph 1 of Schedule 2;

(b) by an order under section 29 or 62.

41. A decision relating to the recovery of a sum payable to OFCOM under section 15 or 24.

42. A decision given effect to by regulations under section 31 and any decision under any such regulations.

43. A decision relating to the making or revision of a statement under—

(a) section 34, or

(b) section 44.

44. A decision to impose a penalty under section 42. (1).

45. A decision for the purposes of section 59.

46. A decision relating to an authority under section 62. (5).]

Schedule 9. Arrangements about carrying on of C4C's activities

Section 199

Notification of requirement to submit proposals

1. (1)It shall be the duty of OFCOM to give a notification under this paragraph to C4. C—
(a) as soon as practicable after the commencement of this Schedule,
[F1. (aa)as soon as practicable after the day on which section 198. A comes into force,] and
(b) as soon as practicable in the last twelve months preceding each date on which the replacement licence granted in accordance with section 231 would expire if not renewed.
(2) A notification under this paragraph is one requiring C4. C to submit proposals to OFCOM in accordance with this Schedule for the relevant licence period.
(3) A notification under this paragraph must specify the period within which C4. C must submit their proposals.
(4) The period specified under sub-paragraph (3) must be a period ending not less than three months after the day of the giving of the notification.
Amendments (Textual)
F1. Sch. 9 para. 1. (1)(aa) inserted (8.6.2010) by Digital Economy Act 2010 (c. 24), ss. 22. (3)(a), 47. (1)
Commencement Information
I1. Sch. 9 para. 1 in force at 29.12.2003 by S.I. 2003/3142, art. 3. (1), Sch. 1 (with art. 11)

Submission of proposed arrangements

2. (1)This paragraph applies where C4. C have received a notification under paragraph 1.
(2) C4. C must, within the period set out in the notification, submit proposals to OFCOM for the arrangements under which they are proposing to secure, so far as reasonably practicable, that all significant risks that their other activities will have an adverse effect on the carrying out, during the relevant licence period, of their primary functions are—
(a) identified;
(b) evaluated; and
(c) properly managed.
(3) The proposals must include proposals for the arrangements that C4. C consider appropriate for securing the transparency objectives during the relevant licence period.
(4) For the purposes of this Schedule the transparency objectives are—
(a) an appropriate financial and organisational separation between the activities of C4. C that relate to the carrying out of their primary functions and their other activities; and
(b) an appropriate degree of transparency in financial and other reporting where resources are shared between separated activities or where there is some other financial or practical connection between otherwise separated activities.
(5) The matters to which the proposals submitted under this paragraph may relate include, in particular, the procedures and other practices to be followed by C4. C in the case of—
(a) the initiation and management of new ventures;
(b) the exercise of particular powers;
(c) the assessment of risks;
(d) the imposition of charges; and
(e) the keeping of records.

(6) The determination of what is appropriate for the purposes of sub-paragraphs (3) and (4) is not to be confined to a determination of what is appropriate for securing the matters mentioned in sub-paragraph (2).

(7) The arrangements proposed by C4. C must contain provision for compliance with the arrangements to be checked regularly by a person appointed in accordance with that provision.

(8) That person must be a person other than the person for the time being holding an appointment for the purposes of paragraph 12. (2) of Schedule 3 to the 1990 Act (C4. C's auditor).

Commencement Information

I2. Sch. 9 para. 2 in force at 29.12.2003 by S.I. 2003/3142, art. 3. (1), Sch. 1 (with art. 11)

Consideration and approval of proposals

3. (1)OFCOM must consider every proposal or revised proposal submitted to them by C4. C under paragraph 2 or this paragraph and may do one of the following—

(a) approve the proposed arrangements;

(b) approve them with such modifications as they may notify to C4. C;

(c) require C4. C to submit revised proposals in accordance with directions given by OFCOM.

(2) Before—

(a) making modifications of proposed arrangements for the purpose of approving them, or

(b) requiring the submission of revised proposals,

OFCOM must consult C4. C.

Commencement Information

I3. Sch. 9 para. 3 in force at 29.12.2003 by S.I. 2003/3142, art. 3. (1), Sch. 1 (with art. 11)

Duration of approval and modification of arrangements

4. (1)Arrangements approved under this Schedule are to remain in force (subject to the following provisions of this paragraph) throughout the licence period to which they relate.

(2) The arrangements for the time being approved under this Schedule for any licence period may be modified, by agreement between OFCOM and C4. C, at any time during the licence period for which they apply.

(3) OFCOM may carry out a review of the arrangements for the time being approved under this Schedule.

(4) The reviews that may be carried out under this paragraph in any one licence period are confined to either—

(a) one review relating to all the arrangements; or

(b) two reviews carried out at separate times as follows—

(i) one (whether the first or second) relating to the arrangements for securing the transparency objectives; and

(ii) the other relating to other matters.

(5) On a review under this paragraph, OFCOM may require C4. C to submit proposals for modifying the arrangements for the time being approved under this Schedule so far as they relate to the matters under review.

(6) Paragraph 3 applies where proposals are submitted to OFCOM under sub-paragraph (5) as it applies where they are submitted under paragraph 2.

Commencement Information

I4. Sch. 9 para. 4 in force at 29.12.2003 by S.I. 2003/3142, art. 3. (1), Sch. 1 (with art. 11)

Publication of approved arrangements

5. (1)OFCOM must publish all arrangements approved by them under this Schedule.

(2) The publication of anything under this paragraph must be in such manner as OFCOM consider appropriate for bringing it to the attention of members of the public.

Commencement Information

I5. Sch. 9 para. 5 in force at 29.12.2003 by S.I. 2003/3142, art. 3. (1), Sch. 1 (with art. 11)

Duty of C4. C to act in accordance with the approved arrangements

6. It shall be the duty of C4. C to act in accordance with the arrangements for the time being in force under this Schedule.

Commencement Information

I6. Sch. 9 para. 6 in force at 29.12.2003 by S.I. 2003/3142, art. 3. (1), Sch. 1 (with art. 11)

nforcement of duties

7. (1)This paragraph applies to—
(a) every duty of C4. C under this Schedule to submit proposals to OFCOM; and
(b) the duty imposed on C4. C by paragraph 6.
(2) Each of those duties shall be enforceable in civil proceedings by OFCOM—
(a) for an injunction;
(b) for specific performance of a statutory duty under section 45 of the Court of Session Act 1988 (c. 36); or
(c) for any other appropriate remedy or relief.

Commencement Information

I7. Sch. 9 para. 7 in force at 29.12.2003 by S.I. 2003/3142, art. 3. (1), Sch. 1 (with art. 11)

Penalty for contravention of the arrangements

8. (1)OFCOM may impose a penalty on C4. C if C4. C have contravened—
(a) a requirement of this Schedule to submit proposals to OFCOM;
(b) a requirement of arrangements for the time being approved under this Schedule.
(2) The amount of the penalty must not exceed 3 per cent. of C4. C's qualifying revenue for their last complete accounting period before the contravention.
(3) Before imposing a penalty on C4. C under this paragraph OFCOM must give C4. C a reasonable opportunity of making representations to OFCOM about their proposal to impose the penalty.
(4) Where OFCOM impose a penalty on C4. C under this paragraph, they shall—
(a) notify C4. C; and
(b) in that notification, fix a reasonable period after it is given as the period within which the penalty is to be paid.
(5) In the case of a continuing contravention—
(a) separate penalties may be imposed in respect of different periods during which the contravention continues;
(b) the notification of the penalty must specify the period in respect of which the penalty is imposed; and
(c) the reference in sub-paragraph (2) to the last complete accounting period before the contravention is a reference to the last complete accounting period before the end of the period in respect of which the penalty is imposed.
(6) A penalty imposed under this paragraph must be paid to OFCOM within the period fixed by them.
(7) Section 19. (2) to (6) of the 1990 Act and Part 1 of Schedule 7 to that Act (calculation of

qualifying revenue), with any necessary modifications, have effect in relation to C4. C for the purposes of this paragraph as they have effect in relation to the holder of a Channel 3 licence for the purposes of Part 1 of that Act.

Commencement Information

I8. Sch. 9 para. 8 in force at 29.12.2003 by S.I. 2003/3142, art. 3. (1), Sch. 1 (with art. 11)

OFCOM's duty to take account of need to support C4. C's primary functions

9. In exercising their powers under this Schedule OFCOM must have regard, in particular, to the need to secure, so far as practicable, that all significant risks that C4. C's other activities will have an adverse effect on the carrying out of their primary functions are—

(a) identified;

(b) evaluated; and

(c) properly managed.

Commencement Information

I9. Sch. 9 para. 9 in force at 29.12.2003 by S.I. 2003/3142, art. 3. (1), Sch. 1 (with art. 11)

Interpretation of Schedule

10. In this Schedule—

"arrangements" means arrangements about the procedures and other practices to be followed by C4. C and about other matters connected with the carrying on by them of any of their activities;

"licence period" means—

- the period for which the replacement licence is granted to C4. C in accordance with section 231; or

- any subsequent period for which it is renewed;

"primary functions" is to be construed in accordance with section 199. (2);

"relevant licence period"—

- in relation to the first notification to be given under paragraph 1, the licence period mentioned in paragraph (a) of the definition of that period;

- [F2in relation to the notification under paragraph 1. (1)(aa), the period beginning on the day on which section 198. A comes into force and ending on the last day of the first licence period to expire after that day;] and

- in relation to [F3any other notification under paragraph 1] , the first licence period to begin after the giving of the notification;

"transparency objectives" is to be construed in accordance with paragraph 2. (4).

Amendments (Textual)

F2. Words in Sch. 9 para. 10 inserted (8.6.2010) by Digital Economy Act 2010 (c. 24), ss. 22. (3)(b), 47. (1)

F3. Words in Sch. 9 para. 10 substituted (8.6.2010) by Digital Economy Act 2010 (c. 24), ss. 22. (3)(c), 47. (1)

Commencement Information

I10. Sch. 9 para. 10 in force at 29.12.2003 by S.I. 2003/3142, art. 3. (1), Sch. 1 (with art. 11)

Schedule 10. Licensing the public teletext service

Section 219

Modifications etc. (not altering text)

C1. Sch. 10 excluded (8.12.2003) by The Office of Communications Act 2002 (Commencement

No. 3) and Communications Act 2003 (Commencement No. 2) Order 2003 (S.I. 2003/3142), art. 8. (1) (with art. 11)

Part 1. Applications for and award of licence

Notice of proposal to grant licence

1. (1)Where OFCOM propose to grant a licence to provide the public teletext service they must publish a notice stating that they are proposing to do so.

(2) The notice must—

(a) specify the digital capacity which is available for the public teletext service on television multiplex services;

(b) specify whether the licence will require the public teletext service to comprise a service to be provided for broadcasting in analogue form;

(c) invite applications for the licence;

(d) specify the closing date for applications;

(e) specify the fee payable on the making of an application for the licence; and

(f) specify the percentage of qualifying revenue for each accounting period of the licence holder which OFCOM have determined to be the percentage of that revenue that will have to be paid to them.

(3) Where the licence is to comprise an analogue teletext service the notice must specify—

(a) the television broadcasting service or services on whose frequency or frequencies the services are to be provided; and

(b) the extent and nature of the spare capacity which is to be allocated by the licence.

(4) For the purposes of sub-paragraph (2)(f)—

(a) different percentages may be determined and specified for different accounting periods; and

(b) the percentages that may be determined and specified for an accounting period include a nil percentage.

(5) A notice under this paragraph is to be published in such manner as OFCOM consider appropriate.

Commencement Information

I1. Sch. 10 para. 1 in force at 29.12.2003 by S.I. 2003/3142, art. 3. (1), Sch. 1 (with art. 11)

Guidance as to applications

2. (1)When publishing a notice under paragraph 1, OFCOM must publish with it some general guidance to applicants about what is likely to make proposals relating to the matters mentioned in paragraph 3. (1)(c) to (e) acceptable to them.

(2) Guidance published under this paragraph must include examples.

Commencement Information

I2. Sch. 10 para. 2 in force at 29.12.2003 by S.I. 2003/3142, art. 3. (1), Sch. 1 (with art. 11)

Applications for the licence

3. (1)An application made in response to a notice under paragraph 1 must be accompanied by—

(a) the fee specified in the notice as payable on the making of the application;

(b) a technical plan complying with sub-paragraph (2);

(c) the applicant's proposals for providing, or securing the provision of, a service that fulfils the public service remit for the public teletext service;

(d) the applicant's proposals for including news items in the service and for securing that the news items included in the service are up to date and regularly revised;

(e) the applicant's proposals for the inclusion in the service of material that is of particular interest to persons living in different parts of the United Kingdom;

(f) the applicant's cash bid in respect of the licence; and

(g) such information as OFCOM may reasonably require about the matters mentioned in sub-paragraph (3).

(2) The technical plan must indicate—

(a) the nature of the public teletext service which the applicant is proposing to provide; and

(b) the nature of any services the provision of which, in accordance with proposals made by another person, would be secured by the applicant in accordance with provision made under section 220.

(3) The matters about which OFCOM may require information under sub-paragraph (1)(g) are—

(a) the applicant's present financial position; and

(b) his projected financial position during the period for which the licence would be in force.

(4) At any time after receiving an application under this Schedule and before disposing of it, OFCOM may require the applicant to furnish additional information about any one or more of the following—

(a) the matters that must be indicated in the technical plan;

(b) the applicant's proposals with respect to the matters mentioned in sub-paragraph (1)(c) to (e); and

(c) the matters mentioned in sub-paragraph (3).

(5) Any information to be furnished to OFCOM under this paragraph must be in such form, and must be verified, in such manner as they may require.

Commencement Information

I3. Sch. 10 para. 3 in force at 29.12.2003 by S.I. 2003/3142, art. 3. (1), Sch. 1 (with art. 11)

Notice inviting public representations

4. (1)As soon as reasonably practicable after the date specified in a notice under paragraph 1 as the closing date for applications, OFCOM must publish—

(a) the name of every person who has made an application to them in response to their notice;

(b) particulars of the technical plan submitted by each applicant;

(c) the proposals submitted by each applicant with respect to the matters mentioned in paragraph 3. (1)(c) to (e);

(d) such other information connected with each application as OFCOM consider appropriate; and

(e) a notice under sub-paragraph (2).

(2) The notice required by this paragraph is one that—

(a) invites representations to be made to OFCOM with respect to the other matters published under this paragraph; and

(b) specifies the manner in which, and the time by which, such representations have to be made.

(3) Publication of any information or notice under this paragraph is to be in such manner as OFCOM consider appropriate.

Commencement Information

I4. Sch. 10 para. 4 in force at 29.12.2003 by S.I. 2003/3142, art. 3. (1), Sch. 1 (with art. 11)

Determination of applications

5. (1)This paragraph applies where, in response to a notice under paragraph 1, a person has made an application for a licence to provide the public teletext service.

(2) OFCOM must not proceed to consider whether to award the applicant the licence in accordance with the following provisions of this paragraph unless it appears to them—

(a) that the applicant's technical plan, in so far as it involves the use of an electronic communications network, contains proposals that are acceptable to them;

(b) that the applicant's proposals with respect to the matters mentioned in paragraph 3. (1)(c) to (e) are acceptable to them; and

(c) that the services proposed to be provided under the licence would be capable of being maintained throughout the period for which the licence would be in force.

(3) In determining whether it appears to them as mentioned in sub-paragraph (2), OFCOM must take account of any representations made to them in response to the invitation published under paragraph 4.

(4) Sections 17 and 17. A of the 1990 Act (award of licence to highest cash bidder and financial conditions) apply in relation to a licence to provide the public teletext service as they apply in relation to a Channel 3 licence, but with the modifications set out in sub-paragraphs (5) and (6).

(5) In the application of section 17 of the 1990 Act in accordance with sub-paragraph (4)—

(a) any reference to an applicant is to be construed as a reference to an applicant in whose case it appears to OFCOM as mentioned in sub-paragraph (2);

(b) the provisions of subsection (4) down to the end of paragraph (b) are to be omitted;

(c) in subsection (7)(a), the reference to section 19. (1) of the 1990 Act is to be construed as a reference to paragraph 7 of this Schedule;

(d) subsection (12) shall have effect with the substitution of the following paragraph for paragraph (b)—

"(b)the name of every other applicant in whose case it appeared to OFCOM as mentioned in paragraph 5. (2) of Schedule 10 to the Communications Act 2003;"

(e) in subsection (14), the references to a notice under section 15. (1) of the 1990 Act and a notice under Part 1 of that Act shall each have effect as a reference to a notice under paragraph 1 of this Schedule.

(6) In the application of section 17. A of the 1990 Act in accordance with sub-paragraph (4)—

(a) the reference in subsection (1)(b) to section 15. (3)(g) of the 1990 Act shall have effect as a reference to paragraph 3. (1)(g) of this Schedule; and

(b) the reference in subsection (3) to a notice under section 15. (1) of the 1990 Act shall have effect as a reference to a notice under paragraph 1 of this Schedule.

Commencement Information

I5. Sch. 10 para. 5 in force at 29.12.2003 by S.I. 2003/3142, art. 3. (1), Sch. 1 (with art. 11)

Revocation of award

6. (1)This paragraph applies if, at any time after a licence to provide the public teletext service has been awarded to a person, but before it has come into force—

(a) that person indicates to OFCOM that he does not intend to provide, or secure the provision of, the licensed service; or

(b) OFCOM have, for any other reason, reasonable grounds for believing that the licensed service will not be provided once the licence has come into force.

(2) OFCOM must revoke the licence by serving a notice of revocation on the person to whom it was awarded.

(3) OFCOM may then award the licence again in accordance with section 17 of the 1990 Act (as applied by paragraph 5 of this Schedule) as if the person whose licence is revoked had not made an application.

(4) Sub-paragraph (3) has effect subject to subsection (14) of section 17 of the 1990 Act (as so applied) (re-publication of invitation to make applications) as if the reference in that subsection to the following provisions of Part 1 of that Act included a reference to that sub-paragraph.

(5) Before acting under sub-paragraphs (2) and (3) in a case falling within sub-paragraph (1)(b), OFCOM must serve a notice on the person awarded the licence stating their grounds for believing that the licensed service will not be provided once the licence has come into force.

(6) Where such a notice is required to be given, OFCOM must not revoke the licence unless they

have given the person to whom it was awarded a reasonable opportunity of making representations to them about the matters by reference to which they are proposing to revoke it.

(7) In the case of a licence to provide a service that must comprise both—

(a) an analogue teletext service, and

(b) a teletext service provided in digital form,

the references in sub-paragraphs (1) and (5) to the licensed service are references to one or both of those services.

Commencement Information

I6. Sch. 10 para. 6 in force at 29.12.2003 by S.I. 2003/3142, art. 3. (1), Sch. 1 (with art. 11)

Part 2. Conditions and enforcement of licence

Payments to be made in respect of the public teletext service

7. (1)A licence to provide the public teletext service must include conditions requiring the licence holder to pay the following amounts to OFCOM (in addition to any fees required to be so paid by virtue of section 4. (1)(b) of the 1990 Act)—

(a) a specified amount in respect of the first complete calendar year falling within the licence period;

(b) in respect of each subsequent year falling wholly or partly within the licence period, that amount increased by the appropriate percentage;

(c) in respect of each accounting period of his falling within the licence period, an amount representing a specified percentage of qualifying revenue for that accounting period.

(2) The amount specified for the purposes of sub-paragraph (1)(a) must be—

(a) in the case of the replacement licence under section 221, the amount proposed in accordance with subsection (5)(a) of that section;

(b) in the case of a licence renewed under section 222, the amount determined under section 223. (1)(a); and

(c) in any other case, the amount specified in the licence holder's cash bid.

(3) The percentage specified for the purposes of sub-paragraph (1)(c) in respect of an accounting period must be—

(a) in the case of the replacement licence under section 221, nil;

(b) in the case of a licence renewed under section 222, the percentage determined under section 223. (1)(b); and

(c) in any other case, the percentage determined and specified for the purposes of paragraph 1. (2)(f) of this Schedule.

(4) A licence to provide the public teletext service may also include conditions—

(a) enabling OFCOM to estimate before the beginning of an accounting period the amount due for that period by virtue of any condition imposed under this paragraph; and

(b) requiring the licence holder to pay the estimated amount by monthly instalments throughout that period.

(5) Such a licence may, in particular, include conditions—

(a) authorising OFCOM to revise an estimate on one or more occasions;

(b) requiring them to alter the amounts of the instalments payable by the licence holder to take account of the revised estimate;

(c) providing for the adjustment of an overpayment or underpayment.

(6) This paragraph has effect subject to sections 225 and 226 and to the requirement in section 221. (5)(b).

(7) In this paragraph "the appropriate percentage" has the same meaning as in section 19 of the 1990 Act.

Commencement Information

17. Sch. 10 para. 7 in force at 29.12.2003 by S.I. 2003/3142, art. 3. (1), Sch. 1 (with art. 11)

Corrections and statements of findings by the public teletext provider

8. (1)Section 40 of the 1990 Act (power to direct correction or a statement of findings) shall have effect in relation to the public teletext service as it has effect in relation to a Channel 3 service but as if the references in subsection (4) to a programme were references to an item.

(2) OFCOM's powers by virtue of this paragraph in relation to any matter are not affected by any prior exercise by them in relation to that matter of their powers under either or both of paragraphs 9 and 10.

Commencement Information

18. Sch. 10 para. 8 in force at 29.12.2003 by S.I. 2003/3142, art. 3. (1), Sch. 1 (with art. 11)

Enforcement of the licence for the public teletext service

9. (1)If OFCOM are satisfied that the holder of the licence to provide the public teletext service has—

(a) contravened a condition of the licence, or

(b) failed to comply with a direction given to him by OFCOM under or by virtue of a provision of the 1990 Act, the 1996 Act or Part 3 of this Act,

they may serve on him a notice requiring him to pay a specified financial penalty to them.

(2) The maximum amount which a person may be required to pay by way of a penalty under this paragraph is 5 per cent. of the qualifying revenue for his last complete accounting period.

(3) Where an accounting period by reference to which the maximum amount of a penalty falls to be calculated has not ended when the penalty is imposed, the amount taken into account in respect of that period is to be the amount estimated by OFCOM.

(4) OFCOM are not to serve a notice under this paragraph on any person unless they have given him a reasonable opportunity of making representations to them about the matters complained of.

(5) A notice requiring a person to pay a penalty under this paragraph must specify the period within which it is to be paid.

Commencement Information

19. Sch. 10 para. 9 in force at 29.12.2003 by S.I. 2003/3142, art. 3. (1), Sch. 1 (with art. 11)

Power to shorten licence period

10. (1)If OFCOM are satisfied that the holder of the licence to provide the public teletext service has—

(a) contravened a condition of the licence, or

(b) failed to comply with a direction given to him by OFCOM under or by virtue of any provision of the 1990 Act, the 1996 Act or Part 3 of this Act,

they may serve on him a notice reducing the period for which the licence is to be in force by a specified period not exceeding two years.

(2) OFCOM are not to serve a notice under this paragraph on any person unless they have given him a reasonable opportunity of making representations to them about the matters in respect of which it is served.

(3) Where a licence is due to expire on a particular date by virtue of a notice served on a person under this paragraph, OFCOM may, on the application of that person, revoke that notice by a further notice served on him at any time before that date.

(4) OFCOM may exercise their power under sub-paragraph (3) only if they are satisfied that, since the date of the earlier notice, the conduct of the licence holder in relation to the operation of the

413

licensed service has been such as to justify the revocation of that notice.

Commencement Information

I10. Sch. 10 para. 10 in force at 29.12.2003 by S.I. 2003/3142, art. 3. (1), Sch. 1 (with art. 11)

Revocation for contravention of condition or direction

11. Section 42 of the 1990 Act (revocation for contravention) shall apply in relation to the licence to provide the public teletext service as it applies in relation to a licence to provide a Channel 3 service.

Commencement Information

I11. Sch. 10 para. 11 in force at 29.12.2003 by S.I. 2003/3142, art. 3. (1), Sch. 1 (with art. 11)

Penalty on revocation

12. (1)Where OFCOM revoke the licence to provide the public teletext service (whether under paragraph 6 or a provision of the 1990 Act or 1996 Act), they must serve on the licence holder a notice requiring him to pay a specified financial penalty to them.

(2) The maximum amount which a person may be required to pay by way of a penalty under this paragraph is the maximum given by sub-paragraphs (3) and (4).

(3) In a case where the licence is revoked under paragraph 6 or the penalty is imposed before the end of the first complete accounting period of the licence holder to begin in the licence period, the maximum penalty is whichever is the greater of—

(a) £500,000; and

(b) 7 per cent. of the amount which OFCOM estimate would have been the qualifying revenue for the first complete accounting period of the licence holder falling within the period for which the licence would have been in force.

(4) In any other case, the maximum penalty is whichever is the greater of—

(a) £500,000; and

(b) 7 per cent. of the qualifying revenue for the last complete accounting period of the licence holder falling within the licence period.

(5) A notice requiring a person to pay a penalty under this paragraph must specify the period within which it is to be paid.

(6) A financial penalty that must be paid by virtue of this paragraph by a body of any description shall also be recoverable—

(a) as a debt due to OFCOM from the person who controls the body; or

(b) if two or more persons control it, as a debt due jointly and severally from them all.

(7) Sub-paragraph (6) is in addition to the provision for the recovery of penalties contained in section 346, but the amount recovered in respect of any one penalty must not exceed the full amount of that penalty.

(8) References in this paragraph to a person controlling a body are references to his controlling it within the meaning of Schedule 2 to the 1990 Act.

Commencement Information

I12. Sch. 10 para. 12 in force at 29.12.2003 by S.I. 2003/3142, art. 3. (1), Sch. 1 (with art. 11)

Power to modify penalties in paragraph 12.

13. (1)The Secretary of State may by order substitute a different sum for the sum for the time being specified in paragraph 12. (3)(a) or (4)(a).

(2) No order is to be made containing provision authorised by this paragraph unless a draft of the order has been laid before Parliament and approved by a resolution of each House.

Commencement Information

113. Sch. 10 para. 13 in force at 29.12.2003 by S.I. 2003/3142, art. 3. (1), Sch. 1 (with art. 11)

Part 3. Interpretation of Schedule

14. In this Schedule "licence period", in relation to a licence, means the period for which the licence is in force.
Commencement Information
114. Sch. 10 para. 14 in force at 29.12.2003 by S.I. 2003/3142, art. 3. (1), Sch. 1 (with art. 11)
15. (1)For the purposes of this Schedule the qualifying revenue for an accounting period of the holder of a licence to provide the public teletext service consists of the aggregate of all the following amounts—
(a) the amounts received or to be received by a person mentioned in sub-paragraph (2) in consideration of the inclusion in the licensed service in that period of advertisements or other items; and
(b) the amounts received or to be received by such a person in respect of the provision of the service from—
(i) a person authorised by the licence holder to provide the whole or a part of the licensed service; or
(ii) a person who is a connected person in relation to a person so authorised.
(2) Those persons are—
(a) the licence holder; or
(b) a person who is a connected person in relation to the licence holder without being a person authorised by the licence holder to provide the whole or a part of the licensed service.
(3) Part 1 of Schedule 7 to the 1990 Act applies for determining qualifying revenue for the purposes of this Schedule as it applies for the purposes of Part 1 of that Act.
(4) Where, in the case of the licence to provide the public teletext service—
(a) the first complete accounting period of the licence holder to fall within the licence period does not begin at the same time as the licence period, or
(b) the last complete accounting period of his to fall within the licence period does not end at the same time as the licence period,
references in this Schedule to an accounting period of the licence holder include references to such part of the accounting period preceding the first complete accounting period, or (as the case may be) following the last complete accounting period, as falls within the licence period.
(5) In this paragraph "connected person" has the same meaning as in Schedule 2 to the 1990 Act.
Commencement Information
115. Sch. 10 para. 15 in force at 29.12.2003 by S.I. 2003/3142, art. 3. (1), Sch. 1 (with art. 11)

Schedule 11. Approval, imposition and modification of networking arrangements

Sections 291 and 294

Application of Schedule

1. (1)This Schedule applies where OFCOM's approval of networking arrangements entered into by the holders of regional Channel 3 licences is required—
(a) for the purposes of conditions included in regional Channel 3 licences in accordance with section 291; or
(b) in order for networking arrangements made by OFCOM to cease to have effect in accordance

with section 292.

(2) This Schedule also has effect as respects—

(a) the imposition by OFCOM under section 292 of networking arrangements;

(b) the modification of such arrangements following a review under section 293; and

(c) the making of proposals for modifications of networking arrangements following such a review.

Commencement Information

I1. Sch. 11 para. 1 in force at 29.12.2003 by S.I. 2003/3142, art. 3. (1), Sch. 1 (with art. 11)

Approval required for modifications

2. (1)Where networking arrangements are approved by OFCOM for purposes mentioned in paragraph 1. (1), those arrangements are not to be modified unless OFCOM have approved the modifications in accordance with this Schedule.

(2) This paragraph does not apply to modifications proposed by OFCOM under section 293.

Commencement Information

I2. Sch. 11 para. 2 in force at 29.12.2003 by S.I. 2003/3142, art. 3. (1), Sch. 1 (with art. 11)

Procedure for giving approval

3. (1)This paragraph applies where arrangements or modifications are submitted to OFCOM for their approval.

(2) OFCOM must publish a description of the arrangements or modifications that have been submitted.

(3) The publication must be in such manner as OFCOM consider appropriate for bringing the matters published to the attention of the persons who, in OFCOM's opinion, are likely to be affected by the arrangements or modifications.

(4) After allowing a reasonable time after the publication for the making of representations, OFCOM must consider the arrangements or modifications and decide whether or not to approve them.

Commencement Information

I3. Sch. 11 para. 3 in force at 29.12.2003 by S.I. 2003/3142, art. 3. (1), Sch. 1 (with art. 11)

Decision of OFCOM whether or not to approve arrangements or modifications

4. (1)The decision made by OFCOM under paragraph 3. (4) has to be one of the following—

(a) a decision to approve the arrangements or modifications unconditionally;

(b) a decision to give a conditional approval to the arrangements or modifications;

(c) a decision to refuse approval.

(2) A conditional approval is one that has effect only if effect is given, in relation to the proposed arrangements or modifications, to changes proposed by OFCOM.

(3) Before deciding to give a conditional approval, OFCOM must consult every holder of a regional Channel 3 licence about the changes they are proposing.

(4) When OFCOM have made their decision, they must prepare a report setting out—

(a) their decision; and

(b) their reasons for that decision.

(5) OFCOM must publish the report and send a copy of it to—

(a) the [F1. Competition and Markets Authority] ; and

(b) every person to whom the relevant arrangements will apply, or do apply.

(6) The relevant arrangements are—

(a) the arrangements for which approval has been sought; or

(b) the arrangements which are the subject of the modifications for which approval has been sought.

Amendments (Textual)

F1. Words in Sch. 11 substituted (1.4.2014) by The Enterprise and Regulatory Reform Act 2013 (Competition) (Consequential, Transitional and Saving Provisions) Order 2014 (S.I. 2014/892), art. 1. (1), Sch. 1 para. 165 (with art. 3)

Commencement Information

I4. Sch. 11 para. 4 in force at 29.12.2003 by S.I. 2003/3142, art. 3. (1), Sch. 1 (with art. 11)

Notification of decisions on imposition of arrangements

5. (1)Where OFCOM impose arrangements they must prepare and publish a report setting out details of the imposed arrangements.

(2) Where OFCOM carry out a review under section 293, they must prepare and publish a report setting out—

(a) their conclusions on the review;

(b) their reasons for those conclusions; and

(c) the modifications (if any) that they are proposing, or intend to make, following the review.

(3) OFCOM must send a copy of a report prepared under this paragraph to—

(a) the [F1. Competition and Markets Authority] ; and

(b) every person to whom the relevant arrangements will apply or do apply.

(4) The relevant arrangements are—

(a) the arrangements which are imposed; or

(b) the arrangements which are the subject of the modifications proposed by OFCOM or to be made by them.

Commencement Information

I5. Sch. 11 para. 5 in force at 29.12.2003 by S.I. 2003/3142, art. 3. (1), Sch. 1 (with art. 11)

Competition tests applying to OFCOM's decisions

6. (1)OFCOM must not—

(a) approve arrangements or modifications,

(b) impose arrangements or modify imposed arrangements, or

(c) propose modifications following a review under section 293,

unless they are satisfied that the arrangements, or the arrangements as proposed to be modified, satisfy the first or second competition test.

(2) Before making a decision about whether a competition test is satisfied OFCOM must consult the [F1. Competition and Markets Authority] .

(3) Arrangements satisfy the first competition test if they do not have as their object or effect the prevention, restriction or distortion of competition within the United Kingdom.

(4) Arrangements satisfy the second competition test if—

(a) they do have such an object or effect; but

(b) they would satisfy the criteria set out in section 9 of the Competition Act 1998 (c. 41) (agreements contributing to improving the production or distribution of goods or to promoting technical or economic progress).

(5) For the purposes of the second competition test, arrangements imposed by OFCOM and modifications of such arrangements are to be treated as if they were given effect to by an agreement between undertakings.

(6) In determining whether arrangements or modified arrangements would satisfy either of the competition tests, OFCOM must act with a view to securing that there is no inconsistency between—

(a) the principles they apply and the decision they reach; and

(b) any principles or decisions referred to in sub-paragraph (7).

(7) Those principles and decisions are—

(a) the principles laid down by [F2the Treaty on the Functioning of the European Union and the European Court, and any decisions of that court, that are relevant to the construction of Article 101 of that Treaty] ; and

(b) any decisions under Part 1 of the Competition Act 1998, and any decisions of a court in the United Kingdom, that are relevant to the construction of a provision of that Act that is equivalent to the provisions of this Schedule imposing the competition tests.

(8) In the case of a conditional approval, the requirements of this paragraph have to be satisfied in relation to the arrangements or modified arrangements as they will be after giving effect to the changes proposed by OFCOM.

(9) In this paragraph, the "European Court" includes a court attached to the European Court.

Amendments (Textual)

F2. Words in Sch. 11 para. 6. (7)(a) substituted (1.8.2012) by The Treaty of Lisbon (Changes in Terminology or Numbering) Order 2012 (S.I. 2012/1809), art. 2. (1), Sch. Pt. 1 (with art. 2. (2))

Commencement Information

I6. Sch. 11 para. 6 in force at 29.12.2003 by S.I. 2003/3142, art. 3. (1), Sch. 1 (with art. 11)

Other matters to be taken into account

7. (1)OFCOM must not—

(a) approve arrangements or modifications,

(b) impose arrangements or modify imposed arrangements, or

(c) propose modifications following a review under section 293,

unless they consider that the arrangements, or the arrangements as proposed to be modified, are satisfactory.

(2) OFCOM's consideration under sub-paragraph (1) must include consideration of the following two factors.

(3) The first factor is whether the arrangements, or the arrangements as proposed to be modified, represent a satisfactory means of achieving the purpose set out in section 290. (4)(c).

(4) The second factor is the likely effect of the arrangements, or the arrangements as modified, on the ability of the persons who will be or are the holders of regional Channel 3 licences, or of any of them, to maintain the quality and range of—

(a) regional programmes included in regional Channel 3 services; and

(b) the other programmes included in such services which contribute to the regional character of the services.

(5) In this paragraph "regional programme", in relation to a regional Channel 3 service, means a programme (including a news programme) which is of particular interest—

(a) to persons living within the area for which the service is provided;

(b) to persons living within a part of that area; or

(c) to particular communities living within that area.

Commencement Information

I7. Sch. 11 para. 7 in force at 29.12.2003 by S.I. 2003/3142, art. 3. (1), Sch. 1 (with art. 11)

Duty to refuse approval in certain cases

8. (1)This paragraph applies to a decision by OFCOM—

(a) to approve arrangements or modifications;

(b) to impose arrangements or to modify imposed arrangements; or

(c) to propose modifications following a review under section 293.

(2) OFCOM must not make that decision if it appears to them that the arrangements, or the

arrangements as proposed to be modified, would be likely to be prejudicial to the ability of holders of regional Channel 3 licences, or of any of them, to comply with—

(a) their public service remits;

(b) conditions imposed on them under section 286;

(c) conditions imposed on them under section 287; or

(d) conditions imposed on them under section 352.

Commencement Information

I8. Sch. 11 para. 8 in force at 29.12.2003 by S.I. 2003/3142, art. 3. (1), Sch. 1 (with art. 11)

Appeals against decisions relating to competition test

9. (1)A person holding a regional Channel 3 licence may appeal to the Tribunal against the following decisions by OFCOM—

(a) a decision on how to dispose of an application for the approval of arrangements or modifications;

(b) a decision to impose arrangements or to modify imposed arrangements; or

(c) a decision to propose modifications following a review under section 293.

(2) An appeal can be made only by sending the Tribunal a notice of appeal within the period specified, in relation to the decision appealed against, in Tribunal rules.

(3) The notice of appeal must set out the grounds of appeal.

(4) The only grounds on which an appeal may be brought are—

(a) that OFCOM have wrongly decided that a competition test is or is not satisfied in relation to arrangements or modifications submitted to them for approval;

(b) that a competition test is not satisfied in the case of arrangements proposed by OFCOM;

(c) that provisions contained in arrangements proposed by OFCOM for satisfying a competition test are not required for that purpose;

(d) that the requirement to satisfy a competition test should be discharged in a different manner from that in which it would be satisfied in accordance with arrangements proposed by OFCOM.

(5) In sub-paragraph (4) "arrangements proposed by OFCOM" means—

(a) arrangements or modified arrangements as they will have effect after giving effect to changes proposed by OFCOM in giving a conditional approval;

(b) arrangements imposed by them;

(c) imposed arrangements as modified by them;

(d) arrangements as modified by proposals made by OFCOM following a review under section 293.

(6) The holder of a regional Channel 3 licence is not required by the conditions of his licence to take steps for giving effect to a decision of OFCOM at any time when an appeal under this Schedule against that decision is pending.

Commencement Information

I9. Sch. 11 para. 9 in force at 29.12.2003 by S.I. 2003/3142, art. 3. (1), Sch. 1 (with art. 11)

Decisions on an appeal

10. (1)Appeals to the Tribunal under paragraph 9 are to be disposed of in accordance with this paragraph.

(2) The Tribunal shall decide the appeal on the merits and by reference to the grounds of appeal set out in the notice of appeal.

(3) The Tribunal shall decide what (if any) is the appropriate decision for OFCOM to have made in relation to the matters to which those grounds relate.

(4) The Tribunal shall then either—

(a) confirm OFCOM's decision; or

(b) remit the matter to OFCOM with such directions (if any) as the Tribunal considers appropriate for giving effect to its decision.

(5) The Tribunal must not direct OFCOM to take any action which they would not otherwise have had power to take in relation to the matter under appeal.

(6) It shall be the duty of OFCOM to comply with every direction given to them under sub-paragraph (4).

(7) In its application to a decision of the Tribunal under this paragraph, paragraph 1. (2)(b) of Schedule 4 to the Enterprise Act 2002 (c. 40) (exclusion of commercial information from documents recording Tribunal decisions) is to have effect as if for the reference to the undertaking to which commercial information relates there were substituted a reference to the person to whom such information relates.

Commencement Information

I10. Sch. 11 para. 10 in force at 29.12.2003 by S.I. 2003/3142, art. 3. (1), Sch. 1 (with art. 11)

Appeals against decisions of the Tribunal

11. (1)A decision of the Tribunal on an appeal under paragraph 9 may itself be appealed.

(2) An appeal under this paragraph

(a) lies to the Court of Appeal or to the Court of Session; and

(b) must relate only to a point of law arising from the decision of the Tribunal.

(3) An appeal under this paragraph may be brought by a party to the proceedings before the Tribunal.

(4) An appeal under this paragraph requires the permission of the Tribunal or of the court to which it is to be made.

(5) In this paragraph references to a decision of the Tribunal include references to a direction given by it under paragraph 10. (4).

Commencement Information

I11. Sch. 11 para. 11 in force at 29.12.2003 by S.I. 2003/3142, art. 3. (1), Sch. 1 (with art. 11)

Information for OFCOM

12. (1)OFCOM may by notice require a person—

(a) to produce to them such documents specified or described in the notice, or

(b) to furnish them with such other information so specified or described,

as they consider necessary in order to determine for the purposes of section 293 or this Schedule whether the competition tests are satisfied.

(2) A requirement imposed by a notice under this paragraph has to be complied with by producing the document, or by furnishing the required information, at the time and place specified in the notice.

(3) If the requirement is one for the furnishing of information otherwise than by the production of a document, the information must be furnished in the manner specified in the notice.

(4) The only documents that a person is required to produce by a notice under this paragraph are those that are in his custody or under his control—

(a) at the time of the notice; or

(b) at a time between that time and the time when the notice must be complied with.

Commencement Information

I12. Sch. 11 para. 12 in force at 29.12.2003 by S.I. 2003/3142, art. 3. (1), Sch. 1 (with art. 11)

Enforcement of information provisions

13. (1)The court may, on an application by OFCOM, enquire into whether any person ("the defaulter") has refused or otherwise failed, without reasonable excuse, to comply with a

requirement contained in a notice under paragraph 12.

(2) An application under sub-paragraph (1) shall include details of the possible failure which OFCOM consider has occurred.

(3) In enquiring into a case under sub-paragraph (1), the court shall hear—

(a) any witness who may be produced against or on behalf of the defaulter; and

(b) any statement which may be offered in defence.

(4) Sub-paragraphs (5) and (6) apply where the court is satisfied, after hearing any witnesses and statements as mentioned in sub-paragraph (3), that the defaulter has refused or failed, without reasonable excuse, to comply with the requirement contained in the notice under paragraph 12.

(5) The court may punish the defaulter as it would have been able to punish him had he been guilty of contempt of court.

(6) Where the defaulter is a body corporate, the power of the court to punish the defaulter includes power to punish a director or officer of the body corporate.

(7) Where the defaulter is a partnership constituted under the law of Scotland, the power of the court to punish the defaulter includes power to punish a member of the partnership.

(8) A person is guilty of an offence if he intentionally alters, suppresses or destroys a document which he has been required to produce by a notice under paragraph 12.

(9) A person is guilty of an offence if—

(a) he supplies information to OFCOM in purported compliance with a notice given to him under paragraph 12;

(b) the information is false or misleading in a material respect; and

(c) he knows that it is false or misleading in a material respect or is reckless as to whether it is false or misleading in a material respect.

(10) A person is guilty of an offence if—

(a) he supplies information to another person knowing that the information is to be used for complying with a notice under paragraph 12;

(b) the information is false or misleading in a material respect; and

(c) he knows that it is false or misleading in a material respect or is reckless as to whether it is false or misleading in a material respect.

(11) A person guilty of an offence under this paragraph shall be liable—

(a) on summary conviction, to a fine not exceeding the statutory maximum;

(b) on conviction on indictment, to imprisonment for a term not exceeding two years or to a fine, or to both.

(12) In this paragraph "the court" means—

(a) in relation to England and Wales, the High Court;

(b) in relation to Scotland, the Court of Session; and

(c) in relation to Northern Ireland, the High Court or a judge of the High Court.

Commencement Information

I13. Sch. 11 para. 13 in force at 29.12.2003 by S.I. 2003/3142, art. 3. (1), Sch. 1 (with art. 11)

Confidentiality and defamation

14. (1)When publishing a report prepared under paragraph 4 or 5, OFCOM must have regard to the need to exclude from the publication, so far as practicable, the matters which are confidential in accordance with sub-paragraphs (2) and (3).

(2) A matter is confidential under this sub-paragraph if—

(a) it relates specifically to the affairs of a particular body; and

(b) publication of that matter would or might, in OFCOM's opinion, seriously and prejudicially affect the interests of that body.

(3) A matter is confidential under this sub-paragraph if—

(a) it relates to the private affairs of an individual; and

(b) publication of that matter would or might, in OFCOM's opinion, seriously and prejudicially affect the interests of that individual.

(4) For the purposes of the law of defamation absolute privilege attaches to every report prepared under paragraph 4 or 5.

Commencement Information

114. Sch. 11 para. 14 in force at 29.12.2003 by S.I. 2003/3142, art. 3. (1), Sch. 1 (with art. 11)

Interpretation of Schedule

15. In this Schedule—

"competition test" is to be construed in accordance with paragraph 6;

"the Tribunal" means the Competition Appeal Tribunal; and

"Tribunal rules" means rules made under section 15 of the Enterprise Act 2002 (c. 40).

Commencement Information

115. Sch. 11 para. 15 in force at 29.12.2003 by S.I. 2003/3142, art. 3. (1), Sch. 1 (with art. 11)

Schedule 12. Restrictions on product placement

Amendments (Textual)

F1. Sch. 11. A inserted (16.4.2010) by The Audiovisual Media Services (Product Placement) Regulations 2010 (S.I. 2010/831), regs. 1. (1), 9

Introductory

1.(1)In this Part "product placement", in relation to a programme included in a television programme service, means the inclusion in the programme of, or of a reference to, a product, service or trade mark, where the inclusion—

(a) is for a commercial purpose;

(b) is in return for the making of any payment, or the giving of other valuable consideration, to any relevant provider or any person connected with a relevant provider; and

(c) is not prop placement.

(2) "Prop placement", in relation to such a programme, means the inclusion in the programme of, or of a reference to, a product, service or trade mark where—

(a) the provision of the product, service or trade mark has no significant value; and

(b) no relevant provider, or person connected with a relevant provider, has received any payment or other valuable consideration in relation to its inclusion in, or the reference to it in, the programme, disregarding the costs saved by including the product, service or trademark, or a reference to it, in the programme.

2.The product placement requirements are—

(a) that the product placement does not fall within any of paragraphs 3 to 6;

(b) that all of the conditions in paragraph 7 are met; and

(c) that, where paragraph 8 applies, the condition in that paragraph is also met.

Prohibitions of product placement

3.(1)Product placement falls within this paragraph if it is in a children's programme.

(2) In sub-paragraph (1) "children's programme" means a programme made—

(a) for a television programme service or for an on-demand programme service, and

(b) for viewing primarily by persons under the age of sixteen.

4.Product placement falls within this paragraph if it is—

(a) of cigarettes or other tobacco products;

(b) by or on behalf of an undertaking whose principal activity is the manufacture or sale of cigarettes or other tobacco products; F2...

[F3. (ba) of electronic cigarettes or electronic cigarette refill containers; or]

(c) of prescription-only medicines.

Amendments (Textual)

F2. Word in Sch. 11. A para. 4. (b) omitted (20.5.2016) by virtue of The Tobacco and Related Products Regulations 2016 (S.I. 2016/507), regs. 1. (2), 45. (2)(a) (with reg. 57)

F3. Sch. 11. A para. 4. (ba) inserted (20.5.2016) by virtue of The Tobacco and Related Products Regulations 2016 (S.I. 2016/507), regs. 1. (2), 45. (2)(a) (with reg. 57)

5.Product placement of alcoholic drinks falls within this paragraph if—

(a) it is aimed specifically at persons under the age of eighteen; or

(b) it encourages immoderate consumption of such drinks.

6.(1)Product placement falls within this paragraph if it is in a programme to which this paragraph applies and—

(a) the programme is a religious, consumer affairs or current affairs programme;

(b) the product placement is of anything within sub-paragraph (2); or

(c) the product placement is otherwise unsuitable.

(2) The following are within this sub-paragraph—

(a) F4... cigarette lighters, cigarette papers or pipes intended for smoking;

(b) medicinal products;

(c) alcoholic drinks;

(d) infant formulae or follow-on formulae;

(e) a food or drink high in fat, salt or sugar;

(f) gambling services.

(3) This paragraph applies to—

(a) a programme that has been produced or commissioned by the provider of the television programme service in which it is included, or by a person connected with that provider, and that is not a film made for cinema; and

(b) a programme that has been produced or commissioned by any other person with a view to its first showing taking place in a television programme service which is provided by a person under the jurisdiction of the United Kingdom for the purposes of the Audiovisual Media Services Directive.

Amendments (Textual)

F4. Words in Sch. 11. A para. 6. (2)(a) omitted (20.5.2016) by virtue of The Tobacco and Related Products Regulations 2016 (S.I. 2016/507), regs. 1. (2), 45. (2)(c) (with reg. 57)

Conditions applying to product placement

7.(1)These are the conditions referred to in paragraph 2. (b).

(2) Condition A is that the programme in which the product, service or trademark, or the reference to it, is included is—

(a) a film made for cinema;

(b) a film or series made for a television programme service or for an on-demand programme service;

(c) a sports programme; or

(d) a light entertainment programme.

(3) Condition B is that the product placement has not influenced the content or scheduling of the programme in a way that affects the editorial independence of the provider of the television programme service in which the programme is included.

(4) Condition C is that the product placement does not directly encourage the purchase or rental of goods or services, whether by making promotional reference to those goods or services or otherwise.

(5) Condition D is that the programme does not give undue prominence to the products, services or trade marks concerned.

(6) Condition E is that the product placement does not use techniques which exploit the possibility of conveying a message subliminally or surreptitiously.

(7) Condition F is that the way in which the product, service or trade mark, or the reference to it, is included in the programme by way of product placement does not—

(a) prejudice respect for human dignity;

(b) promote discrimination based on sex, racial or ethnic origin, nationality, religion or belief, disability, age or sexual orientation;

(c) encourage behaviour prejudicial to health or safety;

(d) encourage behaviour grossly prejudicial to the protection of the environment;

(e) cause physical or moral detriment to persons under the age of eighteen;

(f) directly encourage such persons to persuade their parents or others to purchase or rent goods or services;

(g) exploit the trust of such persons in parents, teachers or others; or

(h) unreasonably show such persons in dangerous situations.

8.(1)This paragraph applies where the programme featuring the product placement has been produced or commissioned by the provider of the television programme service in which it is included or by a person connected with that provider.

(2) The condition referred to in paragraph 2. (c) is that the television programme service in which the programme is included signals appropriately the fact that product placement is contained in a programme no less frequently than—

(a) at the start and end of such a programme; and

(b) in the case of a television programme service which includes advertising breaks within it, at the recommencement of the programme after each such advertising break.

Minor definitions

9.In this Schedule—

"connected" has the same meaning as it has in the Broadcasting Act 1990 by virtue of section 202 of that Act;

[F5"electronic cigarette" has the meaning given in section 368. R;

"electronic cigarette refill container" has the meaning given in section 368. R;]

"film made for cinema" means a film made with a view to its being shown to the general public first in a cinema;

"follow-on formulae" has the meaning given in Article 2 of Commission Directive 2006/141/EC on infant formulae and follow-on formulae and amending Directive 1999/21/EC;

"infant formulae" has the meaning given in Article 2 of Commission Directive 2006/141/EC on infant formulae and follow-on formulae and amending Directive 1999/21/EC;

"medicinal product" has the meaning given in section 130 of the Medicines Act 1968;

"prescription-only medicine" means a medicinal product of a description or falling within a class specified in an order made under section 58 of the Medicines Act 1968;

"producer", in relation to a programme, means the person by whom the arrangements necessary for the making of the programme are undertaken;

"programme" does not include an advertisement;

"relevant provider", in relation to a programme, means—

   - the provider of the television programme service in which the programme is included; and

   - the producer of the programme;

"residual value" means any monetary or other economic value in the hands of the relevant provider other than the cost saving of including the product, service or trademark, or a reference to it, in a programme;

"significant value" means a residual value that is more than trivial;

"tobacco product" has the meaning given in section 1 of the Tobacco Advertising and Promotion Act 2002;

"trade mark", in relation to a business, includes any image (such as a logo) or sound commonly associated with that business or its products or services.]

Amendments (Textual)

F5. Words in Sch. 11. A para. 9 inserted (20.5.2016) by The Tobacco and Related Products Regulations 2016 (S.I. 2016/507), regs. 1. (2), 45. (2)(d) (with reg. 57)

Schedule 13. Corresponding obligations of the BBC and Welsh Authority

Section 338

Part 1. The BBC

Quotas for independent productions

1. (1)It shall be the duty of the BBC to secure that, in each year, not less than 25 per cent. of the total amount of time allocated to the broadcasting of qualifying programmes included in the television broadcasting services provided by the BBC is allocated to the broadcasting of a range and diversity of independent productions.

(2) In this paragraph—

(a) a reference to qualifying programmes is a reference to programmes of such description as the Secretary of State may by order specify as describing the programmes that are to be qualifying programmes for the purposes of this paragraph;

(b) a reference to independent productions is a reference to programmes of such description as the Secretary of State may by order specify as describing the programmes that are to be independent productions for the purposes of this paragraph; and

(c) a reference to a range of independent productions is a reference to a range of such productions in terms of cost of acquisition as well as in terms of the types of programme involved.

(3) The Secretary of State may by order amend sub-paragraph (1) by substituting a different percentage for the percentage for the time being specified in that sub-paragraph.

(4) The Secretary of State may also by order provide for the BBC to have the duty set out in sub-paragraph (5), either instead of or as well as the one set out in sub-paragraph (1).

(5) That duty is a duty to secure that, in each year, not less than the percentage specified in the order of the programming budget for that year for the television broadcasting services provided by the BBC is applied in the acquisition of independent productions.

(6) The power to make an order under sub-paragraph (4) includes power to provide that the BBC are again to be subject to a duty to which they have previously ceased to be subject by virtue of such an order, in addition to or instead of the duty to which they are subject (apart from the exercise of that power) by virtue of this paragraph.

(7) The Secretary of State is not to make an order for the BBC to be or to cease to be subject to the duty mentioned in sub-paragraph (1) or (5) unless—

(a) OFCOM have made a recommendation to him that the BBC should be subject to that duty, or should cease to be subject to it; and

(b) the order gives effect to that recommendation.

(8) Where television broadcasting services are designated by or under the BBC Charter and Agreement—

(a) as services that must be treated separately for the purposes of the duty imposed by sub-paragraph (1) or a duty imposed under sub-paragraph (4), or

(b) as services that must be included in a group of services that must be taken together for the purposes of such a duty,

that duty is to have effect in accordance with sub-paragraph (9).

(9) A duty having effect in accordance with this sub-paragraph is to have effect as if (instead of applying to all the television broadcasting services provided by the BBC, taken together) it applied separately—

(a) in relation to each service that is required to be treated separately; and

(b) in relation to each group of services that are required to be taken together.

(10) The BBC must comply with directions given to them by OFCOM for the purpose of—

(a) carrying forward to one or more subsequent years determined in accordance with the direction any shortfall for any year in their compliance with the duties imposed by virtue of sub-paragraph (1) or (4); and

(b) thereby increasing the percentage applicable for the purposes of those duties to the subsequent year or years.

(11) For the purposes of this paragraph—

(a) the amount of the programming budget for a year, and

(b) the means of determining the amount of that budget that is applied for any purpose,

are to be computed in accordance with such provision as may be set out in an order made by the Secretary of State, or as may be determined by OFCOM in accordance with such an order.

(12) Before making an order under this paragraph the Secretary of State must consult OFCOM and the BBC.

(13) No order is to be made containing provision authorised by this paragraph unless a draft of the order has been laid before Parliament and approved by a resolution of each House.

(14) In this paragraph—

"acquisition", in relation to a programme, includes commissioning and acquiring a right to include it in a service or to have it broadcast; and

"programming budget" means the budget for the production and acquisition of qualifying programmes.

Commencement Information

I1. Sch. 12 para. 1 in force at 29.12.2003 by S.I. 2003/3142, art. 3. (1), Sch. 1 (with art. 11)

Duty to publicise complaints procedures etc.

2. (1)It shall be the duty of the BBC to make arrangements for securing that the matters mentioned in sub-paragraph (2) are brought to the attention of the public (whether by means of broadcasts or otherwise).

(2) Those matters are—

(a) OFCOM's functions under Part 5 of the 1996 Act in relation to services provided by the BBC; and

(b) any procedures established by OFCOM or the BBC for the handling and resolution of complaints about the observance by the BBC of standards set under section 319 [F1or about compliance by the BBC with the requirements imposed by section 368. D] .

Amendments (Textual)

F1. Words in Sch. 12 para. 2. (2)(b) inserted (19.12.2009) by Audiovisual Media Services Regulations 2009 (S.I. 2009/2979), regs. 1. (1), 3. (2)

Commencement Information

I2. Sch. 12 para. 2 in force at 29.12.2003 by S.I. 2003/3142, art. 3. (1), Sch. 1 (with art. 11)

Part 2. The Welsh Authority

Public service remits of the Welsh Authority services

3. (1)It shall be the duty of the Welsh Authority to secure that the public service remits for each of their public television services is fulfilled.

(2) The public service remit for S4. C is the provision of a broad range of high quality and diverse programming in a service in which—

(a) a substantial proportion of the programmes consists of programmes in Welsh;

(b) the programmes broadcast for viewing between 6:30 PM and 10:00 PM on every day of the week consist mainly of programmes in Welsh; and

(c) the programmes that are not in Welsh are normally programmes which are being, have been or are to be broadcast on Channel 4.

(3) The public service remit for S4. C Digital is the provision of a broad range of high quality and diverse programming in a service in which a substantial proportion of the programmes consists of programmes in Welsh.

(4) The public service remit for a television programme service provided by the Welsh Authority with the approval of the Secretary of State under section 205 is the remit set out in the order approving the provision of the service.

(5) The Secretary of State may by order modify sub-paragraphs (2) and (3).

(6) Before making an order specifying or modifying the public service remit for any of the Welsh Authority's public television services, the Secretary of State must consult—

(a) the Authority; and

(b) where the order relates to the inclusion in any service of programmes that are not in Welsh, C4. C.

(7) An order modifying the public service remit for S4. C or S4. C Digital must not contain provision inconsistent with a requirement that each service must—

(a) represent a public service for the dissemination of information, education and entertainment; and

(b) include programmes a substantial proportion of which consists of programmes in Welsh.

(8) No order is to be made containing provision authorised by sub-paragraph (5) unless a draft of the order has been laid before Parliament and approved by a resolution of each House.

Commencement Information

I3. Sch. 12 para. 3 in force at 29.12.2003 by S.I. 2003/3142, art. 3. (1), Sch. 1 (with art. 11)

Statements of programme policy

4. (1)It shall be the duty of the Welsh Authority—

(a) as soon as practicable after the coming into force of this paragraph, and subsequently at annual intervals, to prepare a statement of programme policy; and

(b) to monitor their own performance in the carrying out of the proposals contained in statements made under this paragraph.

(2) Every statement of programme policy prepared under this paragraph must set out the Welsh Authority's proposals for securing that, during the following year—

(a) the public service remit for each of their public television services to be provided during that year will be fulfilled; and

(b) the Welsh Authority's duties under the provisions of this Schedule will be performed.

(3) Every such statement must contain a report on the performance of the Welsh Authority in the carrying out during the period since the previous statement of the proposals contained in that previous statement.

(4) When preparing such a statement, the Welsh Authority must consider—

(a) any guidance by OFCOM that is in force for the purposes of section 266; and

(b) any reports previously published by OFCOM under section 264 or 358.

(5) Every such statement must be published by the Welsh Authority as soon as practicable after its preparation is complete.

(6) OFCOM may direct that any statement of policy which—

(a) was made by the Welsh Authority before the coming into force of this paragraph, and

(b) is specified in the direction,

is to be treated for the purposes of this Act as if it were a statement made in relation to such period as may be so specified in pursuance of this paragraph.

(7) A direction under sub-paragraph (6) cannot contain provision the effect of which is to postpone the time at which the Welsh Authority would otherwise be required to make its first statement of programme policy.

Commencement Information

I4. Sch. 12 para. 4 in force at 29.12.2003 by S.I. 2003/3142, art. 3. (1), Sch. 1 (with art. 11)

Prospective

Must-offer obligations in relation to networks and satellite services

5. (1)It shall be the duty of the Welsh Authority to ensure that each of their public digital services is at all times offered as available (subject to the need to agree terms)—

(a) to be broadcast or distributed by means of every appropriate network; and

(b) to be broadcast by means of every satellite television service that is available for reception by members of the public in Wales.

(2) It shall be the duty of the Welsh Authority to do their best to secure that arrangements are entered into, and kept in force, that ensure—

(a) that each of their public digital services is broadcast or distributed on appropriate networks; and

(b) that the broadcasting and distribution of each of their public digital services, in accordance with those arrangements, result in the service being available for reception, by means of appropriate networks, by as many members of its intended audience as practicable.

(3) It shall be the duty of the Welsh Authority to do their best to secure that arrangements are entered into, and kept in force, that ensure—

(a) that each of their public digital services is broadcast by means of satellite television services that are broadcast so as to be available for reception by members of the public in Wales; and

(b) that the broadcasting, in accordance with those arrangements, of each of the Authority's public digital services by means of satellite television services results in its being available for reception in an intelligible form and by means of those services by as many members of its intended audience as practicable.

(4) The Welsh Authority must secure that the arrangements entered into and kept in force for the purposes of sub-paragraphs (2) and (3) prohibit the imposition, for or in connection with the provision of an appropriate network or a satellite television service, of any charge that is attributable (whether directly or indirectly) to the conferring of an entitlement to receive each of the Authority's public digital services in an intelligible form by means of that network or service.

(5) OFCOM may, by a direction to the Welsh Authority, require arrangements made or kept in force for the purposes of sub-paragraphs (2) or (3) to apply in the case of every service which is an ancillary service by reference to one of their public digital services as they apply to the service itself.

(6) For the purposes of this paragraph a public digital service of the Welsh Authority is to be treated, in relation to particular appropriate networks and satellite television services, as constituting such services comprised in or provided with that public digital service—

(a) as may be determined by agreement between the Welsh Authority and OFCOM; or

(b) in default of agreement, as may be directed by OFCOM.

(7) This paragraph—

(a) so far as it relates to the broadcasting or distribution of any of the Welsh Authority's public digital services by means of appropriate networks, applies only in relation to times when that service is included in the list of must-carry services in section 64; and

(b) so far as it relates to the broadcasting of such a public digital service by means of a satellite television service, applies only in relation to times when that service is included in the list of must-provide services in section 275.

(8) In this paragraph—

"appropriate network" means an electronic communications network by means of which public electronic communications services are provided that are used by a significant number of end-users in Wales as their principal means of receiving television programmes;

"intended audience", in relation to a public digital service of the Welsh Authority, means—

- if the service is one provided only for a particular area or locality of Wales, members of the public in that area or locality;

- if the service is one provided for members of a particular community, members of that community; and

- in any other case, members of the public in Wales;

"public digital service", in relation to the Welsh Authority, means any of their public television services so far as it is provided in digital form; and

"satellite television service" means a service which—

- consists in or involves the broadcasting of television programme services from a satellite; and

- is used by a significant number of the persons by whom the broadcasts are received in an intelligible form as their principal means of receiving television programmes.

(9) For the purposes of this paragraph an electronic communications network is not an appropriate network in relation to so much of a channel or other service as is provided only for a particular area or locality of Wales unless it is a network by means of which electronic communications services are provided to persons in that area or locality

(10) In sub-paragraph (8) "public electronic communications service" and "end-user" each has the same meaning as in Chapter 1 of Part 2.

(11) An order under section 411 must not appoint a day for provisions of this paragraph to come into force that falls less than six months after the day on which the order is made.

Prospective

Supply of services by satellite in certain areas

6. It shall be the duty of the Welsh Authority—

(a) to join with the providers of other must-provide services in entering into and maintaining arrangements satisfying the requirements of section 274; and

(b) to comply with the requirements of any arrangements imposed by OFCOM for the purposes of conditions under subsection (2) of that section.

Programming quotas for independent productions

7. (1)It shall be the duty of the Welsh Authority to secure that, in each year, not less than 25 per cent. of the total amount of time allocated to the broadcasting of qualifying programmes included in their designated public services (taken together) is allocated to the broadcasting of a range and diversity of independent productions.

(2) In this paragraph—

(a) a reference to qualifying programmes is a reference to programmes of such description as the Secretary of State may by order specify as describing the programmes that are to be qualifying programmes for the purposes of this paragraph;

(b) a reference to independent productions is a reference to programmes of such description as the Secretary of State may by order specify as describing the programmes that are to be independent productions for the purposes of this paragraph; and

(c) a reference to a range of independent productions is a reference to a range of such productions in terms of cost of acquisition as well as in terms of the types of programme involved.

(3) The Secretary of State may by order amend sub-paragraph (1) by substituting a different percentage for the percentage for the time being specified in that sub-paragraph.

(4) The Secretary of State may also by order provide for the Welsh Authority to have the duty set out in sub-paragraph (5), either instead of or as well as the one set out in sub-paragraph (1).

(5) That duty is a duty to secure that, in each year, not less than the percentage specified in the order of the programming budget for that year for the designated public services (taken together) is applied in the acquisition of independent productions.

(6) The power to make an order under sub-paragraph (4) includes power to provide that the Welsh Authority are again to be subject to a duty to which they have previously ceased to be subject by virtue of such an order, in addition to or instead of the duty to which they are subject (apart from the exercise of that power) by virtue of this paragraph.

(7) The Secretary of State is not to make an order for the Welsh Authority to be or to cease to be subject to the duty mentioned in sub-paragraph (1) or (5) unless—

(a) OFCOM have made a recommendation to him that the Authority should be subject to that duty, or should cease to be subject to it; and

(b) the order gives effect to that recommendation.

(8) The Welsh Authority must comply with directions given to them by OFCOM for the purpose of—

(a) carrying forward to one or more subsequent years determined in accordance with the direction any shortfall for any year in their compliance with the duties imposed by virtue of sub-paragraph (1) or (4); and

(b) thereby increasing the percentage applicable for the purposes of those duties to the subsequent year or years.

(9) For the purposes of this paragraph—

(a) the amount of the programming budget for a year, and

(b) the means of determining the amount of that budget that is applied for any purpose,

are to be computed in accordance with such provision as may be set out in an order made by the Secretary of State, or as may be determined by OFCOM in accordance with such an order.

(10) Before making an order under this paragraph the Secretary of State must consult OFCOM, the BBC and the Welsh Authority.

(11) No order is to be made containing provision authorised by this paragraph unless a draft of the order has been laid before Parliament and approved by a resolution of each House.

(12) The services that are designated public services for the purposes of this paragraph are—

(a) S4. C;

(b) S4. C Digital; and

(c) any of the Welsh Authority's other public television services which is designated for the purposes of this paragraph by the order under section 205 approving its provision.

(13) In this paragraph—

"acquisition", in relation to a programme, includes commissioning and acquiring a right to include it in a service or to have it broadcast;

"programme" does not include an advertisement; and

"programming budget" means the budget for the production and acquisition of qualifying programmes.

Commencement Information

I5. Sch. 12 para. 7 in force at 29.12.2003 by S.I. 2003/3142, art. 3. (1), Sch. 1 (with art. 11)

Programme quotas for original productions

8. (1)It shall be the duty of the Welsh Authority, in relation to their designated public services

430

(taken together) to secure—

(a) that the time allocated, in each year, to the broadcasting of original productions included in those services is no less than the proportion fixed under sub-paragraph (2) of the total amount of time allocated to the broadcasting of all the programmes included in those services; and

(b) that the time allocated to the broadcasting of original productions is split in the manner so fixed between peak viewing times and other times.

(2) The fixing for the purposes of sub-paragraph (1) of a proportion or manner of splitting allocated time is to be—

(a) by agreement between the Welsh Authority and OFCOM; or

(b) in default of agreement, by a direction given by OFCOM to the Authority fixing the proportion or manner according to whatever OFCOM consider appropriate for ensuring that the service is consistently of a high quality.

(3) The agreement or direction may, for the purposes of sub-paragraph (1)(b), fix a proportion for the purposes of sub-paragraph (1)(a) in terms of the cumulative effect of two different minimum proportions, one applying to peak viewing times and the other to other times.

(4) The agreement or direction may provide that specified descriptions of programmes are to be excluded in determining the programmes a proportion of which is to constitute original productions.

(5) It may also provide that, in determining whether a programme is of a description of programmes excluded by an agreement or direction by virtue of sub-paragraph (4), regard is to be had to any guidance prepared and published, and from to time revised, by OFCOM.

(6) References in this paragraph, in relation to the designated public services of the Welsh Authority, to original productions are references to programmes of such description as the Secretary of State may by order specify as describing the programmes that are to be original productions for the purposes of this paragraph.

(7) The power to specify descriptions of programmes by order under sub-paragraph (6) includes power to confer such discretions on OFCOM as the Secretary of State thinks fit.

(8) Before making an order under this paragraph the Secretary of State must consult OFCOM, the BBC and the Welsh Authority.

(9) No order is to be made containing provision authorised by this paragraph unless a draft of the order has been laid before Parliament and approved by a resolution of each House.

(10) The services that are designated public services for the purposes of this paragraph are—

(a) S4. C;

(b) S4. C Digital; and

(c) any of the Welsh Authority's other public television services which is designated for the purposes of this paragraph by the order under section 205 approving its provision.

(11) In this paragraph—

"peak viewing time", in relation to the designated public services of the Welsh Authority, means a time that is determined in accordance with sub-paragraph (12) to be a peak viewing time for one or more of those services; and

"programme" does not include an advertisement.

(12) The determination for the purposes of this paragraph of peak viewing times is to be—

(a) by agreement between the Welsh Authority and OFCOM; or

(b) in default of agreement, by a direction given by OFCOM to the Authority determining those times.

Commencement Information

16. Sch. 12 para. 8 in force at 1.7.2004 by S.I. 2003/3142, art. 4. (4)(c) (with art. 11) (as amended (4.3.2004) by S.I. 2004/545, art. 2. (2)(3)(c))

News and current affairs programmes

9. (1)It shall be the duty of the Welsh Authority, in relation to their designated public services, to

secure—

(a) that the programmes included in each service include news programmes and current affairs programmes;

(b) that the news programmes and current affairs programmes included in each service deal with both national and international matters; and

(c) that the news programmes so included are broadcast for viewing at intervals throughout the period for which the service is provided.

(2) It shall be the duty of the Welsh Authority, in relation to each of their designated public services, to ensure that the news programmes and current affairs programmes included in each service are of high quality.

(3) It shall also be the duty of the Welsh Authority, in relation to each of their designated public services, to secure that in each year—

(a) the time allocated to the broadcasting of news programmes included in the service, and

(b) the time allocated to the broadcasting of current affairs programmes so included,

each constitutes no less than the proportion fixed under sub-paragraph (5) of the time allocated to the broadcasting of all the programmes included in the service.

(4) It is the further duty of the Welsh Authority, in relation to each of their designated public services, to secure that the time allocated—

(a) to the broadcasting of news programmes included in the service, and

(b) to the broadcasting of current affairs programmes so included,

is, in each case, split, in the manner fixed under sub-paragraph (5), between peak viewing times and other times.

(5) The fixing for the purposes of sub-paragraph (3) or (4) of a proportion or manner of splitting allocated time is to be—

(a) by agreement between the Welsh Authority and OFCOM; or

(b) in default of agreement, by a direction given by OFCOM to the Authority fixing the proportion or manner according to whatever OFCOM consider appropriate.

(6) The agreement or direction may, for the purposes of sub-paragraph (4), fix a proportion for the purposes of sub-paragraph (3) in terms of the cumulative effect of two different minimum proportions, one applying to peak viewing times and the other to other times.

(7) The services that are designated public services for the purposes of this paragraph are—

(a) S4. C;

(b) S4. C Digital; and

(c) any of the Welsh Authority's other public television services which is designated for the purposes of this paragraph by the order under section 205 approving its provision.

(8) In this paragraph "peak viewing time", in relation to a service, means a time that is determined in accordance with sub-paragraph (9) to be a peak viewing time for that service.

(9) The determination for the purposes of this paragraph of a peak viewing time is to be—

(a) by agreement between the Welsh Authority and OFCOM; or

(b) in default of agreement, by a direction given by OFCOM to the Authority determining that time.

Commencement Information

I7. Sch. 12 para. 9 in force at 29.12.2003 by S.I. 2003/3142, art. 3. (1), Sch. 1 (with art. 11)

Code relating to programme commissioning

10. (1)It shall be the duty of the Welsh Authority to draw up and from time to time revise a code of practice setting out the principles that are to be applied when they or an S4. C company are for a relevant purpose agreeing terms for the commissioning of independent productions.

(2) A relevant purpose is a purpose connected with the provision by the Welsh Authority or an S4. C company of a programme service.

(3) It shall also be the duty of the Welsh Authority—

(a) at all times to comply with the code of practice which is for the time being in force under this paragraph;

(b) to take all reasonable steps for securing that the code is complied with by S4. C companies;

(c) to exercise their power to revise that code to take account of revisions from time to time of the guidance issued by OFCOM for the purposes of this paragraph; and

(d) to comply with such directions as may be given to the Authority by OFCOM for securing that they properly perform their duties under paragraphs (a) and (b).

(4) The code for the time being in force under this paragraph must be such as to secure, in the manner described in guidance issued by OFCOM—

(a) that a reasonable timetable is applied to negotiations for the commissioning of an independent production and for the conclusion of a binding agreement;

(b) that there is sufficient clarity when an independent production is commissioned about the different categories of rights to broadcast or otherwise to make use of or exploit the commissioned production that are being disposed of;

(c) that there is sufficient transparency about the amounts to be paid in respect of each category of rights;

(d) that satisfactory arrangements are made about the duration and exclusivity of those rights;

(e) that procedures exist for reviewing the arrangements adopted in accordance with the code and for demonstrating compliance with it;

(f) that those procedures include requirements for the monitoring of the application of the code and for the making of reports to OFCOM;

(g) that provision is made for resolving disputes arising in respect of the provisions of the code (by independent arbitration or otherwise) in a manner that appears to OFCOM to be appropriate.

(5) The Welsh Authority must also ensure that the drawing up or revision of a code by virtue of this paragraph is in accordance with guidance issued by OFCOM as to—

(a) the times when the code is to be drawn up or reviewed with a view to revision;

(b) the consultation to be undertaken before a code is drawn up or revised;

(c) the publication of every code or revised code.

(6) The Welsh Authority must submit to OFCOM for approval a draft of—

(a) every code that is required to be drawn up under this paragraph; and

(b) every revision made by that Authority of such a code.

(7) A code drawn up by the Welsh Authority or a revision of such a code —

(a) is to have effect for the purposes of this paragraph only if approved by OFCOM; and

(b) if approved by OFCOM subject to modifications, is to have effect with those modifications.

(8) OFCOM—

(a) must issue and may from time to time revise guidance for the purposes of this paragraph;

(b) must ensure that there is always guidance for those purposes in force;

(c) must, before issuing their guidance or revised guidance, consult the providers of licensed public service channels, persons who make independent productions (or persons appearing to OFCOM to represent them), the BBC and the Welsh Authority; and

(d) must publish their guidance or revised guidance in such manner as they think appropriate.

(9) Guidance issued by OFCOM for the purposes of this paragraph must be general guidance and is not to specify particular terms to be included in agreements to which the guidance relates.

(10) OFCOM may by a direction to the Welsh Authority specify that a code which—

(a) was drawn up by the Authority before the commencement of this paragraph, and

(b) is identified in the direction,

is to be treated as drawn up in pursuance of this paragraph and approved by OFCOM.

(11) In this paragraph "independent production" has the same meaning as in paragraph 7.

Commencement Information

I8. Sch. 12 para. 10 in force at 29.12.2003 by S.I. 2003/3142, art. 3. (1), Sch. 1 (with art. 11)

Co-operation with the public teletext provider

11. (1)The Welsh Authority must grant access to the public teletext provider to the facilities that are reasonably required by him for the purposes of, or in connection with, the provision of the public teletext service.

(2) The Welsh Authority may require the public teletext provider to pay a reasonable charge in respect of facilities access to which is granted under this paragraph.

(3) In the event of a dispute, the amount of the charge is to be determined by OFCOM.

Commencement Information

I9. Sch. 12 para. 11 in force at 29.12.2003 by S.I. 2003/3142, art. 3. (1), Sch. 1 (with art. 11)

Programme standards

12. It shall be the duty of the Welsh Authority in relation to their public television services to observe the standards set under section 319.

Commencement Information

I10. Sch. 12 para. 12 in force at 29.12.2003 by S.I. 2003/3142, art. 3. (1), Sch. 1 (with art. 11)

13. It shall be the duty of the Welsh Authority to comply with a direction given to them by OFCOM with respect to the establishment of procedures for the handling and resolution of complaints about the observance by the Authority of standards set under section 319.

Commencement Information

I11. Sch. 12 para. 13 in force at 29.12.2003 by S.I. 2003/3142, art. 3. (1), Sch. 1 (with art. 11)

14. (1)It shall be the duty of the Welsh Authority to comply with directions given to them by OFCOM with respect to any of the matters mentioned in sub-paragraph (2).

(2) Those matters are—

(a) the exclusion from any of the Authority's public television services of a particular advertisement, or its exclusion in particular circumstances;

(b) the descriptions of advertisements and methods of advertising to be excluded from the services so provided (whether generally or in particular circumstances); and

(c) the methods of sponsorship to be excluded from those services (whether generally or in particular circumstances).

Modifications etc. (not altering text)

C1. Sch. 12 para. 14. (1) modified (20.7.2004) by Contracting Out (Functions relating to Broadcast Advertising) and Specification of Relevant Functions Order 2004 (S.I. 2004/1975), art. 1, Sch. para. 1. (d) (with art. 5)

Commencement Information

I12. Sch. 12 para. 14 in force at 29.12.2003 by S.I. 2003/3142, art. 3. (1), Sch. 1 (with art. 11)

15. (1)This paragraph applies if OFCOM are satisfied—

(a) that the Welsh Authority have failed in any respect to perform any of their duties under paragraphs 12 to 14 [F2or 23. A, or under section 368. D] [F3except the requirement imposed by section 368. D(1) so far as it relates to advertising, and the requirement imposed by section 368. D(3)(za)] ; and

(b) that the failure can be appropriately remedied by the inclusion in any or all of the Authority's public television services [F4or on-demand programme services] of a correction or a statement of findings.

(2) OFCOM may direct the Welsh Authority to include a correction or a statement of findings (or both) in any one or more of their public television services [F5or on-demand programme services] .

(3) A direction may require the correction or statement of findings to be in such form, and to be included in programmes at such time or times, as OFCOM may determine.

(4) OFCOM are not to give a direction under this paragraph unless they have given the Welsh Authority a reasonable opportunity of making representations to them about the matters appearing to OFCOM to provide grounds for the giving of the direction.

(5) Where the Welsh Authority include a correction or a statement of findings in any of their public television services [F6or on-demand programme services] in pursuance of a direction under this paragraph, the Authority may announce that they are doing so in pursuance of such a direction.

(6) For the purposes of this paragraph a statement of findings, in relation to a case in which OFCOM are satisfied that the Welsh Authority have failed to perform a duty [F7mentioned in sub-paragraph (1)(a)] , is a statement of OFCOM's findings in relation to that failure.

Amendments (Textual)

F2. Words in Sch. 12 para. 15. (1)(a) inserted (19.12.2009) by Audiovisual Media Services Regulations 2009 (S.I. 2009/2979), regs. 1. (1), 4. (2)(a)

F3. Words in Sch. 12 para. 15. (1)(a) inserted (18.3.2010) by The Audiovisual Media Services Regulations 2010 (S.I. 2010/419), regs. 1. (1), 14. (2)

F4. Words in Sch. 12 para. 15. (1)(b) inserted (19.12.2009) by Audiovisual Media Services Regulations 2009 (S.I. 2009/2979), regs. 1. (1), 4. (2)(b)

F5. Words in Sch. 12 para. 15. (2) inserted (19.12.2009) by Audiovisual Media Services Regulations 2009 (S.I. 2009/2979), regs. 1. (1), 4. (2)(b)

F6. Words in Sch. 12 para. 15. (5) inserted (19.12.2009) by Audiovisual Media Services Regulations 2009 (S.I. 2009/2979), regs. 1. (1), 4. (2)(b)

F7. Words in Sch. 12 para. 15. (6) substituted (18.3.2010) by The Audiovisual Media Services Regulations 2010 (S.I. 2010/419), regs. 1. (1), 14. (3)

Modifications etc. (not altering text)

C2. Sch. 12 para. 15. (2) modified (20.7.2004) by Contracting Out (Functions relating to Broadcast Advertising) and Specification of Relevant Functions Order 2004 (S.I. 2004/1975), art. 1, Sch. para. 2. (d) (with art. 5)

Commencement Information

I13. Sch. 12 para. 15 in force at 29.12.2003 by S.I. 2003/3142, art. 3. (1), Sch. 1 (with art. 11)

Directions with respect to advertising

16. (1)The Welsh Authority must comply with directions given to them by OFCOM with respect to any of the matters mentioned in sub-paragraph (2).

(2) Those matters are—

(a) the maximum amount of time to be given to advertisements in any hour or other period;

(b) the minimum interval which must elapse between any two periods given over to advertisements;

(c) the number of such periods to be allowed in any programme or in any hour or day; and

(d) the exclusion of advertisements from a specified part of S4. C or S4. C Digital.

(3) Directions under this paragraph—

(a) may be either general or specific;

(b) may be qualified or unqualified; and

(c) may make different provision for different parts of the day, different days of the week, different types of programmes or for other differing circumstances.

(4) In giving a direction under this paragraph, OFCOM shall take account of such of the international obligations of the United Kingdom as the Secretary of State may notify to them for the purposes of this paragraph.

Commencement Information

I14. Sch. 12 para. 16 in force at 29.12.2003 by S.I. 2003/3142, art. 3. (1), Sch. 1 (with art. 11)

Fairness standards

17. It shall be the duty of the Welsh Authority to secure the observance—

(a) in connection with the provision of their public television services, and

(b) in relation to the programmes included in those services,

of the code for the time being in force under section 107 of the 1996 Act (the fairness code).

Commencement Information

I15. Sch. 12 para. 17 in force at 29.12.2003 by S.I. 2003/3142, art. 3. (1), Sch. 1 (with art. 11)

Party political broadcasts

18. (1)It shall be the duty of the Welsh Authority to include—

(a) party political broadcasts, and

(b) referendum campaign broadcasts,

in every designated public service of theirs.

(2) The Welsh Authority must prepare, publish and from time to time review and revise their policy with respect to—

(a) party political broadcasts and referendum campaign broadcasts; and

(b) the manner in which they propose to perform their duty under sub-paragraph (1).

(3) The Welsh Authority's policy may, in particular, include provision for determining—

(a) the political parties on whose behalf party political broadcasts may be made;

(b) in relation to each political party on whose behalf such broadcasts may be made, the length and frequency of the broadcasts; and

(c) in relation to each designated organisation on whose behalf referendum campaign broadcasts are required to be broadcast, the length and frequency of such broadcasts.

(4) That policy is to have effect subject to sections 37 and 127 of the Political Parties, Elections and Referendums Act 2000 (c. 41) (only registered parties and designated organisations to be entitled to party political broadcasts or referendum campaign broadcasts).

(5) In preparing or revising their policy with respect to the inclusion of party political broadcasts or referendum campaign broadcasts in their designated public services, the Welsh Authority must have regard to—

(a) any views expressed for the purposes of this paragraph by the Electoral Commission; and

(b) any rules made by OFCOM under section 333.

(6) The services that are designated public services for the purposes of this paragraph are—

(a) S4. C;

(b) S4. C Digital; and

(c) any of the Welsh Authority's other public television services which is designated for the purposes of this paragraph by the order under section 205 approving its provision.

(7) In this paragraph—

"designated organisation", in relation to a referendum, means a person or body designated by the Electoral Commission under section 108 of the Political Parties, Elections and Referendums Act 2000 in respect of that referendum; and

"referendum campaign broadcast" has the meaning given by section 127 of that Act.

Modifications etc. (not altering text)

C3. Sch. 12 para. 18 excluded (13.2.2013) by The Scotland Act 1998 (Modification of Schedule 5) Order 2013 (S.I. 2013/242), arts. 2, 4. (3)(c)

Commencement Information

I16. Sch. 12 para. 18 in force at 29.12.2003 by S.I. 2003/3142, art. 3. (1), Sch. 1 (with art. 11)

Duty to publicise complaints procedures etc.

19. (1)It shall be the duty of the Welsh Authority to make arrangements for securing that the matters mentioned in sub-paragraph (2) are brought to the attention of the public (whether by means of broadcasts or otherwise).

(2) Those matters are—

(a) OFCOM's functions under Part 5 of the 1996 Act in relation to services provided by the Welsh

Authority; and

(b) any procedures established by OFCOM or the Authority for the handling and resolution of complaints about the observance by the Authority of standards set under section 319 [F8or about compliance by the Authority with the requirements imposed by section 368. D and section 368. Q(3), except the [F9requirements mentioned in sub-paragraph (3)]] .

[F10. (3)The requirements mentioned in this sub-paragraph are the requirement imposed by section 368. D(1) so far as it relates to advertising and the requirement imposed by section 368. D(3)(za)]

Amendments (Textual)

F8. Words in Sch. 12 para. 19. (2)(b) inserted (19.12.2009) by Audiovisual Media Services Regulations 2009 (S.I. 2009/2979), regs. 1. (1), 4. (3)

F9. Words in Sch. 12 para. 19. (2)(b) substituted (18.3.2010) by virtue of The Audiovisual Media Services Regulations 2010 (S.I. 2010/419), regs. 1. (1), 14. (4)

F10. Sch. 12 para. 19. (3) inserted (18.3.2010) by The Audiovisual Media Services Regulations 2010 (S.I. 2010/419), regs. 1. (1), 14. (5)

Commencement Information

I17. Sch. 12 para. 19 in force at 29.12.2003 by S.I. 2003/3142, art. 3. (1), Sch. 1 (with art. 11)

Monitoring of programmes

20. (1)It shall be the duty of the Welsh Authority—

(a) in respect of every programme included in any of their public television services, to retain a recording of the programme in the form, and for the period, specified by OFCOM;

(b) to comply with any request to produce such recordings to OFCOM for examination or reproduction; and

(c) to comply, to the extent that they are able to do so, with any request to produce to OFCOM a script or transcript of a programme included in any of their public television services.

(2) The period specified for the purposes of sub-paragraph (1)(a) must be a period not exceeding ninety days.

Commencement Information

I18. Sch. 12 para. 20 in force at 29.12.2003 by S.I. 2003/3142, art. 3. (1), Sch. 1 (with art. 11)

Compliance with international obligations

21. (1)OFCOM may give the Welsh Authority such directions as OFCOM consider appropriate for securing that all relevant international obligations are complied with.

(2) It shall be the duty of the Authority to comply with a direction under this paragraph.

(3) Before giving a direction under this paragraph, OFCOM must consult the Authority.

(4) In this paragraph "relevant international obligations" means the international obligations of the United Kingdom which have been notified to OFCOM by the Secretary of State for the purposes of this paragraph.

Commencement Information

I19. Sch. 12 para. 21 in force at 29.12.2003 by S.I. 2003/3142, art. 3. (1), Sch. 1 (with art. 11)

Services for the deaf and visually impaired

22. It shall be the duty of the Welsh Authority to observe the code for the time being in force under section 303 in the provision of—

(a) S4. C Digital; and

(b) so much of any of the Welsh Authority's other public television services as is provided in digital form.

Commencement Information
I20. Sch. 12 para. 22 in force at 29.12.2003 by S.I. 2003/3142, art. 3. (1), Sch. 1 (with art. 11)

Equality of opportunity

23. (1)It shall be the duty of the Welsh Authority to make such arrangements as they consider appropriate for promoting, in relation to employment with the Authority, equality of opportunity—
(a) between men and women; and
(b) between persons of different racial groups.
(2) It shall be the duty of the Welsh Authority to make arrangements for promoting, in relation to employment with the Authority, the equalisation of opportunities for disabled persons.
(3) The Welsh Authority shall also make such arrangements as they consider appropriate for the training and retraining of persons whom they employ in or in connection with—
(a) the provision of one or more of their public services; or
(b) the making of programmes to be included in one or more of those services.
(4) The Welsh Authority—
(a) shall take all such steps as they consider appropriate for making persons affected by any arrangements made in pursuance of sub-paragraphs (1) to (3) aware of the arrangements (including the publication of the arrangements in such manner as they think fit);
(b) shall review the arrangements from time to time; and
(c) shall, from time to time (and at least annually), publish, in such manner as they consider appropriate, their observations on the current operation and effectiveness of the arrangements.
(5) Before making any arrangements in pursuance of any of sub-paragraphs (1) to (3) or determining the manner in which they will comply with sub-paragraph (4), the Welsh Authority must consult OFCOM.
(6) In this paragraph—
"disabled" has the same meaning as in [F11the Equality Act 2010 or, in Northern Ireland,] the Disability Discrimination Act 1995 (c. 50);
"racial group" has the same meaning as in the [F12. Race Relations Act 1976 (c. 74)] [F12the Equality Act 2010] or, in Northern Ireland, the Race Relations (Northern Ireland) Order 1997 (S.I. 1997/869 (N.I. 6)).
(7) The Secretary of State may by order amend sub-paragraph (1) by adding any other form of equality of opportunity that he considers appropriate to that sub-paragraph.
(8) No order is to be made containing provision authorised by sub-paragraph (7) unless a draft of the order has been laid before Parliament and approved by a resolution of each House.

Amendments (Textual)
F11. Words in Sch. 12 para. 23. (6) inserted by virtue of 2010 c. 15, Sch. 26 Pt. 1 para. 56. (a) (as inserted (E.W.S.) (1.10.2010) by The Equality Act 2010 (Consequential Amendments, Saving and Supplementary Provisions) Order 2010 (S.I. 2010/2279), art. 1. (2), Sch. 1 para. 5) (see S.I. 2010/2317, art. 2)
F12. Words in Sch. 12 para. 23. (6) substituted by 2010 c. 15, Sch. 26 Pt. 1 para. 56. (b) (as inserted (E.W.S.) (1.10.2010) by The Equality Act 2010 (Consequential Amendments, Saving and Supplementary Provisions) Order 2010 (S.I. 2010/2279), art. 1. (2), Sch. 1 para. 5) (see S.I. 2010/2317, art. 2)
Commencement Information
I21. Sch. 12 para. 23 in force at 29.12.2003 by S.I. 2003/3142, art. 3. (1), Sch. 1 (with art. 11)

[F13. On-demand programme services

Amendments (Textual)
F13. Sch. 12 para. 23. A and cross-heading inserted (19.12.2009) by Audiovisual Media Services

Regulations 2009 (S.I. 2009/2979), regs. 1. (1), 4. (4)

23. A.(1)It is the duty of the Welsh Authority to comply with a direction given to them by OFCOM in relation to the establishment of procedures for the handling and resolution of complaints about compliance by the Authority with the requirements imposed by section 368. D or section 368. Q(3).

(2) But OFCOM must not give any such direction in relation to the handling and resolution of complaints about compliance with the requirement imposed by section 368. D(1) so far as it relates to advertising [F14or with the requirement imposed by section 368. D(3)(za)] .]

Amendments (Textual)

F14. Words in Sch. 12 para. 23. A(2) inserted (18.3.2010) by The Audiovisual Media Services Regulations 2010 (S.I. 2010/419), regs. 1. (1), 14. (6)

Meaning of Welsh Authority's public services

24. (1)In this Part of this Schedule, references to the Welsh Authority's public services are references to the following—

(a) S4. C;

(b) S4. C Digital; and

(c) the services the provision of which by the Authority is authorised by or under section 205.

(2) References in this Schedule to a public television service of the Welsh Authority are references to any public service of the Authority which is a television programme service.

Commencement Information

I22. Sch. 12 para. 24 in force at 29.12.2003 by S.I. 2003/3142, art. 3. (1), Sch. 1 (with art. 11)

Schedule 14. Financial penalties under the Broadcasting Acts

Section 345

Part 1. Broadcasting Act 1990

Preliminary

1. The 1990 Act shall be amended as follows.

Commencement Information

I1. Sch. 13 para. 1 in force at 29.12.2003 by S.I. 2003/3142, art. 3. (1), Sch. 1 (with art. 11)

Revocation of television services licence

2. (1)In subsection (3) of section 18 (penalty on revocation of television services licence), for "a financial penalty of the prescribed amount" there shall be substituted " a specified financial penalty ".

(2) For subsection (4) of that section (amount of penalty) there shall be substituted—

"(3. A)The maximum amount which a person may be required to pay by way of a penalty under subsection (3) is the maximum penalty given by subsections (3. B) and (3. C).

(3. B)In a case where the licence is revoked under this section or the penalty is imposed before the end of the first complete accounting period of the licence holder to fall within the period for which

the licence is in force, the maximum penalty is whichever is the greater of—

(a) £500,000; and

(b) 7 per cent. of the amount which OFCOM estimate would have been the qualifying revenue for the first complete accounting period of the licence holder falling within the period for which the licence would have been in force.

(3. C)In any other case, the maximum penalty is whichever is the greater of—

(a) £500,000; and

(b) 7 per cent. of the qualifying revenue for the last complete accounting period of the licence holder falling within the period for which the licence is in force.

(3. D)Section 19. (2) to (6) applies for estimating or determining qualifying revenue for the purposes of subsection (3. B) or (3. C) above."

(3) This paragraph applies only in a case of a revocation in relation to which—

(a) the notice required by section 18. (2) of the 1990 Act, or

(b) the notice revoking the licence,

is served after the commencement of this paragraph.

Commencement Information

I2. Sch. 13 para. 2 in force at 29.12.2003 by S.I. 2003/3142, art. 3. (1), Sch. 1 (with art. 11)

Licences for Channel 3 services and for Channels 4 and 5.

3. (1)For subsection (2) of section 41 (penalties for failure by holder of licence for Channel 3 services, Channel 4 or Channel 5 to comply with licence conditions or directions) there shall be substituted—

"(1. A)The amount of a financial penalty imposed on a person in pursuance of subsection (1)(a) shall not exceed 5 per cent. of the qualifying revenue for the licence holder's last complete accounting period falling within the period for which his licence has been in force ("the relevant period").

(1. B)In relation to a person whose first complete accounting period falling within the relevant period has not ended when the penalty is imposed, subsection (1. A) is to be construed as referring to 5 per cent. of the amount which OFCOM estimate to be the qualifying revenue for that accounting period.

(1. C)Section 19. (2) to (6) applies for determining or estimating qualifying revenue for the purposes of subsection (1. A) or (1. B) above."

(2) This paragraph applies in relation to a failure to comply with a condition or direction only if it is one occurring after the commencement of this paragraph.

Commencement Information

I3. Sch. 13 para. 3 in force at 29.12.2003 by S.I. 2003/3142, art. 3. (1), Sch. 1 (with art. 11)

Restricted services licences

4. (1)In subsection (2) of section 42. B (application of sections 40 to 42 to licensing of restricted services), for "subsections (3) and (4)" there shall be substituted " subsections (3) to (3. C) ".

(2) In subsection (3) of that section—

(a) for "subsection (2)" there shall be substituted " subsections (1. A) to (1. C) "; and

(b) for the words from "shall not exceed whichever is the greater" onwards there shall be substituted " is the maximum penalty given by subsection (3. A). "

(3) For subsection (4) of that section (penalties for failure to comply with conditions or directions) there shall be substituted—

"(3. A)The maximum penalty is whichever is the greater of—

(a) £250,000; and

(b) 5 per cent. of the qualifying revenue for the licence holder's last complete accounting period falling within the period for which his licence has been in force ("the relevant period").

440

(3. B)In relation to a person whose first complete accounting period falling within the relevant period has not ended when the penalty is imposed, subsection (3. A)(b) is to be construed as referring to 5 per cent. of the amount which OFCOM estimate to be the qualifying revenue for that accounting period.

(3. C)Section 19. (2) to (6) applies for determining or estimating qualifying revenue for the purposes of subsection (3. A) or (3. B) above."

(4) This paragraph applies in relation to a failure to comply with a condition or direction only if it is one occurring after the commencement of this paragraph.

Commencement Information

I4. Sch. 13 para. 4 in force at 29.12.2003 by S.I. 2003/3142, art. 3. (1), Sch. 1 (with art. 11)

Additional television services licences

5. (1)For subsection (2) of section 55 (penalties for failure by holder of licence for additional television service to comply with licence conditions or directions) there shall be substituted—

"(1. A)The amount of a financial penalty imposed on a person in pursuance of subsection (1) shall not exceed 5 per cent. of the qualifying revenue for the licence holder's last complete accounting period falling within the period for which his licence has been in force ("the relevant period").

(1. B)In relation to a person whose first complete accounting period falling within the relevant period has not ended when the penalty is imposed, subsection (1. A) is to be construed as referring to 5 per cent. of the amount which OFCOM estimate to be the qualifying revenue for that accounting period.

(1. C)Section 52. (2) applies for determining or estimating qualifying revenue for the purposes of subsection (1. A) or (1. B) above."

(2) This paragraph applies in relation to a failure to comply with a condition or direction only if it is one occurring after the commencement of this paragraph.

Commencement Information

I5. Sch. 13 para. 5 in force at 29.12.2003 by S.I. 2003/3142, art. 3. (1), Sch. 1 (with art. 11)

Revocation of national sound broadcasting licence

6. (1)In subsection (3) of section 101 (penalty on revocation of national sound broadcasting licence), for "a financial penalty of the prescribed amount" there shall be substituted " a specified financial penalty ".

(2) For subsection (4) of that section (amount of penalty) there shall be substituted—

"(3. A)The maximum amount which a person may be required to pay by way of a penalty under subsection (3) is the maximum penalty given by subsections (3. B) and (3. C).

(3. B)In a case where the licence is revoked under this section or the penalty is imposed before the end of the first complete accounting period of the licence holder to fall within the period for which the licence is in force, the maximum penalty is whichever is the greater of—

(a) £250,000; and

(b) 7 per cent. of the amount which OFCOM estimate would have been the qualifying revenue for the first complete accounting period of the licence holder falling within the period for which the licence would have been in force.

(3. C)In any other case, the maximum penalty is whichever is the greater of—

(a) £250,000; and

(b) 7 per cent. of the qualifying revenue for the last complete accounting period of the licence holder falling within the period for which the licence is in force.

(3. D)Section 102. (2) to (6) applies for estimating or determining qualifying revenue for the purposes of subsection (3. B) or (3. C) above."

(3) This paragraph applies only in a case of a revocation in relation to which—

(a) the notice required by section 101. (2) of the 1990 Act, or

(b) the notice revoking the licence,

is served after the commencement of this paragraph.

Commencement Information

I6. Sch. 13 para. 6 in force at 29.12.2003 by S.I. 2003/3142, art. 3. (1), Sch. 1 (with art. 11)

Licences for analogue sound services

7. (1)For subsection (2) of section 110 (penalties for failure by holder of national sound broadcasting licence to comply with licence conditions or directions) there shall be substituted—
"(1. A)The maximum amount which the holder of a national licence may be required to pay by way of a financial penalty imposed in pursuance of subsection (1)(a) is the maximum penalty given by subsection (1. B).

(1. B)The maximum penalty is whichever is the greater of—

(a) £250,000; and

(b) 5 per cent. of the qualifying revenue for his last complete accounting period falling within the period for which his licence has been in force ("the relevant period").

(1. C)In relation to a person whose first complete accounting period falling within the relevant period has not ended when the penalty is imposed, subsection (1. B)(b) is to be construed as referring to 5 per cent. of the amount which OFCOM estimate to be the qualifying revenue for that accounting period.

(1. D)Section 102. (2) to (6) applies for determining or estimating qualifying revenue for the purposes of subsection (1. B) or (1. C) above."

(2) In subsection (3) of that section (maximum penalty for failure by holder of a sound broadcasting licence that is not a national licence to comply with licence conditions or directions), for "£50,000" there shall be substituted " £250,000 ".

(3) This paragraph applies in relation to a failure to comply with a condition or direction only if it is one occurring after the commencement of this paragraph.

Commencement Information

I7. Sch. 13 para. 7 in force at 29.12.2003 by S.I. 2003/3142, art. 3. (1), Sch. 1 (with art. 11)

Additional radio services licences

8. (1)For subsection (2) of section 120 (penalties for failure by holder of additional radio services licence to comply with licence conditions or directions) there shall be substituted—
"(1. A)The amount of a financial penalty imposed on a person in pursuance of subsection (1) shall not exceed 5 per cent. of the qualifying revenue for the licence holder's last complete accounting period falling within the period for which his licence has been in force ("the relevant period").

(1. B)In relation to a person whose first complete accounting period falling within the relevant period has not ended when the penalty is imposed, subsection (1. A) is to be construed as referring to 5 per cent. of the amount which OFCOM estimate to be the qualifying revenue for that accounting period.

(1. C)Section 118. (2) applies for determining or estimating qualifying revenue for the purposes of subsection (1. A) or (1. B) above."

(2) This paragraph applies in relation to a failure to comply with a condition or direction only if it is one occurring after the commencement of this paragraph.

Commencement Information

I8. Sch. 13 para. 8 in force at 29.12.2003 by S.I. 2003/3142, art. 3. (1), Sch. 1 (with art. 11)

Power to amend penalties under the 1990 Act

9. (1)The Secretary of State may by order amend any of the provisions of the 1990 Act specified

in sub-paragraph (2) by substituting a different sum for the sum for the time being specified in that provision.

(2) Those provisions are—

(a) section 18. (3. B)(a) and (3. C)(a);

(b) section 42. B(3. A)(a);

(c) section 101. (3. B)(a) and (3. C)(a);

(d) section 110. (1. B)(a) and (3).

(3) No order is to be made under this paragraph unless a draft of the order has been laid before Parliament and approved by a resolution of each House.

Commencement Information

I9. Sch. 13 para. 9 in force at 29.12.2003 by S.I. 2003/3142, art. 3. (1), Sch. 1 (with art. 11)

Part 2. Broadcasting Act 1996

Preliminary

10. The 1996 Act shall be amended as follows.

Commencement Information

I10. Sch. 13 para. 10 in force at 29.12.2003 by S.I. 2003/3142, art. 3. (1), Sch. 1 (with art. 11)

Revocation of television multiplex licences

11. (1)In subsection (5) of section 11 (penalty on revocation of television multiplex licence), the words from "not exceeding" onwards shall be omitted.

(2) For subsection (6) of that section (amount of penalty) there shall be substituted—

"(5. A)The maximum amount which a person may be required to pay by way of a penalty under subsection (5) is the maximum penalty given by subsections (5. B) and (5. C).

(5. B)In a case where the licence is revoked under this section or the penalty is imposed before the end of the first complete accounting period of the licence holder to fall within the period for which the licence is in force, the maximum penalty is whichever is the greater of—

(a) £500,000; and

(b) 7 per cent. of the amount which OFCOM estimate would have been the multiplex revenue for the first complete accounting period of the licence holder falling within the period for which the licence would have been in force.

(5. C)In any other case, the maximum penalty is whichever is the greater of—

(a) £500,000; and

(b) 7 per cent. of the multiplex revenue for the last complete accounting period of the licence holder falling within the period for which the licence is in force.

(5. D)Section 14 applies for estimating or determining multiplex revenue for the purposes of subsection (5. B) or (5. C) above."

(3) This paragraph applies only in a case of a revocation in relation to which—

(a) the notice required by section 11. (2) of the 1996 Act, or

(b) the notice revoking the licence,

is served after the commencement of this paragraph.

Commencement Information

I11. Sch. 13 para. 11 in force at 29.12.2003 by S.I. 2003/3142, art. 3. (1), Sch. 1 (with art. 11)

Attribution of television multiplex revenue

12. (1)In subsection (1) of section 15 (attribution of multiplex revenue for the purposes of section

443

17. (3)), for "17. (3)" there shall be substituted " 17. (2. A) and (2. B) ".

(2) In subsection (2) of that section (attribution for the purposes of sections 23. (3) and 27. (3)), for "section 23. (3) or section 27. (3)" there shall be substituted " sections 23. (2. A) to (5) and 27. (2. A) to (5) ".

(3) This paragraph has effect in relation only to cases in which section 17, 23 or 27 applies as amended by this Schedule.

Commencement Information

I12. Sch. 13 para. 12 in force at 29.12.2003 by S.I. 2003/3142, art. 3. (1), Sch. 1 (with art. 11)

Multiplex licences

13. (1)In subsection (2) of section 17 (penalty for failure by holder of television multiplex licence to comply with licence conditions or directions), for the words from "whichever is the greater" onwards there shall be substituted " the maximum penalty given by subsection (2. A). "

(2) For subsection (3) of that section (maximum penalties) there shall be substituted—

"(2. A)The maximum penalty is whichever is the greater of—

(a) £250,000; and

(b) 5 per cent. of the share of multiplex revenue attributable to the licence holder for his last complete accounting period falling within the period for which his licence has been in force ("the relevant period").

(2. B)In relation to a person whose first complete accounting period falling within the relevant period has not ended when the penalty is imposed, subsection (2. A)(b) is to be construed as referring to 5 per cent. of the amount which OFCOM estimate to be the share of multiplex revenue attributable to him for that accounting period.

(2. C)Section 15. (1) and (3) applies for determining or estimating the share of multiplex revenue attributable to a person for the purposes of subsection (2. A) or (2. B) above."

(3) This paragraph applies in relation to a failure to comply with a condition or direction only if it is one occurring after the commencement of this paragraph.

Commencement Information

I13. Sch. 13 para. 13 in force at 29.12.2003 by S.I. 2003/3142, art. 3. (1), Sch. 1 (with art. 11)

Digital television programme licences

14. (1)In subsection (2) of section 23 (penalty for failure by holder of digital television programme licence to comply with licence conditions or directions), for the words from "whichever is the greater" onwards there shall be substituted " the maximum penalty given by subsection (2. A). "

(2) For subsection (3) of that section (maximum penalties) there shall be substituted—

"(2. A)The maximum penalty is whichever is the greater of—

(a) £250,000; and

(b) 5 per cent. of the aggregate amount of the shares of multiplex revenue attributable to him in relation to television multiplex services and general multiplex services in respect of relevant accounting periods."

(3) In subsection (4) of that section (meaning of "relevant accounting period"), for "subsection (3)(a)" there shall be substituted " subsection (2. A) ".

(4) In subsection (5) of that section, for "not yet ended, then for the purposes of subsection (3)" there shall be substituted " not ended when the penalty is imposed, then for the purposes of this section ".

(5) Before subsection (6) of that section there shall be inserted—

"(5. B)Section 15. (2) and (3) applies for determining or estimating the share of multiplex revenue attributable to a person for the purposes of subsection (2. A) or (5) above."

(6) This paragraph applies in relation to a failure to comply with a condition or direction only if it is one occurring after the commencement of this paragraph.

Commencement Information

I14. Sch. 13 para. 14 in force at 29.12.2003 by S.I. 2003/3142, art. 3. (1), Sch. 1 (with art. 11)

Digital additional television services licences

15. (1)In subsection (2) of section 27 (penalty for failure by holder of digital additional services licence to comply with licence conditions or directions), for the words from "whichever is the greater" onwards there shall be substituted " the maximum penalty given by subsection (2. A). "

(2) For subsection (3) of that section (maximum penalties) there shall be substituted—

"(2. A)The maximum penalty is whichever is the greater of—

(a) £250,000; and

(b) 5 per cent. of the aggregate amount of the shares of multiplex revenue attributable to him in relation to television multiplex services and general multiplex services in respect of relevant accounting periods."

(3) In subsection (4) of that section (meaning of "relevant accounting period"), for "subsection (3)(a)" there shall be substituted " subsection (2. A) ".

(4) In subsection (5) of that section, for "not yet ended, then for the purposes of subsection (3)" there shall be substituted " not ended when the penalty is imposed, then for the purposes of this section ".

(5) Before subsection (6) of that section there shall be inserted—

"(5. B)Section 15. (2) and (3) applies for determining or estimating the share of multiplex revenue attributable to a person for the purposes of subsection (2. A) or (5) above."

(6) This paragraph applies in relation to a failure to comply with a condition or direction only if it is one occurring after the commencement of this paragraph.

Commencement Information

I15. Sch. 13 para. 15 in force at 29.12.2003 by S.I. 2003/3142, art. 3. (1), Sch. 1 (with art. 11)

Power to amend digital television penalties

16. For section 36. (2) and (3) (provisions that may be amended and negative resolution procedure) there shall be substituted—

"(2)The provisions referred to in subsection (1) are—

(a) section 11. (5. B)(a) and (5. C)(a);

(b) section 17. (2. A)(a);

(c) section 23. (2. A)(a); and

(d) section 27. (2. A)(a).

(3) No order is to be made under subsection (1) unless a draft of the order has been laid before Parliament and approved by a resolution of each House."

Commencement Information

I16. Sch. 13 para. 16 in force at 29.12.2003 by S.I. 2003/3142, art. 3. (1), Sch. 1 (with art. 11)

Revocation of radio multiplex licences

17. (1)In section 53. (5) (maximum penalty on revocation of radio multiplex licence), for "£50,000", in both places, there shall be substituted " £250,000 ".

(2) This paragraph applies only in a case of a revocation in relation to which—

(a) the notice required by section 53. (2) of the 1996 Act, or

(b) the notice revoking the licence,

is served after the commencement of this paragraph.

Commencement Information

I17. Sch. 13 para. 17 in force at 29.12.2003 by S.I. 2003/3142, art. 3. (1), Sch. 1 (with art. 11)

Attribution of radio multiplex revenue

18. (1)In subsection (1) of section 57 (attribution of multiplex revenue for the purposes of sections 59. (3)), for "59. (3)" there shall be substituted " 59. (2. A) and (2. B) ".

(2) In subsection (2) of that section, (attribution for the purposes of sections 62. (3) and 66. (3)), for "section 62. (3) or section 66. (3)" there shall be substituted " sections 62. (2. A) to (5) and 66. (2. A) to (5) ".

(3) This paragraph has effect in relation only to cases in which section 59, 62 or 66 applies as amended by this Schedule.

Commencement Information

I18. Sch. 13 para. 18 in force at 29.12.2003 by S.I. 2003/3142, art. 3. (1), Sch. 1 (with art. 11)

Contraventions of conditions of radio multiplex licences

19. (1)In subsection (2) of section 59 (penalty for failure by holder of radio multiplex licence to comply with licence conditions or directions), for the words from "whichever is the greater" onwards there shall be substituted " the maximum penalty given by subsection (2. A). "

(2) For subsection (3) of that section (maximum penalties) there shall be substituted—

"(2. A)The maximum penalty is whichever is the greater of—

(a) £250,000; and

(b) 5 per cent. of the aggregate amount of the share of multiplex revenue attributable to him for his last complete accounting period falling within a period for which his licence has been in force ("the relevant period").

(2. B)In relation to a person whose first complete accounting period falling within the relevant period has not ended when the penalty is imposed, subsection (2. A)(b) is to be construed as referring to 5 per cent. of the amount which OFCOM estimate to be the share of multiplex revenue attributable to him for that accounting period.

(2. C)Section 57. (1) and (3) applies for determining or estimating the share of multiplex revenue attributable to a person for the purposes of subsection (2. A) or (2. B) above."

(3) In subsection (4) of that section (maximum penalty to be imposed on holder of local radio multiplex licences for failure to comply with conditions or directions), for "£50,000" there shall be substituted " £250,000 ".

(4) This paragraph applies in relation to a failure to comply with a condition or direction only if it is one occurring after the commencement of this paragraph.

Commencement Information

I19. Sch. 13 para. 19 in force at 29.12.2003 by S.I. 2003/3142, art. 3. (1), Sch. 1 (with art. 11)

Digital sound programme licences

20. (1)In subsection (2) of section 62 (penalty for failure by holder of digital sound programme licence to comply with licence conditions or directions), for the words from "whichever is the greater" onwards there shall be substituted " the maximum penalty given by subsection (2. A). "

(2) For subsection (3) of that section (maximum penalties) there shall be substituted—

"(2. A)The maximum penalty is whichever is the greater of—

(a) £250,000; and

(b) 5 per cent. of the aggregate amount of the shares of multiplex revenue attributable to him in relation to relevant multiplex services in respect of relevant accounting periods."

(3) In subsection (4) of that section (meaning of "relevant accounting period"), for "subsection (3)" there shall be substituted " subsection (2. A) ".

(4) In subsection (5) of that section, for "not yet ended, then for the purposes of subsection (3)"

there shall be substituted " not ended when the penalty is imposed, then for the purposes of this section ".

(5) After that subsection there shall be inserted—

"(5. A)A determination or estimate for the purposes of subsection (2. A) or (5) above of the share of multiplex revenue attributable to a person in relation to national radio multiplex services is to be in accordance with section 57. (2) and (3).

(5. B)A determination or estimate for the purposes of subsection (2. A) or (5) above of the share of multiplex revenue attributable to a person in relation to television multiplex services or general multiplex services is to be in accordance with section 15. (2) and (3)."

(6) In subsection (6) of that section (maximum penalty where licence is a local digital sound programme licence), for "£50,000" there shall be substituted " £250,000 ".

(7) This paragraph applies in relation to a failure to comply with a condition or direction only if it is one occurring after the commencement of this paragraph.

Commencement Information

I20. Sch. 13 para. 20 in force at 29.12.2003 by S.I. 2003/3142, art. 3. (1), Sch. 1 (with art. 11)

Licences for digital additional sound services

21. (1)In subsection (2) of section 66 (penalty for failure by holder of digital additional sound services licence to comply with licence conditions or directions), for the words from "whichever is the greater" onwards there shall be substituted " the maximum penalty given by subsection (2. A). "

(2) For subsection (3) of that section (maximum penalties) there shall be substituted—

"(2. A)The maximum penalty is whichever is the greater of—

(a) £250,000; and

(b) 5 per cent. of the aggregate amount of the shares of multiplex revenue attributable to him in relation to relevant multiplex services in respect of relevant accounting periods."

(3) In subsection (4) of that section (maximum penalty where licence is a local digital sound programme licence), for "£50,000" there shall be substituted " £250,000 ".

(4) In subsection (5) of that section (meaning of "relevant accounting period") for "subsection (3)" there shall be substituted " subsection (2. A) ".

(5) In subsection (6) of that section, for "not yet ended, then for the purposes of subsection (3)" there shall be substituted " not ended when the penalty is imposed, then for the purposes of this section ".

(6) After that subsection there shall be inserted—

"(6. A)A determination or estimate for the purposes of subsection (2. A) or (6) above of the share of multiplex revenue attributable to a person in relation to national radio multiplex services is to be in accordance with section 57. (2) and (3).

(6. B)A determination or estimate for the purposes of subsection (2. A) or (6) above of the share of multiplex revenue attributable to a person in relation to general multiplex services is to be in accordance with section 15. (2) and (3)."

(7) This paragraph applies in relation to a failure to comply with a condition or direction only if it is one occurring after the commencement of this paragraph.

Commencement Information

I21. Sch. 13 para. 21 in force at 29.12.2003 by S.I. 2003/3142, art. 3. (1), Sch. 1 (with art. 11)

Power to amend digital television penalties

22. For section 69. (2) and (3) (provisions that may be amended and negative resolution procedure) there shall be substituted—

"(2)The provisions referred to in subsection (1) are—

(a) section 53. (5)(a) and (b)(i);

447

(b) section 59. (2. A)(a) and (4);

(c) section 62. (2. A)(a) and (6); and

(d) section 66. (2. A)(a) and (4).

(3) No order is to be made under subsection (1) unless a draft of the order has been laid before Parliament and approved by a resolution of each House."

Commencement Information

I22. Sch. 13 para. 22 in force at 29.12.2003 by S.I. 2003/3142, art. 3. (1), Sch. 1 (with art. 11)

Schedule 15. Media ownership rules

Section 350

Part 1. Channel 3 services

Ban on newspaper proprietors holding Channel 3 licences

1. (1)A person is not to hold a licence to provide a Channel 3 service if—

(a) he runs a national newspaper which for the time being has a national market share of 20 per cent. or more; or

(b) he runs national newspapers which for the time being together have a national market share of 20 per cent. or more.

F1. (2)............................

(3) For the purposes of this paragraph, where there is a licence to provide a Channel 3 service, each of the following shall be treated as holding that licence—

(a) the actual licence holder; and

(b) every person connected with the actual licence holder.

Amendments (Textual)

F1. Sch. 14 para. 1. (2) omitted (15.6.2011) by virtue of The Media Ownership (Radio and Cross-media) Order 2011 (S.I. 2011/1503), arts. 1, 3

Commencement Information

I1. Sch. 14 para. 1 in force at 29.12.2003 by S.I. 2003/3142, art. 3. (1), Sch. 1 (with art. 11)

Restrictions on participation

2. (1)A person who is—

(a) the proprietor of a national newspaper which for the time being has a national market share of 20 per cent. or more, or

(b) the proprietor of national newspapers which for the time being together have a national market share of 20 per cent. or more,

is not to be a participant with more than a 20 per cent. interest in a body corporate which is the holder of a licence to provide a Channel 3 service.

(2) A person who is the holder of a licence to provide a Channel 3 service is not to be a participant with more than a 20 per cent. interest in a body corporate which is a relevant national newspaper proprietor.

(3) A body corporate is not to be a participant with more than a 20 per cent. interest in a body corporate which holds a licence to provide a Channel 3 service if the first body corporate is one in which a relevant national newspaper proprietor is a participant with more than a 20 per cent. interest.

(4) A restriction imposed by this paragraph on participation in a body corporate which is the

holder of a Channel 3 licence applies equally to participation in a body corporate which controls the holder of such a licence.

(5) Any restriction on participation imposed by this paragraph—

(a) on the proprietor of a newspaper, or

(b) on the holder of a licence,

is to apply as if he and every person connected with him were one person.

(6) In this paragraph "a relevant national newspaper proprietor" means a person who runs—

(a) a national newspaper which for the time being has a national market share of 20 per cent. or more; or

(b) national newspapers which for the time being together have a national market share of 20 per cent. or more.

Commencement Information

I2. Sch. 14 para. 2 in force at 29.12.2003 by S.I. 2003/3142, art. 3. (1), Sch. 1 (with art. 11)

National and local newspapers and their respective national and local market shares

3. (1)In this Part of this Schedule references to a national or local newspaper are references to a national or local newspaper circulating wholly or mainly in the United Kingdom or in a part of the United Kingdom.

(2) Where a newspaper is published in different regional editions on the same day, OFCOM have the power to determine whether those regional editions should be treated for the purposes of this Part of this Schedule as constituting—

(a) one national newspaper;

(b) two or more local newspapers; or

(c) one national newspaper and one or more local newspapers.

(3) In the case of a newspaper which would otherwise be neither a national nor a local newspaper for the purposes of this Part of this Schedule, OFCOM have the power to determine, if they consider it appropriate to do so in the light of—

(a) its circulation and influence in the United Kingdom, or

(b) its circulation or influence in a part of the United Kingdom,

that the newspaper is to be treated as a national or as a local newspaper for such of those purposes as they may determine.

(4) For the purposes of this Part of this Schedule, the national market share of a national newspaper at any time is the percentage of the total number of copies of all national newspapers sold in the United Kingdom in the relevant six months which is represented by the total number of copies of that newspaper sold in the United Kingdom in that six months.

F2. (5). . . . .

(6) In [F3sub-paragraph (4)] "the relevant six months" means the six months ending with the last whole calendar month to end before the time in question.

(7) For the purposes of [F4sub-paragraph (4)] , the number of copies of a newspaper sold in the United KingdomF5... during any period may be taken to be such number as is estimated by OFCOM—

(a) in such manner, or

(b) by reference to such statistics prepared by any other person,

as they think fit.

(8) In relation to a newspaper which is distributed free of charge (rather than sold), references in this paragraph to the number of copies sold include references to the number of copies distributed.

Amendments (Textual)

F2. Sch. 14 para. 3. (5) omitted (15.6.2011) by virtue of Media Ownership (Radio and Cross-media) Order 2011 (S.I. 2011/1503), arts. 1, 6. (2)

F3. Words in Sch. 14 para. 3. (6) substituted (15.6.2011) by Media Ownership (Radio and Cross-media) Order 2011 (S.I. 2011/1503), arts. 1, 6. (3)

F4. Words in Sch. 14 para. 3. (7) substituted (15.6.2011) by Media Ownership (Radio and Cross-media) Order 2011 (S.I. 2011/1503), arts. 1, 6. (4)

F5. Words in Sch. 14 para. 3. (7) omitted (15.6.2011) by virtue of Media Ownership (Radio and Cross-media) Order 2011 (S.I. 2011/1503), arts. 1, 6. (4)

Modifications etc. (not altering text)

C1. Sch. 14 para. 3 applied (29.12.2003) by Media Ownership (Local Radio and Appointed News Provider) Order 2003 (S.I. 2003/3299), arts. 1. (2), 4. (4)

Commencement Information

I3. Sch. 14 para. 3 in force at 29.12.2003 by S.I. 2003/3142, art. 3. (1), Sch. 1 (with art. 11)

Construction of references to running a newspaper

4. For the purposes of this Part of this Schedule a person runs a F6... newspaper if—

(a) he is the proprietor of the newspaper; or

(b) he controls a body which is the proprietor of the newspaper.

Amendments (Textual)

F6. Words in Sch. 14 para. 4 omitted (15.6.2011) by virtue of Media Ownership (Radio and Cross-media) Order 2011 (S.I. 2011/1503), arts. 1, 7

Modifications etc. (not altering text)

C2. Sch. 14 para. 4 applied (29.12.2003) by Media Ownership (Local Radio and Appointed News Provider) Order 2003 (S.I. 2003/3299), arts. 1. (2), 4. (4)

Commencement Information

I4. Sch. 14 para. 4 in force at 29.12.2003 by S.I. 2003/3142, art. 3. (1), Sch. 1 (with art. 11)

Coverage area for a Channel 3 service

F75. . . . .

Amendments (Textual)

F7. Sch. 14 para. 5 omitted (15.6.2011) by virtue of Media Ownership (Radio and Cross-media) Order 2011 (S.I. 2011/1503), arts. 1, 8

Commencement Information

I5. Sch. 14 para. 5 in force at 29.12.2003 by S.I. 2003/3142, art. 3. (1), Sch. 1 (with art. 11)

Power to amend Part 1 of Schedule

6. The Secretary of State may by order repeal or otherwise modify any of the restrictions imposed by this Part of this Schedule.

Commencement Information

I6. Sch. 14 para. 6 in force at 29.12.2003 by S.I. 2003/3142, art. 3. (1), Sch. 1 (with art. 11)

F8. Part 2. F8...

Amendments (Textual)

F8. Sch. 14 Pt. 2 omitted (15.6.2011) by virtue of Media Ownership (Radio and Cross-media) Order 2011 (S.I. 2011/1503), arts. 1, 3

F8...

F87. . . . .

Commencement Information

17. Sch. 14 para. 7 in force at 29.12.2003 by S.I. 2003/3142, art. 3. (1), Sch. 1 (with art. 11)

F8...

F88. . . . .

Commencement Information

18. Sch. 14 para. 8 in force at 29.12.2003 by S.I. 2003/3142, art. 3. (1), Sch. 1 (with art. 11)

F8...

F89. . . . .

Commencement Information

19. Sch. 14 para. 9 in force at 29.12.2003 by S.I. 2003/3142, art. 3. (1), Sch. 1 (with art. 11)

F8...

F810. . . . .

Commencement Information

I10. Sch. 14 para. 10 in force at 12.12.2003 by S.I. 2003/3142, art. 2 (with art. 11)

Part 3. Local sound programme services

Restriction on holding of local sound broadcasting licences

11. (1)The Secretary of State may by order impose—
(a) requirements prohibiting the holding at the same time by the same person, in the circumstances described in the order, of more than the number of local sound broadcasting licences that is determined in the manner set out in the order;
(b) requirements prohibiting a person from holding even one local sound broadcasting licence in the circumstances described in the order.
(2) The circumstances by reference to which a person may be prohibited under sub-paragraph (1) from holding a local sound broadcasting licence, and the factors that may be used for determining the number of such licences that he may hold, include, in particular—
(a) whether and to what extent the coverage areas of different services provided by that person under different local sound broadcasting licences would overlap;
(b) the sizes of the potential audiences for those services and the times when those services would be made available;
(c) whether and to what extent members of the potential audiences for those services would also be members of the potential audiences for services provided under local sound broadcasting licences held by other persons;
(d) in a case in which members of potential audiences for services so provided by that person would also be members of the potential audiences for services so provided by other persons—
(i) the number of those other persons;
(ii) the coverage areas of their services;
(iii) the sizes of the potential audiences for their services; and
(iv) the times when their services are or will be made available;
(e) whether that person runs one or more national newspapers, and their national market share;
(f) whether and to what extent the whole or a part of the coverage area for a service for which that person would hold a local sound broadcasting licence is or includes an area in which one or more local newspapers run by him is circulating, and the newspapers' local market share;

(g) whether and to what extent the whole or a part the coverage area for which that person would hold a local sound broadcasting licence is or is included in the coverage area of a regional Channel 3 service for which he also holds a licence.

(3) For the purposes of this paragraph the coverage area for a service provided under a local sound broadcasting licence or a Channel 3 licence is the area in the United Kingdom within which that service is capable of being received at a level satisfying such technical standards as may have been laid down by OFCOM for the purposes of the provisions of an order under this paragraph.

Commencement Information

I11. Sch. 14 para. 11 in force at 29.12.2003 by S.I. 2003/3142, art. 3. (1), Sch. 1 (with art. 11)

Restriction applying to local digital sound programme services

12. (1)The Secretary of State may by order impose requirements, on persons holding local digital sound programme licences, prohibiting the provision by the same person, in the circumstances described in the order, of more than the number of local digital sound programme services that is determined in the manner set out in the order.

(2) The circumstances by reference to which a person may be prohibited under sub-paragraph (1) from providing a local digital sound programme service, and the factors that may be used for determining the number of such services that he may provide, include, in particular—

(a) whether and to what extent the coverage areas of different local digital sound programme services provided by that person would overlap;

(b) the capacity used by those services on the relevant multiplexes;

(c) the sizes of the potential audiences for those services and the times when those services would be made available;

(d) whether and to what extent members of the potential audiences for those services would also be members of the potential audiences for local digital sound programme services provided by other persons;

(e) in a case in which members of the potential audiences for the services provided by that person would also be members of the potential audiences for local digital sound programme services provided by other persons—

(i) the number of those other persons;

(ii) the coverage areas of their services;

(iii) the capacity used by their services on the relevant multiplexes;

(iv) the sizes of the potential audiences for their services; and

(v) the times when their services are or will be made available.

(3) For the purposes of this paragraph the coverage area for a service provided under a local digital sound programme licence is the area in the United Kingdom within which the relevant multiplex is capable of being received at a level satisfying such technical standards as may have been laid down by OFCOM for the purposes of the provisions of an order under this paragraph.

(4) In this paragraph "the relevant multiplex", in relation to a service provided under a local digital sound programme licence, means the local radio multiplex service in which the service provided under that licence is or is to be included.

(5) For the purposes of this paragraph a person who holds a licence to provide local digital sound programme services provides such a service if, and only if—

(a) the service is one provided by him and is included in a local radio multiplex service for which he holds a local radio multiplex licence; or

(b) under a contract between that person and a person who holds a licence to provide a local radio multiplex service, the person holding the licence to provide the radio multiplex service is required to include that local digital sound programme service in that multiplex service.

Commencement Information

I12. Sch. 14 para. 12 in force at 29.12.2003 by S.I. 2003/3142, art. 3. (1), Sch. 1 (with art. 11)

Powers supplemental to powers under paragraphs 11 and 12.

13. (1)An order under paragraph 11 or 12 may make provision for treating—

(a) persons who are connected with a person who holds a licence,

(b) persons who are associates of a person who holds a licence or of a person who is connected with a person who holds a licence, and

(c) persons who (whether alone or together with such persons as may be described in the order) participate in a body which holds a licence or is treated as doing so by virtue of paragraph (a) or (b),

as if each of them were also a holder of the licence for the purposes of a requirement imposed under that paragraph.

(2) An order under paragraph 12 may make provision for treating—

(a) persons who are connected with a person who provides a local digital sound programme service,

(b) persons who are associates of a person who provides such a service or of a person who is connected with a person who provides such a service, and

(c) persons who (whether alone or together with such persons as may be described in the order) participate in a body who provides such a service or is treated as doing so by virtue of paragraph (a) or (b),

as if each of them were also a person providing the service for the purposes of a requirement imposed under that paragraph.

(3) An order under paragraph 11 or 12 may also make provision for treating—

(a) persons who are connected with each other,

(b) persons who are associates of each other, and

(c) persons who (whether alone or together with such persons as may be described in the order) participate in a body,

as if they and such other persons who are connected with, associates of or participators in any of them as may be described in the order were the same person for the purposes of a requirement imposed under that paragraph.

(4) An order under paragraph 11 may make provision—

(a) as to the circumstances in which a newspaper is to be treated as a national newspaper or a local newspaper for the purposes of a requirement imposed under that paragraph;

(b) as to the person or persons who are to be treated for any such purposes as running a newspaper;

(c) as to the determination for any such purposes of the area within which a local newspaper is circulating; and

(d) as to what is to constitute the national market share or local market share of any newspaper or of a number of newspapers taken together;

and provision made by virtue of this paragraph may apply, with or without modifications, any of the provisions of paragraph 3 or 4 of this Schedule [F9or section 5. (6. AA) to (6. AD) of the Broadcasting Act 1990] .

(5) Power to make provision with respect to any matter by any order under paragraph 11 or 12 includes power—

(a) to make provision with respect to that matter by reference to the making or giving by OFCOM, in accordance with the order, of any determination, approval or consent; and

(b) to confer such other discretions on OFCOM as the Secretary of State thinks fit.

(6) Sub-paragraph (5) of paragraph 12 applies for the purposes of this paragraph as it applies for the purposes of that paragraph.

Amendments (Textual)

F9. Words in Sch. 14 para. 13. (4) inserted (15.6.2011) by The Media Ownership (Radio and Cross-media) Order 2011 (S.I. 2011/1503), arts. 1, 9

Commencement Information

113. Sch. 14 para. 13 in force at 29.12.2003 by S.I. 2003/3142, art. 3. (1), Sch. 1 (with art. 11)

Transitional provision for orders under paragraphs 11 and 12.

14. (1)This paragraph applies where—
(a) immediately after the coming into force of an order under paragraph 11 or 12, a person ("the person in contravention") is in contravention, in any respect, of a requirement imposed under that paragraph; and
(b) immediately before the coming into force of the order, that person—
(i) held one or more relevant licences; but
(ii) was not, in that respect, in contravention of a requirement imposed under that paragraph.
(2) This paragraph does not apply in the case of the first order to be made under paragraph 11 or 12 if the person in contravention was, immediately before the coming into force of the order, in contravention, in relation to one or more of the relevant licences, of a requirement imposed under Part 3 or 4 of Schedule 2 to the 1990 Act.
(3) In sub-paragraphs (1) and (2) the reference to a relevant licence is—
(a) in relation to the coming into force of an order under paragraph 11, a local sound broadcasting licence; and
(b) in relation to the coming into force of an order under paragraph 12, a local digital sound programme licence.
(4) The contravention mentioned in sub-paragraph (1)(a), to the extent that it arises by reason of the coming into force of the order, is to be disregarded (in the case of the person in contravention) in relation to any time which falls—
(a) after the coming into force of the order; and
(b) before there is a relevant change of circumstances.
(5) Where the contravention is one arising under paragraph 11 in the case of a person who held one or more local sound broadcasting licences immediately before the coming into force of the order, there is a relevant change of circumstances if—
(a) another person becomes the holder of any of those licences, otherwise than in consequence of a transaction under which the person in contravention ceases to be a holder of the licence; or
(b) the person in contravention becomes the holder of another local sound broadcasting licence.
(6) A change of circumstances is not a relevant change of circumstances by virtue of sub-paragraph (5)(b) unless the licence of which the person in contravention becomes the holder is one the holding of which, with the holding of licences already held by him, would (apart from sub-paragraph (4)) constitute a contravention of a requirement imposed under paragraph 11.
(7) Where the contravention is one arising under paragraph 12 in the case of a person who, under a local digital sound programme licence, was providing one or more local digital sound programme services immediately before the coming into force of the order, there is a relevant change of circumstances if—
(a) another person becomes the holder of that licence, otherwise than in consequence of a transaction under which the person in contravention ceases to be a holder of the licence; or
(b) the person in contravention becomes the provider of another local digital sound programme service provided under that licence.
(8) A change of circumstances is not a relevant change of circumstances by virtue of sub-paragraph (7)(b) unless the service of which the person in contravention becomes the provider is one the provision of which, with the services already provided by him, would (apart from sub-paragraph (4)) constitute a contravention of a requirement imposed under paragraph 12.
(9) For the purposes of this paragraph, in its application in relation to a contravention of a requirement imposed under paragraph 11 or 12—
(a) references to holding a licence or providing a local digital sound programme service are to be construed in accordance with the provision having effect for the purposes of that requirement; and
(b) the persons who are taken to be holding a local digital sound programme licence immediately

before the coming into force of the order include every person who at that time would, in accordance with that provision, be treated as providing local digital sound programme services that were being provided at that time under that licence.

Commencement Information

I14. Sch. 14 para. 14 in force at 29.12.2003 by S.I. 2003/3142, art. 3. (1), Sch. 1 (with art. 11)

Part 4. Religious bodies etc.

Approval required for religious bodies etc. to hold licences

15. (1)A person mentioned in paragraph 2. (1) of Part 2 of Schedule 2 to the 1990 Act (religious bodies etc.) is not to hold a Broadcasting Act licence not mentioned in paragraph 2. (1. A) of that Part unless—

(a) OFCOM have made a determination in his case as respects a description of licences applicable to that licence; and

(b) that determination remains in force.

(2) OFCOM are to make a determination under this paragraph in a person's case and as respects a particular description of licence if, and only if, they are satisfied that it is appropriate for that person to hold a licence of that description.

(3) OFCOM are not to make a determination under this paragraph except on an application made to them for the purpose.

(4) OFCOM must publish guidance for persons making applications to them under this paragraph as to the principles that they will apply when determining for the purposes of sub-paragraph (2) what is appropriate.

(5) OFCOM must have regard to guidance for the time being in force under sub-paragraph (4) when making determinations under this paragraph.

(6) OFCOM may revise any guidance under sub-paragraph (4) by publishing their revisions of it.

(7) The publication of guidance under sub-paragraph (4), or of any revisions of it, is to be in whatever manner OFCOM consider appropriate.

Commencement Information

I15. Sch. 14 para. 15 in force at 18.9.2003 by S.I. 2003/1900, art. 2. (2), Sch. 2 (with art. 5)

Power to amend Part 4 of Schedule

16. The Secretary of State may by order repeal or otherwise modify the restriction imposed by this Part of this Schedule.

Commencement Information

I16. Sch. 14 para. 16 in force at 18.9.2003 by S.I. 2003/1900, art. 2. (2), Sch. 2 (with art. 5)

Part 5. Supplemental provisions of Schedule

Procedure for orders

17. (1)Before making an order under any provision of this Schedule (other than one that is confined to giving effect to recommendations made by OFCOM in a report of a review under section 391), the Secretary of State must consult OFCOM.

(2) No order is to be made containing provision authorised by any provision of this Schedule unless a draft of the order has been laid before Parliament and approved by a resolution of each House.

Commencement Information
I17. Sch. 14 para. 17 in force at 18.9.2003 for specified purposes by S.I. 2003/1900, art. 2. (2), Sch. 2 (with art. 5)
I18. Sch. 14 para. 17 in force at 12.12.2003 in so far as not already in force by S.I. 2003/3142, art. 2 (with art. 11)
I19. Sch. 14 para. 17 in force at 29.12.2003 in so far as not already in force by S.I. 2003/3142, art. 3. (1), Sch. 1 (with art. 11)

Interpretation of Schedule

18. (1)Part 1 of Schedule 2 to the 1990 Act applies for construing this Schedule as it applies for construing Part 2 of that Schedule.
(2) References in this paragraph to an area overlapping another include references to its being the same as, or lying wholly inside, the other area.

Commencement Information
I20. Sch. 14 para. 18 in force at 29.12.2003 by S.I. 2003/3142, art. 3. (1), Sch. 1 (with art. 11)

Schedule 16. Amendments of Broadcasting Acts

Section 360

Part 1. Amendments of the 1990 Act

Licences under Part 1.

1. (1)Section 3 of the 1990 Act (licensing under Part 1) shall be amended as follows.
(2) For "the Commission" and "The Commission", wherever occurring, there shall be substituted " OFCOM ".
(3) In subsection (1), for "Chapter II, III, IV or V of this Part" there shall be substituted " Chapter 2 or 5 of this Part or section 235 of the Communications Act 2003 ".
(4) For subsection (8) (saving for telecommunications licences) there shall be substituted—
"(8)The holding by a person of a licence under this Part shall not relieve him of—
    (a) any liability in respect of a failure to hold a licence under section 1 of the Wireless Telegraphy Act 1949; or
    (b) any obligation to comply with requirements imposed by or under Chapter 1 of Part 2 of the Communications Act 2003 (electronic communications networks and electronic communications services)."

Commencement Information
I1. Sch. 15 para. 1 in force at 29.12.2003 by S.I. 2003/3142, art. 3. (1), Sch. 1 (with art. 11)

General licence conditions

2. (1)Section 4 of the 1990 Act (general licence conditions) shall be amended as follows.
(2) For "the Commission", wherever occurring, there shall be substituted " OFCOM ".
(3) In subsection (1), in each of paragraphs (a) and (c), after "this Act" there shall be inserted " , the Broadcasting Act 1996 or the Communications Act 2003 ".
(4) In subsection (3) (fixing of fees), the words from "and the amount" onwards shall be omitted.
(5) In subsection (5) (provision of false information to be breach of condition)—

(a) for "imposed under this Part" there shall be substituted " contained in the licence "; and

(b) after "and 42" there shall be inserted " or (as the case may be) sections 237 and 238 of the Communications Act 2003 (enforcement of television licensable content service licences) ".

Commencement Information

I2. Sch. 15 para. 2 in force at 29.12.2003 by S.I. 2003/3142, art. 3. (1), Sch. 1 (with art. 11)

Restrictions on licence holding

3. (1)Section 5 of the 1990 Act (restrictions on licence holding) shall be amended as follows.

(2) For "The Commission" and "the Commission", wherever occurring, there shall be substituted " OFCOM ".

(3) In subsection (2) (incidental requirements to provide information), after paragraph (d) there shall be inserted—

"(da)impose conditions in a licence requiring the licence holder, if a body corporate, to give OFCOM notice, after they have occurred and irrespective of whether proposals for them have fallen to be notified, of changes, transactions or events affecting—

(i) shareholdings in the body; or

(ii) the directors of the body;

(db) impose conditions in a licence enabling OFCOM to require the licence holder to provide them with such information as they may reasonably require for determining—

(i) whether the licence holder is a disqualified person in relation to that licence by virtue of Part 2 of Schedule 2; or

(ii) whether any such requirements as are mentioned in subsection (1)(b) have been and are being complied with by or in relation to the licence holder;".

(4) In subsection (6)—

(a) in paragraph (a), for "complained of" there shall be substituted " constituting their grounds for revoking the licence "; and

(b) in paragraph (b)(i), for "Parts III and IV of Schedule 2" there shall be substituted " the requirements imposed by or under Schedule 14 to the Communications Act 2003, ".

(5) In subsection (6. A)—

(a) paragraph (a) shall cease to have effect; and

(b) in paragraph (b), for "Part IV of that Schedule" there shall be substituted " Part 1 of Schedule 14 to the Communications Act 2003 ".

(6) Subsection (6. B) shall cease to have effect.

(7) In subsection (7), for the words from "a failure" to the end of paragraph (c) there shall be substituted " a disqualification under Part 2 of Schedule 2 to this Act or a contravention of a requirement imposed by or under Schedule 14 to the Communications Act 2003 ".

Commencement Information

I3. Sch. 15 para. 3 in force at 29.12.2003 by S.I. 2003/3142, art. 3. (1), Sch. 1 (with art. 11)

Repeal of previous regulatory regime

4. Sections 6 to 12 of the 1990 Act (which contain the mechanism for regulation in relation to licences under Part 1 of that Act) shall cease to have effect.

Commencement Information

I4. Sch. 15 para. 4 in force at 29.12.2003 by S.I. 2003/3142, art. 3. (1), Sch. 1 (with art. 11)

Prohibition on providing television services without a licence

5. (1)Section 13 of the 1990 Act (prohibition on providing television services without a licence) shall be amended as follows.

(2) In subsection (1) (offence of providing such service without a licence), for "service falling within section 2. (1)(a), (aa), (b), (c), (cc) or (d)" there shall be substituted " relevant regulated television service ".

(3) After that subsection there shall be inserted—

"(1. A)In subsection (1) "relevant regulated television service" means a service falling, in pursuance of section 211. (1) of the Communications Act 2003, to be regulated by OFCOM, other than a television multiplex service."

(4) In subsection (2) (exemption orders made after consulting the ITC), for "the Commission" there shall be substituted " OFCOM ".

Commencement Information

I5. Sch. 15 para. 5 in force at 29.12.2003 by S.I. 2003/3142, art. 3. (1), Sch. 1 (with art. 11)

Television broadcasting on Channel 3.

6. In section 14 of the 1990 Act (establishment of Channel 3), for "The Commission" and "the Commission", wherever occurring, there shall be substituted " OFCOM ".

Commencement Information

I6. Sch. 15 para. 6 in force at 29.12.2003 by S.I. 2003/3142, art. 3. (1), Sch. 1 (with art. 11)

Applications for Channel 3 licences

7. (1)Section 15 of the 1990 Act (applications for Channel 3 licences) shall be amended as follows.

(2) For "the Commission" and "The Commission", wherever occurring, there shall be substituted " OFCOM ".

(3) In subsection (2), for "specified in section 16. (2) or (3) (as the case may be)" there shall be substituted "that have to be imposed under Chapter 4 of Part 3 of the Communications Act 2003 by conditions relating to—

　(a) the public service remit for that service,

　(b) programming quotas,

　(c) news and current affairs programmes, and

　(d) programme production and regional programming."

(4) In subsection (3)—

(a) in paragraph (b), for "specified in section 16. (2) or (3) (as the case may be)" there shall be substituted "that have to be imposed under Chapter 4 of Part 3 of the Communications Act 2003 by conditions relating to—

(i) the public service remit for that service,

(ii) programming quotas,

(iii) news and current affairs programmes, and

(iv) programme production and regional programming";

(b) paragraphs (c) to (e) shall be omitted.

(5) After subsection (3) there shall be inserted—

"(3. A)For the purposes of subsection (1)(d)(ii)—

　(a) different percentages may be specified for different accounting periods; and

　(b) the percentages that may be specified for an accounting period include a nil percentage."

(6) In subsection (4), for "paragraphs (b) to (e)" there shall be substituted " paragraphs (b) ".

Commencement Information

I7. Sch. 15 para. 7 in force at 29.12.2003 by S.I. 2003/3142, art. 3. (1), Sch. 1 (with art. 11)

Procedure on consideration of applications for Channel 3 licences

8. (1)Section 16 of the 1990 Act (consideration of applications for Channel 3 licences) shall be amended as follows.

(2) For "the Commission", wherever occurring, there shall be substituted " OFCOM ".

(3) In subsection (1), for "specified in subsection (2) or (3) below (as the case may be)" there shall be substituted "that have to be imposed under Chapter 4 of Part 3 of the Communications Act 2003 by conditions relating to—

(i) the public service remit for that service,

(ii) programming quotas,

(iii) news and current affairs programmes, and

(iv) programme production and regional programming".

(4) Subsections (2) and (3) of that section shall cease to have effect.

(5) In subsection (4) of that section—

(a) for "specified in subsection (2) or (3) (as the case may be)," there shall be substituted "that have to be imposed under Chapter 4 of Part 3 of the Communications Act 2003 by conditions relating to—

    (a) the public service remit for that service,

    (b) programming quotas,

    (c) news and current affairs programmes, and

    (d) programme production and regional programming,";

(b) the words from "and in applying" onwards shall be omitted.

(6) Subsections (5) to (8) shall cease to have effect.

Commencement Information

I8. Sch. 15 para. 8 in force at 29.12.2003 by S.I. 2003/3142, art. 3. (1), Sch. 1 (with art. 11)

Television broadcasting on Channel 3.

9. (1)Section 17 of the 1990 Act (award of licences to person submitting highest bid) shall be amended as follows.

(2) For "the Commission" and "The Commission", wherever occurring, there shall be substituted " OFCOM ".

(3) In subsection (12)(b), for "specified in section 16. (2) or (3) (as the case may be)" there shall be substituted "that have to be imposed under Chapter 4 of Part 3 of the Communications Act 2003 by conditions relating to—

(i) the public service remit for that service,

(ii) programming quotas,

(iii) news and current affairs programmes, and

(iv) programme production and regional programming".

Commencement Information

I9. Sch. 15 para. 9 in force at 29.12.2003 by S.I. 2003/3142, art. 3. (1), Sch. 1 (with art. 11)

Financial conditions of licence and failures to begin a service

10. In sections 17. A to 19 of the 1990 Act (financial conditions in Channel 3 licences and failures to begin a service), for "The Commission" and "the Commission", wherever occurring, there shall be substituted " OFCOM ".

Commencement Information

I10. Sch. 15 para. 10 in force at 29.12.2003 by S.I. 2003/3142, art. 3. (1), Sch. 1 (with art. 11)

Changes of control in period after award of licence

11. (1)Section 21 of the 1990 Act (changes of control in period immediately after award of

licence) shall be amended as follows.

(2) For "the Commission" and "The Commission", wherever occurring, there shall be substituted " OFCOM ".

(3) In subsection (2), in the definition of "associated programme provider", for the words from "appears" to "inclusion" there shall be substituted " is or is likely to be involved, to a substantial extent, in the provision of the programmes included ".

Commencement Information

I11. Sch. 15 para. 11 in force at 29.12.2003 by S.I. 2003/3142, art. 3. (1), Sch. 1 (with art. 11)

Temporary provision of Channel 3 service for an additional area

12. In section 22 of the 1990 Act (temporary provision of regional Channel 3 Service for additional area), for "the Commission", wherever occurring, there shall be substituted " OFCOM ".

Commencement Information

I12. Sch. 15 para. 12 in force at 29.12.2003 by S.I. 2003/3142, art. 3. (1), Sch. 1 (with art. 11)

Appointment of members of C4 Corporation

13. In section 23 of the 1990 Act (appointment of C4. C members), for "the Commission", wherever occurring, there shall be substituted " OFCOM ".

Commencement Information

I13. Sch. 15 para. 13 in force at 29.12.2003 by S.I. 2003/3142, art. 3. (1), Sch. 1 (with art. 11)

Channel 4 licence

14. In section 24. (3) of the 1990 Act (Channel 4 licence), for "the Commission" there shall be substituted " OFCOM ".

Commencement Information

I14. Sch. 15 para. 14 in force at 29.12.2003 by S.I. 2003/3142, art. 3. (1), Sch. 1 (with art. 11)

Channel 5.

15. In section 28 of the 1990 Act (Channel 5), for "The Commission" and "the Commission", wherever occurring, there shall be substituted " OFCOM ".

Commencement Information

I15. Sch. 15 para. 15 in force at 29.12.2003 by S.I. 2003/3142, art. 3. (1), Sch. 1 (with art. 11)

Application to Channel 5 of Channel 3 provisions

16. (1)In section 29 of the 1990 Act (application to Channel 5 of Channel 3 provisions)—
(a) subsection (2)(b) and the word "and" immediately preceding it, and
(b) subsection (3),
shall cease to have effect.

(2) In subsection (2)(a) of that section, for "the Commission" there shall be substituted " OFCOM ".

Commencement Information

I16. Sch. 15 para. 16 in force at 29.12.2003 by S.I. 2003/3142, art. 3. (1), Sch. 1 (with art. 11)

Announcement of programme Schedules

17. In section 37. (1) of the 1990 Act (conditions requiring announcement of programme Schedules), for "the Commission" there shall be substituted " OFCOM ".
Commencement Information
I17. Sch. 15 para. 17 in force at 29.12.2003 by S.I. 2003/3142, art. 3. (1), Sch. 1 (with art. 11)

Enforcement of conditions of Channel 3, Channel 4 and Channel 5 licences

18. (1)In sections 40 to 42 of the 1990 Act (enforcement of licences), for "the Commission" and "The Commission", wherever occurring, there shall be substituted " OFCOM ".
(2) In sections 41. (1) and 42. (1)(a) of that Act (which contain provisions relating to the enforcement of directions under Part 1 of that Act), after "this Part", in each place, there shall be inserted " , Part 5 of the Broadcasting Act 1996 or Part 3 of the Communications Act 2003 ".
Commencement Information
I18. Sch. 15 para. 18 in force at 29.12.2003 by S.I. 2003/3142, art. 3. (1), Sch. 1 (with art. 11)

Restricted services

19. In section 42. B(1) of the 1990 Act (licensing of restricted services), for "the Commission", wherever occurring, there shall be substituted " OFCOM ".
Commencement Information
I19. Sch. 15 para. 19 in force at 29.12.2003 by S.I. 2003/3142, art. 3. (1), Sch. 1 (with art. 11)

Additional television services

20. (1)Section 48 of the 1990 Act (additional services) shall be further amended as follows.
(2) In subsection (1)—
(a) for "telecommunication" there shall be substituted " electronic "; and
(b) for paragraphs (a) and (b) there shall be substituted " on a relevant frequency ".
(3) In subsection (2), for paragraphs (a) and (b) there shall be substituted "any part of the signals which—
(a) is not required for the purposes of the television broadcasting service for the purposes of which the frequency has been made available; and
(b) is determined by OFCOM to be available for the provision of additional services;".
(4) After that subsection there shall be inserted—
"(2. A)For the purposes of this Part, if they consider it appropriate to do so, OFCOM may, while an additional services licence is in force, from time to time modify the determination made under subsection (2)(b) for the purposes of that licence in any manner that does not reduce the amount of spare capacity made available for the licensed services; and when so modified any such licence shall have effect accordingly."
(5) In subsection (3)—
(a) for "The Commission" there shall be substituted " OFCOM "; and
(b) for "(2)(a)" there shall be substituted " (2)(b) "; and
(c) for paragraphs (a) to (c) there shall be substituted—
"(a)to the obligations contained in any code under section 303 of the Communications Act 2003 by virtue of subsection (5) of that section; and
(aa) to any need of the person providing the television broadcasting service in question to be able to use part of the signals carrying it for providing services (in addition to those provided for satisfying those obligations) which—
(i) are ancillary to programmes included in the service and directly related to their contents; or

461

(ii) relate to the promotion or listing of such programmes."

(6) In subsection (4), for paragraphs (a) and (b) there shall be substituted—

"(a)to provide services for the satisfaction in his case of obligations mentioned in subsection (3)(a); and

(b) to provide in relation to his television broadcasting service any such services as are mentioned in subsection (3)(aa)."

(7) For subsection (6) there shall be substituted—

"(6)In this section—

"electronic signals" means signals within the meaning of section 32 of the Communications Act 2003;

"relevant frequency" means a frequency made available by OFCOM for the purposes of a television broadcasting service."

(8) This paragraph does not affect the validity of a licence granted or last renewed before the television transfer date, or the services licensed by any such licence.

Commencement Information

I20. Sch. 15 para. 20. (1)(2)(a) in force at 25.7.2003 by S.I. 2003/1900, art. 2. (1), Sch. 1

I21. Sch. 15 para. 20. (2)(b) (3)-(8) in force at 29.12.2003 by S.I. 2003/3142, art. 3. (1), Sch. 1 (with art. 11)

Licensing of additional television services

21. (1)Section 49 of the 1990 Act (licensing of additional television services) shall be amended as follows.

(2) For "the Commission", wherever occurring, there shall be substituted " OFCOM ".

(3) In subsection (1), for the words from "of the following" to "48. (1)(b)" there shall be substituted " relevant frequency ".

(4) For subsections (2) and (3) there shall be substituted—

"(1. A)An additional services licence is not required for an additional service that is comprised in the public teletext service (within the meaning of Part 3 of the Communications Act 2003)."

(5) In subsection (10), at the end there shall be inserted " and "relevant frequency" has the same meaning as in section 48. "

Modifications etc. (not altering text)

C1. Sch. 15 para. 21. (4) excluded (8.12.2003) by The Office of Communications Act 2002 (Commencement No. 3) and Communications Act 2003 (Commencement No. 2) Order 2003 (S.I. 2003/3142), art. 8. (2) (with art. 11)

Commencement Information

I22. Sch. 15 para. 21 in force at 29.12.2003 by S.I. 2003/3142, art. 3. (1), Sch. 1 (with art. 11)

Applications for additional services licences

22. (1)Section 50 of the 1990 Act (applications for additional services licences) shall be amended as follows.

(2) For "the Commission" and "The Commission", wherever occurring, there shall be substituted " OFCOM ".

(3) In subsection (1)(b)(ii), the words "(subject to the approval of the Secretary of State)" shall be omitted.

(4) Subsection (7) shall cease to have effect.

Commencement Information

I23. Sch. 15 para. 22 in force at 29.12.2003 by S.I. 2003/3142, art. 3. (1), Sch. 1 (with art. 11)

Procedure on application etc. for additional television services

licences

23. (1)Section 51 of the 1990 Act (consideration of applications for licences for additional television services) shall be amended as follows.

(2) For "the Commission", wherever occurring, there shall be substituted " OFCOM ".

(3) In subsection (1), for paragraph (a) (requirement of approval of technical plans) there shall be substituted—

"(a)that the technical plan submitted under section 50. (3)(b), in so far as it involves the use of an electronic communications network (within the meaning of the Communications Act 2003), contains proposals that are acceptable to them; and".

(4) Subsections (2) and (7) shall cease to have effect.

Commencement Information

I24. Sch. 15 para. 23 in force at 29.12.2003 by S.I. 2003/3142, art. 3. (1), Sch. 1 (with art. 11)

Additional payments in respect of additional television services licences

24. In section 52 of the 1990 Act (additional payments in respect of additional television services licences), for "the Commission", wherever occurring, there shall be substituted " OFCOM ".

Commencement Information

I25. Sch. 15 para. 24 in force at 29.12.2003 by S.I. 2003/3142, art. 3. (1), Sch. 1 (with art. 11)

Duration of additional television services licences

25. (1)Section 53 of the 1990 Act (duration and renewal of additional television services licences) shall be amended as follows.

(2) In subsection (1), for the words before paragraph (a) there shall be substituted—

"(1)A licence to provide additional services on a frequency which is a relevant frequency for the purposes of section 48 or (in the case of a licence granted before the television transfer date) was assigned under section 65—".

(3) In subsection (2), after "not later than" there shall be inserted " the day falling three months before ".

(4) In subsections (4) to (11), for "the Commission", wherever occurring, there shall be substituted " OFCOM ".

(5) In subsection (8), for the words from "payable" onwards there shall be substituted " the cash bid of the licence holder were the licence (instead of being renewed) to be granted for the period of the renewal on an application made in accordance with section 50. (3). "

(6) After that subsection there shall be inserted—

"(8. A)For the purposes of subsection (7)(b)—

(a) different percentages may be specified for different accounting periods; and

(b) the percentages that may be specified for an accounting period include a nil percentage."

(7) After subsection (11) there shall be inserted—

"(12)A determination for the purposes of subsection (11)—

(a) must be made at least one year before the date determined; and

(b) must be notified by OFCOM to the person who holds the licence in question.

(13) In this section "the television transfer date" has the same meaning as in the Communications Act 2003."

Commencement Information

I26. Sch. 15 para. 25 in force at 29.12.2003 by S.I. 2003/3142, art. 3. (1), Sch. 1 (with art. 11)

Additional television services not to interfere with other

transmissions

26. (1)Section 54 of the 1990 Act (additional television services not to interfere with other transmissions) shall be amended as follows.

(2) In subsection (1), for "the Commission" there shall be substituted " OFCOM ".

(3) Subsection (2) shall cease to have effect.

Commencement Information

127. Sch. 15 para. 26 in force at 29.12.2003 by S.I. 2003/3142, art. 3. (1), Sch. 1 (with art. 11)

Enforcement of additional television services licences

27. (1)Section 55 of the 1990 Act (further provision in relation to additional television services licences) shall be amended as follows.

(2) For "the Commission" and "The Commission", wherever occurring, there shall be substituted " OFCOM ".

(3) In subsection (4) at the end there shall be inserted " and, in the case of a licence renewed under section 53 as if the reference in section 42. (4) to the end of the period for which the licence is to continue in force were a reference to the end of the period for which it has been renewed. "

Commencement Information

128. Sch. 15 para. 27 in force at 29.12.2003 by S.I. 2003/3142, art. 3. (1), Sch. 1 (with art. 11)

The Welsh Authority

28. (1)Section 58 of the 1990 Act (sources of programmes for S4. C) shall be amended as follows.

(2) In subsection (1), for "comply with their duty under section 57. (2)(b)" there shall be substituted " fulfil so much of their public service remit in relation to S4. C under paragraph 3 of Schedule 12 to the Communications Act 2003 as is contained in sub-paragraph (2)(a) and (b) of that paragraph ".

(3) In subsection (2)(a), for "comply with section 57. (3)" there shall be substituted " fulfil so much of their public service remit in relation to S4. C under paragraph 3 of Schedule 12 to the Communications Act 2003 as is contained in sub-paragraph (2)(c) of that paragraph ".

(4) After subsection (5) there shall be inserted—

"(6)In this section "programme" does not include an advertisement."

Commencement Information

129. Sch. 15 para. 28 in force at 29.12.2003 by S.I. 2003/3142, art. 3. (1), Sch. 1 (with art. 11)

Distribution of licensed public service channels

29. (1)Section 66 of the 1990 Act (requirements relating to transmission and distribution of services) shall be amended as follows.

(2) For "the Commission", wherever occurring, there shall be substituted " OFCOM ".

(3) In subsections (1) and (2), for "for general reception" there shall be substituted " so as to be available for reception by members of the public ".

(4) After subsection (2) there shall be inserted—

"(2. A)In subsections (1) and (2) "available for reception by members of the public" shall be construed in accordance with section 361 of the Communications Act 2003".

Commencement Information

130. Sch. 15 para. 29 in force at 29.12.2003 by S.I. 2003/3142, art. 3. (1), Sch. 1 (with art. 11)

Enforcement of licences held by BBC companies

30. In section 66. A of the 1990 Act (enforcement of licences held by BBC companies), for "the Commission", wherever occurring, there shall be substituted " OFCOM ".

Commencement Information

I31. Sch. 15 para. 30 in force at 29.12.2003 by S.I. 2003/3142, art. 3. (1), Sch. 1 (with art. 11)

Interpretation of Part 1.

31. (1)Section 71 of the 1990 Act (interpretation) shall be amended as follows.

(2) For the definitions of "S4. C" and "on S4. C" there shall be substituted—

""S4. C" has the same meaning as in Part 3 of the Communications Act 2003;".

(3) For the definitions of "television broadcasting service" and "television programme service" there shall be substituted—

""television broadcasting service", "television licensable content service" and "television programme service" each has the same meaning as in Part 3 of the Communications Act 2003;".

Commencement Information

I32. Sch. 15 para. 31 in force at 29.12.2003 by S.I. 2003/3142, art. 3. (1), Sch. 1 (with art. 11)

Licensing functions of OFCOM

32. (1)Section 85 of the 1990 Act (licensing of independent radio services) shall be amended as follows.

(2) In subsections (1) and (2), for "the Authority" and "The Authority", wherever occurring, there shall be substituted " OFCOM ".

(3) In subsection (1), for "such licences to provide independent radio services as they may determine" there shall be substituted " licences to provide relevant independent radio services ".

(4) Subsections (3) and (4) (duty to secure the meeting of a variety of tastes and interests and to ensure fair and effective competition) shall cease to have effect.

(5) After subsection (7) there shall be inserted—

"(8)In this section "relevant independent radio services" means the following services so far as they are services falling to be regulated under section 245 of the Communications Act 2003—

(a) sound broadcasting services;

(b) radio licensable content services;

(c) additional radio services."

Commencement Information

I33. Sch. 15 para. 32 in force at 29.12.2003 by S.I. 2003/3142, art. 3. (1), Sch. 1 (with art. 11)

Licences under Part 3 of the 1990 Act

33. (1)Section 86 of the 1990 Act (licences under Part 3) shall be amended as follows.

(2) For "the Authority" and "The Authority", wherever occurring, there shall be substituted " OFCOM ".

(3) For subsection (9) of that section there shall be substituted—

"(9)The holding of a licence by a person shall not relieve him of—

(a) any liability in respect of a failure to hold a licence under section 1 of the Wireless Telegraphy Act 1949; or

(b) any obligation to comply with requirements imposed by or under Chapter 1 of Part 2 of the Communications Act 2003 (electronic communications networks and electronic communications services)."

Commencement Information

I34. Sch. 15 para. 33 in force at 29.12.2003 by S.I. 2003/3142, art. 3. (1), Sch. 1 (with art. 11)

General licence conditions

34. (1)Section 87 of the 1990 Act (general licence conditions) shall be amended as follows.
(2) For "the Authority", wherever occurring, there shall be substituted " OFCOM ".
(3) In subsection (1), in each of paragraphs (a) and (d), after "this Act" there shall be inserted " , the Broadcasting Act 1996 or the Communications Act 2003 ".
(4) In subsection (2), sub-paragraph (ii) of paragraph (b) and the word "or" immediately preceding it shall be omitted.
(5) In subsection (3) (fixing of fees), the words from "and the amount" onwards shall be omitted.
Commencement Information
I35. Sch. 15 para. 34 in force at 29.12.2003 by S.I. 2003/3142, art. 3. (1), Sch. 1 (with art. 11)

Restrictions on holding licences

35. (1)Section 88 of the 1990 Act (restrictions on the holding of licences) shall be amended as follows.
(2) For "The Authority" and "the Authority", wherever occurring, there shall be substituted " OFCOM ".
(3) In subsection (2) (incidental requirements to provide information), after paragraph (d) there shall be inserted—
    "(da)impose conditions in a licence requiring the licence holder, if a body corporate, to give OFCOM notice, after they have occurred and irrespective of whether proposals for them have fallen to be notified, of changes, transactions or events affecting—
(i) shareholdings in the body; or
(ii) the directors of the body;
    (db) impose conditions in a licence enabling OFCOM to require the licence holder to provide them with such information as they may reasonably require for determining—
(i) whether the licence holder is a disqualified person in relation to that licence by virtue of Part 2 of Schedule 2; or
(ii) whether any such requirements as are mentioned in subsection (1)(b) have been and are being complied with by or in relation to the licence holder;".
(4) In subsection (6)—
(a) in paragraph (a), for "complained of" there shall be substituted " constituting their grounds for revoking the licence "; and
(b) in paragraph (b)(i), for "Parts III and IV of Schedule 2" there shall be substituted " the requirements imposed by or under Schedule 14 to the Communications Act 2003 ".
(5) In subsection (6. A)—
(a) paragraph (a) shall cease to have effect; and
(b) in paragraph (b), for "Part IV of that Schedule" there shall be substituted " Part 1 of Schedule 14 to the Communications Act 2003 ".
(6) Subsection (6. B) shall cease to have effect.
(7) In subsection (7), for the words from "a failure" to the end of paragraph (c) there shall be substituted " a disqualification under Part 2 of Schedule 2 to this Act or a contravention of a requirement imposed by or under Schedule 14 to the Communications Act 2003, ".
Commencement Information
I36. Sch. 15 para. 35 in force at 29.12.2003 by S.I. 2003/3142, art. 3. (1), Sch. 1 (with art. 11)

Disqualification of persons convicted of transmission offences

36. (1)Section 89 of the 1990 Act (offences giving rise to disqualification) shall be amended as follows.

(2) In subsection (1), for paragraph (a) there shall be substituted—

"(a)an offence under section 1. (1) of the Wireless Telegraphy Act 1949 ("the 1949 Act") consisting in the establishment or use of a station for wireless telegraphy, or the installation or use of wireless telegraphy apparatus, for the purpose of making a broadcast (within the meaning of section 9 of the Marine, &c., Broadcasting (Offences) Act 1967);

(aa) an offence under section 1. A of the 1949 Act (keeping wireless telegraphy station or apparatus available for unauthorised use) where the relevant contravention of section 1 would constitute an offence falling within paragraph (a);

(ab) an offence under section 1. B or 1. C of the 1949 Act (unlawful broadcasting offences);".

(3) In subsection (3), for the words from "concerned" onwards there shall be substituted "concerned in—

(a) the provision of the licensed service or the making of programmes included in it; or

(b) the operation of a station for wireless telegraphy used for broadcasting the service."

(4) This paragraph does not impose a disqualification in respect of any offence committed before the commencement of this paragraph.

Commencement Information

I37. Sch. 15 para. 36 in force at 29.12.2003 by S.I. 2003/3142, art. 3. (1), Sch. 1 (with art. 11)

Offence of providing regulated radio services

37. (1)Section 97 of the 1990 Act (prohibition on providing services without a licence) shall be amended as follows.

(2) In subsection (1), for the words from "independent" to "84. (1)(d), (e) or (f)" there shall be substituted " relevant regulated radio service ".

(3) After that subsection there shall be inserted—

"(1. A)In subsection (1) "relevant regulated radio service" means a service falling to be regulated by OFCOM under section 245 of the Communications Act 2003, other than a radio multiplex service."

(4) In subsection (2) (exemption orders made after consulting the Radio Authority), for "the Authority" there shall be substituted " OFCOM ".

Commencement Information

I38. Sch. 15 para. 37 in force at 29.12.2003 by S.I. 2003/3142, art. 3. (1), Sch. 1 (with art. 11)

Applications for national licences

38. (1)Section 98 of the 1990 Act (applications for national licences) shall be amended as follows.

(2) For "the Authority" and "The Authority", wherever occurring, there shall be substituted " OFCOM ".

(3) In subsection (3)(a) (proposals to accompany application)—

(a) the word "both", and

(b) sub-paragraph (ii) and the word "and" immediately preceding it,

shall be omitted.

(4) After subsection (3) there shall be inserted—

"(3. A)For the purposes of subsection (1)(d)(ii)—

(a) different percentages may be specified for different accounting periods; and

(b) the percentages that may be specified for an accounting period include a nil percentage."

(5) In subsection (4) (provision of further information), after "paragraphs (a)," there shall be inserted " (aa), ".

(6) In subsection (6)(b) (publication of details of successful applicant), after "subsection (3)(a)" there shall be inserted " and (aa) ".

Commencement Information

I39. Sch. 15 para. 38 in force at 29.12.2003 by S.I. 2003/3142, art. 3. (1), Sch. 1 (with art. 11)

Consideration of applications for a national licence

39. (1)Section 99 of the 1990 Act (consideration of applications for national licence) shall be amended as follows.
(2) For "the Authority", wherever occurring, there shall be substituted " OFCOM ".
(3) In paragraph (a) of subsection (1) (proposals to accompany application)—
(a) the word "both", and
(b) sub-paragraph (ii) and the word "and" immediately preceding it,
shall be omitted.
(4) In paragraph (b) of that subsection, after "maintain that service" there shall be inserted " and any proposed simulcast radio service corresponding to that service ".
Commencement Information
I40. Sch. 15 para. 39 in force at 29.12.2003 by S.I. 2003/3142, art. 3. (1), Sch. 1 (with art. 11)

Award of national licences

40. In section 100 of the 1990 Act (award of national licences to person submitting highest cash bid), for "the Authority" and "The Authority", wherever occurring, there shall be substituted " OFCOM ".
Commencement Information
I41. Sch. 15 para. 40 in force at 29.12.2003 by S.I. 2003/3142, art. 3. (1), Sch. 1 (with art. 11)

Failure to begin providing licensed service

41. (1)Section 101 of the 1990 Act (failure to begin providing licensed service) shall be amended as follows.
(2) For "the Authority", wherever occurring, there shall be substituted " OFCOM ".
(3) In subsection (1)—
(a) in paragraph (a) for "the service in question" there shall be substituted " the licensed national service or that he does not intend to provide a corresponding simulcast radio service that he is required to provide by a condition imposed under section 100. A "; and
(b) in paragraph (b), for "that service" there shall be substituted " the licensed national service or any such simulcast radio service ".
(4) In subsection (2), for "the service in question" there shall be substituted " the licensed national service or the simulcast radio service ".
Commencement Information
I42. Sch. 15 para. 41 in force at 29.12.2003 by S.I. 2003/3142, art. 3. (1), Sch. 1 (with art. 11)

Additional payments in respect of national licences

42. In section 102 of the 1990 Act (additional payments in respect of national licences), for "the Authority", wherever occurring, there shall be substituted " OFCOM ".
Commencement Information
I43. Sch. 15 para. 42 in force at 29.12.2003 by S.I. 2003/3142, art. 3. (1), Sch. 1 (with art. 11)

Restrictions affecting change in control of holder of national licence

43. (1)Section 103 of the 1990 Act (restrictions on change of control of national licence) shall be

amended as follows.

(2) For "the Authority" and "The Authority", wherever occurring, there shall be substituted "OFCOM ".

(3) In subsection (2) (interpretation)—

(a) in the definition of "associated programme provider", for the words from "appears" to "inclusion" there shall be substituted " is or is likely to be involved, to a substantial extent, in the provision of the programmes included "; and

(b) in the words after the definition of "the relevant period", for the words from "as if" onwards there shall be substituted " as it has effect for the purposes of that Schedule. "

Commencement Information

I44. Sch. 15 para. 43 in force at 29.12.2003 by S.I. 2003/3142, art. 3. (1), Sch. 1 (with art. 11)

Renewal of national licences

44. (1)Section 103. A of the 1990 Act (renewal of national licences) shall be amended as follows.

(2) For "the Authority", wherever occurring, there shall be substituted " OFCOM ".

(3) In subsection (1), for "eight" there shall be substituted " twelve ".

(4) In subsection (2), after "not later than" there shall be inserted " the day falling three months before ".

(5) In subsection (3), paragraph (a) and in paragraph (b) the words "in any other case" shall cease to have effect.

(6) In subsection (4), for paragraph (b) there shall be substituted—

"(b)the applicant gave notice to OFCOM, within the period of one month beginning with the commencement of section 42 of the Broadcasting Act 1996, of his intention to provide a simulcast radio service, and".

(7) For subsection (7) there shall be substituted—

"(7)The amount determined under subsection (6)(b) must be equal to the amount which, in OFCOM's opinion, would have been the cash bid of the licence holder were the licence (instead of being renewed) to be granted for the period of the renewal on an application made in accordance with section 98.

(7. A)For the purposes of subsection (6)(c)—

(a) different percentages may be specified for different accounting periods; and

(b) the percentages that may be specified for an accounting period include a nil percentage."

(8) After subsection (10) there shall be inserted—

"(10. A)In the case of a pre-transfer national licence (including one for a period extended under section 253 of the Communications Act 2003)—

(a) the licence is not to be capable of being renewed under this section if it has already been renewed under this section before the radio transfer date; and

(b) on the renewal of the licence, it shall be the duty of OFCOM to secure that the renewed licence contains only such provision as would be included in a national licence granted by OFCOM under this Part after the radio transfer date."

(9) After subsection (11) there shall be inserted—

"(12)A determination for the purposes of subsection (11)—

(a) must be made at least one year before the date determined; and

(b) must be notified by OFCOM to the person who holds the licence in question."

Commencement Information

I45. Sch. 15 para. 44 in force at 29.12.2003 by S.I. 2003/3142, art. 3. (1), Sch. 1 (with art. 11)

Applications for local licences

45. (1)Section 104 of the 1990 Act (application for local licences) shall be amended as follows.

(2) For "the Authority" and "The Authority", wherever occurring, there shall be substituted "

OFCOM ".

(3) In subsection (6), for the words from the beginning to "shall be made" there shall be substituted " An application for a licence to provide a restricted service shall be made ".

Commencement Information

I46. Sch. 15 para. 45 in force at 29.12.2003 by S.I. 2003/3142, art. 3. (1), Sch. 1 (with art. 11)

Renewal of local licences

46. (1)Section 104. A of the 1990 Act (renewal of local licences) shall be amended as follows.

(2) For "the Authority" and "The Authority", wherever occurring, there shall be substituted " OFCOM ".

(3) In subsection (1), for "eight" there shall be substituted " twelve ".

(4) In subsection (3), after "not later than" there shall be inserted " the day falling three months before ".

(5) After subsection (12) there shall be inserted—

"(12. A)In the case of a pre-transfer local licence (including one for a period extended under section 253 of the Communications Act 2003)—

(a) the licence is not to be capable of being renewed under this section if it has already been renewed under this section before the radio transfer date; and

(b) on the renewal of the licence, it shall be the duty of OFCOM to secure that the renewed licence contains only such provision as would be included in a local licence granted by OFCOM under this Part after the radio transfer date."

(6) In subsection (13)(d), for "paragraph 3. A of Part I of Schedule 2" there shall be substituted " paragraph 8. (2) of Schedule 14 to the Communications Act 2003 ".

(7) After subsection (13) there shall be inserted—

"(14)A determination for the purposes of subsection (13)(c)—

(a) must be made at least one year before the date determined; and

(b) must be notified by OFCOM to the person who holds the licence in question."

Commencement Information

I47. Sch. 15 para. 46 in force at 29.12.2003 by S.I. 2003/3142, art. 3. (1), Sch. 1 (with art. 11)

Special procedure for applications for local licences

47. (1)Section 104. B of the 1990 Act (special procedure for applications for local licences) shall be amended as follows.

(2) For "the Authority", wherever occurring, there shall be substituted " OFCOM ".

(3) After subsection (1) there shall be inserted—

"(1. A)In subsection (1)(c) the reference to the service in question, in relation to a case in which it is a pre-transfer local licence that is due to expire, is a reference to the equivalent local service for which a licence is capable of being granted at times on or after the radio transfer date."

Commencement Information

I48. Sch. 15 para. 47 in force at 29.12.2003 by S.I. 2003/3142, art. 3. (1), Sch. 1 (with art. 11)

Special requirements relating to grant of local licences

48. (1)Section 105 of the 1990 Act (special requirements relating to grant of local licences) shall be amended as follows.

(2) For "the Authority" there shall be substituted " OFCOM ".

(3) For paragraph (d) (duty to have regard to the extent to which proposed service supported by persons living in the area) there shall be substituted—

"(d)the extent to which there is evidence that, amongst persons living in that area or locality, there is a demand for, or support for, the provision of the proposed service."

Commencement Information
I49. Sch. 15 para. 48 in force at 29.12.2003 by S.I. 2003/3142, art. 3. (1), Sch. 1 (with art. 11)

Requirements as to character and coverage of services

49. In subsections (1) to (4) and (6) of section 106 of the 1990 Act (requirements as to character and coverage of services), for "the Authority", wherever occurring, there shall be substituted " OFCOM ".

Commencement Information
I50. Sch. 15 para. 49 in force at 29.12.2003 by S.I. 2003/3142, art. 3. (1), Sch. 1 (with art. 11)

Enforcement of licences

50. In sections 109 to 111. A of the 1990 Act (enforcement of licences), for "the Authority" and "The Authority", wherever occurring, there shall be substituted " OFCOM ".

Commencement Information
I51. Sch. 15 para. 50 in force at 29.12.2003 by S.I. 2003/3142, art. 3. (1), Sch. 1 (with art. 11)

Power to suspend licences to provide radio licensable content services from a satellite

51. (1)Section 111. B of the 1990 Act (power to suspend licence to provide satellite service) shall be amended as follows.

(2) For "the Authority", wherever occurring, there shall be substituted " OFCOM ".

(3) In subsection (1)—

(a) in paragraph (a), for "satellite service" there shall be substituted " radio licensable content service ";

(b) in paragraph (b), for the words from "included in the licence" to the end of the paragraph there shall be substituted " which in compliance with section 263 of the Communications Act 2003 is included in the licence for the purpose of securing the objective mentioned in section 319. (2)(b) of that Act, and ".

Commencement Information
I52. Sch. 15 para. 51 in force at 29.12.2003 by S.I. 2003/3142, art. 3. (1), Sch. 1 (with art. 11)

Additional radio services

52. (1)Section 114 of the 1990 Act (additional radio services) shall be amended as follows.

(2) In subsection (1)—

(a) for "telecommunication" there shall be substituted " electronic "; and

(b) for paragraphs (a) and (b) there shall be substituted " on a relevant frequency ".

(3) In subsection (2), for paragraphs (a) and (b) there shall be substituted "any part of the signals which—

(a) is not required for the purposes of the sound broadcasting service for the purposes of which the frequency has been made available; and

(b) is determined by OFCOM to be available for the provision of additional services;".

(4) After that subsection there shall be inserted—

"(2. A)At any time while an additional services licence is in force, OFCOM may, if they consider it appropriate to do so, modify or further modify the determination made for the purposes of that licence under subsection (2)(b); and where there has been such a modification or further modification, the licence shall have effect accordingly.

471

(2. B)A modification or further modification under subsection (2. A) must not reduce the amount of spare capacity made available for the licensed services."

(5) In subsection (3), for the words from the beginning to "subsection (2)(a)" there shall be substituted " OFCOM shall, when determining under subsection (2) ".

(6) For subsection (6) there shall be substituted—

"(6)In this section "electronic signal" means a signal within the meaning of section 32 of the Communications Act 2003.

(7) In this section and section 115 "relevant frequency" means a frequency made available by OFCOM for the purposes of a sound broadcasting service."

(7) This paragraph does not affect the validity of a licence granted or last renewed before the radio transfer date, or the services licensed by any such licence.

Commencement Information

I53. Sch. 15 para. 52. (1)(2)(a) in force at 25.7.2003 by S.I. 2003/1900, art. 2. (1), Sch. 1

I54. Sch. 15 para. 52. (2)(b) (3)-(7) in force at 29.12.2003 by S.I. 2003/3142, art. 3. (1), Sch. 1 (with art. 11)

Licensing of additional radio services

53. (1)Section 115 of the 1990 Act (licensing of additional radio services) shall be amended as follows.

(2) For "The Authority" and "the Authority", wherever occurring, there shall be substituted " OFCOM ".

(3) In subsection (1), for the words from "of the following" to "114. (1)(b)" there shall be substituted " relevant frequency ".

(4) In subsection (4), at the end there shall be inserted " and who would not be in contravention of the requirements imposed by or under Schedule 14 to the Communications Act 2003 if he held such a licence ".

(5) In subsection (8), for "local, restricted or satellite service" there shall be substituted " local or restricted service or to provide a radio licensable content service ".

Commencement Information

I55. Sch. 15 para. 53. (1) (4) in force at 18.9.2003 by S.I. 2003/1900, art. 2. (2), Sch. 2

I56. Sch. 15 para. 53. (2) (3) (5) in force at 29.12.2003 by S.I. 2003/3142, art. 3. (1), Sch. 1 (with art. 11)

Applications for additional radio services licences

54. (1)Section 116 of the 1990 Act (applications for additional radio services licences) shall be amended as follows.

(2) For "the Authority" and "The Authority", wherever occurring, there shall be substituted " OFCOM ".

(3) In subsection (1)(b)(iii), the words "(subject to the approval of the Secretary of State)" shall be omitted.

Commencement Information

I57. Sch. 15 para. 54 in force at 29.12.2003 by S.I. 2003/3142, art. 3. (1), Sch. 1 (with art. 11)

Procedure for awarding additional radio services licences

55. (1)Section 117 of the 1990 Act (procedure for awarding additional radio services licences) shall be amended as follows.

(2) For "the Authority", wherever occurring, there shall be substituted " OFCOM ".

(3) In subsection (1), for paragraph (a) (requirement of approval of technical plans) there shall be

substituted—

"(a)that the technical plan submitted under section 116. (3)(b), in so far as it involves the use of an electronic communications network (within the meaning of the Communications Act 2003), contains proposals that are acceptable to them; and".

(4) Subsections (2) and (7) shall cease to have effect.

Commencement Information

I58. Sch. 15 para. 55 in force at 29.12.2003 by S.I. 2003/3142, art. 3. (1), Sch. 1 (with art. 11)

Additional payments in respect of additional radio services licences

56. In section 118 of the 1990 Act (additional payments in respect of additional radio services licences), for "the Authority", wherever occurring, there shall be substituted " OFCOM ".

Commencement Information

I59. Sch. 15 para. 56 in force at 29.12.2003 by S.I. 2003/3142, art. 3. (1), Sch. 1 (with art. 11)

Additional radio services not to interfere with other transmissions

57. (1)Section 119 of the 1990 Act (additional radio services not to interfere with other transmissions) shall be amended as follows.

(2) In subsection (1), for "the Authority" there shall be substituted " OFCOM ".

(3) Subsection (2) shall cease to have effect.

Commencement Information

I60. Sch. 15 para. 57 in force at 29.12.2003 by S.I. 2003/3142, art. 3. (1), Sch. 1 (with art. 11)

Enforcement of additional radio services licences

58. In section 120 of the 1990 Act (enforcement of additional radio services licences), for "the Authority" and "The Authority", wherever occurring, there shall be substituted " OFCOM ".

Commencement Information

I61. Sch. 15 para. 58 in force at 29.12.2003 by S.I. 2003/3142, art. 3. (1), Sch. 1 (with art. 11)

Interpretation

59. In subsection (1) of section 126 of the 1990 Act (interpretation of Part 3)—

(a) for the definition of "independent radio service" there shall be substituted—

""independent radio service" means a service falling to be regulated under section 245 of the Communications Act 2003;";

(b) for the definitions of "local service", "national service", "restricted service" and "satellite service" there shall be substituted—

""local service", "national service" and "restricted service" each has the same meaning as in section 245 of the Communications Act 2003;

"pre-transfer local licence" and "pre-transfer national licence" each has the same meaning as in section 253 of that Act;

"radio licensable content service" has the same meaning as in Part 3 of that Act;

"radio transfer date" has the same meaning as in that Act;";

(c) in the definition of "sound broadcasting service" for the words from "(as defined" to the end there shall be substituted " (within the meaning of Part 3 of the Communications Act 2003); ".

Commencement Information

I62. Sch. 15 para. 59 in force at 29.12.2003 by S.I. 2003/3142, art. 3. (1), Sch. 1 (with art. 11)

Duty to provide advance information about programmes

60. In column 1 of the Table in section 176. (7) of the 1990 Act (persons who are the providers of services for the purposes of the obligations to give advance information about programmes)—
(a) for "regulation by the Independent Television Commission" there shall be substituted " regulation by OFCOM ";
(b) for "The television broadcasting service provided by the Welsh Authority and the service referred to in section 57. (1. A)(a)" there shall be substituted " The public television services of the Welsh Authority (within the meaning of Part 2 of Schedule 12 to the Communications Act 2003) ";
(c) for "section 84. (2)(a)(i)" there shall be substituted " section 126. (1) ";
(d) for "the Radio Authority", in both places, there shall be substituted " OFCOM ".
Commencement Information
163. Sch. 15 para. 60 in force at 29.12.2003 by S.I. 2003/3142, art. 3. (1), Sch. 1 (with art. 11)

Proscription of foreign satellite services

61. (1)Section 177 of the 1990 Act (proscription of foreign satellite stations) shall be amended as follows.
(2) In subsection (2), for "the Independent Television Commission or the Radio Authority consider that the quality of any relevant" there shall be substituted " OFCOM consider that the quality of any ".
(3) In subsection (3), for the words from the beginning to "Authority" there shall be substituted " OFCOM ".
(4) In subsection (6), the definition of "relevant foreign satellite service" shall be omitted.
Commencement Information
164. Sch. 15 para. 61 in force at 29.12.2003 by S.I. 2003/3142, art. 3. (1), Sch. 1 (with art. 11)

Financing of Gaelic Broadcasting

62. (1)Section 183 of the 1990 Act (financing of Gaelic Broadcasting) shall be amended as follows.
(2) For "the Commission", wherever occurring, there shall be substituted " OFCOM ".
(3) In subsection (2), for "by them under this section to be" there shall be substituted " by the Independent Television Commission under this section and ".
(4) This paragraph—
(a) so far as it relates to subsection (1) of section 183 has effect in relation only to financial years beginning after the television transfer date; and
(b) so far as it relates to subsection (2) of that section does not apply to amounts paid for earlier financial years.
Commencement Information
165. Sch. 15 para. 62 in force at 29.12.2003 by S.I. 2003/3142, art. 3. (1), Sch. 1 (with art. 11)

Gaelic Broadcasting in Scotland

63. (1)Section 184 of the 1990 Act (broadcasting of programmes in Gaelic on Channel 3 in Scotland) shall be amended as follows.
(2) In subsection (1), for the words "subsection (2)" there shall be substituted " subsection (1)(a) ".
(3) In subsection (3), for the words from "The conditions" to "the purpose of" there shall be substituted " The regulatory regime for a service to which this section applies includes the conditions that OFCOM consider appropriate for ".

(4) After that subsection there shall be inserted—

"(3. A)Section 263 of the Communications Act 2003 (regulatory regime) applies in relation to conditions included by virtue of subsection (3) in the regulatory regime for a licensed service as it applies in relation to conditions which are so included by virtue of a provision of Chapter 4 of Part 3 of that Act."

(5) In subsection (4)(b), for "the Commission" there shall be substituted " OFCOM ".

Commencement Information

I66. Sch. 15 para. 63 in force at 29.12.2003 by S.I. 2003/3142, art. 3. (1), Sch. 1 (with art. 11)

Maintenance of the national television archive

64. (1)In section 185 of the 1990 Act (maintenance of the national television archive)—

(a) for "The Commission" and "the Commission", wherever occurring, there shall be substituted " OFCOM ".

(b) in subsection (5), the definition of "the Commission" shall be omitted.

(2) This paragraph so far as it relates to subsection (1) of that section has effect in relation only to financial years beginning after the television transfer date.

Commencement Information

I67. Sch. 15 para. 64 in force at 29.12.2003 by S.I. 2003/3142, art. 3. (1), Sch. 1 (with art. 11)

Modification of networking arrangements

65. (1)Section 193 of the 1990 Act (modification of networking arrangements in consequence of competition legislation) shall be amended as follows.

(2) In subsection (1), for the words from "the Office of Fair Trading" to "relevant authority')" there shall be substituted " the relevant authority ".

(3) After subsection (2) there shall be inserted—

"(2. A)In subsection (1), "relevant authority" means—

　(a) in relation to a relevant order falling within subsection (2)(a), the Office of Fair Trading, the Competition Commission or (as the case may be) the Secretary of State;

　(b) in relation to a relevant order falling within subsection (2)(b), the Office of Fair Trading, the Competition Commission, the Secretary of State or (as the case may be) OFCOM."

(4) In subsection (4), for "section 39. (1) above" there shall be substituted " section 290. (4) of the Communications Act 2003 ".

Commencement Information

I68. Sch. 15 para. 65 in force at 29.12.2003 by S.I. 2003/3142, art. 3. (1), Sch. 1 (with art. 11)

Search warrants

66. (1)Section 196 of the 1990 Act (grant of search warrant to person authorised by the Independent Television Commission or the Radio Authority) shall be amended as follows.

(2) In subsection (1), for "the relevant authority" there shall be substituted " OFCOM ".

(3) Subsection (2) (definition of "relevant authority") shall be omitted.

Commencement Information

I69. Sch. 15 para. 66 in force at 29.12.2003 by S.I. 2003/3142, art. 3. (1), Sch. 1 (with art. 11)

Notices

67. In section 199. (5) of the 1990 Act (publication of notices), for paragraphs (a) and (b) there shall be substituted " by OFCOM under section 21, 41, 42, 55, 103, 109, 110, 111 or 120 ".

Commencement Information

Interpretation

68. (1)Section 202 of the 1990 Act (general interpretation) shall be amended as follows.

(2) In subsection (1), after the definition of "modifications" there shall be inserted—

""OFCOM" means the Office of Communications;".

(3) After subsection (6) there shall be inserted—

"(6. A)Subsections (2) and (3) of section 362 of the Communications Act 2003 (persons by whom services provided) are to apply for the purposes of this Act as they apply for the purposes of Part 3 of that Act."

Commencement Information

I71. Sch. 15 para. 68 in force at 29.12.2003 by S.I. 2003/3142, art. 3. (1), Sch. 1 (with art. 11)

Disqualified persons

69. (1)Schedule 2 to the 1990 Act (restrictions on the holding of licences) shall be amended as follows.

(2) In paragraph 1. (1) of Part 1, after the definition of "associate" there shall be inserted—

""Broadcasting Act licence" means a licence under Part 1 or 3 of this Act or Part 1 or 2 of the Broadcasting Act 1996;".

(3) In paragraph 1. (6) of Part 1 (meaning of "more than a 20 per cent. interest"), for "20 per cent.", wherever occurring, there shall be substituted " 5 per cent. ".

(4) In Part 2 (disqualified persons), for "a licence granted by the Commission or the Authority", wherever occurring, there shall be substituted " a Broadcasting Act licence ".

(5) In paragraph 1. (1)(i) of Part 2 (bodies controlled by persons falling within paragraphs (a) to (g)), for "(a)" there shall be substituted " (c) ".

(6) In paragraph 3. (1) of Part 2, for "by the Authority" there shall be substituted " under Part 3 of this Act or Part 2 of the Broadcasting Act 1996 ".

(7) In paragraph 4. (1) of Part 2, for "that body" there shall be substituted " OFCOM ".

(8) In paragraph 4. (2) of Part 2—

(a) in paragraph (a), for "by the Commission, means a body" there shall be substituted " under Part 1 of this Act or Part 1 of the Broadcasting Act 1996, means a person "; and

(b) in paragraph (b), for "by the Authority, means a body" there shall be substituted " under Part 3 of this Act or Part 2 of the Broadcasting Act 1996, means a person ".

(9) In paragraph 5. A of Part 2—

(a) in sub-paragraph (1)(a), the words "granted by the Commission",

(b) sub-paragraph (1)(b) and the word "and" immediately preceding it,

(c) in sub-paragraph (2), the words "granted by the Authority",

shall be omitted.

Commencement Information

I72. Sch. 15 para. 69 in force at 29.12.2003 by S.I. 2003/3142, art. 3. (1), Sch. 1 (with art. 11)

C4. C

70. (1)Schedule 3 to the 1990 Act (provision about constitution and management of C4. C) shall be amended as follows.

(2) For "the Commission", wherever occurring, there shall be substituted " OFCOM ".

(3) In paragraph 2. (1) (persons disqualified from membership of the Corporation), for paragraphs (b) to (d) there shall be substituted "or

  (b) a member or employee of OFCOM."

173. Sch. 15 para. 70 in force at 29.12.2003 by S.I. 2003/3142, art. 3. (1), Sch. 1 (with art. 11)

The Welsh Authority

71. (1)Schedule 6 to the 1990 Act (provision about constitution and management of the Welsh Authority) shall be amended as follows.
(2) In paragraph 2 (persons disqualified from membership of the Authority)—
(a) sub-paragraph (1) shall be omitted; and
(b) in sub-paragraph (2)(b), for "the Commission" there shall be substituted " OFCOM ".
(3) In paragraph 12. (1. A), for the words from "the general fund" onwards there shall be substituted " the assets of the Authority that are not comprised in that fund; and accordingly, the statement must deal with liabilities separately according to whether they fall to be met from that fund or from those assets. "
Commencement Information
174. Sch. 15 para. 71 in force at 29.12.2003 by S.I. 2003/3142, art. 3. (1), Sch. 1 (with art. 11)

Computation of qualifying revenue

72. (1)Schedule 7 to the 1990 Act (computation of "qualifying revenue") shall be amended as follows.
(2) In Part 1, for "the Commission" and "The Commission", wherever occurring, there shall be substituted " OFCOM ".
(3) In Part 2, for "the Authority" and "The Authority", wherever occurring, there shall be substituted " OFCOM ".
Commencement Information
175. Sch. 15 para. 72 in force at 29.12.2003 by S.I. 2003/3142, art. 3. (1), Sch. 1 (with art. 11)

The Gaelic Television Committee

73. (1)Schedule 19 to the 1990 Act (Gaelic Television Committee) shall be amended as follows.
(2) For "the Commission" and "The Commission", wherever occurring, there shall be substituted " OFCOM ".
(3) For "Committee", wherever occurring, there shall be substituted " Service ".
(4) In paragraph 8. (c), the words "and (where the expenses relate to the Commission's functions in connection with sound programmes) the Radio Authority" shall be omitted.
(5) In paragraph 11. (4), the words "or the Radio Authority" and "or (as the case may be) the Authority" shall be omitted.
Commencement Information
176. Sch. 15 para. 73 in force at 29.12.2003 by S.I. 2003/3142, art. 3. (1), Sch. 1 (with art. 11)

Part 2. Amendments of the 1996 Act

Multiplex services and digital programme services

74. (1)Section 1 of the 1996 Act (interpretation) shall be amended as follows.
(2) For subsection (1) there shall be substituted—
"(1)In this Part "multiplex service" means (except where the context otherwise requires) a television multiplex service."
(3) In subsection (4), for "for general reception" there shall be substituted " so as to be available

477

for reception by members of the public ".

(4) For subsection (4. A) there shall be substituted—

"(4. A)In subsection (4), "available for reception by members of the public" means available for reception by members of the public (within the meaning of Part 3 of the Communications Act 2003) in the United Kingdom or another EEA State, or in an area of the United Kingdom or of such a State."

(5) For subsection (7) of that section there shall be substituted—

"(7)In this section "broadcast" means broadcast otherwise than from a satellite."

Commencement Information

I77. Sch. 15 para. 74 in force at 29.12.2003 by S.I. 2003/3142, art. 3. (1), Sch. 1 (with art. 11)

Meaning of qualifying service

75. In section 2 of the 1996 Act (meaning of "qualifying service" etc.), for subsections (2) to (6) there shall be substituted—

"(2)In this Part "qualifying service" means any of the following, so far as they are provided with a view to their being broadcast in digital form—

   (a) a television broadcasting service included in Channel 3;

   (b) Channel 4;

   (c) Channel 5;

   (d) S4. C Digital;

   (e) a television programme service provided by the Welsh Authority with the approval of the Secretary of State under section 205 of the Communications Act 2003;

   (f) the digital public teletext service."

Commencement Information

I78. Sch. 15 para. 75 in force at 29.12.2003 by S.I. 2003/3142, art. 3. (1), Sch. 1 (with art. 11)

Licences under Part 1.

76. (1)Section 3 of the 1996 Act (licences under Part 1 of that Act) shall be amended as follows.

(2) In subsection (1), for "the Independent Television Commission (in this Part referred to as the "the Commission")" there shall be substituted " OFCOM ".

(3) In subsections (3) to (7), for "The Commission" and "the Commission", wherever occurring, there shall be substituted " OFCOM ".

(4) For subsection (8) there shall be substituted—

"(8)The holding by a person of a licence under this Part shall not relieve him of—

   (a) any liability in respect of a failure to hold a licence under section 1 of the Wireless Telegraphy Act 1949; or

   (b) any obligation to comply with requirements imposed by or under Chapter 1 of Part 2 of the Communications Act 2003 (electronic communications networks and electronic communications services)."

Commencement Information

I79. Sch. 15 para. 76 in force at 29.12.2003 by S.I. 2003/3142, art. 3. (1), Sch. 1 (with art. 11)

Licence conditions

77. (1)Section 4 of the 1996 Act (general licence conditions) shall be amended as follows.

(2) For "the Commission", wherever occurring, there shall be substituted " OFCOM ".

(3) In subsection (1), in each of paragraphs (a) and (c), for "the 1990 Act or this Act" there shall be substituted " this Act, the 1990 Act or the Communications Act 2003 ".

(4) In subsection (3) (fixing fees), the words from "and the amount" onwards shall be omitted.

Commencement Information
180. Sch. 15 para. 77 in force at 29.12.2003 by S.I. 2003/3142, art. 3. (1), Sch. 1 (with art. 11)

Restrictions on digital licence holding

78. (1)Section 5 of the 1996 Act (restrictions on holding licences) shall be amended as follows.

(2) For "The Commission" and "the Commission", wherever occurring, there shall be substituted " OFCOM ".

(3) In subsection (2) (incidental requirements to provide information), after paragraph (d) there shall be inserted—

"(da)impose conditions in a licence requiring the licence holder, if a body corporate, to give OFCOM notice, after they have occurred and irrespective of whether proposals for them have fallen to be notified, of changes, transactions or events affecting—

(i) shareholdings in the body; or

(ii) the directors of the body;

(db) impose conditions in a licence enabling OFCOM to require the licence holder to provide them with such information as they may reasonably require for determining—

(i) whether the licence holder is a disqualified person in relation to that licence by virtue of Part 2 of Schedule 2 to the 1990 Act; or

(ii) whether any such requirements as are mentioned in subsection (1)(b) have been and are being complied with by or in relation to the licence holder;".

(4) In subsection (6)—

(a) in paragraph (a), for "complained of" there shall be substituted " constituting their grounds for revoking the licence ".

(b) in paragraph (b)(i), for "Parts III and IV of Schedule 2 to the 1990 Act" there shall be substituted " the requirements imposed by or under Schedule 14 to the Communications Act 2003 ".

(5) In subsection (7)—

(a) paragraph (a) shall cease to have effect; and

(b) in paragraph (b), for "Part IV of that Schedule" there shall be substituted " Part 1 of Schedule 14 to the Communications Act 2003 ".

(6) In subsection (8), for the words from "a failure" to the end of paragraph (c) there shall be substituted " a disqualification under Part 2 of Schedule 2 to the 1990 Act or a contravention of a requirement imposed by or under Schedule 14 to the Communications Act 2003, ".

Commencement Information
181. Sch. 15 para. 78 in force at 29.12.2003 by S.I. 2003/3142, art. 3. (1), Sch. 1 (with art. 11)

Multiplex licences

79. (1)Section 7 of the 1996 Act (multiplex licences) shall be amended as follows.

(2) For "the Commission" and "The Commission", wherever occurring, there shall be substituted " OFCOM ".

(3) In subsection (4)—

(a) after paragraph (c) there shall be inserted—

"(ca)the applicant's proposals as to the number (if any) of digital sound programmes services which are to be broadcast, as to the characteristics of each of those services and as to the areas in which they would be provided;"

(b) in paragraph (d) for "those services" there shall be substituted " the services mentioned in paragraphs (c) and (ca) ".

Commencement Information
182. Sch. 15 para. 79 in force at 29.12.2003 by S.I. 2003/3142, art. 3. (1), Sch. 1 (with art. 11)

Award of multiplex licences

80. (1)Section 8 of the 1996 Act (award of multiplex licences) shall be amended as follows.
(2) For "the Commission", wherever occurring, there shall be substituted " OFCOM ".
(3) In subsection (2)(f), after "digital programme service" there shall be inserted " , digital sound programme service ".
Commencement Information
I83. Sch. 15 para. 80 in force at 29.12.2003 by S.I. 2003/3142, art. 3. (1), Sch. 1 (with art. 11)

Power to require two or more multiplex licences to be granted to one person

81. In section 9 of the 1996 Act (grant of two or more multiplex licences to one person), for "The Commission" and "the Commission", wherever occurring, there shall be substituted " OFCOM ".
Commencement Information
I84. Sch. 15 para. 81 in force at 29.12.2003 by S.I. 2003/3142, art. 3. (1), Sch. 1 (with art. 11)

Award of multiplex licences subject to conditions

82. (1)Section 10 of the 1996 Act (award of multiplex licences subject to conditions) shall be amended as follows.
(2) For "The Commission" and "the Commission", wherever occurring, there shall be substituted " OFCOM ".
(3) In subsection (1)(a), for "the 1990 Act or this Act" there shall be substituted " this Act, the 1990 Act or Part 3 of the Communications Act 2003 ".
Commencement Information
I85. Sch. 15 para. 82 in force at 29.12.2003 by S.I. 2003/3142, art. 3. (1), Sch. 1 (with art. 11)

Failure to provide licensed service and revocation

83. In section 11 of the 1996 Act (failure to provide licensed service and revocation), for "the Commission", wherever occurring, there shall be substituted " OFCOM ".
Commencement Information
I86. Sch. 15 para. 83 in force at 29.12.2003 by S.I. 2003/3142, art. 3. (1), Sch. 1 (with art. 11)

Conditions attached to multiplex licences

84. In section 12 of the 1996 Act (conditions attached to multiplex licences), for "the Commission", wherever occurring, there shall be substituted " OFCOM ".
Commencement Information
I87. Sch. 15 para. 84 in force at 29.12.2003 by S.I. 2003/3142, art. 3. (1), Sch. 1 (with art. 11)

Additional payments in respect of multiplex licences

85. In section 13 of the 1996 Act (additional payments in respect of multiplex licences), for "the Commission", wherever occurring, there shall be substituted " OFCOM ".
Commencement Information
I88. Sch. 15 para. 85 in force at 29.12.2003 by S.I. 2003/3142, art. 3. (1), Sch. 1 (with art. 11)

Multiplex revenue

86. (1)Section 14 of the 1996 Act (multiplex revenue) shall be amended as follows.

(2) In subsection (1)—

(a) for "section 13. (1)" there shall be substituted " this Part ";

(b) for "the holder of a multiplex licence" there shall be substituted " the person who is the multiplex provider in relation to any television multiplex service or any general multiplex service ";

(c) in paragraph (a), for "the multiplex service to which the licence relates" there shall be substituted " the relevant multiplex ";

(d) in paragraph (b) for "of any qualifying service by means of the multiplex service" there shall be substituted " by means of the multiplex service of any service which is a qualifying service or which (without being a qualifying service) is provided by the BBC ";

(e) in paragraphs (c) and (d), for "the holder of the multiplex licence" and "the multiplex service", in each place where they occur there shall be substituted, respectively, " the multiplex provider " and " the relevant multiplex ".

(3) In subsections (2) to (8)—

(a) for the words "the holder of the multiplex licence" and "the licence holder", wherever occurring, there shall be substituted, in each case, " the multiplex provider "; and

(b) for "the Commission", wherever occurring, there shall be substituted " OFCOM ".

(4) In subsection (9)—

(a) for "a multiplex licence", in each place, there shall be substituted " a television multiplex service or a general multiplex service ";

(b) for "the multiplex service to which the licence relates", in each place, there shall be substituted " that multiplex service ";

(c) after the definition of "additional services provider" there shall be inserted—

""multiplex provider"—

(a) in relation to a television multiplex service for which a person holds a licence under this Part, means the licence holder; and

(b) in relation to a television multiplex service which is not licensed under this Part or a general multiplex service, means the person who provides that service;"

(d) after the definition of "programme provider" there shall be inserted—

""the relevant multiplex"—

(a) in relation to a multiplex provider falling within paragraph (a) of the definition of that expression, means the television multiplex service to which his licence relates; and

(b) in relation to any other multiplex provider, means the television multiplex service or general multiplex service which is provided by him;

and this section and section 15 shall have effect as if references in this section to digital programme services included references to digital sound programme services and references to digital additional services included references to digital additional services within the meaning of Part 2."

Commencement Information

I89. Sch. 15 para. 86 in force at 29.12.2003 by S.I. 2003/3142, art. 3. (1), Sch. 1 (with art. 11)

Attribution of multiplex revenue to multiplex providers

87. (1)Section 15 of the 1996 Act (attribution of multiplex revenue to licence holder) shall be amended as follows.

(2) In subsection (1)—

(a) for "the holder of a multiplex licence" there shall be substituted " the person who is the multiplex provider in relation to any television multiplex service ";

(b) for "of multiplex services in that period," there shall be substituted " in that period of television multiplex services, ";

(c) for "the holder of the multiplex licence" there shall be substituted, " the multiplex provider ".

(3) In subsection (2)—

(a) for "a multiplex service" there shall be substituted " a television multiplex service or a general multiplex service ";

(b) for "the holder of the multiplex licence", wherever occurring, there shall be substituted " the multiplex provider ".

(4) In subsection (3)—

(a) for "the Commission" there shall be substituted " OFCOM "; and

(b) for "the holder of the multiplex licence" there shall be substituted " the multiplex provider ".

(5) In subsection (4)—

(a) after "additional services provider" there shall be inserted " , 'multiplex provider' "; and

(b) for "a multiplex licence" there shall be substituted " a television multiplex service or a general multiplex service ".

Commencement Information

I90. Sch. 15 para. 87 in force at 29.12.2003 by S.I. 2003/3142, art. 3. (1), Sch. 1 (with art. 11)

Duration of multiplex licences

88. (1)Section 16 of the 1996 Act (duration and renewal of multiplex licences) shall be amended as follows.

(2) For "the Commission", wherever occurring, there shall be substituted " OFCOM ".

(3) In subsection (3), after "not later than" there shall be inserted " the day falling three months before ".

(4) After subsection (12), there shall be inserted—

"(12. A)A determination for the purposes of subsection (12)—

   (a) must be made at least one year before the date determined; and

   (b) must be notified by OFCOM to the person who holds the licence in question."

Commencement Information

191. Sch. 15 para. 88 in force at 29.12.2003 by S.I. 2003/3142, art. 3. (1), Sch. 1 (with art. 11)

Enforcement of multiplex licences

89. In section 17 of the 1996 Act (enforcement of multiplex licences), for "the Commission" and "The Commission", wherever occurring, there shall be substituted " OFCOM ".

Commencement Information

192. Sch. 15 para. 89 in force at 29.12.2003 by S.I. 2003/3142, art. 3. (1), Sch. 1 (with art. 11)

Licensing of digital programme services

90. (1)Section 18 of the 1996 Act (licensing of digital programme services) shall be amended as follows.

(2) In subsections (1) to (4), for "the Commission", wherever occurring, there shall be substituted " OFCOM ".

(3) Subsections (5) and (6) (application of sections 6 to 12 of the 1990 Act) shall cease to have effect.

Commencement Information

193. Sch. 15 para. 90 in force at 29.12.2003 by S.I. 2003/3142, art. 3. (1), Sch. 1 (with art. 11)

Conditions of licences for digital programme services

91. (1)Section 19 of the 1996 Act (conditions of licences for digital programme services) shall be amended as follows.

(2) In subsection (3)—

(a) for "the Commission", wherever occurring, there shall be substituted " OFCOM ";

(b) in paragraphs (a) and (c), for "the holder of a multiplex licence" there shall be substituted, in each case, " the provider of a television multiplex service or general multiplex service ";

(c) in paragraph (a), for "by means of a multiplex service" there shall be substituted " by means of that provider's service "; and

(d) in paragraph (a)(i), for "the identity of the multiplex service" there shall be substituted " the identity of the service by means of which it will be broadcast ".

(3) Subsections (2) and (4) to (10) of that section shall cease to have effect.

Commencement Information

I94. Sch. 15 para. 91 in force at 29.12.2003 by S.I. 2003/3142, art. 3. (1), Sch. 1 (with art. 11)

Duration and enforcement of multiplex licenses

92. (1)Section 23 of the 1996 Act (enforcement of digital programme licences) shall be amended as follows.

(2) For "the Commission" and "The Commission", wherever occurring, there shall be substituted " OFCOM ".

(3) In subsection (4), for the words from "multiplex service" onwards there shall be substituted " television multiplex service or general multiplex service, means the last accounting period of the multiplex provider ".

(4) In subsection (5), for "multiplex service, the first accounting period of the holder of the multiplex licence" there shall be substituted " television multiplex service or general multiplex service, the first accounting period of the multiplex provider ".

(5) After that subsection there shall be inserted—

"(5. A)In subsections (4) and (5) "multiplex provider" has the same meaning as in section 14."

(6) In subsection (8) for "apology" there shall be substituted " statement of findings ".

Commencement Information

I95. Sch. 15 para. 92 in force at 29.12.2003 by S.I. 2003/3142, art. 3. (1), Sch. 1 (with art. 11)

Digital additional services

93. (1)Section 24 of the 1996 Act (digital additional services) shall be amended as follows.

(2) In subsection (1), for paragraphs (a) and (b) there shall be substituted—

"(a)is provided by a person with a view to its being broadcast in digital form (whether by him or some other person) so as to be available for reception by members of the public;

(b) is so provided with a view either—

(i) to the broadcasting being by means of a television multiplex service or by means of a general multiplex service; or

(ii) to the members of the public in question being or including members of the public in an EEA State other than the United Kingdom, or in an area of such a State;

and

(c) is not a Channel 3 service, Channel 4, Channel 5, a public television service of the Welsh Authority, the digital public teletext service, a digital programme service, a digital sound programme service, an ancillary service or a technical service."

(3) In subsection (2) (meaning of ancillary service)—

(a) for "an independent analogue broadcaster" there shall be substituted " a relevant public service broadcaster "; and

(b) for paragraphs (a) and (b) there shall be substituted—

"(a)assistance for disabled people in relation to some or all of the programmes included in a digital programme service or qualifying service provided by him;

(b) a service (apart from advertising) that relates to the promotion or listing of programmes included in such a service or in a digital sound programme service so provided; or

(c) any other service (apart from advertising) that is ancillary to one or more programmes so included, and relates directly to their contents."

(4) In subsection (3)(a), after "digital programme services" there shall be inserted " , digital sound programme services ".

(5) After subsection (3) there shall be inserted—

"(3. A)In this section—

"assistance for disabled people" has the same meaning as in Part 3 of the Communications Act 2003;

"available for reception by members of the public" shall be construed in accordance with section 361 of that Act;

"public television service of the Welsh Authority" means—

(a) S4. C Digital; or

(b) any television programme service the provision of which by the Authority is authorised by or under section 205 of that Act and which is provided in digital form;

"relevant public service broadcaster" means any of the following—

(a) a person licensed under Part 1 of the 1990 Act to provide a Channel 3 service;

(b) the Channel 4 Corporation;

(c) a person licensed under Part 1 of the 1990 Act to provide Channel 5;

(d) the BBC;

(e) the Welsh Authority;

(f) the public teletext provider."

Commencement Information

I96. Sch. 15 para. 93 in force at 29.12.2003 by S.I. 2003/3142, art. 3. (1), Sch. 1 (with art. 11)

Licensing of digital additional services

94. (1)Section 25 of the 1996 Act (licensing of digital additional services) shall be amended as follows.

(2) In subsections (1) to (4), for "the Commission", wherever occurring, there shall be substituted " OFCOM ".

(3) After subsection (4) there shall be inserted—

"(4. A)A digital additional services licence is not required for a service that is or is comprised in a qualifying service."

(4) Subsections (5) and (6) (application of sections 6 to 12 of the 1990 Act) shall cease to have effect.

Commencement Information

I97. Sch. 15 para. 94 in force at 29.12.2003 by S.I. 2003/3142, art. 3. (1), Sch. 1 (with art. 11)

Conditions of digital additional services licence

95. (1)Section 26 of the 1996 Act (conditions of licences for digital additional services) shall be amended as follows.

(2) In subsection (2)—

(a) for "the Commission", wherever occurring, there shall be substituted " OFCOM ";

(b) in paragraphs (a) and (c), for "the holder of a multiplex licence" there shall be substituted, in each case, " the provider of a television multiplex service or general multiplex service ";

(c) in paragraph (a), for "by means of a multiplex service" there shall be substituted " by means of that provider's service "; and

(d) in paragraph (a)(i), for "the identity of the multiplex service" there shall be substituted " the identity of the service by means of which it will be broadcast ".

Commencement Information
I98. Sch. 15 para. 95 in force at 29.12.2003 by S.I. 2003/3142, art. 3. (1), Sch. 1 (with art. 11)

Enforcement of digital additional television services licences

96. (1)Section 27 of the 1996 Act (enforcement of digital additional television services licences) shall be amended as follows.

(2) For "the Commission" and "The Commission", wherever occurring, there shall be substituted " OFCOM ".

(3) In subsection (4), for the words from "multiplex service" onwards there shall be substituted " television multiplex service or general multiplex service, means the last accounting period of the multiplex provider ".

(4) In subsection (5), for "multiplex service, the first accounting period of the holder of the multiplex licence" there shall be substituted " television multiplex service or general multiplex service, the first accounting period of the multiplex provider ".

(5) After that subsection there shall be inserted—

"(5. A)In subsections (4) and (5) "multiplex provider" has the same meaning as in section 14."

Commencement Information
I99. Sch. 15 para. 96 in force at 29.12.2003 by S.I. 2003/3142, art. 3. (1), Sch. 1 (with art. 11)

Digital broadcasting of Gaelic programmes

97. (1)Section 32 of the 1996 Act (digital broadcasting of Gaelic programmes) shall be amended as follows.

(2) In subsection (1), for "the Commission to include in any multiplex licence granted in respect of one frequency to which section 28 applies" there shall be substituted " OFCOM to include in no more than one relevant multiplex licence ".

(3) In subsection (7), for "Comataidh Craolaidh Gaidhlig" there shall be substituted " Seirbheis nam Meadhanan Gàidhlig ".

(4) For subsection (9) there shall be substituted—

"(9)In this section—

"Gaelic" means the Gaelic language as spoken in Scotland;

"relevant multiplex licence" means a multiplex licence in respect of which the Secretary of State has made an order under section 243. (3) of the Communications Act 2003;

"television broadcasting service" has the same meaning as in Part 3 of the Communications Act 2003."

Commencement Information
I100. Sch. 15 para. 97 in force at 29.12.2003 by S.I. 2003/3142, art. 3. (1), Sch. 1 (with art. 11)

Review of digital television broadcasting

98. (1)Section 33 of the 1996 Act (review of digital television broadcasting) shall be amended as follows.

(2) For "the Commission", wherever occurring, there shall be substituted " OFCOM ".

(3) In subsection (1)(a)(ii), for the words "services specified in section 2. (3), S4. C Digital, the qualifying teletext service" there shall be substituted " following services, namely, Channel 3 services, Channel 4, Channel 5, the public television services of the Welsh Authority (within the meaning of Part 2 of Schedule 12 to the Communications Act 2003), the digital public teletext service ".

Commencement Information

Enforcement of licences held by BBC companies

99. In section 35 of the 1996 Act (enforcement of licences held by BBC companies), for "the Commission", wherever occurring, there shall be substituted " OFCOM ".
Commencement Information
I102. Sch. 15 para. 99 in force at 29.12.2003 by S.I. 2003/3142, art. 3. (1), Sch. 1 (with art. 11)

Interpretation of Part 1.

100. In section 39. (1) (interpretation of Part 1)—
(a) after the definition of "digital programme service" there shall be inserted—
""digital public teletext service" has the same meaning as in Part 3 of the Communications Act 2003;
"digital sound programme service" has the same meaning as in Part 2 of this Act;
"general multiplex service" has the same meaning as in that Part;".
(b) for the definition of "public teletext provider" there shall be substituted—
""public teletext provider" means the person for the time being licensed under Part 1 of the 1990 Act to provide the public teletext service (within the meaning of Part 3 of the Communications Act 2003);"
(c) for the definitions of "S4. C" and "on S4. C" and of "S4. C Digital" and "on S4. C Digital" there shall be substituted—
""S4. C" and "S4. C Digital" each has the same meaning as in Part 3 of the Communications Act 2003;".
(d) after the definition of "technical service" there shall be inserted—
""television multiplex service" has the meaning given by section 241 of the Communications Act 2003."
Commencement Information
I103. Sch. 15 para. 100 in force at 29.12.2003 by S.I. 2003/3142, art. 3. (1), Sch. 1 (with art. 11)

Radio multiplex services

101. (1)Section 40 of the 1996 Act (radio multiplex services) shall be amended as follows.
(2) For subsections (1) to (3) there shall be substituted—
"(1)In this Part "radio multiplex service" means a radio multiplex service within the meaning of Part 3 of the Communications Act 2003."
(3) In subsection (4) (local and national multiplex services), the words "provided on a frequency or frequencies assigned to the Authority under section 45. (1)" shall be omitted.
(4) In subsection (5), for "for general reception" there shall be substituted " so as to be available for reception by members of the public ".
(5) For subsection (8) of that section there shall be substituted—
"(8)In this section—
"available for reception by members of the public" shall be construed in accordance with section 361 of the Communications Act 2003;
"broadcast" means broadcast otherwise than from a satellite."
Commencement Information
I104. Sch. 15 para. 101 in force at 29.12.2003 by S.I. 2003/3142, art. 3. (1), Sch. 1 (with art. 11)

Licences under Part 2 of the 1996 Act

102. (1)Section 42 of the 1996 Act (licences under Part 2) shall be amended as follows.

(2) In subsection (1), for "the Radio Authority (in this Part referred to as "the Authority")" there shall be substituted " OFCOM ".

(3) In subsections (2), (5) and (6), for "The Authority" and "the Authority", wherever occurring, there shall be substituted " OFCOM ".

(4) For subsection (3) (variation of licences) there shall be substituted—

"(3)OFCOM may vary a licence by a notice served on the licence holder.

(3. A)OFCOM shall not vary—

(a) the period for which a licence having effect for a specified period is to continue in force, or

(b) increase the total amount of digital capacity specified in a national radio multiplex licence for the purposes of section 48. (1. A),

unless the licence holder consents.

(3. B)OFCOM shall not make any other variation of a licence unless the licence holder has been given a reasonable opportunity of making representations to OFCOM about the variation."

(5) In subsection (4) (exceptions from power to vary licences), for "Paragraph (a) of subsection (3)" there shall be substituted " Paragraph (a) of subsection (3. A) ".

(6) For subsection (7) there shall be substituted—

"(7)The holding of a licence by a person shall not relieve him—

(a) of any liability in respect of a failure to hold a licence under section 1 of the Wireless Telegraphy Act 1949; or

(b) of any obligation to comply with requirements imposed by or under Chapter 1 of Part 2 of the Communications Act 2003 (electronic communications networks and electronic communications services)."

Commencement Information

I105. Sch. 15 para. 102 in force at 29.12.2003 by S.I. 2003/3142, art. 3. (1), Sch. 1 (with art. 11)

General licence conditions

103. (1)Section 43 of the 1996 Act (general licence conditions) shall be amended as follows.

(2) For "the Authority", wherever occurring, there shall be substituted " OFCOM ".

(3) In subsection (1) (conditions may include conditions to give effect to duties imposed by or under 1990 Act or 1996 Act)—

(a) in paragraph (a), for "the 1990 Act or this Act" there shall be substituted " this Act, the 1990 Act or the Communications Act 2003 "; and

(b) in paragraph (d), after "this Act" there shall be inserted " , the 1990 Act or the Communications Act 2003 ".

(4) In subsection (2), sub-paragraph (ii) of paragraph (b) and the word "or" immediately preceding it shall be omitted.

(5) In subsection (3) (fixing of fees), the words from "and the amount" onwards shall be omitted.

Commencement Information

I106. Sch. 15 para. 103 in force at 29.12.2003 by S.I. 2003/3142, art. 3. (1), Sch. 1 (with art. 11)

Restrictions on holding licences

104. (1)Section 44 of the 1996 Act (restrictions on the holding of licences) shall be amended as follows.

(2) For "The Authority" and "the Authority", wherever occurring, there shall be substituted " OFCOM ".

(3) In subsection (2) (incidental requirements to provide information), after paragraph (d) there shall be inserted—

"(da)impose conditions in a licence requiring the licence holder, if a body corporate, to give OFCOM notice, after they have occurred and irrespective of whether proposals for them have

487

fallen to be notified, of changes, transactions or events affecting—

(i) shareholdings in the body; or

(ii) the directors of the body;

(db) impose conditions in a licence enabling OFCOM to require the licence holder to provide them with such information as they may reasonably require for determining—

(i) whether the licence holder is a disqualified person in relation to that licence by virtue of Part 2 of Schedule 2 to the 1990 Act; or

(ii) whether any such requirements as are mentioned in subsection (1)(b) have been and are being complied with by or in relation to the licence holder;".

(4) In subsection (6)—

(a) in paragraph (a), for "complained of" there shall be substituted " constituting their grounds for revoking the licence "; and

(b) in paragraph (b)(i), for "Parts III and IV of Schedule 2 to the 1990 Act" there shall be substituted " the requirements imposed by or under Schedule 14 to the Communications Act 2003 ".

(5) In subsection (7)—

(a) paragraph (a) shall cease to have effect; and

(b) in paragraph (b), for "Part IV of that Schedule" there shall be substituted " Part 1 of Schedule 14 to the Communications Act 2003 ".

(6) In subsection (8), for the words from "a failure" to the end of paragraph (c) there shall be substituted " a disqualification under Part 2 of Schedule 2 to the 1990 Act or a contravention of a requirement imposed by or under Schedule 14 to the Communications Act 2003, ".

Commencement Information

I107. Sch. 15 para. 104 in force at 29.12.2003 by S.I. 2003/3142, art. 3. (1), Sch. 1 (with art. 11)

National radio multiplex licences

105. (1)Section 46 of the 1996 Act (national radio multiplex licences) shall be amended as follows.

(2) For "the Authority" and "The Authority", wherever occurring, there shall be substituted " OFCOM ".

(3) In subsection (1)(d), for "a direction" there shall be substituted " a condition ".

Commencement Information

I108. Sch. 15 para. 105 in force at 29.12.2003 by S.I. 2003/3142, art. 3. (1), Sch. 1 (with art. 11)

Award of national radio multiplex licences

106. In section 47 of the 1996 Act (award of national radio multiplex licences), for "the Authority", wherever occurring, there shall be substituted " OFCOM ".

Commencement Information

I109. Sch. 15 para. 106 in force at 29.12.2003 by S.I. 2003/3142, art. 3. (1), Sch. 1 (with art. 11)

Reservation of capacity for independent national broadcasters

107. (1)Section 48 of the 1996 Act (reservation of digital capacity for independent broadcasters) shall be amended as follows.

(2) For subsections (1) to (3) there shall be substituted—

"(1. A)OFCOM must ensure that the conditions included in national radio multiplex licences (taken together) secure that an amount of digital capacity on the multiplex frequencies is reserved for every independent national broadcaster for the broadcasting of a simulcast radio service provided by that broadcaster.

(1. B)Where the conditions of a licence for a national radio multiplex service reserve capacity on the frequency made available for that service for the broadcasting of a simulcast radio service provided by an independent national broadcaster, those conditions must also include the condition specified in subsection (1. C).

(1. C)That condition is the condition that OFCOM consider appropriate for securing that, in consideration of the making by the independent national broadcaster of the payments which —

(a) are agreed from time to time between him and the licence holder, or

(b) in default of agreement, are determined under this section,

the licence holder uses, for the broadcasting of a simulcast radio service provided by that broadcaster, such of the reserved digital capacity as may be requested, from time to time, by that broadcaster.

(1. D)Where conditions are included under this section in a national radio multiplex licence reserving capacity for an independent national broadcaster, OFCOM may include conditions relating to the broadcasting of the simulcast radio service in the licence for the national service provided by that broadcaster."

(3) In subsections (4) to (6), for "the Authority", wherever occurring, there shall be substituted " OFCOM ".

(4) In subsection (4), for "subsection (3)(a)" there shall be substituted " subsection (1. C) ".

(5) After subsection (6) there shall be inserted—

"(7)In this section "the multiplex frequencies" means the frequencies made available for the purposes of licensed national radio multiplex services."

Commencement Information

I110. Sch. 15 para. 107 in force at 29.12.2003 by S.I. 2003/3142, art. 3. (1), Sch. 1 (with art. 11)

Reservation of digital capacity for BBC

108. (1)Section 49 of the 1996 Act (reservation of digital capacity for BBC) shall be amended as follows.

(2) In subsections (1) to (3) and (6), for "the Authority", wherever occurring, there shall be substituted " OFCOM ".

(3) In subsection (4) (determination of capacity to be reserved), for the words from "If the BBC" to "the Secretary of State, who may" there shall be substituted " If the BBC do not give their consent to the proposals within such period as OFCOM may specify in their notice under subsection (3), OFCOM shall ".

(4) In subsection (5), for words from "the Secretary of State" onwards there shall be substituted " OFCOM shall give the BBC an opportunity of making representations to them about their proposals. "

(5) In subsection (6), after "and the BBC" there shall be inserted " or (in default of agreement) determined under this section ".

(6) After that subsection there shall be inserted—

"(7)Where the holder of the licence and the BBC fail to agree—

(a) the payments to be made under a condition included in the licence in accordance with subsection (6), or

(b) the other terms that are to apply in relation to the use of digital capacity in accordance with such a condition,

either of them may refer the matter to OFCOM for determination.

(8) Before making a determination under subsection (7), OFCOM must give the licence holder and the BBC an opportunity of making representations to them about the matter.

(9) In making any determination under subsection (7), OFCOM shall have regard to—

(a) the expenses incurred, or likely to be incurred, by the licence holder in providing the local radio multiplex service in question, and

(b) the terms on which persons providing local radio multiplex services contract with persons

providing local digital additional services for the broadcasting of those services."
Commencement Information
I111. Sch. 15 para. 108 in force at 29.12.2003 by S.I. 2003/3142, art. 3. (1), Sch. 1 (with art. 11)

Local radio multiplex licences

109. (1)Section 50 of the 1996 Act (local radio multiplex licences) shall be amended as follows.
(2) For "the Authority" and "The Authority", wherever occurring, there shall be substituted " OFCOM ".
(3) In subsection (1)(b), for "the Secretary of State has" there shall be substituted " OFCOM have ".
(4) In subsection (2)(d), for "direction under section 49" substitute " determination under section 49. (4) ".
Commencement Information
I112. Sch. 15 para. 109 in force at 29.12.2003 by S.I. 2003/3142, art. 3. (1), Sch. 1 (with art. 11)

Award of local multiplex licences

110. (1)Section 51 of the 1996 Act (award of local multiplex licences) shall be amended as follows.
(2) For "the Authority", wherever occurring, there shall be substituted " OFCOM ".
(3) In subsection (2), for paragraph (f) there shall be substituted—
   "(f)the extent to which there is evidence that, amongst persons living in that area or locality, there is a demand for, or support for, the provision of the proposed service; and".
Commencement Information
I113. Sch. 15 para. 110 in force at 29.12.2003 by S.I. 2003/3142, art. 3. (1), Sch. 1 (with art. 11)

Power to require two or more local radio multiplex licences to be granted to one person

111. In section 52 of the 1996 Act (power to require two or more local radio multiplex licences to be granted to one person), for "The Authority" and "the Authority" there shall be substituted " OFCOM ".
Commencement Information
I114. Sch. 15 para. 111 in force at 29.12.2003 by S.I. 2003/3142, art. 3. (1), Sch. 1 (with art. 11)

Failure to begin to provide licensed service

112. In section 53 of the 1996 Act (failure to provide licensed service), for "the Authority", wherever occurring, there shall be substituted " OFCOM ".
Commencement Information
I115. Sch. 15 para. 112 in force at 29.12.2003 by S.I. 2003/3142, art. 3. (1), Sch. 1 (with art. 11)

Conditions which may be attached to radio multiplex licences

113. In section 54 of the 1996 Act (conditions which may be attached to a radio multiplex licence), for "the Authority", wherever occurring, there shall be substituted " OFCOM ".
Commencement Information
I116. Sch. 15 para. 113 in force at 29.12.2003 by S.I. 2003/3142, art. 3. (1), Sch. 1 (with art. 11)

Additional payments to be made in respect of national radio multiplex licences

114. In section 55 of the 1996 Act (additional payments to be made in respect of national radio multiplex licences) for "the Authority", wherever occurring, there shall be substituted " OFCOM ".

Commencement Information

I117. Sch. 15 para. 114 in force at 29.12.2003 by S.I. 2003/3142, art. 3. (1), Sch. 1 (with art. 11)

Multiplex revenue

115. (1)Section 56 of the 1996 Act (multiplex revenue) shall be amended as follows.

(2) In subsection (1)—

(a) for "section 55. (1)" there shall be substituted " this Part ";

(b) for "the holder of a national radio multiplex licence" there shall be substituted " the person who is the multiplex provider in relation to a national radio multiplex service ";

(c) in paragraph (a)(i), "to which the licence relates" shall be omitted;

(d) in paragraphs (c) and (d), for "the holder of the radio multiplex licence" there shall be substituted " the multiplex provider ".

(3) In subsections (2) to (8)—

(a) for "the holder of the radio multiplex licence", "the licence holder" and "the holder of the multiplex licence", wherever occurring, there shall be substituted, in each case, " the multiplex provider "; and

(b) for "the Authority", wherever occurring, there shall be substituted " OFCOM ".

(4) In subsection (9)—

(a) for "a national radio multiplex licence", in each place, there shall be substituted " a national radio multiplex service ";

(b) for "the radio multiplex service to which the licence relates", in each place, there shall be substituted " that radio multiplex service ";

(c) after the definition of "additional services provider" there shall be inserted—

""multiplex provider"—

(a) in relation to a national radio multiplex service for which a person holds a licence under this Part, means the licence holder; and

(b) in relation to a national radio multiplex service which is not licensed under this Part, means the person who provides that service."

Commencement Information

I118. Sch. 15 para. 115 in force at 29.12.2003 by S.I. 2003/3142, art. 3. (1), Sch. 1 (with art. 11)

Attribution of radio multiplex revenue

116. (1)Section 57 of the 1996 Act (attribution of radio multiplex revenue) shall be amended as follows.

(2) In subsection (1)—

(a) for "the holder of a national radio multiplex licence" there shall be substituted " the person who is the multiplex provider in relation to a national radio multiplex service "; and

(b) for "the holder of the national radio multiplex licence" there shall be substituted " the multiplex provider ".

(3) In subsection (2), for "the holder of the radio multiplex licence", wherever occurring, there shall be substituted " the multiplex provider ".

(4) In subsection (3)—

(a) for "the Authority" there shall be substituted " OFCOM "; and

(b) for "the holder of the national radio multiplex licence" there shall be substituted " the multiplex provider ".

(5) In subsection (4)—

(a) after "'additional services provider'" there shall be inserted " ', multiplex provider' "; and

(b) for "a national radio multiplex licence" there shall be substituted " a national radio multiplex service ".

Commencement Information

I119. Sch. 15 para. 116 in force at 29.12.2003 by S.I. 2003/3142, art. 3. (1), Sch. 1 (with art. 11)

Duration and renewal of radio multiplex licences

117. (1)Section 58 of the 1996 Act (duration and renewal of radio multiplex licences) shall be amended as follows.

(2) For "the Authority" and "The Authority", wherever occurring, there shall be substituted " OFCOM ".

(3) In subsection (3), after "not later than" there shall be inserted " the day falling three months before ".

(4) Subsection (5) (consent of the Secretary of State for exercise of certain powers in connection with renewal) shall cease to have effect.

(5) After subsection (12) there shall be inserted—

"(12. A)A determination for the purposes of subsection (12)—

(a) must be made at least one year before the date determined; and

(b) must be notified by OFCOM to the person who holds the licence in question."

Commencement Information

I120. Sch. 15 para. 117 in force at 29.12.2003 by S.I. 2003/3142, art. 3. (1), Sch. 1 (with art. 11)

Enforcement of radio multiplex licences

118. In section 59 of the 1996 Act (enforcement of radio multiplex licences), for "the Authority" and "The Authority", wherever occurring, there shall be substituted " OFCOM ".

Commencement Information

I121. Sch. 15 para. 118 in force at 29.12.2003 by S.I. 2003/3142, art. 3. (1), Sch. 1 (with art. 11)

Digital sound programme licensing

119. (1)Section 60 of the 1996 Act (digital sound programme licensing) shall be amended as follows.

(2) For "the Authority", wherever occurring, there shall be substituted " OFCOM ".

(3) After subsection (6), there shall be inserted—

"(6. A)Section 89 of the 1990 Act (disqualification from being licence holder or concerned with the provision of a programme service if convicted of a transmitting offence) shall apply in relation to a licence under this section as it applies to a licence under Part 3 of that Act, but with the omission of paragraph (b) of subsection (3) of that section and of the word "or" immediately before that paragraph."

(4) Sub-paragraph (3) does not impose a disqualification in respect of any offence committed before the commencement of that sub-paragraph.

Commencement Information

I122. Sch. 15 para. 119 in force at 29.12.2003 by S.I. 2003/3142, art. 3. (1), Sch. 1 (with art. 11)

Conditions of digital sound programme licences

120. (1)Section 61 of the 1996 Act (conditions of licences for digital sound programme services) shall be amended as follows.

(2) In subsection (2)—

(a) for "the Authority", wherever occurring, there shall be substituted " OFCOM ";

(b) in paragraphs (a) and (c), for "the holder of a radio multiplex licence", there shall be substituted, in each case, " the provider of a radio multiplex service, of a television multiplex service or of a general multiplex service ";

(c) in paragraph (a) for "by means of a radio multiplex service" there shall be substituted " by means of the multiplex service "; and

(d) in paragraph (a)(i) for "radio multiplex service" there shall be substituted " multiplex service ".

Commencement Information

I123. Sch. 15 para. 120 in force at 29.12.2003 by S.I. 2003/3142, art. 3. (1), Sch. 1 (with art. 11)

Enforcement of digital sound programme licences

121. (1)Section 62 of the 1996 Act (enforcement of digital sound programme licences) shall be amended as follows.

(2) For "the Authority" and "The Authority", wherever occurring, there shall be substituted " OFCOM ".

(3) In subsection (4), for the words from "national radio multiplex service" onwards there shall be substituted " relevant multiplex service, means the last accounting period of the multiplex provider ".

(4) In subsection (5)—

(a) for "national radio multiplex service" there shall be substituted " relevant multiplex service ";

(b) for "holder of the national radio multiplex licence" there shall be substituted " multiplex provider "; and

(c) for "the radio multiplex service" and "that radio multiplex service" there shall be substituted " that relevant multiplex service ".

(5) After subsection (5. A) (inserted by Schedule 13) there shall be inserted—

"(5. B)For the purposes of this section, a service is a relevant multiplex service if it is—

(a) a national radio multiplex service;

(b) a television multiplex service; or

(c) a general multiplex service.

(5. C)In this section, "multiplex provider"—

(a) in relation to a national radio multiplex service, means the multiplex provider within the meaning of section 56; and

(b) in relation to a television multiplex service or a general multiplex service, means the multiplex provider within the meaning of section 14."

(6) In subsection (10) for "apology" there shall be substituted " statement of findings ".

Commencement Information

I124. Sch. 15 para. 121 in force at 29.12.2003 by S.I. 2003/3142, art. 3. (1), Sch. 1 (with art. 11)

Digital additional sound services

122. In section 64 of the 1996 Act (licensing of digital additional sound services), for "the Authority", wherever occurring, there shall be substituted " OFCOM ".

Commencement Information

I125. Sch. 15 para. 122 in force at 29.12.2003 by S.I. 2003/3142, art. 3. (1), Sch. 1 (with art. 11)

Conditions of digital additional sound service

123. (1)Section 65 of the 1996 Act (conditions of licences for digital additional sound services) shall be amended as follows.

(2) In subsection (2)—

(a) for "the Authority", wherever occurring, there shall be substituted " OFCOM ";

(b) in paragraphs (a) and (c), for "the holder of a radio multiplex licence", there shall be substituted, in each case, " the provider of a radio multiplex service or of a general multiplex service ";

(c) in paragraph (a) for "by means of a radio multiplex service" there shall be substituted " by means of the multiplex service "; and

(d) in paragraph (a)(i) for "radio multiplex service" there shall be substituted " multiplex service ".

Commencement Information

I126. Sch. 15 para. 123 in force at 29.12.2003 by S.I. 2003/3142, art. 3. (1), Sch. 1 (with art. 11)

Enforcement of digital additional sound services licences

124. (1)Section 66 of the 1996 Act (enforcement of digital additional services licences) shall be amended as follows.

(2) For "the Authority" and "The Authority", wherever occurring, there shall be substituted " OFCOM ".

(3) In subsection (4), for "national radio multiplex service" there shall be substituted " relevant multiplex service ".

(4) In subsection (5), for the words from "national radio multiplex service" onwards there shall be substituted " relevant multiplex service, means the last accounting period of the multiplex provider ".

(5) In subsection (6)—

(a) for "national radio multiplex service" there shall be substituted " relevant multiplex service ";

(b) for "holder of the national radio multiplex licence" there shall be substituted " multiplex provider "; and

(c) for "the radio multiplex service" and "that radio multiplex service" there shall be substituted " that relevant multiplex service ".

(6) After subsection (6. A) (inserted by Schedule 13) there shall be inserted—

"(6. B)For the purposes of this section, a service is a relevant multiplex service if it is—

    (a) a national radio multiplex service; or

    (b) a general multiplex service.

(6. C)In this section, "multiplex provider"—

    (a) in relation to a national radio multiplex service, means the multiplex provider within the meaning of section 56; and

    (b) in relation to a general multiplex service, means the multiplex provider within the meaning of section 14."

(7) In subsection (10) for "apology" there shall be substituted " statement of findings ".

Commencement Information

I127. Sch. 15 para. 124 in force at 29.12.2003 by S.I. 2003/3142, art. 3. (1), Sch. 1 (with art. 11)

Review of digital radio broadcasting

125. In section 67 of the 1996 Act (review of digital radio broadcasting), for "the Authority", wherever occurring, there shall be substituted " OFCOM ".

Commencement Information

I128. Sch. 15 para. 125 in force at 29.12.2003 by S.I. 2003/3142, art. 3. (1), Sch. 1 (with art. 11)

Interpretation

126. In section 72. (1) of the 1996 Act (interpretation), for the definition of "radio multiplex service" there shall be substituted—

""radio multiplex service" means a radio multiplex service within the meaning of Part 3 of the Communications Act 2003;

"the radio transfer date" has the same meaning as in the Communications Act 2003;".

Commencement Information

I129. Sch. 15 para. 126 in force at 29.12.2003 by S.I. 2003/3142, art. 3. (1), Sch. 1 (with art. 11)

Listed events

127. (1)Section 98 of the 1996 Act (categories of service for the purposes of Part 4 of that Act) shall be amended as follows.

(2) In subsection (3), for the words from "television" onwards there shall be substituted " licence for the purposes of section 363 of the Communications Act 2003 ".

(3) In subsection (5), for "The Commission" there shall be substituted " OFCOM ".

(4) In subsection (6), for "transmission for general reception of television programmes by satellite" there shall be substituted " broadcasting of television programmes from a satellite so as to be available for reception by members of the public (within the meaning of Part 3 of the Communications Act 2003) ".

Commencement Information

I130. Sch. 15 para. 127 in force at 29.12.2003 by S.I. 2003/3142, art. 3. (1), Sch. 1 (with art. 11)

128. In sections 101, 101. B, 102 and 103 of the 1996 Act (restrictions on, and penalties for, televising listed and designated events), for "The Commission" and "the Commission", wherever occurring, there shall be substituted " OFCOM ".

Commencement Information

I131. Sch. 15 para. 128 in force at 29.12.2003 by S.I. 2003/3142, art. 3. (1), Sch. 1 (with art. 11)

129. (1)Section 104 of the 1996 Act (code of guidance) shall be amended as follows.

(2) For "the Commission", wherever occurring, there shall be substituted " OFCOM ".

(3) In subsection (4)(d), the words "by the Commission" and "by them" shall be omitted.

Commencement Information

I132. Sch. 15 para. 129 in force at 29.12.2003 by S.I. 2003/3142, art. 3. (1), Sch. 1 (with art. 11)

130. In section 104. A of the 1996 Act (provision of information about listed and designated events), for "the Commission", wherever occurring, there shall be substituted " OFCOM ".

Commencement Information

I133. Sch. 15 para. 130 in force at 29.12.2003 by S.I. 2003/3142, art. 3. (1), Sch. 1 (with art. 11)

131. In section 105. (1) of the 1996 Act (interpretation of Part 4 etc.), the definition of "the Commission" shall be omitted.

Commencement Information

I134. Sch. 15 para. 131 in force at 29.12.2003 by S.I. 2003/3142, art. 3. (1), Sch. 1 (with art. 11)

Broadcasting standards

132. (1)Part 5 of the 1996 Act (the Broadcasting Standards Commission) shall be amended as follows.

(2) For "the BSC" and "The BSC", wherever occurring in any of sections 107, 110, 111, 114, 115, 118 to 121 there shall be substituted " OFCOM ".

Commencement Information

I135. Sch. 15 para. 132 in force at 29.12.2003 by S.I. 2003/3142, art. 3. (1), Sch. 1 (with art. 11)

133. In section 107. (5)(b) of the 1996 Act (code relating to avoidance of unjust or unfair treatment etc.), for "the service referred to in section 57. (1. A)(a) of the 1990 Act" there shall be substituted " any public service of the Welsh Authority (within the meaning of Part 2 of Schedule

12 to the Communications Act 2003) ".

Commencement Information
I136. Sch. 15 para. 133 in force at 29.12.2003 by S.I. 2003/3142, art. 3. (1), Sch. 1 (with art. 11)

134. In section 115 of the 1996 Act (consideration of fairness complaints)

(a) in subsection (2)(d), for "to (c)" there shall be substituted " or (b) "; and

(b) in subsection (8), for "they shall send a statement of" there shall be substituted " OFCOM shall send a copy of ".

Commencement Information
I137. Sch. 15 para. 134 in force at 29.12.2003 by S.I. 2003/3142, art. 3. (1), Sch. 1 (with art. 11)

135. In section 117 of the 1996 Act (duty of broadcasting body to retain recordings of programmes), for "sections 115 and 116" there shall be substituted " section 115 ".

Commencement Information
I138. Sch. 15 para. 135 in force at 29.12.2003 by S.I. 2003/3142, art. 3. (1), Sch. 1 (with art. 11)

136. (1)For subsections (1) and (2) of section 119 of the 1996 Act there shall be substituted—

"(1)Where OFCOM have considered and adjudicated upon a fairness complaint, they may direct the relevant person to publish the matters mentioned in subsection (3) in such manner, and within such period, as may be specified in the directions."

(2) In that section—

(a) in subsection (4), for "subsection (2)" there shall be substituted " subsection (1) ";

(b) in subsection (5), for "(3)(a), (b) or (c)" there shall be substituted " (3)(a) or (b) ";

(c) in subsection (6), for "broadcasting or regulatory body" there shall be substituted " relevant person " and for "them" there shall be substituted " him ";

(d) in subsection (8), the words "or standards complaint" and in paragraph (c) the words ", a regulatory body" shall be omitted;

(e) in subsection (10), for paragraphs (a) and (b) there shall be substituted " a relevant person "; and

(f) subsection (12) shall cease to have effect.

(3) After subsection (11) of that section there shall be inserted—

"(11. A)In this section "relevant person" means—

(a) in a case where the relevant programme was broadcast by a broadcasting body, that body; and

(b) in a case where the relevant programme was included in a licensed service, the licence holder providing that service."

Commencement Information
I139. Sch. 15 para. 136 in force at 29.12.2003 by S.I. 2003/3142, art. 3. (1), Sch. 1 (with art. 11)

137. In section 130. (1) of the 1996 Act (interpretation of Part 5), for paragraphs (b) and (c) of the definition of "licensed service" there shall be substituted—

"(aa)the public teletext service,

(b) any relevant independent radio service (within the meaning of section 85 of the 1990 Act),

(c) any additional service (within the meaning of Part 1 of the 1990 Act) which is licensed under that Part,".

Commencement Information
I140. Sch. 15 para. 137 in force at 29.12.2003 by S.I. 2003/3142, art. 3. (1), Sch. 1 (with art. 11)

Disqualification on grounds related to political objects

138. (1)Section 143 of the 1996 Act (disqualification on grounds related to political objects) shall be amended as follows.

(2) In each of subsections (1) and (2)—

(a) for "the Independent Television Commission" and "the Commission" there shall be substituted " OFCOM "; and

(b) for "section 5. (1) of the 1990 Act, or as the case may be section 5. (1) of this Act" there shall

be substituted " section 5. (1) or 88. (1) of the 1990 Act or section 5. (1) or 44. (1) of this Act ".
(3) In subsection (1), for "Part I or II of the 1990 Act or Part I of this Act" there shall be substituted " Part 1 or 3 of the 1990 Act or Part 1 or 2 of this Act, ".
(4) In subsection (2), for "Parts I or II of the 1990 Act or Part I of this Act" there shall be substituted " Part 1 or 3 of the 1990 Act or Part 1 or 2 of this Act, ".
(5) Subsections (3) and (4) shall cease to have effect.
(6) In subsection (5), for "to (4)" there shall be substituted " and (2) ".
(7) In subsection (6), for paragraphs (a) and (b) there shall be substituted " the duties imposed on OFCOM by sections 5. (1) and 88. (1) of the 1990 Act and sections 5. (1) and 44. (1) of this Act. "
Commencement Information
I141. Sch. 15 para. 138 in force at 29.12.2003 by S.I. 2003/3142, art. 3. (1), Sch. 1 (with art. 11)

Offence of providing false information

139. (1)Section 144 of the 1996 Act (offence of providing false information) shall be amended as follows.
(2) In subsection (1), for "to the relevant authority a statement", in each place, there shall be substituted " a statement to OFCOM ".
(3) In subsection (2), for "the relevant authority" there shall be substituted " OFCOM ".
(4) Subsection (5) shall cease to have effect.
Commencement Information
I142. Sch. 15 para. 139 in force at 29.12.2003 by S.I. 2003/3142, art. 3. (1), Sch. 1 (with art. 11)

Disqualification for supplying false information

140. (1)Section 145 of the 1996 Act (disqualification for offence of supplying false information) shall be amended as follows.
(2) In subsection (5), for "the relevant authority" there shall be substituted " OFCOM ".
(3) In subsection (7)—
(a) for "5. (1)(a) and 88. (1)(a)" there shall be substituted " 5. (1)(a) and (2)(db), 32. (12) and 88. (1)(a) and (2)(db) "; and
(b) for "5. (1)(a) and 44. (1)(a)" there shall be substituted " 5. (1)(a) and (2)(db) and 44. (1)(a) and (2)(db) ".
(4) In subsection (8) of that section, for the definition of "licence" there shall be substituted—
""licence" means a licence under Part 1 or 3 of the 1990 Act or under Part 1 or 2 of this Act;".
Commencement Information
I143. Sch. 15 para. 140 in force at 29.12.2003 by S.I. 2003/3142, art. 3. (1), Sch. 1 (with art. 11)

Interpretation

141. In section 147. (1) of the 1996 Act (general interpretation), after the definition of "the BBC" there shall be inserted—
""OFCOM" means the Office of Communications;".
Commencement Information
I144. Sch. 15 para. 141 in force at 29.12.2003 by S.I. 2003/3142, art. 3. (1), Sch. 1 (with art. 11)

Computation of qualifying revenue

142. (1)Schedule 1 to the 1996 Act (computation of "multiplex revenue" etc.) shall be amended as follows.
(2) In Part 1, for "the Commission" and "The Commission", wherever occurring, there shall be

substituted " OFCOM ".

(3) In Part 2, for "the Authority" and "The Authority", wherever occurring, there shall be substituted " OFCOM ".

Commencement Information

I145. Sch. 15 para. 142 in force at 29.12.2003 by S.I. 2003/3142, art. 3. (1), Sch. 1 (with art. 11)

Schedule 17. Further amendments in connection with media mergers

Section 389

Competition Act 1980 (c. 21)

1. In section 11. C(1) of the Competition Act 1980 (application of section 117 of the Enterprise Act 2002 (c. 40)) for the words " "the OFT,"" there shall be substituted " "the OFT, OFCOM," ".

Commencement Information

I1. Sch. 16 para. 1 in force at 29.12.2003 by S.I. 2003/3142, art. 3. (1), Sch. 1 (with art. 11)

Gas Act 1986 (c. 44)

2. In section 41. EB(4) of the Gas Act 1986 (application of section 117 of the Enterprise Act 2002) for the words " "the OFT,"" there shall be substituted " "the OFT, OFCOM," ".

Commencement Information

I2. Sch. 16 para. 2 in force at 29.12.2003 by S.I. 2003/3142, art. 3. (1), Sch. 1 (with art. 11)

Electricity Act 1989 (c. 29)

3. In section 56. CB(4) of the Electricity Act 1989 (application of section 117 of the Enterprise Act 2002) for the words " "the OFT,"" there shall be substituted " "the OFT, OFCOM," ".

Commencement Information

I3. Sch. 16 para. 3 in force at 29.12.2003 by S.I. 2003/3142, art. 3. (1), Sch. 1 (with art. 11)

Railways Act 1993 (c. 43)

4. (1)The Railways Act 1993 shall be amended as follows.

(2) In section 13. B(4) of that Act (application of section 117 of the Enterprise Act 2002) for the words " "the OFT,"" there shall be substituted " "the OFT, OFCOM," ".

(3) In section 15. C(2. G) of that Act (application of section 117 of the Enterprise Act 2002) for the words " "the OFT,"" there shall be substituted " "the OFT, OFCOM," ".

(4) In Schedule 4. A to that Act, in paragraphs 10. A(4) and 15. (2. G) (application of section 117 of the Enterprise Act 2002) for the words " "the OFT,"" there shall, in both places, be substituted " "the OFT, OFCOM," ".

Commencement Information

I4. Sch. 16 para. 4 in force at 29.12.2003 by S.I. 2003/3142, art. 3. (1), Sch. 1 (with art. 11)

F1...

Amendments (Textual)

F1. Sch. 16 para. 5 and crossheading repealed (1.4.2013) by Financial Services Act 2012 (c. 21), s. 122. (3), Sch. 19 (with Sch. 20); S.I. 2013/423, art. 3, Sch.

F15. . . . .

Commencement Information

I5. Sch. 16 para. 5 in force at 29.12.2003 by S.I. 2003/3142, art. 3. (1), Sch. 1 (with art. 11)

Postal Services Act 2000 (c. 26)

F26. . . . .

Amendments (Textual)

F2. Sch. 16 para. 6 omitted (1.10.2011) by virtue of Postal Services Act 2011 (c. 5), s. 93. (2)(3), Sch. 12 para. 69; S.I. 2011/2329, art. 3

Commencement Information

I6. Sch. 16 para. 6 in force at 29.12.2003 by S.I. 2003/3142, art. 3. (1), Sch. 1 (with art. 11)

Transport Act 2000 (c. 38)

7. (1)The Transport Act 2000 shall be amended as follows.

(2) In section 12. B(4) (application of section 117 of the Enterprise Act 2002 (c. 40)) for the words " "the OFT,"" there shall be substituted " "the OFT, OFCOM," ".

(3) In section 18. (9) (application of section 117 of the Enterprise Act 2002) for the words " "the OFT,"" there shall be substituted " "the OFT, OFCOM," ".

Commencement Information

I7. Sch. 16 para. 7 in force at 29.12.2003 by S.I. 2003/3142, art. 3. (1), Sch. 1 (with art. 11)

Enterprise Act 2002 (c. 40)

8. (1)Section 43 of the Enterprise Act 2002 (intervention notices under section 42) shall be amended as follows.

(2) In subsection (4)(a) (final determination of matters to which intervention notice relates)—

(a) after the word "OFT" there shall be inserted " or (if relevant) OFCOM "; and

(b) after the word "44" there shall be inserted " or (as the case may be) 44. A ".

(3) After subsection (5) there shall be inserted—

"(6)In this Part "OFCOM" means the Office of Communications."

Commencement Information

I8. Sch. 16 para. 8 in force at 29.12.2003 by S.I. 2003/3142, art. 3. (1), Sch. 1 (with art. 11)

9. In section 45. (1)(b) of that Act (circumstances in which the Secretary of State may make a public interest reference to the Competition Commission) after the words "section 44" there shall be inserted " , and any report of OFCOM which is required by virtue of section 44. A, ".

Commencement Information

I9. Sch. 16 para. 9 in force at 29.12.2003 by S.I. 2003/3142, art. 3. (1), Sch. 1 (with art. 11)

10. After section 50. (2) of that Act (reports on references in public interest cases) there shall be inserted—

"(2. A)Where the report relates to a reference under section 45 which has been made after a report of OFCOM under section 44. A, the Commission shall give a copy of its report (whether or not published) to OFCOM."

Commencement Information

I10. Sch. 16 para. 10 in force at 29.12.2003 by S.I. 2003/3142, art. 3. (1), Sch. 1 (with art. 11)

11. In section 57. (2) of that Act (duty to bring representations to attention of Secretary of State) after the words "the OFT", in both places where they occur, there shall be inserted " , OFCOM ".

Commencement Information

111. Sch. 16 para. 11 in force at 29.12.2003 by S.I. 2003/3142, art. 3. (1), Sch. 1 (with art. 11)

12. In section 58. (4)(b) of that Act (retrospective effect of orders modifying specified considerations) after the word "OFT," there shall be inserted " OFCOM, ".

Commencement Information

I12. Sch. 16 para. 12 in force at 29.12.2003 by S.I. 2003/3142, art. 3. (1), Sch. 1 (with art. 11)

13. In section 60. (4)(a) of that Act (final determination of matters to which special intervention notice relates)—

(a) after the word "OFT" there shall be inserted " or (if relevant) OFCOM "; and

(b) after the word "61" there shall be inserted " or (as the case may be) 61. A ".

Commencement Information

I13. Sch. 16 para. 13 in force at 29.12.2003 by S.I. 2003/3142, art. 3. (1), Sch. 1 (with art. 11)

14. In section 62. (1)(b) of that Act (circumstances in which the Secretary of State may make a special public interest reference to the Competition Commission) after the words "section 61" there shall be inserted " , and any report of OFCOM which is required by virtue of section 61. A, ".

Commencement Information

I14. Sch. 16 para. 14 in force at 29.12.2003 by S.I. 2003/3142, art. 3. (1), Sch. 1 (with art. 11)

15. After section 65. (2) of that Act (reports on references in special public interest cases) there shall be inserted—

"(2. A)Where the report relates to a reference under section 62 which has been made after a report of OFCOM under section 61. A, the Commission shall give a copy of its report (whether or not published) to OFCOM."

Commencement Information

I15. Sch. 16 para. 15 in force at 29.12.2003 by S.I. 2003/3142, art. 3. (1), Sch. 1 (with art. 11)

16. In section 67. (1)(b) of that Act (intervention to protect legitimate interests)—

(a) the words from "which" to "or 33" shall cease to have effect;

(b) for the words "that section" there shall be substituted " section 22 or 33 "; and

(c) after the word "concerned" there shall be inserted " (whether or not there would otherwise have been a duty to make such a reference) ".

Commencement Information

I16. Sch. 16 para. 16 in force at 29.12.2003 by S.I. 2003/3142, art. 3. (1), Sch. 1 (with art. 11)

17. In section 68. (2)(c) of that Act (scheme for protecting legitimate interests)—

(a) the words from "which", where it occurs for the second time, to "or 33" shall cease to have effect; and

(b) for the words "that section" there shall be substituted " section 22 or 33 (whether or not there would otherwise have been a duty to make such a reference) ".

Commencement Information

I17. Sch. 16 para. 17 in force at 29.12.2003 by S.I. 2003/3142, art. 3. (1), Sch. 1 (with art. 11)

18. (1)Section 107 of that Act (further publicity requirements) shall be amended as follows.

(2) In subsection (3) (duties of the Secretary of State to publish), after paragraph (b), there shall be inserted—

"(ba)any report of OFCOM under section 44. A or 61. A which has been received by him;".

(3) In subsection (9)(a) (publication of reports of OFT in public interest cases) after the words "section 44" there shall be inserted " , and any report of OFCOM under section 44. A, ".

(4) In subsection (10)(a) (publication of reports of OFT in special public interest cases) after the words "section 61" there shall be inserted " , and any report of OFCOM under section 61. A, ".

Commencement Information

I18. Sch. 16 para. 18 in force at 29.12.2003 by S.I. 2003/3142, art. 3. (1), Sch. 1 (with art. 11)

19. In section 108 of that Act (defamation) after the words "the OFT," there shall be inserted " OFCOM, ".

Commencement Information

I19. Sch. 16 para. 19 in force at 29.12.2003 by S.I. 2003/3142, art. 3. (1), Sch. 1 (with art. 11)

20. (1)Section 117 of that Act (false or misleading information) shall be amended as follows.

(2) In subsection (1)(a) (offence of supplying false or misleading information to the OFT etc.) after the word "OFT," there shall be inserted " OFCOM, ".

(3) In subsection (2) (offence of supplying false or misleading information to another person for use by OFT etc.) after the word "OFT," there shall be inserted " OFCOM, ".

Commencement Information

I20. Sch. 16 para. 20 in force at 29.12.2003 by S.I. 2003/3142, art. 3. (1), Sch. 1 (with art. 11)

21. In section 118. (1) of that Act (excisions from reports) before the word "or" at the end of paragraph (a) there shall be inserted—

"(aa)a report of OFCOM under section 44. A or 61. A;".

Commencement Information

I21. Sch. 16 para. 21 in force at 29.12.2003 by S.I. 2003/3142, art. 3. (1), Sch. 1 (with art. 11)

22. In section 120. (1) of that Act (review of decisions under Part 3) after the word "OFT," there shall be inserted " OFCOM, ".

Commencement Information

I22. Sch. 16 para. 22 in force at 29.12.2003 by S.I. 2003/3142, art. 3. (1), Sch. 1 (with art. 11)

23. (1)Section 121 of that Act (fees) shall be amended as follows.

(2) In subsection (1)—

(a) after the words "the OFT", where they occur for the second time, there shall be inserted " , OFCOM "; and

(b) the words ", Part V of the Fair Trading Act 1973 (c. 41)" shall cease to have effect.

(3) In subsection (2)—

(a) at the end of paragraph (a) there shall be inserted the word " or "; and

(b) paragraph (b), and the word "or" at the end of the paragraph, shall cease to have effect.

(4) In subsection (4)(c)—

(a) sub-paragraph (i);

(b) the word "and" at the end of the sub-paragraph; and

(c) in sub-paragraph (ii), the words "in any other case,";

shall cease to have effect.

(5) In subsection (8)—

(a) after the words "the OFT", where they occur for the second time, there shall be inserted " , OFCOM "; and

(b) the words ", Part V of the Act of 1973" shall cease to have effect.

(6) Subsection (10) shall cease to have effect.

Commencement Information

I23. Sch. 16 para. 23 in force at 29.12.2003 by S.I. 2003/3142, art. 3. (1), Sch. 1 (with art. 11)

24. (1)Section 124 of that Act (orders and regulations under Part 3) shall be amended as follows.

(2) In subsection (3) after the word "34" there shall be inserted " , 59. (6. A) ".

(3) In subsection (4) after the word "40. (8)," there shall be inserted " 44. (11), ".

(4) In subsection (6) after the word "34," there shall be inserted " 44. (11), 59. (6. A), ".

Commencement Information

I24. Sch. 16 para. 24 in force at 29.12.2003 by S.I. 2003/3142, art. 3. (1), Sch. 1 (with art. 11)

25. (1)Section 130 of that Act (index of defined expressions) shall be amended as follows.

(2) After the entry relating to "Anti-competitive outcome" there shall be inserted—

"Broadcasting | Section 44(9)". |

(3) After the entry relating to "Market in the United Kingdom" there shall be inserted—

"Media public interest consideration | Section 44(8)". |

(4) After the entry for "Modify" there shall be inserted—

"Newspaper | Section 44(10) |

Newspaper enterprise | Section 58A(3)". |

(5) After the entry for "Notified arrangements" there shall be inserted—

"OFCOM | Section 43(6)". |

Commencement Information

I25. Sch. 16 para. 25 in force at 29.12.2003 by S.I. 2003/3142, art. 3. (1), Sch. 1 (with art. 11)

26. In section 180. (2) of that Act (application of section 117 of that Act for the purposes of Part 4 of that Act) after the word "alone" there shall be inserted " and as if the references to OFCOM were omitted ".

Commencement Information

126. Sch. 16 para. 26 in force at 29.12.2003 by S.I. 2003/3142, art. 3. (1), Sch. 1 (with art. 11)

Schedule 18. Minor and Consequential Amendments

Section 406

Interpretation

1. (1)In any Act or instrument amended by this Schedule—

"communications service" means any of the following services—

- an electronic communications service;

- the provision of directory information by means of an electronic communications network for the purpose of facilitating the use of an electronic communications service provided by means of that network;

- the installation, maintenance, adjustment, repair, alteration, moving, removal or replacement of apparatus which is or is to be connected to an electronic communications network;

"electronic communications apparatus" has the same meaning as in the electronic communications code;

"the electronic communications code" has the same meaning as in Chapter 1 of Part 2 of this Act;

"electronic communications code network" means—

- so much of an electronic communications network or conduit system provided by an electronic communications code operator as is not excluded from the application of the electronic communications code by a direction under section 106; and

- an electronic communications network which the Secretary of State or a Northern Ireland department is providing or proposing to provide;

"electronic communications code operator" means a person in whose case the electronic communications code is applied by a direction under section 106;

"electronic communications network" and "electronic communications service" each has the same meaning as in this Act;

"former PTO" means a person—

- who is a provider of a public electronic communications network or a public electronic communications service which, immediately before the date on which the repeal by this Act of section 7 of the Telecommunications Act 1984 (c. 12) comes into force, was designated as a public telecommunication system under section 9 of that Act; and

- who, immediately before that date, was authorised to provide that network or service by a licence to which section 8 of that Act applied;

"operator", in relation to an electronic communications code network, means—

- the electronic communications code operator providing that network; or

- the Secretary of State or a Northern Ireland department, to the extent that they are providing or proposing to provide that network;

"provide" and cognate expressions, in relation to an electronic communications network, an electronic communications service or associated facilities, are to be construed in accordance with section 32. (4) of this Act;

"public electronic communications network" and "public electronic communications service" each has the same meaning as in Chapter 1 of Part 2 of this Act.

502

(2) In this paragraph—

(a) "conduit system" has the same meaning as in the electronic communications code and references to providing a conduit system shall be construed in accordance with paragraph 1. (3. A) of that code;

(b) "electronic communications code", "electronic communications code network", "electronic communications code operator", "public electronic communications network" and "public electronic communications service" each has the meaning given in sub-paragraph (1).

Commencement Information

I1. Sch. 17 para. 1 in force at 25.7.2003 for specified purposes by S.I. 2003/1900, art. 2. (1), Sch. 1 (with art. 3) (as amended by S.I. 2003/3142, art. 1. (3))

I2. Sch. 17 para. 1 in force at 29.12.2003 in so far as not already in force by S.I. 2003/3142, art. 3. (2) (with art. 11)

Official Secrets Act 1911.

2. For the purposes of the Official Secrets Act 1911 (c. 28), any electronic communications station or office belonging to, or occupied by, the provider of a public electronic communications service shall be a prohibited place.

Commencement Information

I3. Sch. 17 para. 2 in force at 25.7.2003 for specified purposes by S.I. 2003/1900, arts. 1. (2), 2. (1), Sch. 1 (with art. 3) (as amended by S.I. 2003/3142, art. 1. (3))

I4. Sch. 17 para. 2 in force at 29.12.2003 in so far as not already in force by S.I. 2003/3142, art. 3. (2) (with art. 11)

Law of Property Act 1925.

3[F1. In section 194. (4) of the Law of Property Act 1925 (c. 20) (exceptions from restrictions on inclosure of commons), for the words from "telecommunication apparatus" onwards there shall be substituted " electronic communications apparatus installed for the purposes of an electronic communications code network. "]

Amendments (Textual)

F1. Sch. 17 para. 3 repealed (E.W.) (1.10.2007 for E., 1.4.2012 for W.) by Commons Act 2006 (c. 26), s. 56, Sch. 6 Pt. 2 (with s. 60); S.I. 2007/2584, art. 2. (d)(ii); S.I. 2012/739, art. 2. (h)

Commencement Information

I5. Sch. 17 para. 3 in force at 25.7.2003 for specified purposes by S.I. 2003/1900, arts. 1. (2), 2. (1), Sch. 1 (with art. 3) (as amended by S.I. 2003/3142, art. 1. (3))

I6. Sch. 17 para. 3 in force at 29.12.2003 in so far as not already in force by S.I. 2003/3142, art. 3. (2) (with art. 11)

Public Health Act 1925.

4. In section 10 of the Public Health Act 1925 (c. 71) (Crown application), for the words from "telecommunication apparatus" to "system" there shall be substituted " electronic communications apparatus kept installed for the purposes of an electronic communications code network ".

Commencement Information

I7. Sch. 17 para. 4 in force at 25.7.2003 for specified purposes by S.I. 2003/1900, arts. 1. (2), 2. (1), Sch. 1 (with art. 3) (as amended by S.I. 2003/3142, art. 1. (3))

I8. Sch. 17 para. 4 in force at 29.12.2003 in so far as not already in force by S.I. 2003/3142, art. 3. (2) (with art. 11)

London Overground Wires, etc Act 1933.

5. (1)The London Overground Wires, etc. Act 1933 (c. xliv) shall be amended as follows.

(2) In section 11 (saving for safety regulations), for "any telecommunication apparatus made" there shall be substituted " any electronic communications apparatus made ".

(3) In section 14 (savings in respect of telecommunications code system)—

(a) for "telecommunication apparatus kept installed for the purposes of a telecommunications code system" there shall be substituted " electronic communications apparatus kept installed for the purposes of an electronic communications code network ";

(b) for the words from "conferred by" onwards there shall be substituted " conferred by or in accordance with the electronic communications code on the operator of any such network. "

Commencement Information

I9. Sch. 17 para. 5 in force at 25.7.2003 for specified purposes by S.I. 2003/1900, arts. 1. (2), 2. (1), Sch. 1 (with art. 3) (as amended by S.I. 2003/3142, art. 1. (3))

I10. Sch. 17 para. 5 in force at 29.12.2003 in so far as not already in force by S.I. 2003/3142, art. 3. (2) (with art. 11)

Wireless Telegraphy Act 1949.

F26. . . . .

Amendments (Textual)

F2. Sch. 17 paras. 6-18 repealed (8.2.2007) by Wireless Telegraphy Act 2006 (c. 36), s. 126. (2), Sch. 9 Pt. 1 (with Sch. 8 Pt. 1)

F27. . . . .

Amendments (Textual)

F2. Sch. 17 paras. 6-18 repealed (8.2.2007) by Wireless Telegraphy Act 2006 (c. 36), s. 126. (2), Sch. 9 Pt. 1 (with Sch. 8 Pt. 1)

Commencement Information

I11. Sch. 17 para. 7 in force at 18.9.2003 by S.I. 2003/1900, art. 2. (2), Sch. 2

F28. . . . .

Amendments (Textual)

F2. Sch. 17 paras. 6-18 repealed (8.2.2007) by Wireless Telegraphy Act 2006 (c. 36), s. 126. (2), Sch. 9 Pt. 1 (with Sch. 8 Pt. 1)

F29. . . . .

Amendments (Textual)

F2. Sch. 17 paras. 6-18 repealed (8.2.2007) by Wireless Telegraphy Act 2006 (c. 36), s. 126. (2), Sch. 9 Pt. 1 (with Sch. 8 Pt. 1)

Commencement Information

I12. Sch. 17 para. 9 in force at 25.7.2003 for specified purposes by S.I. 2003/1900, arts. 1. (2), 2. (1), Sch. 1 (with art. 3) (as amended by S.I. 2003/3142, art. 1. (3))

I13. Sch. 17 para. 9 in force at 29.12.2003 in so far as not already in force by S.I. 2003/3142, art. 3. (1), Sch. 1 (with art. 11)

F210. . . . .

Amendments (Textual)

F2. Sch. 17 paras. 6-18 repealed (8.2.2007) by Wireless Telegraphy Act 2006 (c. 36), s. 126. (2), Sch. 9 Pt. 1 (with Sch. 8 Pt. 1)

Commencement Information

I14. Sch. 17 para. 10 in force at 25.7.2003 for specified purposes by S.I. 2003/1900, arts. 1. (2), 2. (1), Sch. 1 (with art. 3) (as amended by S.I. 2003/3142, art. 1. (3))

I15. Sch. 17 para. 10 in force at 29.12.2003 in so far as not already in force by S.I. 2003/3142, art. 3. (2) (with art. 11)

F211. . . . .

Amendments (Textual)

F2. Sch. 17 paras. 6-18 repealed (8.2.2007) by Wireless Telegraphy Act 2006 (c. 36), s. 126. (2), Sch. 9 Pt. 1 (with Sch. 8 Pt. 1)

Commencement Information

I16. Sch. 17 para. 11 in force at 25.7.2003 for specified purposes by S.I. 2003/1900, arts. 1. (2), 2. (1), Sch. 1 (with art. 3) (as amended by S.I. 2003/3142, art. 1. (3))

I17. Sch. 17 para. 11 in force at 29.12.2003 in so far as not already in force by S.I. 2003/3142, art. 3. (1), Sch. 1 (with art. 11)

F212. . . . .

Amendments (Textual)

F2. Sch. 17 paras. 6-18 repealed (8.2.2007) by Wireless Telegraphy Act 2006 (c. 36), s. 126. (2), Sch. 9 Pt. 1 (with Sch. 8 Pt. 1)

Commencement Information

I18. Sch. 17 para. 12 in force at 29.12.2003 by S.I. 2003/3142, art. 3. (1), Sch. 1 (with art. 11)

F213. . . . .

Amendments (Textual)

F2. Sch. 17 paras. 6-18 repealed (8.2.2007) by Wireless Telegraphy Act 2006 (c. 36), s. 126. (2), Sch. 9 Pt. 1 (with Sch. 8 Pt. 1)

Commencement Information

I19. Sch. 17 para. 13 in force at 29.12.2003 by S.I. 2003/3142, art. 3. (1), Sch. 1 (with art. 11)

F214. . . . .

Amendments (Textual)

F2. Sch. 17 paras. 6-18 repealed (8.2.2007) by Wireless Telegraphy Act 2006 (c. 36), s. 126. (2), Sch. 9 Pt. 1 (with Sch. 8 Pt. 1)

F215. . . . .

Amendments (Textual)

F2. Sch. 17 paras. 6-18 repealed (8.2.2007) by Wireless Telegraphy Act 2006 (c. 36), s. 126. (2), Sch. 9 Pt. 1 (with Sch. 8 Pt. 1)

Commencement Information

I20. Sch. 17 para. 15 in force at 29.12.2003 for specified purposes by S.I. 2003/3142, art. 3. (1)(3), Sch. 1 (with art. 11)

I21. Sch. 17 para. 15 in force at 1.4.2004 in so far as not already in force by S.I. 2003/3142, art. 4. (2), Sch. 2 (with art. 11)

F216. . . . .

Amendments (Textual)

F2. Sch. 17 paras. 6-18 repealed (8.2.2007) by Wireless Telegraphy Act 2006 (c. 36), s. 126. (2), Sch. 9 Pt. 1 (with Sch. 8 Pt. 1)

Commencement Information

I22. Sch. 17 para. 16 in force at 25.7.2003 for specified purposes by S.I. 2003/1900, arts. 1. (2), 2. (1), Sch. 1 (with art. 3) (as amended by S.I. 2003/3142, art. 1. (3))

I23. Sch. 17 para. 16 in force at 29.12.2003 in so far as not already in force by S.I. 2003/3142, art. 3. (2) (with art. 11)

F217. . . . .

Amendments (Textual)

F2. Sch. 17 paras. 6-18 repealed (8.2.2007) by Wireless Telegraphy Act 2006 (c. 36), s. 126. (2), Sch. 9 Pt. 1 (with Sch. 8 Pt. 1)

Commencement Information

I24. Sch. 17 para. 17 in force at 29.12.2003 by S.I. 2003/3142, art. 3. (1), Sch. 1 (with art. 11)

F218. . . . .

Amendments (Textual)

F2. Sch. 17 paras. 6-18 repealed (8.2.2007) by Wireless Telegraphy Act 2006 (c. 36), s. 126. (2), Sch. 9 Pt. 1 (with Sch. 8 Pt. 1)

Commencement Information

I25. Sch. 17 para. 18 in force at 18.9.2003 for specified purposes by S.I. 2003/1900, arts. 1. (2), 2.

(2), Sch. 2 (with art. 3) (as amended by S.I. 2003/3142, art. 1. (3))

I26. Sch. 17 para. 18 in force at 29.12.2003 in so far as not already in force by S.I. 2003/3142, art. 3. (2) (with art. 11)

Coast Protection Act 1949.

19. In section 47 of the Coast Protection Act 1949 (c. 74) (savings), in paragraph (b), for the words from "the telecommunications code" to "system" there shall be substituted " the electronic communications code on the operator of an electronic communications code network ".
Commencement Information

I27. Sch. 17 para. 19 in force at 25.7.2003 for specified purposes by S.I. 2003/1900, arts. 1. (2), 2. (1), Sch. 1 (with art. 3) (as amended by S.I. 2003/3142, art. 1. (3))

I28. Sch. 17 para. 19 in force at 29.12.2003 in so far as not already in force by S.I. 2003/3142, art. 3. (2) (with art. 11)

National Parks and Access to the Countryside Act 1949.

20. (1)The National Parks and Access to the Countryside Act 1949 (c. 97) shall be amended as follows.
(2) In section 20. (2) (byelaws for protection of nature reserves not to interfere with certain rights)—
(a) for "the running of a telecommunications code system" there shall be substituted " the provision of an electronic communications code network ";
(b) for "the telecommunications code" there shall be substituted " the electronic communications code ";
(c) for "such system" there shall be substituted " such network ".
(3) In section 60. (5)(f) (exceptions from rights of public where access agreement etc. in force), for "or a telecommunications code system" there shall be substituted " or an electronic communications code network ".
Commencement Information

I29. Sch. 17 para. 20 in force at 25.7.2003 for specified purposes by S.I. 2003/1900, arts. 1. (2), 2. (1), Sch. 1 (with art. 3) (as amended by S.I. 2003/3142, art. 1. (3))

I30. Sch. 17 para. 20 in force at 29.12.2003 in so far as not already in force by S.I. 2003/3142, art. 3. (2) (with art. 11)

London County Council (General Powers) Act 1949.

21. In section 7. (6) of the London County Council (General Powers) Act 1949 (c. lv) (interference by works etc. for provision of heat), for "telecommunication apparatus kept installed for the purposes of a telecommunications code system" there shall be substituted " electronic communications apparatus kept installed for the purposes of an electronic communications code network ".
Commencement Information

I31. Sch. 17 para. 21 in force at 25.7.2003 for specified purposes by S.I. 2003/1900, arts. 1. (2), 2. (1), Sch. 1 (with art. 3) (as amended by S.I. 2003/3142, art. 1. (3))

I32. Sch. 17 para. 21 in force at 29.12.2003 in so far as not already in force by S.I. 2003/3142, art. 3. (2) (with art. 11)

Local Government (Miscellaneous Provisions) Act 1953.

22. (1)Section 6 of the Local Government (Miscellaneous Provisions) Act 1953 (c. 26)

(supplementary provisions as to omnibus shelters etc.) shall be amended as follows.

(2) For "telecommunication apparatus", wherever occurring, there shall be substituted " electronic communications apparatus ".

(3) In subsection (1)—

(a) for "a telecommunications code system" there shall be substituted " an electronic communications code network ";

(b) for "that system" there shall be substituted " that network ".

(4) In subsection (2), for "system" there shall be substituted " network ".

Commencement Information

I33. Sch. 17 para. 22 in force at 25.7.2003 for specified purposes by S.I. 2003/1900, arts. 1. (2), 2. (1), Sch. 1 (with art. 3) (as amended by S.I. 2003/3142, art. 1. (3))

I34. Sch. 17 para. 22 in force at 29.12.2003 in so far as not already in force by S.I. 2003/3142, art. 3. (2) (with art. 11)

Army Act 1955.

F323. . . . .

Amendments (Textual)

F3. Sch. 17 para. 23 repealed (28.3.2009 for specified purposes, 31.10.2009 in so far as not already in force) by Armed Forces Act 2006 (c. 52), s. 383. (2), Sch. 17; S.I. 2009/812, art. 3. (a)(b) (with transitional provisions in S.I. 2009/1059); S.I. 2009/1167, art. 4

Commencement Information

I35. Sch. 17 para. 23 in force at 25.7.2003 for specified purposes by S.I. 2003/1900, arts. 1. (2), 2. (1), Sch. 1 (with art. 3) (as amended by S.I. 2003/3142, art. 1. (3))

I36. Sch. 17 para. 23 in force at 29.12.2003 in so far as not already in force by S.I. 2003/3142, art. 3. (2) (with art. 11)

Air Force Act 1955.

F424. . . . .

Amendments (Textual)

F4. Sch. 17 para. 24 repealed (28.3.2009 for specified purposes, 31.10.2009 in so far as not already in force) by Armed Forces Act 2006 (c. 52), s. 383. (2), Sch. 17; S.I. 2009/812, art. 3. (a)(b) (with transitional provisions in S.I. 2009/1059); S.I. 2009/1167, art. 4

Commencement Information

I37. Sch. 17 para. 24 in force at 25.7.2003 for specified purposes by S.I. 2003/1900, arts. 1. (2), 2. (1), Sch. 1 (with art. 3) (as amended by S.I. 2003/3142, art. 1. (3))

I38. Sch. 17 para. 24 in force at 29.12.2003 in so far as not already in force by S.I. 2003/3142, art. 3. (2) (with art. 11)

Lough Neagh and Lower Bann Drainage and Navigation Act (Northern Ireland) 1955.

25. In section 17. (2) of the Lough Neagh and Lower Bann Drainage and Navigation Act (Northern Ireland) 1955 (c. 15 (N.I.)) (application of paragraph 23 of telecommunications code)—

(a) for "the telecommunications code" there shall be substituted " the electronic communications code ";

(b) for "telecommunication apparatus" there shall be substituted " electronic communications apparatus ".

Commencement Information

I39. Sch. 17 para. 25 in force at 25.7.2003 for specified purposes by S.I. 2003/1900, arts. 1. (2), 2.

(1), Sch. 1 (with art. 3) (as amended by S.I. 2003/3142, art. 1. (3))

140. Sch. 17 para. 25 in force at 29.12.2003 in so far as not already in force by S.I. 2003/3142, art. 3. (2) (with art. 11)

Naval Discipline Act 1957.

26. F5. . . . .

Amendments (Textual)

F5. Sch. 17 para. 26 repealed (28.3.2009 for specified purposes, 31.10.2009 in so far as not already in force) by Armed Forces Act 2006 (c. 52), s. 383. (2), Sch. 17; S.I. 2009/812, art. 3. (a)(b) (with transitional provisions in S.I. 2009/1059); S.I. 2009/1167, art. 4

Commencement Information

141. Sch. 17 para. 26 in force at 25.7.2003 for specified purposes by S.I. 2003/1900, arts. 1. (2), 2. (1), Sch. 1 (with art. 3) (as amended by S.I. 2003/3142, art. 1. (3))

142. Sch. 17 para. 26 in force at 29.12.2003 in so far as not already in force by S.I. 2003/3142, art. 3. (2) (with art. 11)

Opencast Coal Act 1958.

27. (1)In section 45 of the Opencast Coal Act 1958 (c. 69) (saving for apparatus installed for the purposes of telecommunications code system)—

(a) for "telecommunication apparatus", wherever occurring, there shall be substituted " electronic communications apparatus ";

(b) for "a telecommunications code system", wherever occurring, there shall be substituted " an electronic communications code network ";

(c) for "the telecommunications code", wherever occurring, there shall be substituted " the electronic communications code ";

(d) for "that system" there shall be substituted " that network ".

Commencement Information

143. Sch. 17 para. 27 in force at 25.7.2003 for specified purposes by S.I. 2003/1900, arts. 1. (2), 2. (1), Sch. 1 (with art. 3) (as amended by S.I. 2003/3142, art. 1. (3))

144. Sch. 17 para. 27 in force at 29.12.2003 in so far as not already in force by S.I. 2003/3142, art. 3. (2) (with art. 11)

Pipe-lines Act 1962.

28. In section 40 of the Pipe-lines Act 1962 (c. 58) (avoidance of interference with telecommunications code systems)—

(a) for "telecommunication apparatus", in both places, there shall be substituted " electronic communications apparatus ";

(b) for "a telecommunications code system" there shall be substituted " an electronic communications code network ";

(c) for "such system" there shall be substituted " such network ";

(d) for "the telecommunications code" there shall be substituted " the electronic communications code ".

Commencement Information

145. Sch. 17 para. 28 in force at 25.7.2003 for specified purposes by S.I. 2003/1900, arts. 1. (2), 2. (1), Sch. 1 (with art. 3) (as amended by S.I. 2003/3142, art. 1. (3))

146. Sch. 17 para. 28 in force at 29.12.2003 in so far as not already in force by S.I. 2003/3142, art. 3. (2) (with art. 11)

London County Council (General Powers) Act 1963.

29. In section 17. (4)(a) of the London County Council (General Powers) Act 1963 (c. xvii) (interference from provision of illuminations, floodlighting, etc.), for "telecommunication apparatus kept installed for the purposes of a telecommunications code system" there shall be substituted " electronic communications apparatus kept installed for the purposes of an electronic communications code network ".

Commencement Information

I47. Sch. 17 para. 29 in force at 25.7.2003 for specified purposes by S.I. 2003/1900, arts. 1. (2), 2. (1), Sch. 1 (with art. 3) (as amended by S.I. 2003/3142, art. 1. (3))

I48. Sch. 17 para. 29 in force at 29.12.2003 in so far as not already in force by S.I. 2003/3142, art. 3. (2) (with art. 11)

Harbours Act 1964.

30. In section 53 of the Harbours Act 1964 (c. 40) (application of telecommunications code for certain works)—

(a) for "telecommunications code" there shall be substituted " electronic communications code ";

(b) for "telecommunication apparatus" there shall be substituted " electronic communications apparatus ".

Commencement Information

I49. Sch. 17 para. 30 in force at 25.7.2003 for specified purposes by S.I. 2003/1900, arts. 1. (2), 2. (1), Sch. 1 (with art. 3) (as amended by S.I. 2003/3142, art. 1. (3))

I50. Sch. 17 para. 30 in force at 29.12.2003 in so far as not already in force by S.I. 2003/3142, art. 3. (2) (with art. 11)

New Towns Act (Northern Ireland) 1965.

31. (1)Section 25 of the New Towns Act (Northern Ireland) 1965 (c. 13 (N.I.)) shall be amended as follows.

(2) In subsections (9. A), (9. C) and (9. D)—

(a) for "telecommunication apparatus", wherever occurring, there shall be substituted " electronic communications apparatus ";

(b) for "a telecommunications code system" there shall be substituted " an electronic communications code network ";

(c) for "that system" there shall be substituted " that network ";

(d) for "the telecommunications code", wherever occurring, there shall be substituted " the electronic communications code ".

(3) In subsection (9. B) for "any telecommunications code system" there shall be substituted " any electronic communications code network ".

Commencement Information

I51. Sch. 17 para. 31 in force at 25.7.2003 for specified purposes by S.I. 2003/1900, arts. 1. (2), 2. (1), Sch. 1 (with art. 3) (as amended by S.I. 2003/3142, art. 1. (3))

I52. Sch. 17 para. 31 in force at 29.12.2003 in so far as not already in force by S.I. 2003/3142, art. 3. (2) (with art. 11)

Marine, &c., Broadcasting (Offences) Act 1967.

F632. . . . .

Amendments (Textual)

F6. Sch. 17 paras. 32-38 repealed (8.2.2007) by Wireless Telegraphy Act 2006 (c. 36), s. 126. (2),

Sch. 9 Pt. 1 (with Sch. 8 Pt. 1)

Commencement Information

I53. Sch. 17 para. 32 in force at 18.9.2003 by S.I. 2003/1900, art. 2. (2), Sch. 2

F633. . . . .

Amendments (Textual)

F6. Sch. 17 paras. 32-38 repealed (8.2.2007) by Wireless Telegraphy Act 2006 (c. 36), s. 126. (2), Sch. 9 Pt. 1 (with Sch. 8 Pt. 1)

Commencement Information

I54. Sch. 17 para. 33 in force at 18.9.2003 by S.I. 2003/1900, art. 2. (2), Sch. 2

F634. . . . .

Amendments (Textual)

F6. Sch. 17 paras. 32-38 repealed (8.2.2007) by Wireless Telegraphy Act 2006 (c. 36), s. 126. (2), Sch. 9 Pt. 1 (with Sch. 8 Pt. 1)

Commencement Information

I55. Sch. 17 para. 34 in force at 29.12.2003 by S.I. 2003/3142, art. 3. (1), Sch. 1 (with art. 11)

F635. . . . .

Amendments (Textual)

F6. Sch. 17 paras. 32-38 repealed (8.2.2007) by Wireless Telegraphy Act 2006 (c. 36), s. 126. (2), Sch. 9 Pt. 1 (with Sch. 8 Pt. 1)

Commencement Information

I56. Sch. 17 para. 35 in force at 29.12.2003 by S.I. 2003/3142, art. 3. (1), Sch. 1 (with art. 11)

F636. . . . .

Amendments (Textual)

F6. Sch. 17 paras. 32-38 repealed (8.2.2007) by Wireless Telegraphy Act 2006 (c. 36), s. 126. (2), Sch. 9 Pt. 1 (with Sch. 8 Pt. 1)

Commencement Information

I57. Sch. 17 para. 36 in force at 29.12.2003 by S.I. 2003/3142, art. 3. (1), Sch. 1 (with art. 11)

Wireless Telegraphy Act 1967.

F637. . . . .

Commencement Information

I58. Sch. 17 para. 37 in force at 25.7.2003 for specified purposes by S.I. 2003/1900, arts. 1. (2), 2. (1), Sch. 1 (with art. 3) (as amended by S.I. 2003/3142, art. 1. (3))

I59. Sch. 17 para. 37 in force at 29.12.2003 in so far as not already in force by S.I. 2003/3142, art. 3. (1), Sch. 1 (with art. 11)

F638. . . . .

Amendments (Textual)

F6. Sch. 17 paras. 32-38 repealed (8.2.2007) by Wireless Telegraphy Act 2006 (c. 36), s. 126. (2), Sch. 9 Pt. 1 (with Sch. 8 Pt. 1)

Commencement Information

I60. Sch. 17 para. 38 in force at 25.7.2003 for specified purposes by S.I. 2003/1900, arts. 1. (2), 2. (1), Sch. 1 (with art. 3) (as amended by S.I. 2003/3142, art. 1. (3))

I61. Sch. 17 para. 38 in force at 29.12.2003 in so far as not already in force by S.I. 2003/3142, art. 3. (2) (with art. 11)

F739. . . . .

Amendments (Textual)

F7. Sch. 17 para. 39 repealed (25.6.2013) by Enterprise and Regulatory Reform Act 2013 (c. 24), s. 103. (2), Sch. 21 para. 2

Commencement Information

I62. Sch. 17 para. 39 in force at 29.12.2003 by S.I. 2003/3142, art. 3. (1), Sch. 1 (with art. 11)

Countryside Act 1968.

40. (1)The Countryside Act 1968 (c. 41) shall be amended as follows.

(2) In section 41 (exceptions from powers to make byelaws etc.), in subsections (4) and (12)—

(a) for "the running of a telecommunications code system" there shall be substituted " the provision of an electronic communications code network ";

(b) for "the telecommunications code" there shall be substituted " the electronic communications code ";

(c) for "such system" there shall be substituted " such network ".

(3) In paragraph 6 of Schedule 2 (exceptions from procedure for taking common land)—

(a) for "the telecommunications code" there shall be substituted " the electronic communications code ";

(b) for "a telecommunications code system" there shall be substituted " an electronic communications code network ".

Commencement Information

I63. Sch. 17 para. 40 in force at 25.7.2003 for specified purposes by S.I. 2003/1900, arts. 1. (2), 2. (1), Sch. 1 (with art. 3) (as amended by S.I. 2003/3142, art. 1. (3))

I64. Sch. 17 para. 40 in force at 29.12.2003 in so far as not already in force by S.I. 2003/3142, art. 3. (2) (with art. 11)

Greater London Council (General Powers) Act 1969.

41. In section 7. (6) of the Greater London Council (General Powers) Act 1969 (c. lii) (effect of exercise of power to stop up streets)—

(a) for "the telecommunications code" there shall be substituted " the electronic communications code ";

(b) for "telecommunications code system" there shall be substituted " electronic communications code network ".

Commencement Information

I65. Sch. 17 para. 41 in force at 25.7.2003 for specified purposes by S.I. 2003/1900, arts. 1. (2), 2. (1), Sch. 1 (with art. 3) (as amended by S.I. 2003/3142, art. 1. (3))

I66. Sch. 17 para. 41 in force at 29.12.2003 in so far as not already in force by S.I. 2003/3142, art. 3. (2) (with art. 11)

Harbours Act (Northern Ireland) 1970.

42. In section 37 of the Harbours Act (Northern Ireland) 1970 (c. 1 (N.I.)) (application of telecommunications code for certain works)—

(a) for "telecommunications code" there shall be substituted " electronic communications code ";

(b) for "telecommunication apparatus" there shall be substituted " electronic communications apparatus ".

Commencement Information

I67. Sch. 17 para. 42 in force at 25.7.2003 for specified purposes by S.I. 2003/1900, arts. 1. (2), 2. (1), Sch. 1 (with art. 3) (as amended by S.I. 2003/3142, art. 1. (3))

I68. Sch. 17 para. 42 in force at 29.12.2003 in so far as not already in force by S.I. 2003/3142, art. 3. (2) (with art. 11)

Thames Barrier and Flood Prevention Act 1972.

43. In section 20. (1)(a) of the Thames Barrier and Flood Prevention Act 1972 (c. xlv)(power to make subsidiary works etc.), for "telecommunication installations" there shall be substituted "

electronic communications installations ".

Commencement Information

169. Sch. 17 para. 43 in force at 25.7.2003 for specified purposes by S.I. 2003/1900, arts. 1. (2), 2. (1), Sch. 1 (with art. 3) (as amended by S.I. 2003/3142, art. 1. (3))

170. Sch. 17 para. 43 in force at 29.12.2003 in so far as not already in force by S.I. 2003/3142, art. 3. (2) (with art. 11)

Fair Trading Act 1973.

44. In section 137. (3) of the Fair Trading Act 1973 (c. 41) (meaning of "supply of services"), for paragraph (f) there shall be substituted—

"(f)includes the making of arrangements, by means of such an agreement as is mentioned in paragraph 29 of Schedule 2 to the Telecommunications Act 1984, for the sharing of the use of any electronic communications apparatus, and".

Commencement Information

171. Sch. 17 para. 44 in force at 25.7.2003 for specified purposes by S.I. 2003/1900, arts. 1. (2), 2. (1), Sch. 1 (with art. 3) (as amended by S.I. 2003/3142, art. 1. (3))

172. Sch. 17 para. 44 in force at 29.12.2003 in so far as not already in force by S.I. 2003/3142, art. 3. (2) (with art. 11)

Drainage (Northern Ireland) Order 1973.

45. In paragraph 3 of Schedule 9 to the Drainage (Northern Ireland) Order 1973 (S.I. 1973/69 (N.I. 1))—

(a) for "telecommunication apparatus", wherever occurring, there shall be substituted " electronic communications apparatus ";

(b) for "a telecommunications code system", wherever occurring, there shall be substituted " an electronic communications code network ";

(c) for "telecommunications code", wherever occurring (except in the expression "telecommunications code system"), there shall be substituted " electronic communications code ";

(d) for "any such system" and "that system" there shall be substituted, respectively, " any such network " and " that network ".

Commencement Information

173. Sch. 17 para. 45 in force at 25.7.2003 for specified purposes by S.I. 2003/1900, arts. 1. (2), 2. (1), Sch. 1 (with art. 3) (as amended by S.I. 2003/3142, art. 1. (3))

174. Sch. 17 para. 45 in force at 29.12.2003 in so far as not already in force by S.I. 2003/3142, art. 3. (2) (with art. 11)

Water and Sewerage Services (Northern Ireland) Order 1973.

46[F8. (1)In Article 57. A(3)(b) of the Water and Sewerage Services (Northern Ireland) Order 1973 (S.I. 1973/70 (N.I. 2)) (civil liability of Department for escapes of water)—

(a) for "telecommunications code" there shall be substituted " electronic communications code ";

(b) for "a telecommunication system" there shall be substituted " an electronic communications network ".

(2) In Article 58. (1) of that Order (protection for telegraph and telephone lines), for "telecommunications" there shall be substituted " electronic communications ".]

Amendments (Textual)

F8. Sch. 17 para. 46 repealed (N.I.) (1.4.2007) by The Water and Sewerage Services (Northern Ireland) Order 2006 (S.I. 2006/3336), art. 1. (2), Sch. 13 (with arts. 8. (8), 121. (3), 307); S.R.

2007/194, art. 2. (2), Sch. Pt. 2 (with Sch. 2)
Commencement Information
I75. Sch. 17 para. 46 in force at 25.7.2003 for specified purposes by S.I. 2003/1900, arts. 1. (2), 2. (1), Sch. 1 (with art. 3) (as amended by S.I. 2003/3142, art. 1. (3))
I76. Sch. 17 para. 46 in force at 29.12.2003 in so far as not already in force by S.I. 2003/3142, art. 3. (2) (with art. 11)

Consumer Credit Act 1974.

47. In section 16. (6) of the Consumer Credit Act 1974 (c. 39) (exempt agreements) for "public telecommunications operator specified in the order" there shall be substituted " provider of a public electronic communications service who is specified in the order ".
Commencement Information
I77. Sch. 17 para. 47 in force at 25.7.2003 for specified purposes by S.I. 2003/1900, arts. 1. (2), 2. (1), Sch. 1 (with art. 3) (as amended by S.I. 2003/3142, art. 1. (3))
I78. Sch. 17 para. 47 in force at 29.12.2003 in so far as not already in force by S.I. 2003/3142, art. 3. (2) (with art. 11)

House of Commons Disqualification Act 1975.

48. In Part 2 of Schedule 1 to the House of Commons Disqualification Act 1975 (c. 24) (bodies of which all members are disqualified), in the appropriate place, there shall be inserted— " Seirbheis nam Meadhanan Gàidhlig ".
Commencement Information
I79. Sch. 17 para. 48 in force at 29.12.2003 by S.I. 2003/3142, art. 3. (1), Sch. 1 (with art. 11)

Northern Ireland Assembly Disqualification Act 1975.

49. In Part 2 of Schedule 1 to the Northern Ireland Assembly Disqualification Act 1975 (c. 25) (bodies of which all members are disqualified), in the appropriate place, there shall be inserted— " Seirbheis nam Meadhanan Gàidhlig ".
Commencement Information
I80. Sch. 17 para. 49 in force at 29.12.2003 by S.I. 2003/3142, art. 3. (1), Sch. 1 (with art. 11)

Welsh Development Agency Act 1975.

50. (1)Section 19 of the Welsh Development Agency Act 1975 (c. 70) (the Agency and the media) shall be amended as follows.
(2) In subsection (9), for "the appropriate authority", in both places, there shall be substituted " the Office of Communications ".
(3) In subsection (11), in the definition of "relevant licence" for "the Independent Television Commission or the Radio Authority" there shall be substituted " the Office of Communications ".
Commencement Information
I81. Sch. 17 para. 50 in force at 29.12.2003 by S.I. 2003/3142, art. 3. (1), Sch. 1 (with art. 11)

Building Regulations (Northern Ireland) Order 1979.

51. In paragraph 14 of Schedule 1 to the Building Regulations (Northern Ireland) Order 1979 (S.I. 1979/1709 (N.I. 16)) (building regulations), for "telecommunications services" there shall be substituted " communications services ".
Commencement Information

182. Sch. 17 para. 51 in force at 25.7.2003 for specified purposes by S.I. 2003/1900, arts. 1. (2), 2. (1), Sch. 1 (with art. 3) (as amended by S.I. 2003/3142, art. 1. (3))

183. Sch. 17 para. 51 in force at 29.12.2003 in so far as not already in force by S.I. 2003/3142, art. 3. (2) (with art. 11)

Local Government, Planning and Land Act 1980.

52. (1)Part 3 of Schedule 28 to the Local Government, Planning and Land Act 1980 (c. 65) (provisions about land acquired by urban development corporations) shall be amended as follows.
(2) In paragraphs 5, 6, 13, 14 and 16—
(a) for "the telecommunications code", wherever occurring, there shall be substituted " the electronic communications code ";
(b) for "a telecommunications code system" and "any telecommunications code system", wherever occurring, there shall be substituted " an electronic communications code network ";
(c) for "telecommunication apparatus", wherever occurring, there shall be substituted " electronic communications apparatus ";
(d) for "such system" and "the system", wherever occurring, there shall be substituted, respectively, " such network " and " the network ".

Commencement Information

184. Sch. 17 para. 52 in force at 25.7.2003 for specified purposes by S.I. 2003/1900, arts. 1. (2), 2. (1), Sch. 1 (with art. 3) (as amended by S.I. 2003/3142, art. 1. (3))

185. Sch. 17 para. 52 in force at 29.12.2003 in so far as not already in force by S.I. 2003/3142, art. 3. (2) (with art. 11)

Highways Act 1980.

53. In section 35. (11)(c) and (12) of the Highways Act 1980 (c. 66) (regulation of rights to maintain apparatus on walkways), for "telecommunications code systems" there shall be substituted " electronic communications code networks ".

Commencement Information

186. Sch. 17 para. 53 in force at 25.7.2003 for specified purposes by S.I. 2003/1900, arts. 1. (2), 2. (1), Sch. 1 (with art. 3) (as amended by S.I. 2003/3142, art. 1. (3))

187. Sch. 17 para. 53 in force at 29.12.2003 in so far as not already in force by S.I. 2003/3142, art. 3. (2) (with art. 11)

54. In section 115. D of that Act (limits on powers to restrict access to highways), for paragraph (d) there shall be substituted—

   "(d)as to prevent the operator of an electronic communications code network having access to any electronic communications apparatus kept installed for the purposes of that network under, in, on or over the highway."

Commencement Information

188. Sch. 17 para. 54 in force at 25.7.2003 for specified purposes by S.I. 2003/1900, arts. 1. (2), 2. (1), Sch. 1 (with art. 3) (as amended by S.I. 2003/3142, art. 1. (3))

189. Sch. 17 para. 54 in force at 29.12.2003 in so far as not already in force by S.I. 2003/3142, art. 3. (2) (with art. 11)

55. In section 142. (5) of that Act (protection of telecommunications apparatus by conditions in licences to plant trees etc. in a highway), for "telecommunications code systems" there shall be substituted " electronic communications code networks ".

Commencement Information

190. Sch. 17 para. 55 in force at 25.7.2003 for specified purposes by S.I. 2003/1900, arts. 1. (2), 2. (1), Sch. 1 (with art. 3) (as amended by S.I. 2003/3142, art. 1. (3))

191. Sch. 17 para. 55 in force at 29.12.2003 in so far as not already in force by S.I. 2003/3142, art. 3. (2) (with art. 11)

56. (1)This paragraph applies to the following provisions of that Act—

(a) the definition of "statutory undertakers" in section 144. (6) (power to erect flagpoles etc. on highways);

(b) the definition of "statutory undertakers" in section 169. (4) (control of scaffolding on highways);

(c) the definition of "statutory undertakers" in section 170. (3) (control of mixing mortar etc. on highways);

(d) section 177. (4) and (12) (licence to build over highway not to interfere with telecommunications code systems);

(e) section 178. (5) (exceptions to restriction on placing rails etc. over highways);

(f) section 329. (4. A) (interpretation);

(g) section 334 (savings for operators of telecommunications code systems).

(2) In the provisions to which this paragraph applies—

(a) for "a telecommunications code system" and "any telecommunications code system", wherever occurring, there shall be substituted " an electronic communications code network ";

(b) for "the telecommunications code system" there shall be substituted " the electronic communications code network ";

(c) for "telecommunication apparatus", wherever occurring, there shall be substituted " electronic communications apparatus ";

(d) for "telecommunications code", wherever occurring (except in the expression "telecommunications code system"), there shall be substituted " electronic communications code ";

(e) for "system", wherever occurring (except in the expression "telecommunications code system"), there shall be substituted " network ".

Commencement Information

192. Sch. 17 para. 56 in force at 25.7.2003 for specified purposes by S.I. 2003/1900, arts. 1. (2), 2. (1), Sch. 1 (with art. 3) (as amended by S.I. 2003/3142, art. 1. (3))

193. Sch. 17 para. 56 in force at 29.12.2003 in so far as not already in force by S.I. 2003/3142, art. 3. (2) (with art. 11)

New Towns Act 1981.

57. (1)This paragraph applies to the following provisions of the New Towns Act 1981 (c. 64)—

(a) section 16. (2) (exception to extinguishment of rights over land compulsorily acquired);

(b) section 19. (2) (saving from the power to override certain rights);

(c) section 24 (apparatus kept installed for purposes of telecommunications code system);

(d) section 26. (8) (extinguishment of rights of way and removal of apparatus);

(e) section 39. (7) (power of development corporation to transfer undertakings).

(2) In the provisions to which this paragraph applies—

(a) for "in accordance with the telecommunications code", wherever occurring, there shall be substituted " in accordance with the electronic communications code ";

(b) for "a telecommunications code system" and "any telecommunications code system", wherever occurring, there shall be substituted " an electronic communications code network ";

(c) for "telecommunication apparatus", wherever occurring, there shall be substituted " electronic communications apparatus ";

(d) for "the running of the telecommunications code system" there shall be substituted " the provision of the electronic communications code network ";

(e) for "the running of such a system" there shall be substituted " the provision of such a network ";

(f) for "such system" and "the system", wherever occurring, there shall be substituted, respectively, " such network " and " the network ".

Commencement Information

194. Sch. 17 para. 57 in force at 25.7.2003 for specified purposes by S.I. 2003/1900, arts. 1. (2), 2. (1), Sch. 1 (with art. 3) (as amended by S.I. 2003/3142, art. 1. (3))
195. Sch. 17 para. 57 in force at 29.12.2003 in so far as not already in force by S.I. 2003/3142, art. 3. (2) (with art. 11)

Acquisition of Land Act 1981.

58. (1)The Acquisition of Land Act 1981 (c. 67) shall be amended as follows.
(2) In section 28 (acquisition of land by the creation of new rights), after paragraph (h) there shall be inserted—
    "(i)paragraph 3. (3) of Schedule 4 to the Communications Act 2003."
(3) In section 32. (6. A) (exception to power to extinguish certain public rights of way)—
(a) for the words from "telecommunication apparatus" to "telecommunications code system" there shall be substituted " electronic communications apparatus kept installed for the purposes of an electronic communications code network "; and
(b) in paragraph (a), for "system" there shall be substituted " network ".
Commencement Information
196. Sch. 17 para. 58 in force at 25.7.2003 for specified purposes by S.I. 2003/1900, arts. 1. (2), 2. (1), Sch. 1 (with art. 3) (as amended by S.I. 2003/3142, art. 1. (3))
197. Sch. 17 para. 58 in force at 29.12.2003 in so far as not already in force by S.I. 2003/3142, art. 3. (2) (with art. 11)

Housing (Northern Ireland) Order 1981.

59. In Article 159. A of the Housing (Northern Ireland) Order 1981 (S.I. 1981/156 (N.I. 3)) (application of telecommunications code to the Northern Ireland Housing Executive)—
(a) for "telecommunications code", wherever occurring, there shall be substituted " electronic communications code ";
(b) for "telecommunication apparatus", wherever occurring, there shall be substituted " electronic communications apparatus ";
(c) for "a telecommunications code system" there shall be substituted " an electronic communications code network ";
(d) for "that system" there shall be substituted " that network ".
Commencement Information
198. Sch. 17 para. 59 in force at 25.7.2003 for specified purposes by S.I. 2003/1900, arts. 1. (2), 2. (1), Sch. 1 (with art. 3) (as amended by S.I. 2003/3142, art. 1. (3))
199. Sch. 17 para. 59 in force at 29.12.2003 in so far as not already in force by S.I. 2003/3142, art. 3. (2) (with art. 11)

Civil Aviation Act 1982.

60. In section 48. (7)(b) of the Civil Aviation Act 1982 (c. 16) (Secretary of State to give notice of orders stopping up highways for civil aviation purposes), for "a telecommunications code system" there shall be substituted " an electronic communications code network ".
Commencement Information
I100. Sch. 17 para. 60 in force at 25.7.2003 for specified purposes by S.I. 2003/1900, arts. 1. (2), 2. (1), Sch. 1 (with art. 3) (as amended by S.I. 2003/3142, art. 1. (3))
I101. Sch. 17 para. 60 in force at 29.12.2003 in so far as not already in force by S.I. 2003/3142, art. 3. (2) (with art. 11)

Representation of the People Act 1983.

61. In section 92. (1)(c) of the Representation of the People Act 1983 (c. 2) (broadcasting from outside the United Kingdom), for "the Independent Television Commission or the Radio Authority" there shall be substituted " the Office of Communications ".

Commencement Information

I102. Sch. 17 para. 61 in force at 29.12.2003 by S.I. 2003/3142, art. 3. (1), Sch. 1 (with art. 11)

62. (1)Section 93 of that Act (broadcasting of local items during election period) shall be amended as follows.

(2) In subsection (4), for the words from the beginning to "each" there shall be substituted " The Office of Communications shall ".

(3) In subsection (6)—

(a) in the definition of "broadcasting authority", for "the Independent Television Commission, the Radio Authority" there shall be substituted " the Office of Communications ";

(b) in the definition of "relevant services", for paragraphs (b) and (c) there shall be substituted—

   "(b)in relation to the Office of Communications, means services licensed under Part 1 or 3 of the Broadcasting Act 1990 or Part 1 or 2 of the Broadcasting Act 1996."

Commencement Information

I103. Sch. 17 para. 62 in force at 29.12.2003 by S.I. 2003/3142, art. 3. (1), Sch. 1 (with art. 11)

Telecommunications Act 1984.

63. (1)Sections 44 to 46 of the Telecommunications Act 1984 (c. 12) (offences relating to modification and interception of messages and to assaults on the persons engaged on the business of a telecommunications operator) shall cease to have effect.

(2) No proceedings shall be capable of being begun at any time after the commencement of this paragraph for any offence under any of those sections which was committed before the commencement of this paragraph.

(3) Any proceedings for an offence under any of those sections which have been begun before the commencement of this paragraph but in which there has not yet been a conviction must be discontinued immediately.

Commencement Information

I104. Sch. 17 para. 63 in force at 25.7.2003 for specified purposes by S.I. 2003/1900, arts. 1. (2), 2. (1), Sch. 1 (with art. 3) (as amended by S.I. 2003/3142, art. 1. (3))

I105. Sch. 17 para. 63 in force at 29.12.2003 in so far as not already in force by S.I. 2003/3142, art. 3. (2) (with art. 11)

F964. . . . .

Amendments (Textual)

F9. Sch. 17 paras. 64-69 repealed (8.2.2007) by Wireless Telegraphy Act 2006 (c. 36), s. 126. (2), Sch. 9 Pt. 1 (with Sch. 8 Pt. 1)

Commencement Information

I106. Sch. 17 para. 64 in force at 29.12.2003 by S.I. 2003/3142, art. 3. (1), Sch. 1 (with art. 11)

F965. . . . .

Amendments (Textual)

F9. Sch. 17 paras. 64-69 repealed (8.2.2007) by Wireless Telegraphy Act 2006 (c. 36), s. 126. (2), Sch. 9 Pt. 1 (with Sch. 8 Pt. 1)

Commencement Information

I107. Sch. 17 para. 65 in force at 29.12.2003 by S.I. 2003/3142, art. 3. (1), Sch. 1 (with art. 11)

F966. . . . .

Amendments (Textual)

F9. Sch. 17 paras. 64-69 repealed (8.2.2007) by Wireless Telegraphy Act 2006 (c. 36), s. 126. (2), Sch. 9 Pt. 1 (with Sch. 8 Pt. 1)

Commencement Information

I108. Sch. 17 para. 66 in force at 29.12.2003 by S.I. 2003/3142, art. 3. (1), Sch. 1 (with art. 11)

F967. . . . .

Amendments (Textual)

F9. Sch. 17 paras. 64-69 repealed (8.2.2007) by Wireless Telegraphy Act 2006 (c. 36), s. 126. (2), Sch. 9 Pt. 1 (with Sch. 8 Pt. 1)

Commencement Information

I109. Sch. 17 para. 67 in force at 29.12.2003 by S.I. 2003/3142, art. 3. (1), Sch. 1 (with art. 11)

F968. . . . .

Amendments (Textual)

F9. Sch. 17 paras. 64-69 repealed (8.2.2007) by Wireless Telegraphy Act 2006 (c. 36), s. 126. (2), Sch. 9 Pt. 1 (with Sch. 8 Pt. 1)

Commencement Information

I110. Sch. 17 para. 68 in force at 29.12.2003 by S.I. 2003/3142, art. 3. (1), Sch. 1 (with art. 11)

F969. . . . .

Amendments (Textual)

F9. Sch. 17 paras. 64-69 repealed (8.2.2007) by Wireless Telegraphy Act 2006 (c. 36), s. 126. (2), Sch. 9 Pt. 1 (with Sch. 8 Pt. 1)

Commencement Information

I111. Sch. 17 para. 69 in force at 29.12.2003 by S.I. 2003/3142, art. 3. (1), Sch. 1 (with art. 11)

70. (1)Section 94 of that Act (directions in the interests of national security) shall be amended as follows.

(2) In subsection (1), for "requisite or expedient" there shall be substituted " necessary ".

(3) In subsection (2), for "requisite or expedient" there shall be substituted " necessary ".

(4) After subsection (2), there shall be inserted—

"(2. A)The Secretary of State shall not give a direction under subsection (1) or (2) unless he believes that the conduct required by the direction is proportionate to what is sought to be achieved by that conduct."

(5) In subsection (3), for "this Act" there shall be substituted " Part 1 or Chapter 1 of Part 2 of the Communications Act 2003 and, in the case of a direction to a provider of a public electronic communications network, notwithstanding that it relates to him in a capacity other than as the provider of such a network ".

(6) In subsection (6), for "public telecommunications operators" there shall be substituted " providers of public electronic communications networks ".

(7) In subsection (8), for the words from "the Director" onwards there shall be substituted " OFCOM and to providers of public electronic communications networks. "

Commencement Information

I112. Sch. 17 para. 70 in force at 25.7.2003 for specified purposes by S.I. 2003/1900, arts. 1. (2), 2. (1), Sch. 1 (with art. 3) (as amended by S.I. 2003/3142, art. 1. (3))

I113. Sch. 17 para. 70 in force at 18.9.2003 in so far as not already in force by S.I. 2003/1900, art. 2. (2), Sch. 2

71. (1)Section 98 of that Act (use of conduits for telecommunications purposes) shall be amended as follows.

(2) In subsection (1), for the words "telecommunication apparatus", wherever occurring, there shall be substituted " electronic communications apparatus ".

(3) In subsection (5)(a), for the words "telecommunication purposes" there shall be substituted " the purposes of any electronic communications network or of any electronic communications service ".

Commencement Information

I114. Sch. 17 para. 71 in force at 25.7.2003 for specified purposes by S.I. 2003/1900, arts. 1. (2), 2. (1), Sch. 1 (with art. 3) (as amended by S.I. 2003/3142, art. 1. (3))

I115. Sch. 17 para. 71 in force at 29.12.2003 in so far as not already in force by S.I. 2003/3142, art. 3. (2) (with art. 11)

72. (1)Section 101 of that Act (general restrictions on disclosure of information) shall be amended

as follows.

F10. (2). . . . .

(3) In subsection (2)(a)—

(a) the words "or transferred"shall be omitted; and

(b) for the words ", the Director or the Commission by or under this Act" there shall be substituted " or OFCOM by or under this Act (except functions assigned by or under Part 6) ".

(4) In subsection (2)(b), after "the Rail Regulator" there shall be inserted " , OFCOM ".

(5) In subsection (3), after paragraph (p) there shall be inserted—

"(q)the Communications Act 2003 (excluding the provisions of that Act which are enactments relating to the management of the radio spectrum within the meaning of that Act)."

(6) Subsection (4) shall cease to have effect.

(7) In subsection (6), for "the Director" there shall be substituted " OFCOM ".

Amendments (Textual)

F10. Sch. 17 para. 72. (2) repealed (8.2.2007) by Wireless Telegraphy Act 2006 (c. 36), s. 126. (2), Sch. 9 Pt. 1 (with Sch. 8 Pt. 1)

Commencement Information

I116. Sch. 17 para. 72. (1)-(3)(5)(6) in force at 25.7.2003 for specified purposes by S.I. 2003/1900, arts. 1. (2), 2. (1), Sch. 1 (with art. 3) (as amended by S.I. 2003/3142, art. 1. (3))

I117. Sch. 17 para. 72. (1)-(3) (5) (6) in force at 29.12.2003 in so far as not already in force by S.I. 2003/3142, art. 3. (1), Sch. 1 (with art. 11)

I118. Sch. 17 para. 72. (4) (7) in force at 29.12.2003 by S.I. 2003/3142, art. 3. (1), Sch. 1 (with art. 11)

73. In section 104 of that Act (orders and schemes), after subsection (1) there shall be inserted—

"(1. A)Section 403 of the Communications Act 2003 (procedure for regulations and orders made by OFCOM) applies to every power of OFCOM to make an order under a provision of this Act.

(1. B)The approval of the Secretary of State is required for the making by OFCOM of an order under section 85 or 86 above.

(1. C)A statutory instrument containing an order made by OFCOM under section 85 or 86 above shall be subject to annulment in pursuance of a resolution of either House of Parliament."

Commencement Information

I119. Sch. 17 para. 73 in force at 25.7.2003 for specified purposes by S.I. 2003/1900, arts. 1. (2), 2. (1), Sch. 1 (with art. 3) (as amended by S.I. 2003/3142, art. 1. (3))

I120. Sch. 17 para. 73 in force at 29.12.2003 in so far as not already in force by S.I. 2003/3142, art. 3. (1), Sch. 1 (with art. 11)

74. In section 106. (1) of that Act (general interpretation), after the definition of "modifications" there shall be inserted—

""OFCOM" means the Office of Communications;".

Commencement Information

I121. Sch. 17 para. 74 in force at 29.12.2003 by S.I. 2003/3142, art. 3. (1), Sch. 1 (with art. 11)

75. In paragraph 18. (2) of Schedule 2 to that Act (notices affixed to overhead apparatus), for "paragraph 24. (4)(a)" there shall be substituted " paragraph 24. (2. A)(a) ".

Commencement Information

I122. Sch. 17 para. 75 in force at 25.7.2003 for specified purposes by S.I. 2003/1900, arts. 1. (2), 2. (1), Sch. 1 (with art. 3) (as amended by S.I. 2003/3142, art. 1. (3))

I123. Sch. 17 para. 75 in force at 29.12.2003 in so far as not already in force by S.I. 2003/3142, art. 3. (2) (with art. 11)

Cinemas Act 1985.

76. In section 21. (1) of the Cinemas Act 1985 (c. 13) (interpretation), for the definition of "film exhibition" there shall be substituted—

""film exhibition" means any exhibition of moving pictures other than an exhibition of items

included in a programme service (within the meaning of the Communications Act 2003) that is being simultaneously received (or virtually so) by the exhibitor".
Commencement Information
I124. Sch. 17 para. 76 in force at 29.12.2003 by S.I. 2003/3142, art. 3. (1), Sch. 1 (with art. 11)

Surrogacy Arrangements Act 1985.

77. In section 3 of the Surrogacy Arrangements Act 1985 (c. 49) (advertisements about surrogacy), for "a telecommunication system", wherever occurring, there shall be substituted " an electronic communications network ".
Commencement Information
I125. Sch. 17 para. 77 in force at 25.7.2003 for specified purposes by S.I. 2003/1900, arts. 1. (2), 2. (1), Sch. 1 (with art. 3) (as amended by S.I. 2003/3142, art. 1. (3))
I126. Sch. 17 para. 77 in force at 29.12.2003 in so far as not already in force by S.I. 2003/3142, art. 3. (2) (with art. 11)

Bankruptcy (Scotland) Act 1985.

F1178. . . . .
Amendments (Textual)
F11. Sch. 17 para. 78 repealed (30.11.2016) by The Bankruptcy (Scotland) Act 2016 (Consequential Provisions and Modifications) Order 2016 (S.I. 2016/1034), art. 1, Sch. 2 Pt. 1
Commencement Information
I127. Sch. 17 para. 78 in force at 25.7.2003 for specified purposes by S.I. 2003/1900, arts. 1. (2), 2. (1), Sch. 1 (with art. 3) (as amended by S.I. 2003/3142, art. 1. (3))
I128. Sch. 17 para. 78 in force at 29.12.2003 in so far as not already in force by S.I. 2003/3142, art. 3. (2) (with art. 11)

Housing Act 1985.

79. (1)The Housing Act 1985 (c. 68) shall be amended as follows.
(2) In section 295. (2)(b) (extinguishment of other rights over land acquired), for "telecommunications systems" there shall be substituted " electronic communications networks ".
(3) In section 298. (2) and (3) (telecommunications apparatus)—
(a) for "telecommunication apparatus", wherever occurring, there shall be substituted " electronic communications apparatus ";
(b) for "a telecommunications code system", wherever occurring, there shall be substituted " an electronic communications code network ";
(c) for "the telecommunications code", wherever occurring, there shall be substituted " the electronic communications code ";
(d) for "the system" and "a system" there shall be substituted, respectively, " the network " and " a network ".
Commencement Information
I129. Sch. 17 para. 79 in force at 25.7.2003 for specified purposes by S.I. 2003/1900, arts. 1. (2), 2. (1), Sch. 1 (with art. 3) (as amended by S.I. 2003/3142, art. 1. (3))
I130. Sch. 17 para. 79 in force at 29.12.2003 in so far as not already in force by S.I. 2003/3142, art. 3. (2) (with art. 11)

Airports Act 1986.

80. In section 62 of the Airports Act 1986 (c. 31) (provisions as to telecommunication

apparatus)—

(a) for "the telecommunications code", wherever occurring, there shall be substituted " the electronic communications code ";

(b) for "telecommunication apparatus" and "telecommunications apparatus", wherever occurring, there shall be substituted " electronic communications apparatus ";

(c) for "a telecommunications code system", wherever occurring, there shall be substituted " an electronic communications code network ";

(d) in subsection (3), for "that system" there shall be substituted " that network ".

Commencement Information

I131. Sch. 17 para. 80 in force at 25.7.2003 for specified purposes by S.I. 2003/1900, arts. 1. (2), 2. (1), Sch. 1 (with art. 3) (as amended by S.I. 2003/3142, art. 1. (3))

I132. Sch. 17 para. 80 in force at 29.12.2003 in so far as not already in force by S.I. 2003/3142, art. 3. (2) (with art. 11)

Gas Act 1986.

81. In section 4. AA(4)(b) of the Gas Act 1986 (c. 44) (general duties of Secretary of State and Authority), for sub-paragraph (i) there shall be substituted—

"(i)communications services and electronic communications apparatus, or".

Commencement Information

I133. Sch. 17 para. 81 in force at 25.7.2003 for specified purposes by S.I. 2003/1900, arts. 1. (2), 2. (1), Sch. 1 (with art. 3) (as amended by S.I. 2003/3142, art. 1. (3))

I134. Sch. 17 para. 81 in force at 29.12.2003 in so far as not already in force by S.I. 2003/3142, art. 3. (2) (with art. 11)

Insolvency Act 1986.

82. (1)The Insolvency Act 1986 (c. 45) shall be amended as follows.

(2) In section 233 (supplies of telecommunications services etc. in cases of administration or liquidation)—

(a) in subsection (3), for paragraph (d) there shall be substituted—

"(d)a supply of communications services by a provider of a public electronic communications service.";

(b) in subsection (5), for paragraph (d) there shall be substituted—

"(d)"communications services" do not include electronic communications services to the extent that they are used to broadcast or otherwise transmit programme services (within the meaning of the Communications Act 2003)."

(3) In section 372 (supplies of telecommunications services etc. in cases of bankruptcy)—

(a) in subsection (4), for paragraph (d) there shall be substituted—

"(d)a supply of communications services by a provider of a public electronic communications service.";

(b) in subsection (5), for paragraph (c) there shall be substituted—

"(c)"communications services" do not include electronic communications services to the extent that they are used to broadcast or otherwise transmit programme services (within the meaning of the Communications Act 2003)."

(4) In Schedule 2. A (exceptions to prohibition on appointment of administrative receiver), in paragraph 10, after sub-paragraph (2) there shall be inserted—

"(2. A)For the purposes of section 72. D a business is also regulated to the extent that it consists in the provision of a public electronic communications network or a public electronic communications service."

Commencement Information

I135. Sch. 17 para. 82 in force at 25.7.2003 for specified purposes by S.I. 2003/1900, arts. 1. (2),

2. (1), Sch. 1 (with art. 3) (as amended by S.I. 2003/3142, art. 1. (3))

I136. Sch. 17 para. 82 in force at 29.12.2003 in so far as not already in force by S.I. 2003/3142, art. 3. (2) (with art. 11)

Company Directors Disqualification Act 1986.

83. In section 9. E(2) of the Company Directors Disqualification Act 1986 (c. 46) (interpretation), for paragraph (a) there shall be substituted—

"(a)the Office of Communications;".

Commencement Information

I137. Sch. 17 para. 83 in force at 29.12.2003 by S.I. 2003/3142, art. 3. (1), Sch. 1 (with art. 11)

Channel Tunnel Act 1987.

84. For section 32 of the Channel Tunnel Act 1987 (c. 53), there shall be substituted—

"32. Exclusion of rights under electronic communications code

No rights shall be exercisable by any person by virtue of the electronic communications code in relation to any land comprised in the tunnel system and lying in or under the bed of the sea."

Commencement Information

I138. Sch. 17 para. 84 in force at 25.7.2003 for specified purposes by S.I. 2003/1900, arts. 1. (2), 2. (1), Sch. 1 (with art. 3) (as amended by S.I. 2003/3142, art. 1. (3))

I139. Sch. 17 para. 84 in force at 29.12.2003 in so far as not already in force by S.I. 2003/3142, art. 3. (2) (with art. 11)

85. In paragraph 3. (2)(b) of Schedule 2 to that Act (supplementary provisions as to scheduled works etc.), for "telecommunications" there shall be substituted " electronic communications ".

Commencement Information

I140. Sch. 17 para. 85 in force at 25.7.2003 for specified purposes by S.I. 2003/1900, arts. 1. (2), 2. (1), Sch. 1 (with art. 3) (as amended by S.I. 2003/3142, art. 1. (3))

I141. Sch. 17 para. 85 in force at 29.12.2003 in so far as not already in force by S.I. 2003/3142, art. 3. (2) (with art. 11)

86. (1)Part 10 of Schedule 7 to that Act (protection of telecommunications operators) shall be amended as follows.

(2) In paragraph 1. (1), for "a telecommunications operator" there shall be substituted " an operator of an electronic communications code network ".

(3) In paragraphs 2 to 7—

(a) for "telecommunication apparatus", wherever occurring, there shall be substituted " electronic communications apparatus ";

(b) for "a telecommunications code system", "a telecommunication system" and "any telecommunications code system", wherever occurring, there shall be substituted " an electronic communications code network ";

(c) for "that telecommunications system" there shall be substituted " that network ";

(d) for "the telecommunications operator", wherever occurring, there shall be substituted " the operator ";

(e) for "any telecommunications operator", wherever occurring, there shall be substituted " any operator of an electronic communications code network ";

(f) for "a system" and "that system", wherever occurring, there shall be substituted, respectively, " a network " and " that network ";

(g) for "the system", wherever occurring, there shall be substituted " the electronic communications code network ".

Commencement Information

I142. Sch. 17 para. 86 in force at 25.7.2003 for specified purposes by S.I. 2003/1900, arts. 1. (2), 2. (1), Sch. 1 (with art. 3) (as amended by S.I. 2003/3142, art. 1. (3))

I143. Sch. 17 para. 86 in force at 29.12.2003 in so far as not already in force by S.I. 2003/3142, art. 3. (2) (with art. 11)

Consumer Protection (Northern Ireland) Order 1987.

87. (1)Article 29 of the Consumer Protection (Northern Ireland) Order 1987 (S.I. 1987/2049 (N.I. 20)) (restrictions on disclosure of information) shall be amended as follows.

(2) In paragraph (3), after sub-paragraph (n), there shall be inserted—

   "(o)the Communications Act 2003."

(3) In paragraph (6) for "the Director General of Telecommunications" there shall be substituted " the Office of Communications ".

Commencement Information

I144. Sch. 17 para. 87 in force at 25.7.2003 for specified purposes by S.I. 2003/1900, arts. 1. (2), 2. (1), Sch. 1 (with art. 3) (as amended by S.I. 2003/3142, art. 1. (3))

I145. Sch. 17 para. 87 in force at 29.12.2003 in so far as not already in force by S.I. 2003/3142, art. 3. (2) (with art. 11)

Income and Corporation Taxes Act 1988.

88. In section 567. (2)(b) of the Income and Corporation Taxes Act 1988 (c. 1) (meaning of "construction operations"), for "telecommunication apparatus" there shall be substituted " electronic communications apparatus ".

Commencement Information

I146. Sch. 17 para. 88 in force at 25.7.2003 for specified purposes by S.I. 2003/1900, arts. 1. (2), 2. (1), Sch. 1 (with art. 3) (as amended by S.I. 2003/3142, art. 1. (3))

I147. Sch. 17 para. 88 in force at 29.12.2003 in so far as not already in force by S.I. 2003/3142, art. 3. (2) (with art. 11)

Norfolk and Suffolk Broads Act 1988.

89. In section 25. (1) of the Norfolk and Suffolk Broads Act 1988 (c. 4) (interpretation), in the definition of "statutory undertaker", for paragraph (d) there shall be substituted—

   "(d)any electronic communications code operator;".

Commencement Information

I148. Sch. 17 para. 89 in force at 25.7.2003 for specified purposes by S.I. 2003/1900, arts. 1. (2), 2. (1), Sch. 1 (with art. 3) (as amended by S.I. 2003/3142, art. 1. (3))

I149. Sch. 17 para. 89 in force at 29.12.2003 in so far as not already in force by S.I. 2003/3142, art. 3. (2) (with art. 11)

Malicious Communications Act 1988.

90. In section 1. (2. A)(a) of the Malicious Communications Act 1988 (c. 27) (offence of sending electronic communications with intent to cause distress or anxiety), for "a telecommunication system (within the meaning of the Telecommunications Act 1984)" there shall be substituted " an electronic communications network ".

Commencement Information

I150. Sch. 17 para. 90 in force at 25.7.2003 for specified purposes by S.I. 2003/1900, arts. 1. (2), 2. (1), Sch. 1 (with art. 3) (as amended by S.I. 2003/3142, art. 1. (3))

Copyright, Designs and Patents Act 1988.

91. (1)Section 69 of the Copyright, Designs and Patents Act 1988 (c. 48) (no infringement of copyright by use of recordings for certain supervisory purposes) shall be amended as follows.
(2) In subsection (2)—
(a) for paragraph (a) there shall be substituted—
   "(a)section 167. (1) of the Broadcasting Act 1990, section 115. (4) or (6) or 117 of the Broadcasting Act 1996 or paragraph 20 of Schedule 12 to the Communications Act 2003;";
(b) in paragraph (b), for the words from "by virtue of" to "1990" there shall be substituted " by virtue of section 334. (1) of the Communications Act 2003 ";
(c) in paragraph (c), for "Radio Authority" there shall be substituted " OFCOM ";
(d) after paragraph (c) there shall be inserted—
   "(d)section 334. (3) of the Communications Act 2003."
(3) For subsection (3) there shall be substituted—
"(3)Copyright is not infringed by the use by OFCOM in connection with the performance of any of their functions under the Broadcasting Act 1990, the Broadcasting Act 1996 or the Communications Act 2003 of—
   (a) any recording, script or transcript which is provided to them under or by virtue of any provision of those Acts; or
   (b) any existing material which is transferred to them by a scheme made under section 30 of the Communications Act 2003.
(4) In subsection (3), "existing material" means—
   (a) any recording, script or transcript which was provided to the Independent Television Commission or the Radio Authority under or by virtue of any provision of the Broadcasting Act 1990 or the Broadcasting Act 1996; and
   (b) any recording or transcript which was provided to the Broadcasting Standards Commission under section 115. (4) or (6) or 116. (5) of the Broadcasting Act 1996."
Commencement Information
I152. Sch. 17 para. 91 in force at 29.12.2003 by S.I. 2003/3142, art. 3. (1), Sch. 1 (with art. 11)
92. (1)Section 73 of that Act (no breach of copyright by certain retransmissions of [F12wireless broadcasts by cable]) shall be amended as follows.
(2) In subsection (6)—
(a) for paragraphs (c) and (d) there shall be substituted—
   "(c)the public teletext service,
   (d) S4. C Digital, and";
(b) for the words after paragraph (e) there shall be substituted— " and expressions used in this subsection have the same meanings as in Part 3 of the Communications Act 2003. "
(3) For subsection (7) there shall be substituted—
"(7)In this section "relevant requirement" means a requirement imposed by a general condition (within the meaning of Chapter 1 of Part 2 of the Communications Act 2003) the setting of which is authorised under section 64 of that Act (must-carry obligations)."
Amendments (Textual)
F12. Words in Sch. 17 para. 92. (1) substituted (31.10.2003) by virtue of The Copyright and Related Rights Regulations 2003 (S.I. 2003/2498), reg. 1, Sch. 1 para. 23 (with regs. 31-40)
Commencement Information
I153. Sch. 17 para. 92 in force at 29.12.2003 by S.I. 2003/3142, art. 3. (1), Sch. 1 (with art. 11)
93. (1)Paragraph 17 of Schedule 2 to that Act (no infringement of performance rights by use of recordings for certain supervisory purposes) shall be amended as follows.
(2) In sub-paragraph (2)—

(a) for paragraph (a) there shall be substituted—

"(a)section 167. (1) of the Broadcasting Act 1990, section 115. (4) or (6) or 117 of the Broadcasting Act 1996 or paragraph 20 of Schedule 12 to the Communications Act 2003;";

(b) in paragraph (b), for the words from "by virtue of" to "1990" there shall be substituted " by virtue of section 334. (1) of the Communications Act 2003 ";

(c) in paragraph (c), for "Radio Authority" there shall be substituted " OFCOM ";

(d) after paragraph (c) there shall be inserted—

"(d)section 334. (3) of the Communications Act 2003."

(3) For sub-paragraph (3) there shall be substituted—

"(3)The rights conferred by Part 2 are not infringed by the use by OFCOM in connection with the performance of any of their functions under the Broadcasting Act 1990, the Broadcasting Act 1996 or the Communications Act 2003 of—

(a) any recording, script or transcript which is provided to them under or by virtue of any provision of those Acts; or

(b) any existing material which is transferred to them by a scheme made under section 30 of the Communications Act 2003.

(4) In subsection (3), "existing material" means—

(a) any recording, script or transcript which was provided to the Independent Television Commission or the Radio Authority under or by virtue of any provision of the Broadcasting Act 1990 or the Broadcasting Act 1996; and

(b) any recording or transcript which was provided to the Broadcasting Standards Commission under section 115. (4) or (6) or 116. (5) of the Broadcasting Act 1996."

Commencement Information

I154. Sch. 17 para. 93 in force at 29.12.2003 by S.I. 2003/3142, art. 3. (1), Sch. 1 (with art. 11)

Housing Act 1988.

94. (1)Part 2 of Schedule 10 to the Housing Act 1988 (c. 50) (provisions about land acquired by a housing action trust) shall be amended as follows.

(2) In paragraphs 4, 5, 11, 12 and 14—

(a) for "the telecommunications code", wherever occurring, there shall be substituted " the electronic communications code ";

(b) for "a telecommunications code system" and "any telecommunications code system", wherever occurring, there shall be substituted " an electronic communications code network ";

(c) for "telecommunications apparatus" and "telecommunication apparatus", wherever occurring, there shall be substituted " electronic communications apparatus ";

(d) for "such system" and "the system", wherever occurring, there shall be substituted, respectively, " such network " and " the network ".

Commencement Information

I155. Sch. 17 para. 94 in force at 25.7.2003 for specified purposes by S.I. 2003/1900, arts. 1. (2), 2. (1), Sch. 1 (with art. 3) (as amended by S.I. 2003/3142, art. 1. (3))

I156. Sch. 17 para. 94 in force at 29.12.2003 in so far as not already in force by S.I. 2003/3142, art. 3. (2) (with art. 11)

Road Traffic Act 1988.

95. In section 21. (3)(b) of the Road Traffic Act 1988 (c. 52) (exception from prohibition of driving etc on cycle tracks for statutory undertakers), for the words from "a telecommunications code system" to "1984)" there shall be substituted " an electronic communications code network ".

Commencement Information

I157. Sch. 17 para. 95 in force at 25.7.2003 for specified purposes by S.I. 2003/1900, arts. 1. (2), 2. (1), Sch. 1 (with art. 3) (as amended by S.I. 2003/3142, art. 1. (3))

I158. Sch. 17 para. 95 in force at 29.12.2003 in so far as not already in force by S.I. 2003/3142, art. 3. (2) (with art. 11)

Water Act 1989.

96. (1)Section 174 of the Water Act 1989 (c. 15) (general restrictions on disclosure of information) be amended as follows.
(2) In subsection (2)(d), for sub-paragraph (iv) there shall be substituted—
"(iv)the Office of Communications;".
(3) In subsection (3), after paragraph (ln) there shall be inserted—
    "(lo)the Communications Act 2003;".
Commencement Information
I159. Sch. 17 para. 96 in force at 25.7.2003 for specified purposes by S.I. 2003/1900, arts. 1. (2), 2. (1), Sch. 1 (with art. 3) (as amended by S.I. 2003/3142, art. 1. (3))
I160. Sch. 17 para. 96 in force at 29.12.2003 in so far as not already in force by S.I. 2003/3142, art. 3. (2) (with art. 11)

Road Traffic (Driver Licensing and Information Systems) Act 1989.

97. (1)The Road Traffic (Driver Licensing and Information Systems) Act 1989 (c. 22) shall be amended as follows.
(2) For section 9. (3) (requirement for licence to operate driver information systems) there shall be substituted—
"(3)The holding by a person of a licence under this section shall not relieve him of—
    (a) any liability in respect of a failure to hold a licence under section 1 of the Wireless Telegraphy Act 1949; or
    (b) any obligation to comply with requirements imposed by or under Chapter 1 of Part 2 of the Communications Act 2003 (electronic communications networks and electronic communications services)."
(3) In paragraph 4 of Schedule 4 (application of telecommunications code to licence holders), for the words "(application of telecommunications code)" there shall be substituted " (procedure for works involving alteration of electronic communications apparatus) ".
(4) In paragraph 8 of Schedule 5 (undertakers' works affecting driver information systems)—
(a) in the definition of "relevant undertaker", for paragraph (b) there shall be substituted—
    "(b)any electronic communications code operator;";
(b) in the definition of "undertaker's works", in paragraph (b), for "a telecommunication system run by him" there shall be substituted " an electronic communications code network provided by him ".
Commencement Information
I161. Sch. 17 para. 97 in force at 25.7.2003 for specified purposes by S.I. 2003/1900, arts. 1. (2), 2. (1), Sch. 1 (with art. 3) (as amended by S.I. 2003/3142, art. 1. (3))
I162. Sch. 17 para. 97 in force at 29.12.2003 in so far as not already in force by S.I. 2003/3142, art. 3. (2) (with art. 11)

Electricity Act 1989.

98. In section 3. A(4)(b) of the Electricity Act 1989 (c. 29) (general duties of Secretary of State and Authority), for sub-paragraph (i) there shall be substituted—
"(i)communications services and electronic communications apparatus, or".
Commencement Information

I163. Sch. 17 para. 98 in force at 25.7.2003 for specified purposes by S.I. 2003/1900, arts. 1. (2), 2. (1), Sch. 1 (with art. 3) (as amended by S.I. 2003/3142, art. 1. (3))

I164. Sch. 17 para. 98 in force at 29.12.2003 in so far as not already in force by S.I. 2003/3142, art. 3. (2) (with art. 11)

99. (1)Schedule 4 to that Act (other powers etc. of licence holders) shall be amended as follows.

(2) In paragraphs 3. (1)(d) and 5—

(a) for "telecommunication apparatus", wherever occurring, there shall be substituted " electronic communications apparatus ";

(b) for "a telecommunication system" there shall be substituted " an electronic communications code network "; and

(c) for "telecommunications code", wherever occurring, there shall be substituted " electronic communications code ".

(3) In paragraph 4. (1), for paragraph (c) there shall be substituted—

"(c)any electronic communications code operator or any former PTO; and".

Commencement Information

I165. Sch. 17 para. 99 in force at 25.7.2003 for specified purposes by S.I. 2003/1900, arts. 1. (2), 2. (1), Sch. 1 (with art. 3) (as amended by S.I. 2003/3142, art. 1. (3))

I166. Sch. 17 para. 99 in force at 29.12.2003 in so far as not already in force by S.I. 2003/3142, art. 3. (2) (with art. 11)

Local Government and Housing Act 1989.

100. In section 88. (1)(e)(i) of the Local Government and Housing Act 1989 (c. 42) (electronic communication), for "a telecommunication system (within the meaning of the Telecommunications Act 1984)" there shall be substituted " an electronic communications network ".

Commencement Information

I167. Sch. 17 para. 100 in force at 25.7.2003 for specified purposes by S.I. 2003/1900, arts. 1. (2), 2. (1), Sch. 1 (with art. 3) (as amended by S.I. 2003/3142, art. 1. (3))

I168. Sch. 17 para. 100 in force at 29.12.2003 in so far as not already in force by S.I. 2003/3142, art. 3. (2) (with art. 11)

Insolvency (Northern Ireland) Order 1989.

101. (1)The Insolvency (Northern Ireland) Order 1989 (S.I. 1989/2405 (N.I. 19)) shall be amended as follows.

(2) In Article 197. (3) (supplies of water, electricity, etc.) for sub-paragraph (c) to the end there shall be substituted—

"(c)a supply of communications services by a provider of a public electronic communications service,

and in this paragraph "communications services" do not include electronic communications services to the extent that they are used to broadcast or transmit programme services (within the meaning of the Communications Act 2003). "

(3) In Article 343. (4) (supplies of water, electricity, etc.) for sub-paragraph (c) to the end there shall be substituted—

"(c)a supply of communications services by a provider of a public telecommunications service, and in this paragraph 'communications services' do not include electronic communications services to the extent that they are used to broadcast or transmit programme services (within the meaning of the Communications Act 2003). "

Commencement Information

I169. Sch. 17 para. 101 in force at 25.7.2003 for specified purposes by S.I. 2003/1900, arts. 1. (2), 2. (1), Sch. 1 (with art. 3) (as amended by S.I. 2003/3142, art. 1. (3))

1170. Sch. 17 para. 101 in force at 29.12.2003 in so far as not already in force by S.I. 2003/3142, art. 3. (2) (with art. 11)

Town and Country Planning Act 1990.

102. In section 148. (1) of the Town and Country Planning Act 1990 (c. 8) (interpretation of Chapter 1), in the definition of "statutory undertakers", for "public telecommunications operators" there shall be substituted " electronic communications code operators and former PTOs ".
Commencement Information
1171. Sch. 17 para. 102 in force at 25.7.2003 for specified purposes by S.I. 2003/1900, arts. 1. (2), 2. (1), Sch. 1 (with art. 3) (as amended by S.I. 2003/3142, art. 1. (3))
1172. Sch. 17 para. 102 in force at 29.12.2003 in so far as not already in force by S.I. 2003/3142, art. 3. (2) (with art. 11)
103. (1)This paragraph applies to the following provisions of that Act—
(a) section 236. (2) (exception to extinguishment of rights over land compulsorily acquired);
(b) section 237. (3) (saving from power to override certain rights);
(c) section 256 (Secretary of State's orders affecting telecommunications apparatus);
(d) section 260 (orders by other authorities affecting telecommunication apparatus);
(e) section 272 (extinguishment of rights of telecommunications code system operators);
(f) section 273. (7) and (8) (notices given to developing authority);
(g) section 274. (2) (making of orders);
(h) section 279. (3) (right to compensation).
(2) In each of the provisions to which this paragraph applies—
(a) for "telecommunications code", wherever occurring (except in the expression "telecommunications code system"), there shall be substituted " electronic communications code ";
(b) for "a telecommunications code system" and "any telecommunications code system", wherever occurring, there shall be substituted " an electronic communications code network ";
(c) for "telecommunications apparatus" and "telecommunication apparatus", wherever occurring, there shall be substituted " electronic communications apparatus ";
(d) for "the telecommunications code system", wherever occurring, there shall be substituted " the electronic communications code network ";
(e) for "system", wherever occurring (except in the expression "telecommunications code system"), there shall be substituted " network ".
Commencement Information
1173. Sch. 17 para. 103 in force at 25.7.2003 for specified purposes by S.I. 2003/1900, arts. 1. (2), 2. (1), Sch. 1 (with art. 3) (as amended by S.I. 2003/3142, art. 1. (3))
1174. Sch. 17 para. 103 in force at 29.12.2003 in so far as not already in force by S.I. 2003/3142, art. 3. (2) (with art. 11)
104. In section 280 of that Act (measures of compensation)—
(a) for "a telecommunications code system" there shall be substituted " an electronic communications code network ";
(b) for "the running of the telecommunications code system", wherever occurring, there shall be substituted " the provision of the electronic communications code network ".
Commencement Information
1175. Sch. 17 para. 104 in force at 25.7.2003 for specified purposes by S.I. 2003/1900, arts. 1. (2), 2. (1), Sch. 1 (with art. 3) (as amended by S.I. 2003/3142, art. 1. (3))
1176. Sch. 17 para. 104 in force at 29.12.2003 in so far as not already in force by S.I. 2003/3142, art. 3. (2) (with art. 11)
105. In paragraph 1. (a) of Schedule 13 to that Act (blighted land), for sub-paragraph (ii) there shall be substituted—
"(ii)of the provision by an electronic communications code operator of an electronic

communications code network or the provision by a former PTO of a public electronic communications network or a public electronic communications service, or".

Commencement Information

I177. Sch. 17 para. 105 in force at 25.7.2003 for specified purposes by S.I. 2003/1900, arts. 1. (2), 2. (1), Sch. 1 (with art. 3) (as amended by S.I. 2003/3142, art. 1. (3))

I178. Sch. 17 para. 105 in force at 29.12.2003 in so far as not already in force by S.I. 2003/3142, art. 3. (2) (with art. 11)

Planning (Listed Buildings and Conservation Areas) Act 1990.

106. (1)The Planning (Listed Buildings and Conservation Areas) Act 1990 (c. 9) shall be amended as follows.

(2) In section 51. (2) (saving for ending of rights over land compulsorily acquired), for paragraphs (b) and (c) there shall be substituted—

"(b)to any right conferred by or in accordance with the electronic communications code on the operator of an electronic communications code network, or

(c) to any electronic communications apparatus kept installed for the purposes of any such network."

(3) In section 91. (3) (meaning of "statutory undertakers" in certain sections), in paragraph (a) for "a public telecommunications operator" there shall be substituted " an electronic communications code operator and to a former PTO ".

Commencement Information

I179. Sch. 17 para. 106 in force at 25.7.2003 for specified purposes by S.I. 2003/1900, arts. 1. (2), 2. (1), Sch. 1 (with art. 3) (as amended by S.I. 2003/3142, art. 1. (3))

I180. Sch. 17 para. 106 in force at 29.12.2003 in so far as not already in force by S.I. 2003/3142, art. 3. (2) (with art. 11)

London Local Authorities (No. 2) Act 1990.

107. (1)Section 5 of the London Local Authorities (No. 2) Act 1990 (c. xxx) (crime prevention) shall be amended as follows.

(2) For subsection (1)(b) there shall be substituted—

"(b)providing within their area an electronic communications service which is distributed—

(i) only to persons on a single set of premises; and

(ii) by an electronic communications network which is wholly within those premises and is not connected to an electronic communications network any part of which is outside those premises;".

(3) In subsection (1)(c), for "telecommunications system" there shall be substituted " electronic communications network or electronic communications service ".

(4) After subsection (4), there shall be inserted—

"(4. A)For the purposes of subsection (1)(b)—

(a) a set of premises is a single set of premises if, and only if, the same person is the occupier of all the premises; and

(b) two or more vehicles are capable of constituting a single set of premises if, and only if, they are coupled together."

(5) For subsection (5), there shall be substituted—

"(5)In this section—

"premises" includes a vehicle; and

"vehicle" includes a vessel, aircraft or hovercraft."

Commencement Information

I181. Sch. 17 para. 107 in force at 25.7.2003 for specified purposes by S.I. 2003/1900, arts. 1. (2), 2. (1), Sch. 1 (with art. 3) (as amended by S.I. 2003/3142, art. 1. (3))

I182. Sch. 17 para. 107 in force at 29.12.2003 in so far as not already in force by S.I. 2003/3142,

New Roads and Street Works Act 1991.

108. (1)In the New Roads and Street Works Act 1991 (c. 22)—
(a) paragraph 7 of Schedule 4 (streets with special engineering difficulties), and
(b) paragraph 7 of Schedule 6 (roads with special engineering difficulties),
shall be amended as follows.
(2) For "telecommunication apparatus", wherever occurring, there shall be substituted " electronic communications apparatus ".
(3) In sub-paragraph (3)(c)—
(a) for "a telecommunication system" there shall be substituted " an electronic communications network "; and
(b) for "a system" there shall be substituted " a network ".
Commencement Information
I183. Sch. 17 para. 108 in force at 25.7.2003 for specified purposes by S.I. 2003/1900, arts. 1. (2), 2. (1), Sch. 1 (with art. 3) (as amended by S.I. 2003/3142, art. 1. (3))
I184. Sch. 17 para. 108 in force at 29.12.2003 in so far as not already in force by S.I. 2003/3142, art. 3. (2) (with art. 11)

Coal Mining Subsidence Act 1991.

109. In section 52. (1) of the Coal Mining Subsidence Act 1991 (c. 45) (interpretation) in the definition of "statutory undertakers", in paragraph (b) for "any public telecommunications operator" there shall be substituted " any electronic communications code operator, any former PTO ".
Commencement Information
I185. Sch. 17 para. 109 in force at 25.7.2003 for specified purposes by S.I. 2003/1900, arts. 1. (2), 2. (1), Sch. 1 (with art. 3) (as amended by S.I. 2003/3142, art. 1. (3))
I186. Sch. 17 para. 109 in force at 29.12.2003 in so far as not already in force by S.I. 2003/3142, art. 3. (2) (with art. 11)

Water Industry Act 1991.

110. In section 219 of the Water Industry Act 1991 (c. 56) (general interpretation), in the definition of "accessories", for "telecommunication apparatus (within the meaning of Schedule 2 to the Telecommunications Act 1984)" there shall be substituted " electronic communications apparatus ".
Commencement Information
I187. Sch. 17 para. 110 in force at 25.7.2003 for specified purposes by S.I. 2003/1900, arts. 1. (2), 2. (1), Sch. 1 (with art. 3) (as amended by S.I. 2003/3142, art. 1. (3))
I188. Sch. 17 para. 110 in force at 29.12.2003 in so far as not already in force by S.I. 2003/3142, art. 3. (2) (with art. 11)
111. (1)Schedule 13 to that Act (protective provisions in respect of certain undertakings) shall be amended as follows.
(2) In paragraph 1. (5), for paragraph (c) there shall be substituted—
   "(c)any undertaking consisting in the provision of an electronic communications network;".
(3) In paragraph 4, for "telecommunication apparatus" there shall be substituted " electronic communications apparatus ".
Commencement Information
I189. Sch. 17 para. 111 in force at 25.7.2003 for specified purposes by S.I. 2003/1900, arts. 1. (2),

2. (1), Sch. 1 (with art. 3) (as amended by S.I. 2003/3142, art. 1. (3))

I190. Sch. 17 para. 111 in force at 29.12.2003 in so far as not already in force by S.I. 2003/3142, art. 3. (2) (with art. 11)

112. (1)Schedule 15 to that Act (disclosure of information) shall be amended as follows.

(2) In Part 1, for "The Director General of Telecommunications" there shall be substituted " The Office of Communications ".

(3) In Part 2, after the entry relating to the Enterprise Act 2002, there shall be inserted— " The Communications Act 2003. "

Commencement Information

I191. Sch. 17 para. 112 in force at 25.7.2003 for specified purposes by S.I. 2003/1900, arts. 1. (2), 2. (1), Sch. 1 (with art. 3) (as amended by S.I. 2003/3142, art. 1. (3))

I192. Sch. 17 para. 112 in force at 29.12.2003 in so far as not already in force by S.I. 2003/3142, art. 3. (2) (with art. 11)

Water Resources Act 1991.

113. In section 221 of the Water Resources Act 1991 (c. 57) (general interpretation), in the definition of "accessories", for "telecommunication apparatus (within the meaning of Schedule 2 to the Telecommunications Act 1984)" there shall be substituted " electronic communications apparatus ".

Commencement Information

I193. Sch. 17 para. 113 in force at 25.7.2003 for specified purposes by S.I. 2003/1900, arts. 1. (2), 2. (1), Sch. 1 (with art. 3) (as amended by S.I. 2003/3142, art. 1. (3))

I194. Sch. 17 para. 113 in force at 29.12.2003 in so far as not already in force by S.I. 2003/3142, art. 3. (2) (with art. 11)

114. (1)Schedule 22 to that Act (general provisions protecting undertakings) shall be amended as follows.

(2) In paragraph 1. (4), for paragraph (c) there shall be substituted—

"(c)any undertaking consisting in the provision of an electronic communications network;".

(3) In paragraph 5, for "telecommunication apparatus" there shall be substituted " electronic communications apparatus ".

Commencement Information

I195. Sch. 17 para. 114 in force at 25.7.2003 for specified purposes by S.I. 2003/1900, arts. 1. (2), 2. (1), Sch. 1 (with art. 3) (as amended by S.I. 2003/3142, art. 1. (3))

I196. Sch. 17 para. 114 in force at 29.12.2003 in so far as not already in force by S.I. 2003/3142, art. 3. (2) (with art. 11)

115. (1)Schedule 24 to that Act (disclosure of information) shall be amended as follows.

(2) In Part 1, for "The Director General of Telecommunications" there shall be substituted " The Office of Communications ".

(3) In Part 2, after the entry relating to the Enterprise Act 2002, there shall be inserted— " The Communications Act 2003. "

Commencement Information

I197. Sch. 17 para. 115 in force at 25.7.2003 for specified purposes by S.I. 2003/1900, arts. 1. (2), 2. (1), Sch. 1 (with art. 3) (as amended by S.I. 2003/3142, art. 1. (3))

I198. Sch. 17 para. 115 in force at 29.12.2003 in so far as not already in force by S.I. 2003/3142, art. 3. (2) (with art. 11)

Land Drainage Act 1991.

116. In paragraph 1. (1) of Schedule 6 to the Land Drainage Act 1991 (c. 59) (protection for particular undertakings), for paragraph (c) there shall be substituted—

"(c)any undertaking consisting in the provision of an electronic communications code network;".

Commencement Information
I199. Sch. 17 para. 116 in force at 25.7.2003 for specified purposes by S.I. 2003/1900, arts. 1. (2), 2. (1), Sch. 1 (with art. 3) (as amended by S.I. 2003/3142, art. 1. (3))
I200. Sch. 17 para. 116 in force at 29.12.2003 in so far as not already in force by S.I. 2003/3142, art. 3. (2) (with art. 11)

Planning (Northern Ireland) Order 1991.

117. In Articles 103 (making of orders) and 104 (telecommunication apparatus) of the Planning (Northern Ireland) Order 1991 (S.I. 1991/1220 (N.I. 11))—
(a) for "telecommunications code", wherever occurring (except in the expression "telecommunications code system") there shall be substituted " electronic communications code ";
(b) for "a telecommunications code system" and "any telecommunications code system", wherever occurring, there shall be substituted " an electronic communications code network ";
(c) for "telecommunication apparatus", wherever occurring, there shall be substituted " electronic communications apparatus ";
(d) for "system" (except in the expression "telecommunications code system") there shall be substituted " network ".
Commencement Information
I201. Sch. 17 para. 117 in force at 25.7.2003 for specified purposes by S.I. 2003/1900, arts. 1. (2), 2. (1), Sch. 1 (with art. 3) (as amended by S.I. 2003/3142, art. 1. (3))
I202. Sch. 17 para. 117 in force at 29.12.2003 in so far as not already in force by S.I. 2003/3142, art. 3. (2) (with art. 11)

Charities Act 1992.

118. In section 60. (6)(c) of the Charities Act 1992 (c. 41) (making of payments to professional fund-raisers etc.), for "telecommunication apparatus" there shall be substituted " electronic communications apparatus ".
Commencement Information
I203. Sch. 17 para. 118 in force at 25.7.2003 for specified purposes by S.I. 2003/1900, arts. 1. (2), 2. (1), Sch. 1 (with art. 3) (as amended by S.I. 2003/3142, art. 1. (3))
I204. Sch. 17 para. 118 in force at 29.12.2003 in so far as not already in force by S.I. 2003/3142, art. 3. (2) (with art. 11)

Carriage of Goods by Sea Act 1992.

119. In section 1. (5) of the Carriage of Goods by Sea Act 1992 (c. 50), for "a telecommunication system" there shall be substituted " an electronic communications network ".
Commencement Information
I205. Sch. 17 para. 119 in force at 25.7.2003 for specified purposes by S.I. 2003/1900, arts. 1. (2), 2. (1), Sch. 1 (with art. 3) (as amended by S.I. 2003/3142, art. 1. (3))
I206. Sch. 17 para. 119 in force at 29.12.2003 in so far as not already in force by S.I. 2003/3142, art. 3. (2) (with art. 11)

Electricity (Northern Ireland) Order 1992.

120. The Electricity (Northern Ireland) Order 1992 (S.I. 1992/231 (N.I. 1)) shall be amended as follows.
Commencement Information
I207. Sch. 17 para. 120 in force at 25.7.2003 for specified purposes by S.I. 2003/1900, arts. 1. (2),

2. (1), Sch. 1 (with art. 3) (as amended by S.I. 2003/3142, art. 1. (3))

I208. Sch. 17 para. 120 in force at 29.12.2003 in so far as not already in force by S.I. 2003/3142, art. 3. (2) (with art. 11)

121. In Article 61 (restrictions on disclosure of information)—

(a) for paragraph (2)(b)(vi) there shall be substituted—

"(vi)the Office of Communications;";

(b) after paragraph (3)(u) there shall be inserted—

"(v)the Communications Act 2003;".

Commencement Information

I209. Sch. 17 para. 121 in force at 25.7.2003 for specified purposes by S.I. 2003/1900, arts. 1. (2), 2. (1), Sch. 1 (with art. 3) (as amended by S.I. 2003/3142, art. 1. (3))

I210. Sch. 17 para. 121 in force at 29.12.2003 in so far as not already in force by S.I. 2003/3142, art. 3. (2) (with art. 11)

122. (1)Schedule 4 (other powers etc. of licence holders) shall be amended as follows.

(2) In paragraph 1. (1)—

(a) for "a public telecommunications operator" there shall be substituted " an electronic communications code operator ";

(b) for "telecommunication system" there shall be substituted " electronic communications network ".

(3) In paragraphs 4 and 6 for "public telecommunications operator" there shall be substituted " electronic communications code operator ".

(4) In paragraphs 3. (1) and (2), 5. (1), (2), (3) and (4), 6. (1) and 9—

(a) for "telecommunication apparatus", wherever occurring, there shall be substituted " electronic communications apparatus ";

(b) for "a telecommunication system", wherever occurring, there shall be substituted " an electronic communications network ";

(c) for "telecommunications code", wherever occurring, there shall be substituted " electronic communications code ".

Commencement Information

I211. Sch. 17 para. 122 in force at 25.7.2003 for specified purposes by S.I. 2003/1900, arts. 1. (2), 2. (1), Sch. 1 (with art. 3) (as amended by S.I. 2003/3142, art. 1. (3))

I212. Sch. 17 para. 122 in force at 29.12.2003 in so far as not already in force by S.I. 2003/3142, art. 3. (2) (with art. 11)

F13...

Amendments (Textual)

F13. Sch. 17 para. 123 and crossheading repealed (1.12.2008) by Housing and Regeneration Act 2008 (c. 17), s. 325. (1), Sch. 16; S.I. 2008/3068, art. 5, Sch. (with arts. 6-13)

F13123. . . . .

Commencement Information

I213. Sch. 17 para. 123 in force at 25.7.2003 for specified purposes by S.I. 2003/1900, arts. 1. (2), 2. (1), Sch. 1 (with art. 3) (as amended by S.I. 2003/3142, art. 1. (3))

I214. Sch. 17 para. 123 in force at 29.12.2003 in so far as not already in force by S.I. 2003/3142, art. 3. (2) (with art. 11)

Cardiff Bay Barrage Act 1993.

124. In Schedule 2 to the Cardiff Bay Barrage Act 1993 (c. 42) (supplementary provisions about Development Corporation works)—

(a) in paragraph 1. (c), for "telecommunication" there shall be substituted " electronic communications ";

(b) in paragraph 16, for "telecommunication apparatus" there shall be substituted " electronic communications apparatus ".

Commencement Information

I215. Sch. 17 para. 124 in force at 25.7.2003 for specified purposes by S.I. 2003/1900, arts. 1. (2), 2. (1), Sch. 1 (with art. 3) (as amended by S.I. 2003/3142, art. 1. (3))

I216. Sch. 17 para. 124 in force at 29.12.2003 in so far as not already in force by S.I. 2003/3142, art. 3. (2) (with art. 11)

125. In paragraph 3. (2)(c) of Schedule 4 to that Act (exception to extinguishment of rights over land compulsorily acquired)—

(a) for "the telecommunications code" there shall be substituted " the electronic communications code ";

(b) for "a telecommunications code system" there shall be substituted " an electronic communications code network ";

(c) for "such system;" there shall be substituted " such network. "

Commencement Information

I217. Sch. 17 para. 125 in force at 25.7.2003 for specified purposes by S.I. 2003/1900, arts. 1. (2), 2. (1), Sch. 1 (with art. 3) (as amended by S.I. 2003/3142, art. 1. (3))

I218. Sch. 17 para. 125 in force at 29.12.2003 in so far as not already in force by S.I. 2003/3142, art. 3. (2) (with art. 11)

126. In paragraph 21 of Schedule 7 to that Act (powers of survey etc. in connection with groundwater damage)—

(a) in sub-paragraphs (5)(b)(ii) and (7), for "a relevant telecommunications licenceholder" there shall be substituted " a provider of a public electronic communications network ";

(b) in sub-paragraphs (6) and (7), for "or licenceholder" there shall be substituted " or provider ";

(c) in sub-paragraph (6), for "running of the telecommunication system" there shall be substituted " provision of the public electronic communications network ".

Commencement Information

I219. Sch. 17 para. 126 in force at 25.7.2003 for specified purposes by S.I. 2003/1900, arts. 1. (2), 2. (1), Sch. 1 (with art. 3) (as amended by S.I. 2003/3142, art. 1. (3))

I220. Sch. 17 para. 126 in force at 29.12.2003 in so far as not already in force by S.I. 2003/3142, art. 3. (2) (with art. 11)

Railways Act 1993.

127. (1)Section 145 of the Railways Act 1993 (c. 43) (general restrictions on disclosure of information) be amended as follows.

(2) In subsection (2)(b), for sub-paragraph (iv) there shall be substituted—

"(iv)the Office of Communications,".

(3) In subsection (3), after paragraph (qs) there shall be inserted—

   "(qt)the Communications Act 2003;".

Commencement Information

I221. Sch. 17 para. 127 in force at 25.7.2003 for specified purposes by S.I. 2003/1900, arts. 1. (2), 2. (1), Sch. 1 (with art. 3) (as amended by S.I. 2003/3142, art. 1. (3))

I222. Sch. 17 para. 127 in force at 29.12.2003 in so far as not already in force by S.I. 2003/3142, art. 3. (2) (with art. 11)

Roads (Northern Ireland) Order 1993.

128. (1)This paragraph applies to the following provisions of the Roads (Northern Ireland) Order 1993 (S.I. 1993/3160 (N.I. 15))—

(a) Article 12. (2) (road bridges over railways);

(b) Article 70. (2) (consultation on exercise of power to erect structure on road);

(c) Article 72. (2) (control of scaffolding on roads);

(d) Article 73. (2) (restriction on placing rails etc. over roads);

(e) Article 78. (2) (excavations in a road);

(f) Article 79. (2) (placing of apparatus in or under roads);

(g) Article 82. (3) (excavations near a road);

(h) Article 83. (2) (alteration of wall, fence or drain at the side of a road);

(i) Schedule 9 (savings for telecommunications apparatus).

(2) In each of the provisions to which this paragraph applies—

(a) for "a telecommunications code system" and "any telecommunications code system", wherever occurring, there shall be substituted " an electronic communications code network ";

(b) for "telecommunication apparatus", wherever occurring, there shall be substituted " electronic communications apparatus ";

(c) for "telecommunications code", wherever occurring (except in the expression "telecommunications code system"), there shall be substituted " electronic communications code ";

(d) for "that system", "any such system" and "the system", wherever occurring, there shall be substituted, respectively, " that network ", " any such network " and " the network ";

(e) for "the telecommunications code system" there shall be substituted " the electronic communications code network ".

Commencement Information

I223. Sch. 17 para. 128 in force at 25.7.2003 for specified purposes by S.I. 2003/1900, arts. 1. (2), 2. (1), Sch. 1 (with art. 3) (as amended by S.I. 2003/3142, art. 1. (3))

I224. Sch. 17 para. 128 in force at 29.12.2003 in so far as not already in force by S.I. 2003/3142, art. 3. (2) (with art. 11)

Value Added Tax Act 1994.

129. (1)The Value Added Tax Act 1994 (c. 23) shall be amended as follows.

(2) In section 33 (refunds of VAT in certain cases)—

(a) in subsection (3), for paragraph (j) there shall be substituted—

"(j)the appointed news provider referred to in section 280 of the Communications Act 2003; and";

(b) in subsection (5), for "a nominated" there shall be substituted " an appointed ".

(3) In Part 2 of Schedule 9 (exemptions), in Note (1) in Group 12 (fund-raising events by charities etc.), for "a telecommunications system (within the meaning of the Telecommunications Act 1984)" there shall be substituted " an electronic communications network ".

Commencement Information

I225. Sch. 17 para. 129. (1)(3) in force at 25.7.2003 for specified purposes by S.I. 2003/1900, arts. 1. (2), 2. (1), Sch. 1 (with art. 3) (as amended by S.I. 2003/3142, art. 1. (3))

I226. Sch. 17 para. 129. (1) (3) in force at 29.12.2003 in so far as not already in force by S.I. 2003/3142, art. 3. (1), Sch. 1 (with art. 11)

I227. Sch. 17 para. 129. (2) in force at 29.12.2003 by S.I. 2003/3142, art. 3. (1), Sch. 1 (with art. 11)

Criminal Justice and Public Order Act 1994.

130. (1)Section 163 of the Criminal Justice and Public Order Act 1994 (c. 33) (local authority powers to provide closed-circuit television) shall be amended as follows.

(2) For subsection (1)(b) there shall be substituted—

"(b)providing within their area an electronic communications service which is distributed—

(i) only to persons on a single set of premises; and

(ii) by an electronic communications network which is wholly within those premises and is not connected to an electronic communications network any part of which is outside those premises;".

(3) In subsection (1)(c), for "telecommunications system" there shall be substituted " electronic communications network or electronic communications service ".

(4) After subsection (3), there shall be inserted—

"(3. A)For the purposes of subsection (1)(b)—

(a) a set of premises is a single set of premises if, and only if, the same person is the occupier of all the premises; and

(b) two or more vehicles are capable of constituting a single set of premises if, and only if, they are coupled together."

(5) In subsection (4), for the definition of "telecommunications system" there shall be substituted—

""premises" includes a vehicle; and

"vehicle" includes a vessel, aircraft or hovercraft."

Commencement Information

I228. Sch. 17 para. 130 in force at 25.7.2003 for specified purposes by S.I. 2003/1900, arts. 1. (2), 2. (1), Sch. 1 (with art. 3) (as amended by S.I. 2003/3142, art. 1. (3))

I229. Sch. 17 para. 130 in force at 29.12.2003 in so far as not already in force by S.I. 2003/3142, art. 3. (2) (with art. 11)

Airports (Northern Ireland) Order 1994.

131. In Article 12 of the Airports (Northern Ireland) Order 1994 (S.I. 1994/426 (N.I. 1)) (provisions as to telecommunications apparatus)—

(a) for "telecommunications apparatus", wherever occurring, there shall be substituted " electronic communications apparatus ";

(b) for "the telecommunications code", wherever occurring, there shall be substituted " the electronic communications code ";

(c) for "a telecommunications code system", wherever occurring, there shall be substituted " an electronic communications code network ";

(d) in paragraph (3), for "that system" there shall be substituted " that network ".

Commencement Information

I230. Sch. 17 para. 131 in force at 25.7.2003 for specified purposes by S.I. 2003/1900, arts. 1. (2), 2. (1), Sch. 1 (with art. 3) (as amended by S.I. 2003/3142, art. 1. (3))

I231. Sch. 17 para. 131 in force at 29.12.2003 in so far as not already in force by S.I. 2003/3142, art. 3. (2) (with art. 11)

Merchant Shipping Act 1995.

132. In section 91. (7) of the Merchant Shipping Act 1995 (c. 21) (report of dangers to navigation), in the definition of "controlled station for wireless telegraphy"—

(a) after "Secretary of State" there shall be inserted " or by the Office of Communications "; and

(b) for "by him" there shall be substituted " by the Office of Communications ".

Commencement Information

I232. Sch. 17 para. 132 in force at 29.12.2003 by S.I. 2003/3142, art. 3. (1), Sch. 1 (with art. 11)

Criminal Procedure (Scotland) Act 1995.

133. (1)The Criminal Procedure (Scotland) Act 1995 (c. 46) shall be amended as follows.

(2) In section 302. (9)(a) (interpretation), at the end there shall be inserted " nor an offence to which Schedule 6 to the Communications Act 2003 (fixed penalties for wireless telegraphy offences) applies. "

(3) In Schedule 9 (certificates as to proof of certain routine matters), at the end there shall be inserted—

"The Communications Act 2003

Section 363. (1) and (2) (offence of unauthorised installation or use of a television receiver)

Commencement Information

I233. Sch. 17 para. 133. (1) (3) in force at 1.4.2004 by S.I. 2003/3142, art. 4. (2), Sch. 2 (with art. 11)

British Waterways Act 1995.

134. In section 3. (1) of the British Waterways Act 1995 (c. i) (interpretation), in the definition of "relevant undertaker", in paragraph (f), for the words from the beginning to "in that Act)" there shall be substituted " any provider of an electronic communications network having any electronic communications apparatus ".

Commencement Information

I234. Sch. 17 para. 134 in force at 25.7.2003 for specified purposes by S.I. 2003/1900, arts. 1. (2), 2. (1), Sch. 1 (with art. 3) (as amended by S.I. 2003/3142, art. 1. (3))

I235. Sch. 17 para. 134 in force at 29.12.2003 in so far as not already in force by S.I. 2003/3142, art. 3. (2) (with art. 11)

Street Works (Northern Ireland) Order 1995.

135. (1)Paragraph 7 of Schedule 2 to the Street Works (Northern Ireland) Order 1995 (S.I. 1995/3210 (N.I. 19)) (streets with special engineering difficulties) shall be amended as follows.

(2) For "telecommunication apparatus", wherever occurring, there shall be substituted " electronic communications apparatus ".

(3) In sub-paragraph (3)(c)—

(a) for "a telecommunication system" there shall be substituted " an electronic communications network ";

(b) for "a system" there shall be substituted " a network ".

Commencement Information

I236. Sch. 17 para. 135 in force at 25.7.2003 for specified purposes by S.I. 2003/1900, arts. 1. (2), 2. (1), Sch. 1 (with art. 3) (as amended by S.I. 2003/3142, art. 1. (3))

I237. Sch. 17 para. 135 in force at 29.12.2003 in so far as not already in force by S.I. 2003/3142, art. 3. (2) (with art. 11)

Housing Act 1996.

F14136. . . . .

Amendments (Textual)

F14. Sch. 17 para. 136 repealed (1.4.2010) by The Housing and Regeneration Act 2008 (Consequential Provisions) Order 2010 (S.I. 2010/866), art. 1. (2), Sch. 4 (with art. 6, Sch. 3)

Commencement Information

I238. Sch. 17 para. 136 in force at 25.7.2003 for specified purposes by S.I. 2003/1900, arts. 1. (2), 2. (1), Sch. 1 (with art. 3) (as amended by S.I. 2003/3142, art. 1. (3))

I239. Sch. 17 para. 136 in force at 29.12.2003 in so far as not already in force by S.I. 2003/3142, art. 3. (2) (with art. 11)

Housing Grants, Construction and Regeneration Act 1996.

137. In section 105. (1)(b) of the Housing Grants, Construction and Regeneration Act 1996 (c. 53)

(meaning of "construction operations"), for "telecommunication apparatus" there shall be substituted " electronic communications apparatus ".
Commencement Information
I240. Sch. 17 para. 137 in force at 25.7.2003 for specified purposes by S.I. 2003/1900, arts. 1. (2), 2. (1), Sch. 1 (with art. 3) (as amended by S.I. 2003/3142, art. 1. (3))
I241. Sch. 17 para. 137 in force at 29.12.2003 in so far as not already in force by S.I. 2003/3142, art. 3. (2) (with art. 11)

Channel Tunnel Rail Link Act 1996.

138. In Schedule 6 to the Channel Tunnel Rail Link Act 1996 (c. 61) (planning conditions), in the table in paragraph 6. (4) and the table in paragraph 15. (4), for "telecommunications masts", in each place, there shall be substituted " electronic communications masts ".
Commencement Information
I242. Sch. 17 para. 138 in force at 25.7.2003 for specified purposes by S.I. 2003/1900, arts. 1. (2), 2. (1), Sch. 1 (with art. 3) (as amended by S.I. 2003/3142, art. 1. (3))
I243. Sch. 17 para. 138 in force at 29.12.2003 in so far as not already in force by S.I. 2003/3142, art. 3. (2) (with art. 11)
139. (1)Part 4 of Schedule 15 to that Act (protection of telecommunications operators) shall be amended as follows.
(2) In paragraph 1. (1), for "telecommunications operator" there shall be substituted " an operator of an electronic communications code network ".
(3) In paragraphs 2 to 4—
(a) for "telecommunications code", wherever occurring, there shall be substituted " electronic communications code ";
(b) for "telecommunications apparatus", wherever occurring, there shall be substituted " electronic communications apparatus ";
(c) for "a telecommunications operator", wherever occurring, there shall be substituted " an operator ";
(d) for "any telecommunications operator", wherever occurring, there shall be substituted " any operator of an electronic communications code network ";
(e) for "the telecommunications operator", wherever occurring, there shall be substituted " the operator ";
(f) for "telecommunications system" there shall be substituted " electronic communications code network ".
(4) In paragraph 5—
(a) for "telecommunications apparatus", wherever occurring, there shall be substituted " electronic communications apparatus ";
(b) for "telecommunications operator", in the first place where it occurs, there shall be substituted " operator of an electronic communications code network ";
(c) for "telecommunications operator", in each other place where it occurs, there shall be substituted " operator ".
Commencement Information
I244. Sch. 17 para. 139 in force at 25.7.2003 for specified purposes by S.I. 2003/1900, arts. 1. (2), 2. (1), Sch. 1 (with art. 3) (as amended by S.I. 2003/3142, art. 1. (3))
I245. Sch. 17 para. 139 in force at 29.12.2003 in so far as not already in force by S.I. 2003/3142, art. 3. (2) (with art. 11)

Gas (Northern Ireland) Order 1996.

140. The Gas (Northern Ireland) Order 1996 (S.I. 1996/275 (N.I. 2)) shall be amended as follows.
Commencement Information

I246. Sch. 17 para. 140 in force at 25.7.2003 for specified purposes by S.I. 2003/1900, arts. 1. (2), 2. (1), Sch. 1 (with art. 3) (as amended by S.I. 2003/3142, art. 1. (3))

I247. Sch. 17 para. 140 in force at 29.12.2003 in so far as not already in force by S.I. 2003/3142, art. 3. (2) (with art. 11)

141. In Article 44 (restrictions on disclosure of information)—

(a) in paragraph (3)(b), for head (vi) there shall be substituted—

"(vi)the Office of Communications;";

(b) in paragraph (4), after sub-paragraph (v) there shall be inserted—

    "(w)the Communications Act 2003."

Commencement Information

I248. Sch. 17 para. 141 in force at 25.7.2003 for specified purposes by S.I. 2003/1900, arts. 1. (2), 2. (1), Sch. 1 (with art. 3) (as amended by S.I. 2003/3142, art. 1. (3))

I249. Sch. 17 para. 141 in force at 29.12.2003 in so far as not already in force by S.I. 2003/3142, art. 3. (2) (with art. 11)

142. (1)Schedule 3 (other powers etc. of licence holders) shall be amended as follows.

(2) In paragraph 1. (1)—

(a) for "a public telecommunications operator" there shall be substituted " an electronic communications code operator ";

(b) for "telecommunication system" there shall be substituted " electronic communications network ".

(3) In paragraphs 4 and 6 for "public telecommunications operator" there shall be substituted " electronic communications code operator ".

(4) In paragraphs 3. (1), (2) and (3), 5. (1) and (2), 6. (1) and 8—

(a) for "telecommunication apparatus", wherever occurring, there shall be substituted " electronic communications apparatus ";

(b) for "a telecommunication system", wherever occurring, there shall be substituted " an electronic communications network ";

(c) for "telecommunications code", wherever occurring, there shall be substituted " electronic communications code ".

Commencement Information

I250. Sch. 17 para. 142 in force at 25.7.2003 for specified purposes by S.I. 2003/1900, arts. 1. (2), 2. (1), Sch. 1 (with art. 3) (as amended by S.I. 2003/3142, art. 1. (3))

I251. Sch. 17 para. 142 in force at 29.12.2003 in so far as not already in force by S.I. 2003/3142, art. 3. (2) (with art. 11)

Construction Contracts (Northern Ireland) Order 1997.

143. In Article 4. (1)(b) of the Construction Contracts (Northern Ireland) Order 1997 (S.I. 1997/274 (N.I. 1)) (meaning of "construction operations"), for "telecommunication apparatus" there shall be substituted " electronic communications apparatus ".

Commencement Information

I252. Sch. 17 para. 143 in force at 25.7.2003 for specified purposes by S.I. 2003/1900, arts. 1. (2), 2. (1), Sch. 1 (with art. 3) (as amended by S.I. 2003/3142, art. 1. (3))

I253. Sch. 17 para. 143 in force at 29.12.2003 in so far as not already in force by S.I. 2003/3142, art. 3. (2) (with art. 11)

Waste and Contaminated Land (Northern Ireland) Order 1997.

144. In Article 2. (2) of the Waste and Contaminated Land (Northern Ireland) Order 1997 (S.I. 1997/2778 (N.I. 19)) (meaning of "industrial waste" for "telecommunication services") there shall be substituted " communications services ".

Commencement Information

I254. Sch. 17 para. 144 in force at 25.7.2003 for specified purposes by S.I. 2003/1900, arts. 1. (2), 2. (1), Sch. 1 (with art. 3) (as amended by S.I. 2003/3142, art. 1. (3))

I255. Sch. 17 para. 144 in force at 29.12.2003 in so far as not already in force by S.I. 2003/3142, art. 3. (2) (with art. 11)

Wireless Telegraphy Act 1998.

F15145. . . . .

Amendments (Textual)

F15. Sch. 17 paras. 145-151 repealed (8.2.2007) by Wireless Telegraphy Act 2006 (c. 36), s. 126. (2), Sch. 9 Pt. 1 (with Sch. 8 Pt. 1)

Commencement Information

I256. Sch. 17 para. 145 in force at 29.12.2003 by S.I. 2003/3142, art. 3. (1), Sch. 1 (with art. 11)

F15146. . . . .

Amendments (Textual)

F15. Sch. 17 paras. 145-151 repealed (8.2.2007) by Wireless Telegraphy Act 2006 (c. 36), s. 126. (2), Sch. 9 Pt. 1 (with Sch. 8 Pt. 1)

Commencement Information

I257. Sch. 17 para. 146 in force at 29.12.2003 by S.I. 2003/3142, art. 3. (1), Sch. 1 (with art. 11)

F15147. . . . .

Amendments (Textual)

F15. Sch. 17 paras. 145-151 repealed (8.2.2007) by Wireless Telegraphy Act 2006 (c. 36), s. 126. (2), Sch. 9 Pt. 1 (with Sch. 8 Pt. 1)

Commencement Information

I258. Sch. 17 para. 147 in force at 25.7.2003 for specified purposes by S.I. 2003/1900, arts. 1. (2), 2. (1), Sch. 1 (with art. 3) (as amended by S.I. 2003/3142, art. 1. (3))

I259. Sch. 17 para. 147 in force at 29.12.2003 in so far as not already in force by S.I. 2003/3142, art. 3. (1), Sch. 1 (with art. 11)

F15148. . . . .

Amendments (Textual)

F15. Sch. 17 paras. 145-151 repealed (8.2.2007) by Wireless Telegraphy Act 2006 (c. 36), s. 126. (2), Sch. 9 Pt. 1 (with Sch. 8 Pt. 1)

Commencement Information

I260. Sch. 17 para. 148 in force at 29.12.2003 by S.I. 2003/3142, art. 3. (1), Sch. 1 (with art. 11)

F15149. . . . .

Amendments (Textual)

F15. Sch. 17 paras. 145-151 repealed (8.2.2007) by Wireless Telegraphy Act 2006 (c. 36), s. 126. (2), Sch. 9 Pt. 1 (with Sch. 8 Pt. 1)

Commencement Information

I261. Sch. 17 para. 149 in force at 18.9.2003 for specified purposes by S.I. 2003/1900, arts. 1. (2), 2. (2), Sch. 2 (with art. 3) (as amended by S.I. 2003/3142, art. 1. (3))

I262. Sch. 17 para. 149 in force at 29.12.2003 in so far as not already in force by S.I. 2003/3142, art. 3. (2) (with art. 11)

F15150. . . . .

Amendments (Textual)

F15. Sch. 17 paras. 145-151 repealed (8.2.2007) by Wireless Telegraphy Act 2006 (c. 36), s. 126. (2), Sch. 9 Pt. 1 (with Sch. 8 Pt. 1)

Commencement Information

I263 (as amended by S.I. 2003/3142, art. 1. (3))

I264. Sch. 17 para. 150 in force at 18.9.2003 for specified purposes by S.I. 2003/1900, arts. 1. (2), 2. (2), Sch. 2 (with art. 3) (as amended by S.I. 2003/3142, art. 1. (3))

I265. Sch. 17 para. 150 in force at 29.12.2003 in so far as not already in force by S.I. 2003/3142, art. 3. (1), Sch. 1 (with art. 11)

F15151. . . . .

Amendments (Textual)

F15. Sch. 17 paras. 145-151 repealed (8.2.2007) by Wireless Telegraphy Act 2006 (c. 36), s. 126. (2), Sch. 9 Pt. 1 (with Sch. 8 Pt. 1)

Commencement Information

I266. Sch. 17 para. 151 in force at 29.12.2003 by S.I. 2003/3142, art. 3. (1), Sch. 1 (with art. 11)

Finance Act 1998.

F16152. . . . .

Amendments (Textual)

F16. Sch. 17 para. 152 repealed (with effect in accordance with s. 381. (1) of the amending Act) by Taxation (International and Other Provisions) Act 2010 (c. 8), s. 381. (1), Sch. 10 Pt. 12 (with Sch. 9 paras. 1-9, 22)

Commencement Information

I267. Sch. 17 para. 152 in force at 25.7.2003 for specified purposes by S.I. 2003/1900, arts. 1. (2), 2. (1), Sch. 1 (with art. 3) (as amended by S.I. 2003/3142, art. 1. (3))

I268. Sch. 17 para. 152 in force at 29.12.2003 in so far as not already in force by S.I. 2003/3142, art. 3. (2) (with art. 11)

Competition Act 1998.

153. (1)Schedule 7 to the Competition Act 1998 (c. 41) (members of Commission appointed under certain enactments) shall be amended as follows.

(2) In paragraph 2. (1)(d), for sub-paragraph (iii) there shall be substituted—

"(iii)section 194. (1) of the Communications Act 2003;".

(3) In paragraph 19. A(9), in the definition of "special reference group", after paragraph (n) there shall be inserted "or

(o) section 193 of the Communications Act 2003."

Commencement Information

I269. Sch. 17 para. 153 in force at 25.7.2003 for specified purposes by S.I. 2003/1900, arts. 1. (2), 2. (1), Sch. 1 (with art. 3) (as amended by S.I. 2003/3142, art. 1. (3))

I270. Sch. 17 para. 153 in force at 29.12.2003 in so far as not already in force by S.I. 2003/3142, art. 3. (2) (with art. 11)

154. In paragraph 1 of Schedule 7. A to that Act (procedural rules), in the definition of "special investigation", for "and (n)" there shall be substituted " , (n) and (o) ".

Commencement Information

I271. Sch. 17 para. 154 in force at 25.7.2003 for specified purposes by S.I. 2003/1900, arts. 1. (2), 2. (1), Sch. 1 (with art. 3) (as amended by S.I. 2003/3142, art. 1. (3))

I272. Sch. 17 para. 154 in force at 29.12.2003 in so far as not already in force by S.I. 2003/3142, art. 3. (2) (with art. 11)

Regional Development Agencies Act 1998.

F17155. . . . .

Amendments (Textual)

F17. Sch. 17 para. 155 repealed (1.7.2012 at 0.02 a.m.) by Public Bodies Act 2011 (c. 24), s. 38. (3), Sch. 6 (with Sch. 6 Note 1); S.I. 2012/1662, art. 2. (2)(b)

Commencement Information

I273. Sch. 17 para. 155 in force at 25.7.2003 for specified purposes by S.I. 2003/1900, arts. 1. (2),

2. (1), Sch. 1 (with art. 3) (as amended by S.I. 2003/3142, art. 1. (3))

I274. Sch. 17 para. 155 in force at 29.12.2003 in so far as not already in force by S.I. 2003/3142, art. 3. (2) (with art. 11)

Finance Act 1999.

156. In section 132. (10) of the Finance Act 1999 (c. 16) (power to provide for use of electronic communications), for "a telecommunication system (within the meaning of the Telecommunications Act 1984)" there shall be substituted " an electronic communications service ".

Commencement Information

I275. Sch. 17 para. 156 in force at 25.7.2003 for specified purposes by S.I. 2003/1900, arts. 1. (2), 2. (1), Sch. 1 (with art. 3) (as amended by S.I. 2003/3142, art. 1. (3))

I276. Sch. 17 para. 156 in force at 29.12.2003 in so far as not already in force by S.I. 2003/3142, art. 3. (2) (with art. 11)

Greater London Authority Act 1999.

157. (1)Section 235 of the Greater London Authority Act 1999 (c. 29) (restrictions on disclosure of information) shall be amended as follows.

(2) In subsection (2)(c), for sub-paragraph (iv) there shall be substituted—

"(iv)the Office of Communications,".

(3) In subsection (3), after paragraph (rs) there shall be inserted—

"(rt)the Communications Act 2003;".

Commencement Information

I277. Sch. 17 para. 157 in force at 25.7.2003 for specified purposes by S.I. 2003/1900, arts. 1. (2), 2. (1), Sch. 1 (with art. 3) (as amended by S.I. 2003/3142, art. 1. (3))

I278. Sch. 17 para. 157 in force at 29.12.2003 in so far as not already in force by S.I. 2003/3142, art. 3. (2) (with art. 11)

Electronic Communications Act 2000.

158. In section 15. (1) of the Electronic Communications Act 2000 (c. 7) (general interpretation), in the definition of "electronic communication", for "a telecommunication system (within the meaning of the Telecommunications Act 1984)" there shall be substituted " an electronic communications network ".

Commencement Information

I279. Sch. 17 para. 158 in force at 25.7.2003 for specified purposes by S.I. 2003/1900, arts. 1. (2), 2. (1), Sch. 1 (with art. 3) (as amended by S.I. 2003/3142, art. 1. (3))

I280. Sch. 17 para. 158 in force at 29.12.2003 in so far as not already in force by S.I. 2003/3142, art. 3. (2) (with art. 11)

Television Licences (Disclosure of Information) Act 2000.

159. In section 5 of the Television Licences (Disclosure of Information) Act 2000 (c. 15) (interpretation)—

(a) for the definitions of "the BBC" and "television licence" there shall be substituted—

""the BBC" means the British Broadcasting Corporation;";

(b) after the definition of "prescribed" there shall be inserted—

""television licence" means a licence for the purposes of section 363 of the Communications Act 2003;".

Finance Act 2000. M

160. In paragraph 8 of Schedule 38 to the Finance Act 2000 (c. 17) (regulations for providing incentives for electronic communications), in the definition of "electronic communications", for "a telecommunication system (within the meaning of the Telecommunications Act 1984)" there shall be substituted " an electronic communications service ".

Regulation of Investigatory Powers Act 2000.

161. (1)The Regulation of Investigatory Powers Act 2000 (c. 23) shall be amended as follows.
(2) In section 26. (6)(a) (surveillance carried out for detecting unlicensed TV use), for "section 1 of the Wireless Telegraphy Act 1949)" there shall be substituted " Part 4 of the Communications Act 2003) ".
(3) In Part 1 of Schedule 1 (relevant public authorities for the purposes of sections 28 and 29 of that Act), after paragraph 23 there shall be inserted—
"23. AThe Office of Communications."

Postal Services Act 2000.

162. (1)The Postal Services Act 2000 (c. 26) shall be amended as follows.
(2) In section 125. (2)(a) (communications delivered otherwise than electronically), for "a telecommunication system (within the meaning of the Telecommunications Act 1984)" there shall be substituted " an electronic communications network ".
F18. (3)...........................

Utilities Act 2000.

163. (1)Section 105 of the Utilities Act 2000 (c. 27) (general restrictions on disclosure of information) shall be amended as follows.
(2) In subsection (5), for paragraph (d) there shall be substituted—
  "(d)the Office of Communications;".

(3) In subsection (6), after paragraph (s) there shall be inserted—

"(t)the Communications Act 2003."

Commencement Information

I288. Sch. 17 para. 163 in force at 25.7.2003 for specified purposes by S.I. 2003/1900, arts. 1. (2), 2. (1), Sch. 1 (with art. 3) (as amended by S.I. 2003/3142, art. 1. (3))

I289. Sch. 17 para. 163 in force at 29.12.2003 in so far as not already in force by S.I. 2003/3142, art. 3. (2) (with art. 11)

Freedom of Information Act 2000.

164. In Part 6 of Schedule 1 to the Freedom of Information Act 2000 (c. 36) (public authorities), there shall be inserted at the appropriate place—

"The Consumer Panel established under section 16 of the Communications Act 2003."

Commencement Information

I290. Sch. 17 para. 164 in force at 29.12.2003 by S.I. 2003/3142, art. 3. (1), Sch. 1 (with art. 11)

Countryside and Rights of Way Act 2000.

165. (1)The Countryside and Rights of Way Act 2000 (c. 37) shall be amended as follows.

(2) In section 17. (4) (byelaws not to interfere with certain rights), for paragraph (c) there shall be substituted—

"(c)with the provision of an electronic communications code network or the exercise of any right conferred by or in accordance with the electronic communications code on the operator of any such network."

(3) In paragraph 8 of Schedule 1 (excepted land), for "a telecommunications code system" there shall be substituted " an electronic communications code network ".

Commencement Information

I291. Sch. 17 para. 165 in force at 25.7.2003 for specified purposes by S.I. 2003/1900, arts. 1. (2), 2. (1), Sch. 1 (with art. 3) (as amended by S.I. 2003/3142, art. 1. (3))

I292. Sch. 17 para. 165 in force at 29.12.2003 in so far as not already in force by S.I. 2003/3142, art. 3. (2) (with art. 11)

Transport Act 2000.

166. (1)Paragraph 3 of Schedule 9 to the Transport Act 2000 (c. 38) (air traffic information) shall be amended as follows.

(2) In sub-paragraph (2), for paragraph (d) there shall be substituted—

"(d)the Office of Communications;".

(3) In sub-paragraph (3)—

(a) after paragraph (q) there shall be inserted—

"(qa)the Broadcasting Act 1996;";

(b) after paragraph (ra) there shall be inserted—

"(rb)the Communications Act 2003;".

Commencement Information

I293. Sch. 17 para. 166. (1)(2)(3)(b) in force at 25.7.2003 for specified purposes by S.I. 2003/1900, arts. 1. (2), 2. (1), Sch. 1 (with art. 3) (as amended by S.I. 2003/3142, art. 1. (3))

I294. Sch. 17 para. 166. (1) (2) (3)(b) in force at 29.12.2003 in so far as not already in force by S.I. 2003/3142, art. 3. (1), Sch. 1 (with art. 11)

I295. Sch. 17 para. 166. (3)(a) in force at 29.12.2003 by S.I. 2003/3142, art. 3. (1), Sch. 1 (with art. 11)

Political Parties, Elections and Referendums Act 2000.

167. (1)The Political Parties, Elections and Referendums Act 2000 (c. 41) shall be amended as follows.

(2) In section 11. (3) (broadcasters to have regard to Electoral Commission's views on political broadcasts), for the words from "and Sianel" to "regard" there shall be substituted " shall have regard, in determining its policy with respect to party political broadcasts, ".

(3) In paragraph 4. (6) of Schedule 12 (broadcasters to have regard to Electoral Commission's views on referendum campaign broadcasts), for the words from "and Sianel" to "regard" there shall be substituted " shall have regard, in determining its policy with respect to referendum campaign broadcasts by designated organisations, ".

Commencement Information

I296. Sch. 17 para. 167 in force at 29.12.2003 by S.I. 2003/3142, art. 3. (1), Sch. 1 (with art. 11)

Vehicles (Crime) Act 2001.

168. In sections [F1916. (2)(a),] 31. (2)(a) and 40. (6) of the Vehicles (Crime) Act 2001 (c. 3) (transmission of representations and service of notices etc.), for "a telecommunication system (within the meaning of the Telecommunications Act 1984 (c. 12))" there shall be substituted " an electronic communications network ".

Amendments (Textual)

F19. Word in Sch. 17 para. 168 repealed (E.W.) (1.10.2013) by Scrap Metal Dealers Act 2013 (c. 10), ss. 19. (1)(e), 23. (2); S.I. 2013/1966, art. 3. (r) (with art. 5)

Commencement Information

I297. Sch. 17 para. 168 in force at 25.7.2003 for specified purposes by S.I. 2003/1900, arts. 1. (2), 2. (1), Sch. 1 (with art. 3) (as amended by S.I. 2003/3142, art. 1. (3))

I298. Sch. 17 para. 168 in force at 29.12.2003 in so far as not already in force by S.I. 2003/3142, art. 3. (2) (with art. 11)

Criminal Justice and Police Act 2001.

169. In the table in section 1. (1) of the Criminal Justice and Police Act 2001 (c. 16) (offences leading to penalties on the spot), after the entry relating to section 12 of that Act there shall be inserted—

"Section 127(2) of the Communications Act 2003 | Using public electronic communications network in order to cause annoyance, inconvenience or needless anxiety". |

Commencement Information

I299. Sch. 17 para. 169 in force at 25.7.2003 for specified purposes by S.I. 2003/1900, arts. 1. (2), 2. (1), Sch. 1 (with art. 3) (as amended by S.I. 2003/3142, art. 1. (3))

I300. Sch. 17 para. 169 in force at 29.12.2003 in so far as not already in force by S.I. 2003/3142, art. 3. (2) (with art. 11)

Electronic Communications Act (Northern Ireland) 2001.

170. In section 4. (1) of the Electronic Communications Act (Northern Ireland) 2001 (c. 9 (N.I.)) (interpretation), in the definition of "electronic communication", for "a telecommunication system (within the meaning of the Telecommunications Act 1984)" there shall be substituted " an electronic communications network ".

Commencement Information

I301. Sch. 17 para. 170 in force at 25.7.2003 for specified purposes by S.I. 2003/1900, arts. 1. (2), 2. (1), Sch. 1 (with art. 3) (as amended by S.I. 2003/3142, art. 1. (3))

I302. Sch. 17 para. 170 in force at 29.12.2003 in so far as not already in force by S.I. 2003/3142, art. 3. (2) (with art. 11)

Office of Communications Act 2002.

171. Sections 2, 4, 5 and 6 of the Office of Communications Act 2002 (c. 11) shall cease to have effect.

Commencement Information

I303. Sch. 17 para. 171 in force at 29.12.2003 by S.I. 2003/3142, art. 3. (1), Sch. 1 (with art. 11)

172. (1)The Schedule to that Act shall be amended as follows.

(2) The following shall cease to have effect—

(a) paragraph 1. (4);

(b) paragraph 8. (5);

(c) paragraph 17. (8) and (9); and

(d) paragraph 20.

(3) For paragraph 8. (1) there shall be substituted—

"(1)It shall be the duty of OFCOM so to conduct their affairs as to secure that their revenues so far as they —

(a) derive from the exercise of powers to impose charges or fees in respect of the carrying out of particular functions, and

(b) do not fall to be paid into the Consolidated Fund of the United Kingdom or of Northern Ireland,

are at least sufficient to enable OFCOM to meet the costs of carrying out the functions to which the revenues relate."

(4) After paragraph 14. (3) (executive committees of OFCOM to include member or employee of OFCOM) there shall be inserted—

"(3. A)Sub-paragraph (3) has effect in the case of a committee of OFCOM which—

(a) is not the Content Board, but

(b) has functions that are confined to functions falling within section 13. (2) of the Communications Act 2003 (functions within the Content Board's remit),

as if the reference in that sub-paragraph to a member of OFCOM included a reference to a member of the Content Board who is not a member of OFCOM."

Commencement Information

I304. Sch. 17 para. 172 in force at 29.12.2003 by S.I. 2003/3142, art. 3. (1), Sch. 1 (with art. 11)

Tobacco Advertising and Promotion Act 2002.

173. (1)Section 12 of the Tobacco Advertising and Promotion Act 2002 (c. 36) (exclusion from that Act of advertising on television and radio) shall be amended as follows.

(2) For subsection (3) there shall be substituted—

"(3)This subsection applies to —

(a) a service falling within section 211. (1) of the Communications Act 2003 (independent television services regulated by the Office of Communications) which is not an additional television service (within the meaning of Part 3 of that Act); and

(b) an additional television service comprised in the public teletext service (within the meaning of that Part)."

(3) For subsection (5) there shall be substituted—

"(5)This subsection applies to a service which—

(a) falls within section 245. (1) of the Communications Act 2003 (independent radio services regulated by the Office of Communications); but

(b) is not a digital additional sound service (within the meaning of Part 3 of that Act)."

Commencement Information

I305. Sch. 17 para. 173 in force at 29.12.2003 by S.I. 2003/3142, art. 3. (1), Sch. 1 (with art. 11)

Enterprise Act 2002.

174. (1)The Enterprise Act 2002 (c. 40) shall be amended as follows.

(2) In section 126. (6) (service of documents electronically), for "a telecommunication system (within the meaning of the Telecommunications Act 1984 (c. 12))" there shall be substituted " an electronic communications network ".

(3) In section 128. (5) (supply of services and market for services etc.), for "section 189. (2) of the Broadcasting Act 1990 (c. 42)" there shall be substituted " paragraph 29 of Schedule 2 to the Telecommunications Act 1984 ".

(4) In section 136 (investigations and reports on market investigation references)—

(a) in subsection (7), after paragraph (g) there shall be inserted—

   "(h)in relation to the Office of Communications, sections 370 and 371 of the Communications Act 2003.";

(b) in subsection (8), for "or the Civil Aviation Authority" there shall be substituted " , the Civil Aviation Authority or the Office of Communications ".

(5) In section 168 (regulated markets)—

(a) in subsection (3)(e), for "section 39. (1) of the Broadcasting Act 1990 (c. 42)" there shall be substituted " section 290 of the Communications Act 2003 ";

(b) for subsection (4)(e), there shall be substituted—

   "(e)in relation to any networking arrangements (within the meaning given by section 290 of the Communications Act 2003), the duty of the Office of Communications under subsection (1) of section 3 of that Act to secure the matters mentioned in subsection (2)(c) of that section;";

(c) for subsection (5)(g), there shall be substituted—

   "(g)the Office of Communications;".

(6) In section 234. (5) (supply of services), for "section 189. (2) of the Broadcasting Act 1990 (c. 42)" there shall be substituted " paragraph 29 of Schedule 2 to the Telecommunications Act 1984 ".

(7) In Schedule 15 (enactments conferring functions), in the appropriate place, there shall be inserted— " Communications Act 2003. "

Commencement Information

I306. Sch. 17 para. 174. (1)(2)(4)(6)(7) in force at 25.7.2003 for specified purposes by S.I. 2003/1900, arts. 1. (2), 2. (1), Sch. 1 (with art. 3) (as amended by S.I. 2003/3142, art. 1. (3))

I307. Sch. 17 para. 174. (1) (2) (4) (6) (7) in force at 29.12.2003 in so far as not already in force by S.I. 2003/3142, art. 3. (1), Sch. 1 (with art. 11)

I308. Sch. 17 para. 174. (3) (5) in force at 29.12.2003 by S.I. 2003/3142, art. 3. (1), Sch. 1 (with art. 11)

Income Tax (Earnings and Pensions) Act 2003.

175. (1)The Income Tax (Earnings and Pensions) Act 2003 (c. 1) shall be amended as follows.

F20. (2). . . . .

F21. (3). . . . .

Amendments (Textual)

F20. Sch. 17 para. 175. (2) repealed (19.7.2006 with effect in accordance with Sch. 26 Pt. 3. (6) Note of the amending Act) by Finance Act 2006 (c. 25), Sch. 26 Pt. 3. (6)

F21. Sch. 17 para. 175. (3) repealed (19.7.2006 with effect in accordance with Sch. 26 Pt. 3. (7) Note of the amending Act) by Finance Act 2006 (c. 25), Sch. 26 Pt. 3. (7)

Commencement Information

I309. Sch. 17 para. 175 in force at 25.7.2003 for specified purposes by S.I. 2003/1900, arts. 1. (2), 2. (1), Sch. 1 (with art. 3) (as amended by S.I. 2003/3142, art. 1. (3))

I310. Sch. 17 para. 175 in force at 29.12.2003 in so far as not already in force by S.I. 2003/3142, art. 3. (2) (with art. 11)

Schedule 19. Transitional Provisions

Section 406

General

1. (1)This paragraph applies where, at any time before the coming into force of a transfer made by virtue of section 2—
(a) any subordinate legislation has been made in the carrying out of the transferred functions by the person from whom the transfer is made; or
(b) any other thing has been done by or in relation to that person for the purposes of or in connection with the carrying out of those functions.
(2) The subordinate legislation or other thing—
(a) is to have effect, on and after the coming into force of the transfer, and so far as necessary for its purposes, as if it had been made or done by or in relation to OFCOM; and
(b) in the case of subordinate legislation to which section 403 applies when it is made by OFCOM, shall so have effect as if made in accordance with the requirements of that section.
(3) Where any subordinate legislation, direction, authorisation or notice has effect in accordance with this paragraph—
(a) so much of it as authorises or requires anything to be done by or in relation to the person from whom the transfer is made is to have effect in relation to times after the coming into force of the transfer as if it authorised or required that thing to be done by or in relation to OFCOM; and
(b) other references in the subordinate legislation, direction, authorisation or notice to the person from whom the transfer is made are to have effect, in relation to such times, as references to OFCOM.
Commencement Information
I1. Sch. 18 para. 1 in force at 25.7.2003 for specified purposes by S.I. 2003/1900, arts. 1. (2), 2. (1), Sch. 1 (with art. 3) (as amended by S.I. 2003/3142, art. 1. (3))
I2. Sch. 18 para. 1 in force at 29.12.2003 in so far as not already in force by S.I. 2003/3142, art. 3. (2) (with art. 11)

Steps taken in anticipation of passing or coming into force of Act

2. (1)This paragraph applies where the Secretary of State or OFCOM is or are required—
(a) by a provision of this Act, or
(b) by virtue of an amendment made by this Act,
to take steps before exercising a power or performing a duty.
(2) The requirement is capable of being satisfied by the taking of the steps in anticipation of effect being given to the provision by virtue of which the power or duty is—
(a) conferred or imposed on the Secretary of State or OFCOM; or
(b) transferred to OFCOM.
(3) For the purposes of sub-paragraph (2) it is immaterial—
(a) that the provision by virtue of which the power or duty is conferred, imposed or transferred had not been enacted, or had not come into force, when the steps were taken; and
(b) in the case of steps taken before the enactment of that provision, that the provision the effect of which was anticipated was modified before being enacted.
(4) In relation to provisions brought into force as mentioned in subsection (1) of section 408 for

the purpose of enabling specified functions to be carried out by the Director or the Secretary of State—

(a) this paragraph has effect in relation to steps taken by the Director or the Secretary of State as it has in relation to steps taken by OFCOM; and

(b) subsection (5) of that section applies in relation to steps taken by the Director or the Secretary of State in anticipation of effect being given to those provisions as it would apply to anything done by the Director or the Secretary of State for the purposes of, or in connection with, the carrying out of those functions.

(5) Where a requirement is satisfied by virtue of this paragraph by steps taken in anticipation of effect being given to a provision—

(a) representations made to or other things done in relation to OFCOM, or the Director or the Secretary of State, in consequence of the taking of those steps, and

(b) any requirements framed by reference to the time at which those steps were taken,

are to have effect as if the provision in question had come into force before those steps were taken.

Commencement Information

I3. Sch. 18 para. 2 in force at 25.7.2003 for specified purposes by S.I. 2003/1900, arts. 1. (2), 2. (1), Sch. 1 (with art. 3) (as amended by S.I. 2003/3142, art. 1. (3))

I4. Sch. 18 para. 2 in force at 29.12.2003 in so far as not already in force by S.I. 2003/3142, art. 3. (2) (with art. 11)

Savings for agreements referring to the termination of a 1984 Act licence

3. (1)This paragraph applies where a term or condition of an agreement in force immediately before the abolition of licensing provides—

(a) for the agreement, or a provision of it, to cease to have effect,

(b) for the agreement to become capable of being terminated,

(c) for a requirement to pay or repay an amount (whether liquidated or unliquidated) to arise under the agreement, or to arise earlier than it would otherwise have arisen,

(d) for a security to become enforceable, or

(e) for rights or obligations of a person under the agreement to be different or to be modified,

if a person (whether or not a party to the agreement) ceases to hold a licence under section 7 of the 1984 Act, or ceases to do so in a manner or in circumstances described in the agreement.

(2) Where a person ceases to hold a licence in consequence of the provisions of this Act removing the requirement to hold a licence under section 7 of the 1984 Act—

(a) the term or condition is not to apply; and

(b) the rights and obligations of the parties to the agreement are to be the same (subject to the following sub-paragraphs) as they would have been had the person in question continued to hold such a licence.

(3) In relation to times after the abolition of licensing, that term or condition is to have effect as if the reference in that term or condition—

(a) to a person's ceasing to hold a licence under section 7 of the 1984 Act, or

(b) to his ceasing to do so in a particular manner or particular circumstances,

were a reference to his becoming subject to a direction under this Act by virtue of which he is prohibited from providing the whole or a part of an electronic communications network or electronic communications service.

(4) In sub-paragraph (3) the reference to a person's becoming subject to a direction by virtue of which he is prohibited from providing the whole or a part of an electronic communications network or electronic communications service—

(a) does not include a reference to his becoming subject to a direction imposing a prohibition for a fixed period of less than eighteen months or to a direction that will have to be revoked if not confirmed; but

(b) except in the case of a direction imposing a prohibition for such a fixed period, does include a reference to the confirmation of a direction that would otherwise have had to be revoked.

(5) This paragraph does not apply in the case of a term or condition of an agreement if, on an application to the court by one or both of the parties to the agreement, the court directs—

(a) that this paragraph is not to apply; or

(b) that it is to apply with such modifications, or subject to the payment of such compensation, as the court may specify in the direction.

(6) In determining whether to give a direction under sub-paragraph (5) or what modifications or compensation to specify in such a direction the court must have regard to the following—

(a) whether either or both of the parties to the agreement contemplated the abolition of the licensing requirements of the 1984 Act when they entered into the agreement; and

(b) the extent (if any) to which the provisions of this paragraph represent what it would have been reasonable for the parties to have agreed had they both known at that time what provision was to be made by this Act and when it was to come into force.

(7) For the purposes of this paragraph—

(a) references to ceasing to hold a licence include references to its expiring or being revoked; and

(b) references to a licence under section 7 of the 1984 Act include references to a licence under that section of a particular description.

(8) In this paragraph "the court" means the High Court or the Court of Session.

(9) This paragraph has effect subject to paragraph 14.

Commencement Information

I5. Sch. 18 para. 3 in force at 25.7.2003 for specified purposes by S.I. 2003/1900, arts. 1. (2), 2. (1), Sch. 1 (with art. 3) (as amended by S.I. 2003/3142, art. 1. (3))

I6. Sch. 18 para. 3 in force at 29.12.2003 in so far as not already in force by S.I. 2003/3142, art. 3. (2) (with art. 11)

Saving for agreements with special provision for 1984 Act licence holders

4. (1) This paragraph applies in a case to which paragraph 3 does not apply and in which a term or condition of an agreement in force immediately before the abolition of licensing provides for rights or obligations of a person ("the contracting party") under the agreement to be different or to be modified according to whether or not he or another person (whether or not a party to the agreement)—

(a) is or has become the holder of a licence under section 7 of the 1984 Act; or

(b) is or has become the holder of such a licence in a manner or in circumstances described in the agreement.

(2) In relation to times after the abolition of licensing, that term or condition is to have effect as if the rights and obligations to which the contracting party is entitled or subject under the agreement were, except in a case falling within sub-paragraph (3), those for which the agreement provides in relation to a case in which the person in question—

(a) is or has become the holder of such a licence; or

(b) is or has become the holder of such a licence in that manner or in those circumstances.

(3) The excepted case is where that person is subject to a direction under this Act by virtue of which he is prohibited from providing the whole or a part of an electronic communications network or electronic communications service.

(4) In sub-paragraph (3) the reference to a person's being subject to a direction by virtue of which he is prohibited from providing the whole or a part of an electronic communications network or electronic communications service—

(a) does not include a reference to his being subject to a direction imposing a prohibition for a fixed period of less than eighteen months or to a direction that will have to be revoked if not confirmed; but

(b) except in the case of a direction imposing a prohibition for such a fixed period, does include a reference to his being subject to a direction which would have had to be revoked if not confirmed but which has been confirmed.

(5) This paragraph does not apply in the case of a term or condition of an agreement if, on an application to the court by one or both of the parties to the agreement, the court directs—

(a) that this paragraph is not to apply; or

(b) that it is to apply with such modifications, or subject to the payment of such compensation, as the court may specify in the direction.

(6) In determining whether to give a direction under sub-paragraph (5) or what modifications or compensation to specify in such a direction the court must have regard to the following—

(a) whether either or both of the parties to the agreement contemplated the abolition of the licensing requirements of the 1984 Act when they entered into the agreement; and

(b) the extent (if any) to which the provisions of this paragraph represent what it would have been reasonable for the parties to have agreed had they both known at that time what provision was to be made by this Act and when it was to come into force.

(7) For the purposes of this paragraph references to a licence under section 7 of the 1984 Act include references to a licence under that section of a particular description.

(8) In this paragraph "the court" means the High Court or the Court of Session.

Commencement Information

I7. Sch. 18 para. 4 in force at 25.7.2003 for specified purposes by S.I. 2003/1900, arts. 1. (2), 2. (1), Sch. 1 (with art. 3) (as amended by S.I. 2003/3142, art. 1. (3))

I8. Sch. 18 para. 4 in force at 29.12.2003 in so far as not already in force by S.I. 2003/3142, art. 3. (2) (with art. 11)

General saving for agreements conditional on certain Broadcasting Act licences

5. (1)This paragraph has effect where an agreement in force immediately before the coming into force of a provision of this Act removing a requirement for a relevant Broadcasting Act licence provides—

(a) for the agreement to cease to have effect, or

(b) for it to be capable of being terminated,

if a party to the agreement ceases to hold a relevant Broadcasting Act licence of a particular description, or so ceases in a manner described in the agreement.

(2) In this paragraph "relevant Broadcasting Act licence" means—

(a) a licence under Part 1 of the 1990 Act to provide a satellite television service or a licensable programme service;

(b) a licence under that Part to provide the service mentioned in section 49. (2) of that Act;

(c) a licence under Part 2 of that Act to provide a local delivery service; or

(d) a licence under Part 3 of that Act to provide a formerly regulated radio service (within the meaning of section 251 of this Act).

(3) The agreement is not to cease to have effect, or to be capable of being terminated, by reason only of the coming into force of the provisions of this Act under which the requirement for the licence is removed.

(4) In relation to times after the commencement of the provision of this Act removing the requirement for a licence to provide a satellite television service or a licensable programme service, a reference to such a licence in the provision of the agreement in question is to have effect as a reference to a licence granted or having effect as if granted as a licence to provide a television licensable content service.

(5) In relation to times after the commencement of the provision of this Act removing the requirement for a licence to provide the service mentioned in section 49. (2) of the 1990 Act, a reference to such a licence in the provision of the agreement in question is to have effect as a

reference to a licence to provide the public teletext service.

(6) In relation to times after the commencement of the provision of this Act removing the requirement for a licence to provide a licensable sound programme service, a reference to such a licence in the provision of the agreement in question is to have effect as a reference to a licence to provide a radio licensable content service.

(7) References in this paragraph to a provision having effect if a person ceases to hold a licence include references—

(a) to a provision having effect if a licence of his expires without being renewed; and

(b) to a provision having effect if his licence is revoked.

(8) Expressions used in this paragraph and in Part 3 of this Act have the same meanings in this paragraph as in that Part.

Commencement Information

I9. Sch. 18 para. 5 in force at 29.12.2003 by S.I. 2003/3142, art. 3. (1), Sch. 1 (with art. 11)

Orders under Part 2 of the Deregulation and Contracting Out Act 1994.

F16. . . . .

Amendments (Textual)

F1. Sch. 18 para. 6 repealed (8.2.2007) by Wireless Telegraphy Act 2006 (c. 36), s. 126. (2), Sch. 9 Pt. 1 (with Sch. 8 Pt. 1)

Commencement Information

I10. Sch. 18 para. 6 in force at 29.12.2003 by S.I. 2003/3142, art. 3. (1), Sch. 1 (with art. 11)

Pre-commencement proposals relating to universal service matters

7. (1)Where a proposal for the designation of a person as a universal service provider has been confirmed under regulation 4. (10) of the Electronic Communications (Universal Service) Regulations 2003 (S.I. 2003/33), the designation is to have effect after the commencement of section 66 of this Act as a designation in accordance with regulations under that section.

(2) Where in any person's case a proposal to set a condition has been confirmed under regulation 4. (10) or 5. (4) of those regulations, that condition is to have effect after the commencement of that section as a condition set by OFCOM under section 45 of this Act and applied to that person.

(3) Where an appeal under regulation 6 of those regulations against a decision under them has been brought but not concluded before the commencement of section 192 of this Act—

(a) that appeal is to be stayed or sisted as from the commencement of the section; but

(b) the appellant is to have a new right of appeal under the section against the decision (as it has effect by virtue of this paragraph) as if—

(i) it were the corresponding decision made by OFCOM under Chapter 1 of Part 2 of this Act; and

(ii) it had been made immediately after the commencement of the section.

(4) Tribunal rules (within the meaning of Chapter 3 of Part 2 of this Act) may, in relation to an appeal stayed or sisted under sub-paragraph (3), make transitional provision for requiring steps taken and things done for the purposes of that appeal to be taken into account, to the extent set out in the rules, in the case of an appeal brought by virtue of paragraph (b) of that sub-paragraph.

Commencement Information

I11. Sch. 18 para. 7 in force at 25.7.2003 for specified purposes by S.I. 2003/1900, arts. 1. (2), 2. (1), Sch. 1 (with art. 3) (as amended by S.I. 2003/3142, art. 1. (3))

I12. Sch. 18 para. 7 in force at 29.12.2003 in so far as not already in force by S.I. 2003/3142, art. 3. (2) (with art. 11)

Local loop notifications

8. (1)This paragraph applies where, as a result of a market power determination made by OFCOM for the purposes of a provision of Chapter 1 of Part 2 of this Act, they conclude that a person who is for the time being LLU notified is no longer a person falling to be so notified.

(2) OFCOM must give a notification of their conclusion to—

(a) the Secretary of State; and

(b) the notified person.

(3) On receiving a notification under sub-paragraph (2) the Secretary of State must withdraw the LLU notification of the person in question.

(4) For the purposes of this paragraph a person is LLU notified if he is a person who, for the purposes of Regulation (EC) No. 2887/2000 of the European Parliament and of the Council on unbundled access to the local loop, is notified to the European Commission as having significant market power in an identified market, and "LLU notification" shall be construed accordingly.

(5) Section 192 applies to a decision by OFCOM to give a notification under this paragraph as it applies to a decision by them under Part 2 of this Act.

Commencement Information

I13. Sch. 18 para. 8 in force at 25.7.2003 for specified purposes by S.I. 2003/1900, arts. 1. (2), 2. (1), Sch. 1 (with art. 3) (as amended by S.I. 2003/3142, art. 1. (3))

I14. Sch. 18 para. 8 in force at 29.12.2003 in so far as not already in force by S.I. 2003/3142, art. 3. (2) (with art. 11)

Conditions relating to premium rate services and conditions corresponding to SMP or access-related conditions

9. (1)This paragraph applies where OFCOM give a continuation notice to the holder of a licence granted under section 7 of the 1984 Act.

(2) A continuation notice is a notice that a provision contained in a condition of the licence is to have effect, after the abolition of licensing—

(a) to the extent specified in the notice; and

(b) subject to such modifications (if any) as may be so specified.

(3) OFCOM are not to give a continuation notice except to the extent that they consider that provision to which it will give effect, as modified by the notice, ("the continued provision")—

(a) regulates the provision of premium rate services; or

(b) falls within sub-paragraph (4).

(4) The continued provision falls within this sub-paragraph in so far as it corresponds to provision of one or more of the following descriptions—

(a) provision that OFCOM have power to include in SMP conditions;

(b) provision authorised by section 73. (2) or (4) for inclusion in access-related conditions;

(c) provision relating to matters mentioned in Article 16 of the Universal Service Directive or Article 7 of the Access Directive.

(5) A continuation notice relating to provision corresponding to anything that OFCOM have power to include in SMP conditions—

(a) may identify the market by reference to which an SMP condition replacing the provision would have to be set; and

(b) in so far as the provision corresponds to anything that OFCOM have power to include only in SMP apparatus conditions, must do so.

(6) OFCOM are not to give a continuation notice relating to provision corresponding to anything that OFCOM have power to include only in SMP apparatus conditions except to the extent that it has effect in relation to the supply of electronic communications apparatus of a description supplied in the market identified in the notice as the market by reference to which SMP conditions

replacing the continued provision would have to be set.

(7) The modifications for which a continuation notice may provide—

(a) must be confined to modifications for the purpose of securing that the provision to which they relate continues to have effect for so long as the notice is in force; but

(b) in the case of provision which is expressed to impose a requirement to be met before the abolition of licensing, may include a modification under which that requirement must continue to be met for so long as the notice remains in force.

(8) Notwithstanding any repeal or revocation made by this Act—

(a) the continued provision,

(b) every provision made by a direction, determination or consent given or made for the purposes of the continued provision, and

(c) so far as necessary for giving effect to anything mentioned in paragraph (a) or (b), every provision made by or under the licence under the 1984 Act that is not so mentioned,

are to remain in force for so long as the continuation notice is in force.

(9) A continuation notice shall cease to have effect if OFCOM give a notice to that effect to the holder of the licence.

(10) Where the continued provision is one that OFCOM have power to include only in an SMP apparatus condition, it shall be their duty, as soon as reasonably practicable after giving the continuation notice—

(a) to carry out an analysis of the market which, under sub-paragraph (5), is identified in that notice;

(b) to take all other steps necessary for enabling them to decide whether or not to set an SMP apparatus condition by reference to that market for the purpose of replacing the continued provision; and

(c) to decide whether or not to exercise their power to set such a condition for that purpose.

(11) In the case of every other continued provision falling within sub-paragraph (4), it shall be OFCOM's duty, as soon as reasonably practicable after giving the continuation notice—

(a) to take all steps necessary for enabling them to decide whether or not to set a condition of any other description under Chapter 1 of Part 2 of this Act for the purpose of replacing the continued provision; and

(b) to decide whether or not to exercise their power to set a condition under that Chapter for that purpose.

(12) It shall be the duty of OFCOM—

(a) as soon as reasonably practicable after making a decision required by sub-paragraph (10) or (11), but

(b) in a case where that decision is a decision to set a condition, not before the coming into force of that condition,

to give a notice under sub-paragraph (9) with respect to the continuation notice.

(13) The duties imposed by sub-paragraphs (10) to (12) apply only where OFCOM have not previously given a notice under sub-paragraph (9) with respect to the continuation notice in question.

(14) This paragraph has effect in the case of a licence granted under section 7 of the 1984 Act to persons of a particular class as if—

(a) references to the holder of that licence were references to the members of that class; and

(b) the manner in which a continuation notice or notice under sub-paragraph (9) is to be given to members of that class were by its publication in such manner as, in OFCOM's opinion, is appropriate for bringing it to the attention of the members of that class who are affected by the notice.

[F2. (14. A)Sections 185 to 191 apply to a dispute relating to a provision of a kind mentioned in paragraph (4), other than a dispute relating to provision that OFCOM have power to include in SMP apparatus conditions, as they apply to disputes of a kind mentioned in subsections (1. A) and (2) of section 185.]

(15) Section 192 applies to a decision by OFCOM to give a notice under this paragraph as it

applies to a decision by them under Part 2 of this Act.

(16) In this paragraph "Access Directive", "electronic communications apparatus", "the provision of premium rate services", "SMP condition", "SMP apparatus condition" and "Universal Service Directive" each has the same meaning as in Chapter 1 of Part 2 of this Act.

Amendments (Textual)

F2. Sch. 18 para. 9. (14. A) inserted (26.5.2011) by The Electronic Communications and Wireless Telegraphy Regulations 2011 (S.I. 2011/1210), reg. 1. (2), Sch. 1 para. 100. (a) (with Sch. 3 para. 2)

Commencement Information

I15. Sch. 18 para. 9 in force at 25.7.2003 for specified purposes by S.I. 2003/1900, arts. 1. (2), 2. (1), Sch. 1 (with art. 3) (as amended by S.I. 2003/3142, art. 1. (3))

I16. Sch. 18 para. 9 in force at 29.12.2003 in so far as not already in force by S.I. 2003/3142, art. 3. (2) (with art. 11)

Pre-commencement proposals relating to market power determinations

10. (1)Sub-paragraph (2) has effect where a proposal for—

(a) the identification of a market,

(b) the making of a market power determination, or

(c) the setting of conditions by reference to a proposal for a market power determination,

has been confirmed under regulation 8 of the Electronic Communications (Market Analysis) Regulations 2003 (S.I. 2003/330).

(2) If, at any time after the commencement of section 45, OFCOM—

(a) are satisfied that a procedure has been followed in relation to the proposal that satisfies the requirements of Article 7 of the Framework Directive, and

(b) publish a notification to that effect in such manner as they consider appropriate for bringing it to the attention of the persons who, in their opinion, are likely to be affected by the proposal,

the proposal (with such modifications, if any, as are specified in the notification) is to have effect, from the publication of the notification, in accordance with sub-paragraph (3).

(3) The proposal is to have effect as follows—

(a) in the case of a proposal for identifying a market, as an identification of a services market in accordance with and for the purposes of section 79 of this Act;

(b) in the case of a proposal for the making of a market power determination, as a market power determination made in accordance with and for the purposes of Chapter 1 of Part 2 of this Act; and

(c) in the case of a proposal for setting conditions, as if the conditions were SMP services conditions set under section 45 of this Act and applied to the same person as the condition in the proposal.

(4) Where an appeal under regulation 11 of those regulations against a decision under them has been brought but not concluded before the commencement of section 192 of this Act—

(a) that appeal is to be stayed or sisted as from the commencement of the section; but

(b) the appellant is to have a new right of appeal under the section against the decision (as it has effect by virtue of this paragraph) as if—

(i) it were the corresponding decision made by OFCOM under Chapter 1 of Part 2 of this Act; and

(ii) it had been made immediately after the commencement of the section.

(5) Tribunal rules (within the meaning of Chapter 3 of Part 2 of this Act) may, in relation to an appeal stayed or sisted under sub-paragraph (4), make transitional provision for requiring steps taken and things done for the purposes of that appeal to be taken into account, to the extent set out in the rules, in the case of an appeal brought by virtue of paragraph (b) of that sub-paragraph.

(6) Section 192 applies to a decision by OFCOM to publish a notification under this paragraph as it applies to a decision by them under Part 2 of this Act.

(7) In this paragraph "the Framework Directive" has the same meaning as in Chapter 1 of Part 2 of

this Act.

Commencement Information

I17. Sch. 18 para. 10 in force at 25.7.2003 for specified purposes by S.I. 2003/1900, arts. 1. (2), 2. (1), Sch. 1 (with art. 3) (as amended by S.I. 2003/3142, art. 1. (3))

I18. Sch. 18 para. 10 in force at 29.12.2003 in so far as not already in force by S.I. 2003/3142, art. 3. (2) (with art. 11)

Savings for licence conditions relating to accounting

11. (1)This paragraph applies where a licence granted under section 7 of the 1984 Act contains conditions which impose requirements with respect to—

(a) the keeping of accounts or financial information; or

(b) the provision of accounts and financial information to the Director.

(2) OFCOM may give a notice to the holder of the licence as respects so much of those conditions as relates to—

(a) the keeping of accounts for a period current at the time of the abolition of licensing; and

(b) the provision of accounts and financial information in relation to any such period or in relation to periods ending before the abolition of licensing.

(3) In the case of a licence granted otherwise than to a particular person, a notice under this paragraph may be given to the licence holders by being published in such manner as OFCOM consider appropriate for bringing it to their attention.

(4) Notwithstanding any repeal or revocation made by this Act—

(a) the licence under the 1984 Act is to continue in force to the extent that it imposes requirements as respects which a notice has been given under this paragraph; but

(b) those requirements, so far as they require the provision of accounts or information to the Director, are to have effect in relation to times after the abolition of licensing, as requirements to provide the accounts or information to OFCOM.

(5) Section 192 applies to a decision by OFCOM to give a notice under this paragraph as it applies to a decision by them under Part 2 of this Act.

Commencement Information

I19. Sch. 18 para. 11 in force at 25.7.2003 for specified purposes by S.I. 2003/1900, arts. 1. (2), 2. (1), Sch. 1 (with art. 3) (as amended by S.I. 2003/3142, art. 1. (3))

I20. Sch. 18 para. 11 in force at 29.12.2003 in so far as not already in force by S.I. 2003/3142, art. 3. (2) (with art. 11)

Charges under Telecommunications Act licences

12. (1)Where any amount is required by a licence under section 7 of the 1984 Act to be paid to the Director in respect of a period beginning before the abolition of licensing, that liability is to have effect after the abolition of licensing as a liability to pay to OFCOM so much of that amount as does not relate to times after the abolition of licensing.

(2) For the purpose of determining how much of an amount payable to the Director relates to times after the abolition of licensing, an apportionment is to be made according to how much of that period had expired before the abolition of licensing.

Commencement Information

I21. Sch. 18 para. 12 in force at 25.7.2003 for specified purposes by S.I. 2003/1900, arts. 1. (2), 2. (1), Sch. 1 (with art. 3) (as amended by S.I. 2003/3142, art. 1. (3))

I22. Sch. 18 para. 12 in force at 29.12.2003 in so far as not already in force by S.I. 2003/3142, art. 3. (2) (with art. 11)

Enforcement of breaches of licence conditions

13. (1)This paragraph applies to—

(a) any provision to which effect is given, after the abolition of licensing, by a continuation notice under paragraph 9;

(b) conditions in respect of which notices under paragraph 11 have been given;

(c) liabilities under paragraph 12; and

(d) conditions of a licence under section 7 of the 1984 Act requiring compliance by the licence holder with directions given by the Director under regulation 6 of the Telecommunications (Interconnection) Regulations 1997 (S.I. 1997/2931).

(2) Notwithstanding any repeal or revocation made by this Act, after the abolition of licensing, OFCOM are, for the purpose of enforcing anything to which this paragraph applies, to have all the enforcement powers previously exercisable by the Director under the 1984 Act.

(3) Those powers are to be exercisable in accordance with this paragraph irrespective of whether the contraventions occurred before or after the abolition of licensing.

(4) For the purpose of exercising those powers, references to the likelihood that a person will again be in contravention of a condition include references to whether he will be in contravention of any equivalent obligation imposed—

(a) by section 38 of this Act;

(b) by conditions set under section 45 of this Act; or

(c) by directions under section 190 of this Act.

(5) OFCOM are not to exercise any powers conferred by virtue of this paragraph if they consider that the exercise of those powers would be incompatible with the requirements of the Directives.

(6) In this paragraph "enforcement powers" includes—

(a) the Director's powers under sections 16 to 18 and 53 of the 1984 Act; and

(b) in the case of a licence issued to a particular person, every power of his under the licence to require information for the purpose of computing the amount of the liability to a charge.

(7) In this paragraph "the Directives" means the Authorisation Directive or any of the following Directives (as defined in Chapter 1 of Part 2 of this Act)—

(a) the Access Directive;

(b) the Framework Directive;

(c) the Universal Service Directive.

(8) In sub-paragraph (7) "the Authorisation Directive" means Directive 2002/20/EC of the European Parliament and of the Council on the authorisation of electronic communications networks and services [F3, as amended by Directive 2009/140/EC of the European Parliament and of the Council] .

Amendments (Textual)

F3. Words in Sch. 18 para. 13. (8) inserted (26.5.2011) by The Electronic Communications and Wireless Telegraphy Regulations 2011 (S.I. 2011/1210), reg. 1. (2), Sch. 1 para. 100. (b) (with Sch. 3 para. 2)

Commencement Information

I23. Sch. 18 para. 13 in force at 25.7.2003 for specified purposes by S.I. 2003/1900, arts. 1. (2), 2. (1), Sch. 1 (with art. 3) (as amended by S.I. 2003/3142, art. 1. (3))

I24. Sch. 18 para. 13 in force at 29.12.2003 in so far as not already in force by S.I. 2003/3142, art. 3. (2) (with art. 11)

Saving for agreements having effect by reference to licensing regime

14. (1)This paragraph has effect where an agreement entered into for the purposes of a condition of a licence under section 7 of the 1984 Act has effect immediately before the abolition of licensing subject to a provision which entitles a party to it to terminate the agreement if he or another party ceases to be a Schedule 2 public operator.

(2) The right of termination is not to be exercisable by reason of the effect of the coming into force of any provision of this Act if—

(a) a general condition,

(b) an access-related condition, or

(c) a provision made by or having effect as if made under an SMP condition,

imposes requirements on one or both of the parties to the agreement that correspond to those for the purposes of which the agreement was originally entered into.

(3) In any such case, the agreement shall have effect in relation to times after the abolition of licensing as if references in the agreement to a Schedule 2 public operator were references to the provider of a public electronic communications network.

(4) In this paragraph "Schedule 2 public operator" has the same meaning as in Schedule 1 to the Telecommunications (Licence Modifications) (Standard Schedules) Regulations 1999 (S.I. 1999/2450).

(5) Expressions used in this paragraph and in Chapter 1 of Part 2 of this Act have the same meanings in this paragraph as in that Chapter.

Commencement Information

I25. Sch. 18 para. 14 in force at 25.7.2003 for specified purposes by S.I. 2003/1900, arts. 1. (2), 2. (1), Sch. 1 (with art. 3) (as amended by S.I. 2003/3142, art. 1. (3))

I26. Sch. 18 para. 14 in force at 29.12.2003 in so far as not already in force by S.I. 2003/3142, art. 3. (2) (with art. 11)

Fees for approvals for the purposes of licence conditions

15. (1)This paragraph has effect where a general condition set under section 45 of this Act requires apparatus to be approved by reference to a standard previously designated for the purposes of section 24. (6) of the 1984 Act.

(2) The Secretary of State may by order provide for the charging of fees in respect of the giving of approvals for the purposes of the condition.

(3) Fees charged under this paragraph are be paid to the person giving the approvals and, to the extent authorised by the Secretary of State, may be retained by that person.

(4) To the extent that they are not retained by that person, the fees must be paid into the Consolidated Fund.

(5) Any order made under section 24. (13) of the 1984 Act that is in force immediately before the coming into force of the repeal of section 24 of that Act shall have effect after the coming into force of the repeal as an order made under this paragraph.

Commencement Information

I27. Sch. 18 para. 15 in force at 25.7.2003 for specified purposes by S.I. 2003/1900, arts. 1. (2), 2. (1), Sch. 1 (with art. 3) (as amended by S.I. 2003/3142, art. 1. (3))

I28. Sch. 18 para. 15 in force at 29.12.2003 in so far as not already in force by S.I. 2003/3142, art. 3. (2) (with art. 11)

Allocated telephone numbers

16. (1)Where immediately before the abolition of licensing telephone numbers are allocated to a person holding a licence under section 7 of the 1984 Act for the purposes of the conditions of that licence, those numbers shall be treated, after the abolition of licensing as allocated to that person for the purposes of general conditions such as are mentioned in section 58 of this Act.

(2) An allocation having effect by virtue of sub-paragraph (1) may be withdrawn by OFCOM at any time, but only in accordance with section 61 of this Act.

(3) An allocation shall only continue to have effect in accordance with this paragraph for so long as the person to whom the allocation was made for the purposes of the licence conditions is a communications provider.

(4) The power by virtue of section 58 for general conditions to make provision for the making of periodic payments in respect of the allocation of telephone numbers shall be exercisable, at any time after the coming into force of that section, in relation to an allocation having effect by virtue of this paragraph as it has effect in relation to an allocation made under that section.

(5) Expressions used in this paragraph and in Chapter 1 of Part 2 of this Act have the same meanings in this paragraph as in that Chapter.

Commencement Information

I29. Sch. 18 para. 16 in force at 25.7.2003 for specified purposes by S.I. 2003/1900, arts. 1. (2), 2. (1), Sch. 1 (with art. 3) (as amended by S.I. 2003/3142, art. 1. (3))

I30. Sch. 18 para. 16 in force at 29.12.2003 in so far as not already in force by S.I. 2003/3142, art. 3. (2) (with art. 11)

Electronic communications code

17. (1)Sub-paragraph (2) applies where, immediately before the coming into force of section 106 of this Act, the telecommunications code set out in Schedule 2 to the 1984 Act applies to a person by virtue of the provisions of his licence under section 7 of that Act.

(2) That person shall be treated after the commencement of section 106 of this Act as a person in whose case the electronic communications code applies by virtue of a direction given by OFCOM.

(3) The deemed direction shall be assumed to be one given in relation to so much of any electronic communications network as—

(a) was included immediately before the commencement of section 106 of this Act in the telecommunication system which was the operator's system for the purposes of the application of the code; or

(b) which would have been so included if it had been being provided at that time.

(4) So much of the code in Schedule 2 to the 1984 Act as has effect immediately before the commencement of Schedule 3 to this Act—

(a) in relation to telecommunication apparatus, or

(b) in relation a telecommunication system,

is to have effect after the commencement of that Schedule in relation to so much of the apparatus or system as is electronic communications apparatus or the operator's network for the purposes of the application of that Schedule to this Act by virtue of this paragraph or section 106. (3)(b) of this Act.

(5) A right which for the purposes of the code in Schedule 2 to the 1984 Act has effect immediately before the commencement of Schedule 3 to this Act as conferred for purposes connected with the provision of a telecommunication service is to have effect after the commencement of that Schedule as conferred for the purposes of the corresponding electronic communications service.

(6) Any agreement which, immediately before the repeal of the provisions contained in section 10. (3. A) and (3. B) of the 1984 Act or section 189 of the 1990 Act, is a relevant agreement for the purposes of those provisions shall be deemed in relation to times after the coming into force of that repeal to be a relevant agreement for the purposes of paragraph 29 of the electronic communications code.

(7) In this paragraph "the electronic communications code" has the same meaning as in Chapter 1 of Part 2 of this Act.

Commencement Information

I31. Sch. 18 para. 17 in force at 25.7.2003 for specified purposes by S.I. 2003/1900, arts. 1. (2), 2. (1), Sch. 1 (with art. 3) (as amended by S.I. 2003/3142, art. 1. (3))

I32. Sch. 18 para. 17 in force at 29.12.2003 in so far as not already in force by S.I. 2003/3142, art. 3. (2) (with art. 11)

Saving for guarantees of liabilities of telecommunications code

operators

18. (1)This paragraph applies where, immediately before the abolition of licensing, a person holding a licence under section 7 of the 1984 Act ("the operator") —

(a) is a person to whom the telecommunications code applies in respect of the running of a telecommunications system by him ("the operator's system"); and

(b) in pursuance of a condition of his licence imposed for the purpose of securing that sufficient funds are available to meet code-related liabilities specified in the licence, is a party to any guarantee arrangements.

(2) Arrangements are guarantee arrangements for the purposes of this paragraph if they are arrangements under which a person (the "guarantor") is obliged, in circumstances specified in the arrangements, to make payments in respect of a failure by the operator to meet a code-related liability specified in the licence.

(3) The guarantor's obligation to make payments under the guarantee arrangements is not to arise by reason only of the abolition of licensing.

(4) In relation to times after the abolition of licensing, the guarantee arrangements are to have effect, notwithstanding the operator's licence having ceased to have effect on the abolition of licensing and subject to sub-paragraph (7), as if the following references continued to have effect—

(a) references in those arrangements to the code-related liabilities specified in the licence; and

(b) (subject to sub-paragraph (5)(a)) references, for the purposes of any provision identifying the circumstances in which payments are to be made under the arrangements, to events specified in the licence.

(5) In relation to such times, those arrangements are also to have effect—

(a) as if references (directly or indirectly) to the revocation, or to the expiration without renewal, of the operator's licence were references to his becoming subject to a direction by virtue of which he is prohibited from providing the whole or a part of his network; and

(b) as if references to the telecommunications code were references to the electronic communications code.

(6) In sub-paragraph (5) the reference to a person's becoming subject to a direction by virtue of which he is prohibited from providing the whole or a part of an electronic communications network—

(a) does not include a reference to his becoming subject to a direction imposing a prohibition for a fixed period of less than eighteen months or to a direction that will have to be revoked if not confirmed; but

(b) except in the case of a direction imposing a prohibition for such a fixed period, does include a reference to the confirmation of a direction that would otherwise have had to be revoked.

(7) The guarantor is not to be liable in respect of any liability arising in connection with or as a result of activities carried on after the abolition of licensing except in so far as those activities are activities carried on for the purposes of providing the operator's network.

(8) In this paragraph "code-related liabilities", in relation to the operator, means liabilities arising or incurred by him—

(a) by reason of the application to him of the telecommunications code;

(b) by reason of its ceasing to apply to him; or

(c) otherwise in respect of activities carried on by him in connection with running the operator's system.

(9) In this paragraph—

"the electronic communications code" has the same meaning as in Chapter 1 of Part 2 of this Act;

"the operator's network" means so much of any electronic communications network provided by the operator as is a network in relation to which the electronic communications code applies in the operator's case by virtue of paragraph 17. (3)(a) of this Schedule;

"the telecommunications code" means the code set out in Schedule 2 to the 1984 Act (as it had effect immediately before the abolition of licensing).

Commencement Information

I33. Sch. 18 para. 18 in force at 25.7.2003 for specified purposes by S.I. 2003/1900, arts. 1. (2), 2. (1), Sch. 1 (with art. 3) (as amended by S.I. 2003/3142, art. 1. (3))

I34. Sch. 18 para. 18 in force at 29.12.2003 in so far as not already in force by S.I. 2003/3142, art. 3. (2) (with art. 11)

Compulsory purchase

19. Where—

(a) a compulsory purchase order made under section 34 or 35 of the 1984 Act,

(b) a vesting order, or an application for a vesting order, made under section 36 of that Act, or

(c) an authorisation given by the Secretary of State under section 37, 38 or 39 of that Act,

is effective immediately before the commencement of Schedule 4 to this Act, it is to have effect after the commencement of that Schedule as if made or given under that Schedule.

Commencement Information

I35. Sch. 18 para. 19 in force at 25.7.2003 for specified purposes by S.I. 2003/1900, arts. 1. (2), 2. (1), Sch. 1 (with art. 3) (as amended by S.I. 2003/3142, art. 1. (3))

I36. Sch. 18 para. 19 in force at 29.12.2003 in so far as not already in force by S.I. 2003/3142, art. 3. (2) (with art. 11)

Notices under section 1. D of the Wireless Telegraphy Act 1949.

F420. . . . .

Amendments (Textual)

F4. Sch. 18 para. 20 repealed (8.2.2007) by Wireless Telegraphy Act 2006 (c. 36), s. 126. (2), Sch. 9 Pt. 1 (with Sch. 8 Pt. 1)

Commencement Information

I37. Sch. 18 para. 20 in force at 29.12.2003 by S.I. 2003/3142, art. 3. (1), Sch. 1 (with art. 11)

Notices under regulations under section 3 of the Wireless Telegraphy Act 1998.

F521. . . . .

Amendments (Textual)

F5. Sch. 18 para. 21 repealed (8.2.2007) by Wireless Telegraphy Act 2006 (c. 36), s. 126. (2), Sch. 9 Pt. 1 (with Sch. 8 Pt. 1)

Commencement Information

I38. Sch. 18 para. 21 in force at 18.9.2003 for specified purposes by S.I. 2003/1900, arts. 1. (2), 2. (2), Sch. 2 (with art. 3) (as amended by S.I. 2003/3142, art. 1. (3))

I39. Sch. 18 para. 21 in force at 29.12.2003 in so far as not already in force by S.I. 2003/3142, art. 3. (2) (with art. 11)

Disputes about interconnection

22. (1)Where—

(a) before the revocation by this Act of the Telecommunications (Interconnection) Regulations 1997 (S.I. 1997/2931) a dispute was referred to the Director under regulation 6 of those regulations, and

(b) that dispute has not been resolved when the revocation comes into force,

Chapter 3 of Part 2 of this Act (except sections 189 and 190) is to have effect as if that dispute were a dispute which, immediately after the commencement of section 185 of this Act, was referred to OFCOM under that section.

(2) Where a dispute—

(a) has arisen or arises about anything occurring or existing before the time when the revocation of those regulations comes into force ("the relevant time"),

(b) relates to matters disputes about which would (before that time) have been referable to the Director under regulation 6,

(c) is neither a dispute which was referred to him before that time nor a dispute arising after that time which is referable to OFCOM under section 185, and

(d) is referred to OFCOM after that time either during the transitional period or in a case in which OFCOM are satisfied that the circumstances that prevented the making of a reference before the end of that period are exceptional,

sub-paragraph (1) is to have effect as if the dispute were a dispute arising before the relevant time in the case of which a reference to the Director had been made under regulation 6 before that time.

(3) Where OFCOM make a determination for resolving a dispute falling to be resolved in accordance with sub-paragraph (1) or (2)—

(a) their powers on making that determination are to be those which would have been exercisable by the Director under those regulations (instead of those under Chapter 3 of Part 2);

(b) conditions of a licence under section 7 of the 1984 Act requiring compliance with directions given by the Director under regulation 6 of those regulations are to continue to have effect as if they also applied to directions given by OFCOM by virtue of paragraph (a); and

(c) paragraph 13 of this Schedule has effect as if the reference in sub-paragraph (1)(d) to directions given by the Director under that regulation included a reference to directions given by OFCOM by virtue of paragraph (a) of this sub-paragraph.

(4) But OFCOM are not to give a direction by virtue of sub-paragraph (3)(a) containing provision which they would have no power to include in—

(a) a condition set under Chapter 1 of Part 2 of this Act; or

(b) a direction under section 190.

(5) Where the Director gave a direction under regulation 6 of those regulations at any time before the coming into force of their revocation, the direction is to continue, after the revocation comes into force, to have effect (and be enforceable in accordance with paragraph 13 of this Schedule) to the extent that it is continued in force under this paragraph.

(6) The direction is continued in force under this paragraph only where OFCOM have at any time after the passing of this Act given notice to the persons to whom it applies that it is continued in force.

(7) OFCOM are to give such a notice only if they consider that the direction makes provision corresponding to that which they have power to include in—

(a) conditions set under Chapter 1 of Part 2 of this Act; or

(b) directions under section 190.

(8) OFCOM may at any time by notice to the person to whom it applies revoke (in whole or in part) a direction which—

(a) was given by virtue of sub-paragraph (3)(a); or

(b) is a direction to which a notice under sub-paragraph (6) relates.

(9) Where a direction which OFCOM have power to revoke under sub-paragraph (8) makes provision corresponding to anything that OFCOM have power to include in a condition set under Chapter 1 of Part 2 of this Act, it shall be their duty, as soon as reasonably practicable after giving the direction or as the case may be the notice under sub-paragraph (6)—

(a) to take all steps necessary for enabling them to decide whether or not to set such a condition for the purpose of replacing the direction; and

(b) to decide whether or not to exercise their power to set a condition under that Chapter for that purpose.

(10) It shall be the duty of OFCOM—

(a) as soon as reasonably practicable after making a decision required by sub-paragraph (9), but

(b) in a case where that decision is a decision to set a condition, not before the coming into force of that condition,

to give a notice under sub-paragraph (8) revoking the direction in question.

(11) The duties imposed by sub-paragraphs (9) and (10) apply only where OFCOM have not previously revoked the direction in question.

(12) Section 192 applies to a decision by OFCOM to give a notice under this paragraph as it applies to a decision by them under Part 2 of this Act.

(13) In this paragraph "transitional period" means the period which is the transitional period (within the meaning of section 408) in relation to this paragraph.

Commencement Information

I40. Sch. 18 para. 22 in force at 25.7.2003 for specified purposes by S.I. 2003/1900, arts. 1. (2), 2. (1), Sch. 1 (with art. 3) (as amended by S.I. 2003/3142, art. 1. (3))

I41. Sch. 18 para. 22 in force at 29.12.2003 in so far as not already in force by S.I. 2003/3142, art. 3. (2) (with art. 11)

Appeals against wireless telegraphy and telecommunications decisions

23. (1)This paragraph applies where—

(a) a decision was made before the commencement of section 192;

(b) the decision has effect after the commencement of a provision of this Act as a decision made by OFCOM, or is a decision not to do something which (if done) would so have had effect; and

(c) the decision is one against which an appeal was or could have been brought under—

F6. (i). . . . .

(ii) section 46. B of the 1984 Act.

(2) If no such appeal has been brought before the commencement of section 192 of this Act, that section applies to the decision as it applies to decisions by OFCOM under Part 2 of this Act F7..., but as if that section had been in force when the decision was made.

(3) If an appeal under F8... section 46. B of the 1984 Act—

(a) has been brought against the decision, but

(b) has not been concluded before the commencement of section 192 of this Act,

the court in which it was brought may stay or sist the appeal as from the commencement of that section of this Act.

(4) If the court stays or sists the appeal under sub-paragraph (3), the appellant is to have a new right of appeal under section 192 against the decision as if (subject to sub-paragraph (7)) it were a decision to which that section applies that had been made immediately after the commencement of that section.

(5) Tribunal rules (within the meaning of Chapter 3 of Part 2 of this Act) may, in relation to an appeal stayed or sisted under sub-paragraph (3), make transitional provision—

(a) for requiring steps taken and things done for the purposes of that appeal to be taken into account, to the extent set out in the rules, in the case of an appeal brought by virtue of sub-paragraph (4); and

(b) for enabling the Tribunal in an appeal under sub-paragraph (4) to give directions to OFCOM as to the carrying out of functions of theirs that are the same as or correspond to those in the course of carrying out which the maker of the appealed decision made that decision.

(6) If, in a case falling within sub-paragraph (3), the court does not stay or sist the appeal—

(a) it must determine the appeal in the manner in which the Tribunal is required under section 195 of this Act to determine an appeal under section 192; but

(b) its powers on determining the appeal include a power to give directions to OFCOM as to the carrying out of any functions of theirs that correspond to those in the course of which the appealed decision was made.

(7) On an appeal brought or continued under this paragraph against a decision, the court or the

Tribunal, in determining what was the appropriate action for the maker of the decision to take, must determine that question according to the law in force at the time when the decision was made.

Amendments (Textual)

F6. Sch. 18 para. 23. (1)(c)(i) repealed (8.2.2007) by Wireless Telegraphy Act 2006 (c. 36), s. 126. (2), Sch. 9 Pt. 1 (with Sch. 8 Pt. 1)

F7. Words in Sch. 18 para. 23. (2) repealed (8.2.2007) by Wireless Telegraphy Act 2006 (c. 36), s. 126. (2), Sch. 9 Pt. 1 (with Sch. 8 Pt. 1)

F8. Words in Sch. 18 para. 23. (3) repealed (8.2.2007) by Wireless Telegraphy Act 2006 (c. 36), s. 126. (2), Sch. 9 Pt. 1 (with Sch. 8 Pt. 1)

Commencement Information

I42. Sch. 18 para. 23 in force at 25.7.2003 for specified purposes by S.I. 2003/1900, arts. 1. (2), 2. (1), Sch. 1 (with art. 3) (as amended by S.I. 2003/3142, art. 1. (3))

I43. Sch. 18 para. 23 in force at 29.12.2003 in so far as not already in force by S.I. 2003/3142, art. 3. (2) (with art. 11)

Section 94 of the Telecommunications Act 1984.

24. (1)Subject to sub-paragraph (2), provisions of Schedule 17 to this Act amending section 94 of the 1984 Act do not affect—

(a) the continuation, after the coming into force of the amendment, of any duty of a person previously given a direction under that section to give effect to it; or

(b) the power of the Secretary of State after the amendment comes into force to make grants under subsection (6) of that section to such a person.

(2) A direction under that section which was given to the Director before the relevant transfer date shall have effect in relation to times on and after that date as if it were a direction to OFCOM.

(3) In sub-paragraph (2) "the relevant transfer date" means the date of the coming into force of the provisions of Schedule 17 to this Act substituting " OFCOM " for "the Director" in section 94. (8) of the 1984 Act.

Commencement Information

I44. Sch. 18 para. 24 in force at 25.7.2003 for specified purposes by S.I. 2003/1900, arts. 1. (2), 2. (1), Sch. 1 (with art. 3) (as amended by S.I. 2003/3142, art. 1. (3))

I45. Sch. 18 para. 24 in force at 29.12.2003 in so far as not already in force by S.I. 2003/3142, art. 3. (2) (with art. 11)

Competition Commission: specialist panel members

25. The persons who—

(a) have been appointed as members of the Competition Commission by the Secretary of State under section 13. (10) of the 1984 Act, and

(b) hold office immediately before the date on which section 194 comes into force,

shall continue to hold office as members of the Competition Commission as if they had been appointed to that office by the Secretary of State under section 194. (1).

Commencement Information

I46. Sch. 18 para. 25 in force at 25.7.2003 for specified purposes by S.I. 2003/1900, arts. 1. (2), 2. (1), Sch. 1 (with art. 3) (as amended by S.I. 2003/3142, art. 1. (3))

I47. Sch. 18 para. 25 in force at 29.12.2003 in so far as not already in force by S.I. 2003/3142, art. 3. (2) (with art. 11)

Transitory amendments to telecommunications terms in Broadcasting Act 1990.

26. (1)This paragraph has effect, in the case of each of the provisions of the 1990 Act to which it applies, in relation to times between—

(a) the commencement of Chapter 1 of Part 2 of this Act; and

(b) the commencement of so much of this Act (apart from this paragraph) as amends or repeals that provision.

(2) The provisions of the 1990 Act set out in sub-paragraph (3) shall have effect (subject to sub-paragraph (4)) as if—

(a) for every reference to a telecommunication system there were substituted a reference to an electronic communications network; and

(b) for references to running such a system there were substituted references to providing it.

(3) Those provisions of the 1990 Act are—

(a) section 46 (licensable programme services);

(b) section 51. (1)(a) (procedures for consideration of applications for additional services licences);

(c) section 72 (local delivery services);

(d) section 75 (procedures for consideration of applications for local delivery licences);

(e) section 112 (licensable sound programme services);

(f) section 117. (1)(a) (procedures for consideration of applications for additional services licences);

(g) section 181 (apparatus deemed to be apparatus for wireless telegraphy).

(4) Sections 46. (2) (licensable programme services), 112. (2) (licensable sound programme services) and 201. (2) (programme services) of the 1990 Act shall each have effect as if for paragraph (b) there were substituted—

"(b)a service which satisfies the conditions in section 233. (5) of the Communications Act 2003;".

(5) In sections 48 and 114 of the 1990 Act (additional services), references to electronic signals shall have effect as references to signals within the meaning of section 32 of this Act.

(6) Section 75. (2) of the 1990 Act (consultation with relevant licensing authorities) shall have effect as if in paragraph (b) for the words "would be required to be licensed" there were substituted " is a system which (but for repeals made by the Communications Act 2003) would have been required to be licensed ".

(7) In section 181 of the 1990 Act (apparatus deemed to be apparatus for wireless telegraphy), "connected"—

(a) shall continue to be construed in accordance (notwithstanding its repeal) with section 4 of the 1984 Act; but

(b) shall be so construed as if, in that section of the 1984 Act, a reference to an electronic communications network were substituted for every reference to a telecommunication system.

(8) Part 5 of Schedule 2 to the 1990 Act (restriction on holding of licences by operators of public telecommunication systems) and the Broadcasting (Restrictions on the Holding of Licences) Order 1991 (S.I. 1991/1176) shall have effect as if references to a national public telecommunications operator were references to a person who provides an electronic communications network so as to make it available for use by members of the public in the whole, or substantially the whole, of the United Kingdom.

Commencement Information

I48. Sch. 18 para. 26 in force at 25.7.2003 for specified purposes by S.I. 2003/1900, arts. 1. (2), 2. (1), Sch. 1 (with art. 3) (as amended by S.I. 2003/3142, art. 1. (3))

I49. Sch. 18 para. 26 in force at 29.12.2003 in so far as not already in force by S.I. 2003/3142, art. 3. (2) (with art. 11)

Activities of the Welsh Authority

27. (1)No approval shall be required under section 205 for the continued provision after the commencement of that section of any service that was being provided by the Welsh Authority immediately before the commencement of that section.

(2) Where any activities are being carried on immediately before the commencement of section 206 by the Welsh Authority, no approval is required under that section in respect of the continued carrying on of the activities by the Authority.

(3) Where any activities are being carried on immediately before the commencement of section 206 by an S4. C company, no approval is required under that section in respect of the carrying on after that commencement by that company or another S4. C company of those activities.

Commencement Information

I50. Sch. 18 para. 27 in force at 29.12.2003 by S.I. 2003/3142, art. 3. (1), Sch. 1 (with art. 11)

Gaelic Broadcasting

28. The persons who are members of Comataidh Craolaidh Gaidhlig immediately before the date on which section 208 comes into force—

(a) shall continue to hold office as members of Seirbheis nam Meadhanan Gàidhlig as if they had been appointed to that office by OFCOM;

(b) shall hold and vacate office in accordance with the terms of their appointment by the ITC;

(c) shall hold office for the period for which they were appointed by the ITC; and

(d) after the end of that period, shall be eligible for re-appointment as members of Seirbheis nam Meadhanan Gàidhlig.

Commencement Information

I51. Sch. 18 para. 28 in force at 29.12.2003 by S.I. 2003/3142, art. 3. (1), Sch. 1 (with art. 11)

29. (1)The continuance in force of the Multiplex Licence (Broadcasting of Programmes in Gaelic) Order 1996 (S.I. 1996/2758) made under section 32 of the 1996 Act is not affected by the amendment of that section by Schedule 15 to this Act.

(2) But in relation to times after the television transfer date, that order shall have effect as if—

(a) the reference in that order to the ITC were a reference to OFCOM; and

(b) the reference to the application of section 28 of the 1996 Act to a frequency were omitted.

Commencement Information

I52. Sch. 18 para. 29 in force at 29.12.2003 by S.I. 2003/3142, art. 3. (1), Sch. 1 (with art. 11)

Pre-transfer Broadcasting Act licences

30. (1)Subject to any express provision made by this Act in relation to a particular description of Broadcasting Act licence, neither—

(a) the transfer from a pre-commencement regulator to OFCOM of the function of granting or awarding such licences or of any other power exercisable in relation to such licences, nor

(b) any other modification by or by virtue of this Act of the power to grant or award such licences or of a provision having effect in relation to such licences,

shall affect the continuing validity of a licence by or under which the provision of a service is authorised immediately before the coming into force of the transfer or modification.

(2) Accordingly, such a licence shall continue to have effect, after the coming into force of the transfer or modification—

(a) on the same terms and conditions and for the same period as it would have done if this Act had not been passed; but

(b) as if, in relation to times after the coming into force of any relevant transfer of functions to OFCOM, every reference in the licence to a pre-commencement regulator were a reference to OFCOM.

(3) Sub-paragraph (2) is subject to the following provisions of this Act—

(a) those under which a licence is to have effect as if the period for which it is granted were the period determined under this Act; and

(b) those under which the conditions of a licence fall to be varied for the purpose of imposing a condition required by this Act.

(4) Anything done at any time before the relevant transfer date under or for the purposes of enforcing any provision of a Broadcasting Act licence is to have effect in relation to times on or after that date—

(a) to the extent that it was done by or in relation to the ITC or Radio Authority, and

(b) so far as necessary for preserving its effect or for facilitating the taking of further action by OFCOM,

as a thing done by or in relation to OFCOM.

(5) In sub-paragraph (4) "relevant transfer date"—

(a) in relation to licences under Part 1 of the 1990 Act or Part 1 of the 1996 Act, means the television transfer date; and

(b) in relation to licences under Part 3 of the 1990 Act or Part 2 of the 1996 Act, means the radio transfer date.

Commencement Information

I53. Sch. 18 para. 30 in force at 25.7.2003 by S.I. 2003/1900, art. 2. (1), Sch. 1

Channels 3 and 5.

31. A determination made by the ITC under or for the purposes of section 14 or 28 of the 1990 Act (Channels 3 and 5) is to have effect on and after the television transfer date as a determination under that section by OFCOM.

Commencement Information

I54. Sch. 18 para. 31 in force at 29.12.2003 by S.I. 2003/3142, art. 3. (1), Sch. 1 (with art. 11)

Saving pending replacement of licences for Channels 3 and 5 and the public teletext service

32. (1)The regulatory regime for a Channel 3 service, and that for Channel 5 and the existing teletext service, shall not include the self-regulation conditions in any case in which the service or (as the case may be) Channel 5 is provided under a licence granted before the television transfer date.

(2) In sub-paragraph (1) "the self-regulation conditions" means the conditions which (apart from that sub-paragraph) are included by virtue of sections 265 to 269 of this Act in the regulatory regime for Channel 3 services, for Channel 5 and for the public teletext service.

(3) In relation to a licence granted before the television transfer date for a Channel 3 service, Channel 5 or the existing teletext service, section 263 shall have effect as if the reference in subsection (3)(a) of that section to a corresponding or additional service to be provided in analogue form were a reference to a corresponding or additional service to be provided in digital form.

(4) In this paragraph "the existing teletext service" means the existing service within the meaning of section 221 of this Act.

Commencement Information

I55. Sch. 18 para. 32 in force at 29.12.2003 by S.I. 2003/3142, art. 3. (1), Sch. 1 (with art. 11)

Digital additional licences

33. (1)This paragraph applies where immediately before the coming into force of section 242 of this Act a person holds a digital additional services licence under Part 1 of the 1996 Act in respect of a digital sound programme service and with a view to the inclusion of the broadcasting of that

service by means of a television multiplex service licensed under Part 1 of the 1996 Act.

(2) The licence is to have effect on and after the coming into force of section 242 of this Act as if it were a national digital sound programme licence or (as the case may be) were comprised in any national digital sound programme licence already held by the licence holder for the service in question.

(3) Where a licence has effect in accordance with this paragraph, it shall not (to the extent that it so has effect) authorise the broadcasting of the digital sound programme service in question by means of a radio multiplex service.

(4) In this paragraph—

"digital additional services licence" has the same meaning as in Part 1 of the 1996 Act; and

"national digital sound programme licence" has the same meaning as in Part 2 of that Act.

Commencement Information

I56. Sch. 18 para. 33 in force at 29.12.2003 by S.I. 2003/3142, art. 3. (1), Sch. 1 (with art. 11)

Programme quotas

34. Any order which—

(a) was made under section 16. (5)(a) of the 1990 Act (definitions of "qualifying programmes" and "independent productions"), and

(b) is in force immediately before the commencement of sections 277 and 309 of this Act and paragraphs 1 and 7 of Schedule 12 to this Act,

is to have effect in relation to times after the commencement of those sections and those paragraphs as an order made in exercise of the corresponding powers conferred by those sections and those paragraphs.

Commencement Information

I57. Sch. 18 para. 34 in force at 29.12.2003 by S.I. 2003/3142, art. 3. (1), Sch. 1 (with art. 11)

Continuity in relation to appointed news provider

35. Where a body holds an appointment for the purposes of section 31. (2) of the 1990 Act immediately before the date of the commencement of section 280 of this Act—

(a) that appointment shall have effect in relation to times on and after that date as an appointment for the purposes of arrangements entered into in accordance with conditions imposed under section 280 of this Act;

(b) the arrangements under which that appointment was made shall have effect in relation to such times as arrangements so entered into; and

(c) so much of the appointment or arrangements, or of any agreement to which the body is a party, as makes provision by reference to the body's ceasing to be nominated under section 32 of the 1990 Act shall have effect in relation to such times as if references to ceasing to be so nominated were references to becoming a body falling within section 281. (2) of this Act.

Commencement Information

I58. Sch. 18 para. 35 in force at 29.12.2003 by S.I. 2003/3142, art. 3. (1), Sch. 1 (with art. 11)

Networking arrangements

36. (1)Where arrangements approved for the purposes of section 39 of the 1990 Act (networking arrangements) are in force immediately before the commencement of section 291 of this Act, those arrangements are to have effect for the purposes of this Act, and of any conditions imposed under that section of this Act, as approved networking arrangements.

(2) For the purposes of proceedings in relation to a report under Schedule 4 to the 1990 Act at any time after the commencement of Schedule 11 to this Act, that report is to have effect as if it were a

report under that Schedule to this Act.

Commencement Information

I59. Sch. 18 para. 36 in force at 29.12.2003 by S.I. 2003/3142, art. 3. (1), Sch. 1 (with art. 11)

Determination of qualifying revenue

37. (1)A statement of the ITC that is for the time being in force immediately before the television transfer date for the purposes of—

(a) Schedule 7 to the 1990 Act (statement of principles for determining qualifying revenue), or

(b) Schedule 1 to the 1996 Act (corresponding statement for the purposes of that Act,

is to have effect on and after that date as a statement by OFCOM.

(2) On and after the television transfer date a determination by the ITC under paragraph 2 of Part 1 of either of those Schedules is to have effect as a determination under that paragraph by OFCOM, and sub-paragraph (2) of that paragraph is to have effect accordingly.

Commencement Information

I60. Sch. 18 para. 37 in force at 29.12.2003 by S.I. 2003/3142, art. 3. (1), Sch. 1 (with art. 11)

Rules for political broadcasts

38. Where—

(a) rules made by the ITC for the purposes of section 36 of the 1990 Act (party political broadcasts on Channel 3, Channel 4 or Channel 5), or

(b) rules made by the Radio Authority for the purposes of section 107 of the 1990 Act (party political broadcasts on national radio services),

are in force immediately before the commencement of section 333 of this Act, those rules are to have effect after its commencement as rules made by OFCOM for the purposes of that section of this Act.

Commencement Information

I61. Sch. 18 para. 38 in force at 29.12.2003 by S.I. 2003/3142, art. 3. (1), Sch. 1 (with art. 11)

Functions under section 88 of the 1990 Act

39. A requirement imposed or notice given before the radio transfer date by the Radio Authority under section 88 of the 1990 Act (restriction on holding of licences) is to have effect on and after that date as if it were imposed or given by OFCOM.

Commencement Information

I62. Sch. 18 para. 39 in force at 29.12.2003 by S.I. 2003/3142, art. 3. (1), Sch. 1 (with art. 11)

Notices under section 94 of the 1990 Act

40. A notice given by the Secretary of State or any other Minister of the Crown under section 94 of the 1990 Act (government control over licensed services) is to have effect on and after the radio transfer date as a notice given to OFCOM under section 336 of this Act.

Commencement Information

I63. Sch. 18 para. 40 in force at 29.12.2003 by S.I. 2003/3142, art. 3. (1), Sch. 1 (with art. 11)

Programme standards: television

41. (1)This paragraph applies as respects times on or after the television transfer date and before the first coming into force, in the case of the holder of a licence under Part 1 of the 1990 Act or Part 1 of the 1996 Act, of conditions imposed under section 325 of this Act.

(2) Sections 6 to 12 of the 1990 Act (general provisions about the content of licensed services) are to have effect in the case of that licence holder as if references in those sections to the ITC were references to OFCOM.

(3) A code drawn up by the ITC under section 6, 7 or 9 of the 1990 Act is to have effect as if it had been drawn up by OFCOM.

Commencement Information

I64. Sch. 18 para. 41 in force at 29.12.2003 by S.I. 2003/3142, art. 3. (1), Sch. 1 (with art. 11)

Programme standards: radio

42. (1)This paragraph applies as respects times on or after the radio transfer date and before the first coming into force, in the case of the holder of a licence under Part 3 of the 1990 Act or Part 2 of the 1996 Act, of conditions imposed under section 325 of this Act.

(2) Sections 90 to 96 of the 1990 Act (general provisions about the content of licensed services) are to have effect as if references in those sections to the Radio Authority were references to OFCOM.

(3) A code drawn up by the Radio Authority under section 90, 91 or 93 of the 1990 Act is to have effect as if it had been drawn up by OFCOM.

Commencement Information

I65. Sch. 18 para. 42 in force at 29.12.2003 by S.I. 2003/3142, art. 3. (1), Sch. 1 (with art. 11)

Standards code

43. (1)In relation to any time after the commencement of section 319 of this Act, a code in force immediately before its commencement as a code drawn up under section 6, 7, 9, 90, 91 or 93 of the 1990 Act or section 108 of the 1996 Act is to have effect (subject to sub-paragraphs (2) and (3)) as if it were a code issued by OFCOM for the purpose of setting standards under section 319 of this Act.

(2) A code under the 1990 Act shall have effect by virtue of sub-paragraph (1) in relation only to the following—

(a) in the case of the codes under sections 6, 7 and 9, services the provision of which is authorised by licences under Part 1 of the 1990 Act and S4. C; and

(b) in the case of the codes under sections 90, 91 and 93, services the provision of which is authorised by licences under Part 3 of that Act.

(3) In the case of the code under section 108 of the 1996 Act, the code shall have effect by virtue of sub-paragraph (1)—

(a) in relation only to services provided by the BBC or the Welsh Authority; and

(b) to the extent only that it contains provision that applies to those services and, in the case of services provided by the Welsh Authority, relates to matters other than advertising and impartiality.

Commencement Information

I66. Sch. 18 para. 43 in force at 29.12.2003 by S.I. 2003/3142, art. 3. (1), Sch. 1 (with art. 11)

Local and national radio licences

44. (1)Section 103 of the 1990 Act (restriction on changes of control affecting holders of national licences) is to apply in relation to a pre-transfer national licence as it applies in relation to a national licence within the meaning of Part 3 of the 1990 Act.

(2) Anything done by or in relation to the Radio Authority under any of sections 98 to 102 or 103. A of the 1990 Act, so far as it has been done—

(a) before the radio transfer date, and

(b) for the purposes of, or in connection with, the grant or renewal of a pre-transfer national licence,

is to have effect for the purposes of, and in connection with, the grant or renewal of a licence at times on or after that date as if done by or in relation to OFCOM in connection with or for the purposes of the grant or renewal of national licence (within the meaning of Part 3 of that Act).

(3) Anything done by or in relation to the Radio Authority under any of sections 104 to 105 of the 1990 Act, so far as it has been done—

(a) before the radio transfer date, and

(b) for the purposes of, or in connection with, the grant or renewal of a pre-transfer local licence,

is to have effect for the purposes of, and in connection with, the grant or renewal of a licence at times on or after that date as if done by or in relation to OFCOM in connection with, or for the purposes of, the grant or renewal of local licence (within the meaning of Part 3 of that Act).

(4) In this paragraph "pre-transfer local licence" and "pre-transfer national licence" each has the same meaning as in section 253 of this Act.

Commencement Information

167. Sch. 18 para. 44 in force at 29.12.2003 by S.I. 2003/3142, art. 3. (1), Sch. 1 (with art. 11)

Section 111. B of the 1990 Act

45. (1)Section 111. B of the 1990 Act (power to suspend satellite services) is to have effect in relation to a licence to provide a formerly regulated radio service (within the meaning of section 251) as it applies in relation to a licence to provide a radio licensable content service, but as if the reference in subsection (1)(b) of that section to a condition included in the licence in pursuance of the provisions there mentioned included a reference to a condition included in the licence in pursuance of section 90. (1)(a) of that Act.

(2) In relation to any time falling—

(a) on or after the radio transfer date, and

(b) before the first coming into force, in the case of the holder of a licence under Part 3 of the 1990 Act or Part 2 of the 1996 Act, of conditions imposed under section 325 of this Act,

section 111. B of the 1990 Act is to have effect in relation to a licence to provide a radio licensable content service as if the reference in subsection (1)(b) of section 111. B of that Act to a condition included in the licence in pursuance of the provisions there mentioned were a reference to a condition included in the licence in pursuance of section 90. (1)(a) of that Act.

Commencement Information

168. Sch. 18 para. 45 in force at 29.12.2003 by S.I. 2003/3142, art. 3. (1), Sch. 1 (with art. 11)

Section 185 of the 1990 Act

46. (1)A determination or nomination made for the purposes of section 185 of the 1990 Act (the national television archive) by the ITC is to have effect on and after the television transfer date as a determination or nomination made by OFCOM.

(2) Sub-paragraph (1) applies in the case of a determination so far only as it relates to a financial year beginning on or after the television transfer date.

Commencement Information

169. Sch. 18 para. 46 in force at 29.12.2003 by S.I. 2003/3142, art. 3. (1), Sch. 1 (with art. 11)

Section 28 of the 1996 Act

47. (1)The repeal by this Act of section 28 of the 1996 Act does not affect any power to vary a licence under Part 1 of the 1990 Act which is—

(a) conferred on the ITC by an order under that section; and

(b) transferred to OFCOM by this Act.

(2) Nor does it affect so much of any order under that section in force immediately before the repeal as—

(a) modifies section 16 of the 1996 Act in its application in relation to the renewal of a licence first granted before the television transfer date; or

(b) imposes a prohibition on the use of digital capacity reserved before that date;

but so much of any such prohibition as requires the consent of the ITC for the use of any digital capacity shall have effect after the television transfer date as if the consent required were OFCOM's consent.

(3) Sub-paragraph (1) only saves the power so far as it is exercisable in relation to a licence granted before the television transfer date.

Commencement Information

I70. Sch. 18 para. 47 in force at 29.12.2003 by S.I. 2003/3142, art. 3. (1), Sch. 1 (with art. 11)

Section 48 of the 1996 Act

48. Subsections (4) to (6) of section 48 of the 1996 Act (reservations of capacity for national radio multiplex licences to independent national broadcasters) are to apply in relation to conditions included in pursuance of that section in licences granted before the radio transfer date as they apply in relation to conditions included in licences by virtue of the amendments of that section made by this Act.

Commencement Information

I71. Sch. 18 para. 48 in force at 29.12.2003 by S.I. 2003/3142, art. 3. (1), Sch. 1 (with art. 11)

Applications for extension of pre-transfer licences

49. (1)Section 253. (4)(a) does not prevent the determination by OFCOM of a day falling less than one year after the making of the determination where—

(a) OFCOM consider that the day by which they would need to publish a notice is a day which is not more than 15 months after the commencement date; and

(b) the determination of that day is made as soon as practicable after the commencement date.

(2) Where the day determined by OFCOM for the purposes of paragraph (b) of section 253. (3) is a day in the period of three months beginning with the day after the determination, that paragraph shall have effect as if for the words "three months before" there were substituted " on ".

(3) In this paragraph, the "commencement date" is the date on which section 253 comes into force.

Commencement Information

I72. Sch. 18 para. 49 in force at 29.12.2003 by S.I. 2003/3142, art. 3. (1), Sch. 1 (with art. 11)

Applications for renewal of licences under 1990 Act and 1996 Act

50. (1)A provision set out in sub-paragraph (2) does not prevent the determination by OFCOM of a date falling less than one year after the making of the determination where—

(a) OFCOM consider that the relevant date for the purposes of the section in question is a date which is not more than 15 months after the commencement date; and

(b) the determination of the relevant date is made as soon as practicable after the commencement date.

(2) Those provisions are—

(a) section 53. (12) of the 1990 Act;

(b) section 103. A(12) of the 1990 Act;

(c) section 104. A(14) of the 1990 Act;

(d) section 16. (12. A) of the 1996 Act;

(e) section 58. (12. A) of the 1996 Act.

(3) An application which is made before the commencement date in accordance with a provision set out in sub-paragraph (5) shall be treated after that date as if it had been made in accordance with that provision as amended by this Act.

(4) Where, in a case where a provision set out in sub-paragraph (5) applies, the relevant date for the purposes of the section in question is a date in the period of three months beginning with—

(a) the commencement date, or

(b) the day after the day on which the relevant date is determined,

that provision shall have effect as if the words "the day falling three months before" were omitted.

(5) Those provisions are—

(a) section 53. (2) of the 1990 Act;

(b) section 103. A(2) of the 1990 Act;

(c) section 104. A(3) of the 1990 Act;

(d) section 16. (3) of the 1996 Act;

(e) section 58. (3) of the 1996 Act.

(6) In this paragraph, the "commencement date", in relation to any provision set out in sub-paragraph (2) or (5) is the date on which the provision of Schedule 15 inserting or amending that provision comes into force.

Commencement Information

I73. Sch. 18 para. 50 in force at 29.12.2003 by S.I. 2003/3142, art. 3. (1), Sch. 1 (with art. 11)

Listed events rules

51. (1)Subject to sub-paragraph (2), Part 4 of the 1996 Act (sporting and other events of national interest) is to have effect in relation to times on or after the television transfer date as if anything done before that date by or in relation to the ITC had been done by or in relation to OFCOM.

(2) The code drawn up by the ITC under section 104 of the 1996 Act (code of guidance as to the operation of Part 4) and in force immediately before the commencement of section 301 of this Act is to continue to have effect (notwithstanding the substitutions made by that section of this Act)—

(a) until the code drawn up by OFCOM under that section comes into force; but

(b) in relation to times on or after the transfer date and before the coming into force of OFCOM's code, as if references in section 104. (2) of that Act and in the code to the ITC were references to OFCOM.

(3) If a provision of sections 300 to 302 of this Act comes into force before the television transfer date, a reference to OFCOM in an amendment made by that provision is to be construed in relation to times before that date as a reference to the ITC.

(4) On the date on which section 300 of this Act comes into force, the Secretary of State shall revise the list maintained for the purposes of Part 4 of the 1996 Act in order to allocate each event which is a listed event on that date either to Group A or to Group B.

(5) Where—

(a) the events listed in the list in force immediately before the Secretary of State revises it under sub-paragraph (4) are treated, for any of the purposes of the code in force under section 104 of the 1996 Act at that time, as divided into two categories, and

(b) the Secretary of State's revision under that sub-paragraph makes the same division,

section 97. (2) of the 1996 Act shall not apply in relation to that revision of that list.

(6) In this paragraph "the transfer date" is the date on which paragraph 13 of Schedule 1 comes into force.

Commencement Information

I74. Sch. 18 para. 51 in force at 29.12.2003 by S.I. 2003/3142, art. 3. (1), Sch. 1 (with art. 11)

Complaints to the Broadcasting Standards Commission

52. (1)On and after the transfer to OFCOM under this Act of the functions of the Broadcasting Standards Commission under Part 5 of the 1996 Act, that Part is to have effect in relation to a fairness complaint made to, but not disposed of by, the Commission before the transfer as if—
(a) anything done, or treated as done, by or in relation to the Commission for the purposes of, or in connection with, that complaint had been done by or in relation OFCOM; and
(b) those functions had been functions of OFCOM at the time when it was done.
(2) Where immediately before the commencement of section 327 of this Act a licence to provide a licensed service (within the meaning of Part 5 of the 1996 Act) contains a condition included in that licence by virtue of section 119. (7) of that Act (conditions requiring compliance with BSC directions), that condition is to have effect on and after the coming into force of section 327 of this Act as a condition requiring the licence holder to comply with directions given to him by OFCOM.
(3) In this paragraph "fairness complaint" has the same meaning as in Part 5 of the 1996 Act.
Commencement Information
I75. Sch. 18 para. 52 in force at 29.12.2003 by S.I. 2003/3142, art. 3. (1), Sch. 1 (with art. 11)

Codes of practice drawn up by the Broadcasting Standards Commission

53. The code of practice drawn up by the Broadcasting Standards Commission under section 107 of the 1996 Act (code in respect of unjust and unfair treatment and infringements of privacy) is to have effect on and after the transfer under this Act to OFCOM of the Commission's functions under Part 5 of that Act as if it were the code required to be drawn up under that section by OFCOM.
Commencement Information
I76. Sch. 18 para. 53 in force at 29.12.2003 by S.I. 2003/3142, art. 3. (1), Sch. 1 (with art. 11)

Media ownership provisions

54. (1)Part 4 of Schedule 14 to this Act is to have effect—
(a) in relation to times before the television transfer date as if references to OFCOM were, in relation to licences under Part 1 of the 1990 Act or Part 1 of the 1996 Act, references to the ITC; and
(b) in relation to times before the radio transfer date as if references to OFCOM were, in relation to licences under Part 3 of the 1990 Act or Part 2 of the 1996 Act, references to the Radio Authority.
(2) A determination by the ITC or the Radio Authority under paragraph 2. (2) of Part 2 of Schedule 2 to the 1990 Act which is in force immediately before the commencement of Part 4 of Schedule 14 to this Act is to have effect on and after its commencement as a determination under paragraph 15 of that Schedule to this Act.
(3) Any guidance issued by the ITC and the Radio Authority under paragraph 2. (3) of Part 2 of Schedule 2 to the 1990 Act and in force immediately before the commencement of Part 4 of Schedule 14 to this Act is to have effect on and after its commencement as guidance published under paragraph 15. (4) of that Schedule to this Act.
(4) Anything done under paragraph 15 of Schedule 14 by the ITC or the Radio Authority which is in force immediately before the relevant transfer date is to have effect on and after that date as if done under that paragraph by OFCOM.
(5) The following powers under enactments in force before the relevant transfer date shall be exercisable by OFCOM at all times on or after that date in relation to a pre-commencement contravention of a requirement imposed by or under Parts 3 to 5 of Schedule 2 to the 1990 Act—
(a) all the powers and duties of the ITC under section 5 of the 1990 Act and section 5 of the 1996

Act;

(b) all the powers and duties of the Radio Authority under section 88 of the 1990 Act and section 44 of the 1996 Act; and

(c) all the other powers and duties of the ITC or the Radio Authority in relation to contraventions of conditions imposed under section 5 or 88 of the 1990 Act or section 5 or 44 of the 1996 Act.

(6) For the purpose of determining whether anything occurring after the relevant transfer date is a pre-commencement contravention of a requirement imposed by or under Parts 3 to 5 of Schedule 2 to the 1990 Act, references in those Parts of that Schedule to the ITC or to the Radio Authority are to be construed as including references to OFCOM.

(7) In this paragraph—

"pre-commencement contravention" means a contravention of a requirement which occurred before the coming into force of the repeal by this Act of the provision by or under which the requirement was imposed; and

"the relevant transfer date"—

- in relation to the ITC, means the television transfer date; and

- in relation to the Radio Authority, means the radio transfer date.

Commencement Information

I77. Sch. 18 para. 54. (1)-(4) in force at 18.9.2003 by S.I. 2003/1900, art. 2. (2), Sch. 2

I78. Sch. 18 para. 54. (5)-(7) in force at 29.12.2003 by S.I. 2003/3142, art. 3. (1), Sch. 1 (with art. 11)

TV licences

F955. . . . .

Amendments (Textual)

F9. Sch. 18 para. 55 repealed (8.2.2007) by Wireless Telegraphy Act 2006 (c. 36), s. 126. (2), Sch. 9 Pt. 1 (with Sch. 8 Pt. 1)

Commencement Information

I79. Sch. 18 para. 55 in force at 1.4.2004 by S.I. 2003/3142, art. 4. (2), Sch. 2 (with art. 11)

Functions under the Enterprise Act 2002.

56. (1)This section has effect in so far as, at any time before the coming into force of section 370 of this Act, anything has been done or is treated as done by or in relation to the Director for the purposes of, or in connection with, the carrying out of any of his functions under the Enterprise Act 2002 (c. 40).

(2) That thing is to have effect on and after that date, and OFCOM may carry out their functions and continue anything begun by that Director, as if—

(a) that thing had been done by or in relation to OFCOM for the purposes of, or in connection with, their functions under that Act by virtue of that section; and

(b) the provisions conferring those functions on OFCOM had been in force at the time it was done.

(3) Sub-paragraph (1) does not apply to anything that could not be done by or in relation to OFCOM for the purposes of, or in connection with, the carrying out of their functions under the Enterprise Act 2002 (c. 40).

(4) Where, by virtue of sub-paragraph (3), sub-paragraph (1) does not apply to something, that thing is to have effect instead as if done by or in relation to the Office of Fair Trading

Commencement Information

I80. Sch. 18 para. 56 in force at 25.7.2003 for specified purposes by S.I. 2003/1900, arts. 1. (2), 2. (1), Sch. 1 (with art. 3) (as amended by S.I. 2003/3142, art. 1. (3))

I81. Sch. 18 para. 56 in force at 29.12.2003 in so far as not already in force by S.I. 2003/3142, art. 3. (2) (with art. 11)

Functions under the Competition Act 1998.

57. (1)This paragraph applies in so far as, at any time before the coming into force of section 371 of this Act, anything has been done by or in relation to the Director for the purposes of, or in connection with, the carrying out of any of his functions under the Competition Act 1998 (c. 41).

(2) That thing is to have effect on and after that date, and OFCOM may carry out their functions and continue anything begun by that Director, as if—

(a) that thing had been done by or in relation to OFCOM for the purposes of, or in connection with, their functions under that Act by virtue of that section; and

(b) the provisions conferring those functions on OFCOM had been in force at the time it was done.

(3) Sub-paragraph (1) does not apply to anything that could not be done by or in relation to OFCOM for the purposes of, or in connection with, the carrying out of their functions under the Competition Act 1998.

(4) Where, by virtue of sub-paragraph (3), sub-paragraph (1) does not apply to something, that thing is to have effect instead as if done by or in relation to the Office of Fair Trading Commencement Information

182. Sch. 18 para. 57 in force at 25.7.2003 for specified purposes by S.I. 2003/1900, arts. 1. (2), 2. (1), Sch. 1 (with art. 3) (as amended by S.I. 2003/3142, art. 1. (3))

183. Sch. 18 para. 57 in force at 29.12.2003 in so far as not already in force by S.I. 2003/3142, art. 3. (2) (with art. 11)

58. (1)Where any regulations made under section 54. (4) of the Competition Act 1998 (regulations about concurrent functions of regulators and the Office of Fair Trading) are in force at the coming into force of section 371 of this Act, those regulations—

(a) shall, from that time have effect in relation to functions exercisable concurrently by virtue of section 371 of this Act as they have effect in relation to functions exercisable concurrently by virtue of Part 2 of Schedule 10 to the Competition Act 1998; but

(b) shall so have effect subject to any amendments or revocations coming into force at or after that time.

(2) Where, at any time before the coming into force of section 371, anything has been done by or in relation to the Director under or for the purposes of any regulations made under section 54. (4) of the Competition Act 1998 that thing is to have effect, so far as necessary for the purposes of paragraph 57 of this Schedule, as if done by or in relation to OFCOM.

Commencement Information

184. Sch. 18 para. 58 in force at 25.7.2003 for specified purposes by S.I. 2003/1900, arts. 1. (2), 2. (1), Sch. 1 (with art. 3) (as amended by S.I. 2003/3142, art. 1. (3))

185. Sch. 18 para. 58 in force at 29.12.2003 in so far as not already in force by S.I. 2003/3142, art. 3. (2) (with art. 11)

Newspaper mergers

59. (1)Chapter 2 of Part 5 and any related repeals shall, subject to sub-paragraph (2), not apply in relation to—

(a) a transfer of a newspaper or of newspaper assets (within the meaning given by section 57. (2) of the Fair Trading Act 1973 (c. 41)) which has been made before the coming into force of section 373 of this Act; or

(b) a proposed transfer of a newspaper or of newspaper assets in relation to which an application for the consent of the Secretary of State under section 58 of the Act of 1973 has been made before the coming into force of section 373 of this Act.

(2) Chapter 2 of Part 5 and any related repeals shall apply in relation to a proposed transfer of a newspaper or of newspaper assets if—

(a) an application for the consent of the Secretary of State under section 58 of the Act of 1973 has been made;

(b) the application is expressed to depend on the operation of subsection (3) or (4) of that section;

(c) no consent is given by the Secretary of State under subsection (3) or (4) of that section; and

(d) no further application has been made for the consent of the Secretary of State under that section before the coming into force of section 373 of this Act.

Commencement Information

I86. Sch. 18 para. 59 in force at 29.12.2003 by S.I. 2003/3142, art. 3. (1), Sch. 1 (with art. 11)

60. Chapter 2 of Part 5 and any related repeals shall apply in relation to any transfer of a newspaper or of newspaper assets which is proposed (and not made) before the coming into force of section 373 of this Act and in relation to which no application has been made for the consent of the Secretary of State under section 58 of the Act of 1973 before the coming into force of that section.

Commencement Information

I87. Sch. 18 para. 60 in force at 29.12.2003 by S.I. 2003/3142, art. 3. (1), Sch. 1 (with art. 11)

61. References in paragraphs 59 and 60 to Chapter 2 of Part 5 do not include references to subsections (2) to (4) of section 389 (powers to make transitional and consequential amendments etc.).

Commencement Information

I88. Sch. 18 para. 61 in force at 29.12.2003 by S.I. 2003/3142, art. 3. (1), Sch. 1 (with art. 11)

62. (1)The Secretary of State may, instead of any or all of the conditions attached to a consent given by him (or treated as so given) under section 58 of the Fair Trading Act 1973 (c. 41)), accept undertakings under this paragraph to take, or refrain from taking, action specified or described in the undertakings.

(2) If, and so far as, the Secretary of State accepts an undertaking under this paragraph instead of a condition, that condition shall cease to have effect.

(3) In deciding whether to accept an undertaking under this paragraph, the Secretary of State may, in particular, consult the Office of Fair Trading and OFCOM.

(4) An undertaking under this paragraph—

(a) shall come into force when accepted;

(b) may be varied or superseded by another undertaking; and

(c) may be released by the Secretary of State.

(5) The Secretary of State shall, as soon as reasonably practicable, consider any representations received by him in relation to varying or releasing an undertaking under this paragraph.

(6) Paragraph 10 of Schedule 7 to the Enterprise Act 2002 (c. 40) (order-making power where final undertakings not fulfilled) shall apply in relation to an undertaking under this paragraph as it applies in relation to an undertaking under paragraph 9 of that Schedule to that Act but as if—

(a) in sub-paragraph (2) the words from "for any" to "66. (6)" were omitted; and

(b) sub-paragraph (3) were omitted.

(7) The following provisions of the Enterprise Act 2002 (c. 40) shall apply in relation to an undertaking under this paragraph or an order made by virtue of sub-paragraph (6) as they apply in relation to an undertaking under paragraph 9 of Schedule 7 to that Act or (as the case may be) an order under paragraph 10 of that Schedule to that Act—

(a) section 90 and Schedule 10 (procedural requirements for certain undertakings and orders);

(b) section 91 (register of undertakings and orders);

(c) section 92 (duty of OFT to monitor undertakings and orders);

(d) section 93 (further role of OFT in relation to undertakings and orders); and

(e) section 94 (rights to enforce undertakings and orders).

(8) Section 402 of this Act shall not apply in relation to the power of the Secretary of State to make an order which is exercisable by virtue of sub-paragraph (6) but supplementary provisions of Part 3 of the Enterprise Act 2002 which relate to the making of an order under paragraph 10 of Schedule 7 to that Act shall apply in relation to the making of an order by virtue of sub-paragraph (6).

(9) Section 402 of this Act shall not apply in relation to the power of the Secretary of State to make an order under section 91. (6)(a) of the Enterprise Act 2002 as applied by virtue of sub-

paragraph (7)(b) above but supplementary provisions of Part 3 of the Enterprise Act 2002 which relate to the making of an order under section 91. (6)(a) of that Act shall apply in relation to the making of an order under that provision as applied by virtue of sub-paragraph (7)(b) above.

Commencement Information

I89. Sch. 18 para. 62 in force at 29.12.2003 by S.I. 2003/3142, art. 3. (1), Sch. 1 (with art. 11)

Orders in Council under section 6 of the Continental Shelf Act 1964.

F1063. . . . .

Amendments (Textual)

F10. Sch. 18 para. 63 repealed (8.2.2007) by Wireless Telegraphy Act 2006 (c. 36), s. 126. (2), Sch. 9 Pt. 1 (with Sch. 8 Pt. 1)

Commencement Information

I90. Sch. 18 para. 63 in force at 25.7.2003 for specified purposes by S.I. 2003/1900, arts. 1. (2), 2. (1), Sch. 1 (with art. 3) (as amended by S.I. 2003/3142, art. 1. (3))

I91. Sch. 18 para. 63 in force at 29.12.2003 in so far as not already in force by S.I. 2003/3142, art. 3. (2) (with art. 11)

Interpretation of Schedule

64. In this Schedule—

"the 1984 Act" means the Telecommunications Act 1984 (c. 12);

"the abolition of licensing" means the coming into force of the repeal by this Act of section 7 of the 1984 Act;

"the Director" means the Director General of Telecommunications;

"the ITC" means the Independent Television Commission.

Commencement Information

I92. Sch. 18 para. 64 in force at 25.7.2003 for specified purposes by S.I. 2003/1900, arts. 1. (2), 2. (1), Sch. 1 (with art. 3) (as amended by S.I. 2003/3142, art. 1. (3))

I93. Sch. 18 para. 64 in force at 29.12.2003 in so far as not already in force by S.I. 2003/3142, art. 3. (2) (with art. 11)

Schedule 20. Repeals

Section 406

(1) Enactments

Short title and chapter | Extent of repeal |
Telegraph Act 1899 (c. 38) | The whole Act. |
In section 1—
subsection (1. A);
in subsection (4), the words "other than a television licence" and the words from "; and a television licence" onwards;
subsections (6) and (7).
Section 1. D(1), (2), (7) and (8).
Section 1. F.
Section 2.

In section 3. (1), the words after paragraph (d) from "and different" to "classes of case:".
Section 9.
In section 10. (2), the words after paragraph (b).
In section 11. (1)—
paragraph (i) of the proviso;
in paragraph (ii) of the proviso the words ", and paragraph (i) of this proviso shall not apply".
Section 14. (1. A)(e), (2) and (3)(b).
Section 15. (4)(c) and the word "or" immediately preceding it.
Section 19. (2. A) and (9).
Schedule 2.
Army Act 1955 (3 & 4 Eliz. 2 c. 18) | In section 44B(5), the definition of "telecommunication system" and the word "and" immediately preceding it. |
Air Force Act 1955 (3 & 4 Eliz. 2 c. 19) | In section 44B(5), the definition of "telecommunication system" and the word "and" immediately preceding it. |
Naval Discipline Act 1957 (c. 53) | In section 29B(5), the definition of "telecommunication system" and the word "and" immediately preceding it. |
Opencast Coal Act 1958 (c. 69) | In section 45(3), the word "a" before "telecommunication apparatus". |
Continental Shelf Act 1964 (c. 29) | Section 6. |
Parliamentary Commissioner Act 1967 (c. 13) | In Schedule 2, the entries relating to the Broadcasting Standards Commission and the Office of the Director General of Telecommunications. |
Marine, &c., Broadcasting (Offences) Act 1967 (c. 41) | Section 6(2) and (7). |
Section 4.
In section 7. (5), paragraph (b) and the word "or" immediately preceding it.
Sections 57 to 62.
In section 93. B—
in subsection (1)(b), the words "the Telecommunications Act 1984 or";
in subsection (5), the words "section 13. B of the Telecommunications Act 1984 or".
In Part 2 of Schedule 1, the entries relating to—
the Broadcasting Standards Commission;
Comataidh Craolaidh Gaidhlig;
the Independent Television Commission;
the Radio Authority.
In Part 3 of Schedule 1, the entry relating to the Director General of Telecommunications.
In Part 2 of Schedule 1, the entries relating to—
the Broadcasting Standards Commission;
the Independent Television Commission;
the Radio Authority;
the Tribunal established under Part 2 of the Wireless Telegraphy Act 1949.
In Part 3 of Schedule 1, the entries relating to—
the Director General of Telecommunications;
a Director of the successor company within the meaning of Part 5 of the Telecommunications Act 1984.
Welsh Development Agency Act 1975 (c. 70) | In section 19(11), the definition of "appropriate authority". |
In section 88—
in subsection (1), the words from ", and the special" to "Schedule 5,";
in subsection (2), the words "and 5".
In Schedule 4, paragraphs 2 to 18, 21 and 22.
In Schedule 5, paragraphs 1 and 3 to 22.
Acquisition of Land Act 1981 (c. 67) | In section 28, paragraph (f). |
Sections 1 to 30.

Sections 34 to 49.

In section 50, subsections (2) to (6. A).

Sections 51 to 55.

Section 60.

Section 61. (1) to (6).

Section 62.

Section 63. (1) to (4).

Sections 64 to 67.

Sections 69 to 71.

In section 72—

in subsection (1), the words from the beginning to "this Act," and the words "and development land tax";

subsections (2), (4) and (5).

Section 73.

Sections 80 and 81.

Section 88.

Section 90.

In section 91—

in subsection (2), the words "or section 80. (9)(b) above" and the words "for an offence or (as the case may be) for the forfeiture of any apparatus under that section";

in subsection (4), the words "and in section 80. (9)(b) above".

Section 92. (4).

Section 93.

Sections 95 to 97.

In section 98. (9), the words "and 'telecommunication apparatus'".

In section 101—

in subsection (2)(a), the words "or transferred";

subsection (4).

Section 102.

In section 104—

in subsection (1), the words "2, 27. L 60. (1) or (3), 69. (2) or" and ", or paragraph 1 of Schedule 5,";

subsection (3).

In section 106. (1), the definitions of—

"commercial activities connected with telecommunications";

"consumer", "monopoly situation", "practice" and "supply";

"the Director";

"directory information service";

"disabled person" and "disabled";

"public telecommunications operator";

"public telecommunications system";

"telecommunication apparatus";

"telecommunication service";

"telecommunications operator";

"telecommunication system";

"transitional period".

Section 107. (1), (2) and (4).

In section 109—

subsections (2) and (3);

in subsection (4), the words "and the special transitional provisions with respect to patents for inventions and registered designs contained in Schedule 6 to this Act";

subsections (5) to (7).

Schedule 1.

In Schedule 2—

in paragraph 1. (1), the words from "'telecommunications apparatus' includes any apparatus" onwards;

in paragraph 9. (2), the words "section 11. (1) of this Act,";

in paragraph 10. (2)(b), the words "(within the meaning of section 6 of this Act)";

in paragraph 27. (1), the words "section 109. (2) or (3) of or".

In Schedule 4, paragraphs 2, 3, 12, 16, 28. (2), 40, 55. (1) and (7), 65, 80. (1), 86. (1), 89. (5) and 90.

In Schedule 5—

paragraphs 1 to 7;

paragraph 8. (2) and (4);

paragraphs 9 to 14;

paragraphs 16 to 29;

paragraphs 31 to 33;

paragraph 35;

paragraphs 38 to 42;

paragraph 47;

in paragraph 48, in sub-paragraph (1), the words "Part 1 of the Industry Act 1972 and" and in sub-paragraph (2), the words "Part 1 of the Industry Act 1972 or";

paragraphs 49 to 51.

Schedule 6.

Companies Consolidation (Consequential Provisions) Act 1985 (c. 9) | In Schedule 2, the entries relating to sections 60(3), 61(4), 66, 70 and 73(1) of and Schedule 5 to the Telecommunications Act 1984. |

Surrogacy Arrangements Act 1985 (c. 49) | Section 3(6). |

Interception of Communications Act 1985 (c. 56) | Schedule 2. |

Housing Act 1985 (c. 68) | Section 298(1). |

Airports Act 1986 (c. 31) | Section 62(8). |

Insolvency Act 1986 (c. 45) | In Schedule 2A, paragraph 10(1)(a). |

Consumer Protection Act 1987 (c. 43) | In Schedule 4, in paragraph 9(1), the words "28(6) and". |

Channel Tunnel Act 1987 (c. 53) | In Part 10 of Schedule 7, paragraph 1(2). |

Income and Corporation Taxes Act 1988 (c. 1) | In Schedule 29, in the Table in paragraph 32, the entries relating to sections 62(7) and 72(4) of the Telecommunications Act 1984. |

Legal Aid Act 1988 (c. 34) | In Schedule 5, paragraph 11. |

In section 69. (2), the word "or" at the end of paragraph (b).

In Schedule 2, the word "or" at the end of paragraph 17. (2)(b).

In Schedule 7, paragraph 27.

Housing Act 1988 (c. 50) | In Part 2 of Schedule 10, paragraph 19. |

Electricity Act 1989 (c. 29) | In Schedule 4, in paragraph 12, the definitions of "public telecommunications operator" and of "telecommunication apparatus", "telecommunication system" and "the telecommunications code". |

In Schedule 18, paragraph 28.

In Schedule 20, paragraph 2.

Planning (Consequential Provisions) Act 1990 (c. 11) | In Schedule 2, paragraph 63. |

Courts and Legal Services Act 1990 (c. 41) | In Schedule 10, paragraph 8. |

Sections 1 and 2.

In section 4. (3), the words from "and the amount" onwards.

In section 5—

subsection (6. A)(a);

subsection (6. B).

Sections 6 to 12.

In section 15. (3), paragraphs (c) to (e).

In section 16—

subsections (2) and (3);

in subsection (4), the words from "; and in applying" onwards;

subsections (5) to (8).

Section 20.

Section 21. A.

In section 24, subsections (4) to (6).

Sections 25 to 27.

In section 29—

in subsection (2), paragraph (b) and the word "and" immediately preceding it;

subsection (3).

Sections 30 to 36.

Sections 38 and 39.

In section 42. A, paragraph (b) and the word "and" immediately preceding it.

Chapters 3 and 4 of Part 1.

Section 48. (5).

In section 50—

in subsection (1)(b)(ii), the words "(subject to the approval of the Secretary of State)";

subsection (7).

Section 51. (2) and (7).

In section 53. (4), the words "before the relevant date".

Section 54. (2)

In section 56. (1)(b), the words ", and have the functions conferred by,".

Section 57.

Section 59.

Section 60. (1) to (3) and (6).

In section 61. A—

subsection (1);

in subsection (2) the words "on or after the notified date";

subsections (5) and (6).

Section 62.

Section 65.

In section 66. A(2), paragraphs (c) and (d).

Sections 68 to 70.

In section 71. (1)—

in the definition of "Channel 3", the words "by the Commission";

the definitions of "the Commission", "licensable programme service" and "satellite television service".

Part 2.

Sections 83 and 84.

In section 85, subsections (3) and (4).

In section 87—

in subsection (2)(b), sub-paragraph (ii) and the word "or" immediately preceding it;

in subsection (3), the words from "and the amount" onwards.

In section 88—

subsection (6. A)(a); and

subsection (6. B).

Section 89. (2).

Sections 90 to 96.

In section 98. (3)(a), the word "both" and sub-paragraph (ii) and the word "and" immediately preceding it.

In section 99. (1)(a), the word "both" and sub-paragraph (ii) and the word "and" immediately preceding it.

In section 103. A—

in subsection (3), the words "before the relevant date", paragraph (a) and, in paragraph (b), the words "in any other case";

in subsection (8), the words from "(whether because" to "any other reason)";

subsection (10);

in subsection (11), the definition of "simulcast radio service".

In section 104. A(5), at the end of paragraph (a), the word "and".

In section 104. B—

subsection (1)(b);

subsections (6) and (7).

In section 106. (1), the words from ", except" onwards.

Sections 106. A to 108.

Section 110. (7).

Sections 112 and 113.

Section 114. (5).

In section 116. (1)(b)(iii), the words "(subject to the approval of the Secretary of State)".

Section 117. (2) and (7).

Section 119. (2).

Section 122 to 125.

In section 126. (1), the definitions of "assigned frequency", "the Authority" and "licensable sound programme service".

Section 134.

In section 177. (6), the definition of "relevant foreign satellite service".

Section 180. (2) and (3).

Section 181.

In section 183—

in subsection (3), the words ", which shall be called" onwards;

subsection (3. A);

subsections (6) and (7).

In section 185. (5), the definition of "the Commission".

Section 186.

Section 187. (1) and (2).

In section 188. (2), paragraphs (b), (d) and (e).

Sections 189 to 191.

In section 196—

in subsection (1)(a), the words ", 82";

subsection (2).

Section 197.

Section 199. (1) to (4) and (6).

In section 201. (1), the words "under this Act".

In section 202—

in subsection (1), the definition of "telecommunication system";

in subsection (2)(b), the words "1" and "8";

in subsection (5)(a), the words "for general reception, or".

Schedule 1.

In Part 1 of Schedule 2—

in paragraph 1. (1), the definitions of "coverage area", of "digital programme service", of "local delivery licence" and "local delivery service", of "local digital sound programme service" and "national digital sound programme service", of "local radio multiplex service" and "national radio multiplex service" and of "television multiplex service";

paragraph 1. (8);

paragraph 3. A;

paragraph 3. B;

paragraph 4.

In Part 2 of Schedule 2—

paragraph 1. (1)(a) and (b);

in paragraph 1. (1)(j)(i), the words "(a), (b) or";

paragraph 1. (2) and (3);

in paragraph 5. A(1)(a), the words "granted by the Commission";

paragraph 5. A(1)(b) and the word "and" immediately preceding it;

in paragraph 5. A(2), the words "granted by the Authority";

paragraph 5. A(3).

Parts 3 to 5 of Schedule 2.

Schedule 4.

Schedule 5.

In Schedule 6—

paragraph 2. (1);

in paragraph 13. (2), the words from "and shall include" onwards.

Schedule 8.

Schedule 12.

In Schedule 18—

in Part 1, paragraphs 1. (4) to (6), 2. (1) and (3) and 4;

in Part 2, paragraphs 1. (d) and 5.

In Schedule 19—

in paragraph 8. (c), the words "and (where the expenses relate to the Commission's functions in connection with sound programmes) the Radio Authority";

in paragraph 11. (4), the words "or the Radio Authority" and "or, as the case may be, the Authority".

In Schedule 20—

paragraph 9;

paragraph 24. (c)(ii);

paragraph 38;

paragraph 54.

In Schedule 22—

paragraphs 1 to 3;

in paragraph 4, the words "and 45";

paragraph 5.

In Schedule 4, in paragraph 7. (4), the definitions of "telecommunication apparatus" and "telecommunication system".

In Schedule 6, in paragraph 7. (4), the definitions of "telecommunication apparatus" and "telecommunication system".

Taxation of Chargeable Gains Act 1992 (c. 12) | In Schedule 10, paragraph 7. |

Charities Act 1992 (c. 41) | In section 60(10), the definition of "telecommunication apparatus". |

Sections 1 to 10.

Section 49.

In Schedule 1, paragraphs 1, 2, 3. (b) and 4.

Carriage of Goods by Sea Act 1992 (c. 50) | In section 5(1), the definition of "telecommunication system" and the word "and" immediately preceding it. |

Tribunals and Inquiries Act 1992 (c. 53) | In Part 1 of Schedule 1, the entry at paragraph 45 relating to wireless telegraphy. |

Section 26. (8)(a).

In Schedule 5, the entry relating to the President of the tribunal established under section 9 of the Wireless Telegraphy Act 1949.

In Schedule 6, paragraph 58.

In Schedule 7, paragraph 5. (5)(xxxii).

Leasehold Reform, Housing and Urban Development Act 1993 (c. 28) | In Part 2 of Schedule 20, paragraph 19(1). |

In Schedule 4, in paragraph 3. (2), the words following paragraph (c).

In Schedule 7, paragraph 21. (10).

Local Government (Wales) Act 1994 (c. 19) | In Schedule 16, paragraph 72. |

Vehicle Excise and Registration Act 1994 (c. 22) | In Schedule 3, paragraph 3(a)(i). |

Criminal Justice and Public Order Act 1994 (c. 33) | Section 92. |

Section 8.

In Schedule 4, paragraph 3. (a).

Criminal Procedure (Consequential Provisions) (Scotland) Act 1995 (c. 40) | In Schedule 4, paragraph 48(2) and (3). |

Criminal Procedure (Scotland) Act 1995 (c. 46) | In Schedule 9, the entry relating to the Wireless Telegraphy Act 1949. |

Arbitration Act 1996 (c. 23) | In Schedule 3, paragraph 7. |

Section 1. (1. A) to (3).

Section 2. (1), (6) and (7).

In section 4. (3), the words from "and the amount" onwards.

Section 5. (7)(a).

Section 6.

In section 11. (5), the words from "not exceeding" onwards.

Section 12. (7).

In section 16. (6), the words "before the relevant date".

Section 18. (5) and (6).

Section 19. (2) and (4) to (10).

Sections 20 to 22.

Section 25. (5) and (6).

Section 28.

In section 29. (2), the word "59,".

Sections 30 and 31.

In section 33. (3)(c), the words "or II".

Section 34.

Section 38.

In section 39. (1), the definitions of "the Commission" and "qualifying teletext service".

In section 40. (4), the words "provided on a frequency or frequencies assigned to the Authority under section 45. (1)".

In section 43—

in subsection (2)(b), sub-paragraph (ii) and the word "or" immediately preceding it;

in subsection (3), the words from "and the amount" onwards.

Section 44. (7)(a).

Section 45.

In section 46. (1), paragraph (e).

Section 47. (4).

Section 54. (7).

In section 56. (1)(a)(i), the words "to which the licence relates".

In section 58—

subsection (5);

in subsection (6), the words "before the relevant date".

In section 60, subsections (7) to (10).

In section 61, subsections (3) and (4).

Section 68.

Section 71.

In section 72. (1), the definition of "the Authority".

Sections 74 to 76.

Sections 78 and 79.

Section 80. (2).

Sections 82 to 84.

Section 86. (3).

Sections 87 to 90.

Section 91.

Section 93.

In section 95, subsections (3) to (7).

In section 97. (3)(b), the words "by the Commission" and "by them".

In section 104. (4)(d), the words "by the Commission" and "by them".

In section 105. (1), the definitions of "the Commission" and "live".

Section 106.

In section 107—

subsection (2);

in subsection (4)(a), the words "or regulatory".

Sections 108 and 109.

In section 110—

subsection (2);

in subsection (3), the words from "; and in exercising" onwards;

in subsection (4), the definition of "a standards complaint" and the word "and" immediately preceding it.

Sections 112 and 113.

In section 114—

in subsection (1), the words "or a standards complaint";

in subsection (2), the words "or a standards complaint" and in paragraph (b) the words ", in the case of a fairness complaint,".

In section 115—

in subsection (2), paragraph (c);

in subsection (3), paragraph (b) and the word "and" immediately preceding it.

Section 116.

In section 118, the words "or a standards complaint".

In section 119—

in subsection (3), paragraph (c);

in subsection (8), the words "or standards complaint" and in paragraph (c) the words ", a regulatory body";

in subsection (9), the words "or standards complaint" and ", 113. (1)";

subsection (12).

In section 120. (1), the words "or a standards complaint".

Sections 122 to 129.

In section 130—

in subsection (1), in the definition of "licensed service", the words from ", subject to" to "125. (6),";

the definitions in that subsection of "the appropriate regulatory body", "the BSC", "financial year", "local delivery service", "regulatory body", "sexual conduct" and "standards complaint";

in subsection (2), paragraph (b) and the word "and" immediately preceding it.

Section 142.

Section 143. (3) and (4).

Section 144. (5).

In section 145. (8), the definition of "the relevant authority".

In Schedule 2, paragraphs 1. (2)(d) to (f), 4, 5, 6. (3), 10 and 11.

Schedule 3.

Schedule 4.

In Schedule 8, paragraph 4.

In Schedule 10, paragraphs 1, 3 to 6, 8, 11 to 14, 16, 18 to 20, 22 to 25, 26. (a)(ii) and (b) and 27. (a).

Channel Tunnel Rail Link Act 1996 (c. 61) | In Part 4 of Schedule 15, in paragraph 1(2), the definitions of "telecommunications code", "telecommunications operator" and "operator", "telecommunication apparatus", "telecommunications code system" and "telecommunication system". |

Telecommunications (Fraud) Act 1997 (c. 4) | The whole Act. |

Planning (Consequential Provisions) (Scotland) Act 1997 (c. 11) | In Schedule 2, paragraph 37. |

In section 1. (1), the words "other than a television licence as defined in section 1. (7) of that Act".

In section 1. (3)—

paragraph (a);

in paragraph (b) the words from "or provide" to "the Secretary of State";

paragraph (d) and the word "and" immediately preceding it.

In section 3—

in subsection (1), the words "or determined by him under" and paragraph (a) and the word "and" immediately after it;

subsection (2);

in subsection (3), paragraph (h) and the word "and" immediately preceding it.

Section 5.

Schedule 1.

In Schedule 4—

in paragraph 2. (3), the words "section 6 (wireless telegraphy) and";

paragraph 19.

In Schedule 1, paragraph 3.

In Schedule 7—

paragraph 2. (1)(d)(iii);

in paragraph 19. A(9), in the definition of "merger reference group", the words "section 59 of the Fair Trading Act 1973 (c. 41)," and in the definition of "special reference group" paragraphs (b) and (f) and the word "or" at the end of paragraph (m).

In Schedule 7. A, in paragraph 1, in the definition of "merger investigation", the words "section 59 of the Fair Trading Act 1973 (c. 41),".

In Schedule 10—

paragraph 2. (1) to (6), (8) and (9);

paragraph 9. (2) to (4) and (6).

In Schedule 12, paragraph 14. (3).

In Schedule 13, paragraph 35. (2)(a).

Regional Development Agencies Act 1998 (c. 45) | In Schedule 6, paragraph 16(1). |

Access to Justice Act 1999 (c. 22) | In Schedule 4, paragraph 26. |

Electronic Communications Act 2000 (c. 7) | Sections 11 and 12. |

Section 18. (12)(e).

In Schedule 4, paragraph 3.

Postal Services Act 2000 (c. 26) | In Schedule 7, paragraph 3(2)(g). |

In Part 6 of Schedule 1, the entries relating to—

the Broadcasting Standards Commission;

the Independent Television Commission;

the Radio Authority;

the Scottish Advisory Committee on Telecommunications;

the Welsh Advisory Committee on Telecommunications.

In Part 7 of Schedule 1, the entry relating to the Northern Ireland Advisory Committee on Telecommunications.

Countryside and Rights of Way Act 2000 (c. 37) | In section 45(1), the definitions of "telecommunications code" and "telecommunications code system". |

In Schedule 8, paragraph 14. (2).

In Schedule 9, paragraph 3. (2)(e).

Section 11. (1) and (2).

In Schedule 12, in paragraph 4, sub-paragraphs (1) to (5) and in sub-paragraph (7) the definitions of "the 1990 Act", "licence", "licensed" and "the licensing body".

In Schedule 21, paragraph 8.

Criminal Justice and Police Act 2001 (c. 16) | In the table in section 1(1), the entry relating to section 43(1)(b) of the Telecommunications Act 1984. |

Anti-terrorism, Crime and Security Act 2001 (c. 24) | In Schedule 4, paragraph 29. |

Section 2.

Sections 4 to 6.

In the Schedule, paragraphs 1. (4), 8. (5), 17. (8) and (9) and 20.

Tobacco Advertising and Promotion Act 2002 (c. 36) | Section 12(4). |

In section 22. (3)(a), the words "69. (1),".

In section 33. (3)(a), the words "69. (1),".

In section 46. (1)(a), the words "69. (1),".

In section 62. (4), the words "section 69. (1) or".

In section 67. (1)(b), the words from "which" to "or 33".

In section 68. (2)(c), the words from "which", where it occurs for the second time, to "or 33".

Section 69.

In section 121—

in subsection (1), the words ", Part V of the Fair Trading Act 1973 (c. 41)";

in subsection (2), paragraph (b) and the word "or" at the end of the paragraph;

in subsection (4)(c), sub-paragraph (i), the word "and" at the end of the sub-paragraph and, in sub-paragraph (ii), the words "in any other case,";

in subsection (8), the words ", Part V of the Act of 1973";

subsection (10).

In section 136—

in subsection (7), paragraph (a) and the word "and" immediately preceding paragraph (g);

in subsection (8), the words "the Director of Telecommunications,".

Section 168. (3)(a), (4)(a) and (5)(d).

In Schedule 9, paragraphs 1 and 16.

In Schedule 25, paragraphs 13. (2) to (8), 24. (2) to (6), (8) and (9) and 34.

Income Tax (Earnings and Pensions) Act 2003 (c. 1) | In section 320(7), paragraph (d). |

European Parliament (Representation) Act 2003(c. 7) | In section 12(4), in the definition of "programme services", the words from "(including" to "local delivery services". |

Commencement Information

I1. Sch. 19. (1) in force for specified purposes at 25.7.2003 by S.I. 2003/1900, arts. 1. (2), 2. (1), Sch. 1 (with art. 3) (as amended by S.I. 2003/3142, art. 1. (3))

I2. Sch. 19. (1) in force for specified purposes at 18.9.2003 by S.I. 2003/1900, arts. 1. (2), 2. (2), Sch. 2 (with art. 3) (as amended by S.I. 2003/3142, art. 1. (3))

I3. Sch. 19. (1) in force for specified purposes at 29.12.2003 by S.I. 2003/3142, art. 3. (1), Sch. 1 (with arts. 5, 6, 10, 11)

I4. Sch. 19. (1) in force for specified purposes at 29.12.2003 by S.I. 2003/3142, art. 3. (2) (with art. 11)

I5. Sch. 19. (1) in force for specified purposes at 1.4.2004 by S.I. 2003/3142, art. 4. (2), Sch. 2 (with art. 11)

Note

F11. . . . .
Amendments (Textual)
F1. Sch. 19 Note 1 repealed (8.2.2007) by Wireless Telegraphy Act 2006 (c. 36), s. 126. (2), Sch. 9 Pt. 1 (with Sch. 8 Pt. 1)

2. The repeal of section 63 of the Telecommunications Act 1984 (c. 12) does not affect the power

of the Secretary of State or the Treasury to acquire or subscribe for securities of the successor company or of any subsidiary of the successor company other than pursuant to an enactment.

Commencement Information

I6. Sch. 19. (1) Note 2 in force for specified purposes at 25.7.2003 by S.I. 2003/1900, arts. 1. (2), 2. (1), Sch. 1 (with art. 3) (as amended by S.I. 2003/3142, art. 1. (3))

I7. Sch. 19. (1) Note 2 in force in so far as not already in force at 29.12.2003 by S.I. 2003/3142, art. 3. (2) (with art. 11)

F23. . . . .

Amendments (Textual)

F2. Sch. 19 Note 3 repealed (8.2.2007) by Wireless Telegraphy Act 2006 (c. 36), s. 126. (2), Sch. 9 Pt. 1 (with Sch. 8 Pt. 1)

4. The repeal of paragraph 20 of Schedule 5 to the Telecommunications Act 1984 shall be disregarded for the purposes of Schedule 18 to this Act.

Commencement Information

I8. Sch. 19. (1) Note 4 in force for specified purposes at 25.7.2003 by S.I. 2003/1900, arts. 1. (2), 2. (1), Sch. 1 (with art. 3) (as amended by S.I. 2003/3142, art. 1. (3))

I9. Sch. 19. (1) Note 4 in force in so far as not already in force at 29.12.2003 by S.I. 2003/3142, art. 3. (2) (with art. 11)

5. The repeals of sections 27. A to 27. L and in section 50 of the Telecommunications Act 1984 and the repeal of sections 1 to 10 of the Competition and Service Utilities Act 1992 do not have effect in relation to any dispute or other matter referred to the Director General of Telecommunications before the coming into force of the repeals.

Commencement Information

I10. Sch. 19. (1) Note 5 in force for specified purposes at 25.7.2003 by S.I. 2003/1900, arts. 1. (2), 2. (1), Sch. 1 (with art. 3) (as amended by S.I. 2003/3142, art. 1. (3))

I11. Sch. 19. (1) Note 5 in force in so far as not already in force at 29.12.2003 by S.I. 2003/3142, art. 3. (2) (with art. 11)

6. The repeals of sections 26 and 27 of the 1990 Act have effect subject to section 201. (2) of this Act.

Commencement Information

I12. Sch. 19. (1) Note 6 in force for specified purposes at 25.7.2003 by S.I. 2003/1900, arts. 1. (2), 2. (1), Sch. 1 (with art. 3) (as amended by S.I. 2003/3142, art. 1. (3))

I13. Sch. 19. (1) Note 6 in force in so far as not already in force at 29.12.2003 by S.I. 2003/3142, art. 3. (2) (with art. 11)

(2) Instruments

Title and number | Extent of revocation |

Planning (Northern Ireland) Order 1991 (S.I. 1991/1220 (N.I. 11)) | Article 104(5). |

Electricity (Northern Ireland) Order 1992 (S.I. 1992/231 (N.I. 1)) | In Schedule 4, in paragraph 1(1), the definitions of "public telecommunications operator" and of "telecommunication apparatus", "telecommunication system" and "the telecommunications code". |

Telecommunications (Single Emergency Call Number) Regulations 1992 (S.I. 1992/2875) | The whole regulations. |

Roads (Northern Ireland) Order 1993 (S.I. 1993/3160 (N.I. 15)) | In Article 2(2), the definitions of "telecommunication apparatus", "the telecommunications code" and "telecommunications code system". |

Airports (Northern Ireland) Order 1994 (S.I. 1994/426 (N.I. 1)) | Article 12(7). |

Street Works (Northern Ireland) Order 1995 (S.I. 1995/3210 (N.I. 19)) | In Schedule 2, in paragraph 7(4), the definitions of "telecommunication apparatus" and "telecommunication system". |

Gas (Northern Ireland) Order 1996 (S.I. 1996/275 (N.I. 2)) | In Schedule 3, in paragraph 1, the dcfinitions of "public telecommunications operator" and of "telecommunication apparatus", "telecommunication system" and "the telecommunications code". |

Race Relations (Northern Ireland) Order 1997 (S.I. 1997/869 (N.I. 6)) | Paragraphs 4 and 9 of Schedule 2. |

Telecommunications (Voice Telephony) Regulations 1997 (S.I. 1997/1886) | The whole regulations. |

Telecommunications (Interconnection) Regulations 1997 (S.I. 1997/2931) | The whole regulations. |

Telecommunications (Open Network Provision and Leased Lines) Regulations 1997 (S.I. 1997/2932) | The whole regulations. |

Telecommunications (Open Network Provision) (Voice Telephony) Regulations 1998 (S.I. 1998/1580) | The whole regulations. |

Telecommunications (Licence Modification) (Standard Schedules) Regulations 1999 (S.I. 1999/2450) | The whole regulations. |

Telecommunications (Licence Modification) (Fixed Voice Telephony and International Facilities Operator Licences) Regulations 1999 (S.I. 1999/2451) | The whole regulations. |

Telecommunications (Licence Modification) (Mobile Public Telecommunications Operators) Regulations 1999 (S.I. 1999/2452) | The whole regulations. |

Telecommunications (Licence Modification) (British Telecommunications plc) Regulations 1999 (S.I. 1999/2453) | The whole regulations. |

Telecommunications (Licence Modification) (Cable and Local Delivery Operator Licences) Regulations 1999 (S.I. 1999/2454) | The whole regulations. |

Telecommunications (Licence Modification) (Kingston Communications (Hull) PLC) Regulations 1999 (S.I. 1999/2455) | The whole regulations. |

Telecommunications (Interconnection) (Carrier Pre-section) Regulations 1999 (S.I. 1999/3448) | The whole regulations. |

Telecommunications (Interconnection) (Number Portability, etc.) Regulations 1999 (S.I. 1999/3449) | The whole regulations. |

Telecommunications (Licence Modification) (Satellite Operator Licences) Regulations 2000 (S.I. 2000/1711) | The whole regulations. |

Telecommunications (Licence Modification) (Regional Public Access Mobile Radio Operator Licences) Regulations 2000 (S.I. 2000/1712) | The whole regulations. |

Telecommunications (Licence Modification) (Amendment) Regulations 2000 (S.I. 2000/1713) | The whole regulations. |

Telecommunications (Licence Modification) (Mobile Data Operator Licences) Regulations 2000 (S.I. 2000/1714) | The whole regulations. |

Telecommunications (Licence Modification) (Paging Operator Licences) Regulations 2000 (S.I. 2000/1715) | The whole regulations. |

Telecommunications (Services for Disabled Persons) Regulations 2000 (S.I. 2000/2410) | The whole regulations. |

Telecommunications (Licence Modifications) (Amendment No. 2) Regulations 2000 (S.I. 2000/2998) | The whole regulations. |

Telecommunications (Licence Modifications) (Amendment) Regulations 2001 (S.I. 2001/2495) | The whole regulations. |

Commencement Information

114. Sch. 19. (2) in force for specified purposes at 25.7.2003 by S.I. 2003/1900, arts. 1. (2), 2. (1), Sch. 1 (with art. 3) (as amended by S.I. 2003/3142, art. 1. (3))

115. Sch. 19. (2) in force in so far as not already in force at 29.12 .2003 by S.I. 2003/3142, art. 3. (1)(2), Sch. 1 (with art. 11)

Open Government Licence v3.0

Contains public sector information licensed under the Open Government Licence v3.0. The full licence if available at the following address: http://www.nationalarchives.gov.uk/doc/open-government-licence/version/3/

Printed in Great Britain
by Amazon